Essentials of

INDIAN POLITY

CONSTITUTION & GOVERNANCE

FOR UPSC & STATE CIVIL SERVICES AND OTHER COMPETITIVE EXAMINATIONS

About The Author

Ms. Neeharika Reddy is an alumnus of Gujarat National Law University (GNLU), and is a practising advocate at the High Courts of Andhra Pradesh & Telangana since 2010. She is an expert in Constitutional Law and Writs. She provides coaching and mentoring for Civil Services aspirants in Hyderabad.

Essentials of

INDIAN POLITY

CONSTITUTION & GOVERNANCE

FOR UPSC & STATE CIVIL SERVICES AND OTHER COMPETITIVE EXAMINATIONS

NEEHARIKA REDDY

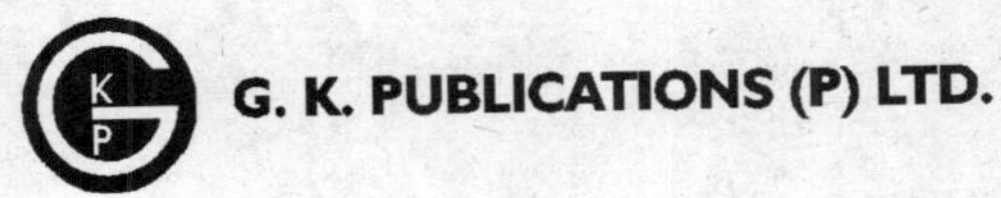

Title : Essentials of Indian Polity : Constitution & Governance

Language : English

Author's Name : Neeharika Reddy

Typeset & Published by :

Career Launcher Infrastructure (P) Ltd.

A-45, Mohan Cooperative Industrial Area, Near Mohan Estate Metro Station, New Delhi - 110044

Marketed by :

G.K. Publications (P) Ltd.

Plot No. 9A, Sector-27A, Mathura Road, Faridabad, Haryana-121003

ISBN : **978-93-5681-277-2**

Printer's Details : Printed in India, New Delhi.

For product information :
Visit ***www.gkpublications.com*** or email to ***gkp@gkpublications.com***

Contents

PART - I : CONSTITUTION & POLITY OF INDIA

PART - II : COMPARISON OF CONSTITUTIONS

PART - III : GOVERNANCE OF INDIA

Dedication

TO MY PARENTS

For raising me to believe that anything was possible

TO MY HUSBAND, BROTHER & SISTER-IN-LAW

For making everything possible

TO MY DAUGHTER

For being my sweetest little sunshine ever

TO MY COUNTRY

To whom my loyalty is pledged

Acknowledgements

My first thanks always goes to Shri Lakshmi Narasimha Bhagwan, for giving me the strength and the conviction to complete the task that is entrusted upon me.

Next, as we all know, there's always a long list of thank-you that comes with any book.

In this instance, my huge thanks are due to:

Smt. Sumathi (amma), Vijaya Chandra Reddy (nanna), Pradeep (husband), Srikanth (brother), Sirisha (best friend cum sister-in-law), Srinath Rao (friend) and to my students.

This book is in fact the brainchild of the conversation between Sirisha and me. Special thanks to my best friend for helping me to kick-start the book-writing process.

Thankful to my dear brother Srikanth for taking out time from his busy schedule to read the manuscript more than once and make any number of highly intelligent and useful suggestions.

I am grateful to my companion and better-half Mr. Pradeep Reddy who never stopped challenging me and helping me develop my ideas. Special thanks to his incredible support.

Deep gratitude to my friend Srinath for academic support and helping me with the best research material.

I am also grateful to GK Publications and to their wonderful team led by Kannath Prakash for showing confidence in my work, and for their patience and help.

Finally, I would like to acknowledge with gratitude, the support and love of my students.

Preface

"What should I read for Governance"?", "How to corelate Constitution with other disciplines?" "What is the significance of the legal doctrines in Constitution and how should I read them?".... As a mentor/ tutor of UPSC civil services aspirants, I keep getting such questions from the aspirants. Popular books on Indian Polity do give a political understanding of the Constitution, but I feel that they sometimes ignore the legal context/understanding. But if one observes keenly the questions asked in the Preliminary and Main examination of the UPSC and State Civil Service Examinations, they clearly indicate that the expectation is that the aspirant must understand the political as well as the legal paradigm and context of the various aspects of our Constitution. In other words, it is not sufficient to just read and understand the provisions of the Indian Constitution. Understanding the background of the provisions of the Constitution, interpreting them in the light of leading case laws and corelating with other disciplines or current developments is very essential. Moreover, legal interpretation of the Constitution is not only necessary to appreciate its nuances, it is also necessary to appreciate the various Acts or legislations which are related to governance. Basic concepts of the Constitution like Constitutionalism, asymmetric federalism, etc. have to be addressed, which helps aspirants with an overall understanding of our polity.

There is also a general perception that books on Indian polity are more information oriented rather than context oriented. Therefore the approach in this book is to fill such contextual gaps and also provide an overall view of our polity, constitution and governance.

While lucidly explaining the constitution, both from a legal and a political perspective, the book also extensively covers governance with various important legislations & case-laws. It comprehensively compares Indian Constitution with other major democratic constitutions of the world. Each chapter in this book contains sample questions for the readers to practise and reinforce their understanding.

The Appendices in the book are important as it contains landmark Supreme Court judgements, important amendments to the constitution, Articles of the constitution etc.

This book will be useful and important not only for the General Studies section of the examination, but also for certain optional subjects such as Political Science, Public Administration, Law and Sociology. It will also serve as a valuable resource for various State Public Service Examinations and other All India competitive examinations.

Happy reading & I wish all readers/aspirants the best in their endeavours towards achieving their aspirations.

Looking forward for your valuable suggestions and feedback!

Neeharika Reddy

Preface

Part - I

CONSTITUTION & POLITY OF INDIA

CHAPTER 1

INTRODUCTION

"Constitution is not a mere lawyers' document, it is a vehicle of Life, and its spirit is always the spirit of Age."

– B.R. Ambedkar

CONSTITUTION : THE FUNDAMENTAL LAW OF THE COUNTRY

The word 'Constitution' is of Latin origin which is generally used for regulation and orders. The Constitution of any country is the fundamental law of the land with greater authority and sanctity. It not only describes the basic principles of the State, the structures and processes of governance and the Fundamental Rights of citizens, but also envisions a path of growth and development for a nation.

After India attained freedom, the dream of the Constitution-makers was to evolve such a viable model of governance that would best serve the nation, keeping the primacy of the people central. It is the farsightedness and visionary leadership of the Founding Fathers of the Constitution which has bestowed our country with an outstanding Constitution that has worked as a beacon for the nation over the last seventy-five years. The country greatly owes the success of the democratic system to the robust edifice and institutional framework that the Constitution of India has laid down.

Definition:

"*Constitution of a State is that body of rules of laws, written or unwritten which determine the organization of government, the distribution of powers to the various government and the general principles on which these powers are to be exercised*"

- Gilchrist

In simple words, we can say a Constitution is the constitutional law of the State. Constitutional law enjoys the position of being the supreme and fundamental law of the State. It lays down the organization and functions of the government of the State. The Government can use only those powers which the Constitution grants to it.

The Constitution lays down the following :

1. Organization and powers of the government,
2. Principles and rules governing the political process,
3. Relations between the people and their government, and
4. Rights and duties of the people.

The government of the State gets organized and works in accordance with the provisions of the Constitution. People get their rights protected from the Constitution. No one, not even the government, can violate the Constitution.

Thus, the Constitution is the supreme law of each State/Country. It lays down rules regarding the organization, powers, and functions of the government. It also defines the basic features of the State and the relation between the citizens and the State. The Constitution is the basic, fundamental law of a State which sets out how that State will be organized and the powers and authorities of the government between different political units and citizens.

Qualities of a Good Constitution

These are the basic features which are necessary in every good Constitution:

1. It should incorporate the constitutional law of the State and enjoy supremacy.
2. It should be systematically written.
3. It should have the ability to develop and change in accordance with the changes in the environment and needs of the people.
4. It should be neither unduly rigid nor unduly flexible.
5. It must provide for Fundamental Rights and freedom of the people.
6. It should clearly define the organization, powers, functions, interrelations of the government of the State, and its three organs.
7. It must provide for the organization of a representative, responsible, limited, and accountable government.
8. It must clearly reflect the sovereignty of the people.
9. The language of the Constitution should be simple, clear, and unambiguous.
10. It also must provide for – Rule of Law, Decentralization of powers, Independent and powerful Judiciary, a system of Local Self-Government, a sound method of Amendment of the Constitution, and a process and machinery for the conduct of Free and Fair elections.
11. It should empower the Judiciary with the power to interpret, protect, and defend the Constitution and the Fundamental Rights and freedoms of the people against the possible legislative and executive excesses.

CONSTITUTIONALISM

Today, constitutionalism has become as important an issue as that of good governance. Constitutionalism is the political philosophy on which the idea that government authority is derived from the people and should be limited by the Constitution that clearly defines the functions of the government is based. The State, i.e., the government is not free to do anything that they want because they are bound by the laws. In a democracy, constitutionalism has become an essential part of good governance. Constitutionalism is defined as the 'Belief in the constitutional government'. A constitutional government refers to the government with a Constitution or a government which is established according to the Constitution or the government acting according to the Constitution.

Having a Constitution alone does not secure or bring the constitutionalism. Almost every country has a Constitution, but it does not mean that all of them practise constitutionalism. That is why constitutionalism is far more important than the Constitution.

In simple words, the nature of any nation's government is, of course, a matter dealt with by a Constitution; yet, the simple existence of a Constitution is no guarantee that constitutionalism will follow. It is entirely possible for a nation to have a Constitution but not constitutionalism in the sense of a limited government. A dictatorship, for instance, may subsist pursuant to a Constitution, but depend more on the dictator's edict/authority rather than on the constitutional framework for its laws. Constitutionalism—being in essence, limited government or the existence of legal limitations on government—represents the antithesis of the arbitrary powers exercised by a dictator[1]. Thus, a country may have the Constitution but not necessarily the constitutionalism. 'Constitutionalism' recognizes the need for a State with powers, but at the same time, insists that limitations be placed on those powers. The antithesis of Constitutionalism is despotism. Unlimited power may cause an authoritarian, oppressive, government which jeopardizes the freedoms of the people.

Historical Background

The roots of the Constitutionalism are from the 13th century. In the year of 1215, King John of England signed a document called 'Magna Carta'. Magna Carta set specific limits on the king's power. The practical importance of the Magna Carta has been exaggerated over the years, but Magna Carta set a precedent for limited government. Later, in the year 1689, the Bill of Rights was signed by King William III and Mary II of England. The Bill of Rights outlines the rights of the English citizens, which placed limits on the Monarch and the Parliament.

Features of Constitutionalism

Constitutionalism represents the antithesis of arbitrary rule, the opposite of despotic government found in the raw will of an individual or a limited group rather than the Rule of Law[2]. It is the limitation of government by law. All modern Constitutions, from the unwritten British to the written American, give space to essentials of constitutionalism; indeed, their very existence (Constitution) is the attempt to limit government.

Henkin identifies following as the essential features of Constitutionalism[3]:

1. Popular sovereignty,
2. Rule of Law,
3. Limited government,
4. Separation of powers (checks and balances),
5. Civilian control of the military,
6. Police governed by law and judicial control,
7. An independent Judiciary,
8. Respect for individual rights, and
9. The right to self-determination.

---

[1]C.H. Mcllwain, *Constitutionalism: Ancient and Modern 21* (Mcilwain [1940] 2008); S.A. De Smith, *Constitutional and Administrative Law 34* (De Smith 1977).

[2]Mcllwain, supra note 1, at 21.

[3]Michael Rosenfeld ed., *Constitutionalism, Identity, Difference and Legitimacy, Theoretical Perspectives 4042* (Durham: Duke University Press, 1994).

Constitutionalism in the Indian Constitution

The Indian Constitution, which came of age in the era of modern written Constitutions, makes constitutionalism a pre-condition of Indian limited government, or a government of law[4]. As such, the written Indian Constitution, in addition to its express provisions for the existence and operation of government, also incorporates well-known principles of constitutionalism which bolster limited government:

- Federalism,
- Secularism,
- Reasonableness,
- An independent judiciary with powers of judicial review,
- The doctrine of the Rule of Law and the Separation of powers,
- Free and fair elections,
- Decentralized, accountable, transparent, democratic government, and Fundamental Rights, and
- Welfare State.

These principles give coherence to the Constitution. They make it an organic whole. Though they are not expressly stated in written provisions, they nonetheless form a part of the government established by the Indian Constitution.

Thus, constitutionalism is the philosophy of the Constitution, which imposes limitations on the exercise of powers.

CONSTITUTIONAL MORALITY

Constitutional morality basically means the adherence to the core principles of the Constitution in a democracy. Constitutional morality is not just limited to following the constitutional provisions in their literal sense, but includes a commitment to an inclusive and democratic political process in which both individual and collective interests of the society are satisfied.

There is no mention of the word "Constitutional morality" in the Constitution. The Judiciary has crafted many inventions that find no express reference in the constitutional text. They read between the lines and come up with new inventions from time to time to safeguard the constitutionalism and spirit and soul of the Constitution – the "Basic Structure" doctrine, the Doctrine of "Eclipse", the old "Arbitrariness," new "Manifest Arbitrariness", the "Classification Test" – all were the examples of same. The most recent addition in the tally of the inventions by the Judiciary, which is gaining prominence and pronounced time and again by the Judiciary, is the Doctrine of Constitutional Morality[5]. The doctrine is not a new discovery. It was invented way back in Greece history, but in the Indian context now, the doctrine has attracted the attention of the Judiciary and the same is talked about in the recent landmark rulings by judges of the Apex court.

The Doctrine of Constitutional Morality is difficult to define as it has many different meanings. It is not defined anywhere as it is a judge-made doctrine for safeguarding the spirit and soul of the Constitution. It is confusing because it is applied by judges in different cases in different ways to give justice. It is subjective and changes with every case.

---

[4] *State of Karnataka Vs. Dr. Praveen Bhai Thogadia, A.I.R. 2004 S.C. 2081* ("Welfare of the people is the ultimate goal of the Constitution").

[5] *Indian Young Lawyers Association Vs. State of Kerala, (2018)* SCC Online SC 1690.

The origin and inception of the Constitutional Morality can be traced back to the 19th century. According to the British historian, George Grote, Constitutional Morality means a culture of reverence among the individual of that nation, which would ensure a peaceful administration and functioning of government. In the Indian context, the word "Constitutional Morality" was first time pronounced by the Father of the Constitution, Dr. B.R. Ambedkar during the Constituent Assembly Debates. A closer examination of the Constituent Assembly Debates reveals that Ambedkar referred to the idea of Constitutional Morality to justify the inclusion of extensive details of the administrative structure in the Constitution which made it a very voluminous document. In that context, Constitutional Morality refers to the respect, reverence, and internalization of the "form" as well as spirit of the Constitution. Till such norms are cultivated, it was necessary to even specify the form of administration in order to preserve the form of the Constitution. So, it is clear that at least when Ambedkar used this expression, it was less about the constitutional values themselves but more about internalization of constitutional values or inculcating the "habit of obedience" of the Constitution and that too, in more of an administrative/ federal context.

Even after our Constitution came into force, the word found a passing reference in some cases here and there with no significance.

The Delhi High Court's reference to Constitutional Morality in *Naz Foundation Vs. Government of NCT of Delhi*[6] is remarkable and unique. In this case, the Delhi High Court applied this doctrine to strike down Section 377 of the Indian Penal Code. The court radically transformed the meaning of the Constitutional Morality and reconstituted its content to suit the present context. In the *Naz case,* the court draws on the notion of Constitutional Morality and in the context of sexual orientation rights affirms:

The Fundamental Rights, therefore, were to foster the social revolution by creating a society egalitarian to the extent that all citizens were to be equally free from coercion or restriction by the State, or by society privately; liberty was no longer to be the privilege of the few. The Constitution of India recognizes, protects and celebrates diversity. To stigmatize or to criminalize homosexuals only on account of their sexual orientation would be against the Constitutional Morality.

It is crucial to notice how the court relates the claim of decriminalization of homosexuality with constitutional value of diversity. It questions the idea of penalizing homosexuality and introduces the idea of different sexual orientation as a value which strengthens the diversity of Indian society and thereby, fosters Constitutional Morality.

In the celebrated case of *Navtej Singh Johar Vs. Union of India*[7], the then Chief Justice of India (CJI) Dipak Mishra, reiterated the Doctrine of Constitutional Morality and stated that the court must not be remotely guided by popular perception or public morality that is backed by the majoritarian populace, but they must be controlled and guided by the Constitutional Morality. The concept of Constitutional Morality is not limited to mere observance of the core principles of constitutionalism as magnitude and sweep of Constitutional Morality is not confined to the provision and literal text that Constitution contained itself. Rather, it embraces within itself virtues of wide magnitudes of ushering of a pluralistic and inclusive society.

Public Morality and Constitutional Morality

It is the moral responsibilities of an individual together with the society to be lawful towards the values enshrined in the Constitution and uphold them with utmost integrity. Equilibrium between

---

[6]WP(C) No.7455/2001, Delhi High Court; Decision on 2nd July, 2009; 160 Delhi Law Times 277.

[7]AIR 2018 SC 4321.

Constitutional Morality and Public Morality should be maintained. The use of Public Morality to curb the Fundamental Rights should be avoided and hence, Constitutional Morality plays the role when Public Morality crosses the limit. Constitutional morality gives assurance of establishment of Rule of Law in the land while integrating the dynamic needs of the society. This doctrine forms to impact and change the persisting Societal Morality. The abolition of *sati* by enactment is an example in this regard, as it leads to a better society. Constitutional Morality is a progressive tool since it recognizes plurality and diversity prevailing in a society and provides scope for improvements and reforms. For instance, decriminalization of criminal offence against homosexuals in *Naz Foundation's case* and again reiterated in *Navtej Singh Johar's case* helped to realize the trauma faced by the LGBT community and helped to reaffirm their rights to live with dignity, identity, and liberty.

Summarising the Doctrine

Thus, the doctrine of Constitutional Morality means adherence to the noble principles of the Constitution. It is the duty of the Judiciary, as the guardian of law, to effectively use this doctrine to overcome the outdated laws and bring reforms with the changing times. Constitutional Morality has meant different things at different points in time. And law needs to cater to the changing needs of the society according to the rights guaranteed under the Constitution. This concept empowers the law-keepers to interpret the Constitution in a moral way (not conceiving the Constitution only in a way what public perceives). Legally, there is no test to determine the Constitutional Morality and hence, a standardized yardstick must be evolved so as to avoid the scope of legal inconsistencies. The term 'morality' is often confused with popular majoritarian morality. There are four key constitutional values – Justice, Liberty, Equality, and Fraternity. The interpretation of morality should be based on the values enshrined in the Constitution. Hence, it is understood that the doctrine of Constitutional Morality is a progressive and transformative tool to evaluate and analyse the various puzzling circumstances keeping the values of the Constitution in mind.

CHAPTER 2

FORMS OF GOVERNMENT

INTRODUCTION

The Government is one of the important components to run the State, and its constituent parts. It is the government which performs major functions of the State. It makes laws and policies to conduct the various affairs of the State and the daily life of the people.

The term 'Government' comes from the term 'govern', which stands for 'to rule, guide, govern and direct'. On the basis of various meanings, it can be said that the term 'government' represents a form of system which exercises control over a society through law and order. At the same time, it can be a way of exercising power. The government exists to operate the various elements of the State. To perform these functions, the government can be divided into three organs—Legislature, Executive, and Judiciary. The primary function of the Legislature is to perform the function of law-making for the State and the people. The main Executive function is to enforce the law. The major function of the government is to run the State, make rules and laws for the State, decision-making, and policy formulation. On the other hand, the Judiciary's major function is to interpret the application of laws to specific cases. The governments have many forms of governance depending on its characteristics.

CLASSIFICATION ON THE BASIS OF DIVISION OF POWER

Based on the division and concentration of powers and the relationship between the Union and States or local bodies, the governments are majorly divided into two forms – Unitary and Federal. The Countries like USA, South Africa, Canada, and Australia have adopted a federal form of government. Whereas, the countries like Britain, Japan, Italy, and France have adopted a unitary form of government.

Unitary Form of Government

Unitary government is the most common form of government. A model unitary government is one in which all governing power including sovereign power, exists in a single government over the entire nations. France, China, Japan, Britain, etc., are examples of unitary governments with power and authority concentrated at the Centre. Such States may have sub-divisions within their boundaries, but these divisions are merely extensions or local offices of the Central government. They, therefore, obtain their powers from the Central authority. These powers are specifically delegated to them from the Central government, which may change or be withdrawn at the discretion of the Central Government.

In other words, regional or local authorities do not derive their powers from the Constitution but from Legislature enactments of the Central Legislature. Sovereign powers are undivided. The Constitution of a unitary State does not admit any other law-making body. Its regimes can legislate on all subjects and administer them without reservation. Thus, the two essential qualities of the unitary State are: the supremacy of the Central Parliament and absence of subsidiary sovereign bodies.

Thus, the British Parliament is sovereign and can regulate the division of powers between authorities within the United Kingdom absolutely. The spirit of nationalism has been the dominant element in the unitary States.

This was the system in India also prior to the enactment of the Government of India Act, 1935. There were well organized provincial governments, but they were not autonomous. They enjoyed delegated powers. France is another very good example of the unitary system. France, from European standards, is a fairly big country. The Central government at Paris is all-powerful, but the country is divided into a number of provinces which are known as 'departments'. Each 'department' is administered by a 'prefect' who is a nominee of the Central Ministry of the Interior. Similarly, the provincial governments in Sri Lanka and other countries are agents of the Centre. Garner, while defining the unitary government, said that in such a system, all powers of the government are vested by the Constitution in one or more Central organs and where the local governments acquire from the Centre little or more authority or autonomy.

Features of a Unitary Form of Government

(a) **The Centre is the reservoir of all powers in a unitary system :** There exists no province or provincial governments in such a system and the Central government has the constitutional powers to legislate, execute, and adjudicate with full might. There is no other institution in this kind of State to share the powers of the Central government. Thus, it rules with no external pressure and runs the State and administration free of any checks and balances. Their power is absolute. What powers are to be centralized and decentralized are also decided by the Central government. Local governments exist but it is the Centre which decides what powers will be given to them. Even these are carried out with Central control or supervision.

(b) **Unicameral legislature :** The Parliament or the Legislature is unicameral. Generally, in federal forms of government, it is bicameral. The Lower House represents the people and the Upper House represents the States or provinces in the federal form of governments. However, there is no Upper House or Chamber in the unitary form government to represent the States or Provinces or local governments. In the unicameral Legislature, the members of the Legislature are generally elected by the people directly. In other words, most unitary systems are defined by the unicameral Legislature where the popular voting is held for the unicameral Legislature. An exception is UK. Even though UK adopted a unitary form of government, it has adopted a bicameral system. Members of the House of Commons (Lower House) are elected by the people. Whereas, the members of the House of Lords (Upper House) are appointed by the Queen on the advice of the Prime Minister. The Upper House in UK is not created for representing the provinces or States.

(c) **Uniformity of laws :** Laws in the unitary system are uniform laws unlike the ones in the federal State. This is one crucial characteristic of a unitary government. Laws are made and executed by the Central government for the entire country. They are enforced without any distinction being made for any State. In contrast, in a federal system, the nature of a law can vary from State to State. But in the unitary system, the laws are made uniform throughout the country. In a federation, however, laws of a similar nature can have sharp contrasts, thus complicating their understanding.

(d) **No distribution of powers :** Within a federation, powers are distributed among the federations and the State. In contrast, in the unitary system, no such distribution of powers is made. All powers rest with the Centre.

(e) **Flexible Constitutions :** Flexibility is what defines the Constitutions of unitary States. The Constitution in the unitary form of governments is easy to be amended and can be amended like an ordinary legislation. There is no special procedure to amend the Constitution. Whereas, in federal systems, the amendment of the Constitution is rigid. There will be a separate and special procedure to amend the Constitution and further, the amendment process will be very difficult in federal systems. In other words, in the federal form of governments, the Constitution generally cannot be amended without the consent of the States, thereby making the amending process difficult.

A flexible Constitution ensures that the desires and changing demands of the people are included in it accordingly and from time to time. It is crucial to the idea of progressiveness. Thus, Constitutions in unitary systems are evolutionary and are strong to respond to contingency situations

(f) **Uncodified or Unwritten Constitution :** The Constitutions can be codified or uncodified. It is very important to have a codified or a written Constitution in a federal form of government because it is necessary to clearly define and maintain the relationship between the Centre and the State. Whereas, there is no such necessity in the unitary form of government to define the powers and relationship between the Centre and the State. Therefore, it is not mandatory to have a codified or written Constitution. France, which has a unitary form of government, has a codified Constitution whereas UK has an uncodified Constitution. The UK is often said to have an 'unwritten' Constitution. This is not strictly correct. It is largely written, but in different documents. But it has never been codified or brought together in a single document. In this respect, the UK is different from most other countries, which have codified constitutions, but not all. For instance, New Zealand which has a unitary form of government lacks a codified Constitution.

(g) **No supreme authority of court :** Constitutions in the federal form of governments provide checks and balances and also provides a dispute resolution mechanism between the Centre and the State. Therefore, there is a need for an independent Judiciary to interpret the Constitution and to resolve the disputes between the Centre and the State. However, there is no such necessity in the unitary form of governments. Therefore, the Judiciary may not be a powerful wing of the State as the powers completely lie with the Parliament or Central government.

(h) **Excessive centralization may lead to despotism :** A unitary State can turn totalitarian or despotic when its rulers do not follow rules or move away from the path of patriotism. Since powers are with the Centre and there is no check on the activities of the government, there are higher chances of misuse. Such a government can become absolute and abuse its powers mainly due to the absence of an internal check system.

Federal Form of Government

Federalism is a form of government where the powers are distributed between the Central and provincial governments and both have their separate and well-defined areas of authority. Here, the totality of government power is divided and distributed by the national Constitution between a Central government and those of the individual States.

Generally, the federal States are the result of an agreement. In other words, several sovereign States combine together and form a big State by entering into an agreement. One of the earliest federal countries USA was formed when the colonies ratified the Constitution. Thus, the federal government can be seen as the creation of an agreement which takes place as a result of a Constitution in which the powers of the federal government and the federating units and the details of their rights are listed. This Constitution is expected to be written and rigid enough so that neither the Centre, nor the federating units may change it at their own will. Also, the Constitution is sovereign in the sense that both the Centre and the units are subordinate to it.

Secondly, an indispensable quality of the federal government is the distribution of powers of government between the Central government and the federating units. Normally, the subjects of national importance such as defence, foreign affairs, railways, communications, and finance are entrusted to the Central government whereas subjects like education, health, agriculture, etc. are looked after by the provincial units. The powers may also be distributed in one of the two ways: either the Constitution states the powers that the federal authority shall have and leave the reminder to the units, or it states those powers the federating units shall possess and leave the reminder to the federal authority. For example, in the American federation, the Constitution defines the powers of the federal authority and leaves the rest to the federating units. In Canada, it is the reverse, i.e., the Constitution prescribes only the powers of the federating units and leaves the rest to the Central government. However, in India, both the powers of the Centre and the units have been listed.

Thirdly, there should be an independent institution to settle the disputes with regard to the jurisdiction of the Centre and the units and among the units. Such an institution can only be the Judiciary/Supreme Court whose function is to see that the Constitution is respected in so far as it distributes the governmental powers between the Centre and the States. In a completely federalised State, the Judiciary is absolutely supreme in its power to decide in cases of conflict between the federal authority and the State authorities.

Features of a Federal State

(a) **Delegation and distribution of power :** In a federal government, the powers are distributed and delegated between the Centre and State (units) and many other local governments too. It is one of the most essential features of the federal government. In a federal State, the Constitution works as a sovereign over both the Central and the State government.

(b) **Written and rigid Constitution :** In a federal government, the power is distributed and divided between the Central and State government. Thus, in such cases, it becomes essential and binding to define the powers in a written and enacted Constitution. The written document can only give the effective distribution and division of power. The unwritten Constitution may generate and bring some misunderstandings, confusion, and disagreements between the Central and State governments. Federal governments in the case of USA, India, and Canada have written Constitutions. In the federal system of government, the written Constitutions are generally rigid.

It is to protect the nature of the federal structure. The Central and State government together will have the power to amend the written Constitution. Under this mutual consent between the Centre and the State, the method followed to amend any part of Constitution related to the federal structure requires a special majority.

(c) **Independence of the Judiciary :** Judiciary plays a very important rcle in a federal form of government. Judiciary plays a pioneering role to protect and promote the federal nature of the State. It is the Judiciary which protects and interprets the Constitution. In India and USA, the Judiciary utilises the power of judicial review over the laws of the Centre and State government. The Judiciary not only interprets or protects the Constitution, but also resolves the disputes between the Centre and State or among the States.

As it has been mentioned by J. S. Mill '*the constitutional authority of limits of each (Central and regional governments alike) should be precisely and clearly defined, but that the power to decide between them in any case of dispute should not reside in either of the governments, or in any functionary subject to it, but in empire independent of both*'. In this regard, it can be found that the Judiciary performs a key role in USA, Canada, and India.

(d) **Dual Administration and Citizenship :** A federal State is featured by the dual administration—at the Central government for the people of the federation and the other at the level of the State government. The nature of functioning of administration at the Centre and State level government is totally independent but both the units mutually support each other in the national interest.

Moreover, in a federal government, each person gets citizenship at the federal level as well as at the State level. In other words, it can be said that people of a federal State get double citizenship—one is common union citizenship of the whole nation and another is the State as unit of which the person is a resident. For example, in USA, the people enjoy the citizenship of USA as well as the citizenship of the respective State.

(e) **Bicameral Legislature :** In a federal State, the Legislature at the Central level will be bicameral (two Houses). In one house—the citizens of the country are represented, while the other house is represented by the units of the federation (i.e., States). The USA and Canada have bicameral Legislature. In USA, the Senate, i.e., Upper House represents the States whereas the House of Representatives represent the citizens of the country. In USA, the Senate and the States are equally represented, irrespective of their size and population. In other words, the total strength of the Senate is 100; two members coming from each State of the USA (Total number of States in the USA are 50).

(f) **Equality to all the unit States :** The federal system of government follows one key principle – i.e., to treat all the States or units equally. It never gives special or extra preference to any State on the basis of its size, population, resources, etc. It is due to this requirement that all the States are given equal seats in one or two houses of the Central Legislature. For example, in the American Senate, each State is represented by two members irrespective of its size or population. As K. C. Wheare mentioned, the framers of the federation must ensure that all the units can maintain their independence within the sphere allotted to them and work for the federation. Principally, it can be said that the federal government takes a neutral or middle path between the Centre and the unit affairs. The system is supported by the method of distribution of power between the Central and State governments.

Comparison Between Unitary and Federal Form of Governments

Comparative Advantages

Advantages	Unitary	Federal
Laws	Laws may be applied uniformly to all throughout the country.	Laws may be made to suit individual needs of the States. Local needs and local aspirations can be taken into consideration.
Government	Efforts seldom duplicate or contradict themselves.	Tyranny can be avoided more easily.
Decision-making	Fast and efficient.	Government is closer to the people.

Comparative Disadvantages

Disadvantages	Unitary	Federal
Power	Concentration of power can lead to tyranny.	Distribution of power may lead to conflict among the States or between Centre and the States.
Unity and integrity	If the country is large, a distant Central government can lose control.	The country has a tendency to split apart. Tendencies of regionalism may grow.
Local needs and resources	Central officials may not always understand the needs of their citizens.	Sub-governments may lack resources that a Central government has.

CLASSIFICATION ON THE BASIS OF LEGISLATIVE–EXECUTIVE RELATIONSHIP: PARLIAMENTARY AND PRESIDENTIAL

The modern democratic governments are classified into Parliamentary and Presidential forms of government on the basis of the Legislature-Executive relationship. In a Parliamentary democracy, the two organs are closely related. The Legislature exercises control over the Executive and the real Executive (Ministers) are bound to function in accordance with the wishes of the Legislature. This system is found in India, Great Britain, Canada, and Australia. The system of American Government, on the other hand, is Presidential. In the Presidential system, the President (Executive) is free from the control of the Legislature, and the government is organized on the principle of separation of powers. In other words, the Parliamentary government is 'responsible', while the Presidential system, though ultimately answerable to the people, is not responsible to the Legislature. The distinction was clearly explained by Walter Bagehot thus as: "The independence and separation of the Legislative and Executive power is the specific feature of the Presidential Form of Government just as fusion and combination is the principle of the Cabinet Government."

Parliamentary Form of Government[1]

The features of the Parliamentary form of government are listed below :

1. **Responsible Government/Cabinet Government :** The Parliamentary government is also known by two other names. These are 'responsible' government, and 'Cabinet' government. It is called

[1] Modes of Classification of Political Regimes; UNIT 13; IGNOU.

Cabinet[2] government because the actual power of the Executive is exercised by the Cabinet. The Cabinet itself is responsible to, and removable by, the Legislature. Hence, this system is known as responsible or Parliamentary government.

2. **Collective Responsibility :** The Principle of Collective Responsibility is another important feature of the Parliamentary systems. This principle denotes that the Council of Ministers as a whole, must support all government decisions publicly as well as in the Legislature. It means that the Council of Ministers are equally responsible for all acts of the government, and therefore no member of the Council of Ministers may castigate actions of the government after a collective policy decision has been taken. Decisions made in the Cabinet are considered as collective decisions which have to be supported by all members. A member of the Council of Ministers who cannot support government decisions in the Legislature or in the public is expected to resign from the Council of Ministers. This principle ensures unity and encourages balance and moderation within the Council of Ministers, the two essential conditions for the survival and efficiency and efficacy of the Cabinet. This principle becomes critical when there is a coalition government, where the Cabinet members belong to different political parties. Moreover, the Principle of Collective Responsibility contributes in arriving at a conclusion about what legislative proposals are to be formally introduced in the Legislature and thereby, enabling the government to get these proposals passed with ease as the members of Cabinet are themselves members of the Legislature and senior leaders of the majority party. However, critics argue that the Principle of Collective Responsibility is basically a means of achieving the goal of a disciplined party rather than encouraging balance and moderation.

3. **Two Executive Heads :** In Parliamentary systems, there are two Executive heads; Head of State and Head of Government. The Head of the State is a symbolic or figurehead representative of the State. His or her role is primarily non-political, formal, symbolic, and ceremonial, with real power lying with the Head of Government. The Head of a State can be either hereditary or elective. In the UK, Spain, Belgium, Denmark, Netherlands, and Japan, the Head of the State is a constitutional monarch, meaning that this position in these States passes by hereditary succession. On the other hand, in other States, such as India, Germany, Italy, Austria, Ireland, and Israel, there is an elected Head of the State known as President (Republic government). The Head of State enjoys and performs a wide range of ceremonial powers and functions, such as appointing Head of Government and other ministers and officials, giving assent to legislation and treaties, representing his or her State in world affairs, awarding honours, and receiving ambassadors, high commissioners, heads of States, and so on. Owing to the ceremonial nature of these powers and functions, the Head of State is a mere non-partisan figurehead. The Head of Government, on the other hand, is the political leader of the government who serves as a real Executive in a State. It is the Head of the government that exercises decision-making and political responsibilities. The Head of State is known as Prime Minister in India, Britain, Australia, Japan and most of the countries, as Chancellor in Germany and Austria, and as Minister-President in Netherlands.

4. **Leadership of the Head of Government :** In Parliamentary systems, the real power on a day-to-day basis resides with the Prime Minsters or Chancellors. As the leader of the Council of Ministers, the Legislature, and the majority party, the Prime Minister exercises a wide range of

---

[2] Council of Ministers who enjoy cabinet rank are called as Cabinet Ministers.

powers, making him or her the most powerful actor in the political system. It is on the advice of the Prime Minister that the titular head (President) of the State appoints ministers and other important officials of the Central government, allocates and reshuffles portfolios among the ministers, dismisses the minister, summons and prorogues the sessions of the Legislature, and dissolves the Legislature (particularly the popular Lower House). Thus, it is the Head of Government who enjoys real power and governs in practice, not the Head of State who simply acts as the titular head. According to Douglas Verney (1966), "As chief Executive, chief legislator and chief administrator, the Prime Minister is potentially a very powerful individual. Everything depends on the use which he chooses to make of his position, and the success with which he delegates some of his responsibilities". However, all Prime Ministers are not equally powerful in all situations. The Prime Minister, for example, enjoys relatively more power in a situation where the government is formed by a single-majority party of which he or she is the leader than in a situation where there is a coalition government. The main determinants of Prime-ministerial power are: legislative strength of his or her party, degree of unity within the party, his or her ability to appoint or remove the minsters and exercise authority in relation to the Council of Ministers, his or her ability to deal with policy-making process and exercise authority in the Legislature, his or her image at the international level, and his or her accessibility to the media.

5. **Fusion of the Executive and Legislature :** In Parliamentary systems, there is no clear-cut separation of powers between the Legislative and Executive branches. On the contrary, there is a fusion of powers, that is, merger of the authority of the two organs of the government. The fusion of Legislature and Executive exists in Parliamentary systems mainly in four forms. Firstly, Executive (the Cabinet or Council of Ministers including the Prime Minister) is drawn from the Legislature and remains accountable to it. A new government (the Prime Minister and his or her Cabinet) is formed only after it secures a '*Vote of confidence*' from the Legislature. The vote of confidence refers to a vote by a majority of the members of Legislature expressing their support for the new Prime Minister and his or her Cabinet. The Executive cannot pass its legislative proposals without the support of the majority of the members of the Legislature. Moreover, the members of the Executive, particularly Cabinet ministers, are responsible to the Legislature. They are answerable to the members of the Legislature about the activities of their respective departments. Secondly, members of the Executive are also the members of the Legislature. Thirdly, the Legislature can remove the government from power before the completion of its term by passing a vote of no confidence, a vote by a majority of the Legislature indicating its lack of confidence in the Prime Minister. Fourthly, the Prime Minister can dissolve the Legislature before the expiry of its term and call for new elections.

6. **Absence of fixed terms :** In Parliamentary systems, there is absence of fixed terms of office. The Legislature (generally the Lower House) can remove the government before the completion of its term via a vote of no confidence and the Prime Minister can dissolve the Legislature (generally the Lower House) before the expiry of its term and call for new elections in order to take advantage of an electoral opportunity for his or her party. This feature is mainly found in the countries characterized by either coalition government or single-party minority governments than in the countries where single-party majority governments are frequently found.

Advantages of a Parliamentary Form of Government

(a) Because of fusion of powers, members of the Legislature are more cooperative in relation to the Executive branch than the Legislature in a Presidential system.

(b) The government is more responsible and accountable in that ministers are individually responsible to the Legislature about the activities of their respective departments and an incumbent government, particularly a coalition one, can remain in office only as long as it enjoys the support of the Legislature.

(c) Because the members of the Executive are themselves the members of the Legislature, there is a strong government and effective policy-making in the sense that the legislative proposals that an incumbent government introduces in the Legislature are easily passed into law by the latter.

(d) The Parliamentary systems are more flexible in the sense that they impel the elected representatives, who have different political views, to negotiate compromises in order to form the government.

(e) The absence of a fixed term of the Executive offers an opportunity to voters to remove incompetent and unpopular representatives at any time.

Disadvantages of a Parliamentary Form of Government

(a) Parliamentary systems tend to create the problem of Executive domination. This usually happens in single-party majority-based Parliamentary governments where the Executive enjoys so much control over the Legislature that the latter serves as a mere talking shop.

(b) Parliamentary systems are associated with a weak government and political instability. This usually exists in coalition governments.

(c) Parliamentary systems are far less efficient than Presidential systems in the sense that the voters do not know in advance (prior to casting a vote) what the composition of the new government will be, which depends on the final electoral results and the subsequent negotiations for forming a coalition government.

(d) In a situation of where no party wins a majority of legislative seats, the preferred policies of the voters may not be actualized as the parties holding different political positions have to compromise their positions in order to form a government.

(e) The Prime Minister can call earlier elections at any time in the interests of his or her party.

Presidential Form of Government

The Presidential system is a form of government in which the Executive and Legislative branches of the government are separate and there is mutual independence between the two. In this system, the Executive and Legislature are elected separately and have independent powers. According to J.W. Garner (1952), Presidential form of government "is that system in which the Executive (including both the head of the State and his ministers) is constitutionally independent of the Legislature in respect to the duration of his or their tenure and irresponsible to it for his or their political policies". The best example of this system is the United States where it emerged and has been adopted by almost all the States of continental Americas such as Argentina, Brazil, Mexico, Chile, Colombia, etc. and in some Asian countries as well, such as Indonesia, Maldives, Philippines, etc.

Features of the Presidential Form of Government

Important features of the Presidential form of government are as follows :

1. **Single Head :** In Presidential systems, a single elected person, known as President, wears what Andrew Heywood called "two hats", both the Head of State and the Head of Government. The President directs the government and exercises the political responsibilities as well as performs the ceremonial duties. However, the President is far weaker than the Prime Minister in a Parliamentary system and has less control over the Legislature and its members than a Prime Minister has in a Parliamentary State. This is primarily because of the "*Doctrine of Separation of powers*"[3].
2. **Separation of Powers :** The defining feature of Presidential forms of government is the principle of separation of powers. There is a clear division of powers and responsibilities among the three branches of the government – Legislature, Executive, and Judiciary. The separation of powers between the Legislature and Executive exists in Presidential systems mainly in the following forms. First, the Executive (President and his Cabinet) is not drawn from the Legislature. Instead, both the President and the Legislature are elected separately in their own elections. Second, the President is directly accountable and responsible to the electorate and not to the Legislature as he or she is elected by the people, either directly or through an Electoral College. Third, the Legislature cannot remove the President before the expiry of his or her term. It can do so only in the exceptional circumstances through a process of impeachment. Fourth, the President cannot dissolve the Legislature before the expiry of its term. Fifth, the members of the Executive, including the President, cannot be the members of the Legislature and vice-versa. A member of the Legislature cannot join the Executive branch and Executive members cannot sit in the Legislature and take part in the legislative process.
3. **President and Cabinet Members :** In the Presidential system, the President has complete freedom in the appointment of Cabinet members and formation of the government, though they cannot be drawn from the Legislature. The Cabinet members appointed by the President serve as his or her policy advisers rather than policy or the Legislature. Since the President is politically responsible to the people, he or she has absolute authority to hire and fire his or her Cabinet members who share no decision-making powers with him or her. In this respect, there is unipersonal Executive responsibility in the Presidential form of government and the Cabinet is a far less important decision-making body.
4. **Law-making Authority :** In a Presidential system, the Executive has far less law-making authority than the Executive in a Parliamentary system. The American President, for example, can veto a legislation passed by the Congress (Legislature of USA), but the latter can override a veto with a

[3]Separation of powers is a doctrine under which the three branches of government (executive, legislative, and judicial) are kept separate. This is also known as the system of checks and balances, because each branch is given certain powers so as to check and balance the other branches. One of the earliest and clearest statements of the separation of powers was given by French social commentator and political thinker Montesquieu in 1748: '*When the legislative and executive powers are united in the same person, or in the same body of magistrates, there can be no liberty... there is no liberty if the powers of judging is not separated from the legislative and executive... there would be an end to everything, if the same man or the same body... were to exercise those three powers.*' Each branch has separate powers, and generally each branch is not allowed to exercise the powers of the other branches. The Legislative branch makes laws. The Executive puts those laws into effect and plans policy. The Judiciary administers justice by interpreting the law when its meaning is in dispute, ensuring the law is upheld.

two-thirds majority vote. Similarly, the President can sign treaties but such treaties are subject to the approval of the Senate (Upper House). Because of mutual independence of the Executive and Legislative branches in terms of their selection, tenure, and membership, the Legislature is a far more independent law-making body than the Legislature in a Parliamentary system.

5. **Fixed Terms of Offices :** Another distinguishing feature of Presidential systems is the presence of fixed terms. Both the President and the Legislature have fixed terms of office, meaning that neither can usually remove the other before the expiry of the given term. The President is elected separately for a fixed term, which varies from four to six years in different Presidential States. The President's term is not dependent on the legislative support as in a Parliamentary system. This means that the Legislature cannot usually remove the President before the expiry of his or her term, except in the exceptional circumstances through a process of impeachment which needs extraordinary measures. Similarly, the President cannot dissolve the Legislature and remove its members who enjoy their own democratic mandates.

Advantages of the Presidential Form of Government

(a) The separation of powers between the Legislative and Executive branches prevents the problem of Executive domination, establishes limited government, and thereby protects individual rights and liberties.

(b) Unlike the Parliamentary system under which each party is likely to represent only its sympathizers, the President in a Presidential system, as a single nationally elected official, tends to represent an entire country and thereby, acts as a symbol of national unity.

(c) Because of fixed terms, the Presidential systems provide greater continuity in the Executive and ensure far more political stability than Parliamentary systems.

(d) In Presidential systems, the voter is likely to have information in advance about who will lead the new government.

(e) The Presidential systems provide voters more opportunities to influence and shape the policy-making process in that they are represented by two separately and independently elected institutions – Legislature and Executive.

Disadvantages of the Presidential Form of Government

(a) Because of separation of powers, the Presidential systems are likely to cause a deadlock between the Legislature and the Executive in the sense that these two institutions on the basis of their equal public legitimacy tend to clash over policy, causing a threat to effective policy-making and effective implementation of policy programmes.

(b) Presidential systems are highly rigid in that both the Executive and the Legislature have fixed terms of office. The President cannot be usually removed from office before the expiry of his or her term, even if he or she is incompetent to face any serious problem, thereby causing a political crisis.

(c) Accountability in Presidential systems becomes blurred in that both the Legislative and Executive branches claim credit for policy success and offload the blame for policy failures.

(d) Because of unipersonal Executive responsibility, the Presidential systems suffer from the problem of weak Cabinet causing far less deliberation than what occurs under Parliamentary systems.

2.1 INDIAN PARLIAMENTARY FORM OF GOVERNMENT

RATIONALE BEHIND ADOPTING PARLIAMENTARY FORM OF GOVERNMENT IN INDIA

India adopted the Parliamentary form of democracy in the year 1947 since India has been familiar with its working during the times of British Rule. The type of government that functioned in India before independence in 1947 was very much similar to the British model of Parliamentary form of government. The framers of the Constitution were greatly influenced by the English system. Therefore, the members of the Constituent Assembly decided to adopt this form of government for the independent India. India is a nation deeply divided into several groups with conflicting interests. All these varied groups are ensured representation in the Parliament through this form of government.

As explained by K.M. Munshi in the Constituent Assembly, "*We must not forget a very important fact that during the last one hundred years Indian public life has largely drawn upon the traditions of the British Constitutional Law. Most of us and during the last several generations before us, public men in India, have looked up to the British model as the best. For the last thirty or forty years, some kind of responsibility has been introduced in the governance of this country. Our constitutional traditions have become Parliamentary and we have now all our Provinces functioning more or less on the British model. As a matter of fact, today, the Dominion Government of India is functioning as a full-fledged Parliamentary government.*"[1]

The Constitution of India rejected the Presidential system as in the USA on the grounds that under such a system, "*the Executive and the Legislatures are separate from and independent of each other, which is likely to cause conflicts between them, which our infant democracy could ill-afford to risk.*"[2]

Therefore, the familiarity of the Indian polity with the working of the British system of government, representation of diverse interest groups, Executive being responsible to the Legislature (responsible form of government), fear of deadlock between the Executive and Legislature – all led to the adoption of the Parliamentary system of government in India by the Constituent Assembly.

THE INDIAN PARLIAMENTARY SYSTEM

(a) **Nominal Head and Real Head of the State :** The Head of the State, i.e., the President in Indian context is titular (*de jure*), while the Prime Minister is the Real Head (*de facto*). This implies

---

[1]Subir K. Bhatnagar, *Need for Structural Changes in Indian Parliamentary Model I*, Central Law Quarterly.

[2]According to Durga Das Basu, *Commentary on The Constitution of India*, (8th Edition 2012, LexisNexis Butterworths Wadhwa, Nagpur).

that the person holding the Presidential post may have great stature, but he does not exercise his power independently. Constitutionally, all the powers belong to him, and every affair of the State runs under his name and assent as articulated in Article 77 of our Constitution, but those powers are actually exercised by the "Council of Ministers" headed by the Prime Minister who is the Head of the Government. This has been provided by the Constitution under Article 74. Thus, there exist two Heads of the Executive, a Real and a Nominal Head. The President must act according to the advice of the Council of Ministers or else, it might be set aside.

(b) **Close nexus between the Executive and Legislature :** The Constitution-makers adopted a partial separation of powers between the Executive and Legislature so that they are not totally independent of each other. Therefore, under this system, the Executive and the Legislature have a close collaboration with each other. This is done by choosing the Council of Ministers from the Legislature, which involves 15% of the strength of the House of the People. The President summons the Legislature and gives his consent to the bills that are initiated and passed by the Legislature to make them Acts.

(c) **Majority Party Rule :** The political party which wins majority seats in the Lower House/ Lok Sabha forms the government. In India, the President invites the leader of the majority party in the Lok Sabha to form the government. Generally, the President appoints the leader of the party as the Prime Minister and the other ministers are appointed by the President on the advice of the Prime Minister. The President may invite a coalition of parties to form the government in case no party has got the majority. In other words, the majority party or a coalition of parties commanding majority in the Lok Sabha forms the government.

(d) **Accountability of the Executive :** The executives must perform all those residuary functions of the government which involve the implementation and administration of various policies and Acts and orders determined by the Legislature and ordered by the Judiciary respectively. In the Parliamentary system, the Executive is responsible and accountable to the Legislature for all its actions since it has the right to seek detailed information about the working of the Ministers. The Council of Ministers remain in office as long as they enjoy the support and confidence of the Lok Sabha, i.e., the House of the People.

(e) **Collective Responsibility :** According to Article 75, the Council of Ministers are collectively responsible to the Parliament in general and to the Lok Sabha specifically. Moreover, the Council of Ministers has Collective Responsibility towards each other, which mean that the Council shares the responsibility for the lapses of each and every Minister. Moreover, the individual minister cannot differ from the decision of the Council, particularly the Cabinet. Thus, in order to oppose the policies or decisions of the Cabinet, the Minister has to resign from the Council and then refute it on the floors of the Legislature. Therefore, the

Ministers "swim and sink together". The other implication of Collective Responsibility is that the Council of Ministers can also be removed by passing the vote of Non-Confidence against them in the Lok Sabha.

(f) **Leadership of the Prime Minister :** J. Laski said, "*Prime Minister is central to formation, central to growth and central to the death of the Council of Ministers.*" Since he is the Head of the Government and also the Real Head of the State, the President appoints and distributes portfolios among the members of the Council of Ministers upon the recommendations of the Prime Minister as enunciated by Article 75 of the Indian Constitution. The Prime Minister has the power to dismiss any Minister any time without assigning any reason. Also, his resignation leads to the resignation of the entire Council of Ministers. He also serves as a "link or pivot" between the Council and the President by conveying the decisions taken by the Council after every meeting. He is not only the Leader of the Council of Minsters but also the Leader of the Parliament.

(g) **Double Role and Double Membership :** Parliamentary democracy is characterised by the fusion of Executive and Legislative powers into a single body. The Executive (the Council of Ministers) sits as Members of Parliament and play a double role in the fusion of executive and legislative powers. Those who recommend legislation as Members of the Council of Ministers also vote on the same legislation as Members of the Parliament/Legislature. In other words, the Council of Ministers are Members of both the Legislature and the Executive. A person who is not a Member of Parliament can become the Minister but in order to continue as the Minister, he has to become the Member of the either of House of Parliament within 6 months.

(h) **Secrecy :** One of the prerequisites for the Parliamentary form of government is the secrecy of the Cabinet meetings and the discussions held therein. In other words, the Council of Ministers cannot reveal any information about their proceedings, meetings, and decisions. They take the Oath of Secrecy before entering their office, which is administered by the President. In the oath taken by the Ministers, they promise to keep the faith and secrecy as given in Article 75 of the Constitution. As per Article 74(2) of the Constitution, the advice given by the Council of Ministers cannot be inquired in any court of India which ensures secrecy.

(i) **Dissolution of the Lok Sabha :** The President can dissolve the Lok Sabha even before the completion of its 5-year term based on the recommendations of the Prime Minister.

(j) **No Fixed Tenure :** In a Parliamentary system, the term or the duration of the Council of Ministers or the ruling government is not fixed. They are dependent on the confidence they enjoy in the Lower House. If the Prime Ministers resigns or the majority party is not able to prove its confidence in the House, then the Council of Ministers has to resign. After that, new election will be conducted and the party having a majority of the members in the Lok Sabha forms the government. In normal circumstances, the tenure of the Lok Sabha is for 5 years, and after that, general elections are held.

DIFFERENCE BETWEEN INDIAN AND BRITISH PARLIAMENTARY FORM OF GOVERNMENT

Although India has primarily adopted the British Model while selecting the Parliamentary form of government, still there are some basic differences between the Parliamentary system of India and Britain. These are:

India	Britain
India adopted the Republican form of government. Hence, India is a Republic. The Head of state in India is the President who is elected on the basis of Proportional Representation.	Britain is not a republic. Britain has a Monarchical system. In other words, the Head of the State in Britain is King or Queen who enjoys the hereditary position and is not elected.
In India, Parliament is not Supreme and neither does India believe in "Parliamentary Sovereignty." The power of the Parliament is limited by the written Constitution, the federal system, judicial review, and Fundamental Rights. In fact, in India, Constitution is considered to be supreme.	The British system is governed by the principle of "Parliamentary Supremacy". In other words, UK believes in Parliamentary sovereignty.
In India, the Prime Minister can be a member of either House of Parliament. In other words, the Prime Ministers can come from either the Lok Sabha or from Rajya Sabha.	In Britain, the Prime Minister should be a member of the House of Commons (Lower House) of the Parliament. In other words, the Prime Minister should invariably come from the Lower House.
In India, a person who is not a member of either House of the Parliament can also become a Minister, but only for a maximum period of 6 months.	In Britain, usually, only the members of Parliament become Ministers.
In India, Ministers do not have any legal responsibility. They only have individual and Collective Responsibility. Individually, they are responsible to the Head of the State and collectively, they are responsible to the Lok Sabha.	In Britain, the Ministers not only have individual and collective responsibility, but also have legal responsibility as well. In Britain, ministers are required to countersign the official Acts of the Head of the State.
India does not have any institution known as "Shadow Cabinet".	There is a concept of 'Shadow Cabinet' in the UK. The Shadow Cabinet is basically a Cabinet formed by the opposition who keeps a check on the activities and policies of the ruling government and can replace it once the ruling party falls.

2.2 QUASI-FEDERAL FEATURES OF THE INDIAN CONSTITUTION

INTRODUCTION

The Indian Constitution can neither be classified as truly federal nor truly unitary in nature. Instead, it is to be classified as "quasi-federal' because it borrows features from both the above-mentioned forms of governance. The Constitution is biased towards the Central government and is also focused on furthering the interests of individual States within the country. This unique structure was adopted by the Constitution-makers to tackle issues faced by other federal countries and to meet diverse needs of the population. The quasi-federal structure adopted by India has been largely successful in achieving its purpose as it has helped reduce conflicts within the country and has helped ensure the unity of States. Furthermore, the country's federal system has also allowed citizens to simultaneously embrace their national and State-based identities. However, it is important to acknowledge that India's federal experiment has failed at times due to the arbitrary use of powers vested in the Centre by the Indian Constitution.

Thus, in the Indian Constitution, there reside the features of both the Federal Structure and the Unitary Structure.

FEDERAL FEATURES OF THE INDIAN CONSTITUTION

(a) **Division of Powers :** The federal form of government contains dual polity – the Union at the Centre and the States at the periphery. Each of the unit is conferred with certain sovereign powers by the Constitution. The powers are divided between the Centre and the States. The division of powers between the Union and the States is the most important characteristic of the federal Constitution. The framers of the Constitution adopted the pattern of the Government of India Act, 1935 and have given predominant power to the Union over the States. The legislative powers are divided under the scheme of the division of powers as under the Lists provided in the 7th Schedule of the Indian Constitution viz., Union List, State List, and Concurrent List. The relation between the Union and the States are governed as under Articles 245-293 of Part XI of the Constitution.

(b) **Supremacy of the Constitution :** Constitution is the supreme law of land in India. A federal State derives its existence from the Constitution. Every type of power; be it legislative, administrative, or judicial – irrespective of it being at the Centre or the State level, is controlled by and subordinated to the Constitution. Every law made by the Parliament and the State Legislature (even the constitutional amendments) are subjected to the interpretation of the Hon'ble Supreme Court and it has the power to nullify the laws which are found beyond or above or violative of the Constitution.

(c) **Written Constitution :** A Federal Constitution cannot exist without a written Constitution. It will be practically impossible to maintain the supremacy of the Constitution and division of powers between the Centre and the States unless the terms of the Constitution have been reduced into writing. In other words, if there were no written Constitution defining the scope of the powers of the Centre and the States, there will be chaos, misunderstandings, and conflicts between the Centre and the States who would seek to cross over each other's line of authority.

(d) **Rigid Constitution :** A natural corollary of a written Constitution is its rigidity. In a rigid Constitution, the procedure of amendment is complicated and difficult. But this does not mean that the Constitution should be legally unalterable. A rigid Constitution, as we know, is one which cannot be changed easily. The Indian Constitution is largely a rigid Constitution. All the provisions of the Constitution concerning federal State relations can be amended only by the joint actions of the State Legislatures and the Union Parliament. Such provisions can be amended only if the amendment is passed by a two-third majority of the members present and by voting in the Parliament, and is ratified by at least one half of the States.

(e) **Independent Judiciary :** For a federation, it is also essential that the Judiciary is impartial and independent. A Federal court is indispensable to a federation. It acts as the guardian of the Constitution. This principle has been playing an important and key role in the working of the federal government. The Constitution has provided for a Supreme Court, and every effort has been made to see that the Judiciary in India is independent and supreme. The Supreme Court of India can declare a law as unconstitutional if it contravenes any provisions of the Constitution. In order to ensure the impartiality of the Judiciary, our judges are not removable by the Executive and their salaries cannot be curtailed by the Parliament.

(f) **Bicameral Legislature :** A bicameral system is considered essential in a federation because it is in the Upper House alone that the federal units can be given equal representation. The Constitution of India also provides for a bicameral Legislature at the Centre consisting of the Lok Sabha and the Rajya Sabha. While the Lok Sabha consists of the elected representatives of the people, the Rajya Sabha mainly consists of representatives elected by State Legislative Assemblies.

UNITARY FEATURES OF THE INDIAN CONSTITUTION

The features that highlight the unitary trend of our Constitution are as follows :

(a) **Absence of the word 'Federation' in the Constitution :** It is important to address the fact that India is referred to as "Union of States" and not a federation, mainly because unlike the USA, India is divided into States for the administrative convenience. Therefore, our Constitution-makers have conspicuously avoided the use of the word 'federation' in the

Constitution. This can be considered as a deliberate attempt on the part of the Constitution-makers to keep India unitary in spirit. India has been described as a 'Union of States' in the Constitution.

(b) **Single Constitution for the Union and the States :** Normally, under a federal set-up, the States have their own Constitutions, i.e., separate from that of the Union. Such is the case in the United States. On the contrary, there is only one Constitution for the Union and the States and there is no separate Constitution for the States in India. Thus, both the Union and State governments derive their authority from a single Constitution.

(c) **Single Citizenship :** India is a country with dual polity with a single citizenship. There is no State citizenship. Every Indian has the same rights of citizenship, no matter in which State he or she resides in. The Indian Constitution does not provide for dual citizenship. Every citizen of India is an Indian by birth. There is only one nationality. Whereas, in other federal States like the USA and Australia, dual citizenship is offered – one at the national level and another at the State level.

(d) **Centre's Supremacy :** Theoretically, in a federation, both the governments should be independent of each other, and none should be allowed to encroach upon the autonomy of the other. In our federation, we have a strong Centre, as compared to the States. Owing to its strong position politically, economically, and financially, the Centre can make inroads into the provincial sphere of action. This does not uphold the federation spirit. It is not just 'distribution of powers' but it is the constitutional guarantee of the State autonomy that makes the 'distribution of powers' the essence of federalism. In the Indian case, a powerful Centre with a large jurisdiction can always show its supremacy over the States.

The Unitary Territories in India are also administered by the Central government. Other than this, the 42nd Constitutional Amendment has empowered the Central government to deploy armed forces in any State to deal with law and order situations.

(e) **Dominance of Parliament :** The Parliament reigns supreme in the following manner:

- As per Article 249, the Rajya Sabha can transfer any of the subjects included in the State List to the Parliament, when viewed from the perspective of national interest.
- Under Article 253, Parliament has got the supreme power to make laws for the whole or any part of the country. Likewise, it can take decisions for implementing any treaty, agreement, and convention with any other country or countries.
- Parliamentary supremacy over the State Legislature is also indicated in Article 3. By virtue of this Article, the Union Government can at any time change the boundaries of any existing State, merge it with some other State, create a new State out of an existing one, or abolish a State altogether.

(f) **Residuary Powers :** Article 248 provides that the residuary power of legislation rests with the Parliament and not the Legislatures of States. This is in contrast with the powers of States in the USA and even Australia, where the residuary power lies with the States.

(g) **Single Unified and Integrated System of Judiciary :** The States of the United States have their own judicial system independent and uncoordinated with the federal Judiciary. Australia also has more or less the same pattern. But in India, the Supreme Court and the High Courts form a single integrated judicial system. The Supreme Court at the top and the High Courts below enforces both the Central as well as State laws. Moreover, the Supreme Court of India is authorized to reverse the decisions of these High courts. The composition of State High Courts is decided by the Centre. The civil and the criminal laws are codified and are applicable to the entire country.

(h) **Appointment of Governors and other High Appointments :**

- The Governors are appointed by the President at the behest of the Centre. State Governors hold office at the Pleasure of President. There is no effective say of a State government in regard to the appointment or removal of a Governor. A Governor merely acts as an agent of the Centre. Apart from the appointment of Governors, the judges of the High Courts who come under the jurisdiction of the State, are appointed by the President of India.
- The Centre also dominates the States in regard to All India Services (AIS) like Indian Administrative Services (IAS) and Indian Police Services (IPS). Members of the AIS are appointed by the President of India. But these AIS work for States as well. The Parliament may also create a new AIS, if the Rajya Sabha passes a resolution by a $2/3^{rd}$ majority of its members present and voting. The manner of posting and promotion of the members of AIS is also decided by the Centre. Disciplinary action against such officers can be initiated by the UPSC alone.
- The Election Commissioner and the Comptroller and Auditor General of India are the Central government employees and they do work for the States also. This reflects that the State governments are virtually run by the high officials of the Union Government.

(i) **Provisions regarding Emergency :** Articles 352, 356, and 360 provide for the emergency powers. They are bestowed on the President of India to be exercised owing to the existence of either condition, that is, when there is threat to sovereignty of the nation or breakdown of constitutional machinery in a State or financial instability and bankruptcy of any government respectively. These powers are so sweeping in their effects that the very nature of the Indian State gets altered into a purely unitary one.

(j) **Inequality of Representation in the Council of States :** There is bicameralism in India but in the Council of States, States have not been given equal representation. Here, population system has been followed and bigger States have been given greater representation than the smaller ones. Whereas in the USA, all the States are equally represented in the Upper House/Senate.

(k) **Flexible Constitution :** Majority of the provisions of the Constitution can be easily amended by the Parliament. The Parliament can amend the majority provisions of the Constitution without the State's consent either with simple majority or with special majority. Whereas, in other federations, the amendment process is very rigid. Moreover, in India, only the Parliament can initiate and amend the Constitution. The States can neither initiate nor propose any amendment like in the USA.

(l) **Veto over State Bills :** Certain State Bills can be reserved by the Governor for the Presidential assent. When State Bills are reserved for the Presidential assent, the President can exercise the absolute veto power. In other words, he can withhold his assent even when the Bill is sent back to him for a second time by the State Legislature after the reconsideration. Whereas, in other federations, there is no such provision of reserving the State Bills for the Presidential assent as the States enjoy complete autonomy with respect to their legislative subjects.

CHAPTER 3

CONSTITUTIONAL HISTORY OF INDIA

INTRODUCTION

The English East India Company was essentially a commercial body. It came to India as a trading Company in the 17th Century. However, to follow the principles of mercantilism and to ensure monopolistic profit, the Company needed political power. Therefore, it enhanced political activities which resulted in acquiring revenue-yielding territories in India. In other words, it obtained Diwani rights, i.e., revenue rights as well as civil justice administration rights. After 1757, it was in a privileged position of yielding political power over a large section of the population of India.

The British Government granted the exclusive trading rights in India to the Company in the 17th century. But the authority (Crown) which controlled the Company was situated far away from India in Britain. The British Government faced many problems because of this situation and relationship.

The Company had become a great empire combining the role of a trader and an overlord. It was now clear that the power and sovereignty of the Indian empire was vested in the Company. The British Government decided that the Company could no longer be allowed to remain outside the ambit of the state after the Sepoy Mutiny in the year 1857. In other words, the British Government started regulating the Company as well as its political activities in India by passing regulating Acts.

Thus, the history of constitutional development of India can be traced back to the 18th century. Since then, a number of constitutional experiments were introduced, aiming at streamlining the British Indian administration. However, the year 1858 serves as a watershed in the Indian administration because the British Parliament took the direct responsibility of administering India. Thus, the period of British Constitutional experiment during the British rule can be divided into two phases –

1. Constitutional Experiment during the rule of East India Company (1773–1857); and
2. Constitutional experiment under the British Crown (1858–1947).

EVOLUTION OF CONSTITUTIONAL DEVELOPMENTS

Acts Between 1773 – 1857[1]

1. **Regulating Act, 1773 :** The British Parliament passed its first important Act in 1773 called as the Regulating Act to control the Company's administration. The Act made changes in the

[1] *Constitutional developments* (1757–1858); Unit 23; eGyanKosh.

Constitution of the Company at home; the whole of the territories in India were subjected to some degree of control. In other words, the Regulating Act was the first step taken by the British Government to control and regulate the affairs of the East India Company in India and also recognised the political and administrative functions of the Company.

Important provisions of the Act :

(a) Laid foundation of central administration in India;

(b) Changes were made in the constitution of the Court of Directors of the Company. It was required that it should submit to the British Government all communications about civil and military affairs received from Bengal and revenues of India;

(c) The status of the Governor of Bengal was raised to Governor-General. His Council would consist of four members. The Governor-General in Council was given the power to superintend and control the presidencies of Madras and Bombay in matters of war and peace. In this body was vested the civil and military administration of the presidency and government of all the territorial acquisitions and revenues in the kingdoms of Bengal, Bihar, and Orissa. Mr. Warren Hastings was the first Governor-General.

(d) The Governors of Madras and Bombay were required to send regularly to the Governor-General, information connected with government, revenues, or interests of the Company. The Governor-General in turn was under the direct control of Court of Directors and kept it fully informed of the affairs concerning the interests of the Company.

(e) The Act also provided for the establishment of a Supreme Court of Justice at Calcutta to give justice to Europeans, their employees, and citizens of Calcutta.

(f) Legislative powers were granted to the Governor-General and Council to make rules, ordinances, and regulations for the civil government of Fort William and subordinate factories.

2. **Act of Settlement/Amending Act of 1781 :** The Amending Act of 1781 was passed by the British Parliament in 1781 to remove the defects of the Regulating Act 1773. It is also known as "Declaratory Act, 1781". The key provision of this Act was to demarcate the relations between the Supreme Court and the Governor-General in Council. One of the biggest problems created by the Regulating Act was the tussle between the Supreme Court and the Governor-General in Council. This was done by curtailing several powers of the Supreme Court in favour of the Governor-General in Council.

Important provisions of the Act :

(a) Under the Regulating Act 1773, the servants of the Company came within the jurisdiction of the Supreme Court, and this brought them under dual control of the Governor-General in Council and the Supreme Court. The 1781 amendment exempted the actions of the public servants in the Company in their official capacity.

(b) Revenue Collectors (including Zamindars) and judicial officers of the Company courts were also exempted from jurisdiction of the Supreme Court. In other words, the court now had no jurisdiction in the revenue matters concerning revenue, or any act done in the collection thereof. The government now became independent of the control of the court in the matter of revenue.

(c) The Supreme Court's geographic jurisdiction became limited to only Calcutta. Moreover, the appellate jurisdiction of the Court was also curtailed. In other words, the Act provided that appeals were to be taken from the provincial courts to the Governor-General in Council but not to the Supreme Court.

(d) The Act empowered the Governor-General and Council to convene as a Court of Record to hear appeals from the provincial courts on civil cases. This means that appeal could be taken from the provincial courts to the Governor-General and Council and that was to be the final court of appeal.

(e) The Act further provided that the Supreme Court shall administer justice based on the personal laws of the parties of the case. In other words, Hindu law will be applicable if the parties are Hindus and Muslim law will be applicable if the parties are Muslims.

(f) Moreover, the Governor-General in Council was empowered to issue rules, ordinances, and regulations.

Thus, this Act made the position of the council very strong so that it could continue to have a good control over the Indian empire. Moreover, it was the first attempt to separate the executive from the judiciary by defining the respective areas of jurisdiction.

3. **Pitts India Act, 1784 :** This Act was passed to remove the defects in the Regulating Act. With the passage of the Act, the Company's public affairs and its administration in India were to come directly under supreme control of the British Government. The right of the Company to territorial possessions was however not touched, so it essentially meant a compromise.

Important provisions of the Act :

(a) Board of Control was established to guide and control the work of the Court of Directors and the Government of India. For political matters, the Board of Control was created and for commercial affairs, the Court of Directors was appointed. The Board of Control also took care of civil and military affairs. It comprised of 6 people:

- Secretary of State (Board President);
- Chancellor of the Exchequer;
- Four Privy Councillors

In this dual system of control, the Company was represented by the Court of Directors and the British government by the Board of Control.

(b) The Governor-General's council's strength was reduced to three members. One of the three would be the Commander-in-Chief of the British Crown's army in India. The Governor-General was given the right of veto.

(c) The Presidencies of Madras and Bombay became subordinate to the Bengal Presidency. In effect, Calcutta became the capital of the British possessions in India.

(d) The Act laid the foundation of a centralised administration–a process which reached its climax towards the close of the nineteenth century. The Company became subordinate to the British government unlike as in the previous Regulating Act of 1773, where the government only sought to 'regulate' matters and not take over.

(e) This Act also made a distinction between the commercial and political activities of the East India Company. In other words, the British Crown's authority was established in the civil and military administration of its Indian territories. Whereas, commercial activities were still a monopoly of the Company. Moreover, for the first time, the term 'British possessions in India' was used.

4. **Charter[2] Act of 1793 :** The Charter of the Company was renewed for 20 years and it was declared that it would be allowed to continue with the possession of all territories for the next 20 years. In other words, the Act was passed to renew the charter of East India Company and authorized the Company to carry on trade with India for next 20 years.

Important provisions of the Act :

(a) The Governor-General's and Governors' powers to overrule their council were emphasised and explained. This power had been given specially to Cornwallis in 1786. The Governor-General's control over the Presidencies was strengthened. He was allowed to issue orders and directions to any Government and Presidency of India during his absence from Bengal without previous consultation with his council. He could exercise all executive power vested in the Central Government.

(b) Even though the Governor-General could override his council, the authority was declared not to apply to the judicial matters, or legislation proper, or taxation.

(c) The Commander-in-Chief was not a member of the Governor-General's council, unless he was specially appointed to be a member by the Court of Directors.

(d) Separation of Executive from Judiciary – The powers vested in the Collector were administrative and judicial as he was also in charge of collection of revenue and for deciding cases arising out of revenue matters. Now, the Collector was only responsible for the collection of revenue. In other words, Revenue Courts/Mal Adalats which exclusively tried cases arising out of revenue matters and presided by the Collector as Judge, was now abolished. All powers and pending suits of the Revenue courts were now transferred to Mofussil Diwani Adalats and thus not tried by the Collector.

(e) Administration of Criminal Justice – The Collectors who also acted as magistrate under the scheme of 1790 were deprived of their magisterial powers. The magisterial power of the Collector was transferred to the Judge of Mofussil Diwani Adalat with the same power and function.

(f) Court fee which was imposed in the judicial plan of 1787 was abolished. The court fee was abolished so that the people could easily access the court for securing justice. In order to ensure efficiency in the administration of justice, Cornwallis organised the legal profession for the benefit of litigants in 1793. In other words, the legal profession was recognised in India for the first time and the person who wanted to join the legal profession was required to obtain a license.

The Charter Act 1793 can be called an Act for consolidation of the Indian Judiciary. This Act reorganized the courts and redefined their jurisdictions.

---

[2]Sanction/Permission.

5. **Charter Act 1813 :** Due to Napoleon Bonaparte's Continental System in Europe (which prohibited the import of British goods into French allies in Europe), British traders and merchants suffered. So, they demanded they be given a share in the British trade in Asia and dissolve the monopoly of the East India Company. But the Company objected to this. Finally, British merchants were allowed to trade in India under a strict licensing system under the Charter Act of 1813.

   Important provisions of the Act :

   (a) This Act asserted the Crown's sovereignty over British possessions in India.

   (b) The Company's rule was extended to another 20 years. Their trade monopoly was ended except for the trade in tea, opium, and with China.

   (c) It empowered the local governments to tax people subject to the jurisdiction of the Supreme Court.

   (d) The Act gave more powers for the courts in India over European British subjects.

   (e) Another important feature of this Act was to grant permission to the missionaries to come to India and engage in religious proselytization. The missionaries were successful in getting the appointment of a Bishop for British India with his headquarters at Calcutta in the provisions of the Act.

   (f) The Act provided for a financial grant towards the revival of Indian literature and the promotion of science.

   (g) The Company was also to take up a greater role in the education of the Indians under them.

6. **Charter Act of 1833 :** The Act of 1833 was a great landmark in the constitutional history on India. The monopoly of tea trade with China was abolished. The Company was to have only political functions/administrative functions. In other words, the Act ended the commercial activities of the Company and restricted it only to the administrative functions. Moreover, the Company territories in India were held by it "in trust for His Majesty, His heirs and successors".

   Important provisions of the Act :

   (a) The Governor-General of Bengal was re-designated as the Governor-General of India. This made Mr. William Bentinck the first Governor-General of India. The Governors of Bombay and Madras lost their legislative powers. The Governor-General had legislative powers over entire British India. Thus, the country's administration was unified under one control.

   (b) The Governor-General in Council had the authority to amend, repeal, or alter any law pertaining to all people and places in British Indian territories whether British, foreign or Indian native. The civil and military affairs of the Company were controlled by the Governor-General in Council.

   (c) For the first time, the Governor-General's government was called Government of India and the council was called India Council.

   (d) The Act added one more member to the Executive council of the Governor-General, the Law member, whose work was fully legislative. He had no vote in the Council and he was to attend meetings on invitation. Macaulay, the Law member, influenced the Educational Policy of the government for a number of years.

(e) The Act mandated that any law made in India was to be put before the British Parliament and was to be called 'Act'. As per the Act, an Indian Law Commission was established. The first Law Commission had Mr. Macaulay as its Chairman. It sought to codify all Indian laws. The Indian Penal Code and Codes of Civil and Criminal Law were enacted by the efforts of the Indian Law Commission.

(f) This was the first Act that gave permission for Indians to have a share in the country's administration. It stated that merit should be the basis of employment to government service and not birth, colour, religion, or race. This was not of much practical importance, since nothing was done and Indians remained excluded from higher posts in civil and military service. The Charter Act of 1833 made no provision to secure the nomination of Indians to the covenanted services of the Company. Yet, the clause proclaiming on discrimination was of great importance, for it became the sheet anchor of political agitation in India towards the end of the century.

7. **Charter Act of 1853 :** The British government renewed the Charter but no term was laid down. The Charter of 1853 was unlike the other previous Charter Acts, as it did not fix any definite time limit for the continuance of the administration of the Company in India. It simply provided that the Indian territories were to remain under the government of the Company, in trust for the Crown, until the Parliament otherwise directed.

Important provisions of the Act :

(a) By the Act of 1853, separation of the executive and the legislative functions was carried a step further by the provision of additional members of council for the purpose of legislation. The Council in its legislative capacity was to consist of 12 members[3]. These included the Governor-General, Commander-in-Chief, four members of his council, and six legislative members. The "Legislative Councillors" were neatly distinguished from the "Executive Councillors" and by doing so, legislation was for the first time treated as a special function of the government requiring special machinery and special procedure. The business of the Council was conducted in public. The procedure it adopted for transaction of business was much the same as in the British Parliament. Questions were put, papers were demanded, information was asked for, and the Government was criticised for its lapses and excesses.

(b) All civil service posts/vacancies in India were to be filled in by competitive examinations. Macaulay Committee of 1854 gave India her first Civil Services.

Acts, Plans, Commissions, and Resolutions Between (1857–1947)

1. **Government of India Act, 1858 :** The Government of India Act, 1858, known as the Act for the Better Government of India was passed in 1858. It marked the end of one chapter and the beginning of new chapter in the constitutional history of India. It took over the administration of the country from the English Company and passed on the same to the Crown.

---

[3] 12 members – (i) the Governor-General, (ii) the Commander-in-Chief, (iii) the four ordinary members of the Governor-General's Council, (iv) the Chief Justice of the Supreme Court (Calcutta), (v) a puisne judge of the Supreme Court, and (vi) four representative members, drawn from Company's servants of ten years' standing, appointed by the local governments of Bengal, Madras, Bombay, and the North-Western Provinces, one from each of the governments.

As the Charter Act of 1853 did not give the East India Company the right to govern India for another 20 years, it gave an opportunity to the Home Government to step in and take the place of the East India Company in India. This process was hastened by the happenings of 1857, or the so-called 'Sepoy Mutiny'.

In other words, "after the First war of Independence of 1857[4]", the British government took direct control of the territories formerly ruled by the English East India Company.

Important provisions of the Act :

(a) The Act provided that India was to be governed directly and in the name of the Crown, acting through a Secretary of State for India (a portfolio that was created in the British ministry and was responsible to the British Parliament). The Secretary of State[5] for India was to exercise the powers which were formerly within the jurisdiction of the Court of Directors and the Board of Control. In discharging his duties, the Secretary of State was to be aided by a Council of fifteen members. The Secretary of State was the President of the Council. The salaries of the Secretary of State for India and his establishment were to be charged on Indian revenues.

(b) The Secretary of State for India was a cabinet minister in the British Government while his agent in India was the Governor-General in India. In India, the Governor-General came to be known as the Viceroy. The Military and Naval forces of the Company were transferred to the Crown. The Viceroy was the direct representative of the British Crown in India and Mr. Canning was appointed as the first Viceroy of India.

(c) The Secretary of State was given the power of sending and receiving secret messages and despatches from the Governor-General without the necessity of communicating them to the Council.

2. **Indian Councils Act, 1861 :** It has been noted that the Charter Act of 1858, which transferred powers from the Company to the Crown, introduced changes in the Home Government only while the administration of India continued to be carried along the old line. The Indian Councils Act of 1861 introduced a number of changes in the administration of India. Moreover, in the aftermath of the Mutiny of 1857, there was a general perception in England that it would be very difficult to secure the government in India without the cooperation of Indians in administration. Therefore, the Act of 1861 was passed to introduce a feature of association of Indians with the legislation work and to make substantial changes in the composition of the Governor-General's council for executive and legislative purposes.

Important provisions of the Act :

(a) The Act made noted changes in the composition of the Governor-General's Council for executive and legislative purposes. The Council of the Governor-General for executive purposes (Executive Council) was expanded by the addition of a fifth member. The fifth

---

[4]The Indian mutiny of 1857 caused by the policy of Mr. Dalhousie of ruthless annexation of the territories of the native princesses through his Doctrine of Lapse, in addition to social and military causes, sounded the death-knell of the Company rule in India.

[5]As the successor of the Company, the Secretary of State-in-Council was rendered able to sue and be sued in respect of contracts and such other matters as could have formed the subject of litigation by or against the Company before its liquidation in India. In other words, the Act declared the Secretary of State-in-Council for India as a corporate body who could sue and be sued in England and in India.

member to the Executive Council was to be "*a gentleman of legal profession, a jurist rather than a technical lawyer*". Mr. Canning, who was the Viceroy at that time, introduced the portfolio system. In this system, each member was assigned a portfolio of a particular department. In other words, there were five members for home, military, law, revenue, and finance. A sixth member for public works was added in 1874.

(b) The Governor-General's Council was further strengthened by adding not less than 6 and not more than 12 members nominated by the Governor-General for the purposes of legislation. In other words, the Legislative Council was created with a minimum of strength of 6 and a maximum of 12. Out of these, at least half of the additional members were to be non-official (British or Indian). Their functions were confined to legislative measures. Mr. Canning nominated three Indians to the Council in 1862–namely, the Raja of Benares, the Maharaja of Patiala, and Sir Dinkar Rao.

(c) The Viceroy had the power to overrule the council if necessary. The Governor-General also had the power to promulgate ordinances without the council's concurrence during emergencies. The life of such an ordinance was six months.

(d) The Secretary of State for India in Britain could also dissolve any Act passed by the Viceroy's Council.

(e) This Act restored the legislative powers of the Governor-in-Councils of the Presidencies of Madras and Bombay (which was taken away by the Charter Act of 1833). In other words, the process of decentralization was initiated with this Act and led to complete decentralization with the 1935 Act.

(f) There was provision made for the formation of legislative councils in other provinces. New provinces could also be created for legislative purposes and Lieutenant Governors could be appointed for them. Legislative councils were formed in other provinces – in Bengal in 1862, North-West Frontier Province in 1886, and Punjab and Burma in 1897.

3. **Indian Councils Act of 1892 :** The passage of the Indian Councils Act, 1892, was influenced by the resolutions of the Indian National Congress adopted in its sessions in 1885 and 1889. In its very first session held in 1885, it adopted a resolution expressing great dissatisfaction at the existing system of government and demanded "the expansion of the Councils by admitting a considerable proportion of elected members".

Important provisions of the Act :

(a) The Act increased the number of additional members in case of the Council of the Viceroy to not less than ten and not more than sixteen. In the case of the Bombay and Madras Councils, to not less than eight and not more than twenty. The maximum for Bengal was fixed at twenty and for the North-Western Province and Oudh at fifteen.

(b) The Governor-General/Viceroy in Council was empowered to make rules for the nomination of the additional members, subject to approval of Secretary of State for India. The rules which were actually made by the Viceroy under these provisions, introduced a system of indirect election for the non-official members, both at the Central Legislative Council as well as the Provincial Legislative Council. The Viceroy used to make the nominations of non-official members to the Central Legislative Council based on the recommendations of bodies like the Provincial Councils, Chambers of Commerce, etc. Whereas, the Governors used to make the nominations to the Provincial Legislative Councils based on the recommendations of the municipalities, district boards, universities, trade associations, chambers of commerce, zamindars, etc. The clause in the Act, which entitled the Viceroy to make the regulations regarding the nomination and in-turn enabled indirect election to be introduced is often known as the "Kimberley Clause[6]".

(c) The Act further enabled the Legislative Councils to discuss the annual financial statement (not to vote the Budget item by item, but to indulge in a full, free, and fair criticism of the financial policy of the government). The members of the Council were given the right of asking questions on matters of public interest (unlike the provisions of the Indian Councils Act, 1861), subject to such conditions and restrictions as might be prescribed in rules formulated by the Viceroy or the Governors.

4. **Morley-Minto Reforms (OR) Indian Councils Act, 1909 :** The Morley-Minto Reforms of 1909 represent the next constitutional advance after the Council Act of 1892. The Act is associated with the names of – Morley, the Secretary of State and Minto, the Viceroy of India.

Important provisions of the Act :

(a) The Act of 1909 enlarged the size of the Central Legislative Council. The additional members of the Governor-General's/Viceroy's were increased up to a maximum of 60, those of Madras, Bengal, Bombay, and United Provinces to a maximum of 50 and those of the Punjab, Burma, and Assam to 30.

(b) Substantial official majority in the Central Legislative Council was maintained whereas, the Act did not provide for any official majority on the provincial legislative councils. The majority of the members were to be non-officials.

(c) The functions of the legislative councils were increased. Elaborate rules were made for the discussion of the budget in the central legislative council. Members were given the right of asking questions and supplementary questions for the purpose of further elucidating any point and were also given the right to ask any supplementary questions or move any resolution relating to any alteration in taxation, any new loan, or any additional grant to local Governments proposed or mentioned in the financial statement.

(d) The Act introduced a separate and discriminatory electorate. The electorate was decided on the basis of class and community. In other words, some seats in the councils were reserved for Muslims to be elected by Muslim voters. This was for the first time that the seats in the legislative bodies were reserved on the basis of religion for Muslims. Separate constituencies were marked for the Muslims and only Muslim community members were given the right to elect their representatives. That's the reason why Lord Minto is known as the "*Father of the Communal Electorate*". The Act also provided for the representation of chambers of commerce, universities, presidency corporations, and zamindars.

(e) The Act for the first time provided for the association of Indians in the Viceroy's executive council. Satyendra Prasanna Sinha was the first Indian to be made a member of the Governor-General's executive council. He was appointed as the Law member.

---

[6]Mr. Kimberley was the then Secretary of State of India.

5. **Government of India Act, 1919/ Montagu-Chelmsford Reforms :** The Government of India Act 1919 aimed at increasing the participation of Indians in the administration of their country. Montagu took over as the Secretary of State for India in July 1917. He is described as "the most liberal Secretary of State since Ripon". Montagu made a historic declaration that British policy in India would have an overall objective of "gradual development of self-governing institutions, with a view to the progressive realization of responsible government in India as an integral part of the British empire". Montagu-Chelmsford reforms came into force in 1921.

Important provisions of the Act :

(a) Provincial Dyarchy (Dual Rule) – The Act provided a dual form of government (a 'dyarchy') for the major provinces. It also relaxed centre's control over provinces by demarcating subjects as 'central subjects' and 'provincial subjects'. Provincial legislatures were authorised to make laws with respect to the subjects falling under the provincial list. Provincial subjects were further divided as *Reserved Subjects* and *Transferred Subjects.* Reserved Subjects are administered by the governor with the help of his 'Executive Council'. Whereas, Transferred Subjects are administered by the Governor with the aid of 'Ministers' responsible for 'Provincial Legislative Council'. The 'Transferred List' included agriculture, supervision of local government, health, and education. This dual system of government was known as 'Dyarchy'[7].

(b) For the first time, 'Direct Elections' was introduced with limited franchise. The franchise was granted on the basis of tax paid, education, property, etc. in the country.

(c) A bicameral system at the centre was introduced. In other words, the Central Legislature would comprise two chambers – the Council of State (Upper House) and the Indian Legislative Assembly (Lower House). The majority of members of both the Houses in this bicameral system were directly chosen. Whereas, at the provincial level, unicameral system was established.

(d) Separate electoral provision of Morley Minto was retained and was further extended to Sikhs, Indian Christians, Anglo-Indians, and Europeans.

(e) The revenue resources were divided between the centre and the provinces, with land revenue going to the provinces, and income tax remaining with the centre. The Act, also for the first time, separated the provincial budgets from the central budget and further authorized the provinces to enact their own budgets.

(f) The Governors were given powers to summon, prorogue, dissolve the Chambers, and to promulgate ordinances. Thus, despite reserved and transferred list, governor's decision was final.

(g) The number of Indians in the Viceroy's Executive Council was increased to three out of eight members.

(h) The Act provided for the establishment of a Public Service Commission in India for the first time.

---

[7]This new system, however, failed to gain popular acceptance and Simon Commission recommended that Dyarchy should be done away with and 1935 Act did the same.

(i) The Act also made a provision that a statutory commission would be set up at the end of 10 years after the Act was passed which shall inquire into the working into the system of the government. The Simon Commission of 1927 was an outcome of this provision.

(j) The Act further created a new office of the High Commissioner for India in London and transferred to him some of the functions of the Secretary of the State for India.

6. **Simon Commission :** The Indian Statutory Commission, commonly referred to as the Simon Commission after its chairman Mr. John Allsebrook Simon, was sent to India in 1928 (February – March and October 1928 – April 1929) to study potential constitutional reform. The Simon Commission was a group consisting of seven members of the British parliament. The Simon Commission was dispatched to India in 1928 to review the Government of India Act 1919. The Commission, appointed by Prime Minister Stanley Baldwin, did not include any Indian delegates. As a result, the Indian National Congress and a faction of the Muslim League, led by Mohammed Ali Jinnah, decided to boycott the Commission. The Simon Report was met with disappointment and condemnation throughout India. In the wake of the Report, a series of Round Table Conferences[8] were set up from 1930 to 1932. The outcome of the Commission and the Conferences was the Government of India Act 1935.

Recommendations of the Simon Commission :

(a) Dyarchy in the provinces should be abolished and ministers should be made responsible to the provincial legislatures in all departments, including the department of law and order.

(b) The Governor was to retain the special powers for the safety and tranquility of the province and for the protection of the minorities. He would also have full powers of intervention in the event of breakdown of the Constitution.

(c) The Franchise was to be extended and legislatures were to be enlarged.

(d) At the centre, a Federal Assembly/National Government Assembly would be constituted on the basis of representation of the provinces and other areas as per the population.

(e) The council of state would continue as the Upper House but its members would be chosen not on the basis of direct election but on the basis of indirect election by the Provincial councils.

(f) No changes in the executive/executive functions of the central government.

(g) The All India Federation was not considered as a practical idea for immediate execution.

(h) Burma should be separated from the British India and should be provided a Constitution of its own.

7. **Poona Pact 1932 :** All India Federation Ramsay Macdonald, the British Prime Minister, announced the Communal Award that gave Depressed Classes (a loose term that referred to Dalits/Untouchables/Scheduled Castes) separate electorates for central and provincial legislatures. Gandhi viewed this as a danger to the Hindu community that would de-link untouchables from Hindus. Ambedkar and other leaders of the Depressed Classes welcomed the award.

---

[8] A 'White Paper on Constitutional Reforms' was drafted based on the discussions and deliberations. And the same was submitted to the Joint Select Committee of British Parliament.

On 20th September 1932, while in prison, Gandhi announced a fast unto death till the time separate electorates were removed from the Award. The British had given the assurance that it would make changes to the Award if these changes were the result of an agreement between the communities concerned. Indian political leaders realised that the best chance to get Gandhi to terminate his fast was to facilitate an agreement between Gandhi and Ambedkar. Initially, Ambedkar was not fazed by Gandhi's fast. But later, he came around and agreed to negotiate. In the end, Gandhi and Ambedkar came to an agreement – the Poona Pact 1932 – that discarded separate electorates.

Important provisions of the Poona Pact, 1932 :

(a) Separate electorates for Depressed Classes did not feature in the document; instead, the Pact put forward a system of the joint electorates with reserved seats. It reserved 148 seats from the general electorate for Depressed Classes, 78 more than what the Award had proposed.

(b) The Pact also called for the non-discrimination of Depressed Classes in public services and urged for efforts towards the fair representation of the community in public services.

(c) It also contained a provision that proposed the earmarking of a portion of the state's educational grant for Depressed Classes.

The Pact influenced the Government of India Act 1935 where separate electorates were given to Muslims, Sikhs, and others, but not to the Depressed Classes. The Pact was a historic moment in India's constitutional and political history. It brought to bear the tensions between and the Depressed Classes and the Hindus, one that would continue to haunt the freedom movement and negotiations between Indians and the British. To a large extent, the Pact further reinforced and augmented the claim that Depressed Classes were a political minority whose interests could not be ignored while drawing up the constitutional future of India.

8. **Government of India Act, 1935 :** The clear intention behind the Government of India Act, 1935 was to set India upon the path of responsible government and promote the complete realization of her ambition in this respect. So, it was the longest Act enacted by the British Parliament at that time. The provisions of the "Government of India Act 1935", although never implemented fully, had a great impact on the Constitution of India. Many key features of the Constitution are directly taken from this Act. It is really a lengthy and detailed document having 321 sections and 10 schedules. The majority of the today's Constitution was drawn from this. The GOI Act, 1935 was based on –

- Simon Commission Report
- The recommendations of the Round Table Conferences
- The White Paper published by the British government in 1933 (based on the Third Round Table Conference)
- Report of the Joint Select Committees (led by Mr. Linlithgow).

Important provisions of the Act :

(a) All India Federation : The Act envisaged, for the first time, to establish an All India Federation. The Federation was to consist of eleven Governors provinces, six chief commissioners' provinces and such other Indian states which would be willing to accede to it. Accession to the Federation under the 1935 Act was compulsory for Governor's provinces and Chief

Commissioner's provinces but optional for the Indian states. The latter were to sign an Instrument of Accession before joining in the proposed All-India Federation. According to this Act, India would become a federation if 50% of Indian states decided to join it. However, the provisions with regards to the federation were not implemented as the required number of Princely States did not join it.

(b) Dyarchy at the Centre : The Act of 1935 abolished dyarchy at the Provincial level and introduced it at the Centre. There were two categories of federal subjects:

- Reserved subjects
- Transferred subjects.

Reserved Subjects : The subjects that are mentioned in this category of federal subjects were to be administered by the Governor-General on the advice of the Executive Councillors and the Executive Council could not exceed its limit of three members. Religious affairs, defence, administration of tribal areas, and external affairs were included in the reserved subjects.

Transferred Subjects : This subject was to be administered on the advice of the Council of Ministers and the number of ministers could not exceed 10. Subjects other than reserved were dealt with under the Transferred Subjects.

Even though these provisions came into effect in 1937, they were discontinued in 1939.

(c) Provincial autonomy : The most remarkable feature of the Act was the cerebrated provincial autonomy. With the abolition of Dyarchy, the distinction between the reserved and transferred subjects as envisaged by the GOI Act, 1919 was removed and the entire provincial administration was entrusted to the responsible ministers who were controlled and removed by the provincial legislatures. The provinces were no more the mere agents of the omnipotent centres. Thus, the provincial autonomy means two things. First, the Provincial Governments were wholly responsible to the provincial legislatures and secondly, provinces, were free from outside control and interference in a large number of matters. Of course, a large array of powers vested in the Governors in guise of discretionary powers, special responsibilities, and safeguards restricted the actual operation of provincial autonomy to a large extent.

(d) Division of subjects : To form the federation and implement provincial autonomy, the subjects are divided between the Centre and the Provinces. The division of subjects that were given by the Government of India Act, 1919 was revised and some more subjects were added to it by this Act of 1935. It included three lists – Federal List (Only central legislature will make laws), Provincial List (Provincial legislatures will make laws), and Concurrent List (Both central and provincial legislatures are authorized to pass laws on those subjects). The Act further authorized the Viceroy to allocate in his discretion the right to legislate on any subject, not included in the lists, either the Centre or the province. In other words, Viceroy does not have the power to make laws with respect to the residuary subjects. He can only authorize either the Centre or the province to make the laws with respect to the residuary subjects.

(e) Bicameral Legislature : Under the Government of India Act, 1935, the Central Legislature was bicameral, consisting of Federal Assembly and Council of States. The Council of States was to be Upper House and a permanent body with one-third of its membership retiring every 3rd year. The Federal Assembly was the Lower House with the tenure of five years.

Election to the Federal assembly was to be indirect. Both the Indian States as well as the provinces were allocated seats in the legislature. The Act also introduced bicameralism in six out of eleven provinces. Thus, the legislatures of Bengal, Bombay, Madras, Bihar, Assam, and the United Provinces were made bicameral consisting of a legislative council (Upper House) and a legislative assembly (Lower House). However, many restrictions were placed on them.

(f) Retention of Communal Electorate : Separate electorates were provided for Muslims, Sikhs, Anglo-Indians, Indian Christians, Europeans, Landholders, Women, Labour, Commerce, and Industry. There was no separate electorate for Depressed classes. In other words, General Seats were reserved for Scheduled Castes. The Muslims got 33 ⅓ percent of the seats in the Federal Legislature although their number was much less than one-third of the total population of British India. Even the workers and women got separate representation although they had not asked for it.

(g) Abolition of Indian Council : The new Act abolished the Indian Council (which was established through Government of India Act, 1858) and provided for the appointment by the Secretary of State and his team of Advisers.

(h) Extension of Franchise : Franchise was expanded to 14% of the population from 3%.

(i) Federal Court : The Act provided for the establishment of a Federal Court which would interpret the Act and adjudicate disputes relating to the federal matters. The Federal Court was given exclusive original jurisdiction to decide disputes between the Centre and constituent units. The provision was made for filing of appeals from High Courts to the Federal Court and from the Federal Court to the Privy Council. The Federal Court also had jurisdiction to grant Special Leave to Appeal and for such appeals a certificate of the High Court was essential. The Federal Court was established in the year 1937.

(j) It provided for the establishment of a Reserve Bank of India to control the currency and credit of the country.

(k) It also provided for the establishment of not only a Federal Public Service Commission, but also a Provincial Public Service Commission and Joint Public Service Commission for two or more provinces.

9. **The Cripps Mission: (Background) :**

- Japan was advancing outside the eastern borders of India and the fall of Burma was a jolt to the British in the war. The threat of a Japanese invasion on India was looming and Indian support was essential for Britain's war efforts.
- When the 2nd World War broke out in 1939, the Viceroy Linlithgow declared India a party to the war as part of the British Empire. This was done without consultation with Indians and this led to massive protests from the Congress Party. The party leaders, who were heading 7 provincial governments resigned from their posts. The Muslim League celebrated it as 'Deliverance Day'.
- Britain was facing pressure from the US and other allied leaders over its own imperial policies in India and also to secure Indian cooperation for the Allied war effort. This also led the British government to send Cripps to India.

Therefore, the Cripps Mission was sent by the British government to India in March 1942 to obtain Indian cooperation for the British war efforts in the 2nd World War. It was headed by Mr. Richard Stafford Cripps, a Labour Minister in Winston Churchill's coalition government in Britain.

Important proposals of Cripps Mission :

- Setting up of an Indian dominion[9] which would have the freedom to remain with the British Commonwealth or to secede from it. It would also be at liberty to take part in international organisations.
- A Constituent Assembly would be formed to frame a new Constitution for the country. This Assembly would have members elected by the provincial assemblies and also nominated by the princes.
- Any province unwilling to join the Indian dominion could form a separate union and have a separate Constitution.
- The transfer of power and the rights of minorities would be safeguarded by negotiations between the Constituent Assembly and the British government.
- In the meantime, until this new Constitution came into force, India's defence would be controlled by the British and the powers of the Governor-General would remain unaltered.

But the Cripps proposals were rejected by almost all the parties and sections in India on different grounds.

10. **Cabinet Mission Plan :** In September 1945, the newly elected Labour government in Britain expressed its intention of creating a Constituent Assembly for India that would frame India's Constitution. The Cabinet Mission was sent to India in March 1946 to make this happen. The Mission had to deal with a major obstacle: the two main political parties – the Indian National Congress and the Muslim League – who had fundamental differences over India's future. While the Muslim League wanted the Muslim majority provinces of India to constitute a separate sovereign state of Pakistan, the Congress wanted a united India. The Mission, at the Shimla Conference, attempted to facilitate an agreement between the Muslim League and the Congress. When this failed, the Mission came out with its own proposals known as the Cabinet Mission Plan. The members of the Cabinet Mission were: Mr. Pethick-Lawrence, Secretary of State for India, Mr. Stafford Cripps, President of the Board of Trade, and A.V. Alexander, First Lord of the Admiralty.

    Main proposals of the Cabinet Mission Plan :

    - Rejection of the Muslims League's demand for a full-fledged Pakistan.
    - Grouping of existing provincial Assemblies into three sections: Section A—Madras, Bombay, Central Provinces, United Provinces, Bihar, and Orissa; Section B —Punjab, North-West Frontier Province, Sind (Muslim majority provinces); Section C—Bengal and Assam; The full autonomy of the provinces and the provisions for grouping were meant to give the Muslim League the 'substance' of Pakistan.

[9]For the first time, the British government acknowledged India's right to be a dominion.

- A Constituent Assembly to be elected by Provincial Assemblies by proportional representation (voting in groups—General, Muslims, Sikhs). This Constituent Assembly to be a 389-member body with Provincial Assemblies sending 292, Chief Commissioner's Provinces sending 4, and Princely States sending 93.
- In the Constituent Assembly, members from groups A, B, and C would sit separately to decide the constitution for provinces and if possible, for the groups also, then the whole Constituent Assembly would sit together to formulate the Union Constitution.
- There would be a common Centre controlling Defence, Communication, and External Affairs.
- Provinces to have full autonomy and residual powers.
- Princely states to be no longer under paramountcy of the British government and would be free to enter into an arrangement with successor governments or the British government.
- An Interim Government to be formed from the Constituent Assembly.

The Cabinet Mission Plan was accepted by the Congress and the Muslim League though with certain reservations (The objection of the Congress to the Plan was mainly its provision of grouping, and that of the League to the rejection of its demand for Pakistan). In the elections to the Constituent Assembly that took place in July 1946, the Congress captured 205 seats and the League 73. The 4 Sikh seats owed allegiance to the Congress; thus Congress had 209 members in an Assembly of 296. However, the 93 seats allotted to Princely States were not filled as they decided not to participate in the Constituent Assembly. Alarmed at the overwhelming majority of the Congress, the Muslim League withdrew its acceptance of the Cabinet Mission Plan on July 29, 1946. Muslim League initiated 'Direct Action Day' (August 16th, 1946) triggering large-scale violence and communal riots across the country.

11. **The Interim Government (September 2, 1946) :** The Viceroy invited the President of the Congress Jawaharlal Nehru to form the Interim Government which assumed office on September 2, 1946. Initially, the Muslim League kept out, but later on October 13, decided to join the Interim Government to safeguard the interests of the Muslims and other minorities.

12. **Constituent Assembly:** The Constitution-making process was organised around the deliberations of the Constituent Assembly. The members of the Constituent Assembly were elected on a limited franchise. The Cabinet Mission Plan, which set up the Constituent Assembly of India, discarded full adult franchise for elections to the Constituent Assembly and instead, suggested indirect elections by members of the then recently elected Provincial Legislative Assemblies. The elected members of the provincial legislative assemblies elected the representatives to the Constituent Assembly by the method of proportional representation by means of single transferrable vote. Seats allocated to each Province were to be divided among the three principal communities (General, Muslims, and Sikhs). In addition to members elected by the Provincial Legislative Assembly (292), the Princely States and the Chief Commissioner's Provinces contributed 93 and 4 members of the Constituent Assembly, taking the total membership to 389. The representatives of the Princely States were to be nominated by the heads of the Princely States. Whether it is a province or the Princely State, the seats were allocated in proportion to the population of such province or the Princely State respectively. Thus, the Constituent Assembly comprised of both

the indirectly elected members as well as the nominated members. When Jinnah called for the 'Direct Action Day', it led to widespread communal rioting in the country. There was a call for the partitioning of the country on account of the riots. Congress leaders also acknowledged the inevitability of the partition as a means to stop the brutal violence.

On 9 December 1946, the Constituent Assembly sat for the first time. Only 211 members attended the session as the Muslim League boycotted the session. Dr. Sachchidananda Sinha, the oldest member, became the temporary President of the Assembly. Later on, Rajendra Prasad was elected as the Chairman of the Constituent Assembly, whereas, H.C. Mukherjee and V.T. Krishnamachari were elected as the Vice-Presidents of the Assembly. Thus, the Constituent Assembly had two Vice-Presidents. The reasons being, in July 1947, following the decision to partition India, the Constituent Assembly modified its rules to have two Vice-Presidents, and there was a suggestion that one of them might be from the Princely States.

After partition, the total number of seats came down to 299 as some Provinces and Princely States became part of Pakistan.

13. **Objectives Resolution :** The Constituent Assembly formally began its task of framing the Constitution of India on the 13th of December, 1946 with Jawaharlal Nehru moving the Objectives Resolution. The Resolution put forth broad principles that would form the basis of the working of the Constituent Assembly. The Constituent Assembly adopted the Resolution on 22 January 1947. The Objectives Resolution reads as follows:

(a) This Constituent Assembly declares its firm and solemn resolve to proclaim India as an Independent Sovereign Republic[10] and to draw up for her future governance a constitution;

(b) WHEREIN the territories that now comprise British India, the territories that now form the Indian States, and such other parts of India as are outside British India and the States as well as such other territories as are willing to be constituted into the Independent Sovereign India, shall be a Union of them all; and

(c) WHEREIN the said territories, whether with their present boundaries or with such others as may be determined by the Constituent Assembly and thereafter according to the law of the Constitution, shall possess and retain the status of autonomous units, together with residuary powers and exercise all powers and functions of government and administration, save and except such powers and functions as are vested in or assigned to the Union, or as are inherent or implied in the Union or resulting therefrom; and

(d) WHEREIN all power and authority of the Sovereign Independent India, its constituent parts and organs of government, are derived from the people; and

[10]The word democracy was not used in the Objectives Resolution. The reason for not using the word democracy in the Objectives Resolution is explained in the words of Jawaharlal Nehru… "Now some friends have raised the question: why have you not put in the word 'democratic' here? Well I told them that it is conceivable, of course, that a republic may not be democratic but the whole of our past is witness to this fact that we stand for democratic institutions. Obviously we are aiming at democracy and nothing less than a democracy….the House will notice that in this Resolution, although we have not used the word "democratic" because we thought it is obvious that the word "republic" contains that word and we did not want to use unnecessary words and redundant words, but we have done something much more than using the word. We have given the content of democracy in this Resolution and not only the content of democracy but the content, if I may say so, of economic democracy in this Resolution.

(e) WHEREIN shall be guaranteed and secured to all the people of India justice, social, economic, and political: equality of status, of opportunity, and before the law; freedom of thought, expression, belief, faith, worship, vocation, association and action, subject to law and public morality; and

(f) WHEREIN adequate safeguards shall be provided for minorities, backward and tribal areas, and depressed and other backward classes; and

(g) WHEREBY shall be maintained the integrity of the territory of the Republic and its sovereign rights on land, sea, and air according to justice and the law of civilized nations; and

(h) This ancient land attains its rightful and honoured placed in the world and make its full and willing contribution to the promotion of world peace and the welfare of mankind.

This Resolution was unanimously adopted by the Constituent Assembly on 22 January 1947. It was a momentous Resolution that outlined the defining ideals of the Constitution of Independent India, and provided the framework within which the work of Constitution-making was to proceed. It proclaimed India to be an "Independent Sovereign Republic", guaranteed its citizens justice, equality, and freedom, and assured that "adequate safeguards shall be provided for minorities, backward, and tribal areas, and Depressed and Other Backward Classes". Even the Preamble and its objectives are influenced by the Objectives Resolution.

14. **Mountbatten Plan :** On February 20, 1947, Clement Attlee, the then British Prime Minister, declared that the British would quit India in June 1948. The statement in the British Parliament by Attlee meant that a deadline was already fixed for the transfer of power even if the Indian politicians had not agreed on a Constitution. Secondly, the British would relinquish control either to some form of central government or in some areas, to the existing provincial governments if the Constituent Assembly was not fully representative, i.e., if the Muslim majority provinces did not join the Assembly. In his statement, Attlee had stated that the British paramountcy on the Princely States would lapse with the transfer of power, but these would not be transferred to any successor government in British India. The statement by Attlee had contained clear hints of partition and even Balkanisation of the country into numerous states. To perform this job, George VI, King of the United Kingdom and the Emperor of British India, sent his cousin "Mountbatten" to India as its last Viceroy. Earl Louis Mountbatten, the last British Viceroy and the Governor-General of India, who arrived in India on March 22, 1947, had his task cut out – to liquidate the British empire and quit India as soon as possible. Initially, he was given time until June 1948 – not 1947 – to complete his mission. To achieve this, he worked out a plan after having long discussions with Congress and the Muslim League leaders. As Mountbatten's efforts to keep India united failed and with increasing communal riots in the country, Mountbatten expedited the process of transfer of power. On 3 June 1947, Mountbatten announced a plan offering a key to the political and constitutional deadlock created by the refusal of the Muslim League to join the Constituent Assembly formed to frame the Constitution of India. The main proposals of the Mountbatten Plan are as follows:

(a) British India was to be partitioned into two dominions – India and Pakistan.

(b) The Constitution framed by the Constituent Assembly would not be applicable to the Muslim-majority areas (as these would become Pakistan). The question of a separate Constituent Assembly for the Muslim-majority areas would be decided by these provinces.

(c) As per the plan, the legislative assemblies of Bengal and Punjab met and voted for the partition. Accordingly, it was decided to partition these two provinces along religious lines.

(d) The legislative assembly of Sindh would decide whether to join the Indian Constituent Assembly or not. It decided to go with Pakistan.

(e) A referendum was to be held on NWFP (North-Western Frontier Province) to decide which dominion to join. NWFP decided to join Pakistan while Khan Abdul Gaffar Khan boycotted and rejected the referendum.

(f) The date for the transfer of power was to be August 15, 1947.

(g) To fix the international boundaries between the two countries, the Boundary Commission was established chaired by Sir Cyril Radcliffe. The commission was to demarcate Bengal and Punjab into the two new countries.

(h) The Princely States were given the choice to either remain independent or accede to India or Pakistan. The British suzerainty over these kingdoms was terminated.

(i) The British monarch would no longer use the title 'Emperor of India'.

(j) After the dominions were created, the British Parliament could not enact any law in the territories of the new dominions.

(k) Until the time the new constitutions came into existence, the Governor-General would assent any law passed by the constituent assemblies of the dominions in His Majesty's name. The Governor-General was made a constitutional head.

15. **Indian Independence Act, 1947 :** The Indian Independence Bill was introduced in the British Parliament on July 4, 1947 and the Indian Independence Act was enacted on July, 18, 1947. This Act merely formalised and gave legal effect to the 3rd June Plan of Mountbatten.

Important provisions of the Act are as follows :

(a) The British government will leave India on 15th August, 1947.

(b) India will be divided into two sovereign states of India and Pakistan and both these states will become sovereign on this very day.

(c) The powers previously exercised by the British government in India will be transferred to both these states.

(d) Punjab and Bengal will be divided and its territories will be demarcated by a Boundary Commission to be headed by Mr. Radcliff.

(e) Office of the Secretary of State for India will be abolished.

(f) Provision was made for the Governor-General for each dominion, who was to be appointed by the Queen of England on the advice of the dominion government. He was not to act in his individual judgment or discretion but will act merely as constitutional Head of the State.

(g) Each dominion was to have a sovereign legislature for rule-making purpose. No law made by British Parliament was automatically to apply to India.

(h) A bill passed by the dominions legislature could not be disallowed by His Majesty.

(i) Both the dominions will have their own Constituent Assemblies, which will act as their legislatures as well.

(j) Till such time as the Constitution was framed by the Constituent Assembly in any dominion, it will work as near the Act of 1935 as possible.

(k) Governors of the Provinces were to act as constitutional heads of the provinces.

(l) Reservation of posts for Secretary of State was to discontinue. Those civil service personnel who wanted to resign after transfer of power to both the dominions were to be allowed to do so.

(m) Paramountcy of Britain over Indian states and tribal areas was to come to an end on15th August, 1947. In their case power was not to be transferred to dominions, but it was left to the states to decide whether they would like to join India or Pakistan.

(n) Relations of the British government with India henceforth were to be conducted through Commonwealth Relations Office.

(o) The King of England was to drop the title of "Emperor of India".

(p) The territories of Pakistan were to include Eastern Bengal, Western Pakistan, Sindh, and British Baluchistan. In case the people of NWFP in a referendum decide to join Pakistan that territory will also join Pakistan.

DRAFTING AND ENACTMENT OF THE CONSTITUTION

The idea of an Indian Constituent Assembly was first put forward by M.N. Roy[11] in 1934. However, the idea did not go beyond the stage of an isolated suggestion. It was not taken up by any political organization in the country, nor did it attract much public attention at the time[12]. The demand was taken up by the Congress Party in 1934 as an official demand. It was adopted by the Congress in the famous resolution of the Congress Working Committee on the White Paper of the British Government, passed at Bombay in June, 1934[13]. The Resolution inter-alia: "*The only satisfactory alternative to the White Paper is a Constitution, drawn up by a Constituent Assembly, elected on the basis of adult suffrage or as near it as possible.....*[14]". In 1938, Jawaharlal Nehru, on behalf of the Indian National Congress, proposed that "*the Constitution of free India must be framed, without outside interference, by a Constituent Assembly elected on the basis of adult franchise.*"

---

[11] A pioneer of Communist Movement in India.

[12] Varma, V. P., Modern Indian Political Thought, Lakshmi Narain Agarwal, Agra, 1985, p. 493.

[13] The idea of the Constituent Assembly entered Indian Politics in 1934 as a counterpoise to the Constitutional proposals of the British Government contained in The White Paper of 1933 based on the work of the Three Round Table Conferences held in London.

[14] Sitaramayya, B. Pattabhi, op. cit., p. 964.

The British accepted this in the August Offer of 1940. The Constituent Assembly of India came into existence as per the provisions of Cabinet Mission Plan of May 1946. The Constituent Assembly was formed for the purpose of writing a Constitution for independent India.

In the span of 2 years and 11 months, it completed its task of framing the Indian Constitution. During this period, the Constituent Assembly had 11 sessions and sat for a total of 166 days. On 26 November 1949, the Constituent Assembly adopted the Constitution of India which came into force on 26 January 1950.

The Constituent Assembly formally began its task of framing the Constitution of India on the 13th of December, 1946 with Jawaharlal Nehru moving the Objectives Resolution. After the first session of the Constituent Assembly, a number of committees were formed to look into and report on various aspects of the Constitution.

B. N. Rau, the Constitutional Advisor to the Assembly, on the basis of the reports of the various sub-committees and discussions in the assembly, prepared a Draft Constitution. The Draft Constitution was ready by October 1947. This was to be scrutinized by the Drafting Committee.

Various Stages of the Enactment of the Constitution

First Draft Constitution (27th October 1947 – 21st February 1948) : The Drafting Committee began to scrutinize the Draft Constitution prepared by the Constitutional Advisor, along with other notes, reports, and memoranda on October 27th, 1947. It proceeded to make changes and it finally submitted its Draft Constitution to the President of the Assembly on the 21st February 1948.

Public Circulation of the Draft Constitution (21st February 1948 – 26th October 1948) : The Draft Constitution once submitted to the President of the Constituent Assembly was published and circulated among the public.

Debates on the Draft Constitution (4thNovember 1948 – 17th October 1949) : The Draft Constitution was presented to the Constituent Assembly on November 4th, 1948 by the Chairman of the Drafting Committee[15], B. R. Ambedkar (who was Law Minister as well as Chairman of the Drafting Committee). The Constituent Assembly proceeded to take up, clause by clause, every part of the Draft Constitution for debate.

---

[15] On 29 August, 1947, the Constituent Assembly set up a Drafting Committee under the Chairmanship of Dr. B.R. Ambedkar to prepare a Draft Constitution for India. While deliberating upon the Draft Constitution, the Assembly moved, discussed, and disposed of as many as 2,473 amendments out of a total of 7,635 tabled. The Drafting Committee took less than six months to prepare its draft. Drafting Committee sat for 141 days to complete the draft. Out of 166 sittings of the Constituent Assembly, 114 were spent debating the Draft Constitution(s). The Drafting Committee had seven members:

- Alladi Krishnaswami Ayyar,
- N. Gopalaswami;
- B.R. Ambedkar;
- K.M. Munshi;
- Mohammad Saadulah;
- B.L. Mitter; and
- D.P. Khaitan.

Revision of the Draft Constitution (17th October 1949 – 14th November 1949) : After the debates around the Draft Constitution concluded, the revised Draft Constitution was submitted to the President of the Constituent Assembly on the 3rd November, 1949 and then introduced it in the Assembly on the 14 November 1949.

Second Reading of the Draft (14th November 1949 – 16th November 1949) : The Assembly undertook a second reading of the Draft Constitution (revised). While many amendments were moved, most of them were negated.

Third Reading of Draft Constitution (17th November 1949 – 26th November 1949) : The third reading of the Draft Constitution began with Ambedkar moving a motion "that the Constitution as settled by the assembly be passed".

On the 26th of November, 1949, the third reading came to an end and the Constitution was adopted on the said day. On the day of adoption, the Constitution contained a Preamble, 395 Articles, and 8 Schedules.

The Constitution was then finally signed by the members[16] of the Constituent Assembly on 24th January 1950 and came into effect on the 26th January 1950.

The Constitution of India came into force on 26th January, 1950. On that day, the Assembly ceased to exist, transforming itself into the Provisional Parliament of India until a new Parliament was constituted in 1952.

Enforcement of the Constitution

Though the Constitution came into force on 26th November 1950, some provisions relating to citizenship, elections, and provisional Parliament were given immediate effect and it came into force on 26th November, 1949[17].

The remaining provisions of the Constitution came into on 26th January 1950. The Indian National Congress, on 19 December 1929, passed the historic 'Purna Swaraj' – (Total Independence) Resolution – at its Lahore session. A public declaration was made on 26 January 1930 – a day which the Congress Party urged Indians to celebrate as 'Independence Day'. During the Constitution-making process during 1946–1950, members of the Constituent Assembly chose 26 January 1950 for the Constitution of India to come into effect to honour the date of the public declaration of Purna Swaraj. Therefore, this day is marked as the day for the commencement of the Constitution and is also celebrated as the "Republic Day".

Repeal of Acts

With the commencement of the Constitution, Article 395 of the Constitution repealed the Indian Independence Act, 1947 and the Government of India Act, 1935, together with all enactments amending or supplementing the latter Act. However, the Abolition of Privy Council Jurisdiction Act, 1949 continues.

---

[16]In all, 284 members actually signed the Constitution.

[17]The Articles which came into force on 26th Nov 1949 include Articles 5, 6, 8, 9, 60, 324, 366, 372, 388, 391, 392, and 393

Constituent Assembly Committees

The Constituent Assembly at various points during the Constitution-making process, appointed a number of Committees on different aspects of the Constitution to conduct preliminary research and deliberations within smaller groups. The work of these Committees took the form of reports which were discussed in the Constituent Assembly. The Constitutional Adviser, B.N. Rau compiled reports of various committees to prepare a Draft Constitution which he submitted to the Drafting Committee. Decision-making in the committees was on the basis of a majority vote and members could record their dissents to decisions taken if they wished.

Major Committees

Name of the Committee	Chairman
Drafting Committee	Dr. B.R. Ambedkar
Union Power Committee	Jawaharlal Nehru
Provincial Constitution Committee	Sardar Vallabhbhai Patel
Union Constitution Committee	Jawaharlal Nehru
Rules of procedure Committee	Dr. Rajendra Prasad
States Committee (Committee for Negotiating with States)	Jawaharlal Nehru
Steering Committee	Dr. Rajendra Prasad
Advisory Committee on Fundamental Rights, Minorities and Tribal and Excluded Areas – Sub-committees under the above Committee –	Sardar Vallabhbhai Patel
1. Fundamental Rights Sub-Committee.	J.B. Kripalani
2. Minorities Sub-Committee	H.C. Mukherjee
3. North-East Frontier Tribal Areas and Assam excluded and partially excluded areas Sub-committee	Gopinath Bordoloi
4. Excluded and Partially Excluded Areas (other than those in Assam) Sub-Committee	A.V. Thakkar

Minor Committees

Name of the Committee	Chairman
Finance and Staff Committee	Dr. Rajendra Prasad
Credentials Committee	Alladi Krishnaswami Ayyar
House Committee	B. Pattabhi Sitaramayya
Order of Business Committee	Dr. K.M. Munshi

Ad-hoc Committee on the National Flag	Dr. Rajendra Prasad
Committee on the Functions of the Constituent Assembly	G.V. Mavalankar
Ad-hoc Committee on the Supreme Court	S. Varadachari (Not a member of the Constituent Assembly)
Committee on Chief Commissioners Provinces	B. Pattabhi Sitaramayya
Expert Committee on the Financial Provinces of the Union Constitution	Nalini Ranjan Sarkar (Not a member of the Constituent Assembly)
Linguistic Provinces Commission	S.K. Dar (Not a member of the Constituent Assembly)
Special Committee to Examine the Draft Constitution	Jawaharlal Nehru
Press Gallery Committee	Usha Nath Sen
Ad-hoc Committee on Citizenship	S. Varadachari (Not a member of the Constituent Assembly)

Miscellaneous Functions of the Constituent Assembly

The Constituent Assembly was constituted to draft, enact the Constitution, as well as to act as a provisional Parliament and enact the ordinary laws. However, the Constituent Assembly performed a few important miscellaneous functions. They are as follows –

- It adopted the National flag on July 22, 1947.
- It accepted and approved India's membership of the British Commonwealth in May, 1949.
- It elected Dr. Rajendra Prasad as the first President of India on January 24, 1950.
- It adopted the National anthem on January 24, 1950.
- It adopted the National song on January 24, 1950.

Nature of the Constituent Assembly

1. It is often argued that the Constituent Assembly of India did not represent the masses of India because its representatives were not elected through the Universal Adult Franchise. Rather, they were indirectly elected by the restricted adult franchise confined to the elite sections of society – the educated and taxpayers. According to Granville Austin[18], the reasons for the restricted franchise and indirect election to the Constituent Assembly members were spelled by the Cabinet Mission Plan. These were to avoid the cumbersome and slow progress in the process of Constitution-making. The Cabinet Mission provided for the indirect election to the Constituent Assembly by the elected members of the provincial legislature. The Indian National

[18]Constitutional historian. Growing up in Norwich, Vermont, United States, and having procured a doctorate in Indian history at Oxford University, Austin developed an interest in the Indian Constitution, which by all accounts was a product of a unique experiment in a world still reeling under the effects of the Second World War, decolonisation, and the beginning of the Cold War.

Congress agreed to this proposal of the Cabinet Mission forsaking the claim of adult franchise to hold election to the Constituent Assembly. Despite having been elected through the restricted adult franchise, the Constituent Assembly represented different shades of opinions and religious communities of India.

2. Though there was a majority of the Indian National Congress in the Constituent Assembly, it had an "unwritten and unquestioned belief" that the Indian National Congress should represent social and ideological diversity. There was also its "deliberate policy" that the representatives of various minority communities and viewpoints should be represented in the Constituent Assembly. The Constituent Assembly consisted of members with different ideological orientations, and three religious communities–Sikhs, Muslims, and General (Hindus and all other communities like the Anglo-Indians, Parsis, etc.). In the words of K. Santhanam, "There was hardly any shade of public opinion not represented in the Assembly"[19].

3. Majority of the Constituent Assembly members belonged to the Indian National Congress[20]. It also included more than a dozen non-Indian National Congress members. Some of these were A.K. Ayyar, H.N. Kunjru, N.G. Ayyangar, S.P. Mukherjee[21], and Dr. B.R. Ambedkar[22].

4. On the gender front, the Assembly was male-dominated; only 15 members were women.

5. The Constituent Assembly sought to address concerns of every person, irrespective of their social and cultural orientations. Before incorporating a provision in the Constitution, it held elaborate deliberations. Thus, the members of the Constituent Assembly could overcome the limitations of having been elected by the restricted franchise.

6. The Constituent Assembly sought to accommodate universal values of democracy. The Constituent Assembly adopted several provisions from different constitutions of world and adapted them to the needs of India. In fact, Austin argues that while incorporating different provisions in the Constitution, including those which were borrowed from other countries, the Constituent Assembly adopted "two wholly Indian concepts" of resolving differences among its members, i.e., consensus and accommodation.

Criticism of the Constituent Assembly

Though the Constituent Assembly did a commendable job in the framing of the Constitution, the assembly is criticized for many valid reasons –

---

[19]see Austin, 2012, p.13, fn.48.

[20]Close to 80% of members were elected on a Congress ticket, but there was great ideological diversity within the party. This can be said of the Constituent Assembly as a whole as well. K.T. Shah was a socialist and came from the left, Syama Prasad Mookerjee, President of the Hindu Mahasabha, was from the right, and so was Thakur Das Bhargava and K.M. Munshi. There were liberals too, like Minoo Masani.

[21]Represented the Hindu Mahasabha.

[22]Dr. Ambedkar was initially elected to the Constituent Assembly from Bengal as member of the Scheduled Caste Federation. But he lost this seat due to the partition of Bengal and was re-elected by the Bombay Indian National Congress (as a non-Indian National Congress candidate) at the request of the Indian National Congress High Command.

(a) The biggest criticism faced by the assembly is that it was not a representative body as its members were not elected directly by the people of India on the basis of Universal Adult Franchise. The members were elected indirectly. Hence, it is argued that those who were making the Constitution were not chosen by the people for whom the Constitution was being made. On the same grounds, it is said that the general public was not given a choice but to accept the Constitution. Hence, as the critics put it, the Constitution was 'imposed' upon the people of India.

(b) The assembly is also criticised on the grounds that it was not a sovereign body. The Constituent Assembly was formed by the proposal of the British government. Furthermore, the sessions of the assembly were held after taking the permission of the British government.

(c) Compared to the many other constitutions, including that of Pakistan, the Constitution of India was drafted in the right amount of time. But, when we compare it to the Constitutions such as that of the United States of America, which took only four months, the time consumed by Indians, which is almost three years, seems to be unduly long[23].

State-wise Membership of The Constituent Assembly of India as on December 31, 1947

Provinces – 229		
S. No.	**State**	**No. of Members**
1.	Madras	49
2.	Bombay	21
3.	West Bengal	19
4.	United Provinces	55
5.	East Punjab	12
6.	Bihar	36
7.	C.P. and Berar	17
8.	Assam	8
9.	Orissa	9
10.	Delhi	1
11.	Ajmer-Merwara	1
12.	Coorg	1

[23]Constitution of USA took less than 4 months to complete the task. Whereas, in Canada it took about 2 years and 6 months; Whereas Australia 9 years; Whereas, South Africa 1 year.

Indian States – 70		
S. No.	State	No. of Members
1.	Alwar	1
2.	Baroda	3
3.	Bhopal	1
4.	Bikaner	1
5.	Cochin+	1
6.	Gwalior	4
7.	Indore	1
8.	Jaipur	3
9.	Jodhpur	2
10.	Kolhapur	1
11.	Kotah	1
12.	Mayurbhanj	1
13.	Mysore	7
14.	Patiala	2
15.	Rewa	2
16.	Travancore	6
17.	Udaipur	2
18.	Sikkim and Cooch Behar Group	1
19.	Tripura, Manipur and Khasi States Group	1
20.	U.P. States Group	1
21.	Eastern Rajputana States Group	3
22.	Central India States Group (including Bundelkhand and Malwa)	3
23.	Western India States Group	4
24.	Gujarat States Group	2
25.	Deccan and Madras States Group	2
26.	Punjab States Group I	3
27.	Eastern States Group I	4
28.	Eastern States Group II	3
29.	Residuary States Group	4
	Total	299

Sessions of the Constituent Assembly[24]

First Session:	9-23 December, 1946
Second Session:	20-25 January, 1947
Third Session:	28 April - 2 May, 1947
Fourth Session:	14-31 July, 1947
Fifth Session:	14-30 August, 1947
Sixth Session:	27 January, 1948
Seventh Session:	4 November,1948 - 8 January, 1949
Eighth Session:	16 May - 16 June, 1949
Ninth Session:	30 July - 18 September, 1949
Tenth Session:	6-17 October, 1949
Eleventh Session:	14-26 November, 1949

Women Members of the Constituent Assembly

1. Ammu Swaminathan
2. Annie Mascarene
3. Dakshayani Velayudhan
4. Begum Aizaz Rasul
5. Durgabai Deshmukh
6. Hansa Jivraj Mehta
7. Kamla Chaudhry
8. Leela Roy
9. Malati Choudhury
10. Purnima Banerjee
11. Rajkumari Amrit Kaur
12. Renuka Ray
13. Sarojini Naidu
14. Sucheta Kriplani
15. Vijaya Lakshmi Pandit

Interim Government (1946)

Members	Portfolio
Jawaharlal Nehru	Vice-President of the Council; External Affairs & Commonwealth Relations
Sardar Vallabhbhai Patel	Home, Information & Broadcasting
Dr. Rajendra Prasad	Food & Agriculture
Dr. John Matthai	Industries & Supplies
Jagjivan Ram	Labour
Sardar Baldev Singh	Defence

[24]The Assembly met once again on 24 January, 1950, when the members appended their signatures to the Constitution of India

C.H. Bhabha	Works, Mines & Power
Liaquat Ali Khan	Finance
Abdur Rab Nishtar	Posts & Air
Asaf Ali	Railways & Transport
C. Rajagopalachari	Education & Arts
I.I. Chundrigar	Commerce
Ghazanfar Ali Khan	Health
Jogendra Nath Mandal	Law

First Government after independence (1947)

Members	Portfolio
Jawaharlal Nehru	Prime Minister, External Affairs & Commonwealth Relations; Scientific Research
Sardar Vallabhbhai Patel	Home, Information & Broadcasting; States
Dr. Rajendra Prasad	Food & Agriculture
Maulana Abdul Kalam Azad	Education
Dr. John Matthai	Railways & Transport
R.K. Shanmukham Chetty	Finance
Dr. B.R. Ambedkar	Law
Jagjivan Ram	Labour
Sardar Baldev Sing	Defence
Raj Kumar Amrit Kaur	Health
C.H. Bhabha	Commerce
Rafi Ahmed Kidwai	Communication
Dr. Shyama Prasad Mukherjee	Industries & Supplies
V.N. Gadgil	Works, Mines & Power

QUESTIONS

1. The distribution of powers between the Centre and the States in the Indian Constitution is based on the scheme provided in the **(UPSC CSE 2012)**

   (a) Morley-Minto Reforms, 1909
   (b) Montagu-Chelmsford Act, 1919
   (c) Government of India Act, 1935
   (d) Indian Independence Act, 1947

   Ans: (a)

2. Who among the following was the chairperson of the Provincial Constitution Committee of the Constituent Assembly?

   (a) Jawaharlal Nehru
   (b) Sardar Vallabhbhai Patel
   (c) Dr. B.R. Ambedkar
   (d) J.B. Kriplani

   Ans: (b)

3. Who among the following was the Constitutional Advisor to the Constituent Assembly?

   (a) Sachidanand Sinha
   (b) B.N. Rau
   (c) H.N. Kunzuru
   (d) Dr. B.R. Ambedkar

   Ans: (b)

4. With respect to the Constituent Assembly, which among the following observations is/are correct?

   i. The members of Constituent Assembly were elected directly by the people
   ii. The basis of seats allocation was population
   iii. Composition of the Constituent Assembly was roughly in line with the suggestions of the Cabinet Mission Plan.

   Select the correct option from the codes given below:

   (a) Only i and ii are correct
   (b) Only ii and iii are correct
   (c) Only i and iii are correct
   (d) i, ii, and iii are correct

   Ans: (b)

5. The philosophy underlying the Indian Constitution was embodied quite early in the Objectives Resolution, which was moved in the first session of the Constituent Assembly (on 13 December 1946) by:

   (a) Pandit Jawaharlal Nehru
   (b) Sardar Vallabhbhai Patel
   (c) Chakravarti Rajagopalachari
   (d) Dr. Bhimrao Ramji Ambedkar

   Ans: (a)

CHAPTER 4

THE INDIAN CONSTITUTION AND WHAT IT EMBODIES

SALIENT FEATURES OF THE INDIAN CONSTITUTION

Indian Constitution: A Modern Constitution

The Indian Constitution was drafted and enacted in the mid-twentieth century. This gave an advantage to our constitutional makers to go through the various constitutions and forms of governments across the world and adopt a system which is suitable to the political, social, and economic conditions in India. However, it is wrong to assume that the Indian Constitution is a mere copywork of other Constitutions. Our Constitution makers while adopting some of the principles and systems from other countries evolved various unique systems, patterns, and principles which are suitable to India. By doing so, the Indian Constitution has turned out to be a very interesting and unique document.

Features Borrowed From Other Constitutions

Country/Source	Features Borrowed
United States of America	Fundamental Rights, Independence of judiciary, Judicial review, Impeachment of the President, Removal of supreme court and high court judges, Post of vice-president
British Constitutional Law[1]	The machinery of government in our Constitution, Parliamentary procedures, Parliamentary form of government, The Civil Services of the Union and the States, Writs, Appointment of the Supreme Court and the High Court Judges, The appointment of the subordinate judiciary
Australian Constitution	Centre-State Financial Relationship, Promoting the concept of freedom of trade and commerce in the country, Concurrent List, Joint Sitting
Irish Constitution	Shaping of Directive Principles of State Policy
Government of India Act, 1935	Proclamation of Emergency, Federal scheme, The distribution of legislative power, Office of Governor, Judiciary, Public Service Commissions, Administrative details, Directive Principles of State Policy

[1] In England, the independence of Supreme Court and the High Court Judges is secured by prescribing that they shall hold office till age and that they can be removed from office only by a process analogous to impeachment. In this respect, the position of the Judges of the Superior Courts in England and the Judges of the Supreme Court and of other Courts which may be established under Art 3, s.1 of the U.S. Constitution, is the same. However, in England and in India, Judges are not appointed by election as they are in a number of States in the U.S.

Canadian Constitution	Unitary bias, Centre's jurisdiction over residuary subjects, Advisory jurisdiction of Supreme Court, Appointment of Governor by the Centre
German Reich	Emergency provisions
Soviet Russia	Fundamental duties and the Ideal of Justice (Social, economic, and political)
French Constitution	Ideals of liberty, equality, and fraternity in the Preamble
Japanese Constitution	Procedure established by law
South African Constitution	Procedure for amendment of the Constitution and election of members of Rajya Sabha

However, among all the other sources, the Constitution of India is heavily influenced by the Government of India Act, 1935.

Lengthiest Written Constitution

Constitutions can be either a written Constitution (For example: American Constitution) or an unwritten Constitution (For example: British Constitution). Indian Constitution is not only a written Constitution, it is also the lengthiest and the most detailed document of all the written constitutions of the world.

The original Constitution (1949) consisted of 395 Articles divided under 22 Parts and 8 Schedules. Today, after various amendments, it has 448 Articles, divided under 25 Parts and 12 Schedules.

Various factors contributed for its gigantic size.

Factors which contributed for the large size of the Constitution:

(a) Indian Constitution not only deals with the organization and structure of the Central Government but also of the State Government.

(b) Many unwritten conventions of the British Constitution have been reduced to writing and was adopted in the Indian Constitution. For example: *The principle or the convention of "Collective responsibility" of the Ministers was adopted under Article 75.*

(c) The Constitution not only contains the fundamental principles of governance but also minute administrative details such as the provisions regarding Citizenship, Election, official language, etc. In other Constitutions, these aspects were left to the ordinary legislation. However, these provisions are included in the Indian Constitution for smooth and efficient working of the government.

(d) Government of India Act, 1935 preceded the Indian Constitution. The said Act was a bulky document and it even contained minute administrative details. Therefore, the Indian Constitution which is heavily influenced by the Government of India Act, 1935 is also the lengthiest Constitution in the world.

(e) Constitution has also provided detailed provisions to protect the interests of the minority groups and vulnerable sections of the society. For example, there are detailed provisions on Fundamental Rights, safeguards to minorities, Scheduled Tribes, Scheduled Castes and Backward Classes[2].

[2] M.P. Jain, *Indian Constitutional Law*, p. 11

INDIAN CONSTITUTION: WHAT IT ENCOMPASSES

Parliamentary Form Of Government

The Constitution of India establishes a parliamentary form of government both at the Centre and the States. We borrowed this system from the United Kingdom. In the Parliamentary form of Government, the real executive power is vested in the Council of Ministers headed by the Prime Minister. Further, the Council of Ministers are collectively responsible to the Lower House, i.e., Lok Sabha, whereas the President is the nominal executive Head and the constitutional Head of the State.

Rule Of Law

The doctrine of Rule of Law is ascribed to Dicey whose writing in 1885 on the British Constitution included the following three distinct ideas in Rule of Law[3]:

(i) *Absence of arbitrary power:* No man is above law. No man is punishable except for a distinct breach of law established. Dicey asserted that wherever there is discretion, there is room for arbitrariness.

(ii) *Equality before law:* Every man, whatever his rank or condition, is subject to the ordinary law and jurisdiction of the ordinary courts. No man is above law.

(iii) *Upholding individual liberties:* Individual liberty means that people of the land have the freedom to make their own choices and do what they want.

Rule of law connotes some higher kind of law which is reasonable, just, and non-discriminatory. Rule of Law today envisages not arbitrary power but controlled power. The Indian Constitution by and large seeks to promote Rule of Law through many of its provisions[4]. Following are a few illustrations:

(a) Parliament and State Legislatures are democratically elected on the basis of adult suffrage.

(b) Constitution contains provisions regarding independence of judiciary and judicial review.

(c) Equality before law is guaranteed under Article 14.

Constitutional Supremacy

The dominant characteristic feature of the British Constitution is the doctrine of 'sovereignty' or 'supremacy' of Parliament. This means that Parliament has the 'right to make or unmake any law', whatever it deems fit. Britain has no doctrine of unconstitutionality of parliamentary legislation—which means a law enacted by the Parliament cannot be questioned or challenged in a court on any grounds. In USA, the courts enjoy judicial supremacy. The concept of judicial supremacy evolved in USA near the end of the 19th century. The concept of judicial supremacy gained traction in USA because of the wider 'Judicial Review' (Due to the process of law as explained in the 'Fundamental Rights' chapter) enjoyed by the courts in USA.

On the other hand, in India, the Constitution is the supreme law of the land; and all state organs including Parliament, Judiciary, States etc. are bound by it. They must act within the limits laid down by the Constitution. This is called as Doctrine of Constitutional Supremacy. The Supreme Court in *Indira Nehru Gandhi Vs. Raj Narain*[5], examined and explained at some length the meaning of the Supremacy of the Constitution. The court held that "Neither of the three constitutionally separate organs of State (i.e., the

---

[3]*Constitutionalism in America*, 13.

[4]M.P. Jain, *Indian Constitutional Law*, P. 8

[5](1976) 2 SCR P 347

Executive, the Legislature, and the Judiciary) can according to the basic scheme of our Constitution today, leap outside the boundaries of its own constitutionally assigned sphere or orbit of authority into that of the other. This is the logical and natural meaning of the principle of Supremacy of the Constitution".

The principle of Constitutional Supremacy is declared as one of the cardinal features, or a part of the 'basic structure' of the Constitution in *Kesavananda Bharati* case[6].

Secular State

The Constitution of India declares India as Secular. There is no universally accepted definition for the word 'Secular'. However, the word 'Secular' implies that there is no official religion in India and there is no state-recognised religion in India. A Secular state treats all religions and religious sects equally. The word 'Secular' has been inserted in the Preamble by the 42nd Constitutional Amendment Act, 1976. It does not mean that India was a theocratic state (For example: Pakistan) before the amendment. Since the inception of the Constitution, there are several fundamental rights which guarantee freedom of worship and religion as well as outlaw discrimination on the grounds of religion. Therefore, the Constitution since its enactment implicitly prohibited the establishment of a theocratic State.

As regards the nature of Indian secularism, it is neither anti-religion like some of the socialist or communist constitutions, nor does it create a wall of separation between the State and religion as in the US. It is based on equal respect for all religions. It embodies the age-old Indian concept of *sarva-dharma-sambhava*[7].

Socialist State

The word 'socialist' was not there in the original Constitution. It was added to the Preamble by the 42nd Constitutional Amendment, 1976. Moreover, the term 'socialist' has not been defined in the Constitution. However, according to the Supreme Court, "the principal aim of socialism is to eliminate inequality of income and status and standards of life and to provide a decent standard of life to the working people[8]".

The Socialism doctrine inducted into our Constitution does not insist on state ownership as a matter of policy. In India, there has always been an emphasis on mixed economy, i.e., along with a public sector, the private sector also has a role to play.

Responsible Government

In a responsible form of government, the executive is responsible to an elected legislature. We borrowed this system from United Kingdom whereas the American system is based on the doctrine of separation of powers between the executive and the legislature. In doctrine of separation of powers, the three branches of government (executive, legislature, and judiciary) are kept separate. Each branch has separate powers, and generally each branch is not allowed to exercise the powers of the other. In India, the responsible form of government is based on co-ordination and co-operation of the executive and the legislature.

---

[6](1976) 2 SCR P 347

[7]V.N. Shukla, *Constitution of India*, A.24

[8]*DS Nakra Vs. UOI, AIR 1983 SC 130.*

Welfare State

"The Welfare State is a compromise between the two extremes of Communism on the one hand, and unbridled Individualism on the other, and as such, in spite of all its imperfections, it sets a pattern for any humane and progressive society[9]".

A welfare state is a concept of government in which the state plays a key role in the protection and promotion of the economic and social well-being of its citizens. Our Constitution explicitly declares that India will be organised as a social welfare state, i.e., a state which renders social services to the people and promotes their general welfare. The concept of a Social Welfare state is reflected in the objectives contained in the Preamble and in the Directive Principles of State Policy.

Fundamental Rights

The Indian Constitution guarantees certain basic human rights and freedoms to its people. These are known as Fundamental Rights. These Fundamental Rights are adopted in a liberal spirit and it seeks to draw a balance between individual freedom and social control. These Rights can be enforced by the Courts against the Legislative and Executive organs of the State. In other words, no law or executive action infringing a Fundamental Right can be regarded valid. However, no Fundamental Right is absolute. Each and every Fundamental Right is subjected to reasonable restrictions.

Directive Principles Of State Policy

These principles are a kind of instructions issued to future legislatures and executives for their guidance. These principles are fundamental in governance. However, these rights are non-justiciable rights, in other words, the courts cannot enforce these rights. Merely because the directive principles are non-justiciable, it does not mean that they are in any way subservient or inferior to the Fundamental Rights. The authorities of the State may not have to answer for the breach of Directive Principles of State Policy in a court of law, but the State certainly has to answer to the electorate at election time. Thus, the idea of a welfare state envisaged in our Constitution can only be achieved if the States endeavour to implement them with a high sense of moral duty.

Fundamental Duties

Fundamental Duties were incorporated into our Constitution by way of the 42nd Constitutional Amendment Act, 1976. The Fundamental Duties serve as a constant reminder to every citizen of their basic duties. It also requires the citizens to observe certain basic norms of democratic conduct and democratic behaviour.

Universal Adult Suffrage

In India, elections to the Lok Sabha and the State Legislative Assemblies is based on adult suffrage. In other words, every citizen of India, who has reached the age of 18 years[10] or over, has a right to vote without any discrimination. It was a very bold step taken by our Constitution-makers to adopt adult suffrage in a country of millions of illiterates. In nearly all Western democracies, suffrage rights broadened only over an extended period of time[11]. An autonomous Election Commission is also constituted under the Constitution of India to ensure free, fair, and impartial elections in the Country.

---

[9]See D.L. Hobman, *The Welfare State (London, 1953), p. 10*

[10]The voting age was reduced to 18 years from 21 years in 1989 by the 61st Constitutional Amendment Act, 1988.

[11]In the United States, the Civil War ended slavery in 1865, yet it took a century for full voting rights to extend to African Americans. In Switzerland, women received the vote only in 1971.

A Federation With Strong Centralising Tendency

Indian Constitution establishes dual polity, i.e., a two-tier governmental system, with the Central Government at one level and the State Government at the other. However, the Indian federal scheme does not strictly follow the conventional or the orthodox federal pattern. In fact, it has incorporated the advantages of a federal structure and avoided the weaknesses of rigidity and legalism.

Instead of the word 'federation', the word 'Union' was deliberately selected by the Drafting Committees of the Constituent Assembly to indicate two things, i.e.,

(a) That the Indian Union is not the result of an agreement by the States

(b) That the component states have no freedom to secede from it

Though the country and the people may be divided into different States for convenience of administration, the country is one integral whole; its people a single people living under a single imperium derived from a single source[12].

The most unique feature of the Indian Constitution is that being a federal Constitution, it acquires a unitary character during the time of emergency. Thus, during the proclamation of emergency, all powers are centralised in the Union Government and the Constitution acquires a unitary character. This combination of federal and unitary systems is a unique feature of the Indian Constitution.

Single Citizenship

Though the Constitution of India is federal and provides for dual polity, i.e., Centre and States, it provides for a single citizenship for the whole of India whereas, the American Constitution provides for dual citizenship, i.e., the Citizen of America and a State Citizenship. Every Indian is the Citizen of India and enjoys the same rights of citizenship no matter in what state he resides, excepting in a few cases like Jammu and Kashmir, tribal areas, etc.

Unified And Independent Judiciary

An independent and impartial judiciary is considered to be the first condition of liberty. It is also the custodian of the rights of the citizens. Moreover, in a federal Constitution, judiciary also determines the limits of the powers of the Centre and the States. Therefore, the Constitution of India accords a dignified and crucial position to the judiciary. Although the Indian and the American Constitutions are both federal in nature, the Indian judicial system differs from that of the USA, inter alia, in one very significant respect. While the USA has a dual system of courts (a federal judiciary with the Supreme Court at the top along with a separate and parallel judicial system in each State), India has a unified and not a dual system of courts. The Supreme Court, the High Courts, and the Lower Courts constitute a single, unified, judiciary having jurisdiction over all cases arising under any law, whether enacted by Parliament or a State Legislature[13].

Unique Blend Of Rigidity And Flexibility

Like any other written Constitution, the Constitution of India also provides for its amendment. Generally, a written federal constitution is said to be rigid. But, unlike many federal constitutions, the amendment procedure in Indian Constitution is much less rigid and is sufficiently flexible.

---

[12] *Hinsa Virodhak Sangh Vs. Mirzapur Moti Juresh Jamat*, (2008) 5 SCC 33.

[13] M.P. Jain, *Indian Constitutional Law*, p. 19.

The main provision with regard to amendment is Article 368. Under Article 368, the Constitution can be amended in two ways:

(a) Certain provisions of the Constitution can be amended by Special Majority. In other words, certain provisions can be amended only if the Amendment Bill is passed by both the Houses of Parliament by a majority of the total membership of the House (i.e., more than 50 per cent) as well as two-thirds of those who participated in the voting and assented by the President.

(b) Certain other provisions can be amended by a Special majority of the Parliament and approval or ratification of at least one-half of the total number of States.

Moreover, there are some provisions which can be amended in the same way as an ordinary legislation, i.e., by a simple majority. However, these amendments are not considered to be a constitutional amendment under Article 368.

Apart from these provisions for formal amendments of the Constitution, the Constitution also gets amended through constitutional practices, conventions, and by judicial interpretation[14].

Minorities And Backward Classes

The Indian society is a heterogeneous society with different religions, languages, cultures, etc. There are sections of people who are socially, economically, and culturally weaker than other sections of the society. Moreover, mutual suspicion and distrust exists between various religious and linguistic groups. In order to promote a sense of security among the Minorities and to improve the conditions of the depressed and Backward Classes, the Constitution provides a liberal scheme of safeguards to Minorities, Backward Classes, and Scheduled Castes & Scheduled Tribes. Thus, provisions have been made to reserve the seats in the Legislature, reservations in services, to promote welfare of the depressed and Backward Classes, and to protect the language and culture of the minorities. The Constitution also sets up effective institutional machinery to oversee that these safeguards are properly effectuated by the various governments in the country.

Emergency Provisions

The Federal form of government that exists during normal times of peace, turns into a unitary form of government during an emergency situation. This is one of the notable features of the Indian Constitution (the normal peace-time federal government adapting to an emergency situation). During an emergency, the centre will enjoy the overriding powers with respect to administration and legislation throughout the country (i.e., Federal form of government turning into unitary with declaration of emergency). Proclamation of an emergency is a very serious issue as it disturbs the normal fabric of the government and adversely affects the rights of the people. Therefore, the proclamation can be issued only in exceptional circumstances.

Three types of emergencies provided by the Constitution

(a) Emergency arising from a threat to the security of India (National Emergency)

(b) Breakdown of constitutional machinery in a State (President's Rule)

(c) Financial Emergency

---

[14]Say for example, through judicial interpretation the Supreme Court has held that the basic structure or framework of the Constitution cannot be changed by an amendment of the Constitution.

Three-Tier Government

At the time of commencement of the Constitution, India had dual polity. The Constitution contained provisions with respect to the Centre and States. Later on, the government realised the quintessence of the idea of democratic decentralization and introduced the 73rd and 74th Constitutional Amendment Acts, 1992. The 73rd Constitutional Amendment introduced Panchayat Raj System and the 74th Constitutional Amendment introduced Municipalities into the Constitution.

CRITICISM OF THE INDIAN CONSTITUTION

1. **Un-Indian & copied Constitution :** A criticism alleges that the Indian Constitution is entirely an alien document, borrowed Article by Article from Western Constitutions and sits uneasily with the cultural ethos of the Indian people. This criticism is often voiced by many. It is also criticized that the Indian Constitution is nothing but a "patchwork" or a "bag of borrowings" from various Constitutions across the world. It is true that the Indian Constitution is modern and partly Western, but it was never a blind borrowing. It was innovative borrowing. This does not make the Constitution or its provisions entirely alien.

   In the words of Dr. B.R. Ambedkar, the Chairman of the Drafting Committee – "*One likes to ask whether there can be anything new in a Constitution framed at this hour in the history of the world. More than hundred years have rolled over when the first written Constitution was drafted. It has been followed by many countries reducing their Constitutions to writing. What the scope of a Constitution should be has long been settled. Similarly, what are the fundamentals of a Constitution are recognized all over the world. Given these facts, all Constitutions in their main provisions must look similar. The only new things, if there can be any, in a Constitution framed so late in the day are the variations made to remove the faults and to accommodate it to the needs of the country. The charge of producing a blind copy of the Constitutions of other countries is based, I am sure, on an inadequate study of the Constitution*"[15].

2. **Copied version of Government of India Act, 1935 :** Another criticism against the Constitution is that it is a copied version of the Government of India Act, 1935. Many provisions of the Act have been borrowed into our Constitution. Hence, the Indian Constitution is sometimes labelled as "Carbon Copy of the 1935 Act". For instance, Mr. Ivor Jennings, a British Constitutionalist, opined that "the Constitution derives directly from the Government of India Act of 1935 from which, in fact, many of its provisions are copied almost textually". However, Dr. B.R. Ambedkar addressed the said criticism in the following way – "*As to the accusation that the Draft Constitution has reproduced a good part of the provisions of the Government of India Act, 1935, I make no apologies. There is nothing to be ashamed of in borrowing. It involves no plagiarism. Nobody holds any patent rights in the fundamental ideas of a Constitution. What I am sorry about is that the provisions taken from the Government of India Act, 1935, relate mostly to the details of the administration*[16].

[15]Constituent Assembly Debates, Volume VII, P. 35-38.
[16]Ibid.

3. **Paradise of Lawyers :** The Constituent Assembly of India that framed the country's Constitution significantly comprised politicians who were also qualified lawyers. Its leading figures, Dr Rajendra Prasad, Jawaharlal Nehru, Sardar Patel, and Dr B.R. Ambedkar, who became India's first President, Prime Minister, Home Minister, and Law Minister, respectively, were all lawyers. They framed the Constitution in the company of other legal stalwarts, such as K.M. Munshi and Alladi Krishnaswamy Iyer. So dominant was the presence of lawyers in the Constituent Assembly that British advocate and academic Mr. Ivor Jennings dubbed the group a "lawyer's paradise". The critics said that the Indian Constitution is too legalistic and very complicated. It's too complex for an ordinary citizen to comprehend the language and the phraseology in the Constitution. In this context, H.K. Maheswari, a member of the Constituent Assembly, observed: "*The draft tends to make people more litigious, more inclined to go to law courts, less truthful and less likely to follow the methods of truth and non-violence. If I may say so, the draft is a lawyer's paradise. It opens vast avenues of litigation and will give our able and ingenious lawyers plenty of work to do*"[17].

4. **Elephantine Size of the Constitution :** Constitution of India is one of the lengthiest Constitutions in the world. Many constitutional experts criticised that the Constitution is too bulky and contains unnecessary, elaborate, or detailed provisions. Ivor Jennings criticized that the Indian Constitution is too long and complicated and also observed that the provisions borrowed were not always well-selected[18].

5. **Un-Gandhian :** The critics have further criticized that – "the spirit of our Constitution was that it has the imprint of the struggle for independence. But that spirit was evasive rendering the Constitution complex, un-Gandhian, and a borrowed one. Our Constitution was amalgamation of the then existing American and British Constitutions". The critics feel that Indian Constitution is un-Gandhian because it does not contain the philosophy and ideals of Mahatma Gandhi who was not only a pivotal figure in the Indian Independence movement but also revered as the "Father of the Nation".

---

[17]Constituent Assembly Debates, Volume VII, P. 293.

[18]Ivor Jennings, *Some Characteristics of the Indian Constitution*, Oxford University Press, Madras, 1953, P. 9-16.

QUESTIONS

Subjective Questions

1. What are the salient features of the Indian Constitution? Elaborate.
2. "It is wrong to suppose that the Indian Constitution is just a carbon copy of other Constitutions and contains nothing new and original". Comment.
3. India's Constitution is a lengthy and elaborate document. Explain the reasons contributing to its prolixity.
4. "India will be organised as a social welfare state, i.e., a state which renders social services to the people and promotes their general welfare". Critically analyse this statement.
5. Indian system is based on the principle of 'Responsible Government', whereas, American system is based on the doctrine of 'Separation of Powers'. Explain and enumerate the differences between 'Responsible form of Government' and the doctrine of 'Separation of Powers'.

Objective Questions

1. Consider the following statements:

   1. The Constitution borrowed provisions from Government of India Act, 1935 and British Constitution only.
   2. Independence of Judiciary is borrowed from the British Constitution.

   Which of the above statements is/are true?

   (a) 1 Only (b) 2 Only

   (c) 1 and 2 Only (d) None of the above

   Ans: (d)

2. Which of the following exercised the most profound influence in framing the Indian Constitution?

   (a) British Constitution (b) U.S. Constitution

   (c) Irish Constitution (d) The Government of India Act, 1935

   Ans: (d)

3. Which of the following are correctly matched?

   1. South African Constitution – Procedure for Amendment
   2. Japanese Constitution – Due process of law
   3. British Constitution – Parliamentary form of Government

   Codes:

   (a) 1 and 2 Only (b) 1 and 3 Only

   (c) 3 Only (d) All of the above

   Ans: (b)

4. The 'Instrument of Instructions' contained in the Government of India Act, 1935 has been incorporated in the Constitution of India in the year 1950 as **(CDS 2012)**

   (a) Fundamental Rights

   (b) Directive Principles of State Policy

   (c) Extent of Executive Power of State

   (d) Conduct of business of the Government of India

   Ans: (b)

5. The Presidential Government operates on the principle of **(SSC Grad 2004)**

   (a) Division of powers between the Centre and States

   (b) Centralization of powers

   (c) Balance of powers

   (d) Separation of powers

   Ans: (d)

6. The concept of Social Welfare state is reflected in the objectives contained in

   (a) Fundamental Rights (b) Preamble

   (c) Directive Principles of State Policy (d) Both (b) and (c)

   Ans: (d)

6. **Assertion (A):** The Constitution of India is bulky.

   Reason (R): The Constitution is common for both the centre and the states and seeks to protect the interests of the diverse population of the country.

   Codes:

   (a) Both A and R are true and R is the correct explanation of A

   (b) Both A and R are true, but R is not the correct explanation of A

   (c) A is true, but R is false

   (d) A is false, but R is true

   Ans: (a)

7. "Appointment of Judges" in the Indian Constitution is similar to

   (a) USA (b) UK

   (c) France (d) South Africa

   Ans: (b)

8. Which of the following is considered as 'Basic Structure of the Constitution'?

   (a) Parliamentary Sovereignty (b) Judicial Supremacy

   (c) Constitutional Supremacy (d) Socialism

   Ans: (c)

9. Match List I to List II and select the correct answer from the codes given below the lists.

List I (Forms of Government)	List II (Principles or Doctrines)
A. Presidential System	1. Separation of Powers
B. Parliamentary System	2. Co-operation and co-ordination between Executive and Legislature
C. Federal System	3. Division of Powers
D. Unitary System	4. Concentration of Power

Codes

	A	B	C	D
(a)	1	2	3	4
(b)	2	1	3	4
(c)	2	1	4	3
(d)	1	2	4	3

Ans: (a)

CHAPTER 5

PREAMBLE OF THE CONSTITUTION

PREAMBLE: AN OVERVIEW

Preamble to an Act or a Statute is a sort of introduction to the statute and sets out the main objectives which the legislation is intended to achieve. Constitutions all over the world generally have a Preamble. However, the USA Constitution was the first to begin with a Preamble. Unlike the Constitutions of Australia, Canada, or the USA, the Constitution of India has an elaborate Preamble.

History Of The Preamble

The Preamble to the Indian Constitution is based on the 'Objectives Resolution' of Jawaharlal Nehru. Jawaharlal Nehru introduced an 'Objectives Resolution' on December 13, 1946, and it was adopted by the Constituent Assembly on 22nd January 1947. The Drafting Committee of the Assembly in formulating the Preamble in the light of the 'Objectives Resolution' felt that the Preamble should be restricted to defining the essential features of the new state and its basic socio-political objectives and that the other matters dealt with in the Resolution could be more appropriately provided for in the substantive parts of the Constitution.

The Preamble represents the values that are incorporated in the Constitution. The fact that it was adopted by the Constituent Assembly after the Draft Constitution had been approved supports that proposition. This was done with a view to ensure conformity of the Preamble with the provisions of the Constitution and express its philosophy and goals.

Scope Of The Preamble

The Preamble of the Constitution sets out the aims and aspirations of the people of India and these have been translated into the various provisions of the Constitution. The purpose of the Preamble is to clarify who has made the Constitution, what is its source, what is the ultimate sanction behind it; what is the nature of the polity which is sought to be established by the Constitution, and what are its goals and objectives. The Preamble of the Indian Constitution does not grant any power but it gives a direction and purpose to the Constitution. It outlines the objectives of the whole Constitution. Therefore, the Preamble is also regarded as 'a key to open the mind of the makers' of the Constitution which may show the general purposes for which they made several provisions in the Constitution.

The Preamble declares:

"WE, THE PEOPLE OF INDIA, having solemnly resolved to constitute India into a [SOVEREIGN SOCIALIST SECULAR DEMOCRATIC REPUBLIC] and to secure to all its citizens:

JUSTICE, social, economic and political;

LIBERTY of thought, expression, belief, faith and worship;

EQUALITY of status and of opportunity;

and to promote among them all

FRATERNITY assuring the dignity of the individual and the [unity and integrity of the Nation];

IN OUR CONSTITUENT ASSEMBLY this twenty-sixth day of November, 1949, do HEREBY, ADOPT, ENACT AND GIVE TO OURSELVES THIS CONSTITUTION".

Role Of The Preamble

(a) It indicates the source of the Constitution, viz. the People of India. Thus, the source of the Constitution are the people themselves from whom the Constitution derives its ultimate sanction.

(b) It declares the basic type of government and polity which is sought to be established in the country. As regards the nature of the Indian polity, the Preamble to the Constitution declares India to be a 'Sovereign Socialist Secular Democratic Republic'. The words 'Socialist' and 'Secular' were added in the Preamble by the Constitution (42nd Amendment) Act, 1976.

i. India is a '**Republic**' because the head of the State is elected and is not a hereditary monarch, but an elected functionary.

ii. India is '**Democratic**' because the Constitution has established a form of Government which gets it authority from the will of the people, through their participation in the formation of the government at regular intervals, on the principle of Universal Adult Franchise.

iii. India is '**Sovereign**' because India is not subjected to any external authority and it has the power to legislate on any subject in conformity with constitutional limitations.

iv. The addition of the word '**Socialist**' indicates the aim of the Constitution to eliminate inequality in income, status, and standard of living.

v. The word '**Secular**' was not present originally in the Preamble. However, the philosophy of 'Secularism' was not new to the Constitution. What was implicit in the Constitution until then became explicit. The word 'Secular' indicates that there is no official religion in India. The State is urged to treat all religions and religious sects equally.

(c) It declares the great rights and freedoms which the people of India intended to secure to all its citizens. The Constitution makers sought to secure to citizens of India the following objectives:

i. *Justice* – Social, Economic, and Political; The Preamble of the Constitution of India professes to secure to all its citizens political, economic, and social justice. Social justice means the abolition of all sorts of inequities which may result from the inequalities of wealth, opportunity, status, race, religion, caste, title, and the like. To achieve this ideal of social justice, the Constitution lays down the Directives for the state in Part IV of the Constitution.

ii. *Liberty* – of thought, expression, belief, faith; and worship; The Preamble of the Constitution of India professes to secure the liberty of belief, thought, expression, faith, and worship which are essential to the development of the individuals and the nation. Liberty or freedom signifies the absence of external impediments of motion. It implies the absence of restraint. Liberty is the power of doing what is allowed by law.

iii. *Equality* – of status and opportunity; Rights carry no meaning if they cannot be enjoyed equally by all members of the community. One of the main tasks of the Constitution makers was to ensure equality of status and opportunity for all and to provide the basis for ultimately establishing an egalitarian society. They proceeded to achieve these objectives by incorporating a set of fundamental principles into the Constitution.

iv. *Fraternity* – to secure the dignity of the individual and the unity and integrity of the Nation; In the words of the Supreme Court—fraternity means a sense of common brotherhood of all Indians. In a country like ours with so many disruptive forces of regionalism, communalism, and linguism, it is necessary to emphasize and re-emphasize that the unity and integrity of India can be preserved only by a spirit of brotherhood. India has one citizenship and every citizen should feel that he is an Indian first, irrespective of other bases.

"The principles of liberty, equality and fraternity are not to be treated as separate items in a trinity. They form a union of trinity in the sense that to divorce one from the other is to defeat the very purpose of democracy".[1]

(d) The Preamble is of considerable legal significance in so far as it embodies an enacting clause. It contains the enacting clause which brings the Constitution into force. The Preamble declares that the people of India adopted, enacted, and gave to themselves the Constitution on 26th November, 1949, but the date of commencement of the Constitution was fixed as 26 January, 1950.

PERTINENT QUESTIONS REGARDING THE PREAMBLE

Is The Preamble A Part Of The Constitution?

The question whether the Preamble is a part of the Constitution or not was dealt with in two leading cases on the subject:

(i) Berubari Union (1), re[2]:

This case was the Presidential Reference "under Article 143(1) of the Constitution of India on the implementation of the Indo-Pakistan Agreement Relating to Berubari Union and Exchange of Enclaves. The Court ruled that the Preamble no doubt is 'a key to open the mind of the makers' which may show the general purposes for which they made the several provisions in the Constitution but nevertheless, the "Preamble is not a part of the Constitution".

---

[1]Dr. Ambedkar observed in his closing speech in the Constituent Assembly on 25 November 1949.

[2]AIR 1960 SC 845: (1960) 3 SCR 250.

(ii) Kesavananda Bharati Vs. State of Kerala[3]

In this case the court after considering the constituent history of the Preamble held that "The Preamble of the Constitution was part of the Constitution and the observations to the contrary in *Berubari Union Case* were not correct". Not only is the Preamble a part of the Constitution, it is also part of its basic structure. However, the court further held that the Preamble is neither a source of power nor a source of limitations or prohibitions. Therefore, the Preamble cannot be enforced in courts of law.

The recognition of the Preamble as an integral part of the Constitution makes the Preamble a valuable aid in the construction of the provisions of the Constitution.

Can The Preamble Be Amended Under Article 368?

This question was raised for the first time before the Supreme Court in the historic case of *Kesavananda Bharati Vs. State of Kerala*[4]. It was held that the Preamble is a part of the Constitution, therefore, it can be amended but subject to the condition that the 'Basic Structure' in the Preamble cannot be amended. The Court further said that, "the edifice of our Constitution is based upon the basic elements mentioned in the Preamble. If any of these elements are removed the structure will not survive and it will not be the same Constitution or it cannot maintain its identity". The Preamble to the Indian Constitution was amended once by the 42nd Amendment Act, 1976 whereby the words 'Socialist', 'Secular', and 'Integrity' were added to the Preamble.

NOTES ON LEGAL TERMINOLOGY

Socialism

Socialism is a social system which is in contrast to capitalism. Socialism generally refers to an economic concept. The term 'socialism' has reflected many different visions and assumed many different forms. Some examples are Utopian Socialism, Marxian Socialism, and 'Democratic Socialism' (which refers to an ideology resting on both economic and political assumptions).

The word 'Socialist'[5] was not there in the Preamble originally. It was added by the 42nd amendment to the Constitution in 1976. Though the term has not been defined in the Constitution, it does not envisage doctrinaire socialism in the sense of insistence of state ownership as a matter of policy. In other words, it does not mean exclusion of private enterprise and complete state ownership of material resources of the nation. Jawaharlal Nehru described socialism as one, which will be based on political liberty, equality, and tolerance. Under democratic socialism we could maintain individual freedom and initiative with centralized social control and planning of the economic life of the people. Hence, he wanted to follow a middle path. He evolved a system of mixed economy as an alternative to both the rival systems, drawing

---

[3](1973)4 SCC 225: AIR 1973 SC 1461.

[4](1973)4 SCC 225: AIR 1973 SC 1461.

[5]In mid 1950s, Nehru got Parliament to accept the "socialist pattern of society" as the aim of economic development, and at the Avadi session of the Indian National Congress (1955), the resolution now known as the Avadi Resolution was passed. This resolution called for establishment of a socialistic pattern of society where the principal means of production are under social ownership or control and there is "equitable distribution of the national wealth".

the positive aspects of each and rejecting their negative aspects. This would be a combination of free private enterprise and state-controlled economy.

According to the Supreme Court, the principal aim of socialism is to eliminate inequality of income and standards of life and to provide decent standards of life to the working people. In ***Samatha Vs. State of Andhra Pradesh***[6], the Supreme Court has stated while defining socialism that "Establishment of the Egalitarian social order through the rule of law is the basic structure of the Constitution". The Court laid emphasis on social justice so as to attain a substantial degree of social, economic, and political equality. The court, to bring about the distribution of material resources of the country and to serve common good furthered the idea of distributive justice.

Secularism

Political secularism may be defined as the separation of religious activities from those of the state, customarily referred to as 'the separation of Church and State' in the West. Secularism in theory then would mean that religion and state cannot occupy the same space. The state in its governmental capacity does not promote any religion or religious group, nor does it intervene in religious affairs. It cannot even be involved in interpretation or 'reform' of any religion, much less favour one over any other. This model of secularism may be characterized as maximum separation between state and religion, except on manifest grounds of morality, health, and public order. Indian secularism did not erect a strict wall of separation, but proposed instead a 'principled distance' between religion and state. This implies 'Equal protection by the state to all religions', in other words, a secular state to be one that "protects all religions but does not favour one at the expense of others and does not itself adopt any religion as the state religion."

Democracy

There are two types of Democracies : Representative or Indirect Democracy and Pure or Direct Democracy. In a representative democracy, politicians in the parliament and government formulate and pass laws on behalf of the voters who have elected them (For example: India). Voters' political will is thus transformed in representative democracy. Whereas, in Direct democracy, in contrast to representative democracy, political decisions on factual issues are taken by the voters themselves (For example: Switzerland). There are various instruments or devices in Direct Democracy. They are as follows:

- ***Referendum :*** This device is mainly used for legislative process. When the government wants to know the opinion of its electorate on a specific constitutional, legislative, or political issue, then referendum is used.
- ***Initiative :*** This device is used when the people or the electorate takes an initiative to get a certain law of its choice to be passed.
- ***Plebiscite :*** This device is used when people are directly consulted on questions of political importance (especially with respect to boundary disputes).
- ***Recall :*** When this device is used the people of a constituency, by their majority, can ask the legislature to send back their representative, and, thus, cancel his/her membership.

---

[6] AIR 1997 SC 3297

QUESTIONS

Subjective Questions

1. Can the Preamble be amended? Explain with relevant case laws.
2. What is the significance of a Preamble to a Constitution? Bring out the philosophy of the Indian polity as enshrined in the Preamble of the Indian Constitution.
3. What are the major commitments of the Constitution of India as incorporated in its Preamble? Discuss.

Objective Questions

1. Consider the following statements regarding the Preamble of the Indian Constitution:
   1. It is based on the 'Objectives Resolution' moved by Jawaharlal Nehru in the Constituent Assembly.
   2. It is not a part of the Constitution.
   3. It can be amended.

   Which of the statements given above is/are correct?

   (a) 1 only (b) 2 and 3 only
   (c) 1 and 3 only (d) All of the above

   Ans: (c)

2. Consider the following statements in the context of the Preamble to the Constitution:
   1. The Preamble states that the Constitution derives its authority from the Constituent Assembly of India.
   2. American Constitution was the first constitution in the world to begin with a Preamble.
   3. The Preamble is neither enforceable in courts of law nor a source of power to the legislature.

   Which of the statements given above is/are correct?

   (a) 1 and 2 only (b) 3 only
   (c) 2 and 3 only (d) 1, 2, and 3

   Ans: (c)

3. Consider the following statements about the Preamble of the Constitution:
   1. In the event of a conflict between the Preamble and a specific provision of the Constitution, the former will prevail.
   2. The Preamble is not a part of the basic structure of the Constitution.
   3. It was held by the Supreme Court as not a part of the Constitution in *Berubari Union Case.*

   Which of the above statements are correct?

   (a) Only 1 and 2 (b) Only 2 and 3
   (c) Only 1 and 3 (d) All of the above

   Ans: (b)

4. Which of the following statements is correct with regard to the Preamble of the Indian Constitution?

   1. The Preamble is a source of power to the legislature.
   2. Preamble is a part of the Constitution.
   3. The Preamble cannot be amended.
   4. It is non-justiciable, i.e., it is not enforceable in courts of law.

   Select the correct answer using the codes given below:

   (a) 2 and 4 (b) 2 only
   (c) 1, 3, and 4 (d) 1, 2, and 4

   Ans: (a)

5. Consider the following statements:

   1. The ideal of justice (social, economic, and political) in our Preamble has been taken from the Russian Revolution (1917–1923).
   2. The ideals of liberty, equality, and fraternity in our Preamble have been taken from the French Revolution (1789–1799).

   Which of the statements given above is/are correct?

   (a) 1 only (b) 2 only
   (c) Both 1 and 2 (d) Neither 1 nor 2

   Ans: (c)

6. The Preamble declares to constitute India into a Republic. In this context 'Republic' means

   1. The President of India is elected.
   2. Political sovereignty is vested in the people.
   3. All public offices are opened to every citizen without any discrimination.
   4. Head of the state has immunity from civil and criminal proceedings during his term of office.

   Which of the statements given above is/are correct?

   (a) All the above (b) 1 only
   (c) 1 and 2 (d) 1, 2, and 3

   Ans: (b)

7. The Preamble of the Indian Constitution serves which of the following purposes?

   1. It indicates that authority of the Government is derived from the people.
   2. It lays down the objectives which the Constitution seeks to accomplish.
   3. It helps the Judiciary to interpret provisions of the Constitution.

   Select the correct answer using the codes given below.

   (a) 1 and 2 only (b) 1 and 3 only
   (c) 2 and 3 only (d) 1, 2 and 3

   Ans: (d)

8. With reference to the Preamble as enshrined in the Indian Constitution, consider the following statements:

   1. 'Equality' means removing all the differences among the citizens of India.
   2. 'Secular' means the government will not interfere at all in the matters of religion.
   3. 'Republic' means the Head of the State is an indirectly elected person.

   Which of the statements given above is/are correct?

   (a) 1 only (b) 3 only

   (c) 1, 2 and 3 (d) None of the above

   Ans: (d)

9. With reference to the Preamble as enshrined in the Indian Constitution, consider the following statements:

   1. The Preamble was the first part of the Constitution to be enacted.
   2. The 42nd Constitutional Amendment added three new words— 'Socialist', 'Secular', and 'Integrity' into the Preamble.

   Which of the statements given above is/are correct?

   (a) 1 only (b) 2 only

   (c) Both 1 and 2 (d) Neither 1 nor 2

   Ans: (b)

10. Who introduced 'Objectives Resolution' in the Constituent Assembly?

    (a) Jawaharlal Nehru (b) Dr. B.R. Ambedkar

    (c) Dr. Rajendra Prasad (d) Sardar Vallabhbhai Patel

    Ans: (a)

CHAPTER 6

INDIA : THE UNION AND ITS TERRITORY

ARTICLES OF THE CONSTITUTION REGARDING THE STATES AND UNION TERRITORIES

Article 1: Name and Territory of the Union

(1) India, that is Bharat, shall be a Union of States.

(2) The States and the territories thereof shall be as specified in the First Schedule. (3) The territory of India shall comprise—

(a) the territories of the States;

(b) the Union territories specified in the First Schedule; and

(c) such other territories as may be acquired.

The Republic of India is described as a union and not a federation. The Constitution makers have purposefully chosen the word 'Union' instead of the word 'Federation'. The Constitutional makers were of the view that the word 'Union' better expressed the fact that the Union of India is not the outcome of an agreement among any existing States, and, therefore, it is not open to any State or a group of States to secede from the Union or to vary the boundary of their States on their own free will[1].

Therefore, Article 1 of the Indian Constitution declares India as a Union of States. And the list of States and Union Territories are specified in the First Schedule of the Constitution. Moreover, the Constitution allows the changes in the territorial limits of the Constituent States and gives no guarantee of their territorial integrity.

The territory of India given under Article 1 sub-clause (3) falls under three categories:

(1) State Territories

(2) Union Territories

(3) Territories which may be acquired by the Government of India.

No parliamentary legislation is required to acquire a foreign territory. It is an inherent attribute of a sovereign State to acquire new territories. Article 1(3)(c), therefore, in including the acquired territory as part of the Indian territory, merely states a factual situation and does not confer a power on Parliament to acquire foreign territory. Moreover, the acquisition can be of any kind. It may be through an agreement or may be by conquest or occupation, etc.

[1] V.N. Shukla, Constitution of India, p. 6.

Admission or establishment of New States

Article 2:Parliament may by law admit into the Union, or establish, new States on such terms and conditions as it thinks fit.

Article 2 confers two important powers to the Parliament with respect to the Admission of New States. They are as follows:

(1) The power to admit into the Union new States—admission of an existing State or organized political communities; and

(2) The power to establish new States—formation of a State which did not exist before.

The first refers to the admission of States which are duly formed and established and are already in existence. The second refers to the admission and formation of a State which was not in existence before. It is to be noted that Article 2 deals with admission or establishment of new 'States' into the Union of India which may be formed of the territories not included in the existing States.

It has to be understood that the territory acquired by the Union becomes Indian territory by virtue of clause (3)(c) of Article 1. No Parliamentary sanction is required for acquisition of territory. Even though a territory acquired by the Government of India factually becomes territory of India from the date of its acquisition, the legal assimilation into India is brought about only by parliamentary legislation made under this article when the acquired territory is established as a new 'State' of the Union, or under Article 3 when the acquired territory is merged into an existing State[2].

Under Article 2,the Parliament has complete discretion to admit or establish new States on such terms and conditions as "it thinks fit"[3]. In other words, the new State does not have any right under the Constitution to claim complete equality with a State existing at the commencement of the Constitution or formed later under Article 3. Various territories such as Dadra and Nagar Haveli, Goa, Daman and Diu, Pondicherry (admitted as Union Territories), and Sikkim (admitted by inserting new Article 2A and later the same was repealedby 36th Constitutional Amendment Act, 1975), have been admitted into the Union since the commencement of the Constitution. But in all these cases, Article 2 was not invoked. Admission in all these cases was done by an amendment of the Constitution under Article 368 (As it is still doubtful whether the expression 'States' in Article 2 includes a Union Territory).

Article 3: Formation of New States and Alteration of Areas, Boundaries, or Names of Existing States

Article 2 relates to admission or establishment of new States which are not part of the Union, while Article 3 provides for the formation of or changes in the existing States including Union territories. Thus, the States do not have any guarantee of their territorial integrity.

The new States may be formed in the following ways:

(a) by separation of territories from any State or

(b) by uniting two or more States, or

(c) by uniting parts of States, or

(d) by uniting any territory to a part of any State.

Parliament under this article can also increase or decrease the area of any State or alter the boundaries or change the name of any State. Moreover, the Parliament is empowered to alter the territory or names, etc., of the States without their consent or concurrence by a law passed by simple majority. However, there are certain conditions that have to be fulfilled before passing such a law. They are as follows:

---

[2]Chandernagore (Merger) Act, 1954

[3]V.N. Shukla, *Constitution of India*, P.8.

(a) No Bill for the formation of new States or the alteration of the boundaries or the names of the existing State shall be introduced in either House of the Parliament except on the recommendation of the President.

(b) If the Bill affects the area, boundaries, or names of the States, President is required to refer the Bill to the Legislature of the States, so affected for expressing its views within the period specified by the President. The President may extend the period so specified. If the State Legislature, to which the Bill has been referred, does not express its views within the period so specified or extended, the Bill may be introduced in the Parliament even though the views of the State have not been obtained by the President. If the State Legislature expresses its views within the time so specified or extended, the Parliament is not bound to accept or act upon the views of the State Legislature. Further, it is not necessary to make fresh reference to State Legislature every time an amendment to the Bill is proposed and accepted.

Thus, it is clear that the very existence of a State depends upon the sweet will of the Central Government.

EXHIBIT 6.1 : CESSATION OF INDIAN TERRITORY

No cession of Indian territory can take place without a constitutional amendment. But settlement of boundary between Indiaand any of its neighbouring countries does not amount to cession of territory. The same was discussed in the case 'InBerubari Union (1), re'.

Berubari Case - After the Partition of British India in 1947, India and East Pakistan were at one point separated by the then princely state of Cooch Behar, which, on account of a number of historical factors, had enclaves (a portion of territory surrounded by a larger territory whose inhabitants are culturally or ethnically distinct) located in both countries. The accession of Cooch Behar to India in 1949 led to a situation where Indian enclaves were located in East Pakistan, and vice-versa.

A series of attempts to resolve some of these issues by demarcating a common boundary in certain parts and exchanging some enclaves, culminated in the signing of the Nehru-Noon Agreement between the Prime Ministers of both countries in 1958. The operationalisation of the Nehru-Noon agreement presented the first significant Constitutional challenge to the resolution of the boundary dispute. The agreement envisaged, inter alia, the transfer of four enclaves of Cooch Behar to Pakistan, along with the southern half of a territory called the Berubari Union, hitherto part of the Jalpaiguri district of West Bengal.

The Parliament attempted to do this by exercising its power under Article 3 of the Constitution, enacting the Acquired Territories (Merger) Bill, 1960. Under the proviso to Article 3, the Bill was referred to the legislature of West Bengal for its opinion. Here it ran into trouble, with the Assembly passing a unanimous resolution rejecting the Bill and opposing the proposed ceding of Berubari and the other territories. Under these circumstances, the President, in exercise of his powers under Article 143, referred the matter to the Supreme Court for its opinion.

The questions to be considered by the Court were as follows:

(1) Is any legislative action necessary for the implementation of the Agreement relating to Berubari Union?"

(2) Is a law of Parliament relatable to Article 3 of the Constitution sufficient for implementation of the agreement relating to Exchange of Enclaves or is an amendment of the Constitution in accordance with Article 368 of the Constitution necessary for the purpose, in addition or in the alternative?"

To the first question, the court concluded that the agreement did involve a factual transfer of territory, specifically a cession of territory by India in favour of Pakistan. Consequently, its implementation would alter the boundaries of the state of West Bengal, as defined in the First Schedule, thereby requiring legislative action for its implementation.

To the second question, the court concluded that the scheme of Article 3, only envisaged acquisition of territory by the Union and not its cession; it was possible, as a sovereign power, for the Union to cede territory. However, the Court held that, any amendment to the First Schedule as a result of the cession of territory would not be saved by Article 3. Therefore, an amendment to the First Schedule involving cession of territory would not be possible by ordinary legislation under Article 3, but only through an Amendment to the Constitution under Article 368. In other words, Parliament has no power under Article 3 to make a law to implement an agreement with the government of a foreign State ceding Indian territory to a foreign State. The diminution of the area of any State to which Article 3(c) refers, postulates that the area diminished from the State in question should and must continue to be a part of the territory of India. This limitation on cession applies as much to Union Territories as to territories of States.

But the court further held that the settlement of boundary between India and another country stands on a different footing. The settlement of a boundary dispute cannot be held to be cession of territory. This matter rests with the Executive.

Since the agreement in respect of both the Berubari Union and the exchange of enclaves involved cession of territory, the Court opined that the same would be possible only through an Amendment to the Constitution. Pursuant to the judgment, Parliament passed the Constitution (9th Amendment) Act, 1960, amending the First Schedule and paving the way for the implementation of the Nehru-Noon agreement and settling the border dispute in respect of some of the enclaves. However, it could not be implemented in its entirety.East Pakistan was eventually liberated as Bangladesh in 1971, and three years later another comprehensive agreement was signed between India and Bangladesh, covering the remaining aspects of the land boundary dispute. This came to be known as the Indo-Bangladesh Land Boundary Agreement of 1974, which envisaged a final boundary demarcation and exchange of enclaves involving a further cession of about 17,160 acres of land to Bangladesh and acquisition of about 7,110 acres by India.

Due to a variety of historical and political factors, this Amendment was never passed. In 2011, the two countries signed a Protocol to the 1974 Agreement, committing to implementing the exchange of enclaves and also lands which were in adverse possession on both sides of the border. To implement the above said agreement, the Parliament passed 100th Constitutional Amendment Act, 2015. The constitutional amendment allowed the exchange of land between the two countries without dislocation of people.

Article 4: Regulation of Laws Made Under Articles 2 and 3

Article 4 deals with the laws made under Articles 2 and 3 to provide for the amendment of the First and the Fourth Schedules and supplemental, incidental and consequential matters.

(1) Any law referred to in Article 2 or Article 3 shall contain such provisions for the amendment of the First Schedule and the Fourth Schedule as may be necessary to give effect to the provisions of the law and may also contain such supplemental, incidental and consequential provisions (including provisions as to representation in Parliament and in the Legislature or Legislatures of the State or States affected by such law) as Parliament may deem necessary.

(2) No such law as aforesaid shall be deemed to be an amendment of this Constitution for the purposes of Article 368.

If the Parliament makes a law under Article 2 or 3, the law must also include necessary provisions for amendment of the First and Fourth Schedules of the Constitution[4]. Clause (2) expressly provides that changes made in the Constitution by such law shall not be deemed to be an amendment of the Constitution for the purposes of Article 368. In other words, any amendments made under Article 2 and

[4]The First Schedule specifies the States which are the members of the Union and their respective territories. The Fourth Schedule specifies the number of seats to which each State is entitled in the Council of States.

3 requires simple majority and does not require special majority and further,it will not be considered as Constitutional amendment under Article 368.

INTEGRATION OF PRINCELY STATES

British India was divided into what were called the UnitedProvinces and the Princely States. The UnitedProvinces were directly under the control of the British government. On the other hand, several large and small states ruled by princes, called the Princely States, enjoyed some form of control over their internal affairs as long as they accepted British supremacy which was called as paramountcy or suzerainty of the British crown. Princely Statescovered one-third of the land area of the British Indian Empire andone out of four Indians lived under princely rule.

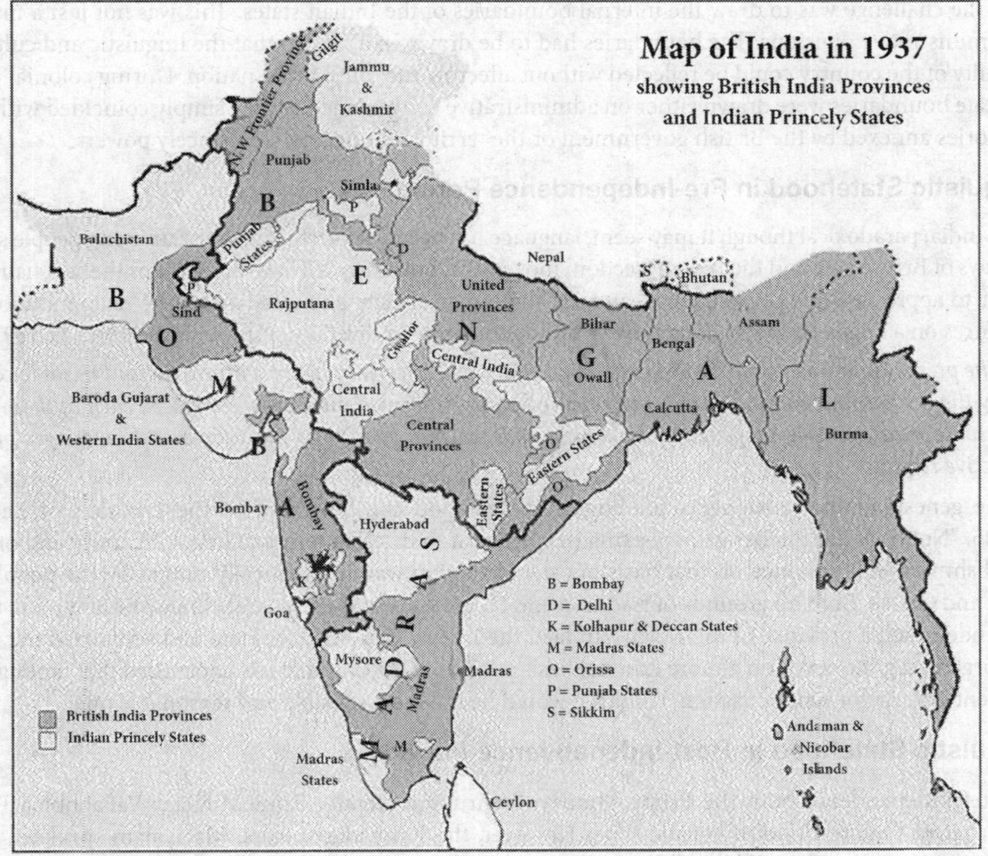

However, with the end of British rule over India, the paramountcy of the British crownover Princely States also lapsed. All the Princely States, as many as 565 Princely States became legally independent. The Princely States were free to join either India or Pakistan or remain independent if they so wished. This decision was left not to the people but to the princely rulers of the sestates. This was a serious threat to the existence of a united India. But the interim government of India took a firm stance against the possible balkanization of India. Sardar Patel who was Deputy Prime Minister and Home Minister of India played ahistoric role in negotiating with the rulers of princely states firmly but diplomatically and bringing most of them into the Indian Union.

Before 15 August 1947, peaceful negotiations had brought almost all states whose territories were contiguous to the new boundaries of India, into the Indian Union. The rulers of most of the states signed a document called the 'Instrument of Accession' which meant that their state agreed to become a part of the Union of India. Accession of the Princely States of Junagadh, Hyderabad, and Kashmir proved more difficult than the rest. The issue of Junagadh was resolved after a plebiscite confirmed people's desire to join India. (Kashmir will be dealt in later chapters). Hyderabad was annexed through Police action against the Nizam and his private army of Razakars.

REORGANISATION OF INDIAN STATES

The process of nation-building did not come to an end with partition and integration of Princely States. Now the challenge was to draw the internal boundaries of the Indian states. This was not just a matter of administrative divisions. The boundaries had to be drawn in a way so that the linguistic and cultural plurality of the country could be reflected without affecting the unity of the nation. During colonial rule, the state boundaries were drawn either on administrative convenience or they simply coincided with the territories annexed by the British government or the territories ruled by the princely powers.

Linguistic Statehood in Pre-Independence Period

In India, paradoxical though it may seem, language has been a powerful factor for unifying people since the days of British rule and the Indian freedom movement. Lokamanya Tilak was perhaps the first national leader to appreciate this conspicuous feature of the Indian society and to advocate the reorganisation of provinces on a linguistic basis with a view to promoting unity in diversity. Hew rote as early as in 1891:

"The present administrative division of India is the result of certain historic processes, and in some cases, purely the result of accident. ... if they are replaced by units formed on a linguistic basis, each of them will have some measure of homogeneity and will provide encouragement to the people and languages of the respective regions"[5].

The genesis of the movements for linguistic statehood can be traced to the Partition of Bengal in1905. "Not only did the Bengali-speaking people learn to think in terms of linguistic unity and of the establishment of a province on that basis but the contagion was automatically caught by the people of Bihar and Orissa. Both on grounds of tradition and on grounds of their separate linguistic affiliation they demanded each a province of their own". In fact, the Indian National Congress had supported the idea of reorganizing the states on a more rational basis as early as 1905 and it was contended that among the different criteria for reorganisation, language would be the most sensible and reasonable one.

Linguistic Statehood in Post-Independence Period

After independence both the Prime Minister Nehru and Deputy PrimeMinister Vallabhbhai Patel were against the creationof linguistic states.However, the Kannadaspeakers, Malayalam speakers, and the Marathi speakers, hadall looked forward to having their own state.

Linguistic Provinces Commission

To advice the Constituent Assembly in its deliberations upon the question of linguistic states a Linguistic Provinces Commission (Dhar Commission) was appointed by the President of the Constituent Assembly in June 1948. S.K. Dhar was the chairman of the commission. The Commission submitted its report on December 1948. It concluded in its report that:

---

[5]"Kesari", Nov. I 7, I 89 I, in Quaerens Veritatem, *Justice Shall Prevail: the Struggle for Samayukta Maharashtra*, J.S. Tilak, Kesari Printing Press, Poona, year not mentioned, P. 7.

(a) The formation of provinces on exclusively or even mainly linguistic consideration is not in the larger interests of the Indian nation and should not be taken in hand.

(b) In the formation of new provinces, whenever such a work is taken in hand, oneness of language may be one of the factors to be taken in consideration along with others; but it should not be the decisive or even the main factor.

The Congress Party was dejected by the report of the Dhar Commission. Therefore, immediately after publication of its report, it formed its own committee in 1949. This was known as JVP Committee (named after first alphabet of the name of its members) at its Jaipur Session in 1948. The Committee consisted of Jawaharlal Nehru, Vallabh bhai Patel, and Pattabhi Sitaramayya.

Like the Dhar Commission Report, the JVP Report too, dismissed the idea of the reorganisation of States on the basis of language. However, there was an optimistic note to it as it conceded that "if public sentiment is insistent and overwhelming, we as democrats, have to submit to it subject to certain limitations in regard to the good of India as a whole."

EXHIBIT 6.2

Formation of Andhra State — A first step towards Linguistic Reorganisation

The agitation for Andhra became acute. At the end of 1952 this agitation for a separate State reached a dramatic climax. A respected Andhra patriot and a veteran of the independence movement, Potti Sriramulu sacrificed his life on 16th of December 1952, by fasting for 58 days. Following this incident many disturbances took place across the State. Ultimately, the Government of India established the State of Andhra by passing the Andhra State Act, 1953.

REORGANISATION OF STATES OF INDIA: CHRONOLOGICAL TRENDS

With the acceptance of the demand of Andhra, the struggle over reorganisation of India on linguistic basis dominated Indian politics from1953 to 1956. Hence, to solve this gigantic problem, the Government of India appointed States Reorganisation Commission. It was a three-member commission under the chairmanship of Fazl Ali to reexamine the whole question. Its other two members were K. M. Panikkar and H. N. Kunzru.

The Commission concluded that creation of linguistic states on the principle of linguistic homogeneity resulted in administrative convenience. The broad principles enunciated by the Commission were:

1. Preservation of unity and integrity of the country
2. Preservation of linguistic and cultural homogeneity
3. Financial, economic, and administrative viability
4. Successful working of the Five-Year Plans

The Government accepted most of the recommendations in the States Reorganisation Act, 1956 leading to the redrawing of the map of India by creating linguistically homogenous States, particularly in the South. The States Reorganisation Act erased the distinction between Parts A, B, C, and D States and reorganized state boundaries on linguistic lines, thereby reducing the number of states from **27** to **14** (plus **6** Union Territories). The Centre had hoped that this reorganisation would pacify the people, nevertheless, demand for the creation of new states continued in a number of states.

Formation of Gujarat (15th State)

In 1960, following widespread agitation the bilingual state of Bombay was bifurcated into two monolingual States—Maharashtra and Gujarat.

Formation of Nagaland (16th State)

In the year 1957, Nagaland was formed as a separate union territory by separation of the Naga Hills and Tuensang area from the State of Assam. In July 1960, the Government of India, in pursuance of an agreement with the leaders of Naga *People's Convention* decided that Nagaland should be formed as a separate state in the Union of India. In 1962, the state of Nagaland was created by the State of Nagaland Act, 1962, and was formally inaugurated in 1963. It comprised of the Naga Hills and Tuensang Area and was given the status of the sixteenth state of the Union.

Formation of States of Haryana (17th) and Himachal Pradesh (18th)

In 1966, Greater Punjab was split between Punjab, Haryana, and Himachal Pradesh (which was initially a union territory and later received full state recognition in 1971).Thus, Haryana became the 17th State and Himachal Pradesh became the 18th state. The Akali Dal led the Punjabi Sub a movement, which led to the creation of a Punjabi-speaking and Sikh-dominated Punjab state, the Hindi-speaking and Hindu-dominated state of Haryana, and Union Territory of Chandigarh in 1966. In 1966, the boundaries of the Union territory of Himachal Pradesh was extended by addition of the certain territories from the state of Punjab. Thus, the Punjab Reorganisation Act, 1966, changed the boundaries of state of Punjab and Union territory of Himachal Pradesh besides creating state of Haryana and Union territory of Chandigarh.

The mountainous parts of erstwhile east Punjab were also merged with the then Himachal Pradesh, to create a Union territory.

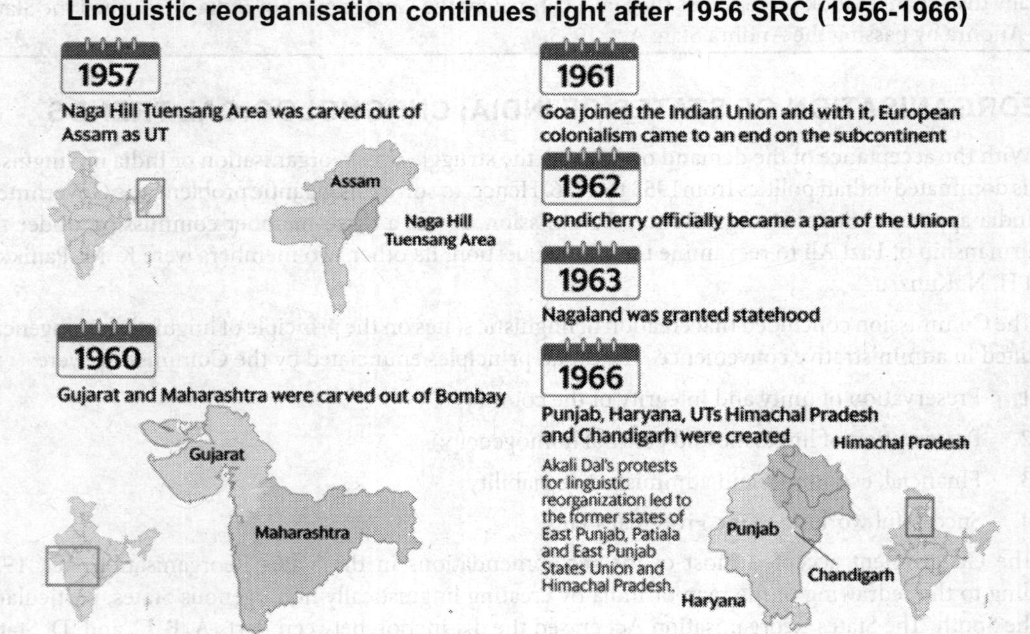

Formation of States of Manipur (19th) and Tripura (20th)

The 70s witnessed several changes in state boundaries along the north-eastern frontier, often to douse the fires of militancy and violence.

In 1972 the Union territory of Manipur and Tripura were granted statehood. There was no change of boundary when the above union territories were given the status of 'State'. Thus, Manipur became the 19th and Tripura the 20th state of the Indian union.

Formation of State of Meghalaya (21st)

In 1969, an autonomous state 'Meghalaya' was created out of the State of Assam, comprising the United Khasi Jaintia Hills District and the Garo Hills district, North Cachar Hills district, the Mikir Hills district, and territories comprised within the municipality of Shillong. Since 1972, Meghalaya has been a full-fledged state. Thus, Meghalaya became the 21st state.

Formation of State of Sikkim (22nd)

Sikkim became the 22nd State of India Vide Constitution (36th Amendment) Act 1975. It was a tiny Himalayan kingdom once ruled by the hereditary monarchy for about 3 centuries from 17 century A.D. In other words, Sikkim was an Indian princely state ruled by Chogyal. In 1950, the kingdom became a protectorate of the Government of India vested with autonomy in its internal affairs while its defence, communications, and external relation came under the responsibility of the protector. A few years later, a referendum held in Sikkim, till then India's protectorate, voted for joining the Indian Union as a state and thus, it became the 22nd state of India.

Formation of State of Mizoram (23rd)

The Union territory of Mizoram was carved out of Assam in 1972 and became a full-fledged 23rd state of India in 1987.

Formation of State of Arunachal Pradesh (24th)

On 20th January, 1972 union territory of Arunachal Pradeshwas formed separating North East Frontier Agency (NEFA) areafrom the State of Assam. In 1987, Arunachal Pradesh was conferred statehood, thus becoming the 24th State.

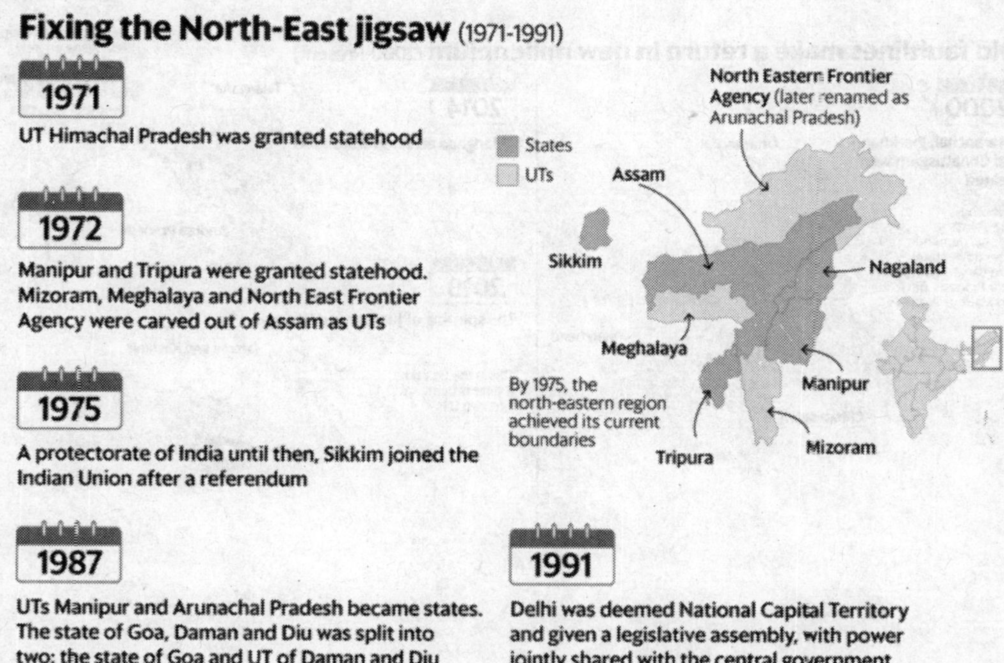

Formation of Goa (25th State)

When India became a free nation, Portugal continued to hold on to Goa, Daman and Diu, and Dadra and Nagar Haveli. With respect to Dadra and Nagar Haveli, the enclave was ruled until its liberation in 1954. Later on, the administration was carried till 1961 by an administrator chosen by the people themselves. Eventually, it was annexed as a union territory of India by the 10th Constitutional Amendment Act, 1961.

With respect to Goa and Daman and Diu, Portugal was unwilling to give up its control over these enclaves. The Indian government eventually authorized its military to launch an operation to take over Goa, and Daman and Diu. After the December 18–19, 1961 military action by India, the enclaves became a part of the Indian Union. They were constituted as a union territory by the 12th Constitutional Amendment Act, 1962. However, in 1987, Goa was conferred a Statehood and Daman and Diu was made a separate union territory in 2020 and was later merged with Dadra and Nagar Haveli.

Formation of New States in the New Millennium

Some major changes to the boundaries happened in the first year of the millennium when Chhattisgarh (26th), Uttarakhand (27th), and Jharkhand (28th) were carved out of Madhya Pradesh, Uttar Pradesh, Bihar, respectively.

Unlike the linguistic basis for states in the 60s, these states were created to address long pending regional demands and inequalities in regional development. Telangana (originally part of Andhra Pradesh) too was formed on the basis of such demands in 2014 and is the 29th state of India.

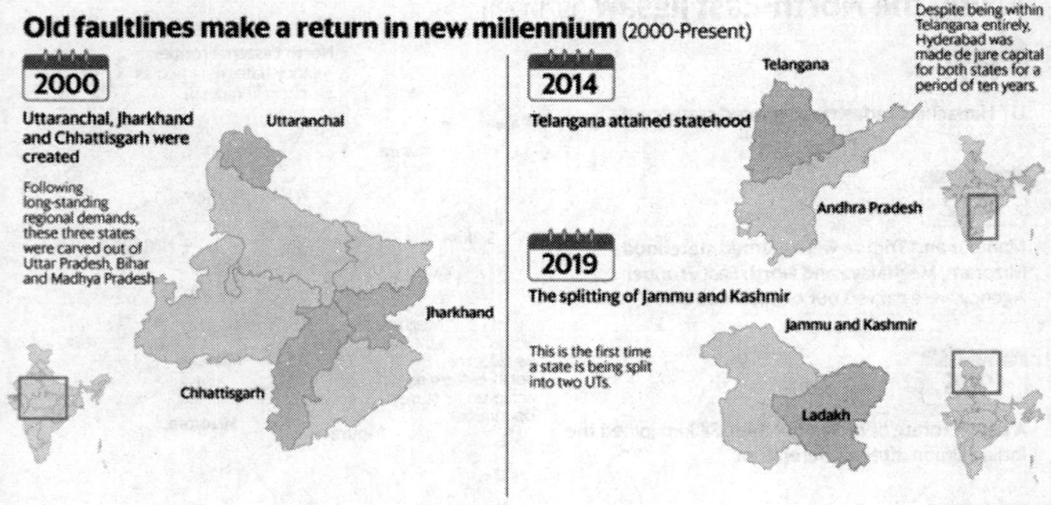

QUESTIONS

Objective Questions

1. Consider the following statements.

   1. To form a new state, the opinion of the state legislature is not binding cn the President.
   2. To form a new state, the opinion of the state legislature is binding on the President.
   3. To form a new state, the Bill needs to be passed by the Parliament with a simple majority.
   4. To form a new state, the Bill needs to be passed by the Parliament with a special majority.

   Which of the above statements is/are correct?

   (a) 1 only (b) 1 and 3 only

   (c) 2 only (d) 1 and 4 only

   Ans: (b)

2. Arrange Himachal Pradesh, Manipur, Kerala, and Maharashtra in correct chronological order of creation.

   (a) Maharashtra, Kerala, Himachal Pradesh, Manipur

   (b) Kerala, Maharashtra, Manipur, Himachal Pradesh

   (c) Kerala, Maharashtra, Himachal Pradesh, Manipur

   (d) Maharashtra, Himachal Pradesh, Manipur, Kerala

   Ans: (c)

3. Preamble declares India as 'sovereign'. What does this imply?

   1. There is no authority above India and it is free to conduct its own affairs.
   2. India can acquire a foreign territory or it can cede a part of its territory in favour of a foreign state subject to limitations (if any) imposed by the Constitution).

   Select the correct answer using the code given below.

   (a) 1 only (b) 2 only

   (c) Both 1 and 2 (d) Neither 1 nor 2

   Ans: (c)

4. Consider the following statements regarding reorganisation of the states:

   1. An Indian territory can be ceded to a foreign country by an executive action.
   2. A boundary dispute settlement between India and another country does not require constitutional amendment.

   Which of the statements given above is/arecorrect?

   (a) 1 only (b) 2 only

   (c) Both 1 and 2 (d) Neither 1 nor 2

   Ans: (b)

5. Which of the statements is correct?

(a) To form a new state, the relevant Bill may be introduced in either house of Parliament only on the recommendation of the President.

(b) To form a new state, the relevant Bill can only be introduced in the Lok Sabha, with the recommendation of the President.

(c) To form a new state, the relevant Bill can only be introduced in the Rajya Sabha with the recommendation of the President.

(d) To form a new state, President's recommendation is not required.

Ans: (a)

CHAPTER 7

CITIZEN AND CITIZENSHIP

INTRODUCTION

The ordinary meaning of the term 'citizen' means an inhabitant of a state or a town. Globally, the term citizen means an individual who pledges his allegiance to the Country's flag and the Constitution of the Country. This term assumes significance since there is a bias in favour of a citizen as compared to the aliens (non-citizens) while asserting one's fundamental rights.

In the Indian context, as discussed in the previous chapter, the Preamble of the Indian Constitution secures to all its 'citizens' justice, social, economic and political, equality of opportunity, and promotes among them fraternity assuring dignity of the individual and the unity and integrity of the Nation.

Terms Relating to Citizens and Citizenship

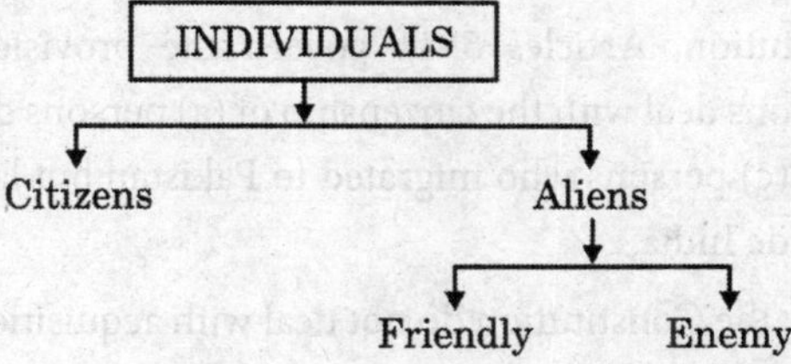

Aliens are individuals who are not citizens of their domiciled country but belong to another country who can be classified as friendly alien (belonging to a friendly nation of the domiciled country) and enemy alien (belonging to an enemy nation).

Citizenship is one's status as a member of a nation, with the right and privileges that status carries with it.

Domicile is where one lives with the intent to stay; it refers particularly to a state, country, and city.

Residence is, broadly, where one's home is, or the building itself. One may have many residences but only one domicile.

SALIENT FEATURES OF INDIAN CITIZENSHIP

Single Citizenship

The Indian Constitution though federal in nature has provided for single citizenship through the Union. No matter where the person resides, he is still a citizen of India. He owes his allegiance to the Indian flag and the Constitution. Unlike in countries like USA where there is separate state citizenship, thereby having dual citizenship concept within the country, India has only single citizenship.

Citizenship Rights of a Foreigner

The Supreme Court has asserted that the power of the Government to expel a foreigner is absolute and unlimited. There is no provision in the Constitution fettering this discretion of the Government. The Government has an unrestricted power to expel a foreigner without assigning any reasons. A foreigner has no right to claim Indian citizenship. No foreigner can claim to stay in India as a matter of right. The Government has an unrestricted right to expel a foreigner[1]. A foreigner can claim the protection to his life and liberty under Article 21, but the right to reside and settle in India as conferred by Article 19(1)(d) is available only to the citizens of India and not to non-citizens[2].

Citizenship Rights of a Refugee

India has an age-old tradition of offering humanitarian assistance to refugees. But India has neither signed the Convention of Refugees, 1951 nor is there any specific refugee law in the country till date. The refugees are dealt with on the basis of a combination of judicial pronouncements and ad hoc executive policies. Different treatment is meted out to different refugee groups. The law relating to entry and exit of foreign nationals, the Foreigners Act, 1946, does not recognize refugees as a special category.

CONSTITUTIONAL PROVISIONS GOVERNING CITIZENS & CITIZENSHIP

Under the Indian Constitution, Articles 5–11 govern the provisions relating to Citizens and Citizenship. The below provisions deal with the citizenship of (a) persons domiciled in India; (b) persons who migrated from Pakistan; (c) persons who migrated to Pakistan but later returned; and (d) persons of Indian origin residing outside India.

The below provisions under the Constitution do not deal with acquisition of citizenship or conditions for granting of citizenship in the future but was limited in its application to:

- the partition of India during 1947 and the consequences of the partition, i.e., migrants from Pakistan and the current residents of India; and
- who are the citizens at the time of the commencement of the Constitution.

---

[1] *Hans Muller of Nuremberg Vs. Superintendent, Presidency Jail, Calcutta*, AIR 1955 SC 367; *Sarbananda Sonawal Vs. UOI, (2005)* 5 SCC 665 at P. 693.

[2] M.P. Jain, Lexis Nexis, P. 847, Eighth Edition.

Citizenship Rights of Certain Individuals in India

Citizenship by Domicile

A person who had his domicile in India and also fulfilled any one of the three conditions, viz., if he was born in India; or if either of his parents were born in India; or if he has been ordinarily resident in India for five years immediately before the commencement of the Constitution, became a citizen of India (Article 5).

Citizenship by Migration

A person who migrated to India from Pakistan became an Indian citizen if he or either of his parents or any of his grandparents was born in undivided India and also fulfilled any one of the two conditions viz., in case he migrated to India before July 19, 1948, and he had been ordinarily resident in India since the date of his migration; or in case he migrated to India on or after July 19, 1948, and he had been registered as a citizen of India. But a person could be so registered only if he had been resident in India for six months preceding the date of his application for registration (Article 6).

A person who migrated to Pakistan from India after March 1, 1947, but later returned to India for resettlement could become an Indian citizen. For this, he had to be resident in India for six months preceding the date of his application for registration (Article 7).

Citizenship by Registration

A person who, or any of whose parents or grandparents, was born in undivided India but who is ordinarily residing outside India shall become an Indian citizen if he has been registered as a citizen of India by the diplomatic or consular representative of India in the country of his residence, whether before or after the commencement of the Constitution. Thus, this provision covers the overseas Indians who may want to acquire Indian citizenship (Article 8).

Other Constitutional Provisions with Respect to Citizenship

Dual Citizenship

No person shall be a citizen of India or be deemed to be a citizen of India, if he has voluntarily acquired the citizenship of any foreign state (Article 9). This provision recognizes the principle that no Indian citizen can claim a dual or plural citizenship. Article 9 applies only to those cases where foreign citizenship had been acquired before and not after, the commencement of the Constitution. The latter type of situation has been dealt with under the provisions of the Indian Citizenship Act, 1955.

Continuance of the Rights of Citizenship

Every person who is or is deemed to be a citizen of India shall continue to be such citizen, subject to the provisions of any law made by the Parliament (Article 10).

Parliament to Regulate the Right of Citizenship by Law

The object of Article 11 is to make it clear that notwithstanding the fact that certain rules relating to citizenship are contained in Part II of the Constitution, Parliament shall have unfettered power to make any provision relating to acquisition, termination, etc. of citizenship.

INDIAN CITIZENSHIP ACT, 1955

Articles 5–10 dealt only with the citizenship at the time of commencement of the Constitution but it does not deal with the acquisition of citizenship or conditions for granting of citizenship after the commencement of the Constitution. To remedy the situation and using the powers bestowed under Article 11 of the Indian Constitution, the Parliament enacted the Indian Citizenship Act, 1955 which came into force with effect from December 30, 1955 to provide for the acquisition and determination of Indian citizenship. It contains 19 Sections.

Acquisition and Determination of Indian Citizenship

The following modes of acquisition of citizenship are prescribed under the Citizenship Act:

Citizenship by Birth (Section 3)

Any person born in India on or after January 26, 1950, but prior to the commencement of the Indian Citizenship (Amendment) Act, 1986 on July 1, 1987, is a citizen of India by birth.

A person born in India on or after July 1, 1987 but before commencement of the Indian Citizenship (Amendment) Act, 2003 on December 3, 2004 is a citizen of India if one of parents was a citizen of India at the time of the birth.

Those born in India on or after December 3, 2004 are considered citizens of India only if both of their parents are citizens of India or if one parent is a citizen of India and the other is not an illegal migrant at the time of their birth.

In September 2013, the Bombay High Court in the matter of Afzal Khan (name changed), gave a judgment that a birth certificate, passport, or even an Aadhaar card alone may not be enough to prove Indian citizenship, unless the parents are Indian citizens.

Citizenship by Descent (Section 4)

Persons born outside India on or after January 26, 1950 but before December 10, 1992 are citizens of India by descent if their father was a citizen of India at the time of their birth.

Persons born outside India on or after December 10, 1992 are considered citizens of India if either of their parents is a citizen of India at the time of their birth.

From December 3, 2004 onwards, persons born outside of India shall not be considered citizens of India unless their birth is registered at an Indian diplomatic mission within one year of the date of birth. In certain circumstances it is possible to register after one year with the permission of the

Central Government. The application for registration of the birth of a child must be made to an Indian diplomatic mission and must be accompanied by an undertaking in writing from the parents of the child that he or she does not hold the passport of another country.

Citizenship by Registration (Section 5)

The Central Government may, on an application, register as a citizen of India under Section 5 of the Citizenship Act, 1955 any person (not being an illegal migrant) if s/he belongs to any of the following categories:

- a person of Indian origin who is ordinarily resident in India for seven years before making application under Section 5(1)(a) (throughout the period of twelve months immediately before making application and for six years in the aggregate in the eight years preceding the 12 months).
- a person of Indian origin who is ordinarily resident in any country or place outside undivided India;
- a person who is married to a citizen of India and is ordinarily resident in India for seven years before making an application for registration; minor children of persons who are citizens of India;
- a person of full age and capacity whose parents are registered as citizens of India.
- a person of full age and capacity who, or either of his parents, was earlier citizen of independent India, and has been residing in India for one year immediately before making an application for registration;
- a person of full age and capacity who has been registered as an overseas citizen of India for five years, and who has been residing in India for one year before making an application for registration.

Citizenship by Naturalization (Section 6)

Citizenship of India by naturalization can be acquired by a foreigner who is ordinarily resident in India for 12 years (throughout the period of 12 months immediately preceding the date of application and for 11 years in the aggregate of 14 years preceding the 12 months) and other qualifications as specified in the Third Scedule of the Indian Citizenship Act, 1955.

Citizenship by Incorporation of Territory (Section 7)

Citizenship is granted to residents of any territory that becomes part of Union of India from a notified date. Examples are Goa, Daman and Diu (Citizenship) Order, 1962, Dadra and Nagar Haveli (Citizenship) Order, 1962, and Citizenship (Pondicherry) Order 1962, in exercise of its powers under Section 7 of the Citizenship Act. For the state of Sikkim, the President extended the Citizenship Act, and the relevant rules under Article 371F of Indian Constitution.

Special Provisions Regarding Citizenship in the Citizenship Act

Persons Covered by the Assam Accord (Section 6A)

The Assam Accord was a Memorandum of Settlement between the Union of India and the leaders of the Assam Movement with a primary objective to identify and deport illegal migrants who entered in the State of Assam from Bangladesh. This was signed on August 15, 1985. To give this demand a salutary effect, the Indian Citizenship Act, 1955 was amended where the following provisions were inserted:

All persons of Indian origin who came before the 1st day of January, 1966 to Assam from the specified territory (including such of those whose names were included in the electoral rolls used for the purposes of the General Election to the House of the People held in 1967) and who have been ordinarily resident in Assam since the dates of their entry into Assam shall be deemed to be citizens of India as from the 1st day of January, 1966.

Every person of Indian origin who :

(a) came to Assam on or after the 1st day of January, 1966 but before the 25th day of March, 1971 from the specified territory; and (b) has, since the date of his entry into Assam, been ordinarily resident in Assam; and (c) has been detected to be a foreigner; shall register himself in accordance with the rules made by the Central Government in this behalf under Section 18 with such authority (hereafter in this sub-section referred to as the registering authority) as may be specified in such rules and if his name is included in any electoral roll for any Assembly or Parliamentary constituency in force on the date of such detection, his name shall be deleted therefrom.

Overseas Citizen of India (Section 7A–7D)

There were demands that people of Indian origin settled abroad should be granted Indian citizenship so that they are connected with their Indian roots. Looking at these demands the Government of India appointed a committee under the Chairmanship of L.M. Singhvi to study the global Indian diaspora in North America and other developed countries to suggest suitable changes in the law to achieve this objective. *The Overseas Citizenship of India (OCI)* scheme was introduced by amending *The Citizenship Act, 1955* in August 2005. The scheme was launched during the Pravasi Bharatiya Divas convention in Hyderabad in 2006. Overseas Citizenship of India is not an actual citizenship of India and thus, does not amount to dual citizenship or dual nationality.

EXHIBIT 7.1 : OCI CARDHOLDER

Eligibility for Registration of OCI Cardholder

The Government of India, on application, may register any person as an Overseas Citizen of India, if the person:

- was a citizen of India on January 26, 1950 or at any time thereafter; or
- belonged to a territory that became part of India after August 15, 1947; or
- was eligible to become a citizen of India on January 26, 1950; or

- is a child or a grandchild or a great-grandchild of such a citizen; or
- is a minor child of such persons mentioned above; or
- is a minor child and whose both parents are citizens of India or one of the parents is a citizen of India; or
- is a spouse of foreign origin of a citizen of India or spouse of foreign origin of an Overseas Citizen of India cardholder registered under Section 7A of the Citizenship Act, 1955 and whose marriage has been registered and subsisted for a continuous period of not less than two years immediately preceding the presentation of the application.

Note : No person, who or either of whose parents or grandparents or great grandparents is or had been a citizen of Pakistan and Bangladesh, is eligible for registration as an Overseas Citizen of India. Persons who served as a member of any foreign military are also ineligible to receive an OCI card.

Privileges and Restrictions of OCI Cardholder

Overseas Citizenship of India allows a holder:

1. Multiple-entry, multi-purpose lifelong visa to visit India;
2. Exemption from foreigner registration requirements for any length of stay in India; and
3. Parity with non-resident Indians in financial, economic, and educational fields, except in the acquisition of agricultural or plantation properties.

Overseas citizens of India are not citizens of India from a constitutional point of view by virtue of Article 9 of the Constitution and will not enjoy the following rights even if resident in India:

1. they do not have the right to vote,
2. they do not have the right to hold the offices of Prime Minister, President, Vice-President, Judge of Supreme Court and High Court, member of Lok Sabha, Rajya Sabha, Legislative Assembly, or Council.
3. they do not have the right to any public services (government jobs).
4. they do not have the right to hold farmland (agricultural property).

EXHIBIT 7.2 : PERSONS OF INDIAN ORIGIN (PIO)

A Person of Indian Origin is a person who or whose any of ancestors was an Indian national and who is presently holding another country's citizenship/nationality, i.e., he/she is holding a foreign passport.

The 'Persons of Indian Origin (PIO)' card was a form of identification issued to an individual (person of Indian Origin) who held a passport in a country other than Afghanistan, Bangladesh, Bhutan, China, Iran, Nepal, Pakistan, and Sri Lanka and could prove their Indian origin up to three generations before.

In early 2011, the then Prime Minister of India, Manmohan Singh, announced that the Persons of Indian Origin card will be merged with the Overseas Citizen of India card. This new card was proposed to be called the Overseas Indian card.

As of January 9, 2015, the PIO card scheme has been discontinued and applicants are to apply for OCI only. All PIO cardholders were advised, from time to time, to convert the PIO card to OCI card.

Types of Loss of Indian Citizenship

Renunciation

Renunciation is covered in Section 8 of the Citizenship Act, 1955. If an adult makes a declaration of renunciation of Indian citizenship, s/he loses Indian citizenship. In addition, any minor child of that person also loses Indian citizenship from the date of renunciation. When the child reaches the age of 18, he or she has the right to have his or her Indian citizenship restored. The provisions for making a declaration of renunciation under Indian citizenship law require that the person making the declaration be 'of full age and capacity'.

Termination

Termination is covered in Section 9 of the Citizenship Act, 1955. The provisions for termination are separate and distinct from the provisions for making a declaration of renunciation.

Section 9(1) of the Act provides that any citizen of India who by naturalization or registration acquires the citizenship of another country shall cease to be a citizen of India. Notably, the termination provision differs from the renunciation provision because it applies to 'any citizen of India' and is not restricted to adults. Indian children, therefore, also automatically lose their claim to Indian citizenship if at any time after birth they acquire a citizenship of another country by, for example, naturalization or registration—even if the acquisition of another citizenship was done as a result of actions by the child's parents.

The acquisition of another country's passport is also deemed under the Citizenship Rules, 1956 to be voluntary acquisition of another country's nationality. It does not matter that a person continues to hold an Indian passport. Persons who acquire another citizenship lose Indian citizenship from the date on which they acquire that citizenship or another country's passport.

Note : *The subtle difference between Renunciation and Termination is that renunciation is made by the person through a declaration whereas termination is by operation of the Citizenship Act.*

Deprivation

Deprivation is covered under Section 10 wherein the Central Government will compulsorily terminate the citizenship so granted if:

- Citizenship was obtained by fraud, false representation, or concealment of material fact; or
- Citizen shows his disloyalty towards the Constitution of India as law established through his speech or his conduct; or
- Citizen has indulged in an unlawful communication with the enemy during period of war; or
- Citizen, within a period of 5 years from naturalization or registration, is convicted of any offence in any country and been sentenced for imprisonment for a term of not less than 2 years; or
- Citizen has been outside India for a period of seven years or more continuously, except for education or in the service of Government of India or is employed with an international organization of which India is a member.

SUMMARY OF AMENDMENTS TO THE CITIZENSHIP ACT, 1955

Citizenship Act has been amended number of times since its enactment. Following is the summary of the key amendments.

Amendment Act	Effective Date	Key Amendments
Citizenship (Amendment) Act, 1986	July 1, 1987	To give effect to Assam Accord Insertion of Section 6A
Citizenship (Amendment) Act, 1992 (Act 39, 1992)	December 10, 1992	Definition change from 'male person' to 'person' in Section 4
Citizenship (Amendment) Act, 2003 (Act 6 of 2004)	December 3, 2004	Requiring that no parent of the child can be an illegal immigrant for the child to qualify for citizenship (Section 3) Grant of Overseas Citizenship to persons of Indian origin of all countries except Pakistan and Bangladesh Insertion of Section 7A to 7D Mandated the Central Government to create and maintain a National Register of Citizens and to issue national identity cards to all the registered citizens. The Central Government may compulsorily register every citizen of India and issue national identity card to him. Insertion of Section 14A and Section 15A
Citizenship (Amendment) Act, 2005 (Act 32 of 2005)	June 28, 2005	Substitution of Section 7A to 7D to expand the scope of OCI and PIO
Citizenship (Amendment) Act, 2015 (Act 1 of 2015)	January 6, 2015	Merging of PIO and OCI and substitution of Sections 7A to 7D with new sections
Citizenship (Amendment) Act, 2019 (Act 47 of 2019)	December 12, 2019	Fast track citizenship for religiously persecuted minorities, namely Hindus, Sikhs, Buddhists, Jains, Parsis, and Christians, from Afghanistan, Bangladesh and Pakistan, who faced 'persecution or fear of persecution' in their countries and entered India on or before 31 December, 2014. Insertion of Section 6B

COMPARATIVE CHART ON NRI/PIO/OCI CARDHOLDER[3]

	NRI	Persons of Indian Origin (PIO)	OCI
1. Who?	An Indian citizen who is ordinarily residing outside India and holds an Indian Passport	A person who or whose any of ancestors was an Indian national and who is presently holding another country's citizenship/ nationality, i.e., he/she is holding a foreign passport	A person registered as Overseas Citizen of India (OCI) cardholder under Section 7A of the Citizenship Act, 1955

[3]https://www.mha.gov.in/PDF_Other/CompNRIPIOOCI_25042017.pdf

2. Who is eligible?			Following categories of foreign nationals are eligible for registration as Overseas Citizen of India (OCI) cardholder:
			(1) Who was a citizen of India at the time of, or at any time after the commencement of the Constitution, i.e., 26.01.1950; or
			(2) who was eligible to become a citizen of India on 26.01.1950; or
			(3) who belonged to a territory that became part of India after 15.08.1947; or
			(4) who is a child or a grand-child or a great grandchild of such a citizen; or
			(5) who is a minor child of such persons mentioned above; or
			(6) who is a minor child and whose both parents are citizens of India or one of the parents is a citizen of India; or
			(7) spouse of foreign origin of a citizen of India or spouse of foreign origin of an Overseas Citizen of India cardholder registered under Section 7A of the Citizenship Act, 1955 and whose marriage has been registered and subsisted for a continuous period of not less than two years immediately preceding the presentation of the application. **Note :** *No person, who or either of whose parents or grandparents or great grand-parents is or had been a citizen of Pakistan, Bangladesh or such other country as the Central Government may, by notification in the Official Gazette, specify, shall be eligible for registration as an Overseas Citizen of India cardholder.*

3. Which nationals are ineligible?			No person, who or either of whose parents or grandparents or great grandparents is or had been a citizen of Pakistan, Bangladesh, or such other country as the Central Government may, by notification in the Official Gazette, specify, shall be eligible for registration as an Overseas Citizen of India cardholder.
4. What benefits one is entitled to?	All benefits as available to Indian citizens subject to notifications issued by the Government from time to time	No specific benefits	(i) Multiple entry lifelong visa for visiting India for any purpose (However OCI cardholders will require a special permission to undertake research work in India for which they may submit the application to the Indian Mission/ Post/ FRRO concerned).
			(ii) Exemption from registration with Foreigners Regional Registration Officer (FRRO) or Foreigners Registration Officer (FRO) for any length of stay in India.
			(iii) Parity with Non-Resident Indians (NRIs) in respect of all facilities available to them in economic, financial, and educational fields, except in matters relating to the acquisition of agricultural or plantation properties.
			(iv) Registered Overseas Citizen of India cardholder shall be treated at par with Non-Resident Indians in the matter of inter-country adoption of Indian children.
			(v) Registered Overseas Citizen of India cardholder shall be treated at par with resident Indian nationals in the matter of tariffs in air fares in domestic sectors in India.
			(vi) Registered Overseas Citizen of India cardholder shall be charged the same entry fee as domestic Indian visitors to visit national parks and wildlife sanctuaries in India.

			(vii) Parity with Non-Resident Indians (NRI) in respect of: (A) entry fees to be charged for visiting the national monuments, historical sites, and museums in India; (B) pursuing the following professions in India, in pursuance of the provisions contained in the relevant Acts, namely: (a) doctors, dentists, nurses, and pharmacists; (b) advocates (c) architects (d) chartered accountants (C) to appear for the All India Pre-Medical Test or such other tests to make them eligible for admission in pursuance of the provisions contained in the relevant Acts.
			(viii) State Governments should ensure that the OCI cardholder registration booklets of OCI cardholders are treated as their identification for any services rendered to them. In case proof of residence is required, Overseas Citizens of India cardholder may give an affidavit attested by a notary public stating that a particular/specific address may be treated as their place of residence in India and may also in their affidavit give their overseas residential address as well as e-mail address, if any. Any other benefits to an OCI cardholder will be notified by the Ministry of External Affairs (MEA) under Section 7B(1) of the Citizenship Act, 1955.

5. Does he/she require visa for visiting India	No	Yes	Can visit India without visa for lifelong
6. Is he/she required to register with the local police authorities in India?	No	Yes, if the period of stay is for more than 180 days	No
7. What activities can be undertaken in India?	All activities	Activity as per the type of visa obtained	All activities except research work for which special permission is required from the Indian Mission/Post/FRRO concerned
8. How can one acquire Indian citizenship?	He/she is an Indian citizen	As per Section 5(1)(a) & 5(1)(c) of the Citizenship Act, 1955, he/she has to be ordinarily resident in India for a period of 7 years before making an application for registration.	As per Section 5(1)(g) of the Citizenship Act,1955, a person registered as an OCI cardholder for 5 years and who is ordinarily resident in India for twelve months before making an application for registration is eligible for grant of Indian citizenship. Central Government, if it is satisfied that special circumstances exist, may after recording the circumstances in writing, relax the period of twelve months, up to a maximum of thirty days which may be in different breaks.

QUESTIONS

Objective Questions

1. Which of the following statements is/are correct with regard to acquisition of Citizenship in India?
   1. The children of foreign diplomats posted in India can acquire Indian citizenship by birth.
   2. A person applying for citizenship by Naturalization should have an adequate knowledge of a language specified in the Eighth Schedule.

   Select the correct answer using the codes given below.

   (a) 1 only (b) 2 only

   (c) Both 1 and 2 (d) Neither 1 nor 2

   Ans: (b)

2. With reference to the citizenship in India, consider the following statements:
   1. Both a citizen by birth as well as a naturalized citizen is eligible to contest for the membership of the Parliament and the state legislature.
   2. Only a citizen by birth and not a naturalized citizen is eligible for the office of the President of India.

   Which of the statements given above is/are correct?

   (a) 1 only (b) 2 only

   (c) Both 1 and 2 (d) Neither 1 nor 2

   Ans: (a)

3. Which of the following is essentially not a feature of Indian federal polity?

   (a) Independent judiciary (b) Dual citizenship

   (c) Written Constitution (d) Bicameral legislature

   Ans: (b)

4. Which of the following are the conditions for acquiring Indian Citizenship as per Citizenship Act, 1955?

   (a) Birth, Descent, and Holding property

   (b) Birth, Descent, Nauralization, Registration, and Incorporation of Territory

   (c) Domicile, Descent, Registration, and Holding property

   (d) None of the above

   Ans: (b)

5. Which among the following Articles deal with single citizenship?

   (a) Article 8 (b) Article 9

   (c) Article 10 (d) Article 11

   Ans: (b)

CHAPTER **8**

FUNDAMENTAL RIGHTS

"Political democracy cannot last unless there lies at the base of it social democracy. What does social democracy mean? It means a way of life which recognizes liberty, equality and fraternity as the principles of life."

Dr. B. R. Ambedkar

INTRODUCTION

Personal liberty is a precious right. The first object of the Founding Fathers of Indian Constitution was to give unto the people a Constitution whereby a Government was established. Their second object, equally important, was to protect the people against the Government. That is why, while conferring extensive powers on the Government, like the power to declare an emergency, the power to suspend the enforcement of Fundamental Rights, or the power to issue ordinances, they assured to the people a Bill of Rights by Part III of the Constitution, protecting the executive and legislative despotism, those rights which they regarded as "fundamental". The imperative necessity to protect those rights is a lesson taught by all history and all human experience[1].

It is, therefore, a mistake to regard Fundamental Rights as a gift from the State to its citizens as individuals possess basic human rights independently of any Constitution by virtue of being members of the human race. Hence, Part III of the Constitution does not confer Fundamental Rights, but confirms their existence and gives them protection. Its purpose is to withdraw certain subjects from the area of political controversy to place them beyond the reach of majorities and officials and to establish them as legal principles to be applied by the courts. A Fundamental Right is a limitation on the power of the State. Fundamental Rights have, in fact, proved to be the most significant constitutional control on the Government, and particularly legislative power.

Thus, Parts III, IV, and IV-A of the Constitution together constitute and concretize the lofty goals of justice, liberty, equality, fraternity, and the "dignity of the individual" set out in the Preamble[2]. Based on the dominant theories of human rights, we may classify these three parts respectively as:

---

[1] *State of Maharashtra Vs. Bhaurao Punjabrao Gawande,* (2008) 3 SCC 613, 624.

[2] For details, see, M.P. Singh, *The Statics and the Dynamics of the Fundamental Rights and the Directive Principles – A Human Rights Perspective* in S.P. Sathe and Sathya Narayan (Eds.), *Liberty, Equality and Justice* (Eastern Book Company 2003)45–58. For similar assertion, see, Ramlila Maidan Incident, re, (2012) 5 SCC 1: (2012) 2 SCC (Civ) 820.

- Negative obligations of the State not to interfere with the liberty of the individual (Part III/ Fundamental Rights);
- Positive obligations of the State to take steps for the welfare of the individual (Part IV/Directive Principles of State Policy); and
- The duties of the individual to society and fellow individuals (Part IV-A/Fundamental Duties).

While in the liberal tradition of constitutionalism the first ones are readily accepted as part of human rights regime, the second ones still invoke some resistance but are fast becoming indistinguishable from the first ones. The last ones are generally associated with socialist tradition as negation of human rights. But as the human rights are fast acquiring horizontal application[3], they also represent a positive step in that direction[4].

EVOLUTION OF FUNDAMENTAL RIGHTS

Since the 17th century, if not earlier, human thinking has been veering round to the theory that man has certain essential, basic, and inalienable rights or freedoms and it is the function of the state to recognize these rights and protect them. The concept of human rights can be traced to the natural law philosophers, such as, Locke and Rousseau. The Declaration of the French Revolution, 1789, may be regarded as a concrete political statement on Human Rights. This was inspired by the Lockeian philosophy which declared:

"The aim of all political association is the conservation of the natural and inalienable rights of man".

Thus, the concept of human rights protects individuals against the excesses of the state.

Evolution of Fundamental Rights in Various Countries

The evolution of Fundamental Rights in various countries is as follows :

(a) **USA :** The modern trend of guaranteeing Fundamental Rights to the people may be traced to the Constitution of the USA drafted in 1787. The US Constitution was the first modern Constitution to give a concrete shape to the concept of human rights by putting them into the Constitution and making them justiciable and enforceable through the instrumentality of the courts. The original US Constitution did not contain any Fundamental Rights. There was huge criticism of the Constitution on this score. Consequently, the Bill of Rights came to be incorporated in the Constitution in 1791 in the form of ten amendments which embody the Lockeian ideas about the protection of life, liberty, and property.

(b) **Britain :** The idea that human beings should have a set of basic rights and freedoms has deep roots in Britain. The Magna Carta, or "Great Charter", was arguably the most significant early influence on the English-speaking world including India. Magna Carta[5] was issued in June 1215 and was the first document to put into writing the principle that the king and his government was not above the law. It sought to prevent the king/executive from exploiting his power, and placed limits of royal authority by establishing law as a power in itself. But unlike the USA and

---

[3]Horizontal rights are applied against private actors while the vertical rights are rights which can be applied only against public authorities.

[4]For some discussion on this point, see, M.P. Singh, *Socio-Economic Rights in India: A Comparative Perspective* (Mohr Siebeck Tübingen 2015) 63 Jahrbuch des Offentlichen Rechts der Gegenwart 643ff.

[5]Magna Carta sought to limit the powers of the Monarch and his government (Executive) by placing the law above them.

India, there is no formal declaration of people's Fundamental Rights in Britain. The orthodox doctrine of the Sovereignty of the Parliament prevailing there does not envisage a legal check on the power of Parliament which is, as a matter of legal theory, free to make any law even though it abridges, modifies, or abolishes any basic civic right and liberty of the people. The power of the executive is however limited in the sense that it cannot interfere with the rights of the people without the sanction of law. Even in Britain, there was an ever-growing realization that guaranteed civil rights do serve a useful purpose and that Britain should also have a written Bill of Rights. Ultimately, the British Parliament enacted the Human Rights Act, 1998. The purpose of the Act is to give effect to the rights and freedoms guaranteed under the European Convention on Human Rights.

(c) **India :** During the British rule in India, human rights were violated by the rulers on a very wide scale. Therefore, the framers of the Constitution, many of whom had suffered long incarceration during the British regime, had a very positive attitude towards these rights. Several demands were made by our freedom fighters during the British rule for the declaration and protection of human rights. Following demands are some of the important milestones in the evolution of Fundamental Rights in India –

- **The Commonwealth of India Bill, 1925[6] :** The Commonwealth of India Bill demanded seven Fundamental Rights for Indians. Among these rights included: individual liberty, freedom of conscience, free expression of opinion, free assembly, and equality before law. The Bill also had provisions for right to free elementary education, equal right to use roads, court of justice, and all other places of business or resorts dedicated to the public.
- **The Nehru Report, 1928 :** The printing of the Commonwealth Bill was followed by the visit of Simon Commission in 1927, which aimed to study the possibility of introducing constitutional reforms in India. In response to the Simon Commission, the Congress passed a resolution to set up a committee in its forty-third annual session held at Madras for the purpose of drafting of "a Swaraj Constitution for India". A declaration of rights was to be the basis of this draft Constitution. The task to draft the Constitution was assigned to a committee. This committee came to be known as Nehru Committee after its chairman, Motilal Nehru. The Nehru Report underlined the need for securing Fundamental Rights that had been denied to them by the colonial government. Indeed, the Fundamental Rights in the Nehru report were a reiteration of the rights mentioned in the Commonwealth of India Bill.
- **The Sapru Report, 1945 :** The Sapru Committee was assigned the task of doing spadework for making the Constitution for future India. The Committee consisted of thirty members. It was known as Sapru Committee after the name of its chairman, Tej Bahadur Sapru, an eminent lawyer. The report was published in 1945. The Sapru Committee is distinguished for making two suggestions about rights. One, it made a distinction between justiciable rights and non-justiciable rights. Two, it suggested that rights of the minorities must be protected.

NEED OF FUNDAMENTAL RIGHTS IN INDIA

Indian society is fragmented into many religious, cultural, and linguistic groups, and it was necessary to declare Fundamental Rights to give to the people a sense of security and confidence. Though democracy was being introduced in India, yet democratic traditions were lacking, and there was a danger that the

[6]Drafted by Annie Besant.

majority in the legislature may enact laws which may be oppressive to individuals or minority groups, and such a danger could be minimized by having a Bill of Rights in the Constitution. Thus, the inclusion of Part III in the Constitution is in accordance with the trends of modern democratic thought.

The Fundamental Rights in India, apart from guaranteeing certain basic civil Rights and freedoms to all, also fulfill the important function of giving a few safeguards to minorities, outlawing discrimination, and protecting religious freedom and cultural rights.

GROUPING OF FUNDAMENTAL RIGHTS

The Fundamental Rights in the Indian Constitution have been grouped under seven heads as follows:

i. *Right to Equality* comprising Articles 14 to 18, of which Article 14 is the most important.
ii. *Right to Freedom* comprising Articles 19 to 22 which guarantee several freedoms.
iii. *Right against Exploitation* consists of Articles 23 and 24.
iv. *Right to Freedom of Religion* is guaranteed by Articles 25 to 28.
v. *Cultural and Educational Rights* are guaranteed by Articles 29 and 30.
vi. *Right to Property* under Articles 19 1(f) and 31 were deleted by 44th Constitutional Amendment Act, 1978. Right to Property is now very much diluted and is secured to some extent by Article 300A.
vii. *Right to Constitutional Remedies* is secured by Articles 32 to 35.

CHARACTERISTICS OF FUNDAMENTAL RIGHTS

1. **Basic inherent human rights :** Fundamental Rights are basic inherent human rights which are justiciable and enforceable by the courts.
2. **Not absolute rights :** The US Constitution declares the Fundamental Rights in broad and general terms. But as no right is absolute, the courts have, in course of time, spelled out some restrictions and limitations on these Rights. The framers of the Indian Constitution, learning from the experiences of the USA, visualized a great many difficulties in enunciating the Fundamental Rights in general terms and in leaving it to the courts to enforce them. Therefore, the Indian Constitution adopted a different approach. In other words, in respect of some Fundamental Rights, the exceptions and qualifications have been formulated and expressed in a comprehensive form in the Constitution itself, while in respect of some other rights, the Constitution confers power on the Legislature to impose the limitations. However, whether such restrictions are reasonable or not is to be decided by the courts. Thus, the Fundamental Rights are not absolute but qualified.
3. **Implied Fundamental Rights :** The Supreme Court has enunciated the doctrine of *Implied Fundamental Rights.* The Supreme Court has asserted that in order to treat a right as Fundamental Right, it is not necessary that it should be expressly stated in the Constitution as a Fundamental Right. There is no rule that unless a right is expressly stated as a Fundamental Right it cannot be treated as one. Over time, the Supreme Court has been able to imply by its interpretative process, several Fundamental Rights, such as, Freedom of Press, Right to Privacy, etc., out of the expressly stated Fundamental Rights.

4. **Fundamental Rights are not mutually exclusive :** The Fundamental Rights are not all distinct and are not mutually exclusive rights. Fundamental Rights are not separate from each other. Each right has some relation with another. No Fundamental Right in the Constitution is to be read in isolation.
5. **Fundamental Rights are protected and guaranteed :** The Supreme Court acts as the protector and the guardian of these rights. The Court acts as the interpreter of the Fundamental Rights. The Supreme Court acts as the "*sentinel on the qui vive*" (watchful guardian) in relation to the Fundamental Rights.
6. **Fundamental Rights are not limited to citizens :** All the Fundamental Rights are enjoyed by the citizens. Whereas, certain Fundamental Rights are equally enjoyed by citizens, aliens, as well as legal persons also.
7. **Fundamental Rights can be suspended :** Except Article 20 and 21, all other fundamental Rights can be suspended during the National Emergency[7]. During emergency, some curtailment of the Fundamental Rights does take place. But all these curtailments of Fundamental Rights are of a temporary nature.
8. **Fundamental Rights are not permanent :** Fundamental Rights are neither sacrosanct nor permanent. The Parliament, subject to the basic structure, can repeal or amend any Fundamental Rights by way of a constitutional amendment.
9. **Fundamental Rights' application can be restricted :** The application of certain Fundamental Rights to the members of military forces, para-military forces, intelligence agencies, etc., can be restricted by the Parliament by passing a law. Further, the application of rights can restricted even while martial law is in force.
10. **Horizontal application of Fundamental Rights :** Generally, the Fundamental Rights are enforceable against the state, whereas, in a few cases, it can be enforceable against the private individuals. In other words, certain Fundamental Rights can not only be enforceable against the state but also against the other individuals as well.
11. **Majority of Fundamental Rights are self-executable :** Majority of the Fundamental Rights are enforceable without any law or an Act. In other words, most of the Fundamental Rights are self-executable. However, certain rights can be executed or enforced only by passing a law. Such law can be passed only by the Parliament according to Article 35.
12. **No waiver of Fundamental Rights :** In *Olga Tellis Vs. Bombay Municipal Corporation*[8], the Supreme Court unanimously held that a person cannot waive any of the Fundamental Rights conferred upon him by the Constitution in Part III, by any act of his. Fundamental Rights being in the nature of a prohibition addressed to the State, none of the Fundamental Rights in our Constitution can be waived by an individual.

ARTICLE 12 – DEFINITION OF STATE

Article 12 – *In this Part, unless the context otherwise requires, "the State" includes the Government and Parliament of India and the Government and the Legislature of each of the States and all local or other authorities within the territory of India or under the control of the Government of India.*

[7]Suspension of Fundamental Rights is explained in a great detail in the "Emergency chapter".

[8]1986 AIR 180.

Article 12 defines the word "State". The present Article gives an extended meaning to the words "the State" wherever they occur in Part III of the Constitution. The framers of the Constitution used the words "the State" in a wider sense to place responsibilities and obligations on the "State". In other words, the normal legal rights are the creation of the State given to the individuals against one another, whereas Fundamental Rights are claimed against the State. The definition of "State" under Article 12, however, is only for the purpose of Part III of the Constitution.

According to Article 12, the term "State" include :

i. The Executive (Government) and Legislature (Parliament) of India;

ii. The Executive (Government) and Legislature (Parliament) of a State;

iii. All local authorities (Urban Local Bodies and Rural Local Bodies); and

iv. Other authorities within the territory of India, or under the control of the Central Government.

The expression "local authorities" usually refers to authorities such as municipalities, District Boards, Panchayats, mining settlement boards, etc. Any body functioning under the state; owned; controlled and managed by the "state" and carrying out a public function is a local authority and comes within the definition of the state.

The term 'other authorities' under Article 12 encompasses those authorities that do not fall within the first three categories. 'Other Authorities' though not defined in the Constitution has been widely interpreted through various judgments and now includes a number of authorities under it. For this purpose, the Supreme Court has developed the concept of an "instrumentality" of the state. Anybody which can be regarded as an "instrumentality" of the State falls under Article 12. Thus, the expression "other authorities" includes instrumentalities or agencies of the state; though such instrumentalities or agencies are not necessarily a "Government Department". Any organization having an independent status distinct from the State (e.g.: government companies, public undertakings, etc.,) falls under the definition of "Other authorities" if it acts like an agency or instrumentality of the state.

Whether "State" includes the Judiciary or not?

Judiciary, though an organ of the state, is not specifically mentioned in Article 12, unlike the executive and the legislature. Whether the judiciary comes under the definition of 'state' or not depends on the type of function carried out by the courts. In the exercise of non-judicial functions such as administrative or legislative, the courts fall within the definition of 'state'. However, in the exercise of judicial functions, the courts cannot be brought within the definition of the state. Therefore, the judiciary for discharge of its judicial functions cannot come under the definition of 'state' and is not amenable to the writ.

ARTICLE 13 – MEANS FOR JUDICIAL REVIEW

Article 13 - Laws inconsistent with or in derogation of the Fundamental Rights –

(1) All laws in force in the territory of India immediately before the commencement of this Constitution, in so far as they are inconsistent with the provisions of this Part, shall, to the extent of such inconsistency, be void.

(2) The State shall not make any law which takes away or abridges the rights conferred by this Part and any law made in contravention of this clause shall, to the extent of the contravention, be void.

(3) In this Article, unless the context otherwise requires, —

(a) "law" includes any Ordinance, order, bye-law, rule, regulation, notification, custom or usage having in the territory of India the force of law;

(b) "laws in force" includes laws passed or made by a Legislature or other competent authority in the territory of India before the commencement of this Constitution and not previously repealed, notwithstanding that any such law or any part thereof may not be then in operation either at all or in particular areas.

[9][(4) Nothing in this Article shall apply to any amendment of this Constitution made under Article 368.]

(a) **Pre-Constitution laws** : Clause (1) of Article 13 deals with pre-Constitution or existing laws, i.e., laws which were in force at the time of the commencement of the Constitution. This clause provides that all "laws in force" at the commencement of the Constitution which violates the Fundamental Rights shall, to that extent, be void. A pre-constitutional law, after the commencement of the Constitution, must conform to the provisions of Part III of the Constitution. But the inconsistent pre-constitutional laws will become void or invalid only after the court holds them inconsistent. So long as the courts do not hold them to be so, they shall continue to remain in force. Sometimes a law may be found against the Fundamental Rights long after the commencement of the Constitution[10].

In applying the rule embodied in Clause (1) of Article 13, the following principles of interpretation has been propounded by the Supreme Court[11]:

i. No retrospective effect : The provisions of the Constitution relating to the Fundamental Rights have no retrospective effect. All inconsistent existing laws, therefore, become void only from the commencement of the Constitution. Acts done before the commencement of the Constitution in pursuance or in contravention of the provisions of any law, which after the commencement of the Constitution become void because of inconsistency with the Fundamental Rights, are not affected.

ii. Doctrine of Severability : Article 13 does not make an entire Act inoperative; it makes inoperative only such provisions of it as are inconsistent with or violative of the Fundamental Rights[12].

iii. Doctrine of Eclipse : An existing law inconsistent with a Fundamental Right, though becomes inoperative from the date of the commencement of the Constitution, is not dead altogether. It is overshadowed by the Fundamental Right and remains dormant, but is not dead. It is a good law if a question arises for determination of rights and obligations incurred before the commencement of the Constitution. The reason is that a pre-Constitutional law was valid when enacted and therefore, was not *void ab initio*

---

[9]Ins. by the Constitution (Twenty-fourth Amendment) Act, 1971, s. 2.

[10]*John Vallamattom Vs. Union of India*, (2003) 6 SCC 611

[11]V.N. *Shukla's Constitution of India*, Thirteenth Edition, EBC Explorer, Pg No.39

[12]In *State of Bombay Vs. F.N. Balsara* (AIR 1951 SC 318), eight sections of the Bombay Prohibition Act, 1949 were held ultra vires on the ground that they infringed the Fundamental Rights of the citizens. But the Act, minus the invalid provisions, was allowed to stand.

(invalid since the beginning), but became void when Constitution came into force. Thus, according to this doctrine, a law made before the commencement of the Constitution, remains eclipsed or dormant to the extent it comes under the shadow of the Fundamental Right, i.e., is inconsistent with it.

(b) **Post-Constitutional laws :** Article 13(2) applies to the post-Constitution laws. The said clause prohibits the making of a law abridging Fundamental Rights. In Article 13(2), the words "the State shall not make any law" indicate that after the commencement of the Constitution, no law can be made so as to contravene a Fundamental Right. Such a law is *void ab initio.*

(c) **Definition of Law :** Article 13(3) defines the terms "law". The word law includes –

- Statutory law/Acts passed by the Parliament or State legislature; or
- Rules, orders, regulations, notifications, bye-laws etc., passed by the executive under the delegated legislative power[13]; or
- Ordinances issued by the President or the Governor; or
- Custom and usage having the force of law[14].

(d) **Court's power and duty to declare a law unconstitutional :** Article 13 expressly confers upon the courts the power of the judicial review, i.e., the power to strike down the law which is violating the Fundamental Rights. Judicial review is the power bestowed upon the judiciary by the Constitution, by virtue of which the judiciary can examine legislative enactments and executive orders of the governments, be it state or central. It is the power of the Court to declare a legislative Act void on the grounds of unconstitutionality (e.g.: violating the Constitution).

The foundation of this power of judicial review, as explained by a nine-judge Bench is the theory that the Constitution, which is the fundamental law of the land, is the will of the "people", while a statute/Act is only the creation of the elected representatives of the people. Therefore, when the will of the Legislature as declared in a stature, stands in opposition to that of the people as declared in the Constitution, the will of the people must prevail[15].

(e) **Constitutional Amendments[16] :** In *Shankari Prasad Singh Deo Vs. Union of India[17]*, the Constitution (1st Amendment Act), 1951 which amended the Fundamental Rights guaranteed under the Constitution, was challenged on the grounds that since the amendment had the effect of abridging the Fundamental Rights, it was not a valid law within the meaning of clause (2) of Article 13. The Supreme Court rejected the contention and held that the word "law" did not include the amendment of the Constitution under Article 368. In other words, the word "law" includes only the law made under the "ordinary legislative power" and not the

[13]Delegated Legislative power/Delegated legislation – means the power given by the legislature to the executive or administration to enact certain laws. In other words, when the function of the legislation is entrusted to organs other than the legislature by the legislature itself, the legislation made by such organs is known as delegated legislation.

[14]In early times, custom was the main source of law but now, to a large extent, it has been superseded by statutory law. However, custom has not wholly lost its law-creating efficacy. A reasonable and certain ancient custom is binding on courts like an Act of the legislature. Even binding customs, if they are in derogation of the Fundamental Rights, shall become inoperative after the commencement of the Constitution.

[15]*SC Advocates on Record Association Vs. UOI, AIR 1994 SC 268.*

[16]V.N. Shukla's *Constitution of India*, Thirteenth Edition, EBC Explorer, Pg No. 47.

[17]AIR 1951 SC 458.

amendments made under the "constituent power" of the Parliament. This interpretation was followed by the majority judgment in *Sajjan Singh Vs. State of Rajasthan*[18]. But in *Golak Nath Vs. State of Punjab*[19], the Supreme Court, held that the word "law" includes amendments to the Constitution and consequently, if any amendment abridged or took away a Fundamental Right guaranteed by Part III of the Constitution, the amending Act itself was void. Subsequently, in *Kesavananda Bharati Vs. State of Kerala*[20], the Supreme Court overruled the *Golak Nath Case,* and unanimously held that the 24th Constitutional Amendment Act, 1971 which inserted clause (4) in Article 13 and clause (3) in Article 368 was valid. The Supreme Court agreed that under Article 368, all provisions of the Constitution including those Fundamental Rights can be amended. However, the "basic structure" of the Constitution cannot be amended. Therefore, even if an amendment of the Constitution is not "law" within the meaning of Article 13, that does not exempt the amendment to violate the basic structure of the Constitution.

ARTICLE 14 – EQUALITY BEFORE LAW

Article 14 – The State shall not deny to any person equality before the law or the equal protection of the laws within the territory of India.

The Constitution of India guarantees the Right to Equality through Articles 14 to 18. Equality is one of the magnificent cornerstones of Indian democracy. Article 14 outlaws discrimination in a general way and guarantees equality before law and equal protection of law to all persons. Article 14 is not only applicable to citizens but it is also applicable to foreigners, and legal persons such as companies, societies, corporations, etc.

(a) **Concepts of Equality**[21] **:** There are two concepts of equality – "formal equality" and "egalitarian equality". Formal equality means that law treats everyone equal and does not favour anyone either because he belongs to the advantaged section of the society or to the disadvantaged section of the society. "Egalitarian equality" is proportional equality. Concept of proportional equality expects the States to take affirmative action in favour of disadvantaged sections of the society within the framework of liberal democracy. Proportional equality is equality "in fact" whereas formal equality is equality "in law".

(b) **Rule of Law :** Rule of law is one of the basic principles of the common law in England. This doctrine is accepted in the Constitution of USA and also in the Constitution of India. Dicey developed this theory in his book "Introduction to the Study of the Law of the Constitution", published in the year 1885. "Rule of law" means that no man is above the law and that every person is subject to the jurisdiction of ordinary courts of law, irrespective of his rank and position. The doctrine of equality before law is a necessary corollary to the concept of the Rule of Law. According to Prof. Dicey, 'Rule of Law' includes three core principles –

- Supremacy of law – According to this principle, Rule of Law means there should be lacking of arbitrariness or wide discretionary power. In other words, every Act will be controlled by law.

---

[18] AIR 1965 SC 845.

[19] AIR 1967 SC 1643.

[20] (1973) 4 SCC 225.

[21] Durga Das Basu, *Shorter Constitution of India*, LexisNexis, 16th Edition, Pg No. 82.

- Equality before Law – This principle emphasizes that everyone, including the government, irrespective of rank, shall be subject to the same law and courts.
- Predominance of Legal Spirit – It means that the source of the right of the individual is not just the written Constitution but the rules as defined and enforced by the courts. This part does not apply to the Indian system as the source of rights of individuals is the Constitution of India. Further, under the principle of 'Predominance of Legal Spirit', Dicey also believed that each man's individual rights are best protected under Common Law rather than a formal Bill of Rights. This reveals his faith in judiciary. Dicey states that many constitutions of the states (countries) guarantee their citizens certain rights (fundamental or human or basic rights) such as right to personal liberty, freedom from arrest, etc. According to him, documentary guarantee of such rights is not enough. Such rights can be made available to the citizens only when they are properly enforceable in the Courts of Law. Thus, the role of Courts in protecting the Fundamental Rights or the concept of Judicial Review is recognized in the Indian Constitution as well.

The Supreme Court in the case of *Indira Nehru Gandhi Vs. Raj Narain*[22] held that the Rule of Law embodied in Article 14 is the 'basic structure' of the Indian Constitution and hence, it cannot be destroyed even by an amendment of the Constitution under Article 368 of the Constitution.

(c) **Equality before Law :** This principle is taken from the English Common Law. It is a declaration of equality of all persons within the territory of India. Equality before law is a negative concept which ensures that –

- There is no special privilege in favour of any one;
- All are equally subject to the ordinary law of the land;
- No person whatever be his rank or condition, is above the law.

This however, is not an absolute rule and there are number of exceptions to it –

- Foreign diplomats enjoy immunity from the country's judicial process. The said diplomatic immunity is enjoyed even by the members of United Nation Organization and its agencies.
- Article 361 extends immunity to the President of India and the State Governors[23].
- Public officers such as MPs[24], MLAs, and judges also enjoy some protection;
- Article 31-C is an exception to Article 14. If a law which is implementing Article 39(b) and (c) violates Article 14, then the said law cannot be challenged on the ground that it is violative of Article 14.

(d) **Equal Protection of Laws :** This concept is positive in content. It means that amongst equals, the law should be equal and should be equally administered and the likes should be treated alike. Thus, what it forbids is discrimination between persons who are substantially in similar circumstances or conditions. It does not forbid unequal treatment of unequals. Equal protection means the right to equal treatment in similar circumstances, both in privileges conferred and in the liabilities imposed[25].

---

[22] AIR 1975 SC 2299.

[23] Kindly, refer to President and Governor chapters for immunities and privileges enjoyed by the President and Governor respectively.

[24] Refer to the Parliament chapter for the privileges enjoyed by the MPs

[25] *T.M.A. Pai Foundation Vs. State of Karnataka*, AIR 2003 SC 355.

(e) **Doctrine of "Reasonable Classification" :** Equality before law and equal protection of laws connote that equality is not an absolute concept. Equals cannot be treated unequally and unequals cannot be treated equally. Article 14 does not provide for equal treatment of all persons without distinction. It permits reasonable classification for the purpose of legislation and administrative decisions. The Rule of Law cannot prevent a certain class of persons from being subject to special laws. Hence, the State has the power to make laws operating differently on different classes of people, in a way that the principle of equality of civil rights and equal protection of law is followed. This is being known as the 'Doctrine of Reasonable Classification'. Article 14 permits Reasonable Classification and not Class Legislation. Class Legislation means making of arbitrary and improper discrimination by conferring certain privileges upon a class of persons arbitrarily selected from a huge number of people. Thus, Class legislation violates equal protection whereas; Reasonable Classification is always based on real and substantial distinction. The classification however must not be "arbitrary, artificial, or evasive" but must bear a reasonable relation to the object sought to be achieved by the legislation.

(f) **Exceptions to Article 14 :**

- Article 31A–31C[26]
- A new part XIV-A has been introduced relating to Administrative Tribunals, by the 42nd Constitutional Amendment Act, 1976, providing that the provisions in these Articles shall override any other provisions of the Constitution (Article 323A and 323B) as a result of which nobody aggrieved by the decisions of such tribunals shall be entitled to invoke Article 14, on the ground that there has been discrimination by having his dispute adjudicated by an administrative tribunal to the exclusion of the ordinary courts of the land.
- A total suspension of Article 14 may be made by an order under Article 359, made by the President.

ARTICLE 15 – SECURING THE CITIZENS FROM EVERY SORT OF DISCRIMINATION BY THE STATE

Article 15 – Prohibition of discrimination on grounds of religion, race, caste, sex or place of birth –

(1) The State shall not discriminate against any citizen on grounds only of religion, race, caste, sex, place of birth, or any of them.

(2) No citizen shall, on grounds only of religion, race, caste, sex, place of birth or any of them, be subject to any disability, liability, restriction or condition with regard to —

(a) access to shops, public restaurants, hotels, and places of public entertainment; or

(b) the use of wells, tanks, bathing ghats, roads, and places of public resort maintained wholly or partly out of State funds or dedicated to the use of the general public.

(3) Nothing in this Article shall prevent the State from making any special provision for women and children.

[27]*[(4) Nothing in this Article or in clause (2) of Article 29 shall prevent the State from making any special provision for the advancement of any socially and educationally backward classes of citizens or for the Scheduled Castes and the Scheduled Tribes.]*

---

[26] Explained in Right to Property Chapter.

[27] Added by the Constitution (First Amendment) Act, 1951, s. 2.

[28][(5) *Nothing in this Article or in sub-clause (g) of clause (1) of Article 19 shall prevent the State from making any special provision, by law, for the advancement of any socially and educationally backward classes of citizens or for the Scheduled Castes or the Scheduled Tribes in so far as such special provisions relate to their admission to educational institutions including private educational institutions, whether aided or unaided by the State, other than the minority educational institutions referred to in clause (1) of Article 30.]*

[29][(6) *Nothing in this Article or sub-clause (g) of clause (1) of Article 19 or clause (2) of Article 29 shall prevent the State from making,—*

(a) any special provision for the advancement of any economically weaker sections of citizens other than the classes mentioned in clauses (4) and (5); and

(b) any special provision for the advancement of any economically weaker sections of citizens other than the classes mentioned in clauses (4) and (5) in so far as such special provisions relate to their admission to educational institutions including private educational institutions, whether aided or unaided by the State, other than the minority educational institutions referred to in clause (1) of Article 30, which in the case of reservation would be in addition to the existing reservations and subject to a maximum of ten percent of the total seats in each category.

***Explanation.** : For the purposes of this Article and Article 16, "economically weaker sections" shall be such as may be notified by the State from time to time on the basis of family income and other indicators of economic disadvantage.]*

Article 14 talks about equality in wider sense, whereas Article 15 promotes equality and prohibits discrimination on specific grounds. While Article 14 is available to all persons, Article 15 is available to citizens only.

(a) Clause (1) of the Article prohibits the State from discriminating against citizens on grounds only of religion, race, sex, caste, place of birth or any of them. The right guaranteed in clause (1) is conferred on a citizen as an individual and is available against his being subjected to discrimination.

(b) Clause (2) provides that no citizen shall on grounds only of religion, race, caste, sex, place of birth or any of them, be subjected to any disability, liability, restriction or condition with regard to :

- Access to shops, public restaurants, hotels and places of public entertainment; or
- The use of wells, tanks, bathing ghats, roads, and places of public resort, maintained wholly or partly out of State funds or dedicated to the use of the general public.

This clause contains a prohibition of a general nature and is not confined to the state only. Attention should be drawn to the word "only" in clauses (1) and (2) of Article 15, i.e., the State shall not discriminate against any person on grounds only of religion, race, caste, sex, place of birth or any of them. In other words, the prohibited ground should not be the only or sole consideration for discriminatory treatment. If sex, religion, etc., is not the only ground for the differentiation, the law will be valid, irrespective of its operation.

---

[28]Inserted by the Constitution (Ninety-third Amendment) Act, 2005, s. 2, (w.e.f. 20-1-2006).

[29]Inserted by the Constitution (One Hundred and Third Amendment) Act, 2019.

(c) Clause (3) enacts that nothing in Article 15 shall prevent the State from making any special provision for women and children. From the reading of clauses (1), (2), and (3) together, it follows that while discrimination on the ground of sex is impermissible, special provisions for women and children are permissible.

(d) Clause (4) was added by the Constitution (1st Amendment) Act, 1951, to override the decision of the Supreme Court in *State of Madras Vs. Champakam Dorairajan*[30]. In the said case, the court struck down the communal order of the Madras government which, with the object of helping backward classes, had fixed the proportion of students of each community that could be admitted into the State medical and engineering colleges[31]. Clause (4) is an exception to clause (1) in so far as it forbids discrimination on the ground of "race" or "caste". The special provisions permissible under Article 15(4) are not confined to "positive action programs" for the advancement of backward classes but would include "reservation" (*positive discrimination*) in education institutions and other walks of life. Article 15(4) envisages the policy of compensatory or protective discrimination but it should be reasonable and consistent with ultimate public interest, i.e., national interest and the interest of community or society as a whole. The expression "Backward classes" in Article 15(4) is qualified by the words "socially and educationally". In other words, in order to satisfy the requirement of Article 15(4), the class must be both socially and educationally backward. Thus, mere educational backwardness is not enough if the class is not socially backward, and *vice versa.* Moreover, Article 15(4) does not make any mandatory provision for reservation in favour of socially and educationally backward classes or for scheduled castes and scheduled tribes and the power of the State to make reservation under Article 15(4) is discretionary and no writ of mandamus can be issued to effect reservation.

(e) The Constitution 93rd Amendment Act, 2005, added clause (5) in Article 15 enabling the State to make special provisions for members of the SCs, STs, and socially and educationally backward classes, for admission to all educational institutions, including private unaided institutions, but except minority institutions.

(f) Clause (6) empowers the state to make special provisions for the advancement of "economically weaker sections[32]" of the society, which would even include the reservations in educational institutes. This sub-clause was added as 103rd amendment in 2019. The amendment further states that 10% of the reservation has to be provided for Economically Weaker Sections. This 10% of reservations is independent of ceilings upon the already existing reservations[33].

---

[30] AIR 1951 SC 226.

[31] V.N. Shukla's *Constitution of India*, Thirteenth Edition, EBC Explorer, Pg No. 95

[32] On January 17th 2019, the government released an official memorandum (OM) informing that families earning a gross annual income below ₹ 8 lakh would be identified as EWS for benefit of reservation. However, the Supreme Court (SC) has questioned the methodology adopted by the government in fixing Rs. 8 lakh as the annual income limit to identify the Economically Weaker Sections (EWS) for providing 10% quota in public jobs and educational institutions.

[33] Several writ petitions have been filed challenging the constitutionality of the Constitution (One Hundred and Third Amendment) Act, 2019. The matter is before the Supreme Court.

(g) Economically Weaker Sections : Persons who are not covered under the scheme of reservation for SCs, STs, and OBCs and whose family has gross annual income below Rs. 8 lakh[34] (Rupees eight lakh only) are to be identified as EWSs for benefit of reservation. Income shall also include income from all sources, i.e., salary, agriculture, business, profession, etc., for the financial year prior to the year of application.

Also, persons whose family owns or possesses any of the following assets shall be excluded from being identified as EWS, irrespective of the family income:-

i. 5 acres of agricultural land and above;

ii. Residential area of 1000 sq ft. and above;

iii. Residential plot of 100 sq. yards and above in notified municipalities;

iv. Residential plot of 200 sq. yards and above in areas other than the notified municipalities.

The property held by a "Family[35]" in different locations or different places/cities would be clubbed while applying the land or property holding test to determine EWS status.

ARTICLE 16 – EQUALITY OF OPPORTUNITY IN MATTERS OF PUBLIC EMPLOYMENT

According to Article 16 –

(1) There shall be equality of opportunity for all citizens in matters relating to employment or appointment to any office under the State.

(2) No citizen shall, on grounds only of religion, race, caste, sex, descent, place of birth, residence or any of them, be ineligible for, or discriminated against in respect of, any employment or office under the State.

(3) Nothing in this Article shall prevent Parliament from making any law prescribing, in regard to a class or classes of employment or appointment to an office[36][under the Government of, or any local or other authority within, a State or Union territory, any requirement as to residence within that State or Union territory] prior to such employment or appointment.

(4) Nothing in this Article shall prevent the State from making any provision for the reservation of appointments or posts in favour of any backward class of citizens which, in the opinion of the State, is not adequately represented in the services under the State.

[37][(4A) Nothing in this Article shall prevent the State from making any provision for reservation [38][in matters of promotion, with consequential seniority, to any class] or classes of posts in the services under the State in favor of the Scheduled Castes and the Scheduled Tribes which, in the opinion of the State, are not adequately represented in the services under the State.]

---

[34]The Supreme Court (SC) has questioned the methodology adopted by the government in fixing Rs. 8 lakh as the annual income limit to identify the Economically Weaker Sections (EWS) for providing 10% quota in public jobs and educational institutions.Following SC's suggestion, the Centre had set up the Pandey Committee.

[35]The term "Family" for this purpose will include the person who seeks benefit of reservation, his/her parents and siblings below the age of 18 years as also his/her spouse and children below the age of 18 years.

[36]Substituted by the Constitution (Seventh Amendment) Act, 1956.

[37]Inserted by the Constitution (Seventy-seventh Amendment) Act, 1995.

[38]Substituted by the Constitution (Eighty-fifth Amendment) Act, 2001, s. 2, for certain words (w.e.f. 17-6-1995).

[39]*[(4B) Nothing in this Article shall prevent the State from considering any unfilled vacancies of a year which are reserved for being filled up in that year in accordance with any provision for reservation made under clause (4) or clause (4A) as a separate class of vacancies to be filled up in any succeeding year or years and such class of vacancies shall not be considered together with the vacancies of the year in which they are being filled up for determining the ceiling of fifty per cent. reservation on total number of vacancies of that year.]*

(5) *Nothing in this Article shall affect the operation of any law which provides that the incumbent of an office in connection with the affairs of any religious or denominational institution or any member of the governing body thereof shall be a person professing a particular religion or belonging to a particular denomination.*

Among Articles 14, 15, and 16, Article 16 is the narrowest of all three. Article 16 talks about equality of opportunity limited to public employment and appointment matters. Article 15 and 16 are instances of Article 14. Article 15 is more general than Article 16, as the latter is confined to matters relating to employment or appointment to any office under the State. It is also worthy to note that Article 15 does not mention "descent" as one of the prohibited grounds of discrimination, whereas Article 16 does.

(a) Clause(1) – lays down the general rule that there shall be equal opportunity for citizens in matters relating to "employment" or "appointment to any office" under the State. It gives the right only to equal opportunity, i.e., the right to be considered for employment to any office under the State. The rule applies only in respect of employment or offices which are held under the State[40].

(b) Clause (2) – is in a negative form. It prohibits discrimination on grounds only of religion, race, caste, sex, descent, place of birth, and residence. However, if the discrimination is on any grounds other than those specified in this clause, then it is not violative of Article 16. E.g.:

   i. A condition in rules for recruitment to the State Judiciary that the candidates must be advocates practicing in the State[41]; or

   ii. Giving linguistic concessions, at an All India Services Examination to residents of North-Eastern territories which are linguistically backward[42].

(c) Clause (3) – Under clause (2), residence in a State cannot be a ground for discrimination in the matter of employment under the State, whereas, an exception is made under clause (3). According to clause (3), Parliament (not any State Legislature) is empowered to make any law prescribing residence in a particular State to be requirement for employment within that State. The power to make such exceptions belongs exclusively to the Parliament. Hence, in the absence of any legislation by the Parliament, the condition imposed by any State Government or local authority that a person shall not be employed unless he is a "local" candidate, would be violative of Article 16(1).

---

[39]Inserted by the Constitution (Eighty-first Amendment) Act, 2000, s. 2 (w.e.f. 9-6-2000).

[40]V.N. Shukla's Constitution of India, Thirteenth Edition, EBC Explorer, Pg No. 111.

[41]Nallanthighal Bhaktavatsalam Iyengar Vs. PSC, AIR 1956 Andhra 14.

[42]Javed Niaz Beg Vs. UOI, AIR 1981 SC 794.

(d) Clause 4 – Article 16(4) is enacted as a remedy for the past historical discrimination against a social class. The said clause enables the State to provide for reservation in cases where it is satisfied on the basis of quantifiable data that there exists backwardness of a class and inadequacy of representation in employment. Therefore, in every case where the State decides to provide for reservation, there must exist two circumstances, namely, "backwardness" and "inadequacy of representation". Article 16(4) is an enabling provision and no citizen can claim reservation as a matter of right[43].

(e) Clause 5 – Article 16(5) is an exception to Article16 (1). According to Article 16(5), the office-bearer of a religious denomination shall be appointed only from amongst persons of that particular religious faith or denomination. Eg: A Christian cannot be appointed as a temple priest and a Hindu cannot be appointed as a church father.

(f) The Mandal Commission Case (*Indra Sawhney Vs. UOI*[44], known as the Mandal Commission case) – The Mandal Commission was appointed by the Government of India in terms of Article 340[45] of the Constitution in 1979 to investigate the conditions of socially and educationally backward classes. One of the major recommendations made by the Commission was that, besides SCs and STs, for Other Backward Classes (OBCs) which constitute nearly 52% component of the population, 27% government jobs should be reserved so that the total reservation for all, SCs, STs, and OBCs, amounts to 50%. No action was taken on the basis of the Mandal Report for a long period after it was submitted. In 1990, the V.P. Singh Government at the Centre issued an office memorandum accepting the Mandal Commission recommendation and announcing 27% reservation for the socially and educationally backward classes in vacancies in civil posts and services under the Government of India. This memorandum led to widespread disturbances in the country. In 1991, the Narasimha Rao Government modified the above memorandum in two respects: one, the poorer sections among the backward classes would get preference over the other sections; two, 10% vacancies would be reserved for other "economically backward sections" of the people who were not covered by any existing reservation scheme. The Mandal Commission report and the official memorandum was challenged before the Supreme Court. *The Supreme Court nine-judge Bench was constituted to finally settle the legal position on reservations. Supreme Court in its majority judgment held that -*

i. Article 16(4) is not an exception to 16(1). It is an instance of classification permitted by 16(1).

ii. While explaining the meaning of "backward classes" in Article 16(4), the Supreme Court elaborated that there is an integral connection between caste, occupation, poverty, and social backwardness. Social, educational, and economic backwardness are closely intertwined in the Indian context. As regards identification of backward classes, caste may be used as a criterion because caste often is a social class in India. But caste cannot be the sole criterion

---

[43]Durga Das Basu, Shorter Constitution of India, 16th Edition, LexisNexis, Page No. 269 & 270.

[44]AIR 1993 SC 477.

[45]Govt. of India appointed the First Backward Classes Commission under Article 340 of the Constitution in 1953. The Commission popularly known as "Kaka Kalelkar Commmission" submitted its report in 1955. Mandal Commission is the Second Backward Class Commission.

for reservation. Reservation is not being made under Article 16(4) in favour of a caste but a backward class.

iii. Backwardness under Article 16(4) need not be social as well as educational as is the case under Article 15(4).

iv. The Court has rejected the reservation of 10% posts in favour of "other economically backward sections of the people" because such category cannot be related to Article 16(4). Moreover, a backward class cannot be identified only and exclusively with reference to economic criterion. A backward class may, however, be identified on the basis of occupation-cum-income without any reference to caste.

v. There is no constitutional bar in the State categorizing the backward classes as 'backward' and 'more backward'.

vi. The Court has left the task of identifying backward classes to the commission/authority to be appointed by the Government.

vii. The Court further recommended the concept of "creamy layer". The socially advanced members of a backward class should be excluded from the benefit of reservation. Such exclusion would benefit the truly backward people and thus, more appropriately serve the purpose of Article 16(4). However, the court directed the Government to determine the criteria for the 'creamy layer'[46].

viii. The total reservation cannot exceed 50% in any one year. Article 16(4) speaks of "adequate representation" and not "proportional representation". Therefore, reservation under Article 16(4) should not exceed 50% of the appointment or posts "barring certain extraordinary situations".

ix. Reserved posts remaining unfilled in one year may be carried forward to the next year but subject to the overall limit that overall reservation in any one year cannot be more than 50%.

x. Under Article 16(4), reservation is permissible only at the stage of entry or appointment and not at the promotional stage.

---

[46]Based on Supreme Court's recommendation, an expert Committee headed by Justice Ram Nandan Prasad was constituted by the Government to determine the criteria for the creamy layer. The recommendations made by the Committee for excluding the Creamy Layer amongst OBCs were accepted by the Government. Following category of people fall under creamy layer and they cannot avail the OBC reservation –

(a) Son(s) and daughter(s) of persons holding Constitutional positions or Group A Officers or are in the rank of Colonel and above in the Army and equivalent posts in the Navy and Air Force and the para-military forces or if both the parents are Group B officers (or)

(b) Son(s) and daughter(s) of persons holding equivalent or comparable posts in PSUs, Banks, Insurance Organizations, Universities, etc.,

(c) Families owning irrigated land, which is equal to or more than 85% of the ceiling limit in terms of irrigated land as per State land ceiling laws; (or)

(d) The persons having gross annual income of Rs. 8.00 lakh or above; (or)

(e) Possessing wealth above the exemption limits prescribed in the wealth Tax Act for a period of three consecutive years (income for salaries or agricultural land shall not be clubbed) are also excluded.

xi. The Court has directed to establish a permanent body or Commission at the Centre and in each State, which can look into the complaints of wrong inclusion or non-inclusion of classes or groups in the OBC lists[47].

In order to modify the proposition and to tone down the impact of the ruling laid down by the Supreme Court in *Indra Sawhney*, various Constitutional Amendments have been incorporated in Article16 –

(g) Article 16 (4A) – The Supreme Court in *Indra Sawhney* opined that the reservations should be confined to initial appointments only and should not permit reservations in the promotion stage. However, the 77th Constitutional Amendment, 1995 added Article 16(4A) permitting reservation even in promotion to the SCs and STs.

(h) Article 16(4B) – The 81st Amendment Act, 2000 provides that the rule of 50% reservation laid down by the Supreme Court is to be applied only to normal vacancies and not to the posts of backlog of reserved vacancies. In other words, the unfilled reserved vacancies are to be carried forward from year to year without any limit, and are to be filled separately from the normal vacancies.

(i) In 2006, the constitutional validity of 77th, 81st, 82nd[48], and 85th[49] amendments were challenged in *M. Nagaraj Vs. Union of India*[50]. In it, the Court validated Parliament's decision to extend reservations for SC/STs to include promotions (reservation in promotion). However, the Court laid down certain conditions to grant such reservations.

- First, the State must show the backwardness of the class.
- Second, it must show that the class is inadequately represented in the position/service for which reservations in promotion will be granted.
- Finally, it must show that the reservations are in the interest of administrative efficiency.

(j) Article 16(6) – is added by 103rd Constitutional Amendment Act, 2019 to provide reservations to people from economically weaker[51] sections in government posts. The reservation is of a maximum of 10% for the economically backward class or economically weaker section in public employment.

---

[47] Based on the Supreme Court's ruling, the National Commission for Backward Classes (NCBC) was initially constituted by the Central Govt. by 'The National Commission for Backward Classes Act, 1993'. The commission was constituted to consider inclusions in and exclusions from the lists of communities notified as backward for the purpose of job reservations and to tender the needful advice to the Central Government. However, the Central Govt. has repealed 'The National Commission for Backward Classes Act in 2018. The Commission has been accorded Constitutional Status and constituted through "The Constitution (One Hundred and Second Amendment) Act, 2018" Act whereby Article 338B has been inserted, forming a Commission for the socially and educationally backward classes to be known as NCBC. The functions of NCBC were further enlarged with the constitutional amendment. The nodal ministry for NCBC is Ministry of Social Justice and Empowerment.

[48] The Constitution (Eighty Second Amendment) Act, 2000 inserted a proviso to Article 335. Article 335 mandates that reservations have to be balanced with the 'maintenance of efficiency'. The 2000 amendment to Article 335 clarified that the Article will not apply to the State relaxing evaluation standards 'in matters of promotion'.

[49] The Constitution (Eighty Fifth Amendment) Act, 2001 added "consequential seniority" for SC/STs under 16(4A).

[50] AIR 2007 SC 71.

[51] "Economic weakness" shall be decided on the basis of "family income" and other "indicators of economic disadvantage."

ARTICLE 17 – ABOLITION OF UNTOUCHABILITY

Article 17 –"Untouchability" is abolished and its practice in any form is forbidden. The enforcement of any disability arising out of "Untouchability" shall be an offence punishable in accordance with law.

Article 17 abolishes untouchability and forbids its practice in any form. Abolition of untouchability is applicable to state action as well as acts or omissions by individuals, institutions, or legal persons.

To give effect to Article 17, Parliament enacted the Untouchability (Offences) Act, 1955, prescribing punishments for practicing untouchability in various forms. In 1976, the Act was renamed as the "Protection of Civil Rights Act, 1955". The word "untouchability" has not, however, been defined by the Act just as there is no definition in the Constitution. A single judge of the Mysore High Court[52] has held that "untouchability" in the Act refers to "the social disabilities historically imposed on certain classes of people by reason of their birth in certain cases and would not include an instigation of social boycott by reason of the conduct of certain persons".

Parliament has also enacted the Scheduled Castes and Scheduled Tribes (Prevention of Atrocities) Act, 1989, in order –

i. To prevent the commission of atrocities against the members of the Scheduled Castes and the Scheduled Tribes;

ii. To provide for setting up of special Courts for the trial of offences under the Act; and

iii. Also to provide for the relief and rehabilitation of victims of such offences.

ARTICLE 18 – ABOLITION OF TITLES

According to Article 18:

(1) No title, not being a military or academic distinction, shall be conferred by the State.

(2) No citizen of India shall accept any title from any foreign State.

(3) No person who is not a citizen of India shall, while he holds any office of profit or trust under the State, accept without the consent of the President any title from any foreign State.

(4) No person holding any office of profit or trust under the State shall, without the consent of the President, accept any present, emolument, or office of any kind from or under any foreign State.

Clause(1) – The framers of the Constitution sought to put an end to the practice followed by the British in respect of conferment of titles. They, therefore, prohibited titles of nobility and all other titles that carry suffixes or prefixes to the names of the holders as they result in creation of a distinct unequal class of citizens. The national awards like "Bharat Ratna", "Padma Vibhushan", etc. awarded by the Government of India, are not 'titles' within the meaning of Article 18(1)[53]. However, awards conferred by the State are not to be used as suffixes or prefixes.

However, the framers did not intend that the State should not officially recognize merit or work of an extraordinary nature. The National Awards are not violative of the principles of equality.

Clause (2) – prohibits citizens of India from accepting any title from a foreign government. It is not clear as to what would happen if a citizen accepts a title in contravention of Article 18(2). It is open to Parliament, under its residuary powers, to make a law prescribing what should be done with regard to an individual who accepts a title contrary to the Article.

---

[52] *Devarajiah Vs. Padmanna*, AIR 1961 Mad 35, p. 39.

[53] *Balaji Raghavan Vs. UOI*, AIR, 1996 SC 770.

Clause (3) – A foreigner holding any office of profit or trust under the state cannot accept any title from a foreign state without the consent of the President.

Clause (4) – No person holding any office of profit under the state is to accept, without the consent of the President, any present, emolument, or office of any kind from or under any foreign state.

ARTICLE 19 – FREEDOM OF SPEECH AND EXPRESSION

Article 19 – Protection of certain rights regarding freedom of speech, etc. :

(1) All citizens shall have the right —

(a) to freedom of speech and expression;

(b) to assemble peaceably and without arms;

(c) to form associations or unions [54]*[or co-operative societies];*

(d) to move freely throughout the territory of India;

(e) to reside and settle in any part of the territory of India;[55]*[and]* [56]*[(f)* Omitted * * * *]*

(f) to practise any profession, or to carry on any occupation, trade, or business.

[57]*[(2) Nothing in sub-clause (a) of clause (1) shall affect the operation of any existing law, or prevent the State from making any law, in so far as such law imposes reasonable restrictions on the exercise of the right conferred by the said sub-clause in the interests of*[58]*[the sovereignty and integrity of India], the security of the State, friendly relations with foreign States, public order, decency or morality, or in relation to contempt of court, defamation or incitement to an offence.]*

(3) Nothing in sub-clause (b) of the said clause shall affect the operation of any existing law in so far as it imposes, or prevent the State from making any law imposing, in the interests of [59]*[the sovereignty and integrity of India or] public order, reasonable restrictions on the exercise of the right conferred by the said sub-clause.*

(4) Nothing in sub-clause (c) of the said clause shall affect the operation of any existing law in so far as it imposes, or prevent the State from making any law imposing, in the interests of [60]*[the sovereignty and integrity of India or] public order or morality, reasonable restrictions on the exercise of the right conferred by the said sub-clause.*

(5) Nothing in [61]*[sub-clauses (d) and (e)] of the said clause shall affect the operation of any existing law in so far as it imposes, or prevent the State from making any law imposing, reasonable restrictions on the exercise of any of the rights conferred by the said sub-clauses either in the interests of the general public or for the protection of the interests of any Scheduled Tribe.*

---

[54]Inserted by the Constitution (Ninety-seventh Amendment) Act, 2011, s. 2 (w.e.f. 8-2-2012).

[55]Inserted by the Constitution (Forty-fourth Amendment) Act, 1978.

[56]Inserted by the Constitution (Forty-fourth Amendment) Act, 1978.

[57]Substituted by the Constitution (First Amendment) Act, 1951

[58]Inserted by the Constitution (Sixteenth Amendment) Act, 1963

[59]Ibid.

[60]Ibid

[61]Substituted by the Constitution (Forty-fourth Amendment) Act, 1978.

Article 19 of the Constitution guarantees to the citizens of India the following six fundamental freedoms –

a. Freedom of Speech and Expression

b. Freedom of Assembly

c. Freedom to form Associations, Unions and Co-operative societies

d. Freedom of movement

e. Freedom to reside and to settle

f. [* Omitted * *][62]

g. Freedom of profession, occupation, trade or business

These six freedoms are however, not absolute. Absolute individual rights cannot be guaranteed by any modern State. If people were given complete and absolute liberty without any social control, the result would be a chaotic society. Liberty has to be limited in order to be effectively possessed. The guarantee of each of the above rights is, therefore, restricted by the Constitution itself by conferring upon the State a power to impose by law, reasonable restrictions as may be necessary in the larger interest of the community. The restrictions on these freedoms are provided in clauses 2 to 6 of Article 19 of the Constitution.

The restriction which may be imposed under any of the clauses must be a reasonable restriction. The restrictions cannot be arbitrary. Hence, a restriction to be constitutionally valid must satisfy the following tests:-

(1) the restriction must be for the purposes mentioned in clauses 2 to 6 of Article 19;

(2) The restriction must be a reasonable restriction.

(a) **Test for 'Reasonable Restriction'** : The restriction on the rights under Article 19(1) can only be imposed by a 'Law' and not executive or departmental instructions. The phrase "reasonable restrictions" in Article 19(6) means that the restrictions imposed on a person in the enjoyment of his right should not be arbitrary or of an excessive nature, beyond what is required in the interests of the public. It is the courts and not the Legislature which has to judge finally whether a restriction is reasonable or not.

(b) **Rights available to 'Citizens only'** : The rights granted by Article 19 are available only to citizens and not to an alien or a foreigner. A foreigner is not a citizen of India and therefore, he cannot claim a right under Article 19. Citizens mean only natural persons and not legal persons, such as corporations or companies.

(c) **Freedom of speech and expression :** Freedom of speech is the bulwark of a democratic government. Freedom of speech plays a crucial role in the formation of public opinion on social, political, and economic matters. The freedom of speech includes the right to express one's views and opinions at any issue through any medium, e.g., by words of mouth, writing, printing, picture, film, movie, etc. It thus includes –

i. Freedom of communication

ii. Right to propagate or publish opinion

[62]Right to Property was repealed by 44th Constitutional Amendment Act, 1978.

iii. Freedom of press[63]

iv. Right to advertise or broadcast

v. Right to acquire and disseminate information

vi. Right to free debate and open discussion

vii. Right to remain silent

viii. Rights of voters to know about their candidates

ix. Right to demonstrate or picketing (not to strike)

x. Right to criticize

But this right is subject to reasonable restrictions being imposed under Article 19(2):

i. Sovereignty and integrity of India;

ii. Security of the State;

iii. Friendly relations with foreign States;

iv. Public order;

v. Decency or morality;

vi. Contempt of court;

vii. Defamation; and

viii. Incitement to an offence.

(d) **Freedom to Assemble :** Article 19(1)(b) guarantees to all citizens of India the right of assembly which includes the right to hold meetings and to take out processions. The Constitution secures this right to the citizens subject to two limitations –

i. The assembly must be unarmed and

ii. It must be peaceful, i.e., it must not be tumultuous and riotous in character.

Further, under clause (3), the State may impose reasonable restrictions as may be deemed necessary in the interests of public order or the sovereignty and integrity of India.

(e) **Right of Association :** Article 19(1)(c) guarantees to the citizens of India the right to form associations or unions or co-operative societies. The words "co-operative societies" were inserted by the 97th Constitution Amendment Act, 2011. Under Article 19(4), reasonable restrictions in the interests of public order, morality, or sovereignty and integrity of India may be imposed on this right by law.

(f) **Freedom of Movement and Residence :** Article 19(1)(d) guarantees to every citizen the right to move freely throughout the territory of India. Article 19(1)(e) guarantees to a citizen the right to reside and settle in any part of India. According to Article 19(5), however, the State may impose reasonable restrictions on these rights by law in the interests of general public or for the protection of the interests of any Scheduled Tribe. These constitutional provisions

---

[63] In the USA, the First Amendment specifically protects a free press. The prime purpose of the free press guarantee is regarded as creating a fourth institution outside the government as an additional check on the three official branches – executive, legislative, and judiciary. In India, freedom of press is implied from the guaranteed freedom of speech and expression. There is no specific provision ensuring freedom of the press as such. The freedom of press is regarded as a "species of which freedom of expression is a genus".

guarantee to the Indian citizens the right to go or to reside wherever they like within the Indian territory. These rights underline the concept that India is one unit so far as the citizens are concerned.

(g) **Right to property :** Articles 19(1)(f) and 19(5) have been repealed by the 44th Constitution Amendment Act, 1978.

Freedom to carry on trade and commerce – Article 19(1)(g) guarantees to all citizens the right to practice any profession, or to carry on any occupation, trade or business. However, the State can impose reasonable restrictions such as in the interests of general public; prescribe professional or technical qualifications necessary for carrying on any profession, trade, or business; and enable the State to carry on any trade or business to the exclusion of private citizens, wholly or partially.

ARTICLE 20 – PROTECTION IN RESPECT OF CONVICTION FOR OFFENCES

According to Article 20 :

(1) *No person shall be convicted of any offence except for violation of a law in force at the time of the commission of the Act charged as an offence, nor be subjected to a penalty greater than that which might have been inflicted under the law in force at the time of the commission of the offence.*

(2) *No person shall be prosecuted and punished for the same offence more than once.*

(3) *No person accused of any offence shall be compelled to be a witness against himself.*

(a) **Ex post facto law (Article 20(1)) :** Imposes a limitation on the law-making power of the Legislature. Ordinarily, a Legislature can make prospective as well as retrospective laws, but clause (1) of Article 20 prohibits the Legislature to make retrospective criminal laws. The first part of the clause provides that an act is not an offence at the date of its commission it cannot be an offence at the date subsequent to its commission. The second part of the clause protects a person from 'a penalty greater than that which he might have been subjected to at the time of the commission of the offence'. However, it does not prohibit imposition of civil liability retrospectively, i.e., with effect from past date. So, a tax can be imposed retrospectively. An *ex post facto* law is a law which imposes penalties retrospectively, i.e., on acts already done and increases the penalty for such acts.

(b) **Protection against Double Jeopardy (20(2)) :** No person shall be prosecuted and punished for the same offence more than once. This clause embodies the common law rule of "*nemo debet bis vexari*" which means that no man should be put twice in peril for the same offence. Thus, following are the essentials of the clause –

i. The person must be accused of an 'offence[64]'.

ii. The proceeding or the prosecution must have taken place before a "court" or "judicial tribunal[65]". Thus, proceedings before departmental and administrative authorities cannot be a proceeding of judicial nature.

---

[64] According to 'General Clauses Act, 1897, the meaning offence – "Any act or omission made punishable by law for the time being in force".

[65] The revenue authorities, like the sea customs authorities, are not judicial tribunals. Likewise, proceedings before a tribunal which entertains departmental or administrative enquiries cannot be considered as proceedings in connection with prosecution and punishment.

iii. The person must have been 'prosecuted and punished' in the previous proceedings.

iv. The 'offence' must be the same for which he was prosecuted and punished in the previous proceedings.

Thus, Article 20(2) will have no application where punishment is not for the same offence.

(c) **Protection against self-incrimination (Article 20(3)) :** Clause (3) of Article 20 provides that a person accused of any offence shall be not be compelled to be a witness against himself. The cardinal principle of criminal law is that an accused must be presumed to be innocent till the contrary is proved. It is the duty of the prosecution to prove the offence. The accused need not make any admission or statement against his own free will. Thus, following are the essentials of the clause –

i. It is a right pertaining to a person who is "accused of an offence".

ii. It is a protection against "compulsion to be a witness".

iii. It is a protection against such compulsion relating to his giving evidence against "himself".

ARTICLE 21 – PROTECTION OF LIFE AND PERSONAL LIBERTY

Article 21 – No person shall be deprived of his life or personal liberty except according to procedure established by law.

Article 21 is one of the luminary provisions in the Constitution. The Article mandates that no person shall be deprived of his life and personal liberty except according to the procedure established by law. Life or personal liberty includes a right to live with human dignity. Enjoyment of a quality life by the people is the essence of the guaranteed right under Article 21 of the Constitution. The protection of the Article extends to all "*persons*".

Article 21 secures two rights:

(1) Right to life, and

(2) Right to personal liberty.

Right to Life

Right to life, enshrined in Article 21, means something more than survival or animal existence. It would include the right to live with human dignity. It would include all those aspects of life which will make a man's life meaningful, complete, and worth living. It would include all that gives meaning to a man's life, e.g.: Right to live with human dignity, Right to livelihood, Right to health, Right to pollution-free air, etc. The 'right to life' included the right to lead a healthy life to enjoy all faculties of the human body in their prime conditions[66]. Thus, the Right to life includes various implicit rights as recognized by the Supreme Court.

(a) **Right to Live with Human Dignity :** In *Maneka Gandhi Vs. Union of India*[67], the Supreme Court gave a new dimension to Article 21. The Court held that the right to live is not merely a physical right but includes within its ambit, the right to live with human dignity.

---

[66]Sunil Batra v. Delhi Administration, AIR 1978 SC 1675.

[67]1978 AIR 597.

(b) **Right Against Sexual Harassment at Workplace :** In *Vishakha Vs. State of Rajasthan*[68], the Supreme Court declared sexual harassment at the workplace to violate the right to equality, life, and liberty.

(c) **Right to Reputation :** Reputation is an essential part of one's life. It is one of the finer graces of human civilization that makes life worth living[69].

(d) **Right to Livelihood :** The *Olga Tellis Vs. Bombay Municipal Corporation*[70], popularly known as the 'Pavement Dwellers Case', is important. Herein, a five-judge bench of the Court implied that the right to livelihood is borne out of the right to life. It said so as no person can live without the means of living, that is, the means of livelihood.

(e) **Right to Die with Dignity :** The Supreme Court in *Common Cause Vs. Union of India*[71] recognized the right of terminally ill persons to die with dignity by refusing prolonged medical treatment. In other words, the Supreme Court has now allowed passive euthanasia under some exceptional circumstances and strict monitoring of the court. In the above judgment, the court has permitted "Living Will" of a patient to withdraw medical support in case if the person concerned goes into an irreversible state of coma. Though active euthanasia (where something is done to end the life of the patient) is not permissible, passive euthanasia (when something is not done that would preserve the patient's life) is held to be a Fundamental Right under Article 21.

(f) **Right to Privacy :** Although not explicitly mentioned in the Constitution, the right to privacy is considered a 'penumbral right'/'implied right' under the Constitution, i.e., a right declared by the Supreme Court as integral to the fundamental right to life and liberty. The same was recognized in *Justice K.S. Puttaswamy (Retd.) Vs. Union of India*[72]. Right to privacy includes telephonic conversation. Therefore, telephone-tapping amounts to its violation unless it is permitted under procedure established by law.

(g) **Right to legal aid and right to speedy trial :** Litigation can become unthinkably expensive affecting the rights of indigent persons to have their just and fair claims adjudicated in the courts of law. In view of the same, the Supreme Court has provided liberty to poor persons to apply to the state for free legal services and it shall be the duty of the state to provide assistance to such poor persons and have their claims adjudicated without burden of legal fees and expenses. Right to free legal aid has been held to be a Fundamental Right and it is the duty and obligation of any trial court to inform the accused about his right to free legal aid. The right to speedy trial has also been held as inalienable right of every citizen of the country (*Husscinara Khatoon Vs. State of Bihar*[73]and Khatri Vs. State of Bihar[74]).

---

[68]AIR 1997 SC 3011.

[69]*Smt. Kiran Bedi v. Committee of Inquiry*, 1989 AIR 714.

[70]AIR 1986 SC 180.

[71]2018 5 SCC 1

[72](2017) 10 SCC 1

[73]AIR 1979 SC 1369.

[74]1981 SCC (1) 627).

(h) **Right to clean environment"** : Article 21 includes the right to live a life of dignity in a healthy environment with proper sanitation system and free of pollution (*Vellore Citizens' Welfare Forum Vs. Union of India*[75]).

(i) **"Right of prisoners and right against illegal detention"** : The Article 21 is available to each and every person and not only to the citizens of India. It recognises the rights of the arrested persons by providing a fair and reasonable mechanism to be followed in confinement of persons so that no person is illegally detained. Even a person convicted of any offence, though deprived of freedom, is well entitled to rights guaranteed under Article 21 of the Constitution. Even solitary confinement of a person in jail was held to be violative of Article 21 (*Sunil Batra Vs. Delhi Administration*[76]).

Implicit Rights Recognized Under Article 21

The other implicit rights recognized under Article 21 are –

i. Right to Social security and Protection of family
ii. Right to Know or be Informed
iii. Right against Solitary Confinement
iv. Right against Delayed Execution
v. Right against Public Hanging
vi. Right to go Abroad
vii. Right to Speedy, Fair, and Open Trial
viii. Right to Education
ix. Right Against Handcuffing
x. Right of Prisoners
xi. Right to Food
xii. Right to choose a Life Partner
xiii. Right to Fair Trial
xiv. Right Against Custodial Violence
xv. Right to Shelter
xvi. Right to Reputation
xvii. Right To Health And Medical Care
xviii. Right to get Pollution Free Water and Air
xix. Right Against Noise Pollution
xx. Right to Sleep
xxi. Right to Opportunity
xxii. Right to Family Pension
xxiii. Right to Water
xxiv Reproductive Rights

[75] 1996 (5) SCC 647).

[76] 1980 SCC (3) 488.

xxv. Right of Victim of an Offence

xxvi.Right to Bail

xxvii. Right to Appeal

xxviii. Right to Development

xxix. Right to Sustainable Development

Personal Liberty

The meaning of the term personal liberty was considered by the Supreme Court in "*Kharak Singh Vs. State of U.P.*"[77] The court held that mere life without movement would be meaningless and without the exercise of human faculties, it would not rise above the levels of animals. 'Personal liberty' includes all the varieties of rights which go to make up a man's personal liberties other than those which are already included in the several clauses of Article 19. In other words, the expression "personal liberty" in Article 21 is of the widest amplitude and it covers a variety of rights which go to constitute the personal liberty of a man and some of them have been raised to the status of distinct Fundamental Rights and given additional protection under Article 19 of the Constitution.

Procedure Established By Law –

(a) **Doctrine of Due Process of Law :** Due process has ancient history which is traceable from the Magna Carta[78]. Section 39 of the Magna Carta of 1215 has led the foundation for the terminology of due process which runs as follows:

"No free man shall be seized, imprisoned, dispossessed, outlawed, exiled or ruined in any way, nor in any way proceeded against, except by the lawful judgement of his peers and the law of the land."

The term 'Due Process of Law' was transplanted to American soil by English colonists[79].

(b) **Indian scenario before Maneka Gandhi case :** In our Constitution, we adopted "*Procedure established by law*" which is borrowed from the Japanese Constitution.

Immediately after the Indian government adopted the Constitution of India, the Supreme Court of India was faced with the task of interpretation of the words used in the Article 21 in the famous *A.K. Gopalan Vs. State of Madras*[80] case in which the validity of the Preventive Detention Act, 1950 was challenged. The petitioner questioned his detention on the grounds that his detention has affected his rights guaranteed under Article 19(1) and the provisions of the Act have imposed unreasonable restrictions on the exercise of those rights. Further, petitioner contended that the freedom of movement is the part of right to personal liberty protected under Article 21. The apex court, by majority, held that 'Procedure established by law' would mean the procedure as laid down in an enacted law. In other words, 'Procedure established by law' says that a law that has been lawfully enacted is valid, even if it violates justice and equitable ideals. So, if Parliament passes a law, even though it is arbitrary, the life or personal liberty of a person can be taken off according to the provisions and procedures of that law. Thus, Article 21 was available against the arbitrary executive action and not against arbitrary law.

---

[77] AIR 1963 SC 1295

[78] Magna Carta was not a statute but was merely a personal treaty between King John and the enraged upper classes.

[79] The Fifth Amendment to the Bill of Rights is most important because it lays down that person's life, liberty, or property would not be deprived without due process of law.

[80] AIR 1950 SC 27.

(c) **From "procedure established by law" to "due process of law" :** *Maneka Gandhi Vs. Union of India*[81] is such a landmark case in the era of Indian legal system that it can be classified as pre- and post-Maneka Gandhi. Maneka Gandhi questioned the constitutional validity of Section 10(3)(c) of the Passport Act, 1967 which empowered the authority to impound the passport of a person on public interest. She contended that this section gives discretionary power to the authority to impound the passport without being heard which is an unjust process and violative of the right to equality and right to personal liberty. The Court upheld the contentions of the petitioner that the procedure established under Article 21 should be just, fair, and reasonable. Further, such procedure should be tested under Articles 14 and 19 of the Constitution. The court further held that the law prescribing a procedure for deprivation of life and personal liberty in Article 21 should neither be arbitrary nor unfair nor unreasonable. Thus, the due process concept is read under Article 21 by articulating that 'Procedure established by law' must be fair, just, and reasonable. In other words, not only arbitrary executive action will be struck down, even the legislative action will be struck down if it is arbitrary, unjust, and unreasonable. The liberal interpretation of procedural established by law in the Maneka Gandhi case marks the beginning of a new dimension of procedural due process especially in the criminal justice system under Article 21 of the Constitution. Now the courts do not hesitate to quash the law if such law offends due process requirements.

ARTICLE 21A – RIGHT TO EDUCATION

Article 21A – The State shall provide free and compulsory education to all children of the age of six to fourteen years in such manner as the State may, by law, determine.

Article 21A was inserted in the Constitution by the 86th Constitutional Amendment Act, 2002. Before the amendment, the court in *Unni Krishnan, J.P. Vs. State of Andhra Pradesh*[82], had recognized the Fundamental Right of every child for free and compulsory elementary education as provided in Article 45. To give further strength, the 86th amendment was added.

Article 21A of the Constitution and Article 51 A(k) of the Constitution cast obligations on the State and the parents respectively to provide education to a child between the age of 6-14 years.

In pursuance of this right, Parliament has enacted the Right of Children to Free and Compulsory Education Act, 2009. The Act entitles a child to free and compulsory education between the age of 6 to 14 years in a neighborhood school. Even the private unaided school shall not charge any capitation fee from any child, nor will they do any screening of the child or its parents. For better social inclusion, every unaided school is under obligation to admit 25% students from weaker sections of the society in the neighborhood. The Supreme Court in *Pramati Education & Cultural Trust Vs. Union of India*[83], has upheld the Act and its provisions subject to the clarification that it shall not apply to unaided as well as aided minority schools[84].

---

[81] AIR 1978 SC 597.

[82] (1993) 1 SCC 645.

[83] (2014) 8 SCC 1.

[84] V.N. Shukla's *Constitution of India*, Thirteenth Edition, EBC Explorer, Pg No. 234.

ARTICLE 22 – PROTECTION AGAINST ARREST AND DETENTION IN CERTAIN CASES

According to Article 22 :

(1) *No person who is arrested shall be detained in custody without being informed, as soon as may be, of the grounds for such arrest nor shall he be denied the right to consult, and to be defended by, a legal practitioner of his choice.*

(2) *Every person who is arrested and detained in custody shall be produced before the nearest magistrate within a period of twenty-four hours of such arrest excluding the time necessary for the journey from the place of arrest to the court of the magistrate and no such person shall be detained in custody beyond the said period without the authority of a magistrate.*

(3) *Nothing in clauses (1) and (2) shall apply —*

(a) to any person who for the time being is an enemy alien; or

(b) to any person who is arrested or detained under any law providing for preventive detention.

(4) *No law providing for preventive detention shall authorize the detention of a person for a longer period than three months unless*

(a) an Advisory Board consisting of persons — who are, or have been, or are qualified to be appointed as, Judges of a High Court has reported before the expiration of the said period of three months that there is in its opinion, sufficient cause for such detention:

Provided that nothing in this sub-clause shall authorise the detention of any person beyond the maximum period prescribed by any law made by Parliament under sub-clause (b) of clause (7); or

(b) such person is detained in accordance with the provisions of any law made by Parliament under sub-clauses (a) and (b) of clause (7).

(5) *When any person is detained in pursuance of an order made under any law providing for preventive detention, the authority making the order shall, as soon as may be, communicate to such person the grounds on which the order has been made and shall afford him the earliest opportunity of making a representation against the order.*

(6) *Nothing in clause (5) shall require the authority making any such order as is referred to in that clause to disclose facts which such authority considers to be against the public interest to disclose.*

(7) *Parliament may by law prescribe —*

[85]*(a) the circumstances under which, and the class or classes of cases in which, a person may be detained for a period longer than three months under any law providing for preventive detention without obtaining the opinion of an Advisory Board in accordance with the provisions of sub-clause (a) of clause (4);*

(b) the maximum period for which any person may in any class or classes of cases be detained under any law providing for preventive detention; and

(c) the procedure to be followed by an Advisory Board in an inquiry under sub-clause (a) of clause (4).

---

[85]Sub-clause (a) shall stand omitted by the Constitution (Forty-fourth Amendment) Act, 1978.

Article 22 prescribes the minimum procedural requirements that must be included in any law enacted by the Legislature in accordance with the procedure established by law. Article 22 deals with two separate matters:

(1) persons arrested under the ordinary law of crimes; and

(2) persons detained under the law of 'preventive detention'.

The first two clauses of Article 22 deal with detention under the ordinary law of crimes and lay down the procedure which has to be followed when a man is arrested and the remaining clauses (3), (4), (5), and (6) deal with persons detained under a preventive detention law and lay down the procedure which is to be followed when a person is detained under the law.

Rights of Arrested Persons Under Ordinary Laws

Clauses (1) and (2) of Article 22 guarantee four rights to a person who is arrested for any offence under an ordinary law –

(a) The right to be informed "as soon as may be" of ground of arrest

(b) The right to consult and to be represented by a lawyer of his own choice

(c) The right to be produced before a Magistrate within 24 hrs of his arrest, excluding the time necessary for the journey from the place of arrest to the magistrate's court. This would enable the arrested person to get a speedy trial. This protection will not apply to a person arrested under a warrant issued by the court on a criminal or quasi-criminal complaint. Article 22 is designed to give protection against the Act of the Executive or order of non-judicial authorities and applies to a person who has been accused of a crime.

(d) No such person is to be detained in custody beyond this period without the authority of a magistrate.

The above Fundamental Rights guaranteed to arrested persons are available to both citizens and non-citizens. Article 22 (1) and (2) do not apply to enemy aliens and to persons arrested or detained under a law providing for preventive detention. Moreover, the protection under (1) and (2) applies to only acts of criminal or quasi-criminal nature or some act prejudicial to the State of public interest. The protection does not apply to arrests made under the Civil Procedure Code, recovery arrears of revenue, or deportation of a foreigner.

Preventive Detention

Clauses (4) to (7) of Article 22 provide the procedure which is to be followed if a person is arrested under the law of "Preventive Detention". In other words, the said clauses lay down a few safeguards, and provide for minimum procedure, which must be observed in any case of preventive detention. If a law of preventive detention, or administrative action relating thereto, infringes any of these safeguards, then the law or the action would be invalid as infringing the Fundamental Right of the detainee.

In preventive detention, a person is detained to prevent him for committing an undesirable act in future. While the object of punitive detention is to punish a person for what he has done, the object of preventive detention is to prevent him from doing something which is unlawful. Preventive detention is thus preventive, not punitive in theory. Preventive detention is an exception to Article 22 (1) and (2). Consequently, a person arrested under a law of preventive detention has no right to be produced before a magistrate within 24 hrs.

Preventive detention in other democratic countries like Britain, USA, and Canada, is invoked through special laws as a war-time and not a peace-time measure. In India, the Constitution itself provides the possibility of a preventive detention. In spite of all the emphasis on individual liberty, it has been found necessary in India to resort to preventive detention during peace-time because of the unstable law and order situation in the country. However, preventive detention laws restricting freedom should be exercised with extra caution and not as a matter of course.

A law for preventive detention can be enacted by Parliament exclusively under entry 9, List I, for reasons connected with defence, foreign affairs, or the security of India. For example, following preventive detention acts were passed by the Parliament –

i. Preventive Detention Act, 1950. (Expired in 1969)

ii. Maintenance of Internal Security Act (MISA), 1971. (Repealed in 1978)

iii. Terrorist and Disruptive Activities (Prevention) Act (TADA), 1985. (Repealed in 1995)

iv. Prevention of Terrorism Act (POTA), 2002. (Repealed in 2004)

v. Prevention of Illicit Traffic in Narcotic Drugs and Psychotropic Substances (PITNDPS) Act, 1988.

vi. National Security Act (NSA), 1980.

Further, under entry 3 List III, Parliament as well as the State Legislatures can concurrently make a law for preventive detention for reasons connected with security, maintenance of public order, or maintenance of supplies and services essential for the community. For example, the Parliament passed "Prevention of Black-marketing and Maintenance of Supplies of Essential Commodities Act (PBMSECA), 1980" under List III. Several States passed statutes authorizing preventive detention for various purposes under List III, such as – The Tamil Nadu Prevention of Dangerous Activities of Bootleggers, Drug Offenders, Forest Offenders, Goondas, Immoral Traffic Offenders, and Slum-Grabbers Act, 1982, the Bihar Control of Crimes Act, 1981 etc. Moreover, Parliament can enact preventive detention laws on any other ground not mentioned in List I and List III by exercising its residuary power. For example, Parliament enacted Conservation of Foreign Exchange and Prevention of Smuggling Activities Act (COFEPOSA), 1974 under its residuary power.

Constitutional Safeguards – Clause (4) to (7)

(a) Review by Advisory Board (clause 4) : The clause embodies following safeguards –

  i. The detenu's case must be referred to an Advisory Board for its opinion (the functions of the Board is advisory), if he is sought to be detained for a period longer than three months. In other words, for preventive detention up to three months[86], no reference to such board is necessary. The board is to consist of persons who are, or have been, or are qualified to act as the High Court judges.

  ii. If the Advisory Board has reported that there is sufficient cause for detention, the detention may continue for a period longer than three months, but not longer than the maximum period prescribed by the Parliament made under clause 7(b).

---

[86] The 44th Amendment Act of 1978 has reduced the period of detention without obtaining the opinion of an advisory board from three to two months. However, the said change or the amendment did not come into force. Therefore, the original period of three months still continues.

(b) Communication of grounds of detention to detenue (clause 5) : The clause provides the following safeguards –

i. The authority making the order of detention must "as soon as may be" communicate to the person detained the grounds of his arrest, that is, the grounds which led to be subjective satisfaction of the detaining authority. However, under Article 22(6,) disclosure of facts which are considered to be against public interest may not be furnished to the detenu. Hence, it follows that both the obligations to furnish particulars and the duty to consider whether the disclosure of any facts involved therein is against public interest are vested in the detaining authority, not in any other.

ii. To give the detenu the "earliest opportunity" of making a representation against the order of detention, that is, to be furnished with sufficient particulars to enable him to make a representation.

Parliament's Power to Dispense with Advisory Boards

(a) Under Article 22(7)(a), Parliament may by law prescribe "the circumstances under which, and the class or classes of cases in which, a person may be detained for a period longer than three months" without referring the case to an advisory board under Article 22(4)(a).

(b) Article 22(4)(a) says that no person can be detained beyond the maximum period prescribed by any law made by the Parliament. Under Article 22(7)(b), Parliament may, by law, prescribe the maximum period of detention for which any person can be detained.

ARTICLE 23 – RIGHT AGAINST EXPLOITATION

Article 23 – Prohibition of traffic in human beings and forced labour –

(1) Traffic in human beings and begar and other similar forms of forced labour are prohibited and any contravention of this provision shall be an offence punishable in accordance with law.

(2) Nothing in this Article shall prevent the State from imposing compulsory service for public purposes, and in imposing such service, the State shall not make any discrimination on grounds only of religion, race, caste or class or any of them.

Article 23 prohibits traffic in human beings and *begar* and other forms of forced labor. "Traffic in human beings" means selling and buying men and women like goods and includes immoral traffic in women and children for immoral or other purposes. Any contravention of this provision shall be an offence punishable in accordance with law. Under Article 35 of the Constitution, Parliament is authorized to make laws for punishing acts prohibited by this Article. In pursuance of this Article, Parliament has passed 'The Immoral Traffic (Prevention) Act, 1956'.

Article 23 prohibits *begar, slavery,* and other forms of forced labor. The term *begar* means compulsory work without any payment. Specific law to prohibit the forced labor system is the "Bonded Labour System (Abolition) Act 1976". The legal framework against bonded labor provided in the Bonded Labour System (Abolition) Act, 1976 is supported by other legislations like the Contract Labour (Regulation and Abolition) Act, 1970, the Inter-State Migrant Workmen (Regulation of Employment and Conditions of Service) Act, 1979, the Minimum Wages Act, 1948, and the Equal Remuneration Act, 1976.

Article 23 protects the individual not only against the State but also private citizens. It is to be noted that the protection of this Article is available to both citizens as well as non-citizens.

Compulsory service for public purposes

Clause (2) of Article 23 contains an exception to the above general rule. Under this clause, the State is empowered to impose compulsory service for public purposes. But in imposing such compulsory service, the State cannot make any discrimination on grounds only of religion, race, caste or class, or any of them. For example, compulsory military service or social services can be imposed because they are neither *begar* nor traffic in human beings.

ARTICLE 24 – PROHIBITION OF EMPLOYMENT OF CHILDREN IN FACTORIES, ETC.

Article 24 – No child below the age of fourteen years shall be employed to work in any factory or mine or engaged in any other hazardous employment.

Article 24 of the Constitution prohibits employment of children below 14 years of age in factories and hazardous employment. This provision is certainly in the interest of public health and safety of children. Children are the assets of the nation.

In pursuance of this Article, the Parliament passed the "Child Labour (Prohibition and Regulation) Act, 1986" to regulate the child labour practices in India. In 2016, the Act was amended. Pursuant to the said amendment, the name of the Child Labour Act has been changed to 'Child and Adolescent Labour (Prohibition and Regulation) Act, 1986'. Further, a complete prohibition has been imposed on employment of child labour (i.e., a person below the age of 14 years) in any establishment whether hazardous or not. A child is permitted to work only to help the family in a family enterprise or as child artist after school hours or during vacations. The amendment also introduced the concept of adolescent labour for the first time. An adolescent has been defined as a person between the ages of 14–18 years. The amendment permits employment of adolescent labour except in hazardous processes or occupations. The violations under the Act provides for increased penalty and imprisonment which shall not be less than 6 months and may extend upto 2 years and fine which may vary between Rs. 20, 000 to Rs. 50,000.

Further, in pursuance of this Article, Commissions for Protection of Child Rights Act, 2005 was enacted. The Commission is mandated to ensure that "all Laws, Policies, Programmes, and Administrative Mechanisms are in consonance with the Child Rights perspective as enshrined in the Constitution of India and the UN Convention on the Rights of the Child". For the purpose of speedy trial of offences against children or of violation of child rights under the Act, the State governments are empowered to establish children's court as special courts.

ARTICLE 25 – RIGHT TO FREEDOM OF RELIGION

India is a pluralistic society and a country of religions. It is inhabited by people of many religions. It is the ancient doctrine in India that the State protects all religions but interferes with none.

The concept of secularism was not expressly incorporated in the Constitution at the stage of making it. However, its operation was visible in the Fundamental Rights and Directive Principles of State Policy. The concept of secularism, though not expressly stated in the Constitution, was, nevertheless, deeply embedded in the Indian Constitution and its constitutional philosophy. In 1976, through the 42nd Amendment of the Constitution, the concept of secularism was made explicit by amending the Preamble. The Constitution does not define the term 'secular'.

A Secular State can have no religion. It should treat all religions equally. In a Secular State, the State is only concerned with the relation between man and man. It is not concerned with the relation of man with God.

In *S.R. Bommai Vs. Union of India*[87], the Supreme Court has held that "secularism is a basic feature of the Constitution". The State treats equally all religions and religious denominations. Religion is a matter of individual faith and cannot be mixed with secular activities. Secular activities can be regulated by the state by enacting law. Justice Ramaswami observed that Secularism is not anti-God.

The Indian Constitution embodies the positive concept of secularism and has not accepted the American doctrine of secularism, i.e., the concept of erecting "a wall of separation between Religion and State". The positive concept of secularism separates spiritualism from individual faith.

Note : *Article 25 to 28 of the Indian Constitution confers certain rights relating to freedom of religion not only on citizens but also on all persons in India. These constitutional provisions guarantee religious freedom not only to individuals but also to religious groups.*

Article 25 – Freedom of conscience and free profession, practice and propagation of religion. –

(1) Subject to public order, morality and health and to the other provisions of this Part, all persons are equally entitled to freedom of conscience and the right freely to profess, practice, and propagate religion.

(2) Nothing in this Article shall affect the operation of any existing law or prevent the State from making any law —

(a) regulating or restricting any economic, financial, political, or other secular activity which may be associated with religious practice;

(b) Providing for social welfare and reform or the throwing open of Hindu religious institutions of a public character to all classes and sections of Hindus.

Explanation I : *The wearing and carrying of kirpans shall be deemed to be included in the profession of the Sikh religion.*

Explanation II : *In sub-clause (b) of clause (2), the reference to Hindus shall be construed as including a reference to persons professing the Sikh, Jaina, or Buddhist religion, and the reference to Hindu religious institutions shall be construed accordingly.*

Article 25(1) guarantees to every person the freedom of conscience and the right to profess, practice, and propagate religion. The right guaranteed under Article 25(1) like other constitutional rights is not absolute. This right is subject to public order, morality, and health and to other provisions of Part III of the Constitution. Thus, under Article 25(1), a person has a two-fold freedom –

(a) Freedom of conscience;

(b) Freedom to profess, practice, and propagate religion.

The freedom of 'conscience' is an absolute inner freedom of the person to mould his own relation with God in whatever manner he likes. When this freedom becomes articulate and expressed in outward form, it is 'to profess[88], practice[89], and propagate[90] religion'. However, the right to propagate one's religion does not give a right to convert any person to one's own religion.

---

[87] 1994 AIR 1918. x

[88] Means to declare freely and openly one's faith and belief

[89] To practice his belief by practical expression in any manner he likes

[90] Means to spread and publicize his religious order in which he believes

Further, under sub-clauses (a) and (b) of clause (2) of Article 25, the State is empowered by law –

(a) To regulate or restrict any economic, financial, political or other secular activity which may be associated with religious practice;

(b) To provide for (i) social welfare and reform, and (ii) to throw open Hindu religious institutions of a public character to all classes and sections of Hindus.

According to Explanation I, wearing and carrying *kirpans* by the Sikhs is included in the profession of the Sikh religion. The term 'Hindu' in this Article, according to Explanation II, includes persons professing the Sikh, Jain or Buddhist religion and the reference to Hindu religious institutions is to be construed accordingly.

ARTICLE 26 – FREEDOM TO MANAGE RELIGIOUS AFFAIRS

Article 26 – Subject to public order, morality and health, every religious denomination or any section thereof shall have the right —

(a) to establish and maintain institutions for religious and charitable purposes;

(b) to manage its own affairs in matters of religion;

(c) to own and acquire movable and immovable property; and

(d) to administer such property in accordance with law.

The right guaranteed by Article 25 is an individual right while right guaranteed by Article 26 is the right of an "organized body" like the religious denomination or section thereof. Article 26 thus guarantees collective freedom of religion. To form a religious denomination, three conditions must be fulfilled:

(1) It must be a collection of individuals who have a system of beliefs which they regard as conducive to their spiritual well-being, that is, common faith;

(2) It must have a common organization; and

(3) It must be designated by a distinctive name.

For instance, the Supreme Court has ruled that Ramakrishna religion (propounded by Shri Ramakrishna) is not different and distinct from the Hindu religion. But 'Ramakrishna Math' is a religious denomination within Hindu religion and can, thus, claim the Fundament Rights conferred by Article 26.

ARTICLE 27 – FREEDOM AS TO PAYMENT OF TAXES FOR PROMOTION OF ANY PARTICULAR RELIGION

Article 27 – No person shall be compelled to pay any taxes, the proceeds of which are specifically appropriated in payment of expenses for the promotion or maintenance of any particular religion or religious denomination.

Article 27 provides that no person shall be compelled to pay any tax for the promotion or maintenance of any particular religion or religious denomination. This Article emphasizes the secular character of the State. The public money collected by way of tax cannot be spent by the State for the promotion of any particular religion. It is against the policy of the Constitution to pay out of public funds any money for the promotion or maintenance of the particular religion or religious denomination. It is to be noted here that what this Article prohibits is the levying of tax and not of fee. The Supreme Court[91] held that

[91]In *Ratilal Vs. State of Bombay*, AIR 1954 SC 388.

a tax is in the nature of a compulsory exaction of money by a public authority for public purposes. The imposition is made for public purpose to meet the general expenses of the State without reference to any special advantage to be conferred upon the taxpayer. Fees are, on the other hand, payments primarily in public interest but for some special service rendered or some special work done for the benefit of those from whom the payments are demanded.

ARTICLE 28 – FREEDOM AS TO ATTENDANCE AT RELIGIOUS INSTRUCTION OR RELIGIOUS WORSHIP IN CERTAIN EDUCATIONAL INSTITUTIONS

According to Article 28 –

(1) No religious instruction shall be provided in any educational institution wholly maintained out of State funds.

(2) Nothing in clause (1) shall apply to an educational institution which is administered by the State but has been established under any endowment or trust which requires that religious instruction shall be imparted in such institution.

(3) No person attending any educational institution recognised by the State or receiving aid out of State funds shall be required to take part in any religious instruction that may be imparted in such institution or to attend any religious worship that may be conducted in such institution or in any premises attached thereto unless such person or, if such person is a minor, his guardian has given his consent thereto.

Article 28 mentions four types of education institutions:

(a) Institutions wholly maintained by the State

(b) Institutions recognized by the State

(c) Institutions that are receiving aid out of the State fund

(d) Institutions that are administered by the State but are established under any trust or endowment

In the institutions of (a) type, no religious instructions can be imparted. In (b) and (c) type institutions, religious instructions may be imparted only with the consent of the individuals. In other words, religious education can be imparted on a voluntary basis; and in case of minors, with the consent of the guardians. In the (d) type of institutions, there is no restriction on religious instructions.

In *Aruna Roy Vs. UOI*[92], the Supreme Court has ruled that Article 28 does not ban a study of religions. The whole emphasis of Article 28 is "against imparting religious instructions". There is no prohibition on study of religious philosophy and culture, particularly for having value-based social life in a society which is degenerating for power, post, or property. In the words of Justice Dharmadhikari "study of religions, therefore, in school education cannot be held to be an attempt against the secular philosophy of the Constitution".

Thus, there is distinction between imparting "religious instruction" that is teaching of rituals, observances, customs, and traditions and other non-essential observances or modes of worship in religions and teaching philosophies of religion with more emphasis on study of essential moral and spiritual thoughts contained in various religions. There is a very thin dividing line between imparting of "religious instruction" and "study of religions".

---

[92] AIR 2002 SC 3176.

ARTICLE 29 – CULTURAL AND EDUCATIONAL RIGHTS

Article 29 – Protection of interests of minorities

(1) Any section of the citizens residing in the territory of India or any part thereof having a distinct language, script or culture of its own shall have the right to conserve the same.

(2) No citizen shall be denied admission into any educational institution maintained by the State or receiving aid out of State funds on grounds only of religion, race, caste, language or any of them.

Articles 29 and 30 protect and guarantee certain cultural and educational rights to various cultural, religious, and linguistic minorities located in India. Article 29(1) guarantees to any section of the citizens residing in any part of India having a distinct language, script, or culture of its own, the right to conserve the same, i.e., language, script, or culture. The right to conserve the language includes the right to agitate for the protection of that language, including political agitation. Hence, political agitation to conserve the language of a section of the citizens cannot be made a "corrupt practice" within the meaning of section 123(3) of the Representation of the People Act.[93]

According to Article 29(2), admission is not to be denied to any citizen into any educational institution maintained by the State, or receiving aid out of the state funds, on the grounds of *only* religion, race, caste, language, or any of them. This provision guarantees the rights of a citizen as an individual, irrespective of the community to which he belongs.

Article 15(1) of the Constitution also prohibits discrimination on grounds of religion, race, caste, sex, or place of birth. However, it differs from Article 29(2). Article 15 protects all citizens against discrimination generally while Article 29(2) is a protection against a particular species of wrongs, namely, denial of admission to any citizen into educational institutions of the types mentioned therein.

ARTICLE 30 – RIGHT OF MINORITIES TO ESTABLISH AND ADMINISTER EDUCATIONAL INSTITUTIONS

According to Article 30 –

(1) All minorities, whether based on religion or language, shall have the right to establish and administer educational institutions of their choice.

[94]*[(1A) In making any law providing for the compulsory acquisition of any property of an educational institution established and administered by a minority, referred to in clause (1), the State shall ensure that the amount fixed by or determined under such law for the acquisition of such property is such as would not restrict or abrogate the right guaranteed under that clause.]*

(2) The State shall not, in granting aid to educational institutions, discriminate against any educational institution on the ground that it is under the management of a minority, whether based on religion or language.

Article 30(1) guarantees to all linguistic and religious minorities the 'right to establish' and the 'right to administer' educational institutions of their own choice. The benefit of Article 30(1) extends only to linguistic or religious minorities and not to any other sections of the citizens of India.

---

[93] *V.R. Sree Rama Rao Vs. Telugudesam Political Party*, AIR 1983 AP 96; *Jagdev Singh Sidhanti Vs. Pratap Singh Daulta*, AIR 1965 SC 183.

[94] The Constitution (44th Amendment) Act, 1978.

Minorities

The term 'linguistic minority' or 'minorities' have not been defined. But the Supreme Court held that, since reorganization of the States of India has been on linguistic lines, therefore, for the purpose of determining the minority, the unit will be the State and not the whole of India. It has been settled in *T.M.A. Pai Foundation Vs. State of Karnataka*[95] that a linguistic minority is determinable with reference to the State as a unit.

With respect to religious minorities, the central government had identified Muslims, Sikhs, Christians, Buddhists, Jains, and Zorastrians (Parsis) as minority communities under Section 2(c) of the National Commission for Minorities Act, 1992. This Act does not define the term 'minorities' but under section 2(c), it says that central government will notify who are minorities. Thus, effectively, the religious minorities are recognized at national level whereas linguistic minorities are recognized at state level.

Article 30(2) mandates that in granting aid to educational institutions, the state shall not discriminate against any educational institution on the grounds that is under the management of a minority, whether based on religion or language.

ARTICLE 32 – RIGHT TO CONSTITUTIONAL REMEDIES

Article 32 – Remedies for enforcement of rights conferred by this Part –

(1) *The right to move the Supreme Court by appropriate proceedings for the enforcement of the rights conferred by this Part is guaranteed.*

(2) *The Supreme Court shall have power to issue directions or orders or writs, including writs in the nature of habeas corpus, mandamus, prohibition, quo-warranto, and certiorari, whichever may be appropriate, for the enforcement of any of the rights conferred by this Part.*

(3) *Without prejudice to the powers conferred on the Supreme Court by clauses (1) and (2), Parliament may by law empower any other court to exercise within the local limits of its jurisdiction all or any of the powers exercisable by the Supreme Court under clause (2).*

(4) *The right guaranteed by this Article shall not be suspended except as otherwise provided for by this Constitution.*

The Constitutional Courts, i.e., the Supreme Court and the High Courts are the sentinels/guards of justice and have been vested with the extraordinary powers of judicial review to ensure that the rights of citizens are duly protected. A right without a remedy does not have much substance. The Fundamental Rights guaranteed by the Constitution would have been worth nothing had the Constitution not provided an effective mechanism for their enforcement.

According to Article 13, Fundamental Rights are enforceable and any law incompetent with a Fundamental Right is void. Article 13 is the key provision as it makes Fundamental Rights justiciable. Article 13 confers a power and imposes a duty and an obligation on the courts to declare a law void if it is inconsistent with a Fundamental Right. This is a power of great consequence for the courts. The Supreme Court has characterized this role of the judiciary as that of a "sentinel on the qui vive" (watchful guardian). Article 32 confers power on the Supreme Court to enforce the Fundamental Rights. The High Courts also have a parallel power under Article 226 to enforce the Fundamental Rights[96].

---

[95] *T.M.A. Pai Foundation Vs. State of Karnataka*

[96] M.P. Jain, *Indian Constitutional Law*, LexisNexis, Eighth Edition, Pg No. 1408.

Article 32 is the very heart and soul of the Constitution.

Article 32(1) guarantees the right to move the Supreme Court for the enforcement of the Fundamental Rights conferred by Part III of the Constitution. The said Article can be invoked only when there is an infringement of a Fundamental Right. Article 32 is in itself a Fundamental Right and, therefore, the existence of an alternative remedy is no bar to the Supreme Court entertaining a petition under Article 32 for the enforcement of a Fundamental Right. When the court is satisfied that the petitioner's Fundamental Right has been infringed, it is not only its right but also its duty to afford relief to the petitioner.

Article 32(2) clause confers power on the Supreme Court to issue appropriate directions or orders or writs (Writ is a form of written command in the name of the court to act in a specific way), including writs in the nature of *habeas corpus, mandamus, prohibition, quo-warranto, and certiorari.*

(a) **Habeas Corpus :** The word 'habeas corpus' literally means to have a body. The writ of Habeas corpus - an effective bulwark of personal liberty – is a remedy available to a person who is confined without legal justification. In other words, this writ is used to release a person who has been unlawfully detained or imprisoned. By virtue of this writ, the Court directs the person so detained to be brought before it to examine the legality of his detention. If the Court concludes that the detention was unlawful, then it directs the person to be released immediately. Circumstances of unlawful detention are:

- The detention was not done in accordance with the procedure laid down. For instance, the person was not produced before a Magistrate within 24 hours of his arrest.
- The arrest has been made without any violation of law done by the person.
- The arrest has been made for an unconstitutional law, i.e., a law against the provisions of the Indian Constitution
- Detention is done with malafide intent, or with the intent to harm the person/s

However, Habeas corpus cannot be granted –

- when a person has been arrested under an order from a competent court;
- When the detention is lawful;
- When the proceeding is for contempt of a legislature or a court;
- Where the person or authority against whom habeas corpus is sought is not within the territorial jurisdiction of the court;

The writ of Habeas Corpus can be sanctioned not only against the State but also against any private individual who is falsely imprisoning the other person. This writ can be applied not only by the person who is detained but it can also be done by some other person on behalf of the detained person. Usually, the detained person and his family members are allowed to file an application for habeas corpus but the court has also allowed such application by strangers if it is done in public interest. For e.g., a writ application can also be made by postcard. In the case of *Sunil Batra Vs. Delhi Administration*[97], the Supreme Court had accepted the application made through a letter by a co-convict (a stranger) due to the inhuman treatment of prisoners. In this case, the letter was accepted as an application and the writ of Habeas Corpus was issued.

---

[97] 1980 AIR 1579.

(b) Mandamus – Mandamus is a Latin word meaning 'we command'. This writ is used by the court to order the public official who has failed to perform his duty or refused to do his duty. Besides public officials, Mandamus can be issued against any public body, a corporation, an inferior court, a tribunal, or government for the same purpose. Simply put, it is a writ issued to a public official to do a thing which is a part of his official duty, but, which, he has failed to do, so far. The primary purpose of this writ is to make the Government machinery work properly or direct the public authorities to some particular thing which is in the nature of public duty. Mandamus may also be issued to a tribunal to compel it to exercise the jurisdiction vested in it, which it has refused to exercise.

This writ can be issued by the Courts when the following grounds are fulfilled:

- The petitioner[98] has a right recognized by law;
- The right of the petitioner has been infringed;
- The petitioner has demanded the authority to perform their duty but there has been non-performance of such duty;
- The last essential ground for Mandamus is the absence of an effective alternative remedy which can be resorted to by the petitioner to enforce the duty of the authority.

The petitioner has to show to the Court that a duty is owed to him by the authority and such authority has not performed their duty. This writ can be issued against all the administrative actions which are unlawful in nature. The authority has many duties, some of which are mandatory while some are left at their discretion to be performed. Thus, if an authority does not perform their mandatory duty, the writ of Mandamus will be issued by the Court. But in cases of discretionary duties, the writ cannot be issued.

Mandamus does not lie –

- When the duty in question is discretionary and not mandatory
- To enforce departmental instruction that does not possess statutory force where the right of the petitioner has lapsed
- To enforce a contractual obligation
- Against the President or the Governor of a State for the exercise of their duties and power (Article 361).
- Against a private individual or body
- Against the Chief Justice of a High Court acting in a judicial capacity

Who can apply for this writ?

Usually, the person whose right is infringed is allowed to apply for the Writs of Mandamus but after the Supreme Court adopted a liberal view and the advent of Public Interest Litigation in India, a public-spirited citizen can also apply for the issuing of the writ of Mandamus on other people's behalf.

(c) **Prohibition :** The literal meaning of 'Prohibition' is 'To forbid.' A writ of prohibition is issued by a Court to prohibit the lower courts, tribunals, and other quasi-judicial authorities from doing something beyond their authority. In other words, it is issued to an Inferior Court preventing the

[98]Petitioner is a person who files the writ.

latter from usurping jurisdiction which is not legally vested in it. When a tribunal or lower court acts without or in excess of jurisdiction, or in violation of rules or law, a writ of prohibition can be asked for. It is generally issued before the trial of the case. For e.g., if a District Court is hearing an appeal against the judgment of the High Court, such an Act is bound to be prohibited because the District Court does not have the power to hear such an appeal. So, a writ of Prohibition will be issued against such an Act of District Court[99]. The said writ can be issued only when –

- The inferior court or tribunal has overstepped its jurisdiction;
- The court or tribunal is acting against the provisions of law;
- In cases where the court is partly acting within its jurisdiction and partly outside it, the writ will be issued against the Act which is partly outside its jurisdiction.
- This writ can be issued only when the proceedings are pending in the inferior court and not when an order has already been passed by that court. Thus, this writ is a pre-emptive remedy which is exercised by the superior court to prevent the inferior court from acting outside its jurisdiction.
- The writ of Prohibition can be issued only against a judicial or a quasi-judicial body and it cannot be issued against any administrative body or legislative authority or private individuals.

Who can file a writ petition?

A writ petition can be filed by any person whose Fundamental Rights have been infringed by the State. Under a Public Interest Litigation, any public-spirited person may file a writ petition in the interest of the general public even if his own Fundamental Right has not been infringed.

(d) **Certiorari :** 'Certiorari' means to 'to be certified'. Certiorari is a curative writ. When the Court is of the opinion that a lower court or a tribunal has passed an order which is beyond its powers or committed an error of law then, through the writ of certiorari, it may transfer the case to itself or quash the order passed by the lower court or tribunal. The writ of Certiorari can be issued by the Supreme Court or any High Court for quashing the order already passed by an inferior court. Although the object of both the writs of prohibition and of certiorari is the same, prohibition is available at an earlier stage whereas certiorari is available at a later stage but in similar grounds, i.e., Certiorari is issued after authority has exercised its powers. The writ can be issued in the following circumstances:

- When a subordinate court acts without jurisdiction or by assuming jurisdiction where it does not exist, or
- When the subordinate court acts in excess of its jurisdiction by way of overstepping or crossing the limits of jurisdiction, or
- When a subordinate court acts in flagrant disregard of law or rules of procedure, or
- When a subordinate court acts in violation of principles of natural justice where there is no procedure specified.

---

[99] https://www.latestlaws.com/articles/analysis-of-types-of-writs-under-Constitution-of-india-landmark-cases/.

The writ lies against –

- Those bodies which are judicial or quasi-judicial in nature. Thus, when anybody or a person is performing a judicial act, their acts can be subjected to the writ of Certiorari.
- Prior to 1991, the writ of Certiorari used to be issued only against judicial and quasi-judicial authorities and not against administrative authorities. Post-1991, the Supreme Court ruled that the certiorari can be issued even against administrative authorities affecting the rights of individuals.
- It cannot be issued against legislative bodies and private individuals or bodies.

Thus, mandamus commands activity, while prohibition commands inactivity.

(e) **Quo-Warranto :** The meaning of the writ of 'Quo-Warranto' is 'By what authority or warrant'. Through this writ, the Court calls upon a person holding a public office to show under what authority he holds that office. If it is found that the person is not entitled to hold that office, he may be ousted from it. Its objective is to prevent a person from holding an office he is not entitled to, therefore preventing usurpation of any public office. It cannot be issued with respect to a private or ministerial office.

The writ can be issued only when the following conditions are fulfilled:

- The public office is wrongfully assumed by the private person;
- The office was created by the Constitution or by any other statute and the person holding the office is not qualified to hold the office under the Constitution or law;
- The term of the public office must be a substantive one and of a permanent nature. And it should not be merely an office at the will and during the pleasure of another.
- The nature of duties arising from the office must be public.

In *Kumar Padma Prasad Vs. Union of India*[100] case, Mr K.N. Srivastava was appointed as a Judge of the Gauhati High Court by the President of India by a warrant of appointment under his seal. A petition was filed for issuing a writ of quo-warranto contending that Mr K.N. Srivastava was not qualified for the office. It was held by the Supreme Court that since Mr K.N. Srivastava was not qualified, quo-warranto could be issued and accordingly, the appointment of Mr K.N. Srivastava was quashed.

ARTICLE 33 – POWER OF PARLIAMENT TO MODIFY THE RIGHTS CONFERRED BY THIS PART IN THEIR APPLICATION TO FORCES, ETC.

Article 33 – Parliament may, by law, determine to what extent any of the rights conferred by this Part shall, in their application to, –

(a) The members of the Armed Forces; or

(b) The members of the Forces charged with the maintenance of public order; or

(c) Persons employed in any bureau or other organisation established by the State for purposes of intelligence or counter intelligence; or

(d) persons employed in, or in connection with, the telecommunication systems set up for the purposes of any Force, bureau or organisation referred to in clauses (a) to (c), be restricted or abrogated so as to ensure the proper discharge of their duties and the maintenance of discipline among them.

[100] AIR 1992 SC 1213.

Article 33 is an exception to the Fundamental Rights conferred by Part III of the Constitution.

A government servant is also entitled to enjoy Fundamental Rights. A person does not lose his Fundamental Rights just by joining government service. But, under Article 33, the Parliament is empowered to restrict or abrogate the Fundamental Rights of a few categories of government servants. Article 33 empowers Parliament to determine, by law, to what extent any of the Fundamental Rights shall be applicable to –

- The members of the Armed Forces; or
- The members of the forces charged with maintenance of public order, or
- Persons employed in any bureau or other organization established by the State for purposes of intelligence or counter intelligence; or
- Persons employed in, or in connection with, the telecommunication systems set up for the purposes of any Force, bureau, or organization referred to in clauses (a), (b), and (c).

Article 33 does not by itself abrogate any rights. Parliament can, in exercise of powers conferred by Article 33, restrict the application of the Fundamental Rights to the armed forces. Therefore, a law enacted by Parliament governing the armed forces cannot be challenged on the grounds that it infringes a Fundamental Right. The power under Article 33 is only exercisable by Parliament and not by State Legislatures. For e.g.:, Maintenance of law and order being a State subject, the law governing the forces charged with the maintenance of public order falls within the State sphere. Nevertheless, such a State law cannot abrogate a Fundamental Right of members of such force. This can only be done by Parliament under Article 33.

In pursuance of this Article, Parliament passed various legislations restricting the Fundamental Rights of armed forces and analogous forces. Few of such acts are – Police Forces (Restriction of Rights) Act, 1966; Army Act; Intelligence Organizations (Restrictions of Rights) Act, 1985, etc.

The expression "members of the Armed forces" used in clause (3) covers such civilian employees of armed forces as barbers, carpenters, mechanics, etc. Although these persons are non-combatants, nevertheless, they are integral to the armed forces, and, therefore, their Fundamental Rights can also be curtailed under Article 33. Article 33 selects only a few services for special treatment, such as, military and para-military forces, police forces, and analogous forces.

The military tribunals or court martial[101]have been excluded from the Supreme Court's appellate jurisdiction under Article 136 (Special Leave Petition)[102]. These tribunals have also been excluded from the power of superintendence vested in a High Court under Article 227. The military tribunals are not, however, exempt from the Supreme Court's writ jurisdiction under Article 32 and the High Court's writ jurisdiction under Article 226. Article 32 can be invoked if there is denial of any Fundamental Right. However, the Fundamental Rights of the armed forces can be curtailed under Article 33 under a Parliamentary law and, to that extent, the courts-martial can be excluded from the purview of Articles 32 and 226[103].

---

[101]Tribunals/courts established under military law.

[102]Discussed in Supreme Court chapter.

[103]M.P. Jain, *Indian Constitutional Law*, LexisNexis, Eighth Edition, Pg No.1436.

ARTICLE 34 – RESTRICTION ON RIGHTS CONFERRED BY THIS PART WHILE MARTIAL LAW IS IN FORCE IN ANY AREA

According to Article 34 –

Notwithstanding anything in the foregoing provisions of this Part, Parliament may by law indemnify any person in the service of the Union or of a State or any other person in respect of any act done by him in connection with the maintenance or restoration of order in any area within the territory of India where martial law was in force or validate any sentence passed, punishment inflicted, forfeiture ordered or other act done under martial law in such area.

This Article merely empowers Parliament to make laws of indemnity to cover illegalities committed by the officers or government personnel during the operation of martial law. Article 34 uses the term 'Martial Law' without defining it. However, martial law can be understood as an action of the military to deal with an emergency amounting to a state of war. Generally, during the martial law, restrictions and regulations are imposed upon civilians. Martial law therefore is a condition of affairs in which absolute power (for the purposes of suppression of invasion, etc.) is assumed by the military authorities who are temporarily placed above the ordinary or civilian law.

Article 34 enables Parliament to enact an Act of Indemnity to protect government and military officers from any liability for action taken by them for restoration of order during the martial law period. Such an Act cannot be questioned on the ground of infringement of Fundamental Rights of a person. Further, under Article 34, Parliament can extend the immunity to any person other than a government servant as well. The reason for this is that during martial law, it is not only the duty of the military officers but of all citizens to help in maintaining law and order. Therefore, if a citizen does any such act, he should also be indemnified in the same way as government servants. The power of Parliament under Art 34 is subject to two conditions:

- The act to be indemnified must have been done in connection with the maintenance or restoration of order; and
- Martial law must be in force in the area where the act was done.

There is no other provision in the Constitution, besides Article 34, referring to martial law. Martial law has not been invoked since the commencement of the Constitution. However, in order to fight terrorism and breakdown of law and order, Parliament has had to enact some drastic laws conferring broad powers on the military personnel but falling short of martial. During the militancy years in certain states, the Armed Forces (Assam and Manipur) Special Powers Act, 1958 (AFSPA) was enacted which conferred special powers on the members of the armed forces in the disturbed areas of Assam, Manipur, Nagaland, Tripura, Meghalaya, and Arunachal Pradesh. The said Act authorizes the civil authorities to call the armed forces to their aid in case of disturbed or dangerous conditions and the army officers are given extensive power to maintain public order.

It is not out of place to mention about The Armed Forces (Punjab and Chandigarh) Special Powers Act, 1983 (*is repealed now)*, which authorized the armed forces to use force, even to the extent of firing and causing death, on any person infringing law and order in the disturbed area.

These laws are no doubt Draconian in nature but may perhaps be justified on the ground that they deal with extraordinary situations and may avoid more drastic measures like martial law to deal with such situations. It is usually complained that a good deal of abuse of power takes places under these special laws. The courts, however, do try to ensure that misuse of power does not take place. For e.g.: in the *Naga People's Movement*, the Apex Court laid down certain guidelines for exercising power under the Armed Forces (Assam and Manipur) Special Powers Act, 1958[104].

What is AFSPA?

The Act in its original form was promulgated by the British in response to the Quit India movement in 1942. After Independence, Prime Minister Jawaharlal Nehru decided to retain the Act, which was first brought in as an ordinance and then notified as an Act in 1958. AFSPA has been imposed on the Northeast states, Jammu & Kashmir, and Punjab during the militancy years. Punjab was the first state from where it was repealed, followed by Tripura and Meghalaya. It remains in force in Nagaland, Manipur, Assam, Jammu & Kashmir, and parts of Arunachal Pradesh.

ARTICLE 35 – GIVING PARLIAMENT THE EXCLUSIVE POWER TO MAKE LAWS RELATING TO ARTICLES 16 (3), 32 (3), 33, AND 34

Article 35 – Legislation to give effect to the provisions of this Part – Notwithstanding anything in this Constitution, –

(a) Parliament shall have, and the Legislature of a State shall not have, power to make laws—

(i) with respect to any of the matters which under clause (3) of Article 16, clause (3) of Article 32, Article 33, and Article 34 may be provided for by law made by Parliament; and

(ii) for prescribing punishment for those acts which are declared to be offences under this Part; and Parliament shall, as soon as may be after the commencement of this Constitution, make laws for prescribing punishment for the acts referred to in sub-clause (ii);

(b) any law in force immediately before the commencement of this Constitution in the territory of India with respect to any of the matters referred to in sub-clause (i) of clause (a) or providing for punishment for any act referred to in sub-clause (ii) of that clause shall, subject to the terms thereof and to any adaptations and modifications that may be made therein under Article 372, continue in force until altered or repealed or amended by Parliament.

Explanation : *In this Article, the expression "law in force" has the same meaning as in Article 372.*

Article 35(a)(i) confers on Parliament, and not on the State Legislatures, the power to make laws for giving effect to certain Fundamental Rights. The relevant provisions are mentioned herein are:

i. Article 16(3): prescribing residence within a State as qualification for employment in the State;

ii. Article 32(3): empowering courts other than the Supreme Court and the High Courts to issue writs and orders to enforce Fundamental Rights;

iii. Article 33: providing for abrogation of, or restriction on, Fundamental Rights of members of armed forces and the police in the interests of disciple and efficiency of armed forces;

iv. Article 34: passing an Act of Indemnity after operation of martial law in any area.

Each of the provisions mentioned above itself confers a similar power on Parliament. Therefore, Article 35 does not contain any additional power for Parliament but only states much more explicitly that the State Legislatures are not entitled to pass any such law.

---

[104] M.P. Jain, *Indian Constitutional* Law, LexisNexis, Eighth Edition, Pg No.1442.

Article 35(a)(ii) confers on Parliament, and not on the State Legislatures, power to makes laws for prescribing punishments for those acts which are declared offences under the Fundamental Rights. Such matters are –

i. Article 17: prescribing punishment for enforcement of any disability arising out of untouchability;

ii. Article 23(1): prescribing punishment for traffic in human beings and imposition of *begar* and other forms of forced labor.

The object of this Article is that if Fundamental Rights shall be uniform and the punishment involved in the breach of such rights also shall be uniform, then that power must be exercised only by Parliament.

Article 35(b), provides that all pre-constitutional laws or Acts which provide punishment for breaches of the Fundamental Rights, or which deal with any of the matters referred to in sub-clause(i) of clause (a) shall continue in force (even though the law is made by the state or provincial legislature) until altered or repealed or amended.

Fundamental Rights available to only citizens and not foreigners

Article Number	Fundamental Right
Article 15	Prohibition of discrimination on grounds of religion, race, caste, sex, or place of birth
Article 16	Equality of opportunity in matters of public employment
Article 19	Six basic freedoms subject to reasonable restrictions
Article 29	Protection of language, script, and culture of minorities
Article 30	Right of minorities to establish and administer educational institutions

Fundamental Rights available to both citizens and foreigners except enemy aliens

Article Number	Fundamental Right
Article 14	Equality before law and equal protection of laws
Article 20	Protection in respect of conviction for offences
Article 21	Protection of life and personal liberty
Article 21A	Right to elementary education
Article 22	Protection against arrest and detention in certain cases
Article 23	Prohibition of traffic in human beings and forced labour
Article 24	Prohibition of employment of children in factories etc.
Article 25	Freedom of conscience and free profession, practice, and propagation of religion
Article 26	Freedom to manage religious affairs
Article 27	Freedom from payment of taxes for promotion of any religion
Article 28	Freedom from attending religious instruction or worship in certain educational institutions

QUESTIONS

Subjective Questions

1. Discuss the importance of 'Right to Life and Personal Liberty' with relevant examples and case laws. **(150 words)**
2. "The Rule of Law" is based on the principle of legality and is opposed to exercise of arbitrary powers". Explain. **(150 words)**
3. Article 13 makes the judiciary, and especially the Apex Court, as a guardian, protector, and the interpreter of the Fundamental Rights. It confers a power as well as imposes an obligation on the Courts to declare a law void if it inconsistent with a Fundamental Right. Discuss. **(200 words)**

Objective Questions

1. Right to vote and to be elected in India is a (UPSC CSE 2017)

(a) Fundamental Right (b) Natural Right

(c) Constitutional Right (d) Legal Right

Ans: (c)

2. Consider the following statements with respect to the Fundamental Rights in India.

(1) Right to Property was deleted from the list of Fundamental Rights by the 44th Amendment Act, 1978.

(2) Right to Elementary Education is only available to the citizens of India.

(3) Article 19 protects the citizen's right to move in and out of the country.

Which of the given statements is NOT correct?

(a) Only 1 (b) Only 3

(c) Both 2 and 3 (d) All of the above

Ans: (c)

3. One of the implications of equality in society is the absence of

(a) Privileges (b) Restraints

(c) Competition (d) Ideology

Ans: (a)

4. Which one of the following statements is correct? (UPSC CSE 2017)

(a) Rights are claims of the State against the citizens.

(b) Rights are privileges that are incorporated in the Constitution of a State.

(c) Rights are claims of the citizens against the State.

(d) Rights are privileges of a few citizens against the many.

Ans: (c)

5. Consider the following Fundamental Rights:

   1. Article 15   2. Article 16

   3. Article 25   4. Article 19

   Which of the above belong to the citizens alone?

   (a) 1, 2, and 4 only   (b) 1, 2, and 3 only

   (c) 2, 3, and 4 only   (d) 1, 3, and 4 only

   Ans : (a)

6. With reference to Protection against arrest and detention under Fundamental Rights, which of the following statement(s) is/are incorrect?

   1. Safeguard in the case of ordinary law is available to all including an alien whereas in the case of preventive detention law, safeguard is available only to citizens and not to aliens.
   2. The 44th Amendment Act of 1978 has reduced the period of detention without obtaining the opinion of an Advisory Board from three to two months which is in force now.
   3. Apart from India, there is no democratic country in the world which has made preventive detention an integral part of the Constitution.

   Select the correct answer using the code given below.

   (a) 1 only   (b) 1 and 2 only

   (c) 2 and 3 only   (d) 1, 2, and 3

   Ans: (b)

7. Which of the following are envisaged by the Right against Exploitation in the Constitution of India?

   1. Prohibition of traffic in human beings and forced labour
   2. Abolition of untouchability
   3. Protection of the interests of minorities
   4. Prohibition of employment of children in factories and mines

   Select the correct answer using the code given below:

   (a) 1, 2, and 4 only   (b) 2, 3, and 4 only

   (c) 1 and 4 only   (d) 1, 2, 3, and 4

   Ans: (c)

8. Which of the following parts/provisions of the Indian Constitution cannot be amended?

   (a) Preamble to the Constitution

   (b) Directive Principles of State Policy

   (c) Fundamental Rights

   (d) Judicial Review

   Ans: (d)

9. Which of the following statements is/are correct regarding Fundamental Rights?

   1. They are sacrosanct in nature and cannot be amended.
   2. They are available against the actions of both State and private individuals.
   3. They operate as checks on tyranny of both Executive and Legislature.

   Select the correct answer using code given below.

   (a) 1 and 3 only (b) 2 only

   (c) 2 and 3 only (d) 1, 2, and 3

   Ans: (c)

10. Dr. Ambedkar called which of the following Fundamental Rights as the most important Article of the Constitution, without which Indian Constitution would be a nullity?

   (a) Right to Constitutional Remedies

   (b) Right to Freedom of Speech and Expression

   (c) Right to Religious and Cultural Freedom

   (d) Right against Exploitation

   Ans: (a)

RIGHT TO PROPERTY

BACKGROUND

The Constitution of India, before the 44th Amendment Act, 1978 provided for the Right to Property as a Fundamental Right, which was later revoked. The Property Right still stands as a constitutional right.

Right to Property as a Fundamental Right created a barrier for both the government and landless people as the government was unable to generate the comprehensive revenue from the land, whereas the landless are unable to cultivate and earn their livelihood aptly. To overcome this issue, the status of the Right to Property was changed from Fundamental Right to constitutional right.

Right to Property was one of the seven Fundamental Rights enshrined in the original Constitution and guaranteed by Article 19(1)(f) and Article 31.

- Article 19(1)(f): Guarantees citizens the right to acquire, hold, and dispose of the property.
- Article 31: Ensures that any person could not be deprived of property except by authority of law. It also mentioned that the State could acquire property only for public purposes and in return of which compensation had to be paid.

At the time when the Indian Constitution was adopted, the organization of land was dominated by Zamindars, intermediaries, Ryotwari settlement, Mahalwari settlement, etc. and a substantial portion of the land was cultivated through tenants at will and sharecroppers who were paying about one-half of the produce as rent for the holdings to the Government were very small. So, for doing justice with the landless or poor people and to uplift them, Indian Government started passing various laws like Zamindari Abolition Act, Land Ceiling Act, and Land Tenure Act. But in these laws, some part becomes contradictory to the Part III of the Constitution, i.e., Fundamental Rights, especially to Article 19(1)(f) and Article 31.

For example:

- Zamindari Abolition Act becomes challengeable in the court because it was contradictory to the Fundamental Rights Article 19(1)(f) and Article 31. These two Articles say that person has a right to acquire, hold, and dispose of property but Zamindari Abolition Act was obstructing people (zamindars) to acquire land and get proper compensation.
- Land Ceiling Act: By this Act, limit of holding land was decided and land beyond the limit would go in the account of the Government, which again became contradictory to Article 19(1)(f) and Article 31.

CONSTITUTIONAL PROVISIONS REGARDING RIGHT TO PROPERTY

Article 31A

After independence, the then Central Government of India decided to launch the abolition of Zamindari Programme in which it abolished the Zamindari system and acquired the lands of the Zamindars. Various land legislations were declared invalid and were challenged under Article 14 and 19(1)(f). *In State of Bihar Vs. Kameshwar Singh*[1], the Bihar Land Reforms Act, 1950, was held invalid under Article 14 for it classified the Zamindars in a discriminatory manner for the purpose of compensation.

---

[1] AIR (1952) Pat 417.

Therefore, finding Zamindari Abolition Programme in danger because of these judicial pronouncements, the central government amended the Constitution and a new provision, i.e., Article 31A[2] was added by the First Amendment, in the year 1951. The said Article in its clauses states that any law -

- made regarding the acquisition of any estate or right by the government or management of any property, or
- creates a merger of any two or more companies,
- receives the benefit of any agreement, lease, or license,

will not be void or null until it has received the assent of the President.

In other words, the Article laid down that no law providing for the acquisition by the State of any estate or of any rights therein, or for the extinguishing or modifying any such rights, would be void on the ground of any inconsistency with any of the Fundamental Rights contained in Article 14, 19, and 31. The only requirement was that such law should receive the assent of the President.

Ninth Schedule (Article 31B)

The 9th Schedule became part of the Constitution in 1951, when the Constitution was amended for the first time. It was created by the new Article 31B, which along with Article 31A was brought in by the government to protect laws related to agrarian reforms and for abolishing the Zamindari system. While Article 31A extends protection to 'classes' of law, Article 31B shields specific laws or enactments.

Article 31B says that any law that is made, which violates any Article or right under Part Three, shall be immune from judicial challenges if this is placed in Schedule Nine. This was done to execute land reforms and protect laws from judicial challenges but the amendment did not mention the nature of laws to be kept in Schedule Nine and that's why it got unlimited scope.

The First Amendment added 13 laws to the 9th Schedule. Subsequent amendments have taken the number of protected laws to 284.

The constitutional validity of the first amendment was upheld in *Sri Sankari Prasad Singh Deo Vs. Union of India and State of Bihar*[3]. The main object of the amendment was to fully secure the constitutional validity of Zamindari Abolition Laws (Article 31A) in general and certain specified Acts (31B/Ninth Schedule) in particular and save those provisions from the dilatory litigation which resulted in holding up the implementation of the social reform measures affecting a large number of people.

---

[2]Notwithstanding anything contained in Article 13, no law providing for —

(a) the acquisition by the State of any estate or of any rights therein or the extinguishment or modification of any such rights, or

(b) the taking over of the management of any property by the State for a limited period either in the public interest or in order to secure the proper management of the property, or

(c) the amalgamation of two or more corporations either in the public interest or in order to secure the proper management of any of the corporations, or

(d) the extinguishment or modification of any rights of managing agents, secretaries and treasurers, managing directors, directors or managers of corporations, or of any voting rights of shareholders thereof, or

(e) the extinguishment or modification of any rights accruing by virtue of any agreement, lease or licence for the purpose of searching for, or winning, any mineral or mineral oil, or the premature termination or cancellation of any such agreement, lease or licence, shall be deemed to be void on the ground that it is inconsistent with, or takes away or abridges any of the rights conferred by [Article 14 or Article 19]

[3](1952) SCR 89.

Thus, upholding the validity of the amendment, it was held in Sankari Prasad case that Article 13(2) does not affect amendments to the Constitution made under Article 368 because such amendments are made in the exercise of constituent power.

Further, the constitutional validity of the Acts added to the Ninth Schedule by the 17th Constitution Amendment Act, 1964 was challenged in Sajjan Singh Vs. State of Rajasthan[4]. Upholding the constitutional amendment, the Supreme Court reiterated the law declared in Sankari Prasad's case.

In I.C. *Golak Nath & Ors. Vs. State of Punjab & Anr*[5&6], a Bench of 11 Judges considered the correctness of the view that had been taken in Sankari Prasad and Sajjan Singh cases. It was held that the constitutional amendment is 'law' within the meaning of Article 13 of the Constitution and, therefore, if it takes away or abridges the rights conferred by Part III thereof, it is void. It was declared that the Parliament will have no power from the date of the decision (27th February, 1967) to amend any of the provisions of Part III of the Constitution so as to take away or abridge the Fundamental Rights enshrined therein. Soon after Golak Nath's case, the Constitution (24th Amendment) Act, 1971, the Constitution (25th Amendment) Act, Act, 1971, the Constitution (26th Amendment)[7] Act, 1971, and the Constitution (29th Amendment[8]) Act, 1972 were passed by the Parliament as a reaction to the judgment.

By Constitution (24th Amendment) Act, 1971, Article 13(4) was added:

"Nothing in this Article shall apply to any amendment of this Constitution made under Article 368".

Article 368 was also amended and in Article 368(1), the words "*in exercise of its constituent powers*" were inserted.

The 25th Amendment Act, 1971 amended the provision of Article 31 dealing with compensation for acquiring or acquisition of properties for public purposes so that only the amount fixed by law need to be given and this amount could not be challenged in court on the ground that it was not adequate or insufficient. The 25th Amendment Act, 1971 further inserted Article 31C.

Constitutional Validity of Article 31B/Ninth Schedule

In *Waman Rao Vs. Union of India*[9], the court held that the laws or the amendments in the Ninth schedule made before the decision of *Keshavananda Bharti Vs. State of Kerala*[10], that is, before 24.04.1973, were beyond challenge, but the amendments made afterwards could be tested on the grounds of amendment of basic structure. Similar views were given by the court in *Minerva Mills Vs. Union of India*[11].

In *IR Coelho Vs. State of Tamil Nadu*[12], the Supreme Court dealt with two new issues –

- The issue was whether an Act or regulation which has been declared to be violative of any of the Articles 14, 19, and 31 by the Supreme Court can be included in the Ninth Schedule? And

---

[4](1965) 1 SCR 933

[5&6](1967) 2 SCR 762

[7]The Constitution (26th Amendment) Act, 1971 omitted from Constitution Articles 291 (Privy Purses) and Article 362 (rights and privileges of Rulers of Indian States) and inserted Article 363A after Article 363 providing that recognition granted to Rulers of Indian States shall cease and privy purses be abolished.

[8]The Constitution (29th Amendment) Act, 1972 amended the Ninth Schedule to the Constitution inserting therein two Kerala Amendment Acts in furtherance of land reforms.

[9]AIR 1981, Supreme Court, 271

[10]AIR 1973 SC 1461.

[11]AIR 1980 SC 1789.

[12]AIR 2007 SC 861

- Whether the First Constitutional Amendment which introduced the Ninth Schedule contradicts the basic structure of the Constitution and whether it should be struck down?

The Court held that –

"If the validity of any Ninth Schedule law has already been upheld by this Court, it would not be open to challenge such law again on the principles declared by this judgment. However, if a law has already been held as violative of any rights in Part III of the Constitution and later on, subsequently incorporated in the Ninth Schedule after 24th April 1973, such an infraction shall be open to challenge on the ground that it damages the basic structure as designated in Article 21 read with Article 14, Article 19, and the ideologies implicit therein."

In other words, even though an Act is put in the Ninth Schedule by a constitutional amendment, its provision would be open to attack on the ground that they affect the basic structure of the Constitution by taking away the Fundamental Rights guaranteed to the people.

The court further held that neither the First Constitutional Amendment Act nor Article 31B violated or damaged the basic structure. Therefore, Article 31B is valid.

Article 31C

Article 31C[13] - This Article protect laws enacted by the Parliament to effectively implement the socialistic Directive Principles under Article 39(b) or 39(c) which stands in conflict with the Fundamental Rights under Article 14 or Article 19.

Thus, the Parliament in order to overcome the Court's judgment, kept on passing various constitutional amendments such as Article 31A, 31B, and 31C. Finally, the Parliament was successful in repealing Article 19(1)(f) and Article 31 as well, by the passing of the 44th Constitutional Amendment Act, 1978 and henceforth, making Right To Property no more a Fundamental Right , but a legal and a constitutional right. In other words, the Right to Property has not been entirely erased from the Constitution. It now sits in Article 300A.

Article 300A

Right to Property was removed from Part III of the Constitution of India and was introduced under Article 300A of the Constitution with the heading 'Right to Property' itself. Article 300A states that "no person shall be deprived of his property save by authority of law". This Article provides restrictions on the State that it cannot take anybody's property without the force of law. The word 'law' here means a validly enacted law which is just, fair, and reasonable. Thus, this right to property secured under Article 300A, will be available against the executive interference and not against the legislative action.

This means that the Right to Property is no longer a Fundamental Right. In other words, the aggrieved individual would not be competent to move to the Supreme court under Article 32, for any violation of Article 300A but under Article 226, individuals can move to the High court. Also, a law will be necessary to deprive a person of his property. Article 300A gives protection against deprivation of property. A person can only be deprived of his property by the authority of law. It means proper compensation shall be given for deprivation according to laws.

Compensation Under Article 300A

In *Kalyani (Dead) Through Lrs. & Ors. Vs. The Sulthan Bathery Municipality & Ors*[14], it was held that the actions of the respondents (State) of acquiring the property of the appellants, all farmers, without

[13] The Constitutional validity of Article 31C is dealt in "Directive Principles of State Policy Chapter". Kindly, refer to the same.

[14] Civil Appeal Nos. 3189 of 2022.

paying any compensation was arbitrary, unreasonable, and clearly a violation of Article 300A of the Constitution. The bench, while relying on its judgment in *K.T. Plantation Private Limited & Anr Vs. State of Karnataka*[15] (2011), observed that under the mandate of Article 300A, the State can only deprive a person of the Right to Property if the same is for a public purpose and the right to compensation is fulfilled, thereby reiterating that the right to compensation is an inbuilt part of Article 300A. Even though Article 300A does not explicitly provide about the compensation, the recent Supreme Court judgments started recognizing compensation as an integral part of Article 300A. Thus, the two requirements are implicit and the pre-condition for the acquisition of any land under Article 300A are as follows:

- The land is need for public purpose.
- The owner of the land has a right to claim compensation for the acquisition of such land.

Right to own Private Property as a Human Right

In *Vidya Devi Vs. The State of Himachal Pradesh & Ors*[16], it was held by the Supreme Court that the Right to own Private Property is a human right and cannot be denied. It further held that the Right to Property is a former Fundamental Right and current human right. Without the sanction of the law and due process, a person cannot be deprived of their right to land. Any unjust acquisition without the proper mechanisms invites the application of the court, for providing compensation on such unjust acquisition.

CONCLUSION

Hence, we can relate the following facts to the Right to Property:

- Right to Property is no more a Fundamental Right under Part III of the Constitution
- Right to Property is a legal, constitutional, as well as a human right
- No action can be taken against legislative orders. Actions are only available against executive orders. In other words, for compulsory acquisition, it should be backed by law. Acquisition without law is invalid. It provides protection to the landowners against the arbitrary action of the executive authorities.
- The Right to Property can now be regulated by the Parliament, i.e., it can abridge, curtail, or modify the said right without undergoing any constitutional amendments.
- No one has the right to approach the Supreme Court under Article 32 as the above right had ceased to exist as a Fundamental Right.
- Constitution explicitly prescribes compensation in the following two cases –
  (a) In a case, where the property of a minority educational institution has been acquired and requisitioned by the State, here the latter is liable to pay adequate compensation to the former[17].
  (b) In a case, where the property of a person owning an agricultural plot, within its statutory ceiling limit, has been acquired or requisitioned by the State, in such a case the State is liable to pay adequate compensation[18].

---

[15] (2011) 9 SCC 1.

[16] SC, DB, Appeal (civil), 60-61 of 2020, Judgement date: Jan 08 2020

[17] Article 30(1A).

[18] Article 31A (Proviso).

CHAPTER 9

DIRECTIVE PRINCIPLES OF STATE POLICY

INTRODUCTION

"In enacting this Part of the Constitution, the Assembly is giving certain directions to the future legislature and the future executive to show in what manner they are to exercise the legislature and the executive power they will have. Surely it is not the intention to introduce in this Part these principles as mere pious declarations. It is the intention of the Assembly that in future both the legislature and the executive should not merely pay lip-service to these principles but that they should be made the basis of all legislative and executive action that they may be taking hereafter in the matter of the governance of the country."

Dr. B.R. Ambedkar (C.A.D. Vol. VII p. 476)

Directive Principles of State Policy are enshrined under Part IV of the Constitution (Articles 36–51). The source of the concept of Directive Principles of State Policy is the Spanish Constitution from which it came in the Irish Constitution. The makers of the Indian Constitution were very much influenced by the Irish nationalist movement and borrowed this concept of Directive Principles of State Policy from the Irish Constitution, 1937. Through these directives, the framers of the Indian Constitution sought to incorporate certain basic principles which they considered essential to be followed by a Welfare State for its social and economic progress. In other words, Part IV contains what may be described as the positive obligations of the State.

Historical Background

The Sapru Committee was assigned the task of doing spadework for making a Constitution for future India. The Committee consisted of thirty members. It was known as the Sapru Committee after the name of its chairman, Tej Bahadur Sapru, an eminent lawyer. The report was published in 1945. The Sapru Committee is distinguished for making suggestions about rights. It made distinction between justiciable rights and non-justiciable rights. The justifiable rights were those enforceable by a court of law. The justiciable rights, as we know, are the Fundamental rights, whereas the non-justiciable ones are the Directive Principles of State Policy.

Reasons for the Non-Justiciability of the Directive Principles of State Policy

The provision to incorporate these DPSPs found wide support in the Constituent Assembly. Dr. B.R. Ambedkar and K.T. Shah were among the few several strong proponents of the Directive Principles. Despite the initial disagreements over the non-enforceable nature of the DPSPs, the Assembly decided on the Directives in their present form for mainly two reasons—firstly, the changing times could put them out of date, and secondly, India did not possess the adequate resources at the time of Independence to enforce all the DPSPs, and thus, it was left to the future Governments to follow them voluntarily[1].

Utility of the Directive Principles

The Directive Principles of State Policy possess two characteristics. Firstly, they are not enforceable in any court and, therefore, if a directive is not obeyed or implemented by the State, its obedience or implementation cannot be secured through judicial proceedings. However, this characteristic has been diluted in practice by court decisions which have enforced some of the Directive Principles in support of the Fundamental Rights. Secondly, they are fundamental in the governance of the country and it shall be the duty of the State to apply these principles in making laws.

The Preamble, the Fundamental Rights, and the Directive Principles can be characterised as the trinity of the Constitution. The Directive Principles seek to give certain directions to the legislatures and governments in India as to how, and in what manner and for what purpose, they are to exercise their power. The reason behind the legal non-enforceability and non-justiciability of these principles is that they impose positive obligations on the State. While taking positive action, government functions under several restraints, the most crucial of these being that of financial resources. The Constitution-makers, therefore, taking a pragmatic view, refrained from giving teeth to these principles. They believed more in an awakened public opinion, rather than in court proceedings, as the ultimate sanction for the fulfilment of these principles. Nevertheless, the Constitution declares that the Directive Principles, though not enforceable by any Court, are 'fundamental' in the governance of the country, and the 'State' has been placed under an obligation to apply them in making laws. The State has to make laws and use its administrative machinery for the implementation and achievement of these Directive Principles.

Fundamental Rights, on the other hand, create negative obligations on the State, i.e., the State is required to refrain from doing something, and it is easier to enforce through a Court as a negative, as compared to a positive, obligation. Accordingly, Article 13 declares that a law inconsistent with a Fundamental Right is void. But there has never been such a provision in the Constitution as regards the Directive Principles. Therefore, a law inconsistent with a Directive Principle cannot be declared invalid.

Thus, the Directive Principles guide the exercise of legislative power but do not control the same.

Interrelationship between Fundamental Rights and Directive Principles

The question of the relationship between the Directive Principles and the Fundamental Rights has caused some difficulty, and the judicial attitude has undergone transformation on this question over time. What if a law enacted to enforce a Directive Principle infringes a Fundamental Right? On this question, the judicial view has changed from irreconcilability to integration between the Fundamental Rights and Directive Principles and, in some of the more recent cases, to giving primacy to the Directive Principles.

Initially, the Courts adopted a strict and literal legal position in this respect. The Supreme Court adopting the literal interpretative approach to Article 37 ruled that a Directive Principle could not override a Fundamental Right, and, that in case of conflict between the two, the Fundamental Right would prevail over the Directive Principle.

---

[1]Surabhi Rao, Constituent assembly debate on Directive Principles of State Policy, National Interest, available at http://logos.nationalinterest.in/2014/07/constituent-assembly-debate-on-directive-principles-of-state-policy/.

This point was settled by the Supreme Court in *State of Madras Vs. Champakam Dorairajan*[2], where a government order in conflict with Article 29(2), a Fundamental Right, was declared invalid, although the government did argue that it was made in pursuance of Article 46, a Directive Principle. The Court ruled that while the Fundamental Rights were enforceable, the Directive Principles were not, and so the laws made to implement Directive Principles could not take away Fundamental Rights. Thus, up to the year 1971, the position was that the Fundamental Rights prevailed over the Directive Principles of State Policy.

In order to overcome this difficulty, Article 31C was inserted by the Twenty-Fifth Constitutional Amendment Act, 1971. This Article provided immunity from any challenge on the grounds of violation of Article 14, 19, and 31 any law enacted for implementing the directives in clause (b) and (c) of Article 39. The second part of the Article further provided that such law made to give effect to the policy under Article 39(b) and (c), would not be open to judicial review[3].

The constitutional validity of Article 31C was challenged in *Kesavananda Bharati Vs. State of Kerala*[4]. The Supreme Court held by a majority that while the first limb of Article 31C was valid, its second limb was invalid. Thus, a declaration as mentioned in the original Article 31C could not be conclusive. The Court must consider, notwithstanding the declaration, whether there was a nexus between the Act and the policy of the Directive Principles in Article 39(b) and (c). If the court came to the conclusion that the declaration was merely a pretence and that the real purpose of the law was the accomplishment of some object other than to give effect to the policy underlying Article 39(b) and (c), the declaration could not debar the Court from striking down any provision therein violating Articles 14, 19, and 31.

Reacting to the Supreme Court's judgment in *Kesavananda Bharati's Case,* the Parliament through the 42nd Constitutional Amendment Act, 1976 further amended Article 31C expanding its scope. The Amended Article provided that "no law giving effect to any of the Directive Principles would be deemed to be void on the ground of its inconsistency with Article 14 and 19". Thus, the 42nd Amendment gave primacy to all the Directive Principles, and not only to Articles 39(b) and (c), over Article 14 and 19.

In *Minerva Mills Limited Vs. UOI*[5], the extended version of Article 31C was struck down by the Supreme Court. The Court ruled that the extension of the shield of Article 31C to all the Directive Principles was beyond the amending power of the Parliament under Article 368, because by giving primacy to all Directive Principles over the Fundamental Rights in Article 14 and 19, the basic or essential feature of the Constitution, viz, judicial review has been destroyed.

Thus, Article 31C is restored to its pre-1976 position so that a Law would be protected by Article 31C only if it has been made to implement the directive in Article 39(b)–(c) and not any of the other Directives included in Part IV. And, there is no antithesis between the Fundamental Rights and the Directive Principles. They are meant to supplement one another. In *Kesavananda Bharati Vs. State of Kerala*[6], the Supreme Court has said that "Fundamental Rights and Directive Principles aim at the same goal of bringing about a social revolution and establishment of a Welfare State and they can be interpreted

---

[2]AIR 1951 SC 226.

[3]Article 31C ran as follows: Notwithstanding anything contained in Article 13, no law giving effect to the policy of the State towards securing the principle specified in clause(b) or clause(c) of Article 39 shall be deemed to be void on the ground that it is inconsistent with, or takes away or abridges any of the rights conferred by Article 14, Article 19 or Article 31; and no law containing a declaration that it is for giving effect to such policy shall be called in question in any Court on the ground that it does not give effect to such policy.

[4]AIR 1973 SC 1461.

[5]AIR 1980 SC 1789.

[6]AIR 1978 SC 1461.

and applied together. They are supplementary and complimentary to each other. It can well be said that Directive Principles prescribed the goal to be attained and the Fundamental Rights lay down the means by which that goal is to be achieved".

Thus, the trilogy of Fundamental Rights, Directive Principles of State Policy, and Fundamental Duties is the bedrock of the Indian Constitution. Granville Austin calls them as 'the conscience of the Constitution'.

DIRECTIVE PRINCIPLES OF STATE POLICY (ARTICLES 36 – 51)

Article 36 (Definition of State)

In this Part, unless the context otherwise requires, "the State" has the same meaning as in Part III.

The word 'State' used in these Directive Principles has the same meaning as has been given to it by Article 12 for the purpose of enforcement of Fundamental Rights unless the context otherwise requires. Since this Article adopts the definition of 'State' in Article 12, it would include courts and statutory tribunals, so that they cannot overlook the objectives of the Directives.

Article 37 (Application of the Principles Contained in this Part)

The provisions contained in this Part shall not be enforceable by any court, but the principles therein laid down are nevertheless fundamental in the governance of the country and it shall be the duty of the State to apply these principles in making laws.

Article 38 (State to Secure a Social Order for the Promotion of Welfare of the People)

1. *The State shall strive to promote the welfare of the people by securing and protecting as effectively as it may a social order in which justice, social, economic and political, shall inform all the institutions of the national life.*
2. *The State shall, in particular, strive to minimise the inequalities in income, and endeavour to eliminate inequalities in status, facilities and opportunities, not only amongst individuals but also amongst groups of people residing in different areas or engaged in different vocations.*

Article 38(1) directs the State to strive "to promote the welfare of the people by securing and protecting as effectively as it may, a social order in which justice—social, economic and political—shall inform all the institutions of national life". The said Article envisages not only legal justice but socio-economic justice as well. This directive only reaffirms what has already been said in the Preamble according to which the function of the Republic is to secure to all its citizens social, economic, and political justice.

The 44th Constitutional Amendment Act, 1978 inserted 38(2), which provides that the State shall, in particular, strive to minimise inequalities in income and endeavour to eliminate inequalities in status, facilities, and opportunities, not only amongst individuals but also amongst groups of people residing in different areas or engaged in different vocations.

Article 39 (Certain Principles of Policy to be Followed by the State)

The State shall, in particular, direct its policy towards securing—

(a) *that the citizens, men and women equally, have the right to an adequate means of livelihood;*

(b) *that the ownership and control of the material resources of the community are so distributed as best to subserve the common good;*

(c) *that the operation of the economic system does not result in the concentration of wealth and means of production to the common detriment;*

(d) *that there is equal pay for equal work for both men and women;*

(e) *that the health and strength of workers, men and women, and the tender age of children are not abused and that citizens are not forced by economic necessity to enter avocations unsuited to their age or strength;*

[7][(f) *that children are given opportunities and facilities to develop in a healthy manner and in conditions of freedom and dignity and that childhood and youth are protected against exploitation and against moral and material abandonment.]*

This Article specially requires the State to ensure for its people adequate means of livelihood, fair distribution of wealth, equal pay for equal work, and protection of children and labor. Article 39(b) and (c) together with other provisions of the Constitution contain the main objectives, namely, the building of a welfare society and an egalitarian social order.

The Minimum Wages Act (1948), Child Labour Prohibition and Regulation Act (1986), The Maternity Benefit Act (1961), Equal Remuneration Act (1976), etc. are the laws which implement this Article.

Article 39A - Equal justice and free legal aid—The State shall secure that the operation of the legal system promotes justice, on a basis of equal opportunity, and shall, in particular, provide free legal aid, by suitable legislation or schemes or in any other way, to ensure that opportunities for securing justice are not denied to any citizen by reason of economic or other disabilities.

Article 39A was added by 42nd Constitutional Amendment Act, 1976. The said Article puts stress upon legal justice. Put simply, the directive requires the State to provide free legal aid to deserving people so that justice is not denied to any one merely because of economic disability.

The Supreme Court has held that Article 39A provides for a holistic approach in imparting justice to the litigating parties. It not only includes providing free legal aid via appointment of counsel for the litigant, but also includes ensuring that justice is not denied to litigating parties due to financial difficulties[8].

The concept of free legal aid is broader than the legal assistance provided to a poor person or indigent accused who is arrested and is put in jeopardy of his life or personal liberty. The Supreme Court has emphasised that under Article 39A, the State Government undoubtedly has an obligation to set up a comprehensive and effective legal aid programme in order to ensure that the operation of the legal system promotes justice on the basis of equality.

Article 39A has been read with Article 21 and, thus, free legal assistance at State cost has been raised to the status of a Fundamental Right of a person accused of an offence which may involve jeopardy to his life or personal liberty. The Court has further ruled that it would make a mockery of legal aid if it were to be left to a poor, ignorant, and illiterate accused person to ask for legal aid. Accordingly, the presiding Judge has been obligated to inform the accused that he can obtain free legal service at the cost of the State if he is unable to engage a lawyer because of his poverty[9].

In pursuance of this Article, the Parliament has passed the Legal Services Authorities Act, 1987.

---

[7]Subs. by the Constitution (Forty-second Amendment) Act, 1976

[8]*Manoharan Vs. Sivarajan*, (2014) 4 SCC 163.

[9]*Suk Das Vs. Union Territory of Arunachal Pradesh, AIR* 1986 SC 991.

Article 40 (Organisation of Village Panchayats)

The State shall take steps to organise village Panchayats and endow them with such powers and authority as may be necessary to enable them to function as units of self-government.

The idea underlying this constitutional provision is to introduce democracy at the grassroots. This provision does not prescribe as to what powers should be given to the Panchayats or what their structure should be.

When Article 40 speaks of village Panchayats as units of self-government, it envisages the organization of the lowest level units of self-governance in the hierarchy of self-governing, democratic, policy-making, and administrative units. In the words of the Supreme Court, "The village Panchayats are envisaged by the Article as the base democratic institutions of a pyramid of the democratically organized and functioning self-governing units".

Articles 243 to 243(O) have been enacted by the Parliament through the 73rd Constitutional Amendment Act, 1992 to give effect to Article 40.

Article 41 (Right to Work, to Education and to Public Assistance in Certain Cases)

The State shall, within the limits of its economic capacity and development, make effective provision for securing the right to work, to education and to public assistance in cases of unemployment, old age, sickness and disablement, and in other cases of undeserved want.

The State is directed by this Article to ensure to the people within the limits of its economic capacity and development:

a. Employment;

b. Education; and

c. Public assistance in cases of unemployment, old age, sickness and disablement, and in other cases of undeserved want.

It is usual to refer to matters specified in this directive as measures of social security. The laws and schemes such as Mahatma Gandhi National Rural Employment Guarantee Act, Pradhan Mantri Vaya Vandana SchemeYojana, etc.etc., implement this provision.

Article 42 (Provision for Just and Humane Conditions of Work and Maternity Relief)

The State shall make provision for securing just and humane conditions of work and for maternity relief.

Article 42 provides the basis of the large body of labor law that obtains in India. The Constitution expresses a deep concern for the welfare of the workers through Articles 42 and 43.

The State is directed to provide just and humane conditions of work and for maternity relief. Laws such as the Industrial Disputes Act, the Minimum Wages Act, the Maternity Relief Act, the Workmen's Compensation Act, the Employees State Insurance Act, etc. implement these provisions.

Article 43 (Living Wage, Etc., for Workers)

The State shall endeavour to secure, by suitable legislation or economic organisation or in any other way, to all workers, agricultural, industrial or otherwise, work, a living wage, conditions of work ensuring a decent standard of life and full enjoyment of leisure and social and cultural opportunities and, in particular, the State shall endeavour to promote cottage industries on an individual or co-operative basis in rural areas.

This Article requires the State to strive to secure work to the worker, a living wage, conditions of work ensuring a decent standard of life and full enjoyment of leisure and social and cultural opportunities.

The last portion of the Article lays emphasis on the promotion of cottage industries on an "individual or cooperative basis in rural areas". This provision enunciates the revolutionary doctrine that employees are entitled as of right to certain reliefs.

A 'living wage' is such a wage as enables the male earner to provide for himself and his family not merely the bare essentials of food, clothing, and shelter, but a measure of frugal comfort including education for children, protection, against ill-health, requirements of essential social needs, and a measure of insurance against the more important misfortunes including old age. A 'minimum wage', on the other hand, is just sufficient to cover the bare physical needs of a worker and his family. Minimum wage is to be fixed in an industry irrespective of its capacity to pay. A 'fair wage' is a mean between 'living wage' and 'minimum wage'. 'Living' and 'fair' wages have to be fixed keeping in view the capacity of the industry to pay.

In pursuance of this Article, various initiatives have been taken to promote the cottage industries in the country. Khadi and Village Industries Commission (KVIC) is the premier organisation charged with the responsibility of developing and promoting cottage and village industries. The other important organisations concerned are All India Handloom Board, Central Silk Board, All India Handicrafts Board, and Coir Board.

Article 43A - Participation of workers in management of industries—The State shall take steps, by suitable legislation or in any other way, to secure the participation of workers in the management of undertakings, establishments or other organisations engaged in any industry.

Article 43A which was introduced by the 42nd Amendment in 1976, has a direct bearing on labour laws, in so far as it provides that the State shall take steps by suitable legislation or any other means to secure the participation of workers in the management of industrial establishments.

The workers' participation in management is not a novel and imported idea from outside. It can be dated as far back as 1920 when Mahatma Gandhi suggested participation of workers in the management on the ground that workers contributed labour and brains while shareholders contributed money to the enterprise and that both should, therefore, share in its property. He said that there should be a perfect relationship of friendship and cooperation among them. For the unions, he said that the aim should be to raise the moral and intellectual height of labour and, thus, by sheer merit, make labour the master of the means of production instead of the slave that it is.

After independence, the first major step in the direction of workers' participation in management in India was the enactment of the Industrial Disputes Act, 1947 with the dual purpose of prevention and settlement of industrial disputes. The Industrial Policy Resolution, 1948 advocated workers' participation in management by suggesting that labour should be involved in all matters concerning industrial production[10].

Article 43B - Promotion of co-operative societies—The State shall endeavour to promote voluntary formation, autonomous functioning, democratic control and professional management of co-operative societies.

The 97th Constitutional Amendment Act, 2011 added Article 43B in the Constitution which provides that the State shall endeavour to promote voluntary formation, autonomous, functioning, democratic control, and professional management of co-operative societies. Article 43B aims at revitalizing co-operative societies with a view to ensuing their contribution to the economic development of the country.

[10]Labour laws & Practice, Module 3, PgNo.21, The Institute of Company Secretaries of India.

Article 44 (Uniform Civil Code for the Citizens)

The State shall endeavour to secure for the citizens a uniform civil code throughout the territory of India.

The object behind this Article is to effect an integration of India by bringing all communities on the common platform on matters which are at present governed by diverse personal laws but which do not form the essence of any religion, e.g., divorce and maintenance for divorced wife.

The Supreme Court has regretted that Article 44 has so long remained a dead letter and recommends early legislation to implement it[11]. The court has observed that the Parliament is still to step in for framing a common civil code in the country which will help the cause of national integration by removing the contradictions based on ideologies.

Article 45 (Provision for Early Childhood Care and Education to Children Below the Age of Six Years)

The State shall endeavour to provide early childhood care and education for all children until they complete the age of six years.

Initially, Article 45 required the State to endeavour to provide, within a period of ten years from the commencement of the Constitution, for free and compulsory education for all children until they complete the age of fourteen years. Article 45 was substituted in 2002 when the right to free and compulsory education was made a fundamental right under Article 21A. Article 45 now provides that the State shall endeavour to provide early childhood care and education for all children until they complete the age of six years.

Article 46 (Promotion of Educational and Economic Interests of Scheduled Castes, Scheduled Tribes and Other Weaker Sections)

The State shall promote with special care the educational and economic interests of the weaker sections of the people, and, in particular, of the Scheduled Castes and the Scheduled Tribes, and shall protect them from social injustice and all forms of exploitation.

Article 46 obligates the State to promote with special care the educational and economic interests of the weaker sections of the people, and, in particular, of the Schedule Castes and the Scheduled Tribes, and to protect them from social injustice and all forms of exploitation. Article 46 supplements Articles 15(2), 15(4), 16, 17, and 29(2). Special social enactments have come into force from time to time for SCs and STs in order to uphold the constitutional mandate and safeguard the interests of these sections of the society.

The major legal enactments at the national level are :

(i) The Protection of Civil Rights Act, 1955

(ii) The Scheduled Castes and Scheduled Tribes (Prevention of Atrocities) Act, 1989

[11] *Jordan Diengdeh Vs. SS Chopra*, AIR 1985 SC 935 (para 7); *Ahmed Khan, Mohd Vs. Shah Bano Begum*, AIR 1985 SC 945 (para 32).

The Protection of Civil Rights Act, 1955 was enacted in furtherance of Article 17 of the Constitution to abolish untouchability and its practice in any form. The Scheduled Castes and Scheduled Tribes (Prevention of Atrocities) Act, 1989 was brought into force from 30th January 1990 in order to check and deter crimes against persons belonging to SCs/STs by persons belonging to other communities. These enactments have extended the positive discrimination in favour of SCs and STs to the field of criminal law in as much as they prescribe penalties that are more stringent than the corresponding offences under Indian Penal Code (IPC) and other laws. Special Courts have been established in major States for speedy trial of cases registered exclusively under these Acts.

This Article further embodies the concept of 'distributive justice' which connotes the removal of economic inequalities and rectifying the injustice resulting from dealings or transactions between unequals in society.

Moreover, the expression 'weaker section' has not yet been defined. The Supreme Court observed that there are millions of other citizens apart from the Scheduled Castes and Scheduled Tribes who also belong to the weaker sections, and directed the Central Government to draw up a guideline for this purpose[12].

In *Indra Sawhney's Case*[13], the Supreme Court has clarified that the expression 'weaker sections' of the people is wide than the expression 'backward class' of citizens, which is only a part of the weaker sections. Backward classes comprise only those which are socially or economically backward. The term 'weaker sections' does not necessarily refer to a group or a class. It connotes all sections of the society which are rendered weaker due to various causes e.g., poverty, natural calamity, or physical handicap.

Article 47 (Duty of the State to Raise the Level of Nutrition and the Standard of Living and to Improve Public Health)

The State shall regard the raising of the level of nutrition and the standard of living of its people and the improvement of public health as among its primary duties and, in particular, the State shall endeavour to bring about prohibition of the consumption except for medicinal purposes of intoxicating drinks and of drugs which are injurious to health.

This Article directs the State to regard the raising of the level of nutrition and the standard of living of its people and the improvement of public health as among its primary duties. Further, the State is required to take steps, to bring about prohibition of the consumption, except for medicinal purposes, of intoxicating drinks and drugs.

In pursuance of this Article various legislations and policies such as National Food Security Act, 2013, Food Safety and Standards Act, 2006, Integrated Child Development Services (ICDS) scheme, Midday Meal Scheme, Targeted Public Distribution Scheme, etc., have been initiated to improve the nutritional status of the Population.

Article 48 (Organisation of Agriculture and Animal Husbandry)

The State shall endeavour to organise agriculture and animal husbandry on modern and scientific lines and shall, in particular, take steps for preserving and improving the breeds, and prohibiting the slaughter, of cows and calves and other milch and draught cattle.

---

[12] *Shantistar Builders Vs. Narayan Khimalal Totame*, AIR 1990 SC 630 (paras 12-13).

[13] (1992) Supp (3) SCC 217.

Article 48 consists of two parts. The first part enjoins the State to "endeavour to organise agricultural and animal husbandry" and that too "on modern and scientific lines". The emphasis is not only on 'organisation', but also on 'modern and scientific lines'. The second part of the Article enjoins the State, to take steps, in particular, "for preserving and improving the breeds, and prohibiting the slaughter, of cows and calves and other milch and draught cattle".

Article 48A - Protection and improvement of environment and safeguarding of forests and wild life—The State shall endeavour to protect and improve the environment and to safeguard the forests and wild life of the country.

This Article was inserted by the 42nd Constitutional Amendment Act, 1976. The Article deals with the 'environment, forests and wildlife'. These three subjects have been dealt with in one Article for the simple reason that these three are interrelated. Protection and improvement of the environment is necessary for safeguarding forests and wildlife, which in turn protect and improve the environment. Forests and wildlife are clearly interrelated and interdependent. They protect each other.

The Environment (Protection) Act, 1986, Wildlife Protection Act, 1972, Forest Conservation Act, 1980, and various other laws providing for the protection of environment, forest, and wildlife are among the steps taken for under this Article.

Article 49 (Protection of Monuments and Places and Objects of National Importance)

It shall be the obligation of the State to protect every monument or place or object of artistic or historic interest, [declared by or under law made by Parliament] to be of national importance, from spoliation, disfigurement, destruction, removal, disposal, or export, as the case may be.

This Article places the State under the duty to protect every monument or place or object of artistic or historic interest, declared by or under a law of Parliament to be of national importance, from spoliation, disfigurement, destruction, removal, disposal, or export, as the case may be. The Ancient Monuments and Archaeological Sites and Remains Act, 1958, was enacted to provide for the preservation of ancient and historical monuments and archaeological sites and remains of national importance, for the regulation of archaeological excavations and for the protection of sculptures, carvings, and other like objects.

Article 50 (Separation of Judiciary From Executive)

The State shall take steps to separate the judiciary from the executive in the public services of the State.

The Constitution has not indeed recognised the doctrine of separation of powers in its absolute rigidity but the functions of different branches of the government have been sufficiently differentiated. Consequently, it can very well be said that our Constitution does not contemplate assumption, by one organ of the government of functions that essentially belong to another. Broadly stated, Article 50 provides that there shall be a separate judicial service free from executive control. This Article is based on the bedrock of the principle of independence of the judiciary.

The separation of the judiciary from the executive is regarded as a very necessary element for proper administration of justice in the country. The separation of powers between the legislature and the executive and the judiciary constitutes one of the basic features of the Constitution.

In pre-independence India, the criminal magistrate was under the direct control of the executive. There was a strong agitation against such a state of affairs. There was a public demand for separating the judiciary from executive at all levels. It was vehemently argued that without such a separation, the independence of the judiciary at the lower level would be nothing more than a mockery. It is this idea, which is incorporated in Article 50.

Code of Criminal Procedure, 1973 clearly separates the judiciary from the executive in line with Article 50.

Article 51 (Promotion of international peace and security)

The State shall endeavour to:

(a) *promote international peace and security;*

(b) *maintain just and honourable relations between nations;*

(c) *foster respect for international law and treaty obligations in the dealings of organised peoples with one another; and*

(d) *encourage settlement of international disputes by arbitration.*

This Article embodies the principles, which the Indian foreign policy is to follow. The Supreme Court has accepted and incorporated provisions of International Conventions ratified by India in a growing number of situations where domestic law was silent or ambiguous.

Article 51(c) does not deal with the enforcement or implementation of treaties. Unless municipal law is changed, an international covenant does not bind. It is only the municipal law that binds the Courts. However, the Supreme Court has referred to several international covenants while interpreting several Fundamental Rights. For example, in *People's Union for Civil Liberties Vs. UOI*[14], the Court referred to Article 17 of the International Covenant on Civil and Political Rights, 1966 and Article 12 of the Universal Declaration of Human Rights, 1948, so as to derive from Article 21 a right to privacy in India.

CLASSIFICATION OF DIRECTIVE PRINCIPLES OF STATE POLICY

The Constitution doesn't differentiate between types of Directive Principles of State Policy but on the basis of their content and direction, they are usually classified into three categories: *Socialistic, Gandhian, and Liberal-Intellectual Principles.*

Socialistic Principles

They emphasis on providing a better structure for economic and social justice and lay down the framework of a democratic socialist State. These also contemplate the ideology of socialism. They direct the State through-

(a) Article 38 - State to secure a social order for the promotion of welfare of the people

(b) Article 39 - Certain principles of policy to be followed by the State

(c) Article 41 - Right to work, to education and to public assistance in certain cases

(d) Article 42 - Provision for just and humane conditions of work and maternity relief

(e) Article 43 - Living wage, etc., for workers

f) Article 43A - Participation of workers in management of industries

(g) Article 47 - Duty of the State to raise the level of nutrition and the standard of living and to improve public health

---

[14] AIR 1997 SC 568.

Gandhian Principles

They reflect the Gandhian philosophy of reconstruction enunciated by Gandhi during the national movement. In order to pursue the path directed by him, some of his ideas are incorporated in DPSP and they direct the State through -

a. Article 40 - Organisation of village Panchayats

b. Article 43 - Provision to promote cottage industries on an individual or cooperative basis in rural areas

c. Article 43B - Promotion of co-operative societies

d. Article 46 - Promotion of educational and economic interests of Scheduled Castes, Scheduled Tribes, and other weaker sections

e. Article 47 - Promotion of steps to improve public health and prohibit consumption of intoxicating drinks and drugs that are injurious to health

f. Article 48 - Prohibition of slaughter of cows, calves, and other milch and draught cattle and to improve their breeds

Liberal-Intellectual Principles

They emphasis on the ideology of liberalism and incline towards the political and moral philosophy-based liberty, consent of citizens, and equality before the law. They direct the State through -

a. Article 39A - Protecting equal justice and free legal aid

b. Article 44 - Endeavouring to secure for the citizen a Uniform Civil Code through the territory of India

c. Article 45 - Providing early childhood care and education for all children until they complete the age of six years

d. Article 48 - Organizing agriculture and animal husbandry on modern and scientific lines

e. Article 48A - Protecting and improving the environment and to safeguard the forests and wildlife of the country

f. Article 49 - Protecting every monument or place of artistic or historic interest

g. Article 50 - Separating judiciary from the executive in the public services of the State

h. Article 51 - Promoting and establishing international peace and security

CRITICISMS OF THE DIRECTIVE PRINCIPLES OF STATE POLICY

Many critics have been very vocal in criticizing the existence of unenforceable pious declarations in the body of the Constitution as stand incorporated in its Part IV (DPSP). They consider these as "*superfluous high sounding principles*" with little scope for actual realization. The major criticisms against the Directive Principles of State Policy are as follows:

1. **Lack of legal force :** The critics hold that since these principles are unenforceable directives, these principles do not carry any weight. Their violation or non-realization cannot be challenged in any court.

   "Non-justiciable and abstract Directive Principles which may be safely ignored by the legislator... do not enhance the true prestige of a written Constitution." – M. Anantnarayan.

2. **Mere declarations :** The Directive Principles are a mere declaration of intentions or instruments of instructions which are to be observed and secured by the State at will. The Constitution does not make them justiciable and neither fixes the time limit within which these are to be secured. The legislature is to secure these as and when it may be possible for it. No wonder then, critics like K.T. Shah describe it as "a cheque payable by the bank at its convenience."

3. **Unsystematic enumeration :** Another point of criticism against the Directive Principles has been that these have been neither systematically slated nor properly classified. These appear to be a collection of pious declarations recorded in the Constitution.

   "These Directives are neither properly classified nor logically arranged. The declaration mixes up relatively unimportant issues with the most vital economic and social questions." – *Srinivasan.*

4. **Lack of Clarity :** Several Directives lack clarity while several have been repeated at different places. *"The formulation of the Directive Principles of State Policy can hardly be considered inspiring. It is both vague and repetitive."* – *Srinivasan.*

5. **Borrowed obsolete philosophical foundations :** The critics criticize Part IV also for the fact that most of the Directive Principles incorporated in it are based on age-old and foreign philosophical foundations which essentially the foundations of Fabian Socialism[15].

[15]Fabian socialism was founded in 1884 in London. It is a variety of socialism. The purpose of the Fabian Socialism was to reach the goals of socialism through evolutionary or parliamentary process and to avoid revolution or armed struggle.

QUESTIONS

Subjective Questions

1. "The harmony and balance between Fundamental Rights and Directive Principles is an essential feature of the basic structure of the Constitution". Discuss. **(20 marks)**

2. The Directive principles of State Policy impose an obligation on the State to take positive action for creating socio-economic conditions in which there will be an egalitarian social order with social and economic justice to all. Explain. **(10 marks)**

Objective Questions

1. Consider the following provisions under the Directive Principles of State Policy as enshrined in the Constitution of India : **(UPSC CSE 2012)**

   1. Securing for citizens of India a uniform civil code
   2. Organizing village Panchayats
   3. Promoting cottage industries in rural areas
   4. Securing for all the workers reasonable leisure and cultural opportunities

   Which of the above are the Gandhian Principles that are reflected in the Directive Principles of State Policy?

   (a) 1, 2, and 4 only (b) 2 and 3 only

   (c) 1, 3, and 4 only (d) 1, 2, 3, and 4

   Ans: (b)

2. 'Economic Justice' has been one of the objectives of the Indian Constitution provided in: **(UPSC CSE 2013)**

(a) the Preamble and Fundamental Rights

(b) the Preamble and the Directive Principles of State Policy

(c) the Fundamental Rights and the Directive Principles of State Policy

(d) None of the above

Ans: (b)

3. In the Constitution of India, promotion of international peace and security is included in the: **(UPSC CSE 2014)**

(a) Preamble to the Constitution (b) Directive Principles of State Policy (DPSP)

(c) Fundamental Duties (d) Ninth Schedule

Ans: (b)

4. With reference to Directive Principles, consider the following statements:

1. The harmony between Fundamental Rights and Directive Principles of State Policy is a part of the basic structure of the Constitution.
2. No law which seeks to implement the Directive Principles under Article 39(b) and (c) shall be void on the ground of contraventions of any of the Fundamental Rights.

Which of the statements given above is/are correct?

(a) 1 only (b) 2 only

(c) Both 1 and 2 (d) Neither 1 nor 2

Ans: (a)

5. Which of the following bodies are expected to follow the Directive Principles of State Policy?

1. Union and State executive organs
2. Union and State legislative organs
3. Local self-government
4. LIC

Select the correct answer using the code given below.

(a) 1 and 2 only (b) 2 only

(c) 1, 2, and 3 only (d) 1, 2, 3, and 4

Ans: (d)

CHAPTER 10

FUNDAMENTAL DUTIES

INTRODUCTION

"Law is not merely right alone. The only real right of man in the society is to do his duty[1]*"*

The original Constitution as enacted did not contain any provisions relating to Fundamental Duties. As rights and duties are two sides of the same coin, it looks rather enigmatic that the framers of the Indian Constitution did not lay down Fundamental Duties for the citizens along with their Fundamental Rights. Such duties are generally not found in the Constitutions based on the Western liberal traditions. They are invariably found in the socialist constitutions[2]. But they are also found in non-socialist constitutions[3]. To some extent, their inclusion in the Constitution may also be associated with cultural traditions of a society[4]. Thus, the Asian and African societies give greater emphasis to duties than the Western societies[5]. Reference to duties, however, finds place even in international instruments such as the Universal Declaration of Human Rights and International Covenant on Civil and Political Rights. Coming to the Indian Constitution, Fundamental Duties are said to be 'borrowed' from the citizen's duties enumerated in the Constitution of the erstwhile Union of Soviet Socialist Republics(USSR). They also intended to bring the Constitution in line with Article 29(1) of the Universal Declaration of Human Rights.

Incorporation of Fundamental Duties : Swaran Singh Committee

In 1976, during National emergency, the then Indira Gandhi's government constituted a committee under the chairmanship of Sardar Swaran Singh (who had been the Minister for External Affairs till 1974). This committee was entrusted with the responsibility to study the Constitution of India and make amendments to them in light of experience gathered for the past 25 years. The committee went through the Constitutions of various countries where a separate chapter on Fundamental Duties was incorporated. Then it recommended to incorporate Fundamental Duties in the Constitution of India and proposed the following Fundamental Duties:

(1) to respect and abide by the Constitution and the laws,

(2) uphold the sovereignty of the nation and function in such a way as to sustain and strengthen its unity and integrity,

---

[1] Arun Sud; Our Fundamental Duties, Journal of Political Studies, V.10.N1;(1977) P.88.

[2] The Constitution of People's Republic of China.

[3] The Constitution of Sri Lanka, 1997; The Constitution of Japan 1947.

[4] V.N. Shukla, *Constitution of India*, Thirteenth Edition, M.P.Jain 392.

[5] W.D. O'Flaherty and J.D.M., Derett, *The Concept of Duty in Asia*; African Charter on Human and People's Right of 1981.

(3) respect the democratic institutions enshrined in the Constitution and not do anything which may impair their dignity or authority,

(4) defend the country and render national service, including military service, when called upon to do so,

(5) adjure communalism in any form,

(6) render assistance and cooperation in the implementation of the Directive Principles of State Policy, and promote the common good of the people, so as to sub serve the interest of social and economic justice,

(7) abjure violence, protect, and safeguard public property, and refrain from doing anything which may cause damage and destruction to such property, and

(8) pay taxes according to law.

The committee has further proposed that Parliament may, by law, provide for the imposition of such penalty or punishment as may be considered appropriate for any non-compliance with or refusal to, and observe any of these duties. To safeguard the Fundamental Duties from being challenged in any court of law, the committee has suggested the inclusion of an explicit provision that "no law imposing such penalty shall be called in question in any court on the ground of infringement of any of the Fundamental Rights or on the ground of repugnancy to any other provisions of the Constitution."

Rejected Recommendations Of The Swaran Singh Committee

Following recommendations of the Swaran Singh Committee were not accepted by the Government:

- Penal provision for non-compliance of Fundamental Duties
- Law by which person is punished (for not observing Fundamental Duties) cannot be taken to the Court of Law as a matter of violations of certain Fundamental Rights
- Duty to pay taxes

CONSTITUTIONAL PROVISIONS REGARDING FUNDAMENTAL DUTIES

Based on the Swaran Singh Committee's recommendations, the Constitution (Forty-second Amendment) Act, 1976, was enacted, whereby Article 51Ain Part IV-A was inserted on Fundamental Duties among a slew of other changes to the Constitution.

Article 51A enumerates that the following shall be the duty of every citizen of India:

1. To abide by the Constitution and respect its ideals and institutions, the National Flag, and the National Anthem;
2. To cherish and follow the noble ideals which inspired our national struggle for freedom;
3. To uphold and protect the sovereignty, unity, and integrity of India;
4. To defend the country and render national service when called upon to do so;
5. To promote harmony and the spirit of common brotherhood amongst all the people of India transcending religious, linguistic, and regional or sectional diversities; to renounce practices derogatory to the dignity of women;
6. To value and preserve the rich heritage of our composite culture;
7. To protect and improve the natural environment including forests, lakes, rivers, wildlife, and to have compassion for living creatures;
8. To develop the scientific temper, humanism, and the spirit of inquiry and reform;

9. To safeguard public property and to abjure violence;
10. To strive towards excellence in all spheres of individual and collective activity so that the nation constantly rises to higher levels of endeavour and achievement;
11. Who is a parent or guardian, to provide opportunities for education to his child, or as the case may be, ward between the age of six to fourteen years.

The eleventh fundamental duty was added by the (Eighty-Sixth Amendment) Act, 2002 of the Constitution.

These Fundamental Duties are essentially taken from the Indian tradition, mythology, religions, and practices. Essentially, these were the duties that are the codification of tasks integral to the Indian way of life.

Hence, these are different kinds of duties prescribed under Article 51A of the Indian Constitution. One set of duties talks about the obligation of a citizen towards the state. Another one refers to code that citizens need to adopt, such as development of scientific temper and achieve excellence so that the community as a whole benefit from the economic and social development. Moreover, Article 51A is confined to 'citizens', unlike some of the articles relating to Fundamental Rights which extend to 'all persons', including aliens.

Enforcement of Fundamental Duties

Article 51A of the Indian Constitution merely declares the Fundamental Duties of the citizens of India. It does not say of the enforcement of these duties. Fundamental duties are criticized on the ground that there is no sanction behind the Fundamental Duties. Like the Directive Principles of State Policy, there has been no provision under the Indian Constitution to enforce the Fundamental Duties.

It is true that there is no legal sanction provided for violation or non-performance of Fundamental Duties. There is neither specific provision for enforceability, nor any specific prohibition. However, Fundamental Duties have an inherent element of compulsion regarding compliance. They are a constant reminder to us of the national goals as well as the basic norms of political order. They may inspire us to inculcate in ourselves a sense of social responsibility. Therefore, it is no longer correct to say that Fundamental Duties enshrined in Article 51A are not enforceable to ensure their implementation and are a mere reminder. Fundamental Duties have the element of compulsion regarding compliance. What is needed is to enact suitable legislation wherever necessary to require obedience of the duties by the citizens, with legal sanctions. There is need for comprehensive legislation in this area to ensure a faithful and effective implementation of the Fundamental Duties.

Once Article 51A was enforced, Shri H.R.Gokhale, the former Union Law Minister, described the Chapter as "by far the most fundamental and very important for the purpose of every generation, the present as well as the future".

Importance of Fundamental Duties

The breach of any Fundamental Duty is not punishable. It therefore, becomes obvious, that the real purpose behind the incorporation of a set of duties in the Constitution was to lay down a system of basic norms, which are 'directory' in nature. Reacting to the question as to how the mere inclusion of a set of duties in the Constitution would be of any help to the nation, the then Prime Minister, Mrs. Indira Gandhi, had observed: *"If people only kept the Fundamental Duties in their mind, we will soon have apeaceful and friendly revolution"*[6].

[6] L.S.Sinha, The Fundamental Duties: Their Importance; Socialist India, V.13, Oct.23, 1976, P.102.

The Fundamental Duties contain noble principles. It is obligatory on the part of every citizen who seeks the enforcement of his Fundamental Rights not to violate the Fundamental Rights of any other person. The Fundamental Duties have no sanction attached. The citizen must introspect and endeavour to perform these duties[7]. The sanction should be self-imposed. They are much of an educational and psychological value for the citizens.

The Supreme Court has held that Article 51A can even be used to interpret ambiguous statutes. Fundamental Duties have been particularly invoked in litigation concerning the environment.

The Apex Court in AIIMS Students' Union v. AIIMS[8], observed as under:

"Almost a quarter century after the people of India have given the Constitution unto themselves, a chapter on Fundamental Duties came to be incorporated in the Constitution". Fundamental Duties, as defined in Article 51A, are not made enforceable by a writ of court just as the Fundamental Rights are, but it cannot be lost sight of that 'Duties' in Part IV-A Article 51A are prefixed by the same word 'Fundamental 'which was prefixed by the founding fathers of the Constitution to 'Rights' in Part III. Every citizen of India is fundamentally obligated to develop a scientific temper and humanism. He is fundamentally duty-bound to strive towards excellence in all spheres of individual and collective activity so that the nation constantly rises to higher levels of endeavour and achievements. State is, all the citizens placed together and hence though Article 51A does not expressly cast any fundamental duty on the State, the fact remains that the duty of every citizen of India is the collective duty of the State".

Grounds for Criticism of Insertion of Fundamental Duties

1. The insertion was merely to create awareness among citizens (who were already aware) about their duties and is not backed by any legal sanction. However, variou slegislations have been enacted covering the various gamut of Fundamental Duties like Flag Code of India, 2002, The Emblems and Names (Prevention of Improper Use) Act, 1950, and the Prevention of Insults to National Honour Act, 1971.
2. The Fundamental Duties enumerated under Article 51A is only a code of conduct. There is no enforcement of these duties or legal sanction. These would have anyway been performed by the citizens and no special chapter was required to be incorporated under the Constitution.
3. Some of the Fundamental Duties are vague since they are qualitative in nature and cannot be measured using some standards like development of scientific temper, composite culture, etc.
4. It did not include certain important duties like 'the duty of state to make the citizens aware of dangers of increasing population and seek their cooperation in birth control of human population, compulsory voting for eligible population, duty to pay taxes', etc.

OPERATIONALISATION OF FUNDAMENTAL DUTIES : JUSTICE VERMA COMMITTEE

The Government of India constituted a committee in the year 1998 under the chairmanship of Justice J.S. Verma, "to work out a strategy as well as methodology of operationalising acountry wide programme for teaching Fundamental Duties in every educational institution as a measure of in-service training". The committee suggested that there is an imperative need for wider dissemination of information and generating greater awareness in regard to the Fundamental Duties of citizens and obligations of citizenship.

---

[7]In *Surya Narain Vs. Union of India*, (AIR 1982 Raj. 1,) the Rajasthan High Court held that the duties under Article 51A were the duties of the individual citizens. They cast no public duties.

[8](2002) 1 SCC 428

The Justice Verma Committee was also conscious of the fact that any non-operation alization of Fundamental Duties might not necessarily be the lack of concern or non-availability of legal and other enforceable provisions; but it was more a case of lacuna in the strategy of implementation. It, therefore, thought it appropriate to list in brief some of the legal provisions already available in regard to enforcement of Fundamental Duties.

Legal Provisions Regarding Fundamental Duties

A summary of the legal provisions suggested by the Justice Verma Committee is given below:

(i) *In order to ensure that no disrespect is shown to the National Flag, Constitution of India, and the National Anthem, the Prevention of Insults to National Honour Act, 1971 was enacted and The Emblems and Names (Prevention of Improper Use) Act, 1950 was enacted to prevent improper use of the National Flag and the National Anthem.*

(ii) *There are a number of provisions in the existing criminal laws to ensure that the activities which encourage enmity between different groups of people on grounds of religion, race, place of birth, residence, language, etc. are adequately punished. Writings, speeches, gestures, activities, exercise, drills, etc. aimed at creating a feeling of insecurity or ill-will among the members of other communities, etc. Have been prohibited under Section 153A of the Indian Penal Code (IPC).*

(iii) *Imputations and assertions prejudicial to the national integration constitute a punishable offence under Section 153B of the IPC.*

(iv) *A Communal organization can be declared unlawful association under the provisions of Unlawful Activities (Prevention) Act, 1967.*

(v) *Offences related to religion are covered in Sections 295–298 of the IPC (Chapter XV).*

(vi) *Provisions of the Protection of Civil Rights Act, 1955 (earlier the Untouchability (Offences) Act. 1955)provides rights to the people of lower caste to exercise their rights.*

(vii) *Sections 123(3) and 123(3A) of the Representation of the People Act, 1951 declares that soliciting of vote on the ground of religion and the promotion or attempt to promote feelings of enmity or hatred between different classes of citizens of India on the grounds of religion, race, caste, community, or language is a corrupt practice. A person indulging in a corrupt practice can be disqualified for being a Member of Parliament or a State Legislature under Section 8A of the Representation of the People Act, 1951.*

Thus, even though the Fundamental Duties are not enforceable, the courts in India have been taking note of the Fundamental Duties in judicial decisions. Being provisions of the Constitution, the courts will have due regard for the Fundamental Duties in interpreting the text of the Constitution. The Fundamental Duties are always taken into account while interpreting any Fundamental Rights.

QUESTIONS

Subjective Questions

1. "If society becomes duty-based, everyone in India should turn attention on performance of duties and through such performance, ensure and be entitled to the rights of a citizen." Critically Analyse. (250 words)

2. "It is the obligation of the State to educate the citizens in the matter of Fundamental Duties so that a right balance between Rights and Duties may emerge". Explain. (250 words)

Objective Questions

1. Which of the following statements is/are true of the Fundamental Duties of an Indian citizen?
   1. A legislative process has been provided to enforce these duties. **(UPSC CSE 2017)**
   2. They are correlative to legal duties.

   Select the correct answer using the code given below:

   (a) 1 only (b) 2 only
   (c) Both 1 and 2 (d) Neither 1 nor 2

   Ans: (d)

2. 'To uphold and protect the Sovereignty, Unity, and Integrity of India' is a provision made in the **(UPSC CSE 2015)**

   (a) Preamble of the Constitution (b) Directive Principles of State Policy
   (c) Fundamental Rights (d) Fundamental Duties

   Ans: (d)

3. Which of the following is/are among the Fundamental Duties of citizens laid down in the Indian Constitution? **(UPSC CSE 2012)**
   1. To preserve the rich heritage of our composite culture
   2. To protect the weaker sections from social injustice
   3. To develop the scientific temper and spirit of inquiry
   4. To strive towards excellence in all spheres of individual and collective activity

   Select the correct answer using the codes given below:

   (a) 1 and 2 only (b) 2 only
   (c) 1, 3, and 4 only (d) 1, 2, 3, and 4

   Ans: (c)

4. Consider the following statements regarding the Fundamental Duties:
   1. Fundamental Duties in the Indian Constitution are inspired by the USSR Constitution.
   2. Fundamental Duties are applicable to all the citizens of India.
   3. Fundamental Duties can be enforced in the court of law if the Parliament passes a law in this regard.

   Which of the statements given above is/are incorrect?

   (a) 1 only (b) 1 and 2 only
   (c) 2 and 3 (d) 1, 2, and 3

   Ans: (b)

5. 'The Protection of Monuments' is covered in the Constitution under which section or part?
   1. Directive Principles of State Policy 2. Fundamental Duties
   3. Union List

   Select the correct answer from the codes given below:

   (a) 2 only (b) 2 and 3 only
   (c) 1, 2, and 3 (d) 1 only

   Ans: (d)

CHAPTER 11

THE CENTRAL EXECUTIVE

The Central Executive or the Union Executive consists of the President, Vice-President, Prime Minister, Council of Ministers, and the Attorney-General of India.

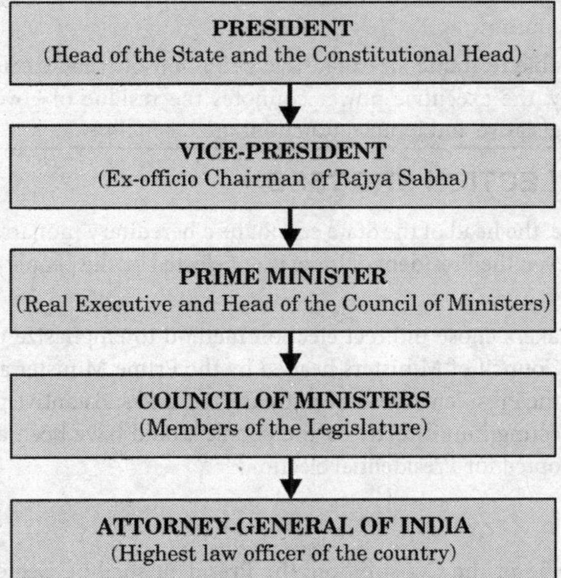

The structure of the Central Executive closely resembles the British model which functions on the basis of unwritten conventions. In India, however, some of these conventions have been written in the Constitution, for example, provisions regarding appointment, tenure and collective responsibility of the Ministers. But some matters are left to conventions, for example, the Cabinet.

11.1 THE PRESIDENT

Office of the President

The President is the head of the State and the Formal Executive. According to Article 53, the executive power of the Union shall be vested in the President and it shall be exercised by him in accordance with the Constitution either directly or through officers' subordinate to him.

EXHIBIT 11.1 : EXECUTIVE POWER

The word "Executive power" is not defined in the Constitution. However, Article 73 of the Constitution provides that *"the executive power of the Union shall extend to the matters with respect to which Parliament has power to make laws and includes the exercise of such rights, authority and jurisdiction as are exercisable by the Government of India by virtue of any treaty or agreement"*. In other words, the executive power of the Union which is exercised in the name of the President is co-extensive or co-terminus with the legislative powers of the Parliament.

Ram Jawaya Kapur Vs. State of Punjab

In *Ram Jawaya Kapur Vs. State of Punjab* case, the Supreme Court held that it is difficult to provide an exhaustive definition of the "Executive Power" in the modern state.

Highlights of the case

- The functions of modern state like the police state are not confined to a mere collection of taxes or maintenance of laws and protection of realm from external or internal enemies. The modern state is expected to engage in all the activities necessary for the promotion of the social and economic welfare of the community.
- It may not be possible to frame an exhaustive definition of what executive function means and implies. Ordinarily, the executive power connotes the residue of governmental functions that remain after the legislative and judicial functions are taken away.

PRESIDENTIAL ELECTION PROCESS

India being a republic, the head of the State cannot be a hereditary monarch. Therefore, the President of India is elected. However, the President of India is not elected by the people directly, but by the method of indirect election.

The Constitution-makers chose indirect election method to emphasize that the effective executive power resides with the Council of Ministers headed by the Prime Minister and not in the President as such. In other words, as the President does not enjoy any real and substantive power in the Parliamentary form of government, electing him directly by the people would have been absurd. Therefore, indirect election method was adopted for Presidential election.

Electoral College

According to Article 54 of the Constitution, the President shall be elected by an Electoral College consisting of:

- The elected members of both Houses of Parliament; and
- The elected members of the Legislative Assemblies of the States.
- The elected members of the Legislative Assemblies of Delhi and Puducherry.

The 70th Constitutional Amendment Act, 1992 added a new explanation to Article 54 which provides that the word "State" includes the National Capital Territory of Delhi and the Union Territory of Puducherry, even though a legislature created by Article 239A is not a legislative assembly as contemplated by Article 54. This means that the MLA's of the Union Territory of Delhi and Puducherry will take part in the Presidential election. Elaborate provisions are made in Article 55 for securing uniformity in the scale or representation of the different states at the election of the President, and also for securing parity between the States as a whole and the Union.

The nominated members of both the Houses of Parliament, the nominated members of the State Legislative Assembly, and both the elected and the nominated members of the State Legislative Council will not take part in the Presidential elections. The Electoral College of the President, therefore, includes not only the elected members of the Parliament but also the elected members of the State Legislative Assembly as well. The framers of the Constitution did not want the President to be elected by Parliament alone as that would have been a very narrow basis, and Parliament being dominated by one political party would have invariably chosen a candidate from that party. In order to command national consensus as the Head of the State, the Constitution-makers felt imperative that the members of the state legislature should also take part in the Presidential elections.

Proportional Representation System

The election of the President shall be held in accordance with the system of Proportional Representation by means of a Single Transferrable Vote. The system adopted for voting is secret ballot. The Constitution provides that as far as practicable, there shall be uniformity in the scale of representation among the State inter se as well as parity between the States as a whole and the Union at the election of the President. However, the votes cast by all members of the Electoral College are not of uniform value. Following are the principles adopted in order to determine the value of each MLA and MP vote:

- **Value of each MLA vote** – In order to bring uniformity in representation among the states the value of each MLA vote is determined in the following manner:

$$\frac{\text{State Population}}{\text{Total Number of elected members in the State Legislative Assembly}} \times \frac{1}{1{,}000}$$

This formula seeks to secure to a member of a State legislative assembly votes in the ratio of the population of the State which he represents in the assembly and thereby to prevent the swamping of votes of a larger State by those of a smaller State having a relatively larger legislature

- **Value of each MP vote** – In order to bring parity of votes between the elected members of the Parliament and the State Legislative Assemblies following formula is used:

$$\frac{\text{Total number of votes assigned to the members of the State Legislative Assemblies in the Electoral College}}{\text{Total number of elected members of the two Houses of Parliament}}$$

According to Article 71, Presidential election cannot be challenged on the ground of existence of vacancy among the members of the Electoral College. The vacancy can be for whatever reason, including dissolution of state assembly; still it cannot be challenged on the grounds of existence of vacancy. The Supreme Court reiterated the same in its advisory opinion to the President of India. In *re, Presidential Poll,* the Supreme Court has ruled that the election of the President can be held even when a State Assembly has been dissolved under Article 356 and its members are unable to participate in the election.

As per Article 55(3) of the Constitution of India, the election of the President shall be held in accordance with the system of proportional representation by means of single transferable vote and the voting at such election shall be by secret ballot. Under this system every voter has one vote and can mark preferences against contesting candidates. To win the election, candidates need to secure a certain quota of votes.

The quota for declaring a candidate as selected is determined by dividing of the valid votes by 2 and adding one to the quotient, ignoring the remainder, if any: For example, assuming the total value of valid votes polled by all candidates is 1,00,001. The quota required for getting elected is:

$$\frac{1{,}00{,}001}{2} + 1 = 50{,}000.50 + 1 \text{(Ignore .50)}$$

Quota = 50,000+1 = 50,001.

If no candidate gets the quota on the basis of first preference votes, then the second round of counting will be started. During this process the candidate having lowest value of votes of first preference is excluded and his votes are distributed among the remaining candidates according to the second preference marked on those ballot papers. This process will continue till one of the candidates secures the requisite quota.

However, Presidential electoral system in India cannot be called as 'Proportional Representation system' in the strict sense because the elections are conducted for one vacancy or seat. Therefore, there is no scope for proportional representation. In other words, the term 'proportional representation' is used to describe an electoral system in which the distribution of seats corresponds closely with the proportion of the total votes cast for each party or individual candidate.

EXHIBIT 11.2: VOTING SYSTEMS OF THE WORLD

There are a variety of voting systems in the world, some of which are currently in use in various countries. These voting systems can be classified under two major families: (a) Plurality System and (b) Proportional Representation System.

- **Plurality System :** This is otherwise called as 'first-past-the-post' or 'winner-take-all' system. According to this system, an individual candidate who secures maximum number of votes will be declared as elected. The candidate need not secure majority (more than 50%) votes to win; so long as he has larger number of votes than all other candidates, he will be declared as winner. In India we have adopted this system for the Lok Sabha, State Legislative Assembly, and Local Bodies' elections. This system was chosen in India to avoid fragmented legislatures and to help the formation of stable governments.

  Characteristic features of plurality system:

  * It is the easiest electoral system for the voter to use and to understand.
  * It requires simple and transparent voting and counting processes
  * This electoral system is based on the principle that the contestant with the most support ought to be elected.
  * There is less opportunity for minority parties to be given power in proportion to their electoral support.

- **Proportional Representation System :**

  This system ensures that the parties or the candidates are represented proportionally (according to the share of the vote they win) in the legislature. Under this system, the candidate should secure majority of votes or pre-determined quota of votes. This system is adopted by certain advanced western democracies. In India this system is adopted for the elections of President, Vice-President, MP's of Rajya Sabha, and State Legislative Council members.

  Characteristic features of proportional representation:

  * It is one of the complex systems; counting and seat determination processes are generally complex and not immediately transparent.
  * This system gives minority parties a fair representation.
  * It offers a greater and more representative choice for voters.
  * It rarely produces an absolute majority for one party, and it can further be argued that this system ensures greater continuity of government and requires greater consensus in policy-making.

However, there are chances of producing weak coalition governments rather than strong majority governments.

Eligibility For Election To The Post Of President

No person shall be eligible for election as President unless he-

- is a citizen of India;
- has completed the age of 35 years; and
- is qualified for election as a member of the House of the People (Article 58).

A person shall not be eligible for election as President if he holds any office of profit under the Government of India or the Government of any State or under any Local or other Authority subject to the control of any of the State Governments. However, a person shall not be deemed to hold any office of profit by reason only that he is the President or Vice-President of the Union or the Governor of any State or is a Minister either for the Union or for any State.

Every candidate contesting for the Presidential election should be proposed by at least fifty electors as proposers and at least fifty electors as seconders. The security deposit for the election is Rs. 15,000/- which will be required to be made along with the nomination paper. This amount can be deposited by the candidate or on his behalf in the Reserve Bank of India or in a Government Treasury. The deposit will be forfeited if the candidate is not elected and he does not secure more than one-sixth of the total votes polled.

Conditions of Office after the Election

- A person who is elected as the President, before entering upon his office has to subscribe to an oath or affirmation given in the Constitution[1]. The said oath shall be administered by the Chief Justice of India, or in his absence, the senior-most judge of the Supreme Court.
- The President cannot be a member of a House of Parliament or a State Legislature. If a member gets elected as the President, then automatically his seat becomes vacant as soon as he assumes charge of the President's office.
- The President cannot hold any other office of profit.
- The President is entitled to his official residence without payment of rent and is also entitled to such emoluments, allowances, and privileges as Parliament may by law determine[2].
- Even though the Parliament has the power to determine the allowances and the emoluments of the President, the same cannot be diminished during his term of office.

Disputes over Presidential Election

- All doubts and disputes arising out of the election of the President are to be decided by the Supreme Court whose decision is final[3].

[1]"I, A.B., do swear in the name of God/ solemnly affirm that I will faith-fully execute the office of President (or discharge the functions of the President) of India and will to the best of my ability preserve, protect and defend the Constitution and the law and that I will devote myself to the service and well-being of the people of India". (Article 60)

[2]Basic Salary of the President is Rs. 5 lakh per month, which is non-taxable; the spouses of Presidents will also get a secretarial assistance of Rs. 30,000 per month.

[3]Article 71.

- An election petition calling in question an election to the office of the President may be presented by any candidate at such election or by any twenty or more electors joined together as petitioners[4]. Therefore, a person who is neither a candidate nor an elector cannot challenge the election of the President through an election petition.
- The Supreme Court has held that it would not entertain any petition challenging the Presidential election before the completion of the election process and declaration of the result[5]. The reason for this stand is that if a doubt or dispute arsing in connection with the election of a President is brought before the Court before the whole election process is concluded, then conceivably, the entire election may be held up till after the expiry of five years' term which will involve a non-compliance with the mandatory provisions of Article 62"[6].
- If the election of the President is declared void by the Supreme Court, all the acts done by the President in his official capacity before the decision of the Supreme Court shall not be invalidated[7].

Time to hold Presidential elections

- *Scenario I* – According to Article 62 (1) - Elections to the President's office must be held before the expiry of the tenure of the President in office. However, due to some reason if elections were not conducted before the expiry of the tenure, then the President whose term has expired can continue to hold office until his successor enters upon his office.
- *Scenario II* – According to Article 62(2) – If the office of the President falls vacant for reasons like death, resignation, or removal etc., in such cases the election for the office of the President shall be held within six months (not more than six months) from the occurrence of such vacancy. In the event of occurrence of such vacancy the Vice-President will act as President for a maximum period of six months. The newly elected president shall hold the office for a full term of five years on which he enters upon his office.

TENURE, VACANCY, AND REMOVAL OF THE PRESIDENT

- The President shall hold office for a term of five years from the date on which he enters upon his office. He shall, however, continue to hold office notwithstanding the expiry of his term, until his successor enters upon his office.
- Article 57 explicitly provided that the person elected as the President is eligible for re-election. He may be elected for any number of times. In other words, there are no term limits for the President[8].
- The President can resign to his office by writing under his hand addressed to the Vice President of India. The Vice President has to communicate the President's resignation without any delay (forthwith) to the Speaker of the Lok Sabha.

---

[4]Section 14 of the Presidential and Vice-Presidential Elections Act, 1952.

[5]M.P. Jain *Indian Constitutional Law* P. 127

[6]*N.B. Khare Vs. Election Commission of India,* AIR 1957 SC 139.

[7]Article 71

[8]US President cannot be elected more than twice. The said term limits to the Presidential office were introduced after 22nd amendment to the U.S.A. Constitution.

- The President can be removed from his office through a process of impeachment on the grounds of "violation of the Constitution". However, the word "violation of the Constitution" is not defined. The concept of impeachment is borrowed from the US constitution.

The Impeachment Procedure Of The President

The impeachment charges against the President can be initiated in either House of Parliament. The said charges should be presented in the form of a resolution. Such a resolution can be moved only after giving fourteen days' written notice signed by not less than one-fourth of the total number of the members of the House. The said resolution must be passed by a majority of not less than two-thirds of the total membership of the House.

When one House prefers a charge, it becomes incumbent on the other House to investigate the same[9]. In other words, the House which passes the resolution to prefer a charge against the President shall not be entitled to investigate the charge; the charge shall be investigated by the other House[10]. Investigation may be made either by the House itself or by some other agency as the House may direct. The President has the right to appear and be represented at such investigation.

If the House which has investigated the charge finds the President guilty; it must pass a resolution to that effect by a majority of two-thirds of the total membership. The resolution shall have the effect of removing the President from his office from the date on which the resolution is passed. Thus, it's a quasi-judicial function performed by the Parliament. The State legislatures or the legislatures of the Union Territories cannot take part in the impeachment proceedings of the President. Moreover, the probability of invoking the impeachment provisions by the Parliaments is very remote because the President cannot act on his own discretion; he acts only on the aid and advice of the Council of Ministers who are in turn collectively responsible to the Parliament. As long as the President acts on the advice of the Council of Ministers the chances of impeachment are less. Only when the President acts independently, or contrary to the ministerial advice can he be impeached.

Comparison of impeachment proceedings of President of India and President of United States

India	United States
The President in India can be impeached only for violation of the Constitution.	The President in the US can be impeached for acts like treason, bribery, or other high crimes and misdemeanours.
Impeachment can be tried by either of House of Parliament.	Impeachments are tried solely by the Senate.
There is no provision for the Chief Justice of India to take part in the proceedings of impeachment.	When the President is being impeached, the Chief Justice of the Supreme Court presides over the sittings.
The impeachment resolution should be passed by 2/3rd of the total membership of the House	The impeachment resolution should be passed by 2/3rd of the members of the Senate present and voting.

[9] M.P. Jain *Indian Constitutional Law* P. 129.

[10] V.N. Shukla's *Constitution of India* P. 408.

POWERS OF THE PRESIDENT

Executive Powers

Executive powers or functions connote the residue of governmental functions that remain after legislative and judicial functions are taken away. Under this category, the President enjoys the following powers:

(a) President is the titular head. The Executive power of the Union is vested in him. This power is to be exercised in accordance with the Constitution[11].

(b) The President can exercise his functions either directly or through officers' subordinate to him. But all the executive functions are executed in the name of the President, authenticated in such manner as may be prescribed by rules to be made by the President. These Rules of Business confers power on the Ministers to carry on the administration and take decisions in their departments. When an order is made in accordance with the Rules of Business made under Article 77, it cannot be challenged on the ground that the President had not personally applied his mind to the matter[12]. In other words, although the executive power of the Union is vested in the President, actually, in practice, it is carried on by the Minsters and other officials and the President's personal satisfaction is not necessary in every case[13].

(c) The President has the power to appoint the Prime Minister and, on his advice, other Council of Ministers. He further has the power to appoint the Governor of the States; the Attorney-General of India; the Comptroller and Auditor-General; the Chairman and the members of the Union Public Service Commission, Finance Commission, National Commission for SC's, ST's and OBC's; and Special Officer for Linguistic Minorities.

(d) The President has the power to administer the Union Territories.

(e) The President can declare any area as a scheduled area and further enjoys powers with respect to the administration of scheduled areas.

(f) The President can appoint Commissions to report on the administration of Scheduled Areas and Commissions to investigate into the conditions of socially and educationally backward classes.

(g) The President can appoint an inter-state council for the strengthening of centre-state and inter-state relations.

Military Powers

President is the Supreme Commander of the Defence Forces. He has powers to declare war and peace. Chiefs of Army, Navy, and Air Force are appointed by the President on the recommendation of the Appointments Committee of the Cabinet. However, this power as the supreme Commander of the defence forces is subjected to two limitations, i.e.,

---

[11]This indicates that the exercise of executive power is subjected to judicial review and an unconstitutional act can be struck down if it is infringing any Constitutional provision.

[12]M.P. Jain, *Indian Constitutional Law*, P. 145.

[13]*Bijoya Cotton Mills Vs. State of West Bengal*, AIR 1967 SC 1145

(a) The military power of the President is subjected to the general executive power of the President and is exercised by him in accordance with the Constitution[14]. In other words, the military power of the President is subordinate to his executive power which is exercisable by him on the advice of the Council of Ministers.

(b) The military power of the President can be regulated by the Parliament by passing a law to that effect.

Diplomatic Powers

(a) All treaties and international agreements are negotiated and concluded in the name of the President though subject to the ratification by the Parliament.

(b) He sends and receives Ambassadors and other diplomatic representatives.

Legislative Powers

The President of India is a part of the Parliament. As a component of the Parliament, he enjoys extensive legislative powers. Legislative powers of the President can be discussed under the following heads:

Participation in the Legislative Process

(i) He can summon and prorogue the Parliament and dissolve the Lok Sabha.

(ii) As enumerated in Article 111, "Every Bill passed by both Houses of Parliament is to be sent to the President for his assent." When the Bill (ordinary Bill) comes to the President:

- He may either give assent or withhold his assent. If he gives assent, the Bill turns into an Act. If the President refuses to give his assent to a Bill in the first instance, the Bill will be dead. (or)
- In the case of a Bill other than a Money Bill, he may return it to House for reconsideration on lines suggested by him. When a Bill is so returned, it is the duty of each House to reconsider it accordingly and if the Bill is again passed by both the Houses of the Parliament with or without amendment, he must give his assent to it when it is sent to him for the second time.

(iii) The President also participates in some extent, in the legislative process in the States:

- Bills passed by the State Legislatures may be reserved for the Presidential consideration by the Governor. In such cases the President can either give assent to the Bill or withhold his assent or send back the Bill for reconsideration. If he gives assent, the Bill turns into an Act. If the President withholds his assent, the Bill comes to an end. If he sends back the Bill (other than Money Bill) for reconsideration of the State legislature, it is not obligatory on the President to give his assent if the Bill is passed by the state legislature with or without amendments.

[14] V.N. Shukla's *Constitution of India* P. 396.

- Governor of a state shall reserve the Bill for consideration of the President if it is affecting the powers of the High Courts[15].
- Bills imposing restrictions on freedom of trade and commerce can be introduced in the state legislature only after the prior sanction of the President.

(iv) If there is a deadlock between the two Houses of Parliament over an ordinary Bill, then he can call for joint sitting of both Houses, to resolve the deadlock.

(v) He can address or send messages to either or both of Houses of the Parliament.

(vi) Money Bills and States' Reorganization Bills can be introduced in the Parliament only on the prior recommendation of the President.

(vii) No demand for grants can be presented in the Lok Sabha without the President's prior approval.

(viii) President's recommendation is required for consideration by a House of a Bill involving expenditure from the Consolidated Fund of India.

(ix) He nominates 12 members of the Rajya Sabha from among persons having special knowledge or practical experience of Literature, Science, Art, and Social Services[16].

(x) He used to nominate two Anglo-Indians to the Lok Sabha, if he is of opinion that the Anglo-Indians community is not adequately represented in that House. The nominations were not meant to last permanently, but depended on the extension through a Constitutional Amendment. However, the 126th Constitutional Amendment Bill, 2019 did not extend the provision for nomination of Anglo-Indians.

Power of Rule-making under the Constitution

Several constitutional provisions confer rule-making powers on the President enabling him to prescribe detailed provisions for several matters:

(i) He has the power to make rules with respect to authentication of orders and instruments made and executed in his name.

(ii) He makes rules for the convenient transaction of the government's business and for the allocation among Ministers of the said business.

(iii) He has the power to make rules to determine the conditions of services, etc. of Audit and Accounts Department, Chairman and Members of the Union and Joint Public Service Commissions, Secretariat, and staff of Houses of Parliament.

(iv) He further makes rules with respect to dual membership of Parliament and State Legislatures; and procedures to be followed at the joint sittings of the two Houses of Parliament.

(v) He also makes rules to regulate the conditions of service of persons appointed to services and posts in connection with the affairs of the Union.

---

[15] Article 200

[16] Article 80(1)(a) read with Article 80(3)

Ordinance-making Power

One of the most important legislative powers of the President is his ordinance-making power under Article 123. The President has the power to promulgate the ordinances or in other words, short duration laws to overcome any unforeseen or urgent situations arising in the country when the Parliament is not in session. An ordinance is a temporary law. The President can promulgate the ordinance only when the following conditions exist:

- The ordinance can be promulgated when both Houses of Parliament are not in session; or when the session of a House comes to an end on its prorogation or dissolution; or if one House is sitting, but the other is not (Because one House cannot pass the Bill);
- The President must be satisfied that the circumstances exist which render it necessary for him to take immediate action.

The Ordinance is promulgated in the name of the President and on the satisfaction of the President. However, in reality, it is promulgated on the advice of the Council of Ministers and on their satisfaction[17]. The power to issue an ordinance is legislative power. Therefore, the ordinance made by the President shall be subject to the same limitations as a law made by the Parliament. Thus, an ordinance cannot violate the Fundamental Rights.

The President can make ordinances related to any subject in respect of which the Parliament has power to legislate. So, an ordinance can repeal or amend any existing laws, or can have prospective or retrospective applicability related to any matters included in List I or List III. In other words, the Ordinance-making power of the President is co-extensive with the legislative power of the Parliament. However, there are a few limitations with respect to the Ordinance-making power of the president in comparison with the legislative power of the Parliament. They are discussed hereunder:

- A Constitutional Amendment under Article 368 cannot be passed through an ordinance.
- Every Ordinance passed must be laid before both Houses and they must be approved by Parliament within six weeks of re-assembling, otherwise they will cease to operate. They will also cease to operate in case resolutions disapproving the ordinance are passed by both the Houses even before the expiration of the six weeks period. If the Houses of Parliament are summoned on different dates, then the period of six weeks will be counted from the later of those dates. Moreover, the ordinance can be withdrawn by the President any time.

  Ordinance-making power of the President is an exceptional law-making power which cannot be used as a substitute to the legislative power of the Parliament. If the ordinance is re-promulgated time and again without being brought before the Parliament, such ordinance will be invalidated by the courts[18].

  The President promulgates the ordinance only on the advice of the Council of Ministers. In other words, theoretically, it is the Presidential satisfaction that is required but in reality, it is the satisfaction of the Council of Ministers that is essential to promulgate an ordinance. However,

---

[17]R.C. Cooper Vs. UOI, AIR 1970 SC 564.

[18]If the ordinance is lapsed for not being placed before Parliament or it is invalidated by the court for re-promulgating time and again without laying down before the Parliament, such ordinance is not void ab initio (to be treated as invalid from the outset). All the acts done and completed under it remains fully valid and effective.

the courts cannot inquire into the reasons for the subjective satisfaction of the President or into the sufficiency of those reasons[19]. This is because inquiring into the motive of the legislature in passing an Act is beyond the scrutiny of the courts. Therefore, the same logic is applied even for the ordinances passed by the President. But the Ordinance-making power of the President is not completely immune from judicial review[20]. The Ordinance-making power of the President can be challenged, if it could be proved or established that the President has not acted in a bona fide manner or there are mala fide intentions behind such promulgation.

The ordinance-making power of the President is unique to India. It is generally not found in any other democratic constitutions in the world. The Ordinance-making power of the President is similar to the Ordinance-making power of the Governor-General under the Government of India Act, 1935. The power to make Ordinances is justified on the ground that the President must be armed with powers to overcome unforeseen circumstances when the Houses of Parliament are not in session.

Judicial Powers

(a) The President appoints the Judges of the Supreme Court and the High Courts.

(b) The President decides on the question of disqualification of a member of House of Parliament on the recommendations of the Election Commission.

(c) The President can seek the opinion of the Supreme Court on any question of law or fact of public importance on which he thinks it expedient to obtain such an opinion.

(d) The President is endowed with *Pardoning Power (as per* Article 72 of the Constitution of India) which provides the President the power to grant pardons, reprieves, respites, or remissions of punishments or to suspend, remit or commute the sentence of any person convicted of any offence in all cases:

- where the punishment or sentence is by a Court Martial;
- where the punishment or sentence is against a person who has committed an offence against a Union Law.
- where the sentence is a sentence of death.

The object of conferring the 'Judicial' power on the President is to correct possible judicial errors, for no human system of judicial administration can be free from imperfections[21]. In other words, The President or a Head of State is granted the power of pardon with the view that there should be provision in the law to save a person from the consequences of a punishment adjudged by mistake against that person by the Judiciary which being a human institution is likely to err. It is for this reason that a provision is made in every Constitution (whether monarchical or democratic), for the power of granting pardon. The scope of the power conferred on the President by Article 72 is very extensive. The pardoning power of the President includes:

---

[19] *T. Venkata Reddy Vs. State of A.P.*, (1985) 3 SCC 198.

[20] The 38th Constitutional Amendment Act, 1975 made the Presidential satisfaction to promulgate the ordinance as final and non-justiciable by inserting Article 123(4). However, the 44th Constitutional Amendment Act, 1978 deleted this provision and restored the status quo.

[21] D. D. Basu: *Introduction to the Constitution of India*, Part II, Page 21, 3rd Edition.

- **Pardon:** Pardon means to forgive or to excuse. If a person is pardoned, he will be released from punishment for some offence. A pardon may be full, limited, or conditional. A full pardon wipes out the offence in the eyes of law; a limited pardon relieves the offender from some but not all consequences of the guilt, and a conditional pardon imposes some conditions for the pardon to be effective[22].
- **Respite:** Respite means awarding a lesser punishment on some special ground, for example, pregnancy of a woman offender. In *State (NCT of Delhi) v. Prem Raj*[23], Supreme Court laid down that the term 'respite' implies awarding a lesser sentence instead of the penalty prescribed in view of the fact that the accused has had no previous conviction or the like. It was held that it is something like a release on probation for good conduct under Section 360 of the Code of Criminal Procedure[24].
- **Reprieve:** Reprieve means a stay of the execution of a sentence or postponement of the execution of a sentence for a temporary period.
- **Commutation:** Commutation means exchange of one thing for another. In other words, commutation substitutes a lesser sentence for a more severe sentence. The most common example is granting life sentence in place of a death sentence.
- **Remission:** Remission means reducing the amount of punishment without changing the character of punishment. For example, remitting the sentence of two years to six months.

Exercise of the Pardoning power

- Pardoning power being an executive power of the President, is to be exercised on the advice tendered by the Council of Ministers[25]. However, there is no time limit as such within which the mercy petition has to be decided.
- Subject to the advice tendered by the Council of Ministers, the President may scrutinise the evidence on record of the criminal cases and come to a different conclusion from that recorded by the Court. The President acts under a Constitutional power, and is entitled to go into the merits of the case. He can take a different view from that of the courts and it does not amount to supersession of judicial review[26].
- The manner of consideration of the petition lies within the discretion of the President. On the basis of the proceeding before the President being of an executive character, the petitioner has no right to insist on presenting an oral argument[27].

[22]M.P. Jain *Indian Constitutional Law* P. 168

[23](2003)7 SCC 121

[24]https://shodhganga.inflibnet.ac.in/bitstream/10603/148889/10/10_chapter%203.pdf

[25]Convict will file mercy petition under Article 72. Such petition will be sent to the Ministry of Home Affairs. The said petition will be discussed by the Home Ministry in consultation with the concerned state government. After the consultation, the Ministry of Home Affairs will send back the petition to the President along with recommendations.

[26]*Kehar Singh Vs. Union of India*, AIR 1989 SC 653.

[27]*Kehar Singh Vs. Union of India*, AIR 1989 SC 653.

- It is an absolute power, conferred by the Constitution and is not subject to any statutory provision or provision in any Act[28].
- The pardoning power of the President is of the widest amplitude and therefore, the court cannot suggest guidelines[29].
- While an earlier mercy petition has been dismissed by the President, the convict cannot obtain an order of staying execution of the death sentence by submitting repeated mercy petitions[30].

Whether pardoning power of the President is subjected to judicial review or not?

In *Epuru Sudhakar & Another Vs Andhra Pradesh and Others*[31], the Supreme Court held that the powers of the President or Governor under Articles 72 and 161 are subject to judicial review. Their decision can be challenged on the grounds that

(a) it was passed without application of mind;

(b) it is mala fide;

(c) it was passed on extraneous or wholly irrelevant considerations;

(d) relevant materials were kept out of consideration;

(e) it suffers from arbitrariness

Thus, the exercise of President's power under Article 72 (also of Governor under Article 161) is subject to the judicial review like any other power of the executive.

When can the Pardoning power exercised by the President?

A plain reading of Articles 72 and 161 would give an impression that the power of pardon can be exercised by the President or the Governor only for persons convicted of an offence and not to undertrials. However, the courts in India, on several occasions, have held otherwise. In *State of Maharashtra Vs. K.M. Nanavati*[32], the Supreme Court held that in view of the language of Articles 72 and 161, which was similar to that used in Section 295(2) of the Government of India Act, 1935, and also similar to that used in Article 2, Section 2 of the American Constitution, the President and the Governors in India had the same powers of pardon both in its nature and effect, as is enjoyed by the King in Great Britain and the President in the United States. Therefore, in India also, the pardoning power can be exercised before, during, or after trial.

PRESIDENT AND THE CONCEPT OF VETO

The power of the President to refuse or approve a Bill passed by the legislature and thus preventing its enactment into law is the veto. Veto power is given to the President to provide a system of checks and balances. Moreover, the presidential veto power is to protect the public against legislation that is blatantly unconstitutional or that has not been enacted in accordance with the proper constitutional procedure.

[28] *State of Punjab Vs. Joginder Singh*, AIR 1990 SC 1396

[29] *Kehar Singh Vs. Union of India*, AIR 1989 SC 653.

[30] *Triveniben Vs. State of Gujarat*, (1990) Cr.L.J. 1341 SC.

[31] (2006) 8 SCC 161

[32] AIR 1961 SC 112.

The President's role is essentially to protect and defend the Constitution; therefore, he has the power to conduct an executive review of proposed legislation (in contrast to the judicial review conducted by the courts). When the President has been forwarded a Bill, which was introduced and passed by both Houses of the Parliament, he can do one of three things which are mentioned in Article 111 of the Constitution of India. These three alternatives are as follows:

- The President may give his approval to the Bill.
- The President may withhold his approval to the Bill.
- The President may return the Bill for reconsideration of the Parliament if he is not satisfied with any one or more of its characteristics.

This indicates that the President can exercise the veto power and reject the Bill that is forwarded to him. Moreover, there is no time limit within which the President has to approve the Bill or is supposed to exercise his veto power.

Types of Veto

The various kinds of veto powers exercised by the President can be classified as follows:

- ***Absolute Veto :*** By using this power the President can withhold his assent to any Bill passed by the Parliament. If the President exercises this veto power, the Bill will come to an end and it does not turn into an Act. Generally, Absolute veto is used in the following cases:
    * The bills which are introduced by any member of the Parliament, who is not a Minister, known as the Private Members' Bills.
    * The bills which are passed by the government but before the President could give his assent, the cabinet has resigned and the new cabinet advises the president not to follow through by giving his assent to those bills.

    In the year 1991, when R. Venkataraman was President of India, he withheld his assent to the Salary, Allowances, and Pension of Members of Parliament (Amendment) Bill because it was passed on the last day before the Lok Sabha was dissolved and introduced without seeking prior recommendation from the President of India.
- ***Suspensive Veto or Weak qualified veto :*** As the name suggests, Suspensive Veto is a power of the President by which the President can suspend the passing of a Bill by returning it to the parliament for reconsideration. If the Bill is again passed by the Parliament either with or without any amendment or changes and then again presented to the President, this time the President has to give his assent. In this case the President can veto a legislation by returning Bill to the legislature for reconsideration, while allowing the legislature to insist on the Bill with the same majority. In a way, the veto power of the President is overridden when the Parliament passes the Bill again by the same simple majority.

    Parliament (Prevention of Disqualification) Amendment Bill 2006 was passed by the Parliament. It enacted a self-serving piece of legislation that protected members from disqualification with retrospective effect. President A. P. J. Abdul Kalam, returned the Bill. However, the Bill was sent back to the President again and was finally approved.

- ***Pocket Veto :*** Pocket veto is the power of the President in which he neither approves a Bill nor does he return it for reconsideration. The president simply keeps the Bill pending for as long as he likes. By doing this the President does not take any positive or negative action on the Bill. This is possible because the Indian Constitution does not provide for any specific period of time in which the President has to take action on a Bill presented to him for his assent. However, in the United States of America, the President is mandated to return the Bill within 10 days of submission for reconsideration. The Pocket Veto of the Indian President is bigger than that of the American President.

  In 1986, the Parliament passed a Bill known as Indian Post Office (Amendment) Bill. This Bill was widely criticised because its restrictions on freedom of press. The then President, Giani Zail Singh, did not take any decision on this Bill. After his term was over, the next President, R. Venkataraman sent the Bill finally back to the Parliament for reconsideration. By that time the new government which came into power did not pursue the Bill further. Thus, the Bill came to an end.

- ***Veto over State Legislations* :** When a Bill is forwarded to the Governor after being passed by the State Legislature, he has the following options under Article 200 of the Constitution:
  * The Governor may give his approval to the Bill; or
  * The Governor may withhold his assent to the Bill; or
  * The Governor may return the Bill to the state legislature for their reconsideration. This can only be done if the Bill is not a Money Bill; or
  * The Governor may reserve the Bill for the consideration of the President.

  Once the Bill is reserved for the Presidential consideration, the President has the following options under Article 201 of the Constitution:
  * The President can give his approval to the Bill; or
  * The President can withhold his assent to the Bill; or

  The President can ask the Governor to return the Bill to the state legislature so that the state legislature can reconsider it. If the state legislature passes the Bill again with or without any amendments or changes, then the Bill will be again presented to the President for his assent. In such a case, the President is not bound to give his approval as he does in the case of Parliamentary bills.

Note: *In addition to the Veto powers discussed earlier, there exists a Qualified Veto or Strong Qualified Veto (with high thresholds for legislative override). A veto that can be overridden by a subsequent decision of the legislature is known as a 'qualified' veto. However, in a qualified veto or strong qualified veto, the legislature can override the decision of the President by repassing the Bill with higher majority and sending it back to the President. In such cases the President has to give his assent to the Bill. The said Qualified veto power is enjoyed by the US President but not by the President of India.*

Emergency Powers of the President

President also enjoys a special and extraordinary power known as "emergency power" along with the other powers mentioned above. The power to proclaim emergency is conferred on the President to overcome the emergent situations in the country. The President is empowered with the power to declare an emergency either in the whole territory of India or in any State or any part of India. He can impose three types of emergencies :

a. National Emergency provided under Article 352 (due to war, external aggression, or armed rebellion).

b. State Emergency provided under Article 356 (due to the failure in constitutional machinery in States).

c. Financial Emergency provided under Article 360 (due to threat to the financial stability in India).

PRIVILEGES OF THE PRESIDENT

Article 361 guarantees the following privileges to the President:

- The President shall not be personally liable for any acts done in his official capacity. In other words, the President shall not be answerable to any court for the exercise of his official powers and duties. The powers and duties of his office include the powers of the President expressly conferred by the Constitution or by any law or statutory rules. However, the conduct of the President may be brought under review by any court, tribunal, or body appointed or constituted by either House of Parliament for the investigation of the charge in impeachment proceedings.
- The legal immunity conferred upon the President will not deprive the citizens of his right to sue the Government of India where he has a right under the law. Thus, the immunity available to the President cannot be extended to the order passed in his name by the Ministers[33].
- No criminal proceedings can be instituted against the President nor can he be arrested or imprisoned during his tenure of office. Moreover, if criminal proceedings were pending against a person on the date of his appointment as President, those proceedings shall remain stayed during his term of office. But on the expiry of his term, the stayed proceedings will be revived[34].
- The civil proceedings can be initiated against the President in respect of his personal liabilities. The only condition is that two months' notice shall be given to the President before initiating the proceedings.

INDIAN PRESIDENT *VS* AMERICAN PRESIDENT

The American President is the real executive head and is directly responsible to the people of his country, while the Indian President is the nominal head, and the real Executive is the Council of Ministers headed by Prime Minister.

The American President has under him Secretaries of State in charge of different executive departments who are appointed by him and who are his personal advisers. He is not bound to accept the advice tendered by them; he enjoys ultimate power of decision and therefore, has complete political responsibility for all executive actions. The Secretaries of State hold offices during the pleasure of the President of America.

---

[33] *Common Cause Vs. Union of India*, (1999) 6 SCC 667.

[34] V.N. Shukla's *Constitution of India* P. 1065.

As has been aptly said, "The cabinet is not a device for sharing responsibility among a group; it is a necessary result of the President's inability to supervise all affairs directly"[35]. In India, the President has no choice but to appoint the Leader of the majority party in the Lok Sabha as the Prime Minister and to appoint the Council of Ministers on the recommendation of the Prime Minister.

Dr. Ambedkar, the Chairman of the Drafting Committee, has summed up the true position of the Indian President in the following words:

"In the Draft Constitution there is placed at the head of the Indian Union a functionary who is called the President of the Union. The title of the functionary reminds one of the Presidents of the United States. But beyond identity of names there is nothing in common between the form of Government prevalent in America and the form of Government proposed under the Draft Constitution. The American form of Government is called the Presidential system of Government, what the Draft Constitution proposes is the Parliamentary System."

Under the Presidential system of America, the President is the Chief Head of the Executive. Administration is vested in him. Under the Indian Constitution, the President occupies the same position as the King under the English Constitution. He is Head of the State but not the Executive. He represents the nation but does not rule the nation. His place in the administration is that of a ceremonial device on a seal by which the nation's decisions are made known[36].

LIST OF PRESIDENTS IN INDIA

S. No.	NAME	PERIOD	IMPORTANT FACTS
1.	Dr. Rajendra Prasad	1950–1962	The first President of India
2.	Dr. Sarvepalli Radhakrishnan	1962–1967	
3.	Dr. Zakir Husain	1967–1969	He died at his post
4.	Shri Varahagiri Venkata Giri	1969 – 1974	Only person to be elected President as an independent candidate.
5.	Dr. Fakhruddin Ali Ahmed	1974–1977	
6.	Neelam Sanjiva Reddy	1977 –1982	The only President of India who was elected unopposed President.
7.	Giani Zail Singh	1982–1987	Prior to becoming the President, he was also the Chief Minister of Punjab. He used Pocket Veto on the Indian Post Office Bill.
8.	R. Venkataraman	1987 –1992	
9.	Dr Shankar Dayal Sharma	1992 –1997	
10.	K. R. Narayanan	1997 – 2002	
11.	Dr. A.P.J. Abdul Kalam	2002 – 2007	He came to be known as 'Missile Man of India'. He was the first scientist who took over the post of President.
12.	Pratibha DeviSingh Patil	2007 – 2012	The first woman president
13.	Pranab Mukherjee	2012 – 2017	
14.	Ram Nath Kovind	2017 –2022	
15.	Droupadi Murmu	2022-	

[35]Bowie and Friedrich, Studies in Federalism, P. 65.

[36]Constituent Assembly Debates, Vol VII, Pgs 33–34.

QUESTIONS

Subjective Questions

1. Instances of President's delay in commuting death sentences have come under public debate as denial of justice. Should there be a time limit specified for the President to accept/reject such petitions? Analyse. **(UPSC 2014)**
2. Explain the legislative powers exercised by the President of India. **(250 words)**
3. Determine the 'value' assigned to the vote of a Member of a State Legislative Assembly and of a Member of Parliament in the Indian Presidential elections. **(UPSC 2012)**
4. 'The exercise of executive clemency is not a privilege but is based on several principles, and discretion has to be exercised on public considerations.' Analyse this statement in the context of the judicial powers of the President of India. **(UPSC 2011)**
5. "The failure to place the ordinance before Parliament is a serious constitutional fraction". Critically analyse the statement in the context of the judicial powers of the President. **(250 words)**

Objective Questions

1. Consider the following statements regarding Ordinances in India:

   1. The President can promulgate an ordinance only when both the Houses of Parliament are not in session.
   2. The decision of the President to issue an ordinance cannot be questioned in a court of law.

   Which of the statements given above is/are not correct?

   (a) 1 only (b) 2 only

   (c) Both 1 and 2 (d) Neither 1 nor 2

   Ans: (c)

2. The Electoral College to elect the President of India consists of:

   1. All the members of Lok Sabha
   2. All the members of Legislative Assemblies of states
   3. All the members of Rajya Sabha
   4. All the members of Legislative Councils of states

   Select the correct answer using the code below.

   (a) 1 and 2 only (b) 1, 2, and 3 only

   (c) 1, 2, and 4 only (d) None of the above

   Ans: (d)

3. Consider the following statements regarding the office of the President:

   1. He should have completed 35 years of age.
   2. He should not hold any office of profit under the Union government or any state government.
   3. He should be qualified for election as a member of the Lok Sabha.

Which of the statements given above is/are correct?

(a) 2 only (b) 1 and 3 only

(c) 2 and 3 only (d) 1, 2, and 3

Ans: (d)

4. Consider the following statements: **(UPSC CSE 2013)**

1. The Council of Ministers in the Centre shall be collectively responsible to the Parliament.
2. The Union Ministers shall hold the office during the pleasure of the President of India.
3. The Prime Minister shall communicate to the President about the proposals for legislation.

Which of the Statements given above is/are correct?

(a) 1 only (b) 2 and 3 only

(c) 1 and 3 only (d) 1, 2, and 3

Ans: (b)

5. Consider the following statements:

1. The President shall make rules for the more convenient transaction of the business of the Government of India, and for the allocation among Ministers of the said business.
2. All executive actions of the Government of India shall be expressed to be taken in the name of the Prime Minister.

Which of the statements given above is/are correct?

(a) 1 only (b 2 only

(c) Both 1 and 2 (d) Neither 1 nor 2

Ans: (a)

11.2 VICE PRESIDENT

INTRODUCTION

The Vice President of India is the second-highest ranked dignitary in the executive branch of the government of India, following the President, and represents the nation in the absence of the President, and also has the legislative functions of actingas the Chairman of the Rajya Sabha.

The only Constitution, among the important democracies of the world, which provides for such an office, is that of the United States of America. But the office of the Vice President of India though analogous to, is not identical with that of the Vice President in the United States of America for the obvious reason that it has a Presidential system of Government and not a Parliamentary one as in India[1].

OFFICE OF VICE PRESIDENT : OVERVIEW

Election

Vice President of India is elected indirectly by the people of India. In other words, the VicePresident of India is elected by the members of an Electoral College consisting of the members of both Houses of Parliament in accordance with the system of proportional representation by means of single transferable vote by secret ballot[2] (Article 66). The election of the Vice President cannot be called in question on the ground that any vacancy exists in the Electoral College electing him.

The Electoral College of the Vice President is different from that of the President in the following aspects:

- The elected members of the State Legislative Assemblies take part in the Presidential elections. On the other hand, the State Legislative members are not included in the Electoral College of Vice President of India.
- The nominated members of Lok Sabha and Rajya Sabha cannot take part in the Presidential elections. However, both the elected members and the nominated members of the Parliament take part in the Vice Presidential elections.

In explaining why the system prescribed for the election of the President has not been made applicable to the election of the Vice President, Dr.Ambedkar, Chairman, Drafting Committee, said:

"The President is the Head of the State and his power extends both to the administration by the Centre as well as to the States. Consequently, it is necessary that in his election, not only Members of Parliament should play their part, but the Members of the State Legislatures should have a voice. But when we come to

[1] http://164.100.47.5/Chairman-Rajyasabha/Ex-officio-position.htm

[2] In the original Constitution, the members of both Houses of Parliament used to assemble in a joint sitting in order to take part in the Vice Presidential elections. However, the said process of joint sitting during the election of Vice President was ended by the 11th Constitutional Amendment Act, 1961.

the Vice President, his normal functions are merely to preside over the Council of States. It is only on a rare occasion and that too for a temporary period, that he may be called upon to assume the duties of President. That being so, it does not seem necessary that the Members of the State Legislatures should also be invited to take part in the election of the Vice President"[3].

Election Disputes

Subject to the provisions of the Constitution, Parliament is empowered to enact legislation to regulate any matter relating to the election of the Vice President[4]. All doubts and disputes arising out of, or in connection with, the election of the Vice President are decided by the Supreme Court whose decision is final[5]. If the Court declares the election of a person as Vice President void, the acts done by him/her while in office before the Court's declaration cannot be invalidated.

No election of Vice President can be called in question except by presenting an election petition to the Supreme Court. Election petition can be filed by any candidate at such election or by ten or more electors joined together as petitioners[6].

Qualifications

As per the Constitution, a candidate for the Vice President's office should fulfil the following conditions :

- Should be a citizen of India; and
- Completed at least thirty-five years of age; and
- Qualified to be elected as a member of the RajyaSabha; and
- Should not be holding any Office of Profit under the Central or State Government or under any local or other authority which is subject to the control of Central or State Government. (However, the President, the Vice President or a State Governor, or a Minister in the Central or a State Government is not disqualified to contest election to this office. This is because these offices will not fall under the definition of Office of Profit).

As per 'The Presidential and Vice Presidential Elections Act, 1952', a candidate contesting for the Vice President's office should fulfil the following conditions:

- Each candidate should be supported by at least 20 electors as proposers and at least another 20 electors as seconders.
- Each candidate has to deposit a sum of Rs. 15,000/- either in the Reserve Bank of India or in a Government Treasury.

Conditions for the Vice President's Office

- Before entering upon his office, the Vice President has to subscribe to an oath or affirmation, before the President or someone appointed by the President for this purpose[7].

---

[3]Constituent Assembly Debates, Vol. VII, 1100-01

[4]Presidential and Vice Presidential Elections Act, 1952.

[5]Article 71 of the Constitution of India.

[6]The Presidential and Vice Presidential Elections Act, 1952

[7]Oath is given in the Article 69 of the Constitution of India - "I, A.B., do swear in the name of God solemnly affirm that I will bear true faith and allegiance to the Constitution of India as bylaw established and that I will faithfully discharge the duty upon which I am about to enter.".

- He cannot hold any other office of profit
- He cannot be a member of any House of Parliament or a State Legislature. If he is a member of any House of Parliament or a State Legislature at the time of Vice Presidential election, then his seat automatically becomes vacant when enters upon the office of Vice President.

Salary and Allowances

The Vice President is entitled to receive salary only as the ex officio Chairman of the Rajya Sabha. He does not get any salary as Vice President. Moreover, the salary and allowances entitled by the Vice President as ex officio Rajya Sabha Chairman will be determined by the Parliament by passing an Act. Till the passage of the Act, Vice President is entitled to the salary specified in the Second Schedule of the Constitution.

Tenure and Removal

- The tenure of the Vice President office is five years from the date on which he enters upon his office. The incumbent Vice President can hold office beyond his term of 5 years until his successor enters upon his office.
- Elections to the office of Vice President will be held before it falls vacant due to expiration of the term. In case vacancy arises for any other reason (in case of resignation, removal, death, etc.), election will be held as soon as after the occurrence of the vacancy.
- The Vice President can resign from his office by writing to the President.
- There is no explicit provision in the Constitution which restricts the re-election of the Vice President. Therefore, a person can be elected as Vice President any number of terms.
- The Vice President can resign from his office by writing to the President. He can also be removed by passing a resolution with effective majority in the Rajya Sabha and simple majority in Lok Sabha. In other words, Vice President's removal resolution can be introduced only in the Rajya Sabha. The removal resolution has to be passed in the Rajya Sabha by a majority of all the then members of the Rajya Sabha (excluding those whose seats are vacant) and agreed to by the Lok Sabha. Moreover, such a resolution can be moved only after giving fourteen days' notice of the intention to move such resolution[8].

Functions and Duties

- He is the ex-officio chairmanof the RajyaSabha.
- He acts as President when the office of President falls vacant due to death, resignation, removal,or otherwise. In such cases, Vice President can act as President for a maximum period of six months, within which Presidential elections should be conducted as per the Constitution.

---

[8]Vice President's removal is not impeachment under the Constitution. There are no grounds mentioned in the Constitution for the removal of the Vice President. In other words, the Vice President can be removed on any ground and without enquiry into the charges against him/her.

- When the President is unable to discharge his functions due to illness, absence, or otherwise, in such cases Vice President discharges the duties of the President till the President is able to resume his duties.
- While acting as or while discharging the functions of the President, the Vice President enjoys all powers and immunities enjoyed by the President and is also entitled to salary and allowances of the President.
- The Parliament is empowered to make provisions to overcome any other contingency not mentioned in the Constitution. In pursuance of this power, Parliament enacted the President (Discharge of Functions) Act, 1969. It provides that when vacancies occur in the offices of both the President and the Vice President, the Chief Justice of India or, in his absence, the senior most judge of the Supreme Court will discharge the functions of the President and the Vice President until a new President or Vice President enters upon their office[9].
- While acting as the President, the Vice President ceases to act as the Chairman of the RajyaSabha and he is not entitled to receive any salary or allowance as RajyaSabhaChairman during that period.

COMPARISON BETWEEN THE VICE PRESIDENT OF INDIA AND THE VICE PRESIDENT OF USA

Subject-Matter	INDIA	USA
Tenure	Five years	Four years
Election	Indirect	Indirect
Functions with respect to Upper Chamber	Chairman of RajyaSabha	President of the Senate
The Vice President acts asPresident if:	• The President dies; (or) • The President resigns; (or) • The President is impeached; (or) • The Presidential election has been declared invalid by the Supreme Court. In all these cases, Vice President acts as President for a maximum period of six months (within which Presidential elections shall be conducted in order to elect a new President).	• The President dies • The President resigns • The President is temporarily incapacitated • The President is impeached. In all these cases, Vice President shall act as the President for the unexpired term of his predecessor.
Removal	No formal impeachment is required. Can be removed by passing a resolution with effective majority in Rajya Sabha and simple majority in the Lok Sabha.	Impeachment

[9] M.P. Jain P. 132

List of Vice Presidents

S. NO.	NAME	PERIOD
1.	Sarvepalli Radhakrishnan	1952–1962
2.	Zakir Husain	1962–1967
3.	Varahagiri Venkata Giri	1967–1969
4.	Gopal Swarup Pathak	1969–1974
5.	Basappa Danappa Jatti	1974–1979
6.	Mohammad Hidayatullah	1979–1984
7.	Ramaswamy Venkataraman	1984–1987
8.	Shankar Dayal Sharma	1987–1992
9.	Kocheril Raman Narayanan	1992–1997
10.	Krishan Kant	1997–2002
11.	Bhairon Singh Shekhawat	2002–2007
12.	Mohammad Hamid Ansari	2007–2017
13.	Muppavarapu Venkaiah Naidu	2017–2022
14	Jagdeep Dhankar	2022–

QUESTIONS

Subjective Questions

1. Who make the Electoral College for election of the Vice President of India?

   (a) Only Members of Parliament

   (b) Members of Parliament and Members of Legislative Assemblies

   (c) Members of Parliament, Members of Legislative Assemblies, and Members of Legislative Councils

   (d) Members of Rajya Sabha only

   Ans: (a)

2. Consider the following statements regarding the election of Vice President:

   1. The Vice President, like the President, is elected not directly by the people but by the method of indirect election.
   2. He is elected by the members of an Electoral College consisting of the Members of both Houses of Parliament.
   3. It consists of both elected and nominated Members of the Parliament (in the case of President, only elected Members).

   Which of the following statement(s) is/are correct?

   (a) Only 1 (b) 1 and 2

   (c) 2 and 3 (d) All of the above

   Ans: (d)

3. Consider the following statements regarding the office of Vice President:

    1. If the election of a Vice President is declared void, acts done by him before the date of such declaration are invalidated.
    2. While acting as President, the Vice President does not perform the duties of the office of the chairman of Rajya Sabha.

    Which of the statements given above is/are correct?

    (a) 1 only (b) 2 only

    (c) Both 1 and 2 (d) Neither 1 nor 2

    Ans: (b)

4. Consider the following statements.

    1. The Vice President acts as the ex-officio chairman of Rajya Sabha.
    2. In the absence of the President, the Vice President acts as President only for a maximum period three months.

    Which of the statement given above is / are correct?

    (a) 1 only (b) 1, 2 only

    (c) Both 1 and 2 (d) Neither 1 nor 2

    Ans: (a)

5. Consider the following statements:

    1. An election petition calling in question an election to the office of Vice President may be presented by a candidate at such election or by any ten or more electors joined together as petitioners.
    2. According to Article 71 of the Constitution, all doubts and disputes arising out of or in connection with the election of the President or Vice President shall be inquired into and decided by the Chief Election Commissioner.

    Which of the above statements is/are correct?

    (a) Only 1 (b) Only 2

    (c) Both 1 and 2 (d) Neither 1 nor 2

    Ans: (a)

11.3 PRIME MINISTER

PRIME MINISTER

The Prime Minister is the Head of the Council of Ministers. He is appointed by the President (Article 75(1)[1]). While reading Article 75(1), it appears that the Constitution has conferred an unfettered discretion on the President to appoint whomsoever he likes to the post of the Prime Minister. However, it is not true in reality. The power of the President to appoint the Prime Minister is regulated by certain Parliamentary conventions and Constitutional provisions.

CONSTITUTIONAL PROVISIONS REGARDING THE PRIME MINISTER

According to Article 75(3)[2], the Council of Ministers shall be collectively responsible to the Lok Sabha. In other words, Council of Ministers including the Prime Minister (who is the Head of Council of Ministers), should enjoy the confidence of the Lok Sabha. It is therefore, essential that the leader of the majority party in the Lok Sabha should invariably be invited to become the Prime Minister. This is the important limitation that regulates the President's choice to appoint the Prime Minister. However, in exceptional cases, the President enjoys some situational discretion with respect to the appointment of the Prime Minister. For instance, if no party has clear majority in the Lok Sabha, or when the Prime Minister dies in his/her office and there is no obvious successor[3], in such cases the President can exercise his discretion and find a person who belongs to the largest political party in the Lok Sabha or who could form a coalition government with the help of two or more parties and command the support of the Lok Sabha. This perhaps is the only occasion where the President can exercise his personal discretion in the appointment of the Prime Minister. Moreover, the Constitution does not require that a person must prove or establish his majority in the Lok Sabha before he is invited to be the Prime Minister. The President may first invite and appoint him the Prime Minister, and then ask him to prove his majority or seek Vote of Confidence in the Lok Sabha within a reasonable time[4] (this is what President Neelam Sanjiva Reddy did in appointing Charan Singh as the Prime Minister in the year 1979, the President Shankar Dayal Sharma did in appointing A.B. Vajpayee as the Prime Minister in 1996, etc.).

Term of the Prime Minister

According to Article 75(2), the ministers shall hold office during the pleasure of the President. Theoretically, there is no fixed tenure for the office of Prime Minister. He shall hold the office during the pleasure of the President. However, this does not give any unfettered right to the President to remove the Prime Minster. As long as the Prime Minister enjoys the majority or confidence in the Lok Sabha, the President cannot remove the Prime Minister. If the Prime Minister loses the majority support or confidence in the Lok Sabha, then the Prime Minister should resign or can be removed by the President.

---

[1] Article 75(1) – The Prime Minister shall be appointed by the President and the other Ministers shall be appointed by the President on the advice of the Prime Minister.

[2] Article 75

[3] In 1984, when Prime Minister Indira Gandhi was assassinated, there was no obvious or recognised successor. Then President Zail Singh immediately appointed her son Rajiv Gandhi as the Prime Minister without waiting for his being formally elected as the leader of the Congress Party.

[4] Dinesh Chandra Pande Vs. Chaudhary Charan Singh, AIR 1980 Del 114.

But the Parliamentary conventions and the real working of the Constitution in all these years shows that the full term of the Prime Minister is five years, which coincides with the normal life of the Lok Sabha. However, the term can end sooner if he/she loses the vote of confidence in the Lower House. So, it can be said that he/she remains in power as long as he/she enjoys the confidence of the Lok Sabha. The Prime Minister can also resign by writing to the President. Moreover, there are no term limits on the office of the Prime Minister and there is also no official retirement age.

Eligibility Criteria to Become the Prime Minister of India

The Constitution does not provide any explicit eligibility criteria for the appointment of the Prime Minister. But a Prime Minister should be a member of a House of Parliament. It is a well-established convention in all countries having a Parliamentary system that the Prime Minister and the Council of Ministers shall invariably be the members of a House of Parliament[5]. However, if a non-member is appointed as a minister, he cannot hold the office for longer than six months without becoming a member of a House of Parliament in the meantime[6]. A minister who for a period of six consecutive months is not a member of a House of Parliament, ceases to be a minister at the expiry of that period (Article 75(5)). Therefore, in order to be eligible for the position of the Prime Minister of India, a person should:

- Be a citizen of India; and
- Be a member of either the Lok Sabha or the Rajya Sabha[7].

Oath of Office and Oath of Secrecy

The Prime Minister of India has to take Oath of Office and Oath of Secrecy before entering upon the office (The Oath of Office and the Oath of Secrecy of the Prime Minister and all the Council of Ministers is the same). All ministers, including the Prime Minister about to assume office, are required to take an Oath of Office and Secrecy as per Article 75(4) in the Third Schedule[8] of the Constitution. In an Oath of Office, the Prime Minister swears allegiance to the Constitution of India and fulfil his or her duties to the best of his/her honesty and integrity for the welfare of the country[9]. An Oath of Secrecy requires the minister-designate to safeguard the secrets and official secrets in their office[10].

Salary of the Prime Minister

The salaries and allowances of the Prime Minster shall be determined by the Parliament from time to time through a law. Until the Parliament so determines, it shall be as specified in the Second Schedule of the Constitution.

---

[5]Sir Ivor Jennings, Cabinet Government, 60 (IIIrd ed).

[6]M.P. Jain P. 141.

[7]In Britain the Prime Minister should invariably come from the House of Commons (Lower House of the Parliament).

[8]Third Schedule of the Constitution provides the form of oaths or affirmations to the Constitutional posts.

[9]Form of oath of office for a Minister for the Union: —

"I, A. B., do swear in the name of God/solemnly affirm that I will bear true faith and allegiance to the Constitution of India as by law established, [that I will uphold the sovereignty and integrity of India,] that I will faithfully and conscientiously discharge my duties as a Minister for the Union and that I will do right to all manner of people in accordance with the Constitution and the law, without fear or favour, affection or ill-will."

[10]Form of oath of secrecy for a Minister for the Union: —

"I, A.B., do swear in the name of God/solemnly affirm that I will not directly or indirectly communicate or reveal to any person or persons any matter which shall be brought under my consideration or shall become known to me as a Minister for the Union except as may be required for the due discharge of my duties as such Minister."

Roles and Responsibilities of the Prime Minister

With Respect to the Council of Ministers

- The Prime Minister is the Head of the Council of Ministers. The Prime Minister in relation to the Council of Ministers is considered to be the 'First among Equals'.
- The President can appoint the Council of Ministers only on the recommendation of the Prime Minister. The Prime Minister can recommend to the President to dismiss a person as minister and the President has to follow suit. If any difference of opinion arises between the Prime Minister and any other minister, the opinion of the Prime Minister prevails.
- The Prime Minister allocates portfolios among the ministers and distributes work among various ministries and offices. The Prime Minister coordinates work among various ministries and departments through the Cabinet Secretariat[11]. He/she further has the power to reshuffle the portfolios of the Council of Ministers.
- The Prime Minister summons and presides over meetings of the Council of Ministers and determines what business shall be transacted in these meetings.
- The Council of Ministers have to resign from their office if the Prime Minister resigns or dies in office.

With Respect to the President

- The President shall exercise his functions only on the aid and advice of the Council of Ministers headed by the Prime Minister[12].
- Article 78 inherited the British Parliamentary convention whereby, like the English monarch, our President has the right to be kept informed. Though the Council of Ministers meeting is never presided over by the President, it is the duty of the Prime Minister to communicate to the President either personally or through his Ministers, all decisions of the Council of Ministers relating to the administration of affairs of the Union and proposals for legislation.
- The Prime Minister is the sole channel of communication between the Council of Ministers and the President. The Constitution enjoins upon the Prime Minister to communicate to the President all the decisions taken by the Council of Ministers and to furnish him information relating to the administration of the country as well as the proposals for legislation as the President may call for[13].

---

[11]The Cabinet Secretariat is responsible for the administration of the Government of India (Transaction of Business) Rules, 1961 and the Government of India (Allocation of Business) Rules, 1961, facilitating smooth transaction of business in Ministries/Departments of the Government.

[12]Article 74

[13]Article 78 - Duties of Prime Minister as respects the furnishing of information to the President, etc. It shall be the duty of the Prime Minister

(a) to communicate to the President all decisions of the council of Ministers relating to the administration of the affairs of the Union and proposals for legislation;

(b) to furnish such information relating to the administration of the affairs of the Union and proposals for legislation as the President may call for; and

(c) if the President so requires, to submit for the consideration of the Council of Ministers any matter on which a decision has been taken by a Minister but which has not been considered by the Council

- Moreover, the President can even ask the Prime Minister to submit any matter for the consideration of the Council of Ministers, provided it has not already been considered by it.
- The Prime Minister advises the President regarding the appointment of high officials such as Governors of the States, Attorney General, UPSC Chairman and its members, CAG, Election Commissioners, etc.

With Respect to Parliament

- The Prime Minister also acts as a link between the Council of Ministers and the Parliament. He/she is the chief spokesperson of the government in the Parliament.
- The Prime Minister is the Leader of the House to which he/she belongs. He/she can also take part in debates in the House of which he/she is not a member.
- The Prime Minister represents the 'Government' in Parliament, so that the government bills are easily adopted, and policies of the Cabinet are explained and approved. He/she also makes sure that the Parliament is kept informed of all important policy developments.
- Based on the recommendations of the Prime Minister, the President summons and prorogues both Houses of the Parliament and even dissolves the Lok Sabha on his/her recommendation.
- He/She assists the Speaker or the Chairman in the House so that Parliamentary business is conducted smoothly.
- The Prime Minister also tries to keep liaison with Opposition parties so that the areas of disagreement are removed as much as possible, and the parties in minority do not feel that they have virtually no role to play in the Parliament[14].

With Respect to the Government

- The Prime Minister of India is the Head of the Government.
- He/She represents the country in various international forums, organizations, etc.
- He/She addresses the nation on various occasions of national importance.
- He/She plays a major role in directing India's foreign policy.
- He/She is the ex-officio Chairman of the NITI Aayog, National Integration Council, Inter-State Council, etc.

Pre-Eminence of the Prime Minister in the Indian Scenario

One can easily conclude that the Prime Minister is really the keystone of the arch of the Union Executive and the Council of Ministers. In England, the position of the Prime Minister has been described by Lord Morley as 'primus inter pares', i.e., 'First among equals'. In theory, all ministers or members of the Cabinet have an equal position, all being advisers of the Crown, and all being responsible to the Parliament in the same manner. Nevertheless, the Prime Minister of the United Kingdom has a pre-eminence, by convention and usage. Similarly, even in India, the Prime Minister is considered to be 'First among equals' and has pre-eminence, by constitutional provisions and conventions.

---

[14]https://shodhganga.inflibnet.ac.in/bitstream/10603/38544/9/09_chapter%204.pdf

LIST OF PRIME MINISTERS OF INDIA

NAME	TENURE
Jawaharlal Nehru	August 15, 1947 – May 27, 1964
Gulzari Lal Nanda (Acting)	May 27, 1964 – June 9, 1964
Lal Bahadur Shastri	June 09, 1964 – January 11, 1966
Gulzari Lal Nanda (Acting)	January 11, 1966 – January 24, 1966
Indira Gandhi	January 24, 1966 – March 24, 1977
Morarji Desai	March 24, 1977 – July 28, 1979
Charan Singh	July 28, 1979 – January14, 1980
Indira Gandhi	January 14, 1980 – October 31, 1984
Rajiv Gandhi	October 31, 1984 – December 01, 1989
Vishwanath Pratap Singh	December 02, 1989 – November 10, 1990
Chandra Shekhar	November 10, 1990 – June 21, 1991
P.V. Narasimha Rao	June 21, 1991 – May 16, 1996
Atal Bihari Vajpayee	May 16, 1996 – June 01, 1996
H.D. Deve Gowda	June 01, 1996 – April 21, 1997
I.K. Gujral	April 21, 1997 – March 18, 1998
Atal Bihari Vajpayee	March 19, 1998 – May 22, 2004
Dr. Manmohan Singh	May 22, 2004 – May 26, 2014
Narendra Modi	May 26, 2014 – Incumbent

QUESTIONS

Subjective Questions

1. Critically analyze the constitutional relation between the President and the Prime Minister of India. **(250 words)**
2. "The Prime Minister is really the keystone of the cabinet arch and until and unless we create that office and endow that office with statutory authority to nominate and dismiss ministers, there can be no collective responsibility". Justify. **(250 words)**

Objective Questions

1. The Prime Minister of India is the chairman of:
   1. NITI Aayog
   2. Inter-State Council
   3. National Integration Council

   Select the correct answer using the codes given below.

   (a) 1 only (b) 1 and 2 only
   (c) 2 and 3 only (d) 1, 2, and 3

   Ans: (d)

2. With reference to Indian Prime Minister, consider the following statements:

   1. He/She allocates portfolios among the ministers and makes rules regarding them.
   2. He/She has no role in the appointment of the Chairman and members of the Union Public Service Commission.

   Which of the statements given above is/are correct?

   (a) 1 only (b) 2 only

   (c) Both 1 and 2 (d) Neither 1 nor 2

   Ans: (a)

3. The Prime Minister of India, at the time of his/her appointment: **(2012 UPSC CSE)**

   (a) need not necessarily be a member of one of the Houses of the Parliament but must become a member of one of the Houses within six months

   (b) need not necessarily be a member of one of the Houses of the Parliament but must become a member of the Lok Sabha within six months

   (c) must be a member of one of the Houses of the Parliament

   (d) must be a member of the Lok Sabha

   Ans: (a)

4. Consider the following statements: (2013 UPSC CSE)

   1. The Council of Ministers in the Centre shall be collectively responsible to the Parliament.
   2. The Union Ministers shall hold the office during the pleasure of the President of India.
   3. The Prime Minister shall communicate to the President about the proposals for legislation.

   Which of the Statements given above is/are correct?

   (a) 1 only (b) 2 and 3 only

   (c) 1 and 3 only (d) 1, 2, and 3

   Ans: (b)

5. Consider the following statements:

   1. The President shall make rules for the more convenient transaction of the business of the Government of India, and for the allocation among ministers of the said business.
   2. All executive actions of the Government of India shall be expressed to be taken in the name of the Prime Minister.

   Which of the statements given above is/are correct?

   (a) 1 only (b) 2 only

   (c) Both 1 and 2 (d) Neither 1 nor 2

   Ans: (d)

11.4 COUNCIL OF MINISTERS

INTRODUCTION

The executive power of the Union is vested in the President and is exercisable by him on the aid and advice of the Council of Ministers headed by the Prime Minister. Though we have an elected President, who is a formal or Constitutional Head of the executive, the real power will be exercised by the Council of Ministers headed by the Prime Minister.

CONSTITUTIONAL PROVISIONS REGARDING THE COUNCIL OF MINISTERS

According to Article 74[1]

(1) [There shall be a Council of Ministers with the Prime Minister at the head to aid and advise the President who shall be, in the exercise of his functions, act in accordance with such advice:]

[2][Provided that the President may require the Council of Ministers to reconsider such advice, either generally or otherwise, and the President shall act in accordance with the advice tendered after such reconsideration.]

(2) The question whether any, and if so what, advice was tendered by Ministers to the President shall not be inquired into in any court.

Article 74(1) makes it mandatory that there shall be a Council of Ministers to aid and advice the President. At no point of time can the President work or exercise his functions without the Council of Ministers. The Council of Ministers remains in office even when the Lok Sabha is dissolved[3]. In Britain, it is a convention that the Monarch acts on the advice of the Ministers. On the other hand, in the original Indian Constitution, the ministerial advice binding on the President was merely directory in nature. To make matters clear beyond doubt, the 42nd Constitutional Amendment Act, 1976, made the advice tendered by the Council of Ministers headed by the Prime Minister binding on the President. However, this amendment was relaxed to a certain extent by the 44th Constitutional Amendment Act, 1978, which provided that the President can ask the Council of Ministers to reconsider the advice tendered by them. And, once the Council of Ministers advice the President based on their reconsideration, such reconsidered advice is binding on the President.

Non-Justiciability of the Council of Ministers' Advice

Article 74(2) protects and preserves the secrecy of the discussions and deliberations between the President and the Council of Ministers. No court can ask the government to disclose the actual advice tendered by the Council of Ministers to the President. The Supreme Court has clarified the implication of Article 74(2) in the *S.R. Bommai Vs. UOI case.*[4]

[1]Subs. by the Constitution (42nd Amendment) Act, 1976, S.13 (w.e.f. 3-1-1977). Subs. cl. (1) read:

(1) There shall be a Council of Ministers with the Prime Minister at the head to aid and advise the President

[2]Ins. by the Constitution (44th Amendment) Act, 1978, S.11 (w.e.f.20-6-1979).

[3]*U.N.R. Rao Vs. Indira Gandhi*, AIR 1971 SC 1002, 1005: (1971) 2 SCC 63.

[4]AIR 1994 SC 1918: (1994) 3 SCC 1

- No court is concerned with what advice was tendered by the minister to the President.
- The court is only concerned with the validity of the order and not with what happened in the inner councils of the President and the ministers.
- An order cannot be challenged on the ground that it is not in accordance with the advice tendered by the Minister or that it is based on no advice.
- If, in a given case, the President acts without, or contrary to, the advice tendered to him, it may be a case warranting his impeachment, but so far as the court is concerned, it is the act of the President.

Appointment, Removal, and Size of the Council of Ministers

According to Article 75

(1) The Prime Minister shall be appointed by the President and the other Ministers shall be appointed by the President on the advice of the Prime Minister.

[5]*[(1A) The total number of Ministers, including the Prime Minister, in the Council of Ministers shall not exceed fifteen per cent. of the total number of members of the House of the People.*

(1B) A member of either House of Parliament belonging to any political party who is disqualified for being a member of that House under paragraph 2 of the Tenth Schedule shall also be disqualified to be appointed as a Minister under clause (1) for duration of the period commencing from the date of his disqualification till the date on which the term of his office as such member would expire or where he contests any election to either House of Parliament before the expiry of such period, till the date on which he is declared elected, whichever is earlier.]

(2) The Ministers shall hold office during the pleasure of the President.

(3) The Council of Ministers shall be collectively responsible to the House of the People.

(4) Before a Minister enters upon his office, the President shall administer to him the Oaths of Office and of Secrecy according to the forms set out for the purpose in the Third Schedule.

(5) A Minister who for any period of six consecutive months is not a member of either House of Parliament shall at the expiration of that period cease to be a Minister.

(6) The salaries and allowances of Ministers shall be such as Parliament may from time to time by law determine and, until Parliament so determines, shall be as specified in the Second Schedule.

Appointment

The first step in the process of forming a Council of Ministers is to find a Prime Minister. Once the Prime Minister is appointed by the President, the other Ministers are appointed by the President on the advice of the Prime Minister. The nomination of Ministers rests with the Prime Minister. Normally speaking, a Minister should be a member of a House of Parliament. If however, a non-member is appointed as a Minister, he cannot hold the office for longer than six months without becoming a member of the House of Parliament in the meantime.

---

[5]Inserted by the Constitution (Ninety-first Amendment) Act, 2003, Section 2 (w.e.f. 1-1-2004).

Removal

Simple reading of Article 75(2) indicates that the Ministers shall hold office during the pleasure of the President and a Minister can be dismissed by the President whenever he likes. However, the power of the President to remove the Council of Ministers is conditioned by the principle that as long as the Council of Ministers enjoy the confidence in the Lok Sabha, they cannot be dismissed by the President. However, the Prime Minister can recommend the President to dismiss a Minister. Since a Minister is appointed on the advice of the Prime Minister, he can get rid of any Minister.

Ordinarily, a Minister whom the Prime Minister no longer wants in the Council of Ministers will himself resign when asked by the Prime Minister to do so. But in an extreme situation, when such a Minister ignores the wishes of the Prime Minister, the latter may request the President to dismiss the undesirable Minister from office. The President, thus, acts on the advice of the Prime Minister and uses his power to maintain the integrity and solidarity of the government without which the Council of Ministers cannot function effectively[6].

Size

The original Constitution did not provide any upper limit on the size of the Council of Ministers. However, in order to curb defections (elected members jumping from one political party to another) and to punish the defectors, the National Commission to Review the Working of the Constitution (NCRWC) in its report of March 31, 2002, recommended that abnormally large Councils of Ministers were being constituted by various Governments at Centre and States to lure the elected members. In order to curb this practice, it has to be prohibited by law and that a ceiling on the number of Ministers in a State or the Union Government has to be fixed. In this way, the incentive to defect a political party would be reduced.

Accordingly, 91st Constitutional Amendment Act, 2003 was introduced. This amendment has added two new Clauses to Article 75, i.e., (1A) and (1B). Article 75 (1A) provides that the total number of ministers, including the Prime Minister, in the Council of Ministers shall not exceed 15 per cent of the total number of members of the House of the People.

Oath

The Council of Ministers before entering upon the office has to subscribe to the Oath of Office and Oath of Secrecy administered by the President. All the Council of Ministers, including the Prime Minister, has to subscribe to the same Oath of Office and Oath of Secrecy as given in the Third Schedule of the Constitution.

Salaries and Allowances

The salaries and allowances of the Council of Ministers shall be determined by the Parliament by way of law, and until determined by the Parliament, it shall be as specified in the Second Schedule.

---

[6] M.P.Jain, *Indian Constitutional Law*, LexisNexis, 2018, P. 144

Responsibility of the Council of Ministers

The 'Principle of Ministerial Responsibility' is a very unique and distinctive feature of the Parliamentary form of government. The Ministerial responsibility to the legislature may again be of two kinds:

- Individual responsibility, and
- Collective responsibility

Individual Responsibility

There are two principles of individual responsibility:

- One, every Minister is individually responsible to the Parliament. In other words, every Minister is responsible individually for the work of his department. Each Minister is the head of one or a few departments. The concerned Minister is responsible for the working of his/her department.

  In case anything wrong happens in his/her department, the Minister is accountable before the Parliament. The Parliament has the power to pass a Censure Motion[7] against him/her.
- Secondly, no person shall be retained in the Council of Ministers if the Prime Minister recommends for his/her dismissal. It is only when the members of the Council of Ministers, both in the matter of their appointment as well as in the matter of their dismissal, are placed under the Prime Minister, that it would be possible to realise the ideal of collective responsibility. It can be achieved only through the instrumentality of the Prime Minister. Therefore, each Minister is individually responsible to the Prime Minister.

Collective Responsibility

The Council of Ministers are responsible to the Lok Sabha or the House of the People not as individuals alone, but collectively also. It is the hallmark of the Parliamentary system that the government acts collectively. The entire Council of Ministers will accept and take the responsibility for the acts of any of its members, so that the censure of one will become the censure of all. Every decision is taken by the government (the Cabinet), and all ministers are responsible for that. They may agree or disagree with the decision. They might have expressed their dissent in the decision-making process, but once the decision is arrived at, all are bound by the decision. The implication of collective or joint responsibility is that all ministers are responsible for all aspects of government policy, as a result of which all ministers swim or sink together. The term 'Collective Responsibility' is well explained by Lord Salisbury thus:

"For all that passes in the Cabinet, every member of it who does not resign is absolutely and irretrievably responsible, and has no right afterwards to say that he agreed in one case to a compromise, while in another he was persuaded by his colleagues... It is only on the principle that absolute responsibility is undertaken by every member of the Cabinet, who, after a decision is arrived at, remains a member of it, that the joint responsibility of Ministers of Parliament can be upheld and one of the most essential principles of Parliamentary responsibility established.[8]

Therefore, the only alternative, for a Minister who is not prepared to defend the policy of the government is to resign. But while he remains a member of the government, he cannot say that he is in disagreement with any of the Cabinet/Council of Ministers' decisions[9].

---

[7]Explained in the Parliament Chapter.

[8]*Life of Robert Marquis of Salisbury*, Vol. II, 219–20.

[9]V.N.Shukla's *Constitution of India*, EBC, 2017, P. 434.

EXHIBIT 11.3: LEGAL RESPONSIBILITY IN BRITAIN

In Britain, along with Individual and Collective Responsibility, the ministers also have Legal Responsibility. It means that every Ministeris legally responsible for every act of the Crown in which he takes part. Every order in the United Kingdom will be passed in the name of the Crown. The Minister of the Crown who thus takes part in giving expression to the order (in the name of the Crown) is legally responsible for the act in which he is concerned, and he cannot get rid of his liability by pleading that he acted in obedience to royal orders. The reason is that the Crown will always act on the aid and advice of the Council of Ministers. Hence, indirectly but surely, the action of every servant of the Crown, and therefore in effect of the Crown itself, is brought under the supremacy of the law of the land. In Britain, behind Parliamentary responsibility lies legal liability, and the acts of ministers, no less than the acts of subordinate officials, are made subject to the rule of law[10].

On the other hand, in India, the Council of Ministers do not have any such legal responsibility.

FACTS REGARDING COUNCIL OF MINISTERS

Types of Council of Ministers

The Indian Constitution does not make any distinction such as a senior or a junior minister, or more or less important Minister. Yet, according to the Parliamentary conventions and practices, there have been in India the following three categories of ministers:

(1) Cabinet Ministers

(2) Ministers of State (Independent charge)

(3) Ministers of State (Junior charge) and Deputy Ministers

A person after getting appointed as the Prime Minister decides who will be the ministers in the Council of Ministers. The Prime Minister allocates ranks and portfolios to the ministers. Depending upon the seniority and political importance, the ministers are given the ranks of Cabinet Minister, Minister of State, or Deputy Minister. There is no qualification or age limit for the above different categories of ministers. It is in the hands of the Prime Minister to decide which Ministry lies under which category and can handle which portfolio. As per the Salaries and Allowances of Ministers Act, 1952, 'Minister' is defined as 'a member of the Council of Ministers by whatever name called, and includes a Deputy Minister'. According to the said Act the ministers are classified as follows:

(a) the Prime Minister;

(b) every other Minister who is a member of the Cabinet;

(c) a Minister of State;

(d) a Deputy Minister.

---

[10] A.V. Dicey, Introduction to the Study of the Law of the Constitution, Liberty Fund, Page No. 210.

Hierarchy of The Council of Ministers

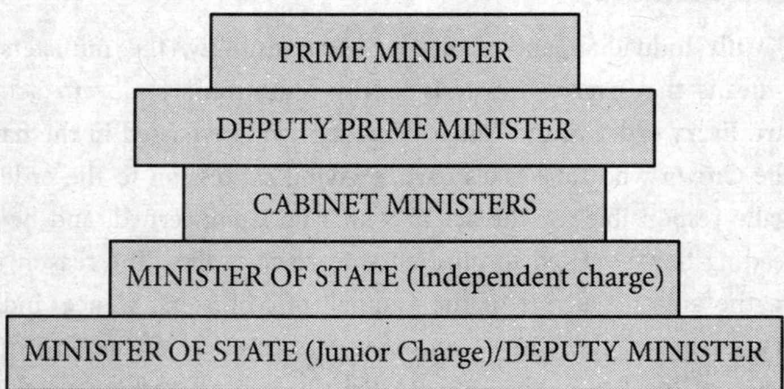

The above hierarchy table depicts the Hierarchy of the Council of Ministers in India. A brief discussion of each category is provided below.

Cabinet Ministers

Union Cabinet includes the Prime Minister and the ministers of Cabinet rank[11]. Each Minister must be a member of one of the Houses of the Parliament of India. The cabinet is headed by the Prime Minister and is advised by the Cabinet Secretary (who also acts as the Head of the Civil Services Board). Though unknown to the Constitution, the Cabinet is the supreme directing authority. It is the highest policy making body in India and takes all the important decisions related to Administration[12]. The most experienced leaders of the party are appointed as the Cabinet Ministers of India so that the portfolios are handled independently with the help of other kinds of Ministers. Their number is between 15–20. The Cabinet generally meets on a specific day of a week to take decisions on all issues brought before it. The cases which shall be brought before the cabinet are defined in the 2nd schedule of the 'The Government of India (Transaction of Business) Rules, 1961'. The Cabinet meetings are only attended by the Cabinet Ministers and other categories cannot attend the meetings unless and until specially invited to do so. The matters brought before the Council of Ministers for their consideration and decision are of the following categories:

- Proposals to summon or prorogue the Houses of Parliament or dissolve the House of the People;
- Matters involving negotiations with foreign and Commonwealth countries on treaties, agreements, etc.
- Addresses and messages of the President to the Houses of Parliament;
- Proposals for legislation, including issue of an ordinance;
- Matters relating to commencement or cessation of a state of war and related matters;
- Proclamation of Emergency under Articles 352 to 360 of the Constitution and other matters related thereto; and
- Such other important issues and policies related to the Union government.

[11] Article 352(2)

[12] Sometimes, the Prime Minister relies more on an inner circle of advisers than on the Cabinet. Such inner circle of the Cabinet is called as 'Kitchen Cabinet'. Every Prime Minister in India has had his `Inner Cabinet'.

Minister Of State

Ministers of State may be in independent charge of Ministries, or of departments within a Ministry under the charge of a Cabinet Minister. Therefore, there can be two types of Minister of State—One, who do not report to a Cabinet Minister (Independent Charge) and the other one, who are junior members who report directly to one of the Cabinet Ministers, often overseeing a specific aspect of the government.

Deputy Minister

Deputy Ministers are helping ministers attached to the Cabinet Ministers or the Ministers of State (Independent Charge). No Deputy Minister holds an independent charge of any Ministry. His function is to help the Minister under whom he works. They are mainly given the responsibility to prepare answers to the Parliamentary questions pertaining to their respective departments and to help the process of getting the government bills passed by the Parliament.

Every Minister irrespective of their category, shall have the right to speak in, and to take part in the proceedings of either House, any joint sitting of the Houses, and any committee of the Parliament one may be named a member, but shall not be entitled to a vote in the House where one is not a member.

Difference between Council of Ministers and Cabinet Ministers

1. Council of Ministers includes Cabinet Ministers, Ministers of State (Independent Charge), Ministers of State (Junior Charge), and Deputy Ministers. On the other hand, the Cabinet Ministers include only the Ministers who hold the Cabinet rank.
2. The Council of Ministers is a larger body, whereas the Cabinet Ministers or the Union Cabinet is comparatively a smaller body.
3. All the members of the Cabinet Ministers represent the Council of Ministers and it is not necessary that every Minister present in the Council of Ministers would be a Cabinet Minister.
4. The Council of Ministers has no collective function, i.e., it never meets as a whole. It is the Cabinet which decides and the Council of Ministers accepts and executes.
5. The major policy decisions of the government are taken by the Cabinet. Once the policy comes into formation, then the whole of the Council of Ministers are responsible for that.
6. The Constitution, under its Article 74, provides for the Council of Ministers and not the Cabinet. The organization and working of the Cabinet rest upon conventions of the Parliamentary system. As per the original Constitution, the Cabinet was, technically, an extra Constitutional body which, nevertheless, is the most powerful single political institution of the Indian political system. However, the word 'Cabinet' was inserted in Article 352(2) of the Constitution in 1978 by the 44th Constitutional Amendment Act[13]. But Article 352(2) does not define the word 'Cabinet'. It only provides that "The President shall not issue a Proclamation under Clause (1) or a Proclamation varying such Proclamation unless the decision of the Union Cabinet (that is to say, the Council consisting of the Prime Minister and other Ministers of Cabinet rank appointed under Article 75) that such a Proclamation may be issued has been communicated to him in writing."

[13]With the said amendment the Cabinet is no more an extra-constitutional body.

EXHIBIT 11.4 : LEGAL RESPONSIBILITY IN BRITAIN

Parliamentary Secretaries are neither ministers, nor are they assigned any administrative work. Their sole function is to help the ministers in the Parliament. As their designation itself indicates, their assistance is mainly in relation to the discharge of the Parliamentary responsibilities of the Minister in Parliament. The Parliamentary Secretaries are not the members of the Council of Ministers as the term 'Minister' appearing in Article 75 of the Constitution does not include Parliamentary Secretaries and they are not appointed by the President. They are appointed by the Prime Minister. As they are not members of the Council of Ministers, they can appear only in that particular House to which they belong. They do not hold any administrative responsibilities in the Ministry. The office of a Parliamentary Secretary is an office used for training 'future ministers'.

QUESTIONS

Subjective Questions

1. "The Cabinet is responsible to the Legislature for every action taken in any of the ministries. That is the essence of joint responsibility". Analyse. (250 words)
2. "The Head of the State should be a President, with a Council of Ministers to aid and advise him in the discharge of his functions". Explain. (250 words)

Objective Questions

1. With reference to the Central Council of Ministers, consider the following statements:

   1. Council of Ministers are collectively responsible to the President.
   2. Council of Ministers are collectively responsible to the House of the People.
   3. Resignation or death of an incumbent Prime Minister dissolves the Council of Ministers.

   Which of the statements given above is/are correct?

   (a) 1 and 3 only (b) 2 only
   (c) 2 and 3 only (d) 3 only

   Ans: (c)

2. In which of the following situations can the President exercise his powers using his own discretion?

   1. While sending back the advice given by the Council of Ministers for its reconsideration
   2. Appointing the Prime Minister when no one party has clear majority in the Lok Sabha
   3. Appointment of the Chief Justice of India

   Select the correct answer using the codes given below.

   (a) 1 and 2 only (b) 2 and 3 only
   (c) 1 and 3 only (d) 1, 2, and 3

   Ans: (a)

3. Consider the following statements regarding the Council of Ministers:
   1. The strength of the Council of Ministers cannot exceed 10 per cent of the total number of members of the Lok Sabha.
   2. The Council of Ministers is collectively responsible to the Lok Sabha.

   Which of the statements given above is/are correct?

   (a) 1 only (b) 2 only

   (c) Both 1 and 2 (d) Neither 1 nor 2

   Ans: (b)
4. There is a Parliamentary System of Government in India because the (2015 UPSC CSE)

   (a) Lok Sabha is elected directly by the people.

   (b) Parliament can amend the Constitution.

   (c) Rajya Sabha cannot be dissolved.

   (d) Council of Ministers is responsible to the Lok Sabha.

   Ans: (d)
5. Consider the following statements: (UPSC CSE 2013)

   (1) The Council of Ministers in the Centre shall be collectively responsible to the Parliament.

   (2) The Union Ministers shall hold the office during the pleasure of the President of India.

   (3) The Prime Minister shall communicate to the President about the proposals for Iegislation.

   Which of the Statements given above is/are correct?

   (a) 1 only (b) 2 and 3 only

   (c) 1 and 3 only (d) 1, 2, and 3

   Ans: (b)

11.5 CABINET COMMITTEES

CABINET COMMITTEES

Overview of Cabinet Committees

Cabinet Committees are extraconstitutional bodies and do not find any reference in any Constitutional provisions and are formed by rules of business. The Union Executive works under the Government of India (Transaction of Business) Rules, 1961. The Rules mandate the minister-in-charge of a department (ministry) to dispose of "all business allotted to a department under" him or her. However, "when the subject of a case concerns more than one department", no decision can be taken "until all such departments have concurred, or, failing such concurrence, a decision thereon has been taken by or under the authority of the Cabinet". Therefore, in order to reduce the workload of the Cabinet and expedite the decision-making process, the Cabinet Committees are set up, either directly by the Prime Minister or vetted by the Cabinet. In other words, the Prime Minister-led Union Cabinet has the powers to constitute committees of Cabinet drawing members from various ministries. Besides permanent members, there could be some special invitees to these Cabinet committees. The Prime Minister heads a majority of the committees.

Role of Cabinet Committees

The Cabinet committees ensure smooth functioning between two departments or ministries of the government. The role of a Cabinet committee is to deliberate and take a final call on important policy issues related to different sectors such as security, politics, and economy, among others. Any decision taken by a Cabinet committee may be reviewed by the Cabinet. The ministries at times are seen holding contrasting views on policy matters or their implementation. Cabinet committees help in ironing out the differences by preparing a common ground. Cabinet committees work as organisations which are instrumental in reducing the workload of the Union Cabinet.

Formation and Assignment of Cabinet Committees

There are basically two types of Cabinet committees—Standing committees and Adhoc committees. The Prime Minister constitutes Standing committees of the Cabinet and sets out the specific functions assigned to them. He can add or reduce the number of committees. Standing committees enjoys permanency when compared to Adhoc committees. Adhoc committees are constituted from time to time arising out of emergency relating to a specific problem before the Government. The Adhoc committees are disbanded once their task is accomplished. Conventionally, while Ministers with Cabinet rank are named as 'Members' of the Standing committees of the Cabinet, Ministers of State, irrespective of their status of having 'Independent charge' of a Ministry/Department, and others 'with rank of' a Cabinet Minister or Minister of State are named as 'Special invitees'.

Composition and Functions of Various Cabinet Committees

As of 2020, following are the Cabinet committees that have been reconstituted by the Government according to the Transaction of Business Rules[1]:

- **Appointments Committee of the Cabinet :** This is one of the most powerful committee which takes decisions with respect to the appointments of several top posts under the Government of India. It is headed by the Prime Minister.
- **Cabinet Committee on Political Affairs :** This is another powerful committee which takes decisions regarding centre–state relations, or economic issues with political implications, or policy matters concerning foreign affairs. The committee is chaired by the Prime Minister.
- **Cabinet Committee on Accommodation :** This committee determines the guidelines or rules with regard to the allotment of government accommodation. It considers the allotment of accommodation from the General Pool to Members of Parliament. It also considers proposals for shifting existing Central Government Offices to locations outside the capital. The Prime Minister is not a member of the Cabinet Committee on Accommodation.
- **Cabinet Committee on Economic Affairs :** This committee is supposed to review economic trends, problems, and prospects for evolving a consistent and integrated economic policy, coordinate all activities requiring policy decisions at the highest level, and deal with fixation of prices of agricultural produce and prices of essential commodities. It is chaired by the Prime Minster.
- **Cabinet Committee on Parliamentary Affairs :** This committee draws the schedule for Parliament sessions and monitors the progress of government business in the Parliament. It scrutinizes non-government business and decides which official Bills and resolutions are to be presented. The Prime Minister is not a member of the said committee.
- **Cabinet Committee on Security :** This committee deals with issues relating to law and order, internal security, and policy matters concerning foreign affairs with internal or external security implications. It is chaired by the Prime Minister.
- **Cabinet Committee on Investment and Growth :** This committee will "identify key projects required to be implemented on a time-bound basis", involving investments of Rs 1,000 crore or more, or any other critical projects, as may be specified by it, with regard to infrastructure and manufacturing. It will prescribe time limits for giving requisite approvals and clearances by the ministries concerned in identified sectors. It will also monitor the progress of such projects. It is chaired by the Prime Minister.
- **Cabinet Committee on Employment & Skill Development :** This committee is supposed to provide "direction to all policies, programmes, schemes, and initiatives for skill development aimed at increasing the employability of the workforce for effectively mseeting the emerging requirements of the rapidly growing economy and mapping the benefits of demographic dividend". It is chaired by the Prime Minister.

[1]Indian Express, June 09, 2019.

11.6 ATTORNEY-GENERAL OF INDIA

ATTORNEY-GENERAL OF INDIA

Constitutional Provisions Regarding Appointment of Attorney-General Of India

Article 76 of the Constitution deals with Attorney-General's office. Attorney-General is the highest law officer in the country. He is part of the Union Executive.

According to Article 76

(1) The President shall appoint a person who is qualified to be appointed a Judge of the Supreme Court to be Attorney-General for India.

(2) It shall be the duty of the Attorney-General to give advice to the Government of India upon such legal matters, and to perform such other duties of a legal character, as may from time to time be referred or assigned to him by the President, and to discharge the functions conferred on him by or under this Constitution or any other law for the time being in force.

(3) In the performance of his duties the Attorney-General shall have right of audience in all courts in the territory of India,

(4) The Attorney-General shall hold office during the pleasure of the President, and shall receive such remuneration as the President may determine.

According to Article 76, the President shall appoint a person who is qualified to be a Supreme Court judge as the Attorney-General for India. However, the age limit of 65 for the judges of the Supreme Court, does not apply to the appointment of Attorney-General of India[1]. The Attorney-General holds office during the pleasure of the President and receives such remuneration as determined by the President. The Constitution does not provide any fixed tenure to the Attorney-General of India. But according to Law Officers (Conditions of Service) Rules, 1987, Attorney-General shall hold office for a term of three years from the date on which he enters upon his office. He can even resign from his office at any time before the end of his term of service by addressing the resignation letter to the President. Moreover, there is a practice that the Attorney-General also resigns on the resignation of the Prime Minister and the Council of Ministers.

Functions of the Attorney-General

Functions As Per The Constitutional Provisions

- To give legal advice to the Government of India on such matters as may be referred to him by the President;
- To perform such other duties of a legal character as the President may assign; and
- To discharge the functions conferred on him by the Constitution or any other law.

[1] State of Uttaranchal Vs. Balwant Singh Chaufal, (2010) 3 SCC 402.

Functions as per the Rules made by the President[2]

- To appear on behalf of the Government of India in all cases in the Supreme Court in which the Government is concerned;
- To represent the Government of India in any reference made by the President to the Supreme Court under Article 143;
- If required, to appear in any High Court in any case in which the Government of India is concerned.

Restrictions[3] on the Attorney-General

Attorney-General shall not –

- Hold any brief or advice against the Government of India;
- Defend an accused person in a criminal prosecution, without the permission of the Government of India;
- Accept appointment to any office in any company or corporation without the permission of the Government of India;
- Advise any Ministry or Department of Government of India or any statutory organization or any Public Sector Undertaking unless the proposal or a reference in this regard is received through the Ministry of Law and Justice, Department of Legal Affairs.

Rights and Privileges of the Attorney-General of India

In the performance of his duties, the Attorney-General has the right of audience in all Courts in India. He has the right to take part in the proceedings of either House of Parliament, or their joint sitting, and any parliamentary committee of which he may be named as a member, without the right to vote[4]. He enjoys all the privileges which are available to a Member of Parliament. In discharge of his functions, the Attorney-General is assisted by Solicitor Generals and Additional Solicitor Generals.

Difference between Attorney-Generals in India and UK

In United Kingdom, the appointment of the Attorney-General is 'political' in nature in the sense that it is conferred on a successful barrister who is a supporter of the party in power. He has sometimes been a member of the Cabinet though "it is generally regarded as preferable that he should remain outside the Cabinet as the Government's chief legal adviser"[5].

On the other hand, in India, the Attorney-General is appointed on the basis of professional competence and not on political considerations. He is a non-party man, appointed because of his competence as a lawyer and he is neither a member of the Cabinet nor the Council of Ministers. According to the Government of India (Allocation of Business) Rules 1961, advice to the ministries on legal matters, including the interpretation of the Constitution and the laws, is the job of the Department of Legal Affairs under the Ministry of Law and Justice.

---

[2]See, Notification No.F. 43/50-c, Gaz. of India, Extra., Vol. VII, 33–34, dt.26-1-1950.

[3]Manual of Office Procedure and the Law Officers (Conditions of Service) Rules, 1987

[4]Article 88

[5]Wade & Philips, opage cit., 333.

EXHIBIT 11.5 :SOLICITOR-GENERAL

The Solicitor-General for India is the second law officer of the country. The Solicitor-General assists the Attorney-General, and is himself assisted by four Additional Solicitor-Generals for India. According to Law Officers(Conditions of Service) Rules, 1987, the Solicitor-General and fourAdditional Solicitor-Generals are appointed for a period of three years.

Unlike the Attorney-General, Solicitor-General does not give legal advice to the Government of India. His workload is confined to appearing in courts on behalf of the Union of India. Moreover, the Solicitor-General office is not a constitutional office like the Attorney-General.

CHAPTER 12

PARLIAMENT

INTRODUCTION

Parliament is the supreme legislative body of India. The Parliament of India is a magnificent manifestation of the democratic ethos of our country. As the national Legislature and repository of the constituent powers of the Union, it occupies a central position in our democratic polity. The federal structure of Indian polity rests on the principle of Parliamentary form of government which makes the Executive accountable to the Legislature.

The Parliament of India was adopted when the Indian Constitution was promulgated in 1950. However, it was formally inaugurated after the first General Election conducted under the Universal Adult Franchise in independent India in 1952. Article 79 of the Constitution of India provides a bicameral Legislature consisting of the President of India, the Rajya Sabha (Council of States), and the Lok Sabha (House of the People). Thus, the Parliament of India has three constituents, i.e., the President of India, Lok Sabha, and the Rajya Sabha. Rajya Sabha is the Upper House and represents the States of India while the Lok Sabha is the Lower House. It is also called Popular House because it represents the people of India.

COMPOSITION OF THE PARLIAMENT

President

The President of India is the constitutional Head of the Executive as well as the constituent part of the Parliament.

While the American President is not a part of the Legislature (Congress), the President of India is an integral part of the Indian Parliament (similar to that of UK Parliament). Though the President of India is a constituent part of Parliament, he does not sit or participate in the discussions in either of the two Houses. The President of India performs certain important roles vis-à-vis the Parliament. The President summons and prorogues the House from one session to another and has the power to dissolve the Lok Sabha. He also summons the joint sittings of both the Houses in the event of disagreement. No bill passed by both the Houses can become a law without the President's assent. Further, certain bills can be introduced only after the recommendation of the President has been obtained. The President also has the power to promulgate ordinances when both the Houses are not in session. These ordinances, though temporary in nature, have the same force and power as a law passed by the Parliament.

Rajya Sabha

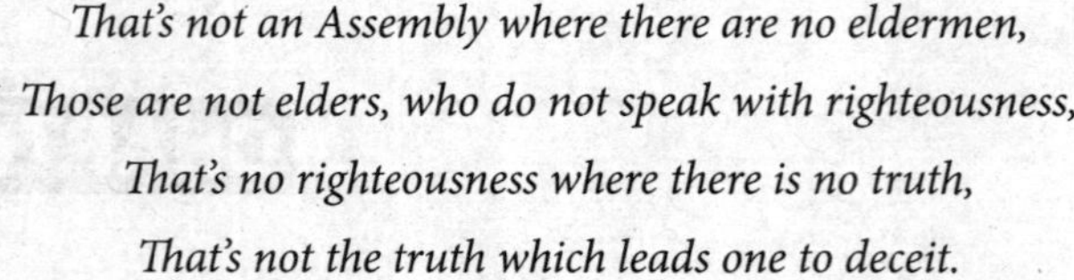

That's not an Assembly where there are no eldermen,

Those are not elders, who do not speak with righteousness,

That's no righteousness where there is no truth,

That's not the truth which leads one to deceit.

Mahabharata[1]

Background

Rajya Sabha or the Council of States as the name suggests represents the interest of the States in the Parliament. The origin of the second Chamber can be traced to the Montagu-Chelmsford Report of 1918. The Government of India Act, 1919 provided for the creation of a 'Council of State' as a second chamber of the then Legislature with a restricted franchise which actually came into existence in 1921. The Governor-General was the ex-officio President of the then Council of State. The Government of India Act, 1935, hardly made any changes in its composition.

Composition

It is a permanent body and is not subject to dissolution but one-third of its members retire on the expiration of every second year by rotation and are replaced by newly elected members. The strength of the Rajya Sabha has been fixed at the maximum of 250 members. Of these, 12 are nominated[2] by the President for their special knowledge or practical experience in such matters as literature, science, art, and social service. The remaining seats are allocated to the various States and Union territories, roughly in proportion to their population; each State is, however, represented by at least one member.

The total number of seats in the Rajya Sabha at present is 245, including 12 members nominated by the President, 229 members representing the States, and 4 members representing the Union Territories. The representatives of each State in Rajya Sabha are elected by the elected members of the Legislative Assembly of the State in accordance with the system of Proportional Representation by means of Single Transferable Vote. The representatives of the Union territories are chosen in such manner as Parliament may by law prescribe. At present, three Union territories, namely, the National Capital Territory of Delhi, Puducherry, and Jammu & Kashmir are represented in the Rajya Sabha[3]. The allocation of seats to the various States is provided in the Fourth Schedule of the Constitution.

---

[1] Sabha Parva

[2] In making nominations to Rajya Sabha, the President acts on the advice of the Council of Ministers. Further, the courts do not interfere with the Presidential power to make nominations. There is no difference of status between the elected and the nominated members of Rajya Sabha, except that the former do and the latter do not participate in the election of the President of India.

[3] The four Rajya Sabha members from the erstwhile state of Jammu and Kashmir had retired in February last year. Since then, the four J&K seats are lying vacant there. The legislative assembly elects the Rajya Sabha members. J&K assembly was dissolved on November 21, 2018 and no fresh elections were held since then, so no new member could be sent to the Upper House. As fresh assembly polls in J&K are yet to be held, the union territory will continue to remain unrepresented in Rajya Sabha for some more time.

Representation of States and Union Territories

Rajya Sabha is the body representing States in the Indian Union. The elected members of the States' Legislative Assemblies elect the members of the Rajya Sabha on the basis of Proportional Representation through the Single Transferable Vote system. But all the States do not send equal number of members to the Rajya Sabha. Their representation is decided on the basis of population of respective States. Thus, the bigger State gets bigger representation and the smaller ones have lesser representation. While a big State like UP has been assigned 31 seats, the smaller States like Sikkim and Tripura send only one member each. Delhi Assembly elects three members of Rajya Sabha and Pondicherry sends one member. Other Union Territories are not represented in the Rajya Sabha. Thus, even though Rajya Sabha is a federal chamber, the States are not equally represented As the State's representation is based on their population. Whereas, in the USA (which is a best example for a federal country), each State is equally represented in the Senate[4] (Upper House of the USA Parliament) by two senators who serve staggered terms of six years. There are currently 100 senators representing the 50 States. The Senators are elected by the popular vote of the people in their States.

Tenure

Unlike the Lok Sabha, the Rajya Sabha is a permanent body and is not subject to dissolution, but one-third of its members retire every two years and their place is taken by new members. That is, a member of Rajya Sabha who is elected for a full term, retains the membership for a period of six years[5]. However, a member elected to a seat rendered vacant due to resignation, etc., serves for the remaining term only. Therefore, the composition of Rajya Sabha changes every second year with one-third of its members retiring and new members getting elected for a period of six years, unlike the members of Lok Sabha, who are elected for a term of five years. Rajya Sabha resembles the American Senate insofar as it is also a continuing body, is not subject to dissolution, and is based on the principle of rotation of members. Rajya Sabha, however, differs from its American counterpart insofar as its members are not elected directly by the people in the States and there is no equality of representation of the constituent States.

Lok Sabha[6]

Unlike Rajya Sabha, Lok Sabha is not a permanent body. Lok Sabha is composed of representatives of the people chosen by direct election on the basis of the Adult Suffrage. Being a House directly elected by popular votes through periodical elections, the Lok Sabha represents 'the people' at the Parliament. Every citizen of India who is not less than 18 years of age is entitled to vote, unless he is otherwise disqualified by law under the Article 326 of the Indian Constitution.

Composition

The maximum strength of the House originally envisaged by the Constitution was 552 (now its 550), which is made up by election of up to 530 members to represent the States, up to 20 members

---

[4]With the passage of time, the original role of the Senate of guarding the interests of the States as political units has largely disappeared. It now functions more as a national institution rather than as a champion of local interests. This transformation has taken place due to several factors, such as, direct election of the Senators by the people on a State wide franchise, development of strong political parties advocating national programmes, development of a national consciousness, and national integration. The Senate is a powerful body and equal representation here gives to the smaller States a voice much greater than what they could otherwise hope to have in federal affairs.

[5]The Constitution has not fixed the term of Rajya Sabha members. It left it to the Parliament. The Parliament by passing the Representation of the People Act, 1951 prescribed the term of Rajya Sabha members as six years.

[6]The Lok Sabha was duly constituted for the first time on 17 April, 1952.

to represent the Union Territories, and not more than two members of the Anglo-Indian Community to be nominated by the President, if, in her/his opinion, that community is not adequately represented in the House. After coming into effect of 'The Constitution (One Hundred and Fourth Amendment) Act, 2019', the provision of special representation of the Anglo-Indian community in the House of the People by nomination has not been extended further. In other words, there is no more nomination of the Anglo-Indian community members by the President. The total elective membership of the House is distributed among the States in such a way that the ratio between the number of seats allotted to each State and the population of the State is, so far as practicable, same for all the States. The qualifying age for membership of the Lok Sabha is 25 years.

Representation of People

The distribution of seats among the States is based on the principle of territorial representation, which means that each State is allotted seats on the basis of its population in proportion to the total population of all the States. For election purposes, each State is divided into territorial units called constituencies which are more or less of the same size with regard to the population.

For the purpose of election from territorial constituencies in the States, a number of seats are allotted to each State in the Lok Sabha in such manner that the ratio between that number and the population of the State is, so far as practicable, the same for all States. Each State is thereafter divided into territorial constituencies in such manner that the ratio between the population of each constituency and the number of seats allotted to it, so far as practicable, is the same throughout the State. This is not, however, applicable to any State as long as the population of that State does not exceed six million[7].

The strength of the Lok Sabha and allocation of seats among the States and Union Territories has been mentioned in First Schedule of the Representation of the People Act, 1950.

Population (With reference to allocation of seats in Lok Sabha)

The expression "population" means the population as ascertained at the last preceding Census of which the relevant figures have been published. Under Article 82 of the Constitution, the Parliament by law enacts a Delimitation Act after every Census. After coming into force of the commencement of the Act, the Central Government constitutes a Delimitation Commission. This Delimitation Commission demarcates the boundaries of the Parliamentary Constituencies as per the provisions of the Delimitation Act. The "Delimitation Commission" is a non-party body. Its decision is immutable and cannot be challenged in any court of law. As per provisions of the Constitution, readjustment and delimitation of constituencies was to be carried out after every 10 years, based on the latest population Census. Accordingly, the delimitation exercise was carried out in 1952, 1963, and 1972. However, the fourth delimitation due in 1981–82 could not take place, as a result of a moratorium placed by the Parliament on further delimitation until the publication of 2001 Census figures. In other words, the 42nd Constitutional Amendment Act, 1976 made a change in the scheme, viz., no fresh adjustment of seats in Lok Sabha (as fixed on the basis of the Census of 1971 was frozen till 2001). By the 84th Amendment Act, 2001, this freeze is to last till 2026. No change in the number of seats for each State in Lok Sabha is to be made till after the first Census held after 2026.

The underlying reason for the above amendment is this: some States have implemented the Family Planning programme more vigorously than others. Accordingly, the population in these States has stabilised while in the other States, the population has increased. If now seats in Lok Sabha were to be reallocated among the States on population basis, the States implementing the Family Planning

[7]The following States and Union Territories have one seat each in the Lok Sabha – Mizoram, Nagaland, Sikkim, Andaman and Nicobar Islands, Chandigarh, Dadra and Nagar Haveli, Daman and Diu, Lakshadweep & Pondicherry.

programme would lose some seats. This may create a setback to the Family Control programme. Hence, it has been decided to extend the freeze on Lok Sabha seats till the year 2026 as a motivational measure to enable the State Governments to pursue the programme of population stabilisation.

However, the readjustment of territorial constituencies within a State without increasing the number of seats in Lok Sabha can be done based on the Census of 2001. Initially, by the 84th Amendment Act of 2001, the Parliament empowered the government to readjust and rationalize the constituencies on the basis of 1991 Census. Later, by the 87th Amendment Act of 2003, it provided for the readjustment of the constituencies based on 2001 Census instead of 1991 Census.

Tenure

The term of the Lok Sabha, unless dissolved, is five years from the date appointed for its first meeting. In other words, the normal term of Lok Sabha is five years. But the President, on the advice of the Council of Ministers, may dissolve it before the expiry of five years. However, while a proclamation of Emergency is in operation, this period may be extended by the Parliament by law for a period not exceeding one year at a time and not extending in any case, beyond a period of six months after the proclamation has ceased to operate.

Reservation of Seats

In Lok Sabha, there is reservation of seats for Scheduled Castes and Scheduled Tribes. Here also, Census figures are taken into account. Allocation of seats for Scheduled Castes and Tribes in the Lok Sabha are made on the basis of proportion of Scheduled Castes and Tribes in the State concerned to that of the total population[8]. Originally the reservation was supposed to operate for ten years from the commencement of the Constitution (i.e., up to 1960), but it has been extended since then by 10 years each time. By the 126th Constitutional Amendment Act, 2019, the reservation is further extended till 2030.

Reservation of seats for the Scheduled Castes or Scheduled Tribes means the persons belonging to SC/ST will represent such reserved seats. That implies that only persons belonging to SC/ST can contest from the reserved constituencies. But we have a joint electorate and all the voters of the reserved constituency vote irrespective of their caste/tribe. There is no separation of voters in terms of caste or tribe.

The 84th Constitutional Amendment Act, 2001 provides for the readjustment of reserved seats of Scheduled Castes and Scheduled Tribes with respect to the total seats in Lok Sabha based on the 1991 Census. Later on, the 87th Amendment Act, 2003 provided for readjustment of reserved seats on the basis of 2001 Census instead of 1991 Census.

PARLIAMENTARY MEMBERSHIP AND FUNCTIONING

Qualifications

The Constitution of India has prescribed certain qualifications to be fulfilled for becoming or getting elected as a member of the Parliament (Article 84) –

(a) Only a citizen of India is qualified to be chosen as a member of a House of Parliament.

(b) He/she should not be less than 30 years of age for Rajya Sabha, and 25 years for Lok Sabha.

[8]Reservations are contained in Article 330 of the Constitution of India read with Section 3 of the R. P. Act, 1950.

(c) He/she should make and subscribe to the prescribed oath or affirmation that "he has true faith and allegiance in the Constitution and that he will uphold the sovereignty and integrity of India", before a person authorized by the Election Commission for this purpose.

(d) He/she should also possess such other qualifications as Parliament may by law prescribe for this purpose.

(e) He/she should not suffer any disqualification prescribed either by the Constitution or a law made by Parliament.

Parliament has prescribed the necessary qualifications and disqualifications for Parliamentary membership in the Representation of the People Act, 1951 –

(a) In order to be qualified as a member of Rajya Sabha (Section 3) - he must be registered as a voter in any constituency in India[9];

(b) In order to be qualified as a member of Lok Sabha (Section 4) – he must be a member of the Lok Sabha, and the person should be an elector for some Parliamentary constituency in India. Also, he should be a member of any Schedule Caste or Scheduled Tribe in any State, if he wants to contest a seat reserved for them. In other words, a person contesting from the reserved seat should belong to the Scheduled Caste or Scheduled Tribe as the case may be. A person belonging to the Scheduled Caste or Scheduled Tribes is not, however, disqualified for being elected to a seat not reserved for these castes or tribes.

Disqualifications

Disqualifications laid down in the Constitution are as follows:

1. Disqualifications under Article 102 :

(a) A competent court has declared him/candidate to be of unsound mind;

(b) He is an undischarged insolvent;

(c) He is not a citizen of India or has voluntarily acquired the citizenship of a foreign State, or is under any acknowledgement of allegiance or adherence to a foreign State;

(d) He holds an *Office of Profit* under the Central or the State Government. The word "office of profit" is not defined in the Constitution. However, in general legal parlance, the "office of profit" ordinarily means an 'office' capable of yielding some profit to the holder of the office. The disqualification arises when a person –

- Holds an office;
- The office is under the Council or State Government; and
- The office if one of profit.

A Minister either in the Central or State Government is not regarded as holding an office of profit. The term 'minister' includes 'Deputy Minister'. The Constitution has conferred on the Parliament the power to declare the offices of profit, the holders of which would not be disqualified for its membership. Accordingly, Parliament has enacted the Parliament (Prevention of Disqualifications) Act, 1959, which lists the various categories of offices the holders of which

[9]Before 2003 RPA amendment – a person is not qualified to be chosen as a member of Rajya Sabha unless he is an elector for a parliamentary constituency in the concerned state or the Union Territory. The 2003 RPA amendment removed such requirement and if a person is an elector in any constituency, he would be eligible to contest the Rajya Sabha elections.

would not be disqualified for membership of Parliament. The Act does not define the term "office of profit". In case of an office other than those exempted under the Act, the final word on whether it is an 'office of profit' or not rests with the courts.

2. **Disqualification on grounds of defection (Xth Schedule) :** It lays down the process by which legislators may be disqualified on grounds of defection by the Presiding Officer of a Legislature based on a petition by any other member of the House. Defection means a member of a political party changes his party voluntarily or on other grounds. A legislator is deemed to have defected if he either –

   (a) voluntarily gives up his membership of such political party;

   (b) disobeys the directions of his political party or votes or does not vote in the Legislature;

   (c) After the election, he joins other political party;

   (d) If nominated member joins any political party after 6 months from the day, he became member of the Legislature;

   (e) If independently elected member joins any political party.

Disqualifications laid down in the Representation of the People Act, 1951 –

(a) Disqualification on conviction[10] for certain offences

i. If a person is convicted for any one of the offences given below, shall be disqualified for a period of six years if only fine is imposed (or) shall be disqualified from the date of such conviction and shall continue to be disqualified for a further period of six years since his release if he is sentenced to imprisonment. Following are the offences –

   - Under Indian Penal Code : Offence of promoting enmity between different groups on ground of religion, race, place of birth, residence, language, etc., and doing acts prejudicial to maintenance of harmony; OR offence of bribery; OR offence of undue influence or personation at an election; OR offences relating to rape; OR offence of cruelty towards a woman by husband or relative of a husband; OR offence of making statement creating or promoting enmity, hatred or ill-will between classes or offence relating to such statement in any place of worship or in any assembly engaged in the performance of religious worship or religious ceremonies; (or)
   - Under the Protection of Civil Rights Act, 1955 : preaching and practice of "untouchability", and for the enforcement of any disability arising therefrom; (or)
   - Under the Unlawful Activities (Prevention) Act, 1967 : offence of being a member of an association declared unlawful, offence relating to dealing with funds of an unlawful association, or offence relating to contravention of an order made in respect of a notified place.
   - Under the Prevention of Insults to National Honour Act, 1971 : offence of insulting the Indian National Flag or the Constitution of India; or offence of preventing singing of National Anthem; (OR)
   - Under : The Commission of Sati (Prevention) Act, 1987; (OR)

[10]Disqualification is applicable only for punitive imprisonment, not for preventive imprisonment. In other words, detention under preventive detention laws is not subject to disqualification.

- Under : The Prevention of Corruption Act, 1988; (OR)
- Under the Representation of the People Act 1951 : offence of promoting enmity between classes in connection with the election; OR offence of removal of ballot papers from polling stations; OR offence of booth capturing; OR offence of fraudulently defacing or fraudulently destroying any nomination paper (In other words, corrupt practices at an election);

ii. A person convicted for the contravention of the following laws and sentenced to imprisonment for not less than six months, shall be disqualified from the date of such conviction and shall continue to be disqualified for a further period of six years since his release. Following are the laws –

- any law providing for the prevention of hoarding or profiteering; or
- any law relating to the adulteration of food or drugs; or
- any provisions of the Dowry Prohibition Act, 1961;

iii. A person convicted of any offence and sentenced to imprisonment for not less than two years other than any offence referred to in (i) or (ii) (referred above) shall be disqualified from the date of such conviction and shall continue to be disqualified for a further period of six years since his release.

(b) **Disqualification for dismissal for corruption or disloyalty :** A person who held an office under the Government of India or under the Government of any State has been dismissed for corruption or for disloyalty to the State shall be disqualified for a period of five years from the date of such dismissal.

(c) **Disqualification for Government contracts :** A person shall be disqualified as long as he is having a subsistence contract for supply of goods to, or execution of any works undertaken by, the government.

(d) **Disqualification for office under Government company :** A person shall be disqualified as long as, for being a managing agent, manager, or secretary of a corporation in which government has not less than 25 per cent share;

(e) **Disqualification for failure to lodge account of election expenses :** If a person fails to lodge an account of election expenses within the time given in the Representation of the People Act, the Election Commission shall by order disqualify such person for a period of three years from the date of the order.

Decision on Disqualification

Under Article 103, once a question arises whether a member has incurred a disqualification, it is only the President who must decide it but only after taking the opinion of the Election Commission. It is the decision of the President taken in accordance with the opinion of the Election Commission that is final. The decision of the President must depend on the opinion of the Election Commission and none else, not even the Council of Ministers. No court has jurisdiction to interfere with this matter as it lies exclusively within the purview of the President and the Election Commission. It has to be noted that the Article 103 becomes applicable when a sitting member of the Legislature becomes subject to a disqualification after his election.

If, however, a disqualified person is elected as a member of the Parliament, his election can be challenged through an election petition in the High Court. When a person is not qualified to be elected a member, there is no doubt that the High Court/election tribunal has got to declare his election to be void.

If a member becomes subject to disqualification after election, then the procedure laid down in Article 103 needs to be followed. But what happens when a person lacking in the basic and fundamental qualification, prescribed by the Constitution for membership of the Parliament, is elected to the House and no election petition is moved against him challenging his election. The person in question knows that he is disqualified and yet he sits in the House and votes as a member. In such case, under Article 103, he is subject to a penalty of Rs. 500 per day for knowingly sitting in the House while being disqualified.

However, the disqualification of a member on the grounds of defection will be decided by the Presiding officer of the House but not the President. The President decides the disqualification on the grounds other than defection.

Other Provisions Regarding Vacation of Parliamentary Seats

1. ***Simultaneous Membership :*** No person can be a member of both Houses of Parliament at one and the same time. Parliament is authorized to provide by law for vacation by a person, who is chosen a member of both the Houses, of his seat in one House. Accordingly, the Parliament in the Representation of People Act, 1951, provided about the consequences of the simultaneous membership.
   - If a person is elected to the both Houses of the Parliament, he may intimate to the Election Commission within ten days from the publication of the results as to the House he desires to serve in, and thereupon his seat in the other House falls vacant. In default of such intimation, his seat in the Rajya Sabha becomes vacant.
   - A sitting member of the Lok Sabha or Rajya Sabha vacates his seat when he is chosen as a member of the Rajya Sabha or Lok Sabha respectively.
   - An individual can contest from two Parliamentary constituencies but, if elected from both, he has to resign one seat within 14 days of the declaration of the result, failing which both his seats shall fall vacant.
   - No person can be a member of Parliament and a State Legislature simultaneously. If a person is so elected, then at the expiry of such period as the President may by rules specify, his seat in Parliament becomes vacant, unless he has previously resigned his seat in the State Legislature. In other words, according to the Prohibition of Simultaneous Membership Rules, 1950, (made by the President) members of State Legislatures who have been elected to Lok Sabha must resign their seats within 14 days "from the date of publication of result in the Gazette of India or in the Official Gazette of the State, whichever is later", failing which their seats in Lok Sabha shall automatically fall vacant.
2. ***Resignation :*** A member of the Rajya Sabha may resign his seat by writing to the Chairman, and that of the Lok Sabha by writing to the Speaker. The seat falls vacant when the resignation is accepted by the Chairman/Speaker who is not to accept the resignation when he is satisfied that it is not voluntary or genuine.

3. ***Absence :*** A House of Parliament may declare a seat vacant if a member absents himself from all its meetings for a period of sixty days without its permission. While computing the sixty days period, no account shall be taken of any period during which the House is prorogued or adjourned for more than four consecutive days.
4. ***Elected as Heads of the State :*** When a member either gets elected to the office of President or Vice-President or is appointed as the Governor of any State, in such cases his seat in the State Legislature gets vacant.
5. ***Election Petition :*** If the election of a member is declared invalid by the court, then the seat of such member gets vacant.

Taking of Oath

A member of a House of Parliament, before taking his seat in the House, has to make and subscribe to an oath or affirmation before the President, or a person appointed by him for this purpose. Until a duly elected candidate takes the oath, he cannot participate in the proceedings of the House and he cannot enjoy the Parliamentary privileges or immunities as he is not regarded a member thereof.

Penalty

A person is liable to a penalty of Rs. 500 for each day he sits or votes as a member in a House :

(a) Before taking the prescribed oath; or

(b) When he knows that he is not qualified to be a member of the House, or is disqualified for being its member; or

(c) When he knows that he is prohibited from sitting or voting in the House by virtue of any law made by Parliament.

Salaries and Allowances

Under Article 106 of the Constitution, Indian lawmakers fix their own salaries by passing laws. The members of Parliament become entitled to certain amenities. These amenities are provided to members with a view to enable them to function effectively as Members of Parliament. Broadly speaking, the amenities provided to the Members relate to salaries and allowances, travelling facilities, medical facilities, accommodation, telephones, etc. These are governed by the Salary, Allowances and Pension of Members of Parliament Act, 1954 and the rules made thereunder.

At present, a Member of Parliament is entitled to Rs. 100,000/- per month as salary, Rs. 70,000/- per month as Constituency Allowance, Rs. 60,000/- per month as Office Expense Allowance out of which Rs. 20,000/- is for meeting expenses of stationery items and postage; and up to Rs. 40,000/- is paid by the Lok Sabha Secretariat to the person(s) as may be engaged by a member for obtaining secretarial assistance. A Member also gets daily allowance of Rs. 2,000 for the period of residence on duty.

PRESIDING OFFICERS OF PARLIAMENT

Each House has its own Presiding Officer who enjoys ample authority and powers under the Constitution and the Rules of Procedure. The Presiding Officer is the custodian of the rights and privileges of the House, its Committees, and Members. It is through him that the decisions of the House are communicated to individuals and authorities outside. He issues warrants to execute the order of the House, wherever necessary. Within the precincts of the House, his authority is supreme. His conduct cannot be discussed, except on a substantive motion.

Presiding Officers of the Lok Sabha - Speaker and Deputy Speaker[11]

The offices of Speaker and Deputy Speaker originated in India in 1921 under the provisions of the Government of India Act of 1919 (Montagu-Chelmsford Reforms). At that time, the Speaker and the Deputy Speaker were called the President and Deputy President respectively and the same nomenclature continued till 1947. The Government of India Act of 1935 changed the nomenclatures of President and Deputy President to Speaker and Deputy Speaker respectively.

Speaker

The Presiding Officer of the Lok Sabha is known as Speaker.

Election of the Speaker : The Speaker is elected by the Lok Sabha from amongst its members (as soon as may be, after its first sitting). Whenever the office of the Speaker falls vacant, the Lok Sabha elects another member to fill the vacancy. The date of election of the Speaker is fixed by the President.

(a) **Qualifications :** There are no formal qualifications for the office of the Speaker. Any sitting member of the Lok Sabha can be elected as Speaker by the House.

(b) **Tenure :** Generally, the tenure of the Speaker is equal to the tenure of Lok Sabha, i.e., 5 years. However, the Speaker continues to be in office even after the dissolution of the Lok Sabha. He/she holds office till the new Lok Sabha elects a new Speaker. The Speaker can resign his office at any time before the completion of his full tenure.

(c) **Method of Removal :** The Speaker automatically ceases to be so if he is disqualified to be a member of Lok Sabha due to reasons whatsoever. He/she can vacate his/her office by addressing a resignation letter to the Deputy Speaker. He can also be removed by the members of the Lok Sabha by a resolution passed by an absolute majority of Lok Sabha. However, a 14 days advanced notice must be given for such resolution. The motion of removal can be considered and discussed only when it has the support of at least 50 members. These provisions make the removal of the Speaker difficult and provide him the security of tenure. When such resolution is under consideration of the House, the Speaker cannot preside over the meeting of the House. However, he is eligible to participate and vote, except the casting vote in case of an equality of votes.

Whenever the office of the Speaker falls vacant either because of removal or resignation or otherwise, in such cases the election for the said office shall be conducted as soon as possible.

(d) **Salary :** The Speaker is paid such salaries and allowances as are fixed by Parliament by law, and until such a provision is made, as specified in the Second Schedule of the Constitution. The salary and allowances are fixed by the Parliament by law and are not subject to the annual vote of Parliament, and they are charged on the Consolidated Fund of India.

---

[11]The first Speaker of the Lok Sabha was G.V. Mavalankar (1952–56). He is known as the Father of Lok Sabha, for his immense contribution in redesigning the country's Parliamentary proceedings with intricate impartiality. Mr. Ananthasayanam Ayyangar was the Speaker of the Second Lok Sabha (1956–62). The first woman Speaker in the history of the Indian Parliament is Meira Kumar, who presided over the 15th Lok Sabha session beginning in 2009. The only Speaker to have presided over the Parliament in two consecutive terms, for the full five-year periods was Balram Jakhar.

(e) **Oath :** There is no oath while assuming the office of the Speaker.

(f) **Functions and Powers of the Speaker :**

- Lok Sabha Speaker is the representative and principal spokesman of Lok Sabha and his decisions in matters of Lok Sabha are final. His powers and functions are derived from the Constitution, Rules of Procedure (Lok Sabha), and Parliamentary conventions.
- The Speaker presides over the meetings of the Lok Sabha and conducts its proceedings. He/she decides who will speak and all speeches of the members of the House are addressed to the Chair.
- Joint Session : Speaker also presides over the joint sittings of the two Houses of the Parliament. A joint session can be called by the President of India. The Speaker of the Lok Sabha is to be consulted along with the Chairman of the Rajya Sabha by the President while making a provision for the joint meetings of the two Houses.
- To maintain discipline in the Lok Sabha : The primary duty of the Speaker is to maintain order and decorum in the Lok Sabha. The Speaker maintains discipline in the House. He can check the indiscipline and disorder and stop members from using irrelevant and unparliamentary language. He can expunge remarks made by any member from the proceeding of the House, if such remarks are derogatory or unparliamentary. If any member disrupts or tries to disrupt the proceedings of the House, the Speaker can warn him or can ask him to leave the House. He can suspend a member from the House whom he finds guilty of violating the discipline and decorum.
- Interpretation of Rules of Procedure : The business of the House is conducted according to definite and settled Rules of Procedure. In case of any dispute regarding the rules of the House, the Speaker interprets and applies these rules. His interpretations of constitutional provisions, rules, and regulations related to Lok Sabha are final and cannot be challenged.
- To conduct the business of the House : The Speaker conducts the business of the House. He allows the members to introduce the bills or to move motions. He fixes a time limit for the debate in the House, puts matters to vote, and announces the results.
- Power to adjourn the House : The quorum to constitute a meeting of the Lok Sabha is one-tenth of the membership of the House. If there is no quorum, the Speaker decides to suspend the meeting. The Speaker can adjourn the meetings of the House if the quorum of the House is not complete or if the conducting of the business of the House is not possible due to disorderly behavior of its members.
- Decisions about a Money Bill : Whether a bill is a Money Bill or not, is decided by Speaker and his decision in this matter is final. Such a decision is final and cannot be challenged inside or outside the House. When a Money Bill is passed in Lok Sabha and sent to Rajya Sabha, the Speaker's endorsement is needed on that.
- To exercise a Casting Vote : The Speaker does not participate in the debates and discussions of the House. He does not even take part in the voting on bills, although as a member he has the right to vote. In case of a tie due to equal votes, the Speaker exercises the "casting vote". Objective of the casting vote is to resolve a deadlock.

- Permission of Secret Meeting : On the request of the Leader of the House, the Speaker may allow a secret meeting. None other than those permitted by the Speaker can be present in a secret meeting.
- Protection of the privileges of the members of the House : The members of the House enjoy several privileges which are protected by the Speaker. All cases of disputes relating to the privileges of the members are referred by the Speaker to the Committee on Privileges. In accordance with the wishes of this committee, the Speaker then decides these matters. The Speaker acts as the guardian of the privileges of the members of the House.
- Role regarding the Committees of the House : A major part of the business of the House is conducted by the Committees of the House. The Speaker plays an important role in the composition of the Committees. He is the Supreme Head of all Parliamentary Committees and he may issue directions to the Chairman of those Committees relating to their efficient working. The Chairmen of all the Parliamentary Committees of the Lok Sabha are appointed by the Speaker, provided such committees don't need elected Chairmen. He is the ex-officio Chairman of some of the important committees such as Business Advisory Committee, Committee on Rules, and a few others.
- Administrative Functions : The Speaker has several administrative responsibilities. He has control over the Lok Sabha Secretariat. He appoints the employees of the Secretariat, determines the service rules for them, and supervises their work. He has the responsibility for the upkeep of the records of the proceedings of the House.
- Disqualify members on the grounds of defection : The Speaker decides the question of disqualification of Lok Sabha members in matters related anti-defection. This decision is subject to judicial review.
- To fix the agenda of the House : The Speaker, in consultation with other members of the Business Committee of the House and the Prime Minister/Leader of the House, fixes the agenda of the meetings of the House. The Speaker determines the order of the business, the time to be allowed for the debates on the President Address, and the days to be devoted to the Private Member's Bills. He is the sole authority for giving priority to anything that may be placed before the House for the national interest. He is not expected to give reasons for his decisions and his decisions are not subject to challenge by any member.
- Miscellaneous : All communications between the Parliament and the President take place through the Speaker. The Speaker signs all bills passed by the Lok Sabha before they are sent to Rajya Sabha or to the President. In short, he is the representative of the House itself in its powers, proceedings, prestige, and dignity. Besides heading the Lok Sabha, the Speaker is also the 'ex-officio' President of the Indian Parliamentary Group. He/she also acts in the capacity of Chairman of the Conference of Presiding Officers of Legislative Bodies in India.

Deputy Speaker

When the Speaker of the Lok Sabha is not available, his duties are carried out by the Deputy Speaker. A Deputy Speaker is elected by the Lok Sabha members from amongst themselves. Election of the Deputy Speaker is done after the election of the Speaker. The date of election of the Deputy Speaker is fixed by the Speaker. Whenever the office of the Deputy Speaker falls vacant, the Lok Sabha elects another member to fill the vacancy. Like the Speaker, there is no oath while assuming the office of the Deputy Speaker.

The Deputy Speaker performs the duties of the Speaker's office when it is vacant. In case the Deputy Speaker's office is also vacant, the Speaker's duties are to be performed by such member of the House as the President may appoint for the purpose till any of the offices is filled by election by the House. The Deputy Speaker acts as the Speaker when the latter is absent from the House. When both the Speaker and the Deputy Speaker are absent from the House, such person as may be determined by the Rules of Procedure of the House (Panel of Chairpersons), and if no such person (Panel of Chairperson) is present, such other person as may be determined by the House, acts as the Speaker.

The Deputy Speakers remains in office so long as they are members of the House and they vacate their offices as soon as they cease to be its members. The Deputy Speaker may resign his office by writing to the Speaker. The Deputy Speaker may be removed from his office by a resolution passed by a majority of all the then members of the House. Such a resolution can be moved only after at least a 14 days' notice has been given to the Deputy Speaker. When such a resolution is under consideration against the Deputy Speaker, he does not preside at the sittings of the House, though he may be present. He can, however, participate in the proceedings of the House at such time and even vote in the first instance, though not when there is an equality of votes.

The Deputy Speaker is paid such salaries and allowances as are fixed by Parliament by law, and until such a provision is made, as specified in the Second Schedule of the Constitution. Even though the salary and allowances fixed by the Parliament by law are not subject to the annual vote of Parliament, they are charged on the Consolidated Fund of India.

The Deputy Speaker is not subordinate to the Speaker and is directly responsible to the Lok Sabha. He can take part in the proceedings of the House and exercise his voting power like any other ordinary member when the Speaker presides over the House. The Deputy Speaker while presiding over the House does not have the right to vote in the first instance. Like the Speaker, he can only exercise a casting vote in the case of a tie. Whenever the Deputy Speaker is appointed as a member of a Parliamentary Committee, he automatically becomes its Chairman.

Thus, the Speakers and the Deputy Speakers are men of reputation and they have brought up a healthy tradition of impartiality and dignity to the office of the Speaker. Owing to the great importance of his office, the Speaker is expected to maintain his impartiality. So, it is a convention in Britain that the Speaker divests himself of his party character by resigning from the party to which he belonged before his election. This convention is not followed strictly in India where the Speaker remains a member of the party, though he does not attend or participate in any party meeting, except on ceremonial or social occasions. Moreover, the Speaker comes from the Ruling party whereas the Deputy Speaker comes from the Opposition party. It is by convention that the position of Deputy Speaker is offered to opposition parties in India. This convention has been developed since the 11th Lok Sabha.

Time frame for Deputy Speaker's election - Article 93 reads: "*The House of the People shall, as soon as may be, choose two members of the House to be respectively Speaker and Deputy Speaker thereof and, so often as the office of Speaker or Deputy Speaker becomes vacant, the House shall choose another member to be Speaker or Deputy Speaker, as the case may be.*"

Generally speaking, the practice in both Lok Sabha and the State Legislative Assemblies has been to elect the Speaker during the (mostly short) first session of the new House. The election of the Deputy Speaker usually takes place in the second session, even though there is no bar on having this election too in the first session of the new Lok Sabha/Assembly. But the election of the Deputy Speaker is generally not delayed beyond the second session without genuine and unavoidable constraints. In Lok Sabha, the election of the Deputy Speaker is governed by Rule 8 of The Rules of Procedure and Conduct of Business in Lok Sabha. According to the Rule, the election "shall be held on such date as the Speaker may fix", and the Deputy Speaker is elected once a motion proposing his name is carried. In other words, there is no fixed time frame within which the election of the Deputy Speaker has to be conducted. It is the discretion of the Speaker to fix a date and conduct the election. In general, the courts do not intervene if there is an inordinate delay in conducting the Deputy Speaker's election because of Article 122(1), which reads: "The validity of any proceedings in Parliament shall not be called in question on the ground of any alleged irregularity of procedure."

Panel of Chairpersons

The Rules of Procedure and Conduct of Business in Lok Sabha provide that at the commencement of the House or from time to time, as the case may be, the Speaker shall nominate from amongst the Members a Panel of not more than ten Chairpersons, any one of whom may preside over the House in the absence of the Speaker and the Deputy Speaker when so requested by the Speaker or, in the absence of the Speaker, by the Deputy Speaker. A Chairperson so nominated, holds office until a new Panel of Chairpersons is nominated, unless he/she resigns earlier from the Panel or is appointed a Minister or elected as Deputy Speaker. The Panel of Chairperson while presiding over the House shall enjoy the same powers as that of the Speaker. When the panel of Chairpersons are also absent, then the House shall choose any other member of the House to act as the Presiding officer/Speaker. However, the Panel of Chairpersons do not get an opportunity to preside over the House when the office of the Speaker or the Deputy Speaker falls vacant. In such case of vacancy, the Speaker's duties shall be performed by such other member of the House as appointed by the President who is known as the "*Pro-tem* Speaker".

Pro-Tem Speaker

Pro-tem is a Latin phrase which translates to 'for the time being' in English and so, the pro-tem Speaker is a temporary Speaker appointed for a limited period of time. The Constitution does not expressly use the term 'Pro-tem Speaker'. Pro-tem Speaker is appointed in the following circumstances –

- Whenever Lok Sabha is dissolved, the Speaker continues to remain in office until immediately before the first meeting of Lok Sabha after it is reconstituted. The President appoints a Pro-tem Speaker for the first meeting of the newly elected Lok Sabha. He is appointed to administer the oath to the new members and enable the House to elect a new Speaker. Usually, the senior-most member is elected as Pro-tem Speaker and the President himself administers the oath to him. In other words, Pro-tem Speaker is ordinarily elected for the first sitting of a new Legislative Assembly where the Speaker is yet to be elected to conduct the works in Lok Sabha or in State Legislatures.
- The law on Pro-tem Speaker is also laid down under Article 95 of the Constitution which provides that when the Speaker or Deputy Speaker positions are vacant, the duties of the Office should be performed by 'such member of the Parliament as the President may appoint for the purpose'. In

other words, when the offices of both the Speaker and the Deputy Speaker fall vacant, the duties of the Office of the Speaker are performed by such Member of the Lok Sabha as the President may appoint for the purpose. The person so appointed is known as the Speaker Pro-tem.

The Speaker *Pro-tem* has all the powers of the Speaker.

Secretary-General of Lok Sabha

Lok Sabha has its own Secretariat and its Secretary-General is appointed by the Lok Sabha Speaker. He is a government servant and remains in office till the age of 60 years. His functions are to provide a link between changing members and keep the records. He summons the members to attend the sessions of Parliament on behalf of the President. He also authenticates the bill in the absence of the Speaker. He is answerable only to the Speaker and his action cannot be criticized in or out of Lok Sabha. The Secretary-General works with anonymity and is readily available to the Presiding Officers for rendering advice on Parliamentary matters. The Secretary-General is also the administrative Head of the Lok Sabha Secretariat and the custodian of the records of the House.

Presiding Officers of Rajya Sabha – Chairman and Vice-Chairman

Chairman

The Vice President of India is the ex-officio Chairman of Rajya Sabha. The Vice-President is not a member of the Rajya Sabha, yet he acts as its Chairman. The Vice-President is elected by the members of an Electoral College consisting of the members of both Houses of Parliament in accordance with the system of Proportional Representation by means of the Single Transferable Vote. The term of office of the Vice-President is for five years from the date he enters upon his office. The Chairman of the Rajya Sabha can be removed from his office only when he is removed as the Vice-President. The Chairman (Vice-President) can be removed from his office by a resolution passed by a majority of all the then members of Rajya Sabha and agreed to by the Lok Sabha. The salaries and allowances of the Chairman are fixed by the Parliament and they are charged on the Consolidated Fund of India. However, the Vice-President is entitled to the salaries and the allowances of the President only while acting as the President.

Powers and functions of the Chairman :

- Principal spokesman of the House;
- Casting of vote by the Chairman of Rajya Sabha : Under the Indian Constitution, the Chairman exercises only a casting vote in the case of equality of votes. Whereas, he can neither vote nor preside over the House while his removal resolution is under consideration. But he can be present and speak in the House and take part in the proceedings without casting the vote during his removal proceedings. Whereas, the Speaker of the Lok Sabha can vote during his removal proceedings because he is the member of the House;
- The Indian Constitution has laid down powers and duties of the Chairman : the Chairman is empowered to adjourn the House or to suspend its sitting the event of absence of quorum;
- Power conferred under the Rules of procedure of the Rajya Sabha : the Chairman may at any time call a sitting of the House before the date or hour to which it has been adjourned, or at any time after the House has been adjourned sine die, but not prorogued by the President. The consent of the Chairman is required to raise an issue of breach of privilege in the House.
- Under the Rules of Procedure of the House, the Chairman enjoys powers to regulate the proceedings of the House. The Chairman enjoys powers to regulate the proceedings of the House similar to those enjoyed by the Speaker in relation to the Lok Sabha.

- In simple words, the Chairman of the Rajya Sabha enjoys similar powers and functions as that of the Speaker of Lok Sabha. However, there are certain powers enjoyed exclusively by the Speaker of the Lok Sabha. They are as follows:
  - The Speaker has the power to decide whether a Bill is a Money Bill or not. The decision of the Speaker is final in this regard.
  - The Speaker has the power to preside over the joint sitting of the two House of the Parliament. Whereas, the Chairman of the Rajya Sabha cannot preside over the joint sitting.

Deputy Chairman

When the Vice-President acts as the President of India or otherwise performs the duties of the President, the duties of the Chairman of the Rajya Sabha are performed by the Deputy Chairman who is elected by the members of the Rajya Sabha from amongst themselves. In other words, the Deputy Chairman presides over the sittings of the Rajya Sabha in the absence of the Chairman.

The Deputy Chairman will be elected from among its members who vacates his office as soon as he ceases to be a member of the House. He may resign his office by writing to the Chairman. He may be removed from his office by a resolution passed by a majority of all the then members of the House. Such a resolution, however, cannot be moved unless at least a fourteen days' notice has been given of the intention to move it. The Deputy Chairman cannot preside over a sitting of the House when a resolution for his removal is under consideration, though he has a right to vote and participate in the proceedings.

The Deputy Chairman while presiding over the House, cannot vote in the first instance. However, like the Chairman, he can exercise a casting vote in case of a tie. The Deputy Chairman is not subordinate to the Chairman. He is directly responsible to the Rajya Sabha. When the Chairman presides over the House, the Deputy Chairman, like any other ordinary member, takes part in the deliberations as well as votes in the proceedings of the House.

The salaries and allowances payable to the Chairman and Deputy Chairman are fixed by the Parliament by law and, until so fixed, are to be as specified in the Second Schedule of the Constitution. The salaries of the Chairman and the Deputy Chairman are charged on the Consolidated Fund of India.

The Deputy Chairman performs the duties of the Chairman when that office is vacant, or when the Vice-President is acting as the President of India. If the office of the Deputy Chairman is also vacant, then the duties of the Chairman are performed by such member of the Rajya Sabha as the President may appoint for the purpose, till any of these offices is filled. In the absence of the Chairman from a sitting of the House, the Deputy Chairman, and if he is also absent, such person as may be determined by the Rules of Procedure of the House, or, if no such person is present, such other person as may be determined by the House, acts as the Chairman.

Panel of Vice-Chairpersons

The Rules of Procedure and Conduct of Business in Rajya Sabha provide that the Speaker shall nominate from amongst the Members a Panel of not more than six Vice-Chairpersons, any one of whom may preside over the House in the absence of the Chairman and the Deputy-Chairman. In other words, a panel of six members of Rajya Sabha nominated by the Chairman, any one of whom may preside over the House in the absence of the Chairman and the Deputy Chairman when so requested by the Chairman, or in his absence, by the Deputy Chairman. A Vice-Chairperson so nominated, holds office until a new Panel of Chairpersons is nominated, unless he/she resigns earlier from the Panel or is appointed a Minister. The Panel of Vice-Chairperson while presiding over the House shall enjoy the same powers as that of the Speaker. When the Panel of Vice-chairpersons are also absent, then the House shall choose any other member of the House to act as the Presiding officer/Chairman. However, the Panel of Vice-Chairpersons do not get an opportunity to preside over the House when the office of the Chairman or the Deputy Chairman falls vacant. In such case of vacancy, the Speaker's duties shall be performed by such other member of the House as appointed by the President.

Secretary General

Similar to Lok Sabha, the Rajya Sabha also has its own Secretariat and its Secretary-General is appointed by the Chairman. The powers and functions of the Secretary-General of Rajya Sabha is similar to that of the Lok Sabha.

Leaders of the House

Leader of the House/Council in Rajya Sabha

Apart from the Chairman and the Deputy Chairman, Leader of the House is another functionary who plays an important role in the efficient and smooth conduct of the business in the House. The Leader of the House in Rajya Sabha is normally the Prime Minister, if he is its member or any Minister who is a member of the House and is nominated by him to so function. His primary responsibility is to maintain coordination amongst all sections of the House for a harmonious and meaningful debate in the House. For this purpose, he remains in close contact not only with the Government, but also with the Opposition, individual ministers, and the Presiding Officer. He occupies the first seat in the Chamber in the first row at the right the side of the Chair so that he is easily available to the Presiding Officer for consultation. Under the rules, the Leader of the House is consulted by the Chairman in regard to the arrangement of Government business in the House, allotment of days or allocation of time for discussion on the President's Address, Private Members' business on any day other than Friday, discussion on No Day-Yet-Named Motions, Short Duration Discussions, and consideration and return of a Money Bill. He is also consulted by the Chairman in the matter of adjournment or otherwise of the House for the day in case of death of an outstanding personality, national leader, or international dignitary. In the era of coalition governments, his task has become more challenging. He ensures that all possible and reasonable facilities are made available to the House for a meaningful discussion on any matter that is brought before it. He works as the spokesperson of the House in expressing a sense of the House and represents it on ceremonial or formal occasions. Leader of the House is mentioned in the Rules of the House. Leader of the Council is mentioned in the Rules of the Rajya Sabha.

Leader of the Opposition in Rajya Sabha

The office of the Leader of the Opposition in a Legislature is of great public importance. Its importance emanates from the central role accorded to the Opposition in a Parliamentary democracy. The role of the Leader of the Opposition (whether in Lok Sabha or in Rajya Sabha), in fact, is more difficult as he has to criticize, find fault, and present alternative proposals/policies with no power to implement them. He has, thus, to perform a special responsibility to the Parliament and to the nation. In Rajya Sabha until 1969, there was no Leader of the Opposition in the real sense of the term. Till then, the practice was to call the Leader of the party in Opposition having the largest number of the members as the Leader of the Opposition, without according him any formal recognition, status, or privilege. The office of Leader of the Opposition was given official recognition through the Salary and Allowances of Leaders of the Opposition in Parliament Act, 1977. This Act defines the Leader of the Opposition in Rajya Sabha, as a member of the Council of States who is, for the time being, the Leader in that House of the party in Opposition to the Government constituting the greatest numerical strength and recognized as such by the Chairman of the Council of States. Thus, the Leader of the Opposition should satisfy three conditions, namely, (i) he should be a member of the House (ii) the Leader in Rajya Sabha of the party in Opposition to the Government having the greatest numerical strength, and (iii) be recognized as such by the Chairman, Rajya Sabha.

Leader of the House (Lok Sabha)

The Prime Minister, who is the Leader of the majority party in the Lok Sabha, functions as the Leader of the House in the Lok Sabha, except when he is not a member of the Lok Sabha. The Leader of the House is an important Parliamentary functionary and exercises direct influence on the course of business. The whole policy of the Government, especially insofar as it is expressed in the inner life of the House and in measures dealing with the course of its business, is concentrated in her/his person. The arrangement of Government business is the ultimate responsibility of the Leader of the House. He makes proposals for the dates of summoning and prorogation of the House for the approval of the Speaker. She/he has to draw up the programme of official business to be transacted in a session of Parliament. Besides, he deals with procedural matters relating to the business of the House and advices the House in case any difficulty arises. The Leader of the House is not mentioned in the Constitution. However, it is mentioned in the Rules of the Lok Sabha.

Leader of the Opposition in Lok Sabha

In 1969, for the first time since independence, the Lok Sabha had a recognised Opposition party and a Leader of the Opposition. Similarly, in the Rajya Sabha also, until 1969, there was no Leader of the Opposition in the real and accepted sense of that expression. The Leaders of the Opposition in the Rajya Sabha and the Lok Sabha are now accorded statutory recognition and given salary and certain other facilities and amenities under the Salary and Allowances of Leaders of Opposition in Parliament Act, 1977.

Until 1977, there were no emoluments and perks attached to the position of Leader of the Opposition. There is no provision in the Constitution or even in the Lok Sabha Rules of Procedure in regard to the recognition of the Leader of Opposition. Right from the first Lok Sabha, the practice has been to recognise the leader of the largest party in Opposition as the Leader of Opposition, provided that party has a strength that is enough to constitute the quorum for a sitting of the House (in other words, one-tenth of the total membership of the House) — at present that comes to 55 members. From the 9th to the 15th Lok Sabha, since the requirement of having a minimum strength of 55 members was fulfilled, the Lok Sabha had duly recognised the Leader of the Opposition.

The 1977 Act defines the Leader of the Opposition as that member of the House who is the "Leader in that House of the party in opposition to the Government having the greatest numerical strength and recognised as such by the Chairman of the Council of States or the Speaker of the House of the People, as the case may be."

However, The Speaker's decisions in this regard have so far been determined by "Directions by the Speaker Lok Sabha[12] - 121(1)(c)" which laid down one of the conditions for recognition of party or group as having "at least a strength equal to the quorum fixed to constitute a sitting of the House, that is one-tenth of the total number of members of the House". The Leaders and Chief Whips of Recognised Parties and Groups in Parliament (Facilities) Act, 1998 also refers to a recognised party in the Lok Sabha as a party that has not less than 55 members.

It's the Speaker discretion to recognize the Leader of Opposition. Since there is no constitutional provision and the 1977 Act does not provide for the requirement of 55 members as an essential prerequisite, it all depends on the Speaker's directions and discretion.

Thus, the Leader of the Opposition is one of the key Parliamentary functionaries whose role, though not defined in any rule, is of very great importance in the functioning of a Legislature.

In the British Parliament, the Leader of the Opposition is referred to as the 'Shadow Prime Minister', so called because he or she is always in a state of readiness to take over the government if the incumbent government falls. There, the Leader of the Opposition forms a Shadow Cabinet too. Thus, the role of this Parliamentary functionary under the Westminster tradition is not only to oppose and criticise the government, but also to take the responsibility of forming an alternate government, should it become possible to do so in the event of the fall of the existing one.

Whip

In the Parliamentary form of Government, a party has its own internal organisation inside Parliament and is served by a number of officials known as the whips, chosen from members of the party itself. The main function of the Whips is to keep members of their party within sound of the Division Bell whenever any important business is under consideration in the House. During sessions, the Whips of different parties send to their supporters' periodic notices, also sometimes called 'Whips', apprising them when important Divisions are expected, telling them the hour when a vote will probably take place, and requesting them to be in attendance at that time.

Realising the vital role played by the Chief Whips and leaders of parties and groups in Parliament as important party functionaries, an Act, namely the "Leaders and Chief Whips of Recognised Parties and Groups in Parliament (Facilities) Act, 1998 has been enacted. The Act, inter alia, provides additional secretarial assistance and telephone facilities to the Leaders and Chief Whips.

Government Chief Whip

The Chief Whip of the Government Party in the Lok Sabha is the Minister of Parliamentary Affairs. In the Rajya Sabha, the Minister of State for Parliamentary Affairs holds this position. The Chief Whip is directly responsible to the Leader of the House. It is part of his duties to advise the Government on Parliamentary business affecting their departments. The Chief Whip is assisted by one or two Ministers of State and at times by the Deputy Minster also.

---

[12]In pursuance of the provisions of Rule 389 and other rules of the Rules of Procedure and Conduct of Business in Lok Sabha, the Speaker of Lok Sabha has been issuing Directions from time to time for regulating, subject to the provisions of the rules, certain matters not specifically provided for in the rules and also certain matters relating to the detailed working of the rules under the inherent powers of the Speaker.

12.1 SESSIONS AND PARLIAMENTARY PROCEDURES

INTRODUCTION

The term of the Lok Sabha is five years. Dissolution of the Lok Sabha may be effected before the expiry of its term by an order made by the President. At the end of its term, Lok Sabha stands automatically dissolved even if no formal order of dissolution is issued by the President. Whereas, the Rajya Sabha is a permanent House which is not subject to dissolution. In other words, while the Rajya Sabha is a continuing body, the power to dissolve the Lok Sabha vests in the President.

SUMMONING OF THE PARLIAMENT

A session of the House comprises the period commencing from the date and time mentioned in the order of the President summoning the Houses and ending with the day on which the President prorogues the Houses. In the case of Lok Sabha, the session of the House can end either on prorogation or on dissolution.

In other words, the Constitution provides that the President shall from time to time summon each House of Parliament to meet at such time and place as he thinks fit, but six months shall not intervene between its last sitting in one session and the date appointed for its first sitting in the next session. The President may from time to time prorogue the Houses or either House. A session of the Rajya Sabha commences on the date and time mentioned in the Summoning Order of the President and ends with the day on which he prorogues the House. Thus, the maximum gap between two sessions should not be more than six months. A minimum of two sessions shall be conducted every year.

It is not necessary that the Lok Sabha and Rajya Sabha should be summoned and prorogued simultaneously or on the same dates. Until 1961, Sessions of the two Houses generally commenced on different dates, except for the first session of every year when the President addresses members of both the Houses assembled together. However, since 1962, generally both the Houses have been meeting simultaneously. This is a departure from the British practice, for in the UK, both the Houses are summoned, prorogued, and dissolved together, even though the House of Lords is a hereditary body and dissolution has no effect on its membership.

A session is the period of time between the meeting of a Parliament and its prorogation. During the course of a session, either House may adjourn to such date as it pleases. The period between the prorogation of Parliament and its reassembly in a new session is termed as a 'recess' while the period between the adjournment of either House and the resumption of its sitting is generally called an 'adjournment'.

Normally, three sessions of the Parliament are held in a year.

- Budget Session (February to May);
- Autumn Session (July to September);
- Winter Session (November to December);

The fixation of dates of summoning and prorogation of the two Houses of Parliament is one of the functions assigned to the Ministry of Parliamentary Affairs under the Government of India (Allocation of Business) Rules made by the President. After assessing the time likely to be required for transaction of Government business and for discussion on topics of public interest as may be demanded from time to time by the Members of Parliament, the Ministry of Parliamentary Affairs places a note before the Cabinet Committee on Parliamentary Affairs for making a recommendation as to the date of the commencement of a session of Parliament and its likely duration. The recommendation, if agreed to by the Prime Minister, is submitted by the Ministry of Parliamentary Affairs to the President for approval of the date(s) of the commencement of a session. The Summoning Order of the President is then published in the Gazette of India.

ADJOURNMENT & ADJOURNMENT *SINE DIE*

During the course of a session, the House may be adjourned from day to day or for more than a day by the Presiding Officer. In other words, Speaker/Chairman of the House is empowered to adjourn the House. Adjournment, as the term implies, is a postponement of the sitting or proceedings of either House from one time to another specified for the reassembling of the House. In other words, during the course of a session, the House may be adjourned from day to day or for more than a day. It may also be adjourned *sine die*. The adjournment of the House means the suspension of the sitting of the House till the following or some later day or hour of time. Adjournment sine die means termination of the sitting of the House without specifying or fixing any definite date for its next sitting.

The power to adjourn the House from time to time or sine die vests in the Presiding Officer. He does so at a fixed hour or at such other hour as he may determine after taking the sense of the House. The Presiding Officer may, if he thinks fit, call a sitting of the House before the date or hour to which it has been adjourned or at any time after the House has been adjourned sine die but before it is prorogued by the President.

PROROGATION OF THE HOUSE

Termination of a session of the House by an order made by the President under Article 85(2) is called 'prorogation'. The President, in exercising the power to prorogue the House, acts on the advice of the Prime Minister. The Prime Minister may consult the Cabinet before the advice is submitted to the President. Prorogation of the House may take place any time, even while the House is sitting. Usually, however, prorogation follows the adjournment of the sitting of the House sine die. The time gap between the declaration of adjournment sine die and its prorogation is generally two to four days, although there are instances when Lok Sabha was prorogued on the same day on which it was adjourned sine die. Thus, "Prorogation means the end of a session (not of a Parliament)". A prorogation terminates a session; an adjournment is an interruption in the course of a single session. A session is terminated only by prorogation and not by adjournment. The period between the prorogation of the House and its reassembly in a new session is also termed as "inter-session" period.

- **Procedure for Prorogation :** After the adjournment of Lok Sabha sine die, the Minister of Parliamentary Affairs (or the Leader of the House, as the case may be) sends a communication to the Secretary-General conveying the intention of the Prime Minister or the Cabinet to prorogue the House. The proposal of the Prime Minister, after being agreed to by the Speaker, is submitted to the President by the Secretary-General. After the President has made the order, it is notified in the Official Gazette.

- *On prorogation, a session of the House terminates. The prorogation affects different categories of business pending before the House as follows:*

(a) **Bills :** Article 107(3) of the Constitution expressly provides that a Bill pending in Parliament shall not lapse by reason of the prorogation of the House. This saving also covers Bills pending before a Select or Joint Committee of the House(s). Notices of intention to move for leave to introduce Bills also do not lapse on prorogation and no fresh notice is necessary in the next session for that purpose, except where any sanction or recommendation granted under the Constitution in respect of a Bill has ceased to be operative.

(b) **Motions and Resolutions :** On the prorogation, all pending notices, except those relating to introduction of Bills as mentioned above, lapse and fresh notices must be given for the next session. This covers notices of motions, calling attention, resolutions, amendments, etc. Motions and resolutions which have been moved and are not disposed in the session also lapse upon prorogation and are not taken up for further discussion in the next session unless a specific motion to that effect is moved and carried or the House agrees by consensus.

(c) **Business pending before Parliamentary Committees :** The Rules of Procedure specifically provide that any business pending before a Committee shall not lapse by reason only of the prorogation of the House and the Committee shall continue to function notwithstanding such prorogation.

DISSOLUTION OF THE HOUSE

The end of the life of Lok Sabha either by an order made by the President under Article 85(2)(b) or on the expiration of the period of five years from the date appointed for its first meeting is termed as 'dissolution of the House'. Once a Legislature is duly constituted, it becomes capable of dissolution though it begins to function only after it has been summoned to meet. Dissolution puts an end to the representative character of the individuals who at the time compose the Lok Sabha. Once dissolved, the Lok Sabha cannot assemble again until after a general election. Rajya Sabha is not subject to dissolution, as also a Legislative Council where the State Legislature is bicameral. The power to dissolve Lok Sabha is vested in the President and he exercises this power on the advice of the Prime Minister. The Prime Minister may consult the Cabinet or inform it of his intention to make a recommendation to the President. The power to advise the President to dissolve the Lok Sabha is a potent weapon in the hands of the Prime Minister to keep his party intact and acts as a deterrent against its break-up.

Effects of Dissolution of Lok Sabha

Once the House has been dissolved, the dissolution is irrevocable. There is no power vested in the President to cancel his order of dissolution and revive the previous House. The consequences of a dissolution are absolute and irrevocable. In Lok Sabha, which alone is subject to dissolution under the Constitution, dissolution "passes a sponge over the Parliamentary slate". All business pending before it or any of its Committees lapses on dissolution. No part of the records of the dissolved House can be carried over and transcribed into the records or registers of the new House. In short, dissolution draws the final curtain upon the existing House.

The Rajya Sabha is not subject to dissolution unlike the Lok Sabha, which alone is subject to dissolution under the Constitution. All business pending before the Lok Sabha House lapses on its dissolution. However, the dissolution of the Lok Sabha affects the business pending before the Rajya Sabha to a certain extent.

The position as to the effect of dissolution upon different categories of business may be stated as follows:

(a) **Bills :** Article 107 lays down the effect of dissolution upon Bills before each House of Parliament in the event of dissolution of Lok Sabha. The present position of the effect of dissolution upon the pending Bills is that — In Lok Sabha, all Bills pending at the time of dissolution, whether originating in the House or transmitted to it by Rajya Sabha, lapse; and In Rajya Sabha, Bills passed by Lok Sabha, but which have not been disposed of and are pending in Rajya Sabha on the date of dissolution, lapse. Only the Bills originating in Rajya Sabha which have not been passed by Lok Sabha but are still pending before Rajya Sabha, do not lapse. If, however, in respect of a Bill upon which the Houses have disagreed and the President has notified his intention of summoning a Joint Sitting of the Houses for the consideration of the Bill prior to dissolution, that Bill does not lapse and may be passed at a Joint Sitting of both Houses, notwithstanding that dissolution has intervened since the President notified his intention to summon the Joint Sitting of the Houses. In short, the effects on the legislative business can be summarized as follows –

- Bills originating in the Rajya Sabha which are still pending in that House do not lapse on the dissolution of the Lok Sabha.
- Bills originating in the Rajya Sabha which having been passed by that House and transmitted to the Lok Sabha and pending there lapse on the dissolution of the Lok Sabha.
- Bills originating in the Lok Sabha which having been passed by that House and transmitted to the Rajya Sabha and still pending there on the date of dissolution of the Lok Sabha, lapse.
- Bills originating in the Rajya Sabha and returned to that House by the Lok Sabha with amendments and still pending there on the date of its dissolution, lapse.
- A Bill upon which the Houses have disagreed and the President has notified his intention to summon a Joint Sitting of the Houses to consider the Bill prior to dissolution does not lapse on the dissolution of the Lok Sabha.
- A Bill passed by the two Houses of Parliament and sent to the President for assent does not lapse on the dissolution of the Lok Sabha.
- A Bill returned by the President to the Rajya Sabha for reconsideration of the Houses does not lapse if the dissolution of the Lok Sabha takes place without the Houses having reconsidered the Bill.

(b) **Other Business, e.g. Motions, Resolutions, etc. :** All other business pending in Lok Sabha, e.g., motions, resolutions, amendments, supplementary demands for grants, etc., at whatever stage, lapses upon dissolution, as also the petitions presented to the House which stand referred to the Committee on Petitions. A motion for approval or modification of statutory rules laid on the Table of both Houses under the provisions of an Act, passed by Lok Sabha and transmitted to Rajya Sabha for concurrence and vice versa also lapses on dissolution of the Lok Sabha. A motion given in pursuance of Section 3(1) of Judges (Inquiry) Act, 1968 for presenting an address to the President praying for removal of a Judge, if admitted, will not lapse on the dissolution of the Lok Sabha . Anything said or done during the "existence" of a House, "cannot be raised as a privilege issue" after that House has been dissolved.

(c) **Business before Committee :** All business pending before Parliamentary Committees of Lok Sabha lapse upon dissolution of Lok Sabha. Committees themselves stand dissolved on dissolution of the Lok Sabha. However, a Committee which is unable to complete its work before the dissolution of the House may report to the House to that effect, in which case any preliminary memorandum or note that the Committee may have prepared or any evidence that it may have taken is made available to the new Committee when appointed.

(d) **Assurances by Ministers :** The assurances given by Ministers on the floor of the House, which are pending for implementation are deemed not to lapse on the dissolution of the Lok Sabha, irrespective of whether a report to that effect has been made by the Committee on Government Assurances.

LAME DUCK SESSION

This session is held when a new Parliament has been elected but the old Parliament meets for the last time before it is dissolved. The lame ducks are the members of the Parliament who have not got re-elected.

YOUTH PARLIAMENT

In order to develop democratic ethos in the younger generation, the Ministry of Parliamentary Affairs conducts Youth Parliament Competitions in various categories of schools and colleges/universities. The Youth Parliament is a programme in which group discussion and role-playing techniques can be effectively used. Citizenship is not a subject; it is a way of living. Therefore, its learning demands appropriate practice in the living of it. Youth Parliament can impart some real citizenship education. *Thus, the purposes of Youth Parliament are as follows:*

1. To make students understand the Parliamentary procedure.
2. To develop in students an insight into the working of the Parliament.
3. To make students consider public issues and form their opinion on them.
4. To train students in the technique of group discussion.
5. To develop in students an ability to arrive at a decision after group discussion.
6. To develop in them respect and tolerance for the views of others.
7. To develop in them an understanding that respect for rules is essential for conducting any discussion systematically and effectively.
8. To train students in group behaviour.
9. To make students aware of various problems facing our society and the country.
10. To develop in students the quality of leadership.
11. To make students understand the common man's point of view and express it in an articulated manner.

PARLIAMENTARY SESSIONS

Quorum

The minimum number of members required to be present at a sitting of the House or the Committee for valid transaction of its business is called quorum. The quorum to constitute a sitting of the House is one-tenth of the total number of members of the House and in respect of a Committee, it is one-third of the total number of members of the Committee. Article 100 of the Constitution requires that at least one-tenth of the total members of the House be present in order to conduct business, and that it shall be the duty of the Speaker of the House to adjourn or suspend the meeting until a quorum is reached.

Languages to be Used by Members in the House

Under Article 120 of the Constitution, the business of the House is transacted in Hindi or English, but Members who cannot adequately express themselves in these two languages can, with the permission of the Speaker, address the House in any of the languages mentioned in the Eighth Schedule to the Constitution. Such a member should soon after taking the allotted seat in the House, inform the Speaker about it in writing. On each occasion, before speaking in the House, at least half-an-hour in advance, a member should furnish a notice to the Officer at the Table or the Parliamentary Notice Office, mentioning the language in which and the business during which the speech would be made. On receipt of such notice, arrangements will be made to interpret simultaneously the speech in English and Hindi.

Question Hour[1]

Generally, the first hour of a sitting of Lok Sabha is devoted to the Questions and this hour is called the Question Hour. It has a special significance in the proceedings of the Parliament. Asking of questions is an inherent and unfettered Parliamentary right of members. It is during the Question Hour that the members can ask questions on every aspect of administration and Governmental activity. Government policies in national as well as international spheres come into sharp focus as the members try to elicit pertinent information during the Question Hour. It is through questions in the Parliament that the Government remains in touch with the people in as much as members are enabled thereby to ventilate the grievances of the public in matters concerning the administration. Questions enable Ministries to gauge the popular reaction to their policy and administration. Questions bring to the notice of the Ministers many loopholes which otherwise would have gone unnoticed. Sometimes, questions may lead to the appointment of a Commission, a Court of Enquiry, or even Legislation when matters raised by Members are grave enough to agitate the public mind and are of wide public importance.

Members have a right to ask questions to elicit information on matters of public importance within the special cognizance of the Ministers concerned. The questions are of four types: —

i. **Starred Questions :** A Starred Question is one to which a member desires an oral answer from the Minister in the House and is required to be distinguished by him/her with an asterisk. Answer to such a question may be followed by supplementary questions by members.

---

[1]Rule 32 of the "Rules of Procedure and Conduct of Business in Lok Sabha" provides that unless the Speaker otherwise directs, the first hour of every sitting of the House shall be available for the asking and answering of Questions. Thus, it is taken up from 1100 hrs to 1200 hrs in every sitting. Normally, there is no Question Hour during the first Session of the new Lok Sabha and also on the day when the President addresses both Houses assembled together or on the day when General Budget is presented in Lok Sabha and on the sittings held during the extended period of session or on Saturdays/Sundays and Holidays.

ii. **Unstarred Questions :** An Unstarred Question is one to which written answer is desired by the member and is deemed to be laid on the Table of the House by the Minister. Thus, it is not called for oral answer in the House and no supplementary question can be asked thereon.

iii. **Short Notice Questions :** A member may give a notice of question on a matter of public importance and of urgent character for oral answer at a notice less than 10 days prescribed as the minimum period of notice for asking a question in ordinary course. Such a question is known as 'Short Notice Question'.

iv. **Questions to Private Members :** A Question may also be addressed to a Private Member[2], provided that the subject matter of the question relates to some Bill, Resolution, or other matter connected with the business of the House for which that Member is responsible. The procedure in regard to such questions is same as that followed in the case of questions addressed to a Minister with such variations as the Speaker may consider necessary.

Zero Hour

The time immediately following the Question Hour and laying of papers and before any listed business is taken up in the House has come to be popularly known as the `Zero Hour'. As it starts around 12 noon, this period is euphemistically termed as `Zero Hour'. For raising matters during the 'Zero_Hour' in Lok Sabha, Members give notice between 8.30 a.m. and 9.00 a.m. every day to the Speaker stating clearly the subject which they consider to be important and wish to raise in the House. It is, of course, for the Speaker to allow or not to allow for raising such matters in the House. While Question Hour is strictly regulated, Zero Hour is an Indian Parliamentary innovation. The phrase does not find mention in the rules of procedure but has been in existence since 1962.

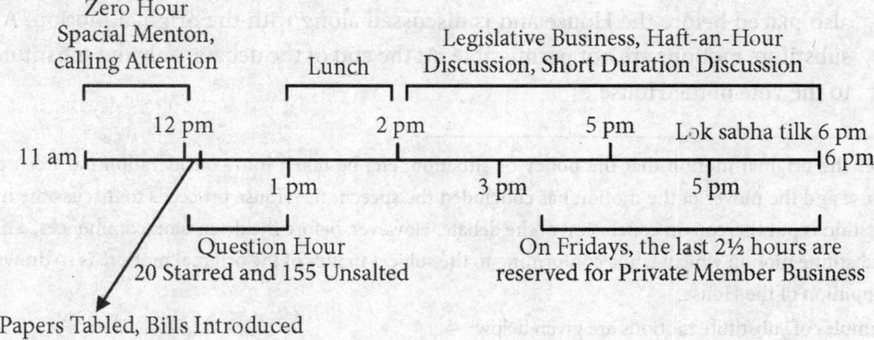

Motions

The House will not consider any matter except on a motion made to that effect. A motion has been defined as a proposal submitted to the House for its consideration and decision. "A motion is simply an expression of the opinion or the will of the Member of the House which he puts before the House so that the House will express the opinion or the will of the whole House". A matter requiring the decision of the House is decided by means of a question put by the Speaker on a motion made by a member. The term 'motion' in its wide sense means any proposal made for the purpose of eliciting a decision of the House. In order to ascertain the will of the House in regard to a matter before it, every question to be decided by the House must be proposed by a member in the form of a motion. Every matter is determined in

[2]Under Rule 40 of the Rules of Procedure and Conduct of Business in Lok Sabha.

the House by means of a question put from the Chair on motion made by a member and resolved in the affirmative or negative, as the case may be.

A debate on a motion passes through the following four stages:

(a) moving the motion;

(b) proposing the question by the Speaker;

(c) the debate or discussion where permissible; and

(d) the vote of decision of the House after the Speaker has put the question. A member shall not speak after the Speaker has collected the voices of Ayes and Noes on the Question.

However, there are certain motions which per se are not put to vote of the House.

All motions moved in the House are classified into three broad categories namely 'Substantive', 'Substitute' and 'Subsidiary' Motions which are defined in the succeeding paragraphs.

(a) **Substantive Motions :** A substantive motion is a self-contained, independent proposal submitted for the approval of the House and drafted in such a way as to be capable of expressing a decision of the House. Example of a substantive motion is: – "That this House expresses its confidence in the Council of Ministers."

(b) **Substitute Motions :** Motions moved in substitution of the original motion for taking into consideration a policy or situation or statement or any other matter are called substitute motions. Such motions, though drafted in such a way as to be capable of expressing an opinion by themselves are not, strictly speaking, substantive motions in as much as they depend upon the original motion[3]. The substitute motion, being in the nature of an amendment to the original motion, is also placed before the House and is discussed along with the original motion. Amendments to substitute motions are not permissible. At the end of the debate, only the substitute motion is put to the vote of the House[4].

---

[3]After the original motion that the policy or situation, etc. be taken into consideration has been placed before the House and the mover of the motion has concluded the speech, the House proceeds to discuss the matter. No further question is put thereon on conclusion of the debate. However, before the discussion commences, a member can move a substitute motion which, while conforming to the subject matter of the original motion, is so drawn up as to express an opinion of the House.

[4]Examples of substitute motions are given below: —

During first session, Tenth Lok Sabha, a government motion namely 'That this House do consider the present international situation' given notice of by Shri Eduardo Faleiro, Minister of State for External Affairs was admitted and listed for discussion in the House on 18 September, 1991.

The following substitute motions giving notices of by the members to the original motion were admitted:—

Shri Jaswant Singh

(1) "This House, having considered the present international situation, do find the conduct of foreign policy by the Government of India as unsatisfactory, particularly in respect of: —

(a) meeting the challenge of rapidly transforming international scene;

(b) ineffective response to events preceding and following the Gulf War;

(c) response to the coup in USSR and its subsequent overturning by the democratic forces in that country; and

(d) inability to counter Pakistan's interference in our internal affairs."

(c) **Subsidiary Motions :** They depend upon or relate to other motion or follow upon some proceedings in the House. They by themselves have no meaning and are not capable of stating the decision of the House without reference to the original motion or proceedings of the House.

Subsidiary motions can be further divided into: —

- Ancillary Motions;
- Superseding Motions; and
- Amendments.

i. **Ancillary Motions :** These are motions which are recognised by the practice of the House as the regular way of proceedings with various kinds of business. Examples of ancillary motions are:

(b) That the Bill be taken into consideration.

(c) That the Bill be passed.

ii. **Superseding Motions :** These are motions which, though independent in form, are moved in the course of debate on another question and seek to supersede that question. In this class fall all motions of dilatory character. The following are superseding motions in relation to the motion for taking into consideration a Bill:

(a) That the Bill be re-committed to a Select Committee.

(b) That the Bill be re-committed to a Joint Committee of the Houses.

(c) That the Bill be circulated for eliciting further opinion thereon.

(d) That consideration of the Bill or the debate on the Bill be adjourned sine-die or to some future date.

Where the Speaker is of the opinion that the superseding motion is of a dilatory character in as much as no unforeseen or new circumstance has arisen to warrant recirculation or recommittal of the Bill, the Speaker is empowered to put the question upon it forthwith or even decline to propose the question. However, when a superseding motion is moved and the Speaker does not hold it to be dilatory, the motion is proposed as a new question superseding the original question and has to be disposed of before the debate upon the original question can be resumed. But the debate upon such a motion must be strictly relevant to the reasons in support of the motion.

iii. **Amendments :** These are subsidiary motions which interpose a new process of question and decision between the main question and its decision. Amendments maybe to the clauses of a Bill, to a resolution or to a motion, or to an amendment to a clause of a Bill, resolution, or motion.

Shri E. Ahmed

(2) "This House, having considered the present international situation, recommends to Government to take immediate necessary steps to realise adequate compensation to those Indian nationals who had to flee to India from Kuwait and Iraq in the face of Gulf War." However, after Minister had replied to the discussion, the members withdrew their substitute motions by leave of the House.

Closure Motion

In order to bring a debate to a close, a member may rise and move "That the question be now put". The acceptance of a closure motion lies within the discretion of the Speaker. Before he accepts it, he considers whether the question before the House has received adequate debate or not, whether or not the views of the Opposition have been adequately expressed before the House. The discretion that the Speaker exercises in the matter of accepting a proposal for closure or in refusing it is entirely absolute and is not open to debate. No debate is allowed on a closure motion. When a closure has been moved and carried, it is not considered to be in order to reflect upon the moving of the closure. Neither time nor motive of closure can be discussed. The effect of a closure is that the original question is put forthwith and decided without further amendment or debate, save as otherwise provided in the rules.

(a) Simple Closure: It is one when a member moves that the 'matter has been sufficiently discussed be now put to vote.

(b) Closure by Compartments: In this case, the clauses of a bill or a lengthy resolution are grouped into parts before the commencement of the debate. The debate covers the part as a whole and the entire part is put to vote.

(c) Kangaroo Closure: Under this type, only important clauses are taken up for debate and voting and the intervening clauses are skipped over and taken as passed.

(d) Guillotine Closure: It is one when the undiscussed clauses of a bill or a resolution are also put to vote along with the discussed ones due to wanting of time (as the time allotted for the discussion is over).

Motion of Thanks on President's Address

It is a formal motion moved in the House expressing its gratitude for the address delivered by the President under Article 87(1) of the Constitution to both Houses of Parliament assembled together. It provides an opportunity for the discussion of the matters referred to the address. In other words, the Constitution provides for an address by the President to both Houses of Parliament assembled together after each general election and before the start of the first session every year. The address is drafted by the government and contains its broad policy plans and legislative agenda for the year. After the address, each House of Parliament discusses the Motion of Thanks, and the Prime Minister responds. Any other Minister may, at his discretion, intervene to explain the Government's point of view on matters concerning his Ministry/Department. The Motion of Thanks is then put to vote of the House. In the motion of thanks, MPs may move amendments to the motion, which are put to vote. If the vote to Motion of Thanks fails or if an amendment to the President's Address is voted successfully, then it is treated as a Vote of No-confidence against the government.

Motions of Confidence & No-Confidence[5]

Collective Responsibility in a Parliamentary system implies that the Council of Ministers is always accountable to the Parliament. For governance, and also for providing legitimacy to its authority, the Executive must, at all times, enjoy the confidence of the House. Article 75 of the Constitution of India

[5] *Cabinet Responsibility to Legislature*, by GC Malhotra, Lok Sabha Secretariat.

provides for the Collective Ministerial Responsibility to the Lok Sabha. The Council of Ministers has to demonstrate its majority support, whenever required, either by winning a Confidence Motion or by defeating a Motion of No-confidence.

(a) ***No-Confidence Motion***[6] **:** A motion of No confidence can be moved against the Council of Ministers. Rule 198 of the Rules of Procedure and Conduct of Business in Lok Sabha lays down the procedure for moving a Motion of No-Confidence in the Council of Ministers. The usual format of such a motion is that "this House expresses its want of confidence in the Council of Ministers". A Motion of No-confidence need not set out any grounds on which it is based. Even when grounds are mentioned in the notice and read out in the House, they do not form part of the No-confidence Motion. Moreover, a motion expressing want of confidence in an individual Minister is not allowed. Under the Rules, only a motion expressing want of confidence in the Council of Ministers as a body is admissible.

A No confidence motion is moved by an MP if according to him/her, the government's activities have not been satisfactory and resignation of the government is demanded. The Speaker will ask MPs who support the motion to rise at their seats, and the leave is granted if at least 50 MPs do so. The motion is then taken up for discussion within ten days from the date of the grant of leave. At the end of such a debate, the motion is put to vote. If the motion is adopted, the government has to resign.

(b) ***Motion of Confidence*** **:** There is no specific rule in the Rules of Procedure relating to the Motions of Confidence in the Council of Ministers. When the rules of the Lok Sabha were framed, motions seeking confidence of the House in the Council of Ministers, to be moved by the Prime Minister at the direction of the President, were perhaps not visualised. The necessity of raising debate through such a motion, which is in the nature of an exercise of demonstrating majority support in the Lok Sabha, arose in the late seventies with the advent of minority Governments caused by split in parties and later formation of coalition Governments as a result of hung Parliaments. In the absence of any specific rule in this regard, such Motions of Confidence have been entertained under the category of motions stipulated in Rule 184 which are meant for raising discussions on matters of public interest. In the case of a Confidence Motion, there is no requirement for seeking leave of the House. The one-line notice of a motion under Rule 184 that "this House expresses its confidence in the Council of Ministers" is given on a Presidential direction. When admitted by the Speaker, it is bulletined. The date and time for its discussion is then fixed in consultation with the Business Advisory Committee. If the Motion of Confidence is voted successfully, then the government will continue in power. But if the confidence motion is negatived, then the Council of Ministers have to resign. In other words, the Government of the day can prove its majority in the House by moving a Motion of Confidence and winning the confidence of the House. The Opposition Parties can move a No-confidence Motion in the Council of Ministers to express the want of confidence of the House and if such motion is carried, the Council of Ministers has to resign.

---

[6]In the 16th Lok Sabha, a no-confidence motion was moved against the government in the Monsoon Session of 2018. The motion was defeated. It was the 27th No-confidence motion since 1952.

Calling Attention Motion[7]

A member may, with the prior permission of the Speaker/Chairman, call the attention of a Minister to a matter of urgent public importance and request him to make a statement thereon. This is a purely India innovation fulfilling the needs felt by members to bring to the notice of the House the matters of urgent public importance without taking recourse to an Adjournment Motion. The test of admissibility decided by the Speaker is urgency and public importance of the subject matter. The Minister may make a brief statement immediately or ask for time to make a statement at a later date. There shall be no debate on such a statement at the time it is made. After the statement, brief clarifications can be sought from the Minister by the Member who has initiated the Calling Attention and other Members whose names appear in the List of Business are called by the Speaker. Only those matters which are primarily the concern of the Union Government can be raised through a Calling Attention notice. The Calling Attention matter is not subject to the vote of the House.

Adjournment Motion

Adjournment Motion is the procedure for adjournment of the business of the House for the purpose of discussing a definite matter of urgent public importance, which can be moved with the consent of the Speaker. The Adjournment Motion, if admitted, leads to setting aside of the normal business of the House for discussing the matter mentioned in the motion. To be in order, an adjournment motion must raise a matter of sufficient public importance to warrant interruption of normal business of the House and the question of public importance is decided on merit in each individual case. The purpose of an Adjournment Motion is to take the Government to task for a recent act of omission or commission having serious consequences. The adoption of an adjournment motion is seen as a censure of the government, although there is no compulsion on the government to resign. Its adoption is regarded as a sort of censure of the Government. Since, it involves censure against the government, it can be introduced only in Lok Sabha. The subject-matter of an Adjournment Motion must relate to the conduct of the Government and must be in the nature of criticism of Governmental action either of omission or commission. An Adjournment Motion is not admissible unless there is a failure on the part of the Government to perform the duties enjoined by the Constitution and the law. An Adjournment Motion can also not be moved on matters where a Minister exercises discretionary powers conferred upon him by a Statute. The normal business of the House is set aside whenever an Adjournment Motion is taken up for discussion In the House and till such time as its disposal.

Some of the grounds on which the Speaker may disallow adjournment Motions are briefly listed as under:

- It does not relate to definite matter;
- It does not relate to a matter urgent enough to warrant interruption of the business of the day;
- It does not relate to a matter of sufficient public importance;
- It does not relate to a matter of recent occurrence which has arisen suddenly but relates to a continuing matter;
- It is not a matter for adjournment motion; other opportunities can be availed of to raise the matter;
- It raises more than one issue;

[7]Lok Sabha Rules – Rule 197; Rajya Sabha Rules – Rule 180.

- It relates to a matter which is likely to be debated in the near future/discussion on which has already been discussed;
- It relates to a matter which is subjudice, in other words, which is under adjudication by a court of law;
- It relates to a State subject;
- It raises a question of privilege;
- It raises a matter entailing legislation;
- It relates to conduct of a foreign Government;
- It relates to an individual case;
- It relates to the affairs of an autonomous corporation/body;
- It relates to unsatisfactory reply given to a question or refusal by Government.

Notice of an adjournment motion is required to be given before 10 am on the day on which the motion is proposed. At least the support of 50 members is required to be admitted. If the adjournment motion is accepted, the House adjourns after voting. The adoption of an adjournment motion is seen as a censure of the government, although there is no compulsion on the government to resign. The debate on adjournment motion should last for not less than two hours and thirty minutes.

Censure Motion

A censure literally means expression of strong disapproval or harsh criticism. It can be a stern rebuke by a Legislature, generally opposition against the policies of Government or an individual minister. However, it can also be passed to criticize or condemn some act. Both censure motion and no-confidence motion can be moved in Lok Sabha or lower House in States. It is pertinent in this context to observe that there is a difference between a motion of No confidence and a censure motion. While it is necessary in the case of a censure motion to set out the ground or charge on which it is based, a motion of No confidence need not set out a ground or charge. A vote of censure presupposes that the persons censured have been guilty of some impropriety or lapse by act or omission. It may, therefore, become necessary to specify the impropriety or lapse while moving a vote of censure. No such consideration arises when a motion of No confidence is moved. Although a ground may be mentioned when passing a motion of No confidence, the existence of a ground is not a prerequisite of a motion of No confidence. There is no legal bar to the passing of a motion of No confidence against an authority in the absence of any charge of impropriety or lapse on the part of that authority. The essential connotation of a No confidence motion is that the party against whom such motion is passed has ceased to enjoy the confidence of the requisite majority of members. Moreover, while censure motion can be moved against individual ministers or members, No confidence motion is moved against the entire Council of Ministers. Finally, there is no impact on the government when a censure motion is passed, but the Council of Ministers have to resign and government collapses when a no-confidence motion is passed.

No-Day-Yet-Named Motion

If the Speaker/Chairman admits a notice of a motion and no day is fixed for its discussion, it is called a 'No-Day-Yet-Named Motion'. All such admitted motions are placed from time to time before the Business Advisory Committee which selects the motions according to the urgency and importance of the subject matter thereof and recommends time for discussion of the same.

Dilatory Tactics And Motions

Dilatory tactics or motions are those tactics used to delay or obstruct business, annoy the deliberative assembly, or, in legislative procedure, to delay consideration of a subject. Unlike using motions for strategic purposes, using them for dilatory purposes is not allowed. Reasonableness is often used as a criterion in deciding whether a motion is dilatory. A motion for the adjournment of the debate or a motion to retard or delay the progress of the business under consideration of the House is known as dilatory motion. (For instance, at any time after a motion has been made, a member may move that the debate on the motion be adjourned. The debate on a dilatory motion must be restricted to the matter of such motion). If the Chairman/Speaker is of opinion that such a motion is an abuse of the Rules of the House, he may either forthwith put the question thereon from the Chair or decline to propose the question.

Point of Order[8]

A point of order is an extraordinary process which, when raised, has the effect of suspending the proceedings before the House. This is meant to assist the Speaker in enforcing the Rules, Directions, and provisions of the Constitution for regulating the business of the House. It should essentially refer to procedure and relate to the business before the House at the moment. Also, it should relate to arrangement of items already included in the List of Business for the day. The test whether a point raised is a point of order or not is based on the fact whether it involves an interpretation of the Rules, Directions, and various provisions of the Constitution which regulate the business of the House and whether it raises a point which the Chair can decide. In other words, a member can raise a point of order when the proceedings of the House do not follow the rules, procedures, or provisions of the constitution. A point of order is not a point of privilege. Further, a member should not seek to have a clarification from a Minister in the garb of a point of order. A point of order cannot be raised:

(a) when a question on any motion is being put to the House; and

(b) during Question Hour.

Moreover, a point of order cannot be raised by a member -

- on rulings given by the Speaker; or
- regarding proceedings of an earlier sitting; or
- to ask for information; or
- to explain one's own position; or
- in academic or hypothetical matter; or
- to point out that Division Bells did not ring or were not heard; or
- on a matter on which the Speaker cannot give any relief; or
- for inserting new or additional item in the List of Business; or
- when a question on any motion is being put to the House.

---

[8] A member who has a point of order should stand up and say 'Point of Order'. She/he should not proceed to formulate it or speak on her/his point of order until the member is identified by the Chair. While formulating her/his point of order, the member should quote the specific rule or the provision of the Constitution relating to the procedure of the House which may have been ignored or neglected or violated. While raising a point of order, a member should not make a speech but come directly to the point of order. A point of order relating to the same matter may not be raised by a member more than once. Further, only one point of order may be raised at a time. There may not be a point of order on a point of order. The decision of the Speaker as to whether a point raised is a point of order or not is final. No debate is allowed on a point of order.

Discussions (Short Duration And Half-An-Hour) :

(a) **Short Duration**[9]**:** In order to provide opportunities to members to discuss matters of urgent public importance, a convention was established in Lok Sabha in March 1953 whereby members could raise discussion for short duration without a formal motion or vote thereon. This procedure was incorporated later into the 'Rules of Procedure and Conduct of Business in Lok Sabha[10] and Rajya Sabha[11]' as 'Short Duration Discussion'. The member who raises the discussion has no right of reply. At the end of the discussion, the Minister concerned gives a brief reply. Notice for raising such a discussion was to be given to the Speaker who would allot time. They can be asked with less than 10 days' notice, with reasons for the short notice. Like starred questions, they are answered orally followed by supplementary questions. These are admitted at the discretion of the Speaker, with the consent of the concerned Minister. The Speaker may allot two sittings in a week during which such matters maybe taken up for discussion and allow such time for discussion not exceeding two hours at or before the end of the sitting, as he may consider appropriate in the circumstances.

(b) **Half-an-Hour Discussion :** Another instrument available to the Members of Lok Sabha for raising issue of public importance is the Half-an-Hour Discussion. Under this, a Member may raise discussion on a matter of sufficient public importance which has been the subject of a recent question, Starred, Unstarred, or Short Notice Question and the answer to which needs further elucidation on a matter of fact. The procedure regarding Half-an-Hour Discussion is regulated by the 'Rules of Procedure and Conduct of Business'. Under this, a Member may give notice to raise a discussion on a matter of sufficient public importance and which has been the subject of a recent question, Starred, Unstarred, or Short Notice Question, and the answer to which needs further elucidation on a matter of fact. A notice is also required to be accompanied by an 'Explanatory Note' stating the reasons for raising the discussion and should also be signed. Normally, only one notice of Half-an-Hour Discussion is put down for a sitting and no formal motion is moved in the House nor does voting take place. The Member who has given notice makes a short statement. Thereafter, the Minister concerned replies briefly. Half-an-Hour Discussions are normally held on three sittings in a week namely, Monday, Wednesday, and Friday. Normally, Half-an-Hour Discussion is not held on the first sitting of the session. Further, normally the Half-an-Hour Discussion is not held till the passage of the Finance Bill by the House. As the name suggests, normally the discussion is for half an hour on the said days and is taken up during the last half an hour of the sitting.

Matters Raised Under Rule 377

Matters which cannot be raised under the rules relating to Questions, Calling Attention, Motions, or during Question Hour, short duration discussion, half-an-hour discussion, adjournment motion, or which is not a point of order can be raised by way of Special Mentions under Rule 377 in Lok Sabha (It is simply referred as "Special Mention" in Rajya Sabha). This procedural device, framed in 1954, provides opportunity to the Members to raise matters of general public interest. At present, the number of matters that can be raised by Members under Rule 377 on a single day is 30.

---

[9] This is a rarely used device; such questions have not been admitted even once in the last 10 years.

[10] Under Rule 193.

[11] Under Rule 176.

Privilege Motion

Parliamentary privileges are certain rights and immunities enjoyed by members of Parliament, individually and collectively, so that they can "effectively discharge their functions". When any of these rights and immunities are disregarded, the offence is called a breach of privilege and is punishable under law of Parliament. A notice is moved in the form of a motion by any member of either House against those being held guilty of breach of privilege. Each House also claims the right to punish as contempt actions which, while not breach of any specific privilege, are offences against its authority and dignity. A member may, with the consent of the Speaker or the Chairperson, raise a question involving a breach of privilege either of a member or of the House or of a Committee thereof. The rules however mandate that any notice should be relating to an incident of recent occurrence and should need the intervention of the House. The Speaker/Chair can decide on the privilege motion himself or herself or refer it to the Privileges Committee of Parliament[12]. A large number of notices are rejected, with penal action recommended in only a few. The most significant case was in 1978 when Indira Gandhi, who had just won the Lok Sabha elections from Chikmaglur, was expelled from the House. The then Home Minister Charan Singh moved a resolution of breach of privilege against her following observations made by the Justice Shah Commission which probed excesses during the Emergency.

Resolutions

Most of the business in Parliament is transacted by means of motions. After a matter has been discussed, the motion is put to the vote of the House, which is technically known as putting the question. "The decision which the putting of the question has thus elicited turns the motion into a resolution of order." Every question, when agreed to, becomes either an order or of a resolution of the House. By its resolutions, the House declares its own opinions and purposes. A member or a Minister may, subject to the Rules of Procedure, move a resolution relating to a matter of general public interest. A resolution or an amendment to resolution once moved by a member cannot be withdrawn, except with leave of the House. A Resolution may be in the form of -

- A declaration of opinion; or
- A recommendation; or
- It may be in the form so as to record either approval; or
- Disapproval by the House of an act or policy of the Government; or
- Convey a message; or
- Commend, urge, or request an action; or
- Call attention to a matter or situation for consideration by the Government;
- Or in such other form as the Speaker may consider appropriate.

Resolutions may be divided into the following categories:

(a) **Private Members' Resolution :** Resolutions which are moved by private members (members other than ministers) are termed as Private Members' Resolutions. The last two and a half hours

---

[12]In the Lok Sabha, the Speaker nominates a Committee of Privileges consisting of 15 members. A report is then presented to the House for its consideration. The Speaker may permit a half-hour debate while considering the report. The Speaker may then pass final orders or direct that the report be tabled before the House. A resolution may then be moved relating to the breach of privilege that has to be unanimously passed. In the Rajya Sabha, the Deputy Chairperson heads the Committee of Privileges, that consists of 10 members.

of a sitting on every alternate Friday in the session are allotted for the discussion of private members' resolutions.

(b) **Government Resolution :** A notice for a resolution given by a member of the Government, i.e., a Minister comes under the category of Government resolutions. Government resolutions can be taken up on any day allotted for Government business.

(c) **Statutory Resolution :** The notice of a Statutory Resolution is given in pursuance of a provision in the Constitution or an Act of Parliament. Such a Resolution, if adopted, is binding on the Government and has the force of law. Statutory Resolution can be moved either by a private member or a minister. There is no particular period for moving a statutory resolution unless the Constitution or the Act of Parliament under which it is tabled so prescribes.

(d) **Resolutions which are expression of opinion by the House :** Since the purpose of such a Resolution is merely to obtain an expression of opinion of the House, the Government is not bound to give effect to the opinions expressed in these Resolutions.

(e) **Resolutions which the House passes in the matter of control over its own proceedings :** It has the force of law and its validity cannot be challenged in any court of law. The House, by such a Resolution, evolves, sometimes, its own procedure to meet a situation not specifically provided for in the Rules.

Distinction Between a Motion and a Resolution[13]

All resolutions are substantive motions. However, all motions need not be of a substantive character that is to say, they may not require to be voted upon in the House. The difference between a resolution and a motion is more of a procedural nature than of content. Quite often both motion and resolution on the same subject are admitted with some slight change of form. The points of distinction between a motion and a resolution are, in short, as follows:

- While all resolutions are substantive motions, a motion need not necessarily be substantive.
- A substitute motion is not to be moved to a substantive motion. As such, a substitute motion is not moved to a resolution. On the other hand, substitute motions can be moved to a motion which is not substantive.
- All resolutions are put to vote. Whereas, all motions are not necessarily put to vote.

PARTICIPATION IN THE PROCEEDINGS OF THE HOUSE

Only a member of the House can participate in its proceedings. However, every Minister or the Attorney-General has a right to speak and otherwise take part in the proceedings of either House, a joint sitting of the two Houses, and any Parliamentary Committee of which he is appointed a member, without being entitled to vote. A right to vote in a House accrues only to its members. The idea underlying the above provision is that a Minister, though member of one House, can participate in the work of the other House without enjoying a right to vote. Further, in India, a person can remain a Minister for six months without being a member of any House. Such a Minister can participate without voting in the proceedings of the House of Parliament.

---

[13]Motions and Resolutions in Parliament; by Lok Sabha Secretariat Published under Rule 382 of the Rules of Procedure and Conduct of Business in Lok Sabha (Fourteenth Edition).

12.2 LEGISLATIVE PROCEDURE

INTRODUCTION

The basic function of Parliament is to make laws. Making laws is Parliament's major pre-occupation. Changing and complex socio-economic problems constantly demand new laws and, thus, Parliament spends a good deal of its time on legislative activity. All legislative proposals have to be brought in the form of Bills before the Parliament. A Bill is a statute/law in draft and cannot become law unless it has received the approval of both the Houses of Parliament and the assent of the President of India. The process of law making begins with the introduction of a Bill in either House of Parliament. A Bill can be introduced either by a Minister or a member other than a Minister. In the former case, it is called a Government Bill and in the latter case, it is known as a Private Member's Bill.

There are four types of bills which are introduced in Parliament :

1. **Constitution Amendment Bills :** These are Bills which seek to amend the Constitution.
2. **Money Bills :** A Bill is said to be a Money Bill if it only contains provisions related to taxation, borrowing of money by the government, and expenditure from or receipt to the Consolidated Fund of India. Bills that only contain provisions that are incidental to these matters would also be regarded as Money Bills.
3. **Financial Bills :** A Bill that contains some provisions related to taxation and expenditure, and additionally contains provisions related to any other matter is called a Financial Bill. Therefore, if a Bill merely involves expenditure by the government, and addresses other issues, it will be a financial Bill.
4. **Ordinary Bills :** All other Bills are called ordinary bills.

ORDINARY BILL

An ordinary Bill may originate in either House of Parliament. The procedure for passage of a Bill in a House is contained in the Rules of Procedure of each House. A Bill undergoes three readings in each House, i.e., the Lok Sabha and the Rajya Sabha, before it is submitted to the President for assent.

(a) **First Reading :** The actual legislative process starts with the introduction of a Bill. An ordinary Bill can be introduced in either by a minister or by a private member. A Bill can be introduced by moving a motion for leave to introduce the Bill. If leave is granted by the House, the Bill is introduced by the mover of the Bill by reading its title and objectives. No discussion on the Bill can take place at this stage. This stage constitutes the First Reading of the Bill. Normally, the motion for introduction of a Bill is not opposed. But if it is opposed, the Speaker/Chairman may in his discretion allow a brief explanatory statement to be made by the member who opposes the motion and the member who moves it. Thereafter, without further debate, the question is put to the vote of the House. However, the motion for leave to introduce a Finance Bill or Appropriation Bill is forthwith put to vote of the House. The question whether leave be granted or not is decided by the majority of the members present and voting.

- **Publication in Gazette :** After a Bill has been introduced, it is published in the Official Gazette. Even before introduction, a Bill might, with the permission of the Speaker, be published in the Gazette. In such cases, leave to introduce the Bill in the House is not asked for and the Bill is straightaway introduced.
- **Reference of Bill to Departmental Standing Committee :** With the introduction of the Department-related Parliamentary Standing Committees, the Bills introduced in Rajya Sabha or Lok Sabha may be referred to the respective Committees by the Chairman, Rajya Sabha or the Speaker, Lok Sabha for examination and report. If a Bill is referred to the Standing Committee, the Committee shall consider the general principles and clauses of the Bill referred to them and make report thereon. The report of the Committee, being of persuasive value, shall be treated as considered advice given by the Committee.

(b) Second Reading : The second reading consists of consideration of the Bill in two stages. The first stage consists of a general discussion on the Bill as a whole, when the principle underlying the Bill is discussed. At this stage it is open for the House to –

- Refer to a select Committee of the House or a Joint Committee of the two Houses; or
- to circulate it for the purpose of eliciting opinion; or
- straightaway take it into consideration.

i. Select Committee or Joint Committee - Most of the bills of complicated, technical, or controversial nature are referred to a Select Committee or a Joint Select Committee. When a Bill is sought to be referred to any Select Committee, the mover of such a proposal himself suggest the names of the members whom he would like to be on that Committee. The consent of the members is sought beforehand. If the Bill is sought to be referred to a Joint Select Committee, the other House is requested to associate its members on such a committee. The Select or Joint Select Committee considers the Bill clause by clause just as the House does. Amendments can be moved to the various clauses by members of the Committee without altering the principles underlying it. After the Bill has been considered, the Committee submits its report to the House which considers the Bill again as reported by the Committee.

ii. If a Bill is circulated for the purpose of eliciting public opinion, such opinions are obtained through the agency of the governments of the State and the union territories. Where a Bill has been circulated for generating opinions and opinions have been received and laid on the table of the House, the next motion on regard to the Bill must be for reference to a Select Committee or a Joint Select Committee. It is not ordinarily permissible at this stage to move a motion for consideration of the Bill, unless the Speaker allows it.

iii. The second stage of the second reading consists of clause-by-clause consideration of the Bill as introduced or as reported by the Select Committee or Joint Select Committee. Discussion takes place on each clause of the Bill and amendments to clause can be moved at this stage. Each amendment and each clause is put to vote in the House. The amendment becomes parts of the Bill, if they are accepted by a majority of members present and voting, after the second reading is deemed to be over.

(c) Third Reading : Thereafter, the Member-in-charge/mover of the Bill can move that the Bill be passed. This stage is known as the Third Reading of the Bill. At this stage, the debate is confined to arguments either in support or rejection of the Bill without referring to the details thereof further than that are absolute necessary. Only formal, verbal, or consequential amendments are allowed to be moved at this stage. In passing an ordinary Bill, a simple majority of members present and voting is necessary.

(d) **Bills in the other House :** After the Bill is passed by one House, it is sent to the other House for concurrence with a message to that effect, and there also it goes through the stages described above, except the introduction stage. The Bill from the other/second House will be sent for the Presidential assent under the following circumstances –

- If the Bill is also passed by the second House as forwarded by the first House; Or
- If the second House suggests some amendments and if the amendments are accepted by the first House.

(e) **Joint Sitting :** If a Bill passed by one House is rejected by the other House, or, the Houses have finally disagreed as to the amendments to be made in the Bill, or more than six months have elapsed from the date of the receipt of the Bill by the other House without the Bill being passed by it, the President may call a joint sitting of the two Houses to resolve the deadlock. If, at the joint sitting of the two Houses, the Bill is passed by a majority of the total number of members of both the Houses present and voting, with the amendments if any, accepted by them, the Bill is deemed to have been passed by both the Houses. Joint sitting of the two Houses is presided over by the Speaker of the Lok Sabha. The difference between the two Houses is cleared at the joint sitting and whatever discussion is taken at the joint sitting is considered as final in the case of the differences.

(f) **Assent of the President :** When a Bill is passed by both Houses, the said Bill will be forwarded for the Presidential assent. The Bill becomes an Act only after the President's assent has been given thereto. The President can either –

- Give his assent. If the President gives his assent, then the Bill will turn into an Act; or
- Withhold his assent to a Bill. If the President withholds his assent the said Bill will not turn into an act; or
- Return the Bill for reconsideration with his recommendations. If the President returns the Bill for reconsideration and if it is passed by both the Houses again with or without amendments and presented again to the President for his assent, the President must give his assent to the Bill.

JOINT SESSION

Joint sitting can be convened only if there is a deadlock with respect to the Ordinary Bills and Financial Bills. There is no joint sitting with respect to Money Bill and the Constitutional Amendment Bill. In the area of ordinary bills, the two Houses of Parliament enjoy equal powers. A Bill has to be passed by the two Houses in an identical form before it can be submitted to the President for his assent. Thus, when a Bill passed by one House and transmitted to the other House –

(a) Is rejected there; or

(b) The two Houses disagree as to the amendments to be made in the Bill; or

(c) If the other House does not pass it for more than six months;

The President may summon a joint session of both the Houses (Article 108). While reckoning the period of six months, no account is to be taken of any period during which the House to which the Bill has been sent is prorogued or adjourned for more than four consecutive days.

After the President notifies his intention to summon a joint session of the two Houses, none of the Houses can proceed further with the Bill. No joint session can be called if the Bill has already lapsed by the dissolution of the Lok Sabha. But the joint session may be held if the Lok Sabha is dissolved after the President has notified his intention to summon such a session.

If the Bill passed by one House is not passed by the other House with amendments and returned to the originating House, no amendments can be proposed to the Bill at a joint sitting other than those which might have become necessary by the delay in the passage of the Bill. If, on the other hand, the Bill has be passed by the other House with amendments and returned to the originating House, then only such amendments, and in addition, such other amendments as are relevant to the matters with respect to which the Houses have not agreed, may be proposed at the joint sitting. In all cases, the decision of the Presiding officer as to what amendments are admissible at the joint sitting is final.

At the joint sitting, the Speaker of the Lok Sabha, or in his absence, such person as may be determined by Rules of Procedure, is to preside. According to the Rules of Procedure – in the absence of the Speaker, the Deputy Speaker shall preside over the joint sitting. If the Deputy Speaker is also absent, then the Deputy Chairman of the Rajya Sabha shall preside over the joint sitting. If the Deputy Chairman is also absent, such other person as may be determined by the members present at the joint sitting, presides over the meeting. Thus, the Chairman of Rajya Sabha will not get an opportunity to preside over the joint sitting as he is not a member of either House of the Parliament. The quorum to constitute a joint sitting is one-tenth of the total number of members of both Houses of the Parliament.

A Bill passed with or without amendments, by a majority of all the members present and voting in the joint session, is deemed to have been passed by both the Houses. Generally, the Lok Sabha with greater number wins the battle in a joint sitting.

So far, joint sittings of the two Houses have taken place on three occasions –

- The first joint sitting was held on 6 May 1961 following a disagreement between the two Houses over certain amendments to the Dowry Prohibition Bill, 1959. This was followed by another sitting on 9 May 1961 when the Bill, as amended, was finally passed.
- The second joint sitting was held on 16 May 1978, following the rejection by the Rajya Sabha of the Banking Service Commission (Repeal) Bill, 1977 and the Bill was passed.
- The third joint sitting was held on 26 March 2002 when the motion to consider the Prevention of Terrorism Bill, 2002, seeking to replace the Prevention of Terrorism Ordinance (POTO) as passed by the Lok Sabha was rejected by the Rajya Sabha. At this sitting held for the purpose of deliberating and voting on the Prevention of Terrorism Bill, 2002, the Bill was passed.

CONTROL OF PUBLIC FINANCE

A government cannot exist without raising and spending money. Parliament controls public finance which includes granting money to the administration for expenses on public services, imposition of taxes, and authorization of loans. The Indian Constitution devises an elaborate machinery for securing Parliamentary control over finances which is based on the following principles –

(a) The first principle regulates the constitutional relation between the Government and the Parliament in matters of finance. The Executive cannot raise money by taxation, borrowing or otherwise, or spend money, without the authority of the Parliament.

(b) The second principle regulates the relation between the two Houses of Parliament in financial matters. The power of raising money by tax or loan and authorising expenditure belongs exclusively to the popular House, i.e., Lok Sabha. Rajya Sabha merely assents to it. It cannot revise, alter, or initiate a grant. In financial matters, Rajya Sabha does not have coordinate/equal authority with Lok Sabha which has the real control in this area. Thus, financial powers have been concentrated in Lok Sabha and Rajya Sabha plays only a subsidiary role in this respect.

(c) The third principle imposes a restriction on the power of Parliament to authorise expenditure. Parliament cannot recommend a new expenditure or vote money for any purpose whatsoever, except on demand by Ministers.

(d) The fourth principle imposes a similar restriction on the power of the Parliament to impose taxation. Parliament cannot impose any tax except upon the recommendation of the Executive.

MONEY BILL

According to Article 110(1) of the Constitution, a Bill is deemed to be a Money Bill if it contains only provisions dealing with all or any of the following matters, namely: the imposition, abolition, remission, alteration, or regulation of any tax;

(a) the regulation of the borrowing of money or the giving of any guarantee by the Government of India, or the amendment of the law with respect to any financial obligations undertaken or to be undertaken by the Government of India;

(b) the custody of the Consolidated Fund or the Contingency Fund of India, the payment of moneys into or the withdrawal of moneys from any such fund;

(c) the appropriation of moneys out of the Consolidated Fund of India;

(d) the declaring of any expenditure to be expenditure charged on the Consolidated Fund of India or the increasing of the amount of any such expenditure;

(e) the receipt of money on account of the Consolidated Fund of India or the public account of India or the custody or issue of such money or the audit of the accounts of the Union or of a State; or

(f) any matter incidental to any of the matters specified above.

A Bill is a Money Bill when it deals only with the matters specified above, and not with any other extraneous matter. Further, A Bill is not deemed to be Money Bill by reason only that

- it provides for the imposition of fines or other pecuniary penalties; or
- for the demand or payment of fees for licences or fees for services rendered; or
- by reason that it provides for the imposition, abolition, remission, alteration, or regulation of any tax by any local authority or body for local purposes.

(a) **Certification of Money Bills :** A Money Bill can be introduced in the Lok Sabha only. If any question arises whether a Bill is a Money Bill or not, the decision of Speaker thereon is final. The Speaker is under no obligation to consult anyone in coming to a decision or in giving certificate that a Bill is a Money Bill. The certificate of the Speaker to the effect that a Bill is a Money Bill is to be endorsed and signed by the Speaker when it is transmitted to Rajya Sabha and also when it is presented to the President for assent.

The Speaker's certificate on a Money Bill once given is final and cannot be challenged. A Money Bill cannot be referred to a Joint Committee of the Houses.

(b) **Introduction of Money Bill :** A Money Bill can be introduced in Lok Sabha only on the recommendation of the President by the Minister. However, no recommendation of the President is necessary for the moving of an amendment taking provision for the reduction or abolition of any tax. Thus, money bills are government bills. After a Money Bill is passed by the Lok Sabha, it is transmitted to the Rajya Sabha for its consideration.

(c) **Role of Rajya Sabha :** Rajya Sabha is required to return a Money Bill passed and transmitted by the Lok Sabha within a period of fourteen days from the date of its receipt. The period of fourteen days is computed from the date of receipt of the Bill in the Rajya Sabha Secretariat and not from the date on which it is laid on the Table of the Rajya Sabha. Rajya Sabha may return a Money Bill transmitted to it with or without its recommendations. If a Money Bill is returned by Rajya Sabha without any recommendation, it is presented to the President for assent. If a Money Bill is returned by Rajya Sabha with recommendations, it is laid on the Table of Lok Sabha. If Lok Sabha accepts the amendment recommended by the Rajya Sabha, the Money Bill is deemed to have been passed by both Houses of Parliament with the amendments recommended by Rajya Sabha and accepted by Lok Sabha. If Lok Sabha does not accept any of the amendments recommended by the Rajya Sabha, the Money Bill is deemed to have been passed by both the Houses of Parliament in the form in which it was passed by Lok Sabha without any of the amendments recommended by Rajya Sabha and it is presented to the President for assent. However, if Rajya Sabha does not return a Money Bill within the prescribed period of fourteen days, the Bill is deemed to have been passed by both Houses of the Parliament at the expiry of the said period of fourteen days in the form in which it was passed by the Lok Sabha and thereafter, it is presented to the President for assent. There is no scope of joint sitting with respect to a Money Bill. In other words, Lok Sabha has more powers than Rajya Sabha with respect to a Money Bill.

(d) **Assent to Money Bills :** The President may either give or withhold assent to a Money Bill. Under the Constitution, a Money Bill cannot be returned to the House by the President for reconsideration. Generally, the President gives assent to a money Bill because the same is introduced on his recommendation.

(e) **Constitution Amendment Bills-not treated as Money Bill :** A Constitution Amendment Bill is not treated as a Money Bill even if all its provisions attract Article 110(1)for the reason that such amendments are governed by Article 368 which overrides the provisions regarding Money Bills.

(f) **Financial Bills—Category-I :** A Bill falling under Clause (1) of Article 117 of the Constitution is called a Financial Bill. It is a Bill which seeks to make provision for any other matters specified in sub-clauses (a) to (f) of clause (1) of Article 110 as also other matters. Whereas a Money Bill deals solely with matters specified in Article 110(1) (a) to (g) of the Constitution, a Financial Bill does not exclusively deal with all or any of the matters specified in the said Article, that is to say it contains some other provisions also. Financial Bill (I) is thus really a Money Bill to which some other matter has also been tacked on. Two incidents are common between a Money and Financial Bill. First, both originate only in Lok Sabha and not in Rajya Sabha. Secondly, neither can be introduced without the recommendation of the President. In all other respects, a Financial Bill is treated like any other ordinary Bill by both Houses; Rajya Sabha has full power to effect amendments in it and a deadlock between the two Houses will have to be resolved through the procedure of the joint session. When the Financial Bill is presented to the President for his assent, he can either give his assent to the Bill or withhold his assent to the Bill or return the Bill for reconsideration of the Houses. Thus, Lok Sabha has much greater control over a Money Bill than a Financial Bill.

(g) **Financial Bills – Category-II :** There is yet another class of Bills which are also Financial Bills under Article 117(3). Such Bills are more in the nature of ordinary Bills rather than the Money Bills and Financial Bills mentioned earlier. The only point of difference between this category of Financial Bills and the ordinary Bills is that such a Financial Bill, if enacted and brought into operation, involves expenditure from the Consolidated Fund of India and cannot be passed by either House of Parliament unless the President has recommended to that House the consideration of the Bill. In all other respects, this category of Bills is just like ordinary Bills, so that such a Financial Bill can be introduced in Rajya Sabha, amended by it, or a joint sitting can be held in case of disagreement between the Houses over such a Bill. There is, in other words, no limitation on the power of Rajya Sabha in respect of such Financial Bills. Thus, those Bills which inter-alia contain provisions which would on enactment involve expenditure from the Consolidated Fund of India are called Financial Bills (II).

(h) **Executive's Responsibility in financial matters :** This rule making the Executive responsible for proposing measures of taxation and spending is concretized through several constitutional provisions. Thus, no demand for a grant can be made except on the President's recommendation (Article 113(3)). Lok Sabha may refuse any demand or reduce its amount but cannot increase it (Article 113(2)). A Financial Bill (I) or a Money Bill, or an amendment thereto, is not to be moved without the President's recommendation, but no such recommendation is necessary to move an amendment to reduce or abolish any tax. Further, a Bill which when enacted and put into operation would involve expenditure from the Consolidated Fund of India is not to be passed by a House unless the President has recommended its consideration to that House (Article 117(3)).

BUDGETARY PROCESS

Governments have to perform manifold functions from maintaining law and order, protecting their territories, to implementation of plans for economic and social betterment. Besides, they provide a variety of social services like education, health, employment, and housing to the people. Needless to say, Government requires adequate resources to discharge these functions effectively. These necessary funds are mobilised from the country's resources by way of taxes – both direct and indirect and loans – both long-term and short-term, to meet the governmental expenditure.

Need For Budget

It is not as if the Government can tax, borrow, and spend money the way it likes. Since there is a limit to the resources, the need for proper budgeting arises to allocate scares resources to various governmental activities. Every item of expenditure has to be well thought out and total outlay worked out for a specific period. Prudent spending is essential for the stability of the government and proper earnings are a pre-requisite to wise spending. Hence, planned expenditure and accurate foresight of earnings are the *sine-qua-non* of sound governmental finance.

Parliamentary Control Over Finance

Ours is a Parliamentary system of Government based on the Westminster model. The Constitution has, therefore, vested the power over the purse in the hands of chosen representatives of the people, thus sanctifying the principle 'no taxation without representation'.

Preparation of Budget for the approval of the Legislature is a constitutional obligation of the Government, both at the Centre and the State levels. Legislative prerogative over taxation, legislative control over expenditure, and executive initiative in financial matters are some of the fundamental principles of the system of Parliamentary financial control.

Annual Appropriations

An important mechanism for securing Parliamentary control over appropriations is the annuality. Most of the appropriations made by the Parliament are on an annual basis. The Executive thus comes before the Parliament every year to ask for grants for the ensuing year so that Parliament gets an opportunity of reviewing, criticizing, and discussing the activities and policies pursued by the Government during the preceding year.

The Parliamentary process to make annual appropriations passes through several stages –

Budget process[5] :

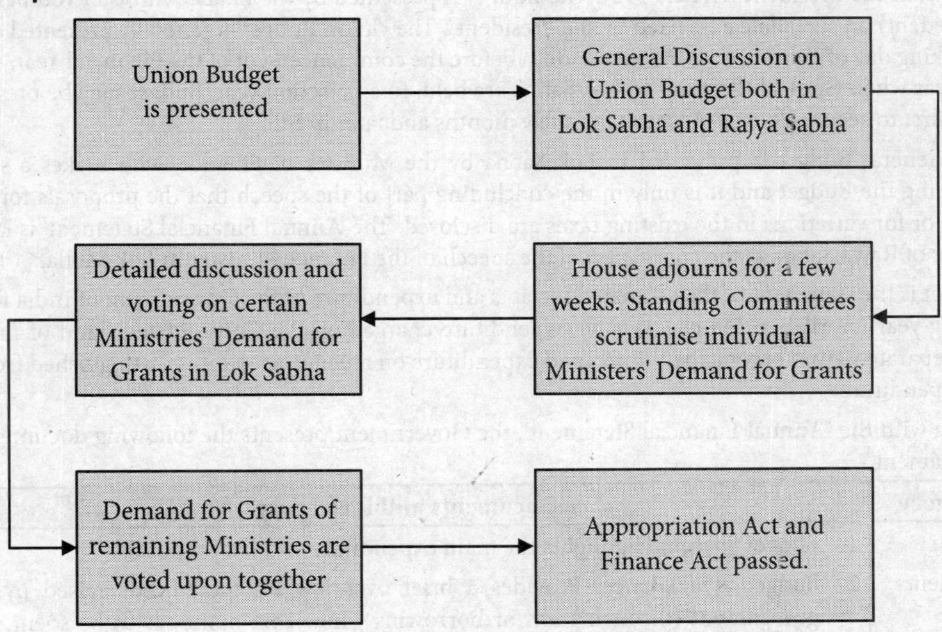

The Annual Financial Statement or the Statement of the Estimated Receipts and Expenditure of the Government of India in respect of each Financial Year is popularly known as the Budget.

Merger Of Railway Budget With Union Budget

Till 2016, the Budget was presented to Lok Sabha in two parts, namely, the Railway Budget pertaining to Railway Finance and the General Budget which gave an overall picture of the financial position of the Government of India, excluding the Railways. Since the year 2017-18, with the merger of the Railway Budget with the General Budget, a single document titled 'Union Budget' is presented by the Minister of Finance.

The practise of presenting a separate Railway Budget was started in the year 1924 under the British regime[1]. The merger of Railway Budget with General Budget is based on the recommendations of the Committee headed by Shri Bibek Debroy, Member, NITI Aayog and a separate paper on 'Dispensing with the Railway Budget' by Shri Bibek Debroy along with Shri Kishore Desai. As per the NITI Aayog recommendations, over the years, the Railway Budget had shrunk significantly, and therefore a separate Budget was not required. The recommendations also stated that the British started this practice in 1924 because a significant part of the government revenues and the country's Gross Domestic Product (GDP) was dependent on Railway revenues.

Presentation of Budget

The "Annual Financial Statement" laid before both the Houses of Parliament constitutes the Budget of the Union Government. This statement takes into account a period of one Financial Year. The Financial Year commences in India on 1st April each year. The statement embodies the estimated receipts and expenditure of the Government of India for the Financial Year.

The formal obligation to cause the Annual Financial Statement[2] to be laid before both Houses has been cast on the President (Article 112). The Budget is presented by the finance minister (on behalf of the President) on such date as is fixed by the President[3]. The Union Budget is generally presented on the last working day of February. i.e., about a month before the commencement of the Financial Year, except in the year when General Elections to Lok Sabha are held. In an election year, Budget may be presented twice – first to secure Vote on Account for a few months and later in full.

The General Budget is presented in Lok Sabha by the Minister of Finance, who makes a speech introducing the Budget and it is only in the concluding part of the speech that the proposals for fresh taxation or for variations in the existing taxes are disclosed. The 'Annual Financial Statement' is laid on the Table of Rajya Sabha at the conclusion of the speech of the Finance Minister in Lok Sabha.

Budget is the statement of the estimated receipts and expenditure of the Government of India for the following year (April 1 to March 31). The Expenditure charged on the Consolidated Fund of India is shown separately from other expenditure, and expenditure on revenue account is distinguished from all other expenditure.

Along with the "Annual Financial Statement", the Government presents the following documents to the Parliament[4]–

Category	Documents in this category
Summary Documents	1. Budget Speech: Highlights the main expenditure and tax proposals; 2. Budget at a Glance: Provides a brief overview on total funds raised by the government (through taxes or borrowing), how that money is to be spent, and budget deficit/surplus; 3. Annual Financial Statement: Similar to 'Budget at a Glance' but organised in a different way to reflect requirements under Article 112 of the Constitution.

[1]On the recommendations of Acworth Committee.

[2]Constitution uses the word "Annual Financial Statement". It doesn't use the term "Budget".

[3]Earlier the Budget speech of the Finance Minister was usually in two parts. First part used to deal with general economic survey of the country, while the second part was related to taxation proposals. Now, the economic survey is presented a day or few days before the presentation of the budget.

[4]Overseeing Public Fund; How to scrutinise budgets; Mandira Kala, Gayatri Mann and Suyash Tiwari; May 2019; PRS Legislative Research.

Expenditure Documents	1. Expenditure Profile: Presents a summary of the total expenditure of all Ministries. Also presents expenditure according to different categories of interest, i.e., summary of funds allocated to schemes for women or minorities; 2. Expenditure Budget: Presents a detailed breakdown of the expenditure of each ministry; 3. Demands for Grants/Appropriation Bill: Two documents required under the Constitution, asking the Parliament to allocate the stated amount of funds to different Ministries and schemes. Parliament votes to pass these two documents.
Receipts Documents	1. Receipts Budget: Presents detailed information on how the government intends to raise money through different sources. 2. Finance Bill: A Bill presented to Parliament (and to be voted on) containing the various legal amendments to bring into effect the tax changes proposed by the government. 3. Memorandum on the Finance Bill: Explains the various legal provisions contained in the Finance Bill and their implications in simple language.
FRBM Documents	1. Macro-Economic Framework: Explains the government's assessment of the growth prospects of the economy. 2. Medium-Term Fiscal Policy: A statement setting limits on the size of the budget deficits for the next three years, as well as targets for tax and non-tax receipts. 3. Fiscal Policy Strategy: A statement explaining the government's efforts to follow sound fiscal policies and reasons for any departure from the targets set by it for deficits under the FRBM Act.

Vote On Account

The discussion on the Budget begins a few days after its presentation. In a democratic set-up, the Government is anxious to give Parliament the full opportunity to discuss the budgetary provisions and the various proposals for taxation. Since Parliament is not able to vote on the entire budget before the commencement of the new Financial Year, the necessity to keep enough finance at the disposal of Government in order to allow it to run the administration of the country arises. A special provision is, therefore, made for "Vote on Account" by which the Government obtains the Vote of Parliament for a sum sufficient to incur expenditure on various items for a part of the year. Normally, the Vote on Account is taken for two months only. But during election year or when it is anticipated that the main demands and Appropriation Bill take longer time than two months, the Vote on Account may be for a period exceeding two months. Vote on Account will be passed by the Lok Sabha after the general discussion on the Budget was over and before the discussion on the demands for grants was taken up.

Procedure After the Presentation of the Budget

After the budget is presented, a general discussion is held in both Lok Sabha and Rajya Sabha. Discussion at this stage is limited to general examination of the budget and proposals of the government. At the end of the discussion, the Finance Minister gives a reply. No voting takes place at this stage. After the general discussion, Parliament may go into recess for a few weeks. At this point, detailed estimates of expenditure of all Ministries, called Demands for Grants, are sent for examination to the Parliamentary Standing Committees, that comprise members of both Lok Sabha and Rajya Sabha.

Role of Standing Committees

One of the functions of the Standing Committees is to scrutinise the allocation of funds to the Ministries under their supervision. At present, there are 24 Standing Committees that together oversee the work of all the Ministries. For instance, the Standing Committee on Defence scrutinises the Demands for Grants of all departments under the Ministry of Defence.

These Committees examine the: (i) amount allocated to various programmes and schemes under the Ministry, and (ii) trends of utilisation of the money allocated to the Ministry. In doing so, officials of the Ministry are required to depose before the Committee to respond to queries and provide additional information in connection with the Demands for Grants being examined. While examining a Ministry's expenditure, the Committees may consult or invite views from experts. Based on these consultations, the Committees submit their reports to the Parliament. The Committees' recommendations are useful for MPs to understand implications of the proposed expenditure across Ministries and allow for informed debate before approving such expenditure.

Typically, Lok Sabha decides to hold a detailed discussion on four or five Demands for Grants. The Ministries identified for discussion vary every year and are decided by the Business Advisory Committee of Lok Sabha. This discussion is followed by voting. The demands which have not been discussed and voted on by the last day are 'guillotined', i.e., they are voted upon together. The graph below shows the share of budget expenditure that has been guillotined from 2000-01 to 2020-21. In 2004-05, 2013-14, and 2018-19, all Demands for Grants were guillotined, i.e., passed without discussion.

Share of Budget Expenditure : Guillotined vs Discussed

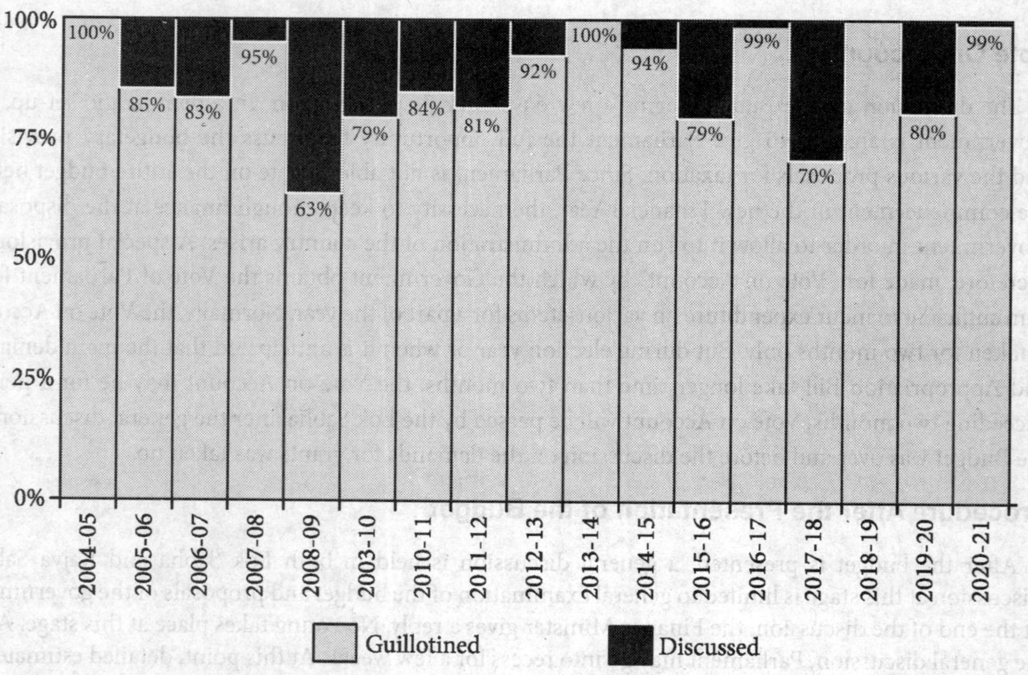

Note : This chart does not include discussion on Demand for Grants for Ministry of Railways

Voting on Demands for Grants

Lok Sabha has the power to assent to or refuse to give assent to any Demand or even to reduce the amount of Grant sought by Government. In Rajya Sabha there is only a General Discussion on the Budget. It does not vote on the Demands for Grants. Only so much of the Grant is subject to the vote of Lok Sabha as is not a "charged" expenditure on the Consolidated Fund of India. The "charged" expenditure includes –

- Emoluments and allowances of the President and other expenditure relating to his office.
- Salaries and allowances of the Chairman and the Deputy Chairman of the Rajya Sabha and the Speaker and the Deputy Speaker of the Lok Sabha.
- Salaries, allowances, and pensions of the Judges of the Supreme Court.
- Pensions of the Judges of High Courts.
- Salary and allowances and pension of the Comptroller and Auditor General of India.
- Salaries and allowances and pension of the Chairman and members of the Union Public Service Commission.
- Administrative expenses of the Supreme Court, the office of the Comptroller and Auditor General of India, and the Union Public Service Commission including the salaries, allowances, and pensions of the persons serving in these offices.
- The debt charges for which the Government of India is liable, including interest, sinking fund charges and redemption charges and other expenditure relating to the raising of loans and the service and redemption of debt.
- Any sum required to satisfy any judgment, decree, or award of any court or arbitral tribunal.
- Sums prescribed by law by Parliament as grants-in-aid for States in need of assistance (Article 275(1)).
- Sums of money required for making loans to the States (Article 293(3)).
- Any other expenditure declared by the Parliament to be so charged.

Discussion in Lok Sabha on 'charged' expenditure is permissible but such expenditure is not voted by the House.

Members have full opportunity to criticise the budgetary provisions during the course of discussion as also to make suggestions for improving the financial position of the country.

Cut Motions

The motions to reduce the amounts of demands for grants are called 'Cut Motions'. The object of a cut motion is to draw the attention of the House to the matter specified therein. During the voting on Demands for Grants, MPs can express their disapproval through 'cut motions'. If a cut motion is passed, it signifies loss of confidence in the government.

Cut Motions can be classified into three categories:

(i) Disapproval of Policy Cut;

(ii) Economy Cut; and

(iii) Token Cut.

(i) **Disapproval of Policy Cut :** A cut motion which says "That the amount of the demand be reduced to Re. 1" implies that the mover disapproves of the policy underlying the demand. And it is open to the mover to advocate an alternative policy.

(ii) **Economy Cut :** Where the object of the motion is to effect economy in the expenditure, the form of the motion is "That the amount of the demand be reduced by Rs...(a specified amount)". The amount suggested for reduction may be either a lump-sum reduction in the demand or omission or reduction of an item in the demand.

(iii) **Token Cut :** Where the object of the motion is to ventilate a specific grievance within the sphere of responsibility of the Government of India, its form is: "That the amount of the demand be reduced by Rs. 100". Discussion on such a cut motion is confined to the particular grievance specified in the motion which is within the sphere of responsibility of the Government of India.

Appropriation Act[5]

No money can be withdrawn from the Consolidated Fund of India without an Appropriation Act being passed in accordance the procedure laid down in the Constitution for the purpose (Article 114). The sanction given by Lok Sabha to the demands for grants does not by itself authorize expenditure without the passage of an Appropriation Act. Therefore, after the demands have been discussed in both Houses of Parliament, and have been assented to in Lok Sabha, an Appropriation Bill is introduced in Lok Sabha.

The Appropriation Bill provides for appropriation out of the Consolidated Fund of all moneys required to meet the grants assented to by Lok Sabha and the expenditure charged on the Consolidated Fund, and in case the amount under each head can exceed what was shown previously in the Budget. No amendments can be proposed to the Bill in any House of Parliament so as to vary the amount of an expenditure charged on the Consolidated Fund. The decision of the Presiding Officer as to whether an amendment is admissible or not under this clause is final. The idea behind these restrictions is that the grants already voted upon in the Lok Sabha should not be disturbed later.

The Appropriation Bill goes before both Houses of Parliament for consideration, but being a Money Bill, the power of Rajya Sabha to deal with it is very restricted. The Appropriation Act plays an important role in the Parliamentary control of public finance. It authorizes the issue of money from the Consolidated Fund of India for the expenditure of the Central Government and limits the expenditure of each department to the sums set out therein, thus ensuring not only that the expenditure does not exceed the sum voted, but that it is incurred only for the purposes authorised.

Finance Act

The last stage in the chain of annual Parliamentary financial procedure is reached when Parliament enacts the Finance Act to effectuate government's taxation proposals for the ensuing year. The government's taxing proposals are first contained in the Budget. The Finance Bill embodying these proposals is introduced in the Lok Sabha immediately after the conclusion of the Finance Minister's Budget speech. The Bill is not proceeded with immediately but is kept pending till the passage of the Appropriation Act. A motion may then be made in the Lok Sabha for referring the Finance Bill to a Select Committee and the scope of discussion on the Finance Bill thereon is vast and members can discuss any action of the Government of India. The Bill is taken up for consideration after the Select Committee has made its report.

---

[5] Authorises Government of India to withdraw funds from the Consolidated Fund of India to meet expenses for a fiscal year.

The passage of the Finance Act is essential to raise the necessary revenue. Ordinarily, the taxes sought to be levied by the Finance Act can be collected only after its enactment, but in order to avoid leakage of revenue, the Government is empowered, under the Provisional Collection of Taxes, Act, 1931 to start collection of duty of customs and excise at the new proposed rates immediately from the date of the Finance Bill is introduced in the Lok Sabha. In view of the provisions of the Provisional Collection of Taxes Act,1931, the Finance Bill has to be passed by Parliament and assented to by the President before the expiry of the seventy-fifth day after the day on which it was introduced.

The procedure in respect of a Finance Bill is the same as in the case of other Money Bills.

If the Government Needs to Spend Additional Money

1. **Supplementary Grant :** It may be that during a Financial Year, the money sanctioned by the Annual Appropriation Act for a particular service may prove to be inadequate. If the amount authorised to be expended for a particular service for the current Financial Year is found to be insufficient for the purpose of that year in such cases, supplementary grants are made by Parliament before the end of the Financial Year.

2. **Additional Grant :** On certain occasions, additional expenditure is needed on some new service not contemplated at the time when the Budget was presented. In other words, when a need has arisen during the current Financial Year for supplementary or additional expenditure upon some new service not contemplated in the annual financial statement for that year, in such cases an estimate is presented before the Parliament for Additional grants. These grants are presented and passed by the Parliament before the end of the Financial Year.

   Thus, if the amount authorised to be expended for a particular service for the current Financial Year is found to be insufficient for the purpose of that year (Supplementary Grant) or when a need has arisen during the current Financial Year for additional expenditure (Additional Grant) upon some 'new service' not contemplated in the Budget for that year, the President causes it to be laid before both the Houses of Parliament another statement showing the estimated amount of that expenditure. The procedure followed in Parliament in regard to Supplementary/Additional Grants is more or less the same as is adopted in the case of estimates included in the General Budget. However, note that, unlike the Demands for Grants presented with the budget, these supplementary demands have never been scrutinised by Standing Committees.

3. **Excess Grant :** Sometimes, a situation may arise when the money has been spent on a service in excess of the amount granted for the year. In other words, Excess Grant is the grant in excess of the approved grants for meeting the requisite expenses of the government. When actual expenditure incurred exceeds the approved grants of the Parliament, the Ministry of Finance presents a Demand for Excess Grant. The Comptroller and Auditor General of India brings such excesses to the notice of the Parliament. The Public Accounts Committee examines these excesses and gives recommendations to the Parliament. The Demand for Excess Grants is made after the actual expenditure is incurred and is presented to the Parliament after the end of the Financial Year in which the expenses were made. But the procedure for passing an excess grant is similar to that of the regular budget.

4. **Exceptional Grant :** Lok Sabha is also authorized to make an exceptional grant which forms no part of the current service of any Financial Year.

5. **Vote Of Credit :** Vote of Credit may be used in times of emergency when the Parliament may vote a lump sum without allocating it to any particular object. Lok Sabha has power to make a grant for meeting an unexpected demand upon the resources of India when on account of the magnitude or indefinite character of the service, the demand cannot be stated with usual details.

Thus, after the Lok Sabha assents to any of the above grants (Exceptional/Vote of Credit), Parliament has to enact a law to withdraw moneys from the Consolidated Fund. In making these grants and passing the law, the procedure prescribed for making annual appropriations is to be followed.

6. **Token Grant :** When funds to meet proposed expenditure on a new service can be made available by reappropriation, a demand for the grant of a token sum may be submitted to the vote of the House and, if the House assents to the demand, funds may be so made available. In other words, token grant is granted when funds to meet the proposed expenditure on a new service can be made available by reappropriation. A demand for the grant of a token sum (of Re 1) is submitted to the vote of the Lok Sabha and if assented, funds are made available. Reappropriation involves transfer of funds from one head to another. It does not involve any additional expenditure.

Budget of a State Under President's Rule

Budget of a State under President's Rule is presented in the Lok Sabha. The procedure followed in regard to the Budget of the Union Government is followed in the case of State Budget also with such variations or modifications, as the Speaker may make.

PRINCIPLES OF BUDGETING

Thus, the essential principles generally observed in government budgeting in India are:

i. Principle of annularity. The budget should be on an annual basis; this leads to another rule – "*the Rule of Lapse*". The operation of this rule leads to a rush of expenditure towards the end of the year. However, it has the merit of enforcing Parliamentary sanction which is always for an amount for a specific period after which it must be obtained again. Thus, the Rule of Lapse implies that if the funds voted are not used by the end of the Financial Year, the unspent balance lapses and moves into the Consolidated Fund.

ii. The government budgets are on cash basis.

iii. There should be one budget for all financial transactions of the government. In the absence of one common budget, it would be difficult to assess the true financial position of the government.

iv. The budgeting should be gross and not net. Gross transactions, both in the case of receipts and expenditure of each department, should be shown. It is not permissible to deduct any receipt accruing to the department from the charges of collection or any other expenditure. This is intended to ensure that the Parliamentary control over expenditure is meaningful. In the absence of this provision, the budget coming up before the Parliament would be reduced only to the net deficit, if any.

v. Budgeting should be close. It should not be a guess work or guess estimates which result in wide fluctuations and can lead to improper allocation of funds.

vi. The form of estimates should correspond to the accounting heads since the estimates eventually get converted into actual accounts of receipts and expenditure.

STRUCTURE OF GOVERNMENT ACCOUNTS AND FUNDS

The accounts of Government of India are kept in three parts: -

- Consolidated Fund of India,
- Contingency Fund of India, and
- Public Account

Consolidated Fund of India

Article 266 of the Constitution provides for the Consolidated Fund of India. The Consolidated Fund is single unified account for all government departments. It is like a reservoir, a national till, into which all government receipts flow.

The Fund is formed of

- all revenue receipts of the Central Government;
- all moneys received by the Central Government in repayment of its loans; and
- any fees or other moneys taken by the Supreme Court.

Thus, practically, all moneys raised by the Central Government for its expenditure form part of the Fund. From the Fund are excluded the sums payable into the Contingency Fund, and the receipts from taxes and duties which have been assigned wholly or partly to the States for their expenditure. The Parliament is empowered to regulate by law such matters as the custody of the Consolidated Fund, payment of money therein, and withdrawal of money therefrom. Till Parliament enacts a law for the purpose, these matters may be regulated by rules made by the President. All Government expenditures are met from the Consolidated Fund of India. However, no moneys can be appropriated out of the Consolidated Fund except in accordance with law and for the purposes and in the manner provided in the Constitution. In other words, appropriation of moneys out of the Consolidated Fund of India is done in accordance with the Constitutional provisions contained in Articles 112 to 117 (Budgetary Process).

Contingency Fund of India

Article 267 of the Constitution authorizes the Parliament to create a "Contingency Fund". Contingency Fund is created as an imprest account to meet some urgent or unforeseen expenditure of the government. Accordingly, the Parliament passed Contingency Fund of India Act, 1950. The Fund is placed at the disposal of the President, who releases the funds on the request of the Union Cabinet at a time when there is a crisis, such as a natural disaster. Any expenditure incurred from this fund requires a subsequent authorisation from the Parliament. And the amount withdrawn is returned to the fund from the Consolidated Fund. In other words, its corpus is always kept intact.

The Union Finance Ministry holds the fund on behalf of the President. And the fund size is enhanced from time to time by the government. In 2005, the corpus of the fund was raised from Rs 5 crore to Rs 500 crore. And again, the government enhanced the Contingency Fund of India from Rs 500 crore to Rs 30,000 crore through the Finance Bill 2021.The fund can be increased through a Finance Bill when the Parliament is in the session. Or through an ordinance if the House is not in session and situation warrants. Withdrawal from the fund takes place with the approval of the Secretary of Department of Economic Affairs, in terms of the Contingency Fund of India Act, 1950.While increasing the corpus in 2021, the government also conferred more powers to the Expenditure Secretary in dealing with the fund.

An amount equivalent to 40% of the corpus has now been placed at the disposal of the Expenditure Secretary (Department of Expenditure). All further Contingency Fund releases beyond this limit will require the approval of the Expenditure Secretary in addition to the Economic Affairs Secretary's approval.

Public Account of India

Besides the Consolidated Fund of India, there is a Public Account of India in which are credited :

- All public moneys, other than those put in the Consolidated Fund, received by or on behalf of the Government of India;
- All moneys received by or deposited with any officer employed in connection with the affairs of the Union, in his capacity as such, other than revenues or public moneys raised or received by the Government of India; and
- All moneys received or deposited with the Supreme Court to the credit of any cause, matter, account or persons.

This fund is constituted under Article 266 (2) of the Constitution. It accounts for flows for those transactions where the government is merely acting as a banker. The receipts into the Public Account and disbursements out of it are not subject to vote by the Parliament. Receipts under this account mainly flow from the sale of Savings Certificates, contributions into General Provident Fund and Public Provident Fund, Security Deposits, and Earnest Money Deposits received by the Government. In respect of such receipts, the Government acts as a Banker or Trustee and refunds the money after completion of the contract/event. The Public Account also includes various suspense and remittance heads. The funds in the Public Account do not belong to the government. They have to be paid back at some time to their rightful owners. Because of this nature of the fund, expenditures from it are not required to be approved by the Parliament.

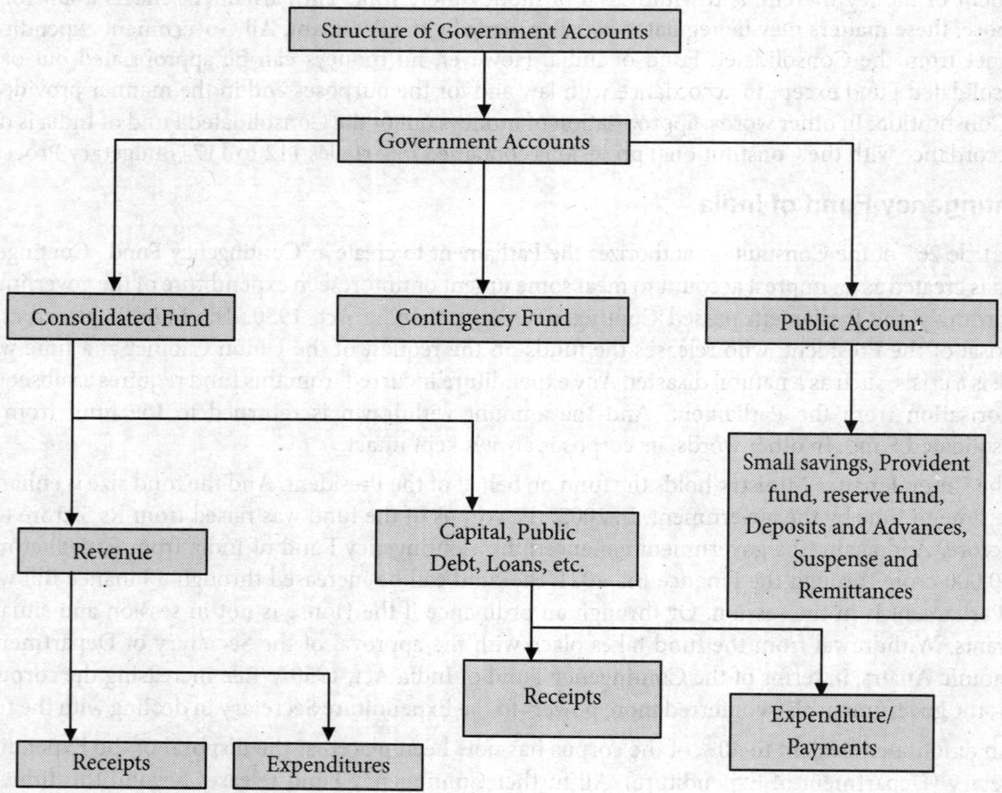

BORROWING

It is not always possible for the Government to find through taxation all the money needed for public expenditure. It may have to resort to borrowing from time to time. Article 292 empowers Central Government to borrow money upon security of the Consolidated Fund of India within such limits, if any, as Parliament may fix from time to time by law and the Government may give guarantees for its loan within the limits so fixed. This constitutional provision is of a permissive nature as it does not obligate the Executive to obtain statutory authorization from Parliament to borrow funds, but it gives the necessary power to Parliament, if it so desires, to control the borrowing activities of the Central Government by fixing quantitative limit thereon. This power has not been exercised by the Parliament so far. The position, therefore, is that the Central Government today borrows money entirely on its Executive authority without seeking a mandate from the Parliament for the purpose.

All borrowings during the year are shown in the Budget and approval of the Budget by Parliament might be regarded as approval of the Government's borrowing programme as well. The money borrowed by the Government becomes part of the Consolidated Fund of India out of which appropriations are made only by Parliament by law.

GOVERNMENT FINANCES

As already discussed above, the Finance Minister presents the Annual Financial Statement of the government for the forthcoming year. The statement consists of estimates of the money the government expects to spend on various Ministries, and how much money will be raised from different sources such as levy of taxes and dividends from public enterprises. The budget also provides an estimate of the borrowing requirements of the government and its overall debt. In addition, the statement also gives an account of how much money the government raised or spent in the previous year, in comparison to the estimates it had given to the Parliament.

Receipts

Government receipts may be broadly categorised under revenue and capital receipts.

(a) **Revenue Receipts :** Revenue receipts of the government comprise tax receipts and non-tax receipts. Tax receipts is the larger component in this category, contributing approximately 80% of the government's own receipts. Taxes such as the Goods and Services Tax (GST), corporation tax ,and income tax generate most of the government's receipts. The government also earns receipts from sources other than taxes. Such non-tax receipts include fees and fines, dividends from public enterprises, royalties from petroleum production, and sale of licenses.

(b) **Capital Receipts :** Some receipts change the government's assets or liabilities. For example, borrowings taken by the government increase its liabilities, whereas receipts from sale of public assets (also known as disinvestment) decreases the government's assets. Such receipts are called capital receipts. Capital receipts (other than borrowings) contribute approximately 5%–6% of the government's receipts. Over the years, disinvestment receipts have been the major part of these capital receipts. The capital receipts also includes loans raised by Government from public, called market loans, borrowings by Government from Reserve Bank and other parties through sale of Treasury Bills, loans received from foreign Governments and bodies, and recoveries of loans from State and Union Territory Governments and other parties.

Expenditure

The government spends its money on items such as the defence forces, implementing its schemes and programmes, providing subsidies, paying interest on the loans it has taken, and administrative expenses including salaries and pension. Government expenditure is categorised into revenue and capital expenditure.

(a) **Revenue Expenditure :** Revenue expenditure is for the normal running of Government departments and various services, interest payments on debt, subsidies, etc. Broadly, the expenditure which does not result in creation of assets for Government of India is treated as revenue expenditure. All grants given to State Governments/Union Territories and other parties are also treated as revenue expenditure even though some of the grants may be used for creation of assets. A large part of government's revenue expenditure goes towards paying interest on the funds that it has borrowed over the years. These interest payments are a form of committed expenditure which the government is obligated to undertake. In addition to this, a part of the government's spending also goes towards providing subsidies and pension.

(b) **Capital Expenditure :** Capital expenditure is that expenditure which goes towards creating assets or reducing liabilities. This would include expenditure on creating infrastructure, such as roads, hospitals, and schools, and repayment of borrowings. Thus, capital payments consist of capital expenditure on acquisition of assets like land, buildings, machinery, equipment, as also investments in shares, etc., and loans and advances granted by Central Government to State and Union Territory Governments, Government companies, Corporations, and other parties.

12.3 PARLIAMENTARY PRIVILEGES

INTRODUCTION

The privileges are certain rights belonging to Parliament collectively and some others belonging to the Members of Parliament individually, without which it would be impossible for the House to maintain its independence of action or the dignity of its position or for the members to discharge their functions. The sole object of Parliamentary privileges is, thus, to protect the rights and dignities of the Members of Parliament or legislative bodies to the extent necessary to enable them to perform their duties unhindered. The privileges of Parliament form a special kind of law of the land administered and interpreted by the Parliament itself without later review from any outside authority. The Parliament can punish anybody inside or outside the House who is guilty of offending against the right and dignity of the House. These privileges are a necessary condition for every legislative body to enable them to discharge their multifarious duties efficiently on behalf of their respective constituencies and even rights of citizens have to be curtailed so far as necessary for this purpose.

Thus, when any of these rights and immunities, both of members, individually and of the House in its collective capacity, which are known by the general name of privileges, are disregarded or attacked by any individual or authority, the offence is called a breach of privileges, and is punishable under the Law of Parliament. Parliament or legislative bodies then act as the highest judicial courts of the land and impose sentences on those who are found guilty of the contempt of the House and deny to the aggrieved party, the right to appeal or recourse to a court of law.

CONSTITUTIONAL PROVISIONS

The Constitution of India specifies some of the Parliamentary privileges. These are:

(a) Freedom of speech in Parliament[1] : Members cannot be held accountable/questioned by an outside body for any speech/disclosure made or a vote given inside the House. This is essential for giving effect to their freedom of speech in the House. Courts have no jurisdiction to take action against a member for his speech made in the House even if it amounts to contempt of the court.

(b) Immunity to a member from any proceedings in any court in respect of anything said or any vote given by him in Parliament or any committee thereof[2];

(c) Immunity to a person from proceedings in any court in respect of the publication by or under the authority of either House of Parliament of any report, paper, votes, or proceedings[3].

(d) Courts are prohibited from inquiring into the validity of any proceedings in Parliament on the ground of an alleged irregularity of procedure[4].

---

[1]Article 105(1)

[2]Article 105(2)

[3]Ibid.

[4]Article 122(1)

(e) No officer or Member of Parliament empowered to regulate procedure or the conduct of business or to maintain order in Parliament can be subject to a court's jurisdiction in respect of exercise by him of those powers[5].

(f) No person can be liable to any civil or criminal proceedings in any court for publication in a newspaper of a substantially true report of any proceedings of either House of Parliament unless the publication is proved to have been made with malice. This immunity is also available for reports or matters broadcast by means of wireless telegraphy[6]. This immunity, however, is not available to publication of proceedings of a secret sitting of the House[7].

(g) Moreover, according to the Constitution, the Parliamentary privileges can be enjoyed even by the persons who are entitled to speak and take part in the proceedings of the House such as Council of Ministers and Attorney General of India. However, the President does not enjoy the privileges even though he is the integral part of the Parliament.

In other respects, the powers, privileges, and immunities of each House of the Parliament and of the members and committees thereof shall be such as may from time to time be defined by Parliament by law and until so defined, shall be those of that House, its members, and committees immediately before the coming into force of Section 15 of the Constitution (Forty-fourth Amendment) Act, 1978.

The framers of the Constitution had provided for the same powers and privileges for members, etc. as were possessed and enjoyed by the House of Commons at the commencement of the Constitution. The reference to the 'House of Commons' in Clause(3) of Article 105 was omitted by the Constitution (Forty-fourth Amendment) Act, 1978. However, no law defining the privileges has been made by the Parliament so far, in actual practice. Hence, the position in this regard remains the same as it existed at the commencement of the Constitution.

STATUTORY PROVISIONS

Apart from the privileges as specified in the Constitution, the Code of Civil Procedure, 1908, provides for freedom from arrest and detention of members under civil process during the continuance of the meeting of the House or of a committee thereof and forty days before its commencement and forty days after its conclusion[8]. The immunity, therefore, has been limited only to civil cases.

PRIVILEGES BASED ON RULES OF PROCEDURE AND PRECEDENTS

- The Speaker/Chairman has a right to receive immediate information of the arrest, detention, conviction, imprisonment, and release of a member on a criminal charge or for a criminal offence.
- Members or officers of the House cannot be compelled to give evidence or to produce documents in courts of law, relating to the proceedings of the House without the permission of the House.
- Members or officers of the House cannot be compelled to attend as witnesses before the other House or a House of a State Legislature or a committee thereof without the permission of the House and without the consent of the member whose attendance is required. In other words, members enjoy exemption from attending as witness in a court.

[5]Article 122(2).

[6]Article 361A.

[7]Article 361A(1), Proviso

[8]Section 135a.

- It is a breach of privilege and contempt of the House to obstruct or molest or assault a member during the execution of his duties, that is, while he is attending the House or when he is coming to, or going from the House. The privilege, however, is not available when the member is not performing any Parliamentary duty.

OTHER PRIVILEGES OF THE HOUSE

(a) The power to commit persons, whether they are members or not, for breach of privilege or contempt of the House;

(b) To compel the attendance of witnesses and to send for persons, papers, and records;

(c) To regulate its procedure and the conduct of its business;

(d) To prohibit the publication of its debates and proceedings;

(e) To exclude strangers from the proceedings of the House and hold secret sittings to debate and discuss on some important matters.

(f) A person found guilty of breach of privilege or contempt of the House may be punished either by imprisonment, or by admonition (warning) or reprimand. Two other punishments may also be awarded to the members for contempt, namely, 'suspension' and 'expulsion' from the House. The House has the power to determine as to what constitutes breach of privilege and contempt. The penal jurisdiction of the House in this regard covers its members as well as strangers and every act of violation of privileges, whether committed in the immediate presence of the House or outside of it.

(g) No member or officer of the House should give evidence in respect of any proceedings of the House or any committee thereof or any document relating to or connected with any such proceedings or in the custody of the officer of the House or produce any such document in a court of law without the leave of the House being first obtained.

(h) No arrest can be made within the precincts of the House nor a legal process, civil or criminal, served without obtaining the permission of the Speaker/Chairman, and this permission is necessary whether the House is in session or not.

(i) It is a breach of privilege and contempt of the House, to make speeches or to print or publish any libels reflecting on the character or proceedings of the House or its committees or on any member of the House for, or relating to his character or conduct, as a Member of Parliament. Such speeches or writings are punished by the House as a contempt on the principle that such acts "tend to obstruct the Houses in the performance of their functions by diminishing the respect due to them".

12.4 FUNCTIONS OF PARLIAMENT[1]

INTRODUCTION

As the Constitution of India adopts a Parliamentary form of government, there is a mixture of legislative and executive organs of the State falling into one. As such, Parliament of India is a multifunctional institution. The most important function of the Indian Parliament is to make and pass laws but there are other equally important functions of the Parliament such as cardinal functions of representation, formation of government, executive and financial control, constituent power, etc. Some of the cardinal roles and functions of the Parliament are discussed in this chapter.

PURPOSE AND ROLE OF THE PARLIAMENT

Representation

The Parliament represents popular will of the people. Members of the Rajya Sabha are elected by the elected members of State Legislative Assembly and are nominated to the Rajya Sabha. The Upper House of the Parliament therefore represents the State. On the other hand, members of the Lok Sabha are elected by popular votes through direct election on the basis of Universal Adult Franchise. Representatives therefore, represent both their constituencies and 'popular will' in the Parliament. As such, the Lok Sabha directly represents the people of India in the Parliament.

Formation of Government

In a Parliamentary form of government, there is a harmonious blending of legislative as well as executive organs of the State. The executives, known as Council of Ministers, are appointed from the Legislatures after every General Election, or a new Lok Sabha is duly elected and constituted. The President of India invites the leader of the majority party or parties to form the Government. Article 75 of the Indian Constitution says that the President shall appoint the Prime Minister and the other Council of Ministers are appointed by the President on the advice of the Prime Minister. The Ministers hold office during the Pleasure of the President. The Council of Ministers are collectively responsible to the Lok Sabha.

Legislative Functions

Law making is the primary function of the Parliament. Under the Constitution of India, Parliament is the supreme legislative body in India. It can make laws on a wide range of subjects mentioned in the Union and Concurrent Lists in the Seventh Schedule of the Constitution. As the Constitution also vests residuary power to the Parliament, it can make laws in areas not specifically assigned to the States. Currently, there are 100 items where the last item is numbered as the 97th Union subject. Few of them are defence, foreign affairs, railways, insurance, communications, currency and coinage, banking, income tax, customs, excise duties, atomic energy, census, etc. Parliament can also make laws on the subjects exclusively reserved for the States under special circumstances such as –

- promulgation of Emergency; or

---

[1]*Parliament of India*, Kshetrimayum Subarta Singh, Department of Political Science, Shyama Prasad Mukherjee College, University of Delhi.

- a resolution passed by the Rajya Sabha with two-thirds special majority; or
- if a resolution is moved by two or more States urging upon the Parliament to make laws for them on certain items of the State list; or
- if there is any international treaty or agreement to be executed.

Every Bill has to be passed by both the Houses and it has to be signed by the President before it becomes law. Moreover, all the ordinances issued by the President must be approved by the Parliament within six weeks after its reassembly. If the ordinance is not approved by the Parliament within the prescribed period, the ordinance shall end.

Controlling The Executives

A significant function of the Parliament is to exercise its control on the Council of Ministers. Article 75(3) of the Indian Constitution states that the Council of Ministers shall hold office as long as they enjoy confidence of the Lok Sabha. Executives are answerable to the House. The Lok Sabha may at any time pass a Vote of No Confidence against the Council of Ministers. If the Lok Sabha conclusively pronounces that the government does not enjoy the confidence of the House, it has no other alternative except to resign. Thus, the Parliament holds the ministers responsible individually and collectively. Parliamentary control over the executive is exercised through a series of mechanisms such as asking questions to the ministers through its members, making ministerial statements, placing documents on the floor, and by raising adjournment motions, cut motions, censure motions, or debates. The ultimate instrument of Parliamentary control is refusing vote supplies or defeating the government on a financial measure or passing a substantive motion of No Confidence in the Council of Ministers. This critical function of the Parliament ensures a responsive and responsible government.

Financial Control

The Parliament of India, especially the Lok Sabha, exercises substantial control in the domain of finance. The executive enjoys the right to formulate the budget. The executive is free to suggest any proposal for expenditure and levying of new taxes to meet the expenditure. Every Financial Year, during the Budget Session of the Parliament, the Finance Minister presents an Annual Budget in the Lok Sabha for its approval. It is the responsibility of the Legislature to ensure that public funds are raised and spent with its consent and control. The executive or the Government of the nation has no authority to spend any money on its own without the approval of the Parliament. Moreover, the Parliament also reviews and scrutinizes the government spending after its approval through various Parliamentary financial committees such as Public Accounts Committee, Committee on Public Undertakings, etc., Thus, the Parliament has pre-budget as well as post-budgetary control on the Executive.

Constituent Power

Parliament is the only authority which can amend the Constitution without changing the 'basic structure' of the Constitution. The amending power of the Parliament is defined under Article 368 of the Indian Constitution. The amending power of Parliament under Article 368 is unlimited and can amend any part of the Constitution, provided it does not alter the basic structure or framework of the Constitution. The amendment of the Constitution undergoes a lengthy process. First, both the Houses of the Parliament can initiate a Constitution Amendment Bill. Most part of Constitution can be amended by a special majority, i.e., a majority of not less than two-thirds of members of each House present and voting. However, some provisions require the approval of at least half of the States after they are passed by the Parliament with required majority. After the Constitution Amendment Bill is passed and ratified, the bill is presented to the President for his/her assent. It is mandatory for the President to sign the bill.

Judicial Power

The Parliament of India enjoys certain judicial functions. It has the power to impeach the President and remove the Vice-President. The Parliament also recommends for the removal of the Supreme Court and High Court Judges. It can also punish its members and officials for contempt. This power cannot be subjected to review of the court.

Approval of Emergencies

The Parliament has the power to approve the three types of emergencies – National Emergency, President's Rule, and Financial Emergency.

Electoral Functions of the Parliament

The Parliament has the power to elect the President and the Vice-President. The Lok Sabha has the power to elect the Speaker and the Deputy Speaker. On the other hand, the Rajya Sabha has the power to elect the Deputy Chairman.

Boundaries and Structure of the Federal Units (States)

The Parliament alone has the power to alter the boundaries of the states, change the names of the States, create or abolish state legislative councils, and establish a common High Court for two or more states.

Rule Making Power of the Parliament

Each House of Parliament has the power to frame its own rules to regulate its own procedure. Parliament can regulate the organisation and jurisdiction of the Supreme Court.

Deliberative Functions of the Parliament

To deliberate upon matters of national importance, public issues, problems, and needs is an important function of a modern Legislature. Through this function, the Legislature reflects the public opinion over various issues. The debates held in the Legislature have a great educative value for the people.

RELATIVE POWERS OF LOK SABHA AND RAJYA SABHA

Instances of Provision of Equal Powers

There are some important matters in respect of which the Constitution has placed both Houses of Parliament on an equal footing as may be seen from the following list:

1. Equal right in the election and impeachment of the President (Articles 54 and 61);
2. Equal right in the election of the Vice-President (Article 66);
3. Equal right in making law defining Parliamentary privileges and also to punish for contempt (Article 105);
4. Equal right in introduction and passage of Ordinary Bills as well as Constitution Amendment Bill;
5. Equal right in creation and abolition of the State Legislative Councils;

6. Equal right in altering the boundaries, changing the names of the States, etc.;
7. Equal right to approve the Proclamation of National Emergency (issued under Article 352), Proclamation of Financial Emergency, and Proclamations regarding failure of the Constitutional machinery in States (issued under Article 356);
8. Equal rights in enlarging the jurisdiction of the Supreme Court;
9. Equal right in enlarging the jurisdiction of the Union Public Service Commission and in setting up of Joint Public Service Commission for two or more States; and
10. Equal right with the Lok Sabha to receive reports and papers from various statutory authorities, namely:
    (a) Audit Reports from the Comptroller and Auditor General of India [Article 151(1)];
    (b) Reports of the Union Public Service Commission. [Article 323(1)];
    (c) Reports of the Special Officer for the Scheduled Castes and Scheduled Tribes [Article 338(2)];
    (d) Report of the Commission to investigate the conditions of the Backward Classes [Article 340(3)];
    (e) Report of the Special Officer for Linguistic Minorities [Article 350 B(2)]; and
11. A Member of the Council of Ministers can be a Member of either House of Parliament;

Special Powers of Lok Sabha

1. Rajya Sabha has a limited role in financial matters. A Money Bill cannot be introduced in the Rajya Sabha. It has to be introduced only in the Lok Sabha and after it is passed by that House, it has to be transmitted to the Rajya Sabha for its recommendation. The Lok Sabha has the power of either accepting or rejecting the recommendations, if any, made by the Rajya Sabha. If a Money Bill is not returned by the Rajya Sabha within fourteen days of its receipt from the Lok Sabha, it will be deemed to have been passed by both Houses after the expiry of the said period.
2. Only the Speaker has the final power to decide whether a Bill is a Money Bill or not.
3. The Annual Budget of the Government of India has to be laid before the Rajya Sabha as well and members have the right to discuss the same like the Lok Sabha. But the Rajya Sabha does not have the power to vote on grants.
4. Financial Bills also cannot be introduced in the Rajya Sabha but there is no other limitation on the power of the Rajya Sabha with respect to Financial Bills.
5. The Executive or the Council of Ministers are responsible to the Lok Sabha and the Government continues in power as long as it enjoys confidence in the Lok Sabha. In other words, the No Confidence motion can be introduced only in the Lok Sabha.
6. The resolution for the discontinuance of the National Emergency can be introduced and passed only by the Lok Sabha.
7. The Speaker can preside over the Joint sitting. Whereas, the Chairman of the Rajya Sabha cannot preside over a Joint sitting. Moreover, in a Joint sitting, the Lok Sabha or the Lok Sabha's premise has higher chances of winning compared to Rajya Sabha because of its strength.

Special Powers of Rajya Sabha

The Constitution vests some special powers in the Rajya Sabha to exercise its federal mandate as it represents the States and Union territories in the Parliament.

1. **Legislation on State matters :** As a federal chamber, Rajya Sabha can initiate Central intervention in the State Legislative field. Article 249 of the Constitution provides that the Rajya Sabha may pass a resolution, by a majority of not less than two-thirds of the Members present and voting, to the effect that it is necessary or expedient in the national interest that Parliament should make laws with respect to any matter enumerated in the State List. If such a resolution is adopted, Parliament will be authorised to make laws on the subject specified in the resolution, for the whole or any part of the territory of India. Such a resolution will remain in force for such period, not exceeding one year, as may be specified therein, but this period can be extended by one year at a time by passing further resolution.
2. **Removal of Vice-President :** The resolution to remove the Vice-President can be introduced or initiated only in the Rajya Sabha.
3. **Creation of All India Services :** Another exclusive power of the Rajya Sabha is contained in Article 312 of the Constitution wherein, if the Rajya Sabha passes a resolution by a majority of not less than two-thirds of the members present and voting declaring that it is necessary or expedient in the national interest to create one or more All India Services common to the Union and the States, Parliament will have the power to create by law such services.
4. **Approval of Proclamation :** Yet another special power of the Rajya Sabha relates to the Proclamation of Emergency. The proviso to Clause (4) of Article 352 of the Constitution, inter alia, provides that if a Proclamation of Emergency is issued when the House of the People remains dissolved and a resolution approving the Proclamation is passed by the Council of States, the Proclamation would be equally effective up to a maximum period of 30 days from the date on which the House of the People first sits after its reconstitution. This provision, therefore, appears to suggest that there might be an occasion when the Council of States could be called into a session at a time when the House of People stands dissolved. The proviso to Clause (3) of Article 356 of the Constitution which relates to the Proclamation to be issued by the President in case of failure of constitutional machinery in a State contains a similar stipulation.

DECLINE OF PARLIAMENTARY GOVERNANCE

1. There has been a consistent decline in the number of days for which both Houses of the Parliament sits every year. As a result of fewer deliberations by the Parliamentarians, most of the work is left for the Executive with full discretion in their hands manifested in increasing promulgation of ordinances. This trend is the serious encroachment on the jurisdiction of the Parliament.
2. Absenteeism of Parliamentarians during the sessions is another major challenge that our Parliament is facing. There is a growing tendency among them to treat the sessions casually.

Moreover, there is decline in terms of the quality of debates in the House. The matters of public importance have been ignored and not discussed while matters requiring least attention are discussed for long durations. For instance, the valuable time of the Parliament was wasted in discussing matters pertaining to corruption issues or opposition parties tend to focus on scandals with immediate political pay-offs rather than on the day-to-day functioning of government, etc., without giving appropriate time to legislative affairs.

3. It is the duty of the Parliament to discuss budget demands of all ministries and other bodies, but in the present session, budget demands of most of the ministries were not even discussed. Hence, demands of only few ministries were discussed while the rest were forwarded for voting without any deliberations.
4. The legislative process is becoming more complex and demands a set of technical skills that few Parliamentarians possess.
5. Much of the inattention to legislative matters is due to Parliament's own predilections and incentive structures.
6. MPs consider their primary function as go-betweens for constituents rather than lawmakers.
7. Most committee reports are never tabled for deliberation and discussion in the Parliament.
8. After a bill has been passed, it does not become a law that can be enforced until a notification is gazetted – a step which is sometimes forgotten, either deliberately or otherwise.

12.5 PARLIAMENTARY COMMITTEES[1]

BACKGROUND

The work done by the Parliament in modern times is not only varied in nature, but considerable in volume. The time at its disposal is limited. It cannot, therefore, give close consideration to all the legislative and other matters that come up before it. A good deal of its business is, therefore, transacted by what are called the Parliamentary Committees.

Types of Parliamentary Committees

Parliamentary Committees are of two kinds:

- Ad hoc Committees; and
- The Standing Committees.

Ad hoc Committees are appointed for a specific purpose and they cease to exist when they finish the task assigned to them and submit a report. The principal Ad hoc Committees are the Select and Joint Committees on Bills. Others like the Railway Convention Committee, the Committees on the Draft Five Year Plans, and the Hindi Equivalents Committee were appointed for specific purposes.

On the other hand, Standing Committees are permanent and regular Committees which are constituted from time to time in pursuance of the provisions of an Act of Parliament or Rules of Procedure and Conduct of Business in Lok Sabha/Rajya Sabha. The work of these Committees is of continuous nature. The Financial Committees, Departmentally Related Standing Committees, and some other Committees come under the category of Standing Committees.

Some of these Standing Committees act as Parliament's 'Watch Dogs' over the Executive. These are the Committees on Subordinate Legislation, the Committee on Government Assurances, the Committee on Estimates, the Committee on Public Accounts, and the Committee on Public Undertakings and Departmentally Related Standing Committees (DRSCs). The Committee on Estimates, the Committee on Public Accounts, the Committee on Public Undertakings, and DRSCs play an important role in exercising a check over governmental expenditure and Policy formulation.

- *The Standing Committees (DRSC)*, aligned with specific Ministries examine their performance and budgets apart from bills or subjects related to their respective Ministries.
- *The Financial Committees* are primarily responsible for scrutinising the expenditure priorities of the government and suggesting measures to improve efficiency in spending and performance of Public Sector Undertakings.
- The Select Committee is formed for analysing a specific legislation/policy and is disbanded after submission of its reports.
- The Administrative Committees are primarily responsible for ensuring day-to-day activities of the Legislature planned in consultation with the members.

---

[1]Source http://164.100.47.193/Loksabha/Committee/Comm_Introductionnew.pdf#page=3

The Membership and tenure of the Parliamentary Committees are discussed in this chapter.

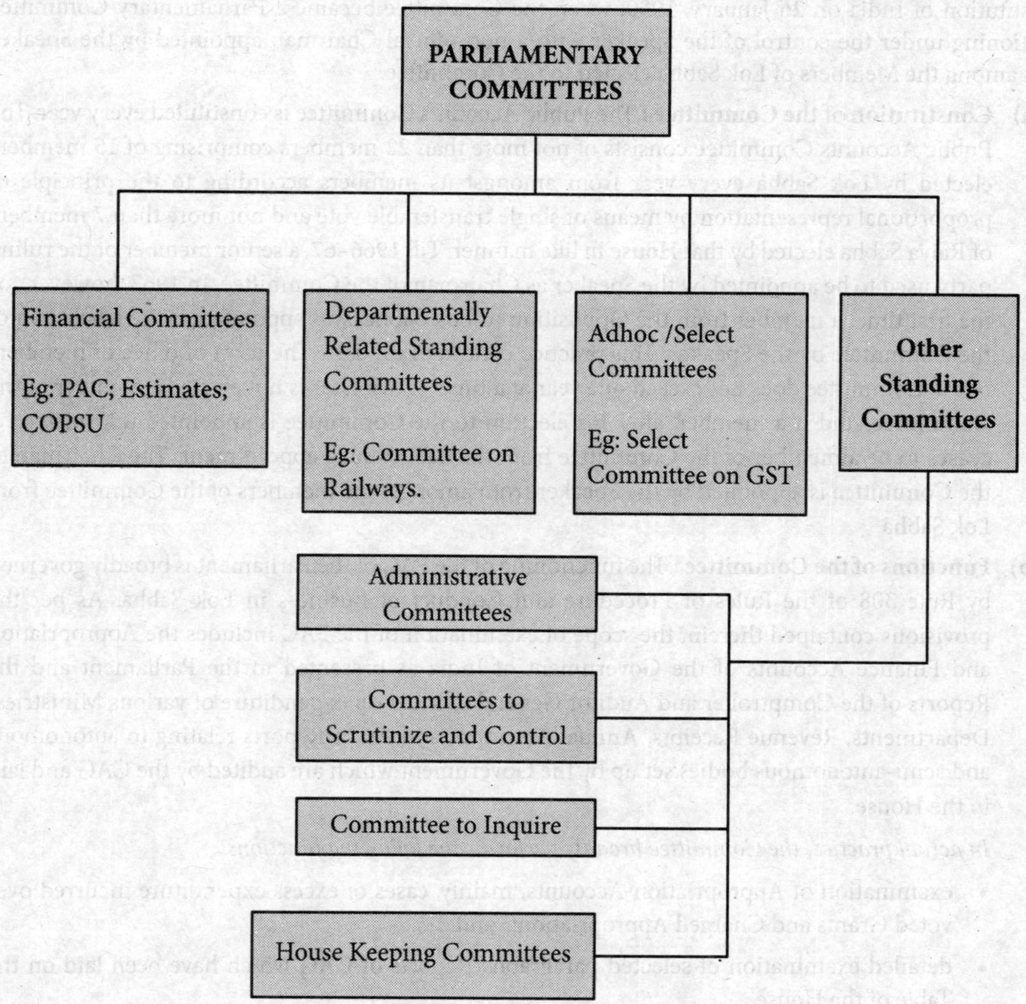

FINANCIAL COMMITTEES

Sl. No.	Name of Committee	No. of Members	Tenure	Members nominated or elected
1	Estimates Committee	30	1 year	Elected by the Lok Sabha
2	Public Accounts Committee	22(15LS+7RS)	1 year	Elected by the two House(s).
3	Committee on Public Undertakings	22(15LS+7RS)	1 year	Elected by the two House(s).

Public Accounts Committee

The Committee on Public Accounts was first set up in 1921 in the wake of the Montagu-Chelmsford Reforms. The Finance Member of the Executive Council used to be the Chairman of the Committee.

The Committee on Public Accounts underwent a radical change with the coming into force of the Constitution of India on 26 January, 1950, when the Committee became a Parliamentary Committee functioning under the control of the Speaker with a non-official Chairman appointed by the Speaker from among the Members of Lok Sabha elected to the Committee.

(a) Constitution of the Committee : The Public Accounts Committee is constituted every year. The Public Accounts Committee consists of not more than 22 members comprising of 15 members elected by Lok Sabha every year from amongst its members according to the principle of proportional representation by means of single transferable vote and not more than 7 members of Rajya Sabha elected by that House in like manner. Till 1966–67, a senior member of the ruling party used to be appointed by the Speaker as Chairman of the Committee. In 1967, however, for the first time, a member from the Opposition in Lok Sabha, was appointed as the Chairman of the Committee by the Speaker. This practice continues till date. The term of office of members of the Committee does not exceed one year at a time. A Minister is not elected a member of the Committee, and if a member, after his election to the Committee is appointed a Minister, he ceases to be a member of the Committee from the date of such appointment. The Chairman of the Committee is appointed by the Speaker from amongst the members of the Committee from Lok Sabha.

(b) Functions of the Committee : The functioning of the PAC of the Parliament is broadly governed by Rule 308 of the Rules of Procedure and Conduct of Business in Lok Sabha. As per the provisions contained therein, the scope of examination of the PAC includes the Appropriation and Finance Accounts of the Government of India as presented to the Parliament and the Reports of the Comptroller and Auditor General of India on expenditure of various Ministries/Departments, Revenue Receipts, Annual Accounts, and Audit Reports relating to autonomous and semi-autonomous bodies set up by the Government which are audited by the CAG and laid in the House.

In actual practice, the Committee broadly performs the following functions:

- examination of Appropriation Accounts, mainly, cases of excess expenditure incurred over voted Grants and Charged Appropriations; and
- detailed examination of selected paragraphs/Reports of CAG which have been laid on the Table of the House.

While examining Accounts/Reports, an important function of the Committee is to ascertain that money granted by Parliament has been spent by the Government within the scope of demand. In other words, it is the duty of the Committee to satisfy itself:

i. that the moneys shown in the accounts as having been disbursed were legally available for, and applicable to the service or purpose to which they have been applied or charged;

ii. that the expenditure conforms to the authority which governs it;

iii. that every re-appropriation has been made in accordance with the provisions made in this behalf under rules framed by competent authority;

iv. that the statement of accounts showing the income and expenditure of State Corporations, trading and manufacturing schemes, concerns and projects together with the balance sheets and statements of profit and loss accounts which the President may have required to be prepared or are prepared under the provisions of statutory rules by the CAG have been examined;

v. that the statement of accounts showing the income and expenditure of autonomous and semi-autonomous bodies, the audit of which may be conducted by the CAG of India either under the directions of the President or by a statute of Parliament have been examined; and

vi. that the report of the CAG in cases where the President may have required him to conduct an audit of any receipts and to examine the accounts of stores and stocks have been considered.

The functions of the Committee extend, however, beyond the formality of expenditure to its wisdom, faithfulness, and economy. The Committee, thus, examines cases involving losses, nugatory expenditure, and financial irregularities. However, the Committee's findings are in the form of recommendations and are not binding on the government.

(c) **Role of CAG :** The Committee examines the Government's accounts in the light of the audit report with the assistance of the CAG. Thus, the exact content of the work of the PAC depends largely on what it receives from the Audit institution. The CAG is "the acting hand of the Committee" and "its guide, philosopher, and friend".

(d) **Limitations of the Committee :** Though the Committee is empowered to act upon the audit reports of the CAG, and also to keep a check on the Union government's expenses, there are still a few limitations on its working. The limitations of the Public Accounts Committee are given below:

i. Broadly, it cannot intervene in the questions of policy.
ii. It can keep a tab on the expenses only after they are incurred, i.e., it has no power to limit expenses.
iii. It cannot intervene in matters of day-to-day administration.
iv. Any recommendation that the Committee makes is only advisory in nature. They can be ignored by the Ministries.
v. It is not vested with the power of disallowance of expenditures by the departments.
vi. Being only an Executive body, it cannot issue an order. Only the Parliament can take a final decision on its findings.

Estimates Committee[1]

The Estimates Committee was first created in April, 1950 on the recommendations of John Mathai, the then Finance Minister. There had been a predecessor of Estimates Committee called as Standing Finance Committee, which was first constituted in 1921 and attached to the Finance Department of the Government of India.

(a) **Composition :** The Estimates Committee is a Committee of Lok Sabha. The Committee consists of 30 members—all from Lok Sabha who are elected by the Lok Sabha every year from amongst its members according to the principle of proportional representation by means of single transferable vote. The Chairperson of the Committee is appointed by the Speaker from amongst the members elected to the Committee. A Minister is not elected to be a member of the Committee, and if a member, after election to the Committee, is appointed a Minister, such member ceases to be a member of the Committee from the date of such appointment. The term of office of the members of the Committee does not exceed one year.

[1]Rule 310 of the Rules of Procedure and Conduct of Business in Lok Sabha.

(b) Functions of the Committee : The Estimates Committee assists the Parliament in overseeing pre-budget estimates of the government, and examines whether the proposed expenditure is within the limits of government policy. It also reports on administrative reforms needed within Ministries, and suggests policies to bring about efficiency in administration. The Committee may select subjects on the estimated expenditure of a part of a Ministry. The Speaker may also refer a subject for examination to the Committee. In other words, the functions of the Committee can be listed as follows:

i. To report what economies, improvements in organization, efficiency, or administrative reform, consistent with the policy underlying the estimates, may be affected;

ii. To suggest alternative policies in order to bring about efficiency and economy in administration;

iii. To examine whether the money is well laid out within the limits of the policy implied in the estimates; and

iv. To suggest the form in which the estimates shall be presented to the Parliament.

However, Public Undertakings allotted to the Committee on Public Undertakings either under the Rules of Procedure of Lok Sabha or by the Speaker do not come under the purview of the Committee on Estimates.

(c) Working of the Estimates Committee : Soon after it is constituted, the Estimates Committee selects such of the estimates pertaining to a Ministry/Department of the Central Government or such of the statutory and other bodies of the Central Government (which do not fall within the purview of the Committee on Public Undertakings for examination during the year) as may seem fit to the Committee. The Committee also examines matters of special interest which may arise or come to light in the course of its work or which are specially referred to it by the House or the Speaker.

The examination by the Estimates Committee for the Ministries/Departments of Government is a continuing exercise throughout the financial year and the Estimates Committee reports to the House as its examination proceeds. That's the reason why "Estimates Committee" is also called as "Continuous economy Committee". It is not incumbent on the Committee to examine the entire estimates in any one year. The Demands for Grants may be finally voted even though the Committee has made no report.

(d) Limitations of the Committee :

- The estimates given by the Executive will be scrutinized by the Estimates Committee after it has been voted by the Parliament. Moreover, in a year, the Committee gets to scrutinize the estimates of only few Ministries/Departments.
- The recommendations of the Estimates Committee are advisory in nature.
- The Estimates Committee cannot question about the policies laid down by the Parliament.
- CAG does not provide any assistance in scrutinizing the estimates of the Ministries or various Departments.

Committee on Public Undertakings

Till April 1964, the affairs of Public Enterprises in India used to be looked after by the two Committees: namely the Estimates Committee and Public Accounts Committee. But in view of huge investments and manifold increase in the activities of public enterprises, it was felt that there should be a separate agency which should look into the working of public enterprises in detail and report to the Parliament. In 1964, on the recommendation of the Krishna Menon Committee, a separate Committee on Public Undertakings was constituted. This Committee, which started functioning from May 1, 1964 took over the work relating to autonomous Public Enterprises from the other two Committees, viz. the Estimates Committee and the Public Accounts Committee.

(a) **Composition :** The Committee On Public Undertakings consists of 22 members – 15 members from Lok Sabha and 7 members from Rajya Sabha. The members of the Committee are elected every year in accordance with the principle of proportional representation by means of single transferable vote. A Minister is not eligible for election to this Committee. The Chairman of the Committee is appointed by the Speaker from amongst the members who are elected from the Lok Sabha.

(b) **Functions of the Committee :** The Principal functions of the Committee are as follows:

i. to examine the reports and accounts of Public Undertakings as specified in the Fourth Schedule of the Rules of Procedure and Conduct of Business in Lok Sabha;

ii. to examine the reports, if any, of the Comptroller and Auditor General of India on the Public Undertakings;

iii. to examine, in the context of autonomy and efficiency of the public undertakings, whether the affairs of the Public Undertakings are being managed in accordance with sound business principles and prudent commercial practice;

iv. to exercise such other functions vested in the Public Accounts Committee and the Estimates Committee in relation to the Public Undertakings as are not covered by clauses (i), (ii), and (iii) above and as may be allotted to the Committee from time to time.

The Committee shall not examine:

i. Matters of major Government policy as distinct from business or commercial functions of public enterprises;

ii. matters of day-to-day administration;

iii. matters for consideration for which machinery is already established by any special statute under which a particular Public Enterprise is established.

(c) **Limitations :**

- Practically, the Committee can scrutinize the reports and accounts of only a few Public Sector Undertakings per year.
- The technical aspects of the Public Sector Undertakings cannot be scrutinized by the Committee as the members of the Committee do not possess the technical expertise to do so.
- The recommendations of the Committee are merely advisory in nature and the work of the Committee is more in the nature of a post-mortem.

DEPARTMENTALLY RELATED STANDING COMMITTEES (DRSCs)

With a view to ensure specialized and Ministry/Department specific scrutiny and oversight of the Executive by the Legislature, the Parliament of India introduced the system of Departmentally Related Standing Committees (DRSCs) in 1993. Initially, consisting of 17 Committees, the DRSCs System was expanded to 24 Committees after reorganization in 2004. Thus, currently there are 24 Departmentally Related Standing Committees covering under their jurisdiction all the Ministries/ Departments of the

Government of India. Each of these Committees consists of 31 Members - 21 from Lok Sabha and 10 from Rajya Sabha to be nominated by the Speaker, Lok Sabha and the Chairman, Rajya Sabha, respectively. The term of Office of these Committees does not exceed one year.

The names of the 24 Committees are as under[2]:

1. Committee on Commerce
2. Committee on Home Affairs
3. Committee on Human Resource Development
4. Committee on Industry
5. Committee on Science & Technology and Environment & Forests
6. Committee on Transport, Tourism and Culture
7. Committee on Health and Family Welfare
8. Committee on Personnel, Public Grievances, Law and Justice
9. Committee on Agriculture
10. Committee on Information Technology
11. Committee on Defence
12. Committee on Energy
13. Committee on External Affairs
14. Committee on Finance
15. Committee on Food, Consumer Affairs and Public Distribution
16. Committee on Labour
17. Committee on Petroleum and Natural Gas
18. Committee on Railways
19. Committee on Urban Development
20. Committee on Water Resources
21. Committee on Chemicals and Fertilizers
22. Committee on Rural Development
23. Committee on Coal and Steel
24. Committee on Social Justice and Empowerment

Till the 13th Lok Sabha, each Standing Committee consisted of not more than 45 members (30 to be nominated by the Speaker from amongst the members of Lok Sabha and 15 to be nominated by the Chairman, Rajya Sabha from amongst the members of Rajya Sabha). However, with restructuring of DRSCs in July, 2004, each DRSC consists of 31 Members – 21 from Lok Sabha and 10 from Rajya Sabha. The Chairman of the first eight Standing Committees is appointed by the Chairman of Rajya Sabha and in respect of the remaining Committees, the Chairman is appointed by the Speaker of Lok Sabha from amongst the members of the Committee. A Minister is not eligible to be nominated as a member of any of the Standing Committees and if a member, after his nomination to any of the Standing

[2]Out of 24 Committees, 8 Committees (Sl. No. 1 to 8) are serviced by the Rajya Sabha Secretariat and 16 Committees (Sl. No. 9 to 24) by the Lok Sabha Secretariat.

Committee, is appointed a Minister, he or she ceases to be a member of the Committee from the date of such appointment. The term of office of each Standing Committee is one year from the date of its constitution.

Functions of DRSCs

With reference to the Ministries/ Departments under their purview, the functions of these Committees are:

(a) To consider the Demands for Grants of the concerned Ministries/Departments and make Reports on the same to the Houses;

(b) To examine such Bills pertaining to the concerned Ministries/Departments as are referred to the Committee by the Speaker, Lok Sabha or the Chairman, Rajya Sabha as the case may be, and make Reports thereon;

(c) To consider Annual Reports of the concerned Ministries/Departments and make Reports thereon; and

(d) To consider national basic long-term policy documents presented to the Houses, if referred to the Committee by the Speaker, Lok Sabha or the Chairman, Rajya Sabha as the case may be, and make Reports thereon.

Procedures of DRSCs

Procedure followed by the Standing Committees relating to consideration of Demands for Grants

After the general discussion on the Budget in the House is over, the Lok Sabha is adjourned for a fixed period. The Committee considers the Demands for Grants (DFGs) of the Ministries/Departments under its jurisdiction during the aforesaid period and presents/lays Reports. There is a separate Report on the Demands for Grants of each Ministry/Department. The Report on Demands for Grants does not suggest anything of the nature of cut motions. The Demands for Grants are considered by the House in the light of the Reports of the Committee.

Procedure followed by the Standing Committees relating to consideration of Bills

The Committee considers only such Bills introduced in either of the Houses as are referred to it by the Speaker, Lok Sabha or the Chairman, Rajya Sabha as the case may be. The Committee considers the general principles and clauses of the Bills referred to it and makes Reports thereon within the given time.

Procedure relating to examination of National Long-Term Policy Documents

The Committee considers national long-term policy documents presented to the Parliament and referred to it by the Speaker, Lok Sabha or Chairman, Rajya Sabha and make Reports on such documents.

These Committees do not consider matters of day-to-day administration of the concerned Ministries/ Departments. The Departmentally Related Standing Committee System is a path breaking endeavor of the Parliamentary surveillance over administration. With the emphasis of their functioning to concentrate on long-term plans and policies guiding the working of the Executive, these Committees are providing necessary direction, guidance, and inputs for broad policy formulations and in achievement of the long-term national perspective by the Executive.

Moreover, the Chairman of a Committee may appoint Study groups/Sub-Committees from amongst the members of the respective Committees with a view to making detailed study/examination of the subject(s) selected by them, scrutinizing the Action Taken[3] replies of the Government on the recommendations contained in the previous reports and for considering procedural and general matters. The Standing Committees may also, if necessary, avail of the expert opinion or the public opinion before preparing the report.

Advantages of Constituting DRSCs[4]

1. First, they help Parliament manage its business better. It is easier to examine a topic in depth by a Committee of 30 than by an assembly of 700.
2. Second, they enable input from experts and those who may be directly affected by a policy or legislation. For example, the DRSCs often invite comments from the public and call people to testify.
3. Third, being outside direct public glare allows members to discuss issues and reach consensus without worrying about Constituency pressures.
4. A related fourth advantage is that the Anti-defection Law does not apply to Committees — therefore, decisions are not usually made on party lines.
5. Finally, these Committees allow members to focus on some specific areas and build their expertise, which helps them scrutinise issues more thoroughly.

Weaknesses of DRSCs

1. There is lack of standing research support. They are backed by the general support staff of Parliament and do not have a dedicated set of researchers associated with them. While they can (and often do) reach out to outside experts, there is no internal expertise that can finesse such opinion.
2. All Committees meet behind closed doors and only the final report is published, with summary minutes. There have been arguments that the meetings should be televised or at least the full transcripts be published. The counter-argument is that Committees work as discussion forums and often reach consensus, as there is no pressure on members to posture for their support base. This would be lost if detailed proceedings were made public. A middle path would be to publish the submissions and evidence given by various experts and members of the public so that any advocacy is made more transparent while keeping the members free from Constituency pressures.

---

[3]Action Taken Reports - The reports of the Standing Committees have persuasive value and are treated as considered advice given by the Committee. The Demands for Grants and Bills are considered by the House in the light of the reports of the Committees. In respect of reports on Demands for Grants and other subjects the Ministry/ Department concerned is requested to take action on the recommendations and conclusions contained in the report and furnish action taken replies thereon within three months. Action taken notes received from the Ministries/Departments are examined by the Committee and Action Taken Reports thereon are presented to the House.

[4]Strengthening India's mini-parliaments; Published on October 10, 2017; Published in www.thehindubusinessline.com; The writer is the President & co-founder of PRS Legislative Research, Delhi, and a CASI Fall 2017 Visiting Scholar. This article is by special arrangement with the Center for the Advanced Study of India, University of Pennsylvania.

Overview of DRSCs

In sum, the DRSC system has been a fairly successful experiment. It is important to further strengthen its ability for detailed scrutiny of issues so that it helps the Parliament work better in its lawmaking and accountability roles. These would include mandatory examination of all Bills, creating research teams, and improving the transparency of input from advocacy groups. Many MPs call these Committees "mini-Parliaments" and strengthening their working will improve Parliament's overall effectiveness.

OTHER STANDING COMMITTEES

Sl. No.	Name of Committee	No. of Members	Tenure	Chairman and Members
1	Business Advisory Committee	15 (Lok Sabha) 11 (Rajya Sabha)	Not fixed. Can continue in office till reconstituted.	Speaker is the ex-officio Chairman in Lok Sabha; Chairman is the ex-officio Chairman in Rajya Sabha; Members are Nominated by the Speaker or the Chairman respectively.
2	Committee of Privileges	15 (In Lok Sabha); 10 (In Rajya Sabha)	Not fixed. Can continue in office till reconstituted.	Members are nominated by the Speaker, Lok Sabha and the Chairman, Rajya Sabha Respectively.
3	Committee on Absence of Members from the Sittings of the House	15	1 year	Members are nominated by the Speaker, Lok Sabha
4	Committee on Empowerment of Women	30 (20 LS+ 10 RS)	1 year	Members are nominated by the Speaker, Lok Sabha and the Chairman, Rajya Sabha respectively.
5	Committee on Government Assurances	15 (In Lok Sabha); 10 (In Rajya Sabha)	1 year	Members are nominated by the Speaker, Lok Sabha and by Chairman, Rajya Sabha respectively.
6	Committee on Papers Laid on the Table	15 (Lok Sabha) 10 (Rajya Sabha)	1 year	Members are nominated by the Speaker, Lok Sabha
7	Committee on Petitions	15	Not fixed. Can continue in office till reconstituted	Nominated by the Speaker, Lok Sabha
8	Committee on Private Members' Bills and Resolutions	15	1 year	Deputy Speaker is the Chairman when nominated as member of the Committee. Members are nominated by the Speaker.

9	Committee on Subordinate Legislation	15 (Lok Sabha) 15 (Rajya Sabha)	1 year	Members are nominated by the Speaker, Lok Sabha and by Chairman, Rajya Sabha respectively.
10	General Purposes Committee	Not fixed	Not fixed.	Chairmanship and Membership is ex-officio.
11	House Committee	12 (In Lok Sabha); 10 (In Rajya Sabha)	1 year	Members are nominated by the Speaker, Lok Sabha and the Chairman, Rajya Sabha Respectively.
12	Joint Committee on Offices of Profit	15 (10 LS + 5 RS)	For the duration of one Lok Sabha	Members are elected by the two Houses.
13	Joint Committee on Salaries and Allowances of MPs.	15 (10 LS + 5 RS)	1 year	Members are nominated by the Speaker, Lok Sabha and the Chairman, Rajya Sabha. The Committee members elects its Chairperson.
14	Library Committee	9 (6 LS + 3 RS)	1 year	Members are nominated by the Speaker, Lok Sabha and the Chairman, Rajya Sabha.
15	Rules Committee	15 (In Lok Sabha) 16 (In Rajya Sabha)	Not fixed. Can continue in office till reconstituted	Speaker is the ex-officio Chairman in Lok Sabha; Chairman is the ex-officio Chairman in Rajya Sabha; Members are nominated by the Speaker, Lok Sabha or the Chairman respectively.
16	Committee on the Welfare of Scheduled Castes & Scheduled Tribes	30 (20 LS + 10 RS)	1 year	Members are elected by the two House(s).

AD HOC COMMITTEES

Sl. No.	Name of Committee	No. of Members	Tenure	Members nominated or elected
1	Railway Convention Committee	18 (12 LS + 6 RS)	For the duration of one Lok Sabha	Nominated by the Speaker, Lok Sabha and by the Chairman, Rajya Sabha
2	Committee on Provision of Computers to Members of Lok Sabha	10	For the duration of one Lok Sabha	Nominated by the Speaker
3	Committee on MP Local Area Development Scheme	24	1 year	Nominated by the Speaker

4	Committee on Ethics	15 (In Lok Sabha); 10 (In Rajya Sabha).	Not fixed. Can continue in office till reconstituted.	Members are nominated by the Speaker, Lok Sabha and by Chairman, Rajya Sabha respectively.
5	Committee on Food Management in Parliament House Complex	15 (10 LS + 5 RS)	1 year	Nominated by the Speaker, Lok Sabha and the Chairman, Rajya Sabha.
6	Committee on Installation of Portraits/Statutes of National Leaders and Parliamentarians	12 (8 LS + 4 RS)	For the duration of one Lok Sabha	Nominated by the Speaker, Lok Sabha and the Chairman, Rajya Sabha.
7	Committee on Security in Parliament House Complex	10 (7 LS + 3 RS)	1 year	Nominated by the Speaker, Lok Sabha and the Chairman, Rajya Sabha.
8	JPC on Maintenance of Heritage Character and Development of Parliament House Complex	10 (7LS + 3 RS) + 3 ex officio members (Dy. Chairman, RS, M/o Urban Development, M/o Home Affairs) + 1 Special Invitee (M/o Parliamentary Affairs	For the duration of one Lok Sabha	Nominated by the Speaker, Lok Sabha and the Chairman, Rajya Sabha.
9	JPC to examine matters relating to allocation and pricing of telecom licences and spectrum	30 (20 LS + 10 RS)	Till submission of Report	Names of Members included in the motion adopted by the House

IMPORTANT: ***A Minister is not eligible for election or nomination to the financial Committees, DRSCs, and Committees on (1) Empowerment of Women, (2) Government Assurances, (3) Petitions, (4) Subordinate Legislation, and (5) Welfare of Scheduled Castes and Scheduled Tribes.***

ADMINISTRATIVE COMMITTEES

Business Advisory Committee

Each House will have its own Business Advisory Committee. It recommends the time that should be allotted for the discussion of such Government, Legislative, and other business as the Speaker/ Chairman, in consultation with the Leader of the House, may direct to be referred to the Committee. The Committee, on its own initiative, may also recommend to the Government to bring forward particular subjects for discussion in the House and recommend allocation of time for such discussions.

Committee on Absence of Members from the Sittings of the House

This Committee considers the applications from members for leave of absence from the sittings of the House and examines every case where a member has been absent for a period of 60 days or more, without permission, from the sitting of the House. Only Lok Sabha has such a Committee. Whereas, in Rajya Sabha, there is no such Committee and such matters are handled by the House itself.

Committee on Private Members' Bills and Resolutions

The said Committee classifies and allots time to Private Members' Bills and Resolutions, examines Private Members' Bills seeking to amend the Constitution before their introduction in the Lok Sabha, and also examines such Private Members' Bills where the legislative competence of the House is challenged. There is no such Committee in Rajya Sabha. The said matters in Rajya Sabha will be taken care by the Business Advisory Committee of Rajya Sabha.

Rules Committee

Each House will have its own Rules Committee. The said Committee considers matters of procedure and conduct of business in the House and recommends any amendments or additions to the Rules of Procedure and Conduct of Business of the House that are considered necessary.

General Purposes Committee

This Committee advises the Speaker on such matters concerning the affairs of the House as may be referred to it by the Speaker from time to time. Each House will have its own Committee. The Speaker/ Chairman is the ex-officio Chairperson of the Committee which consists of the Deputy Speaker/ Deputy Chairman. Members of the Panel include the Chairpersons/Vice-Chairpersons of all Standing Committees of the House, Leaders of recognized parties/groups in the House, and such other members as may be nominated by the Speaker/Chairman. Thus, the Committee considers and advices on such matters concerning the affairs of the House as may be referred to it by the Speaker/Chairman from time to time and which do not appropriately fall within the purview of any other Parliamentary Committee.

COMMITTEES TO SCRUTINIZE AND CONTROL

Committee on Empowerment of Women

It's a common Committee of Lok Sabha and the Rajya Sabha. The Committee was constituted in the year 1997.

Following are the functions of the Committee:

- Consider the reports submitted by the National Commission for Women and to report on the measures that should be taken by the Union Government for improving the status/conditions of women in respect of matters within the purview of the Union Government, including the administrations of the Union Territories;
- Examine the measures taken by the Union Government to secure for women equality, status, and dignity in all matters;
- Examine the measures taken by the Union Government for comprehensive education and adequate representation of women in Legislative bodies/services and other fields;
- Report on the working of the welfare programmes for the women;
- Report on the action taken by the Union Government and administrations of the Union Territories on the measures proposed by the Committee; and
- Examine such other matters as may seem fit to the Committee or are specifically referred to it by the Speaker (Lok Sabha) or the Chairman (Rajya Sabha).

Committee on Government Assurances

This Committee was constituted in the year 1953. Each House has its own Committee. The said Committee scrutinizes the assurances, promises, undertakings, etc. given by Ministers from time to time and to report on the extent to which such assurances, etc. have been implemented and to see whether such implementation has taken place within the minimum time necessary for the purpose.

Committee on Papers Laid on the Table

This Committee was constituted in the year 1975. Each House has its own Committee. The said Committee examines all papers laid on the Table of the House by Ministers (other than those which fall within the purview of the Committee on Subordinate Legislation or any other Parliamentary Committee) and to report to the House –

- whether there has been compliance of the provisions of the Constitution, Act, Rule or Regulation under which the paper has been laid;
- whether there has been any unreasonable delay in laying the paper;
- if there has been such delay, whether a statement explaining the reasons for delay has been laid on the Table of the House, and whether those reasons are satisfactory;
- whether both the Hindi and English versions of the paper have been laid on the Table;
- whether a statement explaining the reasons for not laying the Hindi version has been given and whether such reasons are satisfactory; and
- such other functions in respect of the papers laid on the Table as may be assigned to it by the Speaker from time to time.

However, this Committee does not examine the statutory notifications and orders that fall within the purview of the Committee on Subordinate Legislation.

Committee on Subordinate Legislation

The Committee was constituted in the year 1953. Each House has its own Committee. The Committee scrutinizes and reports to the House whether the powers to make regulations, rules, sub-rules, bye-laws, etc. conferred by the Constitution or delegated by the Parliament are being properly exercised by the Executive within the scope of such delegation.

Committee on the Welfare of Scheduled Castes and Scheduled Tribes

It's a common Committee of both the Houses of Parliament. The functions of the Committee are as follows:

- Considers the reports submitted by the National Commission for the Scheduled Castes and the National Commission for the Scheduled Tribes under Article 338(5)(d) and 338A (5) (d) respectively of the Constitution and to report as to the measures that should be taken by the Union Government in respect of matters within the purview of the Union Government, including the Administration of the Union Territories;
- To report on the action taken by the Union Government and the administrations of the Union Territories on the measures proposed by the Committee;

- To examine the measures taken by the Union Government to secure due representation of the Scheduled Castes and Scheduled Tribes in services and posts under its control (including appointments in the Public Sector Undertakings, Nationalised Banks, Statutory and Semi-Government Bodies, and in the Union Territories) having regard to the provisions of Article 335;
- To report on the working of the welfare programmes for the Scheduled Castes and Scheduled Tribes in the Union Territories; and
- To examine such other matters as may deem fit to the Committee or are specifically referred to it by the House or the Speaker.

Joint Committee on Offices of Profit

It's a common Committee of both Houses of Parliament. The said Committee examines the composition and character of the Committees appointed by the Central and State Governments and recommends what offices should disqualify and what offices should not disqualify a person for being chosen as, and for being a member of either House of Parliament under Article 102 of the Constitution. It also scrutinizes from time to time the Schedule to the Parliament (Prevention of Disqualification) Act, 1959, and recommends any amendments in the said Schedule, whether by way of addition, omission, or otherwise.

COMMITTEES TO INQUIRE

Committee of Privileges

Each House has its own Committee. The Committee examines every question involving breach of privilege of the House or of the members or of any Committee thereof referred to it by the House or by the Speaker. It also determines with reference to the facts of each case whether a breach of privilege is involved and makes suitable recommendations in its report. In other words, the Committee performs quasi-judicial functions.

Committee on Petitions

Each House has its own Committee. The said Committee considers and reports on petitions presented to the House. It also considers representations from various individuals, associations, etc. not covered by the rules relating to petitions and gives directions for their disposal.

Committee on Ethics

The Committee was constituted in the year 1997 in Rajya Sabha and in 2000 in Lok Sabha. Each House has its own Committee. T

he functions of the Committee are as follows:

- Oversee the moral and ethical conduct of members;
- Examine every complaint relating to unethical conduct of member or connected with his Parliamentary conduct referred to it and make such recommendations as it may deem fit;
- Frame rules specifying acts which constitute unethical conduct.

The Committee may also suo moto take up for consideration and investigation matters relating to ethics, including matters relating to unethical conduct by members wherever felt necessary and make such recommendations as it may deem fit. The procedure which shall be followed by the Committee for examining complaints of unethical conduct of members, shall be, so far as maybe, the same as the procedure for inquiry and determination by the Committee of Privileges of any question as to breach of privilege of the House or a member. The provisions of Rules 315 and 316 relating to consideration of report of Committee of Privileges presented to the House and priority for consideration of such Reports by House would be applicable mutatis mutandis to the Reports of Committee on Ethics presented to the House.

HOUSE-KEEPING COMMITTEES

House Committee

Each House has its own Committee. The said Committee deals with all the questions relating to residential accommodation for the members of the House and also exercises supervision over facilities for accommodation, food, medical aid, and other amenities accorded to members in members' residences and hostels in Delhi.

Library Committee

Both the Houses have a combined Committee. The said Committee considers and advises on such matters concerning the library as may be referred to it by the Speaker from time to time. It also considers suggestions for the improvement of the library and assists members of both Houses in fully utilizing the services provided by the library.

Joint Committee on Salaries and Allowances of Members of Parliament

This Committee is constituted under the Salary, Allowances and Pension of Members of Parliament Act, 1954, apart from framing rules in respect of amenities like medical, housing, telephone, postal, constituency, and secretarial facilities.

12.6 PARLIAMENTARY FORUMS[1]

INTRODUCTION

Parliamentary forums were a created for the first time in August 12, 2005 under the aegis of the Lok Sabha Speaker to discuss on the critical issue of water conservation and management. The forum was created to enable the members to discuss the issues related to water management in a structured manner and to place their viewpoints effectively in the House and in the Committee. This laid down the foundation to four more committees covering the issues of Child, Youth, Population and Public Health, and Global Warming and Climate change.

By the time the Fifteenth Lok Sabha was constituted, the following Parliamentary forums were constituted:

1. Parliamentary Forum on Water Conservation and Management
2. Parliamentary Forum on Children
3. Parliamentary Forum on Youth
4. Parliamentary Forum on Population and Public Health
5. Parliamentary Forum on Global Warming and Climate Change
6. Parliamentary Forum on Disaster Management
7. Parliamentary Forum on Artisans and Craftspeople
8. Parliamentary Forum on Millennium Development Goals

OBJECTIVES OF PARLIAMENTARY FORUMS

The key objectives with which the Parliamentary Forums are constituted are as under:

(a) To provide a platform to members to have an interaction with the concerned Minister, experts, and key nodal officers of the Ministry with a view to have a focussed and meaningful discussion on critical issues with a result-oriented approach for speeding up the implementation process;

(b) To sensitize members about the key areas of concern and also about the ground level situation and equip them with the latest information, knowledge, technical know-how, and valuable inputs from experts both from the country and abroad for enabling them to raise these issues effectively on the Floor of the House and in the meetings of the Departmentally-Related Standing Committees (DRSCs); and

(c) To prepare a database through collection of data on critical issues from ministries concerned, reliable NGOs, newspapers, United Nations, Internet, etc. and circulation thereof to the members so that they can meaningfully participate in the discussions of the forums and seek clarifications from experts or officials from the Ministry present in the meetings.

The mandate or objects of these Parliamentary Foras are not to interfere with or encroach upon the jurisdiction of the Departmentally-Related Standing Committees of the Ministry/Department concerned.

---

[1]Source of information: - Lok Sabha Secretariat

COMPOSITION OF PARLIAMENTARY FORUMS

The Speaker of the Lok Sabha is the ex-officio President of all the Forums except the Parliamentary Forum on Population and Public Health wherein the Chairman of Rajya Sabha is the ex-officio President and the Speaker is the ex-officio Co-President. The Deputy Chairman of the Rajya Sabha, the Deputy Speaker of Lok Sabha, the concerned Ministers, and the Chairmen of Departmentally-Related Standing Committees are the ex-officio Vice-Presidents of the respective Forums.

Each Forum consists of not more than 31 members (excluding the President, Co-President, and Vice-Presidents) out of whom not more than 21 are from the Lok Sabha and not more than 10 are from the Rajya Sabha.

Members (other than the President, Co-President and Vice-Presidents) of these forums are nominated by the Speaker/Chairman from amongst the leaders of various political parties/groups or their nominees, who have special knowledge/keen interest in the subject.

The duration of the office of members of the forum is co-terminus with their membership in the respective Houses. A member may also resign from the forum by writing to the Speaker/Chairman.

The President of the forum appoints a member-convener for each forum to conduct regular, approved programmes/meetings of the forum in consultation with the President. The meetings of the forums are held from time to time, as may be necessary, during Parliament sessions.

FUNCTIONS OF PARLIAMENTARY FORUMS

Parliamentary Forum on Water Conservation and Management

The functions are:

- To identify problems relating to water and make suggestions/recommendations for consideration and appropriate action by Government/organizations concerned;
- To identify the ways of involving members of Parliament in conservation and augmentation of water resources in their respective states/constituencies;
- To organize seminars/workshops to create awareness for conservation and efficient management of water;
- To undertake such other related task as it may deem fit.

Parliamentary Forum on Youth

The functions are:

- To have focused deliberations on strategies to leverage human capital in the youth for accelerating development initiatives;
- To build greater awareness amongst public leaders and at the grass-roots level of the potential of youth; for effecting socio-economic change;
- To interact on a regular basis with youth representatives and leaders, in order to better appreciate their hopes, aspirations, concerns and problems;

- To consider ways for improving Parliament's out-reach to different sections of youth, in order to reinforce their faith and commitment in democratic institutions and encourage their active participation therein;
- To hold consultations with experts, national and international academicians, and government agencies concerned on redesigning of public policy in the matter of youth empowerment.

Parliamentary Forum on Children

The functions are:

- To further enhance awareness and attention of Parliamentarians towards critical issues affecting children's well being so that they may provide due leadership to ensure their rightful place in the development process;
- To provide a platform to Parliamentarians to exchange ideas, views, experiences, expert practices in relation to children, in a structured manner, through workshops, seminars, orientation programmes, etc.
- To provide Parliamentarians an interface with civil society for highlighting children's issues, including, *inter-alia*, the voluntary sector, media and corporate sector, and thereby to foster effective strategic partnerships in this regard;
- To enable Parliamentarians to interact, in an institutionalized manner with specialized UN agencies like the UNICEF and other comparable multilateral agencies on expert reports, studies, news and trend-analyses, etc., world-wide, which are germane to developments in the sector;
- To undertake any other tasks, projects, assignments, etc., as the Forum may deem fit.

Parliamentary Forum on Population and Public Health

The functions are:

- To have focused deliberations on strategies relating to population stabilization and matters connected therewith;
- To discuss and prepare strategies on issues concerning public health;
- To build greater awareness in all sections of the society, particularly at the grass-root level, regarding population control and public health;
- To hold comprehensive dialogue and discussion in the matter of population and public health with experts at the national and international levels and to have interactions with multilateral organisations like WHO, United Nations Population Fund, and academicians and government agencies concerned.

Parliamentary Forum on Global Warming and Climate Change

The functions are:

- To identify problems relating to global warming and climate change and make suggestions/ recommendations for consideration and appropriate action by the government/organisations concerned to reduce the extent of global warming;

- To identify the ways of involving members of Parliament to interact with specialists of national and international bodies working on global warming and climate change with increased effort to develop new technologies to mitigate global warming;
- To organise seminars/workshops to create awareness about the causes and effects of global warming and climate change among the members of Parliament;
- To identify the ways of involving members of Parliament to spread awareness to prevent global warming and climate change;
- To undertake such other related task as it may deem fit.

Parliamentary Forum on Disaster Management

The functions are:

- To identify problems relating to Disaster Management and make suggestions/recommendations for consideration and appropriate action by the Government/organizations concerned to reduce the effects of disasters.
- To identify the ways of involving Members of Parliament to interact with specialists of National and International Bodies working on Disaster Management with increased effort to develop new technologies to mitigate the effect of disasters.
- To organize seminars/workshops to create awareness about the causes and effects of disasters among the Members of Parliament.
- To identify the ways of involving Members of Parliament to spread awareness about disaster management.
- To undertake such other related task as it may deem fit.

Parliamentary Forum on Artisans and Craftspeople

The functions are:

- To further enhance awareness and attention to Parliamentarians towards critical issues affecting artisans and craftspeople so as to preserve and promote traditional art and crafts through various mechanisms.
- To provide a platform to Parliamentarians to exchange ideas, views, experiences, expertise, and best practices in relation to artisans and craftspeople, in a structured manner, through Workshops, Seminars, Orientation Programmes, etc.
- To provide Parliamentarians an interface with civil society for highlighting issues related to craftspeople and artisans, including *inter alia*, the Voluntary Sector, Media, and Corporate Sector and thereby to foster effective strategic partnerships in this regard
- To enable Parliamentarians to interact in an institutionalized manner with representatives of various Union Ministries, Government Organizations like Khadi and Village Industries Commission (KVIC), Coir Board, the Council for Advancement of People's Action and Rural Technology (CAPART) and other related organizations/bodies.

- To hold comprehensive dialogue and discussion on the matters relating to preservation of art and traditional craft and the promotion of artisans and craftspeople with experts/organizations at the national and international levels.
- To undertake any other Tasks, Projects, Assignments, etc. as the Forum may deem fit.

Parliamentary Forum on Millennium Development Goals

The functions are:

- To review and enhance awareness and attention of Parliamentarians towards critical issues which have bearing on achievement of goals/targets set under Millennium Development Goals by 2015.
- To provide a platform to Parliamentarians to exchange ideas, views, experiences, expertise and best practices in relation to implementation of Millennium Development Goals in a structured manner, through Workshops, Seminars, Orientation Programmes, etc.
- To provide Parliamentarians an interface with civil society for highlighting issues related to Millennium Development Goals, viz. eradication of poverty; hunger; achievement of universal primary education; promotion of gender equality and empowerment of women; reduction of child mortality; improving maternal health; combating HIV/AIDS; Malaria and other diseases; ensuring environmental sustainability and developing a global partnership for development.
- To enable parliamentarians to interact, in an institutionalized manner with specialized UN Agencies and other comparable Multilateral Agencies, Expert Report, Studies, News and Trend-analyses, etc. regarding achievement of Millennium Development Goals.
- To undertake any other Tasks, Projects, Assignments, etc. as the Forum may deem fit.

12.7 INDIAN PARLIAMENTARY GROUP

INTRODUCTION

The Inter-Parliamentary Union (IPU) is the international organisation of the Parliaments of sovereign States. Its aim is to work for peace and cooperation among peoples and for the firm establishment of representative institutions. The IPU fosters contacts, coordination, and the exchange of experience among Parliaments and Parliamentarians of member countries and contributes to better knowledge of the working of representative institutions. The IPU holds two Statutory Assemblies in a year.

THE INDIAN PARLIAMENTARY GROUP (IPG)

The Indian Parliamentary Group (IPG)[1] is an autonomous body formed in the year 1949 in pursuance of a motion adopted by the Constituent Assembly (Legislative) on 16th August, 1948.

Membership of the Indian Parliamentary Group is open to all Members of Parliament and ex-Members of Parliament. A Member of Parliament can become a life Member of the IPG on payment of life subscription. On ceasing to be a Member of Parliament, a life member of the IPG is designated as 'Associate Life Member'. But, the Associate Members are entitled to limited rights only. They are not entitled to representation at meetings and conferences of the IPU and the Commonwealth Parliamentary Association (CPA)[2]. They are also not entitled to the travel concessions provided to members by certain branches of the CPA.

The management and control of the affairs of the IPG are vested in the Executive Committee. The Speaker, Lok Sabha is the ex-officio President of the IPG. The Deputy Speaker of the Lok Sabha and the Deputy Chairman of the Rajya Sabha are the *ex officio* Vice-presidents of the IPG. The Secretary-General of the Lok Sabha acts as the *ex officio* Secretary-General of the IPG.

The IPG aims to promote personal contacts between Members of Parliament and disseminate information to the Members of Parliament by conducting seminars, etc. on the issues that are likely to come up before Parliament. It arranges lectures on political, defence, economic, social, and educational problems and also arranges visits to foreign countries with a view to develop contacts with Members of other Parliaments.

---

[1]Source http://ipg.nic.in/AboutUs.aspx

[2]The CPA is an Association of Commonwealth Parliamentarians with a mission to promote the advancement of Parliamentary democracy by enhancing knowledge and understanding of democratic governance. The CPA organises annual CPA Conferences, Seminars, Workshops, Study Groups, etc. to provide platform for regular consultation among Commonwealth Members. CPA is organizing new programmes viz. CPA Youth Parliament, CPA Road show, Master Classes, Lecture series, etc.

The IPG acts as a link between the Parliament of India and the various Parliaments of the world by exchange of delegations, goodwill missions, correspondence, documents, etc. with foreign Parliaments. It also functions as the (a) National Group of the Inter-Parliamentary Union and (b) Main Branch of the Commonwealth Parliamentary Association in India.

Objectives of the IPG

The objectives of the IPG are as follows:-

(a) To promote personal contacts between Member of the World's Parliaments;

(b) To work for the establishment and development of democratic institutions and the advancement of the work of peace and international co-operation;

(c) To study and seek solutions for all questions of an international character suitable for settlement by Parliamentary action;

(d) To make suggestions for the development of Parliamentary institutions.

Activities of the IPG

The IPG acts as a link between the Parliament of India and the various Parliaments of the world. This link is maintained through exchange of Delegations, goodwill missions, correspondence, documents, etc. with foreign Parliaments.

The Indian Parliamentary Group functions as the (a) National Group of the Inter Parliamentary Union (IPU) and (b) Main Branch of the Commonwealth Parliamentary Association (CPA) in India.

Addresses to Members of Parliament by the visiting Heads of State and Government of foreign countries and talks by eminent persons are arranged under the auspices of the IPG. Seminars and symposia on Parliamentary subjects of topical interest are organized periodically at national, as well as international level.

The IPG and IPU[3]

Inter-Parliamentary Union global organization of national Parliaments began its journey in the year 1889 as a small group of parliamentarians. It is dedicated to promoting peace through Parliamentary diplomacy and dialogue, and has since grown into a truly global organization of national Parliaments.

As of 2020, its membership inches ever closer to being universal, with 179 Member Parliaments, 13 Associate Members, and increasing numbers of Parliamentarians from all over the world involved in their work.

Its aim is to work for peace and cooperation among peoples and for the firm establishment of representative institutions. It fosters contacts, coordination, and the exchange of experience among Parliaments and Parliamentarians of all member countries and contributes to better knowledge of the working of representative institutions. It also expresses its views on all burning questions of international importance for necessary effective implementation of Parliamentary actions and suggests avenues for improving the working standard and capacity of international institutions.

[3]Source https://www.ipu.org/

The main advantages of membership of the IPG, insofar as its functions as the National Group of the IPU are concerned, are as follows:

1. It helps members of Indian Parliamentary delegations to develop contacts with the Parliamentarians of the member countries of the IPU.
2. The events provide an opportunity to study and understand contemporary changes/reforms taking place in various countries of the world.
3. It provides facilities to meet Parliamentarians in different countries during tours in abroad or in India when visiting Parliamentarians are here.
4. The members of the IPG are eligible to visit foreign countries as members of the Indian Parliamentary delegations to Inter-Parliamentary Conferences.

The IPG and CPA[4]

The Commonwealth Parliamentary Association traces its origin to a world vastly different from today. When the CPA was founded in 1911 as the Empire Parliamentary Association, the world had scarcely two dozen nations which were Parliamentary democracies. The British Empire was composed of one sovereign Parliamentary democracy, five dominions, a handful of tiny protectorates, and a vast array of colonies. Today, the United Nations has 193 member states, 54 of them in the Commonwealth of Nations. The CPA's membership of 180 Branches also includes fourteen Overseas Territories, three Crown Dependencies, and more than 125 sub-national states, provinces, and territories in federal-style countries, all with their own Parliaments or Legislatures. Some of the States and provinces and their Legislatures are far larger and their economies more significant than many independent countries.

The CPA connects, develops, promotes, and supports Parliamentarians and their staff to identify benchmarks of good governance and the implementation of the enduring values of the Commonwealth.

The CPA collaborates with Parliaments and other organizations, including the intergovernmental community, to achieve its Statement of Purpose. It brings Parliamentarians and Parliamentary staff together to exchange ideas among themselves and with experts in various fields, to identify benchmarks of good practices and new policy options they can adopt or adapt in the governance of their societies.

Commonwealth Heads of Government have recognised the Parliaments and Legislatures of the Commonwealth as essential elements in the exercise of democratic governance, and have endorsed the efforts of the Association as the Parliamentary partner of the Commonwealth's governmental and non-governmental sectors.

CPA activities focus on the Commonwealth's commitment to its fundamental political values, including a just and honest government, the alleviation of poverty, fundamental human rights, international peace and order, global economic development, the rule of law, equal rights and representation for all citizens of both genders, the separation of powers among the three branches of government, and the right to participate in free and democratic political processes.

---

[4]Source http://www.cpahq.org/cpahq/

Advantages of Membership of the IPG

The advantages of membership of the IPG, insofar as its functions as the main branch of the CPA in India are concerned, are as follows:

1. **Conferences and Seminars :** Membership provides an opportunity for participation in the plenary and regional conferences, seminars, visits, and exchanges of delegations.
2. **Publications :** All members of the IPG are entitled to receive, free of charge, 'The Parliamentarian' quarterly and the newsletter, 'First Reading', every second month.
3. **Information :** The Parliamentary Information and Reference Centre of the CPA Secretariat provides information to members on Parliamentary, Constitutional, and Commonwealth matters.
4. **Introductions :** The CPA branches readily assist in arranging introductions for members visiting other jurisdictions.
5. **Parliamentary Facilities :** Members visiting other Commonwealth countries are normally accorded Parliamentary courtesies, especially access to debates and local members.
6. **Travel Facilities :** Some branches provide for a designated number of their members annually to undertake study tours of Commonwealth and other countries to compare political and procedural developments. Other branches arrange ad hoc visits.

DURATION OF THE LOK SABHA

LOK SABHA	DURATION
FIRST	1952 -1957
SECOND	1957-1962
THIRD	1962-1967
FOURTH	1967-1971
FIFTH	1971-1977
SIXTH	1977-1980
SEVENTH	1980 -1984
EIGHTH	1985 -1989
NINTH	1989 -1991
TENTH	1991-1996
ELEVENTH	1996 -1997
TWELFTH	1998 -1999
THIRTEENTH	1999 - 2004
FOURTEENTH	2004 - 2009
FIFTEENTH	2009 - 2014
SIXTEENTH	2014 - 2019
SEVENTEENTH	2019 - Present

LOK SABHA SEATS (STATE WISE LIST)

Sl. No.	Name of State	No. of Constituencies	Reserved seats for the Schedule Caste	Reserved Seats for the Scheduled Tribes
1.	Andhra Pradesh	25	7	3
2.	Arunachal Pradesh	2	–	–
3.	Assam	14	1	2
4.	Bihar	40	6	–
5.	Chhattisgarh	11	1	4
6.	Goa	2	–	–
7.	Gujarat	26	2	4
8.	Haryana	10	2	–
9.	Himachal Pradesh	4	1	–
10.	Jharkhand	14	1	5
11.	Karnataka	28	5	2
12.	Kerala	20	2	–
13.	Madhya Pradesh	29	4	6
14.	Maharashtra	48	5	4

15.	Manipur	2		1
16.	Meghalaya	2	–	2
17.	Mizoram	1	–	1
18.	Nagaland	1	–	–
19.	Odisha	21	3	5
20.	Punjab	13	4	–
21.	Rajasthan	25	4	3
22.	Sikkim	1	–	–
23.	Tamil Nadu	39	7	–
24.	Telangana	17	3	2
25.	Tripura	2	–	1
26.	Uttar Pradesh	79	17	–
27.	Uttarakhand	5	1	–
28.	West Bengal	42	10	2

LOK SABHA SEATS (UNION TERRITORY WISE)

Sl. No	Name of State	No. of Constituencies
1.	Andaman and Nicobar Islands	1
2.	Chandigarh	1
3.	Dadra and Nagar Haveli and Daman and Diu	2
4.	Jammu and Kashmir	5
5.	Ladakh	1
6.	Lakshadweep	1
7.	NCT of Delhi	7
8.	Puducherry	1

RAJYA SABHA SEATS

Sl. No	Name of State	No. of Seats	No. Of Members
1.	Andhra Pradesh	11	11
2.	Arunachal Pradesh	1	1
3.	Assam	7	7
4.	Bihar	16	16
5.	Chhattisgarh	5	5
6.	Goa	1	1
7.	Gujarat	11	11
8.	Haryana	5	5
9.	Himachal Pradesh	3	3
10.	Jammu & Kashmir	4	0
11.	Jharkhand	6	6

12.	Karnataka	12	12
13.	Kerala	9	9
14.	Madhya Pradesh	11	11
15.	Maharashtra	19	19
16.	Manipur	1	1
17.	Meghalaya	1	1
18.	Mizoram	1	1
19.	Nagaland	1	1
20.	National Capital Territory of Delhi	3	3
21.	Nominated	12	10
22.	Odisha	10	10
23.	Puducherry	1	1
24.	Punjab	7	7
25.	Rajasthan	10	10
26.	Sikkim	1	1
27.	Tamil Nadu	18	18
28.	Telangana	7	7
29.	Tripura	1	1
30.	Uttar Pradesh	31	31
31.	Uttarakhand	3	3
32.	West Bengal	16	16

LIST OF LOK SABHA SPEAKERS

NAME	FROM	TO
Ganesh Vasudev Mavalankar	1952	1956
M. A. Ayyangar	1956	1957
	1957	1962
Sardar Hukam Singh	1962	1967
Neelam Sanjiva Reddy	1967	1969
Gurdial Singh Dhillon	1969	1971
	1971	1975
Bali Ram Bhagat	1976	1977
Neelam Sanjiva Reddy	1977	1977
K. S. Hegde	1977	1980
Balram Jakhar	1980	1985
	1985	1989
Rabi Ray	1989	1991
Shivraj Patil	1991	1996
P. A. Sangma	1996	1998

G. M. C. Balayogi	1998	1999
	1999	2002
Manohar Joshi	2002	2004
Somnath Chatterjee	2004	2009
Meira Kumar	2009	2014
Sumitra Mahajan	2014	2019
Om Birla	2019	Incumbent

QUESTIONS

Subjective Questions

1. What are Money Bills and how are they different from the Financial Bills. Discuss. **(200 words)**
2. Discuss the Parliamentary Privileges enjoyed by the Members of Parliament. **(200 words)**
3. "Parliament is not only a legislative but also a deliberative body. So far as its deliberative functions are concerned, it will be open to us to make very valuable contributions, and it will depend on our work whether we justify this two Chamber system, which is now an integral part of our Constitution". Evaluate. **(250 words)**

Objective Questions

1. There is a Parliamentary System of Government in India because the **(UPSC CSE 2015)**

   (a) Lok Sabha is elected directly by the people

   (b) Parliament can amend the Constitution

   (c) Rajya Sabha cannot be dissolved

   (d) Council of Ministers is responsible to the Lok Sabha

   Ans : (d)

2. Consider the following statements regarding Parliamentary Forums:

   1. Parliamentary Forums are operational since the first Lok Sabha.
   2. Speaker of the Lok Sabha is the President of all the Forums.
   3. Each Forum consists of 31 Members out of whom not more than 21 are from the Lok Sabha and not more than 10 are from the Rajya Sabha.
   4. The term of the office of members of the Forums is one year.

   Which of the above statements is/are correct?

   (a) 1, 2, 3, and 4 (b) 2, 3, and 4 only

   (c) 3 only (d) 4 only

   Ans: (c)

3. Consider the following statements: **(UPSC CSE 2020)**

1. The President of India can summon a session of Parliament at such place as he/she thinks fit.
2. The Constitution of India provides for three sessions of the Parliament in a year, but it is not mandatory to conduct all three sessions.
3. There is no minimum number of days that the Parliament is required to meet in a year.

Which of the statements given above is/are correct?

(a) 1 only (b) 2 only

(c) 1 and 3 only (d) 2 and 3 only

Ans : (c)

4. Along with the Budget, the Finance Minister also places other documents before the Parliament which include 'The Macro Economic Framework Statement'. The aforesaid document is presented because this is mandated by **(UPSC CSE 2020)**

(a) Long standing Parliamentary convention

(b) Article 112 and Article 110(1) of the Constitution of India

(c) Article 113 of the Constitution of India

(d) Provisions of the Fiscal Responsibility and Budget Management Act, 2003

Ans: (d)

5. Consider the following statements: **(UPSC CSE 2018)**

1. In the first Lok Sabha, the largest party in the opposition was the Swatantra Party.
2. In the Lok Sabha, a "Leader of the Opposition" was recognized for the first time in 1969.
3. In the Lok Sabha, if a party does not have a minimum of 75 members, its leader cannot be recognized as the Leader of the Opposition.

Which of the statements given above is/are correct?

(a) 1 and 3 only (b) 2 only

(c) 2 and 3 only (d) 1, 2, and 3

Ans: (b)

6. With reference to the Parliament of India, which of the following Parliamentary Committees scrutinizes and reports to the House whether the powers to make regulations, rules, sub-rules, by-laws, etc. conferred by the Constitution or delegated by the Parliament are being properly exercised by the Executive within the scope of such delegation? **(UPSC CSE 2018)**

(a) Committee on Government Assurances

(b) Committee on Subordinate Legislation

(c) Rules Committee

(d) Business Advisory Committee

Ans: (b)

7. Regarding Money Bill, which of the following statements is not correct?

(a) A bill shall be deemed to be a Money Bill if it contains only provisions related to imposition, abolition, remission, alteration, or regulation of any tax.

(b) A Money Bill has provisions for the custody of the Consolidated Fund of India or the Contingency Fund of India.

(c) A Money Bill is concerned with appropriation of moneys out of the Contingency Fund of India.

(d) A Money Bill deals with the regulation of borrowing of money or giving of any guarantee by the government of India.

Ans: (c)

8. With reference to the Parliament of India, consider the following statements:

1. A private member's bill is a bill presented by a Member of Parliament who is not elected but only nominated by the President of India.
2. Recently, a private member's bill has been passed in the Parliament of India for the first time in its history.

Which of the statements given above is/are correct? **(UPSC CSE 2017)**

(a) 1 only (b) 2 only

(c) Both 1 and 2 (d) Neither 1 nor 2

Ans: (d)

9. The main advantage of the Parliamentary form of government is that **(UPSC CSE 2016)**

(a) the Executive and Legislature work independently.

(b) it provides continuity of policy and is more efficient.

(c) the Executive remains responsible to the Legislature.

(d) the Head of the government cannot be changed without election.

Ans: (c)

10. The Parliament of India acquires the power to legislate on any item in the State List in the national interest if a resolution to that effect is passed by the **(UPSC CSE 2016)**

(a) Lok Sabha by a simple majority of its total membership

(b) Lok Sabha by a majority of not less than two-thirds of its total membership

(c) Rajya Sabha by a simple majority of its total membership

(d) Rajya Sabha by a majority of not less than two-thirds of its members present and voting

Ans: (d)

CHAPTER 13

INDIAN JUDICIARY AND THE SUPREME COURT

"The primary duty of the Judiciary is to uphold the Constitution and the Laws without fear or favour, without being biased by political ideology or economic theory".

– People's Union for Civil Liberties (PUCL) Vs. UOI[1]

INTRODUCTION

In any country, the Judiciary plays the important role of interpreting and applying the law and adjudicating upon controversies between one citizen and another and between a citizen and the State. It is the function of the courts to maintain Rule of Law in the country and to assure that the government runs according to law.

Especially in a country like India with a written Constitution, courts have the additional function of safeguarding the supremacy of the Constitution by interpreting and applying its provisions and keeping all authorities within the constitutional framework.

Moreover, in a federal country like India, the Judiciary has another meaningful assignment, namely, to decide controversies between the States *inter se*, as well as between the Centre and the States. In addition to the above, the Judiciary also has the significant function of protecting and enforcing the Fundamental Rights of the people guaranteed to them by the Constitution.

Structure of the Indian Judiciary

India has a unified judicial system with the Supreme Court standing at the apex. There are High Courts below the Supreme Court and under each High Court, there exists a system of subordinate courts. The Supreme Court, thus, enjoys the topmost position in the judicial hierarchy of the country. It is the supreme interpreter of the Constitution and the guardian of the people's Fundamental Rights. It is the ultimate court of appeal in all civil and criminal matters and the final interpreter of the law of the land, and thus helps in maintaining a uniformity of law throughout the country.

It is however important to emphasize that unlike other federal systems, for example, that of the United States, we do not have separate hierarchies of federal and State Courts. In India, though the polity is dual, the Judiciary is integrated. For the entire republic of India, there is one unified judicial system – one hierarchy of courts – with the Supreme Court as the highest court and also as the arbiter in matters of relations between the Union and the States and the States inter se.

[1](2003) 4 SSC 399.

SUPREME COURT

History of the Supreme Court of India

The promulgation of Regulating Act of 1773 by the King of England paved the way for the establishment of the Supreme Court of Judicature at Calcutta. The Supreme Court of Judicature at Calcutta was established as a Court of Record, with full power and authority to hear and determine all civil and criminal disputes of the subjects in Bengal, Bihar, and Orissa. The Supreme Courts at Madras and Bombay was established by King George III in 1800 and in 1823 respectively. The appeals from these Supreme Courts used to lie before the "Judicial Committee of the Privy Council" or in other words "Privy Council".

The Privy Council was a judicial body that heard appeals from different British colonies' courts, including India's. During the British period, the Privy Council acted as the highest court of appeal. Cases before the council were adjudicated by the Law Lords of the House of Lords.

Later on, the Indian High Courts Act, 1861 was enacted to create High Courts for various provinces and abolished the Supreme Courts at Calcutta, Madras, and Bombay. And the right to appeal to the Privy Council from these High Courts were granted to the parties. These High Courts had the distinction of being the highest Courts within India for all cases in their respective provinces till the creation of the Federal Court of India under the Government of India Act, 1935.

A Federal Court was established in India by the Government of India Act of 1935, to resolve conflicts between the Centre and the provinces. In other words, the Federal Court was given exclusive original jurisdiction. Appeals from High Courts to the Federal Court and from the Federal Court to the Privy Council were made possible.

After India attained independence in 1947, the Constitution of India came into being on 26 January, 1950. On the 28th of January, 1950, two days after India became a Sovereign Democratic Republic, the Supreme Court came into being. The Supreme Court of India not only replaced the Federal Court but also the Judicial Committee of the Privy Council as the highest court of appeal since 28 January 1950.

Establishment of the Supreme Court

- Article 124 establishes the Supreme Court of India. The Chief Justice of the Supreme Court is designated as the Chief Justice of India.
- Article 130 provides that the seat of the Supreme Court shall be Delhi, or at such other place, as the Chief Justice of India may, with the approval of the President, appoint from time to time. The Supreme Court in *UOI Vs. SP Anand*[2], held that the Article 130 is an enabling provision and does not cast a mandatory obligation on the Chief Justice of India to appoint any place other than Delhi as the seat of the Supreme Court. Whether the Supreme Court should sit at a place other than Delhi involves taking a policy decision by the Chief Justice of India which must receive the approval of the President of India.

Strength of the Judges of the Supreme Court

Originally, under Article 124(1), the strength of the Court was fixed at one Chief Justice and seven other judges. But Parliament has been given power to increase the number of other Judges beyond seven. In the early years, all the Judges of the Supreme Court sat together to hear the cases presented before

---

[2] AIR 1998 SC 2615.

them. As the work of the Court increased and arrears of cases began to cumulate, Parliament increased the number of Judges from 8 in 1950 to 11 in 1956, 14 in 1960, 18 in 1978, and 26 in 1986. As the number of the Judges has increased, they sit in smaller Benches of two and three - coming together in larger Benches of 5 and more only when required to do so or to settle a difference of opinion or controversy. Currently, the maximum sanctioned strength of the Supreme Court is 34 including the Chief Justice of India.

APPOINTMENT OF JUDGES

"The process of appointment of judges to the superior courts was possibly the best kept secret of the country"

- Justice Ruma Pal

Article 124 vests the power of appointment of the Chief Justice of India (CJI) and the Judges of the Supreme Court in the President. The President shall, by warrant under his hand and seal, make the appointment after consultation with such of the judges of the Supreme Court and the High Courts of the States, as he may deem necessary. In the case of appointment of a judge other than the Chief Justice of India, the CJI shall always be consulted. In other words, the CJI is to be consulted in all appointments, except his or her own.

On a plain reading of the provision, the power of appointment vests in the President. The President, of course, means the Executive, i.e., the President acting on the advice of the Council of Ministers. The CJI and other such judges of the Supreme Court and the High Courts shall be consulted by the President, as he may deem necessary.

(a) **Procedure to appoint Judges in the UK and USA :** In the United Kingdom, prior to 2005, the Judges were appointed by the Crown (Executive), without any restrictions. The power of the Executive was curtailed in 2005, by the Constitutional Reform Act, 2005 which established a Judicial Appointments Commission for England and Wales[3] and a Judicial Appointments and Conduct Ombudsman. In the USA, on the other hand, the President appoints the Supreme Court Judges with the consent of the Senate.

(b) **Appointment of CJI :** For long, the practice in India has been to appoint the senior-most judge of the Supreme Court as the Chief Justice whenever a vacancy occurred in that office. In 1958, the Law Commission criticised this practice on the grounds that a Chief Justice should not only be an able and experienced Judge, but also a competent administrator, and therefore, succession to the office should not be regulated by mere seniority. The Government did not act upon this recommendation for long. It continued to appoint the senior-most Judge as the Chief Justice as it was afraid that it might be tampering with judicial independence. A mechanical adherence to the rule at times resulted in the Chief Justice holding office only for a few months before he retired from the Court. In 1973, the Government suddenly departed from this practice and appointed a Judge who was fourth in the order of seniority as the CJI. Thus, three senior Judges were bypassed, who then resigned from the Court in protest. This raised a hue and cry in the country and the Government was accused of tampering with the independence of the Judiciary. Again in

[3]The JAC selects candidates for judicial office on merit, through fair and open competition, from the widest range of eligible candidates. The JAC is an executive non-departmental public body, sponsored by the Ministry of Justice. It consists of judicial as well non-judicial members.

1977, the Government appointed Justice Beg as the Chief Justice bypassing Justice Khanna who was senior to him at that time. Consequently, Justice Khanna resigned in protest. After 1977, the rule of seniority has been followed in the matter of appointment of the CJI. In the context of India, it appears to be best to adhere to the convention of appointing the senior-most Judge as the Chief Justice. This will avoid any suspicion that the Government seeks to tamper with the Judiciary[4].

(c) **Appointment of Judges prior to 1993 :** During the Constitution framing process, many different proposals were mooted for the appropriate method to appoint judges to the Supreme Court and the High Courts. The framers were concerned that the appointment process should ensure that the best candidate was appointed to this high constitutional office, while at the same time ensuring that judicial independence from the other branches of government is maintained. They discussed and discarded proposals such as the President appointing judges on his own initiative, without the aid and advice of the Council of Ministers; appointments being confirmed by one or both Houses of Parliament; setting up of members from various branches of the government to select judges; or giving the Chief Justice of India a veto over judicial appointments. Ultimately, the framework that made it through to the Constitution required the appointment of Supreme Court judges to be made by the President, acting on the aid and advice of the Council of Ministers, in "consultation" with the Chief Justice of India. The President could also consult other Supreme Court and High Court judges as per his/her discretion. The role of the Judiciary in the appointments process was to provide inputs and advice to the President. The President was not bound by the advice of the Chief Justice or any other judge. In practice, recommendations were initiated by the Chief Justice and sent to the Minister of Law and Justice. If the Minister agreed with the suggested name, he/she, with the concurrence of the Prime Minister, would so advise the President, who would make the appointment. If the Minister differed from the views of the Chief Justice, he/she might seek the views of other judges and consult with the Chief Justice on such views or suggest another name to the Chief Justice to secure his/her opinion. Ultimately, however, the Minister of Law and Justice would advise the Prime Minister and with the Prime Minister's concurrence, would advise the President on whom to appoint. This was thus the Executive-led appointment system.

As early as 1958, the Law Commission of India argued that this system of appointment did not allow for the best talent to be appointed to the Court, and that in many cases, "Executive influence exerted from the highest quarters" was responsible for the appointment of some judges. The Law Commission was also critical of the emphasis being placed on "communal and regional considerations" in making appointments to the Supreme Court[5].

In 1981, this system of appointment was challenged on the grounds that it impedes judicial independence. In *S. P. Gupta Vs. Union of India*[6] (also called as First Judges case), petitioners argued that the word "consultation" in the relevant provisions of the Constitution should be read as "concurrence," and that the Judiciary should exercise a veto over judicial appointments. The challenge failed and the Court held that in the event of a disagreement between the Executive and the Chief Justice on whom to appoint as a judge of the Supreme Court, the views of the Executive would prevail.

---

[4]*Indian Constitutional Law*, M.P. Jain, Eighth Edition, LexisNexis, Pg No. 196.

[5]Law Commission of India, 80th Report on the Method of Appointment of Judges, Pgs 16-17.

[6]AIR 1982 SC 149.

(d) **Appointment of Judges post 1993 :** Overturning its previous decision, the Court, in *Supreme Court Advocates-on-Record Association Vs. Union of India*[7] (Second Judges case) held that the 'ultimate power' of appointment vested in the Executive was being abused, and the existing system of appointments had resulted in merit being overlooked due to interference by the Executive. The Court held that judicial independence is part of the unamendable basic structure of the Constitution, and to protect this principle, the Judiciary should have 'primacy' over the appointments process. The term "consultation" with the Chief Justice was interpreted to mean that the Chief Justice had to concur in the appointment of the judge. The opinion of the Chief Justice was, in turn, not his/her individual opinion, but that of the Chief Justice in consultation with a collegium of the two senior-most judges of the Supreme Court. The Chief Justice of India is also expected to ascertain the views of the senior-most Judge of the Supreme Court who comes from the High Court of the candidate. If the government differed in its opinion, it could send the recommendation back to the collegium. However, if the Chief Justice reiterated the decision, the government would be bound by it. Thus, this judgment introduced the collegium-led appointments system.

In the '*In Re: Presidential Reference No. 1 of 1998*[8] (Third Judges case)', the Supreme Court modified and further clarified the appointments system. It held that the collegium for appointment to the Supreme Court would comprise the Chief Justice and the four senior-most judges of the Court. The Court further held that the recommendation made by the Chief Justice of India on the appointment of Judges of the Supreme Court and the High Courts without following the consultation process is not binding on the Government. The consultation process to be adopted by the Chief Justice of India requires consultation of *plurality of judges.* The sole individual opinion of the CJI does not constitute "consultation". The CJI should consult "*a collegium of four senior-most judges of the Supreme Court"* and made it clear that if "two Judges give adverse opinion, the CJI should not send the recommendation to the Government". The collegium must include the successor Chief Justice of India. The opinion of the collegium must be in writing and the CJI should send the recommendation to the President along with his own recommendations. In the IInd and the IIIrd Judges cases, the Court also stated that the inter-se seniority of judges within their High Court and their all-India seniority should be the primary ground for appointment to the Supreme Court. However, other considerations, such as outstanding merit and ensuring regional and other diversity, would be grounds to depart from the seniority norm.

(e) **Criticism of collegium system :** The collegium system has come in for its fair share of criticism. Critics point to the lack of transparency in the system, especially the lack of criteria for appointments and the absence of publicly disclosed reasons for why a person was found suitable for appointment. Further, critics contend that the opaqueness and lack of reasons in the appointments process has meant that the system is rife with corruption and nepotism[9]. Moreover, the two sides–the Executive and the Judiciary–both are trying to assert themselves in a tug of war for supremacy in the matter. However, both the sides have shown their failings

---

[7](1993) 4 SCC 441

[8](1998) 7 SCC 739.

[9]See a recounting of these criticisms in the opinion of Justice Kurian (concurring) and Justice Chelameswar (dissenting) in *Supreme Court Advocates on Record Association vs. Union of India*, 2016 (5) SCC 1.

on the matter. The solution perhaps lies in a practice where neither side enjoys a supremacy. A constitutional body reflecting the aspirations of all sections should be entrusted with the task of bringing harmony between the two conflicting wings of the government (Executive and Judiciary). Justice Bhagwati, in fact, suggested for the appointment of a Judicial Commission on the line of Australian Judicial Commission. Even the Law Commission in 1987, suggested for the Constitution of a National Judicial Service Commission which will have the final say in matters of selection, promotion, and transfer relating to the Judiciary.

(f) **National Judicial Appointments Commission (NJAC)** In 2014, the Parliament amended the Constitution and passed a legislation to overhaul the judicial appointment process. As per the 99th Constitutional Amendment Act, 2014, the National Judicial Appointments Commission Act (NJAC) was passed to replace the collegium system for the appointment of the Supreme Court and the High Court Judges. The National Judicial Appointments Commission comprises of the Chief Justice of India, the two senior-most judges of the Supreme Court after the Chief Justice, the Union Law Minister, and two eminent Persons. The two eminent persons are to be selected by a committee comprising of the Prime Minister, the Leader of the Opposition in the Lok Sabha, and the Chief Justice of India. Such eminent person is to be nominated for a period of three years and cannot be re-nominated again. At least one of the eminent persons would be a member of the Scheduled Castes/Scheduled Tribes/Other Backward Castes/Religious Minorities or a woman. Actions of the National Judicial Appointment Commission cannot be questioned on the ground of existence of error in the Constitution of the commission.

The 99th Constitutional Amendment Act, 2014 and the NJAC were challenged before the Supreme Court in the *Supreme Court Advocates–on-Record Association Vs. Union of India*[10] (Fourth Judges case). The Court, by majority, struck down the amendment for violating the basic structure of the Constitution, on the ground that the new procedure brings in the possibility of political influence, which impede judicial independence. Since judicial independence is part of the unamendable basic structure of the Constitution, the amendment, and consequently the statute framed under it, fail. Recognizing, however, the concerns with the collegium system, the Court held a "consequential hearing," and asked for suggestions from the wider public on the required reforms in the collegium system. The Court opined that reform of the collegium should focus on specifying eligibility criteria for appointments, introducing a transparent process for decision-making, setting up a permanent secretariat to assist the collegium for better management of the appointments system, and a mechanism to entertain complaints against those who are being considered for appointment, among other issues. Thus, the collegium system is continued for the appointment of the judges after striking down the 99th Constitutional Amendment Act, 2014.

Qualification Of Judges

A person to be qualified for appointment as a Judge of the Supreme Court must be a citizen of India. In addition, he may have been –

- Judge of a High Court at least for five years, or
- Has been for at least ten years an advocate of High Court, or
- Is in the opinion of the President, a distinguished jurist.

---

[10] 2016 (5) SCC 1.

Thus, there is no minimum age criteria for becoming the Supreme Court Judge. Secondly, a non-practising or an academic lawyer may also be appointed as Judge of the Supreme Court if he is, in the opinion of the President, a distinguished jurist. This provision has been inspired by the American example where distinguished law teachers have often been appointed to the Supreme Court. However, in India, so far no non-practising lawyer has been appointed as Judge of the Supreme Court.

Oath

Every person who is appointed as a Judge of the Supreme Court, before entering upon his office, has to make and subscribe an oath or affirmation before the President or some other person appointed in that behalf by him.

"I, A.B., having been appointed Chief Justice (or a Judge) of the Supreme Court of India do swear in the name of God/solemnly affirm that I will bear true faith and allegiance to the Constitution of India as by law established, that I will uphold the sovereignty and integrity of India, that I will duly and faithfully and to the best of my ability, knowledge and judgment perform the duties of my office without fear or favour, affection or ill-will and that I will uphold the Constitution and the laws."

Tenure of Judges

A Judge of the Supreme Court shall hold office until he attains the age of 65 years. The age of the Supreme Court Judge shall be determined by such authority and in such manner as Parliament may, by law, provide. In other words, Parliament has to set up an authority for the purpose. However, no such authority has been set up as yet.

The Judge of a Supreme Court even before attaining the age of 65 years can resign from his office by writing to the President.

Removal of Judges

In every democratic country, special provisions are made making removal of judges an extremely difficult exercise. The Constitution of India also makes a provision for the removal of a Supreme Court Judge. A judge of a Supreme Court can be removed by an order of the President on the grounds of "proved misbehaviour" or "incapacity". But the President's power of removal is exercisable only after an address of each House of Parliament, supported by a majority of total membership of that House (more than 50% of the total membership of the house) and a majority of not less than two-thirds of the members of that House present and voting, has been presented to the President in the same session for such removal. In other words, each House of the Parliament should pass a motion with special majority in the same session in order to remove the Judge. Unless such an address is presented to the President in the same session by the two Houses, the President is not empowered to remove a Judge.

The words "proved misbehaviour" or "incapacity" is not defined in the Constitution. The word "proved" in this provision indicates that the address can be presented by the Parliament only after the alleged charge of misbehaviour or incapacity against the Judge has been investigated, substantiated, and established by an impartial tribunal. The Constitution does not prescribe how this investigation is to be carried on. It leaves it to the Parliament to lay down the detailed procedure. The Parliament has enacted the necessary law for the purpose. The Judges (Inquiry) Act, 1968 now regulates the procedure for the investigation and proof of misbehaviour or incapacity of a Supreme Court Judge. The procedure for the purpose is as follows:

- A notice of a motion for presenting such an address may be given by 100 members of the Lok Sabha, or 50 members of the Rajya Sabha.
- The Speaker/Chairman may either admit or refuse to admit the motion.

- If it is admitted, then the Speaker/Chairman is to constitute a committee consisting of a Supreme Court Judge, a Chief Justice of a High Court, and distinguished jurist. If notices for the motion are given on the same day in both the Houses, the Committee of Inquiry is to be constituted jointly by the Speaker and the Chairman.
- The report of the Committee is to be laid before the concerned House or Houses. If the Committee exonerates the Judge of the charges laid against him, then no further action is to be taken on the motion for his removal. If, however, the Committee finds the Judge to be guilty of the charges laid against him, then the House can take up the consideration of the motion.
- The Judge will, however, be supplied a copy of the report by the Speaker before the motion for his removal is taken up in Parliament, in order to refute or rebut the charges levelled against him.
- Once the motion is be passed by each House of the Parliament by special majority, an address is presented to the President for removal of the Judge. Then finally, the President will pass an order removing the Judge.
- Although the address for the removal of the Judge has to be presented in the same session, the proceedings for the investigation and proof can be started earlier, *i.e.,* in a previous session or even in the previous Parliament.
- Parliament is free to drop the removal proceedings at any stage.
- The process of removal started in accordance with the provisions of the Judges (Inquiry) Act, 1968 does not lapse on the dissolution of the Lok Sabha.[11]

How difficult is the process for the removal of a Supreme Court Judge is sufficiently proved by the fact that no judge has ever been removed so far, though six judges have faced attempts to have them removed from office.[12] V. Ramaswami J. was a Judge of the Supreme Court and the first judge against whom impeachment proceedings were initiated. In 1993, the motion was brought up in Lok Sabha but failed to secure the required two-thirds majority.

Salary

Originally, the salary payable to a Supreme Court Judge was specified in the Second Schedule of the Constitution. But then, by the 44th Constitutional Amendment Act, Parliament has been given power to determine the salary payable to a Supreme Court Judge by law. The Parliament is also authorised to determine from time to time, by law, such questions as the privileges, allowances, rights in respect of leave of absence, and pension for these Judges. None of these can, however, be varied by the Parliament to the disadvantage of a Judge after his appointment to the Court. Salaries, gratuity, pension, allowances, etc. in respect of Judges of Supreme Court are governed by the Supreme Court Judges (Salaries and Conditions of Service) Act, 1958. Salaries, etc. of Judges of High Courts are governed by High Court Judges (Salaries and Conditions of Service) Act, 1954. An amendment in the Acts is required whenever there is any proposal for revision of salaries/pension gratuity, allowances, etc. in respect of Judges of Supreme Court and High Courts. Salaries and allowances of Judges of Supreme Court and High Court were last revised w.e.f. 2016.

[11] Sub Committee on Judicial Accountability Vs. Union of India, (1991) 4 SCC 699.

[12] V.N. Shukla's *Constitution of India*, Thirteenth Edition, EBC Explorer, Pg No. 512.

Stop-Gap Arrangement

(a) **Acting Chief Justice :** The President can appoint a Supreme Court Judge as the acting Chief Justice in case the office of the Chief Justice of India falls vacant, or the Chief Justice is unable to perform his duties due to absence or otherwise.

(b) **Ad Hoc Judge :** If at any time there is no quorum of the Judges available in the Court to hold and continue any session of the Court, the Chief Justice of India may, with the previous consent of the President and after the consultation of the Chief Justice of the High Court concerned, request a Judge of the High Court to act as *ad hoc* judge in the Supreme Court for such period as may be necessary. The *ad hoc* judge should be qualified to be appointed as a Judge of the Supreme Court. While so attending the Supreme Court, an *ad hoc* Judge enjoys all the jurisdiction, powers, and privileges of, and discharges all such duties like any other Supreme Court Judges.

(c) **Retired Judge :** A person who has held office as a Supreme Court Judge cannot plead or act in any court or before any authority in India. This disqualification has been placed on the ex-judge with a view to preserve the dignity of the Supreme Court and also to avoid embarrassment to the tribunal or the court before whom he may appear. However, the CJI, with the previous consent of the President, may request any retired Supreme Court Judge to sit and act as a Judge of the Court. If he agrees to do so, then while so sitting and acting, he is entitled to such allowances as may be determined by an order of the President. He will also enjoy all the jurisdiction, powers, and privileges of a Supreme Court Judge, but shall not otherwise be deemed to be a Judge of the Court. The Chief Justice may similarly request a retired High Court Judge, who is duly qualified to be appointed as a Supreme Court Judge, to sit and act as a Judge of the Supreme Court.

JURISDICTION AND POWERS OF THE SUPREME COURT

As the highest court in India, the Supreme Court's judgments are binding on all other courts in the country. It serves both as the final court of appeals and final interpreter of the Constitution. It is a multi-jurisdictional Court and may be regarded as the most powerful Apex Court in the World.

A Court of Record

Article 129 makes the Supreme Court a "Court of Record" and confers all the powers of such a court including the power to punish for its contempt. A court of record is a court –

(a) Whose records are admitted to be of evidentiary value and they are not to be questioned when they are produced before the court.

(b) Who has the power to determine its own jurisdiction; and

(c) Who has the power to punish for its contempt.

- The power to determine its own jurisdiction – In the absence of any express provision in the Constitution, the Apex Court being a court of record has jurisdiction in every matter and if there be any doubt, the court has power to determine its jurisdiction.
- The power to punish for contempt of court has been expressly conferred on the Supreme Court by the Constitution. This is an extraordinary power and is exercised only to uphold the majesty of the judicial system. Such a power is very necessary to prevent interference with the course of justice, to maintain the authority of law as administered in the court, and thus to protect public interest in the purity of the administration of justice[13].

[13] *Indian Constitutional Law*, M.P. Jain, Eighth Edition, LexisNexis, Pg No. 208.

The Contempt of Courts Act, 1971, defines the powers of courts for punishing contempt of courts and regulates their procedure. Contempt of court includes both 'civil' and 'criminal' contempt. 'Civil contempt' means –

- wilful disobedience to any judgment, decree, direction, order, writ other process of a court; or
- wilful breach of undertaking given to a court.

'Criminal contempt' means the publication (whether by words spoken or written by signs or by visible representation or otherwise) of any matter or doing of any act whatsoever which –

- Scandalises or tends to scandalise, or lowers or tends to lower the authority of any court; or
- Prejudices, or interferes or tends to interfere with the due course of any judicial proceeding; or
- Interferes or obstructs with the administration of justice in any other manner.

However, the following acts or publications will not amount to contempt –

- Innocent publications and its distribution;
- Fair and accurate report of judicial proceedings;
- Fair criticism of judicial act;
- Complaint made in good faith against presiding officers of subordinate courts (below High Court);

Delhi Judicial Service Association Vs. State of Gujarat[14] is a landmark judgment where the Supreme Court ruled out that it has the power to punish for contempt not only of itself but also of high courts, subordinate courts, and tribunals functioning in the entire country and is not against the Constitution of India. Both the Supreme Court as well as High Courts are courts of record. The Constitution does not define 'Court of record', but this expression is well recognized in the juridical world. A Court of record is a court whereof the acts and judicial proceedings are enrolled for a perpetual memorial and testimony, and has power of summarily punishing contempt of itself as well as of subordinate courts. The High Court being a court of record has inherent power in respect of contempt of itself as well as of its subordinate courts, even in the absence of any express provision in any Act. The Supreme Court being the Apex court and a superior court of record has the power to determine its jurisdiction under Article 129 and jurisdiction to initiate or entertain proceedings for contempt of the subordinate courts.

Extraordinary/Exclusive Original Jurisdiction

A court has original jurisdiction when it has authority to hear and determine a case in the first instance. It has exclusive jurisdiction when it has authority to hear and determine a case which no other court can hear or determine.

(a) Election of the President and Vice-President : Disputes concerning election of the President or Vice-President are decided exclusively by the Supreme Court and no other court (Article 71).

[14](1991) 4 SCC 406.

(b) Inter-governmental disputes : In a federal or a quasi-federal structure, disputes may arise between the Government of India and one or more States, or between two or more States. A forum should be provided for the resolution of such disputes. The forum should be the highest court so that final adjudication could be achieved expeditiously. Article 131 serves that purpose. Under Article 131, the Supreme Court has exclusive original jurisdiction in any dispute between –

i. The Centre and a State;

ii. The Centre and a State on one side, and a State on the other side;

iii Two or more States.

However, in order to refer a matter to the Supreme Court under Article 131 :

- There must be an inter-State dispute; and
- The dispute must involve a question of law or fact on which the existence of legal right depends. This means that the Court has no jurisdiction in matters of a political nature.

The Supreme Court in its exclusive original jurisdiction cannot entertain any suits brought by private individuals against the Government of India. The exclusive original jurisdiction of the Supreme Court under Article 131, however, does not extend to the following matters:

(a) The Jurisdiction of the Supreme Court shall not extend to a dispute arising out of any treaty, agreement, or other similar instrument which was executed before the commencement of the Constitution and continues to be in operation or which provides that the jurisdiction of the Supreme Court shall not extend to such a dispute.

A dispute involving interpretation of these documents has evidently been left within the exclusive jurisdiction of the Executive. For example, the President may, however, refer any dispute excluded from the court's jurisdiction under Article 131 to the Supreme Court for its advisory opinion under Article 143.

(b) Under Article 262, Parliament may by law exclude the jurisdiction of the Supreme Court in disputes with respect to the use, distribution, or control of the water of any inter-State river or river-valley.

(c) Matters referred to the Finance Commission (Article 280).

(d) The adjustment of certain expenses between the Union and the State (Article 290).

Concurrent Original Jurisdiction :

Article 32 confers original jurisdiction on the Supreme Court to enforce Fundamental Rights. The jurisdiction enjoyed by the Supreme Court under Article 32 is termed as "original concurrent jurisdiction". It is original because the Supreme Court acts as a court of first instance in enforcing the Fundamental Rights. However, both Supreme Court under Article 32 and the High Court under Article 226 have the concurrent powers to enforce the Fundamental Rights.

Article 32 provides a quick remedy for the enforcement of the Fundamental Rights. Under this Article, a person can directly go to the Supreme Court. The Supreme Court has thus been constituted as the protector and guarantor of the Fundamental Rights.

Appellate Jurisdiction

The Supreme Court is the highest court of appeal and enjoys extensive appellate jurisdiction. The Appellate jurisdiction of the Supreme Court can be divided into four main categories –

(a) Appeal in Constitutional Matters : Article 132 deals with questions involving interpretation of the Constitution arising out of any proceedings in a High Court – civil, criminal, or other proceeding. The scheme of the appellate jurisdiction of the Supreme Court clearly indicates that questions relating to the interpretation of the Constitution are placed in which they may arise. The idea is that on questions involving the interpretation of the Constitution, the Supreme Court should have the last say. However, an appeal can lie before the Supreme Court only if the High Court certifies that the case involves a substantial question of law as to the interpretation of the Constitution. There are three conditions for the grant of the Certificate by the High Court –

- Firstly, the order appealed against should be a "judgment, decree or final order made by a High Court".
- Secondly, the case must involve a substantial question of law as to the interpretation of this Constitution, and
- The High Court should certify that the case be heard by the Supreme Court.

(b) Appeal in Civil Matters : Under Article 133, an appeal lies to the Supreme Court from any judgment, decree, or final order in a civil proceeding of High Court if it certifies –

- That the case involves a substantial question of law of general importance; and
- That in the opinion of the High Court, the said question needs to be decided by the Supreme Court.

Prior to 30th Amendment Act, 1972, there was a right of appeal to the Supreme Court from a decision of a High Court if the subject-matter involved in the dispute is valued at Rs, 20,000 or more. The 30th Amendment has removed the condition that an appeal lies only when the amount or value in dispute is not less than Rs. 20,000/-. The result is that now all appeals, irrespective of their monetary value, can be taken to the Supreme Court, provided the case involves substantial question of law. This change has been effected because valuation test is not a true yardstick for the right to appeal to the Supreme Court.

(c) Appeal in Criminal matters : According to Article 134, an appeal lies to the Supreme Court from any judgment, final order, or sentence in a criminal proceeding of a High Court in the following two ways –

(i) Without a Certificate : An appeal lies to the Supreme Court without the certificate of the High Court if the High Court –

- Has on appeal reversed an order of acquittal of an accused person and sentenced him to death[15];

[15]For example, if the Sessions Judge acquits the accused of murder, the government makes an appeal against the judgment of the Sessions judge to the High Court and the High Court sets aside the order of acquittal and sentences the accused to death, an appeal lies to the Supreme Court without any certificate.

- Has withdrawn for trial before itself any case from any court subordinate to its authority and has in such trial convicted the accused person and sentenced him to death;

But if the High Court has reversed the order of conviction and has ordered the acquittal of an accused, no appeal would lie to the Supreme Court.

(ii) With a Certificate : An appeal lies to the Supreme Court if the High Court certifies that it is a fit case for the appeal to the Supreme Court.

In 1970, the Parliament extended the criminal appellate jurisdiction of the Supreme Court, by the words "to imprisonment for life or for a period of not less than ten years" for the words "to death". In other words, under Article 134 of the Constitution, an appeal shall lie to the Supreme Court from any judgment in a criminal proceeding of a High Court in the territory of India if the High Court –

- Has on appeal reversed an order of a acquittal person and sentenced him to imprisonment for life or to imprisonment for a period of not less than 10 years;
- Has withdrawn for trial before itself any case form any court subordinate to its authority and has in such trial convicted the accused person and sentenced him to imprisonment for life or to imprisonment for a period of not less than ten years.

(d) Appeal by Special Leave : Under Article 136, the Supreme Court is authorised to grant in its discretion special leave to appeal from –

- Any judgment, decree, determination, sentence or order;
- In any case or matter;
- Passed or made by any court or tribunal in the territory of India.

The only exception to this power of the Supreme Court is with regard to any judgment of any court or tribunal constituted by or under any law relating to the Armed Forces. In other words, Special Leave Petition cannot lie from the military tribunal.

Articles 132 to 134 of the Constitution deal with appeals to the Supreme Court which a person may avail of as a matter of right so long as the conditions specified in those articles are satisfied. Under Article 136, one may appeal to the court only with its permission or leave. But the power of the court to hear appeals in this Article is much wider and general. It vests in the Supreme Court plenary jurisdiction in the matter of entertaining and hearing appeals by granting special leave against any judgment, decree, determination or order, in any cause or matter, passed or made by any court or tribunal.

Distinction between Article 136 and Articles 132–134:

Articles 132 to 134 permit appeals only against decisions of the High Courts. Article 136 on the other hand, does not impose any such restriction. Under Article 136, the Supreme Court can grant special leave for appeal from "any court or tribunal", viz. from any subordinate court below the High Court.

- Under Articles 132 to 134, appeal can be entertained by the Supreme Court only against the 'final order', but under Article 136, the Supreme Court can hear an appeal even from an interlocutory or interim order as well.

- Article 136 does not define the nature of proceedings from which the Supreme Court may hear appeals, and, therefore, it could hear appeals in any kind of proceedings whether civil, criminal, or relating to income-tax, revenue, or labour disputes, etc. In other words, the Supreme Court can hear appeals in cases which even fall outside the scope of Articles, 132, 133, and 134.
- Article 136 confers no right of appeal upon any party; it only vests a discretion in the Apex Court to grant leave for entertaining the appeal.

Advisory jurisdiction of the Supreme Court

Under Article 143, the Supreme Court has the power of advisory jurisdiction. Article 143(1) provides that if at any time it appears to the President that –

- A question of law or fact has arisen or is likely to arise, and
- The question is of such a nature and of such public importance that it is expedient to obtain the opinion of the Supreme Court upon it, he may refer the question for advisory opinion of the Court and the Court may after such hearing as it thinks fit, report to the President its opinion thereon.

In other words, the Article 143(1) authorises the President to refer to the Supreme Court a question of law or fact which, in his opinion, is of such a nature and of such a public importance that it is expedient to obtain its opinion upon it. Clause (1) of Article 143 empowers the President to refer to the Supreme Court a question of law or fact which has arisen or is likely to arise. In case, the court has already pronounced a judgement on a question of law, then it cannot be said that a doubt exists regarding that question. The President can refer a question of law only when the Supreme Court has not decided it. The advisory jurisdiction under Article 143 is not an appellate jurisdiction of the Supreme Court over its own decisions. The Executive has no power to ask the Supreme Court to revise its decision.

The President can refer any matter to the Supreme Court under the advisory opinion (except those which have already been decided by the Supreme Court earlier). The President has the sole discretion to decide whether the matter referred to the Supreme Court is of such nature which needs urgent attention or not.

The President can also refer the matter to the Supreme Court under Article 143(2) to give its opinion in matters which are arising regarding dispute on any treaty convention, entered into before the commencement of the Constitution.

Is the President bound by the Advice?

The advisory opinion of the Supreme Court under this Article is not binding on the President, though the President honours it and appreciates it. The opinion so rendered by the Supreme Court is not binding on the President for the following reasons –

- Article 143 is not part of the administration of justice. It is part of an Advisory Machinery designed to assist the President.
- The opinion is not law declared by the Court and thus, cannot be bound on the President.

Is Supreme Court bound to give an opinion?

The Supreme Court is not bound to give advice if the President refers any matter to the Supreme Court under Clause 143(1). But the Court is bound to give the advice if the President refers a matter falling under Clause 143(2). There is a reason for this dichotomy between Article 143(1) and 143(2). Whereas it may be possible to approach the courts with respect to the matters falling under Article 143(1) but the matters referred to in Article 143(2) are banned from judicial scrutiny of the Supreme Court, High Court, or any other court because of the operation of Article 131[16].

Thus, while under Clause (2), it is obligatory on the Supreme Court to entertain a reference and to report to the President its opinion thereon, the Court has, under Clause (1), a discretion in the matter and may, in a proper case, decline to express any opinion on the questions submitted to it. For example:

- Where the question referred to is a political one, as distinguished from the constitutional validity of a Bill or Act.
- Where it is incapable of being answered.
- Where the question is hypothetical or speculative or superfluous. But the mere possibility that a pending Bill may undergo changes in the course of legislation, would not make the question of constitutionality of a pending Bill hypothetical.
- Where it is vague unless the vagueness is cleared by the written briefs and submissions of the parties before the court.
- Where the court considers that the question does not arise in the facts and circumstances of the case.

In *Special Reference No. 1/1993 in Ram Janmbhoomi*, which was in relation to the Ayodhya dispute - the President sought the opinion of the Supreme Court with respect to the Ayodhya Temple dispute. In this case, it was held by the Supreme Court that the Supreme Court can decline giving its opinion under Article 143 in cases it does not consider proper or not amenable to such exercise by giving and showcasing proper reason for such denial. Therefore, in the said case, the Supreme Court refused to give its opinion under Article 143, but the same Supreme Court resolved the Ayodhya Issue in *M Siddiq (D) Thr Lrs Vs. Mahant Suresh Das & Ors*[17], under its Civil Appellate Jurisdiction under Article 131.

Power to review its judgments

In India, a binding decision of the Supreme Court can be reviewed in a review petition. A review petition can be filed by the parties aggrieved by the decisions of the Supreme Court.

The normal principle is that a judgment pronounced by the Court is final, and departure from that principle is justified only when circumstances of a substantial and compelling character make it necessary to do so, for instance, if the attention of the Court is not drawn to a material statutory provision during the original hearing. The Court may also reopen its judgment if a manifest wrong has been done and

[16] The Jurisdiction of the Supreme Court shall not extend to a dispute arising out of any treaty, agreement or other similar instrument which was executed before the commencement of the Constitution and continues to be in operation or which provides that the jurisdiction of the Supreme Court shall not extend to such a dispute.

[17] CA 10866 - 10867/2010.

it is necessary to pass an order to do full and effective justice. Power to review its judgments has been conferred on the Supreme Court by Article 137 of the Constitution, and that power is subject to the provisions of any law made by Parliament or the rules under Article 145.

Thus, As per Article 137 of the Constitution of India and the rules made under Article 145, the Supreme Court of India has the power to review its judgment pronounced by it[18]. Review will lie in the Supreme Court on the following grounds:

- Discovery of new important matters of evidence;
- Mistake or error on the face of the record; and
- Any other sufficient reason.

The power of review is distinct from the Court's power to hear appeals, i.e., the appellate jurisdiction. When hearing a review petition filed against its own order or judgment, the Court does not rehear the case at hand, as it would in an appeal. The purpose of a review petition is limited to remedying an apparent error or the resultant grave injustice that has been the consequence of a decision of the Supreme Court.

Curative Petition

Curative petition is the last constitutional remedy available to a person whose review petition has been dismissed by the Supreme Court. Though the Constitution explicitly speaks about the review power of the Supreme Court under Article 137, it is silent about 'curative petition'. The Supreme Court of India evolved the concept of curative petition in the landmark case of *Rupa Ashok Hurra vs. Ashok Hurra and Anr*[19]. In the Rupa Ashoka Hurra case, where the Apex court reconsidered its judgment in exercise of its inherent power to prevent abuse of its process and to cure a gross miscarriage of justice, it was explained in the said decision that the curative power of the Court flows from Article 142 of the Constitution, which gives the Court the power to do complete justice. The Court, to prevent abuse of its process and to cure a gross miscarriage of justice, may reconsider its judgments in exercise of its inherent power.

Except when very strong reasons exist, the court should not entertain an application seeking reconsideration of an order of the Apex Court which has become final on dismissal of a review petition. While acknowledging that it was not possible to enumerate all the grounds on which a curative petition may be entertained, the Court laid down certain broad parameters for exercise of this power.

Conditions to file a curative petition :

- It has to be established by the petitioner that there was a genuine violation of principles of natural justice.
- Wherein the proceedings of a learned Judge failed to disclose his connection with the subject-matter.
- Abuse of the process of the court.
- The curative petition shall be certified by a senior advocate.

[18] As per Supreme Court Rules, 1966, such a petition is to be filed within 30 days of the pronouncement of judgment or order and that petition should be circulated without oral arguments to the same bench that delivered the judgment.

[19] (2002) 4 SCC 388.

- The curative petition is then circulated to the three senior most judges and also to the judges who passed the impugned judgment.
- If majority of the judges agree that the matter needs hearing, then it would be sent to the same bench.
- Exemplary costs could be imposed by the court to the petitioner if his plea lacks merit.

Binding value of the Judgment of the Supreme Court

The judgment of the Supreme Court will be binding on all courts in India. The expression "all courts within the territory of India" clearly means courts other than the Supreme Court. Thus, the Supreme Court is not bound by its own decisions and may in the proper case, reverse its previous decisions. The question was considered in detail by the Supreme Court in the case of Bengal Immunity Co. Vs. State of Bihar[20]. In this case, the Court held that "There is nothing in our Constitution which prevents us from departing from a previous decision if we are convinced of its error and its baneful effect on the general interests of the public."

Miscellaneous Powers

a. ***Doctrine Of Stare Decisis :*** The term 'Stare Decisis' originates from Latin. It means 'to abide by things decided'. Decision taken by a higher court is binding on the lower court and it also stands as a precedent to the lower court judgement, which cannot be distorted by the lower court. This principle is known as stare decisis, which essentially means to stand by the decided matters. In India, it is commonly known as the concept of precedent. Article 141 of the Indian Constitution states that "Any law declared by Supreme Court to be binding on all courts within the territory of India." Article 141 states that only the *ratio decidendi*[21] of a case is binding, not the *obiter dicta*[22] and the mere facts of the cases. Therefore, while applying the decision of the Supreme Court by other courts, what is required is to understand the true principle laid down by the previous decision.

b. ***Transfer of cases :*** Article 139A (1) provides that if cases involving substantially the same questions of law are pending before the Supreme Court and a High Court, or before two or more High Courts, the Supreme Court can withdraw the cases from the High Courts and decide them itself. Once the common issue of law is decided, the cases may be returned to the High Courts under the proviso to Article 139A (1) to decide individual cases in the light of the law so laid down. Moreover, under Article 139A (2), the Supreme Court may also transfer a case from one High Court to another if it deems it expedient to do so for meeting the ends of justice.

c. ***Power to summon witnesses :*** Subject to a law made by the Parliament in this behalf, the Court is empowered to make, as regards the whole of India, any order for the purpose of securing the attendance of any person, the discovery or production of all documents, or the investigation or punishment of any contempt of itself.

d. ***Enforcement of decrees :*** Any decree passed, or order made, by the Supreme Court is enforceable throughout India in such manner as may be prescribed by a law of Parliament.

---

[20] AIR 1955 SC 661.

[21] Ratio decidendi of a judgment may be defined as the principles of law formulated by the Judge for the purpose of deciding the problem before him.

[22] Obiter dicta means observations made by the Judge, but are not essential for the decision reached.

e. ***All authorities bound by court orders :*** All authorities, civil and judicial, in India are under an obligation to act in the aid of the Court. The Court can hold any authority in contempt of Court if he disregards or disobeys any Court order.

f. ***Court's Rule-Making Power :*** The Supreme Court has been given a rule-making power for generally regulating its practice and procedure including such matters as persons practising before it, procedure for hearing appeals, conditions for reviewing its own judgment, fees, grant of bail, stay of proceedings, etc. Rules made by the Court need the approval of the President and they are subject to any law made by Parliament.

g. ***Officers and servants of the Supreme Court*** : Appointment of officers and servants of the Supreme Court are to be made by the Chief Justice, or such other Judge or officer of the Court as the Chief Justice may direct, but the President may, by rules, direct that appointments are to be made after consultation with the Union Public Service Commission.

h. ***Additional Jurisdiction :*** Parliament may confer on the Supreme Court further jurisdiction and powers with respect to any of the matters in the Union List. Under Article 138, the Parliament is authorised to confer on the Supreme Court with additional jurisdiction with respect to the enforcement of any of the matters enumerated in the Union List. The enlargement of powers contemplated here may be in relation to the original or appellate jurisdiction of the Supreme Court. Similarly, Parliament can also confer on the Supreme Court with jurisdiction to decide upon -

- Any matter as the Government of India and the Government of any State may by Special Agreement confer; or
- All matters arising out of treaties, including extradition, between the Union and a foreign State.

INDEPENDENCE OF THE JUDICIARY

Only an impartial and independent Judiciary can protect the rights of the individual and provide equal justice without fear or favour. It is, therefore, very necessary that the Supreme Court should be allowed to perform its functions in an atmosphere of independence and be free from all kinds of political pressures. The Constitution has made several provisions to ensure independence of the Judiciary.

1. **Security of tenure :** The Judges of the Supreme Court have security of tenure. The judges of the Supreme Court serve "during good behaviour" and not during the pleasure of the President. They cannot be arbitrarily removed by the President. They may be removed from office only through impeachment. A Judge can be removed on the ground of proved misbehaviour or incapacity on a report by both Houses of the Parliament supported by a special majority.

2. **Appointment of Judges :** The Constitution does not leave the appointment of the Judges of the Supreme Court to the unguided discretion of the Executive. The Executive is required to consult the Judges of the Supreme Court and High Courts in the appointment of the Judges of the Supreme Court. The independence of the Supreme Court is also emphasised by Article 229 which provides that appointment of officers and servants of the Court shall be made by the Chief Justice or such other Judge or officer as he may appoint.

3. **Salary of the Judges :** The salaries and allowances of judges of the Supreme Court is charged upon the Consolidated Fund of India. They are not subject to the annual vote of the Parliament. Further, the salaries and allowances of the Judges of the Supreme Court cannot be reduced during their tenure, except during a financial emergency under Article 360 of the Constitution.

4. **Conduct of the Judges cannot be discussed in Legislature :** Neither in Parliament nor in a State Legislature a discussion can take place with respect to the conduct of a Judge of the Supreme Court in discharge of his duties, except in case of their removal.

5. **Prohibition on practice after Retirement :** A retired Judge of the Supreme Court is prohibited to appear and plead in any court or before any authority within the territory of India.

6. **Power to punish for its Contempt :** The Supreme Court and the High Court have the power to punish any person for its contempt. This power is very essential for maintaining the impartiality and independence of the Judiciary.

QUESTIONS

Subjective Questions

1. Discuss the procedure for the appointment of judges of the Supreme Court in the light of the 99th Constitutional Amendment Act. **(15 marks)**

2. Explain the various Jurisdictions and powers of the Supreme Court in India. **(15 marks)**

Objective Questions

1. With reference to the Constitution of India, prohibitions or limitations or provisions contained in ordinary laws cannot act as prohibitions or limitations on the constitutional powers under Article 142. It could mean which one of the following? **(UPSC CSE 2019)**

   (a) The decisions taken by the Election Commission of India while discharging its duties cannot be challenged in any court of law.

   (b) The Supreme Court of India is not constrained in the exercise of its powers by laws made by the Parliament.

   (c) In the event of the grave financial crisis in the country, the President of India can declare Financial Emergency without the counsel from the Cabinet.

   (d) State Legislatures cannot make laws on certain matters without the concurrence of the Union Legislature.

   Ans: (b)

2. Consider the following statements:

   i. The motion to impeach a Judge of the Supreme Court of India cannot be rejected by the Speaker of the Lok Sabha as per the Judges (Inquiry) Act, 1968.

   ii. The Constitution of India defines and gives details of what constitutes 'incapacity and proved misbehaviour' of the Judges of the Supreme Court of India.

iii. The details of the process of impeachment of the Judges of the Supreme Court of India are given in the Judges (Inquiry) Act, 1968.

iv. If the motion for the impeachment of a Judge is taken up for voting, the law requires the motion to be backed by each House of the Parliament and supported by a majority of total membership of that House and by not less than two-thirds of total members of that House present and voting.

Which of the statements given above is/are correct? **(UPSC CSE 2019)**

(a) i and ii (b) iii only

(c) iii and iv only (d) i, iii, and iv

Ans: (c)

3. What is the provision to safeguard the autonomy of the Supreme Court of India? **(UPSC CSE 2012)**

i. While appointing the Supreme Court Judges, the President of India has to consult the Chief Justice of India.

ii. The Supreme Court Judges can be removed by the Chief Justice of India only.

iii. The salaries of the Judges are charged on the Consolidated Fund of India to which the Legislature does not have to vote.

iv. All appointments of officers and staffs of the Supreme Court of India are made by the Government only after consulting the Chief Justice of India.

Which of the statements given above is/are correct?

(a) i and iii only (b) iii and iv only

(c) iv only (d) i, ii, iii, and iv

Ans: (a)

4. Which of the following are included in the original jurisdiction of the Supreme Court? **(2012)**

i. A dispute between the Government of India and one or more States

ii. A dispute regarding elections to either House of the Parliament or that of Legislature of a State

iii. A dispute between the Government of India and a Union Territory

iv. A dispute between two or more States

Select the correct answer using the codes given below:

(a) i and ii (b) ii and iii

(c) i and iv (d) iii and iv

Ans: (c)

5. The power of the Supreme Court of India to decide disputes between the Centre and the States falls under its

(a) advisory jurisdiction (b) appellate jurisdiction.

(c) original jurisdiction (d) writ jurisdiction

Ans: (c)

13.1 JUDICIAL REVIEW

JUDICIAL REVIEW

The ultimate power of the Judiciary to review and determine the validity of a law or an order may be described as the powers of "judicial review". In other words, the Supreme Court as well the High Courts in India have the power to check whether the law has been made within the constitutional limits or not. If not, it will be declared unconstitutional.

In India, the Constitution is the supreme law. And if any law passed by the Parliament violates the Constitution, the Higher Judiciary (Supreme Court and High Courts) has the power to nullify that law.

Especially in the written Constitution like India which guarantees individual Fundamental Rights, divides power between the Union and the States, and clearly defines and delimits the powers and functions of every organ of the State including the Parliament, the Judiciary plays a very important role under their powers of judicial review.

The power of judicial review of legislation is given to the Judiciary both by the political theory and the text of the Constitution. There are several specific provisions in the Indian Constitution which deals with judicial review of legislation such as –

Articles	Judicial Review Power
Art. 13 & 32	Supreme Court is constituted as protector & guarantor of the Fundamental Rights. The Supreme Court can strike down the laws violating the Fundamental Rights.
Art. 226	High Courts have the power to issue writs to challenge the Executive as well legislative actions violating the Fundamental Rights or any other constitutional rights.
Art. 131	Exclusive original jurisdiction of Supreme Court. (Disputes between Centre-States & Inter-States).
Art. 132	Appellate Jurisdiction of Supreme Court in Constitutional cases.
Art.133	Appellate Jurisdiction of Supreme Court in civil cases.
Art. 134	Appellate Jurisdiction of Supreme Court in criminal cases.
Art. 134-A	Deals with the certificate for appeal to the Supreme Court from the High Courts.
Art. 135	Confers on the Supreme Court to exercise the jurisdiction and powers of the Federal Court with respect to any pre-constitutional law.
Art. 143	Opinion to the President.
Art. 227	High Courts have the superintendence power over all the courts and tribunals within their respective territorial jurisdiction.
Art. 245	Exclusive power of the Parliament and the State Legislature with respect to the subjects falling under each List. (Union List, State List, Concurrent List).
Art. 254	In case of inconsistency between union and state laws, the state law shall be void.
Art. 372	Deals with the continuance in force of the pre-Constitution laws.

Thus, judicial review is a great weapon in the hands of judges. It comprises the power of a court to hold unconstitutional and unenforceable any law or order based upon such law or any other action by a public authority which is inconsistent or in conflict with the basic Law of the Land. In fact, the study of constitutional law may be described as a study of the doctrine of judicial review in action. The courts have the power to strike down any law, if they believe it to be unconstitutional.

Classification of Judicial Review

Judicial review can conveniently be classified under three heads :

1. *Judicial review of Constitutional amendments* – If any constitutional amendment violates the basic structure of the Constitution, then the said amendment can be struck down by the Supreme Court. The test of validity of Constitutional amendments is that it should conform to the basic features of the Constitution.
2. *Judicial review of legislation of Parliament, State Legislatures, as well as subordinate legislation* – If the Parliament or State Legislature passes any law which violates the Fundamental Rights or any provision of the Constitution or transgresses the limits prescribed in the Constitution, then such laws can be struck down either by the Supreme Court or the High Court for being ultra vires of the Constitution. Even the subordinate legislation or delegated legislation (such as rules and G.O.'s passed by the Executive) can also be struck down by the Higher courts if it is ultra vires of the Constitution.
3. *Judicial review of administrative action of the Union of India as well as the State Governments and authorities falling within the meaning of State* – If any Executive or administrative action or inaction is ultra vires of the Constitution or any law passed by the Legislature, then such action or inaction can be declared null and void by the Higher Courts.

JUDICIAL ACTIVISM

With the framing of the Constitution of India, the three wings of effective governance came into being, namely the Legislature, the Executive, and the Judiciary. The Constitution provides for separation of powers[1] and hence, demarcates the powers and areas of all these three machineries. However, sometimes with the failure of the Legislature and the Executive, the separation of power remains a theory only in the text book and the third wing of governance, the Judiciary assumes unprecedented power under the name and guise of judicial review and turns into an activist.

Origin and Evolution of Judicial Activisms

As far as the origin and evolution of judicial activism goes, there are two theories behind the whole concept. They are: (i) Theory of Vacuum Filling and (ii) Theory of Social Want.

- *Theory of Vacuum* Filling : The Theory of Vacuum Filling states that a power vacuum is created in the governance system due to the inaction and laziness of any one organ. Generally, the

[1]Even though there is no strict separation of powers under Indian Constitution.

vacuum is created by the inactivity, incompetence, disregard of law, negligence, corruption, utter indiscipline, and lack of character among the two organs of governance, viz. the Legislature and the Executive. Hence, the remaining organ of the governance system, i.e., the Judiciary is left with no other alternative but to expand its horizons and fill up the vacuum created by the Executive and the Legislature. Thus, according to this theory, the so-called activism of the Judiciary is a result of filling up of the vacuum or the void created by the non-activism of the Legislature and the Executive.

- *Theory of Social Want* : The Theory of Social Want states that judicial activism emerged due to the failure of the existing legislations to cope up with the existing situations and problems in the country. When the existing legislations failed to provide any pathway, it became incumbent upon the Judiciary to take on itself the problems of the oppressed and to find a way to solve them. The only way left to them within the framework of governance to achieve this end was to provide non-conventional interpretations to the existing legislations, so as to apply them for greater good.

Origin of Judicial Activism in India

Judicial activism is not mentioned in the Constitution. It originated in India in the late 1970s. This origin can be traced to the Theory of Social Want. It was due to Executive abuses and excesses that the Judiciary had to intervene during the course of legal proceedings. Let us look into the rationale behind such intervention. After independence from the British, the Executive has always looked upon the Judiciary as a hostile branch of the State. This view gained more momentum and popularity when the bureaucracy degenerated into a system for personal and not public gains. Exploitation and corruption became inbuilt in the present political system. The masses were oppressed beyond imagination by the unbridled actions by Money power, Muscle power, Media power, and Ministerial power[2]. In this scenario, some emergency situations arose which could not wait for the Parliament for its looking into. Hence, it became a responsibility of the Judiciary to do something to provide relief to the oppressed masses of the society. In *Sunil Batra vs. Delhi Administration*[3], *Justice V. R. Krishna Iyer* described the situation in the following words:

"Though legislation was the best solution, but when lawmakers take for far too long for social patience to suffer. Courts have to make do with interpretation and carve on wood and sculpt on stone without waiting for the distant marble."

The theory of judicial activism received impetus in the case of *Maneka Gandhi vs. Union of India*[4], where the Apex Court substituted the due process clause in Article 21 instead of 'procedure established by law' in order to bypass the absolutism of the Executive and its interference with individual freedom.

---

[2](B. Venkatachalapathi, 1998).

[3]AIR 1978 SC 1548.

[4]AIR 1978 SC 853.

Concept of Judicial Activism

Thus, Judicial activism is not the performance of the function of settling the disputes in accordance with Constitution or Law of the Land. It is the adoption of a pro-active approach by the Judiciary. Judicial activism reflects the situation when the Judiciary comes out of its sphere of traditional roles and becomes active in its working while laying down the policies and programs to ensure the protection of rights and liberties of the people, which otherwise is within the discretion of the Executive and the Legislature.

The activist role of the Judiciary is not only confined to the protection of Fundamental Rights and legal rights, but also tries to implement the socio-economic rights envisaged in the Part IV (DPSP) of the Constitution which are not enforceable in the court of law.

Significance of Judicial Activism

Judicial activism is mainly due to

- Failure on the party of the other organs of governance;
- Growing challenges in front of the Judiciary in the backdrop of new issues;
- Failure of Executive i.e., Corruption, Delay, Non-responsiveness, Inefficiency, etc.;
- Failure of Legislative, that is, Absentee legislator, Legislative's inability to come out with a law in a number of contemporary issues, and Improper addressing of issues through Legislature.

PUBLIC INTEREST LITIGATION

The right to access the courts of justice is available to individuals who are aggrieved by the action of others. It is only when you are the affected or aggrieved person that you are able to approach the court of law for redressal. This means that there is a mechanism to address the violation of individual rights. But the peculiar socio-economic conditions that are unique to India strictly following the rule of locus standi, i.e., whose right is violated alone can approach the court – would result in restricting the access to judicial process. For example, what happens when an individual cannot afford to reach out to the courts? Does his right remain violated forever or is there any other recourse in such situations? Thus, blindly following the rule of locus standi would cause greater injustice. As a result, there is a need for creating new principles and strategies to tackle those cases where the individual representation is either inadequate or impeded due to social, political, and economic constraints. Public Interest Litigation is one of the initiatives by the Indian Judiciary to meet those situations. Public Interest Litigation is a judicial doctrine that has tried not only to address the circumstances in which a person is poor, ignorant, indigent, or illiterate and cannot afford to handle the litigation, but also used in enforcing social rights. The justice delivery system is brought to his doorstep through Public Interest Litigation. The focus is shifted from individual rights to group rights. Any public-spirited person who has interest in pursuing the wrongs done to others or a group of persons, can access the courts of justice and fight for the rights of the disadvantaged and needy group of individuals[5].

---

[5] Access to justice, Public Interest Litigation, ePathshala, An MHRD project under its National Mission on Education through ICT (NME-ICT).

Meaning of Public Interest Litigation[6]

One of the objectives of the Indian legal system is to deliver justice to all. Public Interest Litigation is a tool used to achieve this goal in the society. Preamble to the Constitution of India envisages Social, Economic, and Political justice. In order to achieve this Preambular Goal of Justice, the judicial activism has led to the birth of Public Interest Litigation. Public Interest Litigation is a court proceeding filed by any public-spirited person to voice out the interests of the general public. In this proceeding, the person fighting the litigation may not himself be the aggrieved person. The term 'Public Interest Litigation' is coined by the use of two terms, 'Public Interest' and 'Litigation'. PIL is the manifestation of the Judicial activism.

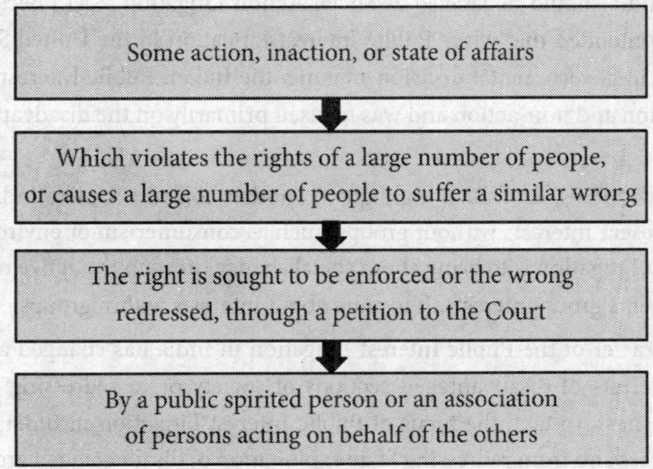

Origin and Development of PIL in India

The concept of Public Interest Litigation originated in the United States of America in late nineteenth century. Whereas in India, till 1960s and seventies, the concept of litigation in India consisted mainly of some action initiated and continued by certain individuals, usually, addressing their own grievances or problems. Thus, the initiation and continuance of litigation was the prerogative of the injured person or the aggrieved party. However, the entire scenario changed during eighties when the Supreme Court of India led the concept of Public Interest Litigation (PIL). The splendid efforts of Justice P. N. Bhagwati and Justice V. R. Krishna Iyer were instrumental for this juristic revolution of the eighties. As a result, any citizen of India or social action groups can approach the apex court of the country seeking legal remedies in all cases where the interests of the general public or a section of the public are at stake. Further, public interest cases could be filed without investment of heavy court fess as required in private civil litigation.

One of the earliest cases of PIL was *Hussainara Khatoon vs. State of Bihar*[7]. This case was concerned with a series of articles published in a prominent newspaper, which exposed the plight of undertrial prisoners in the state of Bihar. A writ petition was filed by an advocate drawing the Court's attention to the deplorable plight of these prisoners. Many of them had been in jail for longer periods than the maximum

[6]IBID.

[7](1980) 1 SCC 81.

permissbile sentences for the offences they had been charged with. The Supreme Court accepted the locus standi of the advocate to maintian the writ petition. Thereafter, a series of cases followed in which the Court gave directions through which the 'right to speedy trial' was deemed to be an integral and an essential part of the protection of life and personal liberty.

PIL in USA and SAL in India[8]

Given that the birth of Public Interest Litigation in India is connected to the evolution of Public Interest Litigation in the United States, it becomes natural to draw comparisons between the US experience and the Indian experience. It was argued by Professor Upendra Baxi that Public Interest Litigation (PIL) in India should be labeled as Social Action Litigation (SAL) because of its distinctive characteristics. He contended that while Public Interest Litigation in the United States has focused on people participation in governmental decision-making, the Indian Public Interest Litigation discourse was against State action and non-action and was focused primarily on the disadvantaged sections of the society.

Writing in the early 1980s, Prof. Baxi highlighted another contrast. Unlike India, PIL in the United States sought to represent interests without groups, such as consumerism or environment. In India, the role of Public Interest Litigation is to bring about social change through the active role of judges wherein the individual represents group interests. It is more about interests within groups.

However, the character of the Public Interest Litigation in India has changed a lot. It is not limited to espousing the interests of disadvantaged sections of society or to redressing State repression and governmental lawlessness. In fact, the focus of Public Interest Litigation in India has shifted from the poor to the middle class and from redressing State exploitation of disadvantaged groups to pleas for civic participation in governance.

Abuse of Public Interest Litigation[9]

The judicial innovation to protect the interest of the underprivileged, disadvantaged, and the needy through Public Interest Litigation has in later stages been abused by the litigants. The misuse of Public Interest Litigation started in 1990s when the nature of filing of such petitions changed. People started using Public Interest Litigation as a means to achieve their personal ends under the guise of Public Interest Litigation. Some petitions were filed with the sole objective to gain popularity in the society as a Public Interest Litigation lawyer. Some PILs were filed to fulfill the politically and financially motivated agendas. Some litigants who specialized in Public Interest Litigation were nothing but blackmailers. The very purpose and concept of Public Interest Litigation has been diluted by such frivolous petitions. An attempt was made by the Government in 1996 by proposing 'The Public Interest Litigation (Regulation) Bill' to punish those who file frivolous PIL. However, the Bill could not receive majority support and lapsed. However, the Judiciary has built its own mechanism through guidelines to treat this self-created problem. Only claims of bonafide individuals are entertained by the Supreme Court and High Courts

[8] Access to justice, Public Interest Litigation, ePathshala, An MHRD project under its National Mission on Education through ICT (NME-ICT).

[9] Ibid.

instead of all Public Interest Litigations. Courts also impose exemplary costs in vexatious litigations. The Supreme Court has cautioned High Courts to be selective in qualifying petitions as Public Interest Litigation.

JUDICIAL OVERREACH

Judicial overreach refers to an extreme form of judicial activism where arbitrary, unreasonable, and frequent interventions are made by the Judiciary into the Legislature's domain, often with the intention of disrupting the balance of powers between the Executive, Legislature, and Judiciary. This is a situation where the court encroaches upon the role of the Legislature by making laws. Cases where the courts encroach upon the role of the Executive by making rules or indulging in censorship can also be termed as judicial overreach.

Characteristics of Judicial Overreach

The line between judicial activism and judicial overreach is very narrow. In simple terms, when judicial activism crosses its limits and becomes judicial adventurism, it is known as judicial overreach. When the Judiciary oversteps the powers given to it, it may interfere with the proper functioning of the Legislative or Executive organs of the government.

Thus, as long as the Judiciary pulls upon the Executive to perform its functions, it is not a controversial issue. While this supervisory function of the Judiciary is and will continue to be desirable; it will be contrary to the notions and theme of the Constitution if the Judiciary was to overstep its mandate and carry the mantle of the Legislature and Executive.

13.2 SUPREME COURT ADVOCATES

There are three categories of Advocates who are entitled to practise law before the Supreme Court of India :

(i) Senior Advocates

These are Advocates who are designated as Senior Advocates by the Supreme Court of India or by any High Court. The Court can designate any Advocate, with his consent, as Senior Advocate if in its opinion, by virtue of his ability, standing at the Bar, or special knowledge or experience in law, the said Advocate is deserving of such distinction. A Senior Advocate is not entitled to appear without an Advocate-on-Record in the Supreme Court or without a junior in any other court or tribunal in India. He is also not entitled to accept instructions to draw pleadings or affidavits, advise on evidence, or do any drafting work of an analogous kind in any court or tribunal in India or undertake conveyancing work of any kind whatsoever, but this prohibition shall not extend to settling any such matter as aforesaid in consultation with a junior.

(ii) Advocates-On-Record

These are the only Advocates are entitled to file any matter or document before the Supreme Court. They can also file an appearance or act for a party in the Supreme Court.

(iii) Other Advocates

These are Advocates whose names are entered on the roll of any State Bar Council maintained under the Advocates Act, 1961 and they can appear and argue any matter on behalf of a party in the Supreme Court, but they are not entitled to file any document or matter before the Court.

CHAPTER 14

THE STATE LEGISLATURE

INTRODUCTION TO THE STATE LEGISLATURE

The basic construct or the structure of the State Legislature follows closely the pattern of the Parliament, but, in the nature of things, there are some significant differences as well[1]. Articles 168 to 212 of the Constitution deal with the State Legislature.

The Constitution provides for a Legislature for every State in India. The Legislatures in the State are either bicameral (consisting of Legislative Assembly/Vidhan Sabha and the Legislative Council/Vidhan Parishad) or unicameral (consisting of Legislative Assembly only). Thus, the Legislature of every State consists of the Governor and Legislative Assembly (or) Governor, Legislative Assembly, and Legislative Council.

LEGISLATIVE COUNCIL

Creation and Abolition of Legislative Council

Under Article 169, Parliament may, by law provide for the creation of the Legislative Council in a State or abolish the Legislative Council in a State where it already exists. The Legislative Assembly of the State shall pass a resolution with special majority[2] either to create or abolish the Legislative Council. Based on the resolution passed by the Legislative Assembly, the Parliament may enact a law for either creation or abolition of the Legislative Council in a State with a simple majority. The law for the creation or abolition of the Legislative Council shall not be deemed to be an amendment of the Constitution and, therefore, it can be passed like an ordinary piece of Legislation. Thus, the creation and abolition of the Legislative Council is left to the Legislative Assembly of the State, which by a resolution, may recommend either for the creation or abolition of the Legislative Council.

The idea of having a second chamber in the States was criticized in the Constituent Assembly on the grounds that it was not democratic as it was not representative of the people, that it delayed legislative process, and that it was an expensive institution. The idea of a second chamber was supported, however,

---

[1] *Indian Constitutional Law*, M.P. Jain, P. 320, Eighth Edition, LexisNexis.

[2] By a majority of total membership and by a majority of not less than two-thirds of its members present and voting.

on the grounds that it would check hasty legislation by the popular chamber[3] and also enable non-elected persons to contribute to the legislative process. However, it was also felt that some of the poorer states could ill-afford the extravagance of two Houses. Therefore, the discretion is vested with the Legislative Assembly in creating and abolishing the Legislative Council.

At present, six States of India are bicameral. These are Andhra Pradesh, Telangana, Uttar Pradesh, Bihar, Maharashtra, and Karnataka. Earlier there were seven states including the State of Jammu and Kashmir. But it had been abolished through the Jammu and Kashmir Reorganization Act, 2019 that reorganized the State into two separate Union Territories of Jammu & Kashmir and Ladakh.

Legislative Councils in the States seem to be a dying institution. The Legislative Councils in Tamil Nadu, West Bengal, and Punjab have since been abolished. The Legislative Council of Andhra Pradesh which had been abolished in 1985 was created again by the Andhra Pradesh Legislature in 2005. The abolition was sought to be justified by the then Government on the grounds that the Legislative Council was redundant and its continuance was a drain on the State exchequer. It is possible that the abolition was dictated by political consideration, since the Legislative Council was dominated by the opposition party, and it posed an obstacle to the passing of controversial legislation and policies. Significantly, when the opposition party came to power, the Legislative Council was revived in the State[4].

Qualifications for Office of State Legislative Council

(a) He/She must be a citizen of India;

(b) He/She should make and subscribe before some persons authorized by the Election Commission an oath or affirmation prescribed in the Third Schedule[5];

(c) He/She must not be less than 30 years in the case of the Legislative Council;

(d) He/She must possess such other qualification as may be prescribed by Parliament by law.

(e) A person to fill an elective seat to a State Legislative Council has to be an elector for an Assembly constituency in that State.

(f) For a person to be qualified for the Governor's nomination, the said person should ordinarily be resident of that State.

Composition of the Legislative Council

The total number of members in the Legislative Council of a State having such a Council shall not exceed one-third of the total number of members in the Legislative Assembly of that State. But the total number of members in the Legislative Council of a State shall, in no case, be less than 40. The Constitution thus fixes the minimum and maximum limits regarding the strength of a Legislative Council. The actual strength of each House is however fixed by the Parliament.

---

[3]IV CAD, 670-688; VII CAD, 1303-1318; IX CAD, 31, 473–492; Austin, op. cit., 158–163.

[4]*Indian Constitutional Law*, M.P. Jain, P. 320, Eighth Edition, LexisNexis.

[5]The oath or affirmation at the time of the presentation of the nomination paper is mandatory.

Moreover, Parliament may by law, provide for the composition of the Legislative Council. Until Parliament passes such a law, the composition of the Legislative Council shall be as follows:

(a) 1/3rd are to be elected by electorates consisting of members of Municipalities, District Boards, and other local authorities in the State as Parliament by law specify;

(b) 1/3rd are to be elected by the members of the Legislative Assembly of the State from amongst persons who are not members of the Assembly.

(c) 1/12th are to be elected by electorates consisting of graduates of any University in India, of at least three years' standing, and residing within the State[6];

(d) 1/12th of its members are elected by teachers of at least three years standing in such education institutions within the State, of a standard not lower than a secondary school, as Parliament may prescribe by law;

(e) The remainder, i.e., 1/6th of its members are nominated by the Governor from amongst those who have a special knowledge or practical experience of literature, science, art, co-operative movement, and social service.

The members of a Legislative Council under heads (a), (c), and (d), mentioned above, are chosen in such territorial constituencies as Parliament may prescribe by law. These, as well as the members under head (b) are elected in accordance with the system of proportional representation by means of the single transferrable vote. The purpose of underlying the Governor's nominations under head (e) is to use the talents of such persons in the State who have achieved distinction in various fields and whose experience and advice may be of value to the State Legislature, but who have neither the time nor inclination to contest elections[7].

All attempts hitherto made to bring the Governor's nominations within judicial purview have proved futile. A writ petition under Article 226 by a member of the Assembly challenging the nomination of C. Rajagopalchari to the Madras Legislative Council in 1952 was rejected on the ground that the petitioner had no personal right "which can be said to have been infringed even in an indirect manner by nomination"[8].

In *Biman Chandra Bose Vs. Dr H.C. Mukherjee*[9], the Calcutta High Court dismissed an action brought personally against the Governor challenging nominations made by him to the Legislative Council because –

(i) Under Article 163, except in cases where the Governor is required to act in his discretion, he is to act on the advice of the Council of Ministers, and so it must be presumed that in making the nomination in question, he must have acted on the advice of the Council of Ministers;

(ii) By reason of Article 163(3), the advice tendered by the Ministers to the Governor cannot be enquired into by the Court.

---

[6]Parliament may by law prescribe any other qualifications as being equivalent to that of a graduate of a University.

[7]*Indian Constitutional Law*, M.P. Jain, P. 321, Eighth Edition, LexisNexis.

[8]Re P. Ramamoorthi, AIR 1953 Mad. 94.

[9]56, CWN 561.

(iii) By virtue of Article 361[10], the validity or invalidity of the nominations could not be inquired into by the court as this Article gives a complete protection to the Governor against a Court action.

It will thus be seen that membership of the Legislative Council is not on an elective basis by the people from territorial constituencies; it is by nomination, indirect election, or by election from teachers' and graduates constituencies. The above-mentioned scheme of composition of a Legislative Council provides for representation in the House of a wide spectrum of interests. But this scheme is tentative in nature and the Parliament may modify the same by law. The Parliament may devise a different scheme for the composition of the upper Houses in the States as may be thought necessary from time to time[11].

Tenure of Legislative Council

The Legislative Council is not subject to dissolution. It is a continuing body. Like the Rajya Sabha, it is a permanent House. As nearly as possible, 1/3rd of its members retire every two years in accordance with the law of Parliament and their places are filled up by fresh elections or nominations, as the case may be[12].

---

[10] The President or the Governor shall not be personally liable for the exercise or purported exercise of their official powers and duties. The Constitution mandates absolute immunity to the office of the President/Governor by virtue of Article 361. The President, however, can be impeached for violation of the Constitution in accordance with the procedure laid down in Article 61. Article 361 - Protection of President and Governors and Rajpramukhs -

(1) The President, or the Governor or Rajpramukh of a State, shall not be answerable to any court for the exercise and performance of the powers and duties of his office or for any act done or purporting to be done by him in the exercise and performance of those powers and duties:

Provided that the conduct of the President may be brought under review by any court, tribunal or body appointed or designated by either House of Parliament for the investigation of a charge under article 61:

Provided further that nothing in this clause shall be construed as restricting the right of any person to bring appropriate proceedings against the Government of India or the Government of a State.

(2) No criminal proceedings whatsoever shall be instituted or continued against the President, or the Governor 1[***] of a State, in any court during his term of office.

(3) No process for the arrest or imprisonment of the President, or the Governor 1[***] of a State, shall issue from any court during his term of office.

(4) No civil proceedings in which relief is claimed against the President, or the Governor 1[***] of a State, shall be instituted during his term of office in any court in respect of any act done or purporting to be done by him in his personal capacity, whether before or after he entered upon his office as President, or as Governor 1[***] of such State, until the expiration of two months next after notice in writing has been delivered to the President or the Governor 2[***], as the case may be, or left at his office stating the nature of the proceedings, the cause of action therefore, the name, description and place of residence of the party by whom such proceedings are to be instituted and the relief which he claims.

[11] M.P. Jain P. 322.

[12] Article 172.

LEGISLATIVE ASSEMBLY

Composition of the Legislative Assembly

- The Legislative Assembly in a State is the popular House.
- The minimum number of seats of the Legislative Assembly is fixed at 60 and the maximum number is fixed at 500.
- The members of Legislative Assembly are chosen directly by the people on the basis of Adult Franchise from territorial constituencies in the State. To elect these members, the State is demarcated into territorial constituencies in such a manner that the ratio between the number of members allotted to a constituency and the population therein, as far as practicable, is uniform throughout the State. Thus, Article 170 incorporates the principle of "fair and effective representation", or the broad democratic principle of "one person one vote". The constituencies ought to be, as far as possible of equal size although this principle cannot be applied with "arithmetical accuracy"[13].
- The representation in the Legislative Assembly is on the basis of the population in respect of each territorial constituency in the State. The 'population' is to be ascertained at the last preceding Census. After the completion of each Census, the number of seats in the Legislative Assembly of each State and the division of each State and the division each State into territorial constituencies is to be readjusted by such authority and in such manner as Parliament may by law determine[14]. Such readjustment is not to affect representation in the Assembly until its dissolution. This is known as delimitation. Delimitation refers to the process of demarcation of the boundaries of Parliamentary or Assembly constituencies.
  * Delimitation Commission : Under Article 170 of the Constitution, the Parliament by law enacts a Delimitation Act after every Census. After coming into force commencement of the Act, the Central Government constitutes a Delimitation Commission. This Delimitation Commission demarcates the boundaries of the Legislative Assembly Constituencies as per provisions of the Delimitation Act. The 42nd Amendment had amended Article 170 and added a new explanation, which provided that the number of seats in State Assemblies would be determined on the basis of the 1971 Census and would be frozen till the year 2000. The 84th Amendment Act, 2001 further extended the deadline from 2000 to 2026. But the said amendment provided for the readjustment and rationalization of territorial constituencies in the States, without altering the number of seats allotted to each State as per the 1991 Census. Further, the 87th Amendment Act, 2003 provided for the readjustment of territorial constituencies on the basis of the population figures of 2001 Census instead of 1991.
- In the Legislative Assembly of every State, seats will be reserved for the Scheduled Tribes and Scheduled Castes on the basis of population. Originally, all such reservations of the seats for the Scheduled Castes and the Scheduled Tribes were to cease after ten years from the commencement of the Constitution, but this provision kept extending for 10 years. Now, the 126th Amendment Act, 2019 extended this provision for another 10 years, i.e., up to 25th January, 2030.

---

[13] R.C. Poudyal Vs. UOI, AIR 1993 SC 1804, 1848.

[14] Delimitation is done on the basis of the preceding Census. The first such exercise in 1950–51 was carried out by the President, with the help of the Election Commission. Following the Delimitation Commission Act in 1952, all such exercises have been conducted by Delimitation Commissions — set up in 1952, 1963, 1973, and 2002.

- As regarding the Anglo-Indian community, the Governor has authority to nominate one member of the community to the State Legislative Assembly of a State if he is of the opinion that the community needs representation in the Assembly and is not adequately represented therein. Even this provision was supposed to cease after the ten years of the commencement of the Constitution. The 126th Amendment Act, 2019 ceases this nomination from January 25th, 2020, i.e., after 70 years of the commencement of the Constitution.

Tenure of Legislative Assembly

The normal tenure of the Legislative Assembly of every State is of five years but it may be dissolved earlier by the Governor even before the completion of five years. During the proclamation of Emergency, the life of the Assembly may be extended by an Act of Parliament for a period of one year at a time but in no case beyond a period of six months after the proclamation has ceased to operate. In other words, the elections have to be conducted within 6 months after the revocation of Emergency.

Qualifications for Membership to Legislative Assembly

The Constitution of India has prescribed certain qualifications for a person to be qualified for being chosen as a member in the State Legislature :

(a) He/She must be a citizen of India;

(b) He/She should make and subscribe before some persons authorized by the Election Commission an oath or affirmation prescribed in the Third Schedule[15];

(c) He/She must not be less than 25 years of age in the case of the Legislative Assembly;

(d) He/She must possess such other qualification as may be prescribed by Parliament by law.

The other necessary qualifications have been prescribed by the Parliament in the Representation of the People Act, 1951 –

A person to be elected to the State Legislative Assembly should be an elector for an Assembly constituency in the State. Also, he/she should be a member of a Scheduled Caste or Scheduled Tribe if he/she wants to contest a seat reserved for such castes and tribes. A person belonging to such castes or tribes is not disqualified for being elected to a seat not reserved for them.

Disqualifications for Membership to Legislative Assembly

According to the Constitution, a person is disqualified for being chosen as a member of the Legislature of a State :

(a) If He/She holds any office of profit under the Central or State Government, or;

(b) If He/She is of unsound mind, or;

(c) If He/She is an undischarged insolvent, or;

(d) If He/She is not a citizen of India or has voluntarily acquired the citizenship of a foreign State or is under any acknowledgement of allegiance or adherence to a foreign State, or;

(e) If He/She is so disqualified by or under any law of Parliament.

---

[15] The oath or affirmation at the time of the presentation of the nomination paper is mandatory.

The other necessary disqualifications have been prescribed by the Parliament in the Representation of People's Act, 1951 :

(a) Disqualification on conviction[16] for certain offences

(i) If a person is convicted for any one of the offences given below, he shall be disqualified for a period of six years if only fine is imposed (or) shall be disqualified from the date of such conviction and shall continue to be disqualified for a further period of six years since his release if he is sentenced to imprisonment. Following are the offences –

- **Under Indian Penal Code :** Offence of promoting enmity between different groups on ground of religion, race, place of birth, residence, language, etc., and doing acts prejudicial to maintenance of harmony; OR offence of bribery; OR offence of undue influence or personation at an election; OR offences relating to rape; OR offence of cruelty towards a woman by husband or relative of a husband; OR offence of making statement creating or promoting enmity, hatred, or ill-will between classes or offence relating to such statement in any place of worship or in any engaged in the performance of religious worship or religious ceremonies; (or)
- **Under the :** Protection of Civil Rights Act, 1955 - preaching and practice of 'untouchability', and for the enforcement of any disability arising therefrom; (or)
- **Under the :** Unlawful Activities (Prevention) Act, 1967 - offence of being a member of an association declared unlawful, offence relating to dealing with funds of an unlawful association, or offence relating to contravention of an order made in respect of a notified place.
- **Under the :** Prevention of Insults to National Honour Act, 1971 - offence of insulting the Indian National Flag or the Constitution of India; or offence of preventing singing of National Anthem; (OR)
- **Under :** The Commission of Sati (Prevention) Act, 1987; (OR)
- **Under :** The Prevention of Corruption Act, 1988; (OR)
- **Under :** The Representation of the People Act 1951 - offence of promoting enmity between classes in connection with the election; OR offence of removal of ballot papers from polling stations; OR offence of booth capturing; OR offence of fraudulently defacing or fraudulently destroying any nomination paper (In other words, corrupt practices at an election);

(ii) A person convicted for the contravention of the following laws and sentenced to imprisonment for not less than six months, shall be disqualified from the date of such conviction and shall continue to be disqualified for a further period of six years since his release. Following are the laws –

- any law providing for the prevention of hoarding or profiteering; or
- any law relating to the adulteration of food or drugs; or
- any provisions of the Dowry Prohibition Act, 1961;

[16] Disqualification is applicable only for punitive imprisonment not for preventive imprisonment. In other words, detention under preventive detention laws is not subject to disqualification.

(iii) A person convicted of any offence and sentenced to imprisonment for not less than two years other than any offence referred to in (i) or (ii) (referred above) shall be disqualified from the date of such conviction and shall continue to be disqualified for a further period of six years since his release.

(b) *Disqualification for dismissal for corruption or disloyalty* : A person shall be disqualified if he held an office under the Government of India or under the Government of any State has been dismissed for corruption or for disloyalty to the State shall be disqualified for a period of five years from the date of such dismissal.

(c) *Disqualification for Government contracts* : A person shall be disqualified as long as he is having a subsistence contract for supply of goods to, or execution of any works undertaken by, the government.

(d) *Disqualification for office under Government company* : A person shall be disqualified as long as, for being a managing agent, manager, or secretary of a corporation in which government has not less than 25 per cent share;

(e) *Disqualification for failure to lodge account of election expenses* : A person shall be disqualified if he fails to lodge an account of election expenses within the time given in the Representation of the People Act. In such cases, the Election Commission shall by order disqualify such person for a period of three years from the date of the order.

Decision on Disqualification[17]

Under Article 192, once a question arises whether a member has incurred a disqualification, it is only the Governor who must decide it but only after taking the opinion of the Election Commission. It is the decision of the Governor taken in accordance with the opinion of the Election Commission that is final. The decision of the Governor must depend on the opinion of the Election Commission and none else, not even the Council of Ministers. No Court has jurisdiction to interfere with this matter as it lies exclusively within the purview of the Governor and the Election Commission. It has to be noted that the Article 192 becomes applicable when a sitting member of the Legislature becomes subject to a disqualification after his election.

If, however, a disqualified person is elected as a member of the State Legislative Assembly, his election can be challenged through an election petition in the High Court. When a person is not qualified to be elected a member, there is no doubt that the High Court/election tribunal has got to declare his election to be void.

If a member becomes subject to disqualification after election, then the procedure laid down in Article 192 needs to be followed. But what happens when a person lacking in the basic and fundamental qualification, prescribed by the Constitution for membership of the State Legislative Assembly, is elected to the House and no election petition is moved against him challenging his election? The person in question knows that he is disqualified and yet he sits in the House and votes as a member. In such cases, under Article 193, he is subject to a penalty of Rs. 500 per day for knowingly sitting in the House while being disqualified.

---

[17] *Indian Constitutional Law*, M.P. Jain, P. 325, Eighth Edition, LexisNexis.

Vacancy of Seats

The seat of the member of State Legislature becomes vacant in the following cases :

(a) **Simultaneous membership :** No one can be a member of both Houses of a State Legislature simultaneously. The State Legislature is authorized to enact a law to provide for the vacation of seats, if a person is elected as a member of both Houses of State Legislature.

(b) **Resignation :** A member of the Legislative Council may resign his seat by writing to the Chairman. A member of the Legislative Assembly may resign by writing to the Speaker. Before the 33rd Constitutional Amendment Act, 1974 was enacted, when a member tendered his resignation, the Speaker/Chairman had no option, and the member's seat fell vacant automatically. The amended Article now directs the Speaker or Chairman not to accept resignations of members automatically, but to inquire about its genuineness and only then accept it. If the Speaker/Chairman finds that the resignation is not voluntary, he shall not accept it. Thus, if a member resigns under any pressure or duress, the resignation is not effective.

(c) **Absence :** A House may declare a member's seat vacant if he absents himself from all its meetings for a period of sixty days, without the permission of the House. If the House is prorogued or adjourned for more than four consecutive days, the same shall not be taken into account while computing these 60 days.

(d) **Disqualification :** A member vacates his seat in a House if he suffers from any constitutional disqualifications or statutory disqualifications (Representation of the People Act, 1951).

(e) **Elected as Heads of the State :** When a member either gets elected to the office of President or Vice President or is appointed as the Governor of any State, in such cases, his seat in the State legislature gets vacant.

(f) **Election Petition :** If the election of a member is declared invalid by the court, then the seat of such member gets vacant.

Oath of Office

Every member of the State legislature has to make and subscribe to an oath or affirmation given in the Third Schedule before the Governor or some person appointed by him for this purpose.

The oath emphasizes that the member shall bear true faith and allegiance to the Constitution of India and that he will uphold the sovereignty and integrity of India and further, that he will faithfully discharge the duty as a member of the Assembly/Council as the case may be[18].

It is compulsory for a member to take an oath. Without doing so, he cannot function as a member of the House. A member who takes part in the proceedings or voting of the House without taking the prescribed oath shall be liable to a penalty of five hundred rupees for each day he sits or votes as a member of the State legislature.

Salaries of the Members

Members of the State Legislature are entitled to receive such salaries and allowances as may from time to time be determined by the State Legislature by law.

---

[18] *Indian Constitutional Law*, M.P. Jain, P. 327, Eighth Edition, LexisNexis.

PRESIDING OFFICERS OF THE LEGISLATIVE ASSEMBLY

Speaker

The position of the Speaker of the State Legislative Assembly is similar to that of the Speaker of the Lok Sabha. The Legislative Assembly is presided over by the Speaker. He is elected by the members of the Assembly from amongst themselves at the beginning of each new State Legislature.

The office of the Speaker gets vacant when:

- He ceases to be a member of the House; or
- He resigns by addressing the resignation letter to the Deputy Speaker; or
- He is removed on a resolution passed by a majority of all the then members of the Assembly. However, such a resolution can be moved only after providing 14 days' notice to the Speaker. In addition to these two conditions laid down in the Constitution, it is open to the House concerned to impose any other condition for moving such resolution. Therefore, it is valid for a House to lay down that such a resolution can be moved only if a certain number of members favor its being moved. When the Speaker's removal resolution is under the consideration in the House, he cannot preside at such sitting of the House, although he is entitled to be present, speak, and defend himself.

The Speaker does not vacate his office on the dissolution of the Legislative Assembly. He continues in office until a new Speaker is elected when the new House meets. Once a member is elected as a Speaker, he has to be above party politics.

Powers and Functions of the Speaker

- He is an impartial and independent presiding officer.
- He presides over the meetings of the House, and regulates proceedings of the House.
- He is vested with the disciplinary powers comparable with those of the Speaker of the Lok Sabha.
- He maintains decorum in the House during debates.
- He interprets the rules of the Assembly and decides all points of order and questions of procedure.
- He can ask a member to withdraw from the House for any violation of the rules of the House. He can suspend him for the whole session if a member disregards the authority and rulings of the Chair (Speaker office).
- He can adjourn or suspend the session of the House in cases of grave disorder.
- He certifies whether a Bill is a Money Bill or not. This decision of the Speaker is considered to be final.
- He is the custodian of the dignity of the House and an impartial arbitrator in its proceedings.
- He decides the question of disqualification of a member of the Legislative Assembly on the grounds of defection given under the Tenth Schedule.
- The rules of the House require the Speaker to decide on the admissibility of motions, resolutions, questions, etc., before they come up in the House.

- The rules further empower the Speaker to constitute various committees of the House. He appoints the Chairman of the committees. The Speaker is the ex-officio Chairman of certain legislative committees such as the Business-Advisory Committee, the General Purposes Committee, and the Rules Committee.
- He determines the order of the Government and other Business in the House.

Thus, the office of the Speaker is of great honor.

The following provisions in the Constitution promote the independence and impartiality of the Speaker :

- Speaker's Salary and allowances are charged on the Consolidated Fund of the State.
- Speaker has no vote except in case of a tie; and
- He can be removed only by a resolution passed by a majority of all the then members of the Assembly.

Deputy Speaker

The position of the Deputy Speaker of the State Legislative Assembly is similar to that of the Deputy Speaker of the Lok Sabha.

The Deputy Speaker performs the duties of the office of the Speaker when it is vacant. If the office of the Deputy Speaker is also vacant at the time, the Speaker's duties are performed by a member of the House whom the Governor may appoint for the purpose till any of the offices is filled by election.

The Deputy Speaker also acts as the Speaker when he is absent from the House. When both the Speaker and the Deputy Speaker are absent from the House, such person may be determined by the rules of the procedure of the House, and in the absence of such person, such other person as may be determined by the House, acts as the Speaker. Generally, the rules of the House enable the Speaker to nominate from amongst the members a panel of Chairmen, any one of whom may preside over the Assembly in the absence of the Speaker and the Deputy Speaker.

Vacancy

The office of the Deputy Speaker falls vacant when :

- He ceases to be a member of the House; or
- He resigns by addressing the resignation letter to the Speaker; or
- He is removed on a resolution passed by a majority of all the then members of the Assembly. However, such a resolution can be moved only after providing 14 days' notice to the Deputy Speaker. When Deputy Speaker's removal resolution is under the consideration in the House, he cannot preside at such sitting of the House, although he is entitled to be present, speak, and defend himself.

Note : *The Speaker and Deputy Speaker receive such salaries and allowances as may be fixed by the Legislature by law. Till such law is passed, they will get the salaries and allowances as specified in the Second Schedule. These salaries etc., are not subject to the annual vote of the Legislature but are charged on the Consolidated Fund of the State. Further, the election of the Speaker or the Deputy Speaker does not require the approval of the Governor. They are not officers subordinate to the Governor. By virtue of Article 212, these presiding officers are immune from the jurisdiction of any court in respect of the powers exercised by them given under the Constitution and rules of the House.*

Chairman of the Legislative Council

The Legislative Council shall have a Chairman. Members of the Council elect the Chairman of the House.

The office of the Chairman gets vacant when:

- He ceases to be a member of the House; or
- He resigns by addressing the resignation letter to the Deputy Chairman; or
- He is removed on a resolution passed by a majority of all the then members of the Council. However, such a resolution can be moved only after providing 14 days' notice to the Chairman. When the Chairman's removal resolution is under the consideration in the House, he cannot preside at such sitting of the House, although he is entitled to be present, speak, and defend himself.

The Chairman of the Legislative Council enjoys similar powers as that of the Speaker. He presides over the sittings of the House. He regulates the debates and proceedings of the House. He is charged with the maintenance of order in the House and enforces the observance of rules by the members. He determines when a member should be called to speak and how long he should be allowed to speak. He can impose time limit on speeches, whenever necessary. The Chairman constitutes various committees and nominates the members and Chairmen of the committees and issues directions for the organization of work and procedure to be followed. However, the Speaker enjoys one special power which is not enjoyed by the Chairman, i.e., to determine whether a Bill is a Money Bill or not.

Salary of Chairman

The Chairman will receive such salaries and allowances as may be fixed by the Legislature by law. Till such law is passed, he will get the salaries and allowances as specified in the Second Schedule. These salaries and allowances are not subject to the annual vote of the Legislature but are charged on the Consolidated Fund of the State.

Deputy Chairman

Members of the Legislative Council elect the Deputy Chairman of the House.

The office of the Deputy Chairman gets vacant when:

- He ceases to be a member of the House; or
- He resigns by addressing the resignation letter to the Chairman; or
- He is removed on a resolution passed by a majority of all the then members of the Council. However, such a resolution can be moved only after providing 14 days' notice to the Deputy Chairman. When the Deputy Chairman's removal resolution is under the consideration in the House, he cannot preside at such sitting of the House, although he is entitled to be present, speak, and defend himself.

The Deputy Chairman performs the duties of the office of the Chairman when it is vacant. If the office of the Deputy Chairman is also vacant at the time, the Chairman's duties are performed by a member of the House whom the Governor may appoint for the purpose till any of the offices is filled by election.

The Deputy Chairman also acts as the Chairman when he is absent from the House. When both the Chairman and the Deputy Chairman are absent from the House, such person may be determined by the rules of the procedure of the House, and in the absence of such person, such other person as may be determined by the House, acts as the Chairman. Generally, the rules of the House enable the Chairman to nominate from amongst the members a panel of Vice-Chairmen, any one of whom may preside over the Assembly in the absence of the Speaker and the Deputy Speaker.

Salary of Deputy Chairman

The Deputy Chairman will receive such salaries and allowances as may be fixed by the Legislature by law. Till such law is passed, he will get the salaries and allowances as specified in the Second Schedule. These salaries and allowances are not subject to the annual vote of the Legislature but are charged on the Consolidated Fund of the State.

RULES OF PROCEDURE

Article 208 provides that the House of the Legislature of a State may make rules for regulating its procedure and the conduct of its business, subject to the provisions of the Constitution. However, until such rules are made, the rules of procedure and standing orders in force immediately before the commencement of the Constitution with respect to the corresponding Province shall have effect in relation to the Legislature of the State, subject to such modifications and adaptation as may be made therein by the Speaker or the Chairman as the case may be.

Moreover, when the State Legislatures do not have a rule on a particular matter, they follow the Lok Sabha rules on that matter. This is a general practise that has been developed.

Further, Article 208 provides that, in a State having a Legislative Council the Governor, after consultation with the Speaker of the Legislative Assembly and the Chairman of the Legislative Council, may make rules as to the procedure with respect to communications between the two Houses.

Sessions and Sittings of the Assembly

The sessions, sittings, and the procedures of the State Legislature are similar to that of the Parliament. Due to the paucity of time and space, only the unique aspects are elucidated under this section.

Summoning and Prorogation

The Governor is empowered under the Constitution to summon the State Legislature from time to time to meet at such time and place as he thinks fit. But, six months should not intervene between its last sitting in one session and the date appointed for its first sitting in the next session. In other words, the State Legislature should at least meet twice a year and the interval between two sessions cannot be more than six months. A session of the legislature consists of multiple sittings.

The Governor is also empowered to prorogue the Assembly. The period from the date of its first sitting in a session to the date of prorogation of the House is called a 'session' of the Assembly.

The Governor addresses the Legislative Assembly or both Houses (if there is bicameral Legislature) at the commencement of the first session after each general election and at the commencement of the first session of the year. This address reflects the policy statement of the government which is to be discussed in the Legislature.

Dissolution of the State Legislature

Legislative Council is a continuing chamber. It is not subject to dissolution. Legislative Assembly on the other hand, is not a continuing chamber. Its normal life is five years from the date of its first meeting after the general elections, and the expiry of this period triggers the dissolution of the House. Dissolution puts an end to the life of the House. The Legislative Assembly can be dissolved by the Governor even before the expiration of 5-year term. However, the Constitution is silent as to when, and in what circumstances, the Governor may dissolve the House. The Governor may not dissolve the House *suo motu,* without ministerial advice to that effect. The five-judge Constitution Bench judgment of the Supreme Court in *Nabam Rebia Vs. Deputy Speaker*[19], held that the Governor's power *"under Article 174 to summon, prorogue, and dissolve the house(s) must be exercised in consonance with the aid and advice of the Chief Minister and his council of ministers". It is a well-recognised principle that, so long as the Council of Ministers enjoys the confidence of the Assembly, its advice in these matters, unless patently unconstitutional must be deemed as binding on the Governor. However, if the advice is rendered by a Chief Minister who doesn't have majority, then the Governor can try to see if an alternate government can be formed and only if that isn't possible, should the House be dissolved.*

Even the Sarkaria Commission in this regard recommended that: *that as long as the Council of Ministers enjoys the confidence of the House, the aid and advice of the Council of Ministers headed by the Chief Minister is binding on the Governor, on the subject of summoning, proroguing or dissolving the House or Houses of the State Legislature. The above position would stand altered, if the Government in power has lost the confidence of the House. As and when the Chief Minister does not enjoy the support from the majority of the House, it is open to the Governor to act on his own, without any aid and advice. Aid and advice sustains and subsists, till the Government enjoys the confidence of the Legislature.*

Life of the Bill

When the Legislative Assembly dissolves, it will have an impact on the life of the Bill. A Bill pending in the Legislature does not lapse because of prorogation of the House.

When the Assembly is dissolved :

- A Bill pending in the Legislative Council, which has not been introduced in the Legislative Assembly, does not lapse.
- A Bill which originated in the Legislative Assembly and is pending in the Legislative Assembly will lapse.
- A Bill which has been passed by the Legislative Assembly and which is pending in the Legislative Council will lapse.
- A Bill passed by the Legislative Council and pending in the Legislative Assembly will lapse.
- A Bill passed by the Legislative Assembly, when there is only one House, or passed by both Houses in a bicameral Legislature, and pending the assent of the Governor or of the President does not lapse.

Language to be Used in the Legislation

According to Article 210 of the Constitution, all the proceedings in the State Legislature like the law-making process should be in the official language of the State or in Hindi or in English. However,

[19] 2016 (1) SCALE 645

the presiding officers can allow the member to use other languages (who cannot express himself/herself either in the official language of the State or in Hindi or in English). Further, it also provided that if the State Legislature does not make any law for using the English language even after fifteen years, then the word English from Article 210 will get eliminated by itself. For certain States like Himachal Pradesh, Manipur, Meghalaya, and Tripura, it is 25 years instead of 15 years. And for States like Arunachal Pradesh, Goa, and Mizoram, it is 40 years instead of 15 years.

LAW-MAKING PROCESS IN THE STATE LEGISLATURE: PASSING ORDINARY BILLS AND MONEY BILLS

The State Legislature performs similar functions for the State as does the Parliament for the whole of India. It makes laws, levies taxes, sanctions funds for the public expenditure, and criticizes and controls the State Executive.

Ordinary Bills

The procedure of legislation in a State Legislature is broadly similar to that in the Parliament under Article 107. All Bills, except a Money Bill or a Financial Bill, may originate in either House of the State Legislature.

In bicameral Legislature, if a Bill has been passed by the Legislative Assembly and transmitted to the Legislative Council, the following three situations can occur:

(a) The Legislative Council rejects the Bill; or,

(b) It does not pass it within three months from the date the Bill is laid before it; or,

(c) The Legislative Council passes it with certain amendments which the Assembly does not accept.

In such cases, the Assembly may pass the Bill again, and transmit the same to the Legislative Council. If the Council

(a) rejects the Bill again, or

(b) does not pass it within one month from the date on which it is laid before it; or,

(c) it passes the Bill with amendments not acceptable to the Assembly, then the Bill is deemed to have been passed by both Houses in the form in which it was passed by the Assembly for the second time.

The starting point for calculating the time of three months or one month as laid down in the Constitution is the date on which the Bill is laid before the Legislative Council. The Legislative Council thus acts as a revising chamber and can hold up legislation for a short time but ultimately, the will of the Legislative Assembly prevails. The procedure to resolve difference between the two Houses in a State differs from the mechanism of Joint Session provided in case of Parliament. There is no concept of Joint Session in the State Legislature. The State Legislative Council has thus been given much less importance than the Rajya Sabha.

Role of the Governor in Passing Ordinary Bills

A Bill passed by the Assembly, or by both Houses in case of bicameral Legislature, is presented to the Governor who has several alternatives:

I. He may give his assent to the Bill; or

II. He may withhold his assent therefrom; or

III. He may return it to the Legislature for reconsideration, or

IV. He may reserve it for the consideration of the President.

If the Governor sends back the Bill for reconsideration, it is the duty of the Legislature to reconsider the Bill accordingly. After reconsideration, if it passed again by the legislature, with or without amendments, and presented to the Governor again for his assent, the Governor shall not withhold assent therefrom. In other words, the Governor has to give his assent in such cases. This is similar to the provision dealing with Presidential assent to the Bills passed by the Parliament. The Constitution does not impose any time limit within which the Governor has to give his assent.

In cases of I, II, and III, the Governor acts on the advice of the Chief Minister and the Council of Ministers. Only in case of IV, he acts in his discretion.

When the Governor reserves a Bill for Presidential consideration, the enactment of the Bill then depends on the assent or refusal of assent by the President. In case of a reserved Bill, the President may

- either assent to, or
- withhold his assent from the Bill, or
- may return it back with message to the Legislature for reconsideration and may even suggest amendments to be made therein. The Bill is then reconsidered within a period of six months from the date of receipt of the message, and if it is again passed by the Legislature, with or without amendments, it is presented again to the President for his consideration. Nothing is said in the Constitution as to what the President may do thereafter. It does not appear that there is any obligation on the President to give his assent to the Bill sent to him after reconsideration. Moreover, once the Bill is reserved for the Presidential Assent, the said Bill will be out of the Governor's purview.

Money Bills

The definition of Money Bill in the State Legislature is similar to the Union Legislation under Article 110. Like the Union Legislature, a Money Bill must originate in the Lower House of the State Legislature (Legislative Assembly). A Money Bill cannot originate in the Legislative Council. After a Money Bill has been passed by the Legislative Assembly, it shall be transmitted to the Legislative Council for its recommendations. The Legislative Council must return the Bill to the Legislative Assembly with its recommendations within a period of 14 days from the date of its receipt of the Bill. The Legislative Assembly may either accept or reject all or any of the recommendations of the Legislative Council. If the Legislative Assembly accepts any of the recommendations of the Legislative Council, the Money Bill shall be deemed to have been passed by both Houses, with the amendments recommended by the Legislative Council and accepted by the Legislative Assembly. If the Legislative Assembly rejects all the recommendations of the Council, the Money Bill shall be deemed to have been passed by both Houses in the form in which it was passed by the Legislative Assembly. But if a Bill is not returned by the Legislative Council within 14 days, it shall be deemed to have been passed by both Houses at the expiration of such period in the form in which it was originally passed by the Legislative Assembly. If any question arises whether a Bill is a Money Bill or not, the decision of the Speaker of the Legislative Assembly shall be final. The Speaker shall certify that a Bill is Money Bill before transmitting it to the Legislative Council. The Supreme Court in *State of Punjab Vs. Sat Pal Dang*[20], held that in the absence of the Speaker, the Deputy Speaker can grant the certificate.

Role of the Governor in Passing Money Bills

Like an ordinary Bill, a Money Bill also needs the Governor's assent to become a law. The position in this connection is the same as in the case of an ordinary Bill, except that the Governor cannot refer back a Money Bill for reconsideration by the Legislature. He either assents, or refuses to assent, or reserves it for Presidential assent. Similarly, the President cannot refer it back for reconsideration by the Legislature. He either gives or refuses to give his assent to the Money Bill[21].

FUNDS OF THE STATE LEGISLATURE

Consolidated Fund of the State

Just as the Centre, every State shall have a Consolidated Fund (Article 266). Money can be with drawn from this Fund only under appropriations made by law, passed by the State Legislature. The Consolidated Fund is formed of all revenues received and all loans raised by the State Government; all money received by the State Government in repayment of loans, and any fees or other money taken by the High Court.

Expenditure Charged on the Consolidated Fund of the State[22]

The following items of expenditure are charged on the Consolidated Fund :

(a) The emoluments and allowances of the Governor and other expenditure relating to his office;

(b) The salaries and allowances of the Speaker and Deputy Speaker of the Assembly, and those of the Chairman and the Deputy Chairman of the Council;

(c) Debt charges for which the State Government is responsible;

(d) Salaries and allowances of the High Court Judges;

(e) Sums needed to satisfy any judgement, decree, or award of any Court or arbitral tribunal;

(f) The administrative expenses of the High Court, including all salaries, allowances, and pensions payable to its officers and servants;

(g) Expenses of the State Public Service Commission, including salaries, allowances, and pensions payable to its members or staff.

(h) Any other expenditure declared by the Constitution or the State Legislature by law to be so charged.

---

[20] AIR 1969 SC 903.

[21] *Indian Constitutional Law*, M.P. Jain, P. 341, Eighth Edition, LexisNexis.

[22] Ibid.

Public Account

All moneys, other than those placed in the Consolidated Fund of the State, received by the State Government, or an officer employed in connection with the affairs of the State, or by any court, is credited to the Public Account of the State.

Contingency Fund

The State Legislature can also create a Contingency Fund by passing a law.

LEGISLATIVE PRIVILEGES OF THE STATE LEGISLATURE

Article 194 (Privileges at the State Legislature level) which applies to the State Legislature and members and committees thereof is an exact reproduction of Article 105, which applies to both Houses of the Parliament and members and committees thereof. Privileges are available not only to the members of the Legislature, but to all those who have a right to speak, or otherwise to participate, in the proceedings of a House or any committee thereof, such as Ministers and the Advocate General of the State. However, these privileges are not enjoyed by the Governor.

Territorial Limitation with Respect to Enforcement of Privileges

A point of interest which arises in case of a State Legislature is the territorial limitation. Suppose a newspaper in Mumbai commits contempt of the U.P. Assembly by pubiishing some material derogatory to it. Can the Assembly issue a warrant to enforce the presence of the Editor before it to answer the charge of contempt, Mumbai being outside the territorial jurisdiction of the U.P. Assembly?

It has been held in *Homi Mistry Vs. Nafisul Hasan*[23], that the Assembly could do so as no territorial limitation has been placed on the power conferred by Article 194.

COMPARISON OF POWERS BETWEEN LEGISLATIVE ASSEMBLY AND LEGISLATIVE COUNCIL

i. *Creation and abolition of the Legislative Council :* The very existence of the Legislative Council depends on the Legislative Assembly. The power to create and abolish the Legislative Council lies in the hands of the Legislative Assembly.

ii. *Ordinary Bill :* An ordinary Bill can originate in either House of the State Legislature and it becomes law only when both Houses pass it in the same form. In case of an inter-House deadlock, the Legislative Assembly ultimately prevails. The Legislative Council cannot do more than holding up the passage of a Bill for some time.

iii. *Money Bill* : Like the Rajya Sabha, the State Legislative Council plays only a subsidiary role in financial matters, the power of the purse having been concentrated in the Legislative Assembly.

iv. *Annual Financial Statement* : Budget will be laid before both the Houses of the Legislature but only the Assembly has the power to vote on the demands for grants.

---

[23]ILR 1957 Bom 218.

v. *Constitutional Amendment Bill* : The Legislative Assembly has an upper hand even with respect to the ratification of the Constitutional Amendment Bill.

vi. *Control of the Executive* : In the area of control of the Executive, the dominant power lies in the Assembly to which the Council of Ministers is constitutionally responsible. Therefore, the Motion of 'No confidence' can be introduced only in the Legislative Assembly.

vii. *Membership of Ministries* : The Council of Ministers including the Chief Minister can be members of either House of the State Legislature.

viii. *Election of President* : Only the elected members of the State Legislative Assembly will take part in the elections of the President. The Legislative Council members cannot take part in the Presidential election.

ix. *Reports* : The reports of constitutional bodies and commissions such as State Public Service Commission, State Election Commission, State Finance Commission, Comptroller and Auditor General of India, etc., which are submitted to the Governor, shall be laid such before both Houses of the State Legislature.

x. *Ordinances* : Both Houses have co-ordinate powers as regards a Governor's ordinance. The Governor's ordinance has to be laid before both Houses of the State Legislature. An ordinance ceases to operate if a resolution it is passed by the Assembly and is agreed by the Legislative Council.

QUESTIONS

Subjective Questions

1. "The Governor is bound by the Council of ministers advice to convene the Legislative Assembly. There is no wriggle room available to the Governor in our federal structure". Discuss.

(250 words)

2. "A State Legislative Assembly can be dissolved only under justifying circumstances". Explain the justifying circumstances. **(150 words)**

Objective Questions

1. With reference to the Delimitation Commission, consider the following statements:

(UPSC 2012)

1. The orders of the Delimitation Commission cannot be challenged in a Court of Law.
2. When the orders of the Delimitation Commission are laid before the Lok Sabha or State Legislative Assembly, they cannot affect any modifications in the orders.

Which of the statements given above is/are correct?

(a) 1 only (b) 2 only

(c) Both 1 and 2 (d) Neither 1 nor 2

Ans: (c)

2. With reference to the Legislative Assembly of a State in India, consider the following statements: **(UPSC 2019)**

   1. The Governor makes a customary address to the members of the House at the commencement of the first session of the year.
   2. When a State Legislature does not have a rule on the particular matter, it follows the Lok Sabha rule on that matter.

   (a) 1 only (b) 2 only

   (c) Both 1 and 2 (d) Neither 1 nor 2

   Ans: (c)

3. When a Bill is reserved by a Governor for consideration of the President, the President shall:

   1. Declare his assent or withhold his assent or return the Bill for reconsideration thereto, within 6 months.
   2. The State Legislature shall reconsider the Bill returned by the President within 6 months of its receipt and, if it is again passed, it shall be presented again to the President for his consideration.
   3. In contrast with the power of the Governor regarding a reconsidered Bill, it is not obligatory for the President to give his assent to a reconsidered Bill.

   Which of the above statements are true?

   (a) 1 and 2 (b) 2 and 3

   (c) 1 and 3 (d) 3 Only

   Ans: (b)

CHAPTER 15

STATE EXECUTIVE

INTRODUCTION

Articles 153 to 167 and 213 of Part VI of the Constitution deal with the structure of the government in the States. The pattern of the State Executive is very similar to that of the Central Executive which is based on the fundamental principle of accountability of the Executive to the Legislature. Like the Centre, the States also have Parliamentary form of government.

The constitutional provisions dealing with the State Executive are more or less word to word similar to the constitutional provisions dealing with the Central Executive, except for some differences arising out of the fact that while the Constitution confers some discretion on the State Governor; it confers none on the President[1].

The State Executive consists of the Governor, who is the Head of the State, the Council of Ministers with the Chief Minister at its Head, and the Advocate General of the State.

GOVERNOR

Appointment of Governor

Each State has a Governor. But two or more states can have a common Governor[2] (Article 153). The Governor of a State is appointed by the President of India by warrant under his hand and seal.[3] He is neither elected by the direct vote of the people, nor by an indirect vote by a specially constituted Electoral College as in the case of President.

The Constituent Assembly fully debated the merits and demerits of an elected Vs. nominated Governor and finally opted for the system of Presidential nomination, rather than direct election of the Governor because of the following reasons[4] –

(a) Constituent Assembly felt that a nominated Governor would encourage centripetal or binding tendencies and thus, promote all-India unity. It was apprehended that an elected Governor would to some extent encourage the separatist provincial tendencies.

---

[1]M. P. Jain, *Indian Constitutional Law*, P. 354, Eighth Edition, 2018, Lexis Nexis.

[2]The provision to have common Governor for two or more states was added by 7th Constitutional Amendment Act, 1956.

[3]Article 155

[4]M. P. Jain, *Indian Constitutional Law*, P. 355, Eighth Edition, 2018, Lexis Nexis.

(b) In a Parliamentary system the Head should be impartial, but a Governor elected by the direct vote of the people would have to be a partyman. On this point, it was stated in the Constituent Assembly:

He should be a more detached figure acceptable to the province; otherwise he could not function, and yet may not be a part of the party machine of the province. On the whole, it would probably be desirable to have people from outside, eminent in something, education or other fields of life who would naturally cooperate fully with Government in carrying out the policy of the Government and yet represent before the public something above politics.

(c) Conflicts might arise between the Governor and the Chief Minister if both were to be elected by the people but vest the whole of executive power only in the Council of Ministers headed by the Chief Minister.

(d) The Governor being only a symbol, a figurehead, there would be no point in spending money in having him elected.

Therefore, the Constitution gives *carte blanche* or complete freedom to the Centre in the matter of appointment of a State Governor. The power of the Centre to appoint the State Governors is similar to that of the Canadian model where the Lieutenant Governors of Provinces are appointed by the Governor General of Canada. On the other hand, in the United States of America, the Governors are elected by the people.

Nature of Governor's office

The office of Governor is an independent constitutional office. The Governor is the Head of the State. In *Hargovind Pant Vs. Dr. Raghukul Tilak*,[5] the Supreme Court held that the office of Governor of a State is not an employment under the Government. The office of the Governor is an independent office and is not under the control of or subordinate to the Government of India.

But the Governor has a dual capacity—he is the Head of the State as well as the representative of the Centre in the State. The Governor works as a channel of communication and contact between the State and the Centre. Therefore, a convention of consulting the State Chief Minister while appointing the Governor is developed with a view to ensure the smooth functioning of the constitutional machinery in the state.

So long as there was one party rule at the Centre as well as in the States, the consultation was merely a formality and no difficulty ever arose in the matter of appointment of the Governor. During this period, the institution of the Governor remained largely dormant. But after the Fourth General Election held in 1967, the political scene underwent a sea change as different political parties came in power in the States and the Centre. The appointment of Governors became a somewhat controversial matter, particularly in those States where the political party in power in the State is different from that at the Centre. Therefore, for a smooth functioning of the Indian federal structure, it is desirable that the person to be appointed as the Governor should be such as to inspire confidence from both the Centre and the State concerned because the office of the Governor is a balancing wheel of the Centre–State relationship[6].

---

[5] AIR 1979 SC 1109.

[6] M. P. Jain, *Indian Constitutional Law*, P. 356, Eighth Edition, 2018, Lexis Nexis

Qualifications, Salary, and Oath of Governor

Eligibility for Appointment as Governor

According to Article 157, a person to be eligible to be appointed as Governor must be:

(a) A citizen of India, and

(b) Must have completed the age of 35 years.

Moreover, the Governor must not be a member of either House of Parliament or of a House of the Legislature of any State. If a member of either House of Parliament or of a House of the Legislature of any such State is appointed as Governor, he shall be deemed to have vacated his seat in the House on the date on which he enters upon his office as Governor. He shall not hold any other office of profit.

Salary and Other Emoluments and Allowances

The Governor is entitled without payment of rent to the use of his/her official residence and such emoluments, allowances, and privileges as may be determined by the Parliament by law. The emoluments and allowances of a Governor cannot be reduced during his term of office. The emoluments and allowances shall be paid by the State. Where one person is appointed Governor of more than one State, his emoluments are allocated amongst the States in such proportion as the President may determine.

Oath of Office

The Governor, before entering upon his office, is required to take an oath[7] or affirmation in the presence of the Chief Justice of the High Court; or if he is not present, in the presence of the senior-most Judge of the High Court.

Tenure and Removal

According to Article 156[8] of the Constitution, the Governor shall hold office during the pleasure of the President. Subject to this rule, a Governor holds office for five years from the date on which he enters upon his office. The five year term provided for the Governors under sub-clause (3) of Article 156 is subject to the exercise of pleasure by the President. If a Governor continues to enjoy the 'pleasure of the President', he or she can be in office for a term of five years; otherwise the Governor can be removed. Therefore, the President can remove the Governor from office at any time without assigning any reason.

However, in *B. P. Singhal Vs. Union of India*[9], the Supreme Court interpreted the powers of the President under Article 156. In this case, the newly elected central government had removed the Governors of

---

[7]"I, A.B., do swear in the name of God/ solemnly affirm that I will faithfully execute the office of Governor (or discharge the functions of the Governor) of ..... (name of the State) and will to the best of my ability preserve, protect and defend the Constitution and the law and that I will devote myself to the service and well-being of the people of .... (name of the State)."

[8]Article 156 – Term of office of Governor

(1) The Governor shall hold office during the pleasure of the President.

(2) The Governor may, by writing under his hand addressed to the President, resign his office.

(3) Subject to the foregoing provisions of this article, a Governor shall hold office for a term of five years from the date on which he enters upon his office:

Provided that a Governor shall, notwithstanding the expiration of his term, continue to hold office until his successor enters upon his office.

[9]TP (Civil) No.663 of 2004

Uttar Pradesh, Gujarat, Haryana, and Goa in July, 2004 after the 14th Lok Sabha Election. When these removals were challenged, the Supreme Court held[10]:

(a) The President, in effect the central government, has the power to remove a Governor at any time without giving him or her any reason, and without granting an opportunity to be heard.

(b) However, this power cannot be exercised in an arbitrary, capricious, or unreasonable manner. The power of removing Governors should only be exercised in rare and exceptional circumstances for valid and compelling reasons.

(c) Further, a Governor cannot be removed on the ground that he is out of sync with the decisions, views, and ideologies of the Union Government or the party in power at the Centre. Nor can he be removed on the ground that the Union Government has lost confidence in him. It thus follows that any modification in government at the Centre should not be taken as a ground for removal of Governors to make way for those who are favoured by the new government.

(d) Lastly, a decision to remove a Governor can be challenged in a court of law. In such cases, first the petitioner will have to make a prima facie case of arbitrariness or bad faith on part of the central government. If a prima facie case is established, the court can require the central government to produce the materials on the basis of which the decision was made in order to verify the presence of compelling reasons.

Thus, the central government enjoys the power to remove Governors of the different states, as long as it does not act arbitrarily, without reason, or in bad faith.

Moreover, according to Article 156, the Governor continues to hold the office even after the lapse of his term till his successor enters upon his office. The President can even transfer a Governor from one State to another State. The Governor may resign at any time by writing to the President. In a contingency where the Constitution makes no provision, such as death of the Governor, the President may make such provision as he thinks fit for discharge of the functions of the Governor of a State. Thus, the Chief Justice of the High Court can be appointed temporarily to discharge the functions of the Governor of the State[11].

Functions and Powers of the Governor

The powers of the Governor of a State are analogous to those of the President, excepting that the Governor has no diplomatic, military, or emergency powers. Moreover, the Governor enjoys the same privileges as the President does under Article 361 and he stands, in this respect, on the same footing as the President. The powers of the Governor can be classified under the following heads:

Executive Powers

The executive power of the State is vested in the Governor and is to be exercised by him directly or through officers subordinate to him[12]. Defining 'executive power', the Supreme Court has stated that "although it cannot be possible to frame an exhaustive definition of what executive functions are, ordinarily they connote the residue of governmental functions that remain after legislative and judicial functions are taken away". The executive functions comprise both the determination of policy as well

---

[10] https://www.prsindia.org/

[11] *Arun Kumar Vs. UOI*, AIR 1982 Raj 67.

[12] Article 154.

as carrying it into execution. This evidently includes the initiation of legislation, the maintenance of order, the protection of social and economic welfare, and the carrying on or supervision of the general administration of the State. However, based on the provisions of the Constitution and the principles of Parliamentary form of the government, the executive powers of the Governor can be enumerated as follows:

(i) The Governor is the Chief Executive in a State. All the executive powers of the State Government are vested upon him and decisions are taken in his name.

(ii) The Governor appoints the Chief Minister and his Council of Ministers. He may dismiss the members of the Council of Ministers on the advice of the Chief Minister. The Governor distributes the portfolios among the members of the Council of Ministers on the recommendations of the Chief Minister. In the States of Chhattisgarh, Jharkhand, Madhya Pradesh, and Odisha, a Minister for Tribal Welfare shall be appointed by the Governors along with other Ministers[13].

(iii) The Governor is authorized to make

(iv) The Governor is the appointing authority in respect of the following authorities:

- Advocate General
- The Lokayukta and Upa Lokayukta
- The State Election Commissioner
- The Chairman and Members of the Human Rights Commission
- The Chairman and Members of Public Service Commission
- The State Chief Information Commissioner and members of Information Commission.

(v) The Governor may call for information from the Chief Minister regarding the activities of state administration and proposals for legislation. If the Governor requires, he may ask the Chief Minister to submit for the consideration of the Council of Ministers any matter on which decision has been taken by a Minister but which has not been considered by the Council.

(vi) The Governor has the powers to recommend President's Rule (Constitutional Emergency) in the state in the event of a breakdown of law and order in the state.

(vii) The Governor acts as the Chancellor of State Universities and appoints Vice-Chancellors of the State Universities[14].

Legislative Powers

Governor and the State Executive participate intimately in the legislative powers. Following are the legislative functions performed by the Governor –

(i) The Governor is an integral part of the State Legislature, even though he is not a member of either house of the State Legislature.

(ii) The Governor can summon a House and may prorogue the House or Houses on the recommendations of the Council of Ministers.

---

[13]Prior to 2006, Governor of Bihar also had to appoint a Tribal Welfare Minister. Later it was removed by 94th Constitutional Amendment Act, 2006.

[14]Governors are not the ex-officio chancellors of the Central Universities in the State.

(iii) The Governor can dissolve the State Legislative Assembly. However, the Constitution is silent as to when, and in what circumstances, the Governor may dissolve the Legislative Assembly. This matter is, therefore, regulated by conventions which evolved in course of time. The following two propositions appear to be well settled in this regard:

- The Governor may not dissolve the House *suo moto,* without ministerial advice to that effect.
- The Governor does not automatically accept the advice of his Council of Ministers to dissolve the House. The matter falls within the area of discretion of the Governor.

(iv) At the commencement of the first session of the Legislative Assembly after each general election, and each year thereafter, the Governor is required to address the Legislative Assembly, or both Houses in a State having two Houses. The Governor is also authorized to address any House, any time of the year. Apart from the right to address the Houses, the Governor also enjoys the right to send messages to any House.

(v) If the office of the Speaker and the Deputy Speaker falls vacant, then the Governor shall appoint a member of the House to discharge the functions of the Speaker till any of the office (Speaker/ Deputy Speaker) is filled by election. Similarly, if the office of the Chairman and the Deputy Chairman of the Legislative Council falls vacant, then the Governor shall appoint a member of the House to discharge the functions of the Chairman.

(vi) A member of any of the Houses of the State Legislature has to make and subscribe, before the Governor or some person appointed by him for this purpose, an oath or affirmation in the prescribed form.

(vii) The Governor of a State has authority to nominate one Anglo-Indian to the Legislative Assembly, if he is of the opinion that they are not adequately represented in the Legislative Assembly.

(viii) The Governor nominates one-sixth of the members of the State Legislative Council from amongst persons having special knowledge or practical experience in literature, science, art, cooperative movement, and social service.

(ix) Rule Making Power/Delegated Legislative Power[15] – The Governor is conferred with several rule making powers by the Constitution. He can makes rules regarding –

- Ways and means by which orders and instruments, made and executed in his name, shall be authenticated;
- Ways for the more convenient transaction of the business of the Government of the State and for its allocation among Ministers.
- Conditions of service of the members of the State Public Service Commission as well as Civil Servants (State);
- Convenient transaction of Government Business;
- Procedure in respect of communication between the Houses of State Legislatures,
- Recruitment of officers, etc., for a High Court;
- Recruitment of secretarial staff of the Legislature.

---

[15]Delegated legislation (sometimes referred as secondary legislation or subordinate legislation or subsidiary legislation) is a process by which the executive authority is given powers to make laws. Such law is the law made by a person or body other than the legislature but with the legislature's authority.

(x) A Bill passed by the Assembly, or by both Houses in case of a bi-cameral Legislature can turn into an Act only when the Governor gives assent to it. Therefore, the Bill passed by the Legislature will be presented to the Governor who has the following alternatives:

(a) He may give assent to the Bill; or

(b) He may withhold his assent; or

(c) He may return it to the Legislature for reconsideration. If the State Legislature after reconsideration sends back the Bill to the Governor with or without amendments, the Governor has to give assent to the Bill; or

(d) He may reserve it for the consideration of the President.

In cases A, B, and C, the Governor acts on the advice of his Cabinet. Only in case of D, he acts in his discretion.

(xi) In case the Governor reserves a Bill for Presidential consideration, the President has the following alternatives:

(a) He may give assent to the Bill; or

(b) He may withhold his assent; or

(c) He may return it back to the Legislature for reconsideration. The State Legislature shall within six months of the receipt of the Bill shall reconsider it and send it back for the Presidential assent. However, there is no obligation on the President to give assent to the Bill sent to him after reconsideration.

(xii) Ordinance making power – The Governor has ordinance-making power similar to that enjoyed by the President. According to Article 213, the Governor may promulgate ordinances when –

- The State Legislative Assembly is not in session; or if the State has two Houses, when one of the Houses is not in session; and
- The Governor is satisfied that circumstances exist which render it necessary for him to take immediate action.

Moreover, the Governor cannot promulgate any ordinance without the instructions from the President, if –

- A Bill which would have required the previous sanction of the President for its introduction in the State Legislature; or,
- The Governor would have deemed it necessary to reserve a Bill to that effect for the President's consideration; or,
- An Act of the State Legislature would have been invalid without receiving the President's assent[16].

Every ordinance must be laid before both Houses of the State Legislature when they assemble, and shall cease to operate at the expiration of six weeks from the reassembly of the Legislature. An ordinance ceases to operate earlier than six weeks, if a resolution disapproving it is passed by the Assembly, and

[16]When a State makes a law containing a provision inconsistent with a Central Law with respect to a matter in the Concurrent List, the State Law has to receive the assent of the President to be valid. Thus, the assent of the President is secured subsequent to the passage of the Bill. However, if an ordinance is being made in the similar circumstances, then the instructions from the President are a condition precedent to the promulgation of the ordinance.

is agreed to by the Council. The Governor may withdraw the ordinance at any time before the expiry of six weeks. An ordinance has the same force and effect as an Act passed by the State Legislature. The ordinance-making power is co-extensive with the legislative power of the State. The power to make ordinances though formally vested in the Governor is, in effect, exercised by the Council of Ministers on whose advice the Governor acts, except when the matter is one in which the Governor has to seek instructions from the President.

Re-promulgation of an ordinance – To re-promulgate simply means to effectively extend the life of an ordinance. An ordinance 'ceases to operate' 6 weeks after the two Houses reassemble, except if it is converted into an Act by then[17]. Re-promulgation sidesteps this limitation. Neither Article 123 nor Article 213 places a cap on ordinances. The President or Governor may promulgate as many ordinances as they desire if the two conditions of — at least one House of the Legislature not being in session and the necessity of an immediate action — are met. The Supreme Court in the case of *Krishna Kumar Singh Vs. State of Bihar*[18] cleared the air regarding the legality of the re-promulgation of the ordinance. In this case, a 1989 ordinance by which the State government took over 429 Sanskrit schools in Bihar was promulgated several times until 1992, but not once tabled in the State Assembly. Therefore, the court ruled that re-promulgation of ordinance is a fraud on the Constitution and concluded that the failure to place an ordinance before the Legislature constitutes abuse of power and a fraud on the Constitution. Laying requirement is mandatory. Its non-observance makes the ordinance unconstitutional and inoperative on the expiry of six weeks of time. Actions taken and concluded under an ordinance are ineffective and invalid if the ordinance is not placed before the Legislature and is allowed to lapse. The Court further held that the satisfaction of the President of India under Article 123 and of the Governor under Article 213 while issuing an ordinance is not immune from judicial review.

Thus, an ordinance has a temporary life and it is not a permanent law like an Act. The very fact that an ordinance lapses automatically after a while, and has to be replaced by an Act of the Legislature shows that the Constitution does not confer the same status on an ordinance as that of an Act.

Judicial Powers

The Constitution confers certain powers on the State Government which may be characterized as 'judicial' in nature:

(i) The appointments of district judges, their posting, and promotion, in any State shall be made by the Governor of the State in consultation with the High Court exercising jurisdiction in relation to such States.

(ii) Appointments of persons other than district judges to the judicial service of a State shall also be made by the Governor in accordance with rules made by him in this behalf after consultation with the State Public Service Commission and with the High Court.

(iii) According to Article 217 of the Constitution, the appointment of High Courts Judges shall be made only after consulting the Chief Justice of India and the Governor of the State.

(iv) Any question regarding the disqualification of a member of a House of the State Legislature shall be decided by the Governor by obtaining the opinion of the Election Commission. Such opinion of Election Commission is binding on the Governor. The decision of the Governor (quasi-judicial power of Governor) regarding the disqualification of members is considered to be final.

[17] So, the maximum life of an ordinance is 6 months 6 weeks. As per the Constitutional provisions, the gap between two sessions of the legislature should not exceed more than 6 months.

[18] 2017 (2) SCJ 136

(v) According to Article 161, the Governor shall have the powers to grant pardons, reprieves, respites, or remissions of punishment or to suspend, remit, or commute the sentence of any person convicted of any offence against law relating to matters which the executive power of the State extends. The executive power of the State extends to matters with respect to which the Legislature of the State has power to make law.

This power of the Governor is very much similar to the power of the President under Article 72. But there are differences between the pardoning power of the President and the pardoning power of the Governor of a State. The President's pardoning power is wider than that of the Governor of States: Firstly, the President has the exclusive power to grant pardon in cases where the sentence is a death sentence while Governor cannot grant pardon in case of a death sentence. Secondly, the President can pardon punishments of sentences inflicted by Court Martial. The Governor has no such power. In respect of suspension, remission, and commutation of sentence of death, both have concurrent powers[19].

The Governor cannot exercise the clemency power in his own discretion but has to act on the advice of his Council of Ministers. Although the pardoning of the power of the Governor is very wide, it is not free from judicial review on certain limited grounds[20]:

- If the Governor is found to have exercised the power himself without being advised by the Government; or
- If the Governor transgresses/exceeds the jurisdiction while exercising the pardoning power; or
- If it is established that the Governor has passed the order without application of mind; or
- If the clemency order in question is a mala fide one or the Governor has passed the order on some extraneous consideration.

Financial Powers

Financial powers enjoyed by the Governor are as follows:

(i) A money Bill cannot be introduced in the Legislative Assembly of the State without the recommendation of the Governor.

(ii) No demand of grants can be made except on the recommendation of the Governor.

(iii) The Governor is required to see that the 'Annual Financial Statements' known as Budget are laid before the House or Houses of the Legislature.

(iv) The Contingency Fund of the State government will be at the disposal of the Governor, who shall release the funds on request of the State Cabinet, which later gets an approval from the State Legislature.

(v) The Governor of a state is required to constitute a State Finance Commission every five years to decide the resource allocation between the state government and the local bodies (Panchayats & Municipalities).

---

[19] *Constitutional Law of India* (2006), J. N. Pandey, P. 491, Central Law Agency.

[20] *Satpal Vs. State of Haryana*, (2000) 5 SCC 170, 174: AIR 2000 SC 1702.

Governor's Discretionary Powers

The concept of Governor acting in his discretion or exercising independent judgment is not alien to the Constitution. The normal rule is that Governor acts on the aid and advice of the Council of Ministers and not independently or contrary to it. But there are exceptions under which the Governor can act in his own discretion.

- The Governor is required to discharge certain functions in his 'discretion' by or under the Constitution. They are termed as 'Specific Discretionary Powers or Constitutional discretionary powers'. However, there are certain Governor's discretionary powers which are not expressly given in the Constitution but are necessarily implied. They are called situational discretionary powers.
- In the discharge of the discretionary functions, he is not required to seek the 'aid and advice' of his Council of Ministers.
- Whether a function falls within the Governor's 'discretion' or not, shall be decided by him in his 'discretion'.
- The Governor is the sole and final judge to decide whether any function is to be exercised in his discretion or on the advice of the Council of Ministers.
- The validity of anything done by the Governor is not to be called in question by any court on the ground that "he ought or ought not to have acted in his discretion".

About the discretionary powers granted to the Governors, Dr. B. R. Ambedkar, the Chairman of Constituent Assembly expressed his views that,

"Because the Provincial Governments are required to work in subordination to the Central Government and therefore, the Governor will reserve certain things in order to give the President the opportunity to see that the rules under which the Provincial Governments are supposed to act according to the Constitution or in subordination to the Central Government are observed[21]".

Thus, it was felt necessary by the makers of the Constitution to confer discretionary power on the Governor for two main reasons:

- The Governor has to serve as an agent of the Central Government in the State; and
- He is an important link between the Centre and the State to maintain the unity and integrity of the country.

Specific Discretionary Powers

Circumstances, which are mentioned in the Constitution, under which the Governor may use his discretion, are called specific discretionary powers. In discharging these responsibilities, he is not bound to seek or accept the advice of his Council of Ministers.

The Articles which give specific discretionary powers to the Governor are as under:

(a) **Article 239 :** Provides that a Union Territory shall be administered by the President through an Administrator with such designation as he may specify or a Governor of a State, adjoining Union Territory, may be appointed as the Administrator of that Union Territory. Where the Governor of a State is appointed as the Administrator of an adjoining Union Territory, he shall exercise his functions as the Administrator without the aid and advice of his Council of Ministers. Or in other words, Governor as an Administrator can act independently without his Council of Ministers.

[21]Vol. VIII, CAD at 502.

(b) **Article 356 :** While recommending to the President regarding the imposition of the President Rule in the state.

(c) **Sixth Schedule**[22] **:** The discretionary power of the Governor in the District Council functioning is enshrined in sub-paragraph 2, Paragraph 9 of the Sixth Schedule[23]. According to the said provision, if any dispute arises between the State Governments (mentioned in the 6th Schedule) and their District Councils regarding the sharing of royalties from extraction of mines and minerals, then the Governor shall take a decision and determine the amount payable. The decision taken by the Governor shall be final.

(d) State Bills Reserved For President's Assent – while reserving the Bills Governor shall act on his personal discretion.

- Article 200 – A State Governor has to reserve for the consideration of the President, any bill passed by a State Legislature, which in his opinion would, prejudicially affect the powers of the High Court. This provision enables the Centre to safeguard the status of the High Courts under the Constitution.
- Article 254(2) – A state law in respect of a matter in the Concurrent List which is repugnant/ contrary to an existing central law on the same matter is validated by the assent of the President. Hence, the Governor should reserve the Bill for President's assent to help a repugnant state law to remain operative.
- Article 31A – State legislations providing for acquisition of property under the said Article, needs the assent of the President in order to become law. The type of laws stated in this Article is exempted from the violation of Fundamental Rights under Articles 14, 19, and 31. The centre's scrutiny at the stage of assent may ensure that the various state laws do not indiscriminately contain provisions violating the Fundamental Rights to equality before law and the right to property. Hence, the Governor has to reserve the Bill for President's assent.
- Article 288(2) – A state law which imposes a tax in respect of any water or electricity stored, generated, consumed, distributed, or sold by any authority established by parliamentary legislation for regulation or developing any inter-state river or river valley, has no effect unless it has received the President's assent. Hence, the Governor has to reserve the Bill for presidential assent.
- Article 304(b) – This Article empowers the state to impose reasonable restrictions on the freedom of trade and commerce with or within that state as may be necessary in the public interest. However, no such bill or amendment is to be introduced or moved in the State Legislature without the previous sanction of the President.
- Article 360: When a proclamation of Financial Emergency is in operation, the central executive authority extends to giving direction to states requiring all money bills or financial bills to be reserved for the consideration of the President after they are passed by the State Legislatures.

---

[22]Sixth Schedule States are Assam, Meghalaya, Tripura & Mizoram.

[23]Part-2 of para nine of 6th schedule provides that if any dispute arises as to the share of such royalties to be made over to a District Council, it shall be referred to the Governor for determination and the amount determined by the Governor in his discretion shall be deemed to the amount payable under Part-1 of para 9 of 6th schedule to the District Council and the decision of the Governor shall be final.

- Article 200 – The omnibus Article 200 further empowers the Governor to reserve any other Bill for the Presidential assent. But Article 200 does not make clear that in which situations and circumstances the Governor may reserve the Bill for the consideration of the President. Some situations when the Governor may be justified in reserving a State Bill are:
  (i) When the State Bill suffers from patent unconstitutionality.
  (ii) When a State Bill derogates from the scheme and framework of the Constitution so as to endanger the sovereignty, unity, and integrity of the country.
  (iii) When the State Bill ex-facie comes in conflict with a central law.
  (iv) When the legitimate interests of another State or its people are being adversely affected.
  (v) When the State Bill is against the Directive Principles of State Policy.

(e) Governor's Responsibility For Certain Regions: Governor enjoys certain special responsibilities regarding certain regions in India. While performing those special responsibilities the Governor shall exercise his discretion.

- Article 371: This Article provides that the President may confer special responsibilities upon the Governor with respect to the State of Maharashtra and Gujarat for the establishment of separate Development Boards for Vidarbha, Marathwada, Saurashtra, Kutch, and the rest of Gujarat with the provision that a report on the working of each of these Boards will be placed each year before the State Legislative Assembly.
- Article 371A: This Article conferred special responsibilities on the Governor of Nagaland for certain purposes. For discharging these responsibilities the Governor shall, after consulting his Council of Ministers, exercise his individual judgement as to the action to be taken. These responsibilities are as follows:
  (i) with respect to law and order so long as internal disturbances occur in some areas of that State.
  (ii) to establish a Regional Council for Tuensang District.
  (iii) to arrange for equitable allocation of money between Tuensang District and the rest of Nagaland
- Article 371F (g) of the Constitution confers special responsibilities upon the Governor of Sikkim for peace and for an equitable arrangement for ensuring the social and economic advancement of different sections of the population of Sikkim.
- Article 371H (a) of the Constitution confers special responsibilities upon the Governor of Arunachal Pradesh with respect to law and order in the State of Arunachal Pradesh.

(f) Article 167: The right of the Governor to seek information from the Chief Minister is again a discretionary one because it would be fallacious to say that the Governor should consult the Chief Minister before seeking information from him. Under Article 167(a), it is the duty of the Chief Minister to keep the Governor informed about the decision of the Council relating to the administration of the affairs of the State and proposals for legislation. Under Article 167(c), the Governor is empowered to ask the Chief Minister to submit for the consideration of the Council of Ministers any matter on which a decision has been taken by a Minister but which has not been considered by the Council. This power is related to the power of asking for information (for while going through the decisions of the government both by the Cabinet and individual Ministers, the Governor may come across a particular decision made by a Minister which, in his opinion, requires reconsideration by the Cabinet as a whole).

Circumstantial/Situational Discretionary Powers

Circumstantial discretionary powers are not defined by the Constitution. These powers are implied powers, which are exercised according to the situations which may vary. The circumstances, in which the he may use his discretionary powers, arise in the following matters:

(a) Appointment of the Chief Minister: In the appointment of the Chief Minister, the Governor can use his discretion. The extent of use of discretion in the appointment of the Chief Minister depends upon the situation that arises. When a single party or group has the majority, the leader of the majority party is invited to form the government. At this time, Governor has not much say in the appointment of the Chief Minister. The problem arises, when no party has a clear-cut majority in the Legislature and in such situation, the role of the Governor becomes very important. Governor uses his discretion in the appointment of the Chief Minister.

(b) Dismissal of the Ministry: The Governor has the discretion to dismiss the ministry. This power has been given to the Governor by the Constitution itself, when it says that ministers hold office during the pleasure of the Governor. Generally, the Governor cannot use his sweet will to dissolve the ministry; there must be some ground to dissolve it. In the following circumstances Governors may use his discretion and dissolve the ministry.

(i) When the 'No Confidence Motion' has been passed against the government and the ministry refuses to resign.

(ii) When the Governor has a reasonable ground to believe that the Chief Minister no longer enjoys the confidence of the Legislative Assembly and he is not prepared to face the Assembly immediately, on one pretext or the other.

(iii) When the Governor believes that the ministry is trying to maintain its majority in the Legislative Assembly by practicing corruption.

(iv) When Governor believes that the ministry is violating the law of the land.

(c) Dissolution of Legislative Assembly: The Governor can use his discretion regarding dissolution of the State Assembly and can refuse to accept the advice of the Council of Ministers who lost their majority to dissolve the Legislative Assembly.

Role of Governor

Thus, the Governor means the Government of State and all executive functions which are exercised by Governor, except where he is required under the Constitution to exercise the functions in his discretion are exercised by him on the aid and advice of the Council of Ministers headed by the Chief Minister. The Governor enjoys both situational as well constitutional discretionary powers, whereas the President enjoys only situational discretionary powers. Moreover, the President can confer on a Governor a function in any contingency not provided in the Constitution.

QUESTIONS

Subjective Questions

1. "The Governor can exercise his discretionary powers only if there is a compelling necessity to do so. The necessity to exercise such powers may arise from the express provision of the Constitution or by necessary implication". Discuss. **(250 words)**
2. "The Governor is essentially a constitutional Head and the Government is run by the Council of Ministers". Comment. **(150 words)**

Objective Questions

1. Which one of the following statements is correct? **(UPSC CSE 2013)**

   (a) In India, the same person cannot be appointed as Governor for two or more States at the same time.

   (b) The Judges of the High Court of the States in India are appointed by the Governor of the State just as the Judges of the Supreme Court are appointed by the President.

   (c) No procedure has been laid down in the Constitution of India for the removal of a Governor from his/her post.

   (d) In the case of a Union Territory having a legislative set-up, the Chief Minister is appointed by the Lt. Governor on the basis of majority support.

   Ans: (c)

2. Which of the following are the discretionary powers given to the Governor of a State?
   1. Sending a report to the President of India for imposing the President's Rule Appointing the Ministers
   2. Reserving certain bills passed by the State Legislature for consideration of the President of India
   3. Making the rules to conduct the business of the State Government

   Select the correct answer using the code given below.

   (a) 1 and 2 only (b) 1 and 3 only

   (c) 2 and 3 only (d) None of these

   Ans: (b)

3. The Governor can reserve a state bill for the consideration of the President if it
   1. Opposes the provisions of Directive Principles of State Policy.
   2. Endangers the position of the State High Court.
   3. Deals with the compulsory acquisition of property under Article 31A.

   Select the correct answer using the code given below.

   (a) 2 and 3 only (b) 1 and 3 only

   (c) 2 only (d) 1, 2, and 3

   Ans: (d)

4. With reference to the office of Governor, consider the following statements:
   1. A person can be appointed as Governor of two states simultaneously.
   2. The Constitution prescribes that the President should consult the Chief Minister of the State while appointing the Governor.

   Which of the statements given above is/are correct?

   (a) 1 only (b) 2 only
   (c) Both 1 and 2 (d) Neither 1 nor 2

   Ans: (a)

5. With reference to the State Finance Commission, consider the following statements:
   1. The Governor constitutes a State Finance Commission once in five years.
   2. It reviews the distribution of revenues between the State and local governments.

   Which of the statements given above is/are correct?

   (a) 1 only (b) 2 only
   (c) Both 1 and 2 (d) Neither 1 nor 2

   Ans: (c)

15.1 REAL EXECUTIVE OF THE STATE

EXECUTIVE FUNCTIONS

Article 162: Extent of Executive Power of State

According to Article 162, 'Subject to the provisions of this Constitution, the executive power of a State shall extend to the matters with respect to which the Legislature of the State has power to make laws:

Provided that in any matter with respect to which the Legislature of a State and Parliament have power to make laws, the executive power of the State shall be subject to, and limited by, the executive power expressly conferred by this Constitution or by any law made by Parliament upon the Union or authorities thereof.'

This Article defines the extent of the executive power of a State. The executive power of the state extends to matters with respect to which the State legislature has authority to make laws, i.e., the subjects enumerated in the State List and the Concurrent List. The proviso to the Article relates to the concurrent sphere. The proviso lays down that the mere fact that the Union Parliament has made a law relating to a matter governed by the Concurrent List will not deprive the State of its executive power relating to that matter. What will happen in such a case is that the executive power of the State relating to that matter shall be subject to the executive power expressly conferred upon the Union or its authorities by the aforesaid law (made by the Union or by the Constitution itself).

However, this Article does not define what the executive functions are and what activities legitimately come within their scope. It is concerned primarily with the distribution of the executive power between the Union and the States. Although it cannot be possible to frame an exhaustive definition of what executive functions are, ordinarily they connote the residue of governmental functions that remain after legislative and judicial functions are taken away. The executive functions comprise both the determination of policy as well as carrying it into execution. This evidently, includes the initiation of legislation, the maintenance of order, and the protection of social and economic welfare (in fact the carrying on or supervision of the general administration of the State). It must not, however, be assumed that the legislative functions are exclusively performed by the legislature, executive functions by the executive, and judicial functions by the judiciary. Even though the Constitution differentiates the functions of the three organs of the government, it has not made an absolute division of functions between the three agencies of the State. Often, the exercise of legislative or judicial function is entrusted to the executive. For instance, power to frame rules, regulations, and notifications which are essentially legislative in character is frequently entrusted to the executive. Similarly, judicial authority is entrusted by legislation to the executive authority. Accordingly, while it may be possible to characterize with precision that an agency of the State is executive, legislative, or judicial, it cannot be predicted that a particular function exercised by any individual agency is necessarily of the character which the agency bears[1].

The executive functions and the administration of the state is carried out in the name of the Governor. But the actual responsibility is that of the Chief Minister and Council of Ministers. Let's discuss about the powers and functions of the Chief Minister and the Council of Ministers who are the real executives of the State.

---

[1]V.N. Shukla's *Constitution of India*, Mahendra Pal Singh, Thirteenth Edition, P. 590, EBC Explorer.

CHIEF MINISTER

The form of government in the States, as at the Centre, is Parliamentary. Accordingly, Article 163, like Article 74, provides for a Council of Ministers with the Chief Minister at its head to aid and advice the Governor in the exercise of his functions. Therefore, each State shall have a Council of Ministers headed by Chief Minister to aid and advice the Governor. The Chief Minister is the real head or real executive of the State. On the other hand, the Governor is the nominal head or nominal executive of the State. The responsibility to the people is of the Council of Ministers headed by the Chief Minister and not of the Governor. Governor's position is the same as that of a King or Queen in England or of the President at the Centre.

Appointment of Chief Minister

The Chief Minister of a state in India is the hub of the wheel around which the administration revolves in a State. He occupies a pivotal position in a state. But, there are no specific Articles in the Constitution which governs the appointment of the Chief Minister. Article 164 merely states that the Governor appoints the Chief Minister and the other ministers are appointed on the advice of the Chief Minister who shall hold office during the pleasure of the Governor. Though in theory it appears that the Chief Minister is an appointee of the Governor, as a matter of a well-established convention, the leader of the majority party in the Legislative Assembly should be appointed as the Chief Minister. However, in the event there are no clear winners in the elections, the Governor may have to exercise his personal judgment in selecting the Chief Minister. The Governor normally invites the leader of the single largest party to form the government and ask him to seek a vote of confidence within a month in the State Legislative. There is no specific provision in the Constitution enabling the Governor to require the Chief Minister to prove his majority on the floor of the House. But it would be preposterous to suggest that there can be no such vote because the Constitution is silent on the point.

It is also interesting to note that the Chief Minister appointed need not be an elected member at the time of swearing in. However, he needs to be elected to either House of the State Legislative within a period of six months, failing which he ceases to be Chief Minister. Under Article 164(4), a person who is not a member of any House may even be appointed as the Chief Minister. Therefore, there have been cases when non-members have been appointed as Chief Ministers. For example, Kamaraj Nadar was appointed as the Chief Minister of Madras in 1954 although he was not a member of the State legislature.[2]

Moreover, there is no convention to the effect that only a member of the Legislative Assembly should be appointed as the Chief Minister. Many a time, members of Legislative Councils have been appointed as Chief Ministers.[3]

Vacancy of the Office of Chief Minister

In the event of the office of the Chief Minister falling vacant on account of death of the Chief Minister or otherwise, the Governor can appoint any person using his judgment where there is no apparent successor. However, the ruling party normally elects a new individual who shall be the Chief Minister in the event of vacancy of the office of Chief Minister on account of death.

---

[2] *Indian Constitutional Law*, M.P. Jain, P. 360, Eighth Edition, LexisNexis.

[3] For example, C Rajagopalachari in Madras and Morarji Desai on Bombay in 1952; C.B. Gupta in UP in 1960 and Mandal in Bihar in 1968.

Oath of Office of the Ministers

Before entering the office of the Chief Minister, the Governor administers to him the prescribed oaths of office and secrecy given in the Third Schedule.

Oath of Office

Form of oath of office for a Chief Minister for a State:—

"I, A.B., do swear in the name of God/solemnly affirm that I will bear true faith and allegiance to the Constitution of India as by law established, that I will uphold the sovereignty and integrity of India, that I will faithfully and conscientiously discharge my duties as a Minister for the State of .... and that I will do right to all manner of people in accordance with the Constitution and the law without fear or favour, affection or ill-will."

It is one of the ten forms of oaths prescribed in the Third Schedule of the Constitution. All of them, except the two oaths of secrecy, require the oath taker to swear that they will "bear true faith and allegiance to the Constitution of India," and "uphold the sovereignty and integrity of India." However, until 1963, no one taking a constitutional oath was required to swear that they would "uphold the sovereignty and integrity of India." But, that changed when the Constitution (Sixteenth Amendment) Act, 1963 came into effect. The Sixteenth Amendment expanded the forms of oath to ensure that "every candidate for the membership of a State Legislature or Parliament, and every aspirant to, and incumbent of, public office" – to quote its Statement of Objects and Reasons – "pledges himself . . . to preserve the integrity and sovereignty of the Union of India." The amendment gave effect to the recommendations of the Committee of National Integration and Regionalism headed by C. P. Ramaswami Aiyar[4]. The committee had been set up to study separatist movements that were prevalent in India and was supposed to report on ways to neutralize them. The Committee was constituted to tackle the threat posed by "separatist," C. N. Annadurai, who had founded the Dravida Munnetra Kazhagam (DMK). A month before the committee was set up, Annadurai had, in his very first speech to the Parliament on 1 May, 1962, demanded the "separation of Dravida Nadu," a demand that the DMK had been making since its founding in 1949. Faced with an ascendant political party using constitutional means to secure separatist ends, Aiyar sought to tackle the threat by proposing the expansion of the oath of office to include a pledge to "uphold the sovereignty and integrity of India." Through the addition of a few words, he had hoped to coerce "separatists" aspiring to, or holding public office into either foregoing their separatist demands, or at least suspending them until they left office. Aiyar's deceptively simple amendment appears to have worked. Soon after the Sixteenth Amendment came into effect, the DMK gave up its demand for an independent Dravida Nadu, despite being the only party to have opposed the Sixteenth Amendment in Parliament[5].

---

[4]Ironically, Ex-Prime Minister Jawaharlal Nehru appointed C. P. Ramaswami Aiyar, a "staunch separatist" as the chairperson of the committee. B. S. Raghavan, the first secretary of the National Integration Council had said that Aiyar had "moved earth and heaven for the continuance of the British Rule" as Dewan of Travancore, "even to the extent of goading the Chamber of Princes to declare the independence of the princely states."

[5]https://theprint.in/opinion/oath-uphold-sovereignty-integrity-india-invented, Srijan Sandip Mandal is on the faculty of the Center for Public History at the Srishti Institute of Art, Design and Technology in Bengaluru.

Oath of Secrecy

Form of oath of secrecy for a Minister for a State:—

"I, A.B., do swear in the name of God/solemnly affirm that I will not directly or indirectly communicate or reveal to any person or persons any matter which shall be brought under my consideration or shall become known to me as a Minister for the State of ………………. except as may be required for the due discharge of my duties as such Minister."

Tenure of the Chief Minister

The Constitution does not provide any fixed tenure for the Chief Minister. The Chief Minister holds office during the pleasure of the Governor. However, it is not the case that the Governor can replace Chief Minister overnight. The Chief Minister cannot be removed from his office so long as he has the trust and confidence of the State Legislative Assembly and he is in majority. However, if the Chief Minister loses this trust and confidence, the Chief Minister would resign or be dismissed by the Governor.

Salary and Allowances of the Chief Minister

The salary and other allowances of the Chief Minister are determined by the State Legislature (as per Article 164 (5)). In the event the same is not determined by the State Legislature, it shall be determined as per Second Schedule to the Constitution of India. Besides the salary, he gets free accommodation, medical facilities, etc.

Powers and Functions of the Chief Minister

The powers and functions of the Chief Minister can be classified as follows:

In Relation with the Governor

The Chief Minister, along with the Council of Ministers, advises the Governor on the various gamuts of the State machinery. They advise the Governor on the appointment of important officials at the State level such as the State Advocate General, Chairman and members of the State Public Commissions, State Election Commissions, etc.

The Chief Minister, being the principal contact, has the duty to communicate to the Governor all the decisions taken by the Council of Ministers relating to the administration of the affairs of the state and proposal for the Legislature. The Chief Minister is also required to furnish all information relating to the administration of the affairs of the state and proposal for the Legislature as required by the Governor. If the Governor so requires, the Chief Minister has to submit for the consideration of the Council of Ministers any matter on which a decision has been taken by a Minister but which has not been considered by the Council of Ministers.

In Relation with the State Legislature

The Chief Minister is the primary spokesman of the Government in the State Legislature, whereby he lays down policies of the government on the floor of the house. He is answerable to the State Legislature on government actions and inactions.

The Chief Minister advises the Governor for summoning and proroguing the sessions of the State Legislature and recommends to the Governor its dissolution and calling for fresh elections at any time.

In Relation with the Council of Ministers

The Chief Minister is the Head of the Council of Ministers. He advises the Governor regarding who are to be appointed as ministers. On a similar power, the Chief Minister can recommend the Governor to dismiss an individual(s) from the post of the minister. He can call upon the individual(s) to tender their resignations as ministers.

It is the Chief Minister who allocates portfolios to the ministers. He can shuffle the portfolios among ministers, whenever the need arises.

The Chief Minister, being the head of the Council of Ministers, presides over the meetings. He guides, influences, directs, controls, etc. the activities of all ministers. He can also engineer a collapse of the Council of Ministers by resigning from the post of Chief Minister. In the event of death of the Chief Minister, the majority party would elect a new person to be the Chief Minister who would then advise the Governor to appoint the ministers and a new Council of Ministers would be formed.

Other Powers of Chief Minister

- Chief Minister is the ex-officio chairman of the State Disaster Management Authority and the State Planning Commission.
- Chief Minister acts as a Vice-chairman of the concerned zonal council in rotation for a period of one year.
- Chief Minister is a member of the Inter-State Council and the Governing Council of NITI Aayog.
- Chief Minister acts as a crisis manager at the political level in the state during emergencies.
- The Chief Minister plays an important role in making policies of the State Government. He has to ensure that the policies of the government do not go against public interest. His voice is final in policy decisions of the State Government.
- He also plays an important role in making higher appointments of the State Government. The Governor appoints different higher officials of the State Government on the advice of the Chief Minister and his Council of Ministers.
- The Chief Minister is the chief administrator of the State. All major decisions of the State Government are taken under his leadership. He is responsible for the overall working of the state departments. He also has to maintain a good and harmonious relation with the Central Government.
- As the leader of the majority party in the Legislative Assembly, the Chief Minister has to see that party discipline is maintained in the House. He has also to defend the ministers of his Council of Ministers on the floor of the House from the criticisms of the opposition.

Deputy Chief Minister

The political parties often adopt the practice of appointing Deputy Chief Ministers for various political reasons. The post of a Deputy Chief Minister does not hold any more significance than that of a Cabinet Minister in the state. The Deputy Chief Minister is not a constitutional post. The Deputy CM is equivalent to the rank of a cabinet minister (in the state) and enjoys pay and perks that a Cabinet Minister is entitled to.

THE COUNCIL OF MINISTERS

Constitutional Provisions Regarding Council Of Ministers

Article 163 - Council of Ministers to Aid and Advice Governor

(1) *There shall be a Council of Ministers with the Chief Minister at the head to aid and advise the Governor in the exercise of his functions, except in so far as he is by or under this Constitution required to exercise his functions or any of them in his discretion.*

(2) *If any question arises whether any matter is or is not a matter as respects which the Governor is by or under this Constitution required to act in his discretion, the decision of the Governor in his discretion shall be final, and the validity of anything done by the Governor shall not be called in question on the ground that he ought or ought not to have acted in his discretion.*

(3) *The question whether any, and if so what, advice was tendered by ministers to the Governor shall not be inquired into in any court.*

Article 163(1) says that there shall be a Council of Ministers with the Chief Minister as the head to *'aid and advise'* the Governor in the exercise of his functions. The Council of Ministers in the State is constituted and functions in the same way as the Union Cabinet.

Article 163(2): Discretionary Powers of the Governor

In exercise of his discretionary powers, the Governor is not required to act on the advice of his ministers or ever to seek advice. This is made clear from Article 163 clause (2) which says that if any question arises whether any matter is or is not a matter as regards the discretion of the Governor, then the Governor's decision shall be final, and the validity of anything done by the Governor shall not be called into question that he ought or ought not have acted in his discretion. The only functions which the Governor may impliedly be called upon to exercise in his discretion, without the aid and advice of the Council of Ministers, are the same as in the case of the President, i.e., the appointment of Chief Minister, dismissal of a Ministry which has lost the confidence of the Legislative Assembly but refuses to resign, and the dissolution of the Legislative Assembly. The other cases of exercise of his discretion are the ones provided in the Constitution itself which are noted in an earlier section of this chapter. But besides them, in a few exceptional cases, the courts have also recognized some other powers which the Governor may exercise in his discretion because of statutory provisions such as grant of sanction to prosecute a Minister, including the Chief Minister, under the Prevention of Corruption Act, 1988. But such exceptions apart, "the Governor is bound to act on the aid and advice of the Council of Ministers", unless he acts, under a particular stature, or acts in his own discretion under the exceptions carved out by the Constitution itself. The other exceptions which are carved out "under" the Constitution are such as taking disciplinary action against a judge of the subordinate judiciary under Article 235 where the Governor must act on the recommendation of the High Court and not of the Council of Ministers if there is any difference of opinion. Nor can he, in this matter, act on the aid and advice of the Council of Ministers without seeking the opinion of the High Court.

Article 163(3) — Bar to Inquiry in Court

This clause includes two propositions:

(a) The question whether any advice was tendered to the Governor by the ministers shall not be inquired into by any court.

(b) The question as to what advice was tendered by the ministers to the Governors shall not be inquired into in any court.

A legal consequence of this provision is that resolutions or other deliberations at the meetings of Council of Ministers or advice finally tendered in pursuance of such deliberations to the Governor are privileged from production in a court of law. If, however, the Government produces the proceedings of the Council of Ministers, without any objection and without any claim or privilege, and they are before the court, there is nothing in Article 163(3) to debar the Court from looking into them.

Article 164 – Appointment of Ministers

(1) *The Chief Minister shall be appointed by the Governor and the other ministers shall be appointed by the Governor on the advice of the Chief Minister, and the ministers shall hold office during the pleasure of the Governor:*

Provided that in the States of Chhattisgarh, Jharkhand, Madhya Pradesh and Orissa, there shall be a Minister in charge of Tribal Welfare who may in addition be in charge of the welfare of the Scheduled Castes and Backward Classes or any other work.

[6]*[(1A) The total number of ministers, including the Chief Minister, in the Council of Ministers in a State shall not exceed fifteen per cent of the total number of members of the Legislative Assembly of that State: Provided that the number of ministers, including the Chief Minister in a State shall not be less than twelve.*

Provided further that where the total number of ministers including the Chief Minister in the Council of Ministers in any State at the commencement of the Constitution (Ninety-first Amendment) Act, 2003 exceeds the said fifteen per cent, or the number specified in the first proviso, as the case may be, then the total number of ministers in that State shall be brought in conformity with the provisions of this clause within six months from such date as the President may by public notification appoint.

[6]Added by 91st Constitutional Amendment Act, 2003.

(1B) A member of the Legislative Assembly of a State or either House of the Legislature of a State having Legislative Council belonging to any political party who is disqualified for being a member of that House under Paragraph 2 of the Tenth Schedule shall also be disqualified to be appointed as a Minister under clause (1) for duration of the period commencing from the date of his disqualification till the date on which the term of his office as such member would expire or where he contests any election to the Legislative Assembly of a State or either House of the Legislarure of a State having Legislative Council, as the case may be, before the expiry of such period, till the date on which he is declared elected, whichever is earlier.]

(2) *The Council of Ministers shall be collectively responsible to the Legislative Assembly of the State.*

(3) *Before a minister enters upon his office, the Governor shall administer to him the oaths of office and of secrecy according to the forms set out for the purpose in the Third Schedule.*

(4) *A minister who for any period of six consecutive months is not a member of the Legislature of the State shall at the expiration of that period cease to be a minister.*

(5) *The salaries and allowances of ministers shall be such as the Legislature of the State may from time to time by law determine and, until the Legislature of the State so determines, shall be as specified in the Second Schedule.*

Article 164(1) – Appointment of Ministers of the Government of a State

Article 164(1) of the Constitution contains provisions regarding the appointment of ministers of the government of a State. The Chief Minister is appointed by the Governor. The other ministers are appointed by the Governor on the advice of the Chief Minister. The ministers hold office during the pleasure of the Governor. The expression "during the pleasure" is used in a rather technical sense. It does not mean that the Governor can dismiss his ministers at his will. The real import of the fact that the ministers hold office during the pleasure of the Governor indirectly strengthens the position of the Chief Minister. In other words, if the Governor is advised by the Chief Minister that a Minister should be dismissed, he should exercise his pleasure and dismiss the Minister.

Article 164(a) – New Clauses

The 91st Constitutional Amendment Act, 2003 added two new clauses, i.e., 1A and 1B to Article 164(a).

(a) Maximum Size of Ministries – Clause (1A) puts a maximum limit of number of ministers to be appointed to the Council of Ministers. It provides that the "the total number of ministers, including the Chief Minister in the Council of Ministers in a State shall not exceed 15% of the total number of members of the Legislative Assembly of that State. However, the number of ministers, including the Chief Minister in a State, shall not be less than 12 for smaller States.

(b) Disqualified to be as a Minister – Clause 1(B) provides that where the member of the original political party defects from the party, their membership of the legislature will automatically come to an end. Such a member cannot be appointed as a minister.

Both these amendments are to be welcomed. The Committee on Electoral Reforms and the Law Commission have recommended for implementation of these reforms. The National Committee to

Review the Working of the Constitution was of the view that the practice of making abnormally large size ministries was a burden on the government exchequer and it should be prohibited. Restricting the size of a council of ministers to not more than 15% of the total strength of the House discourages defections in the lure of becoming ministers.

Article 164(2)

According to Article 164(2), the Council of Ministers shall be collectively responsible to the Legislative Assembly of the State. This provision embodies political responsibility which is distinguished from legal responsibility. Collective responsibility makes each minister responsible to the Legislative Assembly for the acts of other members of the Council of Ministers. The decision is a collective decision from which no Minister can dissociate. Since the Council of Ministers is able to stay in office so long as it commands the support of the majority of the Legislative Assembly, the whole of the Council of Ministers is held politically responsible as one entity and may be compelled to resign for any act done by one particular minister or his department. While collective responsibility is enforced by the Legislative Assembly through the political sanction of removal from office or resignation under pressure of public opinion, each minister is further individually liable for wrongful acts done by him. Thus, the ministers have both collective responsibility for government policy and individual responsibility for their own department's work.

Article 164(3)

Article 164(3) provides that every minister before entering shall make and subscribe to the oath of office and secrecy mentioned in the Third Schedule of the Constitution[7]. The oath shall be administered by the Governor.

Article 164(4)

Article 164(4) provides for two situations:

(a) A person, who is not a member of the Legislature being appointed as a minister, and

(b) Where a person after being appointed as a minister, loses his seat in the Legislature.

In either case, such minister shall cease to be a member if he is not elected as a member of the Legislature within 6 months of his appointment, or the date when he loses his seat in the Legislature (as the case may be).

Salaries and allowances of ministers shall be such as the legislature of the State may from time to time determine; and until these are considered by the legislature, ministers shall be paid such salaries and allowances as specified in the Second Schedule.

Article 166 – Conduct of Business of the Government of a State

(1) *All executive action of the Government of a State shall be expressed to be taken in the name of the Governor.*

[7]The oath of office and secrecy of the Minister is similar to that of the Chief Minister.

(2) *Orders and other instruments made and executed in the name of the Governor shall be authenticated in such manner as may be specified in rules to be made by the Governor, and the validity of an order or instrument which is so authenticated shall not be called in question on the ground that it is not an order or instrument made or executed by the Governor.*

(3) *The Governor shall make rules for the more convenient transaction of the business of the Government of the State, and for the allocation among ministers of the said business in so far as it is not business with respect to which the Governor is by or under this Constitution required to act in his discretion.*

Article 166(1)

Article 166(1) enacts that whenever executive action is to be taken by way of an order or instrument, it shall be expressed to be taken in the name of the Governor in whom the executive power of the State is vested.

Article 166(2)

Under Article 166(2), the orders and instruments made and executed in the name of the Governor shall be authenticated in the manner specified in the rules framed by the Governor. While clause (1) relates to the mode of expression of an executive order or instrument, clause (2) lays down the way in which such order is to be authenticated; and when both these forms are complied with, an order or instrument would be immune from challenge in a court of law on the grounds that it has not been made or executed by the Governor of the State[8].

Article 166(3)

Under our Constitution, the Governor is essentially a constitutional Head. The administration of the State is run by the Council of Ministers. But in the very nature of things, it is impossible for the Council of Ministers to deal with each and every matter that comes before the government. In order to remove that difficulty, the Constitution has authorized the Governor under clause (3) of Article 166 to make rules for the more convenient transaction of business of the government of the State and for the allocation among its ministers of the business of government. All matters excepting those in which the Governor is required to act in his discretion have to be allocated to one or the other of the ministers on the advice of the Chief Minister. Apart from allocating business amongst ministers, the Governor can also make rules on the advice of the Council of Ministers for more convenient transaction of business.

Article 167 – Duties of Chief Minister

It shall be the duty of the Chief Minister of each State —

(a) *to communicate to the Governor of the State all decisions of the Council of Ministers relating to the administration of the affairs of the State and proposals for legislation;*

(b) *to furnish such information relating to the administration of the affairs of the State and proposals for legislation as the Governor may call for; and*

---

[8] *Dattatraya Moreshwar Vs. State of Bombay*, AIR 1952 SC 181, 188:1952 SCR 612.

(c) *if the Governor so requires, to submit for the consideration of the Council of Ministers any matter on which a decision has been taken by a minister but which has not been considered by the Council.*

This Article corresponds to Article 78 which relates to the duties of the Prime Minister in relation to furnishing information to the President. Under Article 167(a), it shall be the duty of the Chief Minister to communicate to the Governor all decisions of the cabinet relating to the administration of State affairs and legislative proposals and under sub-clause (b), the Chief Minister shall furnish such information relating to the administration of State affairs and legislative proposals as the Governor may call for.

Article 167(c) empowers the Governor to require any case on which a decision has been taken by a minister, but has not been considered by the Council of Ministers, to be submitted to the Council of Ministers for its consideration. It is not intended to empower the Governor to reopen any decision already taken by the Council of Ministers. For the successful working of the rule of collective responsibility, it is absolutely necessary that a minister should not take any important action on his own responsibility and without the previous approval of the Council of Ministers.

Article 177 – Rights of Ministers and Advocate General as Respects the Houses

Every Minister and the Advocate General for a State shall have the right to speak in, and otherwise to take part in the proceedings of, the Legislative Assembly of the State or, in the case of a State having a Legislative Council, both Houses, and to speak in, and otherwise to take part in the proceedings of, any committee of the Legislature of which he may be named a member, but shall not, by virtue of this Article, be entitled to vote.

A minister who is a member of Legislative Assembly has the right to speak in and take part in the proceedings of Legislative Council but has no right to vote in Legislative Council and vice-versa. They also have right to speak and take part in the proceedings of any committee of the State Legislature of which he may be named as a member but does have a right to vote. Even the Advocate General (who is not the member of the Legislature) has the right to take part in the proceedings of the State Legislature without the right to vote.

Categories of Ministers

There are no specific provisions governing the categorization of the Council of Ministers. It is a power bestowed upon the Chief Minister to determine the categorization/portfolios of the Council depending upon the requirements of the situation from time to time.

Generally, like at the Centre, the State Council consists of three geneses of the ministers. A point to be noted is that though there is no difference in their membership (all are part of Council of Ministers), they differ only on basis of ranks, salary, entitlements, etc. Ultimately, the entire cadre (ministers) report to the Chief Minister.

- Firstly, there is the Cabinet Minister who is given an independent charge of government department like finance, home, education etc. They form the core of the Council of Ministers and attend all the meetings. They play a very important role in the policy-making and extend their influence over the entire affairs of the state.

- Secondly, there is the Minister of State that is attached to the Cabinet Minister or is given an independent charge of the department/s. However, these ministers are not members of the elite cabinet and do not attend the cabinet meetings unless there are matters relating to their departments on invitation basis.
- Thirdly, there are Deputy Ministers who are attached to the Cabinet Minister to take care of the administrative, political, and Parliamentary duties. They are not members of the elite cabinet and do not attend the cabinet meetings.

EXHIBIT 15.1 : CABINET COMMITTEES

The work of the Cabinet is routed through the Cabinet Committees. They may be ad-hoc or standing. These committees are formed by the Chief Minister according to requirements of the situation; hence, their members and composition vary as per the situation. They play an important role in not only sorting of issues but also in taking decisions. They also formulate proposals for the consideration of the Cabinet.

QUESTIONS

Subjective Questions

1. "In the Parliamentary system, the Chief Executive of the State (Chief Minister) is not elected directly by the people, but he is normally the leader of the majority party in the Legislative Assembly". Discuss. **(250 words)**
2. "There is no harm, but there is a great advantage if the Governor exercises his influence over his cabinet". Critically analyze. **(150 words)**

Objective Questions

1. With reference to the office of Chief Minister, consider the following statements:

   i. He must prove his majority in the State Legislative Assembly before being appointed as Chief Minister.

   ii. He holds office during the pleasure of the Governor.

   Which of the statements given above is/are correct?

   (a) i only (b) ii only

   (c) Both i and ii (d) Neither i nor ii

   Ans: (b)

2. With reference to No-Confidence Motion, consider the following statements:

   i. It can be moved against the entire Council of Ministers as well as against an individual minister.

   ii. If it is passed in the Legislative Assembly, the Council of Ministers must resign from the office.

Which of the statements given above is/are correct?

(a) i only (b) ii only

(c) Both i and ii (d) Neither i nor ii

Ans: (b)

3. There is a constitutional requirement to have a Minister in-charge of Tribal Welfare for the States of:

(a) Nagaland, Manipur, and Tripura

(b) Assam, Nagaland, and Odisha

(c) Madhya Pradesh, Odisha, and Chattisgarh

(d) Jharkhand, Andhra Pradesh, and Maharashtra

Ans: (c)

4. Consider the following statements:

i. The Chief Minister shall communicate to the Governor all the decisions of the Council of Ministers relating to administration.

ii. The Governor can call for information relating to proposals for legislation.

iii. The Governor can direct that any matter on which decision has been taken by a minister should be placed before the State Council of Ministers.

Which of the following statements are true?

(a) Only i (b) Only ii and iii

(c) Only i and iii (d) i, ii, and iii

Ans: (d)

5. **Assertion (A) :** The maximum strength of the State Council of Ministers has been specified in the Constitution of India.

Reason (R) : The strength and the composition of the Council of Ministers at the Union level is mentioned in the Constitution of India.

Consider the following statements:

(a) Both A and R individually true and R is the correct explanation of A.

(b) Both A and R are individually true but R is not the correct explanation of A.

(c) A is true but R is false

(d) A is false but is true

Ans: (c)

15.2 ADVOCATE GENERAL FOR THE STATE

INTRODUCTION

Constitutional Provisions Regarding Advocate General

According to Article 165 –

(1) *The Governor of each State shall appoint a person who is qualified to be appointed a Judge of a High Court to be Advocate General for the State.*

(2) *It shall be the duty of the Advocate General to give advice to the Government of the State upon such legal matters, and to perform such other duties of a legal character, as may from time to time be referred or assigned to him by the Governor, and to discharge the functions conferred on him by or under this Constitution or any other law for the time being in force.*

(3) *The Advocate General shall hold office during the pleasure of the Governor, and shall receive such remuneration as the Governor may determine.*

Parallel to the Attorney General at the Centre, there is an Advocate General in each State. He is formally appointed by the Governor. Needless to say, the Governor exercises this power with the aid and advice of the Council of Ministers.

Qualifications of Advocate General

The Advocate General is a person who is qualified to be appointed as a judge of a High Court. In other words, he must be a citizen of India and must have held a judicial office for ten years or been an advocate of a high court for ten years.

Term of Advocate General

The Advocate General holds his office during the Governor's pleasure. The fact that the Advocate General holds office during the Governor's pleasure means that, unlike a High Court Judge who retires at the age of 62, the Advocate General can hold office even after he attains the age of 62 years.

A State can have only one Advocate General. The Governor may appoint other counsels for looking after the legal matters of the State and may give them any designation, including the designation of Additional Advocate General. But such counsels are appointed and their designation is assigned in the exercise of executive power of the State in Article 162 and not in exercise of its constitutional power under Article 165. The constitutional post of Advocate General in a State is only one and not more[1].

Remuneration of Advocate General

The Advocate General receives such remuneration as the Governor may determine. The relationship between the Advocate General and the State Government is essentially that of an advocate and a client in relation to his appearance in the courts and arguing the case before the courts on behalf of the State. Therefore, the fee for such cases may be settled between the government and the Advocate General by

---

[1] *M.T. Khan Vs. Govt. of A.P.*, (2004) 2 SCC 267.

rules or notifications. In case the fee so settled is not acceptable to the Advocate General, he has the option to resign. But he cannot claim that the fee or remuneration to be paid to him under 165(3) is not subject to change. It may be increased or reduced. There is no rule that it cannot be changed to the disadvantage of the Advocate General[2].

Powers and Functions of Advocate General

(a) The Advocate General gives advice to the State Government upon such legal matters as may be referred to him.

(b) He performs such other duties of a legal character as may be assigned to him by the Governor from time to time or are conferred on him by the Constitution or any other law.

(c) He also has the right to speak and otherwise participate in the proceedings of the House of the State Legislature or of any committee of the Legislature of which he may be named as a member, but he does not have a right to vote under this provision.

(d) He enjoys all legislative privileges which are available to a member of the Legislature.

Article 165 corresponds to Article 76 which deals with the Attorney General of India. The only difference between the two Articles is that Article 76 gives right of audience to the Attorney General in all courts in the territory of India. On the other hand, the Advocate General of a State does not enjoy such rights under Article 165.

Relationship of the Advocate General with the State

The Advocate General and his office defends and protects the interest of State Government and gives invaluable legal guidance to the State Government in the formulation of its policies and execution of its decisions[3].

The Supreme Court in *Joginder Singh Wasu Vs. State of Punjab*[4], held that the Advocate General and his Law officers are basically engaged to deal with court cases in the High Court by the State Government and the relationship between the Government and Law Officers is that of a client and counsel.

---

[2]V.N. Shukla's *Constitution of India*, Mahendra Pal Singh, Thirteenth Edition, P. 597, EBC Explorer.

[3]*State of U.P. & Others Vs. U.P. State Law Officers Association & Others*, (1994) SCC 204

[4](1994) Supreme Court Cases 184

CHAPTER 16

STATE JUDICIARY: HIGH COURTS AND SUBORDINATE COURTS

HIGH COURTS

In India's judicial hierarchy the High Court is second to the Supreme Court. The High Court is the apex court in the State Judicial System. The State Judiciary consists of a High Court and a system of subordinate courts including tribunals. High Courts in India are a legacy of the British Judicial system whereby the Britishers wanted to establish uniformity in administration of justice. The first High Courts were established in India for the first time at the 3 presidency towns of Calcutta (now Kolkata), Madras (now Chennai), and Bombay (now Mumbai) under the Indian High Courts Act, 1861. In course of time, other High Courts also came to be established[1].

Constitution of High Courts

According to Article 214, there shall be a High Court in each State. However, Article 231(1) conferred the power on the Parliament to establish by law a common High Court for two or more States or for two or more States and a Union Territory. Further, a High Court can have one or more Benches of itself within the area of its territorial jurisdiction. The discretion to constitute a Bench of the High Court is an absolute prerogative of the Chief Justice of the High Court, which is not open to challenge before the Supreme Court[2].

Composition of High Court

According to Article 217, every High Court consists of Chief Justice and such other Judges as the President may, from time to time, deem it necessary to appoint. The Constitution does not fix the number of judges of a High Court. The strength of the Judges is settled by the Central Executive from time to time keeping in view the amount of work before a High Court.

In *Supreme Court Advocates-on-Record Association Vs. Union of India*[3] *(Second Judge's Case)*, the court held that the Chief Justice of India (CJI) and the Chief Justice of the High Court concerned must undertake the periodical review of the strength of judges in the interest of effective administration of justice and make recommendations about such strength to the President. The recommendation of the Chief Justice of India in this regard must be acted upon by the President. The courts may even order the President to act on such recommendations if he fails to do so. The Supreme Court's ruling in this regard can be appreciated in the context of the embarrassing situation that every High Court is faced with a load of pending cases.

---

[1] M.P. Jain, *Outlines of Indian Legal and Constitutional History*, 262–289.

[2] *Federation of Bar Association in Karnataka Vs. Union of India*, (2000) 6 SCC 715.

[3] AIR 1994 SC 268.

Qualifications

A person to be qualified for appointment as Judge of a High Court :

- must be a citizen of India; and
- must have held a judicial office for at least ten years, in the territory of India; or
- must have been an advocate of High Court for at least ten years.

There is no minimum age criteria required for the appointment of the High Court Judges.

Appointment of Judges

Article 217 provides that every judge of a High Court shall be appointed by the President. The President appoints the Chief Justice of a High Court after consultation with the Chief Justice of India and the Governor of the State concerned. In case of appointment of a Judge other than the Chief Justice, he may consult even the Chief of the High Court concerned.

In *S.P. Gupta & others Vs. Union of India*[4], (popularly known as *First Judges Case)*, the question was whether in appointing the Judges of the High Court the President was bound by the advice of the Chief Justice of India or not? The majority held that the meaning of the term 'consultation' does not mean concurrence and the President is not bound by it. In other words, the Court held that the Constitutional functionaries (such as the Chief Justice of India, Governor, Chief Justice of the High Court, etc.) had merely a consultative role and that the power of appointment of judges was 'solely and exclusively' vested in the control of the President or the Central Executive. This decision has been rightly criticized on the ground that it would adversely affect the independence and impartiality of the Judiciary.

In *Supreme Court Advocates Vs. UOI*[5], (popularly known as *Second Judges Case)*, the 'First Judges Case' was overruled by a larger Bench and it was held that –

- The process of appointment of Judges to the Supreme Court and the High Courts is an integrated '*participatory consultative process*' for selecting the best and most suitable persons available for appointments; and all the Constitutional functionaries must perform this duty collectively with a view primarily to reach an agreed decision, subserving the Constitutional purpose, so that the occasion of primacy does not arise.
- The proposal for the appointment of the High Court Judges must be initiated by the Chief Justice of that High Court. Whereas, with respect to the proposal for the appointment or the transfer of the Chief Justice of High Court, it has to be initiated by the Chief Justice of India.
- No appointment of any Judge to the High Court can be made unless it is in conformity with the opinion of the Chief Justice of India. In other words, the consultation with the Chief Justice of India is mandatory and it is binding on the President. But the opinion of the Chief Justice of India is not his individual opinion. The opinion of the Chief Justice should be based on the collective views of himself and two senior-most Judges of the Supreme Court who come from the State concerned. All opinions must be expressed in writing.
- The President may not accept the recommendation of the Chief Justice of India only in exceptional cases and that too based on strong reasons disclosed to the Chief Justice of India. However, if the stated reasons are not accepted by the Chief Justice of India and the other Judges of the Supreme Court who have been consulted in the matter, and if the recommendation is reiterated by the Chief Justice of India, then the appointment should be made by the President.

---

[4] AIR 1982 SC 149.

[5] AIR 1994 SC 268.

After the '*Second Judges Case*', the President of India in exercise of his powers under Article 143 made a Presidential Reference[6] to the Supreme Court relating to the consultation between the CJI and the Supreme Court Judges in the matter of appointment of the High Court Judges (popularly known as '*Third Judges Case*'). The Supreme Court reiterated that 'consultation with CJI' implies consultation with a plurality of Judges in the formation of opinion of the CJI. The sole opinion of CJI does not constitute consultation and it is not binding on the President. Only a collegium comprising the CJI and two senior-most Judges of the Supreme Court who come from the State should make the recommendation. The recommendations made by the CJI without complying with the norms and requirements of the consultation process, as aforementioned, are not biding upon the Government of India[7].

National Judicial Appointments Commission (NJAC)

The Parliament passed the 99th Constitutional Amendment Act, 2015 to replace the present collegium system[8] with NJAC for the appointment of the High Court Judges and the Supreme Court Judges. In order to make the appointment of High Court and Supreme Court judges and Chief Justices more transparent, the Union Government intended to create the NJAC. According to the Amendment Act, the judges will be selected by the commission, whose members will be drawn from the Judiciary, Legislature, and civil society. In *Supreme Court Advocates-on-Record Association Vs. Union of India*[9] *(Fourth Judges case/NJAC Case)*, the Court held that, the 99th Constitutional Amendment Act, which provides for the inclusion of 'two eminent persons' as Members of the National Judicial Appointments Commission Act, 2014 was ultra vires the Constitution, for a variety of reasons. The same has also been held as violative of the 'basic structure' of the Constitution. The net effect of this judgment was to 'reaffirm' the supremacy and continuation of the collegium system.

Tenure

A High Court Judge (whether permanent, additional, or acting) retires at the age of 62 years. Any question as to the age of a High Court Judge is to be decided by the President after consulting the Chief Justice of India, and his decision is final. Thus, the jurisdiction to determine the Judges' age is vested exclusively in the President. Consultation with the Chief Justice of India is, however, mandatory, but his advice is not binding on the President.

Additional and Acting Judges

- **Acting Chief Justice :** The President may, under Article 223, appoint one of the Judges of the High Court as acting Chief Justice, when the office of the Chief Justice falls vacant or he is unable to perform his duties by reason of absence or otherwise.
- **Additional Judges :** The President may, under Article 224(1), appoint duly qualified persons to be Additional Judges of the court for a temporary period not exceeding two years, in order to clear the arrears of work in the High Court.
- **Acting Judges :** The President may, under Article 224(2), also appoint an Acting Judge when any Judge of a High Court other than Chief Justice is unable to perform his/her duties by reason of absence or is appointed to act temporarily as Chief Justice or for any other reason. An Acting Judge is to hold office until the permanent Judge resumes his/her duties.

---

[6] Special Reference No.1 of 1998.

[7] Durga Das Basu, *Shorter Constitution of India*, Thirteenth Edition, Wadhwa and Company, 2003 P. 779.

[8] The collegium system evolved after three landmark judgements of the Supreme Court, known as the 'Three Judges Cases': the First, Second, and the Third judges cases.

[9] AIR 2016 SC 117

No person appointed as an additional or Acting Judge of a High Court shall hold office after attaining the age of 62 years[10]

- **Status of an Additional Judge[11] :** The mode of appointment and the qualifications for appointment of an Additional Judge are the same as those for appointment of a Permanent Judge. An Additional Judge discharges functions of the same character as a Permanent Judge. There is no difference in status, allowances, and other incidents of office except that an Additional Judge can hold office only for the period specified in the warrant of his appointment. Additional Judge is entitled to serve for the full period specified in his appointment. However, he can even be removed before the period specified in his appointment in the like manner and on the similar grounds as that of the Permanent Judge of the High Court.

Retired Judges[12]

Article 224A permits appointment of a retired Judge of a High Court to sit and act as Judge of that High Court.

- **Difference between Additional or Acting Judges and Retired Judges :** An Additional or Acting Judge under Article 224 is to be appointed by the President in view of arrears of work in a particular High Court. The President need not consult Chief Justice of India for this purpose[13]. On the other hand, the recall of a retired Judge is made by the Chief Justice of the High Court concerned, but with the consent of the President of India. The Chief Justice of India does not figure in this picture[14].
- The Retired Judge who sits and acts as a Judge of the High Court, is entitled to such allowances as the President may, by order determine. But he enjoys all the jurisdiction, powers, and privileges as that of a Permanent Judge.
- No retired Judge can be recalled until and unless he or she consents to do so.

Resignation of a Judge

A High Court Judge may resign from his office by writing to the President.

Removal of a Judge

A High Court Judge may be removed from his office in the same manner and on the same grounds as a Judge of the Supreme Court, i.e., on the two Houses of Parliament passing a resolution for his removal, by a special majority, for proved misbehaviour or incapacity.

Parliament has enacted the Judges (Inquiry) Act, 1968, to regulate the procedure for investigation of misbehaviour or incapacity of a High Court Judge and also provided the procedure for presenting an address by Parliament to the President for his removal. According to the Judges (Inquiry) Act, 1968 –

- In order to initiate a motion for the removal of a High Court Judge, a notice to that effect must be given by at least 100 members of the Lok Sabha, or 50 members of the Rajya Sabha.
- The Speaker or the Chairman may either admit or refuse to admit the motion. If it is admitted, then the Speaker/Chairman is to constitute a committee consisting of a Supreme Court Judge, a Chief Justice of a High Court, and a distinguished jurist. The Speaker and the Chairman can even jointly constitute a committee if the notices of the motion are given on the same day in both the Houses.

---

[10]Earlier it was 60 years. The age was increased to years by 15th Constitutional Amendment Act, 1963.

[11]Durga Das Basu, *Shorter Constitution of India*, Thirteenth Edition, Wadhwa and Company, 2003 P. 788.

[12]Durga Das Basu, *Shorter Constitution of India*, Thirteenth Edition, Wadhwa and Company, 2003 P. 789.

[13]*Supreme Court Advocates on-Record Association Vs. Union of India*, (1993) 4 SCC 441.

[14]Ibid.

- The committee frames the charges, conducts the inquiry, and prepares a report on the charges.
- The report of the committee must be laid before the Houses concerned.
- If the committee finds the Judge not guilty of the charges, then no further action is to be taken on the motion for his removal. But, if the committee finds the Judge to be guilty of misbehaviour or suffering from incapacity, then the House can take up consideration of the motion.
- If the motion is passed by each House of Parliament by special majority, an address may be presented to the President for removal of the Judge. Once the President passes the removal order, the Judge stands removed.

So far, judicial enquiry or impeachment motion has been initiated against very few Judges in the past. But no judge has so far been removed despite serious charges of misconduct or corruption as the process could not reach the conclusive stage for one or the other procedural reasons.

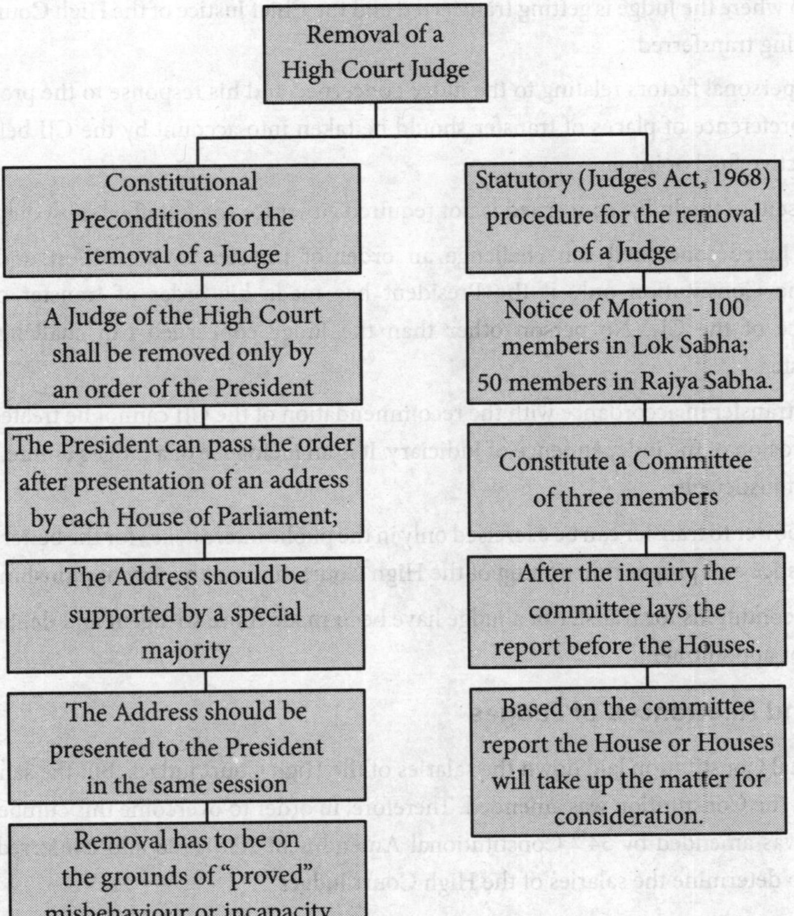

Transfer of a Judge from one High Court to another

Article 222(1) empowers the President after consultation with the Chief Justice of India to transfer a Judge from one High Court to any other High Court. Article 222(2) makes provisions for the grant of compensatory allowance to a Judge who goes on transfer to another High Court.

The Supreme Court of India has provided clarifications regarding the power and procedure regarding the transfer of the High Court Judges in the *Second Judges' case and Third Judges' case* as follows[15]:

- The President of India can transfer a Judge from one High Court to another only based on the recommendation given by the collegium consisting of CJI and four senior-most judges of the Supreme Court. With respect to the transfer of a judge, the opinion of the CJI is final and determinative.
- The CJI shall also form his opinion in consultation with the Chief Justice of that High Court from where the Judge is getting transferred and the Chief Justice of the High Court where a Judge is being transferred.
- The personal factors relating to the judge concerned and his response to the proposal including his preference of places of transfer should be taken into account by the CJI before forming an objective final opinion.
- Consent of the Judge concerned is not required either for the initial or subsequent transfer.
- The Judge concerned can challenge an order of transfer by a petition under Article 226 of the Constitution only if the President has made his order of transfer contrary to the advice of the CJI. No person other than the Judge concerned can challenge the order of transfer.
- Any transfer in accordance with the recommendation of the CJI cannot be treated as punitive or an erosion of the independence of Judiciary. It is an incidence of a Judge's tenure. Such a transfer is not justiciable.
- The power to transfer can be exercised only in the public interest, i.e., for the better administration of justice and proper functioning of the High Courts and not by way of punishment.

Thus, the conditions for transfer of a judge have been made more stringent and demanding than the conditions for appointment.

Salaries and Allowances of Judges

The original Constitution laid down the salaries of the High Court judges. But the same could not be varied unless the Constitution was amended. Therefore, in order to overcome this cumbersome process, Article 221 was amended by 54th Constitutional Amendment Act, 1986 and conferred the power on Parliament to determine the salaries of the High Court Judges[16].

---

[15] V.N. Shukla, *Constitution of India*, Eastern Book Company Thirteenth Edition, 2015, P. 658.

[16] V.N. Shukla, *Constitution of India*, Eastern Book Company, Thirteenth Edition, 2015, P. 656.

Even though the Judges of the High Court are Constitutional functionaries and are not treated as government servants (having no employer), their salaries are taxable under the Income Tax Act[17].

Salaries and allowances of judges are charged on the Consolidated Fund of the State and hence, are non-votable. Their pensions are also charged on the Consolidated Fund of India.

Officers and Expenses of a High Court

The officers and servants of a High Court are appointed by its Chief Justice, or such other judge or officer of the Court, as the Chief Justice may direct. However, this power of the Chief Justice is subject to any rules made by the Governor and any law made by the respective State Legislature.

The administrative expense of a High Court, including all salaries, allowances, and pensions' payable to or in respect of the officers and servants of the court, are charged upon the Consolidated Fund of the State. Further, any fees or other moneys taken by the court, form part of the Consolidated Fund of the State.

Restriction after Retirement

Article 220 prohibits a person who held office as a permanent Judge of a High Court from pleading in any court or before any authority in India, except the Supreme Court and the other High Courts. This prohibition is necessary in order to maintain the independence of the Judiciary.

Oath

Every High Court Judge before entering upon his office shall have to take an oath in the prescribed form administered by the Governor of that State or some person appointed by him for that purpose[18].

Jurisdiction and Powers of High Court

The High Court plays a very significant role in the scheme of administration of justice. Article 225 of the Constitution has laid down that the Jurisdiction and powers of the High Court shall be the same as immediately before the commencement of the Constitution. In other words, pre-constitution jurisdiction of the High Court is preserved. However, the pre-Constitutional jurisdiction of the High Court is subject to the provisions of the Constitution and any law made by the Parliament or the State Legislatures. Therefore, to a major extent, the High Court continues to enjoy the same powers and jurisdictions as they

---

[17] According to The High Court and Supreme Court Judges (Salaries and Conditions of Service) Amendment Act, 2018, the monthly salary of Chief Justice of High Court is Rs. 2,50,000/- and the monthly salary of the High Court Judge is Rs. 2,25,000/-.

[18] Form of oath or affirmation to be made by the Judges of a High Court (As given in the Third Schedule): —

"I, A.B., having been appointed Chief Justice (or a Judge) of the High Court at (or of) ....do swear in the name of God that I will bear true faith and allegiance to the Constitution of India as by law established, that I will uphold the sovereignty and integrity of India,] that I will duly and faithfully and to the best of my ability, knowledge and judgment perform the duties of my office without fear or favour, affection or ill-will and that I will uphold the Constitution and the laws."

used to enjoy before the commencement of the Constitution. But the two major restrictions suffered by the High Court before the commencement of the Constitution have been removed by the Constitution.

Following are the two important changes that have been introduced with respect to the pre-Constitutional jurisdictions of the High Court:

- All or any restrictions imposed on the original jurisdiction of the High Court regarding a revenue matter will cease to operate.
- Prior to the Constitution, only three High Courts at Calcutta, Bombay, and Madras had the powers to issue writs under their original jurisdiction. After the commencement of the Constitution, Article 226 conferred the power to issue writs to all the High Courts within their territorial jurisdiction equally.

Thus, the High Courts in India enjoy Civil as well as criminal, ordinary as well as extraordinary, and original as well as appellate jurisdictions. Following are the powers and jurisdictions enjoyed by the High Courts in India.

Court of Record

According to Article 215, 'A High Court is a Court of record'. As a Court of record, the High Court has the following powers :

- It has the power to preserve its original record in perpetuity;
- It has power to determine the question about its own jurisdiction; and
- It has inherent power to punish for its contempt. The power to punish for contempt under Article 215 is limited to contempt of High Court or its subordinate courts. High Court lacks power under Article 215 to initiate proceedings for contempt of Supreme Court.
- The words 'Contempt of court' is not defined in the Constitution. However, it is dealt by the Contempt of Courts Act, 1971. Contempt can be civil as well as criminal in nature. The Act defines civil contempt as "wilful disobedience to any judgment, decree, order, or other processes of a court, etc. or wilful breach of an undertaking given to a court". Whereas, criminal contempt is defined as "the publication (whether by words, spoken or written, or by signs, or by visible representation, or otherwise) of any matter or the doing of any other act whatsoever which

  (i) scandalises or lowers or tends to lower the authority of, any court; or

  (ii) interferes or tends to interfere with, the due course of any judicial proceeding; or

  (iii) interferes or tends to interfere with, or obstructs or tends to obstruct, the administration of justice in any other manner;"

  However, innocent publication, distribution of matter, and reasonable and fair criticism of judicial acts and comments on the administrative side of the Judiciary does not amount to contempt of the court.

Power of Superintendence

Every High Court under Article 227 has the power of superintendence over all courts and tribunals within its territorial jurisdiction, except those which are related to the armed forces. This power of superintendence and control over all subordinate courts and tribunals is both of administrative and judicial nature, and, such power could be exercised *suo moto* ('on its own'). The power and duty of the High Court under Article 227 is to ensure that the courts and tribunals, inferior to the High Court, have done what they are required to do. The power of superintendence includes the:

- The power to call returns from the courts;
- To make and issue general rules regulating the practice and proceedings of such courts; and
- Prescribe forms in which books, entries, and accounts are to be kept by the officers of such courts.

The power of superintendence does not imply that the High Court can influence the subordinate Judiciary to pass any order or judgment in a particular manner. The power of High Court under Article 227 can be invoked sparingly and when there is no other remedy available. Following can be the grounds for interference –

- Want or exceeding jurisdiction
- Failure to exercise jurisdiction
- Violation of principles of natural justice
- An error apparent on the face of record, etc.

Ordinary Original Jurisdiction

Original jurisdiction in relation to High Court refers to the authority of the High Court to hear and decide cases in the first instance itself, i.e., not by way of an appeal.

Every High Court has ordinary original jurisdiction in the following matters :

(i) Revenue
(ii) Admiralty
(iii) Matrimony
(iv) Probate
(v) Contempt of court
(vi) Election petitions
(vii) Company and
(viii) Guardianship

- **Ordinary Original Civil Jurisdiction**

  In India, only five High Courts, i.e., High Courts of Delhi, Bombay, Calcutta, Madras, and Himachal Pradesh have ordinary original civil jurisdiction in case of higher values. The remaining High Courts only have appellate jurisdiction with respect to civil matters, i.e., they can hear appeals from the subordinate courts.

- **Ordinary Original Criminal Jurisdiction**

  At the time of commencement of the Constitution, certain High Courts such as Bombay, Madras, and Kolkata enjoyed original criminal jurisdiction as well. However, the original criminal jurisdiction of the High Court has been abolished by the Criminal Procedure Code, 1973.

Appellate Jurisdiction

- **Civil Appellate Jurisdiction**
  * In civil cases, appeal can be made to the High Court against the decisions of the District Judges and the Subordinate Judges. These are called 'First Appeals'.
  * When any court subordinate to the High Court decides an appeal from the decision of an inferior court, a 'Second Appeal' can be made to the High Court only on question of law and procedure.
  * Intra-court appeals lie from the decision of a single Judge of the High Court to the Division Bench of the concerned High Court. This power is enjoyed by Bombay, Madras, and Calcutta High Courts.
- **Criminal Appellate Jurisdiction**
  * In criminal cases, appeals lie against the decisions of a Sessions Judge or an Additional Sessions Judge, where the sentence is of imprisonment exceeding 7 years.
  * According to Section 366 of Criminal Procedure Code, 1973, no death sentence imposed by a Sessions Court can be executed unless the punishment is confirmed by the High Court.
  * Appeals can even lie against the decisions of Assistant Sessions Judge, Metropolitan Magistrate, or other Judicial Magistrates in certain specified cases other than 'petty offences' as mentioned in the Criminal Procedure Code, 1973.

Transfer of Certain Cases to High Courts

Under Article 228, the High Court has power to withdraw a case to itself from a subordinate court, if it is satisfied that a case pending in a subordinate court involves a substantial question of law regarding the interpretation of the Constitution. It may then, either dispose of the case itself, or may determine only the Constitutional law point and return the case to the subordinate court for disposal in conformity with the High Court's judgement on the Constitutional point.

Power of Review

There is no provision in the Constitution to confer on the High Court the power to review its own decisions. But the Supreme Court has ruled that a High Court being a Superior Court has inherent power to review its own decisions.

Writ Jurisdiction/Extraordinary Original Jurisdiction

The Writs have been among the greatest safeguards provided by the judicial system for upholding the rights and liberties of the people. It was an act of great wisdom and foresight on the part of the Constitution-makers to introduce the writ system in India, and thus, constitute the High Courts into guardians of the people's rights[19]. Article 226 of the Constitution confers a power on all the High Courts of India which they did not enjoy before the commencement of the Constitution. It enables the High Courts to issue to any person or government authority any order or writs for the enforcement of

[19] M.P. Jain, *Indian Constitutional Law*, LexisNexis, Eighth Edition, P. 424.

any of the Fundamental Rights or for the enforcement of any other legal right. The High Court can issue writs in the nature of Habeas Corpus, Quo Warranto, Mandamus, Certiorari, Prohibition, etc. under Article 226.

Relationship between Article 32 and 226

- Article 226 and 32 exist independently of each other.
- Article 226 is wider in scope than Article 32. Under Article 32, the Supreme Court can issue writs for the enforcement of Fundamental Rights only. Whereas, a High Court can issue a writ under Article 226 not only for the enforcement of Fundamental Rights, but also for any other legal right.

The nature of the proceedings under Article 226 can be either civil or criminal depending upon the questions raised. Under Article 226, the High Court does not sit or act as a court of appeal over the actions of the subordinate courts or authorities or tribunals. The power enjoyed by the High Court under Article 226 is judicial review power and the jurisdiction is supervisory in nature. The said Article confers very wide powers on the High Courts in the matter of issuing writs.

There are only two limitations placed upon the writ jurisdiction of a High Court:

- The writs issued by the Court cannot run beyond the territorial jurisdiction of the concerned state.
- The person or authority to whom the writs are to be issued must be within the territory of the concerned state or the cause of action arose whole or in part, within the territorial jurisdiction of the State.

In a landmark judgment in *L. Chandra Kumar Vs. Union of India*[20], the Supreme Court has held that the writ jurisdiction under Article 226 and the judicial review power of the High Courts are part of the basic structure of the Constitution and therefore, it cannot be amended or ousted even by way of a Constitutional amendment.

Judicial Review

Judicial review is the doctrine under which Legislative and Executive action is subject to invalidation by the Judiciary if and when the action is found to be violative of the provisions of the Constitution and the laws made there under.

The Indian Courts have propounded the doctrine of judicial review in order to:

(a) Check the abuse of power

(b) Guard against discrimination

(c) Ensure equal treatment.

In India, Judicial Review is a part of the basic structure of the Constitution. Therefore, it is inviolable and unamenable to amendment by the Parliament under Article 368 of the Constitution. The Doctrine of Judicial Review is implicit in several Article such as 13, 32, 131–136, 143, 226, and 246.

Broadly speaking, judicial review in India comprises of three aspects :

- judicial review of legislative action,
- judicial review of judicial decisions; and
- judicial review of administrative action.

---

[20] 1995 SCC (1) 400

Thus, the power of judicial review enjoyed by the High Courts and the Supreme Court is important to ensure that the balance of power envisaged by the Constitution is maintained and that the Legislature and the Executive do not, in the discharge of functions, transgress the Constitutional limitations.

Bypassing the High Courts

Bypassing the High Court or debarring it from entertaining a dispute involving the question of Constitutional validity of any law, in other words, taking away the power of judicial review would be directly hitting the basic structure of the Constitution. It would amount to denying a Constitutional remedy to the aggrieved party. The power of judicial review vested in the High Court assumes greater significance when the matters involving the State as one of the litigants are large in number. The High Courts have unquestionable power of superintendence and control over the tribunals under the Constitution.

In *L. Chandra Kumar Vs. Union of India*[21], the Supreme Court ruled that any law or Act, which excludes the jurisdiction of the High Court under Articles 226, 227, and of the Supreme Court under Article 32 of the Constitution as unconstitutional. All decisions of the tribunals in a State will be subject to scrutiny before a Division Bench of the High Court within whose jurisdiction the concerned tribunal falls. The result of this judgment is that an appeal cannot be filed directly before the Supreme Court bypassing the judicial review power and judicial superintendence power of the High Court under Article 226 and 227. The Court held that the power vested in the High Courts to exercise judicial superintendence over the decisions of all Courts and tribunals within their respective jurisdictions is also part of the basic structure of the Constitution.

Independence of the High Courts

Independence of Judiciary is an essential attribute of Rule of Law.

There are various provisions in the Constitution which tries to protect and safeguard the independence of the Judiciary.

- The judges of the High Court are appointed for the fixed tenure and the process to remove them before the age of retirement is difficult and tardy.
- The expenses of a High Court are charged on the Consolidated Fund of the State.
- The conduct of a High Court Judge in discharge of his duties cannot be discussed in the State Legislature or Parliament, except when a motion for his removal is under consideration.
- The allowances, leave, and pension of a High Court Judge are determined by Parliament by law, but these cannot be varied to his/her judgement.
- After retirement, a permanent High Court Judge shall not plead or act in a Court or before any authority in India, except the Supreme Court and a High Court other than the High Court in which he has held office.
- The jurisdiction of a High Court in so far as it is specified in the Constitution, as for example, Article 226, 227, etc., cannot be curtailed by the Legislature. In other respects, however, the matter of jurisdiction has been left to the Parliament and the State Legislature(s).
- If a State law derogates or tries to derogate the Constitutional position of the High Court, then the Bill has to be reserved by the Governor for Presidential Assent. Moreover, the constitution and organization of the High Court fall under the Legislative sphere of Parliament and thus, the High Courts have been largely insulated from local influences.

[21] 1995 SCC (1) 400

LIST OF HIGH COURTS

S. No.	Name	Year	Territorial Jurisdiction	Seat
1.	Kolkata	1862	West Bengal, Andaman & Nicobar Islands	Kolkata (Bench of Port Blair)
2.	Bombay	1862	Maharastra, Dadar, & Nagar Haveli. Goa, Daman Diu	Mumbai (Bench at Panaji, Aurangabad, and Nagpur)
3.	Chennai	1862	Tamil Nadu & Pondicherry	Chennai (Bench at Madurai)
4.	Allahabad	1866	Uttar Pradesh	Allahabad (Bench at Lucknow)
5.	Karnataka	1884	Karnataka	Bengaluru (Bench at Dharwad and Gulbarga)
6.	Patna	1916	Bihar	Patna
7.	Jammu & Kashmir	1928	Jammu & Kashmir, Ladakh	Sri Nagar & Jammu
8.	Punjab & Haryana	1947	Punjab, Haryana, Chandigarh	Chandigarh
9.	Guwahati	1948	Assam, Nagaland, Mizoram, and Arunachal Pradesh	Guwahati (Bench at Kohima, Aizawl, and Itanagar)
10.	Orissa	1948	Orissa	Cuttack
11.	Rajasthan	1949	Rajasthan	Jodhpur (Bench – Jaipur)
12.	Madhya Pradesh	1956	Madhya Pradesh	Jabalpur (Bench - Indore, Gwalior)
13.	Kerala	1958	Kerala & Lakshadweep	Ernakulam
14.	Gujarat	1960	Gujarat	Ahmedabad
15.	Delhi	1966	Delhi	Delhi
16.	Himachal Pradesh	1966	Himachal Pradesh	Shimla
17.	Sikkim	1975	Sikkim	Gangtok
18.	Chhattisgarh	2000	Chhattisgarh	Bilaspur
19.	Uttarakhand	2000	Uttarakhand	Nainital
20.	Jharkhand	2000	Jharkhand	Ranchi
21.	Tripura	2013	Tripura	Agartala
22.	Manipur	2013	Manipur	Imphal
23.	Meghalaya	2013	Meghalaya	Shillong
24.	Andhra Pradesh	2019	Andhra Pradesh	Amaravati
25.	Telangana	2019	Telangana	Hyderabad

QUESTIONS

Subjective Questions

1. Discuss the various kinds of jurisdictions and powers enjoyed by the High Court.
2. 'Any person aggrieved by an order of an appellate tribunal cannot directly appeal to the Supreme Court, side-stepping the High Court'. Critically examine this statement.

Objective Questions

1. With reference to the Constitution of India, consider the following statements:

   1. No High Court shall have the jurisdiction to declare any Central law to be Constitutionally invalid.
   2. An amendment to the Constitution of India cannot be called into question by the Supreme Court of India.

   Which of the statements given above is/are correct?

   (a) 1 only (b) 2 only

   (c) Both 1 and 2 (d) Neither 1 nor 2

   Ans: (d)

2. With respect to the service conditions of the judges of a High Court, consider the following statements:

   1. He subscribes oath before the President of India.
   2. He can resign from office by writing to the Governor.

   Which of the statements given above is/are correct?

   (a) 1 only (b) 2 only

   (c) Both 1 and 2 (d) Neither 1 nor 2

   Ans: (d)

3. With respect to the writ jurisdiction, consider the following statements:

   1. The writ jurisdiction of a High Court is wider than that of the Supreme Court.
   2. A High Court may refuse to exercise its writ jurisdiction in case of violation of a Fundamental Right.
   3. Parliament can empower any court other than the Supreme Court or High Courts to issue writs.

   Which of the statements given above is/are correct?

   (a) 3 only (b) 2 and 3 only

   (c) 1, 2, and 3 (d) 1 and 2 only

   Ans: (c)

4. In India we have an integrated judicial system. It implies:

   1. There is a hierarchy of courts with Supreme Court at the apex.
   2. The High Courts and subordinate courts enforce both the Central and State laws.
   3. President appoints Judges of a High Court.

   Which of the statements given above is/are correct?

   (a) 1 only (b) 1, 2, and 3

   (c) 2 and 3 only (d) 1 and 2 only

   Ans: (b)

5. With reference to the power of judicial review of High Courts, consider the following statements:
   1. High Court can review the laws enacted by state Legislatures only and not the ones enacted by the Centre.
   2. High Court cannot interpret the Constitution while reviewing any law or order passed by the government, as Supreme Court is the sole interpreter of the Constitution.

   Which of the statements given above is/are correct?

   (a) 1 only (b) 2 only
   (c) Both 1 and 2 (d) Neither 1 nor 2

   Ans: (d)
6. With reference to the expenditure 'charged' upon the Consolidated Fund of India, consider the following statements:
   1. It can neither be discussed nor be voted by the Parliament.
   2. Salaries, allowances and pensions of the judges of the High Court are included under it.

   Which of the statements given above is/are correct?

   (a) 1 only (b) 2 only
   (c) Both 1 and 2 (d) Neither 1 nor 2

   Ans: (d)
7. With respect to the powers of a High Court, consider the following statements:
   1. It must confirm a death sentence awarded by a subordinate court even if it is not appealed before it.
   2. It has the power to review and correct its own judgement.

   Which of the statements given above is/are correct?

   (a) 1 only (b) 2 only
   (c) Both 1 and 2 (d) Neither 1 nor 2

   Ans: (c)
8. With reference to appointments of judges to a High Court, consider the following statements:
   1. A distinguished jurist in the opinion of the President can be appointed as a judge of a High Court.
   2. An Indian citizen who has practiced law for ten years as an advocate in one or more High Courts can be appointed as a judge in a High Court.

   Which of the statements given above is/are correct?

   (a) 1 only (b) 2 only
   (c) Both 1 and 2 (d) Neither 1 nor 2

   Ans: (b)
9. The transfer of Judges from one High Court to another is done by:

   (a) Chief Justice of India only
   (b) Governor after consulting Chief Justice of India
   (c) Chief Justice of India after consulting concerned Chief Justice of High Court
   (d) President after consulting Chief Justice of India

   Ans: (d)

STATE JUDICIARY

SUBORDINATE JUDICIARY

Subordinate Judiciary consists of a system of courts in a State below the High Court. Articles 233 to 237 deals with organization of the subordinate courts and also provides provisions to ensure the independence of the subordinate judges.

The subordinate judiciary constitutes a very important segment of the judicial system as it is in these courts that the judiciary comes in close contact with the people. It is therefore, essential to maintain the independence and integrity of the subordinate judiciary and for this purpose, Articles 233 to 237 have been placed in the Constitution. These Articles have been so interpreted by the Supreme Court as to strengthen the control of the High Court on the subordinate judiciary[1]

Before analyzing the provisions in the Constitution regarding the subordinate judiciary, it is necessary to understand the structure and hierarchy of subordinate courts below the High Courts.

SYSTEM OF COURTS IN INDIA

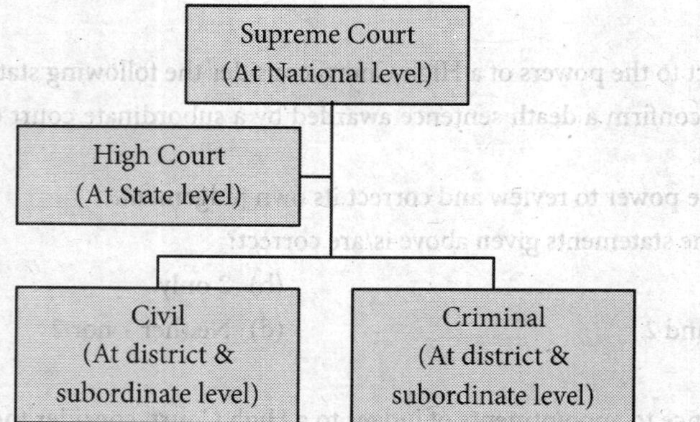

Judicial process involved in the District or subordinate courts :

- A right claimed or a wrong complained by one party against the other.
- Hearing of the parties by the Court.
- Judgment of the Court delivered at the end of the trial.
- Execution of the operative part of the judgment.

Organisation of the Courts Below High Court

Civil Courts subordinate to the High Court	Criminal Courts subordinate to the High Court
Administers civil justice; Civil justice is remedial and is concerned with enforcement of rights.	Criminal Justice is punitive and is concerned with punishing the offenders.
Proceedings in Civil Courts are regulated by Civil Procedure Code.	Proceedings in Criminal Courts are regulated by Criminal Procedure Code.

[1]M.P. Jain P. 487.

Civil Courts Subordinate to the High Court

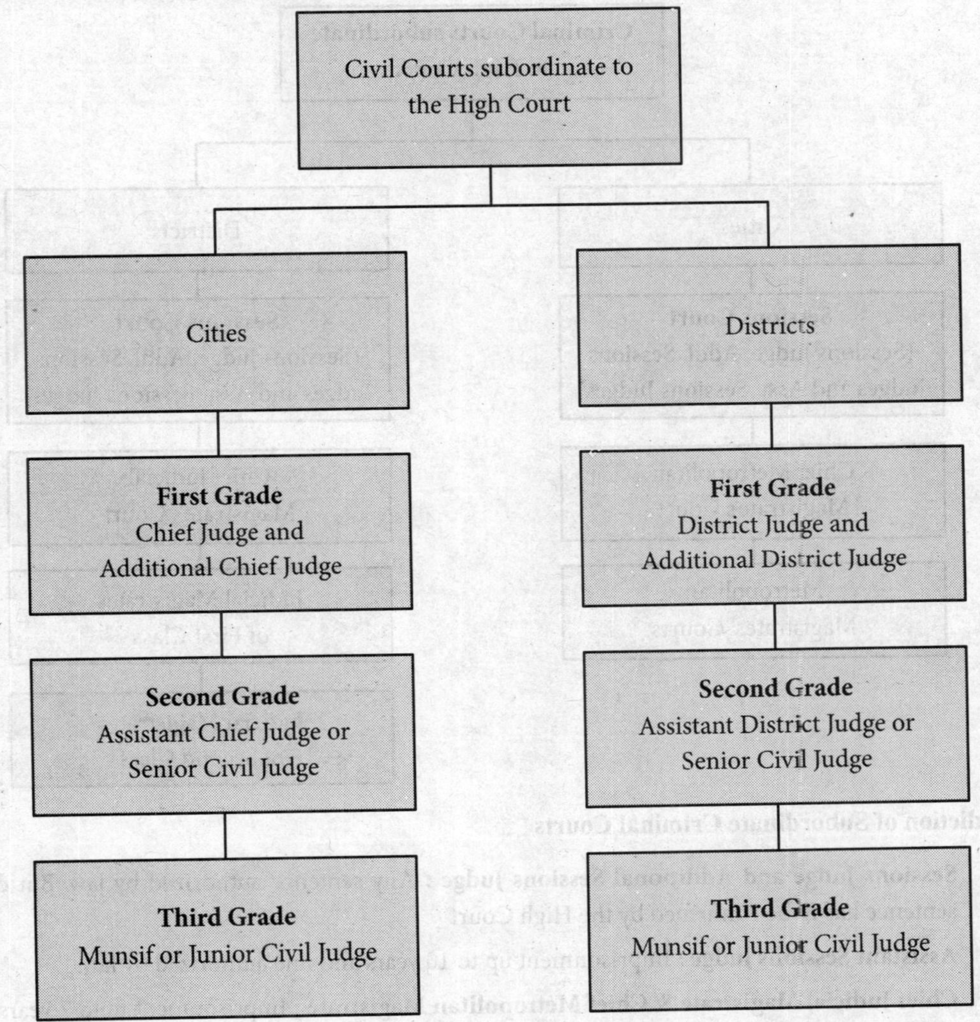

- **District Judge :** Head of civil justice administration in the district.
- **Chief Judge :** Head of civil justice administration in the city.
- **Additional Chief Judges and Additional District Judges :** Assist the Chief Judge and District Judge in administering civil justice.
- Judges of First grade and Second grade possess both original and appellate jurisdiction.
- Judges of First grade may be conferred with revisional powers also.
- Munsif or Junior Civil Judge enjoys only limited pecuniary jurisdiction.
- **Small Cause Courts :** Are constituted under the Provincial Small Cause Courts Act. Matters of small nature, not involving questions of title are tried by Small Cause Courts. Procedures followed by these courts are simpler and shorter than that of an ordinary civil court.

Criminal Courts Subordinate to the High Court

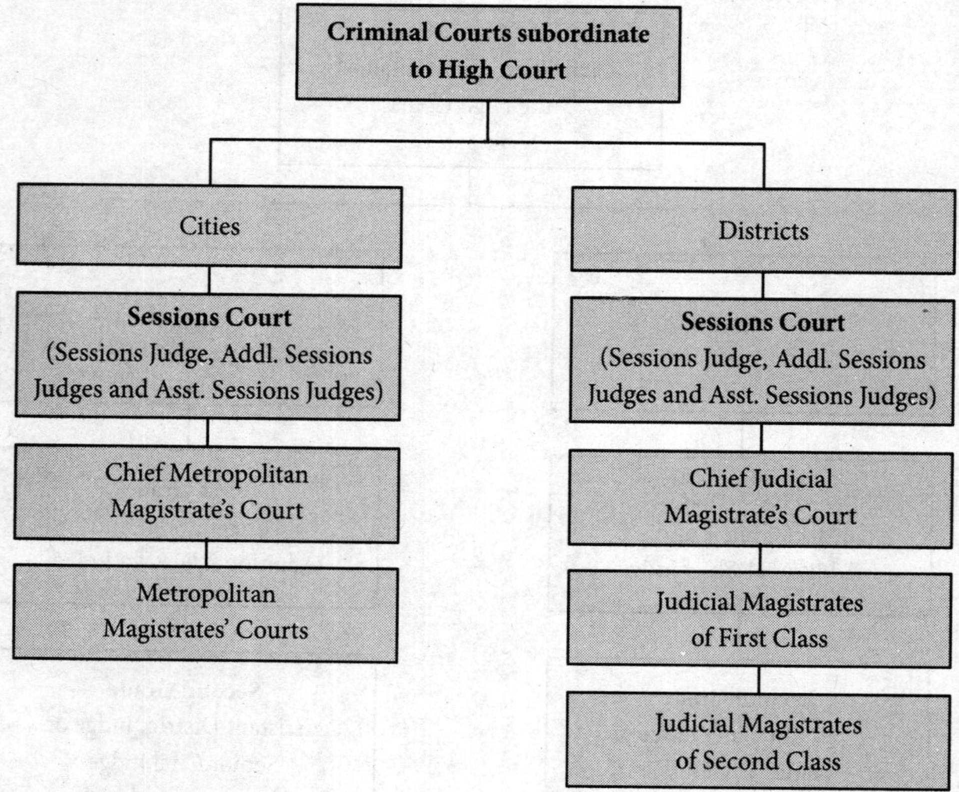

Jurisdiction of Subordinate Criminal Courts

- **Sessions Judge and Additional Sessions Judge :** Any sentence authorized by law. But death sentence has to be confirmed by the High Court
- **Assistant Sessions Judge :** Imprisonment up to 10 years and fine authorized by law.
- **Chief Judicial Magistrate & Chief Metropolitan Magistrate :** Imprisonment upto 7 years and fine authorized by law.
- **Judicial Magistrate of first class & Metropolitan Magistrate :** Imprisonment upto 3 years and fine not exceeding Rs. 10000.
- **Judicial Magistrate of second class :** Imprisonment upto 1 year and fine not exceeding Rs. 5000

Expressions used in Judicial Services

District Judge : The expression 'District Judge' includes judge of a city civil court, Additional District Judge, Joint District Judge, Assistant District Judge, Chief Judge of a small cause court, Chief Presidency Magistrate, Additional Chief Presidency Magistrate, Sessions Judge, Additional Sessions Judge, and Assistant Sessions Judge.

Judicial Service : 'Judicial Service' means a service consisting exclusively of persons intended to fill the post of District Judge and other civil judicial posts inferior to the post of District Judge.

CONSTITUTIONAL PROVISIONS REGARDING STATE JUDICIAL SERVICE

Appointment of District Judges

Article 233 provides that the appointment, posting, and promotion of District Judges shall be made by the Governor of the State in consultation with the High Court.

There are two ways of appointment according to Article 233 –

- Appointing/Promoting a person who is in service of the Union or the State as the District Judge (233(1)).
- Appointing a person who is not in the service of the Union or the State as the District Judge (233(2)).

The initial appointment or initial promotion of a person as a District Judge shall be made by the Governor in consultation with the High Court. But the posting of a District Judge after appointment and subsequent transfers are in the hands of the High Court alone.

Person who is in service

Appointment or promotion of a person who is in service of the Union or the State as the District Judge shall be made on the basis of seniority of officers. Seniority of officers appointed under Article 233(1) will be determined by the Service Rules made under Article 309.

Person who is not in service

A person not already in the service of the Union or of the State shall only be eligible to be appointed as a District Judge if he fulfills two conditions, namely:

- He must be an advocate or a pleader for 7 years; and
- His name is recommended by the High Court for appointment.

In *State of Kerala Vs. A. Lakshmikutty*[2], the Supreme Court has elaborately discussed the respective roles of the Government and the High Court in the matter of appointment of District Judges –

- The power of the State Government to appoint District Judges is not absolute and unfettered but is hedged in with restrictions. The power is conditioned by the requirement of 'consultation' with the High Court.
- The power of appointment is an executive function of the Government.
- The eligibility for appointment as a District Judge by the direct recruitment depends entirely on the High Court's recommendation. The State Government cannot appoint anyone from outside the panel of names forwarded by the High Court.
- 'Consultation' between the High Court and the State Government, must be "real, full, and effective". In other words, there must be an interchange of view between the High Court and the State Government.
- Normally, as a matter of rule, the recommendation of the High Court for appointment as a District Judge should be accepted by the State Government. If, in any particular case, the State Government for "good and weighty" reasons finds it difficult to accept the recommendations of the High Court, the same should be communicated to the High Court by the Government.

Therefore, it can be understood that a person can be appointed to the post of District Judge by the Governor only in consultation with the High Court.

---

[2]AIR 1987 SC 331.

Appointment of Subordinate Judges/other than District Judges

Below the District Courts, there are other subordinate courts. While Article 233 deals with the recruitment of Judges to the District Court, Article 234 deals with the recruitment of members other than District Judge, i.e., judges to the subordinate courts. According to Article 234, appointment of persons, other than District Judges, to the State Judicial Service is made by the Governor in accordance with the rules made by him for the purpose after consultation with the State Public Service Commission and the High Court.

High Courts Control over District and Subordinate Courts

According to Article 235, the control over district and subordinate courts is vested in the High Court, including the posting and promotion of, and the grant of leave to, persons belonging to the State Judicial Service, and holding a post inferior to that of a District Judge.

ALTERNATIVE DISPUTE RESOLUTION

The Judiciary or Courts of law are confronted with four main problems which are as follows:

(i) Low number of courts and judges in all grades

(ii) Increase in the number of cases owing to the various State and Central Acts

(iii) Huge costs involved in prosecuting or defending a case

(iv) Cumbersome and time-consuming process because of the procedural laws and huge number of already pending cases

To overcome the above said problems, Alternative Dispute Resolution (ADR) was developed. ADR provides scientifically developed techniques to the Indian judiciary which helps in reducing the burden on the courts. The ADR aims at checking litigation explosion, making the justice system less expensive and easily accessible to the illiterate and indigent. ADR provides various modes of settlement including arbitration, conciliation, mediation, and negotiation. ADR therefore ensures that only important constitutional matters are dealt by the Superior Courts.

Following are the models of ADR that exist for dispute-redressal at the national level:

- Fast Track Courts
- Lok Adalats
- Tribunals, commissions, boards, etc.
- Gram Nyayalya
- Arbitration
- Conciliation
- Ombudsman
- Family Courts

Fast Track Courts

Fast Track Courts (FTCs) are special kind of courts which have exclusive jurisdiction over a particular category of law. The main objective of fast track courts in India is to provide speedy justice to a large number of pending cases in a specified time. Judges for the Fast Track Courts are appointed on ad hoc basis and retired judges are eligible for selection.

History

Fast track courts were introduced in India in the year 2000 in order to reduce the burden of cases from high courts and district courts and also to provide speedy justice. The 11th Finance Commission recommended the creation of 1734 fast track courts across the country on an experimental period of five years. Out of this, only 1562 were functional by 2005, the year when this experimental scheme was supposed to end. The central government in 2005, decided to continue its support for the 1562 functional FTCs for the next 6 years (till 2011). By the end of 2011, only 1192 FTCs were functional. The December 16, 2012, gang-rape and subsequent death of a young physiotherapy student changed everything. It gave fast track courts a new lease of life. The central government further extended the deadline to March 2015.

Scheme on Fast Track Special Courts (FTSCS), 2019

Heinous crimes against women, especially against minor girls below the age of twelve shook the conscience of the entire nation. To prevent such crimes, stricter laws and harsher punishments were introduced through 'the Criminal Law (Amendment) Act, 2018'. However, in order to create deterrence, the trial in the court should be completed within the time frame and justice should be delivered as expeditiously as possible to the victims. Therefore, the central government proposed to set up 1023 Fast Track Special Courts (FTSCs) as a part of National Mission for Safety of Women (NMSW). FSTCs will be set up in different states based on pendency of subject cases obtained from various High Courts for fast and time- bound trial and disposal of pending cases related to rape and POCSO (Protection of Children from Sexual Offences) Act. Out of 1023 FTSCs, 389 Courts have been proposed to be set up exclusively for POCSO Act related cases in Districts where pendency of such cases are more than 100.

Lok Adalats

The word 'Lok Adalat' means 'People's Court. Lok Adalat is another alternative to judicial justice. This is a strategy for delivering informal, cheap, and expeditious justice to the common man by way of settling disputes, which are pending in courts and also those, which have not yet reached courts by negotiations, conciliation, and by adopting persuasive, common sense, and human approach to the problems of the disputants.

Characteristics of Lok Adalat[3]

- It is one of the alternative dispute redressal mechanisms;
- It is a forum where disputes/cases pending in the court of law or at pre-litigation stage are settled/ compromised amicably;
- Lok Adalats have been given statutory status under the Legal Services Authorities Act, 1987;
- The award/decision made by the Lok Adalats is deemed to be a decree of a civil court and is final and binding on all parties and no appeal against such an award lies before any court of law. If the parties are not satisfied with the award of the Lok Adalat (though there is no provision for an appeal against such an award), the parties are free to initiate litigation by approaching the court of appropriate jurisdiction by filing a case by following the required procedure, in exercise of their right to litigate.

[3] https://nalsa.gov.in/lok-adalat

- There is no court fee payable when a matter is filed in a Lok Adalat. If a matter pending in the court of law is referred to the Lok Adalat and is settled subsequently, the court fee originally paid in the court on the complaints/petition is also refunded back to the parties.
- The persons deciding the cases in the Lok Adalats are called the Members of the Lok Adalats. They have the role of statutory conciliators/mediators only and do not have any judicial role. In other words, they cannot be called as judges. Therefore, they can only persuade the parties to come to a conclusion for settling the dispute outside the court in the Lok Adalat and shall not pressurize or coerce any of the parties to compromise or settle cases or matters either directly or indirectly.

Nature of Cases to be Referred to Lok Adalat

Lok Adalats have the competence to deal with the following cases:

- Compoundable civil, revenue, and criminal cases.
- Motor accident cases
- Partition claims
- Matrimonial and family disputes
- Bonded Labour disputes
- Land acquisition disputes
- Bank's unpaid loan cases
- Arrears of retirement benefits cases
- Cases which are not under the jurisdiction of any court

Powers of The Lok Adalats

The powers bestowed on Lok Adalats are as follows:

- Power to summon and enforce the attendance of any witness and to examine him/her on oath
- Power to enforce the discovery and production of any document
- Power to receive evidence on affidavits
- Power for requisitioning of any public record or document or copy thereof from any court
- Power to specify its own procedure for the determination of any dispute coming before it

Levels and Composition of Lok Adalat – A Four Tier System

- **At the National Level**

  National Level Lok Adalats are held at regular intervals where on a single day. Lok Adalats are held throughout the country, in all the courts right from the Supreme Court till the Taluk levels wherein cases are disposed off in huge numbers. From February 2015, National Lok Adalats are being held on a specific subject matter every month.
- **At the State Authority Level**

  The Member Secretary of the State Legal Services Authority organizing the Lok Adalat would constitute benches of the Lok Adalat, each bench comprising of a sitting or retired judge of the

High Court or a sitting or retired judicial officer and any one or both of—a member from the legal profession; a social worker engaged in the upliftment of the weaker sections and interested in the implementation of legal services schemes or programmes.

- **At District Level**

  The Secretary of the District Legal Services Authority organizing the Lok Adalat would constitute benches of the Lok Adalat, each bench comprising of a sitting or retired judicial officer and any one or both of either a member from the legal profession; and/or a social worker engaged in the upliftment of the weaker sections and interested in the implementation of legal services schemes or programmes or a person engaged in paralegal activities of the area, preferably a woman.

- **At Taluk Level**

  The Secretary of the Taluk Legal Services Committee organizing the Lok Adalat would constitute benches of the Lok Adalat, each bench comprising of a sitting or retired judicial officer and any one or both of either a member from the legal profession; and/or a social worker engaged in the upliftment of the weaker sections and interested in the implementation of legal services schemes or programmes or a person engaged in paralegal activities of the area, preferably a woman.

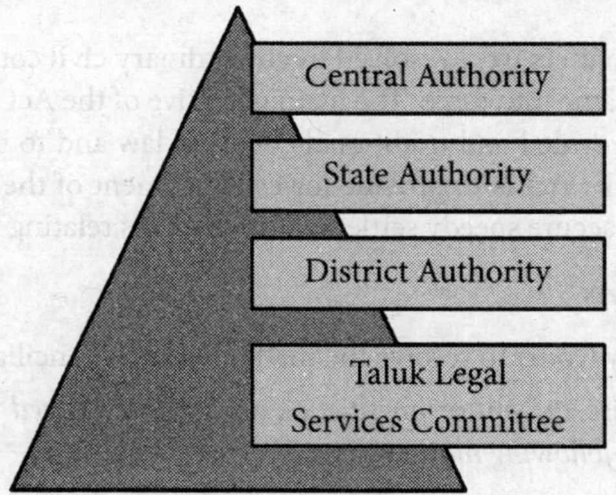

Permanent Lok Adalats

The Legal Services Authorities Act, 1987, which had established Lok Adalats, did not, at first, establish Permanent Lok Adalat. It was the Amendment Act of 2002 that enabled the establishment of the first Permanent Lok Adalat under Section 22B of the Act.

Salient Features of Permanent Lok Adalats

- Permanent Lok Adalats have been set up as permanent bodies with a Chairman and two members for providing compulsory pre-litigative mechanism for conciliation and settlement of cases relating to public utility services.

  The following public utility services come under the preview of Permanent Lok Adalats:

  * transport services of passengers or goods by air, road, and water
  * postal, telegraph, or telephone services
  * supply of power, light, or water to the public by any establishment
  * system of public conservancy or sanitation
  * services in hospitals or dispensaries and
  * insurance services, etc.

- Here, even if the parties fail to reach to a settlement, the Permanent Lok Adalat gets jurisdiction to decide the dispute, provided, the dispute does not relate to any offence.
- The award of the Permanent Lok Adalat is final and binding on all the parties.
- The jurisdiction of the Permanent Lok Adalats is upto Rs. One Crore.
- The Lok Adalat may conduct the proceedings in such a manner as it considers appropriate, taking into account the circumstances of the case, wishes of the parties, like requests to hear oral statements, speedy settlement of dispute, etc.

The basic features of a permanent Lok Adalat are identical to a Lok Adalat. There are, however, certain differences. The key difference is that a typical Lok Adalat can only be summoned occasionally and not on a daily basis. A Permanent Lok Adalat is an established system which is operational throughout just like any other court or Tribunal. Moreover, in Lok Adalats, if the parties fail to arrive at any compromise or settlement, then the parties have a choice to file the case before ordinary courts of law. Whereas, in Permanent Lok Adalats, if the parties fail to reach a settlement, then the Permanent Lok Adalat gets the power to decide and dispose of the case.

Family Courts

Prior to 1984, all family matters were resolved by the ordinary civil court judges. In 1984, the Family Courts Act was passed and came into force. The main objective of the Act was to take family and marital disputes out from the overcrowded and traditional courts of law and to bring them into a sympathetic surrounding. The object of the Act is to provide for establishment of the Family Courts with a view to promote conciliation in and secure speedy settlement of disputes relating to marriage and family affairs.

Jurisdiction of Family Courts

It is the duty of the Family Court to resolve the matter through conciliation and settlement.

The Family Courts exercise the entire jurisdiction which is exercised by any District Court or any subordinate civil court in the following matters -

- Matrimonial cases
- Maintenance and alimony of spouses
- Custody and guardianship of children
- Settlement of spousal property

Power of the Family Court

- The Family Court has the power to make its own procedure.
- They are not required to record the oral statement of the witness at length.
- The Family Court can receive any document or statement even if it is not admissible under Indian Evidence Act, 1872.
- Provisions of the Code of Civil Procedure, 1908 are applied for the enforcement of the order of the Family Court.

Appeal

The appeal from Family Courts lies directly to the High Court within 30 days of passing the order or the judgment. Such appeal can be on both question of law and question of fact. However, no appeal lies against an order which is passed with the consent of the parties.

Gram Nyayalaya

The Gram Nyayalya Act, which was enacted by Parliament in 2008 and came into effect in October 2009, mandates setting up of village courts. The Act aims at making justice easily accessible to the rural population and dealing with the backlog of cases. Besides providing speedy justice which is accessible to the residents of villages, it also aims to provide cost-effective justice. Gram Nyayalaya is a mobile court and exercises the powers of both Criminal and Civil Courts, i.e., the seat of the Gram Nyayalaya will be located at the headquarters of the intermediate Panchayat, but they will go to villages, work there, and dispose of the cases. Moreover, it is for the State Governments to establish Gram Nyayalayas in consultation with the respective High Courts.

Proceedings of a Gram Nyayalaya

The Gram Nyayalayas are supposed to try to settle the disputes as far as possible by bringing about conciliation between the parties and for this purpose, it can make use of the appointed conciliators. The judgment and order passed by the Gram Nyayalaya are deemed to be a decree and to avoid delay in its execution, the Gram Nyayalaya can follow summary procedure for its execution. The Gram Nyayalaya will not be bound by the rules of evidence provided in the Indian Evidence Act, 1872, but shall be guided by the principles of natural justice and subject to any rule made by the High Court.

Presiding Officer of a Gram Nyayalaya

The Gram Nyayalayas are presided over by Nyayadhikari. A Judicial Magistrate of First Class is qualified to hold the post of Nyayadhikari. They are public servants within the meaning of Section 21 of the IPC. Their appointment is done by the State Government in consultation with the High Court.

Territorial jurisdiction of Gram Nyayalaya

The State Government in consultation with the High Court of that respective State establishes Gram Nyayalaya for a group of contiguous Panchayats of villages. They shall decide the extent of territorial jurisdiction of every Gram Nyayalaya accordingly.

Subject-matter Jurisdiction of Gram Nyayalaya

It can try criminal cases, civil suits, claims, or disputes which are specified in the First Schedule and the Second Schedule of the Gram Nyayalaya Act and the scope of these cases can be amended by the Central as well as the State Governments, as per their respective legislative competence.

In which court does the appeals from Gram Nyayalaya lie?

An appeal from Gram Nyayalaya shall lie in the District Court/Sessions Court. From the date of filing of the appeal, it shall be preferred and disposed of within a period of six months. No appeal or revision shall lie thereafter. Needless to say, that person can in all circumstances approach the Supreme Court or the High Court to avail judicial remedies under Article 32 and 226 of the Constitution of India.

Tribunals

With more and more statutes being enacted in specific fields, there arose a requirement for establishment of special courts to deal with the disputes under the statute, hence a Tribunal, and the era is known as Tribunalization. The working of the Tribunals is based on the principles of natural justice and is not bound by the strict procedures laid down under Code of Civil Procedure, 1908 or the Indian Evidence Act, 1872.

An Administrative Tribunal is neither a Court nor an executive body. It stands somewhere midway between a Court and an administrative body. In other words, Tribunals are the bodies which perform quasi-judicial functions. The primary reason for the creation of Tribunals was to overcome the crisis of delays and backlogs in the administration of justice. Therefore, the Administrative Tribunals have been established to overcome the major lacuna present in the Justice delivery system. The Tribunals have the power to adjudicate over a wide range of subjects that impact everyday life. Tribunals function as an effective mechanism to reduce the burden of the judiciary. Particularly in technical cases, it was felt that the nature of the laws/statutes required adjudicatory forums comprising of persons having expert knowledge of the working of these laws. The Tribunals emerged not only with the sole promise of speedy, effective, decentralized dispensation of justice but also the expertise and knowledge in specialized areas that was felt to be lacking in the judges of traditional Courts. The increase in the number of statutory Tribunals mirrors the rise in State activities.

Administrative Tribunals

Original Indian Constitution did not contain any reference to Tribunals. Based on the recommendations of the Swaran Singh Committee, Part XIV-A was added by the Constitution (Forty-second Amendment) Act, 1976, titled as 'Tribunals' which provided for the establishment of 'Administrative Tribunals' under Article 323A and 'Tribunals for other matters' under Article 323B.

Article 323A dealt with establishment of Tribunals in relation to disputes and complaints arising out of recruitment and conditions of service of persons appointed to public services and posts in connection with the affairs of the Union or State or local or other authority within India. In other words, the Tribunals were established to resolve the disputes of public servants of Union or State or Local authorities.

This Article also enabled the Parliament to enact laws for the establishment of Tribunals and to regulate the working of the Tribunals by specifying the jurisdiction it exercised, the powers, the eligibility to become members of the Tribunals, and their employment with the Tribunals, etc.

Invoking the powers of the Article, Parliament enacted the Administrative Tribunals Act, 1985 and set up the Central Administrative Tribunal (CAT) with its principal bench at Delhi. Additional benches were established in various states.

The CAT is headed by a Chairman and has a sanctioned strength of members totaling 65. The members are drawn from the administrative and judicial side. The age of superannuation is 65 years in the case of the Chairman and 62 years in the case of other members with a 5-year tenure. The appointment is based on the recommendation of the selection committee headed by the sitting judge of the Supreme Court duly nominated by the Chief Justice of India.

The CAT exercises original jurisdiction in relation to recruitment and service matters of all public servants appointed through All India Services, Central Civil Services, etc. The CAT does not exercise its jurisdiction on members of Defense Forces, Supreme Court Officials, and Secretarial Staff of the Parliament.

Similarly, Tribunals at State levels have been established, known as State Administrative Tribunals (SAT), to exercise jurisdiction in relation to recruitment and service matters of all State Government employees. In some circumstances, Joint Administrative Tribunals are formed exercising jurisdiction on two or more states. The Chairman and members are appointed by the President of India after consulting the Governor of the State concerned.

According to Article 323B, the Parliament and State Legislatures are empowered to establish Tribunals covering the following matters depending upon their legislative competence:

(i) Matters governing taxation;

(ii) Matters governing foreign exchange, import and export across customs frontiers;

(iii) Matters governing industrial and labour disputes;

(iv) Matters relating to tenancy law;

(v) Matters relating to land reforms;

(vi) Matters relating to elections; and

(vii) Matters relating to foodstuffs.

Distinction between Article 323A & 323B

The subtle distinction between Article 323A & 323B are as follows:

- Article 323A empowers the Parliament to enact laws for Tribunals whereas Article 323B empowers both the Parliament and the State Government to enact laws.
- Article 323A governs matters relating to public servants whereas Article 323B relates to matters for the seven matters discussed earlier.
- Article 323A has no hierarchy of Tribunals since there is only one Tribunal for the Central & All India Services and one Tribunal for the State level Services, whereas, hierarchy of Tribunals can be created under Article 323B.

Appeals from Tribunals

In L. *Chandra Kumar Vs. Union of India,* the Supreme Court held that the Tribunals are not substitutes of the High Court but are supplementary. The Tribunals will function as a supplementary body and all such decisions of the Tribunals will be subject to the scrutiny before a Division Bench of the respective High Courts. To remove the inefficiency of the Tribunals, the Tribunals should be made subject to the supervisory jurisdiction of the High Court. The High Court's Appellate Jurisdiction and the power of judicial superintendence over decisions of all courts and Tribunals within their jurisdiction is the basic structure of the Constitution. Therefore, the Appellate Jurisdiction of the High Courts cannot be curtailed by Parliament through law.

FREE LEGAL AID

It is a common scenario that due to economic barriers the common people may not able to access justice. To preserve 'Rule of Law', 'Legal aid to the poor and weak' is the basic tenet of any policy. Taking into consideration the above aspect, the Legal Aid Scheme was first introduced by Justice P. N. Bhagwati under the Legal Aid Committee formed in1971. Later on, Article 39A was inserted in Part IV of the Constitution through the 42nd Constitutional Amendment Act, 1976 to provide free legal aid to poor, downtrodden, and weaker sections of society. Keeping Article 39A and the Constitutional objective of social justice in view, the Parliament in 1987 enacted the Legal Services Authorities Act, 1987. The Legal Services Authorities Act, 1987 can be conceptually analyzed under the triangle of Legal Aid, Legal Awareness, and Lok Adalat.

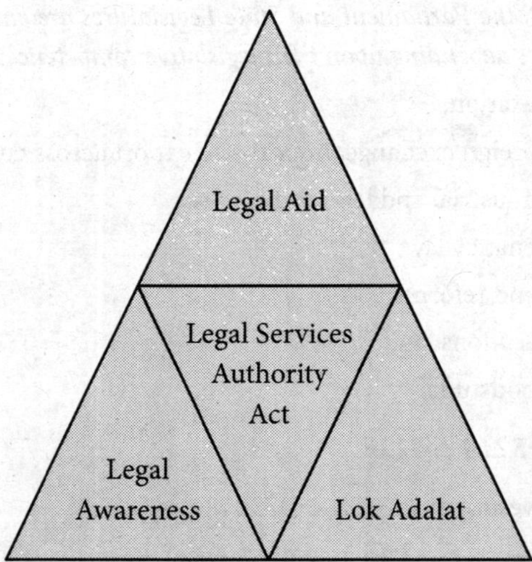

Free Legal Services

The Free Legal Services include:

(a) Payment of court fee, process fees, and all other charges payable or incurred in connection with any legal proceedings;

(b) Providing service of lawyers in legal proceedings;

(c) Obtaining and supply of certified copies of orders and other documents in legal proceedings.

(d) Preparation of appeal, paper book, including printing and translation of documents in legal proceedings.

Who are entitled to Legal Services under The Legal Services Authorities Act, 1987?

Section 12 of the Act prescribes the criteria for giving legal services to the eligible persons.

Every person who has to file or defend a case shall be entitled to legal services under this Act if that person is :

(a) a member of a Scheduled Caste or Scheduled Tribe;

(b) a victim of trafficking in human beings or beggar as referred to in Article 23 of the Constitution;

(c) a woman or a child;

(d) a mentally ill or otherwise disabled person;

(e) a person under circumstances of undeserved want such as being a victim of a mass disaster, ethnic violence, caste atrocity, flood, drought, earthquake, or industrial disaster; or

(f) an industrial workman; or

(g) in custody, including custody in a protective home within the meaning of clause (g) of Section 2 of the Immoral Traffic (Prevention) Act, 1956 (104 of 1956); or in a juvenile home within the meaning of clause (j) of Section 2 of the Juvenile Justice Act, 1986 (53 of 1986) or in a psychiatric hospital or psychiatric nursing home within the meaning of clause (g) of Section 2 of the Mental Health Act, 1987 (14 of 1987); or

(h) in receipt of annual income less than rupees nine thousand or such other higher amount as may be prescribed by the State Government, if the case is before a court other than the Supreme Court, and less than rupees twelve thousand or such other higher amount as may be prescribed by the Central Government, if the case is before the Supreme Court.

Persons who satisfy the criteria specified in Section 12 shall be entitled to receive legal services, provided that the concerned authority is satisfied that such person has a prima facie case to prosecute or to defend.

LEGAL SERVICES AUTHORITY

National Legal Services Authority

The Central Government shall constitute this Authority to exercise the powers and perform the functions conferred on, or assigned to, the Central Authority under this Act.

The Central Authority shall consist of

(a) The Chief Justice of India who shall be the Patron-in-Chief,

(b) A serving or retired Judge of the Supreme Court to be nominated by the President, who shall be the Executive Chairman, and

(c) Such number of other members, possessing such experience and qualifications, as may be prescribed by the Central Government, to be nominated by that Government.

Note : *The Chairman and members must be nominated in consultation with the Chief Justice of India.*

Functions of the National Legal Services Authority

The National Legal Services Authority (NALSA) has been constituted under the Legal Services Authorities Act, 1987 to monitor and evaluate implementation of legal aid programmes and to lay down policies and principles for making legal services available under this Act.

The principal objective of NALSA is to provide free and competent legal services to the weaker sections of the society and to ensure that opportunities for securing justice are not denied to any citizen by reason of economic or other disabilities, and to organize Lok Adalats for amicable settlement of disputes. Apart from the abovementioned, functions of NALSA include spreading legal literacy and awareness, undertaking social justice litigations, etc.

In carrying out all these responsibilities, NALSA works in close coordination with the various State Legal Services Authorities, District Legal Services Authorities, and other agencies for a regular exchange of relevant information, monitoring and updating on the implementation and progress of the various schemes in vogue, and fostering a strategic and coordinated approach to ensure smooth functioning of the various agencies and stakeholders[4].

State Legal Service Authority

The mandate of the Legal Services Authorities Act, 1987 is that the Legal Services Authorities shall be set up in all the States. Every State Government shall constitute a body to be called the Legal Services Authority for the State to exercise the powers and perform the functions conferred on, or assigned to, a State Authority under this Act.

---

[4] https://nalsa.gov.in/about-us/introduction

A State Authority shall consist of –

(a) The Chief Justice of the High Court who shall be the Patron-in-Chief;

(b) A serving or retired Judge of the High Court, to be nominated by the Governor, who shall be the Executive Chairman; and

(c) Such number of other members, possessing such experience and qualifications as may be prescribed by the State Government, to be nominated by that Government.

Note : *The Chairman and members must be nominated in consultation with the Chief Justice of the High Court.*

Functions of Legal Authorities

The State Legal Services Authorities, District Legal Services Authorities, Taluk Legal Services Committees, etc. have been asked to discharge the following main functions on a regular basis:

(i) To Provide Free and Competent Legal Services to the eligible persons;

(ii) To organize Lok Adalats for amicable settlement of disputes; and

(iii) To organize legal awareness camps in the rural areas.

ARBITRATION, CONCILIATION & MEDIATION

Arbitration

Arbitration is a form of dispute resolution, where the parties agree that the civil dispute will not be decided through the regular process of litigation[5] (Regular Dispute Resolution/RDR) but through Alternative, Dispute Resolution. The term alternative dispute resolution is also called out of court dispute settlement. In Arbitration the legal dispute is resolved by a neutral third party known as the "Arbitrator". The concept of arbitration as an alternative dispute resolution mechanism in India is governed by Arbitration and Conciliation Act 1996. As per the mechanism prescribed in the Act, either the parties to the Arbitration, or the Court, appoints an Arbitrator or the Arbitral Tribunal. The order or award passed by the Arbitrator or the Arbitral Tribunals will be binding on both the parties and enforceable in a Court of law similar to a civil decree. The prevalent Arbitration Law in India was the Arbitration and Conciliation Act of 1940 which was later repealed and the Arbitration and Conciliation Act of 1996 was passed. The Act was based on the United Nations Commission on International Trade Law (UNCITRAL) Model Law[6] of the International Commercial Arbitration Council.

Advantages of arbitration

- **Technical experts :** Arbitrators can be appointed based on their knowledge and skill in a particular field so they have the necessary expertise required to adjudicate technical matters/

[5] The act, process, or practice of settling a dispute in a court of law.

[6] ADR is a concept that is recognised globally and various laws are made for resolving international disputes. One of the most recognised and prevalent law is UNCITRAL that deals with ADR in general and arbitration in particular. This law was established by the UN General Assembly in 1966. It is based in Vienna, Austria. Apart from its active role in promoting and making trade related treaties at international level, UNCITRAL has been successful in the field of ADR. It focuses on initiatives that strengthen domestic and international legal authority governing international arbitration (commercial). There are various international treaties and conventions of which UNCITRAL is the central agency for arbitration and conciliation.

issues arising between the parties which a judge presiding over a court of law may not always have.

- **Time & cost effective :** The process of arbitration works more quickly and is more cost-effective than the courts. Moreover, arbitration takes into account the convenience of the parties who are free to choose the arbitrator and the venue and time of the arbitration proceedings.
- **Procedural flexibility :** Arbitration is more flexible in comparison to traditional courts as arbitrators are not bound by strict procedural rules and regulations which are applicable in court proceedings.
- **Privacy & confidentiality:** Privacy and confidentiality of the parties are maintained as there is no unnecessary publicity of the dispute.

Mediation

Mediation is one of the methods of Alternative Dispute Resolution where a neutral third party facilitates communication between parties to help them reach a voluntary agreement. Mediation is more formal than negotiation but less formal than arbitration or litigation. In other words, mediation is a very informal process where the parties themselves do the talking instead of their lawyers. Both sides present their case to the mediator who can then encourage parties to arrive at possible solutions while keeping the other side's interest in mind. Mediation is cost-effective, fast and confidential, and the outcome is not binding like an arbitral award, but can be incorporated into a legally binding contract.

Initiation of mediation

Mediation can either be initiated:

- Voluntarily by the parties through a pre-agreed mediation agreement[7]; or
- During the court proceedings if the parties are willing to resolve the dispute by dialogue, then the court can refer the matter to mediation while putting the court proceedings on hold[8].

Conciliation[9]

Conciliation is a type of ADR where the settlement is made out of court. Conciliation is similar to mediation where parties voluntarily appoint a neutral third party to resolve their disputes. The main difference between mediation and conciliation lies in the role of the mediator. In mediation the mediator facilitates the process and provides a platform for the parties to reach a mutually acceptable solution. Whereas, in conciliation the conciliator may be more proactive and suggest solutions to the parties to resolve their claims and disputes.

OMBUDSMAN

An ombudsman is an official who is appointed by the Government to investigate individual's complaints against a government department, financial institutions, or public entities and attempts to resolve the raised concerns either by process of mediation or by giving recommendations. Ombudsman

---

[7] This is not regulated by law yet.

[8] Regulated by Section 89 of the Civil Procedure Code, 1908, which was amended in 2002.

[9] Conciliation is mentioned in various acts such as Section 89 of the Civil Procedure Code 1908; Arbitration & Conciliation Act, 1996; and the Industrial Disputes Act, 1947.

is an official, who is charged with representing the interests of the public by investigating and addressing complaints reported by individuals. At the national level, most ombudsmen have a wide mandate to deal with the entire public sector, and sometimes also elements of the private sector such as contracted service providers. In some cases, there is a more restricted mandate, for example with particular sectors of society. Ombudsman provide an independent examination of complaints, avoiding conflicts of interest. However, the success of the ombudsman system depends on the selection of an appropriate individual and cooperation from within the State.

QUESTIONS

Subjective Questions

1. "The judiciary has been encouraging parties to take up pre-litigation mediation to settle their dispute before resorting to court proceedings". Discuss. **(200 words)**
2. "Nyaya Panchayats are the judicial components of the Panchayat system, which forms the lowest rung of our judiciary". Critically Analyze. **(200 words)**
3. "Free assistance must be provided to all poor accused, irrespective of the severity of the crime attributed to them, at every stage of the three-tier justice delivery system and should not be restricted to the trial stage only". Discuss. **(200 words)**

CHAPTER 17

SEPARATION OF POWERS

INTRODUCTION TO SEPARATION OF POWERS

The doctrine of Separation of Powers is found in one form or the other in many modern Constitutions. It essentially postulates that powers and responsibilities of the three wings, namely, the Legislature, the Executive, and the Judiciary, should be so delineated that no one wing should exercise the powers of the other. In this, all the three wings are equal and independent and have different powers and functions. The doctrine is opposed to the concentration of state power in a single person or group as this may pose a threat to the ideal of a democratic government.

Baron de Montesquieu, the French satirist and a political philosopher, enunciated the idea of a tripartite system by separating the three branches of government—the Legislature, the Executive, and the Judiciary and stated that one should not encroach on the sphere of the other.

Features of Separation of Powers

A pure form of the separation of powers doctrine has the following features:

(a) The functions of the government are to be divided into the Legislative, the Executive, and the Adjudicative;

(b) Different functions are to be vested in separate and appropriate institutions;

(c) The members of one institution should not be members of any other institution;

(d) The functions of one institution should not encroach on the functions of another.

Therefore, power is divided across three institutions rather than being concentrated into one, and each institution is independent of the other in terms of functioning and personnel.

Significance of Separation of Powers

The hypothesis behind the separation of powers is that when a single person or group has a large amount of power, they can become treacherous to citizens. The separation of powers is a method of removing the abuse of power[1]. The significance of this doctrine can be summed up as follows:

[1] https://www.lawctopus.com/academike/separation-of-powers-a-comparative-analysis-of-the-doctrine-india-united-states-of-america-and-england/ by Dristhi.

- Firstly, it aims to eliminate arbitrariness, totalitarianism, and tyranny and promotes an accountable and democratic form of government.
- Secondly, it aims to safeguard the individual liberty. Separation of powers not only aims to maintain the efficiency in administration, but also protects the people from the arbitrary rule of the Executive.
- Thirdly, it emphasizes on the necessity of independence of Judiciary.
- Fourthly, separation of powers maintains a balance among the three organs of government by dividing the powers among them so that powers do not concentrate on any one branch leading to arbitrariness.
- Fifthly, this principle allows all the branches to specialize themselves in their respective fields with an intention to enhance and improve the efficiency of the government.

SEPARATION OF POWERS IN THE INDIAN CONSTITUTION

The founding fathers of various constitutions have accepted this doctrine with modifications to make it relevant to the changing times. *Montesquieu's* doctrine of separation of powers has also influenced the founding fathers in drafting the Constitution of India. Keeping in mind that the doctrine is an important component of a democratic nation, the founding fathers adopted the doctrine but not in its absolute sense. *Mukherjee*, C. J., speaking for the court in *Ram Jawaya case*[2], observed: "*Indian Constitution has not indeed recognized the doctrine of separation of powers in its absolute rigidity. But the functions of the different parts or branches of the government have been sufficiently differentiated.*"

System of Checks and Balances

The Constitution of India also follows the system of checks and balances to prevent one branch of government from having more power over another. The system limits the powers of the organs in one hand. If there is a complete separation of powers, the government cannot run smoothly and effectively. Smooth running of government is possible only by cooperation and mutual adjustment of all the three organs of the government. It is impossible to put the powers of the three organs in watertight compartments. Therefore, Indian Constitution incorporates a limited separation of powers.

There are no express provisions in the Constitution regarding the Doctrine of separation of powers. But it is considered to be part of the basic structure of the Constitution.

In Kesavananda Bharati Vs. State of Kerala[3], Hon'ble Chief Justice Sikri observed:

"*Separation of powers between the Legislature, the Executive and the Judiciary is a part of the basic structure of the Constitution; this structure cannot be destroyed by any form of amendment.*"

In *Asif Hameed Vs. State of Jammu and Kashmir*[4] the Supreme Court observed:

"*Although the doctrine of separation of powers has not been recognized under the Constitution in its absolute rigidity but the Constitution makers have meticulously defined the functions of various organs of the State. Legislature, Executive and Judiciary have to function within their own spheres demarcated*

---

[2] AIR 1955 SC 549

[3] AIR 1973 SC 1461 at p. 1535

[4] AIR 1989 S.C. 1899

under the Constitution. No organ can usurp the functions assigned to another. The Constitution trusts to the judgment of these organs to function and exercise their discretion by strictly following the procedure prescribed therein. The functioning of democracy depends upon the strength and independence of each of its organs."

The system of checks and balances is essential for the proper functioning of three organs of the government. Different organs of the state impose checks and balances on the other.

Provisions in the Constitution to Illustrate the Checks and Balances

The following provisions in the Constitution illustrate the checks and balances:

- **Judiciary :** The Supreme Court and the High Courts enjoy the power of judicial review. The higher Judiciary has the power to declare the laws passed by the Legislature and actions taken by the Executive as unconstitutional if they violate any provision of the Constitution.
- **Executive :** The President of India who is the supreme Executive authority in India exercises law-making power in the form of ordinances. President appoints the Supreme Court and High Court Judges. He exercises the pardoning power. Various administrative bodies exercise quasi-judicial functions during the course of their work[5].

  Furthermore, in Part XXI of the Constitution dealing with special and temporary Articles, certain special powers, normally attributed to the Legislature have been given to the Governor of the specified states. For instance, the Governor has the power notify that an Act of Parliament may not apply to the concerned state. This and other powers specified in this Part militate against the textual understanding of the separation of powers.
- **Legislature :** The Council of Ministers are selected from the Legislature and this Council is responsible for the Legislature. The Legislature exercises judicial powers in cases of breach of its privileges, impeachment of the President, and removal of judges. The legislative body has the punitive powers under Article 105 (Powers, Privileges, and Immunities of Parliament and its Members).

Relevance of Doctrine of Separation of Powers in the Current Scenario

Thus, it is crucial to understand that the doctrine of separation of powers has come a long way from its theoretical inception. Today, the doctrine in its absolute form is only recognized in letter as it is entirely unfeasible and impractical for usage in the operational practices of a government. With the passage of time, States have evolved from being minimal and non-interventionist to being welfare-oriented by playing the multifarious roles of protector, arbiter, controller, and provider to the people. In its omnipresent role, the functions of the State have become diverse and its problems interdependent; hence, any serious attempt to define and separate the functions in a strict sense would only cause inefficiency in the government[6]. In other words, the principle of separation of powers in the strict sense cannot be applied in any modern Government, may it be either UK, USA, France, India, or Australia.

---

[5]As a general rule, only courts of law have the authority to decide controversies that affect individual rights. One major exception to this general rule is the power of an administrative agency or Executive authority to make decisions concerning the rights of parties. The decision by an agency that has a legal effect is a quasi-judicial action. Eg: Income Tax Appellate Tribunal, Railway Claims Tribunal, etc.

[6]Yadav, Rahul. (2020). *Separation of Powers Law and Practice in India.*

But it does not mean that the doctrine has no relevance nowadays. Government is an organic unity. It cannot be divided into watertight compartments. If there is a complete separation of powers, the government cannot run smoothly and effectively. Smooth running of the government is possible only by cooperation and mutual adjustment of all the three organs of the government. Prof. Garner has rightly said, "the doctrine is impracticable as a working principle of Government." It is not possible to categorize the functions of all three branches of the Government on a mathematical basis[7]. But it is important that each organ of the Government should exercise its power on the principle of "Checks and Balances" signifying the fact that none of the organs of the Government should usurp the essential functions of the other organs. Professor Laski has aptly remarked: "It is necessary to have a separation of functions which need not imply a separation of personnel."[8]

---

[7]J.T.R.I. JOURNAL – Second Year, Issue – 4 & 5 – Year – March, 1996

[8]Ibid.

CHAPTER 18

DEMOCRATIC DECENTRALISATION

INTRODUCTION TO DECENTRALISATION

By definition, decentralisation involves the transfer of power from the central government to actors and institutions at lower levels in a political-administrative and territorial hierarchy[1].

Decentralisation is a process of transferring power to popularly elected local governments. Transferring power means providing local governments with greater political authority (e.g., convene local elections or establish participatory processes), increased financial resources (e.g., through transfers or greater tax authority), and providing more administrative responsibilities. Democratic decentralisation proponents strongly argue that decentralisation should increase citizen voice and participation in the political process, and so make the government more responsive and accountable to the governed. Decentralisation provides an institutional mechanism through which citizens at various levels can organize themselves and participate in the decision-making process.

Local government is one form of a decentralized system which is affected by the transfer of authority or responsibility for decision-making, management, or resources allocation from higher level of government to its subordinate units. The role of local government varies from one country to another, but in every democratic society, local government has some part to play.

Many analyses of decentralisation consider the transfer of powers in three sectors to be necessary for success. Manor, for example, argues, – 'If it is to have significant promise, decentralisation must entail a mixture of all three types: political, fiscal, and administrative'.

TYPES OF DECENTRALISATION

Political Decentralisation

This is the transfer of authority to a local government. Political decentralisation aims to give citizens or their elected representatives more power in public decision-making. Its goal is to introduce more participatory forms of governance by giving citizens, or their representatives, more influence in

---

[1] *Democratic Decentralisation Through A Natural Resource Lens: Countering Central Resistance, Fostering Local Demand*; Anne M. & Jesse C. Ribot; Larson European Journal of Development Research Volume 16, Number 1, Spring 2004

the formulation and implementation of policies and plans. Political decentralisation often requires constitutional law reform as well as changes to other laws. This form of decentralisation is synonymous with democratic decentralisation or devolution.

Fiscal Decentralisation

Financial responsibility is a core component of decentralisation. If sub-national governments or local governments are to carry out decentralised functions effectively, they must have an adequate level of revenues either raised locally or transferred from the national government/state governments. Moreover, they should have the authority to make decisions about their expenditures as well.

Administrative Decentralisation

The functions performed by central government are transferred to geographically distinct administrative units. In other words, in administrative decentralisation there is a transfer of operational responsibility from a higher level to a lower level of organisation.

There are three major forms of administrative decentralisation: De-concentration, Delegation, and Devolution. Each has its own different characteristics.

De-concentration

This is often considered to be the weakest form of decentralisation and is used most frequently in unitary states. In de-concentration, it can merely shift responsibilities from the central government officials in the capital city to those working in regions, provinces, or districts, or it can create strong field administration or local administrative capacity under the supervision of central government ministries.

Delegation

Delegation is a more extensive form of decentralisation. Through delegation, central governments transfer responsibility for decision-making and administration of public functions to semi-autonomous organizations not wholly controlled by the central government, but ultimately accountable to it. Governments delegate responsibilities when they create public enterprises or corporations, housing authorities, etc. These organizations usually have a great deal of discretion in decision-making.

Devolution

A third type of administrative decentralisation is devolution. When governments devolve functions, they transfer authority for decision-making, finance, and management to quasi-autonomous units of local government. Devolution usually transfers responsibilities for services to local authorities that elect their own representatives, raise their own revenues, and have independent authority to make investment decisions. In a devolved system, local governments have clear and legally recognized geographical boundaries over which they exercise authority and within which they perform public functions. It is this type of administrative decentralisation that underlies most political decentralisation.

Decentralisation : A Multi-dimensional Concept[2]

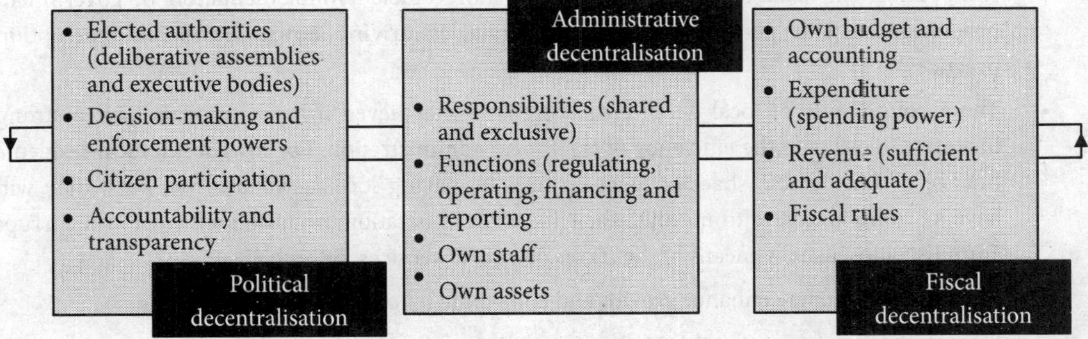

BENEFITS OF DECENTRALISATION[3]

The efficiency and equity of governance can be increased by bringing public decisions closer and making them more open and accountable to local populations. For this to happen, some form of downwardly accountable local representation is necessary. Moreover, local participation in decision-making makes people more likely to have a sense of 'ownership' of those decisions, such as rules for resource use, etc. Because of this 'ownership', they will provide better information and be more engaged in implementing, monitoring, and enforcing such rules. In addition, marginalized groups could have greater influence on local policies because of the open nature of decision-making, thus increasing equity.

Thus, there are reasons for the growth in faith in democratic decentralisation among which are the following:

- A government that is knowledgeable about, and hence responsive to, the needs of the people is better equipped to implement pro-poor policies and outcomes than one that is politically, physically, and mentally distant from the people.
- Democratic decentralisation is also supposed to efficiently address a large number of key issues such as
  (i) the severe limitations of centralized planning and management;
  (ii) the over-concentration of power, authority, and resources at the centre;
  (iii) the weak contact between government and local people, including civil society and the private sector;
  (iv) the lack of equity in the allocation of resources;
  (v) the insufficient representation of various political, religious, ethnic, and tribal groups in the decision-making process;
  (vi) the inadequate exchange of information; and the inefficiency of service delivery modalities).
- Decentralisation provides information advantages as local governments have better insights on citizens' preferences, allowing efficient public services tailored to the population and transfers from the rich to the poor.

---

[2]Source: OECD (2019[1]), Making Decentralisation Work: A Handbook for Policy-Makers, https://dx.doi.org/10.1787/g2g9faa7-en.

[3]Making Decentralisation Work : A Handbook for Policy-Makers; http://www.oecd.org/cfe/regional

- Decentralisation may lead to greater citizens' engagement in local affairs, and political competition can lead to better policies and more efficient implementation of government programmes (with performance-oriented strategies driving down bribes and corruption practices).
- The accountability of local decision-making is best achieved if local residents have a strong incentive to evaluate the efficiency of their local administration. For instance, if local residents finance a considerable share of local services by paying local taxes and user fees, they will have a strong incentive to monitor their local administration, because inefficient and corrupt administration usually means higher taxes or poorer services, or both.
- Decentralisation may enhance growth and contribute to lower regional disparities.
- Decentralisation can strengthen citizen participation in government by bringing governments closer to citizens and by making governments more accessible. Citizen participation is essential for the success of decentralisation as it enables local governments' spending to reflect citizens' preferences and the accountability of public decision-making.

Limitations of Decentralisation

However, the benefits from decentralisation can be limited in the event of inadequate design and implementation of decentralisation reforms. It is important to note that the effects of decentralisation largely depend on implementation. In particular, the policymakers should avoid unclear assignment of responsibilities between levels of government and vague relationships between local and state governments. Unclear assignment of responsibilities can lead to costlier service delivery and democratic deficit because it is difficult for citizens to hold authorities accountable for policy shortcomings due to confusing assignments. Lack of local governments' capacity to deliver public services forms a major threat for successful implementation. This should be tackled with capacity-building programmes and equalisation transfers.

LOCAL SELF-GOVERNMENT

Local self-government refers to the system of subordinate local authorities which has developed in many modern states.

Each unit of local government in any system is assumed to possess the following characteristics:

- A given territory and population;
- An institutional structure for legislative, executive, or administrative purposes;
- A separate legal identity;
- A range of power and functions authorized by delegation from the appropriate central or intermediate legislature; and within the ambit of such delegation, autonomy (including fiscal autonomy).

Thus, local self-governments can elect officials, enact taxes, and do many other things that a national government would do, just on a smaller scale. Local government is the system of electing representatives to be responsible for the administration of public services and facilities in a particular area.

Local Self-Government and Democratic Decentralisation

Local self-government implies the transference of the power to rule to the lowest rungs of the political order. It is a form of democratic decentralisation where the participation of even the grass-root level of the society is ensured in the process of administration.

A democratic polity involves the decentralisation of power through which the affairs of the local people are managed by means of their positive participation. It implies the extension of democracy at the grass-roots level. It signifies marked devolution of power from the higher to the lower levels in a way that the units of local government exercise their authority with the participation of the people of that area with occasional control and supervision of the provincial and central governments.

Democratic decentralisation is that process of decentralisation which conforms to the basic tenets of democracy. It implies a council of elected representatives at the decentralised level of administration which would be accountable to its electorate. It is the very base of the development of the people at the grass-roots level. Democratic decentralisation offers opportunities to the people at grass-roots level to participate in decision-making.

The concept of democratic decentralisation is intimately associated with the idea of local self-government. Democratic decentralisation is a political ideal and local self-government is its institutional form. The institution of local self-government includes both rural and urban local bodies. In India, the Panchayati Raj Institutions (rural) and the Municipal bodies (urban) provide institutional frameworks for democratic decentralisation. The Constitution provides a clear mandate for democratic decentralisation not only through the Directive Principles of State Policy which exhorts the State to promote Panchayati Raj Institutions but more specifically now through the 73rd and 74th Amendments of the Constitution.

18.1 : RURAL LOCAL SELF-GOVERNMENT

INTRODUCTION

In India, most of its population resides in rural areas. The rural areas thus forms the roots for the governance in India and the democracy should start thereon. This is nothing but called as democratic decentralization. Decentralization has been a major feature of the development in India. The local self-governments (Panchayats and Municipalities) in both rural and urban areas are the best instruments of democratic decentralization in India. The 'Panchayat' in rural India and 'Municipalities' in urban India are defined in the Constitution as institutions of local self-government. The popular saying of 'Panch-parmeshwar' (five people are God) or 'Panch-pradhan' (five people are head) from the ancient times connotes that the 'Panchayat' had deep roots in the Indian culture. After the 73rd and 74th Constitutional Amendment to the Indian Constitution, 'Panchayati Raj System' and the urban local governance (Municipalities) has occupied a pivotal place in the Indian democratic system. With this epoch-making amendment, the local governments have become the third tier in our federal system after the Union and the States.

PANCHAYATI RAJ SYSTEM

Panchayats Before Independence

The Panchayats in India have the distinction of a long history, before earning a coveted place in the Indian Constitution. Ancient Indian history has narrated the existence of village Panchayats comprising five informally elected elderly members to settle disputes in the village. A reference to an organized system of rural local self-government (Panchayat) was found in ancient Vedic literature. ***Rig Veda*** has mentioned about '*gramini*', the village head employed by the king for civil and military purposes; while ***Atharva Veda*** envisaged the institution of '*sabha*', '*samiti*', '*sabhapati*', and '*sabhasad*', primarily performing judicial functions. A mention of village institutions had been made in, the ***Ramyana*** and the ***Mahabharata***, where the gramin was responsible for collecting state dues, keeping village records, settling disputes, and controlling crime. ***Kautaliya's Arthashastra*** gives a comprehensive account of the system of village administration prevailing in ancient India. Besides, evidence of the village Panchayats is also discerned in the *Maurya* and *Chola* dynasties and during the golden era of the Guptas[1].

However, the medieval period was the uneventful period in the history of the Panchayat system in India. The system was largely ineffective during Mughal rule in India because of *Shariat laws*. Except Akbar, no other Mughal ruler assigned importance to the Panchayats. In the same vein, during the initial years of British rule, the autonomy of the Panchayats gradually got diluted with the establishment of local civil and criminal courts, revenue, and police organization. However, the British rulers were well cognizant about the role played by self-governing communities at the village level. Mr Charles Metcalfe, a British governor in India during 1852 called Panchayat as 'the little republic'[2]. This is even amply reflected in the East Indian Company Resolution of 1865 which said:

---

[1] Quoted from Das, HH, *Introduction to Panchayati Raj and Community Development in India*, Kalyani Publishers, 1990.

[2] He called panchayats as "Little Republic" but with some reservations because a caste ridden feudal system with power concentrated in the hands of a few landlords would foil the sole mission of decentralization

"The people of this country are perfectly capable of administering their local affairs. The municipal feeling is deeply mooted in them. The village communities are the most abiding of Indian institutions. They maintained the framework of society while successive swarms of invaders swept over the country[3]."

The initiative taken by the former Viceroy, Mr Mayo, in 1870 through a resolution for decentralization of power was aimed at improving administrative efficiency In 1882, the former Governor-General of India, Mr Ripon resolved in favour of progressive extension of local governing bodies with the avowed purpose of imparting political education to the people in general and rural people in particular. The Royal Commission on Decentralization in 1907 recognized the importance of the Panchayats at the village level, which recommended association of the people with the task of local administration. A few subsequent initiatives focused on decentralization during British Raj are Montague Chelmsford Act, 1919; the Simon Commission Report 1925, and Government of India Act, 1935. With these initiatives, by 1925, eight provinces had passed Panchayat Acts and by 1926 six Indian princely states also passed Panchayat laws. By 1948, 20 other native states had Village Panchayat Acts[4].

Panchayati Raj System After Independence

After independence, the process of empowering Panchayats gathered momentum. Mahatma Gandhi, the Father of the Nation, while emphasizing on 'Gram Swaraj' (village autonomy) strongly advocated that:

"Independence must begin at the bottom. Thus every village will be a republic of Panchayat having full power[5]."

Mahatma Gandhi further stressed the need for village swaraj (independent republic): "*My idea of village swaraj is that it is a complete republic, independent of its neighbors for its own vital wants, and yet interdependent for many others in which dependence is a necessity*" (Gandhi 1962, P. 31).

In the immediate post-independence period, during the debates on the drafting of India's Constitution, sharply discrepant views on Panchayats were expressed. In the Constituent Assembly on November 4, 1948, Dr. B. R. Ambedkar, Chairman of the Drafting Committee, called village community "*a sink of localism, a den of ignorance, narrow-mindedness, and communalism*" (Malaviya 1956, 97). Panchayats did not find a place in the first draft of India's Constitution. At the insistence of a few Gandhians, namely Alladi Krishnaswami Aiyar, N. G. Ranga, K. Santhanam, Shibbanlal Saxena, and others, a compromise was arrived at, and Panchayats were included only in the non-justiciable part of the Constitution, under Directive Principles of State Policy, as Article 40, which reads, "*The state shall take steps to organize village Panchayats and endow them with such powers and authority as may be necessary to enable them to function as units of self-government.*" Without any reference to Panchayats, the term local government also crept into Item 5 of the State List in the Constitution. These provisions are, at best, only discretionary[6].

---

[3]Das, HH, *Introduction to Panchayati Raj and Community Development in India*, Kalyani Publishers, 1990.

[4]A Quarterly of local Self Government Institute, Bombay No. 128, PP. 452–53

[5]Mahatma Gandhi's statement was quoted from Harijan, January 18, 1948

[6]Role of Panchayat Bodies in Rural development since 1959, Theme Paper for the Fifty-fifth members' Annual conference., V.N. Alok, Indian institute of Public administration, New Delhi, 2011.

Milestones in the Evolution of Panchayats in India[7]

1687	Royal Charter for the creation of Madras Municipal body
1842	Act X to provide first formal measure of municipal bodies
1857	The aftermath of Mutiny saw severe financial stress. Fiscal decentralization was considered one of the solutions
1870	Lord Mayo's scheme of fiscal and administration devolution. Enactment of Bengal Chowkidari Act
1882	Lord Ripon's Resolution on Local Self-Government
1907	The Royal Commission on Decentralisation was constituted
1948	Debates between Gandhi and Ambedkar on Gram Swaraj (self-rule)
1957	Balwantrai Mehta Commission – Recommended Panchayat structure at district, block, and village levels, elected bodies for 5 year, devolution of powers to Panchayats. Post of Block Development Officer (BDO) was created
1959	Inauguration of first Panchayat in the country at Nagaur district in Rajasthan
1963	K. Santhanam Committee – Recommended limited revenue raising powers of Panchayats to raise revenue and setting up of State Panchayati Raj finance Corporations.
1978	Ashok Mehta Committee – Recommended that the District serve as the administrative unit in the Panchayat structure and two-tier Panchayats be created at district and block levels.
1985	G.V.K. Rao Committee – Recommended that the block development office (BDO) should be strengthened to assume broad responsibility for planning, implementing, and monitoring rural development programmes.
1986	L.M. Singvi Committee – Recommended that local self-government should be constitutionally enshrined, and the Gram Sabha (the village assembly) should be the base of decentralised democracy.
1992	The 73rd Amendment to the Indian Constitution – Panchayats at district, block, and village levels was created through Constitution. Part IX for Panchayats was inserted in the Constitution with 11th schedule that enumerated 29 matters for Panchayats.
1996	PESA – Powers of self-government were extended to tribal communities in 'Fifth Schedule' areas.
2004	Union Ministry of Panchayati Raj was created
2009	The Tenth, Eleventh, and Twelfth Finance Commissions broadly recommended grants for Local Bodies (LBs), amounting to between 1 to 1.5 percent of the Central divisible pool. The Thirteenth Finance Commission broke fresh ground in increasing the allocation to around 2.5 percent of the divisible pool and earmarking a part of the grant for performance, based on the meeting of the conditionalities that it laid down.

POST-INDEPENDENCE COMMITTEES

Before Panchayati Raj Institutions could enjoy the constitutional status that it enjoys today, it had to go through various stages. Committees were constituted by various authorities to advise them on different aspects of decentralization, such as (i) administrative and political decentralization; (ii) fiscal decentralization, etc.

[7]https://www.iipa.org.in

The Balwantrai Mehta Committee (1957)

The earliest committee to study decentralization issues was the Balwantrai Mehta Committee which was appointed in 1957 to study the Community Development Projects and the National Extension Service and to assess the extent 'to which the movement had succeeded in utilizing local initiatives and in creating institutions to ensure continuity in the process of improving economic and social conditions in rural areas'. The report was quite visionary. It offered solutions along two broad axes: (i) administrative decentralization, for effective implementation of the development programme, and (ii) control by elected bodies of this decentralized administrative system. The Balwantrai Mehta committee held that community development would only be deep and enduring when the community was involved in the planning, decision, and implementation process.

It suggested the following:

(a) It highlighted the urgency of democratic and elected institutions at the lowest level and suggested a three-tier system at the district, intermediate, and village levels. In other words, there should be a three-tier structure of local self-government from the village to the district with the village at the bottom and the district at the top with its intermediary link of institutions all organically related to one another;

(b) An early establishment of elected local bodies and devolution to them of necessary resources, power, and authority;

(c) The basic unit of democratic decentralization was to be at the intermediate/block/samiti level since the area of jurisdiction of the local body should neither be too large nor too small. The block was large enough for efficiency and economy of administration, and small enough for sustaining a sense of involvement in the citizens. Such a body must not be constrained by too much control by government or government agencies;

(d) The block level/samiti should be the executive body. Its functions should cover the development of agriculture in all its aspects, the promotion of local industries and other services such as drinking water, road building, etc. while the district/zilla parishad should be the advisory, coordinating, and supervisory body;

(e) The district collector should be the Chairman of the zilla parishad;

(f) There should be a five year term of Panchayati Raj Institutions;

(g) The district and the intermediate levels should be constituted by the indirect elections. The village levels should be constituted by the direct elections;

(h) There should be genuine transfer of power and responsibility to these institutions of local government;

(i) Adequate resources should be transferred to these bodies to enable them to discharge those responsibilities;

(j) All programmes of social and economic development formulated through the network of planning should be channelled through those institutions;

The Committee recommended that while the broad patterns and the fundamentals of the PR institutions might be uniform, there should not be any rigidity in the details of pattern, in view of the vastness of the country, and the complexity of its problems. What really counts is the genuine transfer of power to the people. If this is ensured, the form and pattern could vary according to the conditions prevailing in different states. The National Development Council affirmed the basic principles underlying democratic decentralization. In accordance with the recommendations of the Committee, a number of states created three-tier system of rural local self-government institutions. However, Rajasthan was the first state to establish Panchayati Raj and implement the recommendations on 2nd October, 1959. Some of the states created only one-tier viz. the Village Panchayats (Jammu and Kashmir and Kerala), while others created a two-tier system (Haryana). Even in those states which created three-tier system, there was difference attached to each of them. Even the level at which the three-tier system operates in different states differs.

The Balwant Rai Mehta Committee, the First Administrative Reforms Commission, and successive Five Year Plans emphasised the need to have decentralised development planning to be framed at village, block, and district levels.

K. Santhanam Committee (1963)

K. Santhanam Committee was appointed to look solely at this issue of Panchayati Raj institution finance. The Committee's recommendations have defined the terms of all subsequent discussions.

It suggested that:

(a) Panchayats should have special powers to levy special tax on land revenues, home tax, etc;
(b) People should not be burdened with too many demands;
(c) The PRIs have a deplorable record of tax collections;
(d) All grants and subventions at the state level should be mobilized and sent in a consolidated form to the various PRIs;
(e) A Panchayati Raj Finance Corporation should be set up which would look into the financial resources of PRIs at all three levels, provide loans and financial assistance to these grass-roots level governments, and also provide non-financial requirements of villages.

M.L. Dantwala Committee (1978)

The Planning Commission appointed a working group under the chairmanship of Prof. M.L. Dantwala to draw up guidelines for block level planning. The committee analysed the role of the Panchayati Raj institutions in the planning exercise.

It stated that:

(a) The commitment to democratic decentralisation implies progressive devolution or decision-making on all vital matters effecting people's life to their elected representatives under the Panchayati Raj system. If the main responsibility of development planning at the district or block level is left to the bureaucratic hierarchy under the control or the Ministry at the state level, democratic decentralisation will remain an empty slogan.
(b) The cause for mismatch of financial allocations with location specific needs was the remoteness of planning agencies at the district level from the actual scene of action. The group recommended the Block as the appropriate sub-state planning level for proper appreciation of the needs of the people. It also asserted that the block level provides the vital link between clusters of villages and the district level and thence to the region, State, and National levels.
(c) The need for block level planning and suggested methods for preparing block plans to be implemented in some select blocks in the country. In view of infrastructural difficulties at the block level, the committee assigned the responsibility of block planning to the district-level organization and suggested slow movement towards introduction of effective block planning. The committee proposed the integration of block plans with the district plan and thus, the committee viewed the preparation of both block and district plans to be a part of the same exercise.

Asoka Mehta Committee (1978)

The Asoka Mehta Committee in its report published in the same year as the Dantwala Committee report (1978) endorsed the latter's proposal of locating the planning team at the district stage. The Asoka Mehta Committee gave primacy to the district as the basic unit of decentralization which was a fundamental departure from the system that had developed following the Balwant Rai Mehta Committee recommendations of creation the block and the Panchayat Samiti as the key units of decentralization.

Recognizing that PRIs had failed to live up to their early promise, the Asoka Mehta Committee was appointed to inquire into the working of PRIs and to suggest measures to strengthen them for evolving an effective decentralized system of development. It considered the PRI experience post 1959 as having gone through 3 phases; (i) ascendancy (1959–64), (ii) stagnation (1965–69), (iii) and decline (1969–77). The Asoka Mehta Committee felt that a combination of factors had conspired to undermine PRIs, such as an unsympathetic bureaucracy, absence of political will, lack of involvement in planning and implementation on a sizeable scale, etc.

The Committee's recommendations were as follows:

(a) Two-tier Panchayati Raj Institutions — a district-level Zilla Parishad and a Mandal Panchayat;

(b) The district is a viable administrative unit for which planning coordination and resource allocation are feasible and technical expertise available;

(c) The decentralisation would commence with the district as the first point and further movement below will take place depending upon the situation in each State. Broadly, the Zilla Parishad will handle all the decentralised State programmes and plan for them at the district. The Mandal Panchayat will handle the implementation work;

(d) District planning should take care of the urban–rural continuum;

(e) Participation of political parties in Panchayati Raj elections would ensure clearer orientation towards development programme and facilitate healthier linkages with higher level political process;

(f) The Scheduled Castes and Scheduled Tribes should get representation on the basis of their population;

(g) Co-option of two women as members of both at Zilla and Mandal level. It also recommended for reservation of two seats for women in Panchayats and two co-option women members in case they did not come through elections.

(h) There should be an independent authority to carry out 'Social Audit' of the funds and programmes earmarked for the Scheduled Castes and Scheduled Tribes and ensure that projects designed for them are implemented in a way that the desired impact is not diluted.

(i) The term of all the elected tiers should be 4 years, and, as far as possible, election to all these bodies should be held simultaneously;

(j) Panchayati Raj elections should be conducted by the Chief Election Officer of the State in consultation with the Chief Election Commissioner;

(k) The State Government should not supersede the Panchayati Raj Institutions on partisan grounds and if supersession becomes necessary, these should be replaced by an elected body within six months. The State Governments should not postpone elections of Panchayati Raj Institutions;

(l) All Panchayati Raj Institutions should have compulsory powers of taxation. A select list of taxation powers should be given to the Panchayati Raj Institutions and out of them, some should be made compulsory;

(m) Nyaya Panchayats should be kept as separate bodies and should not be mixed with the people elected for development Panchayats. The members of development Panchayats wield executive powers and there are chances that justice may suffer if the two functions are combined;

(n) There should be a Minister for Panchayati Raj whose main tasks would be to take care of the Panchayati Raj Institutions;

(o) The role of voluntary agencies in mobilizing people's support for Panchayati Raj is crucial. Voluntary organizations should be strengthened and encouraged to supplement the efforts of the Panchayati Raj Institutions;

(p) Constitutional status should be accorded to Panchayati Raj institutions;

(q) Any financial devolution should be committed to accepting that much of the developmental functions at the district level would be played by the Panchayats;

The committee report was discussed at the Conference of Chief Ministers convened during in May, 1979. The Chief Ministers agreed to delegate more financial and administrative powers to PRIs, so that the latter could function as effective instruments of development. The Conference did not accept the recommendations of the Committee regarding a Constitutional Amendment to delegate more powers from State to Panchayat levels and said that State Legislatures would take appropriate action in the matter. The reluctance of the State governments to devolve power to the local bodies failed these recommendations, and therefore no tangible results followed. In fact, thereafter, the decline in the value and performance of PRIs was even more rapid, except in Karnataka, Andhra Pradesh, Maharashtra, Gujarat, and West Bengal.

Hanumantha Rao Committee (1982)

A Working Group on District Planning headed by Dr. C.H. Hanumantha Rao (appointed by the Planning Commission), brought out the fact that planning from below was undermined by different streams of funding the district plan. As States had to prepare their annual plans within the framework prescribed by the government of India, they, in turn, prescribed rigid guidelines, which left little scope for flexibility to District Development Councils in preparation of their annual plans. Substantial funds were also retained at the State level and schemes were formulated by sectoral departments without much consultation with the District Development Council.

The Working Group recommended the following steps to achieve the objective of meaningful district planning:

(a) For good district planning, functions, powers, and finances need to be decentralized. States should outline the sharing of functions with districts.

(b) Each district plan must reflect the basic objectives of the national plan and the divisible plan outlay ought to be distributed to districts on the basis of population, area, and level of development.

(c) District Planning Bodies consisting of a Chairman, Member-Secretary, and about fifty members, in which the Collector is the Chief Co-ordinator should be set up. The District Planning body should be assisted by a Chief Planning Officer assisted by Block level planning officers and technical experts from various disciplines.

Thus, the District Planning Committee is an institution of decentralized planning. Reports of First ARC (1967), Dantwala Committee (1978), and Hanumantha Rao Committee (1983) had recommended its creation. 74th Constitutional Amendment Act, 1992 made it a constitutional obligation to establish the District Planning Committee by the Article 243ZD. But the Hanumantha Rao Committee recommended for conferring more developmental and planning functions to the District Collector. This is where are the other committees such as Ashok Mehta Committee, Administrative Reforms Commission, and G.V.K. Rao Committee differed. These committees wanted to reduce the bureaucratic role in developmental and planning process and confer more such functions to the Panchayat Raj.

G.V.K. Rao Committee (1985)

The 'Committee on Administrative Arrangements for Rural Development and Poverty Alleviation Programmes' which is famously called as 'G.V.K. Rao Committee' was appointed by the Planning Commission to once again look at various aspects of Panchayati Raj Institutions. The committee was of the opinion that rural development has to encompass all economic and social development activities handled by different agencies at the field level. It is not advisable to limit anti-poverty programmes to a few specific schemes. Moreover, government machinery (bureaucracy) alone cannot be assigned the responsibility for achieving economic development and social justice.

Therefore, the committee made the following recommendations:

(a) Panchayati Raj institutions have to be activised and given all the support needed so that they can become effective organisations for handling people's problems. Elections to these bodies should be held regularly;

(b) It is also necessary to encourage voluntary agencies, with informed idealism, operating in rural areas, in every possible way;

(c) The district should be the basic unit for policy planning and programme implementation. The Zilla Parishad should, therefore, become the principal body for management of all development programmes which can be handled at that level;

(d) Panchayati Raj institutions at the district level and below should be assigned an important role in respect of planning, implementation, and monitoring of rural development programmes;

(e) Some of the planning functions at the state level may have to be transferred to the district level for effective decentralised district planning. In this connection, the Committee recommends the introduction of the concept of district budget. It is desirable that it is brought into being as quickly as possible;

(f) The Committee also recommended a post of District Development Commissioner (DDC) be created to look after and coordinate all the developmental activities in the district. The DDC may be made the Chief Executive of the Zilla Parishad who shall hold the responsibility for planning and implementation of various development programmes. The office of the DDC should be of a higher status than that of the District Collector in order to establish the primacy of the Development administration over maintenance administration. In order to reduce the other burden of the Collector, a senior Deputy Commissioner or a junior Deputy Commissioner should be appointed to perform the routine tasks as well as protocol.

(g) The Committee recommends that the Block Development Office should be the sheet anchor of the entire rural development process. For this purpose the status of this office should be upgraded. The Chief Executive Officer of the block/tehsil may be designated as Assistant Development Commissioner (ADC). The ADC should be an officer of the status of Sub-Divisional Officer. There is a need to improve the quality and status of the Block Development Officer. It was felt that as their function is very important, they should be given better status as well as better training

Laxmi Mal Singhvi Committee (1986)

More thinking on PRIs was initiated by the Committee for the Concept Paper on Panchayati Raj Institutions (CCPPRI) also known as the L.M. Singhvi Committee.

The Committee made the following recommendations:

(a) Panchayati Raj Institutions have to be viewed as institutions of self-government which would actually facilitate the participation of the people in the process of planning and development flowing from and as a part of the concept of self-government.

(b) Local self-government should be constitutionally recognized, protected, and preserved by the inclusion of a new chapter in the Constitution. The most important expression of the report may be — "Panchayati Raj institutions should be constitutionally proclaimed as the third tier of Government." This concept of Panchayats as a constitutionally sanctioned third tier was something entirely new and pointed at future developments. Although the L.M. Singhvi Committee made no specific recommendations on the text of a constitutional provision, it suggested that such a provision would help enforcing elections at the local level.

(c) There was introduction and strengthening of Gram Sabhas, corporate village assemblies, as the foundation of democratic self-government.

(d) With respect to the revenue aspect, there should be optional and compulsory levies which should be entrusted to the Panchayati Raj Institutions. For initial years, the State government may levy on behalf of the Panchayati Raj Institutions and disburse money to them. This disbursement should be based upon the recommendations of the State Finance Commission.

(e) For jurisdiction of the Panchayati Raj Institutions, Nyaya Panchayats should be established for a cluster of villages.

(f) Affirming the recognition of Panchayats as political units, the L.M. Singhvi Report acknowledged, in line with the Ashok Mehta Committee Report, the role of political parties. It therefore recommended that there should no prohibition of party politics and party competition in Panchayat elections by law. Nevertheless, the committee did not take a stand for or against the role of political parties. Rather, it suggested that political parties and the government should negotiate the position of party politics in Panchayats among themselves[8].

(g) Judicial tribunals should be established to adjudicate Panchayati Raj election disputes.

[8]This issue of the role of political parties in Panchayats has divided the advocates of PRI into two camps. On the one side are those such as Jayaprakash Narayan, writing within the Gandhian tradition of partyless democracy, who saw 'self government through faction-fighting will not be self-government but self-ruination', and on the other are those such as Asoka Mehta who support the involvement of political parties since it enables candidates, from weak economic backgrounds, to effectively compete because now they have the backing of a strong organization.

Thungon Committee (1988)

This initiative was taken under the leadership of Rajiv Gandhi in 1988. A Sub-Committee of Parliament headed by P.K. Thungon recommended that Panchayati Raj bodies should be constitutionally recognized and the Constitution should have a provision to ensure timely and regular election to these bodies and their term should be five years.

Main Recommendations of Thungon Committee on Panchayati Raj Institutions

(a) Panchayati Raj bodies should be constitutionally recognized.

(b) A three-tier structure for Panchayati Raj with Village Panchayat at the bottom, district Panchayat at the top and mandal Panchayat in the middle, has been recommended where it does not already exist.

(c) The Zilla Parishad as the only planning and development agency in the district.

(d) It advocated setting up of a Planning and Coordination Committee at the State level under the Chairmanship of the Planning Minister. Presidents of the Zilla Parishad would be members of the Committee.

(e) The judicial functions of the village Panchayat are required to be revived so that simple disputes can be sorted out at the village level itself.

(f) The Committee has recommended that MPs and MLAs should be suitably associated with Zilla Parishad.

(g) As regards the procedure for the approval of the District Plan, it has been suggested that the District Planning and Coordination Committee at the Zilla Parishad should be well equipped and should be able to draw upon the latest technology including computer linking the district with the Divisional Headquarters and the State Capital with a two-way querying system.

(h) The suitable constitutional provision should be made to ensure timely and regular elections. The elections could be conducted by the Chief Electoral Officers of the State.

(i) In case a local body does not function in accordance with law; or grossly abuses its powers, it could be suspended or dissolved by the State Government. After any dissolution, the State Government will have to bring a Resolution in the State Legislature before the end of the session or within six weeks of the commencement of the session, whichever is earlier for approval by the House. In any case, a body should not be superseded for a period of more than six months.

(j) The term of Panchayati Raj bodies should be for a period of 5 years. However, the State Government may choose the term depending upon their requirements but this term may not be less than 3 years.

(k) It is recommended that a separate Panchayati Raj Judicial Tribunal should be appointed by the State Government to adjudicate controversies in matters which hamper the functioning of these institutions.

(l) It is recommended that the system of reservation for all the three-tiers of Panchayati Raj bodies should be as per population. In case of areas with the tribal population of more than 30%, the Chairman of the body should be a member from the Scheduled Tribes. Vice-Chairmanship of all the Panchayati Raj bodies should be reserved for a SC or ST member.

(m) It is recommended that as a rule, not less than two women should be members of Panchayati Raj bodies at each level. In case of bodies of small size with membership up to five, there would be only one place reserved for a woman member.

(n) Collector/DC should be the pivotal point for both regulatory as well as development administration. Collector should be the Chief Executive Officer of the Zilla Parishad. The State Government should appoint officers of the rank of Additional Collectors to assist the Collector in development and regulatory administration respectively.

(o) A detailed list of subjects to be dealt with at the district level should be prepared and included in the corresponding schedule of the Constitution.

(p) State Government should set up Finance Commissions to lay down the criteria and guidelines whereby resources would be allocated to the districts. Funds should be allocated to the concerned departments like PWD, Irrigation, Public Health, Rural Water Supply, etc. through the Zilla Parishad.

(q) It envisaged a District Budget where various schemes and projects required in a district are to be taken into account along with contingencies which have not figured in the district budget.

(r) The Sub-Committee felt that the Government of India could also promote Panchayati Raj institutions by giving certain incentives to State Government, e.g., by way of increasing grants-in-aid with reference to financial and other powers devolved upon these institutions by the respective State Government.

(s) The Central Government could organize training programmes for both officials and non-officials of local bodies so that they could be fully familiar with the potentialities of these bodies for development administration.

Gadgil Committee (1988)

Many committees recommended policies and programs for the proper establishment of Panchayati Raj system in India. But the recommendations by the Gadgil committee under the chairmanship of V.N. Gadgil (The Committee on Policy and Programmes)[9] became the basis for drafting an amendment bill aimed at conferring constitutional status to Panchayati Raj institutions.

Following are the recommendations:

(a) The Panchayati Raj bodies should have the responsibility of preparation and implementation of plans for socio-economic development. For this purpose, a list of subjects should be specified in the Constitution.

(b) The Panchayati Raj bodies should be empowered to levy and collect taxes.

(c) The State Finance Commission and State Election Commission should be established for the allocation of finances to the Panchayat and conduction of elections to the Panchayat respectively.

(d) The duration term of Panchayati Raj institutions should be for five years.

(e) The members of the Panchayat at all three levels should be directly elected by the people.

(f) Seats should be reserved for Scheduled Castes/Scheduled Tribes and women.

(g) Constitutional status should be accorded to Panchayati Raj Institutions.

---

[9]Constituted by the Congress Party.

DECENTRALISATION – CHRONOLOGY OF ATTEMPTS AND COMMITTEE REPORTS

Year	Item	Ideas And Concepts
First Plan, 51–56	Community Development Blocks	To break up planning exercise into National, State, District, and Local Community levels
Second Plan, 56–61	District Development Councils	Drawing up of village plans and popular participation in planning through the process of democratic decentralizaton
1957	Balwant Rai Mehta Committee	Village, Block, District Panchayat institutions established
1963	K. Santhanam Committee	Appointed to look solely at the issue of PRI finance
1967	Administrative Reforms Commission	Resources to be given/ local variations accommodated, purposeful plan for area
1969	Planning Commission	Formulated guidelines; detailed the concept of the district plan and methodology of drawing up such a plan in the framework of annual plans, medium term plans, and perspective plans
1978	Prof. M.L. Dantwala	Block level planning to form a link between village and district level planning
1978	Ashok Mehta Committee	Constitutionally recognized two-tier system where seats for SCs and STs should be reserved as per population and inclusion of political parties at all levels of election and formation of Nyaya Panchayat
1984	Hanumantha Rao Committee	Decentralisation of function, powers, and finances; Setting up of district planning bodies and district planning cells
1985	G.V.K. Rao Committee	Administrative arrangements for rural development; district Panchayat to manage all development programmes
1987	L.M. Singhvi Committee	Recommended that the Panchayati Raj should be constitutionally recognized. Recommended for the strengthening of Gram Sabha, Gram Panchayat, and restructuring of village
1988	P.K. Thungon Committee	Recommended for regular and timely Panchayat election
1988	Gadgil Committee	Recommendations of this committee became the basis for the Constitutional Amendment Bill. Panchayati Raj bodies should have the responsibility of preparation and implementation of plans for socio-economic development

The suggestion of giving Panchayati Raj Institutions a Constitutional status was opposed by the Sarkaria Commission but the idea however gained momentum in the late 1980s. In May 1989, Prime Minister Rajiv Gandhi himself introduced the Constitution (64th Amendment) Bill, saying: "Our Bill will ensure that Panchayati Raj has a democratic character similar to the Lok Sabha and the State Assemblies and constitutional protection for their functioning as representative institutions of the people." The Constitution (64th Amendment) Bill was followed in July 1989 with the Constitution (65th Amendment) Bill that sought to endow urban local bodies—from town Panchayats and Municipalities to Metropolitan Councils—with powers similar to those that were sought to be devolved to the rural Panchayats.

Although both Bills received the required two-thirds majority with at least half the members present and voting in the Lok Sabha (on October 13, 1989), the Bills failed to muster—by a handful of votes—the required constitutional majority in the Rajya Sabha. In September 1990, the Government introduced the Constitution (74th Amendment) Bill—a combined Bill on Panchayats and Municipalities—but, before this was taken up for discussion, there was a change of government.

The Government under Prime Minister P. V. Narasimha Rao introduced the 73rd (Panchayats) and 74th (Nagarpalika) Constitution Amendment Bills. During his government the Acts came into force as the Constitution (73rd Amendment) Act, 1992 on April 24, 1993 and the Constitution (74th Amendment) Act, 1992 on June 1, 1993. This added two new parts to the Constitution, namely, Part IX titled 'The Panchayats' and Part IXA titled 'The Municipalities.'

VILLAGE PANCHAYATS (73rd CONSTITUTIONAL AMENDMENT)

Until the enactment of the 73rd Amendment of the Constitution, the Panchayat System was based purely on State laws and the functioning of the system was very sporadic. The Constitutional Amendment seeks to strengthen the system by giving it constitutional protection.

The 73rd Amendment together with 74th Amendment is called 'a silent revolution'. The 73rd Amendment Act has added a new PART IX to the Constitution of India. This part is entitled as 'The Panchayats' and consists of provisions from Art 243 to 243(O). In addition, the Act has also added a new 11th Schedule to the Constitution. This schedule contains 29 functional items of the Panchayats which deals with Article 243G.

This amendment implements the Article 40 of the DPSP which says that "State shall take steps to organise village Panchayats and endow them with such powers and authority as may be necessary to enable them to function as units of self-government" and has upgraded them from non-justifiable to justifiable part of the Constitution and has put constitutional obligation upon states to enact the Panchayati Raj Acts as per provisions of the Part IX. The notable feature of these constitutional provisions is that these are in the nature of basic provisions which need to be supplemented by law made by the respective State Legislature. States have been given enough freedom to take their geographical, politico-administrative and other conditions into account while adopting the Panchayati Raj System. Therefore, the provisions of the 73rd Amendment Act are grouped into 2 categories: Compulsory and voluntary. The compulsory provisions of the Act have to be included in the state laws while creating the new Panchayati Raj system. The voluntary provisions may be included at the discretion of the states. The salient features of Panchayati Raj system under 73rd Constitutional Amendment Act are as follows –

Three-Tier Structure (Article 243B)

Part IX provides for a three-tier Panchayat system, which would be constituted in every state at the village level, intermediate level, and district level. At the base is the 'Gram Panchayat'. A Gram Panchayat covers a village or group of villages. The intermediary level is the Mandal (also referred to as Block or Taluka). These bodies are called Mandal or Taluka Panchayats. However, the states which were having population below 20 lakh are given an option to not to have the intermediate level. At the apex is the Zilla Panchayat covering the entire rural area of the District.

Gram Sabha (Article 243A)

Gram Sabha is a body consisting of all the persons registered in the electoral rolls relating to a village comprised within the area of Panchayat at the village level. Since all the persons registered in electoral rolls are members of Gram Sabha, there are no elected representatives. Further, Gram Sabha is the only permanent unit in Panchayati Raj system and not constituted for a particular period. Although it serves as foundation of the Panchayati Raj, yet it is not among the three-tiers of the same. The powers and functions of Gram Sabha are fixed by state legislature by law.

Duration of Panchayats (Article 243E)

A clear term for 5 years has been provided for the Panchayats and elections must take place before the expiry of the terms. However, the Panchayat may be dissolved earlier on specific grounds in accordance with the state legislations. In that case, the elections must take place before expiry of 6 months of the dissolution. In other words, an election to constitute a Panchayat shall be completed –

(a) Before the expiry of its duration of five years; or

(b) Before the expiration of a period of six months from the date of its dissolution. But, where the remainder of the period (for which the dissolved Panchayat would have continued) is less than six months, it shall not be necessary to hold any election for constituting the new Panchayat for such remaining period.

Moreover, a Panchayat constituted upon the dissolution of a Panchayat before the expiration of its duration shall continue only for the remainder of the period for which the dissolved Panchayat would have continued, had it not been so dissolved. In other words, if there is a premature dissolution of a Panchayat, the new Panchayat which is reconstituted shall continue only for the remainder period, not for full period of five years.

However, no amendment of any law for the time being in force shall cause dissolution of the Panchayat at any level before the expiry of the five years term.

Members of Panchayats (Article 243C)

All levels of Panchayats will consist of persons elected directly from the territorial constituencies in the Panchayat area. The territorial constituencies shall be carved out in such manner that the ratio between the population of each constituency and the number of seats allotted to it should be uniform throughout the Panchayat area as far as practicable.

The Chairperson of a Panchayat at the intermediate and district level shall be elected from among the directly elected members representing the territorial constituencies. In other words, the Chairperson of the Panchayat at the intermediate and district level shall be indirectly elected. But at the village level, the election of chairperson of Panchayat (Sarpanch) may be direct or indirect as provided by the state in its own Panchayati Raj Act.

All members of the Panchayat including the Chairpersons whether or not directly elected shall have the right to vote in the meetings of the Panchayats.

Reservation of Seats (Article 243D)

In the directly elected seats of members in all Panchayats, there will be reservation of seats for Scheduled Castes (SC) and Scheduled Tribes (ST), in proportion to their total population in a Panchayat area, and one-third of these seats will be reserved for women belonging to these groups.

Of the seats to be filled by direct election in every Panchayat, there will be not less than one-third reservation of seats in Panchayats for women[10], including the seats reserved for SC/ST women.

The offices of Chairpersons in the Panchayats at all levels will be reserved for the SC/STs and women as the State legislature may decide, provided that not less than one-third of the Chairpersons' positions shall be reserved for women. Likewise, there will be reservation in the offices of Chairpersons in Panchayats at all levels for members of the SCs and STs, in proportion to their population in the state.

The reservations of seats for SCs and STs (other than the reservation for women) mentioned above ceases to have effect on the expiration of the period specified in Article 334. By 104th Constitutional Amendment Act, 2019 the period has been extended till January 25, 2030.

Further, a State Legislature can make any provision for reservation of seats in any Panchayat or offices of chairpersons in the Panchayat at any level in favour of "backward class of citizens". The expression 'Backward Class' has not been defined. The Patna High Court in *Krishna Kumar Mishra vs. State of Bihar*[11], ruled that it is well within the domain of the Legislature to determine as to who is the Backward Class and the caste can be one of the factors for such determination.

Reservations of Seats in Arunachal Pradesh – Article 243M (3A)

Arunachal Pradesh is a State inhabited fully by indigenous tribal people. The Bengal Eastern Frontier Regulation, 1873 and the Chin Hill Regulations, 1896 provide special protection and safeguard for the peaceful existence of the indigenous tribal people of Arunachal Pradesh. These laws probihit the entry of outsiders in the tribal area without "Inner Line Permit". Only the indigenous tribal people are allowed to participate in the democratic process.

Moreover, the tribal society in Arunachal Pradesh is casteless where social equality among men and women has prevailed over centuries and ages. Since no Scheduled Castes exist in the State and the State of Arunachal Pradesh is singularly free from the caste system, a new clause (3A) in article 243M was added by 83rd Constitutional Amendment Act, 2000, to exempt the State of Arunachal Pradesh from the application of article 243D relating to the reservation of seats in Panchayats for the Scheduled Castes.

In other words, since no Scheduled Castes exist in the State, no reservation of seats for the Scheduled Castes has been made in the State Legislative Assembly and no provisions exist under any law to that effect. There is also no reservation for the Scheduled Castes in State Government services.

Disqualification for Membership (Article 243F)

A person shall be disqualified for being chosen as, and for being, a member of Panchayat :

(a) If he is so disqualified by or under any law for the time being in force for the purposes of elections to the Legislature of the State concerned. Provided that no person shall be disqualified on the ground that he is less than twenty five years of age, if he has attained the age of twenty one years; or

(b) If he is so disqualified by or under any law made by the Legislature of the State.

---

[10] As per the information available with the Ministry of Panchayati Raj (as on September 23rd, 2020), 20 States namely Andhra Pradesh, Assam, Bihar, Chhattisgarh, Gujarat, Himachal Pradesh, Jharkhand, Karnataka, Kerala, Madhya Pradesh, Maharashtra, Odisha, Punjab, Rajasthan, Sikkim, Tamil Nadu, Telangana, Tripura, Uttarakhand, and West Bengal have made provisions of 50% reservation for women in Panchayati Raj Institutions in their respective State Panchayati Raj Acts.

[11] AIR 1996 Pat 112

The main principle followed is that the grounds of disqualification should be the same as applied for elections to the State Legislatures. In other words, any person who is qualified to become an MLA is qualified to become a member of the Panchayat, but for Panchayat the minimum age prescribed is 21 years. Further, the State Legislatures are empowered to provide additional provisions or criteria for disqualifications.

Javed Vs. State of Haryana[12] - In Haryana, a person having more than two living children was disqualified from holding any offices in Panchayats. The purpose was to promote family planning. The petitioners and appellants in the case were individuals who had been disqualified from holding an office in Panchayat due to the reason that they had more than two children. The Supreme Court upheld the provision as constitutional and in keeping with the objective of popularising socio-economic welfare and healthcare of the masses.

If any question arises as to whether a member of a Panchayat has become subject to any of the disqualifications mentioned above, the question shall be referred for the decision of such authority as determined by the State Legislature.

State Election Commission (Article 243K)

This Article provides for Constitution of a State Election Commission in respect of the Panchayats. This State Election Commission would have the power to supervise, direct, and control the elections to the Panchayats and also prepare the electoral rolls.

The State Election Commissioner shall be appointed by the Governor. Subject to the provisions of any law made by the Legislature of a State, the terms, tenure, and conditions of the office of the Election commissioners shall be determined by the Governor. But such conditions of service shall not be varied to his disadvantage.

The Governor of a State shall, when requested by the State Election Commission, make available to the State Election Commission such staff as may be necessary for the discharge of the functions conferred on the State Election Commission.

The Constitution maintains the independence of the Election Commission by making provisions that the State Election Commissioner would be removed only by manner and on same grounds as a Judge of the High Court. In other words, only the President of India can remove the State Election Commissioner in the same manner as he removes the Judge of a High Court. However, the State Election Commissioner can resign from his office by addressing the resignation letter to the Governor.

Further, the State Legislatures are empowered to make laws with respect to all matters relating to, or in connection with, elections to the Panchayats.

Bar to Interference by Courts in Electoral Matters (Article 243O)

As under Article 329, courts shall have no jurisdiction to examine the validity of a law, relating to delimitation of constituencies or the allotments of seats, made under Article 243K.

If there is a dispute in the Panchayat elections, the Courts have no jurisdiction over them. This means that the Panchayat election can be questioned only in the form of an election petition presented to an authority which the State legislature by law can prescribe.

---

[12](2003) 8 SCC 369.

Powers, Authority, and Responsibilities of Panchayats (Article 243G)

State Legislatures have power to confer on the Panchayats such powers and authority as may be necessary to enable them to function as institutions of self-government [Articles 243G–243H]. They may be entrusted with the responsibility of (a) preparing plans for economic development and social justice, (b) implementation of schemes for economic development and social justice, and (c) in regard to matters listed in the Eleventh Schedule (inserted by the 73rd Amendment). The list contains 29 items, e.g., land improvement, minor irrigation, animal husbandry, fisheries, education, women and child development, etc. The 11th Schedule thus distributes powers between the State Legislature and the Panchayat just as the 7th Schedule distributes powers between the Union and the State Legislature.

Thus, Eleventh Schedule gives a list of 29 subjects in respect of which functions, finances and functionaries may be devolved by the State to Panchayati Raj Institutions.

Following are the items given under the Eleventh Schedule:

1. Agriculture, including agricultural extension
2. Land improvement, implementation of land reforms, land consolidation, and soil conservation
3. Minor irrigation, water management, and watershed development
4. Animal husbandry, dairying, and poultry
5. Fisheries
6. Social forestry and farm forestry
7. Minor forest produce
8. Small-scale industries, including food processing industries
9. Khadi, village, and cottage industries
10. Rural housing
11. Drinking water
12. Fuel and fodder
13. Roads, culverts, bridges, ferries, waterways, and other means of communication
14. Rural electrification, including distribution of electricity
15. Non-conventional energy sources
16. Poverty alleviation programme
17. Education, including primary and secondary schools
18. Technical training and vocational education
19. Adult and non-formal education
20. Libraries
21. Cultural activities
22. Markets and fairs
23. Health and sanitation, including hospitals, primary health centres, and dispensaries
24. Family welfare
25. Women and child development

26. Social welfare, including welfare of the handicapped and mentally retarded
27. Welfare of the weaker sections, and in particular, of the Scheduled Castes and the Scheduled Tribes
28. Public distribution system
29. Maintenance of community system

Powers to Impose Taxes and Financial Resources (Article 243H)

A State may by law :

(a) Authorize a Panchayat to levy, collect, and appropriate taxes, duties, tolls, etc. The law may lay down the procedure to be followed as well as the limits of these exactions.

(b) Assign to a Panchayat various taxes, duties, etc. collected by the State Government.

(c) Allocate Grants-in-aids to the Panchayats from the Consolidated Fund of the State.

(d) Provide for Constitution of funds for crediting all moneys received, by or on behalf of the Panchayats, and also for the withdrawal of such moneys there from.

State Finance Commission (Article 243I)

(a) Within one year from the date of commencement of the 73rd Constitutional Amendment and afterwards every five years, the Governor shall appoint a Finance Commission to review the financial position of the Panchayats and to make recommendations as to -

- The distribution between the State and the Panchayats of the net proceeds of taxes, duties, tolls, and fees leviable by the State which may be divided between them and how allocation would be made among various levels of Panchayats;
- The determination of the taxes, duties, tolls, and fees which may be assigned to, or appropriated by the Panchayat;
- The grants-in-aid to Panchayats from the Consolidated Fund of the State;
- The measures needed to improve the financial position of the Panchayats;
- Any other matter referred to the Finance Commission by the Governor in the interests of sound finance of the Panchayats.

The Union Finance Commission also suggests the measures needed to augment the Consolidated Funds of States to supplement the resources of the Panchayats in the states.

(b) Tenure of State Finance Commission : As noted above, a State Finance Commission is appointed at the expiry of every five years. However, there is no fixed term of its working; and it ceases to exist as soon as it submits its report. The experience of most of the states indicates that a State Finance Commission generally works for a period of one year to one and a half years.

(c) Term of Members : Every member of the State Finance Commission holds office for such period as may be specified by the Governor (in order). Members of the Finance Commission are eligible for reappointment. The members can resign from their office by addressing a letter to the Governor.

(d) Composition : The State Legislature may by law, provide for the composition of the commission and the qualifications required for the appointment of the members.

(e) Reports : The report of the Commission, together with a memorandum of action taken on it, shall be laid before the State Legislature by the Governor.

(f) Procedure : The Commission shall determine its own procedure and shall enjoy such powers in the performance of its functions as determined by the State Legislature.

Audit of Accounts (Article 243J)

State Government can make provisions for maintenance and audit of accounts of the Panchayats.

Applications to Union Territories (Article 243L)

Provisions of Panchayats shall be applicable to the UTs in the same way as in case of the states. However, the President by a public notification may make any modifications in the applications of any part.

Exempted Areas and States (Article 243M)

The provisions of Part IX are not applicable to the following:

(a) Fifth Schedule areas (Article 244(1)) and Sixth Schedule areas (Article 244(2)) (However, Parliament may by law extend its provisions to the Scheduled and Tribal Areas subject to such exceptions and modifications as may be specified in such law and no such law shall be deemed to be an amendment to the Constitution. In pursuance of this provision the Parliament passed the Panchayats Extension to Scheduled Areas Act, 1996 and extended the provisions to only Fifth Schedule areas;

(b) Entire states of Nagaland, Meghalaya, and Mizoram (However, the State Legislatures of these States can extend the provisions of Part IX by law to their respective states by passing a resolution with special majority);

(c) Hill areas in the State of Manipur for which District Councils exist;

(d) The district level provisions shall not apply to the hill areas of the District of Darjeeling in the State of West Bengal which affect the Darjeeling Gorkha Hill Council.

(e) The reservation provisions are not applicable to Arunachal Pradesh (as discussed above).

CONTINUANCE OF EXISTING LAWS

Any provision of any law relating to Panchayats in force in a State immediately before the commencement of the Constitution (Seventy-third Amendment) Act, 1992, which is inconsistent with the provisions of this Part, shall continue to be in force until amended or repealed by a competent Legislature or competent authority or until the expiration of one year from the date on which the Amendment Act receives the assent of the President (i.e., within one year from 24th April 1993). In other words, any law made by the states relating to Panchayats which is inconsistent to Part IX shall come to an end within one year of the commencement of the amendment. So the States have to amend or pass Panchayati Raj related laws in accordance with the Constitution.

Mandatory Provisions and Discretionary Provisions

The 73rd Amendment stipulates for certain compulsory provisions which are obligatory on the part of the State Governments to incorporate in their respective Acts. Some aspects have, however, been left at the discretion of State legislatures to make suitable provisions in their Act.

The mandatory provisions are:

(a) There will be establishment of Gram Sabha at village level consisting of people registered in the electoral roll relating to a village falling within the area of the Panchayat.

(b) There will be establishment of three-tier system of Panchayati Raj at village, intermediate, and district level in all States and UTs except those States having a population of less than 20 lakhs.

(c) At all levels, Panchayats will comprise of persons chosen by direct election from the respective territorial constituencies.

(d) All members of Panchayats elected directly or indirectly shall have voting rights in Panchayat meetings.

(e) The Chairpersons of the intermediate and the apex tier of Panchayats will be elected from among the directly elected members.

(f) Reservation for SCs and STs in memberships and offices of chairpersons will be provided based on their population in a Panchayat.

(g) Not less than one-third of the membership and the offices of chairperson will be reserved for women.

(h) Five year term has been decided for all tiers of Panchayats. If a Panchayat dissolves earlier than the above term for whatever reason, fresh elections will be held within 6 months. In case the term remaining is less than 6 months, it is not mandatory to hold election for this period.

(i) There will be constitution of State Finance Commission within one year from the commencement of the Act and thereafter at the expiry of every five years. Sub-Clause "bb" was also inserted in Article 280 of the Constitution. As per this sub-clause, the Central Finance Commission shall recommend to the President, the measures need to augment the Consolidated Fund of a State to supplement the resources of the Panchayats in the State on the basis of the recommendations made by the Finance Commission of the State.

(j) There will be constitution of the State Election Commission for supervision, direction, and control of the preparation of electoral rolls and conducting elections to the Panchayats.

(k) Minimum age for contesting Panchayat elections is 21 years.

(l) The applicability of Part IX is exempted for certain Schedules areas and the tribal areas.

Discretionary Provisions

As the subject of Panchayati Raj Institutions is under the domain of the State List, the 73rd Amendment Act has given discretionary powers to the State on devolution of powers, functions, authority, finance, etc., to the Panchayats.

Following are the enabling provisions given in this Act for the States:

(a) Powers and Functions of the Gram Sabha.

(b) Providing representation of the Chairpersons of Gram/Village Panchayat at intermediate level or, in the case of a State not having Panchayats at the intermediate level, in the Panchayats at district level.

(c) Providing representation of the Chairpersons of the Panchayats at the intermediate level, in the Panchayats at the district level.

(d) Membership of the MP, MLA, and MLCs at intermediate and district levels.

(e) Mode of election of the Chairperson at the Gram/Village Panchayat level.

(f) Reservation of seats in favour of backward classes of citizens in terms of membership as well such chairpersonship, at different tiers of the Panchayati Raj Institutions.

(g) Vesting of power, authority, and responsibility in the Panchayats which may be necessary for them to function as effective institutions of self-government, and to make provisions for devolution of powers and responsibility to Panchayats at the appropriate levels with respect to:

- The preparation of plans for economic development and social justice;
- The implementation of schemes for economic development and social justice entrusted to them including 29 subjects contained in the 11th Schedule of the Constitution

(h) Authorising each tier of the PRS to levy appropriate taxes, duties, tolls, and fees in accordance with a well-defined procedure of levying and allocation of such tax revenue collected by each of three-tiers of the Panchayati Raj Institutions.

(i) Allocation of taxes, duties, tolls, and fees levied by the State government to each tier of the PRS depending on the nature and magnitude of the responsibilities vested in each tier.

(g) Deciding the amount of grant-in-aid to the Panchayats from the Consolidated Fund of the State.

(k) Providing for Constitution of funds for crediting all moneys received, by or on behalf of the Panchayats and also for the withdrawal of such moneys therefrom.

(l) Composition of the State Finance Commission.

ROLE OF PANCHAYATS AS PER THE CONSTITUTION

Thus, the Constitution envisages for Panchayats to function as institutions of self-government and prepare plans and implement schemes for economic development and social justice. Although, the term 'institution of self-government' (ISG) has not been defined in the Constitution, the perception and the connotation are well understood. In order to function as institutions of self-government, the Panchayats have to fulfil three basic conditions, namely[13]:

(a) Institutional existence in the sense that the decisions are taken by the people's representatives;

(b) Institutional capacity, which means that these institutions have clearly defined functions, functionaries, and finances;

(c) Financial viability in terms of sufficiently empowering them in raising resources to meet their responsibilities.

In other words, the Panchayats should enjoy functional, administrative, and financial autonomy at their levels.

Achievements of the 73rd Constitutional Amendment Act

The introduction of Panchayati Raj as the third tier[14] of decentralized administration is indeed one of the most remarkable social and political reforms since independence. The Constitution envisages for Panchayats to function as institutions of self-government and prepare plans and implement schemes for economic development and social justice.

---

[13] Local Self Government vetted via Devolution Index, Dr. Mahi Pal, Kurukshetra, A journal on Rural Development, Vol. 62, No.3, Page 8, 2014.

[14] Panchayati Raj institutions form the third strata of the decentralized structure of the government of India, the two being the Central government and State government.

After the 73rd Constitutional Amendment Act, all states in India initiated the process of radical democratic decentralization. Some states are ahead of other states in implementing the Panchayati Raj Institutions. In some states the system has played a pivotal role in changing the traditional power structure dominated by the local elite bureaucratic network. In other states the system has led to the empowerment of hitherto marginalized sections of society like women, SCs, STs, and other backward classes.

Moreover, soon after the 73rd and 74th Amendments, every state government began the process of creating the requisite layer of Panchayati Raj Institutions and urban local bodies. State election commissions were in charge of the infrastructure required to elect local representatives.

Further, the *Gram Panchayats*' are charged with meeting the basic needs of its residents. All planning and implementation of programme for the social and economic development are carried out by the Gram Panchayats. For example, the *Panchayats (councils)* are responsible for ensuring all basic services for citizens such as drinking water supply, affordable rural housing, public distribution systems for essential commodities, maintenance of community assets, education, women and child development, social welfare, and welfare of vulnerable sections of the society.

In many ways, this has accelerated the process of decentralization of power. Currently[15], India has about 253,400 rural local bodies at the village level (*Gram Panchayats*), and 6613 intermediary or block-level *Panchayats*, and 630 district level Panchayats. There are about 3 million elected representatives of these Panchayats, out of which 1.3 million are women[16]. Thus, 70 per cent of India's population is covered through these local governance institutions. It is fascinating to visualize how the rural community has been mobilized into an electoral process that empowers them to take decisions for themselves.

The Panchayats are also provided requisite funds to manage their own affairs. The Finance Commission, constituted by the Government of India, mandates a certain share in the taxes collected by the central government to automatically flow into these rural local bodies. This is of course, apart from the mandated share that the Panchayats receive from their respective state governments. Also, key central and state government schemes and funds are converged at the *Panchaya* level to allow them to implement projects and to address the needs of the people more effectively.

With the Fourteenth and Fifteenth Finance Commissions' devolution to local bodies (LBs), there is an increase in the share of untied resources available with them. As a result, the Panchayat will now have a larger say in how to spend the money. Moreover, with increased devolution to local governments, the per capita availability of funds has increased. With increased per-capita availability of funding better standard of living of the rural population can be achieved by proper planning relating to expenditure on different sectors pertaining to development of the village.

Further, the Finance Commissions mandate Gram Panchayats to formulate a Gram Panchayat Plan prepared and approved by the Gram Sabhas. Thus, giving Panchayats a greater autonomy to decide on which basic services it wants to spend the allocated funds.

Challenges of 73rd Amendment

The 73rd Amendment introduced local governing bodies across India. This amendment, however, did not require the implementation of local self-governing bodies. In other words, it only mandated the creation of local self-governing bodies, and left the decision to delegate powers, functions, and finances to the state legislatures. And therein lies the gaps and challenges of Panchayati Raj Institutions.

---

[15] As on September 2021.

[16] https://www.unwomen.org/

1. In the State Panchayat and Municipal Acts after 1992, one finds that the states have accepted the letter of the 73rd or 74th Amendments rather than their spirit. In many State Acts, civil servants are indirectly given powers over the elected body. Transfer of activities and functions to Panchayats is taking place very slowly.
2. ***Delay in formulation of Rules & Bye-laws :*** Although all the states have passed conformity Acts, many of them are yet to formulate rules and byelaws for the day-to-day functioning of Panchayats. Added to this, the necessary infrastructural facilities are lacking for Panchayats in many states.
3. ***Lack of Personnel :*** The paucity of Panchayat personnel is also hampering Panchayats' functioning, particularly budget making. In many states one Secretary is in charge of two or three Panchayats.
4. ***Indifferent Attitude of MLA's and MP's :*** The reluctance of state-level politicians to recognize the importance of the lower level of governance – their autonomy, their powers, and their areas of functioning – is creating problems in devolving powers. There are instances where Ministers, MLAs, and senior political leaders are worried that the power they enjoyed so far will diminish if Panchayats and Municipalities become really powerful.
5. ***Lack of coordination between the rural Panchayati Raj Institutions and urban local bodies :*** At present, there is lack of coordination between the Panchayati Raj Institutions and the Urban local bodies. Article 243ZD of the Constitution provides that the municipal bodies are expected to coordinate and work in tandem with other institutions of self-government. The Chairman of the Zilla Parishad is the Chairman of the district planning committee and the mayor of the municipal corporation and president of the municipal councils in the district are members of this constitutional body.
6. ***Weak social auditing :*** Technically, the Panchayats do not have adequate expertise, manpower, and skill to plan and implement development schemes and projects. Thereby, they are increasing their dependence on the state apparatus (Dhaka, 2002). This puts them on the defensive while facing social auditing by the community.
7. ***Politicization of PRIs :*** Many sarpanches contest elections under the patronage of national and regional political parties, as it facilitates their political advancement. This has promoted the use of money and muscle power in Panchayat elections. Politicization of the Panchayats is also responsible for the dismal functioning of gram sabhas.
8. ***Centralization of power in the hands of sarpanches :*** Centralization of power in the hands of sarpanches dilutes the objective of de-concentration of power. In certain States, the power of the village council is totally concentrated in the hands of pradhans (Presidents), for all practical purposes, and the pradhan is a powerful man.
9. ***Growth of parallel bodies :*** The parallel bodies taking away functions of Panchayati Raj Institutions are a growing concern. Water user groups, joint forest management committees, and expert committees are a few examples of the working of parallel institutions in different states. A parliamentary standing committee commented that these parallel bodies were undermining the decision-making powers of the gram sabhas and the gram Panchayats. Even the youth clubs, mahila-mandals, and other village level organizations, that get direct grants from the government were undermining the role assigned to the Panchayati Raj Institutions by the Constitution.
10. ***Inadequate financial resources :*** It has been observed that mere holding of the elections of Panchayats and Municipalities does not mean decentralization. They also require sufficient powers and resources. The financial position of the Panchayati Raj Institutions is also not so good. As a result, they are unable to implement properly and effectively the 29 items assigned

to them. In such a situation, their development goals will remain only on paper. "If the size of funds is minimal in comparison to local requirements, it results in shortage of finds for large number of activities. Normally, PRIs have low level of internal funding as compared to their local requirements. They are mostly dependent on outside funds, which are in the form of grants distributed over a large number of Panchayati Raj Institutions and are quite insufficient to cater to the monumental task of strengthening the local development base. No doubt, states have constituted their respective Finance Commissions but the recommendations given by them have mostly not been given practical shape due to lack of political commitment.

11. ***Non Utilization of Sanctioned Funds*** **:** It has been found that the sanctioned funds are underutilized many times due to delay in planning, delay in release of funds, poor coordination among different administrative bodies, weather conditions like rainy seasons, negative attitude of villagers, and poor support of secretaries appointed by governments in each Panchayats.
12. ***Voting Rights to MLAs and MPs*** **:** Majority of state Acts have provided for representation to MLAs and MPs in the Panchayats along with voting rights. It would lead to over-domination thereof. It is also contrary to the spirit of decentralization.
13. ***Weak Gram Sabhas*** **:** In fact, in some of the States, the Gram Sabhas are not actively involved in planning, programming, implementation, and review of rural development schemes. The voters do not take the Gram Sabha meetings seriously because of the lack of adequate powers and relevance of functions. There is a great need of creating awareness about the role and relevance of this institution so that real democratic value could be imbibed.
14. ***Proxy Presence of Female Gram Pradhans*** **:** Although the 73rd and 74th Amendment Acts provide reservations to women, it only made them representatives, without really empowering them. Male relatives of the women representatives often take power from the women, taking advantage of their position in the artificially fabricated society. Although women representatives in rural areas don't face any kind of formal barriers, the cultural barriers like gender roles and financial constraints, low level of literacy, and non-party affiliation become inextricably knot with their problems.

QUESTIONS

Objective Questions

1. Which of the following is not true about the Village Panchayats?

   1. Election of the Panchayati Raj institutions is conducted under the guidance of the State Election Commission.
   2. The minimum age should be 18 years to contest the election at the Panchayat level.

   Select the correct code:

   (a) 1 only (b) 2 only
   (c) Both 1 and 2 (d) Neither 1 nor 2

   Ans: (b)

2. Consider the following statements: (UPSC CSE 2013)

   1. National Development Council is an organ of the Planning Commission.
   2. The Economic and Social Planning is kept in the Concurrent List in the Constitution of India.

3. The Constitution of India prescribes that Panchayats should be assigned the task of preparation of plans for economic development and social justice.

Which of the statements given above is/are correct?

(a) 1 only (b) 2 and 3 only

(c) 1 and 3 only (d) 1, 2 and 3

Ans: (b)

3. Which of the following is not a recommendation of the Ashok Mehta Committee on Panchayati Raj?

(a) Open participation of political parties in Panchayati Raj affairs

(b) Creation of a three-tier system

(c) Reservation of seats for Scheduled Castes and Scheduled Tribes

(d) Compulsory powers of taxation of Panchayati Raj Institution

Ans: (b)

4. The Constitution (Seventy-Third Amendment) Act, 1992, which aims at promoting the Panchayati Raj Institutions in the country, provides for which of the following? (2011)

1. Constitution of District Planning Committees
2. State Election Commissions to conduct all Panchayat elections
3. Establishment of State Finance Commissions

Select the correct answer using the codes given below:

(a) 1 only (b) 1 and 2 only

(c) 2 and 3 only (d) 1, 2, and 3

Ans: (c)

5. With reference to the Social Audit, consider the following statements:

1. It is a tool which empowers citizens to turn into auditors.
2. It is conducted jointly by the government and the people.
3. Any resident of a Panchayat can do social audit who is part of Gram Sabha.

Which of the statements given above is/are correct?

(a) 1 and 2 only (b) 1 and 3 only

(c) 2 and 3 only (d) 1, 2, and 3

Ans: (d)

Subjective Questions

1. "Resource mobilisation by the PRIs is generally limited. It is imperative to provide PRIs with revenue raising powers of their own in order to reduce their excessive dependence on the State and Central Governments". Discuss. **(250 words)**

2. "In order to accelerate the emergence of Gram Sabhas as bodies to whom the PRIs are accountable, it might be essential to spell out the powers and functions of the Gram Sabha in great detail". Critically analyze. **(150 words)**

18.2 : LOCAL SELF-GOVERNMENT IN SCHEDULED AREAS

EXTENSION TO THE FIFTH SCHEDULED AREAS AND PESA

Local self-governance, interpreted as devolution of powers and functions of the government departments to the Panchayati Raj Institutions (PRIs) is strengthened with the passage of the 73rd Amendment to the Constitution. The States made suitable amendments to existing Panchayat laws where they existed or enacted legislations in accordance with the 73rd Amendment where they did not exist.

The Fifth Scheduled Areas were exempted from the application of the 73rd Amendment for which the Parliament enacted a separate law, Panchayats (Extension to the Scheduled Areas) Act, 1996 (PESA).

Background[1] of PESA

Scheduled areas[2] in India are inhabited by the tribal population who have been managing their natural resources and governing their social, economic, and political life through a well-knit system of ancient customs and practices. However, in the wake of modernisation, these age old institutions of self-governance are fast becoming extinct. It is a challenge to usher the tribals into the mainstream of development efforts without disturbing or destroying their cultural identity and socio-economic milieu. To achieve this objective, Bhuria Committee was constituted in 1994 to examine various dimensions of self-rule for tribals, the constitutional requirements, and to make recommendations for extending the provisions of the Constitution 73rd (Amendment) Act, 1992 to the Scheduled Areas. Following the recommendations of the committee, the Parliament extended the provisions of the 73rd Amendment Act to the Scheduled Areas in the then eight states (now ten states) by passing Provisions of Panchayats (Extension to the Scheduled Areas) Act, 1996 (hereinafter PESA).

PESA legally recognizes the right of tribal communities to govern themselves through their own systems of self-government and also acknowledges their traditional rights over natural resources.

Key Provisions of PESA

'PESA is a unique legislation, often described as a Constitution within the Constitution, which attempts to bring together in a single frame two totally different worlds—the simple system of tribal communities governed by their respective customs and traditions, and the formal system of the State governed exclusively by laws[3]'. The Key provisions of the Act are as follows:

---

[1]PESA Implementation - Some Essential Prerequisites and Suggestions for the State Of Andhra Pradesh; By Enviro Legal Defence Firm, August 2011.

[2]Scheduled Areas are referred to in Article 244 (1) and Schedule V of the Constitution of India. The President has the power to declare an area as a Scheduled Area. Such areas are subject to the provisions of Schedule V and the executive powers of the State. Though no criteria was stipulated under the law for declaring any area as a 'Scheduled Area' under the Fifth Schedule, scheduling an area was on the basis of (a) preponderance of tribal population, (b) compactness and reasonable size of the area, (c) a viable administrative entity such as a district, block or taluk/tehasil, and (d) economic backwardness of the area as compared to the neighboring areas.

[3]Dandekar, Ajay and Chitrangada Choudhury. *PESA, Left-Wing Extremism and Governance: Concerns and Challenges in India's Tribal Districts*, Institute of Rural Management, Anand, Commissioned by Ministry of Panchayati Raj, Government of India, New Delhi 2010, p.5.

(a) **State legislation in consonance with customary law :** The PESA provisions are to be incorporated into the State Panchayat Raj legislations and that such incorporations shall be in consonance with the customary law, social and religious practices, and traditional management practices of community resources. This implies that the state law should have enabling provisions for the tribal peoples and communities to redress their grievances or objections to any provision in any law applicable to Scheduled Areas that are seen as not being in consonance with the customary law, social and religious practices, and traditional management practices of community resources.

(b) **Village :** The 'village' in PESA is the fundamental unit of governance. It can be a habitation/a group of habitation or a hamlet/a group of hamlets. This marks a distinct and most important departure from the existing manner in which a village is defined and notified in the State legislations. The village for the purpose of Panchayat Raj is the notified village for which there exists a Gram Panchayat which is constituted with a number of revenue villages which in turn consists of a number of habitations. Compared to this definition, the PESA definition of village is normally smaller than the revenue village which may, in few instances, be equal to a revenue village. In other words, the 'village' as defined in PESA is not the 'village' under the State Panchayat Raj laws but the habitation.

(c) **Gram Sabha :** As per PESA, every village shall have a Gram Sabha consisting of persons whose names are included in the rolls for the Panchayat at the village level. In other words, Gram Sabha is not the Gram Panchayat. Those who are enrolled in the electoral rolls normally residing in the 'village' shall be the Gram Sabha of the said village. This is to make sure that the Gram Sabha is a manageable assembly of people for it to carry out the core functions in PESA that is entrusted to it. Gram Sabha is compact and small, a face to face community. In contrast, the Gram Panchayat is spread over a vast area in various revenue villages and numerous habitations making it unviable for frequent meetings and regular functioning.

Powers and Functions of Gram Sabha

Gram Sabha shall have the following powers and functions under the Act:

1. ***Responsibilities of Gram Sabha in management of Common Property Resources* :** Conservation and management of all community resources in the village such as water, common land, community forest, pasture land, minor minerals, etc. as per local traditions and customs. Gram Sabha will ensure that community resources are utilised in a manner that there is improvement in means of livelihood and equality among people.

2. ***Responsibility of Gram Sabha in land acquisition* :** Act provides that the Gram Sabha or the Panchayats at appropriate level shall be consulted before making the acquisition of land for development projects or before resettling or rehabilitating persons affected by such projects in the Scheduled Areas.

3. ***Preventing alienation of tribal land* :** PESA empowers Gram Sabha to prevent alienation of land in the Scheduled Areas and take appropriate action to restore unlawfully alienated land of a Scheduled Tribe. The Gram Sabha must ensure that no land belonging to Scheduled Tribes is transferred to non-ST persons. If the Gram Sabha is of the opinion that attempts are being made to alienate land belonging to STs, it may go into details of such cases and pass resolution as to how such attempts should be tackled. If Gram Sabha finds that a non-

ST is in unlawful occupation of any land belonging to an ST member, it shall restore the possession of such land to the original owner as per the laid down procedure. The Gram Sabha adopts traditional dispute resolution methods while adjudicating land conflicts. Concerned department officials shall make available land records for taking correct decision by the Gram Sabha.

4. ***Controlling money lending*** **:** PESA mandates the State Legislatures to empower the Gram Sabha to exercise control over money lending transactions. Gram Sabha may constitute a Debt Relief Committee to deal with money lending transactions and its related issues in relation to STs. A borrower can bring to the notice of the Gram Sabha if he or she is harassed by a money lender or by a lending institution and is being charged exorbitant rates of interests, etc. Gram Sabha can authorise the Debt Relief Committee to conduct an enquiry into such complaints with the support of Gram Sabha/Community Mobilizer and place a report before Gram Sabhas for its decision. Gram Sabha, especially in the case of the tribals, may instruct a bank, society, or any individual money lender that loans be disbursed or repayments made after informing the lending details to the Gram Sabha. Gram Sabha is competent to review agreements of all kinds of labourers in the village and ensure that there is no forced labour in lieu of money borrowed from the lender. However, the concerned State Government is required to make Rules in this regard.
5. ***Minor forest produce*** **:** Under PESA Act, Gram Sabha is endowed with ownership of Minor Forest Produce (MFP). Gram Sabha is competent to ensure protection of trees or plants which yield minor forest produce and also take steps for protection of endangered plant species and impose restrictions on collection or extraction of plant material or products.
6. ***Minor Minerals*** **:** Under PESA Act, it is mandatory to have recommendation of the Gram Sabha and Panchayats at appropriate level prior to grant of prospecting licence or mining lease for minor minerals and for grant of concession for the exploitation of minor minerals by auction in the Scheduled Areas. Consultation should be interpreted as mandatory consultation.
7. ***Dispute resolution as per traditional laws and customs*** **:** There should be collective resolution of disputes on the basis of customs, traditional laws, and religious beliefs of tribal areas. In other words, Gram Sabha is empowered to resolve the disputes through Dispute Resolution as per traditional laws and customs.

Thus, the powers given to Gram Sabha/ Panchayats at appropriate level under the PESA can be summarised as follows:

(i) Safeguard and preserve the traditions and customs of the people, their cultural identity, community resources, and the customary mode of dispute resolution.

(ii) Approve plans, programmes, and projects for social and economic development before such plans, programmes, and projects are taken up for implementation by the Panchayat at the village level.

(iii) Identification or selection of persons as beneficiaries under the poverty alleviation and other programmes.

(iv) Certification of utilisation of funds by the Panchayat for the plans, programmes, and projects for identification or selection of persons as beneficiaries under the poverty alleviation and other programmes.

(v) Right to be consulted before making acquisition of land in the Scheduled Areas for development projects and before re-settling or rehabilitating persons affected by such projects in the Scheduled Areas.

(vi) Right to plan and manage minor water bodies in the Scheduled Areas.

(vii) Power to enforce prohibition or to regulate or restrict the sale and consumption of any intoxicant.

(viii) Power to prevent alienation of land in the Scheduled Areas and to restore any unlawfully alienated land of a Scheduled Tribe.

(ix) Ownership of minor forest produce.

(x) Recommendations prior to grant of prospecting licence or mining lease for minor minerals and for grant of concession for the exploitation of minor minerals by auction in the Scheduled Areas.

(xi) Power to manage village markets.

(xii) Power to exercise control over money lending to the Scheduled Tribes.

(xiii) Power to exercise control over institutions and functionaries in all social sectors.

(xiv) Power to control over local plans and resources for such plans including tribal sub-plans.

(d) **Reservation of Seats :** The Act provides that the reservation of seats in Panchayats at all levels (village, intermediate, and district) should be in proportion to the population of the communities for which it is being sought to be given under Part IX of the Constitution. However, the said reservation is subject to two conditions—The first condition is that of the total number of seats, at least half the number of seats shall be reserved for STs and the second being the reservation of seats of Chairpersons of Panchayats for STs. In other words, half of the seats in the Gram Panchayat, Panchayat Samiti, and Zilla Parishad shall be reserved for STs and all posts of Chairpersons of PanchayatRaj Institutions (in the areas covered under PESA) shall be reserved for tribal community (and only persons belonging to tribal community can contest for these posts).

(e) **Nominated Members :** If any ST community or communities is/are not represented through election to the Panchayat Samiti or the Zilla Parishad, then the State government is to nominate a representative to either the Panchayat Samiti or the Zilla Parishad. This is subject to the provision that the total number of such nominated persons shall not exceed ten percent of the elected members in that Panchayat. This is to ensure that STs who are minorities or dispersed or who are not able to represent through the democratic process of elections should also be represented. This is to bypass the weakness of these communities by virtue of their minority status or social or political marginalization.

(f) **Safeguards :** PESA unambiguously instructs the States to ensure that there is no ambiguity in the powers and authority defined and exercised by the Gram Sabha, the Gram Panchayat, the Panchayat Samiti, and the Zilla Parishad; that the structure above shall not encroach into or subsume or in any way prevent the lower bodies from exercising their power. In other words, it shall be illegal for the Panchayats at the higher level to enter or encroach into the domain of the powers and authority of the Panchayats at the lower level or the Gram Sabha.

(g) **Pattern of the Sixth Schedule :** The administrative arrangement at the district level shall be on the pattern of the powers (legislative, judicial, and executive powers) and structure of the District Councils. This also means the reorganization of the administrative divisions into districts so as to ensure that all the habitations in the Fifth Scheduled Area is organized into districts as far as possible. It would also require the transfer of powers as provided in the Sixth Schedule of the Constitution to the District Councils in Fifth Schedule Area. In other words, PESA envisages that the Fifth Schedule Areas adopt the Sixth Schedule pattern in addition for an autonomous existence.

(h) **Adoption of PESA :** PESA Act requires that all the States having Scheduled Area shall adopt PESA within a year of it coming into force; if not adopted within a year, all provisions in the State legislations that are inconsistent with the provisions of PESA shall stand null and void. However, all the Panchayats that exist at the time of the lapse of one year or at the time of suitable state legislations incorporating the provisions of PESA coming into force, may either be dissolved or allowed to complete its term after which the new provisions shall come into force and operation.

'Village Republic' Concept of PESA

Thus, PESA makes the 'Village Republic' as envisaged in Article 40 to become mandatory for Scheduled Areas. The tribal people, who were unfamiliar with the formal system, were forced under law to approach some authority or the other of an alien 'outside' their world. But now, with PESA, the tribal people are more empowered with the familiar setting of the open assembly of the village formally specified as Gram Sabha to become the centre of governance.

QUESTIONS

Subjective Question

1. Explain the provisions of the Panchayats Extension to Scheduled Areas (PESA) Act, 1996.

(150 words)

Objective Questions

1. The Government enacted the Panchayats Extension to Scheduled Areas (PESA) Act in 1996. Which one of the following is not identified as its objective? (UPSC 2013)
   (a) To provide self-governance
   (b) To recognize traditional rights
   (c) To create autonomous regions in tribal areas
   (d) To free tribal people from exploitation
   Ans: c
2. The Panchayats Extension to Scheduled Areas (PESA) Act in 1996 extends to:
   (a) Only Fifth Scheduled Areas
   (b) Only Sixth Scheduled Areas
   (c) Both Fifth and Sixth Schedules Areas
   (d) Schedules areas recognised by an Act of Parliament
   Ans: a

18.3 : URBAN LOCAL SELF-GOVERNMENT

INTRODUCTION

Local bodies are institutions of the local self-governance, which look after the administration of an area or small community such as villages, towns, or cities. The local bodies in India are broadly classified into two categories. The local bodies constituted for local planning, development, and administration in the rural areas are referred as Rural Local Bodies (Panchayats) (which we have already discussed in the preceding chapter) and the local bodies, which are constituted for local planning, development, and administration in the urban areas are referred as Urban Local Bodies (Municipalities) (which we will discuss hereunder).

Urban Local Bodies in Ancient India

Historical records provide evidence of the existence of organised urban life in India since the ancient period. The origin of local self-government had very deep roots in ancient India. On the basis of historical records, excavations, and archaeological investigations, it is believed that some form of local self-government did exist in the remote past. In the Vedas and in the writings of Manu, Kautilya, and others, and also in the records of some travelers like Megasthenes, the origin of local self-government can be traced back to the Buddhist period. The Ramayana and the Mahabharata also point to the existence of several forms of local self-government such as Paura (guild), Nigama, Pauga, and Gana, performing various administrative and legislative functions and raising levies from different sources[1].

Indus Valley civilization was essentially urban in character. The excavations done at Mohenjodaro, and Harappa and other places in Punjab, Haryana and Rajasthan are authentic proofs of the organized urban life during the ancient period. "They were laid out with wide streets, market places, public offices, community baths and drainage and sewage system. The people of the Indus civilization had the proud distinction of giving to the then contemporary world its earliest cities, its first urban civilization, its first town planning, its first drainage system and its earliest example of city government[2]."

In the Mauryan period followed by the Gupta era and subsequently in the medieval period, the system of local self-government continued to be more or less the same.

Urban Local Governance During the British Rule

British rule in India came to be extended through the East India Company, which was, in its origin, a commercial concern engaged in trade. The unsettled political conditions in India in the eighteenth century and the rivalry between the trading companies representing different European powers led the Britishers to intrigue with the local rulers to protect their trading interests. As a consequence, the East India Company found itself landed suddenly with the liability to rule over vast tracts of land. The company, at

---

[1] http://mospi.nic.in/

[2] Pradeep Sachdeva (2000): *Urban Local Government and Administration in India*; Kitab Mahal, Allahabad, Third Edition, p. 60.

the same time, got concerned also with the health and conveniences of its servants. The basic necessities of a healthy and safe living, i.e., sanitation, light, and roads were almost absent. The Britishers thought it proper to transplant some sort of municipal institutions in areas where the servants of the company and other Europeans had settled. Madras was the first city to have a local government established under a Charter issued by the Company. In other words, the first such Municipal Corporation was set up in the former Presidency Town of Madras in 1688. Then it was followed by similar corporations in the then Bombay and Calcutta in 1726.

In 1863, based on the Royal Commission on the Sanitary State of the Army in India, pinpointing the insanitary state of affairs in Indian towns, a series of Acts were passed, which led to the establishment of city municipalities through the Mayo's (former Governor-General) Resolution of 1870. During the late 19th century, Ripon undertook an evaluation study on the progress of the local self-government since 1870, and the Ripon's[3] resolution of 1882 (also called as 'Magna Carta' of local self-government) came into force, whereby the Government made attempts to divide the functions between the provincial Government and the local bodies in order to raise more income through local sources by the local bodies themselves. Subsequently, based on the recommendations of the Royal Commission on decentralization set up in the year 1907 and the Montague-Chelmsford Report of 1918, the Government of India Act, 1919 was passed wherein, among other things, the system of 'Dyrachy' was introduced. The type of organization, powers, and responsibilities of Urban Local Bodies differed from State to State but there was a similarity in the organizational structure of these Urban Local Bodies.

Post-Independence

Independence brought a new kind of activity in every sphere of public life. It opened a new chapter in the history of local government in India. The Constitution of India has allotted the local self-government to the State List of functions. In other words, the Constitution of India has made detailed provisions for ensuring protection of democracy in Parliament and in State Legislatures. Hence, democracy in these institutions has survived and flourished. However, the Constitution did not make local self-government in urban areas a clear-cut Constitutional obligation. While the Directive Principles of State Policy refer to Village Panchayats, there is no specific reference to municipalities, except implicitly in Entry-5[4] of the State List, which places the subject of local self-government as a responsibility of the State.

As a consequence of inadequate Constitutional provision for local self-government, democracy in municipal governance was not stable. Though the respective municipal Acts of the States provided for regular elections to municipal bodies, they were frequently suspended and superseded for indefinite periods of time. Frequent and indefinite suspensions or supersessions eroded the very basis of local self-government and had a negative effect on democracy at the grass-root level. The general position with regard to financial resources of the municipal bodies was also not satisfactory. Over the years, there was a steady encroachment on the assigned functions and revenues of Urban Local Bodies by specialized agencies of the State Governments. As a result, many Urban Local Bodies became weak and were not able to perform effectively.

---

[3]Hailed as the Father of local self-government.

[4]Local Government, that is to say, the Constitution and powers of municipal corporations, improvement trusts, district boards, mining settlement authorities and other local authorities for the purpose of local self-government or village administration.

Committees and Commissions Appointed for Strengthening Municipal Administration

In order to improve the municipal organizations and their administration, the central government constituted various committees to do in-depth analysis of urban local governance and give recommendations.

The Central Government appointed a committee in 1948 known as the *Local Finance Inquiry Committee*, to report on ways and means for improving the financial resources of local bodies. The report came in 1951. The *Taxation Enquiry Commission*, set up in 1953, was also baffled with this problem. The Centre Council of Local Self-Government constituted by the Central Government, has also played a significant role in labouring on reforms needed in the various aspects of municipal government and administration.

The Central Government though, under the Constitution not charged with the responsibility of local government, has been the principal source of reforms in the municipal field. It is the Central Government, which has been responsible for setting up committees and commissions and other organs devoted to study the problems of the local government.

The other significant committees and commissions appointed were :

1. The Committee on the training of Municipal Employees, 1963;
2. The Committee of Ministers on Augmentation of Financial Resources of Urban Local Bodies, 1963;
3. The Rural Urban Relationship Committee, 1963–1966;
4. Committee on Budgetary Reform in Municipal Administration, 1974;
5. National Commission on Urbanization, 1985–1988.

The Rural–Urban Relationship Committee devoted itself to both functional and financial aspects and was largely microscopic in its approach. Then in 1985, the Central Government appointed the National Commission on Urbanization, which gave its report in 1988. This was the first commission to study and give suggestions on all aspects of urban management.

However, the recommendations of various committees and commissions constituted by the central government with respect to urban local governance were not effectively implemented by the states, thereby weakening the Urban Local Bodies. The need for a Constitutional guarantee to safeguard the interests of Urban Local Bodies was felt in order to strengthen the weakened status of Urban Local Bodies. Accordingly, 74th Constitutional Amendment Act, 1992 was passed.

Evolution of Municipalities in India

Time Period	Developments
Ancient Indian Texts and Periods – Ramayana, Mahabaratha, Buddhist period, etc.	Records of local self-government performing various administrative and legislative functions and raising levies from different sources
2300–1750 BC (Indus Valley Civilisation)	Evidence of organised urban life—wide streets, market places, public offices, community baths, drainage, and sewerage system

Post - Mauryan	Appointment of a chief executive officer to perform various functions related to city administration; responsible for city's sanitation, which included maintenance of drainage system and cleanliness of roads
320–540 AD (Gupta)	Towns administered by a council; Provision of having elected administrative officers
1526–1707 AD (Mughal)	Municipal administration vested in kotwal, who was the city governor possessing powers and duties of the chief of city police, magistrate, and prefect of municipal administration
Between disintegration of Mughal Empire and advent of the British	• Anarchy and military feudalism in most parts of the country • Local institutions perverted or weakened
1688	Setting up of first corporation at Madras
1726	Setting up of corporations at Bombay and Calcutta
1870	• Mayo's Resolution released; provided for decentralisation of administration from the centre to the provinces; emphasised the idea of increased association of Indians in administration; indicated extension of municipal self-government; encouraged the general application of the principle of election • Municipalities established in every town of importance. However, these municipal bodies were completely under the control of the district magistrate and the town people were associated only for raising funds for the maintenance of police, conservancy, and road repairs.
1882	• Ripon's resolution released; advocated for establishment of a network of local self-government institutions; reduction of the official element of not more than a third of the total membership; a large measure of financial decentralisation; adoption of election as a means of constituting local bodies. • Municipal Acts passed; However, Ripon's reforms achieved little success, since they were considered too radical
1914–1919	• National movement for independence gains momentum. • 1917 Declaration released: associate Indians in every branch of administration; gradual development of self-governing institutions. • Montague-Chelmsford reforms introduced to make local self-government representative and responsible. • Government of India Act, 1919 enacted; responsibility for local government transferred from the hands of the district officers to a department controlled by a popular minister; franchise for election to local bodies substantially widened. In some provinces, the municipal bodies were given the power to raise or lower rates of taxes within the statutory limits. The popular ministers of provincial governments proceeded to establish elected councils and gave executive authority to the elected Chairman.

1950	• Enactment and enforcement of Constitution of India. • Contained provisions for rural settlements only; a reference to urban local government observed only in two entries: (a) Entry 5 List II of the Seventh Schedule (the State List); and (b) Entry 209 of List III[5] (Concurrent List). • In the absence of Constitutional recognition and clear statutory delineation of their powers, functions, and resources, urban local governments remain neglected; only few changes made in their structure and functioning.
Post - 1950.	• Numerous committees and commissions appointed by the Central and State Governments to study the functioning of urban local governments and to give recommendations for their improvement. • Central Council of Local Self-Government set up in 1954 to examine the problems of urban local governments
1992	Constitution (74th Amendment) Act finally accepted and enacted; contains provisions for (a) Constitution of a uniform typology of municipalities; (b) composition of municipalities; (c) constitution and composition of wards committees; (d) elections and reservation of seats; (e) duration of municipalities; (f) powers, authority, and responsibilities of municipalities; and (g) constitution of state finance commissions, committees for district planning, and metropolitan planning.

CONSTITUTIONAL PROVISIONS FOR MUNICIPALITIES (PART IX)

Seventy Fourth Constitutional Amendment Act, 1992 has introduced a new Part IXA in the Constitution, which deals with Municipalities in Articles 243P to 243ZG. This amendment, also known as Nagarpalika Act, came into force on 1st June 1993. It has given Constitutional status to the municipalities and brought them under the justifiable part of the Constitution. States were put under Constitutional obligation to adopt municipalities as per the system enshrined in the Constitution. The system/provisions enshrined in Part IX of the Constitution are as follows:

(a) ***Constitution of Municipalities (Article 243Q)***: It provides for Constitution of 3 types of municipalities depending upon the size and area namely:

- Nagar Panchayat: A Nagar Panchayat is for those areas which are transitional areas, i.e., transiting from rural area to urban areas.
- Municipal Council: A Municipal council is for smaller urban area.
- Municipal Corporation: A Municipal Corporation is for larger urban areas.

The Governor will by public notice, define these three areas based upon the population, density of population, revenue generated for local administration, percentage of employment in non-agricultural activities, and such other factors as he may deem fit. Further, a Governor may also if, he fits it necessary, based upon the industrial establishments, specify the industrial townships instead of Municipality by public notice.

[5]Economic and social planning

(b) ***Composition of Municipalities (Article 243R)***: All the members of a Municipality are to be directly elected by the people of the Municipal area. For the purpose of making the electorate, the municipal area will be divided into territorial constituencies known as Wards. However, the manner of election of Chairpersons of municipalities has been left to be specified by the State Legislature.

Besides the seats filled by direct elections, the Legislature of a State may by law provide –

- For nomination of persons having special knowledge and experience in municipal administration (Provided that persons so nominated shall not have the right to vote in the meetings of the Municipality)
- For the representation in a Municipality of members of the House of the People and the members of the Legislative Assembly of the State representing constituencies which comprise wholly or partly the Municipal area
- For the representation in a Municipality of Members of the Council of States and the members of the Legislative Council of the State registered as electors within the municipal area

(c) ***Constitution of Wards Committees (Article 243S) :*** This provides for Constitution of Ward Committees, consisting of one or more wards, within the territorial area of all the municipalities with a population of 3 lakhs or more. A member of a Municipality representing a ward within the territorial area of the Wards Committee shall be a member of that Committee. Where a Wards Committee consists of two or more wards, one of the members representing such wards in the Municipality elected by the members of the Wards Committee shall be the Chairperson of that Committee.

Further, the State legislature may by law, make provision with respect to –

- The composition and the territorial area of a Wards Committee;
- The manner in which the seats in a Wards Committee shall be filled;
- The Constitution of Committees in addition to the Wards Committees.

(d) ***Reservation of Seats (Article 243T) :*** In order to provide for adequate representation of SC/ST and of women in the municipal bodies, provisions have been made for reservation of seats. The proportion of seats to be reserved for SC/ST to the total number of seats shall be same as the proportion of the population of SC/ST in the municipal area. The reservation would be made in respect of seats to be filled by direct elections only (This means no reservation for nominated seats). Not less than one-third of the total number of seats reserved for SC/ST shall be reserved for women belonging to SC/ST.

The reservations of seats for SCs and STs mentioned above cease to have effect on the expiration of the period specified in Article 334. By 104th Constitutional Amendment Act, 2019, the period has been extended till January 25, 2030.

In respect of women, the seats shall be reserved to the extent of not less than one-third of the total number of seats. This includes seats reserved for women belonging to SC/ST. These reservations will apply for direct elections only.

There will be no bar on State Legislatures from making provisions for reservation of seats in any Municipality or office of Chairperson in the municipalities in favour of backward class of citizens.

(e) ***Duration of Municipalities (Article 243U)*** - The Municipality has a fixed term of 5 years from the date appointed for its first meeting. But the Municipality can be dissolved before the completion of the term. However, before dissolving, the Municipality shall be given a reasonable opportunity of being heard and no amendment of any law for the time being in force shall cause dissolution of a Municipality before the expiry of the five years term.

Elections to constitute a Municipality are required to be completed before the expiration of the duration of the Municipality. If the Municipality is dissolved before the expiry of 5 years, the elections for constituting a new Municipality are required to be completed within a period of 6 months from the date of its dissolution. In other words, an election to constitute a Municipality shall be completed –

(a) Before the expiry of its duration of five years; or

(b) Before the expiration of a period of six months from the date of its dissolution. But, where the remainder of the period (for which the dissolved Municipality would have continued) is less than six months, it shall not be necessary to hold any election for constituting the new Municipality for such remaining period.

Moreover, a Municipality constituted upon the dissolution of a Municipality before the expiration of its duration shall continue only for the remainder of the period for which the dissolved Municipality would have continued, had it not been so dissolved. In other words, if there is a premature dissolution of a Municipality, the new Municipality which is reconstituted shall continue only for the remainder period, not for full period of five years.

(f) ***Disqualification of Membership (Article 243V)*** - A person shall be disqualified for being chosen as, and for being, a member of Municipality –

(a) If he is so disqualified by or under any law for the time being in force for the purposes of elections to the Legislature of the State concerned. Provided that no person shall be disqualified on the ground that he is less than twenty five years of age, if he has attained the age of twenty one years; or

(b) If he is so disqualified by or under any law made by the Legislature of the State.

The main principle followed is that the grounds of disqualification should be the same as applied for elections to the State Legislatures. In other words, any person who is qualified to become an MLA is qualified to become a member of the Municipality, but for Municipality the minimum age prescribed is 21 years. Further, the State Legislatures are empowered to provide additional provisions or criteria for disqualifications.

(g) ***Powers and Functions of the Municipalities (Article 243W)*** - All municipalities would be empowered with such powers and responsibilities as may be necessary to enable them to function as effective institutions of self-government. The State Legislature may, by law, specify what powers and responsibilities would be given to the municipalities in respect of – (i) preparation of plans for economic development and social justice, and (ii) for implementation of schemes as may be entrusted to them.

An illustrative list of functions that may be entrusted to the municipalities has been incorporated as the Twelfth Schedule of the Constitution. This schedule defines 18 new tasks in the functional domain of the Urban Local Bodies.

12th Schedule of the Constitution

1. Regulation of land use and construction of land buildings
2. Urban planning, including the town planning
3. Planning for economic and social development
4. Urban poverty alleviation
5. Water supply for domestic, industrial, and commercial purposes
6. Fire services
7. Public health sanitation, conservancy, and solid waste management
8. Slum improvement and upgradation
9. Safeguarding the interests of the weaker sections of society, including the physically handicapped and mentally unsound
10. Urban forestry, protection of environment, and promotion of ecological aspects
11. Construction of roads and bridges
12. Provision of urban amenities and facilities such as parks, gardens, and playgrounds
13. Promotion of cultural, educational, and aesthetic aspects
14. Burials and burial grounds, cremation and cremation grounds, and electric crematoriums
15. Cattle ponds, and prevention of cruelty to animals
16. Regulation of slaughter houses and tanneries
17. Public amenities including street lighting, parking spaces, bus stops, and public conveniences
18. Vital statistics including registration of births and deaths

(h) ***Financial Powers (Article 243X)*** - The Constitution has left it open to the Legislature of a State to specify by law matters relating to imposition of taxes. Such law may specify:

- Taxes, duties, fees, etc. which could be levied and collected by the Municipalities, as per the procedure to be laid down in the State law;
- Taxes, duties, fees, etc. which would be levied and collected by the State Government and a share passed on to the Municipalities;
- Grant-in-aid that would be given to the Municipalities from the State;
- Constitution of funds for crediting and withdrawal of moneys by the Municipality.

(i) ***Finance Commission (Article 243Y) :*** Article 243Y makes provision that the Finance Commission constituted under Part IX for Panchayats shall also review the financial position of the municipalities and will make recommendations to the Governor. The recommendations of the Finance Commission will cover the following:

- Distribution between the State Government and Municipalities of the net proceeds of the taxes, duties, tolls, and fees to be levied by the State;

- Allocation of share of such proceeds between the Municipalities at all levels in the State;
- Determination of taxes, duties, tolls, and fees to be assigned or appropriated by the Municipalities;
- Grants-in-aid to Municipalities from the Consolidated Fund of the State;
- Measures needed to improve the financial position of the Municipalities.

Union Finance Commission also suggests the measures needed to augment the Consolidated Funds of States to supplement the resources of the Panchayats in the states.

(j) ***Audit and Accounts (Article 243Z):*** The maintenance of the accounts of the municipalities and other audit shall be done in accordance with the provisions in the State law. The State Legislatures will be free to make appropriate provisions in this regard depending upon the local needs and institutional framework available for this purpose.

(k) ***Elections to the Municipalities (Article 243ZA):*** As per provisions made in Article 243ZA, the superintendence, direction, and control of the preparation of electoral rolls for, and the conduct of, all elections to the Municipalities are vested in the State Election Commission referred to in article 243K (Part IX). Subject to the provisions of this Constitution, the Legislature of a State may, by law, make provision with respect to all matters relating to, or in connection with, elections to the Municipalities.

(l) ***Application to Union Territories (Article 243ZB):*** The provisions of Municipalities shall be applicable to the UTs in same way as in case of the states but the President by a public notification may make any modifications in the applications of any part.

(m) ***Not applicable to certain areas (Article 243ZC):*** Provisions of Part IXA are not applicable to:

- Fifth and Sixth Schedule areas referred in Article 244. (However, Parliament may, by law, extend its provisions to the Scheduled and Tribal Areas subject to such exceptions and modifications as may be specified in such law and no such law shall be deemed to be an amendment to the Constitution).
- This part is also not applicable to the area covered under Darjeeling Gorkha Hill Council.

(n) ***Committee for District Planning (Article 243ZD):*** Planning and allocation of resources at the district level for the Panchayati Raj institutions are normally to be done by the Zilla Parishad. With regard to urban areas, municipal bodies discharge these functions within their respective jurisdictions. However, some important questions may arise, which would concern the urban-rural interface, and it may be necessary to take an overall view with regard to development of the district as a whole and decide on allocation of investments between the rural and urban institutions. Provision has, therefore, been made for the constitution of a Planning Committee at the district level with a view to consolidating the plans prepared by the Panchayats and the Municipalities and preparing a development plan for the district as a whole.

As per Article 243ZD, there shall be constituted in every State at the district level, a District Planning Committee to consolidate the plans prepared by the Panchayats and the Municipalities in the district and to prepare a draft development plan for the district as a whole. However, the State Legislature may make provisions with respect to the following:

(i) The composition of the District Planning Committees;

(ii) The manner in which the seats in such committees shall be filled. However, there is one condition given in the Constitution with respect to the composition and the election of members, i.e., that not less than four-fifths of the total numbers of members of such committee shall be elected by and from amongst the elected members of Panchayat at the district level and of the municipalities in the district in proportion to the ratio between the population of the rural areas and of the urban areas in the district.

(iii) The functions relating to the district planning which may be assigned to such committees;

(iv) The manner in which the Chairperson of such committees shall be chosen;

Every district planning committee shall prepare the Draft Development Plan. The District Planning Committee in preparing the Draft Development Plan shall have regard to:

- Matter of common interest between the Panchayats and the Municipalities, including spatial planning
- Sharing of water and other physical and natural resources
- Integrated development of infrastructure and environment conservation
- Extent and type of available resources, whether financial or otherwise

Moreover, the District Planning Committee shall consult such institutions and organisations as the Governor may by order, specify. The Draft District Development Plan so prepared and recommended by the District Planning Committee shall be forwarded by the Chairperson of the Committee to the State Government.

(o) ***Committee for Metropolitan Planning (Article 243ZE)*** - As per Article 243ZE of the Constitution, in every Metropolitan area[6], a Metropolitan Planning Committee may be constituted to prepare a Draft Development Plan for the Metropolitan area as a whole. The State Legislature may make provisions with respect to the following:

(i) The composition of the Metropolitan Planning Committee;

(ii) The manner in which the seats in such committees shall be filled. However, there is one condition given in the Constitution with respect to the composition and the election of members, i.e., that not less than two-thirds of the total numbers of members of such committee shall be elected by and from amongst the elected members of the municipalities and chairpersons of the Panchayats in the Metropolitan area in proportion to the ratio between the population of the Municipalities and of the Panchayats in that area;

(iii) Representation of Central Government, State Government, and such other organizations and institutions in such committees for carrying out the functions assigned to such committees;

(iv) The functions relating to the metropolitan planning which may be assigned to such committees;

(v) The manner in which the Chairperson of such committees shall be chosen;

---

[6] An area having a population of 10 lakh or 1 million or more, comprised in one or more districts and consisting of two or more Municipalities or Panchayats or other contiguous areas, specified by the Governor by public notification to be a Metropolitan area.

Every Metropolitan Planning Committee shall, in preparing the Draft Development Plan have regard to

(i) the plans prepared by the Municipalities and the Panchayats in the Metropolitan area;

(ii) matters of common interest between the Municipalities and the Panchayats, including co-ordinated spatial planning of the area, sharing of water, and other physical and natural resources, and the integrated development of infrastructure and environmental conservation;

(iii) the overall objectives and priorities set by the Government of India and the Government of the State; and

(iv) the extent and nature of investments likely to be made in the Metropolitan area by agencies of the Government of India and of the Government of the State and other available resources whether financial or otherwise.

Moreover, the Metropolitan Planning Committee shall consult such institutions and organisations as the Governor may, by order, specify. The Chairperson of every Metropolitan Planning Committee shall forward the development plan, as recommended by such Committee, to the Government of the State.

(p) ***Continuance of Existing laws (Article 243ZF)*** - Any provision of any law relating to Municipalities in force in a State immediately before the commencement of the Constitution (Seventy-fourth Amendment) Act, 1992, which is inconsistent with the provisions of this Part, shall continue to be in force until amended or repealed by a competent Legislature or competent authority or until the expiration of one year from the date on which the amendment Act receives the assent of the President (i.e., within one year from June 1, 1993). In other words, any law made by the states relating to Municipalities which is inconsistent to Part IXA shall come to an end within one year of the commencement of the amendment. So the States have to amend or pass urban local governance related laws in accordance with the Constitution.

(q) ***Bar to interference by Courts in electoral matters (Article 243O):*** As under Article 329[7], courts shall have no jurisdiction to examine the validity of a law, relating to delimitation of constituencies or the allotments of seats, made under Article 243ZA. If there is a dispute in the municipal elections, the Courts have no jurisdiction over them. This means that the municipal election can be questioned only in the form of an election petition presented to an authority which the State Legislature by law can prescribe.

URBAN LOCAL GOVERNANCE UNDER THE CENTRAL MINISTRIES

The matters pertaining to urban development have been assigned by the Constitution of India to the State Governments. The Constitution (74th Amendment) Act has further delegated many of these functions to the Urban Local Bodies. However, Central Ministries have some limited role to play with respect to the Urban Local Bodies.

[7] Article 329 - Bar to interference by courts in electoral matters - (a) The validity of any law relating to the delimitation of constituencies or the allotment of seats to such constituencies, made or purporting to be made under article 327 or article 328, shall not be called in question in any court; (b) No election to either House of Parliament or to the House or either House of the Legislature of a State shall be called in question except by an election petition presented to such authority and in such manner as may be provided for by or under any law made by the appropriate Legislature.

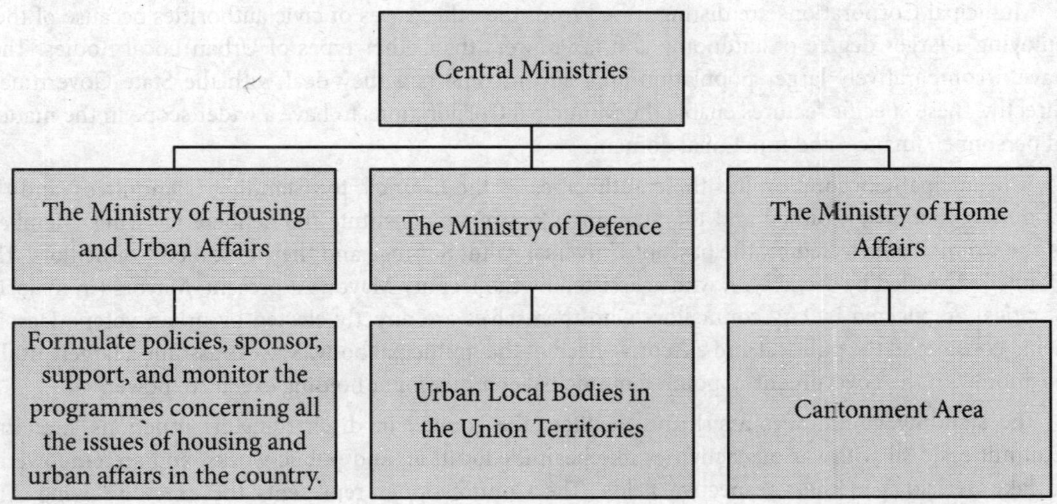

Types of Municipal Organizations

The Constitution provided a framework for urban governance, but states have the prerogative of defining and applying this framework to their territories. While the Constitution does not delve into specific criteria to declare different types of Urban Local Bodies, it provides for states to consider criteria like population size, population density, revenue generated for local administration, the share of the non-agricultural employment, etc. while determining the type of Urban Local Body to be constituted. As a result, the criterion to define an urban area varies significantly among the States. Thus, for the administration of urban areas, several types of municipal bodies are created for the towns and cities, depending on their size, population, industrial or other importance, etc.

By and large, in India we have the following types of municipal organizations:

(i) Municipal Corporation

(ii) Municipality

(iii) Notified Area Committee

(iv) Town Area Committee

(v) Township

(vi) Cantonment Board

(vii) Port Trust

(viii) Special Purpose Agency

Municipal Corporation

A Municipal Corporation is established by the Act of State Government for the big cities of States and by the Act of Parliament for the big cities of Union Territories. It is set up only in the Metropolitan Cities and other larger cities and towns purely at the discretion of the State Governments. However, in a few states, the criteria for constituting it are laid down in the Act itself.

Municipal Corporations are distinguished from the other types of civic authorities because of their enjoying a larger degree of autonomy and tax powers than other types of Urban Local Bodies. They have a comparatively larger population area and income and they deal with the State Government directly. These specific features enable the Municipal Corporations to have a wider scope in the matters of personnel, finance, and functional domain.

A Municipal Corporation has three authorities — the Council, the Standing Committees, and the Commissioner. The Council and the Standing Committee constitute the deliberative wing. Members of the Council are elected on the basis of Universal Adult Suffrage and they are called Councillors. The Council is headed by the Mayor, who is assisted by the Deputy Mayor. At present, Mayors (in majority of cities) are elected by city councillors who themselves are directly elected by urban voters. Despite being considered the political and executive head of the municipal body, Mayors assume a largely titular position with the government-appointed municipal commissioner holding executive power.

The standing committees assist and facilitate the council in discharging its functions. Standing Committees deal with various activities like health, education, and public works, and are empowered to take decisions in their respective fields. The Commissioner represents the executive wing. The Commissioner is an Indian Administrative Services official appointed by the State Government and has the executive powers of the government of Municipal Corporations. The other executives known as the Mayor and Deputy Mayor are political executives generally elected for a period of one year by the members of the Corporation. The Mayor is the titular head of the corporation and presides over the meetings of the corporation.

Municipalities/Municipal Council

They are established by the Acts of the State Legislature for the administration of small cities or towns. It also has three authorities. First, the Municipal Council is the legislative branch of the Municipality, and is headed by the Chairman (also called as President in some states), who in turn is assisted by a Deputy Chairman (also called as Vice-President). The Chairman/President plays a pivotal role in municipal administration and enjoys real deliberative and executive powers. He presides over the meetings of the council, guides the deliberations, and gets the decisions implemented. The President is the administrative head of all the officers of the Municipality.

The standing committees facilitate the work of Municipality/Municipal Council in various fields such as health, taxation, finance, etc.

The third authority of the Municipality is the Chief Executive Officer, who is appointed by the State Government and is responsible for the general administration of the Municipality.

Municipalities have lesser autonomy and smaller jurisdiction. They are subject to comparatively detailed supervisory control and guidance by the State government. Their organizational form varies a great deal from state to state.

Notified Area Committee

Are set up in growing towns not yet fit to have a Municipality. In other words, this may be created either in a town which is fast developing or which may not fulfil the conditions for the creation of a Municipality. It is known as Notified Area Committee because it is created through a notification of the State Government published in the Official Gazette. Notified Area Committees are governed by a special provision in the state Municipal Acts. Generally, it is created in an area which is fast developing and where new industries are being set up. Each notified area elects a notified area committee for its administration where all members as well as the Chairman are nominated by the State Government, which function like a Municipality. There have been various recommendations asking to stop such centralisation in the State Government hands by setting up these areas when they should actually be under the Panchayati Raj Institutions.

Town Area Committee

It is a semi-municipal authority, constituted for small towns. The Town Area Committee is constituted and governed by an Act of the State Legislature and its composition and functions are specified in it. Its membership differs from state to state. The members may be partly elected and partly nominated by the State Government or wholly nominated or wholly elected. The committee is assigned a limited number of functions, such as street lighting, drainage, roads, conservancy, etc. The District Collector in some states has been given powers of surveillance and control over the Town Area Committee.

Cantonment Boards

'Cantonment' is an area where the military is temporarily stationed. However, due to geographic conditions and inadequate road and communications facilities in British India (currently India, Pakistan, and Myanmar), military was permanently stationed at strategic points in our country. In such areas, not only military men and officers used to stay alone, but other civilians also used to stay and provide necessary supporting services to the military. Even after independence the same organizational structure continued.

While all other institutions of urban governance are administered by the State Government, these are the only bodies which are centrally administered by the Defence Ministry.

The Cantonments Act, 1924 makes provisions relating to the administration of cantonments. As cantonments are Central territories under the Constitution, the civic bodies functioning in these areas are not covered under State municipal laws. In view of the present day aspirations and needs of the people residing in cantonment areas and in order to bring in modern municipal management procedures/ techniques in such areas, the Cantonments Act, 1924 was replaced with Cantonments Act, 2006 for greater democratization, better financial management, and management of defence lands and their audit, etc.

As per this Act there are four types of Cantonment Boards

Category of Cantonment Board	Population	Members of the Board	Elected Members	Term of office	President	Vice-President	Term of office of President / Vice Official Members President
Category – I	Exceeding 50,000	Total 16 members - Officer Commanding the station as ex–officio; District Magistrate or an executive magistrate'; Chief Executive officer; the Health officer (ex officio); the Executive Engineer (ex officio) and three military officers; Eight elected members.	8	Five years	Generally officer commanding the station ex-officio or if the Central Government so directs such other Military officer nominated by the General officer commanding in Chief, the Command.	One of the Elected Members elected by the elected Members of the Board	Generally five years. The Vice President is removable by elected Members by passing vote of no confidence by elected Members by 2/3rd majority of the total elected members

Category – II	Exceeding 10,000 but not exceeding 50,000	Total 14 members - Officer Commanding the station as ex –officio; District Magistrate or an executive magistrate'; Chief Executive officer; the Health officer (ex officio); the Executive Engineer (ex officio) and two military officers; Seven elected members.	7	Five years	Generally officer commanding the station ex-officio or if the Central Government so directs such other Military officer nominated by the General officer	One of the Elected Members elected by the elected Members of the Board	Generally five years. The Vice President is removable by elected Members by passing vote of no confidence by elected Members by 2/3rd majority of the total elected members
Category- III	Exceeding 2500 but not exceeding 10,000	Total 12 members –Officer Commanding the station as ex –officio; District Magistrate or an executive magistrate; Chief Executive officer; the Health officer (ex officio); the Executive Engineer (ex officio) and two military officers; Six elected members.	6	Five years	Generally officer commanding the station ex-officio or if the Central Government so directs such other Military officer nominated by the General officer Commanding in Chief, the Command.	One of the Elected Members elected by the elected Members of the Board	Generally five years. The Vice President is removable by elected Members by passing vote of no confidence by elected Members by 2/3rd majority of the total elected members.
Category- IV	Not exceeding 2500	Total 4 members - Officer Commanding the station ex officio; e Chief Executive Officer; two elected members.	2	Five years	Generally officer commanding the station ex-officio or if the Central Government so directs such other Military officer nominated by the General officer Commanding in Chief, the command.	One of the Elected Members elected by the elected Members of the Board	Generally five years. Vice President is removable by vote of no confidence by the Board and in such a situation other elected Member becomes the Vice President.

Thus, the *Cantonment Board (Category I Board)* consists of elected and nominated members and the officer commanding the station is the President of the Board. The Cantonment Board consists of eight elected Members, three nominated Military Members, three Ex-officio Members (Station Commander, Garrison Engineer and senior executive Medical Officer), and one representative of the District Magistrate. An officer of the Indian Defence Estates Services which is a central civil service is posted as the Chief Executive Officer (CEO) as well as the member secretary of the Board. The board is headed by the President Cantonment Board (PCB) who is the Station Commander and also presides over the meetings of the cantonment board. The term of the elected Members is of 5 years. The Vice President is elected from amongst the elected members.

As a local municipal body, the Cantonment strives to ensure that the residents receive all the necessary facilities such as education, sanitation, public health, street lights, water supply, and birth and death registration.

Industrial Townships

In our country, there are many townships which are developed because heavy industries are developed in that area. A well-known industrial township in our country is Jamshedpur in Bihar where Tatas established a Steel Plant due to proximity of raw material required which is also heavy to transport. Likewise, tea estates, steel plants, cement plants, and coal mines are industrial townships. After independence, many States established State-owned and controlled Industries Development Corporations such as Maharashtra Industrial Development Corporation (MIDC), Gujarat Industrial Development Corporation (GIDC), etc.

The distinguishing features of industrial townships are:

a. It is developed because of industry;

b. Municipal services therein are provided by the owners of the industry;

c. Workers of the industry and their families mostly live in the area;

d. Many a times, the services are subsidized;

e. There is a relationship of employer and employee rather than the Municipality and the citizen;

f. A Town Administrator is appointed, who is assisted by a few engineers and technicians.

Thus, the townships are established by a public sector undertaking as its housing colony to provide civil amenities to its employees living in township. It has no elected members and its affairs are managed by a Town Administrator appointed by the public sector undertaking.

Port Trusts

These are the urban bodies created for civic administration of the port areas. Such urban bodies are established by an Act of the Parliament to manage and protect ports and to provide civic amenities to the port area. It is headed by an official appointed by the central government. It has both elected and nominated members.

Special Purpose Agency

The State Governments establish some special purpose agencies to perform some specific functions of municipalities. In other words, along with the above seven types of urban bodies, the states can create certain agencies to look after specific functions which genuinely belongs to municipal authorities. They function as separate bodies not under the control of municipalities. They may be created either by an Act of State Legislature or by an order of the executive. These agencies are function-based and not area-based like the above seven bodies.

Some of these agencies are:

- Housing Board
- Water Supply and Sewerage Undertaking
- Electricity Supply Undertakings
- Urban Development Authorities
- Town Improvement Authorities
- Transport Boards

CHALLENGES FOR URBAN LOCAL GOVERNMENTS IN INDIA[8]

1. **Functional overlap with parastatals[8] for key functions :** The Constitution (74th Amendment) Act, 1992 empowered states to devolve the responsibility of 18 functions including urban planning, regulation of land use, water supply, and slum upgradation to Urban Local Bodies (ULBs). However, in most Indian cities, a majority of these functions are carried out by parastatals. This could create a two-fold challenge in administration. First, if there are multiple agencies performing similar functions, it could lead to a functional overlap, ambiguity, and wastage of resources. Second, and more importantly, the presence of parastatals that are managed by and accountable to the State Government leads to an erosion of the ULB's autonomy. Several experts have highlighted that this lack of autonomy faced by municipal corporations in most Indian cities leads to a challenge in governance, effective service delivery, and development of urban areas.

   A High Powered Expert Committee (HPEC) on Urban Infrastructure (2011) had recommended that activity mapping should be done for the 18 functions. Under this, functions in the exclusive domain of municipalities and those which need to be shared with the state and the central government must be specified. Experts have also recommended that the Municipality should be responsible for providing civic amenities in its jurisdiction and if a parastatal exercises a civic function, it should be accountable to the Municipality.

2. **Stressed municipal finances** : Indian ULBs are amongst the weakest in the world in terms of fiscal autonomy and have limited effective devolution of revenue. They also have limited capacity to raise resources through their own sources of revenue such as property tax. India's municipal revenue as per cent of GDP declined from 1.05 per cent in 2012–13 to 1 per cent in 2017–18[9]. This leads to a dependence on transfers by the state and central

[8]Examining urban local governance in India through the case of Bengaluru, Prachi Kaur and Shruti Gupta- December 24, 2020, https://prsindia.org/

[9]Study prepared by ICRIER for the Fifteenth Finance Commission

government. Experts have recommended that the central government and the respective State Government should provide additional funds and facilitate additional funding mechanisms for ULBs to strengthen their finances. The revenue of ULBs can be augmented through measures including assignment of greater powers of taxation to the ULBs by the State Government, reforms in land and property-based taxes (such as the use of technology to cover more properties), and issuing of municipal bonds (debt instruments issued by ULBs to finance development projects).

3. **Powers of elected municipal officials :** The executive power with state-appointed municipal Commissioners and elected municipal officers differs across states. States like Tamil Nadu and Gujarat, and cities like Chennai and Hyderabad vest the executive power in the Commissioner. In contrast, the executive power of the Corporation is exercised by a Mayor-in council (consisting of the Mayor and up to 10 elected members of the Corporation) in Kolkata and Madhya Pradesh. This is unlike large metropolitan cities in other countries like New York and London, where elected Mayors are designated as executive heads. Experts have noted that charging Commissioners with executive power diluted the role of the Mayor and violated the spirit of self-governance.

   The Expert Committee on Urban Infrastructure (2011) has recommended that the Commissioner should act as a city manager and should be recruited through a transparent search-cum-selection process led by the Mayor. A Model Municipal law, released by the Urban Development Ministry in 2003, provided that the executive power should be exercised by an Empowered Standing Committee consisting of the Mayor, Deputy Mayor, and seven elected councillors.

4. **Management of staff and human resources :** Experts have noted that municipal administration in India suffers from staffing issues which leads to a failure in delivering basic urban services. These include overstaffing of untrained manpower, shortage of qualified technical staff and managerial supervisors, and unwillingness to innovate in methods for service delivery.

   In a majority of cities, the recruitment process is conducted by the respective municipal corporations and the final sanction for hiring staff lies with the State Government.

QUESTIONS

Objective Questions

1. With reference to the Cantonment Boards, consider the following statements:

   1. It is established for municipal administration for the civilian population in the cantonment area.
   2. It is constituted by the State Government by a notification in the Government Gazette.
   3. The members of the board are nominated by the Governor of the state.

   Which of the statements given above is/are correct?

   (a) 1 only (b) 1 and 2 only

   (c) 1 and 3 only (d) 2 and 3 only

   Ans: (a)

2. 74th Constitutional Amendment Act provides for setting up of which of the following types of municipalities in every state?

1. Nagar Panchayat
2. Block Panchayat
3. Municipal Council
4. Municipal Corporation

Select the correct answer using the code given below.

(a) 1 and 2 only
(b) 3 and 4 only
(c) 1, 3, and 4 only
(d) 1, 2, and 4 only

Ans: (c)

3. With regard to elections for local bodies, consider following statements:

1. All the elections to Rural and Urban Local Bodies are compulsorily held on party lines.
2. State Election Commissioner is appointed and removed by the Governor.
3. Seats are reserved for SCs, STs, and Other Backward Castes in local bodies based on the proportion of their population.

Which of the statements given above is/are correct?

(a) 1 and 2 only
(b) 2 and 3 only
(c) 3 only
(d) None of the above

Ans: (d)

CHAPTER 19

ASYMMETRIC FEDERALISM IN INDIA[1]

INTRODUCTION

The Constitution of India describes India, i.e., Bharat, as a Union of States according to Article 1(1). Since its inception, diversity has been an important theme of the Indian Constitution and believes in the underlying theme of 'unity' of people. The Drafting Committee of the Indian Constitution laid emphasis on the term 'Union' as symbol of the determination of the Constituent Assembly to maintain the unity of the country[2]. To further strengthen this unity, a federal system of governance was opted by the Committee as "Federalism offers a way for diverse communities to come together and derive the strength of unity while retaining their identity".

A federal nation is one with a combination of two levels of government, i.e., the Central and the State government, where there is a substantial division of powers among them and both share equal status in a single political system.

Charles Tarlton was the first one to introduce the concept of 'Asymmetric Fecederalism' in his article published in the Journal of Politics in 1965. In order to understand this, it is necessary to draw a distinction between *de facto and de jure asymmetry*. The former refers to asymmetry between different units in terms of wealth, culture, language, etc. As a result, these states differ in terms of autonomy and representation in the union. The latter refers to providing specific units with different number of powers. It is deliberately done as a part of the constitutional design. De facto is the one that existed in all the federations as it refers to the variance in the demographic and geographic sizes of the states and is also known as political asymmetry. The de jure type, also known as constitutional asymmetry, is evident in the design of the Constitution itself as "it refers specifically to differences in the status or legislative and executive powers assigned by the Constitution to the different regional unit. An asymmetrical set-up can be effective when the needs of State are diverse religiously, culturally, and/or ethnically. In such a case, asymmetrical federalism caters to the needs of particular communities by giving them special status or special provisions. In other words, either through the Constitution or legislation, a conscious decision is taken to give special status, powers, and autonomy to some states but not extend it to all. Articles 370 (*now repealed*), 371, and the Armed Forces (Special Powers) Act are perfect examples of this. Since the above-mentioned asymmetries exist in India, it is enough to construe that the Union of States in India is a precise demonstration of asymmetric federalism.

---

[1]India's Union Of States: Asymmetric Federalism; https://www.livelaw.in/lawschoolcolumn/the-constitution-of-india-federalism-asymmetric-federalism-the-armed-forces-special-powers-act-184405?infinitescroll=1

[2]Hinsa Virodhak Sangh v. Mirzapur Moti Kuresh Jamat and Ors., A.I.R. 2008 S.C. 1892.

Asymmetries in India

The asymmetries in India can be seen in various kinds.

- Firstly, representation in the Rajya Sabha is based on the population size of the State and not based on equality among them and due to low levels of population, some Union Territories have no representation at all;
- Differences in administration of tribal areas (5th and 6th Schedule areas), inter-State administration, and law and order of certain states (AFSPA);
- Some UTs like Delhi, J&K, and Puducherry enjoy special powers over other Union Territories;
- The greatest of all the asymmetries is by the provisions of Article 370 which used to provide J&K to have its own Constitution and make its own laws (*was repealed in 2019)* and Article 371 which provides multiple other states such special powers/provisions.

India, Belgium, Canada are examples of asymmetric federalism, whereas, USA and Australia are examples of symmetric federalism.

Union Territories – Sub-State Level Asymmetry

Besides these asymmetries at the State level, there are some sub-State asymmetries in the Indian Constitution. Indian federalism relates to a special kind of unit (unlike States they are not Federal Units) that are called the Union Territories (UTs). The Eight UTs have been created at various points in time. The reasons for their creation were varied. These areas were either too small to be States or too difficult to merge with neighbouring states on account of cultural differences, inter-State disputes, specific needs of the National Capital Territory, or far-flung isolated location on the coasts[3]. Originally, they were all administered directly by the union through a centrally appointed Administrator. None of these had a Legislature but all were represented by at least one seat in the Lower house of Parliament. Two new types of UTs were created, namely Puducherry[4] and Delhi[5]. A common feature of these two territories is that they have been granted unicameral Legislatures whose members are directly elected by the people. The Pondicherry Legislature is partly elected and partly nominated. There is also a Council of Ministers responsible to the Legislature in both the territories. The Head of the State in both Delhi and Pondicherry is a Lieutenant Governor appointed by the union to perform formal executive functions of the government. Both the territories also have governments headed by chief ministers accountable to their respective legislatures. However, the Chief Minister of Delhi is appointed by the President of India on the recommendation of the Lieutenant Governor. This is presumably in view of the fact that Delhi is in the National Capital Territory.

In 2019, two new Union Territories, Jammu and Kashmir and Ladakh were carved out by dissolving the special status of State of Jammu and Kashmir.

To sum up, India is filled with examples of de jure and de facto asymmetries. There is a difference of opinion in scholars whether asymmetric federalism is federalism in real sense or not. But in the case of India, it is its most unique feature. Asymmetric federalism is the need of the hour as federalism in a strict sense is not possible, especially with the cases such as India where there is a huge margin of imbalances between the States with respect to their geographical location and socio-economic status of the residents of the State. In order to bring out parity and inclusive development, certain States needs to have a necessary push so that they could prosper at a pace as others.

---

[3]Rekha Saxena, Is India a Case of Asymmetrical Federalism? Economic and Political Weekly, 2012, accessed on 7 October 2019.

[4]14th Constitutional (Amendment) Act, 1962.

[5]69th Constitutional (Amendment) Act, 1991.

19.1 SCHEDULED AND TRIBAL AREAS

INTRODUCTION

Scheduled Areas are areas in India with a preponderance of tribal population subject to a special governance mechanism wherein the Central Government plays a direct role in safeguarding cultural and economic interests of scheduled tribes in the area. In general, tribal areas are those areas which are culturally different from others and in the past many decades, there were no contact between them and other parts of the country. Scheduled Areas are mentioned in the Fifth Schedule of the Constitution while tribal areas of Tripura, Mizoram, Meghalaya, and Assam are mentioned in the Sixth Schedule.

In other words, even though the Constitution of India seeks to provide a uniform rule over the whole country, certain areas of the country are governed by special provisions. At the time of the framing of the Constitution, the framers of the Constitution took note of the fact that certain areas and communities in the country, on account of their isolated and primitive lifestyle, need special consideration for safeguarding their interests and advancing their socio-economic development. Article 244 in Part X of the Constitution envisages a special system of administration of areas notified as "Scheduled Areas" and "Tribal Areas". According to Article 244(1), the provisions of the Fifth Schedule shall apply to the administration and control of the Scheduled Areas and Scheduled Tribes[1] in any states other than the four North-Eastern states of Assam, Meghalaya, Tripura, and Mizoram. Whereas, as per Article 244(2), the tribal-dominated areas in the above four States of Assam, Meghalaya, Tripura, and Mizoram are to be administered separately under the Sixth Schedule of the Constitution. Under Article 244 and the Sixth Schedule, these areas are specified as "Tribal Areas" which are technically different from the "Scheduled Areas" under the Fifth Schedule. Thus, the Fifth and Sixth Schedules of the Constitution have special provisions related to the administration and control of such areas declared as "Scheduled Areas" and "Tribal Areas" respectively.

Need Of Special Provisions

Culture and identity are an integral part of the tribal people's life. Tribal forms of social organizations, tradition and customs, institutional laws, and land use patterns are different from those of the mainland people. Therefore, special interest should be taken and appropriate mechanisms must be provided to protect their eco-friendly practices in the areas of tribal majority. The preservation of tribal autonomy and culture, and to ensure the socio-economic and political justice is the purpose of the Scheduled and Tribal Areas. Moreover, the framers of the Constitution considered it necessary to introduce some mechanisms to protect their cultural identity, protect them from exploitation, and promote their development. The Fifth and Sixth Schedules are among such mechanisms. Besides, Article 275(1) of the Constitution also guarantees funds to both the Fifth and Sixth Scheduled Areas from the Consolidated Fund of India as grants-in-aid for the purpose of promoting the welfare of the Scheduled Tribes or raising the level of administration of the Scheduled and Tribal Areas. Thus, the provisions of the Fifth and Sixth Schedules were incorporated in order to protect the aspirations of the people of the Scheduled and Tribal areas and simultaneously assimilate them into the mainstream of the country.

---

[1]The reason why they are called Scheduled Tribes is because they included in one of the Schedules of the Constitution of India.

FIFTH SCHEDULE/SCHEDULED AREAS

Fifth Schedule was dubbed as the "Constitution, within the Constitution". Under Article 244(1) of the Constitution, the provisions of the Fifth Schedule shall apply to the administration and control of the Scheduled Areas and Scheduled Tribes in any State other than the State of Assam, Meghalaya, Tripura, and Mizoram. The principal object of these specific provisions in the Fifth Schedule is to protect the interests and rights of the tribals in their land, habitat, and economy; and to preserve the communities' customs and traditions and to ensure a faster socio-economic development in the "Scheduled Areas". The "Scheduled Areas" as defined in Part C of the Fifth Schedule are "such areas as the President may by order declare to be Scheduled Areas".

Important Provisions Of The Fifth Schedule/Scheduled Areas

(a) Criteria for declaration of Scheduled Areas : The Scheduled Area has more than 50 percent tribal population. The criteria for the declaration of any area as a Scheduled Area under the Fifth Schedule as recommended by the First Scheduled Areas and Scheduled Tribes Commission also known as Dhebar Commission are:

- Preponderance of tribal population,
- Compactness and reasonable size of the area,
- Under-developed nature of the area, and
- Marked disparity in the economic standard of the people.

More recently, a viable administrative entity such as a district, block, or taluk, has been also identified as an important additional criterion[2].

According to the Ministry of Tribal Affairs, 'these criteria are not spelt out in the Constitution of India but have become well established'. They embody the principles followed in declaring the `Excluded' and `Partially-Excluded Areas' under the Government of India Act, 1935, as well as those contained in Schedule `B' of recommendations of the Excluded and Partially Excluded Areas Sub Committee of Constituent Assembly and those outlined by the Scheduled Areas and Scheduled Tribes Commission, 1961[3].

It has been held by one of the High Courts that if any guidelines regarding the areas to be included in the Fifth Schedule can be deduced from the provisions of the Constitution, it is that the areas should have a substantial concentration of tribal population[4].

(b) Procedure for declaration of Scheduled Areas : The President may, by order, declare an area to be a Scheduled area. In other words, the Fifth Schedule prescribes the procedure for altering, scheduling, or rescheduling of any Scheduled Areas in any states. The President is the authority to declare any area as a Scheduled Area or increase or decrease the area of a Scheduled Area or renounce a Scheduled Area or part of a Scheduled Area as a non-Scheduled Area in consultation with the Governor of the concerned State.

---

[2] Annual Report 2013–14, Ministry of Tribal Affairs, Government of India.

[3] Special Report: Good Governance for Tribal Development and Administration, National Commission for Scheduled Tribes, May 2012.

[4] Amarendra Nath Dutta vs. State of Bihar, AIR 1983 Patna 151 - "In this case the Presidential Order declaring Dhalbhum Sub Division as part of the Scheduled Areas in Bihar was challenged, and the challenge was rejected by the Patna High Court, stating that the exercise of power by the President is not ultra vires."

(c) Annual reports by the Governor : Under the provisions of the Fifth Schedule, the Governors of the States having Scheduled Areas are empowered to exercise extensive power and functions to discharge for the administration and control of the Scheduled Areas. The Governors of these states are required to submit a report to the President annually or whenever so required by the President, regarding the administration of the Scheduled Areas in that State.

(d) Executive Power of the Union : The executive power of the Union shall extend to the giving of directions to the respective States for the administration of the Scheduled Areas.

(e) Regulations by the Governor : The Fifth Schedule assigns special responsibilities to the Governors for ensuring peace and good governance in the Scheduled Areas. In other words, the Governor is empowered to make regulation for peace and good governance of any area in a state which is for the time being a Scheduled Area. The Governor[5] can make regulations in the Scheduled Areas, particularly for the following purposes:

- to prohibit or restrict the transfer of land by or among the members of Scheduled Tribes in such areas;
- to regulate the allotment of land to members of the Scheduled Tribes;
- to regulate the carrying on of business as money-lenders by persons who lend money to members of the Scheduled Tribes in such area.

In making such regulations, the Governor can repeal or amend any Act of the Parliament or the State Legislature which is for the time being, applicable to the Scheduled Areas. However, the regulations made by the Governor come into effect only when they are accepted by the President.

(f) Acts of the Parliament or the State legislature : The Governor is authorised to direct the State government by public notification not to apply any Act of Parliament or of the State Legislature to a Scheduled Area or apply it subject to exceptions or modifications. In other words, the Governor enjoys the power to modify, annul, or limit the application of any law made by Parliament or State legislature in the areas designated as Schedule Areas.

(g) Tribes Advisory Council : The Fifth Schedule makes the provision to set up the Tribal Advisory Council. In other words, the Tribes Advisory Council is established for the administration and control of the Scheduled Areas and Scheduled Tribes. Each state having Scheduled Areas has the constitutional obligation to constitute a Tribes Advisory Council. A Tribes Advisory Council consists of not more than twenty members of whom nearly three-fourth shall be the representatives of Scheduled Tribes in the State Legislative Assembly. The President may also direct any state having Scheduled Tribes but not Scheduled Areas to create a Tribes Advisory Council. The Tribal Advisory Council has a mandate relating to the matters of welfare and advancement of Scheduled Tribes in the state. As discussed above, the Governor can make

[5]While exercising powers under the Fifth Schedule, there is considerable debate as well as litigation on whether or not the powers conferred upon the Governor by the Fifth Schedule can be exercised without explicit sanction from the State government, and whether he is, in fact, bound by the advice of the Central Government. It has been argued that the Governor, while exercising his powers under the Fifth Schedule, is not bound by the aid and advice of the Council of Ministers and must exercise the function independently. One of the High Courts has affirmed the above position. B.K. Manish & Ors. vs. State of Chhattisgarh & Ors. judgment and order dt. 12th March 2013 in WP (PIL) 23 of 2012, Bilaspur High Court.

regulations which are applicable to Scheduled Areas. The Governor can make such regulation only after consultation with the Tribes Advisory Council of the State. It is to be understood that all such regulation will have effect only after being submitted to and accepted by the President of India.

(h) **Rule-making power of the Governor :** The Governor may make rules prescribing or regulating

- the number of members of the Council, the mode of their appointment; and
- the appointment of the Chairman of the Council and of the officers and servants thereof; and
- the conduct of its meetings and its procedure in general; and
- all other incidental matters.

(i) **Amendment of the Fifth Schedule :** The Parliament through a law can amend any of the provisions of this Schedule by way of addition, variation, or repeal. Any such law is not deemed to be an amendment under Article 368 of the Constitution.

(j) **List of Scheduled Areas :** At present, 10 States namely, Andhra Pradesh, Chhattisgarh, Gujarat, Himachal Pradesh, Jharkhand, Madhya Pradesh, Maharashtra, Odisha, Rajasthan, and Telangana come under Fifth Schedule Areas.

State	Areas
Andhra Pradesh	Visakhapatnam, East Godavari, West Godavari, Srikakulam, Vizianagaram, Prakasam (only some mandals are scheduled mandals)
Jharkhand	Dumka, Godda, Devgarh, Sahabgunj, Pakur, Ranchi, Singhbhum (East & West), Gumla, Simdega, Lohardaga, Palamu, Garwa, (some districts are only partly tribal blocks)
Chattisgarh	Sarbhuja, Bastar, Raigad, Raipur, Rajnandgaon, Durg, Bilaspur, Sehdol, Chindwada, Kanker
Himachal Pradesh	Lahaul and Spiti districts, Kinnaur, Pangi tehsil, and Bharmour sub-tehsil in Chamba district
Madhya Pradesh	Jhabua, Mandla, Dhar, Khargone, East Nimar (Khandwa), Sailana tehsil in Ratlam district, Betul, Seoni, Balaghat, Morena
Gujarat	Surat, Bharauch, Dangs, Valsad, Panchmahl, Sadodara, Sabarkanta (parts of these districts only)
Maharashtra	Thane, Nasik, Dhule, Ahmednagar, Pune, Nanded, Amravati, Yavatmal, Gadchiroli, Chandrapur (parts of these districts only)
Orissa	Mayurbhanj, Sundargarh, Koraput (fully scheduled area in these three districts), Raigada, Keonjhar, Sambalpur, Boudhkondmals, Ganjam, Kalahandi, Bolangir, Balasor (parts of these districts only)
Rajasthan	Banswara, Dungarpur (fully tribal districts), Udaipur, Chittaurgarh, Siroi (partly tribal areas)
Telangana	Adilabad, Komrambheem-Asifabad, Mancherial, Mulug, Warangal (Rural), Mahbubabad, Bhadradri-Kothagudem, Khammam, and Nagarkurnool (only some mandals are scheduled mandals).

(k) Samata Judgment[6] : The Fifth Schedule of the Indian Constitution provides protection to the adivasi (tribal) people living in the Scheduled Areas of ten states in the country from alienation of their lands and natural resources to non-tribals. Samata, an advocacy and social action group working in the southern state of Andhra Pradesh, has been fighting for the rights of tribal communities and for the protection of the environment in the Eastern Ghats region. Samata filed a Special Leave Petition in the Supreme Court. After a four-year legal battle, it won a historic judgment. Known popularly as the 'Samata judgment', it nullified all mining leases granted by the State government in the Scheduled Areas and asked it to stop all mining operations. Only the State Mineral Development Corporation or a cooperative of the tribal people, it ruled, could take up mining activity and that too, in compliance with the Forest Conservation Act and the Environment Protection Act. It also recognised the Constitution (73rd) Amendment and the Panchayat (Extension to Scheduled Areas) Act, under which Gram Sabhas are competent to preserve and safeguard community resources, and reiterated the right of self-governance of Adivasis. Where similar Acts in other States do not prohibit the grant of mining leases in the Scheduled Areas, a committee of Secretaries and State Cabinet sub-committees should be constituted and a decision taken, the judgment said. Before granting leases, it is obligatory for the State government to obtain the concurrence of the Centre, which would, for this purpose, constitute a sub-committee consisting of the Prime Minister and the Union Ministers for Welfare and Environment so that the State's policy is consistent with that of the nation, it said.

Moreover, under Article 339 (1) of the Constitution, the President may also appoint a Commission to report on the administration of the Scheduled Areas and welfare of the Scheduled Tribes in the states. As it was obligatory to appoint such Commission at the end of the first ten years of the implementation of the Constitution, the First Scheduled Areas and Scheduled Tribes Commission was appointed in 1960, with U.N. Dhebar as the Chairman to address the overall situation of the tribals, including the issue of land alienation in the tribal areas. The Commission submitted its report in 1961. And in 2002, the Second Commission was set up under the Chairmanship of Shri Dileep Singh Bhuria (The Bhuria Commission) to review the constitutional mechanisms for the welfare and development of Scheduled Tribes. The Commission submitted its report in 2004.

SIXTH SCHEDULED AREAS/TRIBAL AREAS

The conditions in the Tribal Areas of Assam, Meghalaya, Tripura, and Mizoram are very different from those in the other Tribal Areas. These Tribal Areas are divided into fairly large districts inhabited by single tribes or fairly homogenous groups of tribes with highly democratic and mutually exclusive tribal organizations. The tribes in Assam have not assimilated much the life and ways of the other people in the State. These areas have hitherto been anthropological specimens. The tribal people in other parts of India have more or less adopted the culture of the majority of the people in whose midst they live. These areas are therefore treated differently by the Constitution, and a sizeable amount of autonomy has been given to these people for self-governance. The provisions of the Sixth Schedule apply to the administration of these tribal areas. Article 244(2) of the Constitution, the Sixth Schedule makes special arrangement for the administration of Tribal Areas in the States of Assam, Meghalaya, Mizoram, and Tripura.

---

[6]AIR 1997 Supreme Court 3297.

Important Provisions of the Sixth Schedule

(a) The tribal areas are to be administered as Autonomous Districts and Autonomous Regions. Under the provision of the Sixth Schedule, the Governor of the State is empowered to determine the area or areas as administrative units of the Autonomous Districts and Autonomous Regions[7]. In other words, these areas have been constituted into autonomous districts. If a district has different Scheduled Tribes, autonomous regions may be created therein by the Governor.

(b) The Governor has the power to create a new Autonomous District/Region or alter the territorial jurisdiction or the name of any Autonomous District or Autonomous Regions.

(c) Each Autonomous District shall have a District Council consisting of not more than thirty members, out of which four are nominated by the Governor while the rest are elected on the basis of Adult Franchise (the newly added Bodoland Territorial Council is an exception; it can have up to forty-six members[8]). Nominated members hold office at the pleasure of the Governor, and are removable at his discretion. Whereas, the elected members hold office for a period of five years (unless the council is dissolved before the five-year term). Even the autonomous regions will also have a separate regional council.

(d) The District Councils are conferred with certain Executive, Legislative, and Judicial powers so that they have got the autonomy to make laws of their land, managing their forests (other than the reserved forests), the appointment of traditional chiefs and headman, inheritance of property, marriage, social customs, taxation, etc. The power and functions of District Councils and Regional Councils as given in the Sixth Schedule can be summarised as:

- **Legislative functions :** Para 3 of the Sixth Schedule provides the provision for the District Council and Regional Councils to make rules in respect of lands, management of forest (other than the Reserved Forest), use of canal or water-course for agriculture, regulation of jhum and other forms of shifting cultivation, establishment and administration of village or town committees, appointment or succession of Chiefs or Headmen, inheritance of property, marriage and divorce, and social practices with the prior approval of the Governor. Moreover, under Para 10 of the Schedule, the District Council of an Autonomous District has the power to make law for the regulations and control of money-lending or trading by any person other than Scheduled Tribe residents in that Scheduled District. However, all laws made under this provision shall have no effect until assented by the Governor of the State.
- **Executive functions :** The Sixth Schedule also endowed the District Councils and Regional Councils with extensive executive powers. The District Councils and Regional Councils are given the power to establish, construct or manage primary schools, dispensaries, markets, cattle ponds, fisheries, roads, road transport, and waterways in the districts. The Councils are also authorized to prescribe the language and manner of instruction in the primary schools.
- **Judicial Powers :** The District and Regional Councils are also empowered to constitute Village and District Council Courts for trial of suits and cases where all parties of the dispute belong to Scheduled Tribes within the district. And no other courts, except the High Courts

[7]The power of the Governor to divide areas occupied by Scheduled Tribes is to be exercised on the aid and advice of the Council of Ministers.

[8]Sixth Schedule to the Constitution (Amendment) Act, 2003.

and the Supreme Court, have the jurisdiction over such suits or cases of the Council Courts. However, these Council Courts are not given the power to decide cases involving offences punishable by death or imprisonment for five or more years.

- **Financial Powers :** The provisions of the Sixth Schedule provide certain financial powers to the District and Regional Councils. They are empowered to prepare a budget for their respective Council. Under Para 8 of the Sixth Schedule, District and Regional Councils are empowered to assess and collect land revenue and impose taxes on professions, trades, animals, vehicles, taxes on entry of goods into the market for sale, toll on passengers and goods carried in ferries, and taxes for the maintenance of schools, dispensaries, or roads within their respective jurisdiction. There is a District Fund or a Regional Fund to which all moneys received by the District or Regional Council are credited. And under Para 9 of the Schedule, the Councils are given the power to grant licenses or leases for extraction of minerals within their jurisdiction.

(e) An Act or resolution of a District or Regional Council may be suspended or annulled by the Governor if he is satisfied that it is likely endanger the safety of India. Such an order of the Governor is to be laid before the State Legislature and it remains in force for 12 months unless revoked by the Legislature. The Legislature can pass a resolution to extend the duration of the order further by 12 months at one time.

(f) Acts of the State Legislature dealing with a matter within the purview of the District or Regional Council applies to a district only when the District Councils so directs by public notification. As regards other Acts of the State Legislature, the Governor is authorized to notify that they do not apply to an autonomous district or region, or that they apply subject to such modifications as the Governor may specify in the notification. In case of the State of Meghalaya, the Acts of the Legislature prevail over those made by the District or Regional Council.

(g) In the States of Meghalaya, Mizoram, and Tripura, with respect to the Acts of Parliament, the power vests in the President to extend them, subject to such modifications as he may specify, to the autonomous districts or regions. Whereas, in the case of Assam, the power lies with the Governor with respect to the Acts of the Parliament.

(h) The Governor may appoint a commission to examine and report on any matter relating to the administration of the autonomous districts or regions. The report of the commission and the Governor's recommendations thereon are placed before the State Legislature. A District or Regional Council may be dissolved by the Governor on the recommendation of the commission.

(i) The provisions of the Sixth Schedule may be amended from time to time by the Parliament by making a law for the purpose. Any changes introduced by Parliamentary legislation in the Sixth Schedule are not be deemed to amount to an amendment of the Constitution for the purposes of Article 368.

(j) **List of Autonomous Districts –**

Assam

- The North-Cachar Hills District (Dima Haflong)
- The Karbi-Anglong District
- The Bodoland Territorial Area District

Meghalaya

- The Khasi Hills District
- The Jaintia Hills District
- The Garo Hills District

Tripura

- The Tripura Tribal Areas District

Mizoram

- The Chakma District
- The Mara District
- The Lai District

Difference Between Tribes Advisory Council & Autonomous District Councils

Tribes Advisory Council	Autonomous District Council
Tribal Advisory Councils under the Fifth Schedule are the creation of the State Legislature.	District Councils or Regional Councils under the Sixth Schedule are the product of the Constitution, drawing all their powers and functions from the Constitution itself.
Under the Fifth Schedule, the Tribes Advisory Councils being the creation of the Legislative Assembly of the States have limited powers which are mostly executive in nature. The executive power of the State also extends to the Scheduled Areas.	District Councils under the Sixth Schedule enjoy extensive powers, including executive, legislative, and judicial powers, all derived from the Constitution
The Tribes Advisory Councils established under the provision of the Fifth Schedule are not given the financial power for preparing budget for themselves. There is no mentioning of sources of income or of grant-in-aid in the Fifth Schedule provisions. However, since Tribes Advisory Councils are created by the State Government, it is the moral duty of the State Governments to give financial assistances to the Councils.	In financial matters also, the Sixth Schedule empowers the District and Regional Councils to mobilise resources. They are authorized to levy and collect land revenue and taxes within their respective jurisdiction.
The powers and functions which are to be delegated to the Tribes Advisory Councils in the Fifth Scheduled Areas are minimal and primarily decided by the State Cabinet.	District and Regional Councils are sometimes referred as 'mini-state' or state within a state since they have extensive legislative, executive, financial, and judicial powers.

19.2 UNION TERRITORIES

INTRODUCTION

There exist a few centrally administered units which do not form part of any State but have been kept as separate and distinct entities because of several historical, cultural, or political reasons. These administrative units are designated as Union Territories.

There are at present the following eight Union Territories created at various points of time:

1. Delhi (1956)
2. The Andaman & Nicobar Islands (1956)
3. Lakshadweep (1956)
4. Dadra and Nagar Haveli & Daman and Diu (both the Union territories were merged in the year 2020)
5. Puducherry (1962)
6. Chandigarh (1966)
7. Jammu & Kashmir (2019)
8. Ladakh (2019)

Before 1956, the present-day Union Territories were characterized as Part C States. The States' Reorganisation Commission in its report submitted in 1955 suggested that the Part C States be converted into centrally administered territories as these States were neither financially viable nor function efficient. The States' Reorganisation Act, 1956 and the Seventh Constitution Amendment Act abolished the Part C States and created the present-day Union Territories.

Thus, the Union Territories are formed for varied reasons –

1. Cultural distinctiveness (Puducherry, Daman & Diu and Dadra Nagar Haveli);
2. Strategic location importance (Andaman & Nicobar Islands and Lakshadweep);
3. Administrative and political reasons (Delhi and Chandigarh);
4. Security and growth (Jammu & Kashmir and Ladakh).

A Union Territory is administered directly by the Central Executive. A Union Territory is to be administered by the President acting, to such extent as he thinks fit, through an Administrator to be appointed by him with such designation as he may specify. In other words, the designation of the Administrator can either be Lieutenant or Chief Commissioner or Administrator, as determined by the President. Moreover, a Governor of a State may also be appointed as the Administrator of a Union Territory adjoining to that State. In that capacity, the Governor is to act independently of his Council of Ministers.

Though the Union territories are centrally administered units, they do not become merged with the Central Government. They maintain their distinct constitutional identity.

ADMINISTRATION OF UNION TERRITORIES

1. **Legislation for Union Territories :** The Parliament can make a law for a Union Territory with respect to any matter. With regard to the Union Territories, there is no distribution of legislative power. The three Lists have no relevance so far as the above Union Territories are concerned. The Parliament is however, a busy body and is always pressed for time and it is not, therefore, possible for it enact all the legislation in relation to matters falling in Lists II and III, which may be essential and desirable for the governance of a Union Territory.

   To relieve pressure on the Parliament, therefore, certain other provisions have been made.

   (a) **Regulations :** The President may make Regulations for the peace, progress, and good government of the Union Territories of the Andaman and Nicobar Islands, Lakshadweep, Dadar and Nagar Haveli, and Daman Diu and Puducherry. The President has no Regulation making power with respect to Chandigarh. However, the President shall not make Regulations for Puducherry if a Legislature is established. But the President can make regulations for Puducherry as well if the Legislature there is dissolved or suspended. A Regulation made by the President has the same force and effect as an Act of Parliament. A Regulation may even repeal or amend an Act of Parliament, or any other law, applicable to the Union Territory concerned. The regulation-making power of the President is plenary and a Regulation can be made for a Union Territory on all subjects on which Parliament can make laws. Thus, a Regulation can be made for any matter falling in List I, List II, or List III.

   (b) **The Union Territories laws :** For all the Union Territories, except Andaman & Nicobar Islands and Lakshadweep, various Acts of Parliament (*The Union Territories (Laws) Act, 1950; The Dadra and Nagar Haveli Act, 1961; The Pondicherry (Administration) Act, 1962; The Punjab Re-organization Act, 1966, etc.*), provide that the Central Government may, by notification in the official Gazette, extend with such restrictions and modifications as it thinks fit, to a Union Territory, any enactment which is in force in a State at the date of the notification. The Parliament has thus, delegated some of its legislative power in relation to the Union Territories to the Central Government with a view to lighten its own burden and save its time. This means that the Central Government can extend, after adaptation, to a Union Territory any law in force in any other area in the country.

2. **Executive Directions :** The executive power of the Union Government is co-extensive with the legislative powers of the Parliament. Consequently, the Union Government can validly issue executive directions to the Administrator of a Union Territory. In the case of conflict between a direction issued by the Union Government, and a Presidential Regulation, the Administrator is bound to execute the directions of the Union Government.

3. **High Court For Union Territories :** Parliament may by law, constitute a High Court for a Union Territory or declare any court in any Territory to be a High Court. The constitutional provisions applicable to the High Courts in the State would apply to the High Courts of the Union Territories as well with such modifications or exceptions as Parliament may by law, provide. Parliament may extend or exclude the jurisdiction of any High Court to or from any Union Territory.

Union Territory	High Court Jurisdiction
Andaman & Nicobar Islands	Kolkata High Court
Lakshadweep	Kerala High Court
Chandigarh	Punjab & Haryana High Court
Puducherry	Chennai High Court
Daman & Diu and Dadra Nagar Haveli	Mumbai High Court
Delhi	Has its own High Court
Jammu and Kashmir	Jammu & Kashmir and Ladakh High Court
Ladakh	Jammu & Kashmir and Ladakh High Court

Special Provisions to Puducherry

Article 239A was inserted by the 14th Constitution Amendment Act, 1962. The said Article was added to create a Legislature and Council of Ministers for Puducherry. The Parliament enacted the Government of Union Territories Act, 1963, in pursuance of Article 239A. The object of the Act is to provide for Legislative Assemblies and Council of Ministers for Puducherry. Thus, some form of democracy and Parliamentary government has been introduced by the Act and Article 239A. However, the status of the Union Territory is not affected.

According to the Government of Union Territories Act, 1963, Puducherry enjoys the following special provisions :

(a) Puducherry has an Assembly, which can make laws with respect to matters enumerated in the State List and the Concurrent List. But Parliament's overall power to pass laws for a Union Territory on any subject is unaffected. In case of inconsistency between a law of Parliament and that of the Assembly, the law of Parliament prevails. However, in the area of Concurrent List or the State List, a law made by the Assembly prevails against a Parliamentary law if it has received the assent of the President.

(b) The position of the Administrator/Lieutenant Governor is similar to that of the Governor in the matter of assent to the bills passed by the Legislature.

(c) The Chief Minister is appointed by the President who also makes rules for the conduct of business.

(d) The Union Territory has a Council of Ministers with the Chief Minister at its head to aid and advice the Lieutenant Governor in the exercise of his functions in relation to the matters with respect to which the Assembly of the Union Territory has power to make laws, except in so far as he is required by or under the Act to act in his discretion or by or under any law to exercise any judicial or quasi-judicial functions.

(e) The Administrator and his Council of Ministers function under the general control of the President. They must comply with the directions issued by the President. The Administrator is not bound by the aid and advice of his Ministers when he is acting in his discretion. In case of difference of opinion between the Administrator and the Council of Ministers, the matter is to be referred to the President for decision.

(f) In case of emergency, when the administration of a Union Territory cannot be carried on in accordance with the Act, or for the proper administration of the Union Territory, the President can suspend the operation of all or any provisions of the Act. In such a case, the Administrator administers the Territory as the agent of the President under the provision of Article 239 of the Constitution.

Further, Article 239B[1] empowers the Lt. Governor of Puducherry to promulgate ordinances, except when the Legislature of Puducherry is in session. The Lt. Governor can promulgate the ordinances if he is satisfied that circumstances exist which render it necessary for him to take immediate action. However, no such ordinance shall be promulgated by the Lt. Governor, except after obtaining instructions from the President in that behalf. Moreover, the Lt. Governor cannot promulgate an ordinance whenever the Legislature is dissolved or suspended. In other words, the Administrator can pass an ordinance only during the recess of the Legislative Assembly but not otherwise. Every such ordinance promulgated by the Lt. Governor shall be approved by the Assembly within six weeks from its reassembly. The Lt. Governor can also withdraw the ordinance at any time.

Special Provisions for Delhi[2]

As Delhi is the national capital of India, it is maintained as a Union Territory and has not been given the status of a full-fledged State, because it is felt that Delhi must remain under the effective control of the Union Government. At the same time, it is felt that the people of Delhi ought to enjoy some semblance of democracy. Article 239AA was inserted by the 69th Constitutional Amendment Act, 1991.

By virtue of the said Article, Delhi enjoys following special provisions –

(a) Delhi is called as the "National Capital Territory of Delhi";

(b) The Administrator thereof appointed is designated as the Lt. Governor;

(c) Delhi will have a Legislative Assembly elected directly by the people under the supervision of the Election Commission. The Assembly can make laws with respect to matters enumerated in the State List or the Concurrent List barring certain entries/subjects such as "*Public order, Police, and Land*". In other words, except for "Public order, Police and Land", the Legislative Assembly of Delhi can make laws with respect to any subject falling under State List and the Concurrent List. However, Parliament retains power to make laws with respect to any matter for the Union Territory. In case of repugnancy between a law made by Parliament and a law made by the Legislative Assembly of Delhi, the former prevails over the latter to the extent of the repugnancy. But the law made by the Assembly can prevail over the Central Law if it is assented to by the President. But Parliament can legislate thereafter with respect to the same subject-matter contrary to the Delhi law.

(d) Delhi will have Council of Ministers with the Chief Minister at the head to aid and advise the Lt. Governor, except when he is required to act in his discretion by law. In case of difference of opinion between the Lt. Governor and his Ministers, the matter is to be referred to the President and his decision shall be binding. Pending the decision of the President, if in the opinion of the Lt. Governor the matter is urgent and needs immediate action, he can take such action as he deems necessary.

(e) The Chief Minster is appointed by the President and the other Ministers are appointed by the President on the Chief Minister's advice. They hold office at the pleasure of the President and are collectively responsible to the Assembly.

(f) The strength of the Council of Ministers including the Chief Minister shall not be more than 10% of the total number of members in the Legislative Assembly.

(g) The Lt. Governor of Delhi has power to promulgate ordinances similar to the Administrator of Puducherry.

[1]Inserted by the Constitution (Twenty-seventh Amendment) Act, 1971.

[2]M.P. Jain, *Indian Constitutional Law*, LexisNexis, Eighth Edition, Pg No. 515.

(h) The President has power under Article 239AB[3] to take over the administration in case there is breakdown of the constitutional machinery therein, or for the proper administration of the National Capital Territory. The operation of Article 239AA may be suspended.

(i) Article 239B applies to the Union Territory of Delhi as well. Which means that the Lt. Governor of Delhi enjoys the ordinance-making power similar to that of the Lt. Governor of Puducherry. Thus, the Lt. Governor of Delhi too can promulgate ordinances when the Legislative Assembly of Delhi is in recess. He cannot promulgate ordinances when the House is suspended or dissolved. Moreover, no such ordinance shall be promulgated by the Lt. Governor except after obtaining instructions from the President in that behalf. Every such ordinance promulgated by the Lt. Governor shall be approved by the Legislative Assembly within six weeks from its reassembly. The Lt. Governor can also withdraw the ordinance at any time.

(j) The Parliament passed the Government of National Capital Territory of Delhi Act, 1991, to effectuate and supplement Article 239AA. The said Act has fixed the strength of the Legislative Assembly at 70.

Constitutional Position of Jammu & Kashmir and Ladakh

Situated at the apex of the Indo–Pakistan sub-continent, Jammu and Kashmir is of great strategic importance because to its east lies Tibet; to the north-east, Sinkiang provinces of China; to the north-west, Afghanistan, and to its west lies Pakistan.

Ever since the emergence of the two independent states of India and Pakistan in the Indo-Pakistan continent on August 15, 1947, Jammu and Kashmir has figured as the most critical problems in the relations between them. The issue of Kashmir arises out of its accession to India.

History of Kashmir

Jammu & Kashmir was a princely State ruled by Gulab Singh's Dogra dynasty till 1947. Jammu & Kashmir as a princely State consisted of :

- Jammu & Kashmir (now, the Union Territories of Jammu & Kashmir & Ladakh);
- Pakistan-occupied Kashmir (Azad Kashmir & Gilgit-Baltistan); and
- Aksai Chin (captured by China in 1962 war).

When the Britishers were about to leave India, they partitioned British India into India and Pakistan and further gave an option to the Princely States to either join India or join Pakistan or to be independent. Maharaja Hari Singh (the last ruling Maharaja of the princely State of Jammu and Kashmir) saw an opportunity at the end of British Raj to keep Kashmir as the Switzerland of the East and chose to stay independent. Moreover, Hari Singh tried to sign a Standstill Agreement with India and Pakistan at the time of independence, which Pakistan signed but India declined. When things stood thus, on October 22, 1947, Pakistan unilaterally broke the Standstill Agreement and launched an invasion under codename *Operation Gulmarg* to forcibly capture Jammu and Kashmir using tribal raiders. The raiders, as is well known, looted the State with a ferocity till the Indian Army came to the rescue. The invasion was masterminded and backed by the Pakistan army and led by its senior officer Akbar Khan. The tribesmen transited through Pakistan carrying modern military gear. By October 1947, about, 5,000 tribesmen had entered Kashmir, attacked, and captured most of the parts of the Jammu and Kashmir and they were approaching Srinagar.

Maharaja Hari Singh, made an urgent appeal to the Indian government for help. However, Jawahar Lal Nehru put some conditions, i.e., accession of Jammu & Kashmir into India & release of popular leader

[3] Inserted by 69th Constitutional Amendment Act, 1991.

Shiekh Abdullah. The Maharaja agreed to the conditions and signed the Instrument of Accession, ceding Kashmir to India on October 26, 1947. Indian troops arrived at Srinagar. Even after the Instrument of Accession was signed, Pakistan refused to acknowledge Jammu & Kashmir as an essential part of India. They claimed that the Instrument of Accession was not signed with Maharaja Hari Singh's free permission[4]. Indian and Pakistani forces thus fought their First War over Kashmir in 1947–48. India referred the dispute to the United Nations on 1 January, 1948. In a resolution dated August 13, 1948, the UN asked Pakistan to remove its troops, after which India was also to withdraw the bulk of its forces. Once this happened, a "free and fair" plebiscite was to be held to allow the Kashmiri people to decide their future.

India, having taken the issue to the UN, was confident of winning a plebiscite, since the most influential Kashmiri mass leader, Sheikh Abdullah, was firmly on its side. An emergency government was formed on October 30, 1948 with Sheikh Abdullah as the Prime Minister. Pakistan ignored the UN mandate and continued fighting, holding on to the portion of Kashmir under its control. On January 1, 1949, a ceasefire was agreed, with 65 per cent of the territory under Indian control and the remainder with Pakistan. The ceasefire was intended to be temporary but the Line of Control remains the de facto border between the two countries.

Sheikh Abdullah took charge of an emergency administration in Kashmir. Nehru appointed the former Kashmir Prime Minister N. Gopalswamy Ayyangar as a Cabinet Minister to look after Kashmir affairs. Ayyangar was one of the chief architects of Article 370. In 1957, Kashmir was formally incorporated into the Indian Union. It was granted a special status under Article 370 of India's constitution.

Article 370

Article 370 allowed the State of Jammu and Kashmir a certain amount of autonomy – its own Constitution, a separate flag, and freedom to make laws, etc., while foreign affairs, defence, and communications remained the preserve of the Central Government. As a result, Jammu and Kashmir could make its own rules relating to permanent residency, ownership of property, and Fundamental Rights.

The Rights of Permanent Residents of Jammu and Kashmir are defined in Article 35A[5]. These residents were then entitled for specific privileges and rights granted by the Jammu and Kashmir Legislature which were not enjoyed by the Indians from outside the State.

Jammu & Kashmir Reorganisation Act, 2019

The Reorganisation Act resulted in the division of the State into two union territories: the Union Territory of Jammu and Kashmir, which has a Legislature, and the Union Territory of Ladakh[6], which

[4]Pakistan has managed to spin a narrative that concealed its role in the 1947 invasion calling it a 'spontaneous' attack by the tribals in response to the communal killings in J&K. In addition, it has sought to throw doubts about the genuineness of the accession of J&K to India, labelling the entry of Indian troops on October 27, 1947 in Kashmir as illegal. Pakistan has observed this day as a 'Black Day' for decades in Pakistan, in Pakistan occupied J&K (POJK), and in the diaspora in order to bolster its narrative.

[5]Article 35A was inserted not through Parliamentary assent, which is mandatory for amendments, but through a Presidential proclamation.

[6]For decades, a substantial part of Ladakh (specifically, Leh district) has felt stifled or alienated by J&K's decision-making apparatus, which was centred in Srinagar. The J&K government has often been insensitive to the region's ecological and cultural uniqueness, whose incredible beauty masks the extreme fragility of its cold desert ecosystems and the highly adaptive traditional livelihoods of its people. These are so unlike the topography of the rest of India that people from other parts of the country cannot even understand them. Therefore, the State of Jammu and Kashmir was reorganized into two separate Union Territories and the UT administration in Ladakh is determined to meet the expectations of the people in ensuring protection and development.

does not. Kargil and Leh districts will be part of the Union Territory of Ladakh, while the remaining areas of the existing State of Jammu and Kashmir will be part of the Union Territory of Jammu and Kashmir.

(a) Legislative Assembly consists of a total of 107 seats. Because these seats are in Pakistan Held Kashmir (POK), which is unlawfully occupied by Pakistan, 24 of the 107 seats would stay empty.

(b) Following the repeal of Article 370, some seats in the Union Territory of Jammu and Kashmir would be reserved for Scheduled Castes and Scheduled Tribes in proportion to their population. In addition, if women are underrepresented, the Lieutenant Governor may nominate two women to the Assembly. The Legislative Assembly will have a five-year term instead of the previous six-year term.

(c) The President will manage the Union Territory of Jammu and Kashmir through an Administrator he appoints. Like the New Delhi Union Territory, the Administrator will be known as the Lieutenant Governor. The President, on the other hand, will manage the Union Territory of Ladakh through a Lieutenant-Governor selected by him. The Legislative Assembly has the authority to enact legislation for any area of the Union Territory of Jammu and Kashmir. These laws cover:

- Any item in the Constitution's State List, except "Police" and "Public Order," and
- Any matter in the Concurrent List that applies to Union Territories.

(d) Council of Ministers will assist and advise the Lieutenant Governor of the Union Territory of Jammu and Kashmir. The Minister's council will be no larger than 10% of the Assembly's total membership. Like the Chief Ministers of Delhi and Puducherry, the Chief Minister shall inform the Lieutenant Governor of all Council decisions.

(e) The Jammu and Kashmir High Court will serve as the common High Court for the Union Territories of Jammu and Kashmir as well as Ladakh. Furthermore, an Advocate General would be appointed to provide legal advice for the administration of the Union Territory of J&K.

(f) Following the revocation of Article 370 - 153 State laws of Jammu and Kashmir have been revoked as well. This includes the removal of restrictions on the leasing of land to non-permanent residents of Jammu and Kashmir. On a date set by the Central Government, 106 laws from the Central List would be applicable to the Union Territories of Jammu & Kashmir and Ladakh. *The Right to Education Act of 2009, the Right to Information Act of 2005, the Indian Penal Code of 1860, and the Aadhaar Act of 2016* are among the new laws.

Jammu and Kashmir Reorganisation (Amendment) Act, 2021

The Amendment Act is passed to amend the Jammu and Kashmir Reorganisation Act, 2019. The important features of the Act are as follows:

- The Act provides that Article 239A of the Constitution, which is applicable to the Union Territory of Puducherry, shall also apply to the Union Territory of J&K. Article 239A provides for the constitution of a Union Territory of Puducherry with:

  i. a Legislature, which may be elected, or partly nominated and partly elected, or

  ii. a Council of Ministers.

- The Act states that in addition to Article 239A, any other provision of the Constitution which refers to elected members of a Legislative Assembly of a State and is also applicable to the Union Territory of Puducherry, will apply to the Union Territory of J&K.

- The Reorganisation Act, 2019 provides that the members of the Indian Administrative Service, the Indian Police Service, and the Indian Forest Service serving in the State of J&K would continue to serve in the two union territories, based on allocation decided by the Central Government. Further, in future, postings of officers in the two union territories would be from the Arunachal

Pradesh Goa Mizoram Union Territory (AGMUT) cadre. The AGMUT cadre covers the three states of Arunachal Pradesh, Mizoram, and Goa, as well as all the union territories. The Amendment Act amends these clauses to provide for the merger of the officers in the existing cadre of J&K with the AGMUT cadre.

MINISTRY OF HOME AFFAIRS[7]

The Ministry of Home Affairs (MHA) discharges multifarious responsibilities, the important among them being – internal security, border management, Centre-State relations, administration of Union Territories (UTs), management of Central Armed Police Forces (CAPF), disaster management, etc. Under the Government of India (Allocation of Business) Rules, 1961, Ministry of Home Affairs (MHA) is the nodal Ministry for all matters of UTs relating to legislation, finance & budget, services, and appointment of Lieutenant Governors (LGs) and Administrators.

Administrative Interface

The five UTs without Legislature – Andaman and Nicobar Islands, Chandigarh, Dadra and Nagar Haveli and Daman and Diu, Ladakh, and Lakshadweep – have the forum of Home Minister's Advisory Committee (HMAC)/Administrator's Advisory Committee (AAC). While HMAC is chaired by the Union Home Minister, ACC is chaired by the Administrator of the concerned UT. Members of Parliament and elected members from the local bodies (District Panchayats and Municipal Council) of the respective UTs are the members of these Committees among others. The Committee discusses the general issues relating to social and economic development of the UTs.

Reorganization	Administrator	Area (Sq. km)
Andaman and Nicobar Island	Lt. Governor	8,249
Chandigarh	Administrator	114
Dadra and Nagar Haveli & Daman and Diu	Administrator	Dadra Nagar Haveli District is - 491 sq km; Daman- 72 sq km; Diu - 40 sq km
Delhi	Lt. Governor	1483
Lakshadweep	Administrator	32
Puducherry	Lt. Governor	479
Jammu and Kashmir	Lt. Governor	42,241
Ladakh	Lt. Governor	59,146

[7]Annual Report 2020–21, Ministry of Home Affairs, Government of India, Pg. No. 52.

19.3 SPECIAL PROVISIONS REGARDING CERTAIN STATES

INTRODUCTION

Article 371 of the Indian Constitution is connected to granting special provisions for some states of the Indian Union. As part of XXI and XXII of the Constitution of India, Article 371 grants some temporary, transitional, and special provisions to some states in the country. Ranging from Article 371A to Article 371J, this Article gives special provisions for the states of Maharashtra, Gujarat, Nagaland, Assam, Manipur, Andhra Pradesh, Sikkim, Mizoram, Arunachal Pradesh, Goa, and Karnataka. The main objectives behind the Article 371 granting special provisions to some states are to meet the unique needs of the backward regions of these states, protect the economic and cultural interests of these regions, combat the local challenges, and protect the customary laws in these regions. Article 371 was part of the original Constitution, whereas Articles 371A through 371J were incorporated subsequently through Constitutional amendments.

PROVISIONS OF ARTICLES 371A–371J FOR DIFFERENT STATES OF INDIA

1. **State of Gujarat and Maharashtra (Article 371) :** Article 371(2) enables the President to lay special responsibility on the Governor of Maharashtra and Gujarat for the development of certain areas of that State. In the discharge of the special responsibility so conferred, the Governor has to act according to the directions which may be issued by the President from time to time. The President may, by order made with respect to the State of Maharashtra or Gujarat, provide for any special responsibility of the Governor for:

   (a) The establishment of separate development boards for:

   - Vidarbha, Marathawada, and the rest of Maharashtra.
   - Saurashtra, Kutch, and the rest of Gujarat.

   The order may contain provision requiring that a report on the working of each of these boards will be placed each year before the State Legislative Assembly.

   (b) The equitable allocation of funds for developmental expenditure over the said areas, subject to the requirements of the concerned State as a whole.

   (c) An equitable arrangement providing adequate facilities for technical education and vocational training and adequate opportunities for employment in service under the control of the State Government, in respect of all the said areas, subject to the requirements of the State as a whole.

2. **State of Nagaland (Article 371A) :** Article 371A was added by the 13th Constitutional Amendment Act, 1962. This provision was inserted after a 16-point agreement between the Centre and the Naga People's Convention in 1960, which led to the creation of Nagaland in 1963. Article 371A makes a few special provisions for the State of Nagaland, partly because of the disturbed law and order condition there, and partly because of the prevalence of strong feelings regarding their customs, etc., among the people of the State, known as the Nagas. For long, the territory comprised in the State, Naga Hills – Tuensang Area, has been administered as a Scheduled Area

under the provisions of Schedule VI to the Constitution. Article 371A provides for the following, notwithstanding anything contained in the Constitution:

(a) No Act of Parliament concerning the following matters, shall apply to the State of Nagaland unless the Legislative Assembly of Nagaland by a resolution so decides

- Religious or social practices of the Nagas
- Naga customary law and procedure
- Administration of civil and criminal justice involving decisions according to Naga customary law
- Ownership and transfer of land and its resources

(b) So long as there occur internal disturbances in the State, the Governor of Nagaland shall have special responsibility with respect to law and order, and in the discharge of his functions. The Governor, after consulting the Council of Ministers, exercises his individual judgment as to the action to be taken. In case a question arises whether any matter falls within the Governor's individual judgment or not, the Governor's decision in his discretion is final. The validity of anything done by the Governor is not to be called in question on the ground that he ought or ought to not to have acted in the exercise of his individual judgment. The Governor's special responsibility shall cease when the President makes an order to the effect, on being satisfied, that it is no longer necessary for the Governor to have special responsibility for law and order in the State.

(c) The Governor shall ensure that any money provided by the Government of India for any specific service or purpose is included in the demand for a grant relating to that service or purpose and not in any other demand moved in the State Legislature.

(d) A Regional Council shall be established for the Tuensang district of the State as from such date as the Governor may, by public notification specify. The Council shall consist of 35 members. The Governor shall, in his discretion, make rules providing for:

- The composition of the Council and the manner in which its members shall be chosen. The Deputy Commissioner of the Tuensang District shall be the ex-officio Chairman of the Council and the Vice-Chairman shall be elected by the members of the Council from amongst themselves;
- The qualifications for being chosen as members of the Council.
- The term of office, the salaries, and allowances to be paid to the members.
- The procedure and conduct of business of the Council.
- The appointment of officers and staff of the Council and their conditions of service.
- Any other matter for the proper functioning of the Council.

(e) For a period of ten years from the date of the formation of the State of Nagaland or for such further period, as the Governor may specify on the recommendation of the Regional Council:

- The administration of the Tuensang District shall be carried on by the Governor.
- The Governor shall, in his discretion, arrange for equitable distribution between Tuensang District and the rest of the State, of money provided by the Government of India, to meet the requirements of the State.

- No Act of the Legislature of Nagaland shall apply to Tuensang District unless the Governor so directs on the recommendation of the Regional Council. The Governor may, on the recommendation of the Council, specify exceptions or modifications subject to which such an Act may have application in that District.
- The Governor may make regulations for the peace, progress, and good government of the Tuensang District and any such regulations may repeal or amend any Act of Parliament or any other law, for the time being in force in that District.
- There shall be a Minister for Tuensang affairs in the Council of Ministers, to be appointed by the Governor from amongst the members representing the District and on the advice of the Chief Minister, who in tendering his advice, shall act on the recommendation of the majority of the members from that District; the Minister is to deal with all matters relating to the District and shall have direct access to the Governor for the purpose, but he shall keep the Chief Minister informed about the same and the final decision on all matters relating to the Tuensang District is to be made by the Governor in his discretion.
- Members in the Nagaland Legislative Assembly from Tuensang are not elected directly by the people as in other States but by the Regional Council. Whereas, members from the districts of Kohima and Mokokchung (i.e., rest of the Nagaland) are elected in territorial constituencies.

(f) A change is also incorporated in Article 170 with respect to the State of Nagaland. According to this, the minimum strength of the Legislative Assembly of Nagaland is fixed at 46 members.

3. **State of Assam (Article 371B) :** Article 371B provides that the President may, by order, provide for the Constitution and functions of a committee of the members of the Assam Legislative Assembly elected from the Tribal Areas mentioned in the Sixth Schedule. The Committee is to be constituted with the object to consider Bills introduced in the Assam Assembly from the point of view of the hill people and the well-being of the people inhabiting the other parts of the State of Assam.
4. **State of Manipur (Article 371C) :** Article 371C was added by the 27th Constitutional Amendment Act, 1971. Article 371C says that the President may, by order, provide for the creation of a Committee of the Legislative Assembly of the State of Manipur, consisting of the members of that Assembly elected from the hill areas of that State. The Governor of the State of Manipur is vested with special responsibility to secure the proper functioning of the Committee and to make an Annual Report to the President regarding the administration of the hill Areas in the State. The Union Government may give directions to the State as to the administration of the said areas.
5. **The State of Andhra Pradesh (Articles 371d and 371e) :** Articles 371D and 371E were inserted by the Constitution (Thirty-second Amendment) Act, 1973. The genesis of these Articles is that, for quite some time, the people of Telangana region in Andhra Pradesh were carrying an agitation for the creation of a separate Telangana State. These provisions were, therefore, enacted to meet some of the aspirations of the Telangana people so that they may give up their demand for a separate State.

The primary purpose of Article 371D appears to be two-fold:

- To promote speedy development of the backward areas of the State of Andhra Pradesh with a view to secure balance in the development of the State as a whole; and
- To provide equitable opportunities to different areas of the State in the matter of education, employment, and career prospects in public service.

The provisions of Article 371D are as follows:

(a) The President may, by order provide, having regard to the requirements of the State as a whole, for equitable opportunities for the people belonging to different parts of the State in the matter of public employment and education and different provisions may be made for different parts of the State. In this regard, the President may require the State Government to organize civil posts in local cadres for different parts of the State and provide for direct recruitment to posts in any local cadre.

(b) Provision has also been made for establishing an Administrative Tribunal in the State for redressing grievances of the people *inter alia* in such matters as appointment, allotment, or promotion to civil posts in the State. The President may abolish the tribunal when he is satisfied that its continued existence is not necessary.

(c) The High Court is not to have any powers of superintendence over the Administrative Tribunal. No Court (other than the Supreme Court) is to exercise any jurisdiction, power, or authority in respect of any matter subject to the jurisdiction of the Tribunal.

Article 371E empowers the Parliament to establish a Central University in the State of Andhra Pradesh.

In 2014, the Andhra Pradesh Reorganization Act, 2014[1] extended the provisions of Article 371D to the State of Telangana as well.

6. **State of Sikkim (Article 371f) :** Article 371F was inserted by the Constitution (Thirty-sixth Amendment) Act, 1975 for admitting Sikkim into the Union of India, as a fully-fledged State. The Amendment introduced Article 371F laying down some special provisions applicable to Sikkim to provide for certain peculiar circumstances prevailing there. Important provisions of the Article are as follows:

- The State of Sikkim has one seat each in the Lok Sabha and the Rajya Sabha.
- It confers power on Parliament to provide for the number of seats in Legislative Assembly of Sikkim, which cannot be less than 30 members to be filled by candidates belonging to different sections of the people of the State.
- It also confers special responsibility on the Governor of Sikkim for peace and for an equitable arrangement for ensuring the social and economic advancement of different sections of the State population. In discharge of this responsibility, the Governor is subject to such directions as may be issued by the President from time to time.

[1] AP Reorganisation Act, 2014 bifurcated the State of Andhra Pradesh into States of Andhra Pradesh & Telangana.

- Authorizes Parliament to reserve seats in the Sikkim Legislative Assembly for different sections of the population of Sikkim for the purpose of protecting their rights and interests.
- Empowers the Parliament to provide for the delimitation of the Assembly constituencies from which candidates belonging to such sections alone may stand for election to the State Legislative Assembly.
- Empowers the President to extend (either with or without restrictions/modifications) to Sikkim any law which is in force in any State of the Indian Union.

7. **State of Mizoram (Article 371g) :** Article 371G was inserted by the Constitution (Fifty-third Amendment) Act, 1986 to give effect to a Memorandum of Settlement on Mizoram signed by the Government of India and the Government of Mizoram with the Mizo National Front which envisaged among other things, the conferment of statehood on the Union Territory of Mizoram. Article 371G(a) provides that notwithstanding anything in the Constitution, no Act of Parliament concerning any of the following matters would apply to the State of Mizoram unless the State Legislative Assembly so decides by a resolution:

   - Religious or social practices of the Mizos.
   - Mizo customary law and procedure
   - Administration of civil and criminal justice involving decisions according to Mizo customary law.
   - Ownership and transfer of land.

   Clause (b) of Article 371G further provides that the Legislative Assembly of the State of Mizoram shall consist of not less than 40 members.

8. **State of Arunachal Pradesh (Article 371h) :** Article 371H was added by the Constitution (Fifty-fifth Amendment) Act, 1986. It was proposed to confer statehood on the Union Territory of Arunachal Pradesh. Article 371H (a) provides that notwithstanding anything in the Constitution, the Governor of Arunachal Pradesh shall have special responsibility with respect to law and order in the State. In the discharge of his functions in relation to such responsibility, the Governor shall, after consulting the Council of Ministers, exercise his individual judgment as to the action to be taken. The President can by an order put an end to this special responsibility of the Governor, if after receiving a report from the Governor or otherwise, the President is satisfied that it is no longer necessary for the Governor to have any such responsibility.

   Clause (b) of Article 371H provides that the Legislative Assembly of the State of Arunachal Pradesh shall consist of not less than 30 members.

9. **State of Goa (Article 371i) :** Article 371I inserted by the Constitution (Fifty-sixth Amendment) Act, 1987 provides that the Legislative Assembly of the State of Goa shall consist of not less than 30 members.

10. **State of Karnataka (Article 371j) :** Article 371J inserted by the 98th Constitutional Amendment Act, 2012. This Article gives room for some special provisions to the Hyderabad-Karnataka region. The special provisions aim to establish an institutional mechanism for equitable allocation of funds to meet the development needs over the said region, as well as to enhance

human resources and promote employment from the region by providing for local cadres in service and reservation in educational and vocational training institutions by an amendment to the Constitution of India.

The Legislative Assembly of Karnataka passed a resolution in 2010 and the Legislative Council of the State also passed a similar resolution in the same year, to make special provisions for the Hyderabad-Karnataka areas of the State of Karnataka. The Government of Karnataka has also endorsed the need for special provisions for the region. The resolutions seek to accelerate development of the most backward region of the State and promote inclusive growth with a view to reducing inter-district and inter-regional disparities in the State. It is accordingly proposed to insert a new Article 371J in the Constitution to provide for special provisions for the erstwhile Hyderabad-Karnataka areas of the State of Karnataka which consist of the districts of Gulbarga, Bidar, Raichur, Koppal, and Yadgir and additionally include the Bellary District.

The Article in the form of a special provision seeks to provide for :

(a) establishment of a separate Development Board for the aforesaid region mentioned above and a report on the working of the board would be placed every year before the State Legislative Assembly;

(b) equitable allocation of funds for development over the said region subject to the requirements of the State as a whole;

(c) reservation in public employment through the constitution of local cadres for domiciles of the region; and

(d) reservation in education and vocational training institutions for domiciles of the region.

CHAPTER 20

RELATIONS BETWEEN THE UNION AND THE STATES[1]

"Though the country and the people may be divided into different states for convenience of administration, the country is one integral whole, its people a single people living under a single imperium derived from a single source."

Dr. B.R. Ambedkar

INTRODUCTION

The fabric of the Indian federal system stands on three pillars, viz. a strong Central Government, flexible federal system, and co-operative federalism.

Moreover, the distribution of powers is an essential feature of federalism. The object for which a federal State is formed involves a division of authority between the National Government and the separate States. In fact, the basic principle of federation is that the legislative, executive, and financial authority is divided between the Centre and State not by any law passed by the Centre but by the Constitution itself. The one is not subordinate to the other in its own field; the authority of one is co-ordinate with that of the other. In other words, neither the State is subordinate to the Centre, nor the Centre to the State.

LEGISLATIVE RELATIONS

The legislative relations of the Centre and the State is divided from the point of view of Territory and Subject-matter.

Territorial Jurisdiction to Legislate

According to Article 245(1), Parliament may make laws for the whole of India, or a part thereof. However, a law made by the Parliament shall not be deemed to be invalid on the ground that it has extra-territorial operation. In other words, the laws passed by the Parliament can take effect or is applicable to Indian citizens and their property which are situated even outside the territory of India.

[1] Articles 245 to 255 in Part XI of the Constitution deals with Centre-State Legislative relations.

A State Legislature, on the other hand, may make laws only for the State concerned. A State Legislature has no legislative competence to make laws having extra-territorial operation. A State can legislate effectively only for its own territory. A State law can affect persons, properties, or things within the State and outside the State. In other words, a State law having operation outside the State is not valid.

Doctrine of Territorial Nexus : There is one exception to this general rule of extraterritorial operation of the State law. A State law of extraterritorial operation will be valid if there is sufficient nexus between the object and the State. The doctrine signifies that the object to which the law applies need not be physically located within the territorial boundaries of that State. In other words, if there is a *territorial nexus* between the subject matter of the Act and the State making law, then the Statute in question is not regarded as having *exterritorial operation.* Thus, a State may levy a tax on a person, property, object, or transaction not only when it is situated within it territorial limits, but also when it has a sufficient and real territorial connection with it.

In the case of *State of Bombay Vs. R.M.D.Chamarbaugwala*[2], the Bombay State levied a tax on lotteries and prize competitions. The tax was extended to a newspaper printed and published in Bangalore but this paper had wide circulation in Mumbai. The respondent conducted the prize competitions through this paper. The court held that there existed a sufficient territorial nexus to enable the Bombay State to the tax the newspaper. If there is sufficient nexus between the person sought to be charged and the State seeking to tax him, the taxing statute would be upheld. But the connection between the State and the subject-matter of law must be real and not illusory and the liability sought to be imposed must be pertinent to that connection.

Legislative Power is Plenary : The power of the Legislature under Article 245 to enact laws is a plenary power subject only to its legislative competence and other constitutional limitations. The power to make a law includes the power to give effect to it prospectively as well as retrospectively. The Legislature has power to alter the existing law retrospectively.

Distribution Of Legislative Powers

The distribution of legislative powers between the Centre and the States is the most important characteristic of a federal constitution. The whole structure of the federal system continues to revolve around this central point.

Distribution of legislative powers in other federal Constitutions[3] : In America, the sovereign States which were keen to federate, did not like complete subordination to the Central Government; hence they believed in entrusting subjects of common interest to the Central Government, while retaining the rest with them. Thus, the American Constitution only enumerates the powers of the Central Government and leaves the residuary power to the States. Australia followed the American pattern of only one enumeration of powers, i.e., of the Central Government, leaving the residuary powers to the States because their problems were similar to the Americans. In Canada, there is double enumeration – Federal and Provincial – leaving the residue for the Centre. The Canadians were conscious of the unfortunate happenings in USA culminating in the Civil War of 1891. They were aware of the shortcomings of the weak Centre. Hence, they opted for a strong Centre.

---

[2]AIR 1958 SC 699.

[3]Constitutional Law of India, J.N. Pandey,42nd Edition, Central Law Agency, P. 578.

INDIAN SCENARIO OF FEDERAL SET-UP

The foundation for a federal set-up was laid in the Government of India Act, 1935. Though in every respect, the distribution of legislative power between the Union and the States as envisaged in the 1935 Act has not been adopted in the Constitution, the basic framework is the same. Thus, the Constitution adopted the method followed by the Government of India Act, 1935, and divides the powers between the Union and the States in three Lists – the Union List, the State List, and the Concurrent List. The Seventh Schedule under Article 246 of the Constitution deals with division of powers between the Union and the States.

- **Union List :** Article 246(1) confers on Parliament an 'exclusive power' to make laws with respect to any of the matters in the Union List. The entries in this List are such which need a uniform law for the whole country because they are of national importance. For example, defence, foreign affairs, banking, currency, coinage, etc. are a few entries under List I. The Union List originally had 97 subjects. Now, it has 100 subjects.
- **State List :** Article 246(3) confers an exclusive power on the States to make laws with respect to the matters enumerated in the State List/List II. These are matters which admit of local variations and, from an administrative point of view, are best handled at the State level and, therefore, the Centre is debarred from legislating with respect to these matters[4]. List II originally had 66 subjects but now consists of 61 subjects and it consists of subjects like public order, prisons, public health, production, manufacture, transport, purchase and sale of intoxicating liquors, agricultural education and research, fisheries, State public services, etc.
- **Concurrent List :** Article 246(2) confers a concurrent power of legislation on both the Centre and the States with respect to the matters enumerated in the Concurrent List/List III. It is a unique feature of the Indian scheme of division of powers which provides a large concurrent field for both the Centre and the States. Certain matters, it was felt, could not be allocated exclusively either to the Centre or the States, and though the States might legislate with respect to them, it was also necessary that the Centre should also have a legislative jurisdiction. Moreover, in order to secure uniformity in the law throughout the country and also to provide remedies for mischief arising in the State sphere but whose impact may be felt beyond the boundaries of a single State, the Centre is also given the legislative power[5]. The Concurrent List originally consisted of 47 subjects, but currently it has 52 subjects such as criminal law, criminal procedure, preventive detention, forests, protection of wild animals and birds, trade unions, industrial and labour disputes, population control and family planning, etc. As both the Centre and the State can make laws with respect to the Concurrent List, there are chances of conflict. In case of conflict between the Central and the State law on Concurrent subjects, the Central law will prevail.

  Further, Article 246(A) was inserted by the 101st Constitutional Amendment Act, 2016. According to the said amendment, both the Union and the States will have the "concurrent powers" to make laws with respect to Goods and Services Taxes. The Intra-State trade now comes under the jurisdiction of both the Union and the States.
- **Residuary Powers :** Article 248 vests the residuary powers in the Parliament. It says that Parliament has exclusive power to make any law with respect to any matter not enumerated in the Concurrent List or the State List. Entry 97 in the Union List also lays down that the

[4] M. P. Jain: Indian Constitutional Law, Wadhwa, Eighth Edition, P. 535.

[5] Ibid.

Parliament has exclusive power to make laws with respect to any matter not mentioned in the State List or the Concurrent List, including any tax not mentioned in either of these Lists. Thus, the Indian Constitution makes a departure from the practise prevalent in USA, Switzerland, and Australia where residuary powers are vested in the States. This reflects the leanings that the Constitution makes towards a strong Centre.

- **Composite Legislation :** Many a time, a Legislature may enact composite legislation which may be based on more than one legislative entry. In other words, there is no bar against the Parliament or the State Legislature enacting a statute, the subject-matter of which calls for exercise of powers under two or more entries in the same List or different Lists of which they have legislative competence.

Predominance of the Union List

Article 246 expressly secures the predominance of the Union List over the State List and the Concurrent List and that of the Concurrent List over the State List. Thus, in case of overlapping between the Union List and the State List, it is the Union which is to prevail over the State List. In case of overlapping between the Union List and the Concurrent List, it is again the Union List which will prevail. In case of conflict between the Concurrent List and State List, it is the Concurrent List that shall prevail.

Repugnancy Between a Central and State Law

Doctrine of Repugnancy deals with conflict between two pieces of legislation which when applied to the same facts produce different results. Repugnancy arises when the provisions of two laws are so inconsistent and irreconcilable that it is impossible to do one without disobeying the other.

The constitutional provision relevant for solving questions of repugnancy between a Central law and a State law is to be found in Article 254 :

- According to Article 254(1), if any provision of a State law is repugnant to a provision in a law made by the Parliament which it is competent to enact, or to any existing law with respect to one of the matters in the Concurrent List, then the Parliamentary or the existing law prevails over the State law. Moreover, it does not matter whether the Parliamentary law has been enacted before or after the State law. To the extent of repugnancy, the State law is void. In other words, Article 254(1) is applicable when both the Central law and the State law happen to be with respect to the same matter in the Concurrent List and there is repugnancy between them. When there is such kind of repugnancy, then the Central law shall prevail.
- Article 254(1) lays down the general rule, while exception to Article 254(1) is given in Article 254(2). Article 254(2) provides that when there is a repugnancy between the Central law and State law with respect to a matter in the Concurrent List, in such cases the State law can prevail if it has been reserved for the consideration of the President and has received his assent. The result of obtaining the assent of the President would be that so far as the State Act is concerned, it will prevail in the State and overrule the provisions of the Central Act in its application to that State only. However, both laws should deal with a Concurrent subject.
- Article 254(2) becomes applicable only when the State law is repugnant to an earlier law enacted by the Parliament. When a State Act becomes repugnant to a Central law enacted thereafter, Article 254(2) does not apply. In other words, when the Parliament has already enacted a law

earlier than the State law, and the State law is enacted thereafter after receiving the Presidential assent, then the State law will prevail because the law made by the Parliament was the earlier law. But if the State law which is repugnant to the Central law is passed before the Central law or the Parliament passed the Central law again or after the State law, then in such cases the Central law shall prevail (it doesn't matter whether the State law has received the Presidential assent or not).

Principles of Interpretation of Lists

Scientific division of powers and subjects between the Centre and the States is not possible. Questions constantly arise whether a particular subject falls in the sphere of one or the other government. This duty is vested in the Supreme Court.

The Supreme Court has evolved the following principles of interpretation in order to determine the respective power of the Union and the States under the three Lists:

(a) **Each entry to be interpreted broadly :** Subject to the overriding predominance of the Union List, entries in the various lists should be interpreted broadly. The "widest possible" and "most liberal" interpretation should be given to the language of each entry.

(b) **Doctrine of Harmonious interpretation of entries :** Article 246 confers exclusive power on the Parliament to legislate relating to matters in List I 'notwithstanding anything in List II and List III'. This is known as the *non-obstante* clause and its effect is to make the Union power prevail in case the Union and State powers overlap. The *non-obstante* clause is the ultimate rule which is to be invoked only as a last resort, in case of *inevitable or irreconcilable* conflict between the entries in different Lists. However, before applying the above rule, the Court should make an attempt to reasonably and practically construe the entries so as to reconcile the conflict and avoid overlapping. This is nothing but called as harmonious interpretation of the various entries. Thus, the important principles of the "Doctrine of Harmonious Construction" implies:

- The courts must avoid a head-on clash of seemingly contradicting provisions and they must construe the contradictory provisions so as to harmonize them;
- The provision of one section cannot be used to defeat the provision contained in another unless the court, despite all its efforts, is unable to find a way to reconcile their differences;
- When it is impossible to completely reconcile the differences in contradictory provisions, the courts must interpret them in such a way so that effect is given to both the provisions as much as possible;
- Courts must also keep in mind that interpretation that reduces one provision to a useless number or dead is not harmonious construction;
- To harmonize is not to destroy any statutory provision or to render it fruitless.

(c) **Doctrine of Pith and Substance :** Within their respective spheres, the Union and the State Legislatures are made supreme and they should not encroach into the sphere reserved for the other. If a law passed by one encroaches upon the field assigned to the other, the Court will apply the doctrine of pith and substance to determine whether the Legislature concerned was competent to make it. If the 'pith and substance' of law, i.e., the true object of the legislation or a stature, relates to a matter with the competence of the Legislature which enacted it, it should be held to be *intra vires*[6] even though it might incidentally touch on matters not within the competence of the Legislature. In order to ascertain the true character of the legislation, one must have regard to the enactment as a whole, to its object, and to the scope and effect of its provisions.

---

[6]Within the legal power or authority.

(d) **Doctrine of Colourable Legislation :** 'The doctrine of colourable legislation' signifies only a limitation of the law-making power of the Legislature. It comes into picture when the Legislature purports to act within its power, but in reality, it has transgressed those powers. So, the doctrine becomes applicable whenever any legislation seeks to do in an indirect manner what it cannot do directly. In *K.C.G. Narayan Deo Vs. State of Orissa*[7], the Supreme Court explained the meaning and scope of the doctrine in the following terms:

"Legislative transgression may be patent, manifest or direct, but it may also be disguised, covert or indirect, or and it is this latter class of cases that the expression colourable legislation has been applied in judicial pronouncements. The idea conveyed by the expression is that although apparently a Legislature in passing a stature purported to act within the limits of its powers, yet in substance and in reality it transgressed these powers...In other words, it is the substance of the Act that is material and not merely the form or outward appearance and if the subject-matter in substance is something which is beyond the powers that Legislature to legislate upon the form in which the law is clothed cannot save it from condemnation. The Legislature cannot violate the constitutional prohibitions by employing indirect methods".

In "*State of Bihar Vs. Kameshwar Singh*"[8], a law has been declared invalid on the ground of colourable legislation.

Thus, the whole doctrine of colourable legislation is based upon the maxim "that you cannot do indirectly what you cannot do directly".

Parliament's Power to Legislate on State Subjects[9]

Though in normal times the distribution of powers must be strictly maintained and neither the State nor the Centre can encroach upon the sphere allotted to the other by the Constitution, yet in certain exceptional circumstances, the general system of distribution is either suspended or the powers of the Union Parliament are extended over the subjects mentioned in the State List. In other words, a number of constitutional provisions enable the Parliament to legislate in the State sphere from time to time. These constitutional provisions are discussed below –

1. **Power of Parliament to legislate in the national interests :** According to Article 249, if the Rajya Sabha declares, by a resolution supported by two-thirds of the members present and voting, that it is necessary or expedient in the national interest that Parliament should make laws with respect to a matter in the State List specified in the resolution, it becomes lawful for Parliament to make laws for the whole or any part of India with respect to that matter so long as the resolution is in force. Such a resolution normally lasts for a year; it may be renewed as many times necessary but not exceeding a year at a time. These laws of Parliament will, however, cease to have effect on the expiration of the period of six months after the resolution has ceased to operate.

   Article 249 has been used very sparingly so far. It may be underlined that there are four inbuilt safeguards against the misuse of power :

   - Parliament can assume jurisdiction to legislate only if two-thirds of the members of the Rajya Sabha present and voting pass the necessary resolution;
   - The resolution must specify the matter enumerated in the State List with respect to which Parliament is being authorised to legislate in the national interest;

[7] AIR 1953 SC 375.

[8] AIR 1953 SC 375.

[9] M. P. Jain: *Indian Constitutional Law*, Wadhwa, Eighth Edition, Pg. no. 609.

- The resolution passed by the Rajya Sabha remains in force for one year; and
- The law enacted by the Parliament in pursuance of this resolution remains in force only six months after the resolution ceases to remain in force.

However, the State Legislature continues to enjoy power to make laws which it is empowered to make under the Constitution, even after the Rajya Sabha passes a resolution under Article 249. This is, however, subject to the rule of repugnancy. In other words, the State Legislature can make laws, but if it is in conflict with the law passed by the Parliament, then in such case the Parliamentary law shall prevail.

2. **During a Proclamation of Emergency :** While a proclamation of emergency is in operation in the country under Article 352, Parliament is empowered under Article 250 to legislate with respect to any matter in the State List. Under Article 250, the Parliament is empowered to make laws for the whole or any part of the territory of India with respect to all matters in the State List. Such a law, however, shall cease to have effect on the expiration of six months after the proclamation of emergency ceased to operate. Article 250 does not restrict the power of a State Legislature to make a law which it is entitled to make under the Constitution. However, in case of repugnancy between a State law and a Parliamentary law enacted under Article 250, the latter is to prevail and the State law, to the extent of repugnancy, and so long as the Parliamentary law continues, is to be inoperative.

3. **Parliament's power to legislate with the consent of the States :** Article 252 provides for delegation of powers by two or more States to Parliament so as to enable it to legislate with respect to a matter in the State List in relation to such States. In other words, if the Legislature of two or more States pass a resolution to the effect that it is desirable to have a law passed by Parliament on any matters in the State List, it shall be lawful for Parliament to make laws regulating that matter. Such law can only be amended or repealed by the Act of Parliament. In the context of Article 252, the term 'State Legislature' means only House or Houses of the Legislature without including the Governor. Therefore, Governor's assent is not necessary for the resolution to be passed by the House or Houses.

   When the State Legislature passes a resolution under Article 252, Parliament becomes entitled to legislate, and the State Legislature ceases to share the power to make law with respect to that matter. The resolution operates as "abdication or surrender" of the State power with respect to that matter which is the subject matter of the resolution, and it is placed solely in the hands of the Parliament which alone can then legislate with respect to it. It is as if such matter is lifted out of List II and placed in List I of the Seventh Schedule of the Constitution.

   Article 252 has been used a few times. For example, in order to have a uniform law for the control and regulation of prize competitions, several States passed resolutions authorising the Parliament to enact the requisite legislation. The need for a Central law was felt because these competitions were run by out-of-State journals which a State law could not effectively control. Parliament then enacted the Prize Competitions Act, 1955.

4. **Parliament's power to legislate for giving effect to treaties and international agreements :** Article 253 confers on Parliament the capacity to legislate, irrespective of the scheme of distribution of powers, to implement a treaty or a decision made at an international conference.

5. **In case of failure of constitutional machinery in a State :** Under Article 356, the Parliament is empowered to make laws with respect to all matters in the State List when the Parliament declares that the Government of the State cannot be carried on in accordance with the provisions of the Constitution. Such a law made by the Parliament continues to be operative even after the President's Rule, until and unless it is repealed or re-enacted or amended by the concerned State Legislature.
6. **Expansive nature of some Union/List I Entries :** Lastly, it may also be noted that certain entries in the Union List, such as – 7[10], 23[11], 27[12], 52[13], 53[14], 54[15], 56[16], 62[17], 63[18], and 67[19] are so worded as to make their ambit expansive. For example, under entry 52, Parliament can take any industry under Central control by declaring that its control by the Union is 'expedient in the public interest'. This is a flexible provision because an industry can stay in the State sphere until need is felt to bring it under Central control.

Centre's Control Over State Legislation[20]

In addition to the Parliament's power to legislate directly on the State subjects under the foregoing Articles, the Constitution also provides for the President's consent before a Bill passed by a State Legislature can become a law.

The following Articles give the Centre a control over State legislation –

(a) Article 31A grants immunity to laws providing for agrarian reforms from Articles 14 and 19. The immunity of Article 31A will not be available to a State law unless it has received the assent of the President.

(b) Article 200 (second proviso of the Article) directs the Governor of a State to reserve a Bill passed by a State Legislature for the consideration of the President if in his opinion, if passed into law, would derogate the power of the High Court so as to endanger the position which the Court is designed to fulfil under the Constitution.

---

[10] Atomic energy and mineral resources necessary for its production.

[11] Highways declared by or under law made by Parliament to be national highways.

[12] Ports declared by or under law made by Parliament or existing law to be major ports, including their delimitation, and the constitution and powers of port authorities therein.

[13] Industries, the control of which by the Union is declared by Parliament by law to be expedient in the public interest.

[14] Regulation and development of oilfields and mineral oil resources; petroleum and petroleum products; other liquids and substances declared by Parliament by law to be dangerously inflammable.

[15] Regulation of mines and mineral development to the extent to which such regulation and development under the control of the Union is declared by Parliament by law to be expedient in the public interest.

[16] Regulation and development of inter-State rivers and river valleys to the extent to which such regulation and development under the control of the Union is declared by Parliament by law to be expedient in the public interest.

[17] The institutions known at the commencement of this Constitution as the National Library, the Indian Museum, the Imperial War Museum, the Victoria Memorial and the Indian War Memorial, and any other like institution financed by the Government of India wholly or in part and declared by Parliament by law to be an institution of national importance.

[18] The institutions known at the commencement of this Constitution as the Benares Hindu University, the Aligarh Muslim University and the Delhi University; the University established in pursuance of Article 371E;any other institution declared by Parliament by law to be an institution of national importance.

[19] Ancient and historical monuments and records, and archaeological sites and remains, declared by or under law made by Parliament to be of national importance.

[20] M. P. Jain: Indian Constitutional Law, Wadhwa, Eighth Edition, P. 614

(c) Under Article 254, when there is a repugnancy between a State law and a Central law with respect to a matter in the Concurrent List, it may be cured by the assent of the President to the State legislation.

(d) Article 288 authorises a State to tax in respect of water or electricity stored, generated, consumed, distributed, or sold by any authority established by law made by Parliament. But it makes clear that no such law shall be valid unless it has been reserved for the consideration of the President and has received his assent.

(e) Article 304 authorises a State Legislature to impose reasonable restriction on the freedom of trade, commerce, and intercourse within the State in the "Public interest". But such laws cannot be introduced in the State Legislature without the previous sanction of the President. It may however be mentioned that in the absence of prior sanction of the President, the defect can be cured under Article 255 by subsequent assent of the President to the State law in question.

(f) When a proclamation of Financial Emergency is in operation under Article 360, the President, i.e., the Central Executive, can direct the States to reserve all Money or Financial Bills for the President's consideration after they are passed by the State Legislature.

(g) Besides the above specific situations where State legislation compulsorily needs Central assent for its validity, there is Article 200 which makes a general provision enabling the State Governor to reserve a Bill passed by the State Legislature for Presidential consideration and assent. However, it is not clear in what situations and circumstances the Governor may do so. It needs to be said that the Governor should exercise his discretionary power to reserve a Bill for President's assent not liberally but exceptionally, i.e., only in rare and exceptional cases.

Some of the situations when the Governor may be justified in reserving a State Bill are :

- When the State Bill suffers from patent unconstitutionality;
- When the State Bill derogates from the scheme and framework of the Constitution so as to endanger the sovereignty, unity, and integrity of the country;
- When the State Bill ex facie comes in conflict with a Central law;
- When the legitimate interests of another State or its people are being adversely affected.

20.1 ADMINISTRATIVE RELATIONS[1]

INTRODUCTION

The Indian Constitution contains more elaborate provisions regarding administrative relations between the Centre and the States than are to be found in any of the three Federations of the USA, Canada, and Australia. The Constitution lays down a flexible and permissive, and not a rigid, scheme of allocation of administrative responsibilities between the Centre and the States. The scheme is so designed as to permit all kinds of co-operative administrative arrangements between the two levels of government. Along with distribution of legislative and financial powers, the executive power has also been divided between the Centre and States. Subject to a few exceptions, the general principle followed in this connection is that the executive power is coextensive with legislative power.

The scope and extent of the executive power of the Centre and States are as follows –

i. The executive power of the Centre extends to the whole of India in respect of matters in List I. However, the Centre is not obligated to administer by itself all matters in its exclusive domain. It can, if it so desires, entrust administrative responsibility in any matter to the States.

ii. The executive power of the Centre also extends to the rights, authority, and jurisdiction conferred on it by any treaty or agreement.

iii. A State's executive power extends to its territory in respect of matters in List II.

iv. In respect of matters in which both the Centre and the States have legislative power (Concurrent List), ordinarily, the executive power rests with the States, except when either the Constitution, or a law of Parliament, expressly confers it on the Centre. In the Concurrent field, ordinarily the authority to execute laws rests with the States even when the law is passed by the Centre. In exceptional cases, however, Parliament may prescribe that the execution of a Central law shall be with the Centre alone, or with both the Centre and the States. In the Concurrent List, even after the Centre assumes executive power under its law, the residuary execution power under the entry may still rest with the States.

CENTRAL-STATE ADMINISTRATIVE CO-ORDINATION

To mitigate rigidity which might arise from Centre-State division of administrative power, the Indian Constitution makes provisions for inter-governmental delegation of administrative power. Inter-governmental delegation may happen either under an agreement between the governments or by legislation. While the Centre can use both the methods to delegate administrative power to the States, a State can use only the first method to delegate administrative power to the Centre.

(a) **Centre's delegation to the States through Agreement:** According to Article 258(1), the President may, with the consent of the State Government, entrust either conditionally or unconditionally, to the State Government, or its officers, any function in relation to a matter to which the Centre's executive power extends. This provision authorises entrustment to a State Government, with its consent, of any function of the Central Government. However, this constitutional provision does not authorise the President to delegate those powers and functions with which he is, by the express provisions of the Constitution, invested as the President.

[1]Articles 256 to 263 of Part XI of the Constitution deals with Centre-State administrative relations.

(b) **Centre's delegation to the States by law :** According to Article 258(2), a law made by Parliament, even if it relates to a matter in the Union List, with respect to which the State has no power to legislate, may confer power and impose duties, or authorise the conferring of powers and the imposition of duties, upon a State, its officers, and authorities. Therefore, a Central law, whether pertaining to a matter in List I or List III, may confer powers and impose duties on the States, their officers, and authorities. In other words, through a law is made by Parliament, powers can be conferred and duties can be imposed on a State Government or its officers, even though the State Legislature has no power to make a law with respect to the subject-matter of the Union law. Unlike Article 258(1), under Article 258(2), the conferment is made by Parliament by law and no consent of the State Government is required for the purpose[2].

(c) **Entrustment of State functions to the Centre :** According to Article 258A, a State Government may, with the consent of the Central Government, entrust either conditionally or unconditionally to the Central Government or its officers, functions in relation to any matter to which the executive power of the State extends. Article 258A was inserted in the Seventh Constitution Amendment Act, 1956 to ease the execution of certain development works in the States.

States' Obligations Towards the Centre

The Constitution places certain restrictions and obligations on the States in order to ensure that the Centre can exercise its powers unimpeded by them. As it is necessary to ensure that no State by its action or inaction interferes with legislative and administrative functions of the Centre, the Constitution provides certain provisions with regards to the same:

(a) Article 256 imposes a general obligation on the States to exercise their executive powers in such way that they would comply with the laws made by the Parliament. Moreover, the said Article enables the Centre under its executive power to give directions to the States as may appear necessary by the Centre for the enforcement of any law made by the Parliament.

(b) Article 257 imposes an obligation on the States that the executive power of a State is to be so exercised as not to impede or prejudice the exercise of the Centre's executive power. The Centre can give such directions to a State as may appear to the Central Government to be necessary for that purpose. In other words, the power of the Centre to give directions is limited to such situations only where some State executive action impedes or prejudices the valid exercise of the Central executive power.

It is obligatory on the part of the State Government to comply with the directions issued by the Central Government under Articles 256 and 257. The sanction to enforce the directions is enshrined in the Article 356[3]. In other words, if the States fail to comply with the directions given by the Centre under Articles 256 and 257, then it is lawful for the President to impose President's Rule under Article 356.

---

[2]When powers and duties are entrusted by the Centre to the States or their officers, the Centre is to compensate the States in respect of any extra costs of administration incurred by the States in connection with those power and duties.

[3]Katya Co-op Building Society Ltd. Vs. Government of Andhra Pradesh, AIR 1985 AP 242.

Centre's Directives to the States

Apart from the above Articles, a few other Constitutional provisions authorise the Centre to issue directives to the States in several matters, such as :

(a) 'Communications' is a State subject. However, the Centre may give directions to a State as to the construction and maintenance of means of communication declared in the direction to be of national or military importance. This however, does not restrict the power of the Parliament to declare highways or waterways to be national; nor is the Centre's power restricted with respect to the national highways or waterways, nor its power to construct and maintain means of communication as part of its functions with respect to naval, military, and air force works.

(b) The Centre can give directions to a State regarding the measures to be taken for the protection of the railways within the State. 'Railways' is a Central subject but 'Police' is a State subject and, consequently, the protection of railway property lies within the field of the State Government.

(c) The Central Government has power to issue directives to the States regarding the drawing up and execution of schemes to be essential for the welfare of Scheduled Tribes in the States.

(d) A State is obligated to provide facilities for instruction in the mother-tongue at the primary stage of children belonging to a linguistic minority and the President has been empowered to issue such directions to any State as he considers necessary.

(e) The President may issue directions in regard to the official language of the Union, and with regard to the recognition in a State of the language spoken by a substantial proportion of the State population.

(f) During an emergency under Article 352, the Centre gets some overriding powers with respect to the States. It can give directions to the States as to the way they should exercise their executive power. During a financial emergency, the Centre can give directions to a State, and, under Article 356, the Centre can take over a State Government when it cannot be carried on in accordance with the Constitution.

Article 365 lays down the sanction behind the Central directives to the States, In case of failure of a State to comply with, or give effect to, the Central direction given under any constitutional provision, the President may hold that a situation has arisen in which the State Government cannot be carried on in accordance with the provisions of the Constitution. Thereafter, the Centre can take over the administration of the State as provided in Article 356. Without Article 365, there would have been no sanction to ensure enforcement of Central directions issued to the States, under any constitutional provision in exercise of its executive power. However, taking recourse to Article 365 is a measure of last resort.

ALL INDIA SERVICES IN CENTRE-STATE ADMINISTRATIVE RELATIONS

The All India Services (AIS) are a unique feature of our federal polity. It is the view of many constitutional exports that the Indian Constitution though federal in form, is unitary in substance. The All India Services scheme is a part of this general policy or making the Centre strong in the overall constitutional arrangements. The Constitution adopted the system of unified higher administrative service, which existed during the British regime in India. The British constituted the Indian Civil Service

(ICS) to man administrative posts not only at the Centre, but also at State and district levels. Subsequently, the Indian Police (IP) was formed to take charge of the maintenance of law and order. Also, other All India Technical Services were formed. The officers were allocated to the provinces permanently, the Centre borrowing them as and when required. With the grant of autonomy to the provinces and on the recommendation of the Lee Commission in 1924, All India Services with the exception of the ICS and the IP were abolished. Therefore, at the time of independence, ICS and the IP were the two residuary All India Services still in existence. Soon thereafter, the Indian Administrative Service was constituted to absorb the pre-existing service known as Indian Police. The Constitution retained these two All India Services and empowered the Parliament to create other All India Services, provided that the Rajya Sabha passes a resolution supported by not less than two-thirds of the members present and voting that this was necessary in the national interest. The purpose behind this provision was to permit greater cohesion in administration and to maintain the standard of administration at a fairly high minimum.

In the initial stages of independence, the States were not enthusiastic about the creation of new All India Services. But with the accelerated pace of industrial and economic development, there seems to have been a realisation that the States are not in a position of procure technically trained manpower. With a view to correcting particularistic trends, and also to secure greater inter-State co-ordination for efficient implementation of All India policies, efforts have been undertaken towards creation of a few more All India Services, especially for technical departments, for "the Central and State Governments have to work in very close co-operation in executing important development projects, which necessitates that technical personnel should be trained and recruited on a common basis". Consequently, in 1961, the Chief Ministers' Conference accepted in principle the creation of three new All India Services in the field of engineering, forestry and medicine, and public health. After the adoption of a resolution under Article 312(1) by the Rajya Sabha, these services were created by amending the All India Services Act, 1951 in 1963[4].

Whatever might have been the aim of the British in creating the All India Services, the continued retention of the existing services and even creation of more services in the fields of economic and social administration seems to be essential at the present time. All India recruitment makes available the best talent in the country which is sorely needed in a developing economy. Further, the fact that the services are manned by personnel drawn from all the States promotes national integration and the unity of India. These services give cohesion to the federal structure and help in achieving greater efficiency in the administration of the Union and the States. The All India basis of recruitment attracts the best available talent in the country to these services. Moreover, it is desirable that the States have officers who will not be influenced by parochial and regional considerations in tackling the various administrative problems. As the control of these officers vest jointly in the Centre and the States, the officers are in a position to fulfil their responsibilities without being unduly subjected to the influence of local politicians.

The provision of All India Services appears to be unusual in a federal system. The States have not voiced concerted opposition to the retention of All India Services and is unlikely that they will. For reasons already stated, it would be in the national interest that these services be continued.

---

[4]The State Government has also agreed to the creation of two more All India Services, viz., the Indian Educational Service and the Indian Agricultural Service. The necessary resolution under Article 312 was also adopted by the Rajya Sabha. After the fourth general elections, a few State Governments modified their stand and refused to participate in these two services and, consequently, the matter was deferred.

OTHER ASPECTS OF CENTRE-STATE ADMINISTRATIVE RELATIONS

(a) **Deployment of Military and Para-military Forces :** These can be deployed in a State by the Union, if situation warrants, even against the wishes of the State government.

(b) **Public Service Commission:**

- There can be creation of Joint State Public Service Commission (JSPSC) for two or more States on the request by the State Legislatures through a resolution to that effect. The Chairman and members of the JSPSC are appointed by the President.
- The Chairman and members of a State Public Service Commission, though appointed by the Governor of the respective State, can be removed only by the President.
- UPSC can extend its support and expertise in recruitment, etc., to any State on the request of the Governor of the State and with the approval of the President. Moreover, UPSC can also assist the States when requested by them in framing and operating schemes of joint recruitment for any services for which candidates possessing special qualifications are required.

(c) **Office of Governor :** He is appointed and removed by the President. The Governor does not enjoy any fixed term as he holds office during the Pleasure of the President. The Governor is not only the Head of a State, but also he is an agent of the Centre. The Governor submits reports to the Centre about the administrative affairs of the State and also has the power to recommend about the imposition of the President's Rule.

(d) **State Election Commissioners :** Are appointed by the Governors of the State, but can be removed only by the President.

20.2 CENTRE-STATE FINANCIAL RELATIONS

INTRODUCTION

In a federation, the Centre and State financial relations are considered to be vital and critical for the working of a federal polity. Moreover, in order to maintain the legislative and administrative authority of the constituent units in the federation, the financial autonomy is imperative. The Indian Constitution incorporates a very elaborate scheme of Centre-State financial relations. The scheme of distribution of sources of revenue between the Centre and the States is based on the scheme laid down in the Government of India Act, 1935.

The two most salient features of the scheme are:

(i) A complete separation of Central-State taxing powers, and

(ii) Massive transfer of funds from the Centre to the States.

Allocation of Taxing powers between Centre and States

The legislative power to make a law for imposing a tax is divided between the Centre and the States by means of three separate lists (Union List, State List, and Concurrent List) provided in the Constitution. In other words, the taxes enumerated in the Union List are leviable by the Centre exclusively while those mentioned in the State List are leviable by the States exclusively. In order to avoid the problems of overlapping and multiple taxations between the Union and the States, very few taxes are contained in the Concurrent List. On the other hand, the residuary power of taxation belongs to the Parliament (Entry 97 of List I).

Moreover, the sources of revenue allocated to the Union are not meant entirely for the purposes of the Union and they do not form part of the Consolidated Fund of India. The revenue allocated to the Union has to be shared with the States. The question of distribution of the revenue between the Union and the States and amongst the States and the principles governing them, as also the principles governing grants-in-aid are matters which have to be decided by a high-powered Finance Commission.

Principles of Taxation

(i) The original Constitution of India provided a clear distinction between the legislative power to levy a tax and the power to appropriate the proceeds of a tax so levied. In other words, a tax can be levied by one constituent unit; however, the same tax which has been levied can be appropriated by a different constituent unit.

For Example : According to Article 268, stamp duties and duties of excise on medicinal and toilet preparations provided in the Union List shall be levied by the Central Government. However, these duties are collected and appropriated by the States within which such duties are leviable.

(ii) The Constitution of India does not contain any prohibition against double taxation. In other words, a subject can be taxed twice over if the Legislature provides a clear intention to do so.[1]

[1] M. P. Jain, Indian Constitutional Law, Wadhwa, Eighth Edition, P. 627

TAX SHARING SCHEME OR DISTRIBUTION OF REVENUE BEFORE 2000

The Central Tax Resources

From the point of view of tax-sharing, all Central taxes were arranged in the following five categories:

(i) **Duties levied by the Union but collected and appropriated by the States (Article 268) :** Stamp duties on bills of exchange, cheques, promissory notes, policies of insurance, transfer of shares, excise duties on medicinal and toilet preparations containing alcohol and narcotics – will fall under this category.

The proceeds from these duties, except those collected by the Government of India for the Union Territories, do not form part of the Consolidated Fund. The States themselves collect the duties, though under a Central law, and appropriate them for their own purposes.

(ii) **Taxes levied and collected by the Union, but assigned to the States within which they are leviable (Article 269) :** Duties on succession to property other than agricultural land; Estate duty in respect of property other than agricultural land; Terminal taxes on goods or passengers carried by railway, air, or sea; Taxes on railway fares and freights; Taxes on stock exchange other than stamp duties; Taxes on sales of and advertisements in newspapers; taxes on sale or purchase of goods other than newspapers, where such sale or purchase takes place in the course of inter-State trade or commerce; Taxes on inter-State consignment of goods – fall under this category.

The net proceeds in a financial year of these taxes, except the proceeds attributable to the Union Territories, do not form part of the Consolidated Fund of India, but were to be distributed among the States in accordance with the principles formulated by law made by the Parliament.

(iii) **Taxes levied and collected by the Centre, and used by it as a whole :** Customs, Corporation Tax, Capital Gains Tax, Surcharges on taxes mentioned in sub-clause (2) and (4) of Article 271, and residuary taxes fall under this category. The taxes falling under this category exclusively belongs to the Centre.

(iv) **Taxes levied and collected by the Centre, but the net proceeds of which had to be compulsorily shared by it with the States (Article 270) :** The tax on non-agricultural income falls under this category. The Centre has to hand over a part of the revenue accruing to it from the levy of income tax to the States. This divisible pool of the income tax did not even form part of the Consolidated Fund of India. The percentage to be shared with the States was based on the recommendations of the Finance Commission. The Parliament need not pass a law for the said purpose.

(v) **Taxes levied and collected by the Centre but a portion of the net proceeds of which 'may be assigned' by it to the States by its own law (Article 272) :** The Central excises (other than on medicinal and toilet preparations) fell in this category. Unlike the income tax which must be shared, Centre-State tax sharing in this area was not compulsory but optional for the Centre. The revenue accruing from the Central Excises formed part of the Consolidated Fund of India out of which payments were to be made to the States when Parliament passed a law for this purpose.[2]

The State Tax Resources

(i) **Taxes belonging to the States exclusively :** Land Revenue; Income tax on agricultural income; Estate duty; Succession duty; Taxes on lands and buildings, mineral rights; Taxes on entry of goods into local areas; Sales Tax (Except sale on purchase of goods other than newspapers & taxes on inter- State trade and commerce belong to the States); Tolls; Taxes on professions,

[2]M.P. Jain, Indian Constitutional Law, Wadhwa, Eighth Edition, Pg No missing.

trades, etc., not exceeding Rs. 2500 per annum; Stamp duty except in documents included in the Union List; Taxes on passengers and goods carried on inland waterways – are the taxes which fall in this category. These taxes are levied by the States and collected by them (all taxes enumerated in List II).

(ii) *Taxes levied by the Centre but collected by the States*

(iii) *Taxes levied and collected by the Centre, the whole of the proceeds of which belonged to the States*

(iv) *Taxes levied and collected by the Centre but voluntarily shared with the States*

(v) *Taxes levied and collected by the Centre but compulsorily shared by it with the States.*

DISTRIBUTION OF NON-TAX REVENUE

Non-tax Revenue Receipts are those revenue receipts which are not generated by taxing the public. For example, money which the government earns as "Dividends and Profits" from its profit-making Public-Sector Enterprises (PSUs) are considered to be non-tax revenue.

The Central Government's Non-tax Revenues – Railways, Posts and Telegraphs; Broadcasting; Opium; Currency and Mint; Industrial and Commercial Undertakings of the Central Government relating to the subjects over which the Union has jurisdiction (Steel Authority of India; the Hindustan Shipyard Ltd, etc.)

The State Non-tax Revenues – Forests, Irrigation, and Commercial Enterprises (like Road, Electricity, etc.) and Industrial Undertakings.

Grants-in-Aid

As discussed above, the Constitution had devised a flexible and elaborate scheme of tax-sharing between the Centre and the States. Even after allocating the taxes to the States, the resources of all the States may not be adequate enough. Therefore, the Constitution provides for another expedient system to affect the transfer of revenue from the Centre to the States in the form of Grants-in-aid.

The various forms of grants envisaged by the Constitution are as follows:

(a) Fiscal Need Grants : Article 275 makes provision for 'Fiscal need' grants. These grants are fixed by Parliament every five years on the basis of recommendations of the Finance Commission constituted under Article 280. These grants are not given to every State but only to those States as may be in need of assistance. Moreover, the amount of money payable to the States by way of fiscal need grants is also unconditional and the recipient States can use the said money as they like. The Constitution, therefore, provides that grants-in-aid shall be made in each year by the Union to such States as Parliament may determine to be in need of assistance; particularly, for the promotion of welfare of tribal areas, including special grants to Assam in this respect.

(b) Specific Purpose Grants : These grants given under Article 282 are also known as "Conditional Grants" or "Discretionary Grants". These grants are given at the discretion of the Centre for supporting such activities as the Centre may wish to promote to achieve the desired national goals. Unlike the "Fiscal need grants" under Article 275, these grants lie outside the purview of the Finance Commission (rationale is further explained in Inter-governmental transfers section). Another important difference between Article 275 and 282 is that the funds flowing to the States through the Finance Commission are unconditional, and may even be regarded as coming to the States as a matter of right, whereas the grants under Article 282 may be conditional and tied to specific purposes.

(c) **Other Grants :** Provision is made in Article 273 for grants-in-aid of the revenues of the State of Assam, Bihar, Orissa, and West Bengal in lieu of their share of the net proceeds of the jute export duty. In other words, a portion of the export duty imposed on jute and jute-products by the Union government will be allocated to the States in which jute was grown. The percentage and manner of allocation of the export duty to the States were to be determined by Parliament through legislation based on the recommendations of the Finance Commission. These sums or grants which are made to the States shall be charged on the Consolidated Fund of India. The grants under Article 273 are for a temporary period only, i.e., only for a period of 10 years from the commencement of the Constitution.

SCHEME OF TAX-SHARING AFTER 2000

Till the year 2000, only a few Central taxes were shareable between the Centre and the States. Later on, the Tenth Finance Commission recommended for the replacement of the present system of tax sharing by a new scheme in which the States shared in the total tax revenue of the Centre. The Commission further suggested that the share of the States in the gross receipts of Central taxes be fixed at 29% and that this ratio be reviewed after 15 years.

Based on the recommendations made by the Tenth Finance Commission, the Parliament enacted the Eightieth Constitutional Amendment Act, 2000.

Changes Introduced by 80th Constitutional Amendment Act, 2000

(i) Article 272 has been repealed.

(ii) A new Article 270 has been substituted for the old one. The new Article 270 provides that the net proceeds of all taxes and duties referred to in the Union List shall be distributed between the Centre and the States except a few. The above said few taxes or duties which will not be distributed between the Centre and State are as follows:

(a) Duties and taxes referred to in Article 268, 268-A, and 269 respectively;

(b) Surcharge on Taxes and duties referred to in Article 271;

(c) Any cess levied for specific purposes under a law made by Parliament.

The new Article 270 does not fix the percentage of the net proceeds of the Central taxes which must be distributed among the States. The prescription of the distributable percentage of the Central taxes has been left to be settled by the Finance Commission.

The Fourteenth Finance Commission has fixed this percentage at 42%. The recommendation of tax devolution at 42% is a huge jump from the 32% recommended by the 13th Finance Commission. The Commission has also worked out the scheme of *inter se* distribution of this tax revenue among the States keeping in view a number of considerations, such as Income Distance, Population (1971), Area, Demographic change, and Forest cover.

(iii) In 2003, Article 268-A was introduced in the Constitution by the Eighty-eighth Amendment Act, 2003, which provides that taxes on services shall be charged by the Union of India and shall be appropriated by the Union of India and the States.

Changes Introduced by 101st Constitutional Amendment Act, 2016

The 101st Constitutional Amendment Act, 2016 amended the Constitution to introduce the Goods and Services Tax (GST). The GST is a Value added Tax (VAT) and it is a comprehensive indirect tax levied on manufacture, sale, and consumption of goods as well as services at the national level which will replace all indirect taxes levied on goods and services by a single tax on the supply, right from the manufacturer to the consumer. As per the amendment Act, both the Parliament and State legislatures will have concurrent powers to make laws on GST.

In order to introduce this new tax regime, i.e., GST in the Constitution, several Articles have been either amended or repealed. Following are the important amendments made to the Constitution to accommodate the changes in the financial relations between the Centre and the States.

The following Articles have been inserted :

(a) **Article 246A** : Both the Union and the States will have the "concurrent powers" to make laws with respect to goods & services. The intra-State trade now comes under the jurisdiction of both Union and the States, while inter-State trade and commerce "exclusively" falls under the jurisdiction of the Union government.

(b) **Article 269A** : In case of inter-State trade, the amount collected by the Centre is to be apportioned between the Centre and the States as per recommendations of the GST Council. The Article further makes it clear that the proceeds such collected will not be credited to the Consolidated Fund of India or to the State but their respective shares shall be assigned to that State or the Centre.

(c) **Article 279A** : This Article provides for the Constitution of a GST Council by the President of India within sixty days from this Act coming into force. The GST Council will comprise the following members:

- Union Finance Minister as the Chairman of the Council
- Union Minister of State in charge of Revenue
- One nominated member from each State who is in charge of finance or taxation.

The following Article has been repealed :

Article 268A of the Constitution, as inserted by Eighty-eighth Constitutional Amendment Act, 2003 relating to Service tax levied by the Union and collected and appropriated by the Union and the States has been repealed.

The following Articles have been amended :

(i) The residuary power of legislation of Parliament under **Article 248** is now subject to Article 246A.

(ii) **Article 249** has been amended so that if 2/3rd majority resolution is passed by Rajya Sabha, the Parliament will have powers to make necessary laws with respect to GST also in national interest.

(iii) **Article 250** has been amended so that the Parliament will have powers to make laws related to GST during emergency period.

(iv) **Article 268** has been amended so that excise duty on medicinal and toilet preparation will be omitted from the State list and will be subsumed in GST.

INTER-GOVERNMENT TAX IMMUNITIES

The doctrine of inter-governmental tax immunity seeks to ensure that government at one level in a federation operates without unduly restricting the operations of the government at the other level. Though the doctrine has general application, yet its application is most significant in the area of taxation. The said doctrine restricts to some extent, the taxing powers of the governments in a federation.

Exemption of Union Property from State Taxation

According to Article 285, the Union property is exempted not only from "State Taxation", but also from tax imposed by any other local body or authority like municipality or Panchayat, etc. However, only Parliament can relax this ban to the extent it likes by making a law. Moreover, the word "Property" under Article 285 is a generic term without any qualifications. In other words, the word "Property" includes every kind of property including moveable, immoveable, tangible, or intangible. And there is no distinction being made between the Union property devoted to commercial purposes or that used for governmental functions.

Property and Income of the States and the Union Taxing Powers

According to Article 289, the property and the income of a State shall be exempted from the Union taxation. The word "income" of the State includes both from governmental and non-governmental or commercial activities. However, there is an exception to the above said provision. The Union government, by way of law, is authorized to impose a tax in respect of the income derived by a State government from trade or business carried on by it. This can be done only by the Parliament by making a law to that effect.

The Supreme Court has held by a majority, in an advisory opinion, that the Centre can levy customs duty on goods imported or exported, or an excise duty on goods produced or manufactured by a State Government, irrespective of whether or not it is used for purpose of trade or business. Article 289(1), the Court has held, bars Central taxes directly on property or income of the States and not those taxes which may indirectly affect, or are in respect of, income or property. The customs duty is a tax on 'import or export', and excise on 'production or manufacture' and none of these taxes is levied on property or income as such, and therefore, none of these taxes fall within the purview of Article 289(1).[3]

BORROWING POWER

Borrowing Power of the Central Government

According to Article 292, the Central Government can borrow upon the security of the Consolidated Fund of India, within such limits, if any, as may be fixed by the Parliament by law. However, no quantitative restrictions on loans have yet been fixed by the Parliament.

Borrowing Power of the State Government

According to Article 293, the State Government can borrow within in India upon the security of its Consolidated Fund, within such limits, if any, as may be fixed by the State Legislature by law. However, no quantitative restrictions on loans has yet been fixed by any State Legislature. The States are barred from raising any loan out of India. Only the Central Government enjoys the privilege of raising the Foreign loans. Moreover, the Central Government can either make loans to any State, subject to the conditions

[3] Re Sea Customs Act (1963), Section 20(2), AIR 1963 SC 1760.

laid by the Parliament by law or the Central Government can give guarantees for loans raised by a State, within the amounts fixed by the Parliament. The above said sums which are required for making such loans are charged on the Consolidated Fund of India. Another important aspect with respect to the State's borrowing power is that the State cannot raise any loan without the Centre's consent if any loan made by the Centre to the State is outstanding.

INTERGOVERNMENTAL TRANSFERS

The Constitution of India provides for decentralization of revenue and expenditure at two levels of the Federation, the Union and the States. It specifies the revenue raising power and areas of expenditure broadly on considerations of efficiency based on comparative advantage of the governments at the two levels. An imbalance arises in this process since the Union (Central) government is assigned most of revenue raising power while the State governments are expected to carry out most of the development and welfare-oriented expenditure. Hence, the Constitution provides for devolution of part of the Union revenue to the States.

Fiscal imbalance at different levels of the government is a common feature in many federal countries. The lower levels of government are generally confronted with inadequate resources for meeting their expenditure needs. In the Indian case, the Centre has the authority to decide on broad-based and buoyant taxes such as income tax, corporation tax, and custom duties while the States have the authority on items like stamp duties, entertainment tax, and land revenue – most of which are not as buoyant as the Central taxes. In terms of expenditure decentralization, the central government is entrusted with the responsibilities of provision of nationally important areas like defense, foreign affairs, foreign trade and exchange management, money and banking, and cross-state transport and communication. The State governments are given the responsibility of facilitating agriculture and industry, providing social sector services such as health and education, police protection, State roads, and infrastructure. The third level local self-governments–municipalities and Panchayats–provide public utility services such as water supply and sanitation, local roads, electricity, etc. In addition to these, both Central and State governments are responsible for provisioning services in the Concurrent list. The resultant vertical fiscal gap, which also occurs in India, necessitates intergovernmental revenue transfer. The observed imbalance is not entirely due to revenue instruments and functions assigned in the Constitution, but it is partly an outcome of fiscal choices exercised by different levels of government in practice.

Thus, revenue decentralization results in the sharing of revenue raising powers and the use of instruments, especially various types of taxes, by different levels of government. The Indian government has been undertaking tax reforms on a continuous basis aimed at increasing the tax base of both direct and indirect taxes, reduction in tax evasion, and a resultant increase in the revenues of both State and central governments. The Central government has greater revenue raising powers in India, keeping in view considerations such as administrative efficiency in collecting taxes with a nationwide base. However, expenditure decentralization gives freedom to States to spend according to State-specific needs, given the huge diversity in preferences of citizens in different States and in levels of their economic and social development.

The possibility of fiscal imbalance is well-recognized in the Indian Constitution which provides for an institutional mechanism to tackle the imbalance in the form of the Finance Commission (FC) (constituted under Article 280) which makes recommendations on the magnitude of transfer of resources from the Centre to the States for a period of 5 years.

Terms of Reference (ToR) of the FCs

The Constitution stipulates the primary Terms of Reference (ToR) of the FCs:

(a) Distribution of net proceeds of Union divisible taxes between Union and States and among States inter-se – In other words, the devolution of taxes levied and collected by the Union, between the Union and the States, which has been dealt with under Article 270.

(b) Grants-in-aid from Union revenue to be given to States – Under Article 275 of the Constitution, Finance Commissions are mandated to recommend the principles as well as the quantum of grants to those States which are in need of assistance and that different sums may be fixed for different States. Thus, one of the pre-requisites for grants is the assessment of the needs of the States. Additionally, Article 282 of the Constitution permits the Union and the State governments to make grants for any public purpose.

(c) A third ToR has been added later after the 73rd and 74th Constitutional Amendments in 1992 which relates to recommendation of measures needed to augment the Consolidated Funds of States to supplement resources for rural and urban local governments in the States based on recommendations of the State Finance Commissions.

(d) Besides, the President may include additional ToR for the FC on any other matter in the interest of sound finance of the governments. These additional matters are normally context-specific and vary from one FC to another.

While the tax devolution and grants recommended by the FC forms bulk of Central transfers to the States, it may also be noted that transfers from Union to States are not limited to FC recommendations. Other channels include specific-purpose transfers by Central Ministries and grants transferred earlier by the erstwhile Planning Commission. Thus, intergovernmental fiscal transfers in India are made from the Union to the States through the sharing of central tax revenue with the States under Article 270 of the Constitution, as well as through grants under Articles 275 and 282 of the Constitution. Through the years, transfers have been recommended by various agencies including the Finance Commission, Planning Commission, and the Central Ministries of the Government of India.

Other Aspects of Intergovernmental Transfers

Grants-in-aid of Revenue under Article 275 of the Constitution : Article 275(1) of the Constitution provides that such sums as Parliament may by law provide, shall be charged on the Consolidated Fund of India each year, as 'grants-in-aid' of the revenue of such States. This is determined by the Parliament on various parameters, including considering States that are in need of assistance; with different sums being fixed for different States. Further, the proviso to Article 275(1) and Article 275(1)(a) specifically deal with grants for promoting the welfare of Scheduled Tribes, and to autonomous States.

Article 275(2) provides that until such provision is made by the Parliament, the powers conferred on the Parliament will be exercised by the President, who will be obliged to consider the recommendations of the Finance Commission. Article 280(3)(b) of the Constitution provides that it shall be the duty of the Finance Commission to make recommendations on the principles which should govern the grants-in-aid of the revenue of the States out of the Consolidated Fund of India. These grants have not only been restricted to address revenue deficits, but have also been released to facilitate the upgradation of standards of administrative and social services, and to ensure minimum expenditures on such services across the country, to meet the special needs, burdens, and obligations of the States, address the specific sectors of national importance, and lastly for augmenting expenditures, rather than for substituting what a State government is already spending.

While grants that are aimed at addressing revenue deficits would by their very nature be unconditional, grants that are aimed at more specific purposes, under Article 275, have had conditions attached to them. Such conditions include the receiving State having to "match" or contribute some proportion of the money received from the Union. This was intended to prevent the misuse of the grant and to ensure performance. This would also provide the grant recipient State an incentive to utilize the funds towards a particular purpose. Attachment of conditions has thus been seen as depending on the economic purpose of the transfer. Since the First Finance Commission, conditional grants have been considered permissible under Article 275 of the Constitution, and these grants have recently grown in importance in Indian fiscal federalism. The Fourteenth Finance Commission however avoided making sector-specific grants under Article 275, and instead suggested a new mechanism (under the Inter-State Council) for the same.

Thus, the scheme of the Constitution, the open-ended nature of Article 275 (not specifying types of grants-in-aid to States), and consistent practice of Finance Commissions in this regard means that it is now well-settled that conditional transfers may be made under Article 275.

Grants under Article 282 of the Constitution : Article 282 of the Constitution is an omnibus provision that allows the Union and States to make grants for any public purpose, notwithstanding that the purpose is not one with respect to which the Parliament and State Legislatures may make laws. As opposed to the other provisions of the Constitution, the language of Article 282 gives a lot of flexibility in making transfers to the States. Prior to the abolition of the Planning Commission (PC), transfers for plan expenditure used to be made under Article 282, and even transfers by Central Ministries for various schemes of the Union Government were justified under Article 282. Thus, Article 282 has been used to justify both Central Ministry transfers, as well as Planning Commission transfers. Whether this is truly within the intended Constitutional mandate has been a matter of debate, with constitutional law experts such as Nani Palkhivala stating that Article 282 is only a residuary Article to enable the Union or a State to make a grant for any public purpose.

The Supreme Court of India in *Bhim Singh Vs. Union of India*[4] observed that while both Articles 275 and 282 were sources of spending funds/monies under the Constitution, Article 282 was normally meant for special, temporary, and ad-hoc schemes. In practice, however, Article 282 has been used to justify all manners of discretionary grants with the attachment of conditions. The Supreme Court also noted that the wording of Article 282 allowed both the Union and the States to make grants for any purpose that could be identified as "public purpose" within the meaning of the Constitution. It is clear from a reading of the text of Article 282 and its interpretation that conditional transfers may be made as there is no fetter on the exercise of power under this Article. One such example of a transfer which is made by the Union to the States is that of Centrally Sponsored Schemes.

[4](2010) 5 SCC 538.

Legality of Conditional Transfers in India : From the constitutional analysis in the preceding section, it can be concluded that the Constitution permits conditional transfers made under Article 275 and Article 282. No conditions can be imposed for devolution under Article 270. Further, it is found that the power of the Finance Commission in recommending grants-in-aid under Article 275 is not restrictive in nature, and they can be given for both general and special purposes, as well as for capital or revenue grants. As such, conditions may or may not be imposed on any of such grants, and may include earmarking such grants for particular sectors, or requiring performance of certain actions as a precondition to receipt. Lastly, there are no limitations given in the Constitution on the extent to which grants-in-aid may be made conditional, i.e., that the Constitution does not prescribe the proportion of the grant that maybe made conditional.

Overview

However, in practice, the role of the Finance Commission as envisaged in the Constitution was curtailed when the Planning Commission was created through a cabinet resolution. The Planning Commission took over the powers to issue grants to the States for planning purposes. The scope of the Finance Commissions' review was confined to assessing the non-plan requirements of the States and making tax devolution and grants to meet these requirements.

However, as the Fourteenth Finance Commission's (FFC) Terms of Reference did not restrict its scope to assessing non-plan requirements, the commission made recommendations to cover the entire general-purpose transfers. Thus, when it was announced in August 2014 that the Planning Commission would be abolished, it did not create any discontinuity. However, even as the Finance Commission is empowered by the Constitution to give all transfers – general or specific – given its temporary nature (Specific Purpose Grants), the Fourteenth Finance Commission itself decided that it would refrain from giving specific-purpose transfers, which require continuous monitoring.

After the FFC made the recommendations, the entire architecture of the transfer system was changed (Ministry of Finance, 2015). With the Finance Commission making recommendations on tax devolution and blocking grants and refraining from making any specific-purpose grants, a clear distinction has emerged between general and specific-purpose transfers. All general-purpose transfers are now recommended by the Finance Commission, and all specific-purpose transfers are given by the respective Central Ministries. Although the FFC made a recommendation that the design and implementation of specific-purpose transfers should be decided by a committee comprising the representatives of central and State governments, as well as domain experts, the central government has continued the practice of making decisions on these transfers at the relevant Central Ministry level.

Thus, over the years, the transfers through the institution of the Planning Commission (Planned expenditure) and for the purpose of Centrally Sponsored Schemes acquired a disproportionate importance in the overall transfers to States, according to many analysts. With the abolition of the Planning Commission in 2015–16, this route automatically shrunk. Furthermore, because of the higher share of the States in the tax devolution formula, the Central Ministries have cut down on their allocations on various schemes. Thus, the magnitude of flows through the non-Finance Commission channel is substantially reduced, as was the intention of the 14th Finance Commission.

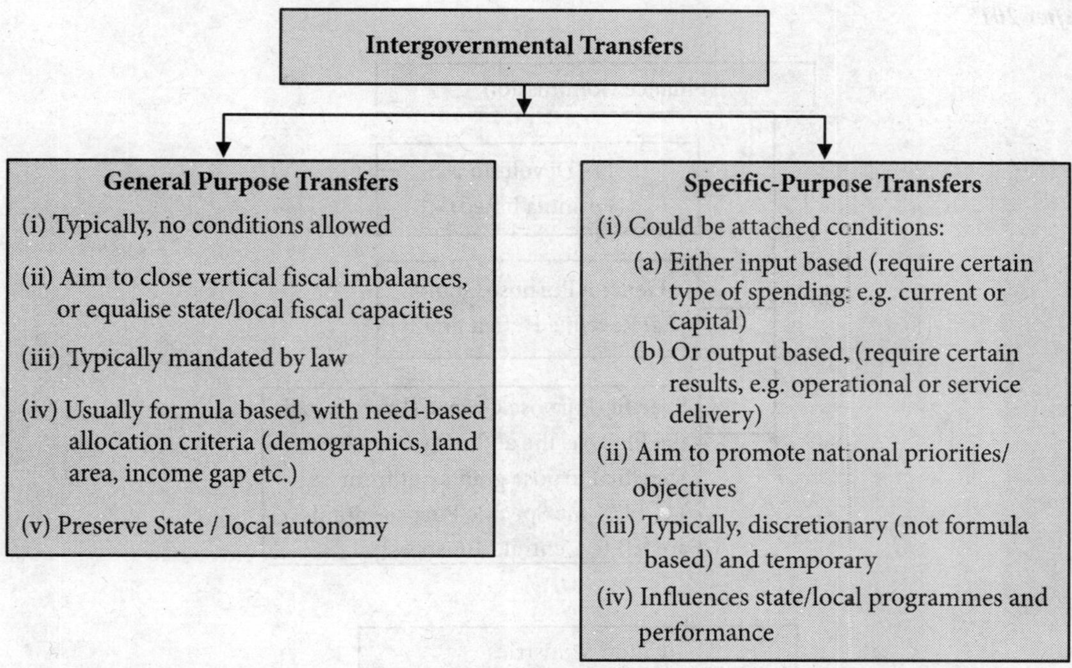

Institutional Structure of Intergovernmental Transfers in India

Before 2015

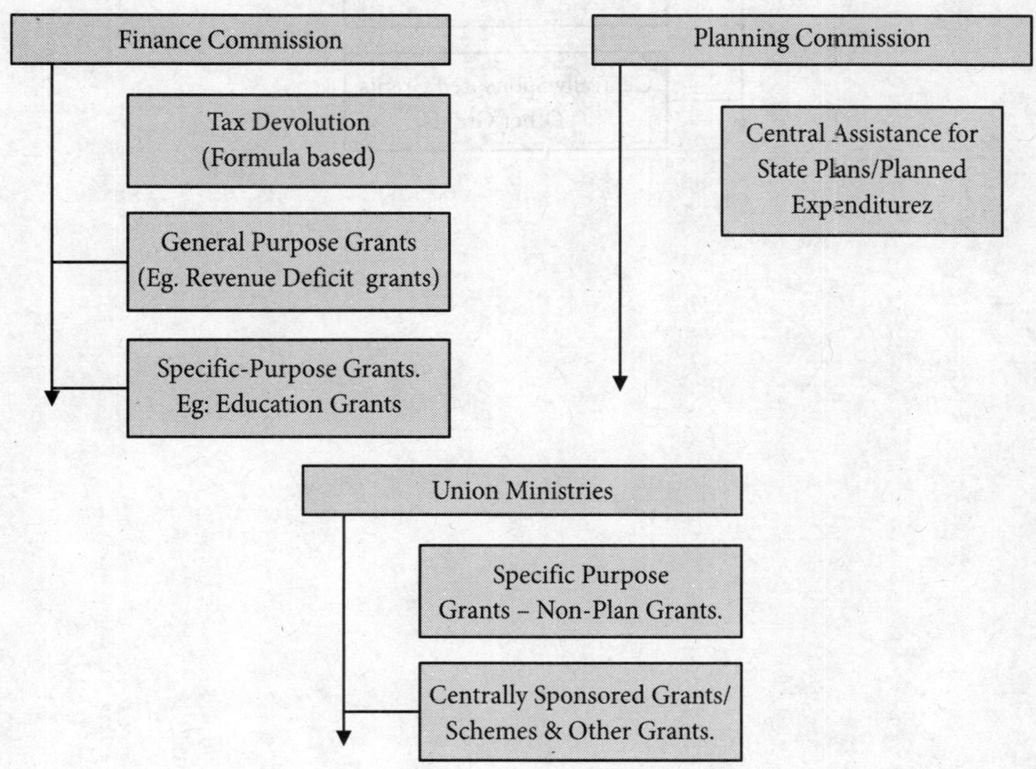

After 2015

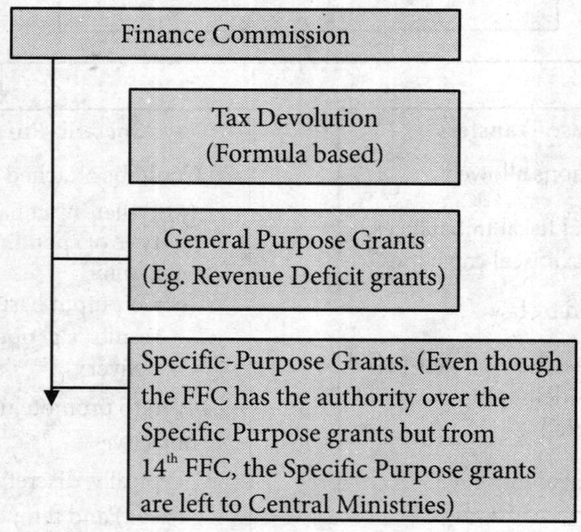
Finance Commission
Tax Devolution
(Formula based)
General Purpose Grants
(Eg. Revenue Deficit grants)
Specific-Purpose Grants. (Even though the FFC has the authority over the Specific Purpose grants but from 14th FFC, the Specific Purpose grants are left to Central Ministries)

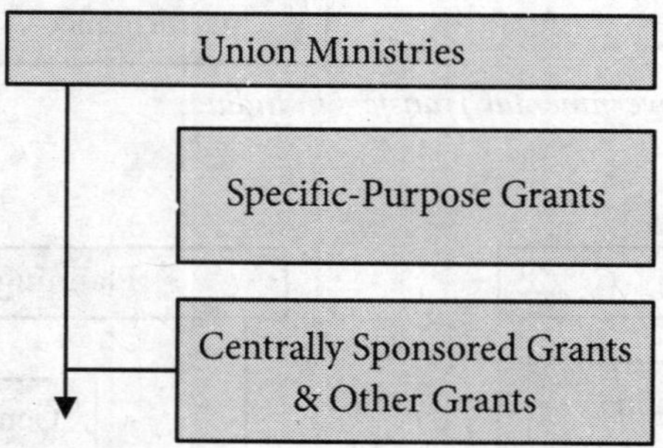
Union Ministries
Specific-Purpose Grants
Centrally Sponsored Grants
& Other Grants

20.3 COOPERATIVE & COMPETITIVE FEDERALISM IN INDIA

"I do believe that the future for India is cooperative and competitive federalism. Competitive federalism provides the dynamism that needs to be unleashed. We need cooperative federalism to balance competitive federalism. We are developing new institutions to enhance cooperative federalism—the Niti Aayog is one, the finance commission and now we have the GST"

– Arvind Subramanian[1]

INTRODUCTION

Though there is division of functions between the Centre and the units in a federation, and the respective areas of competence of each is earmarked, yet it would not be correct to assume that the various governments act in water-tight compartments. As these governments act side by side in the same country, inevitably many types of relations arise amongst them and many instrumentalities to promote intergovernmental co-operation come into existence.

In the three older federations of the USA, Canada, and Australia in the formative stages of development, the dominant operative concept was that of "competitive federalism" which denoted a spirit of competition and rivalry between the Centre and the States. The formative stages were, therefore, marked by intergovernmental disputes; the units were very conscious of their powers and rights and thus, resented the growth of the Centre's powers and any encroachment by it on their domain. With the passage of time, however, the concept of 'competitive federalism' slowly gave way to 'cooperative federalism'. The concept of 'cooperative federalism' helps the federal system, with its divided jurisdiction, to act in unison. It minimises friction and promotes co-operation among the various constituent governments of the federal union so that they can pool their resources to achieve certain desired national goals.

The framers of the Indian Constitution took due note of the emerging trend of cooperative federalism in the older federations. They realised that governments in a federation were arranged not hierarchically or vertically but horizontally, that no line of command runs from the Centre to the States, and that common policies among the various governments can be promoted not by dictation but by a process of discussion, agreement, and compromise.

TYPES OF FEDERALISM

Cooperative Federalism

The cooperative federalism involves the Centre and States governments co-operating with each other for the pan development of the country. It involves the participation of all the States in the creation and implementation of the national policies of the nation. It is the horizontal relationship between the Centre and the States. The Constitution of India has provided for the cooperative federalism in the Inter-State Council, Zonal Council, Schedule VII, etc. The Schedule VII of the Indian Constitution requires the States and the Centre to co-operate among each other. The concept of cooperative federalism is further strengthened with the creation of Niti Aayog and enactment of the Goods and Services Tax.

---

[1] Former Chief Economic Advisor to the Government of India.

Competitive Federalism

The competitive federalism involves the competition amongst the States and also the Centre for the economic benefits, in respect of economic affairs. This concept became more prominent during post-1990's Economic Reforms. When India opened its doors and windows for Globalization, there is now increasing competition between the States for the limited resources. This resulted in the imbalance and inequalities among the States. However, in recent times, competitive federalism has become an effective tool to enhance the economic development of each State.

CONSTITUTIONAL ASPECTS PROMOTING COOPERATIVE FEDERALISM

The concept of cooperative federalism which considerably influenced the working of the traditional federal Constitutions of the United States, Canada, and Australia after the depression of the 1930s and the Second World War, was given effect to by the Constitution of India which created the machinery for achieving comity between the various units of the federal system. Though the division of powers is the essence of federalism, both the Centre and the State govern the same people. Hence, there is a great need for intergovernmental cooperation for minimising friction between the constituent units of the federal union.

Article 261 (Full Faith and Credit)

Article 261 declares that full faith and credit shall be given throughout the territory of India to public acts, records and judicial proceedings of the Union and every State. Under Article 261(3), a final judgment or order delivered or passed by a civil court in any part of India is capable of execution anywhere within India according to law. The clause applies to civil and not to criminal courts.

Inter–State Council

Article 263 provides that the President may by order appoint an Inter-State Council if it appears to him that public interest would be served by its establishment.

The President may define the organization, procedures, and duties of the Council. Generally, it may be charged with the duty of:

- Inquiring into and advising upon disputes which may have arisen between States;
- Investigating and discussing subjects in which some or all of the States, or the Union and one or more of the States, have a common interest;
- Making recommendations upon any subject and, in particular, recommendations for the better co-ordination of policy and action with respect to that subject.

It appears from the above that the Council is envisaged to be an advisory body having no authority to give a binding decision. The Council's function to inquire and advise upon Inter-State disputes is complementary to the Supreme Court's jurisdiction under Article 131 to decide a legal controversy between the governments. The Council can deal with any controversy whether legal or not, but its function is advisory, unlike that of the Court which gives a binding decision. The Supreme Court can decide intergovernmental disputes of a legal nature. But there may arise intergovernmental disputes of a non-legal character and the Council can play a role in settling such disputes. The Council may be appointed either on a permanent basis or from time to time on an ad hoc basis. It is also possible to appoint not only one but any number of such bodies to deal with various matters as Article 263 is of general nature. This power has been used to constitute a *Central Council of Health and Family Welfare, a Central Council of Local Government, and four regional Sales Tax Councils in the North, East, West, and South Zones.*

Establishment of Inter-State Council

Sarkaria Commission on Centre-State Relations (1983–88) has strongly recommended for the establishment of a permanent Inter-State Council under Article 263 to effect co-ordination between States. The Sarkaria Commission recommended that in order to differentiate the Inter-State Council from the other bodies set up under the Article, it must be called Intergovernmental Council. The President of India in exercise of the powers under Article 263 has constituted the Inter-State Council in 1990.

It consists of the following members:

- Prime Minister;
- Chief Ministers of all States;
- Chief Ministers of Union Territories having a Legislative Assembly and Administrators of Union Territories not having a Legislative Assembly;
- Six Ministers of Cabinet Rank in the Union Council of Ministers to be nominated by the Prime Minister.
- Four Ministers of Cabinet rank as Permanent Invitees Members
- Other Ministers and Ministers of State having independent charge in the Union Government may be invited as permanent invitees, if so nominated by the Chairman of the Council, or as and when any item relating to a subject under their charge is to be discussed.

The Prime Minister shall be the Chairman of the Inter-State Council and preside over its meetings. In his absence, he may nominate any Union Minister of Cabinet Rank to preside over the meeting. The Council will meet at least thrice in a year. Its meetings are held in camera and all questions are decided by consensus.

Inter-State Council is a recommendatory body with duties to :

- investigate and discuss the subjects of common interest between the Union and State(s) or among the States;
- making recommendations, particularly for better coordination of policy and action on these subjects; and
- deliberating upon such other matters of general interest to the States which may be referred to it by its Chairman.

The Council also deliberates upon such other matters of general interest to the States as may be referred by the Chairman of the Council. A Standing Committee of the Inter-State Council has been constituted for continuous consultation and processing of matters for the consideration of the Council. The Standing Committee comprises of Union Home Minister as Chairman and 5 Union Ministers of Cabinet Rank and 9 Chief Ministers of States as Members nominated by the Chairman of the Inter-State Council. The Inter-State Council is assisted by a Secretariat. The Secretariat is headed by a Secretary to the Government of India, assisted by two Advisers in the rank of Additional Secretary to the Government of India, two Directors, and three officers each in the rank of Deputy Secretary and Under Secretary. Even the secretarial functions of the Zonal Councils also have been transferred to the Inter-State Council Secretariat since 2011.

Resolution of River Water Disputes

The waters of an inter-State river pass through several States. Such waters cannot be regarded as belonging to any single riparian State. Therefore, the Constitution confers legislative power over such rivers to the Parliament. The Constitution also makes special provisions for creating a suitable machinery for resolving such disputes. Article 262(1) authorises the Parliament to provide by law for adjudication of any dispute or complaint with respect to the uses, distribution or control of the waters of any Inter-State rivers and river valleys. Under Clause(2) of this Article, Parliament may by law provide that neither the Supreme Court nor any other Court shall have any jurisdiction in respect of such disputes and complaints relating to water of Inter-State rivers and river valleys. Under Article 262, Parliament has passed the *River Board Act, 1956* and the *Inter-State River Water Disputes Act, 1956*. The River Board Act is meant for the regulation and development of Inter-State rivers and river valleys. This is established on the request of the State Government to advise the Government. The Water Disputes Act empowers the Central Government to set up a Tribunal for the adjudication of such disputes.

Important features of the Water Disputes Act are as follows :

- A State Government which has a water dispute with another State Government may request the Central Government to refer the dispute to a Tribunal for adjudication.
- The Central Government, if it is of the opinion that the dispute cannot be settled by negotiation, shall refer the dispute to a Tribunal.
- The Tribunal's composition is laid down in the Act. It consists of a Chairman and two other members, nominated by the Chief Justice of India from among persons who, at the time of such nomination, are Judges of the Supreme Court.
- The Tribunal can appoint assessors to advise it in the proceedings before it.
- On the reference being made by the Central Government, the Tribunal investigates the matter and makes its report, embodying its decision. The decision is to be published and is to be final and binding on the parties.
- Jurisdiction of the Supreme Court and other courts in respect of the dispute referred to the Tribunal is barred.
- The Central Government may frame a scheme, providing for all matters necessary to give effect to the decision of the Tribunal. The scheme may, inter alia, provide for establishing an authority for implementing the decision of the Tribunal.

A lacuna in the scheme of Inter-State Water Disputes Act is that it lays down no principles or guidelines to be followed by the Tribunal. The reason to take these disputes out of the purview of the courts and appoint Tribunals to solve them is that rules of law based on the analogy of private proprietary interests in water do not afford a satisfactory basis for settling these disputes where the interests of the public at large in the proper use of water supplies are involved[2].

National Water Development Agency (NWDA)

NWDA was set up in July 1982 as a non-statutory body with all State Irrigation Ministers as its members. The Agency was constituted to carry out surveys, investigations, and studies for the peninsular rivers' development component of the national water plan. The Agency is to promote optimum utilization of the country's water resources. This envisages the use of surplus waters of all rivers in the country. In the year 1990, NWDA was also entrusted with the task of Himalayan Component of National Perspective Plan[3]. In 2006, it was decided that NWDA will explore the feasibility of Intra-State links and take up the work for preparation of a Detailed Project Report of river link proposals under National Perspective Plan (NPP).

---

[2]M.P. Jain, *Indian Constitutional Law*, Wadhwa, Eighth Edition, P. 768.

[3]National Perspective Plan (NPP) envisages inter-basin transfer of water from surplus basins to deficit ones with a view to minimize the regional imbalances and optimally utilize the available water resources. National Perspective Plan comprises of two components, viz. Himalayan Rivers Development and Peninsular Rivers Development.

National Water Resources Development Council

The Prime Minister is the Chairman and all State Chief Ministers are its members. The main functions of the Council are to bring up a national consensus in the proper utilization of water resources and to identify the strategic policy planning. The NWDA will submit its reports to the Council for clearance.

The details of the Tribunals set up so far by the Government to settle water disputes among the States under the Inter-State River Water Disputes (ISRWD) Act, 1956 are as under:

S. No.	Name of Tribunal	Year of Constitution	The Concerned States
1.	Godavari Water Disputes Tribunal	1969	Maharashtra, Andhra Pradesh, Karnataka, Madhya Pradesh, and Odisha
2.	Krishna Water Disputes Tribunal -I	1969	Maharashtra, Andhra Pradesh, and Karnataka.
3.	Narmada Water Disputes Tribunal	1969	Rajasthan, Madhya Pradesh, Gujarat, and Maharashtra
4.	Ravi & Beas Water Tribunal	1986	Punjab, Haryana, and Rajasthan
5.	Cauvery Water Disputes Tribunal	1990	Kerala, Karnataka, Tamil Nadu, and Puducherry
6.	Krishna Water Disputes Tribunal -II	2004	Karnataka, Andhra Pradesh, Telangana, and Maharashtra
7.	Vansadhara Water Disputes Tribunal	2010	Andhra Pradesh and Odisha
8.	Mahadayi Water Disputes Tribunal	2010	Goa, Karnataka, and Maharashtra
9.	Mahanadi Water Disputes Tribunal	2018	Chhattisgarh and Odisha

Freedom of Trade, Commerce, and Intercourse

The framers of the Indian Constitution were fully conscious of the importance of maintaining the economic unity of the Union of India. Free movement and exchange of goods throughout the territory of India was essential for the economic unity of the country which alone could sustain the progress of the country. Thus, the main object of Article 301 was obviously to break down the border barriers between the States and to create one unit with a view to encourage the free flow of stream of trade and commerce throughout the territory of India. Article 301[4] of the Constitution of India declares that trade, commerce, and intercourse throughout the territory of India shall be free. Article 301 applies not only to inter-State trade but also intra-State trade, commerce, and intercourse. However, the Constitution itself lays down the restrictions on Article 301, as no freedom is absolute.

The restrictions for Article 301 are contained in Article 302 to 305 :

- Parliament has the power impose such restrictions on the freedom of trade, commerce, or intercourse between one State and another or within any part of the territory of India as may be required in the public interest. But the Parliament cannot give preference to one State over another or discriminate between the States, except in the case of scarcity of goods in any part of India (Articles 302 and 303).

[4] Article 301 of the Indian Constitution is modelled on Section of the Australian Constitution.

- The States are empowered to impose any tax on goods imported from other State if similar goods in the State are subject to similar tax so as not to discriminate between goods so imported and goods manufactured or produced in the State. In other words, a State cannot treat imported goods worse than it treats its own goods (Article 304(a)).
- The State legislature is authorized to impose such reasonable restrictions on the freedom of trade, commerce, and intercourse as may be required in the public interest. But no Bill or amendment for this purpose can be introduced in the Legislature of State without the previous sanction of the President (Article 304(b)).
- All State monopolistic laws/nationalization laws which provide for "the carrying on by the State, or by a corporation owned or controlled by the State, of any trade, business, industry or service, whether to the exclusion, complete or partial, of citizens or otherwise" are protected and cannot be challenged under Article 301. In other words, a State or Centre can run any business on a monopolistic basis or nationalize any business without infringing Article 301 (Article 305).

Article 307 empowers the Parliament to appoint such authority as it considers appropriate for carrying out purposes of Articles 301 to 304. Parliament can further confer on such authorities such powers and duties as it thinks necessary[5]. No body as envisaged in Article 307 has been set up so far. The Sarkaria Commission reporting in 1988 strongly recommended the setting up of an expert body under Article 307.

GST Council

Before the 1st July, 2017, Indian indirect tax regime was highly fragmented. The Centre and the States were separately taxing goods and services. There were many taxes like excise duty, service tax, VAT, CST, purchase tax, entertainment tax, and octroi. In addition, there was multiplicity of rates, laws, and procedures. This caused heavy compliance burden. Imposition of tax on tax was another serious problem[6]. Input tax credit chain broke as goods moved from one State to another, resulting in hidden cost for the business. Further, pre-GST, there were tax nakas at every inter-State border, creating bottlenecks in inter-State transport of goods. As a result, logistics sector remained inefficient and it adversely impacted the businesses. Every State was effectively a distinct market for the industry as well as the consumer. The industry's choice of locating factories or warehouses was heavily influenced by the prevailing tax regime rather than pure business consideration. This made our industry uncompetitive. Therefore, it was a momentous occasion when the Goods and Services Tax (GST), the biggest tax reform, was rolled out on July 1, 2017. GST removed the inefficiencies and complexities of the erstwhile archaic taxation system and helped in accelerating growth.

The GST regime subsumed all the indirect taxes. Article 246A which was introduced by the 101st Constitution Amendment Act, 2016 vests the Parliament and the State legislatures with the concurrent power to make laws with respect to GST. Article 246A entrusts the Parliament and State legislatures with the power to legislate on the GST. The power of the States is, however, subject to the conferment of an exclusive domain to the Parliament to levy the GST where the supply of goods or services takes place in the course of inter-State trade and commerce. Article 279A of our Constitution gave birth to a new constitutional body called the GST Council. According to Article 279A, it is on the part of the President

---

[5]The origins of the idea contained in Article 307 can be traced to the Australian Constitution which contemplates the establishment of an Inter-State Commission.

[6]For example, VAT was levied on a value that included excise duty.

to give the order to constitute the Council of GST within 60 days from the 12th of September 2016, which is already notified by the Government.

Composition of the GST Council

- The Union Finance Minister who will be the Chairman of the Council;
- The Union Minister of State in charge of Revenue or Finance who will be the Member of the Council;
- One Member from each State who is Minister in charge of Finance or Taxation or any other Minister and any one of them will be Vice Chairman of the GST Council who will be mutually elected by them.
- The Secretary of Revenue Department will work as Ex-Officio Secretary to the GST Council,
- The Chairperson of the Central Board of Excise and Customs will be the Permanent Invitee in all the proceedings of the GST Council who will not have voting rights.

Quorum and Decision-Making of the GST Council

- For a valid meeting of the members of the GST Council, at least 50 per cent of the total number of members should be present at the meeting.
- Every Decision made during the meeting should be supported by at least 75 per cent or three-fourth majority of the weighted votes of the members who are present and voting at the meeting. In "Article 279A", a principle is there which divides the total weighted vote cast between the Central Government and State Governments as follows: -
  * The vote of the Central Government shall have the weight of one-third of the total votes, cast in the meeting
  * The votes of the State Government shall have the weight of two-thirds of the total votes, cast in the meeting
- Any Act, decision, or proceeding shall not be declared invalid on the basis of any remaining deficiency at the time of the establishment of the GST Council, i.e.,
  * if there is any vacancy remaining in the Council
  * if there is any defect in the constitution of the Council
  * if there is any defect in the appointment of a person as a member of the Council
  * if there is any procedural non-compliance.

Functions of the GST Council

The GST Council will be supposed to make the recommendations to the Union and State on the following matters :

- Principles of levy, model Goods and Services Tax Laws, the appointment of Goods and Services Tax levied on supplies in the course of Inter-State trade or commerce under article 269A, and the principles that govern the place of supply;
- Raising resources during any natural calamity or disaster, or any special rate or rates for a specified period, to raise additional resources.
- Any other matter relating to the goods and services tax as the Council may decide.
- Subsuming various taxes, cess, and surcharges in GST.

- Details of services and goods that will be subjected to GST or which will be exempted from GST.
- Determination of the threshold limit below which, services and goods will be exempted from GST.
- Determination of GST rates including floor rate with bands of GST and any special rate for time-being to arrange resources to face any natural calamity.
- Making special provisions with respect to Arunachal Pradesh, Assam, Jammu and Kashmir, Manipur, Meghalaya, Mizoram, Nagaland, Sikkim, Tripura, Himachal Pradesh, and Uttarakhand.
- Model law on GST, Principal of levy of GST, and the principles which will govern the Place of Supply.
- The GST Council shall also recommend the date on which GST will be levied on petroleum crude, high speed diesel, motor spirit (commonly known as petrol), natural gas, and aviation turbine fuel.

Dispute Handling by the GST Council

The GST Council is also charged with the duty to create a mechanism with which the following disputes would be settled :

- Disputes between the Central Government and the State Government of a State;
- The disputes between the Central Government and one or more States on one side and one or more States on the other side;
- Disputes between two or more States which occurred due to any recommendation of the GST Council or due to the implementation of the recommendation of the Council.

Recommendations by the GST Council

The GST Council is a constitutional body which is entrusted with the duty to make recommendations on a wide range of areas concerning GST. The GST Council has plenary powers under Article 279A (4) (h) where it could make recommendations on 'any other matter' related to GST as the Council may decide. The GST Council has to arrive at its recommendations through harmonised deliberation between the federal units as provided in Article 279A. Unlike the other provisions of the Constitution which provide that recommendations shall be made to the President or the Governor, Article 279A States that the recommendations shall be made to the 'Union and the States'. The recommendation of the GST Council made under Article 279A is non-qualified. That is, there is no explanation on the value of such a recommendation. The Supreme Court's in the case of *Union of India versus M/s Mohit Minerals Pvt. Ltd*[7]., held that the GST Council's decisions are not binding on the Centre or the States. In other words, the GST Council is a recommendatory body aiding the Government in enacting legislation on GST.

Cooperative Federalism Through GST

Implementation of GST would be a step towards the largest-ever tax reform in the fiscal history of India. It charts a new course of federalism in India that emphasises more on cooperation instead of self-interest. Cooperative federalism requires both the Union and the State governments to function simultaneously for the development of the nation. Because of GST, both the Centre and State governments have to sacrifice their fiscal autonomy in favour of a collective and single decision-making process. Moreover,

[7]SLP(C) No. 7708 of 2018.

GST creates a unified national market and brings an end to tax wars and economic distortions. The tax reform's chief slogan is "GST—One Nation One Tax One Market".

The GST Council is a unique institution. What makes the GST Council unique is that it is envisaged as functioning on the principles of cooperative federalism. Both its decision-making process and its enforcement mechanisms require the participation and cooperation of the Centre and the States. In essence, the entire GST structure in India depends on the successful running of a Centre-State body founded on collaboration and interdependence. Cooperative federalism is a system by which State and national (Central) governments supplement each other, and jointly and collaboratively perform a variety of functions. It does not replace the legal framework of federalism; rather, it supplements and corrects that framework. Cooperative federalism embraces the realization that the promotion of general welfare is the common goal of all governmental units, and those units should work in concert, not in complete isolation, to reach that goal. It sees the two levels of government as partners, not rivals.

EXTRA-CONSTITUTIONAL ASPECTS PROMOTING COOPERATIVE FEDERALISM

Niti Aayog

Since 1950, Government of India has attempted to bring about a rapid social and economic growth in the entire country through planned effort. The prime institution to carry out this task was the Planning Commission, which was launched in 1950 and was functioning till the end of 2014. Thereafter, on January1, 2015[8], the Planning Commission got replaced by the National Institution for Transforming India, known as, Niti Aayog. NITI Aayog overviews the monitoring and adoption of 'Sustainable Development Goals' (SDGs) and promotes competitive and cooperative federalism among the States and Government undertakings. This is a Government of India policy 'think tank' that aims 'to foster involvement and participation in the economic policy making process by the State Governments of India'.

Composition of NITI Aayog

The composition of the NITI Aayog is, as follows:

(1) Chairperson : Prime Minister of India

(2) Vice-Chairperson : Appointed by the Prime Minister

(3) Governing Council comprising the Chief Ministers of all the States and Lt. Governors of Union Territories

(4) Regional Councils that are formed to address specific issues or contingencies impacting more than one State or region. These are formed for a specified tenure. The Regional Councils are chaired by the Prime Minister and comprise of the Chief Ministers and Lt. Governors of the respective States/region.

(5) Full time members

(6) Part-time members : Maximum of 2 members from any leading universities/research organizations/other relevant institutions in an ex-officio capacity. Part-time members are appointed on a rotational basis.

(7) Ex-officio members : Maximum of 4 members of the Union Council of Ministers nominated by the Prime Minister.

---

[8]On 1 January 2015, a Cabinet resolution was passed to replace the Planning Commission with the newly formed NITI Aayog (National Institution for Transforming India).

(8) Chief Executive Officer : Appointed by the Prime Minister for a fixed tenure and is of the rank parallel to the Secretary to the Government of India.

(9) Experts, specialists, and practitioners with relevant domain knowledge, as special invitees nominated by the Prime Minister

(10) Secretariat

The Seven Pillars of NITI Aayog

Pro-People	Pro-Activity	Participation	Empowerment	Inclusion of all	Equality	Transparency
Fulfils aspirations of society as well as individuals	In anticipation of and response to citizens needs.	Involvement of Citizenry	Women in all aspects	SC, ST,OBC, minorities, poor, and disadvantaged	Opportunity for the Youth	Making Government visible and responsive

Functions of NITI Aayog

The NITI Aayog plays an integrative role with the active involvement of States, civil society, and other think tanks in the development of a shared vision of national priorities and strategies in critical areas of human and economic development. One of the main objectives of NITI Aayog is 'to design strategic and long-term policy and programme frameworks and initiatives, and monitor their progress and their efficacy'. The NITI Aayog is taking the lead in setting up sectoral targets and fostering an environment of innovation and cooperation. The target is to bring innovation, technology, enterprise, and efficient management together at the core of policy formulation and implementation.

The functions of the NITI Aayog can be summarised as follows :

1. To provide a 'think tank' which provides Governments at the Central and State levels with relevant strategic and technical advice across the key elements of policy.
2. To overview monitoring and adoption of 'Sustainable Development Goals' (SDGs) and promote competitive and cooperative federalism among States and Government undertakings.
3. To provide advice and encourage partnerships between key stakeholders, and national and international like-minded 'think tanks', and educational and policy research institutions.
4. To create knowledge, innovation, and entrepreneurial support system via collaborative community of national and international experts, practitioners, and other partners.
5. To evolve a shared vision of national development priorities, sectors, and strategies with the active involvement of States.
6. To foster cooperative federalism through structured support initiatives and mechanisms with the States continuously recognizing that strong States make a strong nation.
7. To provide a critical direction and strategic input to the development process.
8. To replace Centre-to-State one-way flow of policy (that was the hallmark of Planning Commission era) by a genuine and continuing partnership of the States of India.
9. To end the slow and tardy implementation of policy by fostering better inter-Ministry coordination and better Centre-State coordination.

10. To develop mechanisms to formulate credible plans at the village level and aggregate these progressively at higher levels of the Government.
11. To provide a framework for preparing plans to the States and the latter, in turn, to the lower levels of Government.
12. To ensure that the interests of national security are incorporated in economic strategy and policy on the specifically concerned areas.
13. To pay special attention to those sections of society that may be at risk of not benefitting adequately from economic progress.
14. To design strategic and long-term policy and programme frameworks and initiatives, and monitor their progress and their efficacy.
15. To monitor and evaluate implementation of programmes, initiatives, and identification of needed resources, so as to strengthen the probability of success and scope of delivery.
16. To focus on technology upgradation and capacity building for implementation of programmes and initiatives.
17. To offer a platform for resolution of inter-sectoral and inter-departmental issues in order to accelerate the implementation of development agenda.
18. To maintain 'State-of-the-Art Resource Centre', be a research repository on good governance and practices in development, and to help their dissemination to stakeholders.
19. To have an administration paradigm in which the Government is an 'enabler' rather than a 'provider of first and last resort'.
20. To progress from 'food security' to a mix of agricultural production, as well as actual returns that farmers get from their produce.
21. To facilitate the exchange of information and experiences, and promote healthy intergovernmental competition through monitoring and regulation.
22. To deal with the rationalisation of 'Centrally Sponsored Schemes' (CSS) as there is considerable resentment by the States on them.
23. To undertake other activities as may be necessary in order to further the execution of the national development agenda, and the objectives of NITI Aayog.

Role and Objectives of NITI Aayog

1. **Cooperative and Competitive Federalism :** Primary platform for operationalizing cooperative federalism by enabling States to have active participation in the formulation of national policy, as well as achieving time-bound implementation of quantitative and qualitative targets.
2. **Shared National Agenda :** Evolve a shared vision of national development priorities and strategies, with the active involvement of States. This will provide the framework 'national agenda' for the Prime Minister and Chief Ministers to implement.
3. **State's Best Friend at the Centre :** Support States in addressing their own challenges, building on strengths and comparative advantages. This will be through coordination with Ministries, championing their ideas at the Centre, providing consultancy support, and building-capacity.
4. **Decentralised Planning :** Support a planning process in bottom-up model empowering States and guiding local governments to plan at village level, progressively aggregating up the higher levels of government.

5. **Vision & Scenario Planning :** A design of medium- and long-term strategic framework giving India's big picture. It will address overall domestic and global environment evolving trends and emerging challenges. This would be a fundamental transition from where the nation's money goes, to planning where we want the nation to go.

6. **Network of Expertise :** Mainstream external ideas and expertise into government policies and programmes through a collaborative community of national and international experts, practitioners, and other partners. This would entail being Government's link to the outside world.

7. **Knowledge and Innovation hub :** Be an accumulator as well as disseminator of research and best practices on good governance, through a Resource Centre which identifies, analyses, shares, and facilitates replication of the same.

8. **Harmonization :** Facilitate harmonization of actions across different layers of government through communication, coordination, collaboration, and convergence amongst all stakeholders. The emphasis will be on bringing all together on an integrated and holistic approach to development.

9. **Conflict Resolution :** Provide a platform for mutual resolution of inter-sectoral, inter-departmental, inter-State, as well as Centre-State issues.

10. **Coordinating interface with the World :** Be the nodal point for strategically harnessing global expertise and resources from multilateral platforms, nations, etc.

11. **Internal Consultancy :** Offer an internal consultancy function to Central and State governments on policy and program design and specialised skills such as structuring and executing Public Private Partnerships.

12. **Capacity-building :** Enable capacity-building and technology upgradation across governments, benchmarking with latest global trends and providing managerial and technical know-how.

13. **Monitoring and Evaluation :** Monitor the implementation of policies and programmes to evaluate their impact. This will track the weaknesses and will help to take necessary correction.

NITI Aayog's Role in Cooperative and Competitive Federalism

NITI Aayog has been constituted to actualise the important goal of cooperative federalism and to enable good governance in India. On the premise that strong States make a strong nation, NITI Aayog acts as the quintessential platform for the Government of India by bringing States together as 'Team India' to work towards the national development agenda.

In view of this, a number of steps have been taken by NITI Aayog to foster cooperative federalism through structured support initiatives and engagement with the States/UTs on a continuous basis. These include meetings between the Prime Minister/Cabinet Ministers and all Chief Ministers and subgroups of Chief Ministers on subjects of national importance; sharing of best practices; policy support and capacity development of State/UT functionaries; launching of the Aspirational Districts Programme for development of backward districts; theme-based extensive engagements in various sectors; framing model laws for land leasing and agriculture marketing reforms; and area-specific interventions for the North-Eastern and Himalayan States and island development.

NITI Aayog also endeavours to promote competitive federalism by facilitating improved performance of States/UTs. It encourages healthy competition among States through transparent rankings in various sectors, along with a hand-holding approach. Some of the indices launched by NITI Aayog are School

Education Quality Index, State Health Index, Composite Water Management Index, Sustainable Development Goals Index, India Innovation Index, and Export Competitiveness Index. NITI Aayog also releases delta rankings for the performance of Aspirational Districts every month.

The ranking of States in various social sectors based on quantitative objective criteria encourages them, and even districts, to improve their performance. NITI Aayog works closely with all stakeholders, including the State/UT Governments and concerned Ministries/Departments in developing indicator frameworks, review mechanisms, and capacity-building.

Thus, NITI Aayog has called for a mix of cooperative and competitive federalism.

Erstwhile Planning Commission

The Planning Commission was constituted in March, 1950 by a Resolution of the Government of India, and worked under the overall guidance of the National Development Council.

The following functions were assigned to the Planning Commission as per Allocation of Business Rules:

- Assessment of the material, capital, and human resources of the country, including technical personnel, and formulation of proposals for augmenting such of these resources as are found to be deficient;
- Formulation of Plans for the most effective and balanced utilisation of the country's resources;
- Definition of stages in which the Plan should be carried out on a determination of priorities and allocation of resources for completion of each stage;
- Determination of the nature of the machinery necessary for the implementation of the Plan in all its aspects;
- Appraisal from time to time of the progress achieved in the execution of each stage of the Plan;
- Public cooperation in National Development;
- Hill Area Development Programme;
- Perspective Planning;
- Labour Employment and Manpower.

The Planning Commission consisted of a Chairman, Deputy Chairman, and six members. The Prime Minister is its Chairman. The Deputy Chairman was the full-time functional Head of the Commission.

Erstwhile National Development Council (NDC)

The National Development Council was the product of the Planning Commission's recommendations. In the draft outline of the First Five Year Plan, the Commission recommended the need for a body comprising the Central and State governments to enable the plans to have a national character. The National Development Council was set up in August 1952 on the basis of a resolution of the Government of India. The Council composed of the Prime Minister, the Chief Ministers of States, and the members of the Planning Commission. However, other Central Ministers who are not members of the Planning Commission have also attended the Council's meetings. Sometimes, outside experts have also been invited to the Council's meetings whenever considered necessary.

The functions of the National Development Council (NDC) as laid down in the Government of India resolution were as follows:

- to review the working of the national plan from time to time;
- to consider important questions of social and economic policy affecting national development; and

- to recommend measures for the achievement of the aims and targets set out in the national Plan, including measures to secure the active participation and cooperation of the people, improve the efficiency of the administrative services, ensure the fullest development of the less advanced regions and sections of the community and, through sacrifice borne equally by all citizens, build up resources for national development.

The decisions of the NDC have been in the nature of policy formulation. It would not be an exaggeration to call it the highest policy-making body in the country. Though the NDC is a non-statutory advisory body which makes recommendations to the Central and State governments, the very stature of the NDC has ensured that these 'recommendations' have the prestige of directives which are usually followed and obeyed.

Zonal Councils

The idea of the creation of Zonal Councils was mooted by the first Prime Minister of India, Pandit Jawahar Lal Nehru in 1956 during the State reorganization. He suggested that the States which were proposed to be reorganised should be grouped into four or five zones having an Advisory Council 'to develop the habit of cooperative working" among these States. This suggestion was made by Pandit Nehru at a time when linguistic hostilities and bitterness as a result of reorganisation of the States on linguistic patterns was threatening the very fabric of our nation. As an antidote to this situation, it was suggested that a high-level advisory forum should be set up to minimise the impact of these hostilities and to create a healthy Inter-State and Centre-State environment with a view to solving Inter-State problems and fostering balanced socio-economic development of the respective zones. In the light of the vision of Pandit Nehru, five Zonal Councils were set up vide the States Re-organisation Act, 1956.

The present composition of each of these Zonal Councils is as under:

- The Northern Zonal Council, comprising the States of Haryana, Himachal Pradesh, Punjab, Rajasthan, Union Territories of National Capital Territory of Delhi, Chandigarh, Jammu & Kashmir, and Ladakh;
- The Central Zonal Council, comprising the States of Chhattisgarh, Uttarakhand, Uttar Pradesh, and Madhya Pradesh;
- The Eastern Zonal Council, comprising the States of Bihar, Jharkhand, Orissa, Sikkim, and West Bengal;
- The Western Zonal Council, comprising the States of Goa, Gujarat, Maharashtra, and the Union Territories of Daman & Diu and Dadra & Nagar Haveli;
- The Southern Zonal Council, comprising the States of Andhra Pradesh, Karnataka, Kerala, Tamil Nadu, and the Union Territory of Puducherry.

The North Eastern States, i.e., (i) Assam (ii) Arunachal Pradesh (iii) Manipur (iv) Tripura (v) Mizoram (vi) Meghalaya, and (vii) Nagaland are not included in the Zonal Councils and their special problems are looked after by the North Eastern Council, set up under the North Eastern Council Act, 1972. The State of Sikkim has also been included in the North Eastern Council vide North Eastern Council (Amendment) Act, 2002. Consequently, action for exclusion of Sikkim as member of Eastern Zonal Council has been initiated by the Ministry of Home Affairs.

Organisational Structure of Zonal Councils

- Chairman : The Union Home Minister is the Chairman of each of these Councils.
- Vice Chairman : The Chief Ministers of the States included in each zone act as Vice-Chairman of the Zonal Council for that zone by rotation, each holding office for a period of one year at a time.
- Members : Chief Minister and two other Ministers as nominated by the Governor from each of the States and two members from Union Territories included in the zone.
- Advisers : One person nominated by the Planning Commission (now NITI Aayog) for each of the Zonal Councils, Chief Secretaries, and another Officer/Development Commissioner nominated by each of the States included in the zone.
- Union Ministers are also invited to participate in the meetings of the Zonal Councils depending upon necessity.

Role and Objectives of Zonal Councils

The Zonal Councils provide an excellent forum where irritants between the Centre and States and amongst States can be resolved through free and frank discussions and consultations. Being advisory bodies, there is full scope for free and frank exchange of views in their meetings. Though there are a large number of other fora like the Inter-State Council, Governor's/Chief Minister's Conferences, and other periodical high-level conferences held under the auspices of the Union Government, the Zonal Councils are different, both in content and character. They are regional fora of cooperative endeavour for States linked with each other economically, politically, and culturally. Being compact high-level bodies, specially meant for looking after the interests of respective zones, they are capable of focusing attention on specific issues taking into account regional factors, while keeping the national perspective in view.

The main objectives of setting up of Zonal Councils are as under:

- Bringing out national integration;
- Arresting the growth of acute State-consciousness, regionalism, linguism, and particularistic tendencies;
- Enabling the Centre and the States to co-operate and exchange ideas and experiences;
- Establishing a climate of co-operation amongst the States for successful and speedy execution of development projects.

Functions of the Zonal Councils

Each Zonal Council is an advisory body and may discuss any matter in which some or all of the States represented in that Council, or the Union and one or more of the States represented in that Council, have a common interest and advise the Central Government and the Government of each State concerned as to the action to be taken on any such matter.

In particular, a Zonal Council may discuss and make recommendations with regard to:

- any matter of common interest in the field of economic and social planning;

- any matter concerning border disputes, linguistic minorities, or Inter-State transport;
- any matter connected with or arising out of, the reorganization of the States under the States Reorganisation Act.

CONCLUSION

Thus, cooperative federalism signifies a horizontal relationship between the Centre and the State. This means the two entities cooperate and tackle shared issues to serve the larger public interest. Competitive federalism, on the other hand, professes a vertical relationship between the States and the Central government while States compete among themselves. Though cooperative and competitive federalism seem to be at loggerheads, they aim towards the common objective of economic growth and welfare of the nation in an equal and equitable manner. When our Constitution was first created, it only comprised the notion of cooperative federalism through mechanisms like the Inter-State Council, Zonal Council, and 7th Schedule. But in the course of time, when States competed to attract capital and investment to facilitate and stimulate economic activity and improve administrative efficiency, the need for competitive capitalism was founded. It ensures minimum waste and maximum resource usage by stimulating healthy competition among States in creating a physical and social infrastructure.

Achieving both cooperation as well as competition on a national level is a difficult task; thus, it mandates a Collective Responsibility of the Central and State governments. While prosperous States may be able to execute the policies effectively, economically backward States would require the Centre's support to achieve their goals. Even after giving the needed financial support, we cannot expect all the States to perform uniformly due to the differences in their literacy levels, skilled workforce, and other prerequisites for development. For the States to compete in a truly fair fashion, there is a need to provide a level-playing field. Allocating resources balancing demographic management, growth inequality, needs of States, and performance incentives for progress by the Fifteenth Finance Commission is a step in the right direction. Moreover, it is imperative to implement the 74th Constitutional Amendment in its true letter and spirit. It will allow for greater independence in decision-making to local governments which will further improve the nation's competitiveness[9].

---

[9]View : Cooperative competitive federalism, Economic Times, Author - Amit Kapoor is chair, Institute for Competitiveness and visiting lecturer, Stanford University. Ayushi Pundir is researcher, Institute for Competitiveness.

20.4 NATIONAL INTEGRATION COUNCIL

BACKGROUND

The then Prime Minister, Shri Jawaharlal Nehru, convened the National Integration Conference in September–October, 1961 to find ways and means to combat the evils of communalism, casteism, regionalism, linguism, and narrow-mindedness, and to formulate definite conclusions in order to give a lead to the country. This Conference decided to set up a National Integration Council (NIC) to review all matters pertaining to national integration and to make recommendations thereon. The NIC was constituted accordingly and held its first meeting in 1962.

Objectives of the Council

The NIC declared its objectives in the meeting held in 1968.

The declaration of objectives as adopted by the NIC is as follows:

"The foundation of our national life is common citizenship, unity in diversity, freedom of religions, secularism, equality, justice-social-economic and political, and fraternity among all communities. The National Integration Council reiterates its faith in these values and dedicates itself to their achievement.

The National Integration Council, however, notes with concern the increase in communal incidents in different parts of the country over the last few years. The Council emphasizes that notwithstanding sporadic occurrences of communal and other divisive conflicts, the vast majority of common men and women, irrespective of their religious affiliations, live in peace and harmony and have no interest in violence and disorders.

The National Integration Council condemns tendencies that strike at the root of national solidarity and calls upon all political parties, voluntary organizations, other citizen groups, the press, leaders of opinion and indeed all men of goodwill to bring them to a halt:

- by discouraging communal ill-will and regional animosities and weaning the misguided elements of society from paths of violence;
- by active and energetic propagation of the principles, especially of tolerance and harmony for which this nation stands;
- by mobilizing constructive forces of the society in the cause of national unity and solidarity and giving them leadership, encouragement, and articulation; and
- by devising suitable community activities and programmes for fostering fellow feeling, emphasizing the privileges of common citizenship and in general, raising the quality of national life.

The council wishes to emphasize that this task is not of governments alone although governments have to play a major role in strengthening the forces of integration and in implementing expeditiously and effectively the recommendations that this council makes. This task is the collective responsibility of all citizens – politicians, educationists, artists, writers, teachers, parents and students, intellectuals, businessmen, and trade union leaders. This council most earnestly invites all Indians, regardless of their linguistic, religious, ethnic, or cultural affiliations to join in this great and urgent task ofpromoting national unity and solidarity".

National Integration Council Meetings

The National Integration Council has held 16 meetings so far. The last meeting of the NIC was held in September 2013. Meetings of the National Integration Council are convened as per requirement from time to time. There is no regular or specified time interval for convening meetings of the NIC.

Composition

NIC is chaired by the Prime Minister. It consists of other members such as Cabinet ministers, Chief Ministers of states, political leaders, Chairman of the University Grants Commission, Commissioner for Scheduled Castes and Scheduled Tribes, and representatives of industry, business, and trade unions.

20.5 COMMISSIONS TO REFORM CENTRE-STATE RELATIONS

INTRODUCTION

Federal relations in India have always been a question for debate. Till the period of the early 1970's, Indian federalism remained centralized and Central government executed the policy of centralized federalism. However, most of the States criticized this trend in the wake of the rise of regional parties and raised voices against centralization in many parts of India. However, the voices were focused more on the partisan role of the Governor in acting as an agent of the Central government, regarding the fiscal subjects and sharing of taxation and revenue, etc. Therefore, attempts have been made to review and reform the Center-State relations.

The following committees and commissions were instituted for different periods in connection with the Centre-State relations –

- P.V. Rajamannar Committee
- Anandpur Sahib Resolution
- West Bengal Memorandum
- Vijayawada Conclave
- R.S. Sarkaria Commission
- M.M. Punchhi Commission
- National Commission to Review the Working of the Constitution (Justice M.N. Venkatachaliah Commission)
- First Administrative Reforms Commission
- Second Administrative Reforms Commission

RECOMMENDATIONS OF COMMITTEES/COMMISSIONS FOR CENTRE-STATE RELATIONS

Important recommendations of the various committees are discussed hereunder –

P.V. Rajamannar Committee

The Government of Tamil Nadu constituted a Committee in 1969, to examine the entire question regarding the relationship that should subsist between the Centre and the States in a federal set-up, with reference to the provisions of the Constitution of India, and to suggest suitable amendments to the Constitution so as to secure to the States the utmost autonomy.

The Committee made the following recommendations:

- There should be immediate constitution of the Inter-State Council;
- Union Government should not take any decision without consulting the Inter-State Council when such decision can affect the interests of one or more States;
- Every bill which affects the interest of the States should be first referred to the Inter-State Council before it is introduced in Parliament;

- Articles 356 and 357 may be totally omitted. In the alternative, sufficient safeguards should be provided in the Constitution itself to secure the interests of the States;
- Residuary power of taxation should be vested with the States.
- The Planning Commission should be placed on an independent footing by giving a statutory status to it.
- The Governor should always be appointed in consultation with the State Cabinet.

The recommendations of the Rajamannar Committee were completely ignored by the Central Government.

Anandpur Sahib Resolution

Shiromani Akali Dal, known as Akali Dal, is a regional party in Punjab with a strong base among the Sikhs in Punjab. Master Tara Singh, a Sikh political and religious leader, was instrumental in organising the Shiromani Gurdwara Prabhandak Committee. Under the leadership of Tara Singh, Akali Dal demanded a sovereign State for Sikhs till the early 1960s. Under the Leadership of Sant Fateh Singh, several movements took place for Punjabi Suba, a separate State for Punjabi speakers in India. He started a fast-unto-death for the demand of Punjabi Suba. The Central Government accepted the demand for Punjabi Suba. However, this did not satisfy all the Sikhs; the Shiromani Akali Dal passed a resolution for greater autonomy to the States in the Batala Conference in 1968. Again, in October 1973, Akali Dal adopted a resolution containing both religious and political demands at a meeting held at Anandpur Sahib, popularly known as the 'Anandpur Sahib Resolution'. The Anandpur Sahib Resolution demanded that the Center's powers be restricted only to defence, foreign affairs, communications, currency, etc., and entire other powers should be vested in the States. Akali Dal leader Gurnam Singh moved this resolution, and when he became the Chief Minister of Punjab, he invited DMK Leader Karunanidhi to Ludhiana to discuss autonomy to the States. This duo is considered to lead the way in seeking greater autonomy for the State.

West Bengal Memorandum

The Left Front Government in West Bengal had adopted a Memorandum in 1977 seeking a rearrangement of Centre-State relations and submitted it to the Centre for consideration. The Memorandum pointed out how the Centre had made encroachments into the powers of the States, and the autonomy of the States was gradually eroded. The West Bengal Memorandum stated that Article 356 of the Constitution is the anti-federal instrument for undermining the federal system and the autonomy of States. Therefore, Articles 356 and 357, which gives the President the power to dissolve a State government or its Legislative assembly, should be deleted. Therefore, the Constitution should be amended to include the word 'Federal' in the description of the Republic of India. Likewise, the word 'Union' in the Constitution should be replaced by the word 'Federal'.

Telugu Desam Party (TDP) – Vijayawada Conclave

The dominance of the Congress Party in the political history of Andhra Pradesh continued uninterrupted for three decades till it was upset by the Telugu Desam Party (TDP) in the 1983 elections. The TDP succeeded in ending the Congress hegemony in Andhra Pradesh within a short time. The Telugu Desam Party was founded on 29 March 1982 by N.T. Rama Rao, a famous film star. He played the roles of Hindu mythological characters such as Lord Srirama, Krishna, Karna, etc., and as a moral figure who championed the cause of the weaker sections of the society. The TDP has stressed the need for greater financial decentralisation and State autonomy by transferring more powers to the States. It also demanded the abolition of the post of the Governor. The TDP leader N.T. Rama Rao hosted an opposition parties' meeting at Vijayawada in May 1983. After the meeting, opposition leaders issued a joint statement endorsing the call made during the conclave of southern Chief Ministers in Bangalore organised by Ramakrishna Hegde to review Union-State relations.

National Conference - Srinagar Conference

In October 1983, around fifty leaders from seventeen political parties met in Srinagar Conclave hosted by Farooq Abdullah, the then Chief Minister of Jammu and Kashmir State (which was bifurcated into two Union Territories – Jammu and Kashmir and Ladakh, on October 31, 2019). The Srinagar Conclave brought together parties like the DMK, TDP, Akali Dal, the Republican Party of India, the Asom Jatiyatabadi Dal and National Conference, and the Left Parties. All the parties present were united by the cause of federalism and more autonomy to the States.

Sarkaria Commission

The demand for restructuring Centre-State relations continued unabated by non-Congress States like Andhra Pradesh, Karnataka, West Bengal, Kerala, Assam, Tripura, Tamil Nadu, and Jammu & Kashmir. This forced the Government of India to set up a commission under the Chairmanship of Justice R.S. Sarkaria (retired Judge of the Supreme Court) to go into the question and recommend appropriate changes within the constitutional framework in June 1983. The Commission took four years to complete its deliberations and submitted its report on October 27, 1987.

The important recommendations of the Commission are as follows:

Legislative Relations :

- In the Concurrent list, if the Union Government proposes to make a law, it shall consult the State Government and Intergovernmental Council.
- Legislation passed by the Parliament regarding the creation or abolition of a Vidhana Parishad in a State shall be passed within a reasonable time as desired by the resolution of the State Assembly.
- Residuary power regarding taxation should continue with the Parliament.

Administrative Relations :

- In the event of non-compliance of the Union's directions by a State, sanctions issued under Article 365 should be used as a last resort. Prior to its use, all efforts should be made to settle conflict by all available means.

Financial Relations :

- In order to raise the resources from agricultural income, political consensus should be forged to levy tax in consultation with the National Economic Development Council.
- The net proceeds of Corporation Tax should be shared with the States.
- The surcharge on Income Tax should not be levied, except for a specific purpose, that too for a limited period.

Role of the Governor :

- Article 155 should be amended so as to ensure effective consultation with the CM before the selection of a person for the Governor's post.
- The Vice-President of India and Speaker of Lok Sabha may be consulted by the PM in selecting a Governor.

- A politician in the ruling party at the Union level should not be appointed as the Governor of a State, if there is a different party in power at the State level.
- Governors' tenure should not be disturbed for 5 years and as a matter of convention, he should not occupy any other position after his retirement.

The Governor should appoint the CM guided by the following principles :

* Leader of the majority party or parties,
* Should seek the Vote of Confidence in the assembly within 30 days of his appointment as the CM,
* As long as the Council of Ministers possess a majority in the Assembly, he cannot use his discretionary powers.

Reservation of Bills by Governor for President's Consideration :

- Needless reservation of bills for President's consideration should be avoided (Article 200).
- Governor should not act contrary to the advice of his Council of Ministers even if he does not like the policy embodied in the bill.
- President could withhold assent to the bill only if it subverts the constitutional system. Governor's assent should not be withheld on the ground that the Union is contemplating to legislate on it in future.

Promulgation of Ordinances :

- The State governments should give up the practice of repeated promulgation without trying to get it passed by the Legislature.
- The decision to promulgate ordinances should be based on the collective decision of the Union Council of Ministers.

Emergency Provisions :

- Article 356 should be used very rarely as a measure of last resort, only when all available alternatives are used.
- Unless the proclamation of State Emergency is approved by the Parliament, the Governor should not dissolve the Assembly.
- The facts and grounds on which State Emergency was proclaimed should be an integral part of the proclamation.

Deployment of the Union Armed Forces in a State :

- Before deploying Armed Forces, the Union government should consult the State government for declaring an area within the State as disturbed.

All India Services :

- The Commission understood the need of the All India Services in maintaining the unity of the country.
- It discouraged the move to disband All India Services in any State.
- It encouraged the strengthening of the All India Services in order to play a greater role in improving the efficiency in administration.

Intergovernmental Council :

- It recommended for setting up of a permanent Interstate Council or Inter governmental Council to discuss subjects of common interest to all States[1].
- It recommended for constituting Zonal Councils under Article 263.

Social and Economic Planning :

It recommended many measures to improve the working of the Finance Commission, Planning Commission, and National Development Council.

- It recommended for decentralization of the planning process in order to improve efficiency.

Languages :

- Official or State language policy can be a very counter-productive and divisive force;
- Three language formula should be enforced scrupulously and uniformly.

Changes in the Constitution :

- It felt that drastic changes are not required in the Constitution and the amendment process is sufficient to meet the changes and adjust itself.
- It is neither advisable nor necessary to make any drastic changes in the basic character of the Constitution.

Thus, the Commission made a total of 247 recommendations of which 24 were rejected, 10 were not considered wholly relevant, and 36 were accepted with modifications. One hundred and nineteen recommendations are reported to have won the government's full acceptance.

National Commission to Review the Working of the Constitution (NCRWC)

On 26th January 2000, the Constitution of India completed fifty years of functioning. The BJP-led National Democratic Alliance (NDA) government on 22nd February 2000 appointed a National Commission to Review the Working of the Constitution of India, under the Chairmanship of justice M.N. Venkatachalaiah, former Chief Justice of the Supreme Court, in the light of the experience of the past fifty years, as to how the Constitution can respond to changing needs of the time in the best possible way. Pertinent to mention here is that Justice R.S. Sarkaria is one of the members of the NCRWC.

The Commission submitted its report on 31st March 2002 which made several recommendations on Center-State relations.

- Individual and collective consultation with the States should be undertaken through the Inter-State Council established under Article 263 of the Constitution.
- Management of Disasters and Emergencies, Natural or 'Man-Made' should be included in List III of the Seventh Schedule.
- The powers of the President in the matter of selection and appointment of Governors should not be diluted. However, the Governor of a State should be appointed by the President only after consultation with the Chief Minister of that State. Normally, the five-year term should be adhered to and removal or transfer should be by following a similar procedure as for appointment, i.e., after consultation with the Chief Minister of the concerned State.

[1]On the Sarkaria Commission's recommendations, the National Front Government established the Inter-State Council in1990.

- Suitable amendment should be made in the Constitution so that the assent given by the President should avail for all purposes of relevant Articles of the Constitution.
- Article 356 should not be deleted. But it must be used sparingly and only as a remedy of the last resort.
- In order to reduce tension or friction between States and the Union and for expeditious decision-making on important issues involving the States, the desirability of prior consultation by the Union Government with the Inter-State Council may be considered before signing any treaty vitally affecting the interests of the States regarding matters in the State List.
- As river water disputes are important disputes between two or more States and/or the Union, they should be heard and disposed by a bench of not less than three Judges and if necessary, a bench of five Judges of the Supreme Court for the final disposal of the suit.

Madan Mohan Punchhi Commission

On 27th April 2007, the Government of India constituted a Commission on Centre-State Relations under Justice Madan Mohan Punchhi, former Chief Justice of India, to examine Centre-State relations. The Commission examined and reviewed the legislative, administrative, and financial relations, role of Governors, emergency provisions, economic and social planning, Panchayati Raj institutions, and sharing of resources, including Inter-State river water. The Commission made 273 recommendations in its report presented to Government on 30th March 2010.

Following are the important recommendations of the Commission :

- For cultivating better Centre-State relations and to facilitate effective implementation of the laws on List III subjects, it is necessary that some broad agreement is reached between the Union and States before introducing legislation in Parliament on matters in the Concurrent List.
- The period of six months prescribed in Article 201 for the State Legislature to act when the Bill is returned by the President can be made applicable for the President also to decide on assenting or withholding assent to a Bill reserved for consideration of the President.
- Governors should be given a fixed tenure of five years and their removal should not be at the sweet will of the Government at the Centre. Moreover, it is necessary to provide for impeachment of the Governor on the same lines as provided for impeachment of the President in Article 61 of the Constitution. The dignity and independence of the office warrants such a procedure.
- To be able to discharge the Constitutional obligations fairly and impartially, the Governor should not be burdened with positions and powers which are not envisaged by the Constitution and which may expose the office to controversies or public criticism.

  Following eligibility criteria should be adopted while appointing the Governors (the said criteria have been proposed by the Sarkaria Commission) :

  i. He should be eminent in some walk of life;

  ii. He should be a person from outside the State;

  iii. He should be a detached figure and not too intimately connected with the local politics of the States; and

  iv. He should be a person who has not taken too great a part in politics generally and particularly in the recent past.

- Making the Governor the Chancellor of the Universities and thereby, conferring powers on him which may have had some relevance historically has ceased to be so with change of times and circumstances. Therefore, appointing the Governor as the Chancellor of the Universities should be discontinued.
- Governor should not be assigned functions casually under any Statute. His role should be confined to the constitutional provisions only.

  Following guidelines shall be followed by the Governor while appointing the Chief Minister :

  * The party or combination of parties which commands the widest support in the Legislative Assembly should be called upon to form the Government.
  * If there is a pre-poll alliance or coalition, it should be treated as one political party and if such coalition obtains a majority, the leader of such coalition shall be called by the Governor to form the Government.
  * In case no party or pre-poll coalition has a clear majority, the Governor should select the Chief Minister in the order of preference indicated below:

    – the group of parties which had pre-poll alliance commanding the largest number
    – the largest single party staking a claim to form the government with the support of others
    – A post-electoral coalition with all partners joining the government
    – A post-electoral alliance with some parties joining the government and the remaining including independents supporting the government from outside.

- On the question of dismissal of a Chief Minister, the Governor should invariably insist on the Chief Minister proving his majority on the floor of the House for which he should prescribe a time limit.
- On the question of granting sanction for prosecution of a State Minister in situations where the Council of Ministers advised to the contrary, the Commission would endorse the interpretation given by the Supreme Court to the effect that "if the Cabinet decision appears to the Governor to be motivated by bias in the face of overwhelming material, the Governor would be within his rights to disregard the advice and grant sanction for prosecution".
- Article 356 should be used only after exhausting all other options and it should be limited strictly to rectifying a "failure of the Constitutional machinery in the State".
- Though States have raised objections to the power exercisable by the Union under Articles 256 and 257 on the ground that they are destructive of not only the autonomy of States, but also inimical to the very foundation of a federal arrangement, the Commission is of the considered view that there is no case for amendment of these provisions. It must, however, be clarified that favouring the retention of these provisions is entirely different from advocating easy or quick resort to them. Articles 256 and 257 may be viewed as a safety valve, one which may never come into play but which is nevertheless required to be retained.
- Inter-State Council is an extremely useful mechanism for consensus- building and voluntary settlement of disputes and the body shall be staffed by technical and management experts and given the autonomy required for functioning as a constitutional body independent of the Union and the States.

- On the issue of creating a forum for co-ordination of intergovernmental relations, the Inter-State Council (ISC) needs to be substantially strengthened and activised as the key player in intergovernmental relations. It must meet at least thrice a year on an agenda evolved after proper consultation with the States.
- If decision by consensus does not work in the Inter-State Council, it may be taken by a majority in matters of national concern. In other areas, an Empowered Committee of ministers may be asked to study and report a more acceptable way of resolving the problem within a prescribed timeframe. The Inter-State Council must be empowered to follow up the implementation of its decisions for which appropriate statutory provisions should be made.
- The Zonal Councils should meet at least twice a year with an agenda proposed by the States concerned to maximize coordination and promote harmonization of policies and action having inter-state ramification.
- It strongly recommended the constitution of a few other All India Services in sectors like Health, Education, Engineering, and Judiciary. They existed prior to Independence which contributed significantly to the quality of administration.
- It also recommended proper integration of All India Services in the context of the introduction of the third tier of governance. The local bodies are in dire need of building capacities and strengthening the planning process for which the officers of All India Services can play a lead role.
- The factors inhibiting the composition and functioning of the Rajya Sabha as a representative forum of States should be removed or modified even if it requires amendment of the constitutional provisions.
- It recommended the Rajya Sabha to be a Chamber to protect States' rights.
- It also recommended equality of seats to States in the Rajya Sabha, irrespective of their population size.
- The scope of devolution of powers to local bodies to act as institutions of self-government should be constitutionally defined through appropriate amendments, lest decentralised governance should elude realization indefinitely.
- The State Government should confine itself only to matters of policy that cut across the entire domain of local governments.
- The Central Government must make an assessment of the number of courts needed for efficient adjudication of disputes arising out of Central laws and establish the required number of Additional Courts.
- It proposed balancing of powers and functions (between Centre and States) which assumed added significance after the introduction of the 73rd and 74th constitutional amendments. It can largely be accomplished through administrative arrangements supported by adequate devolution of finances.
- It recommended strengthening of the constitutional scheme of fiscal transfers through Finance Commissions and reduce the scope of other forms of devolution which leads to complaints from States.
- Parliament should make a law on the subject of Entry 14 List I (treaty making and implementing it through Parliamentary legislation) to streamline the procedures involved. The exercise of the power obviously cannot be absolute or uncharted in view of the federal structure of legislative and executive powers.

QUESTIONS

Subjective Questions

1. Discuss the doctrine of 'Pith and Substance' relating to the distribution of legislative powers between the Centre and the States with the help of landmark judicial decisions. **(150 words)**
2. From the resolution of contentious issues regarding distribution of legislative powers by the courts, 'Principle of Federal Supremacy' and 'Harmonious Construction' have emerged. Explain. **(150 words)**

Objective Questions

1. Consider the following statements about NITI Aayog:
   1. It is a statutory body.
   2. It has power to allocate funds for different sectors.
   3. The CEO of NITI Aayog is appointed by the PM.

   Which of the statements given above is/are correct?

   (a) 1 and 2 only (b) 2 and 3 only
   (c) 3 only (d) None

   Ans: (c)
2. With respect to the adjudication of Inter-State water disputes, consider the following statements:
   1. The Constitution provides for the formation of a separate tribunal to deal with such cases.
   2. The Parliament can exclude any court from exercising jurisdiction in such a matter.

   Which of the statements given above is/are correct?

   (a) 1 only (b) 2 only
   (c) Both 1 and 2 (d) Neither 1 nor 2

   Ans: (d)
3. Consider the following statements about the Zonal Councils.
   1. Zonal Councils have been established under the provision of the Constitution.
   2. For the purpose of creation of Zonal Councils, the territory of India has been divided into five zones.
   3. The Zonal Councils provide an excellent forum where irritants between Centre and States and amongst States can be resolved through free and frank discussions and consultations.

   Which of the above statements are correct?

   (a) Only 1 and 2 (b) Only 2 and 3
   (c) Only 1 and 3 (d) All of the above

   Ans: (a)

4. Which of the following is/are the constitutional provisions facilitating Union control over the States?

   1. All India Services
   2. National Development Council
   3. Zonal Councils
   4. Grants-in-aid

   Select the correct answer using the code given below.

   (a) 1 only (b) 1, 2, and 4 only

   (c) 2 and 3 only (d) 1, 3, and 4 only

   Ans: (b)

5. The Prime Minister of India is the Chairman of:

   1. NITI Aayog
   2. Inter-State Council
   3. National Integration Council

   Select the correct answer using the code given below.

   (a) 1 only (b) 1 and 2 only

   (c) 2 and 3 only (d) 1, 2, and 3

   Ans: (d)

CHAPTER 21

CONSTITUTIONAL BODIES

FINANCE COMMISSION

The Constitution devised a flexible scheme for transfer of Central revenue to the States—a scheme which can be amended or adjusted based on the contemporary economic situation or financial position of the Centre and the states; and the same which can be reviewed periodically and can be worked automatically without causing any inter-governmental friction[1]. The said objectives are achieved by making provisions in the Constitution for a periodic appointment of a Finance Commission, a 'non-political' body and by leaving it the task of making inter-governmental financial adjustments from time to time[2].

The Finance Commission is a Constitutionally mandated body that is at the centre of fiscal federalism. Set up under Article 280 of the Constitution, its core responsibility is to evaluate the state of finances of the Union and State Governments, recommend the sharing of taxes between them, and lay down the principles determining the distribution of these taxes among States. Its working is characterized by extensive and intensive consultations with all levels of governments, thus strengthening the principle of cooperative federalism. Its recommendations are also geared towards improving the quality of public spending and promoting fiscal stability[3].

CONSTITUTIONAL PROVISIONS

Constitutional Provisions regarding Finance Commission

Appointment of Finance Commission

Article 280(1) provides for the appointment of a Finance Commission by the President every five years, or earlier, if he considers it necessary. The Commission is to consist of a Chairman and four other members appointed by the President. However, the qualifications and disqualifications of the

[1]This approach was adopted by our constitutional makers after witnessing the experiences of Canada and Australia where the formula laid down in the respective constitutions for Central grants to the units soon proved to inadequate and new bases had to be evolved from time to time for the purpose.

[2]M.P. Jain, *Indian Constitutional Law*, LexisNexis 8th Edition, 2018, P. 699

[3]https://fincomindia.nic.in/

members of the Finance commission is not given in the Constitution. Instead, under Article 280(2), Parliament is empowered to determine by law the requisite qualifications for appointment as members of the Commission[4].

Qualifications and Disqualifications of the Members

According to the Finance Commission (Miscellaneous Provisions) Act, 1951, the Chairman of the Finance Commission is to be a person having experience in public affairs. Its other four members are to be selected from among persons qualified to be appointed as the High Court Judges, having special knowledge of government finances and accounts, having wide experience in financial matters and administration, or having special knowledge of economics.

A person is disqualified to be appointed as a member of the Commission if he or she –

- Is of unsound mind; or
- Is an undischarged insolvent; or
- Has been convicted of an offence involving moral turpitude; or
- Has financial or other interests prejudicially affecting his functions as a member of the Commission.

Term of Office of Members

As per the Finance Commission (Miscellaneous Provisions) Act, 1951, every member of the Commission shall hold office for such period as may be specified in the order of the President while constituting the Finance Commission. The members of the Finance Commission are eligible for reappointment.

Procedure Governing the Finance Commission

According to Article 280(4), the Commission is to determine its procedure and is to have such powers as Parliament may by law confer on it. According to the Finance Commission Act, it has all the powers of a civil court for summoning the witnesses, requiring production of any document, requiring any person to furnish information on any point which the commission regards as useful or relevant to any matter under its consideration[5].

Functions of the Finance Commission

The functions of the Commission, are prescribed under Article 280(3).

The Finance Commission makes recommendation to the President with regard to the following matters:

(a) the distribution between the Union and the States of the net proceeds of taxes which are to be, or may be, divided between them and the allocation between the States of the respective shares of such proceeds;

(b) the principles which should govern the grants-in-aid of the revenues of the States out of the Consolidated Fund of India;

[4]Accordingly, the Finance Commission (Miscellaneous Provisions) Act, 1951 has been enacted by Parliament.

[5]The Commission during the course of its work hold discussion, receives memoranda and hears evidence not only from the Central Government and the various State Governments, but even from private individuals and bodies who might be interested in placing their views before it on the questions under its review.

(c) the measures needed to augment the Consolidated Fund of a State to supplement the resources of the Panchayats in the State on the basis of the recommendations made by the Finance Commission of the State;

(d) the measures needed to augment the Consolidated Fund of a State to supplement the resources of the Municipalities in the State on the basis of the recommendations made by the Finance Commission of the State;

(e) any other matter referred to the Commission by the President in the interests of sound finance.

Therefore, the Finance Commission can be characterised as the ***balance wheel*** of the Indian federal financial relationship between the Centre and the States. Thus, the question of devolution of resources from the Centre to the States has been taken out of the arena of political bargaining and entrusted to an objective body and the matter is to be settled on merits and not on the basis of political horse-trading[6].

Finance Commission: An Advisory Body

The Finance Commission is an advisory body and its recommendations are not binding on the Central Government. However, under Article 281, the President shall cause every recommendation made by the Finance Commission together with an explanatory memorandum as to the action taken thereon. Moreover, a convention has been developed over time under which the Central Government invariably accepts the recommendations of the Commission as regards the funds to be transferred to the States under the various heads.

EXHIBIT 21.1 : COMMONWEALTH GRANTS COMMISSION OF AUSTRALIA

The idea of the Finance Commission has been adopted from the model of the Commonwealth Grants Commission of Australia. However, there are lot of differences between these two bodies. The Indian Commission is a constitutional body and is not a continuing body, but sits only once in five years. The Australian Commission, on the other hand, is a statutory body, is a continuing body, and recommends grants to the deficit States every year. While in Australia, members are appointed for three years at a stretch, in India they are appointed for nearly a year, and the Commission becomes *functus officio* after completing its assigned work. In other words, no continuity is provided for in India in the Commission's work[7].

List Of Finance Commissions And Their Heads

S. No.	Finance Commission	Year of Establishment	Chairman	Operational Duration
1.	First	1951	K. C. Neogy	1952–57
2.	Second	1956	K. Santhanam	1957–62
3.	Third	1960	A. K. Chanda	1962–66
4.	Fourth	1964	P. V. Rajamannar	1966–69
5.	Fifth	1968	MahaveerTyagi	1969–74

[6] 6M.P. Jain, *Indian Constitutional Law*, LexisNexis 8th Edition, 2018, P. 582

[7] M.P. Jain, *Indian Constitutional Law*, LexisNexis 8th Edition, 2018, P. 700

6.	Sixth	1972	K. Brahmananda Reddy	1974–79
7.	Seventh	1977	J.M. Shelat	1979–84
8.	Eighth	1983	Y.B. Chavan	1984–89
9.	Ninth	1987	N.K.P. Salve	1989–95
10.	Tenth	1992	K.C. Pant	1995–2000
11.	Eleventh	1998	A.M. Khusro	2000–2005
12.	Twelfth	2002	C. Rangarajan	2005–2010
13.	Thirteenth	2007	Dr. Vijay L. Kelkar	2010–2015
14.	Fourteenth	2013	Dr. Y.V. Reddy	2015–2020
15.	Fifteenth	2017	N.K. Singh	2020-2025

QUESTIONS

Subjective Questions

1. Discuss the role played by the Finance Commission in strengthening the co-operative federalism in India.
2. Explain the roles and functions played by the Finance Commission

Objective Questions

1. As per the Constitution of India, which of the following is/are the function/duty of the Finance Commission of India?
   1. To provide measures to augment the resources of the Consolidated fund of the state.
   2. It has all the powers of a civil court.
   3. To decide the distribution of resources between States and Panchayats.

   Select the correct answer from the codes given below.

   (a) 1 only (b) 1 and 3 only
   (c) 2 and 3 only (d) 1, 2, and 3

   Ans: (a)

2. The Finance Commission makes recommendations with respect to which of the following matters?
   1. Distribution of taxes between the Centre and states.
   2. Expenditure from the Contingency Fund of India.
   3. Grants-in-aid to the states by the Centre.

   Select the correct answer using the code given below.

   (a) 1, 2, and 3 (b) 1 and 3 only
   (c) 1 and 2 only (d) 2 and 3 only

   Ans: (b)

3. With respect to the Finance Commission, consider the following statements:

   1. It can be constituted by the President even before the normal time gap of 5 years.
   2. Its members are not eligible for reappointment.
   3. Its report is laid before both the Houses of the Parliament by the President.

   Which of the statements given above is/are correct?

   (a) 1 and 3 only (b) 3 only
   (c) 1, 2, and 3 (d) 1 and 2 only

   Ans: (a)

4. With reference to the Finance Commission of India, which of the following statements is correct? (2011 UPSC CSE)

   (a) It encourages the inflow of foreign capital for infrastructure development
   (b) It facilitates the proper distribution of finances among the Public Sector Undertakings
   (c) It ensures transparency in financial administration
   (d) None of the statements (a), (b), and (c) given above is correct in this context

   Ans: (d)

5. Which one of the following statements about the Finance Commission is not correct?

   (a) The Commission comprises a Chairman and four other members.
   (b) The Parliament is authorised to determine by law the qualifications of the members of the Constitution.
   (c) All the appointments are made by the President of India.
   (d) All the members have to be from Indian Economic Service or Indian Statistical Service.

   Ans: (d)

21.2 ELECTION COMMISSION OF INDIA

INTRODUCTION

In order to ensure free, fair, and impartial elections, the Constitution establishes an independent and autonomous body, i.e., Election Commission of India, which shall be insulated from all political pressures or executive influence.

Election Commission is a permanent body constituted under Article 324 of the Constitution. It is an all-India body having jurisdiction to conduct elections to the Parliament, State Legislatures, and offices of President and Vice-President.

'The reason for having an all-India body to supervise and conduct of elections, rather than separate bodies to conduct elections in each State, is that some States have a mixed population, as there are native people as well as others who are racially, linguistically or culturally different from the native people. A State Government could discriminate against outsiders by managing things so as to exclude them from the electoral rolls and thus deprive them of their suffrage which is a basic right in democracy. In order to prevent injustice being done to any section of the people, it was thought best to have one central body which would be free from local influences and have control over the entire machinery in the country'[1].

The Structure of Election Commission

Article 324(2) of the Constitution of India envisages that the Election Commission shall consist of the Chief Election Commissioner and such number of other Election Commissioners as may be fixed from time to time by the President.

Further, under 324(3), it is provided that when any other Election Commissioner is appointed, the Chief Election Commissioner will act as the Chairman of the Election Commission.

It is clear from these constitutional provisions that the Election Commission consists of the Chief Election Commissioner (CEC) and the Election Commissioners appointed by the President. The office of the CEC is envisaged to be a permanent feature, but that cannot be said for the Election Commissions, as their appointment is optional with the Central Executive. There cannot be an Election Commission without the Chief Election Commissioner, but the same is not the case with the Election Commissions. Their number can vary from time to time.

Originally, the commission had only a Chief Election Commissioner. It currently consists of one Chief Election Commissioner and two Election Commissioners.

For the first time, two additional Commissioners were appointed by the President on 16th October, 1989[2], but they had a very short tenure till 1st January, 1990. Later, on 1st October 1993, two additional Election Commissioners were appointed. The concept of multi-member Commission has been in operation since then, with decision-making power by majority vote.

---

[1]See Dr. Ambedkar's speech, VII CAD, 905-7.

[2]When the workload of the Election commission increased on account of lowering the age of voting form 21 years to 18 years (61st Constitutional Amendment Act, 1988).

The President may appoint, after consultation with the Election Commission, such Regional Commissioners as the President may consider necessary to assist the Election Commission in the discharge of its functions (Article 324(4)). Generally, the Regional Commissioners are appointed before each general election to the Lok Sabha and the State Legislative Assemblies, and also before the biennial election to the State Legislative Councils.

As the Regional Commissioners are appointed by the President in consultation with the Commission to assist it to perform its functions, the Election Commissioners are placed on a higher pedestal than the Regional Commissioners. While the Election Commissioners are members of the Election Commission; the Regional Commissioners are not its members.

Appointment and Tenure of Election Commissioners

The President appoints Chief Election Commissioner and other Election Commissioners. Further, as per Article 324(5), the President shall make rules to determine the conditions of service and tenure of office of the Election Commissioners and the Regional Commissioners. However, this power of the President is subject to any law made by the Parliament. Accordingly, the Parliament passed an Act to determine the tenure and service conditions of the Election Commission[3]. As per the Act, the Chief Election Commissioner and other Election Commissioners have tenure of six years, or up to the age of 65 years, whichever is earlier. They enjoy the same status and receive salary and perks as available to Judges of the Supreme Court of India. Moreover, as per the Constitution, the Election Commissioners are not barred from any further appointment by the government or re-appointment as Election Commissioners.

Qualifications of Election Commissioners

The Constitution has not prescribed any pre-requisite qualifications to become Election Commissioner or the Chief Election Commissioner.

Removal of Election Commissioners

- The tenure of the Chief Election Commissioner is independent of the executive discretion. In other words, according to Article 324(5), the Chief Election Commissioner can only be removed from his office in the same way and on the same grounds as a Judge of the Supreme Court. Thus, the Constitution provides a security of tenure to the Chief Election Commissioner (similar to a Judge of the Supreme Court). Therefore, he can discharge his functions independently and without any external influence.
- The tenure of other Election Commissioners and the Regional Commissioners is also free from the executive control but it is not similar to that of Chief Election Commissioner. In other words, the Election Commissioners and the Regional Commissioners can be removed by the President only on the recommendation of the Chief Election Commissioner.
- The conditions of service of the Chief Election Commissioner cannot be varied to his disadvantage after his appointment. However, there are no such safeguards provided to the Election Commissioners.

---

[3]The Election Commission (Conditions of Service of Election Commissioners and Transaction of Business) act, 1991

Position of Chief Election Commissioner wrt other Election Commissioners

The Constitution is silent on the position of the Chief Election Commissioner with respect to the other Election Commissioners. In a multi-member Commission, the Chief Election Commissioner has to act as the Chairman. The Chief Election Commissioner and other Election Commissioners enjoy equal voting rights. In other words, the Election Commission will take all the decisions based on majority vote.

The Chief Election Commissioner and the two Election Commissioners draw salaries and allowances at par with those of the Judges of the Supreme Court of India as provided by the Chief Election Commissioner and Other Election Commissioners (Conditions of Service) Act, 1991.

Therefore, the Chief Election Commissioner and other Election Commissioners enjoy equal status while discharging the functions, in terms of salary, allowances, and other perquisites. But the Chief Election Commissioner's tenure and service conditions are safeguarded in the Constitution. The same is not enjoyed by the other Election Commissioners.

POWERS AND FUNCTIONS OF THE ELECTION COMMISSION

The powers and functions of the election Commission flow from Article 324. The superintendence, direction, and control of the entire electoral process in the country is vested in the Election Commission. The words 'superintendence, direction, and control' are of wide amplitude. These words are enough to include all powers necessary for the smooth and effective conduct of elections so that the will of the people may be expressed[4].

According to the Constitution of India, Registration of Electors Rules, 1960 and the Conduct of Elections Rules, 1961, the Election Commission of India performs various functions which are administrative, quasi-judicial, and advisory in nature.

Functions Performed by the Election Commission of India

(a) **Registration of Political Parties and Allotment of Symbols:** Election Commission of India recognizes political parties as the All-India or State Political Parties and allocates symbols to them. The Election Commission registers the political parties in accordance with the provisions of Representation of the People Act, 1951. While discharging these functions, Election Commission of India acts quasi-Judicially and follows principles of natural justice.

(b) **Preparation of Electoral Rolls:** Election Commission prepares the electoral rolls and revises them from time to time. It registers all the eligible voters. Article 325 of the Constitution lays down that there shall be one general electoral roll for every territorial constituency. The preparation of electoral rolls based on religion, race, caste, or sex is forbidden.

(c) **Conduct of Polls:** The work of the Election Commission regarding the conduct of elections begins with the notification of the election and up to the declaration of the result. It has the power to issue a code of conduct to be observed by all the political parties and people at the time of the election. The Election Commission has not only the power to hold elections but also to cancel it and order re-poll if it is rigged. It is also the responsibility of the Election Commission to hold bye-election whenever there is a mid-term vacancy.

---

[4]Election Commission of India Vs. Ashok Kumar, (2000) 8 SCC 216.

Powers of Election Commission of India

(a) **Power to Disqualify the Candidates :** Under the Representation of the People Act, 1951, after every general election, each candidate should file election returns. If a candidate fails to do so within a prescribed time period, the Election Commission has the power to disqualify such a candidate.

(b) **Advisory Jurisdiction :** Under the Constitution of India, the Election Commission has advisory jurisdiction in the matters of post-election disqualification of sitting members of Parliament and State Legislatures. The opinion of the Commission in all such matters is binding on the President or as the case may be, the Governor to whom such opinion is tendered. Further, the Election Commission advises the President on the feasibility of conducting elections in the States under President's Rule in order to continue the President's Rule for more than a year.

Even with respect to the cases of persons found guilty of corrupt practices at elections which come before the Supreme Court and High Courts are also referred to the Commission for its opinion on the question as to whether such person shall be disqualified and if so, for what period.

(c) **Delimitation of Constituencies :** Under Section 11 of the Delimitation Act of 1972, the Election Commission is empowered to correct any printing mistake in any of the orders made by the Delimitation Commission. The Election Commission maintains delimitation orders up-to-date and makes amendments in the Delimitation of Parliamentary and Assembly Constituencies[5]. Sometimes, the work relating to the delimitation of Constituencies arises as a result of the formation of new States, and is generally entrusted to the Election Commission.

(d) **Miscellaneous Powers:**

- Fixes the limits on the amount of money which a candidate can spend during the election campaign.
- Prepares rosters for publicity of political parties on TV and radio during elections.
- Develops a comprehensive policy for media: In order to bring as much transparency as possible to the electoral process, the media are encouraged and provided with facilities to cover the election, although subject to maintaining the secrecy of the vote.
- Deploys requisite poll personnel: The gigantic task of conducting a countrywide general election requires nearly five million polling personnel and civil police forces. This huge election machinery is deemed to be on deputation to the Election Commission and is subject to its control, superintendence, and discipline during the election period, extending over a period of one and half to two months. (Based on the request made by the Election Commission the President or the Governor will depute the requisite staff necessary for conducting the elections).

---

[5]Section 9(1) of the Representation of the People Act,1950

- India is a founding member of the International Institute for Democracy and Electoral Assistance (IDEA), Stockholm, Sweden. In the recent past, the Commission has expanded international contacts by way of sharing of experience and expertise in the areas of Electoral Management and Administration, Electoral Laws, and Reforms. Election Officials from the national electoral bodies and other delegates from the several countries—Russia, Sri Lanka, Nepal, Indonesia, South Africa, Bangladesh, Thailand, Nigeria, Namibia, Bhutan, Australia, the United States, Afghanistan, etc. have visited the Election Commission for a better understanding of the Indian Electoral Process. The Election Commission has also provided experts and observers for elections to other countries in co-operation with the United Nations and the Commonwealth Secretariat[6].

Acting as a Quasi-Judicial Authority

- The Election Commission has power to allot symbols for purposes of elections to political parties and to adjudicate upon disputes with regard to recognition of political parties and rival claims to a particular symbol for purposes of elections.
- While deciding the question of disqualification of a sitting member of a House of Parliament, or of a State Legislature, the Commission not only acts as an advisory body but also acts in a quasi-judicial capacity.

ORGANISATIONAL SET-UP OF THE ELECTION COMMISSION

In order to assist the Election Commissioner, two or three Deputy Election Commissioners and Director Generals are appointed. They are generally appointed from the national Civil Service of the country and are selected and appointed by the Commission with tenure.

At the state level, the election work is supervised, subject to overall superintendence, direction, and control of the Commission, by the Chief Electoral Officer of the State, who is appointed by the Commission from amongst senior civil servants proposed by the concerned state government. He is, in most of the States, a full-time officer and has a small team of supporting staff.

At the district and constituency levels, the District Election Officers, Electoral Registration Officers, and Returning Officers, who are assisted by a large number of junior functionaries, perform election work[7].

---

[6] https://eci.gov.in/about/about-eci/the-setup-r1/

[7] Collector & District Election Officer is overall Controlling Authority of all the elections in the District. He is Returning Officer for Parliamentary Constituency and officer not below the rank of Deputy Collectors are designated as Returning Officers for Legislative Assembly Constituencies. Generally, Returning Officers for Legislative Assembly Constituencies are designated as Assistant Returning Officer for Parliamentary Constituency election.For conducting Lok Sabha, Election Collector is usually appointed as Returning Officer, and Deputy Collectors are appointed as Asst. Returning Officers to assist the Collector.For conducting election of Legislative Assembly, Collector is overall controlling authority as a District Election Officer and Deputy Collector & Sub Divisional Officers are appointed as Returning Officer for each Legislative Assembly Constituencies.

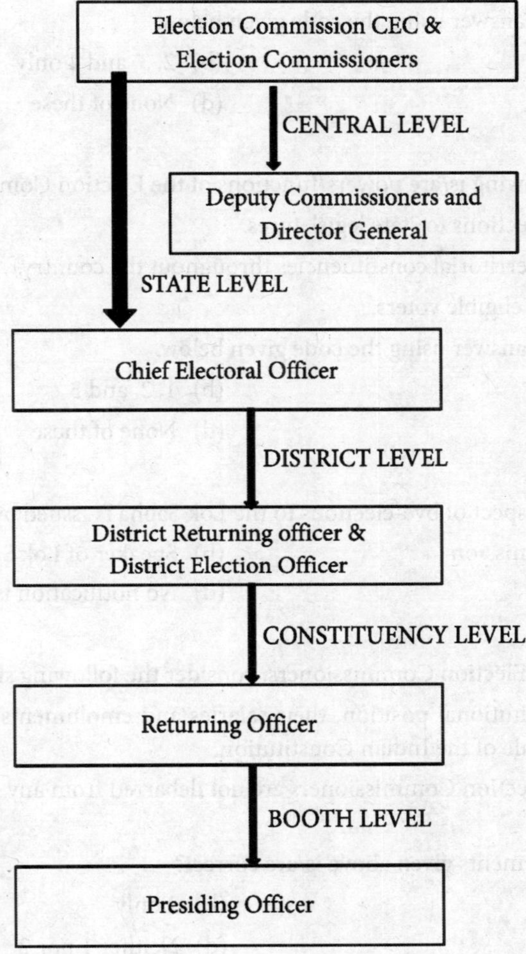

QUESTIONS

Subjective Questions

1. Discuss the role played by the Election Commission of India in conducting 'free and fair' elections.
2. 'The Provisions of the Constitution related to the appointment of the Election Commissioners of India are not sufficient to safeguard the independence and the autonomy of the Election commission of India.' Critically analyse the statement.

Objective Questions

1. The Election Commission of India is responsible for holding elections for which of the following entities?

   1. Municipality elections
   2. Office of President
   3. Office of Vice-President
   4. Speaker of Lok Sabha

Select the correct answer using the code given below.

(a) 2 and 3 only (b) 2, 3, and 4 only

(c) 1 only (d) None of these

Ans: (a)

2. Which of the following is/are powers/functions of the Election Commission of India?
   1. Conducting elections to state legislatures.
   2. Determining territorial constituencies throughout the country.
   3. Registering all eligible voters.

   Select the correct answer using the code given below.

   (a) 2 only (b) 1, 2, and 3

   (c) 1 and 3 only (d) None of these

   Ans: (b)

3. Notifications in respect of bye-elections to the Lok Sabha is issued by the:

   (a) Election Commission (b) Speaker of Lok Sabha

   (c) The Whip (d) No notification is required for bye-election

   Ans: (a)

4. With reference to Election Commissioners, consider the following statements:
   1. Being a Constitutional position, their salaries and emoluments are determined as per the Second Schedule of the Indian Constitution.
   2. The retiring Election Commissioners are not debarred from any further appointment by the government.

   Which of the statements given above is/are correct?

   (a) 1 only (b) 2 only

   (c) Both 1 and 2 (d) Neither 1 nor 2

   Ans: (b)

5. Which of the following directives can be used by the Election Commission of India (ECI) to ensure 'free and fair' elections in India?
   1. The Election Manifesto should be in consonance with the Model Code of Conduct.
   2. Manifestos should broadly reflect the financial means to fulfil the promises.
   3. ECI can declare the election of a candidate null and void on grounds of corruption even after the election process is over.

   Select the correct answer from the codes given below:

   (a) 1 only (b) 1 and 2 only

   (c) 2 and 3 only (d) 1, 2, and 3

   Ans: (b)

21.3 COMPTROLLER AND AUDITOR GENERAL OF INDIA

INTRODUCTION

"The Comptroller and Auditor General of India will be the most important under the Constitution of India official. He should be the guardian of the public purse and it is your duty to see that not a penny the Fund has not spent ... Consolidation of India or a state without the authority of the appropriate legislative power."

Dr. B.R. Ambedkar

The Comptroller and Auditor General of India is a constitutional authority created under Article 148 of the Constitution to protect public money. CAG is the Head of Indian Audit and Accounts Department and he has the authority to audit all income and expenses of the Government of India and State governments, including agencies and authorities substantially financed by the government.

Appointment, Tenure, and Removal of Comptroller and Auditor General of India

- CAG is appointed by the President by warrant under his hand and seal.
- He shall subscribe to the oath administered by the President or some person appointed in that behalf[1].
- The salary and other conditions of service of CAG shall be determined by the Parliament by law but cannot be varied to his disadvantage after his appointment[2]. Accordingly, Parliament passed the Comptroller and Auditor-General's (Duties, Powers and Conditions of Service) Act, 1971. The said Act fixed the tenure of his office at six years.
- The CAG is not eligible for further office either in Central or State government after his retirement.
- Neither the Constitution nor the CAG Act, 1971 prescribed any qualification or experience required for the appointment of the CAG.
- The CAG can be removed from his office in like manner and on the grounds as a Judge of the Supreme Court.

Service Conditions, Salary, and Allowances of Comptroller and Auditor General of India

- According to the CAG Act, 1971, the salary of CAG is equal to that of a Supreme Court Judge.
- The Administrative expenses of the office of CAG, including all salaries, allowances, and pensions payable to him or in respect of persons serving in his office are charged upon the Consolidated Fund of India.
- The President may make rules, after consultation with the CAG, regulating the conditions of service of persons serving in the Indian Audit and Accounts Department.

---

[1] Oaths are set out in the Third Schedule of the Constitution.

[2] The Comptroller and Auditor-General (Duties, Powers and Conditions of Service) Act, 1971.

Duties and Powers of the CAG

In Relation to Accounts[3]

The Constitution did not specifically prescribe the functions of CAG but left the matter to be dealt with by Parliament. According to Article 149, *CAG has to perform such duties and exercise such powers in relation to the accounts of the Union and the States and of any other authority or body as may be prescribed by law by Parliament and until provision in that behalf is so made, shall perform such duties and exercise such powers in relation to the accounts of the Union and of the States as were exercisable by the Auditor General of India before the commencement of the Constitution in relation to the accounts of the Dominion of India and of the provinces respectively.* Under these transitional provisions, the Comptroller and Auditor General continued to perform the duties and exercise the powers in relation to the Accounts of the Union and of the States as provided in the Government of India (Audit and Accounts) Order, 1936, till the Comptroller and Auditor-General's (Duties, Powers and Conditions of Service) Act, 1971 was enacted by the Parliament.

The CAG Act, 1971 authorised the President to relieve the Comptroller and Auditor General, after consultation with him, by an order, from the responsibility of compiling the accounts of the Union or the accounts of any particular service or department of the Union. The Act further authorized the Governor of a State to relieve the Comptroller and Auditor General, with the previous approval of the President and after consultation with the Comptroller and Auditor General, by an order, from the responsibility of compiling the accounts of the State and the accounts of any particular service or department of the State. In 1976, in exercise of powers under the Act, Comptroller and Auditor General has been relieved of the responsibility of compiling and keeping the accounts of various Departments/Ministries of the Union Government by the President.

In Relation to Audit

CAG has the duty to audit all expenditure from the Consolidated Fund of India, of each State and of each Union Territory having a Legislative Assembly. Audit plays an important role in the scheme of Parliamentary financial control. Parliament allots specific sums for specific purposes. Audit ensures that the Executive keeps within the sums allotted and the purposes authorized. Audit is directed towards discovering waste or extravagance. CAG can even disallow any expenditure violating the Constitution or any law. CAG helps in making legislative control over the Executive more effective by a sort of retrospective (an *ex post facto*) examination of the expenses incurred.

Comptroller and Auditor General has the duty to audit all transactions of the Union, of the States, and of the Union Territories having a Legislative Assembly, relating to the Contingency Funds and Public Accounts and to audit all trading, manufacturing, profit and loss accounts and balance sheet, and other subsidiary accounts kept in any department of the Union or of a State or a Union Territory.

The reports of the CAG relating to the accounts of the Union are submitted to the President, who must place the same before each House of Parliament. The reports relating to the accounts of a State are submitted to the Governor, who must place them before the legislature of the State.

In Relation to Audit of Bodies and Authorities

CAG has the duty to audit the accounts of:

- Authorities and bodies receiving financial assistance in the form of grants or/and loans or substantially financed from the Union or State Revenue; or

[3]https://cag.gov.in/content/commentary

- Any other authority or body as may be prescribed by or under any law made by Parliament[4]; or
- Authorities or bodies entrusted by the President/Governor of a State/Administrator of a Union Territory having Legislative Assembly.
- The Supreme Court in the case of Association of Unified Tele Services Providers & Others Vs. UOI[5] has expanded the scope of CAG audit to private companies who are responsible to share the revenue with the Government for using spectrum. This decision of the Supreme Court has expanded the scope of the CAG audit to the books of accounts of private entities in cases where Government earns revenue share on usage of natural resources by them.

In Relation to Government Companies

The auditor of a Government Company (Central Government or State Government) shall be appointed by the CAG. The CAG shall direct the manner in which the accounts of the Government Company are required to be audited and further have the right to conduct a supplementary audit of the financial statements of the Company by such person or persons as the CAG may direct.

In Relation to Parliamentary Committees

The CAG reports are taken into account by the Public Accounts Committee (PAC) and the Committee on Public Undertakings, which are special committees in Parliament of India and the State Legislatures. CAG acts as a guide, friend, and philosopher for PAC.

In Relation to Form of Accounts

The accounts of the Union and of States shall be kept in such form as the President may on advice of the CAG, prescribe (Article 150).

In Relation to Net Proceeds of Taxes

The CAG also plays a fiduciary role in federal financial relations. The CAG determines and certifies the 'net proceeds' of taxes levied and collected by the Union and assigned to the States or distributed between the Union and the States (Article 279). 'Net proceeds' in relation to any tax or duty means the proceeds thereof reduced by the cost of collection. The certificate issued by CAG in this regard shall be final.

In Relation to Local Bodies

CAG is entrusted with audit of Panchayat Raj Institutions and Urban Local Bodies and provides technical guidance and support.

CAG: Miscellaneous Information

Organisations Subject to the Audit of the CAG[6]

- All the Union and State Government departments, including the Indian Railways, Defence, and Posts and Telecommunications.

---

[4]No law of State Legislature can cast any duties or confer any powers upon the CAG or his representatives. Likewise, the duties and powers of the CAG prescribed by law made by the Parliament cannot be superseded or abridged by or be under any law made by the State Legislature.

[5](2014) 6 SCC 110

[6]https://cag.gov.in/faq#:~:text=The%20Audit%20Reports%20of%20the,legislation%2C%20reports%20on%20the%20 Financial

- About 1500 public commercial enterprises controlled by the Union and State governments, i.e., government companies and corporations.
- Around 400 non-commercial autonomous bodies and authorities owned or controlled by the Union or the States[7].
- Bodies and authorities substantially financed from the Union and some of the local bodies and Panchayati Raj Institutions which are critical grassroot agencies for implementation of developmental programmes and delivery of services.

Unique Position of CAG

The CAG of India has a unique position because unlike most countries, the CAG has been assigned both accounting and auditing functions. He is not an officer of the Parliament even though he serves the Parliament and the State Legislature. Thus, CAG is the dignitary who occupies a unique place in Indian Democracy.

CAG's office has been given a dual role. Firstly, it is the agency that functions along with the Legislature and ensures that the Executive obeys the laws passed by the Legislature and enhances the Executive's accountability towards the Legislature. The second role is that it functions as an agency that ensures obedience by subordinate authorities with respect to regulations issued by the Executive. Hence, it is rightly said, "The CAG is as supreme as the Judges of the Supreme Court, perhaps even more so[8]".

CAG's Role in India in Comparison with UK

In Britain, the Comptroller and Auditor General not only audits and examines the Government accounts but as Comptroller, he also controls issue of money out of the Consolidated Fund by ensuring that nothing is taken out of it without due Parliamentary authority.

In India, CAG acts mainly as an auditor and points out the irregularities after the expenses have been incurred. He does not have that preliminary control over the issue of public money as his British counterpart has. Therefore, CAG in India cannot be called as Comptroller in its strict sense.

To sum up, CAG of India acts as a custodian and trustee of public money, and exercises his powers in consonance with the Constitution and within the rules framed by the government from time to time, to ensure that there is no loss, leakage of revenue, avoidable expenditure, and embezzlement.

QUESTIONS

Subjective Questions

1. "Comptroller and Auditor General's report is always subject to scrutiny by the Parliament and it is for the Parliament to decide whether after receiving the report to make its comments on the CAG's report". Analyse. **(250 words)**
2. "Comptroller and Auditor General examines the propriety, legality, and validity of all expenses incurred by the Government and exercises effective control over the Government accounts". Examine. **(250 words)**

---

[7]Certain institutions or bodies like RBI, LIC FCI, SBI, etc. are outside the purview of CAG audit.

[8]http://www.iosrjournals.org/iosr-jbm/papers/Conf.17037-2017/Volume-3/12.%2067-70.pdf

Objective Questions

1. With regard to the Comptroller and Auditor General of India (CAG), consider the following statements:

   1. The reports of the CAG are examined by the Estimates Committee of Lok Sabha.
   2. He has no control over the issue of money from the Consolidated Fund of India.

   Which of the statements given above is/are correct?

   (a) 1 only (b) 2 only

   (c) Both 1 and 2 (d) Neither 1 nor 2

   Ans: (b)

2. With reference to the Comptroller and Auditor General of India (CAG), consider the following statements:

   1. He submits all its reports to the President.
   2. He compiles and maintains the accounts of the State governments.
   3. Governor of a State can request the CAG to audit local bodies.

   Which of the statements given above is/are correct?

   (a) 1 and 2 only (b) 2 and 3 only

   (c) 3 only (d) 1, 2, and 3

   Ans: (b)

3. The reports of the Comptroller and Auditor General (CAG) is/are examined by which of the following committees?

   1. Public Accounts Committee
   2. Committee on Public Undertakings
   3. Estimates Committee

   Select the correct answer using the code given below.

   (a) 1 only (b) 1 and 2 only

   (c) 2 and 3 only (d) 1, 2, and 3

   Ans: (b)

4. Consider the following statements:

   1. The Comptroller and Auditor General of India has no control over the issue of money from the Consolidated Fund of India.
   2. The term of the office of the Comptroller and Auditor General of India has been fixed by an Act enacted by Parliament.

   Which of the statement(s) given above is/are correct?

   (a) Only 1 (b) Only 2

   (c) Both 1 and 2 (d) Neither 1 nor 2

   Ans: (c)

5. To whom does the Comptroller and Auditor General of India submit his resignation letter?

   (a) Finance Minister (b) Lok Sabha Speaker

   (c) President of India (d) Prime Minister

   Ans: (c)

21.4 NATIONAL COMMISSION FOR SCHEDULED CASTES & SCHEDULED TRIBES

BACKGROUND

For effective implementation of various safeguards provided in the Constitution for the SCs & STs and various other protective legislations, the Constitution provided for appointment of a Special Officer under Article 338 of the Constitution. The Special Officer who was designated as Commissioner for SCs & STs was assigned the duty to investigate all matters relating to the safeguards for SCs and STs in various statutes and to report to the President upon the working of these safeguards. In order to facilitate effective functioning of the office of the Commissioner for SCs & STs, 17 regional offices of the Commissioner were set up in different parts of the country where percentage of Scheduled Castes were relatively high.

There was a persistent demand by SCs & STs representatives, particularly the Members of Parliament, that the Special Officer under Article 338 should be replaced by an effective multi-member Commission with increased functions and powers. The Government decided to set up a Multi-Member Commission through an administrative decision (executive resolution). The first Commission for SCs & STs was, therefore, set up in 1978 with Shri Bhola Paswan Shastri as Chairman and four other Members. However, this step was taken without abolishing the office of the Special Officer for SCs & STs (constituted under Article 338).

The functions of the Commission for SCs & STs broadly corresponded and sometimes overlapped with those of the Commissioner for SCs & STs. The functions of the Multi-Member Commission set up in 1978 were modified and the Commission for SCs & STs was renamed as the National Commission for Scheduled Castes and Scheduled Tribes (NCSCST) in 1987. It was an unsatisfactory situation with the constitutional office of the Special Officer for SCs & STs and the non-constitutional Commission for SCs & STs co-existing, charged with the same functions. In the year 1992, through 65th Constitutional Amendment Act of 1990, the arrangement of one-member system (Special Officer) was replaced with a multi-member commission and the constitutional body status was conferred to the National Commission for Scheduled Castes and Scheduled Tribes. It was set up as a National Level Advisory Body to advise the Government on broad policy issues and levels of development of Scheduled Castes and Scheduled Tribes.

Consequent upon the 89th Constitutional Amendment Act, 2003 coming into force in 2004, the erstwhile National Commission for Scheduled Castes & Scheduled Tribes was replaced by

(1) National Commission for Scheduled Castes (Article 338), and

(2) National Commission for Scheduled Tribes respectively (Article 338A).

Composition of National Commission for Scheduled Castes

The National Commission for Scheduled Castes consists of:

- A Chairperson,
- A Vice-Chairperson, and
- Four other members.

They are appointed by the President by warrant under his hand and seal. The Commission has been given the power to regulate its own procedure. The Chairperson has the status of Union Cabinet Minister, while Vice-Chairperson has the status of Minister of State and Members have the Status of Secretary to the Government of India. The tenure and the conditions of service of the members are determined by the President. According to the said terms/rules, the members of the commission hold their office for a term of 3 years.

Functions, Duties, and Powers of the Commission

The functions of the Commission are briefly discussed here :

(a) The Commission is required to investigate and monitor all matters relating to the safeguards provided for SCs under the Constitution or under any other law for the time being in force or under any order of the Government and to evaluate the working of such safeguards.

(b) The Commission is required to inquire into specific complaints with respect to the deprivation of rights and safeguards of SCs.

(c) The Commission is required to participate in and advise on the planning process of socio-economic development of SCs and to evaluate the progress of their development under the Union and any State. The role of the Commission in these areas will be at various levels, the Central Ministries, and the State Governments.

(d) The Commission is required to present to the President, annually and at such other times as the Commission may deem fit, reports of the working of the safeguards provided for SCs under the Constitution, various laws, and orders. These reports shall contain recommendations as to the measures that should be taken by the Union or any State for the effective implementation of those safeguards and other measures for the protection, welfare, and socio-economic development of SCs. The President shall cause all such reports to be laid before each House of the Parliament along with a memorandum explaining the action taken or proposed to be taken on the recommendations relating to the Union and the reasons for the non-acceptance, if any, of any of such recommendations.

Where any such report, or any part thereof, relates to any matter with which the State Government is concerned, a copy of such report shall be forwarded to the Governor of the State who shall cause it to be laid before the Legislature of the State along with a memorandum explaining the action taken or proposed to be taken on the recommendations relating to the State and the reasons for the non-acceptance, if any, of such recommendations.

(e) **Powers of the Commission to act as a Civil Court :** While investigating any matter referred to in clause (a) above or inquiring into any complaint referred to clause (b) above, the Commission shall have the powers of a Civil Court trying a suit and in particular, in respect of the following matters:

- summoning and enforcing the attendance of any person from any part of India and examining him on oath,
- requiring the discovery and production of any document,
- receiving evidence on affidavits,
- requisitioning any public record or copy thereof from any court or office,

- issuing commissions for the examination of witnesses and documents,
- any other matter which the President may, by rule, determine.

The Commission does not have any power to give any verdict or direction. It can only give its findings and recommendations.

(f) **Consultative Role of the Commission :** The Constitution has made it mandatory for the Union and every State Government to consult the Commission on all major policy matters affecting the SCs. This is a very important function of the Commission which has to keep track of all the major policy decisions taken by the Government of India or any State Government. These decisions could be legislative or executive.

(g) **Inquiry into cases of atrocities :** Whenever information is received by the Commission about any incident of atrocity on a person or persons belonging to SCs & STs, the Commission would inquire into it to determine the circumstances that led to the occurrence of the incident and see if the law and order and other State machinery have taken proper action, including distribution of relief to the affected persons or their families. The Commission would lay down detailed procedure for conducting such inquiries at different levels. Such inquiries may be conducted directly by the Members of the Commission or through the investigating teams from the Headquarters office of the Commission or the field officers of the Commission. All the concerned authorities at the Centre or in the States would be expected to render assistance to the Commission in such inquiries.

(h) The Commission is also required to provide safeguards against the exploitation of Anglo-Indian communities to promote and protect their social, educational, economic, and cultural interests. In other words, the Commission is supposed to discharge similar functions with regard to the Anglo-Indian Community as it does with respect to the SCs.

(i) The Commission is also required to discharge such other functions in relation to the protection, welfare, development, and advancement of the SCs as the President may specify.

21.5 NATIONAL COMMISSION FOR SCHEDULED TRIBES

INTRODUCTION

The National Commission for Scheduled Tribes (NCST) has been created by amending Article 338 and inserting a new Article 338A in the Constitution through the Constitution (89th Amendment) Act, 2003. By this amendment, the erstwhile National Commission for Scheduled Castes and Scheduled Tribes was replaced by two separate Commissions namely-

(i) National Commission for Scheduled Castes (NCSC), and

(ii) National Commission for Scheduled Tribes (NCST) w.e.f. February 2004.

Rationale

The framers of the Constitution had realised that geographically, socially, and culturally, the needs and problems of the Scheduled Tribes were different from those of Scheduled Castes and, therefore, a special approach was required to bring about all-round development of Scheduled Tribes. It was in recognition of these considerations that the framers of the Constitution made special provisions for Scheduled Tribes in Article 244 (Fifth and Sixth Schedule States), Article 275(1) (Grants from the Union to certain States), and Article 339 providing for appointment of a Commission to report on the administration of Scheduled Areas and the welfare of Scheduled Tribes in the States. Accordingly, the first such Commission was set up in the year 1960 under the Chairmanship of Shri U.N. Dhebar. Subsequently, in October, 1999, a new Ministry of Tribal Affairs was created to provide a sharp focus to the welfare and development of Scheduled Tribes. It was felt necessary that the Ministry of Tribal Affairs should coordinate all activities in relation to Scheduled Tribes as it would not be administratively feasible for the Ministry of Social Justice and Empowerment to perform this role. Another important step was the creation of a separate National Commission for Scheduled Tribes to monitor the implementation of the Constitutional safeguards for the Scheduled Tribes more effectively.

Composition

Article 338A provides that the National Commission for Scheduled Tribes shall consist of a :

- A Chairperson,
- A Vice-Chairperson, and
- three other Members.

They shall be appointed by the President by warrant under his hand and seal. The conditions of service and tenure of office shall be such as the President may, by rule[1], determine. According to the said rules the Chairperson, the Vice-Chairperson, and Members shall hold office for a term of three years from the date on which they assume such office. The Chairman and the Vice-Chairman of the Commission have been conferred the rank of Union Cabinet Minister and Minister of State, respectively. The Members of

[1]The National Commission for Scheduled Tribes Chairperson, Vice-Chairperson and Members (Conditions of Service and Tenure) Rules, 2004.

the Commission have been given the rank of a Secretary to the Government of India. The Commission has been given the power to regulate its own procedure.

Functions, Duties, and Powers

The functions, duties, and powers of the National Commission for Scheduled Tribes have been laid down in the Article 338A of the Constitution :

(a) to investigate and monitor all matters relating to the safeguards provided for the Scheduled Tribes under the Constitution or under any other law for the time being in force or under any order of the Government and to evaluate the working of such safeguards;

(b) to inquire into specific complaints with respect to the deprivation of rights and safeguards of the Scheduled Tribes;

(c) to participate and advise on the planning process of socio-economic development of the Scheduled Tribes and to evaluate the progress of their development under the Union and any State;

(d) to present to the President, annually and at such other times as the Commission may deem fit, reports of the working of those safeguards. The President shall cause all such reports to be laid before each House of Parliament along with a memorandum explaining the action taken or proposed to be taken on the recommendations relating to the Union and the reasons for the non-acceptance, if any, of any of such recommendations. Moreover, where any such report, or any part thereof, relates to any matter with which any State Government is concerned, a copy of such report shall be forwarded to the Governor of the State who shall cause it to be laid before the Legislature of the State along with a memorandum explaining the action taken or proposed to be taken on the recommendations relating to the State and the reasons for the non-acceptance, if any, of any of such recommendations.

(e) to make in such reports recommendations as to the measures that should be taken by the Union or any State for the effective implementation of those safeguards and other measures for the protection, welfare, and socio-economic development of the Scheduled Tribes; and

(f) to discharge such other functions in relation to the protection, welfare, and development and advancement of the Scheduled Tribes as the President may, subject to the provisions of any law made by Parliament, by rule, specify.

(g) The Commission shall, while investigating any matter referred to in clause (a) above or inquiring into any complaint referred to in clause (b) above, have all the powers of a civil court[2] trying a suit and in particular in respect of them following matters, namely: -

- summoning and enforcing the attendance of any person from any part of India and examining him on oath,
- requiring the discovery and production of any documents,
- receiving evidence on affidavits,

[2]The Commission does not have any power to give any verdict or direction. It can only give its findings and recommendations.

- requisitioning any public record or copy thereof from any court or office,
- issuing commissions for the examination of witnesses and documents,
- any other matter which the President may, by rule, determine.

(h) The Union and every State Government shall consult the Commission on all major policy matters affecting Scheduled Tribes.

Expanded Terms of Reference of the Commission

The President expanded the terms of reference in respect of the National Commission for Scheduled Tribes to incorporate the following :

i. Measures that need to be taken over conferring ownership rights in respect of minor forest produce to Scheduled Tribes living in forest areas;

ii. Measures to be taken to safeguard rights of the tribal communities over mineral resources, water resources, etc., as per law;

iii. Measures to be taken for the development of tribals and to work for more viable livelihood strategies;

iv. Measures to be taken to improve the efficacy of relief and rehabilitation measures for tribal groups displaced by development projects;

v. Measures to be taken to prevent alienation of tribal people from land and to effectively rehabilitate such people in whose case alienation has already taken place;

vi. Measures to be taken to elicit maximum cooperation and involvement of tribal communities for protecting forests and undertaking social afforestation;

vii. Measures to be taken to ensure full implementation of the provisions of Panchayats (Extension to Scheduled Areas) Act, 1996;

viii. Measures to be taken to reduce and ultimately eliminate the practice of shifting cultivation by tribals that lead to their continuous disempowerment and degradation of land and the environment.

21.6 NATIONAL COMMISSION FOR OTHER BACKWARD CLASSES

BACKGROUND OF THE COMMISSION

The first backward class commission was appointed in 1950's chaired by Kaka Kalelkar under Article 340[1] of the Constitution of India and later in 1970's, another commission for backward classes was appointed chaired by B.P. Mandal. Article 340 of the Constitution of India only provides for the creation of temporary commissions. In the Indra Sawhney case, the Supreme Court made the following observations: the Central and State government shall in four months constitute a permanent body to entertain, examine, and recommend the inclusion and exclusion of backward classes for protection and benefit.

Relying on the judgment, the National Commission for Backward Classes Act was enacted in 1993 (under the Ministry of Social Justice and Empowerment) and the Commission for Backward Classes was constituted, and the authority was given to them to examine the request for including the classes as a backward class in the Central List. However, the Parliament also constituted a committee under the chairmanship of B.K. Handique for the welfare of the other backward classes, whose first report was presented in 2012 which recommended that constitutional status should be given to the National Commission for Backward Classes. The committee in its second report recommended the inclusion of new Article 338B.

CONSTITUTIONAL PROVISIONS REGARDING THE COMMISSION

The 102nd Amendment Act, 2018

The 102nd Amendment Act, 2018 inserted three new articles, that is, 342A, 366 (26C), and 338B in the Constitution. While Article 338B has constituted the National Commission for Backward Classes, Article 342A has dealt with the Central List of the socially and educationally backward classes (commonly known as the Other Backward Classes), and Article 366 (26C) has defined the socially and educationally backward classes.

Article 338B gave constitutional status to the National Commission for Backward Classes (NCBC) and the Article also talks about the composition of NCBC and the duties and role of NCBC in monitoring and safeguarding the rights of socially and educationally backward classes. Article 338B along with Article 342A authorize the President to list socially and educationally backward classes in the State and Union Territories in consultation of the Governor of the concerned State. However, to make any amendment in the Central List of backward classes, a law shall be enacted by Parliament to do so.

---

[1]Under Article 340(1) of the Indian Constitution, the President has a power to designate a Commission for the purpose of conducting inquiries with regard to the condition of socially and educationally backward classes.

Jaishri Laxmanrao Patil Vs. Chief Minister of State of Maharashtra[2] (Maratha Reservation Case)

Since 1993, there always existed separate lists of "Socially and Educationally Backward Classes" of the Central Government and that of the State Governments and Union territories. In other words, the States had the power to make their Other Backward Castes (OBC) lists. The 102nd Amendment Act, 2018 which introduced Article 342A provided as follows –

342A(1): The President may with respect to any State or Union territory, and where it is a State, after consultation with the Governor thereof, by public notification, specify the socially and educationally backward classes which shall for the purposes of this Constitution be deemed to be socially and educationally backward classes in relation to that State or Union territory, as the case may be.

342A(2): Parliament may by law include in or exclude from the Central List of socially and educationally backward classes specified in a notification issued under clause (1) any socially and educationally backward class, but save as aforesaid a notification issued under the said clause shall not be varied by any subsequent notification.

The Supreme Court while interpreting the implications of Article 342A held that the Amendment/ Article 342A took away States' powers to identify 'socially and educationally backward classes' (SEBC). States could only make suggestions with the President who will have the exclusive authority to notify the list of SEBC.

In order to rectify as well as clarify the Centre's position with regard to Article 342A, the 105th Constitutional Amendment Act, 2021 was passed.

105th Constitutional Amendment Act, 2021

The 105th Constitutional Amendment Act clarifies that Article 342A deals with the Central List of the socially and educationally backward classes (SEBCs). It further clarifies that the States and Union territories may continue to have their separate State List/Union territory List of SEBCs. The castes or communities included in such State List or Union List of Backward Classes may differ from the castes or communities included in the Central List of SEBCs.

COMPOSITION OF THE COMMISSION

The Commission shall consist of

- a Chairperson,
- a Vice-Chairperson and
- three other Members

All the members of the Commission shall be appointed by the President by warrant under his hand and seal. The conditions of service and tenure of office of the Chairperson, Vice-Chairperson, and other Members so appointed shall be such as the President may, by rule, determine. The said rules provide that the Chairperson shall be appointed from amongst eminent socio-political workers belonging to the socially and educationally backward classes. And of the Vice-Chairperson and all

---

[2]Civil Appeal No..3123 of 2020.

other Members out of whom, at least two shall be appointed from amongst persons belonging to the socially and educationally backward classes. At least one other Member shall be appointed from amongst women.

FUNCTIONS OF THE COMMISSION

(a) To investigate and monitor all matters relating to the safeguards provided for the socially and educationally backward classes under this Constitution or under any other law for the time being in force or under any order of the Government and to evaluate the working of such safeguards;

(b) To inquire into specific complaints with respect to the deprivation of rights and safeguards of the socially and educationally backward classes;

(c) To participate and advise on the socio-economic development of the socially and educationally backward classes and to evaluate the progress of their development under the Union and any State;

(d) To present to the President, annually and at such other times as the Commission may deem fit, reports of the working of those safeguards. The Commission is also supposed to make in such reports the recommendations as to the measures that should be taken by the Union or any State for the effective implementation of those safeguards and other measures for the protection, welfare, and socio-economic development of the socially and educationally backward classes. The President shall cause all such reports to be laid before each House of Parliament along with a memorandum explaining the action taken or proposed to be taken on the recommendations relating to the Union and the reasons for the non-acceptance, if any, of any of such recommendations;

(e) To discharge such other functions in relation to the protection, welfare, and development and advancement of the socially and educationally backward classes as the President may, subject to the provisions of any law made by Parliament, by rule specify.

(f) Powers of the Commission to act as a Civil Court - The Commission shall, while investigating any matter referred to in clause (a) above or inquiring into any complaint referred to in (b) above, shall have all the powers of a civil court trying a suit and in particular in respect of the following matters, namely:—

- summoning and enforcing the attendance of any person from any part of India and examining him on oath;
- requiring the discovery and production of any document;
- receiving evidence on affidavits;
- requisitioning any public record or copy thereof from any court or office;
- issuing commissions for the examination of witnesses and documents;
- any other matter which the President may, by rule, determine.

21.7 UNION PUBLIC SERVICE COMMISSION

INTRODUCTION

For proper and efficient working of a democracy, it is very necessary that civil service be free of political pressures and personal patronage. It is therefore necessary to ensure that the best available person be selected for appointment to a post so as to avoid arbitrariness and nepotism in the matter of appointment. To achieve these objectives, the Constitution creates Public Service Commissions which are autonomous bodies. Article 315 of the Constitution envisages three categories of Public Service Commissions – the UPSC to serve the Union, an SPSC for services of a State, and a Joint PSC for the services of two or more than two States. While UPSC and SPSCs are constitutional bodies, a Joint Public Service Commission is to be created by an Act of Parliament. Article 315 to 323 of Part XIV of the Constitution deals with Union Public Service Commission.

The Constitution visualises the Union Public Service Commission to be the 'Watchdog of merit system'.

Background

The Government of India Act of 1919 provided for the setting up of a Public Service Commission. With the Lee Commission strongly backing it, a Central Public Service Commission was set up in 1926. Owing to the recommendations of the Simon Commission, it was renamed as the Federal Public Service Commission in 1937. In 1947, India achieved independence and the Commission continued to work till 1950 with the same nomenclature. Thereafter, with the Constitution of India coming into effect in 1950, the Commission was renamed as the Union Public Service Commission (UPSC) of India.

Composition

The UPSC is headed by a Chairperson and has other members appointed by the President. The Constitution of India does not specify the number of members but authorizes the President of India to determine the number of members. The strength usually varies between nine to eleven members, including the Chairman. No qualifications are prescribed for the Commissions' membership except that, as nearly as may be, one-half of the members should be persons who have held offices for at least ten years either under the Government of India or that of a State. A member of the Commission is to hold office for six years from the date he takes charge of his officer, or until he attains the age of 65 years, whichever is earlier. A member may, however, resign from his office by writing to the President.

The President may appoint an acting Chairman of the Commission if the office of the Chairman falls vacant, or if the Chairman is unable to discharge his functions due to absence or some other reason. The acting Chairman functions till a person is appointed as the Chairman or when the original Chairman is able to resume his duties.

The President has the powers to make regulations to determine the number of members of the Commission and their conditions of service. However, the regulations so made cannot vary the conditions of service of members to their disadvantage after the appointment.

Removal of the Officers of the Commission

The Chairman or member may be removed from office by the President if he is an adjudged insolvent or engages in any paid employment outside the duties of his office or, is in the opinion of the President, infirm in mind or body. In addition to the above said grounds, the member can also be removed on the ground of 'misbehaviour'. However, the President can remove a member on the grounds of 'misbehaviour' only after referring the matter to the Supreme Court.

In other words, the following conditions have to be fulfilled in order to remove a member on the grounds of 'misbehaviour' -

- The President makes a reference to the Supreme Court, and
- The Court, after holding an inquiry, reports to the President that the person concerned ought to be removed from office.

The word 'misbehaviour' has been explained in the Constitution.

A member shall be deemed to be guilty of misbehaviour if

i. he is interested or concerned in any contract or agreement made on behalf of the Government of India or of a State or

ii. if he participates in any way in the profit of such contract or agreement in common with the other members of an incorporated company

The advice tendered by the Supreme Court in this regard is binding on the President. Moreover, during the course of enquiry by the Supreme Court, the President can suspend the Chairman or the member.

Functions of the Commission

The functions of the UPSC as specified under Article 320 of the Constitution is to be a resemblance to those of the Federal Public Service Commission as specified in Government of India Act 1935.

1. To conduct examination for appointment to the services of the Union. In other words, it conducts examinations of All-India Services, Central Services, and Public Services of the Union Territories. The Commission must scrupulously follow the statutory rules during recruitment and in making appointment. Under this provision the UPSC conducts many written examinations for different categories of posts annually, besides the holding of interviews for selection of candidates for specialised and other categories of positions. Here too, it may be noted that the Commission's jurisdiction is narrowly restricted to gazetted officers who constitute an insignificant proportion of the total number of government employees. Moreover, UPSC is not concerned with cadre management, training, classification of services, etc. There matters are handled by the Department of Personnel and Training (DoPT)[1].
2. The Commission, if requested for the purpose by two or more States, has to assist those States in framing and operating schemes for joint recruitment for any services for which candidates possessing special qualifications are required.
3. The Commission, if requested by a State Governor to do so, may, with the approval of the President, agree to serve all or any of the needs of a State.

[1]Thus, UPSC is only a central recruiting agency whereas DoPT is referred to as a central personnel agency.

4. Under Article 320, the Commission has many advisory functions to discharge. It is consulted on the following matters –
   - All matters relating to methods of recruitment to civil services and for civil posts. The provision is directory and not mandatory and any appointment by the Government without consulting the Commission would not be invalid.
   - The principles to be followed in making appointments to civil services and posts, in making promotion and transfers from one service to another, and on the suitability of candidates for such appointments, promotions or transfers.
   - Matters related to grant of extension of service and re-employment of certain retired civil servants.
   - Matter of temporary appointments for period exceeding one year and on regularization of appointments.
   - All disciplinary matters affecting a person serving under the Government in a civil capacity, including memorials or petitions relating to such matters.
   - Any claim by or in respect of a person in government service in a civil capacity, that any costs incurred by him in defending proceedings instituted against him in respect of acts done or purported to be done in execution of his duty should be paid out of the Consolidated Fund of India.
   - Any claim for the award of a pension in respect of injuries sustained by a person while in a government service, in a civil capacity, and any question as to the amount of any such award.
5. It is the duty of the Commission to advise the President on any matter referred to it by him. However, the President is empowered to frame regulations specifying the matters in which either generally, or in any particular class of cases or circumstances, it is not necessary to consult the Commission. Such regulations are to be laid before each House of Parliament for not less than 14 days as soon as possible after they have been made.
6. Parliament may, by law, confer additional functions on the Commission regarding services of the Union, public institution, or corporation created by law. It has been held that besides the functions conferred on the Commission by the Constitution, other functions can be conferred on the Commission only by way of legislation and not by way of a departmental arrangement between the Government and the Commission.
7. The Commission will present annually to the President, a report of the work done by the Commission. It shall be the duty of the President to lay before each House of Parliament the report of the Commission, together with a memorandum of the cases where the advice of the Commission was not accepted, and the reason for non-acceptance.

The consultation of UPSC prescribed above is only to afford proper assistance to the Government. But, for the omission of or irregularity in such consultation, the aggrieved officer has no remedy in a court of law. In other words, if the Government does not consult UPSC with regards to above mentioned matters, no officer or public servant can claim it as a right and nor does enjoy any remedy in any court. Moreover, a selection by the UPSC does not confer any right upon the post by the candidate. However, the government is supposed to act fairly and without arbitrariness or malafides.

Advisory Role of UPSC

Though the Commission has been entrusted with important constitutional duties and functions, it has been assigned only an advisory and consultative role. Under the Government of India Act 1935, the position of the Federal Public Service Commission also was advisory in nature. It was then felt that vesting of excessive authority with the Commission would lead to its interference with the powers of the Executive. The function of the UPSC is just to advice the government and the Executive is under no legal obligation to accept its advice. Thus, the recommendations made by the Commission are only advisory and it is for the Government to accept them or not. The only safeguard is Article 323 which makes the Government answerable to the Legislature for departing from the Commission's recommendation.

Limitations of the Functions of the UPSC

There are certain matters which have been kept outside the scope of the functions of the UPSC. These include:

(a) The Commission has no right to be consulted in the matter of reservation of posts for backward classes nor can itself make any such reservation.

(b) The Constitution of India, under Article 335, requires the government to take into consideration the claims of the members of the Scheduled Castes and Tribes in the matters of appointment to various posts. As per Article 320(4), the UPSC need not be consulted as regards the extent to which the reservations are to be made for the candidates belonging to the Scheduled Castes and Tribes. But once these conditions are determined by the Government, the Commission as a recruiting agency proceeds with the process of selection.

(c) The President has been empowered to make regulations excluding matters from the purview of consultation with UPSC. All such regulations must be laid before each House of Parliament for approval for a period of not less than fourteen days. The Parliament, if necessary, can modify or annul them.

(d) The posts, the recruitment of which does not require the advice of UPSC include membership or chairmanship of tribunals, commissions, high powered committees, posts of highest diplomatic nature, Group C and D services, posts of a highly technical and administrative nature, and filling up of temporary positions where appointments are made for less than a year.

Salaries and Allowances

The expenses of the Union Public Service Commission, including salaries, allowances, and pensions, payable to the members or staff of the Commission, shall be charged on the Consolidated Fund of India.

Independence of the Commission

Independence of the Commission is protected with the help of the following constitutional provisions :

(a) The Chairman of the UPSC shall be ineligible for further employment either under the Government of India or under the Government of the State;

(b) The Chairman of the UPSC is not eligible for second-term or re-appointment after serving his/ her first term as the Chairman of the Commission;

(c) A member other than the Chairman of the UPSC shall be eligible for appointment as the Chairman of the UPSC or as the Chairman of a State Public Service, but not for any other employment either under the Government of India or under the Government of a State;

(d) The expenses of the Commission, including salaries, allowances and pensions, payable to the members are charged on the Consolidated Fund of India. Thus, they are not subject to the annual vote of the Parliament.

(e) The President can remove the Chairman and members of the Commission only according to the constitutional provisions.

(f) Even though the conditions of service of the Chairman and the members of the Commission are determined by the President, they cannot be varied to their disadvantage after their appointment.

DUALITY OF AUTHORITY – CENTRAL VIGILANCE COMMISSION (CVC) & UPSC

CVC is a statutory body whereas UPSC is a constitutional body. But the Chairmen of both these bodies enjoy the same rank. With respect to the disciplinary proceedings against the officers of All-India Services, Group A services, etc., both CVC and UPSC are consulted by the Government, because of which there was overlapping of functions and thereby delay due to duality of authority. Therefore, the practice of referring to CVC's opinion while approaching UPSC had been done away with in December 2012 to avoid "difference of opinion" and "delay due to duality of authority".

In other words, the apex vigilance body (CVC) is consulted at two stages in vigilance cases/disciplinary proceedings, which involves "first-stage advice" on the investigation reports, and "second-stage advice" before a final decision is taken at the conclusion of the proceedings. The Department of Personnel and Training (DoPT) had issued guidelines in 2011 asking to dispense with "second-stage advice" of CVC in disciplinary cases involving consultation with UPSC. The UPSC is consulted for the quantum of penalty against the concerned officer along with CVC, but the latter had taken a backseat for the past eight years due to DoPT guidelines.

However, it was observed that the move did not obtain the desired result and there were considerable delays in finalisation of disciplinary proceedings in those cases as well, wherein the proceedings were initiated on the advice of the apex vigilance body. "One of the reasons noticed for delay in such cases is that while approaching UPSC for advice about quantum of penalty on the charged officer concerned, the fact that the disciplinary proceedings were initiated on the advice of CVC in that particular case, is not highlighted by the organisations". Therefore, according to CVC, it is desired that the authorities concerned, at the time of approaching the UPSC for advice, with respect to such cases, "must highlight the fact that the particular case was based on the First Stage Advice given by the CVC, so that the cases receive due attention with the authorities in UPSC and its advice is tendered on priority basis". "It may be done by superscribing the file cover of cases being referred to the UPSC with the words 'Vigilance Case' on a red sticker, similar to process being followed in respect of important files pertaining to urgent/time-bound Parliamentary matters and Lok Sabha/Rajya Sabha questions, etc."

21.8 STATE PUBLIC SERVICE COMMISSION

INTRODUCTION

At the State level in India, not one but two distinct sets of Civil Services operate. One of these is the Civil Services recruited by the respective State governments to handle a diverse range of governmental activity at the State level. These are known as the State Civil Services or simply State Services. The second set of Civil Services serving the States is the All India Services. All India Services officers are recruited to perform a varied range of jobs, both at the State level as well as at the Centre. It is this feature of the All India Services, which renders them clearly distinguishable from the State Services. Among the best-known examples of the All India Services are the Indian Administrative Service (IAS) and Indian Police Service (IPS).

State Services are recruited by the respective State governments through their Public Service Commissions. Thus, like UPSC at the Central level, there are State Public Service Commission at the State level. Articles 315 to 323 of Part XIV of the Constitution deals with the Union Public Service Commission and State Public Service Commission (SPSC).

Composition of SPSC

The Constitution established a Public Service Commission in each State. The composition of the State Commission is governed by the same constitutional provisions that apply to the UPSC. Thus, a State Public Service Commission consists of a Chairman and several members who are appointed by the Governor. The number of members which an SPSC may have is not fixed. The Constitution stipulates that this shall be determined by the Governor of the concerned State. At least half of the members of a SPSC should be persons with a minimum of ten years of experience under the Central or a State government.

The Governor of a State may, by regulation, determine the number of members of the Commission and their conditions of service. The conditions of service of a member cannot be varied to his disadvantage after his appointment. All provisions regarding the tenure of a member of the UPSC apply to a member of a State Commission, except with the following differences:

- The age of retirement of a member of a State Commission is 62 years instead of 65 years as in the case of a member of the UPSC. Thus, the tenure of members is six years or until the age of sixty-two years, whichever, is earlier.
- To resign, a member of a State Commission writes to the Governor.

Moreover, the Governor may appoint an acting Chairman of the Commission if the office of the Chairman falls vacant, or if the Chairman is unable to discharge his functions due to absence or some other reason. The acting Chairman functions till a person is appointed as the Chairman or when the original Chairman can resume his duties.

Removal of SPSC

It is interesting to note that the Chairman and the members of the SPSC are appointed by the Governor but the power to remove any of these members vests with the President and not with the Governor. The Chairman or member of the SPSC may be removed from office by the President if he is an adjudged insolvent or engages in any paid employment outside the duties of his office or, is in the opinion of the President, infirm in mind or body. In addition to the above said grounds, the member can also be removed on the grounds of 'misbehaviour'. However, the President can remove a member on the grounds of 'misbehaviour' only after referring the matter to the Supreme Court.

In other words, the following conditions have to be fulfilled in order to remove a member on the grounds of 'misbehaviour' -

- The President makes a reference to the Supreme Court, and
- The Court, after holding an inquiry, reports to the President that the person concerned ought to be removed from office.

The word 'misbehaviour' has been explained in the Constitution. A member shall be deemed to be guilty of misbehaviour if

(i) he is interested or concerned in any contract or agreement made on behalf of the Government of India or of a State or

(ii) if he participates in any way in the profit of such contract or agreement in common with the other members of an incorporated company

The advice tendered by the Supreme Court in this regard is binding on the President. Moreover, the Governor has power to suspend a member/Chairman of the State Public Service Commission in respect of whom a reference has been made to the Supreme Court by the President.

Functions of SPSC

A State Public Service Commission discharges all those functions in respect of the State services as does the Union Public Commission in relation to the Union Services.

(a) As recruiting agencies, the principal function of the State PSCs is to conduct examination for appointment to Civil Services.

(b) The Commission has many advisory functions to discharge. It is consulted on the following matters –

- All matters relating to methods of recruitment to Civil Services and for civil posts. The provision is directory and not mandatory and any appointment by the Government without consulting the Commission would not be invalid.
- The principles to be followed in making appointments to Civil Services and posts, in making promotion and transfers from one service to another, and on the suitability of candidates for such appointments, promotions, or transfers.

- All disciplinary matters affecting a person serving under the Government in a civil capacity, including memorials or petitions relating to such matters.
- Any claim by or in respect of a person in government service in a civil capacity, that any costs incurred by him in defending proceedings instituted against him in respect of acts done or purported to be done in execution of his duty should be paid out of the Consolidated Fund of State.
- Any claim for the award of a pension in respect of injuries sustained by a person while in a government service, in a civil capacity, and any question as to the amount of any such award.
- To tender advice to the State government on a matter so referred to it by the Governor.
- To exercise such additional functions as may be provided for by an act of the Legislature. These may be with respect to the State Civil Service or the services of a local authority or other corporate bodies.
- To present annually to the Governor, a report about the work done by it. The Governor places such report before State Legislature, along with a memorandum explaining the cases where advice of the Commission was not accepted and the reasons for such non-acceptance.

The consultation of SPSC prescribed above is only to afford proper assistance to the Government. But, for the omission of or irregularity in such consultation, the aggrieved officer has no remedy in a court of law. In other words, if the Government does not consult SPSC with regards to the above mentioned matters, no officer or public servant can claim it as right and nor does it enjoy any remedy in any court. Moreover, a selection by the SPSC does not confer any right upon the post upon the candidate. However, the government is supposed to act fairly and without arbitrariness or malafides.

Advisory Role of SPSC

Though the Commission has been entrusted with important constitutional duties and functions, it has been assigned only an advisory and consultative role. The function of the SPSC is just to advice the government and the executive is under no legal obligation to accept its advice. Thus, the recommendations made by the Commission are only advisory and it is for the Government to accept them or not. The only safeguard is Article 323 which makes the Government answerable to the Legislature for departing from the Commission's recommendation.

Limitations of the Functions of the SPSC

There are certain matters which have been kept outside the scope of the functions of the SPSC. These include:

(a) The Commission has no right to be consulted in the matter of reservation of posts for Backward Classes nor can it itself make any such reservation.

(b) The Constitution of India, under Article 335, requires the government to take into consideration the claims of the members of the Scheduled Castes and Tribes in the matters of appointment to various posts. As per Article 320, the SPSC need not be consulted as regards the extent to which the reservations are to be made for the candidates belonging to the Scheduled Castes and Tribes.

But once these conditions are determined by the Government, the Commission as a recruiting agency proceeds with the process of selection.

(c) The Governor has been empowered to make regulations excluding matters from the purview of consultation with the SPSC. All such regulations must be laid before each House of State Legislature for approval for a period of not less than fourteen days. The State Legislature, if necessary, can modify or annul them.

Salaries and Allowances of SPSC

The expenses of the State Public Service Commission, including salaries, allowances, and pensions, payable to the members or staff of the Commission, shall be charged on the Consolidated Fund of the State.

Independence of SPSC

The Constitution also incorporates well-designed safeguards to foster the Commission's independence. These are:

(a) As a check against a possible abuse of power, the appointing and removing authority is vested in different functionaries. The power to appoint the Chairperson and members of a Commission vests with the Governor, but the power of removal is vested in the President.

(b) Removal can be affected only in the manner and on the grounds prescribed in the Constitution.

(c) Salaries and other conditions of service of a member cannot be revised to his disadvantage after his appointment.

(d) The expenses of the Commission are charged on the Consolidated Fund of the State.

(e) A person holding office as a member of a State Commission or the Chairman is not to be re-appointed on expiry of his term. The Chairman of a State Commission can be appointed as the Chairman or member of the UPSC, or as the Chairman of any other State Commission, but not to any post under the Central or the State Government[1]. A member, other than the Chairman of a State Commission is eligible for appointment as the Chairman or member of the UPSC, or as the Chairman of that State Commission, or of any other State Commission, but is not eligible for any other employment either under the Central or the State Government.

Recommendations of the Administrative Reforms Commission (1966) with Respect to SPSC

(a) Regarding the composition, it said that while appointing members of the State Public Service Commissions, the Governor should consult the Chairman of the UPSC and the Chairman of the concerned State Public Service Commissions.

[1] A member of a State Public Service Commission can be appointed as the Governor of a State. The main reason for this ruling is that the office of the Governor is a high constitutional office and cannot be said to be an employment under the Government.

(b) The Administrative Reforms Commission also observed that Research Cells should be set up in the Public Service Commissions to analyse trends in the skill market and in the educational sphere.

State Vigilance Commission & SPSC

The Constitution visualizes the SPSC to be the 'Watchdog of merit system' in the State. It is concerned with the recruitment to the State Services and advises the government, when consulted, on promotion and disciplinary matters. The emergence of State Vigilance Commission (SVC) in 1964 affected the role of SPSC in disciplinary matters. It is so because both are consulted by the government while taking disciplinary action against a civil servant. The problem arises when the two bodies tender conflicting advice. However, the SPSC, being an independent constitutional body, has an edge over the SVC.

JOINT PUBLIC SERVICE COMMISSION

It is possible for two or more States to have a Joint Public Service Commission. The basic policy of the Constitution is that each State should have its own Public Service Commission, but if for administrative or financial reasons it is not possible for each State to have a Commission of its own, two or more States may have a Joint Public Service Commission.

In other words, two or more States may agree that there should be one Public Service Commission for them. If a resolution to that effect is passed by the House or by each House of Legislature (where there are two Houses) of the respective States, Parliament may, by law, provide for the appointment of a Joint State Public Service Commission to serve the needs of those states[2]. Even the UPSC, if requested by a State Governor to do so, may with the approval of the President, agree to serve all or any of the needs of a State.

Thus, the JSPSC is created by an Act of Parliament, whereas UPSC and SPSC are directly created by the Constitution itself. The President shall appoint members of the Commission.

Composition of JSPSC

The composition of the Commission and their service conditions are determined by the President. However, like any other Public Service Commission, even in JSPSC, at least half of the members of a Commission should be persons with a minimum of ten years of experience under the Central or a State government. The Chairman and members of the Commission are appointed by the President. They hold office for a term of six years or 62 years, whichever is earlier.

[2]Say, for example, Punjab and Haryana had a JSPSC for a brief period, after the creation of a new State called "Haryana" from Punjab in 1966.

Removal of Members of JSPSC

The Chairman and members of the Commission can be removed or suspended by the President. The grounds and procedure for the removal of the Chairman and the members of the JSPSC is the same as that of the UPSC and SPSC. The Chairman and the members can also resign from their office at any time by submitting their resignation letters to the President.

JSPSC prepares and submits the annual report on its performance to each of the concerned State Governors. Each Governor has to place the report before the respective State Legislature.

21.9 LINGUISTIC MINORITIES

A civilization can be judged by the way a society treats its minorities.

– Mahatma Gandhi

LINGUISTIC MINORITIES IN INDIA

The Constitution has divided the minorities on the following basis:

1. Religion;
2. Caste; and
3. Language.

A peek into the Fundamental Rights guaranteed under Part III, Articles 29 and 30 deals with the minorities and their interest besides Article 14 (Equality before Law). This is because at the time of drafting of the Constitution, majority of the states were multilingual. Therefore, it became imperative to safeguard certain rights and interests of minorities. Accordingly, certain provisions were incorporated in the Constitution to safeguard the interests of the linguistic minorities.

At the time of drafting of the Constitution, majority of the States were multilingual. Therefore, it became imperative to safeguard certain rights and interests of minorities. Accordingly, certain provisions were incorporated in the Constitution to safeguard the interests of the linguistic minorities.

What is a 'Linguistic Minority' for Purposes of Constitutional Guarantees?

The Constitution recognises minorities based on religion, culture, language, or script.

Article 29 : has the word 'minorities' in its marginal heading but speaks of 'any sections of citizens... having a distinct language, script or culture'. This may be a whole community generally seen as a minority or a group within a majority community. The said Article guarantees to minorities having distinct language, script, or culture the right to conserve it.

Article 30 : confers on the minorities based on religion or language the right to establish and administer educational institutions of their choice.

However, the Constitution neither defines the term 'minority' nor delineates the criteria for determining a minority. Based on various Supreme Court Judgements, the word linguistic minority can be defined as a '*group of people having mother-tongue different from that of the majority in a state or part thereof. These observations are of decisive significance for the formulation and implementation of safeguards for all linguistic minorities in general and for those linguistic groups which have no distinct script of their own in particular*'. The language of the minority group need not be one of the twenty-two languages mentioned in the Eighth Schedule of the Constitution.

Provisions Protecting the Interests of Linguistic Minorities[1]

The provisions provided for the linguistic minorities are unique in their thoroughness and seeks to accommodate the interest of linguistic minorities. The sole purpose of these provisions is to give linguistic minorities the right to preserve and develop their language and to facilitate teaching in mother tongue to their children in early ages[2].

Article 347 : Deals with special provision relating to language spoken by a section of the population of a State — 'On a demand being made in that behalf the President may, if he is satisfied that a substantial proportion of the population of a State desire the use of any language spoken by them to be recognized by that State, direct that such language shall also be officially recognized throughout that State or any part thereof for such purpose as he may specify'.

Article 350 : Deals with the Language to be used in representations for redress of grievances — 'Every person shall be entitled to submit a representation for the redressal of any grievance to any officer or authority of the Union or a State in any of the languages used in the Union or in the State, as the case may be'.

Note : *On the recommendations of the States Reorganisation Commission, the 7th Constitutional (Amendment) Act, 1956 was enacted, whereby Articles 350A & 350B were included in the Constitution. The States Reorganisation Commission 1955, recommended for creation of a mechanism to address the grievances of the linguistic minorities.*

Article 350A : Relates to facilities for instruction in mother-tongue at primary stage. It shall be the endeavour of every State and of every local authority within the State to provide adequate facilities for instruction in the mother-tongue at the primary stage of education to children belonging to linguistic minority groups; and the President may issue such directions to any State as he considers necessary or proper for securing the provision of such facilities.

Article 350B : Provides for a Special Officer for the Linguistic Minorities to be appointed by the President (who would be acting as a **Commissioner** for **Linguistic Minorities** in India). It shall be the duty of the Special Officer to investigate all matters relating to the safeguards provided for linguistic minorities under this Constitution and report to the President upon those matters at such intervals as the President may direct, and the President shall cause all such report to be laid before each House of the Parliament, and sent to the Governments of the State concerned.

COMMISSIONER FOR LINGUISTIC MINORITIES

Functions of Commissioner for Linguistic Minorities[3]

The functions of Commissioner for Linguistic Minorities are listed below:

a. To investigate all matters related to safeguards provided to the linguistic minorities.

---

[1]https://shodhganga.inflibnet.ac.in/bitstream/10603/195026/4/13_chapter4.pdf

[2]Constitutional and Legislative Provisions Regarding the Minorities – Justice Ranganath Misra Report, 2007, p. 36.

[3]52nd Report of the Commissioner for Linguistic Minorities, July 2014 to June 2015, P. 155.

b. To report to the President of India through the Union Minority Affairs Minister, regarding the status of implementation of the Constitutional and the nationally agreed Scheme of Safeguards for the linguistic minorities.

c. To monitor status of implementation of Safeguards through Questionnaires, Visits, Conferences, Seminars, Meetings, Review Mechanism, etc.

Key Objectives of Commissioner for Linguistic Minorities[4]

a. To submit to the President of India, the Reports as mandated under Article 350B (2) of the Constitution on the status of implementation of the Constitutional and the nationally agreed Safeguards for the linguistic minorities.

b. To provide equal opportunities to the linguistic minorities for inclusive development and national integration.

c. To spread awareness amongst the linguistic minorities about the Safeguards available to them.

d. To ensure effective implementation of the Safeguards provided for the linguistic minorities in the Constitution and other Safeguards, which are agreed to by the States/UTs.

e. To take up the representations for redress of grievances related to the Safeguards for linguistic minorities with the States/UTs.

CONSENSUAL SAFEGUARDS FOR LINGUISTIC MINORITIES[5]

In addition to Constitutional safeguards mentioned earlier, following the reorganization of the states on the linguistic basis, there emerged some safeguards on consensual basis for linguistic minorities. These have been agreed to by the Central and the State Governments through a series of meetings of Chief Ministers of all the states. Following are the safeguards:

1. Instruction through minority languages at the Secondary stage of education;
2. Translation and publication of important rules, regulations, notices, etc., into all languages, which are spoken by at least 15% of the total population at district or sub-district level;
3. No insistence upon knowledge of State's Official Language at the time of recruitment. Test of proficiency in the State's Official Language to be held before completion of probation.

Note : *The Constitution is silent about the qualifications, tenure, and removal of the Commissioner for Linguistic Minorities.*

[4]Ibid.

[5]https://shodhganga.inflibnet.ac.in/bitstream/10603/195026/4/13_chapter4.pdf

CHAPTER 22

EMERGENCY PROVISIONS

INTRODUCTION

A unique feature of the Indian Constitution is the way in which the normal peace-time federalism can be adapted to an emergency situation. The framers of the Constitution felt that, in an emergency, the Centre should have overriding powers to control and direct all aspects of administration and legislation throughout the country.

TYPES OF EMERGENCIES

The Constitution of India provides for three types of emergency:

(a) **National Emergency (Article 352) :** Can be declared on the grounds of war or external aggression or armed rebellion.

(b) **President's Rule (Article 356) :** Can be imposed in States due to the failure of constitutional machinery in States.

(c) **Financial Emergency (Article 360) :** Can be declared when the financial stability or credit of the country gets affected.

EMERGENCY PROVISIONS IN INDIA

The provisions of the emergency are provided in the Constitution to make a temporary arrangement to meet an extraordinary circumstance. These provisions have no application in the usual peace-time. Nevertheless, these provisions, especially for their serious consequences, are often regarded as out of place in a democratic and federal set-up. Moreover, such emergency provisions do not exist in the Constitutions of other federations like Canada, the USA, and Australia. But, that does not mean that they dealt with World Wars-I and II- by adopting ordinary peace-time arrangements to run the functions of the Governmental organs. Why does a country, especially a federation, require such emergency provisions? The reason is that according to many jurists, including a renowned British jurist and Constitutional theorist A.V. Dicey, "federalism means distribution of powers of a state among the number of coordinate bodies originating and controlled by the constitution"[1]. That's the reason why

[1](Nevertheless, in due course of time, it has been well settled that even the federal forms of Government can be potent sometimes more than the unitary forms of Government and the federations like the USA, Canada, and Australia have proved it time and again).

our constitutional forefathers felt the need of emergency provisions to overcome the extraordinary circumstances. The Centre becomes all-powerful during the emergency and the States will be under the Centre's control. In other words, in the case of war, external aggressions, or other types of exigencies, the peace-time arrangements to run the functions of the Governmental organs are practically incapable of dealing with such exigencies. Extraordinary circumstances always demand extraordinary solutions.

However, proclamation of an emergency not only weakens the federal form of government but also disturbs the normal fabric of the Constitution and adversely affects the rights of the people. Such a proclamation should therefore, be issued only in exceptional circumstances and not merely to keep an unpopular government in office as happened in 1975 when an emergency was declared on the grounds of 'internal disturbance' without there being adequate justification for the same.

As a consequence thereof, the emergency provisions (especially Article 352 and 356) have been extensively amended by the 44th Constitutional Amendment Act, 1978, with a view to introduce a number a safeguards against abuse of power by the executive in the name of emergency. Amendments have thus been made by the 44th Amendment to the emergency provisions of the Constitution to make the repetition of the 1975 situation extremely difficult, if not impossible[2].

PROCLAMATION OF NATIONAL EMERGENCY[3]

Grounds for Proclamation of Emergency

Constitution does not use the term "National Emergency". Instead, it is provided as "Proclamation of Emergency".

A Proclamation of Emergency under Article 352 may be issued by the President on any of the following grounds :

i. War; or

ii External Aggression; or

iii. Armed rebellion.

Such a proclamation may be made in respect of the whole of India, or such part of the Indian Territory as may be specified in the proclamation. In other words, the proclamation need not extend to the whole of India. It may be restricted to a part of the Indian Territory. Moreover, the proclamation may be issued not only when the war or external aggression or armed rebellion has actually occurred or ensued, but before the actual occurrence also when there is an imminent danger. If the emergency is proclaimed on the grounds of war or external aggression it is called as "External Emergency". Whereas, emergency declared on the grounds of armed rebellion is called as "Internal Emergency".

Before 1978, an emergency could be declared because of war, external aggression, or 'internal disturbance'. The expression 'internal disturbance' was too vague and broad. The 44th Constitutional Amendment Act, 1978 substituted the word 'armed rebellion' for 'internal disturbance' with a view to exclude the possibility of an emergency being proclaimed on the grounds of 'internal disturbance' only

[2]M.P. Jain Pg No. 728.

[3]Constitution does not use the term "National Emergency". It is just mentioned as "Proclamation of Emergency".

not involving armed rebellion as happened in 1975. As the Supreme Court explained in *Naga People's Movement of Human Rights vs. UOI*[4], the expression "internal disturbance" has a wider connotation than "armed rebellion" in the sense that "armed rebellion" is likely to pose a threat to the security of the country, or a part thereof, while "internal disturbance", though serious in nature, would not pose a threat to the security of the country, or a part thereof.

Procedure for Making a Proclamation

i. The President may proclaim emergency only when he is satisfied as to the existence of threat or an imminent danger to the security of India or any part thereof caused by war, external aggression, or armed rebellion. This satisfaction of the President shall not, however, be his personal satisfaction. He (according to the amended Article 352(3)) can be so satisfied only if the Union Ministers of Cabinet rank, headed by the Prime Minister, recommended to him, in writing, that such a proclamation should be issued. This means that the decision to issue such a proclamation has to be arrived at collectively by the Cabinet and not by the Prime Minister alone without consulting the Cabinet. It so happened in 1975 that the President proclaimed emergency on the advice of the Prime Minister alone and the Council of Ministers were informed about the decision later. It is to avoid any such situation in future that the 44th Constitutional Amendment Act added Article 352(3) in the Constitution.

ii. The power conferred on the President to proclaim emergency shall include the power to issue different proclamations on different grounds, either war or external aggression or armed rebellion or imminent danger thereof, whether or not there is a proclamation already issued by the President and such proclamation is in operation.

iii. Every proclamation of Emergency shall be laid before each House of the Parliament. A proclamation will automatically cease after one month if not approved by Parliament in the meantime. Formerly, the period allowed for parliamentary approval of the proclamation was two months. The 44th Amendment has reduced it to one month. If the proclamation of Emergency is issued at a time when the Lok Sabha has been dissolved or the dissolution of the Lok Sabha takes place during the period of 'one' month period referred above, without approving, then in such cases, the proclamation has to be approved by the Rajya Sabha. And the proclamation shall cease to operate at the expiration of 30 days from the date on which the Lok Sabha sits after fresh election, unless before the expiry of the above period of thirty days a resolution, approving the proclamation has been passed by the Lok Sabha. A resolution approving the proclamation must be passed by *special majority,* which is by a majority of the total members of each House and also by a majority of not less than 2/3rd of the members present and voting in each House. Prior to the 44th amendment, such resolution could be passed by the Parliament by a simple majority. Approving the proclamation with special majority is a wholesome safeguard. The reason being, a proclamation of emergency ***virtually*** results in amending the Constitution for the period of the emergency (Fundamental Rights are suspended and, from the legislative point of view, it becomes practically unitary), it is desirable that the proclamation of emergency be approved by the same majority in Parliament as is required for amendment of the Constitution[5].

---

[4] AIR 1988 SC 431.

[5] *Indian Constitutional Law*, M.P. Jain, Eighth Edition, LexisNexis, Pg No. 730.

iv. A proclamation of emergency once approved by Parliament shall remain in force for a period of *six months* unless revoked earlier. For continuance of the emergency beyond that period, Parliamentary approval is needed again. Thus, each time Parliament approves the proclamation; its life is extended for six months. In this way, the question whether the emergency should continue in force or not must periodically come before both the Houses of the Parliament. This periodic approval by the Parliament was added by the 44th Constitutional Amendment Act. Before that, the proclamation once approved by the Parliament, was to remain in force as long as the executive desired. There was no provision for periodical Parliamentary review. With 44th Constitutional Amendment Act, each resolution of approval is to be passed by Parliament by the special majority. It may, however, be noted that the Central Executive can revoke the proclamation at any time it likes. Moreover, if the dissolution of the Lok Sabha takes place during the period of six months without approving the further continuance of emergency, but it has been approved by the Rajya Sabha, the proclamation shall cease to operate at the expiry of 30 days after the Lok Sabha sits after fresh election unless before the expiry of the of the 30-day period, it is approved by the Lok Sabha.

Procedure for Revocation of Proclamation

A proclamation of emergency can be revoked by the President at any time on the recommendation of the Prime Minister and the Council of Ministers. But the President is obliged to revoke a proclamation of emergency if the Lok Sabha passes a resolution with simple majority disapproving the same (proclamation of emergency). Formerly, the power to revoke the proclamation was vested in the Executive only and the Lok Sabha had no say in the matter. Now, the executive has to withdraw the emergency if the Lok Sabha so desires. However, there is a special procedure prescribed by the 44th Amendment Act, for convening a special sitting of the House of the People for passing such a resolution of disapproval. The power has been given to not less than one-tenth (1/10th) of the Members of the House to give a notice in writing to the Speaker (when the House in session) or to the President (when the House is not in session) to convene a special sitting of the House for this purpose. Session must be convened for considering the resolution within 14 days from the date on which such a notice is received by the Speaker of the President. Thus, it is not left to the discretion of the Government to convene or not to convene a session of the Lok Sabha, for considering whether continuance of emergency is necessary or not.

Judicial Review of the President's Discretion

i. Now the question arises about whether the proclamation of emergency by the President is subjected to judicial review or not? In *Bhut Nath Mete Vs. State of West Bengal*[6], the Supreme Court refusing to hold the continuance of the emergency under Article 352 'void' stated that the question is a "political, not justiciable issue and the appeal should be to the polls and not to the courts". Nevertheless, to put the matter beyond any shadow of doubt, the 38th Constitutional Amendment Act, 1975 amended the Constitution by adding clause 5 to Article 352 which declared that the "satisfaction" of the President mentioned in Article 352 "shall be final and conclusive" and "shall not be questioned in any court on any ground".

[6] AIR 1974 SC 806.

ii. However, the 44th Constitutional Amendment Act repealed Article 352(5). The position has thus been restored to what it was before the 38th amendment. In *Minerva Mills Ltd. Vs. Union of India*[7], Justice Bhagwati held that there is no bar to judicial review of the validity of a proclamation of emergency issued by the President under Article 352. If the President while proclaiming emergency has acted outside his powers, or his satisfaction is *absurd, perverse, or mala fide,* or wholly based on extraneous conditions and irrelevant grounds, then it would be liable to be challenged before a court of law.

Consequences of Proclamation of Emergency[8]

The following drastic consequences follow from the issue of the proclamation of emergency under Article 352 :

i. **Centre-State Legislative Relations :** The normal fabric of the Centre-State relations undergoes a fundamental change. Parliament becomes empowered to make a law with respect to any matter in the State List, and such a law operates till six months after the proclamation ceases to operate. In other words, a law enacted by Parliament during an emergency in the exclusive State sphere (List II) ceases to exist six months after the emergency comes to an end. This means that six months after the ending of the emergency, the normal scheme of distribution of legislative powers is fully restored. Thus, the normal peace-time distribution of legislative powers is practically suspended so far as Parliament is concerned. The State Legislatures continue to function as usual and may make any law in their assigned area, i.e., List II and List III, but Parliament becomes empowered to legislate even in the exclusive State sphere (List II) as a result of the proclamation of emergency.

ii. **Center–State Executive Power :** During the operation of a proclamation of Emergency, the executive power of the Union extends to giving directions to any State as to the manner in which the executive power of the state is to be exercised. Since Parliament can make a law even in the exclusive State field, it means that it can give directions even in the area normally allotted to the States.

Further, the Parliament can confer powers and impose duties upon the Centre or its officers and authorities even though the law pertains to a matter not in the Union List.

Moreover, the 42nd Constitutional Amendment Act, provided that when emergency is declared not in the whole of India but only in a part of India, the executive power of the Centre to give directions, and the power of the Parliament to make laws as mentioned above, can be extended not only to the State in which the emergency is in force but also to any State other than the State where emergency is in force.

iii. **Centre-State financial Powers :** The President may, while a proclamation of emergency is in operation, by an order, alter the financial arrangement between the State and the Union as provided in Articles 268 to 279 (Distribution of revenue between the Union and the States). Every such order is to be laid before each House of the Parliament and will come to an end by the end of the financial year in which the proclamation of emergency ceases to operate.

---

[7] Air 1980 SC 1789.

[8] *Indian Constitutional Law*, M.P. Jain, Eighth Edition, Lexis Nexis, Pg No. 731.

During an emergency, Parliament can also levy any tax which ordinarily falls in the State List. Thus, although the State Governments continue to operate during emergency, the Central Government becomes omnipotent and the normal distribution of legislative, executive, and taxing powers, and the scheme of distribution of revenue between the Centre and the States, all are undone so far as the Centre is concerned. The reason is that during an emergency, the Central financial needs become greater than its peace-time commitments and, therefore, the normal financial arrangements between the Centre and the States cannot continue to function.

(a) **Extension of life of Lok Sabha :** While the proclamation of emergency is in operation, the Parliament may, by law, extend the life of the Lok Sabha beyond its normal life of five years of the Lok Sabha by a year each time up to a period not exceeding beyond six months after the proclamation ceases to operate.

(b) **Extension of life of State Legislative Assembly :** Parliament may, by law, extend the life of the State Legislature by one year each time during an emergency, subject to a maximum period of six months after the emergency ceases to operate.

(c) **Suspension of Fundamental Rights :** Emergency has a debilitating effect on the rights of the people in a democratic country. For example, in the USA, which has constitutionally guaranteed Fundamental Rights comparable to those in India, the privilege of the writ of *habeas corpus* can be suspended when in case of rebellion or invasion, and public interest requires it. No other Fundamental Right can be suspended in the USA, but during extraordinary situations, courts do give somewhat restrictive interpretation to these rights than they do during the normal days.

In Britain, during the two World Wars, drastic discretionary powers were conferred on the Executive to interfere with the rights of property and liberty of the people. This drastic interference with people's rights received judicial sanction in several cases. The theory is that when the country is engaged in a war of survival, the people have to sacrifice their rights to some extent so that the State may live. If the State goes down, the people also go down[9].

Effect of Article 352 (National Emergency) on Fundamental Rights

In India, a proclamation of emergency under Article 352 affects the Fundamental Rights of the people very drastically due to the following :

i. **Suspension of Article 19 :** Under Article 358, before the 44th Constitutional Amendment Act, 1978, there was an automatic suspension of Article 19 as soon as an emergency was declared under Article 352. In other words, if the Legislature made a law or the Executive committed acts which are inconsistent with or violating the Fundamental Rights guaranteed by Article 19, their validity cannot be challenged in the courts either during the continuance of the emergency, or even thereafter. As soon as the proclamation ceased to operate, the legislative enactments passed, and the executive action taken, during the course of the said emergency becomes inoperative to the extent that they are in conflict with Article 19. However, the 44th Amendment Act added two safeguards to Article 358. First, Article 19 will be suspended only when a proclamation of emergency is declared on the grounds of war or external aggression and not when emergency is declared on the ground of armed rebellion. Secondly, Article 358 will only protect emergency

[9]Wade & Bradley, *Constitutional Law*, Page Nos 716–25.

laws or executive action under those emergency laws from being challenged in a court of law and not other laws which are not related to the emergency. Prior to this, the validity of even other laws, which are not related to emergency, could not be challenged under Article 358.

ii. **Suspension of other Fundamental Rights :** Under Article 359 as it stood prior to 1978, the enforcement of all Fundamental Rights (other than Article 19 which is the subject matter of Article 358), could be suspended during an emergency by an executive order. Under Article 359, Fundamental Rights as such are not suspended; what is suspended is their enforcement. In other words, under Article 359, the Fundamental Rights are "theoretically alive" but what gets affected is their enforcement or the liberty to file a case or approach the court for their violation. When a proclamation of emergency is in operation, the President could, by an order, declare that the right to move any court for the enforcement of any Fundamental Right "shall remain suspended for the period during which the proclamation is in force or for such shorter period as may be specified in the order". For instance, when the emergency was proclaimed in 1962 in the wake of a conflict between India and China, the President issued an order suspending the right to move any Court to enforce Articles 14, 21, and 22. In 1975, when emergency was declared on the grounds of internal disturbance, a Presidential Order was issued suspending Article 14. But to curtail the vast power vested in the executive, the 44th Amendment has made two significant changes in Article 359. Firstly, it provides that under Article 359, the President does not have the power to suspend the enforcement of the Fundamental Rights guaranteed in Articles 20 and 21 of the Constitution. Secondly, the laws not related to the emergency or the executive action not related to emergency laws can be challenged in a court of law even during emergency. Thus, laws other than those passed for the purpose of the emergency will no longer be protected by the Presidential Order issued under Article 359.

Difference between Article 358 and 359

Supreme Court in *Makhan Singh Vs. State of Punjab*[10], while construing Article 359, compared the provisions of Articles 358 and 359:

- Under Article 358, as soon as the emergency is proclaimed, Article 19 gets suspended. There is no automatic suspension of Fundamental Rights under Article 359. Under Article 359, the rights are not suspended, but the citizens are deprived of their rights to move any court for their enforcement. Article 359 merely authorizes the President to issue an order declaring that the right to move any court remains suspended if the Fundamental Rights mentioned in the Presidential Order are violated.
- Article 358 suspends or is limited only to Article 19. Whereas, Article 359 can be applied to all the Fundamental Rights, except Articles 20 and 21.
- While the suspension of Article 19 under Article 358 applies to the whole of the country and so covers all legislatures and States, the order under Article 352(1) may extend to the whole of India or may be confined to any part of the territory of India. Whereas Article 359 may extend to the entire country or a part of it depending on the Presidential Order.
- Article 358 can be invoked only when the emergency is proclaimed on the grounds of war or external aggression (External Emergency) and it cannot be invoked on the grounds of armed rebellion (Internal Emergency). Whereas, Article 359 can be invoked irrespective on which grounds the emergency has been declared.

---

[10]AIR 1964 SC 381.

- While the suspension of Article 19 under Article 359 continues for the entire period of the emergency, the suspension of the right to move any court for the violation of Fundamental Rights can be declared for the entire period of emergency, or for a shorter period, as specified by the Presidential Order.
- Article 358 provides immunity to the legislative action and execution action for violating Article 19 whereas Article 359 provides immunity to the legislative action and executive action for violating those Fundamental Rights whose enforcement is suspended by the Presidential Order. However, both under Article 358 as well as under 359, the legislative or executive action will get the above said immunity from being challenged only if the actions/laws are related to emergency and not otherwise.

Invocation of Article 352

Article 352 has been invoked three times so far. A proclamation of emergency was issued under Article 352, for the first time, in 1962, in the wake of the conflict with China. It remained in force during the Indo-Pakistan conflict in 1965, and was revoked in January, 1968. Emergency was proclaimed again in December 1971, as a result of the Indo-Pakistan dispute, on the grounds of external aggression. While the 1971 proclamation was still effective, another proclamation was issued on 26th June 1975. This time, the proclamation was issued on the grounds of "Internal disturbance" threatening the security of India. Both these proclamation were revoked in March 1977. Thus, from June 1975 to March 1977, two emergency proclamations were in force simultaneously. The proclamation of 1975 on the grounds of internal disturbance proved to be the most controversial. There was violation of the Fundamental Rights of the people on a large scale, drastic press censorship was imposed, and a large number of persons were put in preventive detention. The general public perception was that issuing of this proclamation amounted to misuse of power on the part of the Central Government. The public reaction to the proclamation was so intense that when general elections were held after the revocation of the proclamation in 1977, the Congress Party, which was responsible for the proclamation, lost its majority and the Janata Government came to power. The Janata Government appointed the Shah Commission to probe into the circumstances which led to the declaration of the emergency in 1975. This Commission in its report held that there was no evidence of any circumstances which could justify the imposition of the emergency The Janata Government accepted the observations and findings of the commission and amended Article 352 by the 44th Constitutional Amendment Act, to introduce some more safeguards and to ensure that what happened in 1975 is not repeated in future.

PRESIDENT'S RULE

Centre's Duty to Protect the States[11]

Article 355 imposes a two-fold duty on the Centre :

i. To protect every State against external aggression and internal disturbance, and
ii. To ensure that the government of every State is carried on in accordance with the provisions of the Constitution.

[11] *Indian Constitutional Law*, M.P. Jain, Eighth Edition, LexisNexis, Pg No. 730.

The two limbs of Article 355 are not interdependent as constitutional breakdown can take place in a State even without there being a situation of "external aggression" or "internal disturbance".

i. **To protect every State against external aggression and internal disturbance :** A provision of this type is to be found in other federal constitutions as well. The American Constitution places a duty on the Central Government to protect a State against invasion, and, on application of the State against domestic violence. The Australian Constitution also provides in express terms that the Centre shall protect every State against invasion, and, on application of the State against domestic violence. However, there is an important distinction between American and Australian provisions on one hand and the Indian provision on the other. In case of America and Australia, the State shall apply to the Centre for necessary protection against domestic violence. Whereas, in India, there is no such condition laid down. Protecting the States under Article 355 does not require any request from the State to the Centre, especially to send the forces into a State to counter the breakdown of law and order therein.

ii. **Government of every State is carried on in accordance with the provisions of the Constitution** : Article 355 also imposes another duty on the Centre, i.e., to "ensure that the government of every State is carried on in accordance with the provisions of the Constitution". This provision stipulates, in essence, that the form of the government prescribed in the Constitution must be maintained in the States. It is in fulfillment of this obligation that the Centre takes over the government of a State under Article 356 in case of breakdown of the Constitutional machinery therein. A parallel provision is to be found in the American Constitution which places the Centre under a duty to maintain the republican form of the government in each State, or in the Australian Constitution which provides that the central executive power extends to the execution and maintenance of the Constitution. There is, however, no specific provision in any of the two (USA and Australia) federal constitutions enabling the Centre to take over the government of a State in case of breakdown of the constitutional machinery therein.

Proclamation of President's Rule for Failure of Constitutional Machinery in States[12]

President's Rule refers to the suspension of a State Government and the imposition of direct rule of the Centre. The central government takes direct control of the State in question. Article 356 of the Constitution of India gives the President of India the power to impose this rule on a State on the advice of the Union Council of Ministers. Article 356 provides that if the President, on receipt of a report from the Governor of a State or otherwise is satisfied that a situation has arisen in which the government of the State cannot be carried on in accordance with the provisions of the Constitution, he may issue a proclamation. Thus, under Article 356, the President acts on a report of the Governor or on information received otherwise. However, the Governor makes his report under Article 356 in his discretion. On the

[12]Article 356, is inspired by section 93 of the Government of India Act, 1935. (Section 93 of the 1935 Act provided that if a Governor of a province was satisfied that a situation has arisen in which the government of the province cannot be carried on in accordance with the provisions of the said Act, he could, by proclamation, assume to himself all or any of the powers vested in or exercisable by a provincial body or authority including the Ministry and the Legislature and to discharge those functions in his discretion). Even though Article 356 was patterned upon the controversial section 93 of the 1935 Act with this difference that instead of the Governor, the President is vested with the said power.

face of it, it may seem to be somewhat incongruous that the Governor, who as the constitutional head of the State, acts on the aid and advice of his Ministers, also reports against them to the President. This is a case of the Governor reporting against his own government. But, under the Constitution, the Governor has a dual capacity – he is the constitutional head as well as the Centre's representative in the State. He is appointed by the President and he takes oath to preserve, protect, and defend the Constitution. It is this obligation which requires him to report to the President when the State government is not being carried on in accordance with the constitutional provisions and which, as the constitutional head, he is not able to check.

By that proclamation under Article 356 :

i. The President may assume to himself all or any of the powers vested in or exercisable by the Governor to any body or authority in the State.
ii. The President may declare that the powers of the Legislature of the State shall be exercised by or under the authority of the Parliament.
iii. The President may make such incidental and consequential provisions as may appear to him to be necessary or desirable for giving effect to the object of proclamation, including suspending in whole or in part, the operation of any provisions of this Constitution relating to any body or authority in the State. The President cannot, however, assume to himself, any of the powers vested in the High Court or suspend the operation of any provisions of the Constitution relating to the High Court.

Proclamation of President's Rule for not Complying with the Directions Given by the Centre

When any State disobeys or does not comply with any directions given by the Union, it will be lawful for the President to hold that a situation has arisen in which the government of the State cannot be carried on in accordance with the provisions of the Constitution. On the President taking such a decision, the provisions of Article 356 will come into operation. Thus, Article 365 can be invoked only if –

- Any direction is given by the Union in the valid exercise of its executive power under any of the provisions of the Constitution; and
- Such direction has not been complied with or given effect by the States.

Procedure to be Followed at the Time of Proclamation under Article 356

i. Every proclamation issued under Article 356 shall be laid before each House of Parliament and shall remain in operation for "two months" unless before the expiry of that period, it has been approved by both Houses of the Parliament by passing a resolution of simple majority. Any such proclamation may be revoked or varied by a subsequent proclamation.
ii. If at the time of issuing the proclamation, or thereafter, the Lok Sabha is dissolved without approving it, and if the Rajya Sabha approves the proclamation, then it ceases to operate thirty days after the date on which the Lok Sabha first sits after the general elections, unless a resolution approving the proclamation is passed by it before that period.

iii. If the proclamation is approved by the Parliament, it will remain in operation for "six months". Parliament may extend the duration of proclamation for "six months" at a time, but no such proclamation shall in any case remain in force for more than three years. After the expiry of the maximum period of three years, neither the Parliament nor the President shall have power to continue the proclamation and the constitutional machinery must be restored to the State.

iv. Thus, the proclamation issued under Article 356 expires in any of the following scenarios –

- The date on which the President issues a proclamation of revocation;
- After two months of its making if it is not presented for approval before both Houses of the Parliament;
- Even before two months, if the proclamation on presentation to the Houses of Parliament fails to get approval from the Houses;
- After 6 months from the date of the proclamation, in case no further resolution is passed by the House of Parliament after the passage of the initial resolution approving the said proclamation.
- After the expiry of 6 months from the passage of the last resolution of approval passed by the two Houses of Parliament subject to an overall maximum limit of 3 years from the date of proclamation.

Restraints Regarding Proclamation Under Article 356

44th Constitutional Amendment Act, 1978 was an amendment Act which introduced a new provision to put restraint on the power of the Parliament to extend a proclamation issued under Article 356 beyond one year. No House of Parliament is to pass a resolution approving continuance of such a proclamation beyond one year unless the following two conditions are satisfied:

- There is a proclamation of National Emergency in operation at the time of passing of such a resolution in the whole of India, or the concerned State, or a part of the State; and
- The Election Commission certifies that the continuance in force of the proclamation under Article 356 during the period specified in such resolution is necessary on account of difficulties in holding general elections to the concerned State Legislative Assembly.

Thus, the effect of the 44th amendment Act is that normally a proclamation under Article 356 remains in force in a State for one year at the most, but, under special circumstances mentioned above, it can remain in force up to three years which is the maximum upper limit.

Consequences of Invoking Article 356

i. **Legislative powers of the State :** The powers of the State Legislature are to be exercised by or under the authority of Parliament. Parliament can then confer on the President the power of the State Legislature to make laws. The President may also be authorized by the Parliament to delegate the power so conferred on him, to any other authority specified by him, subject to such conditions as he may impose. Parliament being a busy body finds it extremely burdensome to itself exercise the legislative power for the concerned State, and pass all the legislative measures needed for the State concerned. Therefore, Parliament passes an Act and delegates the legislative power for the State concerned for the duration of the emergency to the President, i.e., Central Executive. The life of the law made by Parliament or the President during the operation of President's Rule is not co-terminus with the subsistence of the proclamation. The law does not come to an end automatically as soon as the proclamation is revoked. In other words, the law made by the Parliament or the President during President's Rule shall continue to remain in force until they are altered or repealed by the State Legislature.

ii. **Confer powers or duties upon the Union Officers :** A law made during the President's Rule by the Parliament or the President, or the authority in which the power to make laws are vested, may confer powers and impose duties upon the Union officers or authorities.

iii. **Consolidated Fund of the State :** The President may authorize, when the Lok Sabha is not in session, expenditure from the State Consolidated Fund pending its sanction by the Parliament.

iv. **Life of the Legislative Assembly :** During the President's Rule, the President can assume the powers of the Governor. One of the Governor's powers is to dissolve the Legislative Assembly. Consequently, when the President issues a proclamation and assumes the Governor's powers, the power to dissolve the Assembly and hold fresh elections is automatically transferred to the President. But it is not mandatory to dissolve the State Legislature whenever President's Rule is imposed. Several times, the State Legislature has been kept in suspended animation rather than dissolving it.

v. **Executive Powers of the State :** As mentioned earlier, the President may assume to himself all or any functions of the State government and all or any of the powers exercisable by the Governor. Usually, the President, after assumption of the powers of the State government, exercises these powers through the State Governor. The administration of the State, during the President's Rule is carried on by the State Governor as a delegate of the Centre.

vi. **Fundamental Rights :** The Fundamental Rights of the people in the concerned State does not get affected due to the President's Rule. During the President's Rule, only the administration and relation between the Centre and the State concerned gets affected. President's Rule has nothing to do with the individual rights of the citizens.

Invocation of Article 356

When the Constituent Assembly discussed the need to incorporate the Article 356 in the Constitution, strong opposition to it was put forth by some members and it was argued that if power was given to the Centre to intervene, there was a possibility of it "being abused or used for political purposes." But it was hoped by Dr. B.R. Ambedkar that "*such Articles will never be called into operationand that they would remain a dead letter.*" However, this Article has been invoked many times during the last seven decades. Since 1950, the President's Rule has been proclaimed for 132 times in various States/Union Territories, i.e., on an average, twice a year. Many times, the President's Rule was imposed unlawfully in various States for political reasons and vested interests. According to the critics, the first use of Article 356 was itself a great misuse. The Congress Party, unhappy with Punjab Chief Minister Gopi Chand Bhargava in 1951, dismissed him even though he enjoyed a majority in the assembly. There was significant misuse of Article 356. Unfortunately, however, it so happened that over the years, the Centre has not always kept in mind the concept of co-operative federalism or the spirit and object with which the Article was enacted while dealing with the States and has indeed grossly abused the power under Article 356 on many occasions. One should not forget what was affirmed by Dr. B.R. Ambedkar. In the words of Dr. B.R. Ambedkar, the "States are 'Supreme' or 'Sovereign' in the field allotted to them and that notwithstanding a bias in favour of the Centre in our Constitution, ours is a federation – that too a democratic federation".

The number of times Article 356 has been invoked in each state so far

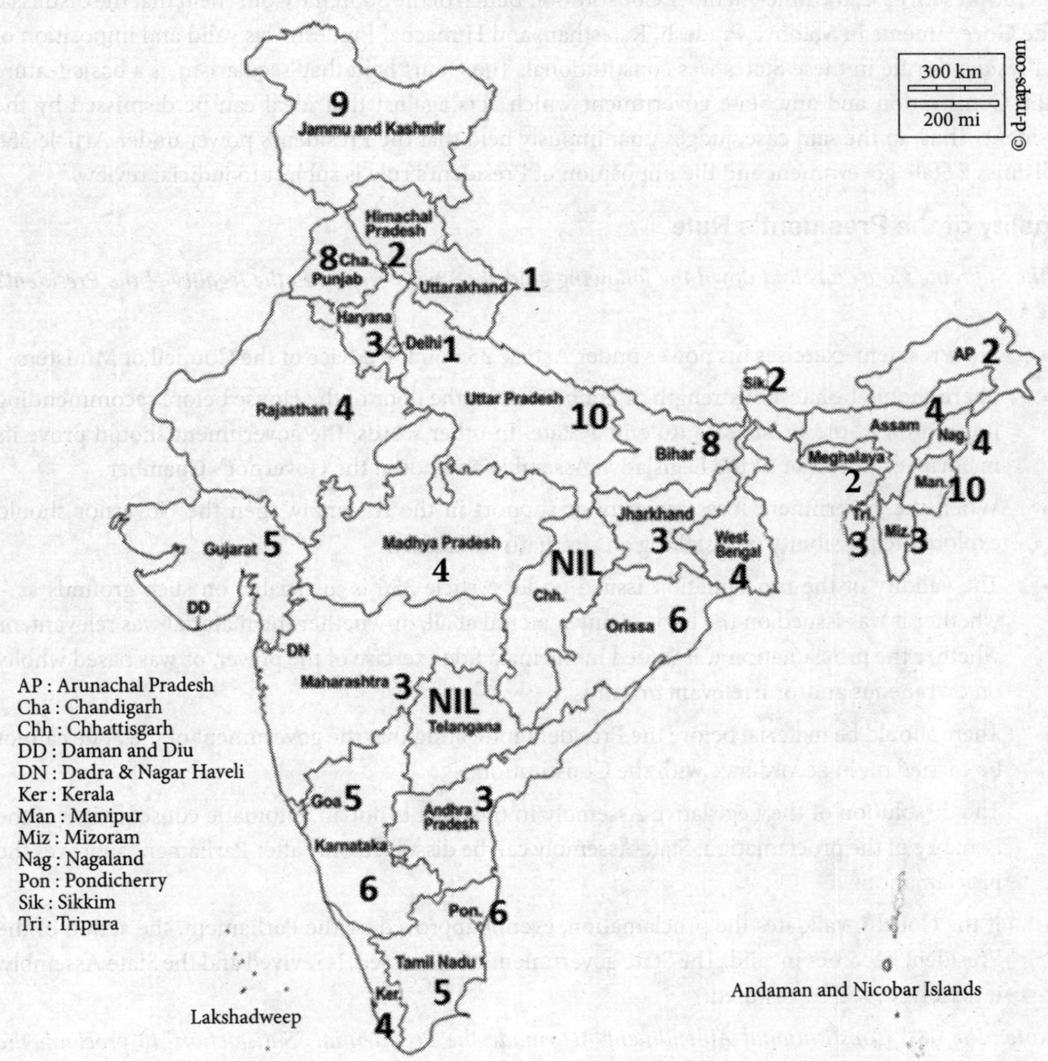

Judicial Review of President's Rule

In *S.R. Bommai Vs. Union of India*[13], all the judges unanimously held that the exercise of power under Article 356 was subject to judicial review. Satisfaction of the President to impose the President's Rule must be formed on relevant materials. It could be stuck down by the court if it was based on wholly irrelevant or extraneous grounds. The action could also be struck down if it was found to be mala fide. The President is under an obligation to produce the material on which the action under Article 356 is based. The court could not go into the correctness of the material or its adequacy, but it could see whether it was relevant to the action.

In the present case, the nine-member Constitution Bench of the Supreme Court held that the dismissal of the Governments in Madhya Pradesh, Rajasthan, and Himachal Pradesh was valid and imposition of the President's rule in these States was constitutional. The Court held that 'secularism' is a basic feature of the Constitution and any State government which acts against that ideal can be dismissed by the President. Thus, in the said case, judges unanimously held that the President's power under Article 356 to dismiss a State government and the imposition of President's rule is subject to judicial review.

Legality of the President's Rule

The Supreme Court has laid down the following guidelines with respect to the legality of the President's Rule :

- The President exercises his power under Article 356 on the advice of the Council of Ministers.
- There should be a test of strength or confidence on the floor of the House before recommending imposition of the President's Rule in a State. In other words, the government should prove its majority on the floor of the Legislative Assembly and not in the Governor's Chamber.
- When the government loses majority or support in the Assembly, then the Governor should explore the possibility of installing an alternative Ministry.
- The validity of the proclamation issued under Article 356 is justiciable on such grounds as – whether it was issued on the basis of any material at all, or whether the material was relevant, or whether the proclamation was issued in the mala fide exercise of the power, or was based wholly on extraneous and/or irrelevant grounds.
- There should be material before the President indicating that the government of the State cannot be carried on in accordance with the Constitution.
- The dissolution of the Legislative Assembly in the State is not an automatic consequence of the issuance of the proclamation. State Assembly can be dissolved only after Parliament approves the proclamation.
- If the Court invalidates the proclamation, even if approved by the Parliament, the action of the President becomes invalid. The State government, if dismissed, is revived and the State Assembly, if dissolved, will be restored.

***Note:** The 38th Constitutional Amendment Act, made the Presidential "Satisfaction" to proclaim the President's Rule as final and conclusive and not subjected to judicial review. However, the above said amendment has been deleted by the 44th Constitutional Amendment Act, 1978. Thus, the Presidential 'satisfaction' or the declaration of financial emergency is subjected to judicial review.*

---

[13](1994) 3SCC 1.

Instances of Proper and Improper Grounds for the Application of Article 356[14]

Proper Application of Article 356	Improper Application of Article 356
Where a Ministry having resigned, the Governor finds it impossible to form an alternative government.	Where after the resignation of a Chief Minister, or after the dismissal of the Ministry on losing the majority support in the Assembly, the Governor recommends dissolution under Article 356 without probing the possibility of the formation of an alternative government.
Where, after election, no party is able to secure a working majority in the Legislative Assembly.	If the dissolution of a State Assembly is sought on the grounds that the Chief Minister belongs to a particular caste or creed[15].
Gross mismanagement of the affairs of a State Government, or abuse of its powers.	A duly constituted Ministry, so long as it enjoys the support of the Assembly, cannot be revoked under Article 356, merely for the sake of securing a good government.
Where a State Government fails to comply with the directions issued by the Union even after warning (Article 365).	Every non-compliance with a particular provision of the Constitution, however does not call for exercise under Article 356. The non-compliance shall be such as to give rise to such a situation where the government of the State cannot be carried on in accordance with the provisions of the Constitution.
When a new State is created as a result of territorial reorganization and there is no legislature for such State until election is held, therefore, resort may be had to Article 356, as a stop-gap arrangement.	The Union Government cannot dismiss a duly elected State Government on the sole grounds that the ruling party in State is different from the ruling party in the Centre.

Differenece Between Article 352 & 356[16]

Article 352	Article 356
Proclaimed on the grounds of war, external aggression, or armed rebellion.	Proclaimed when the constitutional machinery of the State fails.
Under Article 352, the Centre cannot suspend the Legislature/Constitution in a State. The State Governments and Legislatures continue to function normally and exercise the powers assigned to them under the Constitution.	Under Article 356, the State Legislatures ceases to function as it is either dissolved or kept in suspended animation.
The Centre gets concurrent powers of legislation in State matters and thus, it can make the States follow a uniform all-India policy.	Laws for the State are made by Parliament and the Governor administers the State on behalf of the President.
Affects Fundamental Rights	No effect on Fundamental Rights

[14]Durga Das Basu, *Shorter Constitution of India*, Volume 2, 16th Edition, LexisNexis, Pg Nc. 2285.

[15]*State of Rajasthan Vs. UOI*, AIR 1977 SC 1361.

[16]*Indian Constitutional Law*, M.P. Jain, Eighth Edition, LexisNexis, Pg No. 730.

The relationship of all the States with the Centre undergoes a change	The relationship of only one State (where the action is taken) with the Centre is affected.
Proclamation has to be approved by Parliament within a month and thereafter every six months, but there is no maximum duration prescribed for the operation of such a proclamation.	Proclamation has to be approved by the Parliament within two months, and thereafter every six months, and the maximum period for which it can be remain in force is three years.
The proclamation of emergency can be revoked by initiating a resolution in Lok Sabha.	The proclamation of President's Rule cannot be revoked by initiating a resolution in Lok Sabha. It can be revoked only by the Central Executive.

FINANCIAL EMERGENCY

Article 360 provides for financial emergency.

(a) **Proclamation of Financial Emergency :** The President can proclaim financial emergency if he is satisfied that a situation has arisen whereby the financial stability or credit of India or of any part thereof is threatened. The satisfaction of the President is not his personal satisfaction. He has to act upon the advice of the Prime Minister and the Council of Ministers.

(b) **Procedure for proclamation of emergency :** The proclamation of financial emergency shall cease to be in operation at the expiry of two months unless it has been approved by both Houses of Parliament. But if the Lok Sabha is dissolved during the period of two months and resolution is approved by the Rajya Sabha, but not by the Lok Sabha, the proclamation shall cease to operate at the expiry of 30 days from the date on which the new Lok Sabha sits, unless before the expiry of 30 days a resolution approving proclamation is passed by the Lok Sabha. Such a proclamation may be revoked or varied by the President by a subsequent proclamation.

(c) **Consequences of proclamation of Emergency :** During the period of financial emergency, the executive authority of the Union shall extend to –

- Giving direction to any State to observe such canons of financial propriety which are deemed necessary for maintaining financial stability and credit of the State.
- Directing the States as may be required by the Union to reduce the salaries and allowances of all or any class of persons employed by the State.
- Directing the States to reserve all money or financial bills for consideration of the President after they are passed by the legislature of the State.
- Giving such other directions to any State as the President may deem necessary and adequate for the purpose.
- The President can issue directions for the reduction of salaries and allowances of all or any class of persons serving the Union, including Judges of the Supreme Court and the High Courts.

Thus, the proclamation of financial emergency increases the supervision of the Centre on the States in financial matters. Perhaps, the framers of the Constitution adopted the idea of underlying Article 360 from the experiences of the federations of the USA, Canada, and Australia during the Depression of the 1930's when the Central Government found itself very much handicapped in taking effective action to meet the situation. In fact, the argument given in the Constituent Assembly to support this constitutional provision was that during the Depression, the US legislature had passed the National Industrial Recovery

Act which was declared unconstitutional by the Supreme Court (it was declared invalid because the President was conferred wide legislative and financial powers by the Legislature/Congress), and the Central Government of India should not face such situation while coping with the economic crises. Thus, the Government of India can take effective action under Article 360 whenever an occasion arises for the same. However, till now, neither has such an occasion arisen, nor has Article 360 been invoked.

The 38th Constitutional Amendment Act made the Presidential 'satisfaction' to declare the financial emergency as final and conclusive and not subjected to judicial review. However, the above said amendment has been deleted by the 44th Constitutional Amendment Act, 1978. Thus, the Presidential 'satisfaction' or the declaration of financial emergency is subjected to judicial review.

SUMMING UP OF EMERGENCY PROVISIONS

Points For Comparison	National Emergency	President's Rule	Financial Emergency
Articles enabling the proclamation.	Article 352	Article 356 and 365	Article 360
Grounds for declaration	War, Armed rebellion, and External aggression.	Failure of Constitutional machinery; Not complying with the directions given by the Centre.	Threat to financial stability or credit facility
Parliamentary Approval	Must be approved by both the Houses within One month	Must be approved by both the Houses within Two months.	Must be approved by both the Houses within Two months
Majority required	Special Majority	Simple Majority	Simple Majority
Time period	Continues for 6 months; with periodical approval (every 6 months); can be extended for an indefinite period	Continues for 6 months; with periodical approval (every 6 months); can be extended for a maximum period of One year	Once approved continues for an indefinite period without any periodical approval from the Parliament
Revocation	President or the resolution can be initiated by the Lok Sabha.	Only President	Only President

QUESTIONS

Objective Questions

1. Consider the following statements with regard to National Emergency:
   1. National emergency can be imposed by the President when the country is threatened by war or external aggression or internal disturbance.
   2. During the National Emergency, Fundamental Rights under Articles 19 and 22 are suspended automatically.

Which of the statements given above is/are correct?

(a) 1 only (b) 2 only

(c) Both 1 and 2 (d) Neither 1 nor 2

Ans : (d)

2. In the context of Indian federalism during Emergency, consider the following statements:
   1. Parliament can dissolve the Legislative Assembly of a State.
   2. Parliament can legislate on the State List.
   3. Centre can give directions to any State with respect to the executive power.

   Which of the statements given above is/are correct?

   (a) 1 and 2 only (b) 3 only

   (c) 2 and 3 only (d) 1, 2, and 3

   Ans: (d)

3. Consider the following statements about Emergency Provisions:
   1. All types of emergency proclaimed by the President have to be approved by the Parliament.
   2. In the case of National emergency, Parliamentary approval must be given within 1 month from the date of proclamation.
   3. The proclamation of Financial emergency remains in operation for 6 months.

   Which of the statements given above is/are correct?

   (a) 1 only (b) 1 and 2 only

   (c) 2 and 3 only (d) 1, 2 and 3

   Ans: (b)

4. Which of the following can be invoked or affected when the President's Rule is imposed in a State?
   i. The President can authorize expenditure from the Consolidated Fund of the State.
   ii. The President can assume the powers of the High Court of the State.
   iii. The President can declare that the powers of the Legislature of the State shall be exercised by the Parliament.
   iv. The President can suspend the operation of any provision of the Constitution relating to a body or authority in the State if he feels it desirable to do so for attaining the objectives of the emergency.

   Which of the statements given above are correct?

   (a) Only i and iii (b) Only i, iii, and iv

   (c) Only iii and iv (d) All of the above

   Ans: (b)

5. Financial Emergency is declared under –

   (a) Article 365 (b) Article 356

   (c) Article 360 (d) Article 355

   Ans: (c)

CHAPTER 23

OFFICIAL LANGUAGE

India is a multilingual country. Multilingual nations share a common feature of having an official language. An official language is a language that is declared by a country's government, with legal backing.

INTRODUCTION: PRE-CONSTITUTIONAL SCENARIO

On achieving independence, India was confronted with the issue of having an official language for the Union. For a long time, the administration in India was in English under the British rule. The Constituent Assembly had the task of determining whether to continue functioning in the same way for official work or to abandon it for a different language, mainly Hindi. Since the people in the southern states were more confident in English than they were in the most spoken language in India, i.e., Hindi[1], the provisions in the Constitution attempted to represent a compromise between the conflicting views held by the Hindi enthusiasts and others.

CONSTITUTIONAL PROVISIONS RELATING TO THE OFFICIAL LANGUAGE

According to Article 343 :

- Hindi written in Devanagiri script is to be the 'official language' of the Union. The reason for designating Hindi as the 'official' and not the 'national' language, is that not only Hindi but all regional languages are regarded as the national, and not foreign languages[2].
- However, for a period of 15 years (till 1965) from the commencement of the Constitution, the English language shall continue to be used for all the official purposes of the Union. The Constitution does not, however, regard the 15-year period as the final deadline. Some flexibility has been introduced in the arrangement. According to Article 343, the Parliament has the power to permit the use of the English language beyond the 15-year period for some or all official purposes of the Union.
- The form of numerals to be used for the official purposes of the Union shall be the international form of Indian numerals.

---

[1]https://lexlife.in/2020/06/12/official-language-act-1963/

[2]M.P. Jain, *Indian Constitutional Law*, P. 823.

Intergovernmental Communication

According to Article 346, the official language of the Union authorised for the time being, (i.e., English) shall be the official language for communication between one State and another and between a State and the Union, although two or more States may agree to have Hindi as the Official language for communication amongst them.

Official Language of States

According to Article 345, the legislature of a State can adopt Hindi or one or more languages in use in the State as its official language. Until, the legislature adopts an official language by law, the English language shall be continued to be used for those official purposes within the State for which it was being used before the commencement of the Constitution.

Development of Hindi

Article 351 places the Central Government under an obligation to take steps to promote the spread and development of Hindi. In order to develop Hindi, sources should be drawn primarily from Sanskrit and from other languages of India specified in the Eighth Schedule, for new words necessary to develop and enrich Hindi.

Language of Law and Courts

India has a unified judicial system and there exists a basic unity in the laws prevailing in the country. The problem of the language of the law thus assumes a special significance. Difficulties would arise in the functioning of the Supreme Court if the High Court were to adopt different languages. Similarly, problems would arise in regard to the language of the legislation, as it would be difficult to interpret the law enacted in a State in its own official language by the Supreme Court. Therefore, in order to establish a basic unity in the language of the law and courts throughout the country, the Constitution under Article 348 provides that:

- Until Parliament otherwise provides, the proceedings in the Supreme Court and in a High Court are to be in the English language.
- The State Governor, with the previous consent of the President, may authorise the High Court to use Hindi or any other language in its proceedings. However, the judgements, decrees, or orders passed or made by the High Court shall be in English language. Therefore, the Constitution recognizes English as the primary language of the Supreme Court and the High Courts, with a condition that when some other language is used in the proceedings of High Courts, judgments of the High Courts must be delivered in English. Whereas, with respect to the Supreme Court the language shall be English only until the Parliament otherwise provides.
- Until the Parliament otherwise provides, all the Bills introduced, Acts passed by the Parliament or the State Legislature, and all ordinances promulgated by the President or the Governor of a State shall be in the English language. However, the State can prescribe use of any language, other than English, for purposes of Bills, Acts, or Ordinances. But a translation of the same in the English language shall be published in the Official Gazette.

Official Language Commission

Article 344 provides for the appointment of a Commission on Official Language by the President after five years of the commencement of the Constitution, and thereafter at the expiry of ten years from such commencement. The Commission shall comprise of a Chairman and such other members representing the various regional languages mentioned in the Eighth Schedule to the Constitution as the President may appoint. The Commission shall make recommendations on the following aspects:

- The progressive use of the Hindi language for the official purpose of the Union;
- Restrictions on the use of the English language for all or any of the Union's official purposes;
- The language to be used for proceedings in the Supreme Court, High Courts, and for Central and State legislations;
- Form of numerals to be used for the official purposes of the Union;
- Any other matter which the President may refer to it regarding the official language of the Union and the language of communication between the Union and a State, or between one State and another.

Further, according to Article 344, a Parliamentary Committee shall be constituted to examine the recommendations of the Official Language commission. The Parliamentary Committee shall consist of 30 members of which 20 shall be the members of the Lok Sabha and 10 shall be the members of the Rajya Sabha. The members of the Parliamentary Committee will be elected by way of proportional representation by single transferrable vote.

In furtherance of Article 344, the President appointed an Official Language Commission under the chairmanship of B.G. Kher in 1955. The Commission report was examined by a Parliamentary Committee under the chairmanship of Gobind Ballabh Pant. However, another Official Language Commission was not appointed in the year 1960.

CONSTITUTIONAL PROVISIONS RELATING TO LANGUAGES IN THE EIGHTH SCHEDULE[3]

The Constitutional provisions relating to the Eighth Schedule occur in Article 344(1) and 351 of the Constitution.

- Article 344(1) provides for the Constitution of a Commission by the President on expiration of five years from the commencement of the Constitution and thereafter at the expiration of ten years from such commencement, which shall consist of a Chairman and such other members representing the different languages specified in the Eighth Schedule to make recommendations to the President for the progressive use of Hindi for official purposes of the Union.
- Article 351 of the Constitution provides that it shall be the duty of the Union to promote the spread of the Hindi language to develop it so that it may serve as a medium of expression for all the elements of the composite culture of India and to secure its enrichment by assimilating without interfering with its genius, the forms, style, and expressions used in Hindustani and in the other languages of India specified in the Eighth Schedule, and by drawing, wherever necessary or desirable, for its vocabulary, primarily, on Sanskrit and secondarily on other languages.

It would thus appear that the Eighth Schedule was intended to promote the progressive use of Hindi and for the enrichment and promotion of that language. Therefore, a balance was established between Hindi and other regional languages granting equal status to all languages.

List of Languages in the Eighth Schedule

The Eighth Schedule to the Constitution consists of the following 22 languages:

(1) Assamese, (2) Bengali, (3) Gujarati, (4) Hindi, (5) Kannada, (6) Kashmiri, (7) Konkani, (8) Malayalam, (9) Manipuri, (10) Marathi, (11) Nepali, (12) Oriya, (13) Punjabi, (14) Sanskrit, (15) Sindhi, (16) Tamil, (17) Telugu, (18) Urdu (19) Bodo, (20) Santhali, (21) Maithili and (22) Dogri.

---

[3]https://www.mha.gov.in/sites/default/files/EighthSchedule_19052017.pdf

Of these languages, 14 were initially included in the Constitution. Sindhi language was added in 1967. Thereafter, three more languages viz., Konkani, Manipuri, and Nepali were included in 1992. Subsequently, Bodo, Dogri, Maithili, and Santhali were added in 2004.

Demands of Languages for Inclusion in the Eighth Schedule

At present, there are demands for inclusion of 38 more languages in the Eighth Schedule to the Constitution. These are:

(1) Angika, (2) Banjara, (3) Bazika, (4) Bhojpuri, (5) Bhoti, (6) Bhotia, (7) Bundelkhandi (8) Chhattisgarhi, (9) Dhatki, (10) English, (11) Garhwali (Pahari),(12) Gondi, (13) Gujjar/Gujjari (14) Ho, (15) Kachachhi, (16) Kamtapuri, (17) Karbi, (18) Khasi, (19) Kodava (Coorg), (20) Kok Barak, (21) Kumaoni (Pahari), (22) Kurak, (23) Kurmali, (24) Lepcha, (25) Limbu, (26) Mizo (Lushai), (27) Magahi, (28) Mundari, (29) Nagpuri, (30) Nicobarese, (31) Pahari (Himachali), (32) Pali, (33) Rajasthani, (34) Sambalpuri/Kosali, (35) Shaurseni (Prakrit), (36) Siraiki, (37) Tenyidi, and (38) Tulu.

Present Status on Inclusion of Languages in the Eighth Schedule

Government of India believes that - "As the evolution of dialects and languages is dynamic, influenced by socio-eco-political developments, it is difficult to fix any criterion for languages, whether to distinguish them from dialects, or for inclusion in the Eighth Schedule to the Constitution of India. Thus, both attempts, through the Pahwa (1996) and Sitakant Mohapatra (2003) Committees to evolve such fixed criteria have not borne fruit. The Government is conscious of the sentiments and requirements for inclusion of other languages in the Eighth Schedule and will examine the requests keeping in mind these sentiments, and other considerations such as evolution of dialects into language, widespread use of a language, etc."

STATUTORY PROVISIONS RELATING TO THE OFFICIAL LANGUAGE

The provisions mentioned in the Constitution failed to solve the language problem once for all. Therefore, in order to fulfil the aspirations of non-Hindi speaking people, the Official Languages Act, 1963 was passed.

- The Act provided that the English language will continue to be used in addition to Hindi even after the 15-year deadline, for all official purposes of the Union and for transaction of business in Parliament until all the non-Hindi speaking states agreed to the changeover.
- The English language is to be used for the purpose of communication between the Centre and non-Hindi State and Hindi State and non-Hindi State.
- If Hindi is used for communication between a Hindi and a non-Hindi State, then an English translation of the communication is to accompany the Hindi version.
- Both Hindi and the English languages are to be used for:

(i) Resolutions, rules, notifications, etc issued by the Central Government and the contracts, licences, etc. executed by the Central Government.

(ii) Reports and official papers laid before the Parliament.

The above discussed provisions of the Act would remain in force until resolutions for the discontinuance of the use of the English language have been passed by all the non-Hindi States and also by the two Houses of Parliament. In other words, the decision to continue English has now been left not to the legislatures of the Hindi-speaking States but to the legislatures of other States which have not adopted Hindi as their official language.

The Committee of Parliament on Official Language[4]

The Official Languages Act, 1963 provided for the setting up of a Committee on Official Language to review the progress made in the use of Hindi for the official purpose of the Union. This Committee was to be constituted after ten years of the promulgation of the Act. This Committee shall comprise of 30 members of Parliament, 20 from Lok Sabha and 10 from Rajya Sabha elected indirectly by way of proportional representation by single transferrable vote. This Committee was constituted for the first time in 1976 and later on reconstituted every time after the Lok Sabha polls till 2004.

Following are the powers and functions of the Committee:

- After the expiration of ten years from the date of commencement of the Act, there shall be constituted a Committee on Official Language, on a resolution to that effect being moved in either House of Parliament with the previous sanction of the President and passed by both Houses.
- It shall be the duty of the Committee to review the progress made in the use of Hindi for the Official purposes of the Union and submit a report to the President making recommendations thereon and the President shall cause the report to be laid before each House of Parliament and send it to all the State Governments.
- The President may, after consideration of the report submitted by the Committee and the views if any expressed by the State Government thereon, issue directions in accordance with the whole or any part of the report.
- The Chairman of the Committee is elected by the members of the Committee. As a convention, the Union Home Minister has been elected as Chairman of the Committee from time to time.
- The Committee is required to submit its report along with its recommendations to the President after reviewing the position regarding the use of Hindi in Central Government Offices on the basis of its observations.
- Further, in order to assess the use of Official Language for various purposes and other matters connected therewith, eminent persons from various fields such as from education, judiciary, voluntary organizations, and the Secretaries of the Ministries/Departments etc., are invited for oral evidence.

Medium of Education/Medium of Instruction

The Constitution did not prescribe any policy or principle, and did not make any provision regarding the medium of education or instruction. The matter was to left to the discretion of the legislatures.

Later on, the governments felt that too much stress on regional languages as medium of instructions may create a kind of isolationism in the country and weaken the channels of communication between the various language groups. To mitigate this difficulty the National Education Policy 2020 (NEP 2020) reiterated the three-language formula as was prescribed in the earlier Education Policy of 1968 and 1992 with certain changes.

---

[4]https://rajbhasha.nic.in/sites/default/files/cpolreport9-chapter1eng.pdf

Following are the provisions relating to the medium of instruction under NEP 2020:

- Wherever possible, the medium of instruction until at least Grade 5, but preferably till Grade 8 and beyond, will be the mother tongue/ local language/ home language/ regional language. Thereafter, the home/local language shall continue to be taught as a language wherever possible. This will be followed by both public and private schools.
- Even Section 29(1)(f) of the Right to Education Act, 2009 (RTE Act), provides that the "medium of instruction shall, as far as practicable, be in child's mother tongue", just like NEP 2020.
- Both NEP 2020 and RTE Act have made it desirable without making it mandatory to provide the medium of instruction in the mother tongue or local language, etc. According to Mr. K. Kasturirangan, (Chairman of the committee that recommended NEP 2020):

"There is no question of any imposition. This is a free country; education is a concurrent subject and states are free to decide on the matter. The policy does recommend mother tongue/local language/regional language as the medium of instruction as it is found best suited for better understanding and learning in children. However, nowhere is this binding."

CLASSICAL LANGUAGES

The concept of Classical languages is not provided in the Constitution. The same is created by the Central Government. Following are the criteria adopted by the Government to determine the eligibility of a language for granting classical language status:

- High antiquity of its early texts/ recorded history over a period of 1500–2000 years;
- A body of ancient literature/ texts, which is considered a valuable heritage by generations of speakers;
- The literary tradition be original and not borrowed from another speech community;
- The classical language and literature being distinct from modern, there may also be a discontinuity between the classical language and its later forms or its offshoots.

Current Classical Languages

Tamil was the first Classical Language of India. The government declared Tamil in 2004 and Sanskrit in 2005 as the Classical Languages. Later, the government declared Kannada (2008), Telugu (2008), Malayalam (2013), and Odia (2014) as the classical languages.

Once a language is notified as a Classical language, the Human Resource and Development Ministry provides certain benefits to promote it:

- Two major annual international awards for scholars of eminence in classical Indian languages are awarded;
- A Centre of Excellence for studies in Classical Languages is set up;
- The University Grants Commission is requested to create, to start with at least in the Central Universities, a certain number of Professional Chairs for the Classical Languages so declared;
- The University Grants Commission (UGC) also awards research projects for promoting these languages.

CHAPTER 24

ELECTION SYSTEM IN INDIA

"Remember, for your progress, for your welfare, your happiness, never fail to cast your vote in elections".

– Dr. A.P.J. Abdul Kalam

INTRODUCTION TO ELECTIONS

India is the largest democratic country in the world. Democracy is a government of the people. Fair elections, freedom of thought, expression, freedom of press, and independency of judiciary are the main pillars on which the edifice of democracy stands. Elections are the cornerstone of democracy. They lie at the heart of the democratic process. It is based on the popular will. In fact, democracy is based on the active and intelligent interest of the people in their national affairs. The voters come in the picture during an election because it is through elections that sovereignty of the people is institutionalized and realized. The process of elections is shouldered by the responsible executive authorities.

India has been characterised as the biggest democracy in the world because of the colossal nature of the elections held in the country. At a general election, an electorate of millions goes to the polls to elect members for the Lok Sabha, State Legislative Assemblies, and the Legislatures of the Union Territories. Thus, free and fair elections have been held to be a basic feature of the Constitution.

Fundamental Principles of Elections[1]

A few fundamental principles underlie elections to the Lok Sabha and the State Legislative Assemblies :

1. There is one general electoral roll for every territorial constituency (Article 325). The Constitution abolishes separate electorates and communal representation which divided the Indian people and retarded the growth of Indian nationalism in the Pre-Constitution era.
2. No person is ineligible for inclusion in the electoral roll on the grounds only of religion, race, caste, sex or any of them (Article 325). Equality has thus, been accorded to each citizen in the matter of franchise and the electoral roll is prepared on a secular basis.
3. Elections are held on the basis of Adult Suffrage, that is to say, every person who is –
   - A citizen of India;
   - Not less than 18 years of age on a date prescribed by the Legislature, and;

[1]*Indian Constitutional Law*, by M.P. Jain, Eight Edition, LexisNexis, Pg. No. 851.

- Is not otherwise disqualified under the Constitution, or any law made by the Legislature, the ground of non-residence, unsoundness of mind, crime, corrupt or illegal practice, is entitled to be registered as a voter at any such election (Article 326).

It is clear from these provisions that only a citizen of India can be enrolled as a voter. When the name of the person is to be entered in the electoral roll, he may be required to satisfy the Electoral Registration that he is a citizen of India. Moreover, no person is entitled to be registered in the electoral roll for more than one constituency, or of any constituency more than once.

4. No reservation of seats has been made in any House for any community, section, or religious group of the Indian population, except for Scheduled Castes and Scheduled Tribes.

Voting Rights

The Right to Vote is one of the most important rights in a democratic country and it is imperative for the functioning of the electoral system of the country in a free and fair manner. This right can be divided into two parts, i.e., active voting rights and passive voting rights. The term active voting rights refer to the right of the citizens of the country to elect representatives to the legislative bodies of the country and the term passive voting rights deals with the Right to Vote for those individuals who are standing in the elections.

The right to vote is not a Fundamental Right but Article 326 defines the right, which is given in the Representation of the People Act, 1951. Article 326 states that elections to Parliament and Legislative Assemblies would be conducted on the basis of adult franchise and every adult citizen could register in the electoral rolls to vote. In other words, under Article 326, the adult citizens who were above 21 years old had the right to vote. But post the 61st Amendment Act of 1988, the voting age was lowered from 21 years to 18 years. It is the Universal Adult Suffrage that gives the adult citizens the right to vote.

Right to Vote: Constitutional Right or a Mere Statutory Right?

In *N.P. Ponnuswami Vs. Returning Officer*[2], the Supreme Court held that the right to vote is a statutory right. Section 61 of the Representation of the People Act, provides for the right to vote, making it more of a statutory right rather than a constitutional one. It is a creation of statute and subject to limitations contained in it.

However, in *People's Union of Civil Liberties Vs. Union of India*[3], the Supreme Court held that this right is recognized by our Constitution and it is given effect to in specific form by the Representation of the People Act. The Constituent Assembly debates reveal that the idea to treat the voting right as a Fundamental Right was dropped; nevertheless, it was decided to provide for it elsewhere in the Constitution. This move found its expression in Article 326 which enjoins that "the elections to the House of the People and to the Legislative Assembly of every State shall be on the basis of adult suffrage". Thus, the right to vote originates from the Constitution and in accordance with the constitutional mandate contained in Article 326 and the right has been further shaped by the statute.

[2] AIR 1952 SC 64

[3] (2003) 4 SCC 399

24.1 ELECTION LAWS IN INDIA

INTRODUCTION

Part XV of the Indian Constitution deals with Elections, which includes Articles 324 to 329. This part of the Constitution provides for Election Commission (Article 324), Universal Suffrage (Article 325), and Adult Suffrage (Article 326). Article 327 enables the Parliament to enact provisions for the elections and Article 328 provides that States can enact provisions for a House or Houses of the State Legislature, if the Centre has not provided for the same.

Further, the Parliament is empowered to determine by law the manner in which and the authority by which, each State is to be divided into territorial constituencies after each Census for purposes of election to the Lok Sabha and the State Legislative Assembly. Under Article 329, courts are barred from questioning the Delimitation Act brought by the Parliament and it also mentions that disputes related to elections can be called in question only by an election petition in a manner provided by and to the authority decided by the appropriate Legislature.

CONSTITUTIONAL PROVISIONS FOR ELECTION LAWS

The Parliament under Article 327 enacted certain provisions for election laws, among others, namely:

1. The Representation of the People Act, 1950, which provides for allocation of seats and delimitation of constituencies of the Parliament and State Legislature, officers related to conduct of elections, preparation of electoral rolls, and manner of filling seats in the Council of States allotted to Union Territories.
2. The Representation of the People Act, 1951, which provides for the conduct of elections of the Houses of Parliament and to the House or Houses of the Legislature of each State, the qualifications and disqualifications for membership of those Houses, the corrupt practices and other offences at or in connection with such elections, and the decision of doubts and disputes arising out of or in connection with such elections.
3. Delimitation Commission Act of 1952, which provides for the readjustment of seats, delimitation, and reservation of territorial constituencies, and other related matters.
4. The Presidential and Vice-Presidential Elections Act, 1952, which provides for the conduct of Presidential and Vice-Presidential elections and mechanism for the settlement of any dispute arising out of such elections.

The Supreme legislative power in relation to various elections is thus vested in the Parliament but this power is subject to the provisions of the Constitution. Further, subject to the Constitutional provisions, and in so far as provisions have not been made by Parliament with respect to all matters in relation to, or in connection with, the elections to either of its Houses, including the preparation of electoral rolls and all matters necessary for securing the due Constitution of such House or Houses.

The Representation Of The People Act, 1950

Representation of the People Act, 1950 provides for the following :

(a) It lays down procedures for delimitation of constituencies.

(b) It provides for the allocation of seats within the House of the People and within the Legislative Assemblies.

(c) It lays down the procedure for the preparation of electoral rolls and therefore, the manner of filling seats.

(d) It lays down the qualification of voters.

(e) The President of India has been conferred the facility to amend orders delimiting constituencies only after consulting the ECI.

(f) In Lok Sabha, there's a reservation of seats for Scheduled Castes and Scheduled Tribes.

(g) The ECI has the facility to work out the constituencies to be reserved for scheduled tribes within the states of Meghalaya, Mizoram, Nagaland, and Tripura.

(h) Under Article 82 of the Constitution, the Parliament by law, enacts a Delimitation Act after every Census. After the Act came into force, the Central Government constitutes a Delimitation Commission. This Delimitation Commission demarcates the boundaries of the Parliamentary Constituencies as per the provisions of the Delimitation Act. After the delimitation, all the delimitation orders shall be consolidated by the Election Commission (according to the Representation of the People Act, 1950) into a single order and it would be forwarded to the Central Government and to the Government of each State Legislative Assembly.

(i) The present delimitation of constituencies has been done on the idea of the 2001 Census figures under the provisions of the Delimitation Act, 2002. Notwithstanding the above, the Constitution of India was specifically amended in 2002 to not to have delimitation of constituencies till the primary Census after 2026. Thus, these constituencies carved out on the idea of the 2001 Census shall still be operational till the primary Census after 2026.

(j) As far as possible, every state gets representation within the Lok Sabha in proportion to its population as per the Census figures.

Representation Of The People Act, 1951

The Act was enacted by the provisional Parliament under Article 327 of the Indian Constitution, before the first general election. Article 327 states that subject to the provisions of our Constitution, the Parliament is empowered to make provisions by law, with respect to all matters relating to, or in connection with, elections to either House of Parliament or to the House or Houses of the State Legislature including preparation of electoral rolls and all other necessary matters.

The Representation of the People Act, 1951or RPA is an Act of the Parliament of India, which provides for the following:

(a) Conduct of elections of the Houses of Parliament and to the House or Houses of the Legislature of each State;

(b) Notification of elections, general procedure for elections, as well as bye-elections, counting, and declaration of election result;

(c) Registration of political parties;

(d) Nomination of candidates, declaration of assets and liabilities, as well as the election expenses by the candidates;

(e) Details about the structure of administrative machinery for the conduct of elections;

(f) Qualifications and disqualifications for membership of the Houses of Parliament and State Legislatures;

(g) Corrupt practices and other offences at or in connection with such elections;

(h) The decision of doubts and disputes arising out of or in connection with such elections (election disputes);

(i) Powers of the Election Commission in connection with inquiries as to disqualifications of members.

DELIMITATION ACTS

Delimitation literally means the act or process of fixing limits or boundaries of territorial constituencies in a country or a province having a legislative body. The job of delimitation is assigned to a high-powered body. Such a body is known as Delimitation Commission or a Boundary Commission.

In India, such Delimitation Commissions have been constituted 4 times – in 1952 under the Delimitation Commission Act, 1952, in 1963 under Delimitation Commission Act, 1962, in 1973 under Delimitation Act, 1972, and in 2002 under Delimitation Act, 2002.

The Delimitation Acts provide for the appointment of the Delimitation Commission for making adjustment of seats in, and division of seats into territorial constituencies for elections to the Lok Sabha and State Legislative Assemblies after each Census. The Commission is appointed by the Central Government and consists of three members – two sitting or retired Judges of the Supreme Court or High Courts, and the Chief Election Commissioner *ex-officio*. In performance of its duties, the Commission is to be assisted by two to seven associate members for each State drawn from amongst the members of the Lok Sabha representing the State, and the State Legislative Assembly. Every final order of the Commission after publication in the Gazette of India becomes final and cannot be called in question in any court. In other words, the Delimitation Commission in India is a high-powered body whose orders have the force of law and cannot be called in question before any court. These orders come into force on a date to be specified by the President of India in this behalf. The copies of its orders are laid before the House of the People and the State Legislative Assembly concerned, but no modifications are permissible therein by them.

24.2 CORRUPT AND ELECTORAL OFFENCES

INTRODUCTION

Purity of elections is very important for democracy. Purity of elections is based on the following diction: "Not only the end must be pure; the means to achieve the end should also be fair". If elections are not free and fair, and if they suffer from grievous distortions, democratic principles are bound to wilt and decay. With it, the entire political system degenerates and becomes directionless, buffeted by swirling ambitions of self-seeking politicians.

ACTS OR LEGISLATIONS AGAINST CORRUPT AND ELECTORAL OFFENCES

There are legislations which criminalises the corrupt practices and electoral offences. Following are the Acts or legislations which deals with corrupt practices and electoral offences–

Representation of the People Act, 1951

Chapter I of Part VII of RPA, 1951 deals with corrupt practices which are quite large in number. Even a single proven act of corrupt practice committed by a candidate or his agents or workers with his consent or knowledge is enough to vitiate his election. He might incur disqualification for standing as a candidate at future elections for a specified period. There are also certain corrupt practices which are also electoral offences under Chapter III of Part VII of RPA.

Corrupt Practices

Following are the corrupt practices mentioned in Section 123 of RPA 1951.

1. Bribery;
2. Undue influence;
3. Appeal on ground of religion, etc.;
4. Promotion of feelings of enmity or hatred on ground of religion, etc.;
5. Publication of false and defamatory statements;
6. Illegal hiring of vehicles for free conveyance of voter;
7. Excessive election expenditure;
8. Obtaining or procuring any assistance from the government servant, other than giving of vote;
9. Booth capturing.

Electoral Offences

In addition to the corrupt practices at election, various acts of commission and omission have been termed as electoral offences. A candidate may be unseated if it is proved that he has committed a corrupt practice but he may suffer penal consequences for commission of an electoral offence. Further, a person committing an electoral offence is liable for punishment, irrespective of the fact of whether such act was done by him with the consent of the candidate or not.

1. Promoting enmity between classes in connection with election;
2. Prohibition of public meetings during the specified period - The electoral propaganda in the form of public meetings in the polling is to end 48 hours before the time fixed for the conclusion of the poll for any election. Any person violating the provisions commits an electoral offence;
3. Disturbance at election meetings;
4. Restriction on the printing of pamphlets, posters, etc.;
5. Maintenance of secrecy of voting is important. Any person who violates the above provisions commits an electoral offence;
6. Officers, etc. at elections not to act for candidates or to influence voting;
7. Prohibition of canvassing in or near polling station;
8. Penalty for disorderly conduct in or near polling station;
9. Misconduct at the polling station;
10. Penalty for failure to observe voting procedure;
11. Penalty for illegal hiring or procuring of conveyance at elections;
12. Breach of official duty in connection with Elections;
13. Removal of ballot papers from polling station;
14. Fraudulently defacing or fraudulently destroying any nomination paper;
15. Fraudulently defacing, destroys, or removing any list, notice, or other document affixed by or under the authority of a Returning Officer;
16. Fraudulently defacing or fraudulently destroying any ballot paper or the official mark on any ballot paper or any declaration of identity or official envelope used in connection with voting by postal ballot.

Indian Penal Code (IPC)

Other than the electoral offences under electoral law, the IPC also provides certain offences regarding elections as criminal offences.

1. **Bribery and undue influence :** Bribery and undue influence at an election also constitute criminal offences under the IPC;
2. **Personation :** Any person who impersonates at an election for obtaining a voting paper or voting in the name of any other person, whether living or dead or in a fictious name, etc., commits an offence of personation;
3. **False Statement in connection with an Election :** Any person who makes a false statement in connection with an election in relation to the personal character or conduct of the candidate commits a criminal offence;

4. **Illegal payments in connection with an election :** If without the general or special authority in writing of a candidate incurs or authorises expenditure on account of the holding of any public meeting or upon any advertisement, circulation, or publication, or in any other way whatsoever for the purpose promoting or procuring the election of such candidate, commits a criminal offence;
5. **Failure to keep election accounts :** The failure to keep the accounts of election expenses is a criminal offence;
6. **Statements conducting the public mischief and prejudiced to maintenance of harmony :** The corrupt practice of promoting feelings of enmity hatred or ill will between different classes of citizens of India on the grounds of religion, race, etc., amounts to a criminal offence punishable with an imprisonment extending to 3 years or with fine or with both. The commission of the above offence in any place of worship or in any assembly engaged in the performance of religious worship or religious ceremonies is visited with harsher punishment of imprisonment which may extend to 5 years and also with fine.

DISPOSAL OF ELECTION CASES

Article 329(b) of the Indian Constitution provides that no election to either House of Parliament or to the House or either House of the Legislature of a state shall be called on question, except by an election petition presented to such authority and in such manner as may be provided for by and under the law made by the appropriate Legislature.

The mandate that the election petition is the only remedy for calling in question an election is based on the sound public policy that having regard to the important functions which the Legislatures have to perform in democratic countries, it has always been recognised to be a matter of first importance. Hence, elections should be completed as early as possible according to the time schedule and all controversial matters and all disputes arising out of elections should be postponed till after the "elections" are over so that the election proceedings may not be unduly retarded or protracted.

An election covers the entire process from the issue of notification to calling the election to the declaration of result and does not refer only to the last stage at which a candidate is declared elected.

No court has jurisdiction to interfere at any intermediary stage of the electoral process once it is set in motion by the issue of Presidential notification calling upon the constituencies to elect members to constitute a new Lok Sabha. Any remedy or relief which an aggrieved person may like to have is necessarily postponed till after the election is complete. Any irregularity or illegality taking place in the course of an election shall not be called in question till the election is over and even then; it shall be called in question only by an election petition challenging the election.

Conditions for Filing Election Petitions

Election petitions are presented to the High Court having jurisdiction over the area in which election was held and appeals against the order of the High Court lie to the Supreme Court both on question of fact and law.

The right to file an election petition has been conferred only on two categories of persons, namely a defeated candidate or an elector for that election. An elector who wants to challenge the election must be a person who was entitled to vote at the election to which the petition relates, but it is immaterial whether he had voted at such election or not.

An election petition calling in question an election shall be filed within 45 days from, and not earlier than the date of election of the returned candidate. Limitation for filing the election petition runs from the date of declaration of result by the Returning Officer and not from the date of publication of result in the Official Gazette. The election petition must be presented within the specified period and the courts have no power to condone any delay, even of a day, in the filing of an election petition.

An election petition calling in question any election may be presented on any one or more of the following grounds contained in the Section 100(1) of RPA 1951 :

(a) That on the date of his election, a returned candidate (the expression "returned candidate" means a candidate who has been declared as duly elected) was not qualified or was disqualified to be chosen to fill the seat under the Constitution;

(b) that any corrupt practice has been committed by a returned candidate or his election agent or by any other person with the consent of a returned candidate or his election agent;

(c) that any nomination has been improperly rejected;

(d) The result of the election, in so far as it concerns a returned candidate has been materially affected by (i) by improper acceptance of a nomination (ii) by any corrupt practice committed in the interest of the returned candidate by an agent other than election agent (iii) by improper reception refusal or rejection of any vote or the reception of any vote which is void (iv) by any non-compliance with the provision of the Constitution of this Act or any of the rules or orders made under this Act.

24.3 POLITICAL PARTIES

"The ignorance of one voter in a democracy impairs the security of all".

– John F. Kennedy

INTRODUCTION

Political parties are one of the most visible institutions in a democracy. The political parties play an essential role in a democracy. Generally speaking, a political party can be defined as an organized group of citizens who profess to share the same political views and who come together to contest elections and hold power in the government. The word "political party" is not defined in the Constitution. However, it is defined in the Election Symbols (Reservation and Allotment) Order, 1968 and in the Representation of the People Act, 1951. According to Para 2(h) of the Election Symbols (Reservation and Allotment) Order, 1968, and Section 2(f) of the RPA,1951, a political party refers to an association or body of individual citizens of India registered with the Election Commission of India as apolitical party under Section 29A of the RPA of 1951.

PROVISIONS UNDER THE ELECTION SYMBOLS (RESERVATION AND ALLOTMENT) ORDER, 1968

In 1968, the Election Commission (EC) promulgated this order, which provides for the following :

(a) Registration and recognition of political parties as state and national parties;

(b) Specification, reservation, choice, and allotment of symbols at elections in Parliamentary and State Assemblies' constituencies;

(c) Resolution of disputes in cases involving splits in recognized parties or merger of two or more political parties;

(d) Classification of political parties into regional or state and national parties, or registered and unregistered parties.

i. **Election Symbols :** Election symbols are simple images that are easily recognizable by the general mass of voters. Each symbol represents either a political party or an independent candidate and helps the voter to identify the contender that they intend to vote for. This is essential because not all voters are literate, and it helps people to rely on the symbol instead and easily identify the party to vote for. The symbols are allotted to parties by the Election Commission of India.

In every contested election, a symbol will be allocated to a contesting candidate according to the provisions of the Symbols Order and different symbols will be allocated to different candidates at an election in the same constituency. Symbols are classified as reserved and free symbols. A reserved symbol is a symbol reserved for a recognized political party for its exclusive allotment to contesting candidates set up by that recognized party. Whereas, a free symbol is a symbol other than a reserved symbol, which is available to be allocated to unrecognized parties and independent candidates.

ii. Disputes in Election Symbols[1] **:** The dispute regarding election symbols erupts when there is a conflict within a political party which leads to a split of the party. Then, both the factions fight for the reserved symbol of the party. It was held in *Sadiq Ali and Another Vs. Election Commission of India*[2] that an election symbol is not a property that can be simply divided between two owners. So, the dispute regardsing electoral symbols is resolved by the Election Commission of India when the Commission is satisfied that there are rival factions within a recognized political party, each of whom claim to be that party. The Commission, on the basis of relevant facts and circumstances of the case and hearing the representatives from both the factions, decides that one such rival faction or no such faction is that recognized party and the decision of the Commission is final on all such sections. However, the Supreme Court decided that the EC is a tribunal and its decision regarding de-recognition of a party or allocation of symbols in case of dispute could be challenged by way of an appeal to the High Courts and the Supreme Court.

iii. Registration of Political Parties *:* The issue of registration and de-registration of political parties has always been in question. In 1988, the Representation of the People Act was revised to include Section 29A, which says that the parties, in order to enjoy the benefits of the Act, need to register themselves with the Election Commission within the period described in the statute. The compelling parties seeking registration need to furnish documents along with the particulars of their policies and programmes.

The registration of political parties is assessed by Section 29A of the Representation of the People Act, 1951. The sub-section (1) says that if anybody of individual citizens or association, intends to call itself a political party and avail itself of the benefits under the provisions of this part, it must register itself by filing an application to the Election Commission. It further states the conditions needed to be followed in order to register themselves as political parties. It says that if the body of individuals or association is in existence before or at the commencement of the Representation of People's (Amendment) Act, 1988, then the application must be made within the next sixty days following the commencement. It also mentions that if the association is formed after such commencement, then the application must be filed within the next 30 days following its formation.

---

[1] Election Commission's decision on election disputes - The EC decides disputes among rivals' factions of a recognized political party staking claim to its symbol and name. Initially, the Election Commission ascertains the support enjoyed by a claimant within a political party in its organizational and legislative wing. For the organizational wing, the Commission studies the constitution of the party and also the list of office-bearers submitted when the party was still united. It identifies the apex committee in the organization and examines how many delegates, members, and office-bearers support the rival claim. If the Commission fails to test the support strength to any faction based on the organizational support, then it goes for the legislative wing. For this wing, the Commission goes by the number of MLAs and MPs in the rival faction. It considers the affidavits filed by them to examine where they stand. The ECI may decide in favour of the rival section who claims the majority in the organizational and legislative wing, and the winning faction becomes entitled to the symbol and name of the said political party while it may allow the other faction to register itself as a separate political entity. Where the party is vertically divided and it is not feasible to establish majority through these wings, then the Commission may freeze the party's symbol and permit the factions to register themselves with new names or they may add suffixes and prefixes to their party's name.

[2] AIR 1972 SC 187.

After considering all the particulars and also the other necessary factors and also giving the representatives of the association or body reasonable opportunity of being heard, the Commission shall decide either to register the association as a political party or not to register it and the decision of the Commission shall be conveyed to the association. No association or body of individuals will be registered as a political party unless its Memorandum of Rules and Regulations conform to Section 29A of RPA, 1951. The decision of the Commission is final and binding.

iv. **Recognition of Political Parties :** After seeking registration, the next thing that political parties seek is recognition. Recognition of political parties as State or National Party is endowed with several benefits like getting a reserved symbol, placement of their names at the top of the ballot paper, and other economic benefits. The recognition of political parties is governed through the Symbols Order. The political parties are divided into recognized and unrecognized political parties. A recognized political party is either a recognized National Party or a recognized State Party.

A political party, to become a State Party, must fulfil any of the following conditions:

- To the Legislative Assembly of that state, the candidates nominated by that party must secure not less than 6% of the total valid votes polled in that state; and, in addition, the party should have won at least two seats to the Assembly of that state at such election; or
- To the House of the People from that state, the candidates set up by that party must have secured not less than 6% of the total valid votes polled in that state; and the party must have won 1 seat to the House of the People from that State; or
- To the Assembly of that State, the party must have secured at least 3% of the total number of seats in the Assembly or at least three seats, whichever is more; or
- To the House of the People from that state, the party must win at least 1 one seat to the House for every 25 seats or any fraction allotted to that state; or
- To the House of the People from that State, or at the last general election to the assembly of the State, the candidates nominated by the party must have secured not less than 8% of the total valid votes polled from that State.

To become a National Party, the registered party must fulfil any of the following conditions:

- The candidates nominated by the party in any 4 or more states, at the last general election to the House of People or the Assembly of the concerned state, have secured not less than 6% of the total valid votes polled in that state; and the party must have won at least 4 seats to the House of People at the last general election from any state(s); or
- At the last general election to the House of People, the party must have secured not less than 2% of the total number of seats in the House; and the candidates have been elected to the House from not less than 3 states; or
- The party is a recognized State party in at least 4 states.

If the political parties fulfil these conditions, then they become recognized State or National Parties. The benefits provided to them are enormous but they need to perform well during the succeeding general elections to retain their status as a National or State Party. The Symbols Order mentions the conditions for continued recognition as either a State or a National Party.

It says that if a political party is a recognized State party or a National party, the question of its continued recognition after any subsequent elections to the House of People or Legislative Assemblies depends upon the fulfilment of the conditions mentioned above. If the parties fail to fulfil these conditions, they can be declared as derecognized by the Election Commission of India. However, this provision was amended in 2018 and it stated that the review of the status of recognized parties will be done after every two consecutive State Assembly or Lok Sabha elections, instead of after every election. This amendment brought a sigh of relief to parties like Nationalist Congress Party, Bahujan Samaj Party, and Communist Party of India-Marxist, who were on the prospect of losing their national status.

v. **Advantages of being recognized as a state or national party :**

There are certainly many benefits of being a recognized state or national party.

- The biggest advantage of being recognized is getting the reserved symbol.
- Recognized parties need only one proposer for filing the nomination and they also get two sets of electoral rolls free of cost at the time of the revision of rolls. Their candidates also get one copy of the electoral roll free during General Elections.
- They are also entitled to broadcast or telecast facilities over Akashvani or Doordarshan during elections. The telecast and radio facilities can be best used to address the people and convey their message to the masses.
- Political parties, be it recognized or unrecognized, can nominate Star Campaigners during elections. A recognized National or State Party can have a maximum of 40 Star Campaigners while registered unrecognized parties can have a maximum of 20 Star Campaigners. The travel expenses of these Star Campaigners are not included in the election expense accounts of the candidates of these parties.
- They also get subsidized land for their party offices at the national or state capitals.
- The candidates set up by the recognised parties are arranged alphabetically and presented on the top of the ballot paper followed by candidates of registered unrecognized parties and lastly, the independent candidates.
- If the candidate nominated by a recognized party dies before the polling begins, then the elections in that constituency are adjourned and that party is given an additional time of a week to nominate another candidate.

FUNCTIONS AND ROLE OF POLITICAL PARTIES

Political parties perform vital functions in every political system. They provide effective links between the citizens and the governments on the one hand, and the electorates and their representatives on the other. They try to cater to people's demands on public matters, and mobilize political participation. Elections without parties would have almost been impossible. In fact, a democracy needs strong and sustainable political parties with the capacity to represent citizens and provide policy choices that demonstrate their ability to govern for the public good.

The functions performed by the political parties, especially in the context of India, can be summarized as follows:

- they nominate candidates during elections;
- they campaign to obtain support for their candidates in the elections;
- they place objectives and programmes before the voters through their manifestos;

- those securing the majority in elections form the government and enact and implement the policies;
- those not in power form the opposition and keep a constant check on the government;
- they form opposition when they are in minority in the Legislature and constantly put pressure on the government for proper governance;
- they educate people and help in formulating and shaping public opinion;
- they articulate peoples' demands and convey them to the government; and
- they provide a linkage between the people and governmental institutions.

TYPES OF PARTY SYSTEMS[3]

Party systems may be classified into the following four types:

1. **Two-party system :** A two-party system is one where only two parties, despite the presence of other parties, have substantial support of the electorate. One of them is the ruling party, and the other is the opposition. It depends on which party gets the majority in the elections. The United States and the United Kingdom are examples of the two-party system. In the US, the Democratic and Republican parties are the main parties, and in the UK, the Labour Party and the Conservative Party are the two main parties.
2. **Multi-party system :** Multi-party system indicates existence of several parties in a political system. India and many European countries have a multi-party system. In a multi-party system, several parties come together to form a coalition government and adopt a common minimum programme for governance. The multi-party system is of two types: unstable and working. The unstable party system does not provide stability, and the best example of this system can be seen in India during 1996–98. The working multi-party system behaves like a two-party system and thereby tends to provide stability to the government, even though they have more than two major political parties. The multi-party system promotes the coalition government, and since the 1990s, India has been governed by the coalition governments. The drawback of this system is that the members of the Council of Ministers, instead of working under the leadership of the Prime Minister, seek guidance from their party heads, and even a single Member of Parliament tries to blackmail or manipulate the government by threatening to withdraw its support. Government instability is a major problem in this kind of party system.
3. **One-party system :** The one-party system or single party system is ruled by only one party; there is no opposition. This authoritarian principle was first found in monarchies and later in a dictatorship, and now this system exists in a few democratic countries. However, elections are conducted even in such regimes only to show the façade of popular support, since the voter's choice is limited to only one candidate. The essential function of the one-party system is not to elicit decisions from the mass electorate on the issues concerning people, but to ensure discipline and obedience among them. In a system ruled by a single party, the governance is marked by a totalitarian system and that curtails democratic rights: the hand of the ruling party or king. In many cases, this system involves the abolition of the freedom of speech and expression, press, and associations. In this system, there is no opposition, in terms of opposition party or other means of opposing voice against the ruling government. China has a one-party system.

[3] *Party Systems in India*, Dr. Divya Ravi, Consultant, Faculty of Political Science, SOSS, IGNOU, New Delhi.

4. **One-party dominant system :** It is a system in which other parties exist legally but for reasons largely unrelated to legal questions of government coercion, find themselves unable to challenge effectively the dominant party's hold on public power. India is considered to be the classical example of a one-party dominant system. It is in this context that Gcpal Krishna Gokhale characterises this system by stating[4]:

"the continued dominance of one party (Congress), claiming to represent the nation and holding the monopoly of power, internecine factional disputes within it, and a persistent tendency for it either to take over the programmes of the opposition parties or to make timely concessions on issues taken up by them, so preventing them from acquiring much permanent strength. The role of the opposition parties has generally been restricted to influencing the policies of the ruling party rather than challenging its monopoly of power..."

Therefore, one-party dominant system is not the same as the one-party system. It consists of more than one party and the same party will be in power continuously enjoying a comfortable majority. Unlike the one-party system, the one-party dominant system is one which legally permits the existence of other parties. A strong, dominant party results from low competitiveness, and, if the competitiveness is low, it follows that the variable "ideological distance" does not carry much weight in the electoral arena. Due to prolonged domination of one party, the opposition is reduced to impotence. The opposition also becomes irresponsible because of lack of opportunity to exercise power.

CHARACTERISTICS OF THE INDIAN PARTY SYSTEM

(a) **A Multi-party system :** Currently, the Indian political system can be characterised as a multi-party system. It has various national parties and state parties. Because of the multi-party system, coalition governments have become a common feature in India. However, in spite of the multi-party system in India, for many years, single/one party dominance was present. In other words, the Congress political party was dominating the political scene in India for decades together.

(b) **Lack of Ideological Commitment :** In India, politics has become issue-oriented rather than based on ideology. Since 1971, elections have been won not on the basis of the inherent strength of the ideology of a political party, but on the basis of issue of immediate concern to the electorate.

(c) **Lack of strong opposition :** Indian political system lacks a strong well-organised opposition party. A strong opposition is essential for the success of the Parliamentary democracy. The main function of the opposition is to highlight the shortcomings of the government and to compel it to become responsive to the public opinion.

(d) **Communalism and Casteism :** The role of communalism and casteism in politics have increased. Communalism is not a phenomenon confined only to India. It is prevalent in other countries in Asia as well as in Europe. Communalism has divided our society for long. Appeasement politics and communal attitude has been increasing in the political system.

---

[4]Krishna, Gopal, "*One party Dominance:, Development and trends*", in Kothari, Rajni, & Others, Party System and Election Studies, Allied Publishers, New Delhi, 1967, p.22.

Casteism is peculiar to India. In electoral politics, the role of the caste in politics has become powerful. This can be seen at all levels of the political process of the country. All political parties tend to give party tickets to candidates for contesting elections from amongst the numerically or otherwise dominant caste in every constituency. Thus, major caste groups get representation in the Council of Ministers. Be it elections, political appointments, or even formation of political parties, caste has been the major consideration. The influence of caste, however, varies depending upon the level of election and the region. Its influence is far more at the local and state-level political process than at the national level. Caste plays a greater role in the rural areas than in the urban areas.

(e) **Factions within parties :** A political faction is a group of individuals that share a common political purpose but differs in some respect to the rest of the entity. Factions, splits, mergers, etc., are a common phenomenon in the Indian political system. Factions, splits, etc., causes instability in the political system.

(f) **Resurgence of cult personality :** After Independence, Indian politics saw a slew of political leaders who relied on their personal charisma to arouse the masses, and to reap rich political dividends – Indira Gandhi, N.T. Rama Rao (Former Chief Minister of united Andhra Pradesh), MGR (Former Chief Minister of Tamil Nadu), Kanshi Ram (Hero of the Dalits), and many more. Today, Indian politics is seeing a resurgence of the 'cult personality' after an extended lull of over two decades. The best example is the Prime Minister Narendra Modi, who is seen as the representation of strong nationalism and the aspirations of an upwardly mobile middle class.

THE SPECTRUM OF POLITICAL ATTITUDES

The political spectrum is the range of political attitudes of the public, going gradually from extreme to moderate to extreme: radical, liberal, moderate, conservative, and then reactionary. Every individual lies somewhere along this political spectrum, but many do not know exactly where they lie, or they label themselves as something that they may not be entirely. Some even think that they lie nowhere on the political spectrum, because they label themselves as not involved or not feeling strongly about political issue. But the fact is that they are most likely moderate, or maybe they do feel strongly about many political issues but don't really know it.

Political attitude tells us which party someone votes for, what kind of political ideology someone prefers most, which social, economical, cultural, or international policy someone prefers, etc., The terms *radical, liberal, moderate, conservative, and reactionary* are among the most often used words in political discourse.

(a) **Liberals :** Liberalism is one of the intellectual by-products of the Enlightenment, of the Scientific method, and ultimately of the Industrial Revolution. During the medieval era in Europe, people looked heavenward for Divine relief from their wretched earthly existence. Faith in human potential, as well as esteem for humankind in general, was very low. However, the discoveries of inquisitive people such as Copernicus, Galileo, and Newton revolutionized people's attitudes toward themselves and their function in life. Through use of the Scientific method, people began to make improvements in their material existence, and in so doing, they began to develop confidence in their ability to solve many problems. It was not long before people began to conclude that if physical difficulties could be solved through the use of human reason, perhaps the same could be done with social and political problems. This speculation led to the keystone of liberalism – *Optimism about people's ability to solve their problems through the use of reason.* In simple words, "Liberal" refers to someone who advocates change, new philosophies, and new ideas. They are supportive of individual rights but also lots of government intervention and control.

(b) Conservatives : Conservatives are the most supportive of the status quo and therefore are reluctant to see it changed. Being content with things as they are does not suggest that conservatives are necessarily happy with the existing system, however. Conservatives are often accused of lacking vision, but this charge is unfair. The difference between conservatives and liberals is not founded on the fact that the latter dream of achieving a better world, whereas the former think the status quo is the best conceivable existence. In fact, conservatives may desire a future no less pleasant than that of the liberals–a future free of human conflict and suffering. The essential difference between the two viewpoints rests on their respective confidence in when (or indeed, whether) the ideal can be accomplished. Conservatives support the status quo not so much because they like it but because they believe that it is the best that can be achieved at the moment. Put differently, conservatives oppose change because they doubt that it will result in something better, not because they do not desire improvement. Lacking confidence in society's ability to achieve improvements through bold policy initiatives, most conservatives support only very slow, incremental, and superficial alteration of the system. The most cautious of them often resist even seemingly minor changes. They tend to see an intrinsic value in existing institutions and are unwilling to tamper with them, claiming that to do so might seriously damage that which tradition has perfected. In simple words, conservatives seek to promote and to preserve traditional social institutions and practices. "Radical" and "reactionary" are extreme versions of "liberal" and "conservative," respectively.

A radical is extremely far left, or an ultra-liberal or extremist, and a reactionary is extremely far right, or an ultra-conservative or extremist.

(c) Reactionary : Reactionaries are so conservative that they want to reverse political progress or change. Reactionaries favour a policy that would return society to a previous condition or even a former value system. For instance, the Taliban emergence and takeover of Afghanistan in 2021 is also quite reactionary, as is the extreme Islamism movement.

(d) Radicals : Radicals favour drastic political, economic, or social reforms and often advocate these uncompromisingly. In general terms, a radical may be defined as a person who is extremely dissatisfied with the society as it is and therefore, is impatient with less than extreme proposals for changing it. Hence, all radicals favour an immediate and fundamental change in the society. In other words, all radicals favour revolutionary change. The criterion that distinguishes one radical from another most clearly is the methods he/she would use to bring about a particular change.

(e) Moderate : Moderates are those who reject radical or extreme views. Moderates are fundamentally satisfied with the society, although they agree that there is room for improvement and recognize several specific areas in need of modification. However, they insist that changes in the system should be made gradually and that no change should be so extreme as to disrupt the society.

Political Spectrum

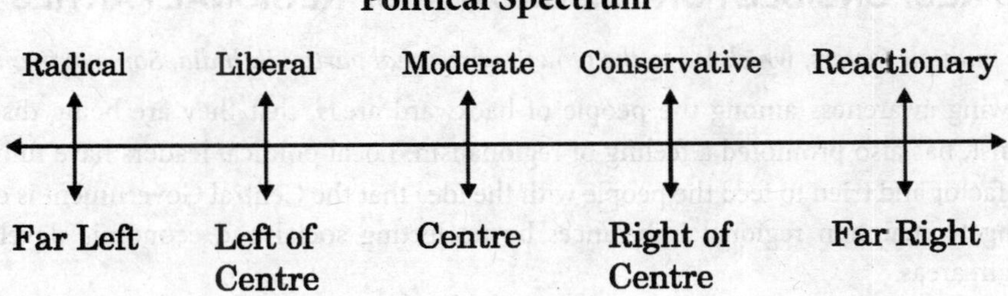

24.4 REGIONAL PARTIES

"The regional parties have emerged as a strong force, and they, too, deserve a place in national politics".

– Atal Bihari Vajpayee

INTRODUCTION

One of the most important political developments in Independent India has been the rise of regional political parties. Regional parties are parties restricted to a particular state and rooted in both regional aspirations and grievances. The support base of the party is limited to a particular state because it identifies itself with the region's culture, language, religion, etc. It also presents the regional perspective vis-à-vis the Centre and often other states.

India has a multi-party system. Earlier, the regional parties were unable to play a major role at the Centre due to the dominance of the Congress Party. But of late, the emergence of regional parties have posed the most powerful challenge to India's 'One-Party Dominant System'. Since 1967, the regional parties are emerging with greater political appeal to control most of the state politics. They emerged as a powerful force and played a vital role in the formulation of governments at the Centre.

The presence of a number of ethnic, cultural, linguistic, religious, and caste groups within the Indian society is greatly responsible for the origin and growth of regional parties. Though the regional parties operate within limited areas and pursue only limited objectives, they have played a significant role both in the state as well as in the national politics. These parties have formed the government in several states and have tried to implement their policies and programmes. Some of the regional parties are also partners in the coalition government at the Centre. In the eighth Lok Sabha Elections (1984), the Telgu Desam Party, a regional party of Andhra Pradesh, emerged as the main opposition party.

Further, in this new era of coalition politics, regional parties have emerged as active actors in the Indian political system. The new scenario in which coalition politics has come to emerge as a reality of Indian politics since 1996, has brought home the fact that the national parties must join hands with regional parties to strengthen their role and position in the Indian political system. Even the Congress has now realised and accepted the necessity of forging alliances with the regional parties, with the result that it was able to form coalition governments at the Centre with the help of regional parties in 2004 and 2009.

FACTORS RESPONSIBLE FOR THE GROWTH OF REGIONAL PARTIES IN INDIA

There are multiple factors, which led to the growth of regional parties in India. Some of them are:

1. Growing awareness among the people of backward areas, that they are being discriminated against, has also promoted a feeling of regionalism. Local political leaders have fully exploited this factor and tried to feed the people with the idea that the Central Government is deliberately trying to maintain regional imbalances by neglecting social and economic development of certain areas.

2. The desire of the various units of the Indian federal system to maintain their sub-cultural regions and greater degree of self-government has promoted regionalism and given rise to demand for greater autonomy.
3. To protest the policy actions of the central government, when central government tries to impose a particular ideology, language, or cultural pattern on all people and groups. For example, the southern states of India, resisted imposition of Hindi as an official language because of the apprehension that this would lead to domination of the North. Similarly, in Assam, Anti-Foreigners Agitation was launched by the Assamese to preserve their own culture.
4. The desire to capture the power. It is well known that political parties like DMK, AIADMK, Akali Dal, Telugu Desam, YSRCP, Asom Gana Parishad, Janata Dal(s), etc., have contested the election by putting forth the local problems and promising solution to those, if they come to power.
5. Continuous neglect of an area or region by the ruling parties and concentration of administrative and political power has given rise to the demand for decentralization of authority and bifurcation of unilingual states. On occasions, the 'Sons of soil' theory has been put forth to promote the interests of neglected groups or areas of the state.
6. Various groups have failed to identify their group interests with national interests; hence the feeling of regionalism has persisted.

Positive Impact of Regional Parties

1. Regional parties have helped in the development of participatory political culture and provided a check against the overshadowing tendencies of the Central government.
2. The regional parties have made a strong impact on the nature of Centre-State relations in India. They are a natural consequence of a democratic system based on adult franchise in multi-ethnic, multi-racial, multi-religious, and multi-linguistic societies like India.
3. Regional parties are even trying to influence the foreign policy as well. For example, the Dravida Munnetra Kazhagam Party of Tamil Nadu quit the ruling coalition over the center's support for what the party considered to be a weakly worded UN resolution on the Sri Lankan government's treatment of its Tamil minority. Moreover, since the opening up of the Indian economy in 1991, states have consistently exercised their newfound economic policy latitude to craft their own strategies to woo foreign investors, irrespective of New Delhi's outlook.
4. Regional parties have provided a place for better representation of local issues, like Mizo National Front putting forward the demands of tribes. Regional parties also have strengthened the federal axis of the Indian democracy by providing voice and bargaining powers to the state.
5. Regional parties have made the political process more competitive and brought the leadership role out of the clutches of major parties only. It has challenged the One-Party Dominant system, especially the Congress Era and thus, helps in breaking the monopoly of one party, apart from helping in widening the choices for the voters. Now a voter can vote for the party representing the interests of his/her state.

Negative Impact of Regional Parties

1. The local parties which are part of the coalition government at the Centre use their power to stall the development activities of the Centre that are genuinely intended for the growth of the country.
2. The local parties for their political benefits divide the people of different states on the lines of language, culture, traditions, etc. This affects the overall unity and integrity of the country.
3. Sometimes, serious issues like "India's foreign policy" will be influenced and compromised by the "coalition dharma". This will affect India's credibility in the global front and portray India as unreliable in terms of sticking to its long-held policies. Eg: In 2011, the Chief of Trinamool Congress Party and the then Chief Minister of West Bengal Ms. Mamata Banerjee scuttled a water-sharing agreement that New Delhi had negotiated with Bangladesh over the Teesta River. The treaty had been a critical component of the central government's plans to improve relations with its neighbour in the east.
4. The local parties in the small states like in North-Eastern India will not get much support from the Centre in terms of development and security of its people even if they are part of the coalition, since they send only a handful of members to the Parliament. The fact that they don't affect the national politics as much as the larger states result in such states getting smaller aid in terms of funds and other development activities.
5. The state governments that get more funds can use these funds for subsidising more and more basic necessities, thereby making the people lethargic and killing the motivation to work hard. Subsidising the scant resources in a particular state can impact the prices in other states.

24.5 PRESSURE GROUPS

INTRODUCTION

The society has become highly complex and in the vastness of its various activities and interactions, the individual seems to have lost his identity. The individual feels that he cannot achieve anything by his own efforts as nobody would give any importance to him. Thus, in order to gain greater bargaining power and make his point of view effective and forceful, he joins with other people who share his ideas and values and constitutes a particular group. For the purpose of achieving their objectives, individuals organize themselves into various kinds of groups.

Pressure groups are an association of interest groups as well as influence groups which are formed to promote the interest of their members by exercising all sorts of direct and indirect pressure on the government. They are different from political parties.

A distinguishing feature of interest/pressure groups is that they seek to influence public policy-makers, but without attempting to take over directly the control and conduct of the government. Political parties, on the other hand, are primarily concerned with governance – to contest elections and to try to secure majority of seats in the Legislature, or the office of the Chief Executive, and govern the country.

DIFFERENCE BETWEEN PRESSURE GROUPS AND POLITICAL PARTIES

S. No.	Pressure Group	Political Party
1.	Pressure groups are the representation of homogeneous interests seeking influence. The interest group is strong and effective when it has a directed specific purpose.	Political parties, on the other hand, seeking office and directed towards policy decisions, combine heterogeneous groups. In fact, it is one of their major themes to reconcile the diverse forces within the political society. Theirs is an integrative function which is not the domain of the interest groups.
2.	Pressure groups do not participate directly in the acquisition of power or in its exercise; they act to influence power and while remaining apart from it, they exert pressure on it.	Political parties strive to acquire power and exercise it—by electing and choosing Cabinet Ministers and the Head of State.
3.	Pressure groups seek to influence the men who wield power, and not to place their own men in power (at least not officially).	Political parties seek to place their own men in power.
4.	Pressure has a narrower focus. It is primarily to articulate specific demands that it comes into existence.	Political parties are committed to a wide-range of issues and policies; their goal is political power.

Thus, political parties are directly engaged in political activity, including selection of candidates for election, presenting formally formulated policies and a clear platform for seeking popular votes, and if successful, to run the affairs of the State. Those who get lesser number of votes and seats sit in the opposition and offer constructive opposition to the ruling party. None of them come within the role of the pressure groups. The interest/pressure groups are essentially non-political associations. Their primary functions may be economic, social, religious, or humanitarian. Exerting pressure is not their main business. They do so if it is necessary for the promotion of the interests of their members.

TYPES OF PRESSURE GROUPS IN INDIA

(a) **Big Business Group :** Business groups/associations are among the largest and the most powerful of all Indian pressure groups. These include a large number of business associations, industrial associations, regional associations, and all Indian organisations connected with trade and commerce. Most important of these are the Federation of Indian Chambers of Commerce and Industry (FICCI), the Associated Chambers of Commerce and Industry (ASSOCHAM), All India Manufacturers' Organisation (AIMO), and Federation of Indian Export Organisation (FIEO). FICCI has been in existence since 1927 and its aims have been the protection and promotion of indigenous Indian interests in trade and industry. For securing their interests, these groups lobby with legislators, ministers, bureaucrats, and various economic institutions like the Planning Commission. The big business interest groups also use their money power in politics for securing their interests. Over the years, the big businesses have emerged as a major force in the Indian economy and politics. Their influence often outweighs the influence of the labour unions.

(b) **Trade Unions :** There are about 16000 Trade Unions in India. Some of these have been sponsored by the political parties, while others have come to develop naturally out of the necessity for protecting the interests of the workers vis-à-vis the capitalists. Active among these are: All India Trade Union Congress (AITUC), the Indian National Trade Union Congress (INTUC), the Hind Mazdoor Sabha (HMS), the United Trade Union Congress (UTUC), the United Trade Union Congress (UTUC), the Hind Mazdoor Prishad (HMP), the Centre of Indian Trade Unions (CITU), the All-India Bank Employees' Association, the National Federation of Indian Railwaymen, and the National Federation of Postal and Telegraph Workers. These trade unions are very conscious of their rights and these try to protect the interests of their members. Almost all the trade unions, particularly their federations, have links with political parties. INTUC is pro-Congress, AITUC is pro-Communists, UTUC is backed by CPM, HMS is pro-Socialist, and HMP is pro-BJP. The existence of so many trade union organizations cut at the root of unity of the working class in India.

(c) **Peasant Organisations :** With nearly 50 per cent of the available Indian workforce engaged in agriculture, it is but natural for the agricultural groups, associations, unions, and Organisations to play an important role in the process of politics. All India Kisan Sabha, Hind Kisan Panchayat, United Kisan Sabha, Workers and Peasants Party, Shetkari Sangathan, Bhartiya Kisan Union, and Bhartiya Kamgar Union are the important peasant Organisations which are active in the Indian political system. These Organisations are active in different regions of the country but these try to put pressure on the Central Government because important agricultural policies and decisions are annually fixed by the Central Government.

(d) **Caste Groups :** Of all the groups based upon the traditional structure of the Indian society, the caste groups are the most politically significant groups. Caste continues to be the most important political force in India. Caste continues to be a determinant of political behaviour of the Indians. In particular, it is a major determinant of electoral behaviour and voting behaviour. The Caste Organisations like Scheduled Castes Federation, Vanniyakula Kshatriya Sangam, Jat Mahasabha, Aggarwal Sabha, Gujjar Sabha, Gujarat Kshatriya Sabha, etc., are active actors in the Indian politics. Caste associations play a useful role in providing channels of communication and basis of leadership and organization to all such people who continue to follow the traditional way of life.

(e) **Student Organisations :** Since 1928, when a student organization was formed in Punjab by Lala Lajpat Rai, several student groups and Organisations have been active in India. In contemporary times, several such Organisations –National Students' Union of India, Students' Federation of India, Akhil Bharatiya Vidyarthi Parishad, Progressive Students Union, Bharatiya Janata Yuva Morcha, Indian Youth Congress, All India Sikh Students Federation, Jamaat-e-Tulba, and several others, are actively involved in the political process. The lowering of the voting age from 21 to 18 years has further encouraged them to play a more active role. Most of the student Organisations have committed links with the political parties.

(f) **Linguistic Pressure Groups :** Several pressure groups in India have been organized mainly for furthering the development of a particular language. The Tamil Sangam. the Anjuman Taraqqi Urdu, the Vishwa Hindu Parishad, the Punjabi Sahit Shabha, the Sahitya Sammelan, etc. are linguistic pressure groups.

(g) **Professional Groups :** Several professional interest groups, like All India Bar Association, Medical Council of India, All India Federation of University and College Teachers' Organisations, etc., are also active in India. These professional groups put forward their problems and needs before the government and try to secure favourable governmental policies that can help them to protect and develop their professional interests.

(h) **Religious Groups :** India is a land of several religions. The multi-religious character of the society has been instrumental in giving rise to several religious pressure groups and Organisations. Anglo-Indian Christian Association, Jamaat-e-Islami, Arya Samaj, Catholic Bishops' Conference of India , Hindu Mahasabha, and others are religious pressure groups. These have always tried to influence the government policy. These have become highly self-conscious and politically conscious groups and some of these have even started fielding their candidates in elections.

LIMITATIONS OF PRESSURE GROUPS

1. The pressure groups are criticized for their particularistic and selfish attitude and their mischievous role in the political process of the country. They undermine the normal functions of the elected representatives.
2. Pressure groups undermine and distort the political process through highly objectionable and unfair methods.
3. It may prejudice the decisions of the government in favour of particular interests as against the general interest of the people.
4. They encourage divisive forces and sharpen group antagonism and conflict, which may destroy the very basis of a political system.
5. It is interesting to note that the pressure groups very often seek judicial intervention in favour of their particularistic interests, which they try to project as matters of fundamental constitutional and national importance. The pressure groups have highly paid agents who act as the lobbyists who work secretly, and are beyond the glare of the public eye to achieve their objectives. Most of the work done by the pressure groups is not purely legal or moral, and these works are performed under some kind of a cover.
6. Large number of people who are not members of pressure groups or whose groups are not as well organized as the groups of some other people are likely to be totally neglected by the government.

24.6 COALITION GOVERNMENT

INTRODUCTION

A coalition government is a cabinet of a Parliamentary government in which several political parties cooperate. The usual reason given for this arrangement is that no party of its own can achieve a majority in Parliament. A coalition government might also be created in a time of national difficulty or crisis, for example during wartime, to give a government the high degree of perceived political legitimacy it desires whilst also playing a role in diminishing internal political strife. In such times, parties have formed all-party coalitions. If a coalition collapses, unless the government itself quits, a Confidence vote is held or a Motion of No Confidence is taken to test whether the government can survive. Thus, a coalition government is one in which several political parties must cooperate in order to run a country, region, state, or province.

Meaning of Coalition Government

When several political parties join hands to form a government and exercise political power on the basis of a common agreed programme/agenda, we can describe the system as coalition politics or coalition government. Coalitions usually occur in modern parliaments when no single political party can muster a majority of votes.

COALITION GOVERNMENT IN INDIA

India also has a multi-party system. However, for a long period following independence, the Indian political system was dominated by one single party – the Congress. It virtually ruled as a monolith party not only at the centre but in almost all states as well. This is because India lacked a strong opposition party, a forceful alternative that could be appealing enough across a vast country. It remained so till late 1980s and further during 1990s.

Currently, the experts as well as the proponents and opponents of the coalition government all agree on one point and that is, coalition governments have become a norm in the present-day Indian polity, both at the centre and in most of the states. This is because India has a multi-party system, where there are a number of national as well as regional parties. Also, the lack of homogeneity in the Indian population causes division between different sections of the people based on religion, region, language, caste, and race. This has led to the rise of a large number of political parties with only a local or regional support base. Some parties openly profess their focus on a particular group. For example, the Dravida Munnetra Kazhagam on the Dravidian population, Shiv Sena on a pro-Marathi agenda, etc.

Features of Coalition Government

The features or implications of coalition politics or coalition government are very well summarised by J.C. Johari in the following way:

1. Coalitions are formed for the sake of some reward, material, or psychic.
2. A coalition implies the existence of at least two partners.
3. The underlying principle of a coalition system stands on the simple fact of temporary conjunction of specific interest.

4. Coalition politics is not a static but a dynamic affair as coalition players and groups dissolve and form new ones.
5. The keynote of coalition politics is compromise, and rigid dogma has no place in it.
6. A coalition government works on the basis of a minimum programme, which may not be ideal for each partner of the coalition.
7. Pragmatism and not ideology is the hallmark of coalition politics. In making political adjustments, principles may have to be set aside.
8. The purpose of a coalition adjustment is to seize power.

Arguments in Favour of the Coalition Government

1. Advocates of proportional representation suggest that a coalition government leads to more consensus-based politics, in that a government comprising differing parties, often based on different ideologies, would need to concur in regard to governmental policy.
2. A coalition government better reflects the popular opinion of the electorate within a country. This is because in almost all coalitions, a majority of citizens voted for the parties which form the government and so their views and interests are represented in political decision-making. Coalition government, therefore, is more democratic, and hence fairer, because it represents a much broader spectrum of public opinion than government by one party alone.
3. Coalition government creates a more honest and dynamic political system, allowing voters a clearer choice at election time. In countries where coalition government is very rare, such as the UK or USA, the main parties straddle a wide spectrum of opinions and can be seen as coalitions of competing interest groups and ideologies. At elections, however, such parties present themselves, perhaps fraudulently, to voters as united behind particular views and policies, whereas in power, their internal divisions may have a serious and often unseen impact upon decision-making.
4. In countries with coalition governments, the greater number of political parties gives the voter a more honest choice and brings differences of opinion out into the open for debate. It is also easier for parties to split, or new ones to be formed, as new political issues divide opinion, because new parties still have a chance of a share in political power.
5. The coalition government is an open government. The Cabinet meets regularly where all decisions are preceded by keen debate. Everyone is consulted. The individual ministers look after their departments and the Prime Minister rarely overrules them. There is hardly any complaint of interference by the Prime Minister or his office. The role of the Cabinet Secretariat is that of a coordinator between the ministries. This is in complete contrast to a majority government where ministries simply follow the instructions issued by the Prime Minister or his office.

Arguments Against the Coalition Government

1. Those who disapprove of coalition governments believe that such governments have a tendency to be fractious and prone to disharmony. This is because coalitions would necessarily include different parties with differing beliefs and who, therefore, may not always agree on the correct path for governmental policy.
2. Coalition breeds instability. The consensus government or the coalition government in India has resulted in a weak Cabinet and even weaker Prime Minister. Both depend upon the precarious support of parties, each of whom may change its stand every time any new issue emerges.

3. Experience shows that coalition governments have mostly been formed due to political opportunities and personal selfishness. Governments formed on these considerations joined hands without taking into consideration principles, ideologies, or programmes. Hence, mixed governments containing communal, secular, capitalist, communists, progressive, and traditional elements all joined together but immediately began fighting on its implementation. Defections also became the reason for the downfall of coalition governments, even after the enactment of Anti-defection Law. Money and Cabinet berth propelled legislators to change sides. The most striking role in this regard has been that of the independent legislators. This led to the process of political bargaining.
4. Due to the agglomeration of several parties, a coalition government is often times, considered a very weak form of government because there is no majority party. In such cases, the only way a policy gets approved is by making concessions to coalition partners or the parties sitting in the opposition.
5. Coalition government is less transparent. Because a party has no real chance of forming a government alone, the manifestoes they present to the public becomes irrelevant and often wildly unrealistic. Real decisions about political programmes are made after the election, in a process of secretive backroom negotiations from which the public is excluded. This undermines accountability, as voters cannot expect individual parties in a coalition to deliver upon their particular manifesto promises, unlike the single-party governments. Accountability is also absent when a coalition government falls, either after an election or through the defection of some of its supporters. Any new administration will tend to include most of the parties and politicians from the previous government, with just a little shuffling of coalition partners and ministerial jobs.

When Can a Coalition Government Work?

Coalition government can work, provided it is formed by like-minded parties. Before forming a coalition government, parties should at least have some amount of matching of their economic, social, political, industrial, and agricultural policies. In case of the Central government, one can also add foreign and defence. These are the major functional areas of the government. If these do not match, then the coalition will not work.

Indian experience has also shown that those coalitions in which the biggest party leads have been more successful. Thus, NDA and UPA have been more successful because it was led by the BJP and the Congress respectively. In contrast, Charan Singh's, Chandra Shekhar's, Deve Gowda's, and Inder Kumar Gujral's governments were short-lived because the largest parties in the coalition were only supporting them from outside. This also is not good for the country and democracy because if the party having the PM is very small, it will have a weak hold over the coalition. It is necessary in a democracy that the government should be stable and for this, it should be led by the largest party in it.

24.7 ANTI-DEFECTION LAW

INTRODUCTION

Initially, the Constitution of India did not have any mention about the political parties. But gradually, when the multi-party system evolved, there have been defections in the Indian Parliamentary System where there has been shift of people from one political party to another, which resulted in breaking down of public confidence in a democratic form of Government.

The term 'defection' simply means desertion or abandonment or running away from duty. However, in politics, its ramifications include many situations like shifting of loyalty or allegiance from one party or group to another.

Defection causes government instability. A government may be toppled over due to defection of some of its supporters to the opposition party, converting the opposition party from a minority into a majority party. Defection is undemocratic as it negates the electoral verdict. A party which fails to get majority in the House through elections may yet be able to manoeuvre a majority in the House and form the government by inducing defections from other parties. Thus, the party which may have won a majority through election, and got the mandate from the people to form the government, may yet fail to do so because a few members defect from the party.

It is one thing for a member to change his political affiliation out of conviction because he may conscientiously disagree with the policies of the party to which he belongs. In such a case, if he leaves the party with whose support he has been elected to the House, he ought to resign from his membership, and seek fresh election to the House. But such principled defections are rare. Most of the defections take place out of selfish motives as the defectors hope to be appointed as Ministers in the Council of Ministers to be formed with their support[1]. This practice of elected members switching the political sides to get office is also known as Horse-Trading. It is also known as "Floor Crossing" in UK.

In order to curb the menace of political defections in India, the Parliament by the 52nd Amendment Act, 1985, appended the Tenth Schedule to the Indian Constitution, prominently known as the Anti-Defection Law. The intention of this law is to secure political stability and prevent the legislatures from defecting their unique political party.

CONSTITUTIONAL PROVISIONS REGARDING ANTI-DEFECTION LAW (TENTH SCHEDULE)

The 52nd Amendment Act, 1985 led to an amendment in the Articles 101, 102, 190, and 191 of the Constitution to provide the grounds for vacation of seats for the disqualification of the members; and also inserted the Tenth Schedule.

The Tenth Schedule lays the grounds for disqualification of the members, i.e.,

1. If a member of a House belonging to a political party:

   (a) Has voluntarily given up his membership of such political party, or

[1] *Indian Constitutional Law*, M.P. Jain, Eighth Edition, LexisNexis, Pg No. 46.

(b) Votes, or abstain from voting in such House, contrary to the direction of his political party. However, if the member has taken prior permission, or is condoned by the party within 15 days from such voting or abstention, the member shall not be disqualified.

2. If an independent candidate joins a political party after the election.
3. If a nominated member of a House joins any political party after the expiry of six months from the date when he becomes a member of the Legislature.

Exemptions Under Anti-Defection Law

However, there are exemptions provided for the defection under the Tenth Schedule:

1. A member of the House shall not be disqualified where his original political party merges with another political party, and he and any other member of his political party: -

   (a) Have become members of the other political party, or of a new political party formed by such merger. Merger is subject to the condition that at least two-third of the members of the Legislature party concerned has agreed to such merger. In other words, merger is when it is supported by 2/3rd of the party members/merging party); or

   (b) Have not accepted the merger and opted to function as a separate group.

2. There will be no disqualification of members if they represent a faction of the original political party, which has arisen as a result of a split in the party. A defection by at least one-third members of such a political part was considered as a spilt which was not actionable. In other words, no disqualification would be incurred in cases where there is a split of at least one-third of the members of the original party. However, this exemption has been omitted from the Tenth Schedule by the 91st Constitutional Amendment Act, 2003.

   Thus, the Anti-Defection Law protects mergers of parties, provided that the decision to merge is supported by not less than two-thirds of a merging party but not splits in the party.

3. If a person is elected as Speaker or Chairman, then he could resign from his party, and re-join the party if he demitted that post. There will be no disqualification in this case.

Role of the Presiding Officer

The question of disqualification under Tenth Schedule is to be determined by the Speaker of the Lok Sabha, or the Chairman of the Rajya Sabha, as the case may be, but he is to take notice of an alleged defection not *suo motu,* but only when a petition in writing is received from a member[2]. The Tenth Schedule renders the decision of the Speaker as final. But before taking the final decision on defection, the Presiding Officer shall give an opportunity of being heard to the defector.

Moreover, the Speaker or the Chairman of the House is empowered to make rules to give effect to the provisions of the Tenth Schedule. All such rules must be placed before the House for 30 days. The House may accept or amend or reject the rules. Once the rules come into force, all the members of the House have to abide by the rules and if not, action for breach of privileges can be initiated against the concerned person.

---

[2]Provided in the Rules of the House.

Kihoto Hollohan Vs. Zachillhu[3] **:** The Supreme Court upheld the Constitutional validity of the Anti-Defection Law. But, at the same time, the Court has ruled that the Speaker's order under the law disqualifying a member of the Legislature on the ground of defection is subject to judicial review. In the words of the Supreme Court,

"The Speakers/Chairmen while exercising powers and discharging functions under the Tenth Schedule act as "Tribunal", adjudicating rights and obligations under the Tenth Schedule and their decisions in that capacity are amenable to judicial review".

The court further held that the Speaker's order would be open to judicial review on the grounds of jurisdictional errors based on violation of Constitutional mandate, *mala fides,* and non-compliance with rules of natural justice and perversity.

Moreover, the plain reading of the Tenth Schedule indicates that the judicial review of the court is possible only after the final adjudication by the Speaker. The question arises whether the court has the power to issue interim orders during the pendency of the disqualification proceedings. The Supreme Court in *Speaker Haryana Vidhan Sabha Vs. Kuldeep Bishnoi*[4] case held that – Prior to final adjudication, judicial review is permissible only on two grounds carved out in *Kihoto Hollohan* case, that is:

(a) Speaker suspending or taking action during the pendency of disqualification proceedings, and

(b) Grave immediate irreversible repercussions.

Merits and Demerits of the Anti-Defection Law

Like every other law, Anti-Defection Laws too come with their own merits and demerits. Looking at the positive side, the law aims at providing stability to the Government by punishing members in case of any party shifts on their parts. Also, Anti-Defection Laws try to bring about a sense of loyalty of the members towards their own party. Thus, it tries to achieve this by ensuring that the members selected in the name of the party support the party manifesto and its policies[5] and remain loyal to the political party of which he is a member.

With respect to the demerits of the law :

- It interferes with the member's freedom of speech and expression by curbing dissent against party policies[6].
- By preventing Parliamentarians from changing parties, it reduces the accountability of the government to the Parliament and the people.
- The provision relating to mergers, whereby it exempts members from disqualification if they defect in large numbers, i.e., two-third, is irrational. In other words, retail defections are not allowed, whereas wholesale defections are allowed. The Anti-Defection law should give more importance to the reasons for defection rather than to the numbers. Therefore, making the reason for defection as the basis for exemption from disqualification rather than mere numbers would be more rational.

---

[3]AIR 1993 SC 412.

[4](2015) 12 SCC 381.

[5]G.C. Malhotra, Anti-Defection Law In India And The Commonwealth (Lok Sabha Secretariat, 2005).

[6]However, it has been held in various judgments that the freedom of speech provided under Article 105 and 194 is not absolute.

- The independent member cannot join any party after being elected to the House. Whereas, a nominated member can join any political party within six months of the nomination. This kind of unwarranted difference between an independent member and a nominated member with respect to defection is irrational.

Recommendations of Various Bodies on Anti-Defection Law[7]

Body/Committee	Main Reforms Suggested/Recommended
Dinesh Goswami Committee on Electoral Reforms (1990)	• Disqualification should be limited to cases where (a) a member voluntarily gives up the membership of his political party, (b) a member abstains from voting, or votes contrary to the party whip in a motion of vote of Confidence or motion of No-confidence. • The issue of disqualification should be decided by the President/ Governor on the advice of the Election Commission.
Halim Committee on Anti-Defection Law (1998)	• The words 'voluntarily giving up membership of a political party' be comprehensively defined. • Restrictions like prohibition on joining another party or holding offices in the government be imposed on expelled members. • The term 'political party' should be defined clearly.
Law Commission (170th Report, 1999)	• Provisions which exempt splits and mergers from disqualification to be deleted. • Pre-poll electoral fronts should be treated as political parties under Anti-Defection law. • Political parties should limit issuance of whips to instances only when the government is in danger.
Election Commission	• Decisions under the Tenth Schedule should be made by the President/Governor on the binding advice of the Election Commission.
Constitution Review Commission (2002)	• Defectors should be barred from holding public office or any remunerative political post for the duration of the remaining term. • The vote cast by a defector to topple a government should be treated as invalid.

[7]R. Kothandaraman, *Ideas for an alternative Anti-Defection law*, 2006; PRS.

24.8 ELECTORAL REFORMS

INTRODUCTION

In Parliamentary democracy, representation is linked with elections at regular intervals. Elections are the only mechanism through which representation, government formation, control on government, and changes in ruling political parties are conducted. Therefore, elections are essential features of a Parliamentary democracy. But only elections are not the criteria to fulfil the aspirations of the people. Free and fair elections are necessary for healthy democracy. Democracy and "free and fair" elections are inseparable twins[1]. In this regard, electoral reforms have paved the way for free and fair elections. Electoral reforms refer to the introduction of best practices in ensuring better responsible Parliamentary democracy, removal of structural flaws, clean politics, honest politicians, maintenance of citizens' trust, true representation, and so on. We need electoral reforms, and need them urgently, if we wish to ensure a healthy democracy, at least in a workable form, if not in its ideal form[2].

ELECTORAL REFORMS IN INDIA

The need for electoral reforms was increasingly felt towards the late 1960s in India. Till then, the electoral system had functioned quite satisfactorily, except for a few of the aberrations in the form of some malpractices like rigging or violence, which are rather small in number.

Committees for Electoral Reforms

A Parliamentary Committee was constituted for the first time in 1970 to suggest amendments to the Election Law from all angles. But with the dissolution of the Lok Sabha in December 1970, the life of this Committee also came to an end. Subsequent to the constitution of a new Lok Sabha in 1971, the Parliament formed a Joint Parliamentary Committee on Amendments to Election Law headed by Shri Jagannath Rao.

In subsequent years, a number of Committees were constituted, such as:

- The Tarkunde Committee (1974);
- The Dinesh Goswami Committee (1990);
- The Vohra Committee Report (1993);
- V.R. Krishna Iyer Committee (1994);
- The Indrajit Gupta Committee on State Funding of Elections (1998);
- Law Commission Report on Reform of the Electoral Laws (1999);
- National Commission to Review the Working of the Constitution (2001);
- Election Commission of India - Proposed Electoral Reforms (2004);
- The Tankha Committee (2010);
- J.S. Verma Committee Report on Amendments to Criminal Law (2013);
- Law Commission Report on Electoral Disqualifications (2014);
- Law Commission Report on Electoral Reforms (2015).

---

[1]Baruah 2018, p. 1.

[2]Chhokar 2010, p. 3977.

PROBLEMS DETERIORATING THE ELECTORAL SYSTEM

In spite of so many committees and reports of the government, the concern on electoral reforms still continues, mainly because, except for bringing some procedural changes in the electoral system, most of the suggestions of these committees and reports have not been implemented by the Government. The question of electoral reforms acquires importance in India at the present day due to the growing deterioration in electoral politics. Widely held views among the public with regard to criminalisation of politics, the use of money power in securing votes, and the paid news disease are some of the issues that are enlarging the trust deficit with regard to our electoral process.

Some of the problems which deteriorate our electoral system are:

(a) **Criminalisation of politics :** The criminalisation of our political system has been observed almost unanimously by all recent committees on politics and electoral reforms. Criminalisation of politics has many forms, but perhaps the most alarming among them is the significant number of elected representatives with criminal charges pending against them. It has been seen that most of the major political parties field a high number of candidates with a criminal record, i.e., those undergoing trial in some court or the other.

(b) **Financing of Elections :** It is widely believed that in many cases, successful contesting of an election costs a significant amount of money that is often much greater than the prescribed limits. But the problem with extravagant spending of money is that the person who wins the election spends all of his or her time recovering the money that he or she spent during the election and in returning favours to those who funded him or her, rather than focusing on real issues of governance. In addition to this, the citizens are directly affected because apart from compromised governance, the huge money spent on elections pushes up the cost of everything in the country and in return, the general citizen has to face the real hurdles. Moreover, it has been seen that electoral compulsions for funds become the foundation of the whole structure of corruption.

(c) **State Funding of Elections :** This refers to the government funding of the political parties or candidates contesting the elections. This would ensure an equal playing field to all and also eliminate outside pressure over government policies and functioning by various lobbies. The move is also bound to help in controlling the flow of unaccounted money and muscle power during elections and hence, control the levels of corruption in public life.

(d) **Registration and de-registration of political parties** *:* Proliferation of political parties is also one of the root causes for the deterioration of electoral process. Section 29A of the Representation of the People Act, 1951, allows for small groups of people to form political parties by making only a simple declaration. According to the Election Commission, a large number of non-serious parties create an excessive load on the electoral system. The Commission was of the view that there are numerous political parties which did not contest election but are registered as political parties in order to get relief in income tax. The Commission also recommends that the power to register or de-register a political party should be vested in the Election Commission in order to eliminate these parties and also, if any political party violates any provision of the law.

(e) **Simultaneous Assembly and General elections :** The massive size of the Indian electorate makes general elections an enormous and daunting exercise. According to the Election Commission of India, the size of the electorate for the 2019 elections to the 17th Lok Sabha was approximately 900 million. The National Commission to Review the Working of the Constitution, 2000, stated in its report that holding of general elections in India is equal to holding of elections for Europe, the United States, Canada, and Australia (if all are put together). In order to administrate the electoral process successfully, it requires more than 50 lakh personnel and almost 1 million (10 lakh) polling booths. Millions of security personnel are required to promote a peaceful and incident-free voting experience. Therefore, conducting the simultaneous general and assembly elections would be cost-effective as well as efficacious.

(f) **Paid News as Electoral Offence :** Paid news is sale of editorial space by media organisations in favour of political parties. This is essentially an advertisement in the guise of news to gain votes. Though the practice has been prevalent for years, it gained limelight during 2009 Lok Sabha elections when the Press Council of India investigated the media coverage of candidates. The Election Commission wants the paid news to be made an electoral offence with not less than two years of imprisonment so that such individuals are disqualified from contesting elections.

(g) **Preparation and Use of Common Electoral Rolls :** The Law Commission endorses the ECI's suggestions regarding the introduction of common electoral rolls for Parliamentary, Assembly, and local body elections.

IMPORTANT ELECTORAL REFORMS IN INDIA

The following are some of the important electoral reforms that have been introduced in our electoral system over the last years in India:

1. **Electronic Voting Machines :** In 1982, EC issued directions for use of Electronic Voting Machines (EVMs) for the first time in a by-election to North Paravur Assembly Constituency in Kerala. Later on, the Representation of the People Act, 1951, was amended to facilitate the use of Electronic Voting Machines (EVM) in elections with effect from 1989. Consequently, electronic Voting Machines (EVMs) were first used after the amendment in November, 1998 in various constituencies in the State elections of Rajasthan, Madhya Pradesh, and Delhi. The 2004 Lok Sabha election was conducted entirely on EVMs.
2. **Anti-Defection Law :** Anti-Defection law was introduced by the 52nd Constitutional Amendment Act, 1985 by amending the Constitution. Under Anti-defection law, an MP or MLA will be declared defected if they either voluntarily resign from the party or disobey the directives of the party leadership on a vote. The Anti-Defection law helps to avoid instability in the government by ensuring that the concerned members do not switch political parties.
3. **Lowering of voting age :** By 61st Constitutional Amendment Act, 1988, the voting age was lowered from 21 years to 18 years for the General as well as Assembly Elections. Lowering of the age provided a greater number of youth an opportunity to actively participate in the electoral process.

4. **Model Code of Conduct :** MCC is a set of guidelines issued by the Election Commission to regulate political parties and candidates prior to the elections. As per the ECI, the Model Code of Conduct was first observed during the 1960 polls. According to the ECI manual, "Historically, the credit of giving the idea of a model code of conduct for political parties should go to the State of Kerala, which adopted, for the first time, a code of conduct for observance for Political Parties during the general election to the State Legislative Assembly in February 1960". In 1996, the ECI enforced the MCC. Even though MCC is not directly enforceable, it can be enforced by invoking the corresponding provisions present in various Acts such as IPC, RPA (1951), etc., which enjoys a statutory backing.

5. **Full disclosure :** In 2002, the Supreme Court of India, while striking down the Section 33B of the Representation of the People Act, held that that all the contesting candidates will have to furnish all personal information, including the criminal record, at the time of filing nomination papers. Non-disclosure (non-filing of affidavits) of the requisite information will clearly be a ground for rejection of nomination. In other words, the candidates at the time of nomination shall disclose the following information:
   - All convictions, charges framed, and cases of which cognizance was taken should be revealed.
   - Statement of assets, liabilities, and dues to public financial institutions in respect of themselves, spouses, and members of their families.
   - Disclosure of educational qualifications.

6. **Restriction on exit polls :** Exit polls are conducted by researchers asking voters how they have voted just after they have left the polling station after casting their ballot. Such polls are aimed at predicting the result of an election based on the information collected from voters on election day. They are conducted by several organisations in India. An opinion poll is a voter behaviour survey conducted in order to find out the opinion of the people, including those who may or may not vote, before voting takes place. An exit poll is done right after people have voted on an election day. The EC approached the Union law ministry along with the endorsement of six national and 18 regional parties in 2004, as it sought an amendment to the Representation of the People Act for a ban on both exit and opinion polls during a period specified by it. Restrictions were imposed only on exit polls through the introduction of Section 126(A) in the Act after the recommendation was accepted in part in February 2010. Section 126A of the Representation of the People Act, 1951, bans exit polls from the beginning of the polls until half an hour after the final phase of voting has been held.

7. **NOTA :** "None of the Above", is the option which enables the voter to officially register a vote of rejection for all candidates who are contesting. If a voter chooses to press NOTA, it indicates that the voter has not chosen to vote for any of the parties. The Supreme Court in *PUCL Vs. UOI*[3], has held that "a provision of negative voting would be in the interest of promoting democracy as it would send clear signals to political parties and their candidates as to what the electorate thinks about them" and directed the ECI to provide option of NOTA in all EVMs. In other

[3] [(2013) 10 SCC 1].

words, the Supreme Court of India ruled that the right to register a "None of the Above" vote in elections should apply, while ordering the Election Commission to provide a button for the same in the electronic voting machines. The ECI introduced a particular symbol for 'None of the Above' option to allow the voters to exercise NOTA. This symbol appears in the last panel on all Electronic Voting Machines (EVMs). The very purpose of introducing this option is to empower the voter to reject all candidates if they do not like any and all the candidates listed in the EVM (electronic voting machine). The political parties would be left with no option other than to nominate clean candidates on their behalf in the elections. Candidates with criminal or immoral backgrounds would have no option but to abstain from contesting elections. The provision of the NOTA button was first implemented in the State Assembly Elections of Chhattisgarh, Mizoram, Rajasthan, Delhi, and Madhya Pradesh in 2013. In 2014, NOTA was first introduced in the Lok Sabha Elections.

8. **Deadline to complete trial against MPs :** The Supreme Court in 2014 ruled that trials of members of Parliament (MPs) and State Legislatures accused of serious crimes should be time-bound and directed lower courts to conclude the proceedings within a year. And if a trial court fails to complete the process within a year of framing charges, it will have to submit an explanation to the Chief Justice of the high court. Any relaxation of the deadline will be decided by the Chief Justice of the high court. Effectively, this decision tries to close the option for politicians to use delays in legal trials to hold on to public office.

9. **Voter Verifiable Paper Audit Trail (VVPAT) :** In a meeting of all political parties held in 2010, the parties requested the Election Commission to consider introducing Voter Verifiable Paper Audit Trail for further transparency and verifiability in poll process. The Government of India notified the amended the Conduct of Elections Rules, 1961 in 2013, enabling the Commission to use VVPAT with EVMs. The Commission used VVPAT with EVMs first time in bye-election from 51-Noksen (ST) Assembly Constituency of Nagaland. Thereafter, VVPATs have been used in selected constituencies in every election to Legislative Assemblies and 8 Parliamentary Constituencies in General Election to the House of the People-2014. Voter Verifiable Paper Audit Trail is an independent system attached with the Electronic Voting Machines that allows the voters to verify that their votes are cast as intended. When a vote is cast, a slip is printed on the VVPAT printer containing the serial number, name, and symbol of the candidate and remains exposed through a transparent window for 7 seconds. Thereafter, this printed slip automatically gets cut and falls in sealed drop box of the VVPAT. VVPAT consists of a Printer and a VVPAT Status Display Unit (VSDU).

10. **Corporate Funding :** To harmonise the efforts to curb flow of cash and unaccounted money into the political system, in 2017, the Company's Act was amended allowing for unlimited corporate donation to political parties. This will also facilitate the broadening of political funding channels. The amendment, besides removing the cap for contributions, also allows companies to keep the names of political parties confidential in their accounts.

11. **Electoral Bonds :** The Government notified the scheme of Electoral Bonds in 2017 to cleanse the system of political funding in the country. Electoral Bond would be a bearer instrument in the nature of a Promissory Note and an interest-free banking instrument. A citizen of India or a body incorporated in India will be eligible to purchase the bond. Electoral bond would be issued/purchased for any value, in multiples of Rs. 1,000, Rs. 10,000, Rs. 1,00,000, Rs. 10,00,000, and Rs. 1,00,00,000 from the specified branches of the State Bank of India (SBI). There is no limit on the number of bonds an individual or company can purchase. Only political parties registered under Section 29A of the Representation of the People Act, 1951 and which secured not less than 1 percent of votes polled in the last general election to the House of the People or the Legislative Assembly of the State, are eligible to receive electoral bonds. But the electoral bonds are being opposed by some activists because even though the political parties reveal the amount of donations received to the Election Commission every year, they don't need to disclose the details of the donors. Thus, the voters cannot know which individual or company has funded the political party.

12. **Disclosure of income sources :** Before 2018, the candidates were required to disclose the details of assets and liabilities for themselves, spouse, and three dependents in Form 26 while filing the nomination paper but not the source of income. However, the Supreme Court in 2018 in *Lok Prahari Vs. Union of India & others*[4], made it mandatory for candidates contesting elections to declare the sources of income for them, their spouses, and dependants in an aim to ensure the probity among politicians.

13. **Foreign funding for political parties :** The Foreign Contribution Regulation Act regulates foreign donations and ensures that such contributions do not adversely affect internal security. First enacted in 1976, it was amended in 2010 when a slew of new measures were adopted to regulate foreign donations. The FCRA is applicable to all associations, groups, and NGOs which intend to receive foreign donations. Registered associations can receive foreign contribution for social, educational, religious, economic, and cultural purposes. But the Members of the Legislature and political parties, government officials, judges, and media persons are prohibited from receiving any foreign contribution. However, in 2018, during the budget session (through a Finance Bill), the FCRA,1976 was repealed, paving the way for political parties to receive funds from the Indian subsidiary of a foreign company or a foreign company in which an Indian holds 50% or more shares.

---

[4]Writ Petition (C) NO.784 OF 2015.

LIST OF RECOGNISED NATIONAL POLITICAL PARTIES (2022)

S.No.	Name of the Party	Symbol Reserved[5]	Founding Date
1.	Bharatiya Janata Party	Lotus	6 April 1980
2.	Bahujan Samaj Partys	Elephant	14 April 1984
3.	Communist Party of India	Ears of Corn & Sickle	26 December 1925
4.	Communist Party of India (Marxist)	Hammer, Sickle and Star	7 November 1964
5.	Indian National Congress	Hand	28 December 1885
6.	Nationalist Congress Party (NCP)	Clock	10 June 1999
7.	National People's Party (NPP)	Book	6 January 2013
8.	Trinamool Congress	Flowers and Grass	1 January 1998

List of Recognised State Political Parties (2022)

S.No	Name of the Party	Foundation Year	States/UT
1.	Aam Aadmi Party	2012	Delhi, Punjab
2.	All India Anna Dravida Munnetra Kazhagam	1972	Puducherry, Tamil Nadu
3.	All India Forward Bloc	1939	West Bengal
4.	All India Majlis-e-Ittehadul Muslimeen	1927	Telangana
5.	All India N.R. Congress	2011	Puducherry
6.	All India United Democratic Front	2004	Assam
7.	All Jharkhand Students Union	1986	Jharkhand
8.	Asom Gana Parishad	1985	Assam
9.	Biju Janata Dal	1997	Odisha
10.	Bodoland People's Front	1985	Assam
11.	Desiya Murpokku Dravidar Kazhagam	2005	Tamil Nadu
12.	Dravida Munnetra Kazhagam	1949	Puducherry, Tamil Nadu
13.	Indian Union Muslim League	1948	Kerala
14.	Hill State People's Democratic Party	1968	Meghalaya
15.	Indian National Lok Dal	1999	Haryana
16.	Indian Union Muslim League	1948	Kerala
17.	Jammu & Kashmir National Conference	1932	Jammu & Kashmir
18.	Jammu & Kashmir National Panthers Party	1982	Jammu & Kashmir
19.	Jammu and Kashmir People's Democratic Party	1998	Jammu & Kashmir

[5]In all States/U.T.s except in Assam, where its candidates will have to choose a symbol out of the list of free symbols specified by the Election Commission.

20.	Janata Dal (Secular)	1999	Karnataka, Kerala
21.	Janata Dal (United)	1999	Bihar
22.	Jharkhand Mukti Morcha	1972	Jharkhand
23.	People's Democratic Front	2017	Meghalaya
24.	Kerala Congress (M)	1979	Kerala
25.	Lok Janshakti Party	2000	Bihar
26.	Maharashtra Navnirman Sena	2006	Maharashtra
27.	Maharashtrawadi Gomantak Party	1963	Goa
28.	United People's Party Liberal	2015	Assam
29.	Mizo National Front	1959	Mizoram
30.	Mizoram People's Conference	1972	Mizoram
31.	Naga People's Front	2002	Manipur, Nagaland
32.	Nationalist Democratic Progressive Party	2017	Nagaland
33.	Pattali Makkal Katchi	1989	Puducherry, Tamil Nadu
34.	People's Party of Arunachal	1977	Arunachal Pradesh
35.	Rashtriya Janata Dal	1997	Bihar, Jharkhand
36.	Rashtriya Loktantrik Party	2020	Rajasthan
37.	Zoram Nationalist Party	1997	Mizoram
38.	Revolutionary Socialist Party	1940	Kerala, West Bengal
39.	Samajwadi Party	1992	Uttar Pradesh
40.	Shiromani Akali Dal	1920	Punjab
41.	Shiv Sena	1966	Maharashtra
42.	Sikkim Democratic Front	1993	Sikkim
43.	Sikkim Krantikari Morcha	2013	Sikkim
44.	Telangana Rashtra Samithi	2001	Telangana
45.	Telugu Desam Party	1982	Andhra Pradesh, Telangana
46.	United Democratic Party	1972	Meghalaya
47.	YSR Congress Party	2011	Andhra Pradesh, Telangana
48.	Samajwadi Janata Party (Rashtriya)	1990	Uttar Pradesh
49.	Communist Party of India (Marxist–Leninist) Liberation	1974	Bihar
50.	Goa Forward Party	2016	Goa
51.	Indigenous People's Front of Tripura	2009	Tripura
52.	Janta Congress Chhattisgarh	2016	Chhattisgarh
53.	Jan Nayak Janta Party	2018	Haryana

Lok Sabha General Elections Since Independence

S. No.	Election Year	Lok Sabha	Total Seats	Turnout	Single Largest Party	Seats won by the single largest party	Prime Minister
1.	1951-52	First	489	45.07%	Indian National Congress	364	Jawaharlal Nehru
2.	1957	Second	494	55.02%	Indian National Congress	371	Jawaharlal Nehru
3.	1962	Third	494	55.42%	Indian National Congress	361	Jawaharlal Nehru
4.	1967	Fourth	520	61.04%	Indian National Congress	283	Indira Gandhi
5.	1971	Fifth	518	55.27%	Indian National Congress	352	Indira Gandhi
6.	1977	Sixth	542	60.49%	Indian National Congress	295	Moraji Desai
7.	1977	Seventh	529	56.92%	Indian National Congress	353	Indira Gandhi
8.	1984	Eighth	541	64.01%	Indian National Congress	414	Rajiv Gandhi
9.	1989	Ninth	529	61.95%	Indian National Congress	197	V.P.Singh
10.	1991	Tenth	521	55.88%	Indian National Congress	244	P.V.Narasimha Rao
11.	1996	Eleventh	543	57.94%	Bharatiya Janata Party	161	Atal Bihari Vajpayee
12.	1998	Twelfth	543	61.97%	Bharatiya Janata Party	182	Atal Bihari Vajpayee
13.	1999	Thirteenth	543	59.99%	Bharatiya Janata Party	182	Atal Bihari Vajpayee
14.	2004	Fourteenth	543	58.07%	Indian National Congress	145	Manmohan Singh
15.	2009	Fifteenth	543	58.21%	Indian National Congress	206	Manmohan Singh
16.	2014	Sixteenth	543	66.44%	Bharatiya Janata Party	282	Narendra Modi
17.	2019	Seventeenth	543	67.40%	Bharatiya Janata Party	303	Narendra Modi

Women in Lok Sabha Elections

General Elections (Year)	Contested	Elected
First (1952)	---	22
Second (1957)	45	27
Third (1962)	70	34
Fourth (1967)	67	31

Fifth (1971)	86	22
Sixth (1977)	70	19
Seventh (1980)	142	28
Eighth (1984)	164	44
Ninth (1989)	198	27
Tenth (1991)	325	39
Eleventh (1996)	599	40
Twelfth (1998)	274	43
Thirteenth (1999)	284	49
Fourteenth (2004)	355	45
Fifteenth (2009)	556	59
Sixteenth (2014)	668	62
Seventeenth (2019)	724	78

Largest Five Parliamentary Constituencies in Terms of Number of Electors (2014)

SI. No.	State	Parliamentary Constituency	Total No. of Electors
1.	Andhra Pradesh	Malkajgiri	29,53,915
2.	Uttar Pradesh	Ghaziabad	22,63,961
3.	Karnataka	Bangalore North	22,29,063
4.	Uttar Pradesh	Unnao	21,10,388
5.	NCT of Delhi	North West Delhi	20,93,922

Smallest Five Parliamentary Constituencies in Terms of Number of Electors (2014)

SI. No.	State	Parliamentary Constituency	Total No. of Electors
1.	Lakshadweep	Lakshadweep	47,972
2.	Daman & Diu	Daman & Diu	1,02,260
3.	Jammu & Kashmir	Ladakh	1,59,949
4.	Dadra & Nagar Haveli	Dadra & Nagar Haveli	1,88,783
5.	Andaman & Nicobar Islands	Andaman & Nicobar Islands	2,57,856

Largest Parliamentary Constituency in Terms of Number of Electors (2019)

State	Parliamentary Constituency	Total No. Of Electors
Telangana	Malkajgiri	3150313

Smallest Parliamentary Constituency in Terms of Number of Electors (2019)

State	Parliamentary Constituency	Total No. Of Electors
Lakshadweep	Lakshadweep	55189

Top Ten Parliamentary Constituencies with Highest Historical Poll Percentage[6]

Rank	Year	Constituency	State	Poll %
1	2004	Nagaland	Nagaland	91.77
2	2019	Dhubri	Assam	90.66
3	2009	Tamluk	West Bengal	90.32
4	2009	Nagaland	Nagaland	89.99
5	2009	Kanthi	West Bengal	89.97
6	1996	Panskura	West Bengal	89.88
7	1996	Tamluk	West Bengal	89.80
8	1996	Cooch Behar	West Bengal	89.56
9	1996	Basirhat	West Bengal	89.20
10	1984-85	Barpeta	Assam	89.04

Top Ten Parliamentary Constituencies with Lowest Historical Poll Percentage

Rank	Year	Constituency	State	Poll%
1	1989	Anantang	Jammu and Kashmir	5.07%
2	1989	Baramulla	Jammu and Kashmir	5.48%
3	2019	Anantang	Jammu and Kashmir	8.98%
4	1991-92	Tarn Taran	Punjab	9.50
5	1991-91	Sangrur	Punjab	10.90
6	1999	Srinagar	Jammu and Kashmir	11.93
7	1962	Bhajanagar	Odisha	12.04
8	1962	koraput	Odisha	12.17
9	1962	Phulbani	Odisha	13.92
10	1991-92	Bathinda	Punjab	13.92

[6]Excluding the bye-elections.

Year-Wise Top Three Parties, Seats Won and Vote Share

Year	1st Position			2nd Position			3rd Position		
	Party	Seats Won	Vote%	Party	Seats Won	Vote%	Party	Seats Won	Vote%
1952	INC	364	44.99	CPI	16	3.29	SP	12	10.59
1957	INC	371	47.78	CPI	27	8.92	PSP	19	10.41
1962	INC	361	44.72	CPI	29	9.94	SWA	18	7.89
1967	INC	283	40.78	SWA	44	8.67	BJS	35	9.31
1971	INC	352	43.68	CPM	25	5.12	CPI	23	4.73
1977	BLD	295	41.32	INC	154	34.52	CPM	22	4.29
1980	INC(I)	353	42.69	JNP(S)	41	9.39	CPM	37	6.24
1984-85	INC	414	48.12	TDP	30	5.72	CPM	22	4.06
1989	INC	197	39.53	JD	143	17.79	BJP	85	11.36
1991-92	INC	244	36.4	BJP	120	20.07	JD	46	8.08
1996	BJP	161	20.29	INC	140	28.8	JD	46	8.08
1998	BJP	182	25.59	INC	141	25.82	CPM	32	5.16
1999	BJP	182	23.75	INC	114	28.3	CPM	33	5.4
2004	INC	145	26.53	BJP	138	22.16	CPM	43	5.66
2014	BJP	282	31	INC	44	19.31	ADMK	37	3.27
2019	BJP	303	37.3	INC	52	19.48	DMK	24	2.34

Recognised National Parties and State Parties (First to Seventeenth General Elections)

General Elections (Year)	Number of National Parties	Number of State Parties
First (1952)	14	39
Second (1957)	4	11
Third (1962)	6	11
Fourth (1967)	7	14
Fifth (1971)	8	17
Sixth (1977)	5	15
Seventh (1980)	6	19
Eighth (1984)	7	19
Ninth (1989)	8	20
Tenth (1991)	9	28
Eleventh (1996)	8	30
Twelfth (1998)	7	30
Thirteenth (1999)	7	40
Fourteenth (2004)	6	36
Fifteenth (2009)	7	40
Sixteenth (2014)	6	47
Seventeenth (2019)	7	52

Cost of Lok Sabha Elections

General Elections (Year)	Cost incurred by the Election Commission (in crores and in Indian rupee)
First (1952)	10.45
Second (1957)	5.90
Third (1962)	7.81
Fourth (1967)	10.95
Fifth (1971)	14.43
Sixth (1977)	29.81
Seventh (1980)	37.07
Eighth (1984)	85.51
Ninth (1989)	154.22
Tenth (1991)	359.10
Eleventh (1996)	597.34
Twelfth (1998)	626.40
Thirteenth (1999)	900
Fourteenth (2004)	1100.00
Fifteenth (2009)	1483.00
Sixteenth (2014)	3426.00
Seventeenth (2019)	N.A.

Coalition Governments at Centre Since Independence

SI. No.	Year	Coalition	Prime Minister	Partners
1.	1977-1979	Janata Party	Moraji Desai (Congress (O))	Congress (O), Bharatiya Jana Sangh, Bharatiya Lok Dal, Socialist Party, Congress for Democracy, Chandra Shekhar Group (former congressmen) and others.
2.	1979-1980	Janata Party (Secular)	Charan Singh	Janata (S) and Congress (U) Congress (I) supported from outside.
3.	1989-1990	National Front	V.P. Singh	Janata Dal, TDP, DMK, AGP and Congress (Socialist) BJP and Left Parties supported from outside.
4.	1990-1991	Janata Dal (Socialist) or Samajwadi Party	Chandra Shekhar (Janata Dal (S) or Samajwadi Janata Party)	Janata Dal (S) and Janata Party. Congress (I) supported from outside.

5.	1996-1997	United Front	H.D. Deve Gowda (Janata Dal)	Janata Dal, CPI, Congress (T), DMK, TDP, TMC, AGP, SP and others Congress and CPM supported from outside.
6.	1997-1998	United Front	I.K Gujral (Janata Dal)	Janata Dal, CPI, TMC, SP, DMK, AGP, TDP and others Congress supported from outside.
7.	1998-1999	BJP – led Coalition	A.B. Vajpayee (BJP)	BJP, AIADMK, BJD, Shiv Sena, Lok Shakti, Arunachal Congress, Samata, Akali Dal, PMK, TRC and others. TDP and Trinamool Congress supported from outside.
8.	1999-2004	National Democratic Alliance (NDA)	A.B. Vajpayee	BJP, JD(U), Trinamool Congress, Shiv Sena, BJD, LJP, DMK, INLD, MDMK, National Conference, Akali Dal, RLD, AGP and others.
9.	2004-2009	United Progressive Alliance (UPA)	Manmohan Singh (Congress)	Congress, NCP, DMK, RJD, LJP, PMK, and others. CPI and CPM supported form outside.
10.	2009-2014	United Progressive Alliance (UPA – II)	Manmohan Singh (Congress)	Congress, NCP, DMK, Trinamool Congress, National Conference and others.
11.	2014-2019	National Democratic Alliance (NDA)	Narendra Modi (BJP)	BJP, LJP, TDP, Shiv Sena, Akali Dal, Rashtriya Lok Samata Party, Apna Dal (S) and others. TDP left NDA in 2018.
12	2019-till date	National Democratic Alliance (NDA)	Narendra Modi (BJP)	BJP, Akali Dal, LJP, Shiv Sena and others Shiv Sena left NDA IN November 2019.

CHAPTER **25**

SAFEGUARDS TO SCHEDULED CASTES, SCHEDULED TRIBES, OBCs, & ANGLO-INDIANS

Indian society, besides being religion-based, is also divided on the basis of the caste system. To make India progressive and in order to bring equity in the socio-economic and political system, certain safeguards and protective measures have been provided in the Constitution for the deprived, weaker, and vulnerable sections of the society, such as SCs, STs, & Other Backward Classes. The safeguards are in the field of social, economic, political, educational, cultural, and services sphere under the State for the people belonging to these communities for their development.

SCHEDULED CASTES & SCHEDULED TRIBES

The Constitution treats the Scheduled Castes in India with special favour and affords them with some valuable safeguards. The Scheduled Castes are not strictly, a racial, linguistic, or religious minority. They are part and parcel of the Hindu society. They are the depressed sections of the Hindus[1].

The term, 'Scheduled Tribes' is of recent origin which came into being with the commencement of the Constitution. Prior to that, Scheduled Tribes were variously termed as 'Aboriginals', 'Adivasis', 'Forest tribes', 'Hill Tribes', 'Primitive Tribes', etc. The term 'tribe' came to be used in denotation of a particular stage of socio-political evolution of a community of people within a given territory and language. The Scheduled Tribes have remained backward because of the fact that they live in inaccessible and hilly regions and have thus been cut off from the main currents of national life.

Identification of SCs and STs

The Constitution has not provided any set criteria for the identification of Scheduled Castes or Scheduled Tribes. The power is left to the President to identify the castes falling under the Scheduled Castes and Scheduled Tribes category.

According to Article 341, the President may, by public notification, specify what castes or groups thereof in each State and Union Territory would be regarded as the Scheduled Castes for the purposes of the Constitution in relation to that State or Union Territory. In the same way, according to Article 342, the President may by public notification specify what tribes or tribal communities would be regarded as Scheduled Tribes for the purposes of the Constitution in relation to that State or Union Territory. In other words, the list of the Scheduled Castes and Scheduled Tribes may vary from State to State and from one Union Territory to another.

---

[1]*Indian Constitutional Law*, M.P. Jain, LexisNexis, Eighth Edition, P. 1506.

Moreover, under Articles 341 and 342, once the notification is issued by the President, any modification to the notification either by inclusion or exclusion of a caste or a tribe from the list can be done only by the Parliament by way of law and not by the Presidential notification. However, it is a Constitutional mandate that the President has to consult the Governors of the respective states before releasing the list of Scheduled Castes and Tribes by a public notification. Thus, it means that once the Presidential notification is issued under Articles 341 and 342, it is considered to be final, until and unless it is altered by Parliament by law. Even the court cannot modify, add, or remove any entry in the Presidential Order[2].

Social Safeguards[3]

- **Article 17** – relates to abolition of untouchability being practised in society. The Parliament enacted the Protection of Civil Rights Act, 1955 and the Scheduled Castes and Scheduled Tribes (Prevention of Atrocities) Act, 1989 to tackle the problem of untouchability, which is being practised against Scheduled Castes.
- **Article 23** – prohibits traffic in human beings and 'begar' and other similar forms of forced labour and provides that any contravention of this provision shall be an offence punishable in accordance with law. Although there is no specific mention about the SCs in this Article, majority of the bonded labour come from SCs. Thus, this Article has a special significance for them. The Parliament enacted Bonded Labour System (Abolition) Act, 1976 for identification, liberation, and rehabilitation of bonded labourers.

Economic Safeguards[4]

- **Article 46** – provides, "The States shall promote with special care the educational and economic interests of the weaker sections of the people, and in particular, of the Scheduled Castes and the Scheduled Tribes, and shall protect them from social injustice and all forms of exploitation."

Educational Safeguards[5]

- **Article 15(4)** – empowers the State to make special provisions for the advancement of any socially and educationally backward classes of citizens and for SCs. This provision has enabled the State to reserve seats for SCs in educational institutions in general and professional courses, etc.

Political Safeguards[6]

- **Article 330**: Seats are to be reserved for the Scheduled Castes and the Scheduled Tribes in Lok Sabha. Originally, this reservation was to operate for ten years from the commencement of the Constitution. But this duration has been extended continuously since then by 10 years each time. The reservation for Lok Sabha seats for the Scheduled Castes and Scheduled Tribes has to be made in each State and Union Territory on population basis.
- **Article 332**: Seats are to be reserved for the Scheduled Castes and the Scheduled Tribes in the State Legislative Assemblies. The reservation has to be made on population basis.

---

[2] *State of Maharashtra Vs. Mana Adim Jamat Mandal*, (2006) 4 SCC 98.

[3] http://ncsc.nic.in/files/ncsc/new3/201.pdf

[4] Ibid.

[5] Ibid.

[6] Ibid.

Originally, the above said reservations were supposed to operate for ten years from the commencement of the Constitution. But this duration has been extended continuously since then by 10 years each time. Now, under the 104th Constitutional Amendment Act, 2019, this reservation is to last until 25 January 2030. It is felt that the disabilities under which Scheduled Castes and Scheduled Tribes live have not yet been removed completely and therefore, the Central Government decided to continue the reservation for some time so that their condition may be ameliorated and they may catch up with the rest of the nation[7].

- **Article 243D** : Provides for reservation of seats for the Scheduled Castes and Scheduled Tribes in every Panchayat in proportion to the population in the Panchayat area.
- **Article 243T** : Seats are reserved for Scheduled Castes and Scheduled Tribes in every municipality and further, the Article also mandates that the offices of Chairpersons in the municipalities shall be reserved for the Scheduled Castes and Scheduled Tribes as the legislature of a State may, by law, provide.

Service Safeguards

- **Article 16(4)**: This is an enabling provision conferring power on the State to make reservation of posts in favour of any backward class of citizens who, in the opinion of the State Government, are not adequately represented in the State services[8].
- **Consideration of Efficiency**: The general principle adopted as regards government service is merit, but in case of the Scheduled Castes and the Scheduled Tribes, some relaxation is needed because of their backwardness. Therefore, Article 335 provides that the claims of the members of the Scheduled Castes and the Scheduled Tribes are to be taken into consideration, consistently with the maintenance of efficiency of administration, in making appointments to services and posts in connection with the affairs the Union or of a State. Article 335 insists on drawing a balance between reservation of government posts and maintenance of efficiency in the administration, in making appointments to services and posts in connection with the affairs of the Union or of a State.

Additional Provisions for Scheduled Tribes

- Under Article 339 of the Constitution, the President can appoint a Commission at any time, and must appoint it after ten years of the commencement of the Constitution, to report the welfare of the Scheduled Tribes in the State and the administration of the Scheduled Areas. So far, only two commissions have been set up. The first commission, appointed in 1960 under the chairmanship of U.N. Dhebar, had gone into the circumstances leading to tribal land alienation and had observed that there was an urgent need to scrutinise legislations on transfer of tribal lands. The Second Scheduled Areas and Scheduled Tribes Commission, under the Chairmanship

[7] *Indian Constitutional Law*, M.P. Jain, LexisNexis, Eighth Edition, P. 15013.

[8] Ibid

of Dilip Singh Bhuria was formed in 2002 and it had submitted its report in July 2004. The Dileep Singh Bhuria-led Commission had made several recommendations for tribal welfare, including amendments to the Fifth Schedule of the Constitution to give powers to the Governors to regulate trade and commerce in Scheduled Areas.

- Moreover, under the said Article, the Centre has the power to issue directions to any States regarding the drawing up and execution of schemes for the welfare of the Scheduled Tribes in the State.

Appointment of National Commission for SCs & STs[9]

OTHER BACKWARD CLASSES

Identification of Other Backward Classes

The Constitution does not provide the list of Other Backward Classes. The 102nd Constitutional Amendment Act made the formation of the National Commission for Socially and Educationally Backward Classes mandatory and gave the President and Parliament the right to identify the list of Other Backward Classes. According to the Article 342-A, which was inserted through the 102nd Constitutional Amendment Act, 2018, the President shall notify the list of socially and educationally backward classes of that State/Union Territory. In other words, the list of the Other Backward Classes may vary from State to State and from one Union Territory to another. However, it is a constitutional mandate that the President has to consult the Governors of the respective states before releasing the list of Other Backward Classes. Once the Presidential notification is issued under Article 342-A, it is considered to be final, until and unless it is altered by Parliament by law.

Educational Safeguards

- **Article 15(4)** : The State is empowered to make any special provision for the advancement of any socially and educationally backward class besides the Scheduled Castes and the Scheduled Tribes. The expression 'special provision for the advancement' has a wide connotation. It may include many things, such as reservation of seats in educational institutions, financial assistance, scholarships, free housing, and so on[10].

Service Safeguards

- **Article 16(4):** This empowers the State to make provisions for the reservation of appointments or posts in favour of any backward class of citizens which, in the opinion of the concerned Government, is not adequately represented in the services of the State or the Central Government.

---

[9]Dealt in Chapter No. 24

[10]*Indian Constitutional Law*, M.P. Jain, LexisNexis, Eighth Edition, Page No. 15016.

Appointment of National Commission for Backward Classes[11]

ANGLO-INDIANS

Anglo-Indians constitute a religious, social, as well as a linguistic minority who fall under the Anglo-Indian community as defined in the Constitution. According to Article 366(2), this refers to a person whose father, or any of whose other male progenitors in the male line, is or was of European descent but who is domiciled within the territory of India and is or was born within such territory of parents habitually resident therein and not established there for temporary purposes only.

Political Safeguards

- **Article 331:** The President, if he is of opinion that the Anglo-Indian community is not adequately represented in the Lok Sabha, may nominate thereto not more than two members of the community.
- **Article 333:** The Governor of a State, if he is of opinion that the Anglo-Indian community needs representation in the State Legislative Assembly, and is not adequately represented there, may nominate one member of the community to the Assembly.

  According to the above said Articles, the reservation of seats for the representation of the Anglo-Indian community is supposed to operate for ten years from the commencement of the Constitution. However, this duration has been extended continuously since then by 10 years each time. Now with the 104th Constitutional Amendment Act, 2019, the provision for nomination of Anglo-Indians to the Lok Sabha and Assemblies was ended seventy years after the commencement of the Constitution.
- **Article 336(1)**: At the time of the Commencement of the Constitution, Anglo-Indians were also enjoying some special privileges in services in Railways, Customs, and Posts and Telegraph under Article 336(1). All such reservations provided under Article 336(1) came to an end by 25 January 1960.
- **Article 337:** Even before independence, Anglo-Indian educational institutions were getting special grants from the government. After the commencement of the Constitution, Article 337 protected these grants for the first three years after the beginning of the Constitution. Thereafter, during each succeeding year, these grants could be reduced by ten per cent as compared to the grants in the preceding three years, so that ten years after the commencement of the Constitution, such grants, to the extent to which they were a special concession to the Anglo-Indian community, were to cease. Thus, Article 337 has now exhausted itself[12].

---

[11] Dealt in Chapter No. 25

[12] *State of Bombay Vs. Bombay Education Society*, AIR 1954 SC 561.

QUESTIONS

Subjective Questions

1. Explain the Constitutional safeguards provided for the Scheduled Tribes. **(250 words)**
2. Caste system and reservations—Are they a Boon or Bane to a progressive India? Discuss. **(250words)**

Objective Questions

1. Which Constitutional amendment has the provision of reservation of seats for SCs/STs in public service and legislatures until 2030?

   (a) 96th Amendment (b) 95th Amendment

   (c) 89th Amendment (d) 104th Amendment

   Ans: (d)

2. Who has the right to decide who will be included in the list of Scheduled Caste and Scheduled Tribes?

   (a) Parliament (b) President

   (c) Supreme Court (d) Governor of the State

   Ans: (b)

3. What does the term Anglo-Indian mean?

   (a) Such persons whose mothers or their female or their male ancestors were of European origin but settled permanently in India and their next generation was born here.

   (b) A person whose father or any of whose other male progenitors in the male line is or was of European descent but who is domiciled within the territory of India and is or was born within such territory of parents habitually resident therein and not established there for temporary purpose only.

   (c) All British origin persons whose parents had settled permanently in India before 1947.

   (d) None of the above.

   Ans: (b)

CHAPTER 26

SAFEGUARDS TO WOMEN[1]

"You can tell the condition of a nation by looking at the status of its women".

– Jawaharlal Nehru

INTRODUCTION

Women, as a class, neither belong to a minority group, nor are they regarded as forming a Backward Class. India has been a male-dominated society since many years and therefore, presently women suffer from many social and economic disabilities and handicaps. It thus becomes necessary that such conditions be created, and necessary ameliorative steps be taken, so that women as a class may make progress and are able to shed their disabilities as soon as possible.

Constitutional Provisions for Women

The Constitution does not contain many provisions specifically favouring women as such. A few provisions are as follows:

- Article 15(3) – is an enabling provision which merely states that the State is not prevented from making any special provision for women.
- General provisions such as Article 14 and 15(2) outlaw any kind of gender discrimination against women.
- Article 21 spells out some safeguards for women.

Safeguards to Women by the Supreme Court

The Supreme Court has, in course of time, by its interpretative process of these various Constitutional provisions, extended some safeguards to women. Reference may be made to a few of these judicial pronouncements –

- Recognizing that women in India need to be liberated from unjust social, political, and economic suppression, the Supreme Court has declared in *Bodhisattwa Gautam Vs. Subhra Chakraborty*[2], that rape is a heinous crime against women and amounts to violation of the Fundamental Right guaranteed to a woman under Article 21.

[1]Indian Constitutional Law, by M.P. Jain, LexisNexis Publications, Eighth Edition, Pg No.1531

[2]AIR 1996 SC 922.

- In *Vishaka Vs. State of Rajasthan*[3], the Supreme Court has come down heavily on sexual harassment of women at workplaces and has declared the same to be violation of women's rights under Article 21.
- The Supreme Court has used the Directive Principles continued in Articles 39(a), 39(d), and 39(e) to confer economic empowerment on women.

NATIONAL COMMISSION FOR WOMEN

To ameliorate the general social condition of the women in the country, the Parliament has enacted the National Commission for Women Act, 1990, to establish the National Commission for Women (NCW).

Composition of National Commission for Women (NCW)

The Commission consists of the following:

(a) A Chairperson, committed to the cause of women;

(b) Five members nominated from amongst persons having experience in law, trade unionism, management of an industry, administration, economic development, health, education, social welfare, and women's voluntary organisations;

(c) A Member Secretary who is either a member of a Civil Service under the Centre, or an expert in the field of management/sociological movement.

All these persons hold office for three years and are appointed by the Central Government.

Powers of the NCW

(a) The Commission has power to constitute Committees as may be necessary to deal with special issues taken up by the Commission from time to time.

(b) The Commission has powers to regulate its own procedure and has power of a Civil Court in matters like summoning witnesses.

Functions of the NCW

(a) Investigate and examine all matters relating to the safeguards provided for women under the Constitution and other laws;

(b) Present to the Central Government, annually and at such other times as the Commission may deem fit, reports upon the working of those safeguards;

(c) Make in such reports recommendations for the effective implementation of those safeguards for improving the conditions of women by the Union or any State;

(d) Review, from time to time, the existing provisions of the Constitution and other laws affecting women and recommend amendments thereto, so as to suggest remedial legislative measures to meet any lacunae, inadequacies, or shortcomings in such legislature;

(e) Take up the cases of violation of the provisions of the Constitution and of other laws relating to women with the appropriate authorities;

[3] AIR 1997 SC 3011.

(f) Look into complaints and take *suo motu* notice of matters relating to –

- Deprivation of women's rights;
- Non-implementation of laws enacted to provide protection to women and also to achieve the objective of equality and development;
- Non-compliance of policy decisions, guidelines, or instructions aimed to mitigating hardships and ensuring welfare and providing relief to women; and take up the issues arising out of such matters with appropriate authorities;

(g) Call for special studies or investigations into specific problems or situations arising out of discrimination and atrocities against women and identify the constraints so as to recommend strategies for their removal.

(h) Undertake promotional and educational research so as to suggest ways of ensuring due representation of women in all spheres and identify factors responsible for impeding their advancement, such as lack of access to housing and basic services, inadequate support services and technologies for reducing drudgery and occupational health hazards, and for increasing their productivity;

(i) Participate and advice on the planning process of socio-economic development of women;

(j) Evaluate the progress of the development of women under the Union and any State;

(l) Inspect jails, remand homes, women's institution, or other place of custody where women are kept as prisoners or otherwise, and take up with the concerned authorities for remedial action, if found necessary;

(l) Fund litigation involving issues affecting a large body of women;

(m) Make periodical reports to the Government on any matter pertaining to women and in particular, various difficulties under which women toil;

(n) Any other matter which may be referred to it by the Central Government.

Annual Reports of NCW

The Commission presents an annual report of its activities. The Central Government is required to lay before the two Houses of Parliament the reports sent to it by the Commission along with a Memorandum explaining the action taken or approved to be taken on the recommendations and the reasons for non-acceptance, if any, of such recommendations. If a recommendation relates to a State Government, the Commission sends the same to that government which lays the same before the State Legislature along with an explanatory memorandum.

CHAPTER 27

SAFEGUARDS TO RELIGIOUS MINORITIES

In this vast country of ours, people profess different religions, speak different languages, dress differently and observe different customs; but we are one nation; the history of our struggle for independence and our faith in our future development are our common bonds.

– Lal Bahadur Shastri

INTRODUCTION

India has a composite population, having a number of groups based on religion, language, caste, etc. The minority problem very much influenced and coloured the political life of the country before independence. That diluted to some extent, the Muslim minority problem, but did not solve completely the minority problem, as such, because a number of other minority groups, as well as a large number of Muslims, are still present in the country. The framers of the Indian Constitution took care to safeguard the interests of the minorities, to give them a sense of security, to protect them against any discrimination, and to help them to get integrated into the mainstream of national life. With this in view, a number of provisions have been incorporated in the Constitution for safeguarding specifically the social, economic, and educational interests of minority groups. In addition, certain general Constitutional provisions, for example, the Fundamental Rights, protect some of the rights of the minority groups[1]. One of the policy objectives of the Constitution is to make the government secular. The Constitution does not recognise any religion for any kind of favoured treatment, but treats all religions alike, and protects the cultural or religious practices of all people from State interference.

The Constitution does not define the term 'Minority'. The Constitution uses the term 'Minority' only twice. The first occurrence is in Article 29, which emphasises on linguistic and cultural minorities and the second is in Article 30, which refers to linguistic or religious minorities. The National Minorities Commission initially notified five religious communities, i.e., Muslims, Christians, Sikhs, Buddhists, and Zoroastrians (Parsis) as religious minorities at the national level because their numerical strength as compared with the rest of the Indian citizens is smaller. Further, vide notification in 2014; Jains were also notified as another minority community.

[1] *Indian Constitutional Law*, by M.P. Jain, LexisNexis Publications, Eighth Edition, Pg No. 1505.

NATIONAL COMMISSION FOR MINORITIES

As a further step to safeguard the interests of the religious and linguistic minorities, to preserve the country's secular traditions, to promote national integration, and remove any feeling of inequality and discrimination amongst various sections of the people, the Government of India appointed a Minorities Commission in 1978 under an administrative resolution. The Commission was charged with the function of evaluating the various safeguards provided in the Constitution for the protection of the minorities and in the laws passed by the Parliament and the State Legislatures. The Commission made periodical reports at prescribed intervals to the Central Government. In course of time, the Commission suggested that its position be strengthened by conferring on it powers of enquiry and it be given a constitutional status so that it could function more effectively. Accordingly, the Parliament enacted the National Commission for Minorities Act, 1992, to establish the National Commission for Minorities on a statutory basis.

An interesting feature of the Act is that it does not define the term 'Minority' but leaves it to the Central Government to notify minorities for the purposes of the Act.

Composition of the Commission

The Commission consists of:

(a) Chairperson;

(b) Vice-Chairperson; and

(c) Five members.

All the members of the Commission, including the Chairperson, are nominated by the Central Government from time to time from amongst persons of eminence, ability, and integrity, subject to the rider that five members, including the Chairperson, must belong to the minority communities. The Chairperson and the other members hold office for three years from the date he/she assumes office. The Government has the power to remove the Chairperson or any member on a few specified grounds, such as, insolvency, moral turpitude, unsoundness of mind, abuse of power, etc.

Powers of the Commission

The Commission meets as and when necessary. It has power to regulate its own procedure, and enjoys powers of a Civil Court for purposes of summoning witnesses, receiving evidence on affidavits, etc.

Functions of the Commission

(a) Evaluate the progress of the development of minorities under the Union and States;

(b) Monitor the working of the safeguards provided in the Constitution and in the laws enacted by the Parliament and the State Legislatures;

(c) Make recommendations for the effective implementation of safeguards for the protection of the interests of minorities by the Central government or the State Governments;

(d) Look into specific complaints regarding deprivation of rights and safeguards of the minorities and take up such matters with the appropriate authorities;

(e) Cause studies to be undertaken into problems arising out of any discrimination against educational development of minorities;

(f) Suggest appropriate measures in respect of any minority to be undertaken by the Central Government or the State Government;

(g) Make periodical or special reports to the Central Government on any matter pertaining to minorities and in particular, difficulties confronted by them; and

(h) Any other matter which may be referred to it by the Central Government.

The Central Government is required to lay the recommendations as well as the Annual Report made by the Commission before both the Houses of the Parliament along with an explanatory Memorandum of Action taken on the recommendations contained in the report and the reasons for the non-acceptance, if any, of such recommendations. If any such recommendation concerns a State Government, the Commission forwards it to that government which follows the same procedure as mentioned above in the State Legislature.

CHAPTER **28**

GOVERNMENT SERVICES UNDER THE UNION AND THE STATES

"It is recognised that in every country there are certain posts in its administrative set-up which might be called strategic from the point of view of maintaining the standard of administration.... There can be no doubt that the standard of administration depends upon the calibre of the civil servants who are appointed to the strategic posts . . . The Constitution provides that, there shall be All India Services, the members of which alone could be appointed to these strategic posts throughout the Union."

– Dr. B.R. Ambedkar

INTRODUCTION

The civil servant is indispensable to the governance of the country in the modern administrative age. Ministers frame policies and Legislatures enact laws, but the task of efficiently and effectively implementing these policies and laws falls on the civil servants. The bureaucracy, thus, helps the political executive in the governance of the country. The Constitution, therefore, seeks to inculcate in the civil servant a sense of security and fair play so that he may work and function efficiently and give his best to the country. Nevertheless, the overriding power of the government to dismiss or demote a servant has been kept intact, even though safeguards have been provided, subject to which only such a power can be exercised[1]. Articles 309 to 323 of the Constitution deals with the Central and State services.

Terms Relating to Central and State Services

Civil Servant : The term civil servant includes members of a Civil Service of the Centre or a State, or of an All India Service, or all those who hold civil posts under the Centre or a State. A 'civil post' means an appointment or office on the civil side and includes all personnel employed in the civil administration of the Union or a State. The term 'civil servant' does not include a member of a defence service or even a civilian employee in defence service who is paid salary out of the estimates of the Ministry of Defence. A member of the Police Force, however, is a 'civil servant.'

[1]M. P. Jain: *Indian Constitutional Law*, Wadhwa, Eighth Edition, Pg. 1536.

All India Services : The Constitution provides for the creation of All India Services (AIS) common to the Union and the States. The All India Services Act, 1951 provides that the Central Government may make rules for regulating the recruitment and the conditions of service of persons appointed to the All India Services. Presently, only the Indian Administrative Service, the Indian Police Service, and the Indian Forest Service have been constituted as All India Services. Recruitment to these services is made under the corresponding AIS Recruitment Rules and may be done by direct recruitment (through Competitive Examinations) and by promotion from the State Service.

The Central Government is the Cadre Controlling Authority for the three All India Services. In terms of the provisions of the respective IAS/IPS/IFS Promotion Regulations, the Central Government means Ministry of Personnel, Public Grievances & Pensions, Department of Personnel & Training for IAS, Ministry of Home Affairs for IPS, and Ministry of Environment, Forest and Climate Change for IFS. The vacancies to be filled under the Promotion Quota for each year are determined by the Central Government in consultation with the respective State Government and the final appointments are also made by the Central Government.

Thus, the Centre enjoys a preponderance of powers when it comes to the AIS officers. However, the immediate control lies with the State Governments, whereas, the ultimate control lies with the Central Government.

Central Services : Unlike the All India Services, the Central Civil Services are under the exclusive control of the Central Government, with its member positions only in the Central Government. The Civil Services of the Central Government comprise established services known as Central Civil Service as well as civil posts created outside the established services, which constitute the General Central Service. Both the established Central Civil Services and the civil posts are classified in the descending order of importance into Group A, Group B, Group C, and Group D. Some important examples of Central Services under Group A are as follows – Indian Foreign Service, Indian Revenue Service, etc.

State Services : State Services work under the exclusive jurisdiction of the respective States. State service personnel work under the various departments of the State Governments. The State Services are also classified as Group A, Group B, Group C, and Group D. Road Transports Service, Revenue Service, etc. are State Services.

CONSTITUTIONAL PROVISIONS

Legislative Power

Article 309 empowers the Parliament and the State Legislatures to regulate the recruitment and the conditions of service of the persons appointed to public services and posts under the Union and the States, respectively. Until provision in that behalf is made by an appropriate Legislature under Article 309, the President and the Governors may make rules for regulating the recruitment and conditions of service of persons appointed to such services and posts. The Constitution itself provides for the creation of the Public Service Commission for the Union and the States to assist in the recruitment of the Public Services. The mode of recruitment and the category from which the recruitment to a service should be made are all matters which are exclusively within the domain of the Executive.

Employment under the Government is a matter of status and not a contract, even though the acquisition of such a status may be preceded by a contract, namely, an offer of appointment which is accepted by the employee. The rights and obligations are not determined by the contract of the two parties but by the statutory rules which are framed by the Government in exercise of power conferred by Article 309 of the Constitution and the service rules can be unilaterally altered by the rule-making authority, namely, the Government[2].

Conditions of Service of Civil Servants

Generally speaking, subject to the rules governing the services of the civil servants, following are the conditions of service applicable to them:

i. Salary or wages
ii. Subsistence allowance during suspension
iii. Periodical increments
iv. Leave
v. Provident fund
vi. Gratuity
vii. Promotion
viii. Seniority
viii. Tenure or Termination of service
ix. Superannuation
x. Pension
xi. Transfer
xii. Deputation
xiii. Disciplinary proceedings

Doctrine of Pleasure

In England, the normal rule is that a civil servant of the Crown holds his office during the pleasure of the Crown. This means that his services can be terminated at any time by the Crown, without assigning any reason. Even if there is a contract of employment between the civil servant and the Crown, the Crown is not bound by it. In other words, if a civil servant is dismissed from service, he cannot claim arrears of salary or damages for premature termination of his service. The Doctrine of Pleasure is based on the public policy.

[2] *Union Public Service Commission Vs. Girish Jayanti Lal Vaghela*, AIR 2006 SC 1165.

Indian Perspective of Doctrine of Pleasure

Article 310 of the Indian Constitution incorporates the Common Law Doctrine of Pleasure. It expressly provides that all persons who are members of the Defence Services or the Civil Services of the Union or of All India Services, hold office during the Pleasure of the President. Similarly, members of the State Services hold office during the Pleasure of the Governor. But this rule of English Law has not been fully adopted in our Constitution. In other words, the Doctrine of Pleasure under Article 310 is restricted or limited by Article 311.

The two main limitations on the Doctrine of Pleasure are as follows –

i. A civil servant cannot be dismissed by any disciplinary authority which is subordinate to the authority by which the appointment in question was made (Article 311(1)).

ii. A civil servant cannot be dismissed, removed or reduced in rank until he has been given a reasonable opportunity of being heard/showing cause against the action proposed to be taken in regard to him (Article 311(2)).

Originally, the opportunity to defend was given to a civil servant at two stages: (1) at the enquiry stage, and this is an accord with the rule of natural justice that no man should be condemned without hearing; and (2) at the punishment stage, when as a result of enquiry, the charges have been proved and any of the three punishments, i.e., dismissal, removal, or reduction in rank were proposed to be taken against him. The 42nd Constitution Amendment Act, 1976 has abolished the right of the Government servant to make representation at the second stage of the inquiry.

Dismissal and removal are synonymous terms, but in law, they acquired technical meanings by long usage in Service Rules. In case of dismissal, a person is debarred from future employment, but in case of removal, he is not debarred from future employment. 'Reduction in rank' means reduction from a higher rank or post to a lower rank or post and not losing place in rank or cadre. In *State of Punjab Vs. Kishan Das*[3], the Supreme Court held that a mere reduction in the salary in the same cadre is not reduction in rank.

It is mandatory under Article 311(2) to make an inquiry before the dismissal, removal, or reduction in rank of a civil servant. In that inquiry, the civil servant has to be 'informed of the charges' against him and should be given a reasonable opportunity of being heard in respect of those charges. 'Informed of the charges' means serving of a chargesheet explaining the reasons for the charges levelled against the concerned officer and statement of allegations against each charge. Thus, Article 311 is available only where dismissal, removal, or reduction in rank is proposed to be inflicted by way of punishment and not otherwise[4].

However, the protection of Article 311(2) for giving 'reasonable opportunity' is not available in the following circumstances (Article 311 proviso) –

i. Where a person is dismissed or reduced in rank on the ground of misconduct which has led to conviction or criminal charges;

---

[3]AIR 1971 SC766.

[4]Suspension is not punishment. It is neither dismissal or removal nor reduction in rank. So, the employee cannot claim a reasonable opportunity to be heard.

ii. Where it is impracticable to give the civil servant an opportunity to defend himself but the authority taking action against him shall record the reasons for such action;

iii. Where in the interest of the security of the State, it is not expedient to give such an opportunity to the civil servant.

Reasonable Opportunity of Being Heard

In *Khem Chand Vs. Union of India*[5], the Supreme Court held that the 'reasonable opportunity' means:

(a) An opportunity to deny his guilt and establish his innocence, which he can do only if he is told what the charges levelled against him are and the allegations on which such charges are based.

(b) An opportunity to defend himself by cross-examining the witness produced against him and by examining himself in support of his defiance.

(c) An opportunity to make his representation as to why the proposed punishment should not be inflicted on him.

LAWS REGARDING ALL INDIA SERVICES

Article 312 empowers the Parliament to create a new All India Services common to the Union and the States. The Parliament can create such services if the Rajya Sabha, by a resolution supported by not less than two-thirds of the members present and voting, declares that it is necessary and expedient in the national interest to create such service.

The services known at the commencement of the Constitution as the IAS and the IPS shall be deemed to be services created by the Parliament under Article 312. Until other provisions are made under the Constitution, all the laws in force immediately before the commencement of the Constitution and applicable to any public service or any post which continues to exist under the Constitution, as an All India Service, or as service or post under the Union or a State, shall continue in force, so far as convenient with the provisions of this Constitution.

The 42nd Amendment has amended Article 312 of the Constitution which provides for the creation of an All India Judicial Service by a Parliamentary law. It further provided that All India Judicial Service shall not include any post inferior to that of a District Judge. Moreover, a law providing for the creation of the All India Judicial Service shall not be deemed to be an amendment of the Constitution for the purpose of Article 368. However, no such law has been passed till now.

Power of Parliament to Vary or Revoke Conditions of Service of Officers of Certain Services

Article 312A was inserted and Article 314 was omitted, by the 28th Constitution Amendment Act, 1972. Article 314 was placed in the original Constitution in order to safeguard the rights of members of the ICS and other civil servants appointed by the British Crown, who continued in the service of the Government of India after the commencement of the Constitution. As a result of this provision, special

[5] AIR 1958 SC300.

privileges were enjoyed by members of these services as compared to members of corresponding rank, appointed after Independence. In order to overcome such arbitrariness arising out of the constitutional protection of the special privileges of these Government servants, which were *prima facie* against the Principle of Equality, Article 314 was repealed and Article 312A was inserted, by the 28th Amendment Act.

By Article 312A, Parliament was empowered to revoke the conditions of service enjoyed by this class of covenanted services (pre-independence officers) and to legislate to regulate their conditions of service, unhampered by any interference from any court.

Other Provisions (Article 313)

Under the Constitution, the Union and State Legislatures have power to make laws to regulate the respective Services under the Union and the State Government. But until such laws are made, the existing laws relating to the Services shall continue to be in force.

CHAPTER 29

SUCCESSION TO RIGHTS & OBLIGATIONS

INTRODUCTION

Articles 294 to 297 deal with succession by the Central and State Governments to the property, rights, liabilities etc., of the various governments functioning in India in the pre-Constitution era.

- **Article 294 :** By virtue of Article 294(a), all property and assets which were vested in British, immediately before the commencement of the Constitution, for the purposes of the Government of the Dominion of India, or a Governor's Province, became vested in the Union and the corresponding State respectively under the present Constitution. Article 294(b) vests in the Government of India, and the corresponding State, all rights, liabilities, and obligations of the Government of the Dominion of India, or of a Governor's Province, whether arising out of contract or otherwise.
- **Article 295 :** The said Article deals with the devolution of liability. The liabilities of an Indian State existing prior to the commencement of the Constitution shall be the liabilities of the Government of India. Article 295 not only denotes transference of the rights, liabilities, and obligations to the Government of India, or to the State Government concerned, but also binds it to the obligations transferred to it and it is duty-bound to discharge them.
- **Article 296 :** The said Article deals with property accruing by escheat or lapse or as bona vacantia. Escheat literally means "to revert to the State". This event happens in default of heirs or devises. When there is no owner of property, it vests in the State and this is known as bona *vacantia.* Consequently, the property of an intestate dying without leaving lawful heirs, and the property of a dissolved corporation pass to the Government as escheat or *bona vacantia.*
- **Article 297 :** The said Article asserts India's sovereign rights over sea wealth. All lands, minerals, and other things of value underlying the ocean within the territorial waters, or the continental shelf of India vest in the Union and are held for the purpose of the Union.

CONTRACTUAL LIABILITY OF A STATE

Indian Government, being a Welfare State, has been increasingly adopting various economic activities to provide large benefits to the general public. Today, a large number of individuals and business organizations enjoy tons of benefits in the form of government contracts, licenses, quotas, mineral rights, tenders, jobs, etc. This raises the possibility of exercise of power by a government to dispense largess in an arbitrary manner and the need was felt to regulate and protect the interests of an individual and what they would be entitled when the contract is breached by the government. Even when the government, as an entity entering into contracts with corporations, assumes the same rights and obligations as that of B2B (business to business) or individual to business contracts, their liability and requirements change.

Contractual liability of the State means a liability of the State for the acts done by the State in exercise of its power as a Sovereign as well as in other capacities in the same manner as an individual does.

Provisions Regarding Contractual Liability

Provided below are the provisions which recognize the contractual liability in the Constitution.

- **Article 294 :** Government contracts have been accorded constitutional recognition. Article 294 states that "all rights, liabilities and obligations of the Government of the Dominion of India and of the Government of each Governors Province, whether arising out of any contract or otherwise, shall be the rights, liabilities and obligations respectively of the Government of India and the Government of each corresponding State".
- **Article 298 :** This Article clearly lays down that the executive power of the Union and of each State extends to "the carrying on of any trade or business and to the acquisition, holding and disposal of property and the making of contracts for any purpose". In other words, this Article gives the government the executive power to enter into contracts with corporations and individuals to carry on any trade or business, acquire, hold, and dispose property and make contracts.
- **Article 299 :** Article 299(1) lays down the manner of formulation of a Government contract. Article 299 provides that all contracts in the exercise of the executive power of the Union or of a State shall be expressed to be made by the President or by the Governor of the State, as the case may be, and all such contracts and all assurances of property made in the exercise of that power shall be executed on behalf of the President or the Governor by such persons and in such manner as he may direct or authorize. Article 299(2) makes it clear that neither the President nor the Governor shall be personally liable in respect of any contract or assurance made or executed for the purposes of this Constitution or for the purposes of any enactment relating to executing any such contract or assurance on behalf of any of them be personally liable in respect thereof. Subject to the provisions of Article 299(1), the other provisions of the general law of contract apply even to the Government contract. A contract with the Government of the Union or State will be valid and binding only if the following conditions are followed:

  1. The contract with the Government will not be binding if it is not expressed to be made in the name of the President or the Governor, as the case may be.
  2. The contract must be executed on behalf of the President or the Governor of the State, as the case may be. The word 'executed' indicates that a contract with the Government will be valid only when it is in writing.
  3. A person duly authorized by the President or the Governor of the State, as the case may be, must execute the contract.

  In other words, Article 299 provides the formal requirements that need to be fulfilled for a contract entered into by the government be held valid and enforceable. If the formal requirements required by Article 299(1) are complied with, the contract can be enforced against the Union or the States. Whereas, Article 299(2) immunises the President, or the Governor, or the person executing any contract on his behalf, from any personal liability in respect of any contract executed for the purposes of the Constitution, or for the purposes of any enactment relating to the Government of India in force. This immunity is purely personal and does not immunise the government, as such, from a contractual liability.

- **Article 300 :** This Article states that the Government of India may sue or be sued by the name of the Union of India and likewise, the State government may sue or be sued by the name of the State or of the Legislature of a State. Thus, the Constitution expressly confers the legal personality upon the State and recognizes it as a juristic person capable of holding and acquiring property, making contracts, carrying on trade or business, and bringing and defending legal action, just as a private individual.

TORTIOUS LIABILITY OF STATE

Tort means a civil wrong. When anyone commits a tort, he/she shall be liable for the same, which is nothing but called as tortious liability. In other words, tortious liability arises from a breach of duty fixed by law.

The concept of tortious liability of State means that the State is liable for the acts of its servants. The State must act through human agencies in carrying out various functions. So, the important question which arises is whether the State can be held vicariously liable for the acts of its employees. Under the English law, the old position was that the Crown enjoyed immunity from the wrongs committed in tort. In other words, the Crown could not be sued for the torts of its servants. This was largely based on the concept 'King can do no wrong.' However, with increase of government's function, this concept was abolished in UK by the Crown Proceedings Act, 1947. This Act placed the government in the same position as the subjects. As far as the Indian position is concerned, the doctrine of 'King can do no wrong' was never accepted in India. Liability of the government is fixed under Article 300 of the Constitution. According to Article 300, the Union of India and the State can sue and be sued in the same way as the Dominion of India and Provinces before the commencement of the Constitution. In order to effectively appreciate the concept of tortious liability of the State, the concept of sovereign and non-sovereign functions is to be understood.

Sovereign and Non-Sovereign Functions

When the East India Company arrived in India, it was essentially a trading entity. The purpose of the company was to trade in India. Subsequently, it obtained the Diwani rights from Mughals and acquired dual character, i.e., (1) trading company (commercial) and (2) sovereign. Later, the Company was granted the right to acquire territories and maintain the Army on behalf of the Crown. The Company could be sued for any tortious liability in its commercial capacity but was exempted from any tortious liability in its sovereign capacity. By virtue of the Government of India Act, 1858, the Crown took sovereignty from the Company. The Act allowed the Secretary of the State in Council (as successor to the Company) to sue and be sued, except for those acts done in the exercise of sovereign powers. Similar provisions were found in Government of India Act, 1915 and 1935. Because of the dual character of the East India Company, there was distinction between sovereign and non-sovereign functions. In respect of sovereign functions, the Company was not liable, while in respect of non-sovereign functions, the Company was liable.

The leading case in the area is *P & O Steam Navigation Company Vs. Secretary of State*[1]. The P & O Steam Navigation Company made a claim for damages for injury caused to its horse by the negligence of some workmen in the Government Dockyard. The Bombay High Court ruled that where an act was done in the exercise of sovereign powers, which could not be lawfully exercised except by a sovereign or private individual delegated by a sovereign to exercise them, no action would lie. On the other hand, the Secretary of State would be liable for non-sovereign acts by its employees. Thus, the court classified the acts of the Secretary of State in two functions – (1) sovereign functions and (2) non-sovereign functions. The court clarified that in respect of sovereign functions, the Secretary of State was not liable. This observation of the court was followed in a catena of decisions.

After the commencement of the Constitution, the Supreme Court was confronted with this question in the case of *State of Rajasthan Vs. Vidyawati*[2]. In this case, the jeep was owned by the State of Rajasthan for the official use of the Collector. The driver of the jeep while bringing the jeep back from the workshop drove it negligently and injured a pedestrian who subsequently died. The court held the State vicariously liable for the rash and negligent act of the driver. The Supreme Court rejected the notion that 'King can do no wrong' and stated that such notion is not applicable in India. Keeping in mind the socialistic pattern of society and the large number of functions of the Government, the State should be held vicariously liable for the tortious acts of its servants. However, later in *Kasturi Lal Ralia Ram Jain Vs. State of U.P*[3]., the Supreme Court diluted the observation in the Vidyawati case. The Court categorically held that if the tortious act is committed by a public servant in exercise of sovereign functions, then the State will not be liable. However, if the act is done in exercise of non-sovereign functions, the State will be liable in tort.

The law laid down in Kasturi Lal's case held ground for quite some time. However, in later decisions, the Supreme Court did not follow the law laid down in Kasturi Lal's case. The Court always distinguished the facts of this case from other cases. Nevertheless, it is pertinent to note that Kasturi Lal's case has not been specifically overruled till date. In *N. Nagendra Rao Vs. State of Andhra Pradesh*[4], Supreme Court held that the concept of sovereign immunity cannot be a defence where the State is involved in commercial activities. Such concept can also not apply where officers of the State are guilty of interfering with life and liberty of citizens. In all such cases, the State should be held vicariously liable and constitutionally bound to compensate and indemnify the wronged person. The Court observed that the distinction between sovereign and non-sovereign functions does not exist anymore. This distinction is contrary to modern thinking. Thus, the demarcating line between sovereign and non-sovereign functions has disappeared. It must be noted that after expansion of the scope of Article 21 and evolution of compensatory jurisprudence[5] under Article 32 and 226, the concept of sovereign and non-sovereign function has become outdated. Kasturi Lal's case, though not specifically overruled, has lost its vigour and has been significantly eroded. Recent judicial trend is in favour of holding the State liable for tortious acts committed by its servants.

---

[1] 5 Bom HCR App 1.

[2] AIR 1962 SC 933.

[3] AIR 1965 SC 1039.

[4] (1994) 6 SCC 205.

[5] Pecuniary compensation (Compensation to victims) is a judicially recognised and an endorsed mode of enforcing Fundamental Rights by the courts of law for serving the lawful entitlements of persons on being victimized of crimes-offences-human rights' abuse.

CHAPTER 30

AMENDMENT OF THE CONSTITUTION

INTRODUCTION

The Constitution of a country, like any other legislation, must change with the changes in the needs of a political society. Especially, a democratic Constitution has to be particularly responsive to changing conditions, since a government founded on the principle of popular sovereignty "must make possible the fresh assertion of the popular will as that will change". Therefore, formal modification of the Constitution is made by using the amending process provided in the Constitution.

Rigid or Flexible Constitution

Constitutions are usually classified as 'flexible' or 'rigid' depending upon the process through which they can be amended. Flexible constitutions are those which can be amended in the same way as ordinary laws/legislations of the country. On the other hand, in rigid constitutions, the Constitution or the Fundamental laws cannot be changed in the same way as ordinary laws. The United Kingdom which has an unwritten Constitution, is the best example of an extremely flexible Constitution as there is no distinction between the legislative power and the constituent power. The British Parliament has the power to change the Constitution by the ordinary process of legislation. As opposed to the UK system, the constitutional amendment has an important place under a written Constitution like that of the USA[1]. Its importance increases where the system is federal. In most of the written Constitutions, the power to amend the Constitutions is either vested in a body other than the ordinary Legislature or it is vested in the ordinary Legislature, subject to a special procedure. In a federal system, additional safeguards like the involvement of the Legislatures at the State level, are also provided for with a view to ensure that the federal set-up does not get altered only at the will of the Federal Legislature.

---

[1] The process of constitutional amendment involves two separate stages: initiation and ratification. An amendment may be proposed or initiated either – (i) by vote of two-thirds of each House of Congress; or (ii) by a constitutional convention called together by Congress on the application of the legislatures of two-thirds of the States. An amendment proposed may be ratified either – (i) by vote of the legislature of three-fourths of the States; or (ii) by a constitutional convention called together by Congress on the application of the legislatures of two-thirds of the States. The procedure of the Constitutional amendment in the USA has proved to be quite difficult. That's the reason why during its (constitution of USA) tenure of over 200 years, only 27 Constitutional amendments could be passed.

The framers of the Indian Constitution were keen to avoid excessive rigidity. They were anxious to have a document which could grow with a growing nation, and adapt itself to the changing needs and circumstances of a growing people. At the same time, the framers were also aware of the fact that if the Constitution was too flexible, it would be playing to the whims and caprices of the ruling party. They were, therefore, anxious to avoid flexibility of the extreme type. Hence, they adopted for a middle course. It is neither too rigid to admit necessary amendment, nor too flexible for undesirable changes.

PROCEDURE FOR AMENDMENT IN THE CONSTITUTION

The Constitution of India provides for a distinctive amending process as compared to the leading Constitutions of the world. It may be described as partly flexible and partly rigid. Different degrees of rigidity are attached to different portions of the Constitution, depending on their importance and significance.

The Constitution, accordingly provides for the following three classes of amendments of its provisions:

1. **Articles that can be amended by Parliament by simple majority as that required for passing of any ordinary law :** Constitutional provisions of comparatively less significance can be amended by the simple legislative process as is adopted in passing ordinary legislation in Parliament. Several Articles of the Constitution make provisions of a tentative nature, and Parliament has been given power to make laws making provisions different from what these Articles in the Constitution provide for. Such a law can be made by the ordinary legislative process, and ***is not*** to be regarded as an "***amendment of the Constitution***" as it is not subject to the special procedure prescribed in Article 368. In most of the cases, the Constitutional text remains intact but the Parliament makes different provisions.

   A *few of these Articles of the Constitution are as follows:*

   (a) Article 124(1) prescribes that the Supreme Court shall have a Chief Justice and seven Judges until Parliament increases the strength of the Judges.

   (b) When Parliament admits a new State under Article 2, it can affect consequential amendments in Schedules I and IV defining territory and allocating seats in the Rajya Sabha amongst the various States respectively.

   (c) Establishment of new States, formation of new States, and alteration of areas, boundaries, or names of existing States by Parliament (Articles 2, 3, and 4);

   (d) Citizenship Acquisition and Termination (Article 10);

   (e) Creation or abolition of Legislative Councils in the States (Article 169);

   (f) Creation of a Legislature or a Council of Ministers for the Union territory of Puducherry (Article 239A);

   (g) Special provisions with respect to Delhi (Article 239AA);

   (h) Amendments in Second Schedule – Emoluments, allowances, privileges, etc., of President, Governors, Judges, Speakers, etc.

   (i) Extension of provisions of Part IX to Scheduled Areas and Tribal Areas referred to in Article 244 (Article 243M);

   (j) Extension of provisions of Part IX-A to Scheduled Areas and Tribal Areas referred to in Article 244 (Article 243ZC);

(k) Formation of an autonomous State comprising certain tribal areas in Assam and creation of local Legislature or Council of Ministers or both therefore (Article 244A);

(l) Creation of All-India Judicial Service (Article 312);

(m) Administration and control of Scheduled Areas and Scheduled Tribes (Para 7 of the Fifth Schedule);

(n) Administration of Tribal Areas in the States of Assam, Meghalaya, Tripura, and Mizoram (Para 21 of the Sixth Schedule);

(o) Use of Official language (Article 343);

(p) Election of MPs and MLAs; and

(q) Parliamentary Procedures and Rules;

2. **Amendment by Special Majority :** Articles of the Constitution which can be amended by special majority are laid down in Article 368 in Part XX. All constitutional amendments, other than those referred to above, (i.e., in (1) with simple majority) come within this category and must be effected by a majority of the total membership of each House of Parliament as well as by a majority of not less than 2/3 of the members of that House present and voting[2].

   Taking a strict interpretation of the Constitutional provision, the special majority prescribed may be required only for voting at the third reading stage, but by way of caution, the requirement of special majority has been provided for in the Rules of Procedure and Conduct of Business in Lok Sabha in respect of all the effective stages of the Bill[3].

3. **By Special Majority and Ratification by States :** There are Articles which require, in addition to the special majority mentioned above, ratification by not less than ½ of the State Legislatures. The States are given an important voice in the amendment of these matters. There are federal matters where States have important power under the Constitution and any unilateral amendment by the Parliament may vitally affect the fundamental basis of the system built up by the Constitution.

   The following provisions require such ratification by the States:

- Election of the President (Articles 54 and 55).
- Extent of the Executive powers of the Union and States (Articles 73 and 162).
- Articles dealing with judiciary, Supreme Court, High Court in the States, and Union Territories (Articles 124 to 147, 214 to 231, 241).
- Distribution of Legislative powers between the Centre and the State (Articles 245 to 255).
- Any of the Lists of the VIIth Schedule.

---

[2]The expression "total membership" means the total number of members comprising the House irrespective of whether there are vacancies or absentees on any account. The expression "present and voting", means members who vote for "a yes" or for "noes". Members who are present in the House and vote "abstention" either through the electronic vote recorder or on a voting slip or in any other manner, are not treated as "present and voting".

[3]i.e., motion that the Bill be taken into consideration, motion that the Bill, as reported by the Select or Joint Committee, be taken into consideration, motion that the Bill, as passed by Rajya Sabha, be taken into consideration, motion for adoption of clauses and schedules to the Bill and finally for the adoption of the motion that the Bill be passed. However, Motions that the Bill be circulated for eliciting opinion thereon or that the Bill be referred to a Select or Joint Committee are passed by simple majority.

- Goods and Services Tax Council.
- Representation of States in Parliament (IVth Schedule).
- Article 368 itself.

Thus, only amendments under Article 368, i.e., either by special majority or by special majority and ratification by States are considered as "Constitutional Amendments". Amendments in the Constitution by way of simple majority are not considered as constitutional amendments. Therefore, the Bills introduced in this regard are not considered as "Constitutional Amendment Bills".

PROCEDURE FOR CONSTITUTIONAL AMENDMENTS

The Constitutional Amendment procedure is laid down in Article 368 as follows:

1. An amendment of the Constitution can be initiated only by the introduction of a Bill for the purpose in either House of Parliament and not in the State Legislatures.
2. The Bill can be introduced either by a minister or by a private member[4] and does not require prior permission of the President.
3. The Bill must be passed in each House by a special majority, that is, a majority (that is, more than 50 per cent) of the total membership of the House and a majority of two-thirds of the members of the House present and voting.
4. Each House must pass the Bill separately. In case of a disagreement between the two Houses, there is no provision for holding a joint sitting of the two Houses for the purpose of deliberation and passage of the Bill.
5. If the Bill seeks to amend the federal provisions of the Constitution, it must also be ratified by the legislatures of half of the States by a simple majority, that is, a majority of the members of the House present and voting.
6. No specific time limit for the ratification of an amending Bill by the State Legislatures is laid down; the resolutions ratifying the proposed amendment should, however, be passed before the amending Bill is presented to the President for his assent.
7. After duly passed by both the Houses of Parliament and ratified by the State Legislatures, where necessary, the Bill is presented to the President for assent.
8. The President must give his assent to the Bill. He can neither withhold his assent to the Bill nor return the Bill for reconsideration of the Parliament.
9. After the President's assent, the Bill becomes an Act (i.e., a constitutional amendment Act) and the Constitution stands amended in accordance with the terms of the Act.
10. The Constitution can be amended: (1) only by Parliament; and (2) in the manner provided. Any attempt to amend the Constitution by a Legislature other than the Parliament and in a manner different from that provided for, will be void and inoperative.

---

[4] If sponsored by a Private Member, the Bill has to be examined in the first instance and recommended for introduction by the Committee on Private Members' Bills and Resolutions before it is included for introduction in the List of Business. Motions for introduction of the Bills are decided by simple majority.

Scope of Parliament's Power to Amend the Constitution

In *Shankari Prasad Singh Deo Vs. The Union of India*[5], the Supreme Court unanimously held: The terms of Article 368 are perfectly general and empower the Parliament to amend the Constitution without any exception whatsoever. In the context of Article 13, "law" must be taken to mean rules or regulations made in exercise of ordinary legislative power and not amendments to the Constitution made in exercise of constituent power, with the result that Article 13(2)[6] does not affect amendments made under Article 368.

In *Sajjan Singh Vs. The State of Rajasthan*[7], the Supreme Court (by a majority of 3:2) held: When Article 368 confers on the Parliament the right to amend the Constitution, the power in question can be exercised over all the provisions of the Constitution. It would be unreasonable to hold that the word "Law" in Article 13(2) takes in Constitution Amendment Acts passed under Article 368.

Thus, until the case of *I.C. Golaknath Vs. State of Punjab*[8], the Supreme Court had been holding that no part of the Constitution was unamendable and that the Parliament might, by passing a Constitution Amendment Act in compliance with the requirements of Article 368, amend any provision of the Constitution, including the Fundamental Rights and Article 368. But in Golaknath's case, the Supreme Court (by a majority of 6:5) reserved its own earlier decisions.

In Golaknath's case, the Court held that an amendment of the Constitution is a legislative process. A Constitution amendment under Article 368 is "law" within the meaning of Article 13 of the Constitution and therefore, if a Constitutional amendment "takes away or abridges" a Fundamental Right conferred by Part III, it is void. The Court was also of the opinion that Fundamental Rights included in Part III of the Constitution are given a transcendental position under the Constitution and are kept beyond the reach of the Parliament. The incapacity of the Parliament to modify, restrict, or impair Fundamental Freedoms in Part III arises from the scheme of the Constitution and the nature of the freedoms.

The decision of the eleven-judge bench in *Golaknath* led to a spate of constitutional amendments. The 24th Constitution Amendment Act, on the one hand, amended the most problematic Article 13 by inserting clause (4), which provides that nothing in that Article "shall apply to any amendment of this Constitution made under Article 368", and on the other, amended Article 368 by inserting the words "in exercise of its constituent power" in clause (1).

Thus, the 24th Constitutional Amendment Act has amended the Constitution to provide expressly that Parliament has power to amend any part of the Constitution, including the provisions relating to Fundamental Rights. This has been done by amending Articles 13 and 368 to make it clear that the bar in Article 13 against abridging or taking away any of the Fundamental Rights does not apply to Constitution amendment made under Article 368.

In *His Holiness Kesavananda Bharati Sripadagalvaru Vs. State of Kerala*[9], the Supreme Court reviewed the decision in the Golaknath's case and went into the validity of the 24th (and other constitutional amendments such as 25th, 26th, and 29th Constitutional Amendments (which are discussed in the "Right

---

[5](A.I.R. 1951 S.C. 458)

[6]Article 13(2): The State shall not make any law which takes away or abridges the right conferred by this Part and any law made in contravention of this clause shall, to the extent of contravention, be void.

[7]A.I.R. 1965 S.C. 845.

[8]A.I.R. 1967 S.C. 1643.

[9]A.I.R. 1973 S.C. 1461.

to Property" chapter)). The case was heard by the largest ever Constitution Bench of 13 Judges. The majority of the Full Bench upheld the validity of the Constitution (Twenty-fourth Amendment) Act and overruled the decision of the Golaknath's case holding that a Constitution Amendment Act is not "law" within the meaning of Article 13. Upholding the validity of clause (4)[10] of Article 13 and a corresponding provision in Article 368(3), inserted by the Twenty-fourth Amendment Act, the Court settled in favour of the view that the Parliament has the power to amend the Fundamental Rights also. However, the Court affirmed another proposition which was also asserted in the Golaknath's case. The Court held that the expression 'amendment' of this Constitution in Article 368 means any addition or change in any of the provisions of the Constitution within the broad contours of the Preamble and the Constitution to carry out the objectives in the Preamble and the Directive Principles. Applied to Fundamental Rights, it would be that while Fundamental Rights cannot be abrogated, reasonable abridgement of Fundamental Rights could be affected in the public interest. The true position is that every provision of the Constitution can be amended, provided the basic foundation and structure of the Constitution remains the same.

Thus, the principle of inviolability of Fundamental Rights laid down in the *Golaknath case* was reversed. Thenceforth, that is, after *Kesavananda Bharathi case,* the Parliament shall have the power to amend each and every part of the Constitution, including Fundamental Rights, but subject only to the principle that in the exercise of such power, basic features or basic structure shall not be damaged or destroyed. The basic structure of the Constitution has, thus, become the juristic principle for effectively controlling the unlimited power to amend the Constitution.

The theory of basic structure of the Constitution was reaffirmed and applied by the Supreme Court in *Smt. Indira Nehru Gandhi Vs. Raj Narain*[11] case and certain amendments to the Constitution were held void.

DOCTRINE OF BASIC STRUCTURE

The "Basic Structure" doctrine is the judge-made doctrine whereby certain features of the Constitution of India are beyond the limits of the amending powers of the Parliament. Though the Court held that the power of the Parliament to amend the Constitution was impliedly limited by the doctrine of basic structure, it did not clearly define or explain what constitutes the basic structure.

Thus, it is for the courts to determine whether a particular feature is a basic structure in each case that comes before it.

So far, the Supreme Court has recognized the following as basic features:

1. The Rule of Law
2. The Principle of Equality
3. The Doctrine of Separation of powers
4. The Supremacy of the Constitution
5. Federalism
6. Secularism
7. The sovereign democratic republican nature of polity

---

[10] Article 13(4)-No amendment of this Constitution (including the provisions of Part III) made or purporting to have been made under this Article [whether before or after the commencement of section 55 of the Constitution (Forty-second Amendment) Act, 1976] shall be called in question in any court on any ground.

[11] A.I.R. 1975 S.C. 2299.

8. Parliamentary system of Government
9. Free and fair Elections
10. Independence of Judiciary (Independent Judicial System)
11. Powers of the Supreme Court under Arts. 32, 136, 142, and 147
12. Fundamental Rights in certain cases
13. Limited power of Parliament to amend the Constitution
14. Power of Judicial Review
15. Republican and Democratic form of Government.

The above-mentioned features are in no way exhaustive. Whether a feature is "basic" or not is to be determined from time to time by the court as and when the question arises.

QUESTIONS

Subjective Question

1. Explain the origin and evolution of the "Doctrine of the Basic Structure". **(250 words)**

Objective Questions

1. With reference to the procedure for the amendment of the Constitution as laid down in Article 368, consider the following Statements:

   1. The Bill can be introduced by a minister only and not by a private member.
   2. The provisions of the Constitution which can be amended by a simple majority are outside the scope of Article 368.
   3. The Constitution Amendment Bill does not require a prior permission of the President.

   Which of the Statements given above is/are correct?

   (a) 1 and 2 only (b) 2 only
   (c) 1 and 3 only (d) 2 and 3 only

   Ans: (d)

2. Which of the following options is/are available to the President when the Constitution Amendment Bill is presented to him/her for assent?

   1. Give assent to the Bill
   2. Withhold assent to the Bill
   3. Return the Bill for reconsideration of the Parliament

   Select the correct answer using the code given below.

   (a) 1 only (b) 1 and 2 only
   (c) 3 only (d) None of these

   Ans: (a)

3. Which among the following Statements is/are correct regarding the amending procedure of the Constitution?

   1. All amendments to the Constitution are initiated only in the Parliament.
   2. A private member can introduce a Bill to amend the Constitution.

   Select the correct answer using the code given below.

   (a) 1 only (b) 2 only

   (c) Both 1 and 2 (d) Neither 1 nor 2

   Ans: (c)

4. Consider the following Statements regarding Parliament's power to reorganise the States:

   1. A Bill contemplating reorganisation of any State requires prior recommendation of the Governor of the State before introduction in the Parliament.
   2. The law made for reorganising the States is not considered to be a constitutional amendment under Article 368.

   Which of the Statements given above is/are correct?

   (a) 1 only (b) 2 only

   (c) Both 1 and 2 (d) Neither 1 nor 2

   Ans: **(b)**

5. With reference to a Constitution Amendment Bill, consider the following Statements:

   1. The Bill must be passed in each House by a majority of two-thirds of the members of the House present and voting.
   2. A deadlock due to disagreement between the two Houses on such Bill must be resolved by a joint sitting of the two Houses.

   Which of the Statements given above is/are correct?

   (a) 1 only (b) 2 only

   (c) Both 1 and 2 (d) Neither 1 nor 2

   Ans: (a)

CHAPTER 31

COOPERATIVE SOCIETIES

"Cooperation is always more powerful than competition"

- Bob Proctor

INTRODUCTION

The concept of cooperatives is not new to man. It actually dates back to man himself and today, they are a universal form of organisation, which is found in almost all the countries.

As we know that the word 'cooperation' means working together, similarly a 'cooperative' is, when isolated and powerless individuals come together and combine their resources to achieve common economic and social goals. The basic philosophy behind a cooperative is self-help through mutual help which also fosters a feeling of fellowship amongst their members and inculcates moral values in them for better living. In literal terms, cooperatives are an autonomous association of persons who come together voluntarily to meet their common economic, social, and cultural needs and aspirations through a jointly-owned and democratically-controlled enterprise. For example: AMUL (Anand Milk Union Limited) is the trademark of one of the milk cooperatives of Gujarat and it is considered as one of the biggest cooperatives of India today. Dairy farmers of the Anand Union collect their milk which is then used to make pouch milk and other products and the profits from selling these products are distributed amongst the farmers. Each dairy farmer is a shareholder of the cooperative and they earn on the basis of their milk investment[1].

Role of Cooperative Societies

The cooperatives play an important part in the development of our country, as India consists of both urban and developed parts, and rural and underdeveloped parts. In fact, most of the population belongs to the rural areas and engages in agricultural activities and without their development, India can never really develop. The cooperatives have always strived to alleviate poverty and help the poor by providing them agricultural credits and funds, and to meet their consumption requirements at concessional rates. The Rural Credit Cooperatives set up under NABARD (National Bank for Agriculture

[1] https://www.lexquest.in/understanding-cooperatives-constitution-97th-amendment-act-2011/

and Rural Development) are one of the major sources of rural financing in India. Cooperatives are always preferred over private banks as the main goal of a cooperative is not to earn profits but to help its members[2].

But the cooperatives which were essentially formed to help people overcome their financial problems were infected due to various reasons. There were instances wherein the elections were postponed for an indefinite period of time and the incumbent remained in charge and many a times, people who were/are in control of the cooperatives were/are actually the people who have joined cooperatives for personal gains. This causes conflict of personal interests with the interest of the cooperatives and subsequently affects the performance of the cooperatives in a negative way. Earlier, inadequate professionalism on the part of the cooperatives was observed to a great extent, which resulted in low productivity and poor services. There was also a lack of active participation of members in the management of cooperatives. Members are the fundamental stakeholders of any cooperative as the growth of the organisation solely depends on their patronage. But unfortunately, neither the members are aware of their role; nor are the other stakeholders like the management committee, employees, government, etc. ready to recognise and respect this role[3].

According to Luzzati, a famous Italian cooperator, "A cooperative with vigilant members and a weak financial base will be preferred to a cooperative with casual members having strong financial base". The government could be blamed at the outset, as it gave too many benefits to cooperatives, for e.g., reservation of items, some extra benefits like finance facilities, but no accountability, which led to these cooperatives becoming more and more lethargic. They became over-dependent on government assistance which led to outside interference, in turn ruining the quality and essence of the cooperatives. Hence, there was a need for uniformity in cooperative legislation, particularly in respect of aspects crucial for autonomous and democratic functioning of cooperatives. But the structure, performance, and crucial aspects of cooperatives varied from state to state. There was no uniformity of cooperatives across the country. The reason was that the Cooperative Societies is a State Subject under Entry 32 of the State List of Seventh Schedule of the Constitution of India. That is when the Parliament amended the Constitution and brought the 97th Constitutional Amendment Act, 2011 into force.

Evolution of Cooperative Societies in India

The cooperative societies of today have a direct nexus with the 19th century's Cooperative movement. The Industrial Revolution had nearly shut down the village industries and drove the villagers towards agriculture, the last resort for livelihood. In Madras, the cooperation of Mutual-Loan Associations was formed. In Punjab, cooperatives for controlling the common lands in the village were formed. These efforts by the citizens were wholly voluntary and non-official. In 1915, Sir Edward Maclagan formed the Maclagan Committee. This committee was appointed to study and report whether the cooperative movements functioning across the country were economically stable and financially sound.

In 1919, the cooperation during the Montague-Chelmsford Reforms became a provincial subject that boosted the movement's success. Individual states did their acts to promote trade, mutual cooperation, etc. The numbers of cooperative societies and their respective numbers increased rapidly.

---

[2]Ibid.

[3]Ibid.

After Independence, cooperative societies continued to function, and were considered balancing factors between public and private sectors. Post-Independence, cooperatives became an integral part of the following Five-Year program under the tenure of Pandit Nehru as Prime Minister. The National Cooperative Development Corporation (NCDC) was formed as a statutory corporation under the National Cooperative Development Corporation Act, 1962. Therefore, we can see that the word 'cooperative' is not a new term. It has been embedded in our Indian Constitution and society for a very long time.

Types of Cooperative Societies

Consumer's Cooperative Society : These societies safeguard the interests of general consumers by manufacturing and selling goods at a reasonable price.

Producers' Cooperative Society : These societies protect the interests of small producers by making the resources like raw materials, tools, equipment, and other things readily available to the producers.

Cooperative Credit Society : These societies provide monetary support to their members. These societies grant loans at reasonable rates of interest in times of need.

Farming Cooperative Society : These societies provide small farmers the opportunity to work jointly in large-scale farming.

Multi-State Cooperative Societies : Cooperatives are usually under state control, but there are many cooperative societies such as those for sugar, milk, banks, unions, etc. whose members and areas of operation are spread across more than one state. Administrative and financial control of these societies is with the Centre. In other words, the multi-state cooperative societies are under the Centre's control.

CONSTITUTIONAL PROVISIONS RELATED TO COOPERATIVE SOCIETIES (97TH CONSTITUTIONAL AMENDMENT ACT, 2011)

In December, 2004, a conference of Ministers dealing with cooperatives in various States resolved to amend the Constitution to ensure democratic, autonomous, and professional functioning of cooperatives; to address key issues of empowerment of cooperatives through voluntary formation, autonomous functioning, democratic control, and professional management; and for regular and timely conduct of elections, general body meetings, and professional audit. After various consultations by the Centre with State Governments, the Constitution (97th Amendment) Act, 2011 was passed.

Thus, the 97th Amendment Act gave a Constitutional status and protection to Cooperative societies. It made 3 major changes to the Constitution :

(a) It inserted the term "or cooperative societies" in Article 19(1)(c) as a part of Freedom to form associations or unions.

(b) It added Article 43-B as DPSP to promote cooperative societies.

(c) Lastly, it added a new part IX-B in the Constitution which was entitled "The Cooperative Societies" [Article 243-ZH to 243-ZT].

Part IX-B

Part IX-B of the Constitution provides for the following aspects –

(a) **Incorporation of Cooperative Societies :** The State Legislature may make provisions for the incorporation, regulation, and winding-up of cooperative societies based on the principles of voluntary formation, democratic member control, member economic participation, and autonomous functioning.

(b) **Strength of the Board :** The Board shall consist of such a number of Directors as may be provided by the State Legislatures. However, the maximum number of Directors of a cooperative society shall not exceed twenty-one.

(c) ***Tenure*** **:** The term of the members of the Board shall be for five years.

(d) **Election of Cooperative Societies :** The election of a Board shall be conducted before the expiry of the term of the Board. The superintendence, direction, and control of the preparation of electoral rolls and conduct of elections to a cooperative society shall vest in such body, as may be provided by the State Legislatures.

(e) **Supersession and Suspension of the Board :** Board can be superseded or kept under suspension for a period not more than six months –

- If there is a persistent default;
- If there is negligence in the performance of its duties;
- If it commits any act which is prejudicial to the interests of the cooperative society or its members;
- If there is a stalemate in the Constitution or functions of the Board;
- If the elections are not conducted regularly.

(f) **Audit and Accounts :** The State Legislature may make provisions for the maintenance of accounts by the cooperative societies and the auditing of such accounts at least once in each financial year. The audit report of the accounts of an apex cooperative society shall be laid before the State Legislature.

(g) **Convening General Body meeting :** The State Legislature may provide that the Annual General Body Meeting of every cooperative society shall be convened within a period of six months of the close of the financial year.

(h) **Returns :** Every cooperative society shall file returns, within six months of the close of every financial year, to the authority designated by the State Government.

(i) **Offences and Penalties :** The State Legislature may make provisions for the offences relating to the cooperative societies and penalties for such offences.

Constitutional Validity of the 97th Amendment

Part IX-B was the bone of contention between the Central and State government. This part defined powers of the State Legislature and the Centre to regulate incorporation, elections, and governing of these cooperative societies. It gave Parliament the power to issue regulations for multi-state cooperatives and UTs. The question was raised before the SC that whether such amendment can be enforced without being ratified by at least half the states.

In *Union of India Vs. Rajendra N Shah & Anr*[4], the Supreme Court observed that the exclusive legislative power given is to states in matters under the Second List of the 7th Schedule. There can be no doubt that our Constitution has been described as quasi-federal in that, so as far as legislative powers are concerned, there is a tilt in favour of the Centre vis-à-vis the States, given the federal supremacy principle. On the contrary, it is clear that by curtailing the width of Entry 32, List II of the 7th Schedule, Part IX-B seeks to effect a significant change in Article 246(3) read with Entry 32 List II of the 7th Schedule in as much as the State's exclusive power to make laws concerning the subject of cooperative societies is significantly curtailed. It thereby, directly impacts the quasi-federal principle contained therein. The bench also mentioned that during the introduction of Municipal Corporations and Panchayats under the 73rd and 74th amendments, they were also sent for ratification by the states. The court further held that, "We reiterate that our judgment is confined to the procedural aspect of Article 368(2) proviso, there being no substantive challenge to Part IX-B on the ground that it violates the basic structure doctrine as laid down in Kesavananda Bharati's case".

But the court upheld the following provisions of the 97th Amendment Act :

- Validity of Provisions related to Multi-State Cooperative Societies : It did not strike down the portions of Part IX-B of the Amendment concerning 'Multi-State Cooperative Societies (MSCS)' due to the lack of ratification. When it comes to MSCS with objects not confined to one State, the legislative power would be that of the Union of India which is contained in Entry 44 List I (Union List). In other words, it is declared that Part IX-B of the Constitution is operative only in so far as it concerns Multi-State Cooperative Societies both within the various States and in the Union Territories.
- Fundamental Rights to form cooperative societies : Article 19(1)(c).
- DPSP to promote cooperative societies : 43-B.

Although, part of the amendment was struck down due to the technicality, still, it can't be ignored that the amendment was a necessary one. It gave the cooperative societies a proper structure and ideals to strive for. Owing to this amendment, it is now our Fundamental Right to form a cooperative society which has huge implications. However, the amendment impacted the exclusive legislative power of the State Legislatures which is struck down by the Supreme Court.

---

[4] 2021 SCC Online SC 474.

Part - II

COMPARISON OF CONSTITUTIONS

CHAPTER 32

TYPES OF CONSTITUTIONS

INTRODUCTION

The Constitution is a fundamental or basic codified legal document which contains organized rights and obligations of the government and citizens. A Constitution further has been defined as a body of rules established to regulate the system of government within a state.

The nature of a Constitution of a country determines the name ascribed to it. This will also determine the category it belongs to for the purposes of critical analysis, comparison, and better understanding of the characteristic features of the type and nature of government operated under the Constitution. The following categorization that will be discussed hereunder is not sacrosanct. As a matter of fact, a country may fall into more than one of the types due to the practices of its government. In other words, all or few of these below categories are combinable in a particular system of government.

Categories of the Constitution

Codified and Un-codified Constitution

Codified or Written Constitution can be described as one in which one or more than one legal documents duly enacted in the form of laws is found. It is precise, definite, and systematic. It is the result of the conscious and deliberate efforts of the people. It is usually documented and framed by a representative body duly elected by the people at a particular period in history A written Constitution is adopted on a specific date in history which is supposed to reflect in the Preamble of the Constitution. The Constitution of India and United States to mention just two, for example, are both written constitutions. They were first framed by a nominated or elected Constituent Assembly made up of representatives and were subsequently promulgated or adopted on a definite date. A written Constitution may also be termed as an enacted Constitution.

An unwritten Constitution is one in which most of the principles of the government have never been enacted in the form of laws. It consists of customs, conventions, traditions, and some written laws bearing different dates. It is unsystematic, indefinite, and un-precise. Such a Constitution is not the result of conscious and deliberate efforts of the people. It is generally the result of historical development. It is never made by a representative Constituent Assembly at a definite state of history, nor is it promulgated on a particular date. It is therefore, sometimes called an *evolved or cumulative Constitution.* The Constitution of England is a classic example of an unwritten Constitution. It is mainly the result of historical growth[1].

The reason for drafting a codified Constitution is usually associated with the time in which a particular State is formed or associated with a major change that has taken place at the national level. For instance, Italy drew up a new Constitution in 1948 and Germany did the same in 1949 following their defeat in World War II and also to mark the destruction of their previous regimes. The United States drafted a codified Constitution upon independence from Britain in 1787, and India drafted a Constitution after independence from Britain in 1950.

In Britain, the Constitution remains un-codified; the reasons for this are both historical and conceptual. The former reflects the fact that British history has remained continuous since 1689, and there has not been an obvious break which would have called for drafting a codified Constitution. As such, Britain has lacked a 'constitutional moment'. Conceptually, the reason for not having a codified Constitution in Britain is because the basis of the government is the sovereignty of the Parliament; this concept seems incompatible with a codified Constitution simply because a codified Constitution would limit the sovereignty of the Parliament[2].

That difference between a codified and un-codified Constitution is also reflected on the fact that what is written in the constitutional document becomes a superior law that can only be judged by a Constitutional Court. This brings us to another classification of constitutions as 'flexible', such as the British Constitution that can be amended with ease, and 'rigid', such as the US Constitution, which contains entrenchments that make it very difficult to make constitutional changes. In constitutions of the rigid type, it is the Constitution, not the Legislature that is supreme. Arguably, codified constitutions provide mechanisms to effect constitutional changes. However, making those changes is not necessarily easy. In the Canadian Constitution of 1982, the whole of Part V of the constitutional document lays down the procedures for constitutional amendment, and as a consequence, the Constitution is criticised for being at a standstill[3].

Rigid and Flexible Constitution

By definition, a rigid Constitution is one which cannot be amended in the manner in which ordinary laws are passed, amended, or repealed. If a special procedure or organ is needed for its amendment, it is a rigid Constitution. Moreover, a rigid Constitution is the supreme law of the land and ordinary Legislature cannot pass laws to amend or vary what is contained in the Constitution. As a matter of fact, other legislations derive their sources and validity under a rigid Constitution. The authority of other laws is limited and can only be validated by the Constitution; otherwise, it will be null and void. The Constitutions of USA, Switzerland, France, and Australia fall in this category. It cannot be amended in the manner in which ordinary laws are passed, amended, or repealed. Distinction is maintained between a Constitution and an ordinary law. There is a special procedure for constitutional amendment.

---

[1] Lecture Note by Akin Olawale Oluwadayisi Esq., Constitutional Law Lecturer, Adekunle Ajasin University, Akungba-Akoko, Ondo State, Nigeria.

[2] Vernon Bogdanor, *The New British Constitution* (Hart 2009) 8 –14

[3] *Ibid.*

Ordinary law in USA can be passed by a simple majority of the Congress, whereas the constitutional laws can be amended only by the agreement of two-thirds majority of the Congress and three-fourths of the States.

The Swiss Constitution is still more rigid. An amendment whether proposed by the Federal Assembly or through initiative needs to be approved by the Cantons and the electorate through referendum. It must be, thus approved by majority of all the voters casting their vote and by majority of such votes in the majority of Cantons.

A flexible Constitution is one which can easily be amended by perhaps an ordinary legislative process by the ordinary resolution. Both constitutional laws and an ordinary law are treated alike since all constitutional amendments can be made by a simple majority of the Legislature. No distinction is made between the Constitution-making authority and the ordinary law-making authority. No law is unconstitutional if passed by the Parliament. It is a sovereign body, enjoying the ordinary law-making powers and constitutional law-making powers at the same time.

The Constitution of England is a typical example of a flexible Constitution. The British Parliament is competent to pass, amend, or repeal any constitutional law in an ordinary legislative process as both constitutional laws and ordinary laws are treated alike. As A.V. Dicey[4] rightly pointed out, "strictly speaking, there is no constitutional law in Great Britain."

Monarchical and Republican Constitutions

In the Monarchical form of government, the Monarch is the Head of state. However, in Britain, the powers of the Monarch are limited, and the Queen reigns in accordance with the Constitution. The political power lies with the Prime Minister. Accordingly, a constitutional monarchy is a limited monarchy. A republican Constitution (Indian Constitution, American Constitution, etc.,) on the other hand, provides for the election of a President who is the Head of state and the Head of the government.

Arguably, the modern concept of a Constitution has been attributed to the American Constitution of 1787, which includes a Bill of Rights, and also to the French Declaration of Rights of 1789. Both Constitutions were created as a consequence of liberation from colonialism and the monarchy respectively, in order to promote the Republic, and they had behind them violent revolutions. No longer was a Constitution a body of law, institutions, and customs forming the State, but it contained the concept of republicanism—the people constituting a State[5].

Unitary and Federal Constitutions

Like governments, Constitutions may also be classified as unitary and federal on the grounds of concentration and distribution of powers. A unitary Constitution is one that vests all powers in a central government, but a federal Constitution distributes powers "between the central and regional governments". The units of the local government do not enjoy autonomy under a unitary Constitution as they live and work under the control of the central government, but the units or regional governments enjoy autonomy under a federal Constitution in the sphere allotted to them by the Constitution.

---

[4]British Jurist

[5]Brian Christopher Jones, *Preliminary warnings on "constitutional" idolatry* (2015) Jan, Public Law, 74–92.

In a federal system, such as the one in the US, it can also be said that the Constitution is a 'federal' Constitution, instead of a 'unitary' one. In the former, apart from a central government, there is also a government at the state level, with legislative competence under the constitutional arrangements. This is the case not just in India and the US but also in Australia, Canada, and South Africa. In a federal Constitution, it is essential to specify the powers of both the governments (central government and state government) so that there is, as far as possible, no chance of conflict between the two. Its process of amendment is made rigid so that it may not be easily amendable by the unilateral action of the central government. Further, an independent and impartial judiciary is also set up to act as an umpire between the two governments and to interpret the provisions of the Constitution when required.

The unitary and federal constitutions have their merits and demerits. A unitary Constitution makes the central government strong so that it may meet any critical situation, but it does not work well in a big country or where there is marked diversity in respect of religions, cultures, languages, and ways of life of the people. The federal Constitution makes the central government weak by dividing the powers between the centre and the units, but it suits big countries like USA, Russian Federation, and Canada and it is invariably required in countries marked by religions, social, and cultural diversities like India, Switzerland, and South Africa. The element of centralism has made its place in every federal system of the world as a result of which the inherent weakness of a federal Constitution has been done away with. A peculiar arrangement has been devised in India where the Constitution operates as a federal mechanism in normal times and becomes unitary during times of Emergency.

Britain has a unitary Constitution and it is centrally governed. However, this point may now be challenged because due to devolution of powers to Scotland, Wales, and Northern Ireland, perhaps there is an incipient federal aspect to the British Constitution[6].

Presidential and Parliamentary Constitutions

The defining attributes that separate presidential and parliamentary constitutions is the type of government which is followed.

- *Presidential System of Government*

A presidential system of government is a government where all executive powers are vested in a President who is the Head of state and Head of the government. The President may exercise the executive powers of government either directly by himself or through the Vice-President, ministers, or other officers in the public service of the federation. The powers of the President is to maintain the Constitution, to apply all the laws made by the Legislature for the time being in force, to implement party programmes, and generally uphold the interest of the nation and the welfare of the people at all times.

The President is elected directly by the people or indirectly through an Electoral College. The President and the Cabinet of ministers appointed by him are not members of the Legislature. The President is free to choose his ministers from within and outside his party. The President is a member of the ruling party. The party advises and supports him and he implements the programmes of the party. The ministers are first responsible to the President who appointed them and he is primarily responsible to discipline the

[6]Parpworth (n1) 8

ministers or otherwise call them to order. The Legislature and the Executive may be controlled by different political parties. The President is responsible to the Legislature which may investigate and impeach him for gross misconduct and he is also responsible to the people who are the sovereign power in a country and who may not renew his mandate at election.

The United States of America and South Africa are examples of countries operating a presidential system of government. There are many checks and balances under the presidential system of government. While the Legislature may refuse to vote for taxes, thus checking a difficult Executive, the Executive President in turn may veto a bill which has been passed by an uncompromising Legislature.

But, if the bill is passed the second time by two-thirds majority, it becomes law. If however the Bill/ Law is challenged on questions of illegality/constitutionality in court, the judiciary may declare it as unconstitutional, thus acting as a check though the judges are appointed by the Executive. One can then say that the Presidential model government is in essence a government of separation of powers coupled with checks and balances.

- *Parliamentary System of Government*

A Parliamentary or Cabinet system of government is a government where all the executive powers of government are vested in a Prime Minister who is the Head of government and Head of the majority party or ruling party, but is not the Head of state. In this system of government, the Head of state who exercises only ceremonial functions may be a Monarch or President who is the figurehead. The Prime Minister and the entire ministers in his Cabinet are all members of the same party or coalition of parties. In a Cabinet system of government, there is no complete separation of powers, nor a complete fusion of powers.

Apart from the doctrine of collective ministerial responsibility and the doctrine of individual ministerial responsibility to the Parliament, the Prime Minister as Head of the government or Executive arm has the power to dismiss any minister and he is primarily responsible for the discipline of his Cabinet. The stability of the government depends a lot on the ruling party controlling a reasonable majority in the Parliament or being able to form a coalition government with another party or parties.

There is an official opposition party in the Parliament, which is usually the party having the highest number of votes next to the ruling party in the Parliament. The members of the Parliament and the Executive arm are one. The Prime Minister is subject to his party and is controlled by the party. He remains in office as long as his party has the majority of members in the Parliament. However, when a vote of 'no confidence' is passed on him and his Cabinet by the Parliament, the Prime Minister and his entire Cabinet is obliged to resign. The United Kingdom is the origin and home of this system of government. Other countries operating a Parliamentary system of government include India, Canada, Israel, Australia, and so on.

ministers or otherwise call them to order. The Legislature and the Executive may be controlled by different political parties. The President is responsible to the Legislature which may investigate and impeach him for gross misconduct and he is also responsible to the people who are the sovereign power in a country and who may not renew his mandate at election.

The United States of America and South Africa are examples of countries operating a presidential system of government. There are many checks and balances under the presidential system of government. While the Legislature may refuse to vote for taxes, thus checking a difficult Executive, the Executive President in turn may veto a bill which has been passed by an uncompromising Legislature.

But if the bill is passed the second time by two-thirds majority, it becomes law. If however, the Bill/Law is challenged on questions of illegality/constitutionality in court, the judiciary may declare it as unconstitutional, thus acting as a check though the judges are appointed by the Executive. One can then say that the Presidential model government is in essence a government of separation of powers coupled with checks and balances.

4. Parliamentary System of Government

A Parliamentary or Cabinet system of government is a government where all the executive powers of government are vested in a Prime Minister who is the Head of government and Head of the majority party or ruling party but is not the Head of state. In this system of government, the Head of state who exercises only ceremonial functions may be a Monarch or President who is the figurehead. The Prime Minister and the other ministers in his Cabinet are all members of the same party or coalition of parties. In a Cabinet system of government, there is no complete separation of powers, nor a complete fusion of powers.

Apart from the doctrine of collective ministerial responsibility and the doctrine of individual ministerial responsibility to the Parliament, the Prime Minister as Head of the government or Executive arm has the power to dismiss any minister and he is particularly responsible for the discipline of his Cabinet. The stability of the government depends a lot on the ruling party controlling a reasonable majority in the Parliament or being able to form a coalition government with another party or parties.

There is an official opposition party in the Parliament which is usually the party having the highest number of votes next to the ruling party in the Parliament. The members of the Parliament and the executive arm are one. The Prime Minister is subject to his party and is controlled by the party. He remains in office as long as his party has the majority of members in the Parliament. However, when a vote of no confidence is passed on him and his Cabinet by the Parliament, the Prime Minister and his entire Cabinet is obliged to resign. The United Kingdom is the origin and home of this system of government. Other countries operating a Parliamentary system of government include India, Canada, Israel, Australia, and Japan.

CHAPTER 33

INDIAN AND AMERICAN CONSTITUTIONS

INTRODUCTION TO THE CONSTITUTION OF AMERICA

Written in 1787, ratified in 1788, and in operation since 1789, the United States Constitution is the world's oldest and longest surviving written charter of the government[1]. The Constitution of the United States of America consists of a Preamble and seven Articles. The said Constitution has been amended 27 times, most recently in 1992. The first ten amendments constitute the Bill of Rights.

The Constitution sets up a federal system by dividing powers between the national and state governments. It also establishes a balanced national government by separating powers among three independent branches—the executive, the legislative, and the judicial.

Features of the USA Constitution

Salient features of the USA Constitution can be listed as follows:

1. **Goals of the Constitution :** In the Preamble to the Constitution, the framers stated the six goals they wanted the national government to accomplish:
2. **A Written Constitution :** It is the oldest, briefest written Constitution in the world. It consist of a Preamble and 7 Articles running into 4000 words with 10 to 12 pages to be read within half an hour. It has also unwritten elements like conventions. Statutes of the Congress, judicial decisions, and executive decrees also enlarged the Constitution.
3. **A Democratic Government :** It is a representative democracy. The Congress is a representative body of the American people. The President is also elected by the people. The real power is vested with the people. It establishes a republican state where the Head of the state is elected by the people.
4. **Popular Sovereignty :** The concept that government gets its authority from the people and that ultimate political power remains with the people is known as popular sovereignty. The framers made popular sovereignty the foundation upon which the Constitution rests.

[1]The present Constitution of USA was adopted at the Philadelphia Convention held in 1787.

Preamble to the USA Constitution, 1787

Form a more perfect Union	Strengh then the relationship among the states as part of a union and between the states and the national government as part of a federal system.
Establish Justice	Provide laws that are reasonable, fair and impartial and make sure that the administration of those laws is also reasonable, fair and impartial.
Ensure domestic tranquility	Keep peace and maintain order within the country.
Promote the general welfare	Allow all states and citizens to benefit militarily & economically from the protection of a strong national government and defend the nation against foreign enemies.
Provide for the common defence	To promote the general welfare.
Secure the blessings of liberty	Protect the liberties recently won in the American Revolution and preserve them for the generations to come.

"We the People of the United States….do ordain and establish this Constitution for the United States of America"

By creating a republic (a national government in which people exercise their sovereignty by electing others to represent them), the Constitution firmly established the people's authority.

5. **Limited Government :** This is the principle that the powers and functions of government are restricted by the US Constitution and other laws. This principle is also known as the Rule of Law, the concept that every member of society, including the ruler or government, must obey the law and is never above it. The principle of limited government is spread throughout the Constitution.

6. **Bicameral Legislature :** The US legislature is constituted of two houses. The Lower House is known as the House of Representatives and the Upper House is the Senate. The Lower House represents the American people while the Senate is representing the federating units, namely the states. The Senate is the strongest second chamber in the world.

a. House of Representatives:

The House of Representatives has 435 members who are elected by the people for a period of two years on population basis, i.e., state with larger population gets more seats in this house (for example, California has 53 members).

b. Senate:

The members of the Senate are elected by the State Legislatures. Each state has two senators; which means each state has two votes in the senate. These senators are elected for a period of six years. The total number of senators is 100.

7. **Separation of Powers :** Under the principle of Separation of Powers, the duties of governing are divided among three branches—legislative, executive, and judicial. The first three Articles of the Constitution list the responsibilities and powers of each branch.
   - Legislative Branch : Congress, the nation's law-making body, is made up of the House of Representatives and the Senate. Although the two houses of the Congress share responsibility for passing laws, each has its own special powers.
   - Executive Branch : The executive branch comprises of the President, Vice-President, and many executive departments. The executive branch implements, or carries out laws passed by the legislative branch. The President is also Commander-in-Chief of the nation's military.
   - Judicial Branch : It is the function of the judicial branch to interpret and apply the law, i.e., to say what the law is.
8. **Checks and balances :** The framers constructed a system of checks and balances among the three branches of the government. Checks and balances refer to the system that gives each branch of the government the power to change or cancel the acts of another branch. The system prevents any branch from exerting too much power. For example, Congress can check the executive branch by controlling taxes and spending. The executive branch has a check on the legislative branch by way of the President's power to veto or reject legislation. The judicial branch can check the powers of the legislative and executive branches by declaring their acts as unconstitutional.
9. **Judicial Review :** Courts exercise judicial review, which is the power to determine whether the actions of the legislative and executive branches of the government are constitutional. Any law or government action that is found to violate a part of the Constitution is said to be unconstitutional.
10. **Federal System :** The US Constitution provides for a federal system of government. It is the first Constitution which adopted a federal system of government. It is a system of government that divides power between a central government having authority over the entire country and a series of local governments collectively covering the entire territory. The Constitution of USA is an indestructible union within destructible states. The national government is given charge of matters of national importance and the subjects of local importance are taken care of by the state

governments. In the US federation, residuary powers are vested with the state governments. It is a federation of 50 states. It is the most perfect of the federal constitutions as quoted by C.F. Strong. States are autonomous bodies and the centre cannot interfere in their affairs. In case of conflict, Supreme Court decides or settles the dispute.

11. **Rigid Constitution :** Another feature of the American Constitution is that it is rigid, which means that it cannot be amended by the Congress through the ordinary procedure. The procedure is very intricate and difficult.

    The procedure to amend the Constitution consists of 2 steps;

    a. Proposal for Amendment:

       There are two ways to propose for amendment. Either two-thirds (67%) of both the houses (Senate and House of Representatives) shall propose for amendment to the Constitution or on the application of legislatures of two-thirds (67%) of states shall call a convention for proposing amendment.

    b. Ratification of Proposal:

       The amendment shall be ratified by the legislatures of three-fourth (75 %) of all states or by the convention of three-fourth of states. It is because of this rigidity that the American Constitution has been amended only 27 times in over 200 years. It is, therefore, rightly remarked that *"if the founding fathers were to return to life today, they would find it difficult to recognize their handiwork"*.

12. **Bill of Rights :** The original Constitution did not contain a Bill of Rights. But the first 10 amendments passed within the first 2 years of its inauguration provided for a Bill of Rights. It contained the following rights:

    a. Freedom of religion,
    b. Freedom of speech and expression,
    c. Freedom of assembly and petition,
    d. Right to keep and bear arms for security,
    e. Freedom of profession,
    f. Right to private property,
    g. Right to legal equality,
    h. Right of voting irrespective of their color, race or sex,
    i. No person can be compelled to be a witness against himself,
    j. No person can be deprived of his life, liberty or property without the due process of law,
    k. Slavery should be abolished,
    l. No property can be taken for public use without just compensation,

m. The right to speedy and public trial by an impartial judiciary,

n. No state shall make or enforce laws which abridge the privileges and immunities of the citizens of USA.

These rights and liberties are not absolute; it can be modified only with an amendment to the Constitution, and these rights are enforceable in the courts of law.

13. **Dual Citizenship :** The concept of citizenship was not defined in the original Constitution. The 14th Amendment Act clearly provided for double citizenship. Citizenship of the USA and the citizenship of respective state in which one resides are the double citizenship an individual enjoys in USA.

14. **Presidential form of Government :** It provides for a Presidential form of government. There is only one executive—the President. The President is neither elected by the Congress and nor is he responsible to it. This system of government functions on the basis of the theory of Separation of Powers. President's Secretariat or Cabinet does not belong to the Congress. The President is the Head of the nation and all executive powers are vested in his name. He enjoys a fixed tenure of 4 years.

15. **Judicial Supremacy :** Judiciary has been granted supremacy over other organs of the government in USA because Judiciary interprets and protects the Constitution and also resolves the disputes between the centre and the states.

COMPARATIVE ANALYSIS OF INDIAN AND USA CONSTITUTIONS[2]

India and the United States (US) are the two largest democracies in the world. In addition to being democracies, the two nations are also constitutional republics, bound by a written Constitution. However, there are various differences between the USA and Indian Constitutions.

A Study in Contrast: India and USA

- The American Constitution is just 4,543 words long. Even if one includes the 27 amendments since 1789, we get to 7,591 words. In contrast, the Indian Constitution has 145,000 words.
- The American Constitution has just seven Articles and has been amended a mere 27 times since its ratification in 1789. The 27 amendments include the 'Bill of Rights' (the first 10 amendments) that were ratified as early as 1791. The Indian Constitution had 395 Articles at its commencement and 448 Articles in its present form. It has been amended more than 100 times.
- The scope of the American Constitution is primarily the description of the structure and powers of the federal government. Unlike the minimalist style of the American document, the Indian Constitution goes above and beyond describing the constitution of each arm of the government. Take the subject of 'Languages'. The Indian document has eleven Articles (343–350, 350A/B, 351) dedicated to discussing 'Languages'. The Indian Constitution's discussion on Languages alone comprises of more Articles than the number of Articles in the US Constitution as a whole. In

[2] *American And Indian Constitutions: A Study In Contrast*, by Shrikanth Krishnamachary-Aug 25, 2018, *https://swarajyamag.com.*

contrast, the American Constitution does not discuss 'Language' at all. The United States has no 'official' or 'national' language. While this is partly understandable given the greater lingual heterogeneity in India, it underscores the fact that the Indian Constitution ventures into areas that the American document steers clear of. While the Indian document caters to the heterogeneity of the land, the American document desists from it, notwithstanding the increase in lingual and ethnic heterogeneity in the US over the past 200 years.

- The other major difference in the two Constitutions lies in the degree of 'federalism' in the two countries, at least in a formal sense. In the US, every state has its own Constitution, unlike in India.

The state constitutions are much more voluble than the federal Constitution. The Alabama Constitution for instance, is the longest and has 345,000 words. That's much longer than the Indian Constitution. But one of the reasons the state Constitutions can be very long in the US is because they go beyond outlining the structure and powers of the government. As an example, Amendment 520 in the Alabama Constitution authorises one of the counties (Madison County) to provide for the excavation of human graves.

The Indian Constitution does not incorporate such specific state-level legislations. So its extraordinary length cannot be explained away by citing the absence of State Constitutions as a reason. But it is a fact that much of the bulk in the Indian Constitution is on account of discussions of centre–state relations.

CHAPTER **34**

SALIENT FEATURES OF THE CONSTITUTION OF THE UNITED KINGDOM

INTRODUCTION

The United Kingdom has never had a written Constitution embodied in a single document. The foundational constitutional text for UK is the Magna Carta issued by King John of England in 1215. Since then, the Constitution has evolved organically over time in response to political, economic, and social changes.

Britain is unusual in that it has an 'unwritten' Constitution, unlike the great majority of countries. There is no single legal document which sets out in one place the fundamental laws outlining how the state works. Britain's lack of a 'written' Constitution can be explained by its history. In other countries, many of whom have experienced revolution or regime change, it has been necessary to start from scratch or begin from first principles, constructing new state institutions, and defining in detail their relations with each other and their citizens. By contrast, the British Constitution has evolved over a long period of time, reflecting the relative stability of the British polity. It has never been thought necessary to consolidate the basic building blocks of this order in Britain. What Britain has instead is an accumulation of various statutes, conventions, judicial decisions, and treaties which collectively can be referred to as the British Constitution. It is thus, more accurate to refer to Britain's Constitution as an 'un-codified' Constitution, rather than an 'unwritten' one.

Salient Features of the British Constitution

The salient features of British Constitution are as follows:

a. **Unwritten Constitution :** Britain's Constitution is un-codified (unwritten) Constitution. This is not to say that it doesn't exist; rather, *there is no single document* which explains the framework of the government. To find out about the British Constitution you would have to refer to a mixture of Statute Law (Acts of Parliament), Common Law (derived from precedents and customs), Conventions (long-established procedures), Works of Authority (text books by constitutional scholars like Bagehot and Dicey, and now European Union Law.

b. **Flexibility of the Constitution :** Though the Constitution is not in a proper codified form, it has a great adaptability of character. It is very easy to amend and make new laws. It requires a simple majority to pass an amendment. Regardless of its flexibility, there have been a very few changes made till date.

c. **Rule of Law :** Rule of Law constitutes one of the fundamental principles of the British Constitution. In Britain, unlike in the United States or India, the Constitution does not grant specific rights to its citizens. Nor is there any Parliamentary Act laying down the Fundamental Rights of the people. In spite of that, there is maximum liberty in Britain. This, according to Dicey, is due to the existence of the Rule of Law. It implies, firstly, that no one in the United Kingdom can be punished arbitrarily. The powers of the government are exercised according to settled and binding rules. It guarantees security of life, liberty, and property. Secondly, Rule of Law implies that no one is above the law. It means that irrespective of their social and official status, all citizens are equal before law and that everyone is amenable to the ordinary court for any violation of the law.

d. **Unitary System of Government :** The British Constitution is unitary and not a federal one like that of the United States of America or India. Although there is devolution, yet all authority flows from the Central Government centered at London. Devolution process transfers varying levels of power from the UK Parliament to the UK's nations (Scotland, Wales, and Northern Ireland) — but has kept authority over the devolved institutions in the UK Parliament itself. Scotland, Wales, and Northern Ireland all held successful referendums on devolution in the late 1990s. This led to the establishment of separate Parliaments or Assemblies and the democratic election of officials. Devolution in the UK has created a national Parliament in Scotland, a Welsh Parliament (Senedd Cymru), and a national Assembly in Northern Ireland.

e. **Constitutional Monarchy :** Constitutional Monarchy is another feature of the British Constitution. The King is the Head of the state and government and all governmental functions are performed in his name. But his powers are only nominal. In reality, all powers belong to the Cabinet and the Parliament. The King cannot be held responsible for any act done in his name.

f. **Bicameralism :** The division of the British Parliament into two houses, the House of Lords and the House of Commons, took place in the 14th century as a result of division among the representatives of the Nobility. In this, the higher nobility joined hands with the clergy to form the House of Lords and the lower nobility and the commonality combined to form the House of Commons. Since that time, the British Parliament has continued to be a bicameral legislature.

The House of Lords is historically the first house. It has a hereditary, nominated, permanent, and class character. It is a permanent house which has never been and which can never be dissolved. However, in respect of powers, it is almost a powerless house — a house which performs mostly revising and delaying functions.

The House of Commons is publicly elected. The party with the largest number of members in the Commons forms the government. Members of the Commons (MPs) debate the big political issues of the day and proposals for new laws. It is one of the key places where government ministers, like the Prime Minister and the Chancellor, and the principal figures of the main political parties, work.

The Commons alone is responsible for making decisions on Financial Bills, such as proposed new taxes. The Lords can consider these Bills but cannot block or amend them.

g. **Supremacy of Parliament :** Parliamentary supremacy is another feature of the British Constitution. The powers of the British Parliament are absolute. Parliamentary supremacy implies two principles. First, Parliament has unlimited legal power to enact and amend any statute and to override any decision of the courts. Secondly, none can question the authority of the Parliament. According to *De Loeme*, "British Parliament can do everything except to make a man into a woman".

h. **Mixed Government :** The Constitution of UK is regarded as being a mixture of Monarchy, aristocracy, and democracy, because the supreme legislature was composed of the Crown, the House of Lords, and the House of Commons. The Crown represents the Monarchy, the House of Lords and Privy Council the Aristocracy, and the House of Commons represents the Democracy.

i. **Difference between Theory and Practice :** The gradual evolution of the British Constitution and the English habits of retaining traditional forms have resulted in a marked difference in theory and practice. The government in the United Kingdom in ultimate theory is an absolute Monarchy, in form, a limited constitutional Monarchy, and in actual character, a democratic republic. In theory, the government of the UK is vested in the Crown (Nominal Executive). All officers of the State, civil and military, are appointed and dismissed in the name of the Crown. The Ministers are Her Majesty's Ministers and they remain in office during the Royal pleasure. The Monarch is the source of law and fountain of justice. The Monarch summons, dissolves, and prorogues the Parliament. No law is effective without the Crown's consent. No parliamentary election can be held without the Royal writ. The Monarch is the Commander-in-Chief of all British forces during peace and war. The Monarch alone can declare war and all treaties are negotiated and concluded in the name and on behalf of the Monarch. In a nutshell, every act of the government is attributed to the Monarch's name. But all this is in theory. In practice, the Monarch has become merely a nominal executive. Britain today is a 'limited Monarchy'. The Monarch reigns but does not rule. The real powers of the government rest with the British Cabinet headed by the Prime Minister (Real Executive). The members of the Cabinet are members of the Parliament. They remain responsible to its Lower house, namely, the House of Commons, for all their acts. All this means the supremacy of the House of Commons and ultimately, that of the people, for it is the people who elect the members of the House of Commons. Accordingly, no government can remain oblivious of public opinion, if it is to continue in office. Thus, the British Constitution is marked by a difference between theory and practice. Britain presents one of the most democratic systems of government in the world.

j. **Independence of Judiciary :** The judiciary is the guardian of the liberties of the people. Necessary safeguards have been provided against all sorts of interference in the judicial process. Judges are paid liberal salaries and ensured the security of service.

k. **Limited Separation of Power :** In British, there is limited 'Separation of Power'. There is a concentration of political powers in the Parliament while the Cabinet which exercises executive power is just a committee of the Parliament, or in other words, it is part of the Parliament. Nevertheless, many safeguards have been provided to secure the independence of the Judiciary from the influence on the part of the other two branches of the Government.

CHAPTER 35

SALIENT FEATURES OF THE FRENCH, AUSTRALIAN AND SOUTH AFRICAN CONSTITUTIONS

THE FRENCH CONSTITUTION

Since the French revolution in 1789, France has witnessed thirteen constitutions. The current Constitution has been in operation since October 4, 1958, which is also termed as the Constitution of the Fifth Republic. The Constituent Assembly under the inspiration of General Charles De Gaulle, who was also the first President of the Fifth Republic, had framed the Constitution. One of the prime motives of the Constitution was to eradicate any chance of constitutional instability which used to be the drawback of the previous Constitutions. Therefore, one can say that the Constitution of the Fifth Republic has been successful in achieving constitutional stability in France.

Features of the French Constitution

a. **Written and Rigid Constitution :** The French Constitution is a written, brief, and enacted Constitution. The Constitution is rigid in nature as the amendment process is complex. The initiative for amending the Constitution belongs both to the President of the Republic on the proposal of the Prime Minister and to the members of the Parliament. But an amendment must be submitted to a referendum unless it has been carried by a three-fifths majority in a joint sitting of both Houses – the National Assembly and the Senate.

b. **Popular Sovereignty :** Like the Constitutions of India and the USA, the French Constitution of 1958 affirms belief in the sovereignty of the people. Article 3 declares: "National Sovereignty belongs to the people, who exercise it through their representatives and by way of referendum. No section of the people and no individual may claim to exercise it…." Further, the Constitution in its Article 2 declares: "Its principle is Government of the people by the people and for the people."

c. **Unitary :** France has a unitary Constitution which means that all powers of administration have been vested in the central government. Local governments derive their powers from the central government and not from the Constitution.

d. **Secular State :** France, like India, is a secular polity. Article 2 declares: "France is an indivisible, secular, democratic and social Republic. It ensures equality of all citizens before law without distinction of origin, race or religion. It respects all beliefs...... The motto of the Republic is liberty, equality and fraternity."

e. **Bicameral Legislature :** "Parliament is composed of the National Assembly and the Senate". National Assembly is the lower, more powerful, and a directly elected house while Senate is the upper, less powerful, and indirectly elected house. The Parliament is a law-making body which meets for single nine month long session each year. The term of the National Assembly is five years but can be dissolved by the President before the completion of the term. The National Assembly can overthrow the government by a motion of 'no confidence'. The Senate members are elected indirectly by officials including regional councilors, department councilors, mayors, municipal councilors, etc. Each senator enjoys a six-year term.

f. **The Economic and Social Council :** The Constitution of the Fifth Republic has created a new council — The Economic and Social Council— but now after an amendment in 2008, it is called the Economic, Social and Environmental Council. This Council gives advice to the government and Parliament on matters related to social and economic importance.

g. **Mixture of Parliamentary and Presidential Systems of Government :** The French Constitution provides for a mixed type of government in France. It combines the features of both Parliamentary and Presidential forms. The President is the Head of the state but he is neither a purely nominal Head of the state like the Indian President, nor an all-powerful executive like the US President.

The President has a power to choose the Prime Minister but cannot dismiss him or her. He can appoint as well as dismiss the members of the Cabinet on the advice of the Prime Minister and make most of the appointments with the consent of the Cabinet. The President may dissolve the lower house of the French Parliament, i.e., the National Assembly. The President is the Commander-in-Chief of the Armed Forces. The President has a right to grant pardon.

The President appoints the Prime Minister, who is not a member of the Parliament. The Prime Minister remains in office as long as he enjoys the confidence of the National Assembly. In other words, he cannot be dismissed by the President. The Prime Minister and the other members of the Cabinet are not the members of the Parliament but are responsible towards the Parliament. The Prime Minister selects the members of the Cabinet who are appointed by the President. The ministers can be dismissed by the President on the advice of the Prime Minister. Despite not being the member of any of the houses of the Parliament, ministers participate in the sessions of the Parliament and members of Parliament also ask questions to the ministers.

h. **French Judiciary :** The judicial system of France is unique in a sense that it works under the government (which means there is no separation of power in France). However, some measurements have been taken in order to ensure a free and impartial justice system. A feature of the French Judiciary is that France has codified laws which are of five types—penal code, civil code, commercial code, criminal procedure code, and civil procedure code. There are no separate courts for civil and criminal cases. There are ordinary and administrative courts in France. Ordinary courts decide case involving ordinary citizens while administrative courts decide cases involving government servants.

i. **Constitutional Council :** In France, judicial review is vest with a separate body called the Constitutional Council. Constitutional Council consists of nine members, each having a tenure of nine years. One-third of the members retire after every three years. The President of France and the Presidents of both the houses of the Parliament nominate three members each to the Constitutional Council. In addition, all the former Presidents of France are the ex-officio life members of the Constitutional Council. The President of the Council is appointed by the President of France. This Council has been given the power to judge the constitutionality or unconstitutionality of laws before their promulgation and the laws and the rules of procedure of the parliamentary assemblies before their application. This Council also acts as the Election commission and the Election tribunal in Parliamentary elections.

j. **Constitution recognition of Political Parties :** A specific feature of the French Constitution is that, unlike the American Constitution or Indian Constitution, it recognizes the role of political parties. Article 4 of the Constitution states that Political parties "shall be formed freely and shall carry on their activities freely" but "they must respect of national sovereignty and of democracy."

k. **Bill of Rights :** Like the American and Indian Constitutions, the Constitution of the Fifth Republic of France provides for some basic rights of the Frenchmen. A statement of such rights is contained in the Preamble and Section 1 of the Constitution. The Preamble to the Constitution begins:

"The French people solemnly proclaim its attachment to the Rights of Man and to the principles of national sovereignty as defined by the Declaration of 1789 and as confirmed and completed by the preamble to the Constitution of 1946".

The Rights of Man refer to the historic Declaration of the Rights of Man and of the Citizen issued by the French Constituent Assembly in 1789, which asserted that the sovereignty resided in the nation and not in the Monarchy or anybody else, that there should be no class distinction or privileges, and that all men were entitled to personal freedom and to equality before the law.

The Constitution of 1946 confirmed and completed the aforesaid Rights of Man by enlisting the following rights:

(1) right to equality for women;

(2) right to work;

(3) right to belong to trade unions;

(4) right to strike;

(5) right to education;

(6) right to social welfare;

(7) right to racial equality;

(8) right to conditions necessary for family development.

The Preamble to the Constitution of the Fifth Republic covers all these matters. Article 2 of the said Constitution "guarantees equality before the law of all citizens without distinction of birth, race or religion. Article 3 lays down that all adult French nationals, of either sex, are electors and are "capable of exercising their civil and political rights".

The basic rights are upheld by the courts in France, and by a Constitutional Council which keeps watch over the constitutional validity of laws passed by the Parliament. But its rulings are advisory and not binding as in the case of the rulings given by the Supreme Court of the United States and the Supreme Court of India. The French system, however, "is at its best", as Professors G.M. Carter and John H. Herz have observed, "in the protection it offers to individual liberties through its system of administrative jurisdiction, headed by the Council of State, which takes infinite care to protect and indemnify individuals injured by unjust or unfair acts committed by Government officials in the name of the state".

THE AUSTRALIAN CONSTITUTION

Creation of the Australian Constitution

Before 1901 the present Australian States were separate colonies of the then British Empire. When the colonies decided to join together in a federation, representatives from each colony were elected to attend meetings (called constitutional conventions) to draw up a constitution for the new nation. The draft constitution was later approved by a vote of the people in referendums held in each colony.

The new Australian nation was established on January 1, 1901 following the passing of the Commonwealth of Australia Constitution Act by the United Kingdom Parliament. The purpose of the Act was 'to constitute the Commonwealth of Australia'.

The Constitution drawn up at the conventions was included as part of this Act, which declared that 'The Constitution of the Commonwealth shall be as follows:

Federation

Australia is a federation of states which each have their own constitution, government and laws. The Australian Constitution originated as an agreement under which the former colonies came together as states in a federation. In brief, the Constitution establishes the form of the federal government (that is, the Commonwealth, national or central government) and sets out the basis for relations between the Commonwealth and the states.

Distribution of Powers between Federal Government & Provincial Government

The Constitution established a federal system of government, which distributed powers between the central government (the Commonwealth) and regional governments (the six former colonies which became autonomous States). The Constitution expressly mostly enumerates the legislative powers of the Commonwealth Government. Subject to a few exceptions, the States retain the power to legislate on all other matters.

Doctrine of Separation of Powers

The Constitution has separate chapters on the Legislature, Executive and Judiciary, preserving the doctrine of separation of powers. Separation of powers doctrine is an essential feature of the Australian system of government.

Legislature of Australia

The legislative or law-making power of Australia is held by the federal Parliament. The Parliament consists of two Houses—the Senate and the House of Representatives—and the King (represented by the Governor-General).

The appointment of the Governor-General and the Governor-General's powers to summon and dissolve Parliament.

The composition of the Senate : Each state is represented equally and there must be at least six Senators from each state. Senators serve for six years, except following a dissolution of the Senate (brought about by disagreement between the two Houses).

The composition of the House of Representatives : The House of Representatives represents the people of each state in proportion to their numbers—that is, there are more Members from the states with the largest populations. The total number of Members must be, as nearly as practicable, twice the total number of Senators. After election the House of Representatives may last not more than three years, but can be ended (dissolved) sooner by the Governor-General.

Union Executive

Under the Australian Constitution, executive power is exercised by the Governor-General as the King's representative. The Governor-General is appointed by the King on the advice of the Prime Minister of Australia. The Prime Minister is Head of Government. Thus, the union executive consists of the Governor-General, Prime Minster & the Council of Ministers.

Judiciary

Constitution establishes the High Court of Australia and empowers parliament to create other federal courts and to vest federal judicial power in state and territory courts. The High Court of Australia-external site is the highest court and the final court of appeal in Australia. It hears matters involving a dispute about the meaning of the Constitution, as well as final appeals in civil and criminal matters from all courts in Australia. Each state and territory has their own laws and court system. State and territory courts fall within the responsibilities of the relevant state. Judiciary is independent from the other arms of government. judicial officers act independently and without interference from the parliament or the executive. The constitutional guarantees of tenure and remuneration assist in securing judicial independence. Federal judicial officers are appointed by the government of the day and cannot be removed from office except on the grounds of proved misbehaviour or incapacity. The remuneration of judicial officers cannot be reduced while the judge holds office.

Amendment of the Constitution

The Constitution may be altered only by a law passed by the Commonwealth Parliament following a referendum. There have been 44 referenda since 1901 and only eight of these have resulted in an amendment.

Bill of Rights

It is notable that the Constitution contains no Bill of Rights and few express guarantees of individual rights.

THE SOUTH AFRICAN CONSTITUTION

South Africa's Constitution is one of the most progressive in the world and enjoys high acclaim internationally. Human rights are given clear prominence in the Constitution.

The highest law in the land, the Constitution of South Africa serves as the foundation for democratic South Africa, a country free of oppression and discrimination. South Africa had several constitutions prior to the current incarnation. The 1910 Constitution granted independence to South Africa from Britain, the 1961 Constitution declared the country a republic, and the 1983 Constitution established a tri-cameral parliament. All iterations barred black South Africans from voting and from political and everyday rights.

Constitutional Development in the 1990s

In 1990, mounting international and domestic pressure, and, growing evidence and realization among the white political class that the apartheid system was unsustainable, forced the ruling government (Nationalist Party Government – NP) towards dismantling the system. The first step was the lifting of the ban on political organizations - in particular the African National Congress (ANC) and the release of veteran opposition leader, Nelson Mandela, after 27 years in prison. This was followed by a repeal of the apartheid legislation. Between these developments and in 1993, and against a backdrop of intense political violence, the NP, the ANC and other political organizations, engaged in a series of negotiations under the umbrella of the Convention for a Democratic South Africa (CODESA). These negotiations eventually led to the adoption of an interim constitution to govern the transition to a new South Africa. This came after an all-white referendum in which over 60 percent of whites voted in favour of absolute reforms.

- **The Interim Constitution of 1993 :** Promulgated by the Constitution of South Africa Act of 1993, it provided for a Government of National Unity, a five-year transition. It also provided for a Constituent Assembly consisting of a combined Senate and National Assembly to draft a new constitution. It is under the terms of this constitution that Mandela would become president in May 1994. This constitution remained in force until 1996 when the current constitution of South Africa was adopted.

- **The Constitution of 1996 :** Promulgated as the Constitution of South Africa Act, it has been described as a masterpiece of post conflict constitutional engineering in the post-cold war era. Designed in the context of South Africa's transition to democratic rule which started with the release of Mandela in February 1990, the constitution completely reconfigured South Africa's political institutions, injecting new dynamics and transformative changes across its political landscape. It effectively ended decades of oppressive white minority rule. The constitution has since been amended sixteen times but remains the basic law of the nation.

Founding Provisions of the Constitution

South Africa is a sovereign, democratic and republic state founded on the following values :

- Human dignity, the achievement of equality and the advancement of human rights and freedom;
- Non-racialism and non-sexism;
- Supremacy of the Constitution;
- Universal adult suffrage;
- A national common voters' roll, regular elections and a multiparty system of democratic government to ensure accountability, responsiveness and openness.

Fundamental Rights/Bill of Rights

The fundamental rights are provided in the Constitution. They seek to protect the rights and freedom of individuals. The Constitutional Court guards these rights and determines whether actions by the state are in accordance with constitutional provisions. South African Constitution is unique because it includes what constitutional scholars call "positive rights". It requires the state to enact policies that minimise inequality. It frees South Africans from discrimination and redresses historical inequalities over personal choice, whether about who you love or reproductive rights. Apartheid legislation denied people the right to vote, to work, to access education, to move freely, to love whomever they wanted to, to not be imprisoned without trial. South Africa's ground breaking Bill of Rights, of the Constitution changed all that. South African's Constitution is the only constitution that includes "third generation rights"[1].

These Rights go beyond the mere civil and social eg:

- Group and collective rights
- Right to self-determination
- Right to a healthy environment
- Right to communicate and communication rights
- Right to participation in cultural heritage

Quasi Federal Form of Government

South Africa has a (quasi) federal model defined in the 1996 Constitution as a co-operative government. The constitution does not define South Africa's government system as strictly federal. Some political systems, like that of South Africa, are hybrid systems. These systems combine the elements of unitary form of government as well as the federal form of government.

Three tier structure

South Africa is a constitutional democracy with a three-tier system of government and an independent judiciary. The national, provincial and local levels of government all have legislative and executive authority in their own spheres, and are defined in the Constitution as distinctive, interdependent and interrelated. Operating at both national and provincial levels are advisory bodies drawn from South Africa's traditional leaders.

---

[1]First generation rights include civil and political rights such as free speech and conscience and freedom from torture and arbitrary detention. In other words, first generation human rights command governments to stand back from the citizen; they are "non-derogable," meaning that they establish bright line rules about which governments have no discretion. Second generation rights are social, economic and cultural and include the rights to reasonable levels of education, healthcare, and housing and minority language rights. Second generation rights require governments to take affirmative action; they are incremental and discretionary because they have a direct financial bearing upon the provision of government services. Most recently third generation rights have shifted focus from the individual person (first generation rights) and the communities in which they live (social, economic and cultural rights) to the natural world, such as the right to a clean and healthy environment, and the right to species biodiversity. Third generation rights can also be identified as the 'solidarity rights', rights which cannot be exerted only by an individual, but only collectively. The Fourth Generation of Subjective Rights the so called "rights related to genetic engineering", rights which are on the doctrinal debate in what regards their recognition or prohibition of certain activities. We can even put in the same category the so called rights of "future generations", as well as rights that cannot belong to an individual nor to social groups, including nations, they belong only to humanity as a whole.

Parliament

Parliament is the legislative authority of South Africa and has the power to make laws for the country, in accordance with the Constitution. It consists of the National Assembly (NA) and the National Council of Provinces (NCOP). Parliamentary sittings are open to the public. The role of Parliament, as the representative of the people, is to promote and oversee adherence to the values of human dignity, equality, non-racialism, non-sexism, and all other rights enshrined in the Bill of Rights, and to oversee the implementation of constitutional imperatives.

National Assembly

The National Assembly is elected to represent the people and to ensure democratic governance as required by the Constitution. It does this by electing the President, providing a national forum for public consideration of issues, passing legislation, and scrutinising and overseeing executive action. The National Assembly, which is elected for a term of five years, is presided over by the Speaker, assisted by the Deputy Speaker.

National Council of Provinces

The National Council of Provinces is mandated to represent the provinces to ensure that provincial interests are taken into account in the national sphere of Government.

Executive Authority

The head of state is the President and he/she leads the Cabinet. The National Assembly elects one of its Members to be President during the first sitting of the National Assembly. Once elected as President, the President ceases to be a Member of Parliament and must be sworn into office within five days. The executive also consists of the Deputy President and the Cabinet ministers at national level, and the Premier and Members of the Executive Councils (MECs) at provincial level. It also includes government departments and civil servants.

Judiciary

The Judicial System establishes the following courts:

- **The Constitutional Court :** The Constitutional Court is South Africa's highest court on constitutional matters. Its jurisdiction - the scope of its authority to hear cases - is restricted to constitutional matters and issues connected with decisions on constitutional matters.
- **The Supreme Court of Appeal :** Except for the Constitutional Court, it is the highest court in South Africa and it only deals with cases sent to it from the High Court;
- **The High Courts :** A high court has jurisdiction in its own area over all persons residing or present in that area. These courts hear matters that are of such a serious nature that the lower courts would not be competent to make an appropriate judgment or to impose a penalty.

Part - III

GOVERNANCE OF INDIA

CHAPTER 36

CONCEPT OF GOVERNANCE AND GOOD GOVERNANCE

CONCEPT OF GOVERNANCE

Governance is the act or manner of governing or the way of control. The concept of 'governance' is not new. It is as old as human civilization. Theories on governance and the question of government's role in encouraging growth is one of the oldest in economics.

In *Rig Veda*, it is mentioned that "*The public good should be the welfare of the society*".

Kautilya's *Arthashastra*, written in the 4th B.C., is one of the first known Indian treatise on public administration. He positioned the State as an institutional necessity for human advancement. Based on this premise, he outlines almost everything that the State should do and described how it should be managed for the maximum happiness of its citizens. The commonly believed Philosophy is — public welfare lies in the happiness of the masses. Therefore, not only the administrators but all the individuals and institutions should keep the happiness and welfare of the society in proper perspective in all their deeds or decisions[1].

Governance is a highly contextual term. Although governance has been defined variously by different people depending upon the context and perspective, there is agreement over the broad elements of governance. Simply put 'governance' means: *The process of decision-making and the process by which decisions are implemented (or not implemented)*[2]. It is a process of governing by which all governmental, as well as non-governmental organizations, civil societies, and private sectors are involved in the process of policymaking and the process of implementation of those policies. Even though government forms the predominant part of the governance environment, it is only one part of several parts of governance.

'Governance' is a broader notion than government. "Governance involves interaction between the formal institutions and those in civil society. Organizations or individuals other than the government, security forces and the military can be grouped together as part of the 'civil society'[3]. Governance refers to a process whereby elements in society wield power, authority and influence and enact policies and decisions concerning public life and social upliftment."

[1]http://hdl.handle.net/10603/145110

[2]https://www.unescap.org/sites/default/files/good-governance.pdf

[3]UNESCAP, what is Good Governance, n.d.http://www.unescap.org/pdd/prs/ProjectA tivities/Ongoing/gg/governance.asp.

TYPES OF GOVERNANCE

Governance depends on the type or nature of the organization's work. Their governance is also different because of the differences in their activities. Various types of governance are as follows:

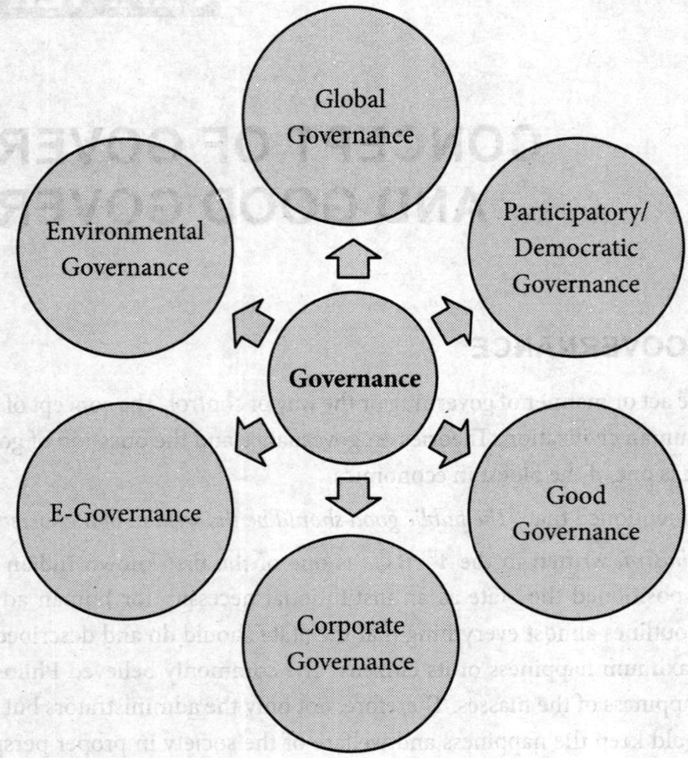

Global Governance

There is no global government or government for the world. In spite of that there exists cross-border movement of people, goods, services, etc. without much disruption, because of global governance. Global governance is collective management of common transnational or global problems — those that were created or exacerbated by globalization, and which cannot be managed at the nation/state level (Example: COVID-19 Pandemic). Global governance encompasses activity at the international, transnational, and regional levels, and refers to activities in the public and private sectors that transcend national boundaries.

The idea of global governance has its roots in the fact that today the states exist with non-state actors. Today, alongside states, we have the presence of international institutions like the United Nations (UN), International Monetary Fund (IMF), the World Bank, World Trade Organization (WTO), and the World Health Organization (WHO). We also have powerful non-state actors like multinational corporations (MNCs), global civil society, and non-governmental organizations (NGO).

Participatory Governance or Democratic Governance

It is a form of governance in which citizens and other non-state actors are empowered to influence and share control in processes of public decision-making and policy making that affect their lives.

In traditional systems of representative democracy, citizens frequently lack access to information, have inadequate opportunities for meaningful dialogue and negotiation with public actors, and are excluded from processes of public deliberation and decision-making. However, the goal of participatory democracy is not to have every citizen participate in every decision, but rather to ensure an equitable representation of different interests and societal groups, especially disadvantaged or marginalized groups, in those decisions and processes that most directly affect people's lives.

Therefore, some level of influence and shared control is required, which is something beyond just information-sharing or consultation in participatory governance.

Good Governance

Good governance is an ideal concept or normative concept. This concept is born when ethics and values are included in the discussion of governance. Now the question is — When will we call any governance as good governance?

When governance is characterized by Participation, Rule of Law, Transparency, Responsiveness, Consensus Oriented, Equity and Inclusiveness, Effectiveness and Efficiency, and Accountability, then we called it good governance[4].

Corporate Governance

Corporate governance is a process and system through which businesses are run. As the businesses grow, the complexities of managing a business also increase. This will lead to various governance issues like providing justice to all the stakeholders of the business, maintaining high ethical standards, and most importantly running a sustainable business in the long run. To achieve these objectives, a strong system and process needs to be in place which is termed as corporate governance.

According to OECD (Organization for Economic Cooperation and Development), "The corporate governance structure specifies the distribution of rights and responsibilities among different participants in the corporation, such as the board, managers, shareholders and other stakeholders, and spells out the rules and procedures for making decisions on corporate affairs".

E-Governance

E-Governance is the use of the ICT to provide services and information on a real-time basis to citizens. E-Governance is composed of information technology, people, and the government. E-Governance is the application of electronic means to improve the interaction between the government and citizens, and to increase the administrative effectiveness and efficiency in the government operations. It is the application of information technology for efficient and effective functioning of government processes in order to establish Simple, Moral, Accountable, Responsive and Transparent (SMART) government[5].

---

[4]https://schoolofpoliticalscience.com

[5]Abramson A.M. and Means E.G. (2001), "e-Government", PriceWaterhouseCoopers Endowment for the Business of Government, Rowman & Littlefield Publishers Inc.

Environmental Governance

Environmental Governance comprises the rules, practices, policies, and institutions that shape how humans interact with the environment. It controls the management of environment and natural resources for proper utilization of the resources and securing sustainable development.

CONCEPT OF GOOD GOVERNANCE

Governance is the act or manner of governing or the way of control. Good governance is, therefore, that system which is accepted as good. Good governance comprises the existence of effective mechanisms, processes, and institutions through which citizens and groups articulate their interests, exercise their legal rights, meet their obligations, and mediate their differences. Although there is a multitude of views regarding good governance, the important dimensions of good governance are discussed here.

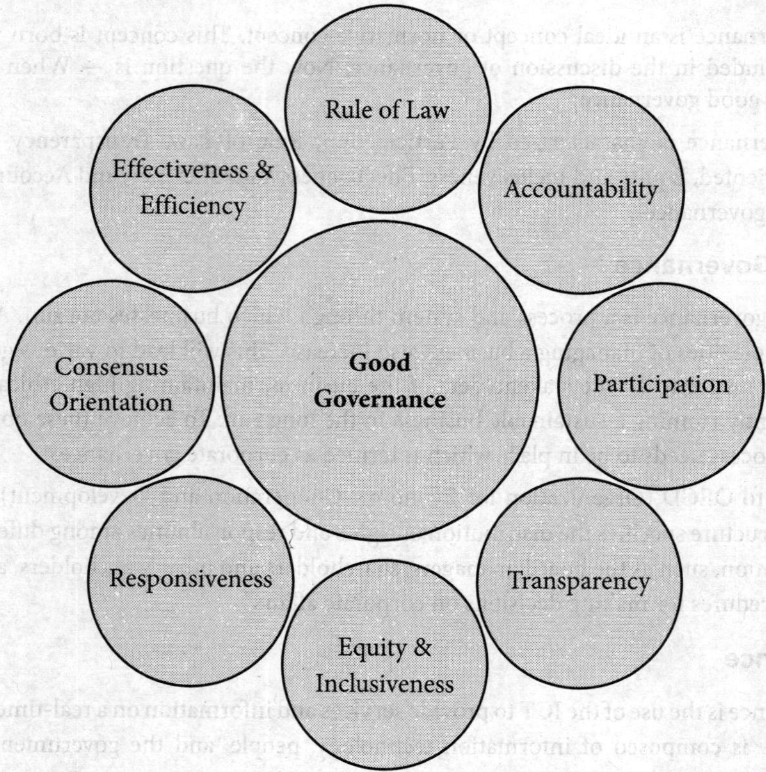

Rule of Law

The Rule of Law is a cornerstone for good governance. A free and fair political system, protection of human rights, a vibrant civil society, public confidence in the police and the courts, and economic development of all depend upon accountable governments, fair and accessible application of the law, and respect for International Human Rights standards. The judicial system should be independent of the government so that it can serve the interests of its citizens rather than a particular political party. In this way it protects the civil rights of its citizens against a predatory state.

Participation

All men and women should have a voice in decision-making, either directly or through legitimate intermediate institutions that represent their interests. Both men and women should have the equal right to participate in society. It is important to point out that representative democracy does not necessarily mean that the concerns of the most vulnerable in the society would be taken into consideration in decision-making. Participation needs to be informed and organized. Such broad participation can be built on freedom of association and expression on one hand and an organized civil society on the other.

Accountability

Accountability is a key requirement of good governance. Generally, accountability means 'holding officials responsible for their action'. However, not only governmental institutions but also the private sector and civil society organizations must be accountable to the public and to their institutional stakeholders. Who is accountable to whom, varies depending on whether decisions or actions taken are internal or external to an organization or institution. In general, an organization or an institution is accountable to those who will be affected by its decisions or actions. Accountability cannot be enforced without transparency and the rule of law[6].

Transparency

Transparency means that decisions taken and their enforcement are done in a manner that follows rules and regulations. It also means that information is freely available and directly accessible to those who will be affected by such decisions and their enforcement. Transparency ensures that enough information is provided and that it is provided in easily understandable forms and media. Transparency is a fundamental element of abolishing corruption[7].

Transparency of decision-making, particularly in budget, regulatory, and procurement processes, is also critical to the effectiveness of resource use and the reduction of corruption and waste.

Equity and Inclusiveness

A society's well-being depends on ensuring that all its members feel that they have a stake in it and do not feel excluded from the mainstream of society. This requires all groups, but particularly the most vulnerable, to have opportunities to improve or maintain their well-being.

Effectiveness and Efficiency

Good governance means that processes and institutions produce results that meet the needs of the society while making the best use of resources at their disposal. The concept of efficiency in the context of good governance also covers the sustainable use of natural resources and the protection of the environment.

Consensus Orientation

There are several actors and as many viewpoints in a given society. Good governance requires mediation of the different interests in the society to reach a broad consensus on what is in the best

---

[6]https://www.unescap.org/sites/default/files/good-governance

[7]https://www.cgg.gov.in

interest of the whole community and how this can be achieved. It also requires a broad and long-term perspective on what is needed for sustainable human development and how to achieve the goals of such development. This can only result from an understanding of the historical, cultural, and social contexts of a given society or community.

Responsiveness

Good governance requires that institutions and processes try to serve all stakeholders within a reasonable time frame.

SUBJECTIVE QUESTIONS

1. 'Good Governance cannot remain merely a philosophy. Concrete steps have to be taken for realizing its goals'. Comment.
2. 'Responsive government makes a good government at every level'. Discuss.

CHAPTER 37

IMPORTANCE OF PEOPLE'S PARTICIPATION IN GOOD GOVERNANCE

"Success of democracy is impossible without participation of the people."

– Hon'ble Prime Minister Shri Narendra Modi

PEOPLE'S PARTICIPATION

People's participation is a key cornerstone of good governance. It is only in a democracy that people can be empowered to demand and shape better policies, express grievances, seek justice, and hold the government to account. Good governance is essential to achieve development while true participatory democracy ensures that development is equitable and sustainable[1]. People's participation is thus, not only the essence of good governance, but the very backbone of the democratic process. Besides being informed citizens of the country, only when people express their views and opinions, does it become possible for a government to effectively execute and sustain the essence of democracy.

CITIZEN'S PARTICIPATION

According to United Nations Development Programme (UNDP), "Participation means that people are closely involved in economic, social, cultural and political process that affects their lives". People's participation in the election is what makes our democracy a representative and participatory democracy. But the meaning of peoples' or citizens' participation does not begin and end with their voting in elections. In fact, participation comprises all those actions of citizens by which they seek to influence, support, or criticize the government and its policies. They do so to ensure that their representatives respond to their needs and aspirations[2]. Using the term 'citizens' in the broadest sense includes individuals, groups, non-profit organisations, and even business corporate citizens.

[1]Meenu (2015). Importance of people's participation in good governance. Internat. J. Appl. Soc. Sci., 2 (7&8): 236-240.

[2]Ibid.

Citizens' participation in governance involves a shift in the development paradigm from citizens as the recipients of development, to one that views them as active participants in the development process. Equally, it involves a shift from a 'top-down' to a 'bottom-up' approach to development involving increasing decentralization of power away from the Union Government, and closer to grassroots levels, i.e., 'subsidiarity' or 'local governance'.

Citizens' participation refers to the mechanism and modalities by which citizens can influence and take control over resources and decision-making that directly impacts their lives. At the ideological level, direct citizens' participation in governance is seen as contributing to a healthy democracy, because it enhances and improves upon the traditional form of representative democracy to transform it into more responsive and thus, a participative grassroots democracy.

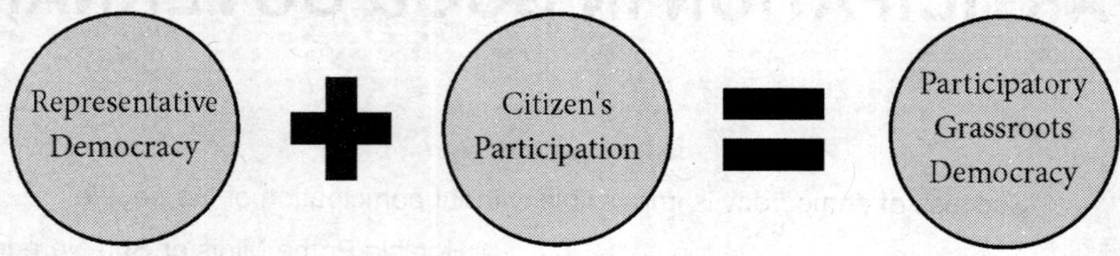

Citizens' Participation and its Contribution to Good Governance

Citizen's participation can contribute to good governance in the following ways[3]:

- It enables citizens to demand accountability and helps to make the government more responsive, efficient, and effective.
- It helps to make government programmes and services more effective and sustainable.
- It enables the poor and marginalized to influence public policy and service delivery to improve their lives.
- It helps to promote a healthy, grassroots democracy

Citizens' participation in governance is a bilateral engagement wherein it is essential both for government agencies as well as the citizens to be fully involved in order for such participation to lead to improved outcomes such as better service delivery, change in public policy, redressal of grievances, etc.

The Second Administrative Reforms Commission's View

The Second Administrative Reforms Commission is of the view that mechanisms for citizens' participation in governance could be conceptualized in the following main forms[4] :

i. **Citizens seeking information :** Access to information is a fundamental pre-requisite for ensuring citizens' participation in governance. Making information available (on procedures, prices, application forms, officers to be contacted for grievance redressal, etc.) is the first step in any strategy to empower citizens for their interaction with the government. The Right to Information Act, 2005 in India has in essence already laid down the ground-work for ensuring this pre-requisite for citizens' participation in governance but it is only by greater citizens' awareness of their rights under this Act that its vision of transparency can be realized.

---

[3]Second Administrative Reforms Commission, Twelfth Report.

[4]Ibid.

ii. **Citizens giving suggestions :** Listening to the voice of citizens not just during periodic elections but, on an on-going basis, is the starting point of participation of citizens in governance. Such listening could be done through public hearings, surveys, referenda, etc. where citizens can give their suggestions with regard to their problems as well as the possible solutions. Citizens are in the best.Position to articulate their needs and suggest the appropriate solutions; which is why there is often need to complement local knowledge and skills with governmental expertise. Such participation can lead to proactive engagement with the policy-making process, thus creating entry points for further participation and mobilization of citizens to enter the arena of governance.

To illustrate, the **MyGov** portal provides citizens the opportunity to exchange their ideas and views, and includes them in various significant policy and decision-making processes undertaken by the government. At the same time, it keeps the people updated about the schemes and activities undertaken for public welfare, and how they can draw the benefits from them. People from all over the country can now reach out directly to the government to voice their concern, share their perspective, or bring to the forefront their knowledge, which in turn can be transformed into actionable agenda by the respective departments[5].

iii. **Citizens demanding better services :** The objective of citizens' participation is to ensure that government organizations work for the constituencies which they are meant to serve. For this to happen, government servants should be accountable not only to their superiors, but also to citizens. It is only when this is realised by government agencies that citizens can voice their grievances with assurance that due attention is given to them.

For example, in 1999, Hyderabad Metropolitan Water Supply and Sewerage Board (HMWSSB) created a campaign called the 'Customer Meets Campaign' which compelled senior managers to leave the comfort and security of their offices to interact directly with citizens in neighbourhoods throughout the city. The campaign not only provided valuable customer feedback to the Metro Water Management, but also sparked pressure from citizens for further reform by raising expectations. The campaign was covered extensively in the media, thereby magnifying its impact. It was followed by the establishment of a Metro Customer Care (MCC) centre located at the Head Office.

According to Second Administrative Reforms Commission, the efficiency of a government organization is best judged by its responsiveness to complaints/demands from its clients. Every government organization must ensure the following:

(i) a fool-proof system for registration of all complaints,

(ii) a prescribed time schedule for response and resolution, and

(iii) a monitoring and evaluation mechanism to ensure that the norms prescribed are complied with.

The heads of all government organizations should be made responsible for ensuring the development of such a system for responding to the complaints of citizens on a time-bound basis.

---

[5]https://blog.mygov.in/journey-towards-empowerment-with-mygov/

iv. **Citizens holding service providers and government agencies accountable :** Citizens should be given the opportunity to rate the services provided by government organizations, on a periodic basis. Mechanisms such as Regular Citizens' Feedback and Citizens' Report Cards[6] should therefore be evolved by all departments for this purpose. This would not only give a voice to the citizens, but also enable the agencies concerned to judge satisfaction ratings and the need for improvement.

Social Audit is another important tool or mechanism that measures, evaluates, and identifies gaps in service delivery and makes the service providers accountable with the direct participation of intended beneficiaries in this process. Social audits are conducted in partnership with civil society organisations, with auditors emerging from among scheme beneficiaries, who are trained over a period of time on how to conduct a social audit. Social audits have been adapted very organically into the implementation process of a number of schemes in India.

For instance, the National Rural Employment Guarantee Act, 2005 (NREGA) has mandated social audits every six months to monitor whether works are in consonance with the annual village plans. Meghalaya became the first state in India to legislate a Social Audit law which makes social audit of state-run schemes mandatory[7].

v. **Active citizens' participation in administration/decision-making :**

Giving citizens on-going access to the decision-making process, beyond periodic consultations, is a more mature and intensive form of citizens' participation in governance which can help them negotiate with the government for better policy, better plans, better projects, etc. At this stage, the citizens no longer merely voice their grievances with the government, but it involves the government to actually work with the citizens.

Examples of such participation would include participatory municipal budgeting, allowing citizens to vote directly through a referendum on specific proposals for changes in public policies, projects, and laws; mandatory public hearings before approval of projects or decisions such as changes in land use plans, that affect the environment and/or the local community, giving citizens' representation on management committees for local hospitals and schools, empowering the Gram Sabha to decide on issues of implementation in government welfare schemes, etc.

Challenges in Citizen Engagement[8]

i. **Apolitical societies :** Most members of the society are reluctant to be political and acts of public engagement are often seen as political. Often, participation in general elections alone is perceived to be public engagement rather than participation in all aspects of policy-making processes with the goal of effecting change.

[6]The Citizens' Report Card in Bangalore was a civil society initiative undertaken in 1993 to monitor government services in terms of efficiency and accountability. The exercise gathered citizen feedback on performance of public agencies and disseminated the findings to the citizenry, thus exerting public pressure on the agencies to initiate reforms. A seven-point rating scale facilitated quantification of citizen satisfaction levels with regard to service delivery, dimensions of corruption, staff behaviour, and so forth. The report card exercise was repeated in 1999 & 2003, to provide a comparative assessment of the progress since 1993.

[7]https://accountabilityindia.in/blog/social-audits-the-indian-experience/

[8]Page No. 8, Framework for Citizen Engagement in NeGP, Department of Information Technology.

ii. **Lack of capacity to engage :** There is usually only limited knowledge within the society regarding policy-making processes and limited knowledge and skills to communicate constructively with decision makers.

iii. **Limited commitment :** The commitment and continuity to act to effect intended changes is usually limited, since creating an environment for meaningful participation can be a long struggle with few resources.

iv. **Low public trust :** There exists low public trust in the government for not fully taking into consideration community ideas on priority basis for development. Citizen participation often means mobilizing attendance; community members or representatives of community groups are invited to meetings only to fulfill the requirement of consultation with communities, but not really to obtain input to improve government priorities.

v. **Exclusion :** Many consultative processes are seen to be ways of reinforcing the view of the dominant groups and exclusion of most marginalized and vulnerable groups, which are often left out of political processes.

SUBJECTIVE QUESTIONS

1. What do you understand by the term 'Participatory Democracy'? What are the initiatives taken by government in this regard? Discuss.
2. 'Citizens need to participate more in making policy decisions related to their own surroundings'. Critically analyse.

CHAPTER 38

RIGHT TO INFORMATION – A STEP TOWARDS TRANSPARENCY AND ACCOUNTABILITY

"Where a society has chosen to accept democracy as its creedal faith, it is elementary that the citizens ought to know what their government is doing."

– Justice P. N. Bhagwati

RIGHT TO INFORMATION

Access to official information held by government and public authorities is the touchstone of a strong and efficient representative democracy. Access to information can empower the poor and the weaker sections of society to demand and get information about public policies and actions, thereby leading to their welfare. Without good governance, no amount of developmental schemes can bring improvements in the quality of life of the citizens.

The four important elements of good governance — transparency, accountability, predictability, and participation can be achieved with the help of free access to information held by the public authorities.

Transparency refers to availability of information to the general public and clarity about functioning of governmental institutions. Right to information opens up government's records to public scrutiny, thereby arming citizens with a vital tool to inform them about what the government does and how effectively, thus making the government more accountable. Transparency in government organisations makes them function more objectively, thereby enhancing predictability. Information about functioning of the government also enables citizens to participate in the governance process effectively. In a fundamental sense, right to information is a basic necessity of good governance[1].

Right to Information as a Fundamental Right

Right to Information (RTI) in India was developed through judicial pronouncements, thereby distinguishing itself as a Fundamental Right under Article 19 (1)(a). The journey in India towards open, transparent governance begun in the early 1970's and the Supreme Court of India through its judgments has played an important role. By interpreting Article 19 (l)(a) of the Constitution to necessarily include freedom of information, the Supreme Court of India gave access to information, the status of a 'Fundamental Right'.

[1]Right to Information: Master Key to Good Governance, First Report, Second Administrative Reforms Commission, Government of India.

By several decisions, including *Bennett Coleman & Co. Vs. Union of India*[2], *S.P. Gupta Vs. Union of India*[3], *State of Uttar Pradesh Vs. Raj Narain*[4], and more particularly, *Centre for PIL Vs. Union of India*[5], the Supreme Court supported and accelerated the movement for a national law on freedom of information. The enactment of Right to Information Act, 2005 in India has also been hailed as one of the examples of vigilant citizenry and civil society working towards openness. Consequently, the Right to Information Act was enacted in the year 2005[6].

SALIENT FEATURES OF RIGHT TO INFORMATION ACT

1 The Act gives every citizen to seek information from any public authority, whether owned, controlled, or substantially financed by the government.

2. Information means any material in any form, including records, documents, memos, e-mails, opinions, advices, press releases, circulars, orders, logbooks, contracts, reports, papers, samples, models, and data material held in any electronic form.

3. Section 2(h) of the Act defines the word 'Public Authority'. Public Authority means any authority or body or institution of self-government established or constituted -

   (a) by or under the Constitution;

   (b) by any other law made by Parliament;

   (c) by any other law made by State Legislature;

   (d) by notification issued or order made by the appropriate Government, and includes any -

      (i) body owned, controlled, or substantially financed;

      (ii) non-Government organisation substantially financed, directly or indirectly by funds provided by the appropriate Government.

Who Can Apply?

Only the citizens of India are entitled to access information under the RTI Act. NRIs or Non-resident Indians are also eligible to seek information under the Act. There is no prescribed format of application for seeking information. A citizen who wants the information just needs to make a request in writing in a plain paper or through electronic means in English or Hindi or in the official language of the area in which the application is being made. The citizen can get assistance from the Central/State public information officers in writing down the application for request and filing of the application[7].

Giving Reason for Seeking Information

Any applicant who wishes to seek information from the public authority is not required to give reasons for seeking information.

[2] AIR 1973 SC 106.

[3] AIR 1982 SC 149.

[4] AIR 1975 SC 865.

[5] (2000) 9 SCC 39

[6] https://www.cusb.ac.in

[7] Every government has prescribed its own fee rules under the RTI Act, 2005. Insofar as Central government is concerned, Rs 10 is the standard RTI application fee.

Exemption from Disclosure of Information

Sub-section (1) of Section 8 of the Act enumerates the types of information which is exempt from disclosure of information regarding information:

- which would cause a breach of privilege of Parliament or the State Legislature;
- which would prejudicially affect the sovereignty and integrity of India, the security, strategic, scientific, or economic interests of the State, relation with foreign State, or lead to incitement of an offence;
- which has been expressly forbidden to be published by any court of law or Tribunal or the disclosure of which may constitute contempt of court;
- which includes commercial confidence, trade secrets, or intellectual property or the disclosure of which would harm the competitive position of a third party;
- which is available to a person in his fiduciary relationship;
- which would weaken confidence of the Foreign Government;
- which would endanger the life or physical safety of any person or identify the source of information or assistance given in confidence for law enforcement or security purposes;
- which would impede the process of investigation or apprehension or prosecution of offenders;
- which would disclose the Records of deliberations of the Council of Ministers, Secretaries, and other Officers; and
- which relates to personal information which has no relationship to any public activity or interest, or which would cause unwarranted invasion of the privacy of the individual.

Sub-section (2) of section 8, however, provides that information exempted under sub-section (1) or exempted under the Official Secrets Act, 1923 can be disclosed if Central Public Information Officer or the State Public Information Officer or the appellate authority, as the case may be, is satisfied that the larger public interest justifies the disclosure of such information or involve infringement of copyright.

Organisations Exempt from Providing Information

Intelligence and security organisations specified in the Second Schedule are exempted from providing information, excepting the information pertaining to the allegations of corruption and human rights violations.

Suo Motu or Voluntary Disclosure of Information

Under Section 4 of the Act, every public authority within 120 days of the enactment of the Act has to voluntarily disclose information through Annual Reports and websites, which includes the particulars of the organisation, functions, duties, budget allocated, proposed expenditures, disbursement reports, plans, directory of its officers, their remuneration, functions, list of beneficiaries of government schemes, minutes of board meetings, and other updated information. Further, the public authorities shall maintain all the records in a manner which facilitates the right to information and can be computerized within a reasonable time and shall also provide information suo motu at regular intervals through various means of communications, including Internet.

Designation of PIOs, APIOs, and Appellate Authorities

Every public authority is required to designate Public Information Officers in all the administrative units or offices under it and also required to designate Assistant Public Information Officers at each sub-divisional level.

All the public authorities should also designate the First Appellate Authorities and publish their particulars alongwith the particulars of the Public Information Officers.

Public Information Officer

Public authorities shall designate some of its officers as Public Information Officers. They are responsible to give information to a person who seeks information under the RTI Act.

Assistant Public Information Officer

These are the officers at sub-divisional level to whom a person can give his RTI application or appeal. These officers send the application or appeal to the Public Information Officer of the public authority or the concerned appellate authority. An Assistant Public Information Officer is not responsible to supply the information.

Time Period for Supply of Information

In normal course, information to an applicant shall be supplied within 30 days from the receipt of application by the public authority. If information sought concerns the life or liberty of a person, it shall be supplied within 48 hours.

Appeals

If an applicant is not supplied information within the prescribed time of thirty days or 48 hours, as the case may be, or is not satisfied with the information furnished to him, he may prefer an appeal to the first appellate authority who is an officer senior in rank to the Public Information Officer. Such an appeal should be filed within a period of thirty days from the date on which the limit of 30 days of supply of information is expired or from the date on which the information or decision of the Public Information Officer is received. The appellate authority of the public authority shall dispose of the appeal within a period of thirty days or in exceptional cases, within 45 days of the receipt of the appeal.

If the first appellate authority fails to pass an order on the appeal within the prescribed period or if the appellant is not satisfied with the order of the first appellate authority, he may prefer a second appeal with the Information Commission within ninety days from the date on which the decision should have been made by the first appellate authority or was actually received by the appellant.

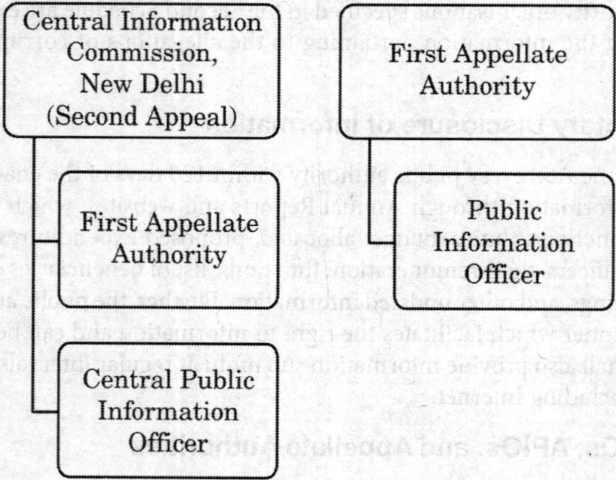

Penalty Provisions

Every PIO will be liable for fine of Rs. 250 per day, up to a maximum of Rs. 25,000/-, for

- not accepting an application;

- delaying information release without reasonable cause;
- malafidely denying information;
- knowingly giving incomplete, incorrect, and misleading information;
- destroying information that has been requested; and
- obstructing furnishing of information in any manner.

The Information Commission (IC) at the Centre and the State levels will have the power to impose this penalty. The Information Commission can also recommend disciplinary action for violation of the law against an erring PIO.

Jurisdictions of Courts

Lower Courts are barred from entertaining suits or applications against any order made under this Act. However, the writ jurisdiction of the Supreme Court and High Courts under Articles 32 and 226 of the Constitution remains unaffected.

Right to Information Vis-a-Vis other Acts

The RTI Act has overriding effect vis-à-vis other laws. It implies that if any of the provisions of the RTI Act are not consistent with any other law for the time being in force including the Official Secrets Act, 1923, the provisions of the RTI Act would have effect.

CENTRAL INFORMATION COMMISSION

Constitution of Central Information Commission

Under the provision of Section 12 of RTI Act, 2005, the Central Government shall, by notification in the Official Gazette, constitute a body to be known as the Central Information Commission. The Central Information Commission shall consist of the Chief Information Commissioner (CIC) and such number of Central Information Commissioners not exceeding 10 as may be deemed necessary.

Eligibility Criteria

Chief Information Commissioner/Information Commissioners must be persons of eminence in public life with wide knowledge and experience in law, science and technology, social service, management, journalism, mass media, or administration and governance.

Chief Information Commissioner/Information Commissioners shall not be a Member of Parliament or Member of the Legislature of any State or Union Territory. He shall not hold any other office of profit or connected with any political party or carrying on any business or pursuing any profession.

Appointment of Chief Information Commissioner/Information Commissioners

The Chief Information Commissioner and Information Commissioners shall be appointed by the President on the recommendation of a committee consisting of the Prime Minister, who shall be the Chairperson of the committee; the Leader of Opposition in the Lok Sabha[8]; and a Union Cabinet Minister to be nominated by the Prime Minister.

[8]Where the Leader of Opposition in the House of the People has not been recognised as such, the Leader of the single largest group in opposition of the Government in the House of the People shall be deemed to be the Leader of Opposition.

Terms and Service Conditions

CIC and IC shall be appointed for a term as may be prescribed by the Central Government[9] or till he attains the age of 65 years, whichever is earlier. CIC and IC's are not eligible for reappointment. However, IC is eligible for appointment as CIC but will not hold office for more than a total of five years including his/her term as IC.

Salary of Chief Information Commissioner and the Information Commissioners shall be such as may be prescribed by the Central Government[10]. The salaries of CIC and IC will not be varied to their disadvantage during their service.

Removal of CIC and IC

The President may, by order, remove from office the Chief Information Commissioner or any Information Commissioner if the Chief Information Commissioner or an Information Commissioner, as the case maybe

(a) Is adjudged an insolvent; or

(b) Has been convicted of an offence which, in the opinion of the President, involves moral turpitude; or

(c) Engages during his term of office in any paid employment outside the duties of his office; or

(d) Is, in the opinion of the President, unfit to continue in office by reason of infirmity of mind or body; or

(e) Has acquired such financial or other interest as is likely to affect prejudicially his functions as the Chief Information Commissioner or an Information Commissioner.

Further, the President can also remove the CIC/IC on the grounds of proved misbehavior or incapacity. However, in such cases, the President has to refer the matter to the Supreme Court for an inquiry. Based on the inquiry and report of the Supreme Court, the President can remove CIC/IC on the grounds of proved misbehavior[11] or incapacity.

Powers and Functions of Central Information Commission

The Central Information Commission has a duty to receive complaints from any person :

(a) who has not been able to submit an information request because a Central Public Information Officer has not been appointed;

(b) who has been refused information that was requested;

---

[9] The department of personnel and training (DoPT), the nodal agency for Right to Information (RTI) Act matters, notified RTI Act rules fixing the tenure of the CIC and ICs for a term of three years. The power to fix the tenure is given to DoPT by RTI Amendment Act, 2019. Prior to the said Amendment Act, the tenure of CIC and IC's were fixed at 5 years by the Act.

[10] Prior to the RTI Amendment Act, 2019 the salary of the CIC and ICs were equivalent to the salary paid to the Chief Election Commissioner and Election Commissioners respectively.

[11] The CIC/IC is deemed to have committed misbehaviour if he is, concerned or interested in any contract or agreement made by or on behalf of the Government of India or participates in any way in the profit thereof or in any benefit or emolument arising therefrom otherwise than as a member and in common with the other members of an incorporated company.

(c) who has received no response to his/her information request within the specified time limits;

(d) who thinks the fees charged are unreasonable;

(e) who thinks information given is incomplete or false or misleading;

(f) any other matter relating to obtaining information under this Act.

The Central Information Commission can even order inquiry if there are reasonable grounds.

Powers of Civil Courts of the Central Information Commission

The Central Information Commission will have the powers of Civil Courts such as -

(a) summoning and enforcing attendance of persons, compelling them to give oral or written evidence on oath and to produce documents or things;

(b) requiring the discovery and inspection of documents;

(c) receiving evidence on affidavit;

(d) requisitioning public records or copies from any court or office;

(e) issuing summons for examination of witnesses or documents; and

(f) any other matter which may be prescribed.

Central Information Commission's Power to Secure Compliance of its Decisions from the Public Authority

(a) Providing access to information in a particular form

(b) Directing the public authority to appoint a PIO/APIO where none exists

(c) Publishing information or categories of information

(d) Making necessary changes to the practices relating to management, maintenance, and destruction of records

(e) Enhancing training provision for officials on RTI

(f) Seeking an Annual Report from the public authority on compliance with this Act

(g) Requiring it to compensate for any loss or other detriment suffered by the applicant

(h) Imposing penalties under this Act

(i) Rejecting the application

Reporting Procedure of CIC

- Central Information Commission will send an Annual Report to the Central Government on the implementation of the provisions of this law at the end of the year.
- Each Ministry at the Central level has a duty to compile reports from its Public Authorities and send them to the Central Information Commission or State Information Commission, as the case may be. Each report will contain details of number of requests received by each Public Authority, number of rejections and appeals, particulars of any disciplinary action taken, amount of fees and charges collected, etc.
- Central Government will table the Central Information Commission report before the Parliament after the end of each year.

STATE INFORMATION COMMISSION

Constitution of State Information Commission

The State Information Commission will be constituted by the State Government through a Gazette notification. It will have one State Chief Information Commissioner (SCIC) and not more than 10 State Information Commissioners (SIC) to be appointed by the Governor.

Eligibility Criteria

State Chief Information Commissioner/State Information Commissioners must be persons of eminence in public life with wide knowledge and experience in law, science and technology, social service, management, journalism, mass media, or administration and governance.

State Chief Information Commissioner/State Information Commissioners shall not be a Member of Parliament or Member of the Legislature of any State or Union Territory. He shall not hold any other office of profit or connected with any political party or carrying on any business or pursuing any profession.

Appointment of State Chief Information Commissioner/State Information Commissioners (SICs)

The State Chief Information Commissioner and Information Commissioners shall be appointed by the Governor on the recommendation of a committee consisting of the Chief Minister, who shall be the Chairperson of the committee; the Leader of the Opposition in the Legislative Assembly, and one Cabinet Minister nominated by the Chief Minister.

Terms and Service Conditions

SCIC and SIC shall be appointed for a term as may be prescribed by the Central Government[12] or till he attains the age of 65 years, whichever is earlier. SCIC and SICs are not eligible for reappointment. However, SIC is eligible for appointment as SCIC but will not hold office for more than a total of five years including his/her term as SIC.

Salary of State Chief Information Commissioner and the State Information Commissioners shall be such as may be prescribed by the Central Government[13]. The salaries of SCIC and SIC will not be varied to their disadvantage during their service.

Removal of SCIC and SIC

The Governor may, by order, remove from office the State Chief Information Commissioner or any State Information Commissioner if the State Chief Information Commissioner or a Information State Commissioner, as the case maybe

[12]The department of personnel and training (DoPT), the nodal agency for Right to Information (RTI) Act matters, notified RTI Act rules fixing the tenure of the SCIC and SICs for a term of three years. The power to fix the tenure is given to DoPT by RTI Amendment Act, 2019. Prior to the said Amendment Act, the tenure of SCIC and SIC's were fixed at 5 years by the Act.

[13]The salaries of the SCIC and SICs were equivalent to the salary paid to the Election Commissioners and the Chief Secretary to the state government.

(a) Is adjudged an insolvent; or

(b) Has been convicted of an offence which, in the opinion of the Governor, involves moral turpitude; or

(c) Engages during his term of office in any paid employment outside the duties of his office; or

(d) Is, in the opinion of the Governor, unfit to continue in office by reason of infirmity of mind or body; or

(e) Has acquired such financial or other interest as is likely to affect prejudicially his functions as the State Chief Information Commissioner or a State Information Commissioner.

Further, the Governor can also remove the SCIC/SIC on the grounds of proved misbehavior or incapacity. However, in such cases, the Governor has to refer the matter to the Supreme Court for an inquiry. Based on the inquiry and report of the Supreme Court, the Governor can remove SCIC/SIC on the grounds of proved misbehavior[14] or incapacity.

Powers and Functions of State Information Commission

The State Information Commission has a duty to receive complaints from any person :

(a) who has not been able to submit an information request because a State Public Information Officer has not been appointed;

(b) who has been refused information that was requested;

(c) who has received no response to his/her information request within the specified time limits;

(d) who thinks the fees charged are unreasonable;

(e) who thinks information given is incomplete or false or misleading;

(f) any other matter relating to obtaining information under this Act.

The State Information Commission can even order inquiry if there are reasonable grounds.

Powers of Civil Courts of the State Information Commission

State Information Commission will have the powers of Civil Courts such as :

(a) summoning and enforcing attendance of persons, compelling them to give oral or written evidence on oath, and to produce documents or things;

(b) requiring the discovery and inspection of documents;

(c) receiving evidence on affidavit;

(d) requisitioning public records or copies from any court or office;

(e) issuing summons for examination of witnesses or documents; and

(f) any other matter which may be prescribed.

State Information Commission's Power to Secure Compliance of its Decisions from the Public Authority

(a) Providing access to information in a particular form

(b) Directing the public authority to appoint a PIO/APIO where none exists;

[14]The SCIC/SIC is deemed to have committed misbehaviour if he is, concerned or interested in any contract or agreement made by or on behalf of the Government of the State or participates in any way in the profit thereof or in any benefit or emolument arising therefrom otherwise than as a member and in common with the other members of an incorporated company.

(c) Publishing information or categories of information

(d) Making necessary changes to the practices relating to management, maintenance, and destruction of records

(e) Enhancing training provision for officials on RTI

(f) Seeking an Annual Report from the public authority on compliance with this Act

(g) Requiring it to compensate for any loss or other detriment suffered by the applicant

(h) Imposing penalties under this Act

(i) Rejecting the application

Reporting Procedure of SIC

- State Information Commission will send an Annual Report to the State Government on the implementation of the provisions of this law at the end of the year.
- Each Ministry at the State level has a duty to compile reports from its Public Authorities and send them to the State Information Commission. Each report will contain details of number of requests received by each Public Authority, number of rejections and appeals, particulars of any disciplinary action taken, amount of fees and charges collected, etc.
- The State Government will table the report of the State Information Commission before the Vidhan Sabha and the Vidhan Parishad (wherever applicable).

SUBJECTIVE QUESTIONS

1. 'RTI Act should not become a tool to obstruct the national development and integration'. Critically Analyze. (150 words)
2. Is it necessary for public institutions to make their orders available online as part of good governance? Comment in the context of RTI Act, 2005. (150 words)
3. How does one achieve the pillars of good governance with RTI Act, 2005? Discuss. (250words)

CHAPTER 39

CITIZEN'S CHARTER

"A customer is the most important visitor to our premises. He is not dependent on us. We are dependent on him. He is not an interruption in our work. He is the purpose of it".

– Mahatma Gandhi

CITIZEN'S CHARTER

Citizen's Charter is a document of commitments made by a Government organization to the citizens regarding the services or schemes provided to them by the Government organization. The objective of Citizen's Charter exercise is to build bridges between citizens and administration and to streamline administration in tune with the needs of citizens. In a nutshell – "the concept of Citizen's Charter enshrines the trust between the service provider and its users".

Historical Background[1]

Citizens' charters were introduced for the first time in the UK by former Prime Minister John Major in the early 1990s. Growing dissatisfaction with public services, the need to transform the country's large, but non-responsive bureaucracy, and the resource crunch facing the government, were key factors that led Major to assign a high priority to this reform.

His Citizen's Charter initiative had a threefold objective:

(1) to ensure that government agencies clearly specify the services and service quality they will provide to the public and the terms on which they will be delivered;

(2) to empower citizens with information on services so as to enable them to claim their entitlements; and

(3) to make government more trans-parent and accountable to citizens.

The UK's Citizens' Charter initiative aroused considerable interest around the world and several countries implemented similar programmes.

The Indian Scene

Over the years, in India, significant progress has been made in the field of economic development. This, along with a substantial increase in the literacy rate, has made Indian citizens increasingly aware of their rights. Citizens have become more articulate and expect the administration not merely to

[1]https://www.epw.in/journal/2008/07/notes/indias-citizens-charters-search-champion.html

respond to their demands, but also to anticipate them. It was in this climate that since 1996 a consensus had evolved in the Government on effective and responsive administration. In a Conference of Chief Ministers of various States and Union Territories held on 24 May, 1997 in New Delhi, presided over by the Prime Minister of India, an 'Action Plan for Effective and Responsive Government' at the Centre and State levels' was adopted. One of the major decisions at that Conference was that the Central and State Governments would formulate Citizens' Charters, starting with those sectors that have a large public interface (e.g., Railways, Telecom, Posts, and Public Distribution Systems)[2]. These Charters were required to include standards of service and time limits that the public can reasonably expect avenues of grievance redress and a provision for independent scrutiny with the involvement of citizens and consumer groups.

Department of Administrative Reforms and Public Grievances (DARPG) in Government of India initiated the task of coordinating, formulating and operationalizing Citizens' Charters. Guidelines for formulating the Charters as well as a list of do's and don'ts were communicated to various government departments/organizations to enable them to bring out focused and effective charters.

Attributes of Citizen's Charter

1. Citizen's Charter initiative is a response to the quest for solving the problems which a citizen encounters, day in and day out, while dealing with the organizations providing public services.
2. The term Citizen in the Citizen's Charter includes not only the citizens, but also all the stakeholders, i.e., citizens, customers, clients, users, beneficiaries, other Ministries/ Departments/ Organisations, State Governments, UT Administrations, etc. In other words, it includes all the stakeholders whose interests and values are addressed by the Citizen's Charter.
3. The Citizen's Charter is not legally enforceable and, therefore, is non-justiciable. However, it is a tool for facilitating the delivery of services to citizens with specified standards, quality, and time frame, etc. with commitments from the organization and its clients.
4. The Charters are expected to incorporate the following elements:
   (i) Vision and Mission Statement;
   (ii) Details of business transacted by the organization;
   (iii) Details of clients;
   (iv) Details of services provided to each client group;
   (v) Details of grievance redress mechanism and how to access it and expectations from the clients.
   (vi) Additional commitments such as compensation in the event of failure of service delivery.

Problems Faced in Implementing the Charters[3]

Introduction and implementation of the concept of Citizen's Charter in the Government of India was much more difficult due to the old bureaucratic set-up/procedures and the rigid attitudes of the work force.

The major obstacles encountered in this initiative are:

1. The general perception of organizations which formulated Citizens' Charters was that the exercise was to be carried out because there was a direction from the top. The consultation process was minimal or largely absent. It thus became one of the routine activities of the organization and had no focus.

[2]https://darpg.gov.in/citizens-charters-historical-background

[3]Ibid.

2. For any Charter to succeed, the employees responsible for its implementation should have proper training and orientation, as commitments of the Charter cannot be expected to be delivered by a workforce that is unaware of the spirit and content of the Charter. However, in many cases, the concerned staff were not adequately trained and sensitized.
3. Sometimes, transfers and reshuffles of the concerned officers at the crucial stages of formulation/implementation of a Citizens' Charter in an organisation severely undermined the strategic processes which were put in place and hampered the progress of the initiative.
4. Awareness campaigns to educate clients about the Charter were not conducted systematically.
5. In some cases, the standards/time norms of services mentioned in Citizen's Charter were either too lax or too tight and were, therefore, unrealistic and created an unfavourable impression on the clients of the Charter.
6. The concept behind the Citizen's Charter was not properly understood. Information brochures, publicity materials, and pamphlets produced earlier by the organisations were mistaken for Citizens' Charters.

Impact of Citizen's Charter on Governance

The significance and potential impact of this reform in India cannot be over-emphasized. For the first time, the GOI had directed all government agencies/departments to make information easily accessible to the citizens on the services and rights they are entitled to, the standards of the services and the remedies in case the services were not delivered. The information was to be provided through websites in all public offices. This was to be done "suo motu", without the citizen having to apply for the information, paying a fee, and applying in a given format, as is the case with the Right to Information (RTI) Act. The impact of this reform would have been enormous, if the numerous public agencies with which citizens interact on a daily basis across the country, had faithfully implemented their Charters. Though this happened well before the RTI Act became law, however, this reform was a low-key affair, almost as if it was a purely internal matter of the government[4].

SUBJECTIVE QUESTIONS

1. Can Citizen's Charter be a game changer in India's governance? Discuss. (150 words)
2. Good Governance is the technology and citizen's charter is the tool and response to quest for solving the administrative problems. Analyze. (250 words)

[4]https://www.epw.in/journal/2008/07/notes/indias-citizens-charters-search-champion.html

CHAPTER 40

CORRUPTION AND LAWS RELATED TO CORRUPTION

"It is impossible to know when and how much water a fish drank; similar is the act of stealing government money by officials.

– *Kautilya, Chanakya Niti*

CORRUPTION

The term 'corruption' refers to the misuse of resources or power for private gain. Transparency International defines corruption as 'the abuse of entrusted power for private gain.' Corruption comes under many different guises like bribery, extortion, fraud, embezzlement, misappropriations of public goods, nepotism (favouring family members for jobs and contracts), cronyism, and influence peddling.

Corruption in India

The economy of India was under socialist regime for an entire generation from the 1950s until the 1980s. During the said period, the economy was shackled by extensive regulation, protectionism, and public ownership, leading to pervasive corruption and slow growth. Since 1991, economic liberalization in India has reduced red-tapism and bureaucracy to a certain extent, and supported the transition towards a market economy and transformed the economy with high growth rate. However, there is no denying the fact that there is widespread corruption in India. Petty corruption which affects the basic rights and services of the common man is highly rampant, besides the grand corruption scandals which break out every now and then. Corruption is a serious economic issue as it adversely affects the country's economic development and achievement of developmental goals. It promotes inefficiencies in utilisation of resources, distorts the markets, compromises quality, destroys the environment, and of late has become a serious threat to national security[1]. If corruption, graft, and nepotism are not checked in time, there is no doubt that the future of the democracy is in peril.

Causes of Corruption

The important causes of corruption in India are :

(i) Exclusivist process of decision-making aggravated by discretion and official secrecy;

(ii) Rigid bureaucratic structures and processes;

(iii) Absence of effective internal control mechanism;

[1]https://cvc.gov.in/sites/default/files/CEO.pdf

(iv) Poor regulatory framework;

(v) Social acceptability and tolerance for corruption;

(vi) Absence of a formal system of inculcating the values of ethics and integrity.

ANTI-CORRUPTION LAWS IN INDIA

Indian Penal Code, 1860 (IPC)

It is one of the first legislations in India which deals with corruption by the public servants. The IPC defines 'public servant' as a government employee, officers in the military, navy, or air force; police, judges, officers of Court of Justice, and any local authority established by a Central or State Act.

The IPC criminalised various activities including taking bribes[2], influencing a public servant through corrupt and illegal means[3], and public servants accepting valuables in the form of gifts[4]. However, all these provisions (Section 161 of the IPC to Section 165A of the IPC) were repealed by the Prevention of Corruption Act, 1988.

Currently under the Act, the following provisions continue to deal with corruption by the public servants :

- Section 169 relates to a public servant unlawfully buying or bidding for property. The public servant shall be punished with imprisonment of upto two years or with fine or both. If the property is purchased, it shall be confiscated.
- Section 409 relates to criminal breach of trust[5] by a public servant. The public servant shall be punished with life imprisonment or with imprisonment of upto 10 years and a fine.

Prevention Of Corruption Act, 1988 (POCA)

In 1988, POCA was enacted to consolidate all laws relating to offences by public servants.

- In addition to the categories included in the IPC, the definition of 'public servant' includes office bearers of cooperative societies receiving financial aid from the government, employees of universities, Public Service Commission, and banks.
- If a public servant takes gratification other than his legal remuneration in respect of an official Act or to influence public servants, he is liable to minimum punishment of six months and maximum punishment of five years and fine. The Act also penalizes a public servant for taking gratification to influence the public by illegal means and for exercising his personal influence with a public servant.
- If a public servant accepts a valuable thing without paying for it or paying inadequately from a person with whom he is involved in a business transaction in his official capacity, he shall be penalized with minimum punishment of six months and maximum punishment of five years and fine.

---

[2]Section 161 - Public Servant taking gratification other than legal remuneration in respect of an official act.

[3]Section 162 - Taking gratification in order by corrupt or illegal means to influence public servant.

[4]Section 165 - Public servant obtaining valuable thing without consideration from person concerned in proceeding or business transacted by such public servant.

[5]Criminal Breach of Trust - 'dishonest misappropriation' or 'conversion to own use' another person's property.

However, it is necessary to obtain prior sanction from the Central or State government in order to prosecute a public servant.

Therefore, it is clearly understood that POCA criminalised various corrupt acts of public servants and middlemen seeking to influence public servants. However, the bribe givers as well as private entities taking bribes were excluded.

The Prevention of Corruption Act, 1988 was enacted to prevent corruption in Government departments and to prosecute and punish public servants involved in corrupt practices. As the Act saw limited success, an amendment was enacted (Amendment Act) and brought into force in 2018. The Amendment Act attempted to bring the POCA in line with United Nations Convention against Corruption (2005), which was ratified by India in 2011.

Prevention Of Corruption (Amendment) Act, 2018[6]

Key provisions of the Amendment Act are as follows:

- **'Definition of 'Undue Advantage'** : The Amendment Act provides that any public servant who accepts or attempts to accept from any person, any 'undue advantage', either for himself or for any other person, in lieu of performance of a public duty, shall be punishable with imprisonment for a minimum term of 3 (three) years and maximum of 7 (seven) years. The Amendment Act has defined 'undue advantage' to mean any gratification other than legal remuneration that a public servant is permitted to receive. Further, 'gratification' is not limited to pecuniary gratifications or to gratifications estimable in money. By virtue of such an expansive definition, even non-monetary considerations such as a better posting, post-retirement benefits, gifts, and favours not estimable in money can also be covered under the ambit of undue advantage.
- **Persons liable for offering a bribe to public servants** : Previously, the POCA did not contain a separate provision for a person who gives or promises to give an undue advantage, but the Amendment Act makes giving an undue advantage by a person to a public servant, a specific offence punishable by 7 (seven) years imprisonment or fine, or both. However, if a person is forced/ coerced to give an undue advantage but reports the same to the concerned authority within 7 (seven) days of doing so, he shall not be liable for the same. Further, as per the POCA, during a corruption trial, if a person made a statement that he gave an undue advantage to a public servant; it would not be used to prosecute him for the offence of abetment. The Amendment Act omits this provision. Effectively, it may become a potential risk for bribe givers to testify against the corrupt, and they may be discouraged from appearing as witnesses in a trial against public servants.
- **Offering of bribes by commercial organizations :** The Amendment Act has defined 'commercial organisation' to mean not just a company or partnership incorporated in India and carrying on business in India or outside India, but also a body or partnership incorporated or formed outside India but carrying on business in India. The Amendment Act provides that if a commercial organisation commits any of the offences listed out in the POCA with the intention to obtain or retain business or obtain or retain an advantage in the conduct of its business, then such commercial organisation shall be punishable with fine, quantum of which is not prescribed in the Amendment Act.

[6]"Prevention of Corruption (Amendment) Act 2018 - Booster for the honest or the corrupt"?, Khaitan & Co, lexology.com.

Protection from Prosecution Under the POCA

A commercial organisation can defend itself when accused of any offence under the POCA, if it proves that it had adequate procedures in place to ensure compliance with such guidelines issued by the Central Government to prevent persons associated with the commercial organisation from undertaking such conduct. The corporate sector in India will have to be swift in enacting its internal guidelines and ensure that its employees are well-informed and abide by these guidelines to protect itself from any kind of prosecution under the POCA, in the event of any associated person being charged with the act of giving a bribe.

Further, if such an offence is proved to have been committed with the consent or connivance of any director, manager, secretary, or other officer of the organisation, then such person shall also be prosecuted under the POCA.

Redefining Criminal Misconduct

Under the POCA, criminal misconduct by a public servant inter alia included:

(i) Using illegal means to obtain any valuable thing or monetary reward for himself or any other person;

(ii) Abusing his position as a public servant to obtain a valuable thing or monetary reward for himself or any other person; and

(iii) Obtaining a valuable thing or monetary reward without public interest, for any person.

However, the Amendment Act replaces this section with a truncated definition of criminal misconduct to include only the following two acts:

(i) Misappropriation or conversion for his own use, any property entrusted to or under the control of a public servant: and

(ii) Amassing assets disproportionate to known sources of income. To prove the latter, the intention to acquire assets disproportionate to income must also be proved, in addition to possession of such assets. Thus, the scope of criminal misconduct has been narrowed and the threshold to establish the offence of possession of disproportionate assets has been increased by the Amendment Act.

Prior Sanction of Appropriate Government for Investigation and Prosecution

The POCA required prior sanction of the appropriate government for prosecution of serving public officials. The Amendment Act extends this protection of requirement of prior approval to investigation prior to prosecution. Further, such protection is extended to former officials as well, for offences done while in office. Moreover, the Amendment Act provides for a directory (not mandatory) time period of 3 (three) months within which the appropriate government must convey the decision on such sanction.

Guidelines for Grant of Sanction for Prosecution

Additionally, the Central Government may prescribe guidelines for grant of sanction for prosecution.

- **Attachment of property :** The Amendment Act has provided for attachment and administration of property procured by means of an offence under the POCA.

- **Time frame for trial :** The POCA did not provide a time frame within which the trial was to be completed. However, the Amendment Act now prescribes that the Special Judge shall endeavour to complete the trial within 2 (two) years. This period can be extended by 6 (six) months at a time and up to a maximum of 4 (four) years in aggregate subject to proper reasons for the same being recorded. The wording of the Section is directory in nature and not mandatory, making it less likely that the courts will abide by such timelines.
- **Enhancement of Punishment :** Punishment has been increased from a minimum imprisonment term of 6 (six) months to 3 (three) years, and from a maximum of 5 (five) years to 7 (seven) years, with or without fine. Punishment for abetment of offences has also been increased by the same quantum.

Review of Prevention Of Corruption (Amendment) Act, 2018

The Prevention Of Corruption (Amendment) Act can be considered as a positive development in respect of anti-graft regime as it includes various provisions relating to commercial organisations and persons who give an undue advantage. It has also modified and enhanced the definitions and penalties for offences related to accepting an undue advantage, being a habitual offender, and abetting an offence.

Despite bringing about the much-needed changes, the Amendment Act has created additional hurdles for investigation and prosecution. The Amendment Act provides for the requirement to obtain prior sanction from appropriate Government to initiate a probe on serving as well as former public servants. While the intent was to prevent victimisation of honest officers, the Amendment Act seemingly strengthens the shield available to officials accused of corruption.

Further, under the POCA, the guilt of the person was presumed for the offences of accepting an undue advantage, being a habitual offender, or abetting an offence. In other words, the burden of proof lies on the accused for the offences of accepting an undue advantage, being a habitual offender, or abetting an offence. This presumption now only applies to the offence of accepting an undue advantage. Burden of proof is shifted to the prosecution for persons accused of being habitual offenders and abetting an offence.

Prevention Of Money Laundering Act, 2002 (PMLA)

Money laundering, as the name itself suggests, is cleaning the money received through illegal source, or concealing the illegal source of money. The process of money laundering involves cleansing of money earned through illegal activities like extortion, drug trafficking, firearm supply, organised crime, etc. Normally, it is a three-step transaction. First, a criminal places the crime money into the formal financial system (Placement). Secondly, the money, which has been injected into the financial system, is layered or spread out into several transactions within the financial system so that the origin or original identity of the crime money be lost or disappeared (Layering). Thirdly, the money gets integrated into the financial system in such a way that the original association with the crime is totally lost and the money could be used by the criminal and his accomplices who get it as clean money (Integration).

History of the Act

Money laundering is a cross-border activity and it has adverse impacts on the economic and political stability of a country. Before 1980s, money laundering was rarely treated as a crime. But in 1980s, there was a sudden surge in the volume of money laundering, mainly due to flow of drug money into the US financial system. The US authorities, therefore, initiated several legislative and regulatory measures at the domestic level to prevent flow of drug money into the US financial system. This was followed by several actions taken at global level to criminalise money laundering. And finally, in 1990, the General Assembly of United Nations, in a resolution, called upon the member states to enact money laundering legislation and programmes. Indian Parliament has enacted Prevention of Money Laundering Act, 2002 to give effect to the said resolution.

Objectives of the Act

- Preventing and controlling money laundering;
- Confiscation and seizure of the property obtained from the laundered money; and
- Dealing with any other issue related with money laundering

Offence of Money Laundering and its Punishment

An offence of money laundering is said to be committed when a person in any way deals with the proceeds of crime[7]. The proceeds of the crime referred above include the normal crimes[8] and the scheduled crimes[9]. The prescribed punishment is 3–7 years rigorous imprisonment for an offence of money laundering with fine. In case of an offence related to narcotics drugs and psychotropic substances, imprisonment would extend up to 10 years.

Other Provisions relating to PMLA

(a) **Powers of attachment of tainted property :** Appropriate authorities can provisionally attach property believed to be 'proceeds of crime' for 180 days. Also, such an order needs to be confirmed by an independent Adjudicating Authority.

(b) **Adjudicating Authority :** The Adjudicating Authority is the authority whose appointment is made by the Central government of India by way of a notification. The Adjudicating Authority decides whether the property related or seized is involved in money laundering. Further, the Adjudicating Authority shall not be bound by any of the procedures specified by the Code of Civil Procedure, 1908, but shall be instructed by the principles of natural justice and subject to the other provisions of the PMLA, 2002.

(c) **Burden of proof :** When a person is accused of having committed the offence of money laundering, the burden of proving that proceeds of crime are untainted property shall be on the accused.

(d) **Special Court :** The Central Government shall, for the purpose of trial of offences under the Act, by notification, assign one or more Courts of Session as the Special Court(s) for such area(s) or for such case(s) as may be specified in the notification. However, such assignment is made in prior consultation with the Chief Justice of the appropriate High Court.

(e) **Administering Agency :** The Directorate of Enforcement under the Department of Revenue, Ministry of Finance is responsible for administering the Prevention of Money Laundering Act.

Benami Transactions (Prohibition) Act

Benami literally means 'without a name'. Therefore, an asset without a legal owner or a fictitious owner is called 'benami'. It can be a property of any kind, whether movable or immovable, acquired by way of benami transaction.

The original Benami Act was introduced in 1988 for prevention of black money but due to some inherent limitations of the Act, it could not be implemented with full force, and therefore, an amendment was introduced in 2016 to ensure the successful enforcement of the Act.

---

[7]Proceeds of Crime - Any property derived or obtained, directly or indirectly, by any person as a result of criminal activity relating to a scheduled offence or the value of any such property or where such property is taken or held outside the country, then the property equivalent in value held within the country.

[8]Crimes which are not mentioned specifically in the schedule of the Act.

[9]The crimes which are mentioned in the Schedule attached to the Act.

An amendment was issued instead of a new Act because if a new Act were introduced, then the transactions entered from 1988 to 2016 would get immunity as the law does not allow retrospective penalization.

The aim of the Benami Transaction Act is to prohibit benami transactions. It states that any person entering into a benami transaction shall be liable for prosecution[10].

What is a benami transaction?

I. A transaction or an arrangement –
   (a) where a property is transferred to, or is held by, a person, and the consideration for such property has been provided, or paid by, another person; and
   (b) the property is held for the immediate or future benefit, direct or indirect, of the person who has provided the consideration,

II. A transaction or an arrangement in respect of a property carried out or made in a fictitious name;

III. A transaction or an arrangement in respect of a property where the owner of the property is not aware of, or, denies knowledge of, such ownership;

IV. A transaction or an arrangement in respect of a property where the person providing the consideration is not traceable or is fictitious.

Property Which Comes Under The Scope of the Benami Act

Banami Act encompasses all kinds of properties whether movable or immovable. The following type of transactions will not be treated as Benami transactions:

- Property is held by a member of the Hindu Undivided Family (HUF) for the benefit of the HUF and the consideration is paid from the known sources of income of such HUF;
- A person who holds the property in a fiduciary capacity for the other person — for example, a trustee for the trust, a director for his company, a depository/depository participant for a trader (holder of shares in demat form), etc.;
- An individual holding property in the name of his spouse or child and where the consideration is paid from the known sources of such individual;
- An individual holding property jointly with a brother, sister, or lineal ascendant/descendant and where the consideration is paid from the known sources of such individual.

Punishment for entering into a Benami Transaction

The various forms of punishment under the Benami Act are as follows:

- Confiscation of benami property

  Where a benami transaction has been entered into to defeat the provisions of any law, avoid payment of statutory dues, or avoid payment to creditors, any person who enters or abets/induces another person to enter into such a transaction would be punishable with:

  * Imprisonment between 1 to 7 years and
  * Fine up to 25% of the fair market value of the property

  Where a person who is required to provide information under this Act provides false information, he shall be punishable with:

- Imprisonment between 6 months to 5 years and
- Fine up to 10% of the fair market value of the property

[10]https://www.charteredclub.com/benami/

Who can take Action?

An Initiating Officer (assistant commissioner or deputy commissioner of income tax), after getting a go ahead from the Approving Authority (Additional Commissioner or Joint Commissioner of Income Tax) can investigate the alleged benami transactions. A notice has to be issued to the benamdar as well as the actual owner, if the identity is known.

The officer can also attach the property being investigated for a maximum of ninety days. If it needs to be attached for a longer period, the matter has to be referred to a three-member Adjudicating Authority. The Adjudicating Authority decides on whether or not a property is benami, after giving a fair hearing to those accused of a benami transaction. When the Adjudicating Authority declares a property benami, the property will pass into the custody of an Administrator.

Appeals against the order of the Adjudicating Authority can be made to a three-member Appellate Tribunal within 45 days. The Appellate Tribunal has to deliver its order within one year.

Criminal Proceedings

The Adjudicating Authority only has the power to determine whether a transaction is benami and initiate attachment/confiscation of property. However, criminal proceedings are to be initiated by one of the authorities mentioned above or an officer of the Central Government or State Government who is authorised by written order. Cognizance may be taken by a Sessions Court which has been especially designated in this regard. Determination by the Adjudicating Authority for confiscation and attachment will not be a final determination for the purpose of criminal punishment — an independent determination by the criminal court in accordance with Criminal Procedure Code and the Indian Evidence Act will be made.

Impact of the 2016 Amendment Act

The 1988 Benami Act did not specify a detailed definition or exclusions for benami transactions. Detailed investigative or adjudicative machinery was not prescribed either. Apart from forfeiture of property, there was simple imprisonment for 3 years or fine or both. Thus, there was an option for a criminal court to sentence an offender with imprisonment or fine.

In comparison, the 2016 Amendment prescribes mandatory rigorous imprisonment for entering into benami transactions and a mandatory penalty which is fairly hefty, at 25% of the market value of the property.

A detailed investigative process and adjudicative machinery are set up, and the government authorities who may assist in the process are also clarified. The law now has teeth.

Fugitive Economic Offenders Act, 2018

The Act provides a method of deterrence for those fraudsters who commit crimes in India and hide in a safe haven in a foreign country. This Act empowers the authorities to confiscate and sell the properties in question to realize the money in default in the fastest method possible. The Act has also included within its ambit, the properties which are situated in abroad as well as those which are a part of the benami transactions, thus hastening the process of recovery and realization[11]. The Act, defines the term 'fugitive economic offender' (FEO).

Definition of FEO

The FEO Act lays down that a person is a FEO if he satisfies the following ingredients of the definition :

- He is an individual;
- An arrest warrant has been issued against him; and

[11]2018 IJLMH | Volume 2, Issue 1 | ISSN: 2581-5369

- He is a fugitive, i.e., he has left India so as to avoid criminal prosecution, or being abroad, and refuses to return to India to face criminal prosecution.

From the definition, it is clear that only an individual can be declared by the Special Court as a FEO for the purposes of the Act.

Procedures to Declare an Individual as FEO

The Act also provides for the following procedures to declare an individual as FEO :

- The Director or the Deputy-Director as defined under the Prevention of Money Laundering Act, 2002 may make an application before the Special Court for a declaration that an individual is a fugitive economic offender; and
- Where an application has been duly filed by the Director or the Deputy Director, the Special Court shall issue a notice to the individual alleged to be a fugitive economic offender;

Additional Provisions of the FEO Act

The Act further provides for the attachment as well confiscation of the property of a fugitive economic offender and proceeds of crime. Moreover, an Administrator will be appointed to manage and dispose of the confiscated property under the Act. The FEO will be disentitled from defending any civil claim.

The Authorities appointed for the purposes of the Prevention of Money Laundering Act, 2002 shall be the Authorities for the purposes of this Act. Moreover, the Fugitive Economic Offenders Act has been enacted to facilitate the functioning of the Prevention of Money Laundering Act, 2002. The proceedings commenced under the former will come to an end as soon as the economic offender submits himself before the jurisdiction of the Indian Courts. Thus, this is an Act to bring back the economic offenders to the country. The Act facilitates the recovery of dues from these economic offenders by empowering the investigative agencies to confiscate and sell the properties. It has come as a ray of hope for the banks and financial institutions who are the primary victims of such offences. The Prevention of Money Laundering Act also provides for reciprocal arrangements and agreements with foreign countries to bring back these absconders. The primary setback behind the already existing law is that the same is very cumbersome and slow. As a result, the recovery is delayed and banks are left with Non-Performing Assets for years. On the other hand, with the enactment of the FEO Act (2018), the same process has been expedited[12].

WHISTLEBLOWING

"Whistleblowing occurs when an employee informs the public of inappropriate activities going on inside the organization."

– Koehn (2003)

Among other things, Whistleblowing can be an act of free speech, an anti-corruption tool, and an internal management dispute mechanism.

Types of Whistleblowing

- **Internal Whistleblowing :** When the whistleblower reports the wrong doings to the officials at higher position in the organization.

---

[12]Ibid.

- **External Whistleblowing :** Where the wrongdoings are reported to the people outside the organization like media, public interest groups, or enforcement agencies
- **Alumini Whistleblowing** : When the whistleblowing is done by the former employee of the organization
- **Open Whistleblowing :** When the identity of the whistleblower is revealed
- **Government Whistleblowing :** When a disclosure is made about wrongdoings or unethical practices adopted by the officials of the Government
- **Corporate :** When a disclosure is made about the wrongdoings in a business corporation

Laws Governing Whistleblowing

Whistleblowers are essentially employees or concerned stakeholders who disclose information about an illegal or unethical conduct within an organization. The laws governing whistleblowing in India are spread over a number of schemes and Acts, i.e., the Companies Act, 2013, the 'Protected Disclosures Scheme for Private Sector and Foreign Banks' ('PD Scheme'), SEBI (Listing Obligations and Disclosure Requirements) Regulations, 2015, and the Whistleblowers Protection Act, 2014. The Whistleblowers Protection Act, 2014 exclusively applies to complaints against corruption and willful misuse of office by a public servant. For corporate whistleblowers, obligations relating to the setting up of whistleblowing mechanisms for certain categories of companies have been provided by the SEBI regulations, Companies Act (2013), and the relevant rules. For those falling outside the categories mandated by SEBI and Companies Act 2013, there is no mandatory requirement under Indian law to ensure adequate whistleblowing mechanisms and protection to whistleblowers. This highlights the inadequacy of whistleblower's protection regime in the private sector in India.

The Whistleblowers Protection Act, 2014[13]

This Act enables any person (i.e., a whistleblower) to report an act of corruption, wilful misuse of power or discretion, or criminal offence by a public servant. This includes all public servants, including Ministers, Members of Parliament, the lower judiciary, regulatory authorities, Central and State government employees, etc. Such disclosures are made to a specified Competent Authority who must conduct a discreet inquiry and conceal the identity of the complainant and public servant. The Act specifies the Competent Authority for each category of public servant. For example, it would be the Prime Minister for a Union Minister; Speaker/Chairman for Members of Parliament; the Chief Justice of the High Court for district court judges, and the Central or State Vigilance Commission for government servants. The Bill amends the Act to prohibit the disclosure of 10 categories of information to a Competent Authority. The table below compares the provisions of the Bill with the Act.

Even though the Act received the President's assent, it remains yet to be implemented[14].

---

[13]https://prsindia.org

[14]Although the Act has received the President's assent, it is yet to be implemented. The government wanted to prohibit two categories of information from being disclosed before the Act is brought into force. Therefore, The Whistleblowers Protection (Amendment) Bill, 2015 was introduced to prohibit two categories of information from being disclosed. This included information related to: (i) sovereignty, strategic, scientific or economic interests of India, foreign relations, or the incitement of an offence; and (ii) proceedings of the Council of Ministers.

Comparison of Whistleblowers Protection Act, 2014 with the Amendment Bill, 2015

Whistleblowers Protection Act, 2014	Whistleblowers Protection (Amendment) Bill, 2015
The Act states that any person, including a public servant or NGO, may make a public interest disclosure before a Competent Authority. This would apply, irrespective of the provisions of the Official Secrets Act, 1923.	A disclosure is prohibited if it contains information related to: (i) The sovereignty, strategic, scientific, or economic interests of India, or the incitement of an offence; (ii) Records of deliberations of the Council of Ministers; (iii) That which is forbidden to be published by a court or if it may result in contempt of court; (iv) A breach of privilege of legislatures; (v) Commercial confidence, trade secrets, intellectual property (if it harms a third party); (vi) That relayed in a fiduciary capacity; (vii) That received from a foreign government; (viii) That which could endanger a person's safety, etc.; (ix) That which would impede an investigation, etc.; (x) Personal matters or invasion of privacy. However, if information related to (ii), (v), (vi), and (x) is available under the Right to Information Act, 2005, then it can be disclosed under the Bill. Disclosures cannot be made if it is prohibited by the Official Secrets Act, 1923
Procedure to determine prohibited disclosures	
Not applicable, as the Act does not prohibit any type of information from being disclosed.	Once a disclosure is made, the Competent Authority will refer it to a government authorised authority. This government authority will take the final decision on whether the disclosure is prohibited.
Certain issues that are exempt from being addressed during an inquiry	
The Act provides that no person is required to answer any question, produce any document, or render any assistance in any inquiry under the Act under certain circumstances. These circumstances are matters that relate to i) security of India, ii) foreign relations; iii) public order and morality; iv) contempt of court; defamation, incitement to an offence; and v) Cabinet proceedings.	Circumstances under which no person is required to answer any question, produces any document, or render any assistance in any inquiry under the Act include the ten conditions discussed earlier, under which public disclosures cannot be made. A certificate by any authority of the State or Central government with regard to the above will be binding.

Impact of 2015 Amendment Bill[15]

- The Statement of Objects and Reasons of the 2015 Bill states that the prohibited categories have been modelled on the 10 categories of information that cannot be revealed under the Right to Information (RTI) Act, 2005. However, this comparison may not be appropriate. The purpose of the RTI Act is to make information with public authorities accessible to all citizens in order to promote transparency and accountability. There may be circumstances where it may not be desirable for public institutions to reveal all types of information to citizens.
- In contrast, the Whistleblowers Act provides for corruption related information to be given by an individual to a Competent Authority. The Competent Authority, in all cases, is a high level Constitutional or Statutory Authority. This information is not made public and the inquiry into the allegation is required to be discreet, with the identity of the complainant, public servant, and related documents being kept secret.

SUBJECTIVE QUESTIONS

1. Does the Prevention of Corruption Act, 2018 envisage to combat commercial bribery or private sector bribery? Explain. **(250 words)**
2. The Prevention of Money Laundering Act, 2002 (PMLA) is a proactive legislation keen on curbing money laundering and bringing violators to justice. Critically Analyze. **(250 words)**
3. "Good faith whistleblowers represent the highest ideals of public service and challenge abuses of power". Explain the importance and the need for 'Whistleblowers' and the laws that protect victimization of whistleblowers. **(250 words)**

[15]https://prsindia.org

CHAPTER 41

ANTI-CORRUPTION AGENCIES IN INDIA

"Without strong watchdog institutions, impunity becomes the very foundation upon which systems of corruption are built"

Rigoberta Menchu` Tum (Nobel Prize Laureate)

ANTI-CORRUPTION AGENCIES IN INDIA

As discussed in the previous chapter on corruption, the Government has established anti-corruption agencies to streamline national anti-corruption efforts, and to investigate and also to prosecute criminal offences in corruption matters (depending on their mandate). Anti-corruption agencies therefore, assume a crucial role in combating corruption.

Following are the important anti-corruption agencies in India:

1. Central Bureau of Investigation (CBI)
2. Central Vigilance Commission (CVC)
3. Enforcement Directorate (ED)
4. Lokpal and Lokayukta
5. Serious Fraud Investigation Office (SFIO)

Central Bureau of Investigation

Central Bureau of Investigation traces its origin to Special Police Establishment (SPE) which was set up in 1941 by the Government of India. The functions of the SPE then were to investigate cases of bribery and corruption in transactions with the War & Supply Department of India during World War II. Superintendence of the SPE was vested with the War Department. Even after the end of the War, the need for a Central Government agency to investigate cases of bribery and corruption by Central Government employees was felt. The Delhi Special Police Establishment Act (DSPE Act) was, therefore, brought into force in 1946. This Act transferred the superintendence of the SPE to the Home Department and its functions were enlarged to cover all departments of the Government of India.

A further growing need was felt for a Central Police Agency at the disposal of the Central Government which would investigate not only cases of bribery and corruption, but also violation of Central fiscal laws, major frauds relating to Government of India departments, public joint stock companies, passport frauds, crimes on the high seas, crimes on the Airlines, and serious crimes committed by organised gangs and professional criminals. Therefore, the Government of India set up Central Bureau of Investigation (CBI) by a resolution dated 1st April, 1963. The Delhi Special Police Establishment acquired its popular current name, Central Bureau of Investigation (CBI), through the aforesaid resolution.

Jurisdiction of CBI

- Initially, the offences that were notified by the Central Government related only to corruption by Central Government servants. In due course, with the setting up of a large number of public sector undertakings, the employees of these undertakings were also brought under CBI purview. Similarly, with the nationalization of the banks in 1969, the Public Sector Banks and their employees also came within the ambit of the CBI.
- The jurisdiction of CBI stretches over the Union Territories as well.
- States – According to Section 5 of DSPE Act, the Central Government may extend the jurisdiction of CBI to any State. The powers vested with the Central Government shall have to be exercised with the consent of the respective State Governments.

In other words, the State Police organizations will have original jurisdiction over a crime that takes place in a State. But CBI can get operative jurisdiction by way of 'General Consent' notifications issued by various State Governments and subsequently further notified by DoPT, Government of India under Section 5 and 6 of DSPE Act respectively. The general consent is given by the States to CBI only for investigation of offences related to loss of revenue to the Government of India and corrupt acts committed by public servants of Government of India or Central Government PSUs. State Government public servants in general do not come under the jurisdiction of CBI. Apart from this, CBI can also take up the investigations when State Governments transfer specific cases in view of their political sensitivity, those attracting large media attention, etc., by issuing specific case-wise notification to transfer the already registered case from State Police Organization to CBI with the consent of the Government of India. The Constitutional Courts like Hon'ble High Courts and Hon'ble Supreme Court can also direct CBI to take up investigation afresh or by way of transferring cases from the State Police organizations.

Thus, CBI is a Specialized Investigating Agency that can exercise powers and jurisdiction in the union territories and the States (of course, with their consent).

Composition of CBI

CBI is headed by a Director. He is assisted by a Special Director or an Additional Director. Additionally, it has a number of joint directors, deputy inspector generals, superintendents of police, and all other usual ranks of police personnel.

The Director of the CBI is the final authority in the organization. He supervises all the work in the CBI and is responsible for constitution of investigating teams for probing cases. Hence, protecting the functional autonomy of the CBI Director and limiting the extent of executive discretion in the matter of appointment of this key functionary is necessary. Therefore, the Delhi Special Police Establishment (DSPE) Act, 1946 was amended in 2003 vide the Central Vigilance Commission (CVC) Act, 2003 to state that the Director of CBI shall be appointed by the Central Government on the recommendations of the Central Vigilance Commissioner, the Vigilance Commissioners, and two Secretaries to the Government of India.

As the above mechanism was not found sufficient to insulate the CBI Director, Section 4A of the DSPE Act, 1946 was further amended vide the Lokpal and Lokayuktas Act, 2013 (the Lokpal Act) to provide that the CBI Director shall be appointed by the Central Government on the recommendations of a committee comprising a) the Prime Minister (Chairperson), b) the Leader of Opposition (Member), and c) the Chief Justice of India or any Judge of Supreme Court nominated by him (Member). The DSPE Act was further amended on 29.11.2014 to include the Leader of the single largest Opposition party in the said committee when there is no recognized Leader of Opposition.

Thus, the appointment of the CBI Director has to be made on the recommendation of the Prime Minister, leader of the single largest opposition party, and the Chief Justice of India (or any Judge of Supreme Court nominated by CJI).

Divisions of CBI

At present, CBI has the following Divisions:

(1) **Anti-Corruption Division :** It investigates cases of corruption and frauds committed by public servants of all the Central Government Departments, Central Public Sector Undertakings, and Financial Institutions;

(2) **Economic Offences Division :** It investigates economic crimes, including bank frauds, cheating, financial frauds, Import, Export and Foreign Exchange violations, large scale smuggling of narcotics, antiques, and other contraband items;

(3) **Special Crimes Division :** It investigates into cases of terrorism, bomb blasts, sensational homicide, kidnapping, murder, and crimes committed by the mafia/underworld;

(4) **Directorate of Prosecution :** Following the Supreme Court judgment in the Vineet Narain case[1], the Directorate of Prosecution was set up in CBI in 2001. This Directorate is responsible for conducting prosecution of CBI cases in courts and giving legal advice to CBI officers. One of the important jobs of the Directorate of Prosecution is preparation of panel of Counsels to conduct prosecution;

(5) **Policy and Coordination Division :** CBI, through its Policy and Coordination Division, coordinates investigation for the members of INTERPOL. The CBI has also set up a Cyber Crime Investigation and Research Cell which, besides doing research in this field, caters to the long felt need of the investigating agencies also. It has also set up a Criminal Intelligence Cell;

(6) **Administration Division;**

(7) **Central Forensic Science Laboratory.**

Thus, CBI is the supreme agency of investigation in the country which registers and investigates the complaints of corruption. It enquires and recommends actions on allegations of corruption against the Government and public servants. CBI advices and guides on internal vigilance in Government departments. It further advices public on the course of action on matters of corruption.

---

[1] *Vineet Narain & Others vs. Union of India* & Another, 1 SCC 226

Central Vigilance Commission

Incorruptibility is an essential requirement for public confidence in the administration of Government departments. The government, in order to strengthen the existing mechanisms, created Central Vigilance Commission (CVC) through an executive resolution in 1964, as an apex body for exercising general superintendence and control over vigilance administration. The main mandate of the Commission was based on the report of the Committee on Prevention of Corruption, popularly known as the Santhanam Committee. The CVC was accorded statutory status in 2003 only after a directive in the judgment of the Supreme Court in *Vineet Narain Vs. Union of India*[2].

CVC has the status of an autonomous body. It is free of control from any executive authority, and is charged with monitoring all vigilance activity under the Central Government of India, advising various authorities in central Government organizations in planning, executing, reviewing, and reforming their vigilance work.

Organizational Structure

The CVC is headed by a Central Vigilance Commissioner who is assisted by two vigilance commissioners. The Central Vigilance Commission has its own Secretariat, Chief Technical Examiners' Wing[3] (CTE), and a Wing of Commissioners for Departmental Inquiries[4] (CDI).

Tenure

The Central Vigilance Commissioner and the Vigilance Commissioner shall hold office for a term of four years from the date on which he/she enters upon his/her office or till he/she attains the age of 65 years, whichever is earlier.

---

[2]In *Vineet Narain Vs. Union of India*, Court gave several directions to make the CBI and CVC more efficient and effective. Some of the main directions are given below –

- The CVC be given statutory status.
- Appointment of the Central Vigilance Commissioner is to be made by the President on the recommendations of the Committee consisting of P.M., Home Minister and Leader of Opposition. The Committee has to recommend persons who are on the panel suggested by Cabinet Secretary and are Civil Servants or others but are of impeccable integrity.
- CVC be made responsible for the effective functioning of CBI. CBI must report to the CVC about the cases taken up by it for investigation and their progress.
- The director of CBI shall have a minimum tenure of 2 years regardless of the date of superannuating. He shall have full freedom for allocation of work within the agency as also for constituting teams for investigation.
- The Supreme Court also gave directions for the establishment of Enforcement Directorate.
- It also gave directions for the establishment of the Nodal Agency for coordinating actions in cases having politic-bureaucrat criminal nexus.

[3]The main functions assigned to this organisation are:

- Technical audit of construction works of Governmental organisations from a vigilance angle;
- Investigation of specific cases of complaints relating to construction works;
- Extension of assistance to CBI in their investigations involving technical matters and for evaluation of properties in Delhi; and Tendering of advice/assistance to the Commission and Chief Vigilance Officers in vigilance cases involving technical matters.

[4]The CDI's function as Inquiry Officers to conduct Oral inquiries in departmental proceeding initiated against public servants.

Appointment

The Central Vigilance Commissioner and the Vigilance Commissioners shall be appointed by the President by warrant under his hand and seal. The President shall appoint only after obtaining the recommendation of a Committee consisting of - Prime Minister (Chairperson), Minister of Home Affairs (Member), and Leader of the opposition in the House of People[5] (Member). No appointment of a Central Vigilance Commissioner or a Vigilance Commissioner shall be invalid merely by reason of any vacancy in the Committee.

The Central Vigilance Commissioner, on ceasing to hold the office, shall be ineligible for reappointment in the Commission. The Vigilance Commissioner, however, on ceasing to hold the office, shall be eligible for appointment as the Central Vigilance Commissioner, provided that the term of the Vigilance Commissioner, if appointed the Central Vigilance Commissioner, shall not be more than four years in aggregate as the Vigilance Commissioner and the Central Vigilance Commissioner.

Salaries and Allowances

The expenses of the Commission, including any salaries, allowances, and pensions payable to or in respect of the Central Vigilance Commissioner, the Vigilance Commissioners, Secretary, and the staff of the Commission, shall be charged on the Consolidated Fund of India.

The salary and allowances payable to and other conditions of service of the Central Vigilance Commissioner shall be the same as those of a Chairman of the Union Public Service Commission and that of the Vigilance Commissioner shall be the same as those of a Member of the Union Public Service Commission.

Removal

The Central Vigilance Commissioner and other Commissioners can be removed from the office by the order of the President on the grounds of proved misbehavior or incapacity, but only after the Supreme Court has held an inquiry and recommended action against him. Despite the exception of involvement of the Supreme Court in the removal process of the Commissioner, the President may also order the removal of the Central Vigilance Commissioner or the Vigilance Commissioner if –

- They are adjudged as an insolvent.
- They have been convicted of an offence which involves the question of moral turpitude.
- They have indulged in any paid employment during the term of their office, outside their duty.
- They are unfit to hold the post and continue in office by the reason of infirmity of mind or body according to the opinion of the President.
- They have acquired such financial or other interest as is likely to affect prejudicially his functions as a Central Vigilance Commissioner or a Vigilance Commissioner.
- They are or have become in any way, concerned or interested in any contract or agreement made by or on behalf of the Government of India.
- They participate in any way in the profit thereof or in any benefit or emolument arising therefrom otherwise than as a member and in common with the other members of an incorporated company.

---

[5]For the purpose of this provision - "The Leader of the Opposition in the House of the People" shall, when no such Leader has been so recognised, include the Leader of the single largest group in opposition of the Government in the House of the People.

Jurisdiction of CVC

Though the advisory jurisdiction of the Commission extends to all organizations to which the executive control of the Union extends, however, for practical reasons, the Commission presently advises only on vigilance cases pertaining to the following categories of employees:

- Members of All India Service serving in connection with the affairs of the Union and Group A officers of the Central Government
- Officers of the rank of Scale V and above in the Public Sector Banks
- Officers in Grade D and above in Reserve Bank of India, NABARD, and SIDBI
- Chief Executives and Executives on the Board and other officers of E-8 and above in Schedule 'A' and 'B' Public Sector Undertakings
- Chief Executives and Executives on the Board and other officers of E-7 and above in Schedule 'C' and 'D' Public Sector Undertakings
- Managers and above in General Insurance Companies
- Senior Divisional Managers and above in Life Insurance Corporations

Powers and Functions of CVC

- *With respect to vigilance :*
  * To undertake an inquiry or cause an inquiry or investigation to be made into any transaction in which a public servant working in any organization, to which the executive control of the government of India extends, is suspected or alleged to have acted for an improper purpose or in a corrupt manner. CVC is not an investigating agency. The CVC either gets the investigation done through the CBI or through the Departmental Chief Vigilance Officers in government offices. The CVC orders investigation into cases of officials of Central Government Departments/Companies/Organisations only.
  * To tender independent and impartial advice to the disciplinary and other authorities in disciplinary cases, involving vigilance angle at different stages, i.e, investigation, inquiry, appeal, review, etc.
  * To exercise a general check and supervision over vigilance and anti-corruption work in Ministries or Departments of the government of India and other organisations to which the executive power of the union extends;
  * To undertake or cause an inquiry into complaints received under the Public Interest Disclosure and Protection of Informer (PIDPI) resolution and recommend appropriate action.
  * To respond to Central Government on mandatory consultation with the commission before making any rules or regulations governing the Vigilance or disciplinary matters relating to the persons appointed to the public services and posts in connection with the affairs of the union or to members of the All India Services.
  * To make rules and regulations governing the vigilance and disciplinary matters relating to the members of Central Services and All India Services in consultation with the Central Government.
  * To apply all the powers of a civil court while conducting any inquiry.

* To recommend to the Central Government concerning appointment of the Director of Enforcement (by the Central Vigilance Commissioner (CVC) who is the Chairperson and the Vigilance Commissioners who are Members of the Committee).

- *With respect to CBI :*
  * To exercise superintendence over the functioning of the Delhi Special Police Establishment (DSPE)(i.e., CBI) with respect to investigation under the Prevention of Corruption Act, 1988; or offences under Criminal Procedure Code (CrPC) for certain categories of public servants and to give directions to the DSPE for purpose of discharging this responsibility;
  * To give directions and to review the progress of investigations conducted by the DSPE into offences alleged to have been committed under the Prevention of Corruption Act;
  * To recommend to the Central Government regarding appointment of the Director of Prosecution.
  * To recommend regarding the appointment of officers to the post above the level of SP except Director and also recommend the extension or curtailment of tenure of such officers in the DSPE (CBI). This is done by the Central Vigilance Commissioner (CVC) who is also the Chairperson and the Vigilance Commissioners who are Members of the Committee empowered to recommend for the aforementioned posts after consultation with the Director (CBI).

- *With respect to Lokpal ;*

  Lokpal and Lokayuktas Act, 2013[6] provides that if Lokpal, decides to proceed with the preliminary inquiry, it shall refer the complaints or a complaint received by it in respect of public servants belonging to Group A or Group B or Group C or Group D to the Central Vigilance Commission. The Central Vigilance Commission in respect of complaints referred to it in respect of public servants belonging to Group A and Group B, after making preliminary inquiry, shall submit its report to the Lokpal. In case of public servants belonging to Group C and Group D, the Commission shall proceed in accordance with the provisions of the Central Vigilance Commission Act, 2003.

Annual Report

CVC shall present annually to the President a report as to the work done by the Commission. The President shall cause the same to be laid before each House of the Parliament.

The Annual Report of the CVC not only gives the details of the work done by it, but also brings out the system failure which leads to corruption in various Departments/Organisations, system improvements, various preventive measures, and cases in which the Commission's advises were ignored, etc.

The report shall also contain a separate part on the functioning of the Delhi Special Police Establishment insofar as it relates to investigation of offences alleged to have been committed under the Prevention of Corruption Act, 1988.

---

[6]Amendments carried out in the CVC Act, 2003, through the Lokpal and Lokayuktas Act, 2013.

Limitations of CVC

- CVC is only an advisory body; Central Governments are free to either accept or reject CVC's advice incorruption cases.
- CVC does not have adequate resources compared with number of complaints that it receives. It is a very small set-up with sanctioned staff strength of 299. However, it is supposed to check corruption in more than 1500 central government departments and ministries.
- CVC cannot direct CBI to initiate inquiries against any officer of the level of Joint Secretary and above on its own. Such permission has to be obtained from the concerned Department and Ministries.
- CVC does not have power to register criminal cases. It deals only with vigilance or disciplinary cases.
- CVC has supervisory powers over CBI. However, CVC does not have the power to call for any file from CBI or to direct CBI to investigate any case in a particular manner. CBI is under administrative control of the Department of Personnel and Training (DoPT) which means that, the powers to appoint, transfer, and suspend CBI officers lie with DoPT.
- As a result, although CVC is relatively independent in its functioning, it has neither resources nor power to inquire and take action on complaints of corruption that may act as an effective deterrence against corruption.

Enforcement Directorate

The responsibility for enforcing economic laws and fighting economic crime in India is empowered to The Directorate of Enforcement[7] (ED) which is the law enforcement agency and economic intelligence agency. It is part of the Department of Revenue, Ministry of Finance, Government of India. The Directorate was established in 1956, when an 'Enforcement Unit' was formed, in Department of Economic Affairs with an object to oversee 'Exchange Control Laws' violations under Foreign Exchange Regulation Act, 1947. In the year 1957, this Unit was renamed as 'Enforcement Directorate'.

After FERA, 1973, which was a regulatory law was repealed and its place was taken by Foreign Exchange Management Act, 1999 (FEMA). The ED is a multi-disciplinary association delegated with the task of securing proceeds of crime under various financial laws, such as Foreign Exchange Management Act, 1999 (FEMA) and Prevention of Money Laundering Act, 2002 (PMLA), and more recently the Fugitive Economic Offenders Act, 2018 (FEOA).

The main functions of ED under these laws are:

- To collect, develop, and disseminate intelligence relating to violations of FEMA, 1999, the intelligence inputs are received from various sources such as Central and State Intelligence agencies, complaints, etc.
- To Investigate the contravention of provisions of any law resulting in financial fraud/crimes like Hawala transactions, money laundering, financing terrorist activities, or others affecting the sovereignty and integrity of the nation;
- To confiscate or attach the properties and other proceeds of crime on sufficient evidences under the FEMA and PMLA;

[7]Besides directly recruiting personnel, the Directorate also draws officers from different Investigating Agencies, viz., Customs & Central Excise, Income Tax, Police, etc. on deputation.

- To prosecute the suspected offenders and bringing them to justice under all the laws;
- To render cooperation to the foreign countries regarding fugitive economic offenders according to the recently enacted law of FEOA.
- To use other powers of investigation like summons, search and seizure, etc., conferred on an Income Tax Authority under the IT Act, 1961.
- To realize penalties imposed on conclusion of adjudication proceedings.
- To provide and seek mutual legal assistance to/from contracting states in respect of attachment/confiscation of proceeds of crime as well as in respect of transfer of accused persons under PMLA.
- To process and recommend cases for preventive detention under the Conservation of Foreign Exchange and Prevention of Smuggling Activities Act (COFEPOSA).

Difference between Enforcement Directorate and CBI[8]

1. The CBI is a central investigation agency that investigates crimes that violate the Prevention of Corruption Act 1988 (POCA) or crimes that are referred to it by the Central Government or State Governments. On the other hand, the ED enforces statutes such as the Foreign Exchange Management Act (1999), the Prevention of Money Laundering Act (2002), and the Fugitive Economic Offenders Act, 2018. The civil enforcement arm of the ED investigates cases relating to violations of foreign exchange control laws. The criminal arm of the ED investigates cases relating to money laundering. Enforcement Directorate or ED is committed to prevent money laundering offences.
2. The CBI operates under the Ministry of Personnel, Public Grievances and Pensions whereas the ED is a part of Ministry of Finance.
3. Enforcement directorate cannot register a case on its own; it is required by the agencies such as CBI or State police to register an offence based on which an Enforcement Case Information Report[9] is filed by Enforcement Directorate. Whereas, the CBI can register a complaint on its own or by request of the Courts.

Lokpal and Lokayukta

World over, several countries have established independent 'ombudsman[10]' institutions to effectively channelize complaints against the public officials in relation to corruption, and to undertake investigations and/or prosecutions in respect of such public officials. Typically, such ombudsman institutions act as nodal agencies to supervise the investigative agencies responsible for investigating the complaints regarding corruption[11].

---

[8]https://lawtimesjournal.in

[9]Just like the police registers a First Information Report (FIR) before starting investigation in a cognizable offence, similarly the ED registers an ECIR upon receiving information of the commission of the offence of money laundering. Unlike the Criminal Procedure Code, 1973 (CrPC), where an FIR is registered by the police under Section 154 before initiating investigation into a cognizable offence, there is no legal compulsion of registering an ECIR before beginning investigation under the Prevention of Money Laundering Act (PMLA).

[10]Ombudsman is Scandinavian word. It is taken to mean officer or commissioner. It means a commissioner who has the duty of investigating and reporting to Parliament on citizens' complaints against the Government.

[11]https://www.amsshardul.com/overview-of-the-lokpal-and-lokayukta-act-2013-in-light-of-the-recent-appointments-and-amendments-made-thereunder/

In 1966, the Government of India had constituted a committee, Administrative Reforms Commission under the chairmanship of Morarji Desai, later taken over by K. Hanumanthaiya. The central goal of the commission was to lay out guidelines for better governance. This committee went on to recommend the establishment of an Ombudsman or otherwise called as the Lokpal at the centre and Lokayuktas at the State level.

This complex mechanism was brought forth to curb the escalation of corruption in all domains and realms of administrative and governmental organisations of India. In the following decades, multiple Acts were passed, all of which fell flat owing partially to the incessant political pressure. Finally, the Second Administrative Reforms Commission was constituted under the chairmanship of Verappa Moily in the year 2005.

Owing to the increasing rates of corruption, in the year 2011, Anna Hazare had undertaken a fast until death to demand for a concrete body that would monitor the corruption levels. Following these protests, Anna Hazare and other anti-corruption protesters were welcomed to help prepare the Jan Lokpal Bill. Within two years, this was replaced by the Lokpal and Lokayuktas Act of 2013[12].

In India, prior to introduction of the Lokpal Act, various Lokayukta institutions had been established at the State level to act as anti-corruption ombudsman institutions empowered to deal with cases/ allegations of corruption and maladministration by State government officials/bodies. The Lokpal Act was brought into effect in order to set up an anti-corruption ombudsman at the center/federal level in India, and to mandate the creation of Lokayuktas at the State level, by all the remaining States in India that so far had not set up Lokayuktas. Therefore, while there had been similar ombudsman institutions functioning at the state level prior to the year 2013, the Lokpal Act sought to establish a nodal agency at the Center to act in relation to allegations/cases of corruption against its central government functionaries and to supervise the overall anti-corruption regulatory framework in India[13].

Constitution and Composition of Lokpal

- Section 3 of the Lokpal Act, 2013 provides for the establishment of Lokpal.
- The members of Lokpal are appointed by the President on the recommendation of a selection committee. The selection committee is composed of the Prime Minister who is the Chairperson; Speaker of Lok Sabha, Leader of Opposition in Lok Sabha, Chief Justice of India or a Judge nominated by him/her, and one eminent jurist.
- Lokpal is a multimember body, made up of one chairperson and a maximum of eight members. The person who is to be appointed as the Chairperson of the body should be either the former Chief Justice of India or the former Judge of Supreme Court or an eminent person with impeccable integrity and outstanding ability, having special knowledge and experience of minimum 25 years in the matters relating to anti-corruption policy, public administration, vigilance, finance including insurance and banking, law, and management.
- Out of the maximum eight members, half will be judicial members. Minimum fifty percent of the Members will be from SC/ST/OBC/Minorities and women. The judicial member of the body should be either a former Judge of the Supreme Court or a former Chief Justice of a High Court. The non-judicial member should be an eminent person with impeccable integrity and

[12]https://lexlife.in

[13]https://www.amsshardul.com/overview-of-the-lokpal-and-lokayukta-act-2013

outstanding ability, having special knowledge and expertise of a minimum of 25 years in matters relating to anti-corruption policy, public administration, vigilance, finance including insurance and banking, law, and management.

- Moreover, the Chairperson or a Member shall not be –
  - i. a member of Parliament or a member of the Legislature of any State or Union territory;
  - ii. a person convicted of any offence involving moral turpitude;
  - iii. a person of less than forty-five years of age, on the date of assuming office as the Chairperson or Member, as the case may be;
  - iv. a member of any Panchayat or Municipality;
  - v. a person who has been removed or dismissed from the service of the Union or a State; and shall not hold any office of trust or profit (other than his office as the Chairperson or a Member) or be affiliated with any political party or carry on any business or practice any profession.

  Further, before entering upon his office, a person appointed as the Chairperson or a Member, as the case may be, shall, if –

  (a) He holds any office of trust or profit, resign from such office; or

  (b) He is carrying on any business, sever his connection with the conduct and management of such business; or

  (c) He is practicing any profession, cease to practice such profession.

Term of office of Chairperson and Members

The Chairperson and every member shall be appointed by the President by warrant under his hand and seal for a term of five years from the date on which he enters upon his office or until he attains the age of seventy years, whichever is earlier.

Reappointment and Restrictions

On ceasing to hold office, the Chairperson and every Member shall be ineligible for :

i. Reappointment as the Chairperson or a Member of the Lokpal;

ii. Any diplomatic assignment, appointment as administrator of a Union territory, and such other assignment or appointment which is required by law to be made by the President by warrant under his hand and seal;

iii. Further employment to any other office of profit under the Government of India or the Government of a State;

iv. Contesting any election of President or Vice-President or Member of either House of Parliament or Member of either House of a State Legislature or Municipality or Panchayat within a period of five years from the date of relinquishing the post.

Notwithstanding anything contained in the above said provision, a Member shall be eligible to be appointed as a Chairperson, if his total tenure as Member and Chairperson does not exceed five years. If the Member is appointed as the Chairperson, his term of office shall not be more than five years in aggregate as the Member and the Chairperson.

Salaries, Allowances, and other Conditions of Service

The Chairman of the body shall enjoy the same salary and allowances as of Chief Justice of India while members shall receive the same salary and allowance as those enjoyed by the justices of the Supreme Court[14].

The salary, allowances, and pension payable to and other conditions of service of the Chairperson or a Member shall not be varied to his/her disadvantage after his/her appointment.

Removal

- The Chairperson or any Member shall be removed from his office by order of the President on grounds of misbehavior[15]. However, to remove on grounds of misbehavior, the President has to firstly refer the matter to the Supreme Court through a petition signed by at least one hundred Members of Parliament. After referring the matter to the Supreme Court, the same shall be investigated by it. If the Supreme Court finds the charges to be true, it shall suggest for their removal.
- The President may, by order, remove from the office, the Chairperson or any Member if the Chairperson or such Member, as the case may be
  (a) Is adjudged an insolvent; or
  (b) Engages, during his term of office, in any paid employment outside the duties of his office; or
  (c) Is, in the opinion of the President, unfit to continue in office by reason of infirmity of mind or body

Jurisdiction and Functions of Lokpal[16]

As per the Lokpal Act, upon receipt of a Complaint, the Lokpal is tasked to conduct a preliminary inquiry to ascertain whether there is any prima facie case to proceed against such public official or to direct an investigation upon such ascertainment.

Such Complaints can inter alia be made against the following persons:

- Prime Minister (including a former one),
- Union Ministers,
- Members of Parliament,
- Groups A, B, C, and D officers of the Central Government.
- Any member or employee of any organisation or trust established by an Act of Parliament or partly financed by the Central Government; and
- Any officer of a society or association or trust, which is in receipt of any donation from any foreign source under the Foreign Contribution (Regulation) Act, 2010[17] in excess of Rs. 10 lakh in a year or such higher amount as the Central Government may notify.

---

[14]Provided that if the Chairperson or a Member is, at the time of his appointment, in receipt of pension (other than disability pension) in respect of any previous service under the Government of India or under the Government of a State, his salary in respect of service as the Chairperson or a Member, be reduced by the amount of that pension.

[15]Misbehaviour - If the Chairperson or any Member becomes, in any way concerned or interested in any contract or agreement made by or on behalf of the Government of India or the Government of a State or participates in any way in the profit thereof or in any benefit or emolument arising therefrom otherwise than as a member and in common with the other members of an incorporated company, shall be deemed to be guilty of misbehaviour.

[16]https://www.amsshardul.com

[17](42 of 2010)

Inquiry into Complaints by Lokpal

Essentially, in terms of the Lokpal Act, Lokpal shall deal with a Complaint in the following manner:

- Upon receipt of a Complaint, Lokpal may pass an order directing its own Inquiry Wing[18] or any other agency[19] to conduct a preliminary inquiry in respect of such Complaint to ascertain whether there is a prima facie case for acting upon such Complaint.
- The inquiry wing of the Lokpal or any other agency that the Lokpal asks to investigate a matter shall submit its report relating to the preliminary inquiry within 60 days, but in no event later than 90 days. On the basis of this report, if the Lokpal decides to investigate further, it shall direct any agency to carry out additional investigation and submit another report within six months from the date of that order.
- Upon receipt of such report from the investigating agency, Lokpal shall decide whether there exists a prima facie case to proceed against the concerned public official after giving due opportunity to such official. If the Lokpal determined that there exists a prima facie case against the public official, Lokpal may:
  * Order an investigation by any agency[20] in respect of the Complaint;
  * Order initiation of department inquiry against the public official;
- Once the Lokpal decides that there is no prima facie case against the public official in terms of the Complaint and the preliminary inquiry, it shall direct the closure of proceedings against such public official and to proceed against the complainant for false complaint in terms of Section 46 of the Lokpal Act.
- In case the Lokpal passed an order for an investigation, the said investigation is required to be completed within a period of six months.
- The investigating agency is required to submit the investigation report to the Special Court and also forward a copy of such report to Lokpal.
- Upon examination of the investigation report, Lokpal may issue the following directions:
  * Grant sanction to prosecute the concerned public official before the Special Court to such investigating agency or its own prosecution wing[21] and file a charge sheet against such public official before the concerned jurisdictional court;
  * Pass an order to initiate department inquiry against such public official.

---

[18]Lokpal shall constitute an Inquiry Wing headed by the Director of Inquiry for the purpose of conducting preliminary inquiry into any offence alleged to have been committed by a public servant punishable under the Prevention of Corruption Act, 1988. Till such time the Inquiry Wing is constituted by the Lokpal, the Central Government shall make available such number of officers and other staff from its Ministries or Departments, as may be required by the Lokpal, for conducting preliminary inquiries under this Act.

[19]The Lokpal will have the power of superintendence and direction over any investigation agency including CBI for cases referred to them by the ombudsman.

[20]Including CBI.

[21]The Lokpal shall, by notification, constitute a Prosecution Wing headed by the Director of Prosecution for the purpose of prosecution of public servants in relation to any complaint by the Lokpal under this Act. However, till such time the Prosecution Wing is constituted by the Lokpal, the Central Government shall make available such number of officers and other staff from its Ministries or Departments, as may be required by the Lokpal, for conducting prosecution under this Act. The Director of Prosecution shall, after having been so directed by the Lokpal, file a case in accordance with the findings of investigation report, before the Special Court and take all necessary steps in respect of the prosecution of public servants in relation to any offence punishable under the Prevention of Corruption Act, 1988.

- However, if Lokpal considers that there exists no merit in proceeding with the prosecution against the public official upon examining the report of the investigating agency, it may direct closure of the proceedings against the public official.
- The Lokpal has other wide ranging powers, including: supervision of certain investigating agencies; the authority to order search and seizures; powers akin to a civil court, such as issuing summons, discovery and production of documents, requisitioning public records, etc.; the power to provisionally attach assets for a maximum of 90 days; and the authority to recommend the transfer or suspension of a public servant in connection with alleged corruption.
- Special courts[22] are to be set up to try cases under the Act. These courts are required to ensure completion of trial within a period of one year from the date of filing the case. Provided that in case the trial cannot be completed within a period of one year, the Special Court shall record reasons therefore and complete the trial within a further period of not more than three months or such further periods not exceeding three months each, for reasons to be recorded in writing before the end of each such three months period, but not exceeding a total period of two years.
- Frivolous and false complaints may be punished criminally with imprisonment of up to one year and a fine of up to Rs. 1 lakh. Additionally, the public servant who has been targeted by such wrongful complaints may be entitled to receive compensation.
- The Lokpal shall not inquire or investigate into any complaint, if the complaint is made after the expiry of a period of seven years from the date on which the offence mentioned in such complaint is alleged to have been committed.

It is relevant to note that in furtherance of the its objective of providing an effective and efficient mechanism to deal with anti-corruption cases in India, the Lokpal Act mandates that upon initiation of the prosecution against the concerned public official, the concerned jurisdictional court ought to complete the trial within a period of one year. Furthermore, besides ensuring fair and prompt investigation, Lokpal Act requires the Lokpal to publish a list of complaints and the status of such complaints in terms of whether they are pending or disposed of, thereby promoting transparency in the entire investigation process.

Shortcomings of the Act[23]

- The Lokpal and Lokayuktas Act of 2013 appear to focus heavily on the Lokpal. To elaborate, the Act only mandates the setting up of Lokayuktas in the respective states within the timeframe of one year. That is, it could be observed that the Act does not adequately delve into the functions of the Lokayuktas. In other words, clear demarcations of powers were not marked. Additionally, the make-up of this State-level body has not been specified clearly in the Act.
- It could be observed that only a handful of states had implemented the setting up of the Lokayuktas. Additionally, various states have enacted various Acts, which lay out different powers for the Lokayuktas. This shows the haphazard execution of the said Act. Moreover, it could be observed that in many states such as Karnataka and Madhya Pradesh, the Lokayuktas have actively taken various initiatives to tackle instances of malfeasance; however, other states seem to lack the resources to bring forth even minutiae of changes.

---

[22]Special Court means the court of a Special Judge appointed under the Prevention of Corruption Act, 1988.

[23]https://lexlife.in

- The jurisdiction of Lokpal does not extend to the judiciary of the country, which could also be plagued with corruption. Consequently, little power is given to the body to deal with the malpractices that creep into the judiciary. In fact, the jurisdiction of the Lokpal does not even extend to the armed forces of the country.
- It is further observed that the Lokpal and Lokayuktas so established are heavily dependent upon bodies, such as Central Bureau of Investigation (CBI) to carry out even preliminary investigations. It has been time and again debated that these ombudsman institutions require some autonomy to carry out their functions in a more efficient manner, without the unnecessary intervention of political parties.
- There is no proper system of proceedings to appeal or reconsider or review the Lokpal order if anyone is not satisfied with its decision, as of now.
- The Act provides no protective armour to the whistleblowers who expose the various malpractices at several governmental levels.

Serious Fraud Investigation Office (SFIO)

The Serious Fraud Investigation Office (SFIO) is an organisation established under the aegis of the Ministry of Corporate Affairs (MCA) — for investigation and prosecution of white-collar crimes. The SFIO was constituted in July 2003 following the recommendations of the Naresh Chandra Committee based on the Serious Fraud Office of the UK, which was established in 1988 under the UK Criminal Justice Act, 1987. In 2002, the Naresh Chandra Committee had recommended setting up a 'Corporate Serious Fraud Office', to uncover corporate fraud, and supervise prosecutions under various economic legislations. The SFIO was granted statutory force for the first time through the Companies Act, 2013. To combat the rising number of corporate fraud cases in India, the 2013 Act introduced Section 447, which, for the first time, provided a definition of fraud as well as punishment for such an offence. It was felt that the MCA should have the powers to investigate serious frauds without depending on police investigation under the IPC.

Investigation into the Affairs of a Company Assigned to SFIO by the Government

The Central Government may assign the investigation into the affairs of a company to the Serious Fraud Investigation Office :

(a) On receipt of report of the Registrar or Inspector under Section 208 of the Companies Act;

(b) On intimation of a special resolution passed by a company requesting an investigation into its affairs;

(c) In public interest;

(d) On the request of any Department of Central Government or State Government.

Composition of SFIO

The Serious Fraud Investigation Office headquarters is in New Delhi. The agency is headed by a Director and consists of experts from different fields such as banking, corporate affairs, taxation, forensic audit, capital market, information technology, law, etc.

The SFIO has 4 regional offices located at Hyderabad, Mumbai, Kolkata, and Chennai.

QUESTIONS

Subjective Questions

1. "CBI has grown over the years in its role, power, and importance and today has become the premier investigative and prosecution agency of the country." Discuss. **(250 words)**
2. "The enactment of Lokpal and Lokayuktas Act, 2013 will help Central Vigilance Commission work in an independent and assertive manner". Comment. **(150 words)**
3. "Bringing synergies in anti-corruption agencies is important to eradicate corruption". Elaborate. **(250 words)**

CHAPTER 42

E-GOVERNANCE

"Transparency is the key to good governance & e-Governance is the only effective way of transparent governance."

– Hon'ble Prime Minister Shri Narendra Modi

INTRODUCTION TO E-GOVERNANCE

The "e" in e-Governance stands for 'electronic'. e-Governance is basically associated with carrying out the functions and achieving the results of governance through the utilization of what has today come to be known as ICT (Information and Communications Technology).

The reason why countries around the world are increasingly opting for 'e-Governance' is that governance per se has become more complex and varied in the last few decades and more importantly, citizens' expectations from government has increased manifold. ICT facilitates efficient storing and retrieval of data, instantaneous transmission of information, processing information and data faster than the earlier manual systems, speeding up governmental processes, taking decisions expeditiously and judiciously, increasing transparency, and enforcing accountability. It also helps in increasing the reach of government — both geographically and demographically[1].

Definition of e-Governance[2]

There is no standard definition for the term 'e-Governance'. Different governments and organizations define this term to suit their own aims and objectives.

- According to World Bank : "*E-Government[3] refers to the use by government agencies of information technologies (such as Wide Area Networks, the Internet, and mobile computing) that have the ability to transform relations with citizens, businesses, and other arms of government. These technologies can serve a variety of different ends: better delivery of government services to citizens, improved interactions with business and industry, citizen empowerment through access to information, or more efficient government management. The resulting benefits can be less corruption, increased transparency, greater convenience, revenue growth, and/or cost reductions.*"

---

[1]Promoting e-Governance, The SMART Way Forward, Eleventh Report, Second Administrative Commission, Government of India.

[2]Ibid.

[3]Sometimes, the term 'e-government' is also used instead of 'e-Governance'.

- Dr. A.P.J. Abdul Kalam, former President of India, has visualized e-Governance in the Indian context to mean:

"*A transparent smart e-Governance with seamless access, secure and authentic flow of information crossing the interdepartmental barrier and providing a fair and unbiased service to the citizen.*"

Stages of e-Governance[4]

It is evident that e-Governance is intrinsically linked with the development of computer technology, and networking of computers and communication systems. In developing countries, such technologies and systems became available with a perceptible time lag as compared to developed nations. However, in the case of India, with the liberalization of the economy from the early 1990s onwards, there has been a convergence in the availability of cutting edge technologies and opportunities in the field of e-Governance. During the initial stages of introduction of ICT in governance, there was resistance from some quarters. Some felt that computerization cannot work in the complex government system and that introduction of computers would lead to unemployment. There were also serious doubts whether government employees at all levels would be able to handle computers. Fortunately, all these misgivings have proved wrong. Today, new software tools have enough flexibility to accommodate the most complex situations. The new technology makes the human-machine interface very user-friendly. The Information Technology (IT) and Information Technology Enabled Services (ITES) sectors have created millions of jobs, besides improving vastly on the services provided by government undertakings like Banks, Airlines, Railways, etc. Generally speaking, the Indian experience demonstrates that the onset of e-Governance proceeded through the following phases:

(a) **Computerization :** In the first phase, with the availability of personal computers, a large number of Government offices got equipped with computers. The use of computers began with word processing, quickly followed by data processing.

(b) **Networking :** In this phase, some units of a few government organizations got connected through a hub leading to sharing of information and flow of data between different government entities.

(c) **Online presence:** With increasing Internet connectivity, a need was felt for maintaining a presence on the Web. This resulted in maintenance of websites by government departments and other entities. Generally, these web pages/websites contained information about the organizational structure, contact details, reports and publications, objectives, and vision statements of the respective government entities.

(d) **Online interactivity:** A natural consequence of online presence was opening up of communication channels between government entities and the citizens, civil society organizations, etc. The main aim at this stage was to minimize the scope of personal interface with government entities by providing downloadable forms, instructions, Acts, rules, etc. In some cases, this has already led to online submission of forms. Most citizen-government transactions have the potential of being put on e-Governance mode.

---

[4]Promoting e-Governance, The SMART Way Forward, Eleventh Report, Second Administrative Commission, Government of India.

Types of Interactions in e-Governance

e-Governance facilitates interaction between different stakeholders in governance.

These interactions may be described as follows:

- **G2G (Government to Government)** : In this case, ICT is used to increase the flow of information and services within and between different entities. This kind of interaction is only within the sphere of government and can be both horizontal, i.e., between different government agencies as well as between different functional areas within an organization, or vertical, i.e., between national, provincial, and local government agencies as well as between different levels within an organization. The primary objective is to increase efficiency, performance, and output.
- **G2C (Government to Citizens)** : In this case, an interface is created between the government and citizens which enables the citizens to benefit from efficient delivery of a large range of public services. This expands the availability and accessibility of public services on the one hand and improves the quality of services on the other. It gives citizens the choice of when to interact with the government (e.g., 24 hours a day, 7 days a week), from where to interact with the government (e.g., service centre, unattended kiosk, or from one's home/workplace) and how to interact with the government (e.g., through Internet, fax, telephone, email, face-to-face, etc). The primary purpose is to make government citizen-friendly.
- **G2B (Government to Business)** : Here, e-Governance tools are used to aid the business community — providers of goods and services — to seamlessly interact with the government. The objective is to cut red tape, save time, reduce operational costs, and to create a more transparent business environment when dealing with the government. The G2B initiatives can be transactional, such as in licensing, permits, procurement, and revenue collection. They can also be promotional and facilitative, such as in trade, tourism, and investment. These measures help to provide a congenial environment to businesses to enable them to perform more efficiently.
- **G2E (Government to Employees)** : Government is by far the biggest employer and like any organisation, it has to interact with its employees on a regular basis. This interaction is a two-way process between the organisation and the employee. Use of ICT tools helps in making these interactions fast and efficient on the one hand and increase satisfaction levels of employees on the other.

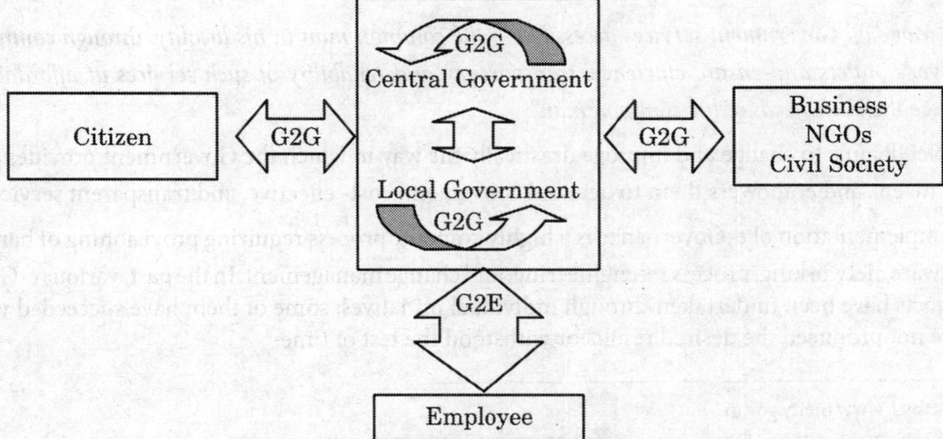

Source: Ministry of Electronics and Information Technology, Government of India

Goals of e-Governance

The goals of e-Governance are:

a. Providing better service delivery to citizens
b. Ushering in transparency and accountability
c. Empowering people through information
d. Improving efficiency within Governments
e. Improving interface with business and industry

MAJOR STEPS TOWARDS E-GOVERNANCE IN INDIA[5]

The establishment of the National Informatics Centre (NIC) in 1977 was the first major step towards e-Governance in India as it brought information and its communication in focus. National Informatics Centre (NIC) is playing a vital role in the implementation of e-Governance by designing and launching various types of web portals and online Management Information Systems (MIS)[6]. The main thrust for e-Governance was provided by the launching of National Satellite-Based Computer Network called NICNET in 1987. A National Task Force on Information Technology and Software Development was constituted in May 1998. In 1999, the Union Ministry of Information Technology was created. In the year of 2000, IT Act was passed and e-Governance got its legal reorganization. After implementation of RTI Act, 2005, Government information such as various Cabinet Decisions, forms, procedures, programs, projects, schemes, tenders, quotation calls, notices, etc. started being displayed in the State Portal for reference and use by the public. Designated Information Officers in individual departments and offices are now responsible to provide all information needs[7].

National E-Governance Plan (NEGP)

The NeGP plan (2003–2007) was formulated by the Department of Information Technology (DIT), Ministry of Communications and Information Technology, Government of India to initiate and provide for long-term growth of e-Governance in our country with the following vision:

"*Make all Government services accessible to the common man in his locality, through common service delivery outlets and ensure efficiency, transparency and reliability of such services at affordable costs to realize the basic needs of the common man*".

NeGP aims to change and improve drastically the way in which the Government provides services to its citizens and empowers them to demand convenient, cost- effective, and transparent services.

Implementation of e-Governance is a highly complex process requiring provisioning of hardware and software, networking, process re-engineering, and change management. In the past, various e-Governance projects have been undertaken through individual initiatives; some of them have succeeded while some have not produced the desired results or withstood the test of time.

---

[5]https://www.meity.gov.in

[6]Puneet Kumar, Prateek Bhanti, *Prospects of E-Governance in India*, 2012.

[7]Nilotpal Chakraborty, 2013.

Elements of NeGP

A prudent approach and methodology is adopted for NeGP and it contains the following elements:

(a) ***Common Support Infrastructure*** : NeGP implementation involves setting up of common support IT infrastructure such as: State Wide Area Networks (SWANs), State Data Centres (SDCs), Common Service Centres (CSCs), and Electronic Service Delivery Gateways.

(i) State Wide Area Networks (SWANs): Under this scheme, technical and financial assistance is being provided to States/UTs for establishing state-wide area networks to connect all headquarters right from the State to the block level in a vertical hierarchical structure with a minimum bandwidth capacity of 2mbps per link. Each State/UT can enhance the bandwidth to 34 Mbps between State headquarter and up to 8 Mbps between District headquarter and Block headquarter depending on the utilization. SWAN implementation can be done in two ways –

- **Public-Private Partnership Model :** There are different models such as Build-operate-transfer (BOT) model where the private entities build it and then return it to the government and Build-own-operate-transfer (BOOT) model where the private entities build it and own it for an extended time period through a lease. An appropriate agency is selected through a suitable competitive process for outsourcing establishment, operation, and maintenance of the network.
- **NIC Model :** The state designates NIC as the prime implementation agency for establishment, operation, and maintenance of the network.

(ii) State Data Centre (SDC) : NeGP envisions the creation of State Data Centre to consolidate services, applications, and infrastructure to provide efficient electronic delivery of Government-to-Government, Government-to-Citizen, and Government-to-Business services. Some of the key functionalities provided at the SDC are Secured Data Storage, Citizen information/services portal, and State Intranet Portal. These services can be supported by core connectivity infrastructure such as statewide area network and common service center connectivity extended upto village level.

(iii) Common Service Centre (CSC): CSC are ICT-enabled front-end service delivery points at the village level for the delivery of government, financial, social, and private sector services in the areas such as agriculture, health, education, entertainment, banking, and insurance. The scheme is being implemented in a public-private partnership framework with a focus on rural entrepreneurship. To facilitate the successful implementation of the scheme, a Special Purpose Vehicle named CSC e-Governance Services India Limited has been set up.

(b) ***Centralized Initiative, Decentralized Implementation*** : e-Governance is being promoted through a centralized initiative to the extent necessary to ensure citizen-centric orientation, to realize the objective of interoperability of various e-Governance applications and to ensure optimal utilization of ICT infrastructure and resources while allowing for a decentralized implementation model. It also aims at identifying successful projects and replicating them with required customization, wherever needed.

(c) *Public-Private Partnerships (PPP):* This model is to be adopted wherever feasible to enlarge the resource pool without compromising on the security aspects.

(d) *Integrative Elements*: Adoption of unique identification codes for citizens, businesses, and property is to be promoted to facilitate integration and avoid ambiguity.

(e) *Programme Management Structure*: For effective management of NeGP, a programme management structure has been created to accord credibility to the programme, to provide a forum to solicit view of stakeholders, to oversee the programme and resolve inter-ministerial/inter-departmental issues, and to ensure speedy sanctioning of projects.

The key components of the Programme Management structure are –

(i) **Apex Body (headed by the Prime Minister)**: A body under the Chairpersonship of Prime Minister with representation drawn from relevant Ministries/Departments, the National Knowledge Commission, experts, etc., to provide leadership, prescribe deliverables and milestones, and monitor periodically the implementation of NeGP.

(ii) **Apex Committee**: This committee is constituted with the Cabinet Secretary as its Chairman and Secretary, Department of Information & Technology (DIT)[8] as its Member Convener. It has been constituted to oversee the NeGP programme. It provides policy and strategic directions for its implementation, resolves inter-ministerial issues; moderates and drives services, and processes re-engineering and service levels of each Mission Mode Project (MMP), wherever required. Further, it is empowered to add or delete MMPs as considered appropriate and to resolve all inter-ministerial issues. DIT acts as the Secretariat for Apex Committee.

(iii) **Cabinet Committee on Economic Affairs (CCEA):** This is a committee for programme level policy decisions.

(iv) **National e-Governance Advisory Group**: This is headed by the Minister of Communications & Information Technology, to solicit views of external stakeholders and to provide inputs to the CCEA, and advise the government on policy issues and strategic interventions necessary for accelerating introduction of e-Governance across Central and State Government Ministries/Departments.

(v) **State level Apex Committees**: This is headed by Chief Secretaries to allocate State level resources, set priority amongst projects, and resolve inter-departmental issues.

Mission Mode Projects of NeGP

A Mission Mode Project is an individual project within NeGP that focuses on one aspect of e-Governance. There are 33 Mission Mode Projects (MMPs) under the NeGP with 11 Central MMPs, 13 State MMPs, and 7 Integrated MMPs. While the respective governments implement Central and State MMPs, both implement integrated MMPs.

---

[8]DIT is the facilitator and catalyst for the implementation of NeGP by various Ministries and State Governments and also provides technical assistance. DIT is also implementing pilot/infrastructure/technical/special projects and support components.

No.	Projects	Line Ministry /Dept. Responsible	Project Brief
		Mission Mode Projects - Central Sector	
1.	Passport	Ministry of External Affairs/Ministry of Home Affairs	The Passport Seva Project was launched by the Ministry of External Affairs with the objective of delivering Passport Services to the citizens in a comfortable environment with wider accessibility and reliability
2.	Visa & Immigration	Ministry of External Affairs/Ministry of Home Affairs	In order to Modernize and upgrade the Immigration services, "Immigration, Visa and Foreigners Registration & Tracking (IVFRT)" has been identified and included as one of the MMPs to be undertaken by the Ministry of Home Affairs under the National e-Governance Plan (NeGP). The core objective of this Project is to develop and implement a secure and integrated service delivery framework that facilitates legitimate travellers while strengthening security.
3.	MCA21	Ministry of Corporate Affairs	The projects aims to provide electronic services to the Companies registered under the Companies Act. Various online facilities offered includes allocation and change of name, incorporation, etc.
4.	Insurance	Department of Banking	MMP aims at facilitating customer services, automating grievance redressal mechanisms, and creating a holistic database of insurance users.
5.	Income Tax	Ministry of Finance/ Central Board of Direct Taxes	Various important e-services being offered under this MMP includes facility for downloading of various forms, online submission of applications for PAN and TAN, etc.
6.	National Citizen Database/UID	Ministry of Home Affairs/ Registrar General of India (RGI)/ NITI Aayog	This MMP aims towards creating a Central database of resident information and assigns a Unique Identification number to each such resident in the country, to facilitate efficient delivery of social and welfare services.
7.	Goods and Services Tax	Department of Revenue/ Central Board of Indirect Taxes & Customs	This MMP aims towards facilitating availability of e-services related to indirect taxation for industry, importers and exporters, inbound travellers, etc.
8.	Pensions	Department of Pensions & Pensioners' Welfare and Department of Expenditure	This MMP provides updated information on government pension rules and regulations; helps facilitating registration of pensioners' grievances, etc.

9.	Banking	Department of Banking	This MMP aims towards streamlining various e-services initiatives undertaken by individual banks.
10.	e-Office	Department of Administrative Reforms & Public Grievances	This MMP aims at significantly improving the operational efficiency of the Government by transitioning to a "Less Paper Office"
		Mission Mode Projects - State Sector	
1.	Land Records	Ministry of Rural Development	The project National Land Records Modernization Programme (NLRMP) aims towards providing integrated land related information and services to citizens.
2.	Road Transport	Ministry of Road Transport & Highways	The project aims to induct technology in transport offices across India to offer vehicle registration, driving licenses, and Smart Card based RCs (Registration Certificates) to citizens
3.	Agriculture	The Department of Agriculture, Co-operation and Farmers' Welfare	The MMP aims at providing information regarding farm practices, market trends, agricultural and technical know-how, etc., and other related services to the farming community.
4.	Treasuries	Ministry of Finance	This MMP aims at computerisation of treasuries involving a common set of standards for seamless integration of participating agencies.
5.	Municipalities	Ministry of Urban Employment and Poverty Alleviation	The MMP aims at providing various services offered by Urban Local Bodies (ULBs) to residents electronically
6.	Gram Panchayats	Ministry of Panchayati Raj	This MMP aims at improving governance at the grassroots and providing various e-services at the Panchayat level
7.	Commercial Taxes	Ministry of Finance (at State level)	This MMP, which aims at providing electronic services to commercial taxes payers, is being formulated.
8.	Police (CCTNS)	Ministry of Home Affairs	This MMP of the Police – Crime and Criminal Tracking Network System (CCTNS) – is aimed at facilitating the process of civil policing and law enforcement by utilizing ICT effectively
9.	Employment Exchanges	Ministry of Labour & Employment	This MMP of the Ministry of Labour aims at providing e-services to employment seekers and employers.
10.	E-District	Department of Information Technology	The MMP aims at delivery of high volume, citizen-centric services at the District level such as issue of birth/death certificate, income and caste certificate, old age and widow pension, etc.

Mission Mode Projects - Integrated Category			
1.	EDI (e-Commerce)	Ministry of Commerce & Industry/ Department of Commerce	The MMP aims at facilitating Electronic Data Interchange amongst various agencies involved in the process of imports and exports.
2.	e-Biz	Department of Industrial Policy & Promotion / Department of Information Technology	The project aims to provide comprehensive Government-to-Business (G2B) services to business entities with transparency, speed, and certainty
3.	Common Services Centres	Department of Information Technology	This MMP is a part of the core and support infrastructure of NeGP and aims towards offering e-Governance services to rural citizens.
4.	India Portal	Department of Information Technology and Department of Administrative Reforms & Public Grievances	This MMP aims towards providing a single window access to information and services of Government at all levels, in a multilingual form.
5.	National e-Governance Service Delivery Gateway (NSDG)	Department of Information Technology	This MMP aims at providing a common interface between the service seekers and service providers (Government Department)
6.	e-Courts	Department of Justice, Ministry of Home Affairs	This MMP aims at utilising technology for improved provisioning of judicial services to citizens.
7.	E-Procurement	Ministry of Commerce & Industry/DGS&D	This MMP of the Ministry of Commerce aims at rolling out IT-enabled procurement by Government Departments.

e-Governance initiatives of NeGP

The NeGP has enabled many e-Governance initiatives like Digital India, Aadhar, myGov.in, Digital Locker, DBT, and NOFN.

i. **Digital India** was launched in 2015 to empower the country digitally. Its main components are:
   - Developing a secure and stable digital infrastructure
   - Delivering government services digitally
   - Achieving universal digital literacy

ii. **Aadhar** is a unique identification number issued by UIDAI that serves as proof of identity and address on the basis of biometric data. It is being used to provide many benefits to the members of the society. One can e-sign[9] documents using Aadhar.

iii. **myGov.in** is a national citizen engagement platform where people can share ideas on and be involved with matters of policy and governance.

iv. **DigiLocker (Digital Locker)** is an Indian digitization online service which helps citizens to digitally store important documents like mark sheets, PAN, Aadhar, and degree certificates. This reduces the need for physical documents and facilitates easy sharing of documents.

[9]E-signatures are not legally valid yet.

v. **Direct Benefit Transfer (DBT)** is a scheme where consumers will receive subsidies directly into their bank accounts, while the subsidized goods will be sold at market prices. This will reduce pilferage, adulteration, and other malpractices, while ensuring that subsidies reach the people who need them. Linking of bank accounts with Aadhar for DBT will allow efficient tracking and monitoring of benefits transfer. It will also reduce leakages and duplication of beneficiaries.

vi. **National Optical Fibre Network (NOFN)** is an ambitious initiative to trigger a broadband revolution in rural areas. At present, OFC (Optical Fibre Cable) connectivity is available in all State Capitals, Districts, HQs, and upto the Block Level. There is a plan to connect all the 2,50,000 Gram panchayats in the country. This will be done by utilizing existing fibres of PSUs (BSNL, Railtel, and Power Grid) and laying incremental fibre to connect to Gram Panchayats, wherever necessary. Dark fibre network thus created will be lit by appropriate technology, thus creating sufficient bandwidth at the Gram Panchayats. This will be called the National Optical Fibre Network (NOFN). Thus, connectivity gap between Gram Panchayats and Blocks will be filled.

Non-discriminatory access to the NOFN will be provided to all the service providers. These service providers like Telecom Service Providers (TSPs), ISPs, Cable TV operators, and Content providers can launch various services in rural areas. Various categories of applications like e-health, e-education, and e-Governance, etc. can be provided by these operators. The Bharat Broadband Network Limited has been set up for the establishment and management of the NOFN programme.

Thus, e-Governance is about reform in governance, facilitated by the creative use of Information and Communications Technology. e-Governance would lead to better access to information and quality services for citizens. Further, it ensures simplicity, efficiency, and accountability in the government by expanding the reach of governance.

SUBJECTIVE QUESTIONS

1. How does the e-Governance and Digital India empower Indian citizens through technology? Explain. **(250 words)**
2. "Development of any country can be judged by the scope of e-Governance in that country". Discuss. **(150 words)**
3. "e-Governance not merely provides information about various activities of a Government but also involves citizens to participate in government's decision-making process." Elaborate. **(250 words)**

CHAPTER 43

HUMAN RIGHTS AS THE FOUNDATION OF GOOD GOVERNANCE

"To deny people their Human Rights is to challenge their very humanity."

– Nelson Mandela

HUMAN RIGHTS

Good governance and Human Rights are mutually reinforcing. Human Rights principles provide a set of values to guide the work of Governments and other political and social actors. They also provide a set of performance standards against which these actors can be held accountable. Without good governance, Human Rights cannot be respected and protected in a sustainable manner. The implementation of Human Rights relies on a conducive and enabling environment. This conducive and enabling environment includes appropriate legal frameworks and institutions, as well as political, managerial, and administrative processes responsible for responding to the rights and needs of the population[1].

Human Rights Under Indian Constitution

Promulgation of the Constitution by the people of India in January, 1950 is a watershed in the history of development of the concept of Human Rights in India. The Preamble, Fundamental Rights, and the Directive Principles together provide the basic Human Rights for the people of India. Moreover, India being the signatory of Universal Declaration of Human Rights (UDHR), 1948, the Indian Constitution was greatly influenced by it. Fundamental Rights and Directive Principles of State Policy bear a close resemblance to the Universal Declaration of Human Rights.

THE PROTECTION OF HUMAN RIGHTS ACT

Background[2]

The United Nations Educational Scientific and Cultural Organization (UNESCO) mooted the idea of the creation of an impartial institution for the protection of Human Rights in the States as early as 1946. In pursuance of the resolution of the General Assembly adopted in 1966, the Economic and Social

[1]UN Office of the High Commissioner for Human Rights, Good Governance Practices for the Protection of Human Rights, 2007, HR/PUB/07/4, available at: http://www.unhcr.org/refworld/docid/47ea6c842.html.

[2]https://police.py.gov.in/NHRC

Council requested the Human Rights Commission of the United Nations to consider the question of creating a National Commission of Human Rights to perform certain functions related to the observance of the International Covenants on Human Rights. The question was taken up by the Commission in 1970 and it recommended that the question of establishment of National Commission of Human Rights in each Member State of the United Nations ought to be decided by each Government of the Member State keeping in view the traditions and institutions of each country. The Commission in 1978 again emphasized the need for the creation of a National Institution. But all these attempts, however, were fruitless.

Realizing the importance of such an institution or commission, the World Conference on Human Rights in 1993 urged the Government to strengthen national structures and institutions of society, which play a role in promoting and safeguarding Human Rights. The Vienna Declaration and Programme of Action adopted by the World Conference prompted a number of States to establish such institutions.

The Western countries, America in particular, criticized India on the violation of Human Rights by Indian armed forces and para-military forces, especially, in the State of Jammu and Kashmir. In the early 1990's, India felt the need for establishing a commission as a positive response to the criticism of the foreign Governments in the context of political unrest and violence in Punjab, Jammu and Kashmir, the North-East, and Andhra Pradesh[3]. In addition to the pressure from foreign countries, there was a strong element from the domestic front as well for the creation of a National Human Rights Commission. All these led the Government to enact a law in the year 1993 to establish the National Human Rights Commission.

Objectives of the Act

The main objective of the Protection of Human Rights Act, 1993 is protecting human beings from violations. The Act also provides for establishment of National Human Rights Commission, State Human rights Commission, and Human Rights Courts which seeks to prevent and punish any gross violation of Human Rights.

Definition of Human Rights under the Act

Section 2(d) of the Act defines Human Rights as the rights relating to life, liberty, equality, and dignity of the individual guaranteed by the Constitution or embodied in the International Covenant[4] and enforceable by courts in India.

A pertinent question naturally arises here — Why was the Commission established for the protection of Fundamental Rights when they are being constitutionally guaranteed and are enforceable by the courts? It appears that the main purpose of the enactment was to provide a better protection of Human Rights[5].

---

[3]Though it is now a well-recognized fact that terrorism is a serious violation of Human Rights, America never missed the opportunity to criticize India, whenever Indian security forces sought to deal sternly with extremists and ultras. America claims to be the champion of Human Rights all over the world. America's practices of Human Rights are discriminatory. They use Human Rights as an instrument of harass and even coerce other States. At the same time, American criticizes India for alleged violation of Human Rights. America has adopted a liberal and biased attitude regarding Human Rights violations in Pakistan, even though Pakistan's records of upholding Human Rights is not only unsatisfactory, but also deplorable.

[4]International Covenants are not directly enforceable as law by the Indian courts. These covenants are enforceable only when they are incorporated in Indian laws.

[5]https://police.py.gov.in/NHRC

NATIONAL HUMAN RIGHTS COMMISSION

Section 3 of the Act lays down that the Central Government shall constitute a body known as the National Human Rights Commission.

Composition[6]

The NHRC comprises of:

- The Chairperson of the NHRC is a person who has been a Chief Justice of the Supreme Court, or a Judge of the Supreme Court.
- One Member who is, or has been a judge of the Supreme Court
- One Member who is, or has been, the Chief Justice of a High Court.
- Three Members to be appointed from amongst persons having knowledge of, or practical experience in, matters relating to Human Rights of which at least one will be a woman.

Besides these, the Commission shall include the following members as the ex-officio members:

- The Chairperson of National Commission for Scheduled Castes
- The Chairperson of National Commission for Scheduled Tribes
- The Chairperson of National Commission for Minorities
- The Chairperson of National Commission for Women
- The Chairperson of National Commission for Backward Classes
- The Chairperson of National Commission for the Protection of Child Rights
- The Chief Commissioner for Persons with Disabilities.

Appointment of Chairperson and Other Members

The President appoints the Chairperson and other members of the Commission by warrant under his hand and seal after obtaining the recommendations of the Committee consisting of:

- Prime Minister (Chairperson)
- Speaker of the House of People
- Minister in charge of Ministry of Home Affairs in the Government of India
- Leader of the Opposition in the House of the People
- Leader of the Opposition in the Council of States
- Deputy Chairperson of the Council of States

Term of Office of Members[7]

The person appointed as Chairperson and the members shall hold the office for a term of three years from the date of their appointment or until he or she attains the age of seventy years, whichever is earlier. They are eligible for reappointment.

---

[6] According to the Human Rights Act, 1993, the Chairperson of the NHRC is a person who has been a Chief Justice of the Supreme Court. However, the same was amended in the year 2019 allowing even a retired judge of the Supreme Court to be the Chairman of the NHRC.

[7] Human Rights Act 1993, prescribed the term of the Chairperson and members of the NHRC as five years or till the age of seventy years, whichever is earlier. However, the Amendment Act, 2019 reduced the term of office to three years or till the age of seventy years, whichever is earlier.

Resignation and Removal of a Member of the Commission

The Chairperson or any member may resign from his or her office by addressing the resignation letter to the President.

The Chairperson or any other member of the Commission may be removed from his office by an order of the President on the ground of proved misbehavior or incapacity. However, they can be removed on the said charges only based on the recommendations of the Supreme Court.

Moreover, the President may also, by order, remove the Chairman and other members if:

- Adjudged as insolvent or
- Engaged during his term of office in paid employment outside the duties of his office or
- Unfit to continue in office by reason of infirmity of mind or body or of unsound mind and stands so declared by a competent court or
- Convicted and sentenced to imprisonment for an offence which in the opinion of the President involves moral turpitude.

Functions of the Commission

Commission shall perform all or any of the following functions:

- Inquire, suo moto, or on a petition presented to it by a victim or any person on his behalf or on a direction or order of any court into complain of
  - (i) violation of Human Rights or abetment thereof; or
  - (ii) negligence in the prevention of such violation by a public servant;
- Intervene in any proceeding involving any allegation of violation of Human Rights pending before a court with the approval of such Court.
- Visit, any jail or other institution under the control of the State Government, where persons are detained or lodged for purposes of treatment, reformation, or protection, for the study of the living conditions of the inmates thereof and make recommendations thereon to the government.
- Review the safeguards provided by or under the Constitution or any law for the time being in force for the protection of Human Rights and recommend measures for their effective implementation.
- Review the factors, including acts of terrorism that inhibit the enjoyment of Human Rights, and recommend appropriate remedial measures.
- Study treaties and other international instruments on Human Rights and make recommendations of their effective implementation.
- Undertake and promote research in the field of Human Rights.
- Spread Human Rights literacy among various sections of society and promote awareness of the safeguards available for the protection of these rights through publications, the media, seminars, and other available means.
- Encourage the efforts of non-governmental organizations and institutions working in the field of Human Rights.
- Such other functions as it may consider necessary for the promotion of Human Rights.

Complaints not Entertained by NHRC

- Complaint in regard to events which happened more than one year before the making of the complaint;

- Complaint with regard to the matters which are subjudice or pending before a state commission or any other commission duly constituted under any law for the time being in force;
- Complaints which are of frivolous nature;
- Complaints which are outside the purview of the Commission.

Powers of NHRC

Powers to Inquire

NHRC enjoys the powers of a civil court while inquiring into a matter.

Following are the powers of a civil court enjoyed by the NHRC -

- Summoning and enforcing the attendance of witnesses and examining them on oath;
- Discovery and production of any document;
- Receiving evidence on affidavits;
- Requisitioning any public record or copy thereof from any court or office;
- Issuing Commissions for the examinations of witnesses or documents;
- Any other matter which may be prescribed

The Powers of the NHRC Relating to Investigation

- The Commission may, while conducting the investigation, utilize the services of any officer or investigation agency of the Central Government or any State Government with the concurrence of the respective governments.
- For the purpose of investigation, any officer

  (a) may be summoned and enforce the attendance of any person;

  (b) require the discovery and production of any document; and

  (c) requisition any public record or copy thereof from any office.
- The officer or agency, whose services are utilized, shall investigate into any matter pertaining to the inquiry and submit a report thereon to the Commission within such period as may be specified by the Commission in this behalf.

The Powers of the NHRC in Relation to Armed Forces

While dealing with complaints of violation of Human Rights by members of armed forces, the Commission :

- may, either on its own motion or receipt of a petition, seek a report from the Central Government. After the receipt of the report, it may, either not proceed with the complaint, or makes recommendations to the Central Government.
- The Central Government shall inform the Commission of the action taken on the recommendations within three months or such further time as the Commission may allow.
- The Commission shall publish its report together with its recommendations made to the Central Government and the action taken by that Government on such recommendations.

Annual and Special Reports of the Commission

- The Commission shall submit an Annual Report to the Central Government and to the State Government concerned, and may at any time submit Special Reports if the commission feels the urgency.

- The Central Government and the State Government, as the case may be, shall cause the Annual and Special Reports of the Commission to be laid before each House of Parliament or the State Legislature respectively, along with a memorandum of action taken or proposed to be taken on the recommendations of the Commission and the reason for non-acceptance of the recommendations, if any.

Role of the National Human Rights Commission

- NHRC is a unique independent institution. It plays an advisory, supportive, and supplementary role to the existing institutions.
- The NHRC does not replace the role of the already existing legal and administrative framework in the form of courts, legislature, and executive bodies and other institutions.

STATE HUMAN RIGHTS COMMISSION (SHRC)

A State Government may constitute a body to be known as the State Human Rights Commission.

Composition of SHRC

The SHRC comprises of:

- a Chairperson who has been a Chief Justice of a High Court or been a Judge of a High Court;
- one Member who is, or has been, a Judge of a High Court or District Judge in the State with a minimum of seven years' experience as District Judge;
- one Member to be appointed from amongst persons having knowledge of, or practical experience in, matters relating to Human Rights

Appointment of Chairperson and Members

The President appoints the Chairperson and other members of the Commission by warrant under his hand and seal after obtaining the recommendations of the Committee consisting of:

- the Chief Minister (Chairperson)
- Speaker of the Legislative Assembly
- Minister in-charge of the Department of Home
- Leader of the Opposition in the Legislative Assembly

Provided that where there is a Legislative Council in a State, the Chairman of that Council and the Leader of the Opposition in that Council shall also be members of the Committee. Moreover, no sitting Judge of a High Court or a sitting District Judge shall be appointed, except after consultation with the Chief Justice of the High Court of the concerned State.

Term of Office of Members[8]

The person appointed as Chairperson and the members shall hold the office for a term of three years from the date of their appointment or until he or she attains the age of seventy years, whichever is earlier. They are eligible for reappointment.

---

[8]Human Rights Act, 1993, prescribed the term of the Chairperson and members of the SHRC as five years or till the age of seventy years, whichever is earlier. However, the Amendment Act, 2019 reduced the term of office to three years or till the age of seventy years, whichever is earlier.

Resignation and Removal of Chairperson and Members

The Chairperson or any member may resign from his or her office by addressing a resignation letter to the Governor.

The Chairperson or any other member of the Commission may be removed from his office only by an order of the President on the ground of proved misbehavior or incapacity. However, they can be removed on the said charges only based on the recommendations of the Supreme Court.

Moreover, the President may also, by order, remove the Chairman and other members if:

- Adjudged as insolvent or
- Engaged during his term of office in paid employment outside the duties of his office or
- Unfit to continue in office by reason of infirmity of mind or body or of unsound mind and stands so declared by a competent court or
- Convicted and sentenced to imprisonment for an offence which in the opinion of the President involves moral turpitude.

Functions of the Commission

The State Commission is empowered to perform all those functions, which have been entrusted to the National Human Rights Commission. However, the Act excludes the study of treaties and other International Instruments on Human Rights from the purview of State Human Rights Commission. The study of such treaties and the eligibility to make recommendations for their effective implementation are the exclusive domain of the National Human Rights Commission.

The State Commission may inquire into violations of Human Rights only in respect of matters related to any of the entries enumerated in List II and List III in the Seventh Schedule of the Constitution. However, the State Human Rights Commission shall not enquire into any matter which is pending before a National Commission or any other statutory Commission duly constituted under any law in force.

Annual and Special Reports of the State Commission

The State Commission shall submit an Annual Report to the State Government and may at any time submit Special Reports if the commission feels the urgency.

The State Government shall cause the annual and special reports of the State Commission to be laid before each House of State Legislature where it consists of two Houses, or where such legislature consists of one House, before that House.

Setting up of Human Rights Courts

The setting up of Human Rights Courts in every District of the country for the speedy trial of offences arising out of violation of Human Rights is a novel provision of the Act.

State Governments, with the concurrence of the Chief Justice of the High Court by notification may specify for each District a Court of Sessions to be a Human Rights Court. For every Human Rights Court, the State Government shall appoint a Public Prosecutor or an advocate who has been in practice as an advocate for not less than seven years for the purpose of conducting cases in the Human Rights Courts; such a person shall be designated as a 'Special Public Prosecutor'. Even though it is not mandatory for the States to create Human Rights Courts in each and every district, it is desirable that States establish such courts in each district.

Functions Related to Union Territories

The Central Government may confer upon State Commissions, the functions relating to Human Rights being discharged by the Union territories, other than the Union territory of Delhi, which will be dealt with by the National Human Rights Commission.

IMPORTANT INTERVENTIONS BY NHRC[9]

There are a number of instances where the Commission intervened to safeguard the Human Rights of the citizens.

A few of the major interventions of the Commission are:

- High suicide rates by debt-ridden farmers continued in some States, including Maharastra despite some relief measures. The Commission took suo motu cognizance of the reports about suicide by farmers. The Government of Maharashtra in its report informed the Commission that it had appointed a Committee at District level under the Chairmanship of the District Collector to monitor and supervise the implementation of various schemes, to assist farmers, and to curb and dissuade them from committing suicide. Families of farmers who had committed suicide were being provided financial assistance as per norms laid down by the State Government. The Government of Andhra Pradesh had also constituted a Commission on Farmers' Welfare to go into the causes of suicide. The Commission has set up a Committee to study the problem and suggest solutions.
- The NHRC took cognizance of issue of inadequate access to health care in *Adivasi* communities of south Orissa. Keeping the plight of these communities in mind, the Commission recommended for improvement of manpower in rural areas followed by other systemic recommendations on Right to Health.
- Violence against *Adivasis* by Maoists and Salwa Judum in Dantewada, Chattisgarh was brought to the notice of the Commission. The Commission called for a report from the State Government. While the matter was under consideration of the Commission, the Supreme Court on the basis of a writ petition filed before it, directed the Commission to examine/verify allegations relating to violation of Human Rights by Naxalites and Salwa Judum and the living conditions in the refugee settlement colonies. The Supreme Court asked the Commission to appoint an appropriate Fact Finding Committee and submit a report. In compliance with the directions of the Apex Court, a team from Investigation Division in the Commission visited remote tribal and forest areas of Chattisgarh and the adjoining State of Andhra Pradesh, for collecting facts. There were incidents of attack on the police by some groups during the visit of the team. Threat to their lives did not deter the team from performing their assigned task and they completed the purpose of their visit. The report of the team is being finalized for submission before the Apex Court for its consideration.

SUBJECTIVE QUESTIONS

1. Explain the powers and functions of the National Human Rights Commission. **(150 words)**
2. Discuss the role of National Human Rights Commission in upholding the Human Rights in India. **(250 words)**

[9]https://nhrc.nic.in/press-release/some-important-interventions-nhrc

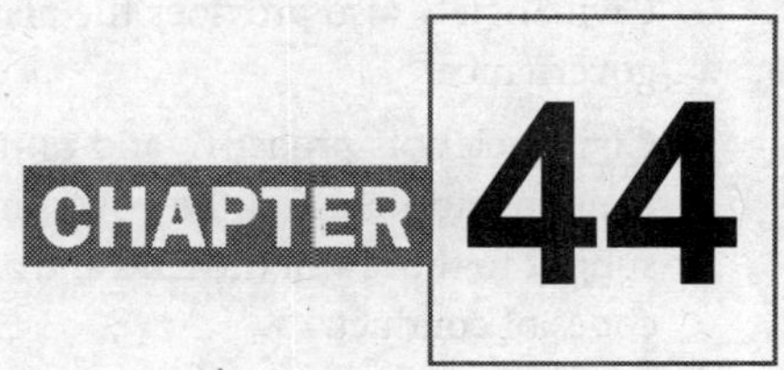

CIVIL SOCIETY

"If we want any significant development, we must co-opt civil society".

– Nelson Mandela

INTRODUCTION TO CIVIL SOCIETY

Civil society is the backbone of democracy. Civil society can be understood as a social and public space and sphere that is above the domain of family and below the State. Migdal considers 'civil society' as a group that is freely created on the basis of common interest to serve as a bridge between the society and government (Migdal, 1988:13).

Thus, civil society includes charities, development NGOs, community groups, women's organizations, faith-based organizations, professional associations, trade unions, social movements, coalitions, and advocacy groups. Civil society can also be understood as the space outside the family, market, and State. Civil society organisations function outside the conventional space of both the State and market, but they have the potential to negotiate, persuade, and pressurise both these institutions to make them more responsive to the needs and rights of the citizens. Civil society is often also referred to as the 'Third Sector' (existing alongside the Public and Private sectors). However, civil society is not homogeneous and the boundaries between civil society and government or civil society and commercial actors can be blurred.

Role of Civil Society in Good Governance[1]

Civil societies do not seek political power for themselves. It can do various works to nurture the concept of democracy. Further, an active civil society is necessary for the prevalence and institutionalization of good governance in the country.

The role of civil society in good governance is as follows:

- Civil Society helps people to appraise their Fundamental Rights and responsibilities[2];
- Civil Society is instrumental in making people aware about the role of the government and State institutions, as well as the responsibilities of State functionaries. Without that knowledge, most people are unaware of governance, public issues, and the administrative structures and functions;
- Civil Society provides the forums to the people to debate and discuss their issues and communicate them to the rulers and administrators;

[1]https://tribune.com.pk/story/1637755/6-civil-society-good-governance

[2]Informed citizenry is a sine qua non for accountability in the governance system and structures of the governance.

- Civil Society also provides the platforms to the people to maximally participate in the process of governance.
- Civil society is proactive and under its influence, an informed citizenry constantly reminds the State institutions and the government servants and makes them realize that they are very much subject to the law of the land and all their actions are conditioned by official rules, procedures, and codes of conduct.

Thus, an active civil society and through it an informed citizenry play a critical role in empowering communities and ensuring good governance.

Categories of Civil Society Groups

Civil society groups in India can be classified into following broad categories[3]:

(a) Registered Societies formed for specific purposes (eg: NGO)

(b) Charitable Organisations and Trusts (eg: Ramakrishna Mission)

(c) Local Stakeholders Groups, Microcredit and Thrift Enterprises, SHGs

(d) Professional Self-Regulatory Bodies (eg: Bar Council of India, Medical Council of India)

(e) Cooperatives

(f) Bodies without having any formal organisational structure

(g) Government promoted Third Sector Organisations

NON-GOVERNMENTAL ORGANIZATIONS/VOLUNTARY ORGANIZATIONS

Voluntary action encompasses the participation of citizens in all aspects of associational life. India has a long history and tradition of voluntary action, providing services to the sick, needy, and destitute. Rather, it is a part of our cultural heritage and way of life. Voluntarism in India is as old as the emergence of organized society itself. It originated as pure philanthropy of charity and this motivation sustained the voluntary efforts all through history in the ancient[4] and medieval period[5]. Indian culture also placed great emphasis on charity. Constructions of temples, dharmashalas, and anna-satrams (centers to serve food free of cost) were some manifestations of charity[6].

During the colonial period, voluntary efforts received a boost with new religious, cultural, and social surroundings. The Laissez Faire policy[7] of the British Government in economic, religious, and social matters left no other avenue of development open to the 'natives' than resort to the 'self-help' form of voluntarism.

---

[3]Social capital - A shared destiny, Ninth Report, Second Administrative Reforms Commission, August 2008, Government of India.

[4]The Upanishads also indicate the gradation of daanam which are Shramdaan , Anna-Daan, Vastra-Daan and Gyan-Daan.

[5]Guru Nanak, the founder of the Sikh religion began work in the Kartarpur Community in present day Pakistan. Here the traditions of Kar Seva based on the principles of Shramdaan were born. The base of volunteerism and volunteering has been built on this tradition.

[6]http://mpbou.edu.in

[7]Laissez-faire is French for "let do" or "leave us alone". It is defined as a situation with minimal government intervention and leaving economies to the invisible hand of the market.

Non-governmental organizations, or NGOs, were first called such in Article 71 in the Charter of the newly formed United Nations in 1945. While NGOs have no fixed or formal definition, they are generally defined as non-profit entities independent of governmental influence (although they may receive government funding).

The term 'NGOs' specifies the organizations undertaking voluntary social action. The term is negative as it seeks to give a meaning that NGOs possess the characteristics/features not possessed by the government, and undertake activities otherwise normally not undertaken by the government.

Definition of NGOs

The World Bank defines NGOs as *"Private organisations that pursue activities to relieve suffering, promote the interests of the poor, protect the environment, provide basic social services, or undertake community development."* In a wider usage, the term, 'NGO' can be applied to any non-profit organisation which is independent from government. NGOs are typically value-based organisations which depend, in whole or in part, on donations and voluntary service[8].

Characteristics that Distinguish NGOs[9]

An organization may be correctly labelled as an NGO if it has the following four characteristics:

1. **Voluntary :** NGOs are formed voluntarily by citizens with an element of voluntary participation in the organization, whether in the form of small numbers of board members or large numbers of members or time given by volunteers.
2. **Independent :** NGOs are independent within the laws of society, and controlled by those who have formed them or by elected or appointed boards. The legal status of NGOs is based on freedom of association—one of the most basic human rights as well as the Fundamental Right.
3. **Not-for-profit :** NGOs are not for private personal profit or gain. NGOs may, in many countries, engage in revenue-generating activities, but must use the revenue solely in pursuit of the organization's mission. Like other enterprises, NGOs have employees who are paid for what they do. Boards are not usually paid for the work they perform, but may be reimbursed for expenses they incur in the course of performing their board duties.
4. **Not self-serving in aims and related values :** The aims of NGOs are to improve the circumstances and prospects of people and to act on concerns and issues detrimental to the well-being, circumstances, or prospects of people or society as a whole.

Types of NGOs (By Orientation)

1. **Charitable orientation :** This often involves a top-down paternalistic effort with little participation by the 'beneficiaries'. It includes NGOs with activities directed toward meeting the needs of the poor—distribution of food, clothing, or medicine; provision of housing, transport, schools, etc. Such NGOs may also undertake relief activities during a natural or man-made disaster.
2. **Service orientation :** As the name suggests, these NGOs provide vital services such as medical, housing, education, family planning, and other assistance which people may need but do not have access to. Under this typology, the programme is designed by the NGO and people are expected to participate in its implementation and in receiving the service.

---

[8]https://www.lkouniv.ac.in/

[9]http://mpbou.edu.in/

3 **Participatory orientation :** In this kind of NGO, the local people who are being targeted are allowed to actively participate in implementing the project. For instance, if they are executing a house building task, it is the people on the ground who do the work. Thus, these NGOs are characterized by self-help projects where local people are involved, particularly in the implementation of a project by contributing cash, tools, land, materials, labour, etc.

4. **Empowering orientation :** These kinds of NGOs are dedicated to empowering communities to be aware of the social, political, and economic issues which are affecting them, and how they can rise from oppression. Sometimes, these groups develop spontaneously around a problem or an issue; at other times outside workers from NGOs play a facilitating role in their development.

Legislation on NGO Activity in India

NGOs are not required to register with the government. However, registration allows an NGO to deduct expenses from income for tax purposes, receive foreign contributions, and be considered for government grant-in-aid schemes. Registration also facilitates domestic fundraising, as the Income Tax Act[10] permits donors to deduct contributions made to registered NGOs.

Registration

A voluntary organization or a NGO in India can either be registered as a charitable trust (subject to Public Trusts Act (1976)), or society (subject to Societies Registration Act, 1860), or Section 8 company[11] (subject to Companies Act, 2013). Irrespective of the fact that whether a NGO is a charitable trust or society or Section 8, it is subject to Income-Tax Act of 1961. Moreover, organizations receiving foreign funds must abide by the Foreign Contribution (Regulation) Act of 2010, and are regulated by the Ministry of Home Affairs.

Therefore, we can conclude that there is no dedicated legislation in India which governs NGOs and its activities.

Advantages of NGO Movement[12]

1. **Adopt innovative and participatory approaches :** The programmes of NGOs tend to be innovative and emphasize on participatory approaches. NGOs are constantly designing innovative participatory approaches to elicit and enable the people to participate in the programmes. Because of these techniques and other people-centered practices, communities actively participate in the programmes and this contributed to the development activities being relevant to the people's needs and aspirations. The participation of the people also contributed to the reduction in costs. For instance, the innovative Credit Management Programme of MYRADA influenced many NGOs to start similar programmes in their project areas. This programme also influenced the NABARD to introduce Bank-SHG (Self-Help Group) linkage programme on a pilot basis, and is now prevalent all over the country.

---

[10] Section 80G allows voluntary organizations working in specified areas deemed to be charitable to register with the income tax authority. This enables donors (individuals and companies) to claim tax relief on 50% of the amount donated, up to 10% of the donor's income. The beneficiary organizations are required to issue a receipt or certificate in a prescribed format to the donor to enable the donor to claim tax deduction. This is the most widely used tax benefit for charitable giving.

[11] A company is referred to as Section 8 Company when it registered as a Non-Profit Organization (NPO) i.e. when it has motive of promoting arts, commerce, education, charity, protection of environment, sports, science, research, social welfare, religion and intends to use its profits (if any) or other income for promoting these objectives.

[12] Non-Governmental Organizations (NGOs) in India: Opportunities and Challenges, D. Rajasekhar, Institute for Social and Economic Change, 2000.

2. **Effective in development work :** The NGO development programmes are relatively more successful to reach the poor and contribute towards poverty alleviation. NGOs have succeeded in:

   (i) breaking the isolation of the poor;

   (ii) enhancing the productivity of assets and labour;

   (iii) improving marketing opportunities for the produce such as milk, handicrafts, etc; and

   (iv) enhancing access to food, health, education, and drinking water.

   But, in some of the development NGOs, the benefits reach only those poor with some initial endowment base. The NGOs are, however, not very successful to enable the poorest among the poor with very little endowment base to begin with, to expand the means to overcome poverty (Murthy and Rao, 1997).

3. **Flexible in methods and practices :** NGOs exhibit a high degree of flexibility in their functioning, methods, and practices because they tend to be local and small. The geographical area of the NGOs tends to be small. Such a small geographical area enables the NGOs to be flexible in methods and practices of formulation, implementation, and monitoring of the programmes. Further, the style of working can easily be changed to suit the needs and aspirations of the community within which they are working. Being small (in terms of staff), NGOs face less problems of lack of coordination convergence that restrict the government departments. NGOs can respond swiftly and efficiently to local demands. Being locally based, they are aware of the local environment and are responsive to it.

4. **More actor-oriented :** NGOs, especially empowerment NGOs, tend to take up need-based activities. Through studies relating to situations and needs of the people, they seek to find out answers to the problems. For instance, NGOs try to find the answers to the questions such as — Who are the poor? Why are they poor? What is to be done to alleviate poverty? — and so on. The rigour with which these studies are carried out may vary, but a starting point in the case of most of these NGOs is to articulate and address the problems of the poor and the marginalized communities such as women, dalits, adivasis, etc. For instance, LEPRA Society, established in 1988 at Hyderabad, brought into focus the Indian Government's National Leprosy Eradication Programme (NLEP). Today, it operates across various states in India. Lepra Society had a systematic approach to dealing with the chronic disease of leprosy. Its prime objective was to first identify its patients within an area via mass contact and school surveys and then treat them with multidrug therapy (MDT). LEPRA Society's success encouraged them to extend a helping hand to victims of other maladies as well. Today, they also work towards helping patients of malaria, tuberculosis, and AIDS. They also help the Indian government in the National Anti-Malaria Programme (NAMP) and have extensively contributed to eye care and prevention of needless blindness.

5. **Speed of execution :** One of the advantages of an NGO is its flexibility and speed of action. Unlike governments, they are not hampered by bureaucratic red tape. They can mobilize the population for rapid action when a crisis breaks out in a given country.

6. **Advocacy and lobbying :** NGOs play an important role to influence the State policies by advocacy and lobbying[13] through their networks. It is now recognized that a part of the requirement of a successful democracy is a strong civil society, which can counterbalance the interests and actions of the State where it is necessary. Civil society is the arena in which the interests of different groups within the social formation can be presented through a wide variety of means and actions. NGOs are important organizations within civil society adding to its ability to influence and strengthen the process of development. NGOs are, therefore, important not just for the fact that they can do development better, but also because they can influence the perception, including that of the State, of what constitutes better development. NGOs play a significant role in influencing the policies of the State at various levels, and counterbalance the interests and actions of the State.

Weaknesses of NGO Movement[14]

1. **Spatial Limitation :** An important problem of most of the NGOs is spatial limitation, that is, NGO development projects remain little more than dots on a map. The territorial space under the NGO is defined by a number of factors: these include the obvious such as the amount of finance available, the physical characteristics of the project, and the organizational size and structure of the NGO. Another important factor is that the poor located beyond the project area of NGOs are not provided with any development assistance. In addition, there is the spatial dimension determined by the definition of the target group. Not all poor or marginalized groups will be covered within the territorial location.
2. **Lack of good governance and transparency :** NGOs need to have good governance. However, in the absence of constant pressure from below, NGOs can assume the paternalistic role and a shift in priorities. As the NGO expands the area and scope of activities, the leaders begin to dominate the NGO. The NGOs become semi-bureaucratic and hierarchical where initiative and decision-making gets confined to the leaders. This will have an adverse impact not only on flexible functioning, but also on the development of new leadership. Often, the views and concerns of young staff members in the organization are overlooked or even suppressed. The young staff members either leave the organization and/or remain as non-entities. In a majority of the NGOs, there are no budget transparency in proposal, sanction, and utilization.
3. **Antagonistic attitude towards the State :** NGOs, especially development and charity NGOs, often seek to supplant the State as the provider of basic services and development programmes and thereby, weaken the political relationship between people and their government.

---

[13]Lobbyists provide governments with valuable policy-related information and expertise but if the activity is not transparent, public interest may be put at risk in favour of specific interests. India currently does not have a law to regulate lobbying. It is worth noting that no country in the world, including India, has banned lobbying. In fact, only a few countries even regulate the activity, prominent among these are the US, Canada, Australia, Germany and Taiwan. These countries treat lobbying as a legitimate right of citizens. Regulations serve as a tool to enhance transparency in the policymaking process rather than restricting access to policymakers. In fact, that is one of the key reasons why the UK regulates the lobbied rather than lobbying. Therefore, the thrust of the Indian law should be to incentivize lobbyists to identify themselves and ensure that competing groups have reasonably equal access to policymakers. (Kaushiki Sanyal, Harsimran Kalra, 2013).

[14]Non-Governmental Organizations in India: Opportunities and Challenges, D. Rajasekhar, Institute for Social and Economic change, 2000.

4. **Limited ability to influence macro-policies :** Individual NGOs are rarely in a position to influence government policies at various levels. In addition, rarely do they seek to influence policy, because their existence and tolerance by the State is based upon a non-controversial, apolitical involvement in development. Furthermore, NGOs rarely cooperate and liaise with one another, tending instead to view each other as competitors for donor funding, State tolerance, and occasionally for local influence and space. Consequently, they fail to emerge as genuine macro actors at regional or at national levels, seeking to represent their members' interest in the political process of governance and more general development.
5. **Lack of Accountability :** Accountability should not be equated with accountancy. The term accountability implies the extent to which NGO activities and programmes seek to fulfill the objectives with which NGOs were started. Accountability can be upwards (i.e., to the government, donors, and governing board), sideways (to the interested public, media, etc.), and downwards (to the people, staff, etc.). It is also observed that some NGO projects do not emerge on the basis of situations and needs of the poor with whom they work, but are influenced by donor priorities and policies.
6. **Vested interests :** An influential argument made by a number of observers is that foreign funding has vested interest: one of the interests mentioned is that they should invest money in those countries where the markets are growing. If a proportion of the population in largely populous countries like India remains poor, the multinational companies will be considerably affected in the long run due to low demand for their products. That the foreign funding has a vested interest of developing markets and market-based economy is borne out by a statement of Ms. Hillary Clinton after her visit to India in the late 90's. She is reported to have stated to the representatives of business houses in the USA that they should donate money liberally for development and poverty alleviation in India as this would be a growing and large market in the new millennia.
7. **Inadequate funding :** Many NGOs find it difficult to garner sufficient and continuous funding for their work. Gaining access to appropriate donors is a major component of this challenge. They may have limited resource mobilization skills locally, so instead they wait for international donors to approach them. Current donors may shift priorities and withdraw funding. The NGO might suffer from a general lack of project, organizational, and financial sustainability.

SELF-HELP GROUPS (SHGs)

Villages are faced with problems related to poverty, illiteracy, lack of skills, health care, etc. These are problems that cannot be tackled individually but can be better solved through group efforts. Today, these groups known as Self-help groups have become the vehicle of change for the poor and marginalized. Self-help groups (SHGs) is the brain child of Nobel Peace Prize Winner Prof. Muhammad Yunus who started Grameen Bank of Bangladesh as early as in 1976.

Self-help group is a method of organising the poor people and the marginalized to come together to solve their individual problems. The SHG method is used by the government, NGOs, and others worldwide.

Structure of SHG

A SHG is a group of about 10 to 20 people, usually women, from a similar class and region, who come together to form a savings and credit organization. They pool financial resources to make small interest bearing loans to their members. This process creates an ethic that focuses on savings first. The setting of terms and conditions and accounting of the loan are done in the group by designated members. Further, the members of the SHG collect their savings and save it in banks. In return, they receive easy access to loans with a small rate of interest to start their micro enterprises units.

Principles of SHG

The concept of SHG is based on the following principles:

- Self-help supplemented with mutual help can be a powerful vehicle for the poor in their socio-economic development;Participative financial services management is more responsive and efficient;
- The poor not only need credit support, but also savings and other services;
- SHGs' role as clients to the banks help in widening the outreach of the banks, lowering the transaction cost and risk costs for the banks;
- Creation of a common fund by contributing small savings on a regular basis;
- Flexible democratic system of working;
- Loaning done mainly on trust with a bare minimum documentation and without any security;
- Amounts loaned are small, frequent, and for short duration;
- Defaults are rare mainly due to group pressure; and
- Periodic meetings and non-traditional savings[15].

In the decade of nineties, National Agriculture Bank for Rural development (NABARD), Government Organizations, Non-government Organizations (NGOs), and Micro Finance Institutions (MFIs) initiated and started Self-help groups for microfinance and micro credit activities for the objectives of poverty alleviation, women empowerment, and financial inclusion.

SHG–Bank Linkage Model

Microfinancing is a poverty eradication revolution which is prevailing not only in India but all over the World in full swing. Since independence in 1947, successive governments have emphasized the link between improving access to finance and employment generation tending to reduction in poverty. The creation of a nationwide network of rural cooperative banks in the 1950s was an effort to improve financial access to the Indian rural poor. It was furthered by the nationalization of 20 Commercial banks. Following the success of Grameen Bank experiment in Bangladesh, the strategy of forming SHGs and extending micro-credit through these SHGs has been strictly and successively followed in India. SHG-Bank Linkage Programme was launched by NABARD (National Bank for Agriculture and Rural Development) in 1991–92, as an experiment in providing hassle-free institutional credit to rural poor, including women. It has achieved spectacular success over

[15] *Rural Development in India: A Role of Self-Help Group*, Prof. Mahadev. S. Terdal, International Journal of Advanced Research in Education & Technology (IJARET), Vol. 5, Issue 3 (July - Sept. 2018).

the last two decades, which is now acclaimed as the biggest micro credit programme in the World. Currently, 75 percent of the total microfinance credit supply is via the Self Help Group-Bank linkage route, largely financed by the National Bank for Agriculture and Rural Development. The remaining part of microfinance credit comes from MFIs, increasingly backed by commercial banks. The role of micro finance institutions (MFIs) and cooperative banks has taken shape of an umbrella under which various NGOs and social organizations are operating employment generation programmes for poverty alleviation.

Socio-economic Impacts of Self-Help Groups[16]

(a) **Microfinancing benefit for rural poor households :** Self-help has aimed at enhancing profitability for rural people. The low economic growth of this country was perceived to be due to lack of capital resources, especially in rural areas. A vicious cycle of low capital, low productivity, low incomes, low savings, and weak capital base was perceived to be operating, perpetuating a permanent poverty syndrome. Therefore, cheap rural credit policies like microfinancing by the SHGs were designed to provide the rural poor with access to adequate capital. Microfinance through SHGs has become a ladder for the poor to bring them up not only economically, but also socially, mentally, and attitudinally and above all, help them break through the stronghold of exploitative money lenders.

(b) **Economic Empowerment of Women :** Empowerment of women is a crucial factor in the eradication of poverty as they are the key contributors to the economy at all levels. Self-help groups' microfinance activities helps the poor women in not just obtaining loans, but also inculcating in them the habits of savings, credit, and investing in micro insurance and money transfer services. Members of self-help groups participate and improve access to micro credit management, marketing skills, and capacity-building to promote financial inclusion and empowerment.

(c) **Social Empowerment of Women :** SHGs ensure the equality of status of women as participants, decision-makers, and beneficiaries in the democratic, economic, social, and cultural spheres of life.

(d) **Political Empowerment :** SHGs as active, articulate, and organized citizenry act on a range of issues, holding the Panchayats accountable in terms of the use, production, and distribution of public resources for the common public good. SHGs enable women to develop their communication skills by speaking at the Grama Sabha, public meetings, etc. A SHG functions through its regular meetings, where members perform transactional activities and discuss over different related issues. Social mobilization through SHGs is inevitable for political empowerment.

(e) **SHGs and Rural Development :** In order to change the face of socio-economic scenarios, microenterprises and SHGs are playing a significant role in the self-employment by raising the level of income and standard of living of the rural people. In this framework, one of the most vital aspects of rural self-employment is the formation of SHGs which is a valuable investment in human capital through training and capacity-building measures. From dairy to mechanized

[16]The Impact Of Self-Help Groups On The Socio-Economic Development Of Rural Household Women In Tamil Nadu - A Study; [Saravanan *, Vol.4 (Iss.7: SE): July, 2016] International Journal of Research – Granthaalayah.

farming, weaving, poultry, food processing units, and mushroom cultivation; rural India has been busy setting up micro-enterprises by forming SHGs. The group members use collective wisdom and peer pressure to ensure appropriate use of funds and its timely repayment. These are informal groups in nature where members come together towards collective action for a common cause. The common need is meeting their emergent economic needs without depending on external help. SHG movement is supposed to build economic self-reliance of rural poor, overcome misuse, and create confidence, predominantly among women who are mostly unseen in the social structure.

Thus, SHG Programme clearly plays a central role in the lives of the poor. Microfinance to the rural SHGs is a way to raise the income level and improve the living standards and economic independence of the rural women. The impact on their lives is not just an economic one; gaining more self-confidence is often a more lasting achievement that forms the basis for social and economic improvements.

SUBJECTIVE QUESTIONS

1. Why is accountability important for NGOs' growth, efficiency, and the creation of hegemony? Discuss. **(250words)**
2. "Self-Help Groups play a significant role in alleviating poverty and rural development". Explain. **(250 words)**

CHAPTER 45

ROLE OF CIVIL SERVICES IN PARLIAMENTARY DEMOCRACY

"With bad laws and good civil servants it's still possible to govern. But with bad civil servants even the best laws can't help".

– Otto von Bismarck

THE CIVIL SERVICE

Civil Service refers to the body of government officials who are employed in civil occupations that are neither political nor judicial. In other words, Civil Service means a group of people who share in the exercise of the sovereign power of the state by discharging the various functions of the executive branch of the government other than military responsibilities as a life career which is paid from government treasury[1].

The concept of Civil Service was prevalent in India from ancient times. The Mauryan administration employed civil servants in the name of *adhyakshas* and *rajukas*. The examination for civil servants in those days too was very stringent (as quoted by Kautilya's *Arthashastra*). The expanse of the territory and the need to hold it intact made it imperative for the Mauryan administration to recruit Civil Servants based on merit. The concept of Civil Service again came into prominence when the British, in search of creating a framework to hold the territories of India, created the much coveted 'Indian Civil Service[2]' or the ICS[3].

Indian Administration During British Regime[4]

The main objectives of the Indian administration in the pre-independence era were maintenance of law and order and the promotion of the development of the colonial economy, complementary to that

---

[1] *Indian Civil Services and their changing role in the context of Globalisation* - A Pragmatic Approach, by Dr. M. Ramana Reddy, Volume 6 I Issue 1 I JAN. – March 2019, IJRAR - International Journal of Research and Analytical Reviews.

[2] The foundations for Civil Services in British India were laid by Warren Hastings.

[3] Civil Service Reforms, M. Satish, Knowledge Manager (Human Development), Centre for Good Governance, Hyderabad.

[4] Tyagi, A. R. "Role of Civil Service in India." The Indian Journal of Political Science, vol. 19, no. 4, 1958, pp. 349–356. JSTOR, www.jstor.org/stable/42753636. Accessed 28 June 2021.

of the ruling country. In social matters it followed a policy of non-interference. This meant that administration was largely a police and judicial system for the protection of life and property and also a simple system of transport and communication for the export of raw material to England. It also meant some regulation of trade and industry so as to give protection to the British trade. The principal agency for the performance of these activities was the Indian Civil Service which was a centralized and neatly-integrated hierarchy of permanent officials which provided "a clear and uninterrupted line of command from the Governor-General at the apex to the lowest official at the base, so that at the pressing of a button, the current of authority could be transmitted through successive layers".

Thus, its functions were mainly regulatory which did not call for any technical skill or inventive and enterprising minds. All its activities were tied down in set rules and regulations and an individual Civil Servant had little to think upon, but to follow the rules and precedents in deciding all issues that came before him.

Need for Civil Services in Independent India

A professionally competent and politically neutral bureaucracy is a sine qua non for the smooth and efficient function of a democratic polity. We have not adopted the 'spoils system' which had prevailed, and which prevails in the United States under which appointments are made as a reward for the political party. Such appointments may be lost on the change of government. The Federal Government of the United States, after great effort, has to a great extent eliminated the spoils system in the Civil Services. Our Civil Service has been based on the British model. Thanks to the foresight and wisdom of the founding fathers, our Constitution provides the framework for a strong administrative structure. The All India Services and the higher Civil Services constitute the very core of India's administrative fabric. These services owe their existence to the administrative acumen and vision of Sardar Vallabhbhai Patel. He envisioned India having a centralized, nationwide administrative structure to aid the integration of many culturally and linguistically diverse states, thus granting the Indian Administrative Service a prime position at the apex of the bureaucracy.

Civil Service constitutes a pool of national talent recruited, trained, and developed on a uniform basis. They hold important posts in the State and Central Governments and have a variety of field experience. Their competence and experience are required for formulation of policy in our federal polity. Especially, the All India Services act as the cementing force and are likely to be less subject to domination by political or other local pressure groups.

Role of Civil Services in our Parliamentary Democracy

(a) A permanent Civil Service is the *sine qua non* of a Parliamentary democracy. In the midst of change of governments due to periodic elections, the Civil Service provides an element of stability and continuity without which orderly government would be impossible.

(b) Our Constitution vests the executive power of the Union and the State in the President and the Governor respectively, and enjoins that this executive power shall be exercised by them directly or through officers subordinate to them in accordance with the Constitution. These officers belong to the permanent Civil Service. In effect, it is the Council of Ministers with the Prime Minister or the Chief Minister at their head, who exercise the executive power of the State through officers of the Civil Service.

(c) The relationship between the Ministers and the civil servants in a Parliamentary democracy such as ours is not amenable to any precise definition.

However, some of the broad parameters of the relationship could be summed up as follows:

(i) Formulation of policy of the Government is the legitimate task of the Minister. At the stage of formulation of policy, the Civil Servant is expected to give his free and frank advice but once the Minister, after giving due consideration to advice of the civil servant, gives the policy a final shape, it is the duty of the Civil Servant to carry out the policy diligently and faithfully though he may be having his own views about the soundness of the policy. Warren Fisher has described the role of civil servants in the following words:

"*Determination of policy is the function of Ministers, and once a policy is determined, it is the unquestioned and unquestionable business of the Civil Servant to strive to carry out that policy with precisely the same energy and precisely the same goodwill, whether he agrees with it or not. That is axiomatic and will never be in dispute. At the same time, it is the traditional duty of civil servants, while decisions are being formulated, to make available to their political chiefs all the information and experience at their disposal, and to do this without fear or favor, irrespective of whether the advice thus tendered may accord or not with the Minister's initial view. The proper discharge of this duty on the part of the Civil Servant requires qualities of a highly moral order, such as, 'presentation of integrity, fearlessness and independence of thought and utterance*'."

(ii) The preservation of integrity, fearlessness, and independence of the Civil Servant is an essential condition of a sound Parliamentary system of Government. One of the important functions of the Civil Service is to "speak truth to power", as once asserted by a Head of the Canadian Public Service.

(iii) There must be trust and mutual respect between the Minister and the Civil Servant as without them, unity of action in the higher echelons of government will be difficult to achieve.

(iv) Both the Minister and the Civil Servant must perform their roles in accordance with the Constitution and the laws as even a minor transgression there of can ultimately be subversive of good governance and rule of law.

(d) In our country, the Ministers and the Civil Servants are more than mere major players of government. "They are the custodian of a nation's ideals, of the belief it cherishes, of its permanent hopes, of the faith which makes the nation out of a mere aggregation of individuals".

Comparative Analysis of the Role of Civil Servants in Pre- & Post-Independence Era[5]

Independence has, however, brought about political changes of such a far-reaching character that they completely transformed the character and role of our Civil Service.

One can witness the following changes:

(a) The Civil Servant is no longer the ruler of the country, but only its administrator, the policy-formulation being now the function of the representatives of the people. His sole duty is to carry out the public will, as expressed in the laws passed by the legislature.

---

[5]Tyagi, A. R. "Role of Civil Service in India." The Indian Journal of Political Science, vol. 19, no. 4, 1958, pp. 349–356. JSTOR, www.jstor.org/stable/42753636. Accessed 28 June 2021.

(b) In a Parliamentary democracy, as India is, a Civil Servant has two roles to play. In the first place, he is an expert advisor to the Minister, and in the second, manager of his administrative unit.

(c) The Civil Servant in a democratic administration stands to the people in the relationship of a servant. Under the old regime, they had been in the habit of looking down upon the people and of treating them with indifference. It may be said that the Civil Servants as a whole have turned with the wind. Although the day when they would treat the humblest of the citizens with respect and impartiality is yet very far, still an average Civil Servant is responsive to public opinion.

(d) Another impact of democracy on the Civil Service is on its internal relationship. The old concepts of hierarchy and unity of command are ill-suited to a democratic system. In democracy, the administration becomes a cooperative partnership in which every officer and employee performs willingly and carefully his part of the appointed duty. There is no doubt that the gradation of posts still exists. But it is a division of responsibilities rather than the creation of classes. Even the line of authority remains intact. But it is not the fear of higher authority that moves employees to action, but a self-created inner urge.

(e) India after independence adopted the policy of welfare pattern of society in place of the Laissez Faire principle. This means a change from a police state to a welfare state, under which the state assumes the responsibility for securing to every citizen their fundamental needs such as housing, education, insurance against sickness, accident, old age, and unemployment. In such a dynamic democratic state, the Civil Servant's role also has become more creative than sedative, and more positive than negative.

(f) During colonial rule, civil servants were governed by principles such as neutrality and objectivity, which made them indifferent to individual human needs and dogmatic about their departmental traditions and procedures. However, in a democratic welfare state, civil servants are social scientists in action. They have to be fully conversant with the social background and natural temperament. They must know the world outside their own department not only with their heads, but also with their hearts, because the implementation of welfare programmes requires not only intellectual excellence, but also human understanding and sympathies.

CRITICISM AND PUBLIC PERCEPTION OF CIVIL SERVICE

Since Civil Services are considered as the most important element of the Indian administrative system that has the responsibility to fulfill the development objectives of the welfare state, any failure or shortcomings in fulfillment of these objectives are attributed to the failure of Civil Services.

Government of India in its report on 'Committee on Civil Service Reforms, 2004' elucidated the observations, criticisms, and public perception of higher Civil Service in India as follows:

(a) Corrupt practices have become prevalent in the higher civil services.

(b) The higher Civil Servants, particularly, officers of the IAS, IPS, and IFoS working in different States of the country do not have fixed tenure in any post and hence, are not able to achieve the targets fixed for them in their assignments. In the absence of any fixed tenure, these officers of the All India Services are not able to function as effective instruments of public policy and are simply wasted due to frequent transfers from one post to the other.

(c) A majority of civil servants are considered to be arrogant and are not perceived as people-friendly and by and large, they have lost touch with ground realities. There is a sharp decline in their field visits and inspections of field programmes. Civil Servants in the States have almost given up their earlier practice of sustained tours of remote areas and night halts in those areas which are so essential to understand and redress problems of the poor and the weaker sections of the community.

(d) There is 'groupism' among higher civil servants and increasingly, they have been divided along sectarian lines—an extremely unfortunate development.

(e) Some Civil Servants develop an unhealthy nexus with power brokers and do not hesitate to resort to questionable means to get good postings in India or abroad.

(f) The vigilance organization in States and the Central Bureau of Investigation in Government of India have created such a fear psychosis that Civil Servants are afraid of taking bold decisions in the public interest, i.e., decisions involving expenditure of big amounts and important commercial decisions.

(g) Article 311 of the Constitution is meant to protect honest and efficient civil servants and not to shield the corrupt and the inefficient. Article 311 of the Constitution should be amended to remove corrupt officials from service and give them an opportunity to defend themselves in a post-decision hearing only after their removal from service. If the Civil Servant is exonerated in the post-decisional hearing, he may be restored his entre service benefits including arrears of pay and allowances.

(h) Most of the Civil Servants fail to achieve results because they are not given targets of performance or the infrastructural support to achieve them. A reality check is essential through which performance of every Department and Ministry should be reviewed and the corrective action is applied. Without performance targets, the Civil Service degenerate into a closed priesthood with no accountability.

(i) There is a case for giving the higher Civil Servants a more liberal package of compensation which bears a fair comparison with what is available outside the government for similar functionaries. This higher package would ensure that Civil Servants are free of financial worries and would not succumb to temptations while holding high public offices.

(j) Unless civil society is proactive, democracy cannot be rid of money power, and the Civil Service cannot be insulated from undue and unwholesome pressures.

(k) Those who deviate from the core values of the Civil Service such as honesty, integrity, and political neutrality must be ostracized by the general body of Civil Servants. Service Associations/ Department of Government of India and Government of States should be encouraged to identify the corrupt and the inefficient in a secret ballot. The list of such officials may be forwarded to the Government of India and the respective State Government for follow up action to remove the identified officers from service if such removal is justified on facts of the case.

(l) Workload of the Civil Service has increased manifold. Workload has increased in government because paperwork has increased and government is trying to do too many things at the same time. Government must re-orient itself to perform only core functions.

(m) Officers of the All India Service in the States, particularly District Magistrates and Collectors and Superintendents of Police are spending too much time in protocol and security duties. To ensure that District Magistrates and Collectors and other senior officers in field formation get time to interact with the common people and solve their problems, protocol and security duties of these officials must be reviewed to limit their ceremonial functions.

(n) A Civil Service should comprise honest and efficient officers who are kind and compassionated. Tools and technology—including Information Technology— may enhance the competence of the Civil Service but the people of India respect a Civil Servant only if he takes personal interest in the welfare of the poor and the downtrodden. For a Civil Servant to succeed in India, he not only has to honest and dedicated but also pro-poor and should display a personal concern for the downtrodden.

(o) The Civil Service should be politically neutral to inspire confidence in their functioning under different political masters, often belonging to diverse political parties. To ensure that they remain politically neutral, they should not be given any post-retirement appointments as members/chairman of statutory commissions, quasi-judicial tribunals, or even in constitutional authorities such as the State Public Service Commission, Union Public Service Commission, Comptroller and Auditor General of India, and Election Commission of India.

(p) A retired Civil Servant/a Civil Servant who has resigned should not be appointed to the high constitutional office of Governor of State unless there is a gap of at least two years between his resignation/retirement and appointment.

(q) A government servant on resignation or on retirement should not be allowed to join a political party and contest any election for a political office on the ticket of a political party or even as an independent candidate. A period of two years must elapse before he is allowed to do so.

(r) Officers of different services who are some of the brightest when they enter the service do not feel motivated to excel in performance as they grow in the service. They stop reading books and journals so necessary to increase their domain knowledge. As issues in public administration are becoming increasingly complex and some of these issues are scientific and technical in character, officers of the higher Civil Service, particularly officers of the IAS, as leaders of multi-disciplinary teams, must acquire more domain knowledge as they go into senior positions.

(s) Training of officers both in the foundational course and also in professional course must be given adequate importance. At periodic intervals, every officer of the higher Civil Service must spend a few months under training in Management Development or in other areas of skill formation. Compulsory visits to inaccessible rural areas and preparation of reports on the problems of such areas should be made part of the training course.

(t) As the age on entry into a Civil Service has risen in recent years, most of the late entrants are no more amenable to be moulded through training.

Making the Civil Service Transparent, Accountable, and Ethical

The Report of the 'Committee on Civil Service Reforms, 2004' has provided the following ways and means to make the Civil Service transparent, accountable, and ethical:

(a) **Emphasis on Service Delivery :** In order to make the Civil Service citizen-friendly, services to the common people, which are expected to be delivered by the office/Department/Ministry, need to be identified in consultation with the beneficiaries. The office/Department/Ministry will also have to benchmark the quality of services and the period within which services can be delivered. The grievance redressal mechanism should be strengthened and held accountable.

(b) **Empowerment of Citizens :** It is necessary that Departments/Ministries direct offices under them, who are service providers, to build partnerships with local groups and organizations representing the citizens not only for formulating the programmes, but also for their proper implementation.

(c) **The Official Secrets Act :** In the past, several Committees have recommended that the Official Secrets Act should be reviewed to include only the essential minimum requirements of national security, public order, and individual privacy. Other than the items included in a negative list, information on all other items in the government should be placed in the public domain and the burden of proving whether any information not disclosed relates to the negative list should be on the government.

(d) **Job Description :** Government functionaries take most of the decisions collectively. The duties, functions, and responsibilities of most of them are neither set out in precise terms, nor widely publicized for information of the general public. Consequently, it is difficult to pinpoint non-performance on the part of these functionaries and hold any one of them accountable. Detailed job description of every post in Civil Service along with the annual performance targets should, therefore, be prepared at the beginning of every financial year so that the performance of each incumbent of the post can be judged against the objectives.

(e) **Sensitizing Civil Servants to Citizens' Problems :** In order to give the Civil Servants an idea of how common man transacts business with government, it would be useful for each Civil Servant to be made familiar with problems being faced by the common man in relation to government departments. It is recommended that every five to seven years in service, at least one month/two months should be spent by a Civil Servant with a non-governmental organization, academic institution, or private sector. It would be worthwhile for the government to identify such institutions to which civil servants can be attached.

(f) **Building Institutional Memory :** Valuable experience and knowledge are lost with the departing officer which could have been useful for his/her successor. Though there are instructions that each officer should leave behind a handing over note to his successor, in practice, the system of a 'Note to Successor' has been virtually discontinued. Therefore, it is recommended that it should be mandatory for the transferred official to leave behind a 'Note to Successor' covering the initiatives he had introduced and the support required to carry them through.

(g) **Property Returns :** All public servants, including members of Civil Service, should make their property returns available on the website for the information of the general public so that any ordinary person familiar with the details of property owned by a public servant can compare the reported figures with the actual situation and report to the government wherever there is a major discrepancy.

(h) **Amendment of Article 311 :** It is recommended that Article 311 of the Constitution be amended to provide that if there are allegations against a Civil Servant/person holding a civil post of accepting illegal gratification or of having assets disproportionate to his known sources of income and the President or the Governor is satisfied that the Civil Servant/person holding a civil post should be removed from service forthwith in the public interest, the President or the Governor may pass an order removing the Civil Servant/person holding the civil post from service and give him/her an opportunity in a post-decision hearing to defend himself.

LATERAL ENTRY[6] INTO CIVIL SERVICES

Keeping bureaucracy, the permanent executive, insulated from the influence of the political executive has always been the focus of administrative reforms. A transparent and fair system of recruitment based on meritocracy is a key to shield administrators from political influence. However, the lack of administrative reform in India has frustrated many stakeholders for a long time. One of the key focus areas of such reforms is enabling lateral entry into an otherwise 'permanent' system of administrators. The current recruitment procedure at the entry level is aimed towards selecting individuals with the best calibre.

However, over time, these bright people get lost in the vortex of a generalist system. Moreover, times are changing. Lack of domain knowledge has become a hindrance for effective policy formulation. This has led to situations where policy decisions have become skewed. It is in this backdrop that the government is intending to allow lateral entry into the departments and ministries.

Lateral entry into the administrative services is not a new idea. It is a widely applied practice, with the governments of the US, the UK, Australia, and New Zealand as well as several members of the European Union doing the same.

Inducting private talent in a somewhat cloistered government environment in India is work in progress. Its roots go back to the 1980s, the heydays of the Rajiv Gandhi administration, but its strongest manifestation can be felt now, with the Narendra Modi government determined to reform bureaucracy, thwarted and frustrated by the officialdom's slow pace of implementing government programmes and plans, which otherwise sound great on files. In fact, even the first Administrative Reforms Commission (ARC) had also advocated the need for specialization all the way back in 1965. Then, in 2005, the Second Administrative Reforms Commission (ARC) recommended that an institutionalized, transparent process be established for lateral entry into central and state government administrative positions. The year after that, the Justice B. N. Srikrishna-headed Sixth Central Pay Commission Report reiterated the recommendation, stating that lateral entry could also 'ensure entry and retention of talent in the Civil Services'.

[6]Lateral entry means the appointment of specialists from the private sector in government organisations.

Pros of Lateral Entry

1. The lack of specialization across the top tier of Indian bureaucracy is a concern that has remained unaddressed until now. The primary arguments in favour of lateral entries are regarding the urgent need for expertise and efficiency in the field of administration. Critics argue that most Civil Servants, as opposed to being specialists, tend to be 'generalists,' i.e., they are not necessarily experts in a particular area — say, finance, agriculture, labour, etc. — but rather have a limited understanding of a wider range of areas. Gulzar Natarajan (IAS) and Duvvuri Subbarao (Ex-RBI governor & retired IAS officer) ascribe this to the fact that the colonial era Indian Administrative Service (IAS) was modelled as a generalist service to deliver two core functions of the state: collect taxes and maintain law and order. Over the years, economic reforms, especially the expansion of the market, led to a transformation in the very nature of administration, demanding domain knowledge at the policy level so as to assess the impact of various policies at the level of the private sector, the non-government sector, and the public at large. Thus, there was a need felt for experts/specialists who will add efficiency to the process of policy decision-making[7].
2. Career promotions in the Civil Services move along seamlessly with few impediments along the way. Attempts to introduce 'meritocracy' hasn't quite worked out. Bringing in experts from the professional sphere is expected to shake the Civil Servants out of their comfort zone[8].
3. There is also a notable precedent for highly qualified professionals being laterally inducted into the top echelons of administration. The list includes heavyweights such as former Prime Minister Manmohan Singh, Urjit Patel, Arvind Panagariya, Arvind Subramanian, and Nandan Nilekani, among several others.

Concerns with Lateral Entry

1. The civil servants who are promoted to top echelons such as Joint Secretary, etc., have years of grassroots experience—being posted in far-flung blocks, tehsils, and districts. Experts in different fields who join government departments through lateral entries may lack this exposure and thus, be devoid of a larger connect with the masses for which they need to design and implement different policies.
2. Lateral entrants from the private sector and academia may not work well with the bureaucracy. The same pretty much goes for any inter-sector scenario. Differences in work culture, turf wars, and systemic inertia often come in the way[9].
3. Another important criticism of lateral entries is that it may institutionalize nepotism. Critics fear that lateral entries may undermine the transparency of recruitments and usher in a form of Spoils System: a mechanism through which friends and supporters of the party in power are employed and promoted in the ranks of Civil Service.[10]

---

[7]Lateral Entry into Civil Services: Boon or Bane? RGICS POLICYWATCH, Volume: 6, Issue-39.

[8]https://www.thebetterindia.com/145021/ias-lateral-entry-civil-service-pros-cons/

[9]Ibid.

[10]Lateral Entry into Civil Services: Boon or Bane? RGICS POLICYWATCH, Volume: 6, Issue-39.

Thus, lateral entry in Civil Services is a welcome step as long as the process is transparent, merit-based, and not done based on political connections. Lateral entry is especially needed in fields of administration which entail specific domain expertise. As noted by Gulzar Natarajan and Duvvuri Subbarao, "The lateral entrants should, therefore, have mandatory 'district immersion', serving at least five of their first ten years in field postings. The hard grind of such field postings will make lateral entry self-selecting, drawing in only those with commitment and aptitude."

SUBJECTIVE QUESTIONS

1. Seva Paramo Dharma" should be the mantra of civil services. Discuss (150 words)
2. "Should lateral entry be ingrained in India's Civil Service"? Comment. (200 words)

APPENDIX-I

(i) ABOUT CONSTITUTION AMENDMENT

(ii) LIST OF SOME IMPORTANT AMENDMENTS TO THE INDIAN CONSTITUTION

(i) How to Amend the Constitution?

- Constitution of India is a combination of flexibility and Rigidity
- Constitution must be amended if so required, but it must be protected from unnecessary and frequent changes.
- Constitution to be 'flexible' and at the same time 'rigid'.
- Flexible means open to changes and rigid means resistant to changes.

Constitutional makers' thoughts of flexibility

- Aware that there may be some faults or mistakes in the Constitution
- Constitution could not be totally free of errors.
- Whenever such mistakes would come to light it can easily amended

Constitutional makers' thoughts on Rigidity

- Strong centre
- Constitution was framing a federal polity
- The rights and powers of the States could not be changed without the consent of the States.
- Tough process of amendment

Amending Article of the Constitution

1. By a simple law of the Parliament (Example : Article 2 and 3)
2. By applying provisions of Article 368
    - The procedure of amendment in the constitution is laid down in Part XX (Article 368) of the Constitution of India.
    - It was borrowed from the South African constitution

Article 368 of Part XX of Constitution of India provides for two types of amendments.

1. Amendment can be made by special majority of the two houses of the Parliament.
2. It requires special majority of the Parliament and consent of half of the State legislatures.

Types of Amendments:

1. Simple Majority
    - This refers to the majority of more than 50% of the members present and voting.
2. Special Majority
    - A bill is said to be passed, if it is supported by a majority of 2/3rd members present and voting supported by over 50% of the total strength of the House.

Special Majority of Parliament and Consent of States

- This type of majority is required when federal structures need to be amended
- Apart from special majority by both the houses of the parliament, it requires consent of half of the state legislature by a simple majority
- There is no time limit within which states should give their consent to the bill

Kesavananda Bharati judgment

- Parliament cannot amend those parts which are part of the 'Basic Structure' of the constitution.
- Article 368: "Parliament under Article 368 can amend any part of the Constitution including the Fundamental Rights but without affecting the 'basic structure' of the Constitution".

(ii) List of Some Important Amendments to the Indian Constitution

1st Amendment, 1950

Amend Articles/Schedules

- 15, 19, 85, 87, 174, 176, 341, 342, 372 and 376.
- Insert articles 31A and 31B
- Insert schedule 9.

Provisions

- Three more reasons for restricting freedom of speech and expression have been added: public order, friendly relations with foreign states, and incitement to an offence.
- It also made the restrictions 'reasonable' and, therefore, in nature, justiciable.
- Right to practice any profession or to carry on any trade or business as contained in Article 19 of the Constitution
- The Ninth Schedule along with Articles 31A and 31B were inserted in the Constitution to protect laws, such as the land reform and other laws, from being challenged in the courts on the ground of violation of fundamental rights.

7th Amendment, 1956

Amend articles/schedules

- 1, 3, 49, 80, 81, 82, 131, 153, 158, 168, 170, 171, 216, 217, 220, 222, 224, 230, 231 and 232.
- Insert articles 258A, 290A, 298, 350A, 350B, 371, 372A and 378A.
- Amend part 8.
- Amend schedules 1, 2, 4 and 7.

Provisions

- Reorganisation of states on linguistic lines
- Abolition of Class A, B, C, D states
- Introduction of Union territories.
- States reorganized into 14 states and 6 federal territories.
- Establishment of new High Courts, High Court Judges etc.

10th Amendment, 1961

Amend Article/Schedule

- Amend article 240.
- Amend schedule 1.

Provisions

- Incorporation of Dadra and Nagar Haveli as a Union Territory, consequent to acquisition from Portugal.

11th Amendment, 1961

- Amend articles 66 and 71.
- Proposed that election of President or Vice President could not be challenged on the ground of any vacancy in the appropriate electoral college.

12th Amendment, 1962

- Amend article 240 and Amend schedule 1
- Included Goa, Daman and Diu as a Union Territory and to amend Article 240 for the purpose.

13th Amendment, 1962

- Amend article 170.
- Insert new article 371A.
- Nagaland was formed with an agreement between Government of India and Naga People's Convention.

14th Amendment, 1962

- Amend articles 81 and 240.
- Insert article 239A.
- Amend schedules 1 and 4
- Pondicherry was included in the First Schedule as a Union Territory
- Creation of Legislature by Parliamentary law for Himachal Pradesh, Manipur, Tripura, Goa, Daman and Diu and Pondicherry

22nd Amendment, 1969

- Amend article 275.
- Insert articles 244A and 371B
- New autonomous state of Meghalaya with in the state of Assam.

24th Amendment, 1971

- Amend articles 13 and 368.
- Removed all doubts regarding the power of Parliament to amend the Constitution including the Fundamental Rights.
- Enable parliament to dilute fundamental rights through amendments to the constitution
- The President's assent to Constitutional Amendment Bill was made compulsory

25th Amendment Act, 1971

- Fundamental Right to Property was curtailed

26th Amendment Act 1971

- Amend article 366.
- Insert article 363A.
- Remove articles 291 and 362.
- Abolition of privy purse paid to former rulers of princely states which were incorporated into the Indian Republic.

31st Amendment, 1973

- Amend articles 81, 330 and 332.
- Increase size of Parliament from 525 to 545 seats.
- Reduced the upper limit for the representation of union territories from 25 members to 20.

35th Amendment, 1974

- Amend articles 80 and 81.
- Insert article 2A.
- Insert schedule 10.
- Conferred Sikkim the status of an associate State of Indian Union.

36th Amendment, 1975

- Amend articles 80 and 81.
- Insert article 371F.
- Amend schedules 1 and 4.
- Made Sikkim a full-fledged State of Indian Union and to include it in the First Schedule to the Constitution

40th Amendment Act, 1976

- Parliament was empowered to specify from time to time the limits of the territorial waters, the continental shelf, the exclusive economic zone (EEZ) and the maritime zones of India.

42nd Amendment, 1976

- Amend articles 31, 31C, 39, 55, 74, 77, 81, 82, 83, 100, 102, 103, 105, 118, 145, 150, 166, 170, 172, 189, 191, 192, 194, 208, 217, 225, 226, 227, 228, 311, 312, 330, 352, 353, 356, 357, 358, 359, 366, 368 and 371F.
- Insert articles 31D, 32A, 39A, 43A, 48A, 131A, 139A, 144A, 226A, 228A and 257A.
- Insert parts 4A and 14A.
- Amend schedule 7.
- Amendment passed during internal emergency
- Provides for curtailment of fundamental rights, imposes fundamental duties and changes to the basic structure of the constitution by making India a "Sovereign Socialist Secular Democratic Republic".

- The Supreme Court, in Minerva Mills v. Union of India, quashed the amendments to Articles 31C and 368 as it was in contravention with the basic structure of the Constitution.
- Ideals of socialism, secularism and the integrity of the nation were adopted
- Directive Principles were given precedence over Fundamental Rights
- Inserted a new chapter on the Fundamental Duties of citizens

44th Amendment, 1978

- Amend articles 19, 22, 30, 31A, 31C, 38, 71, 74, 77, 83, 103, 105, 123, 132, 133, 134, 139A, 150, 166, 172, 192, 194, 213, 217, 225, 226, 227, 239B, 329, 352, 356, 358, 359, 360 and 371F.
- Insert articles 134A and 361A.
- Remove articles 31, 257A and 329A.
- Amend part 12.
- Amend schedule 9.
- Amendment passed after revocation of internal emergency in the Country.
- Right to property from the list of fundamental rights and made it a legal right
- Provided armed rebellion· as one of the circumstances for declaration of emergency

52nd Amendment, 1985

- Amend articles 101, 102, 190 and 191.
- Insert schedule 10.
- Suitable provisions were made with respect to splits in and merger of political parties.
- Anti Defection Law - Provide disqualification of members from parliament and assembly in case of defection from one party to other.
- However, parts of the 10th Schedule to the Constitution of India was struck down by the Supreme Court in the case of KihotoHollohan v. Zachillhu 1992 SCR (1) 686, for being in contravention with Article 368 of the Constitution.

53rd Amendment, 1986

- Insert article 371G.
- Mostly revolved around the state of Mizoram.

55th Amendment, 1986

- Insert article 371H
- Conferred statehood on the Union Territory of Arunachal Pradesh

56th Amendment, 1987

- Insert article 371I.
- Union Territory of Daman and Diu and the formation of the state of Goa.

61st Amendment, 1989

- Amend article 326
- Reduction of the voting age from 21 to 18 years by amending Article 326

65th Amendment, 1989

- Amend article 338.
- National Commission for Scheduled Castes and Scheduled Tribes formed and its statutory powers specified in The Constitution.

66th Amendment, 1990

- Amend schedule 9
- Place land reform acts and amendments to these act under Schedule 9 of the constitution
- Andhra Pradesh, Bihar, Gujarat, Himachal Pradesh, Karnataka, Kerala, Madhya Pradesh, Maharashtra, Orissa, Rajasthan, Tamil Nadu, Uttar Pradesh, West Bengal and administration of the Union Territory of Puducherry were added to the Ninth Schedule
- Relating to land reforms and ceiling on agricultural land holdings)

69th Amendment, 1991

- Insert articles 239AA and 239AB.
- Union territory of Delhi was renamed as the National Capital Territory of Delhi

70th Amendment, 1992

- Amend articles 54 and 239AA.
- Included the elected members of the legislative assemblies of union territories (National Capital Territory of Delhi and Union Territory of Pondicherry)in the electoral college for the election of the President under Article 54 of the Constitution.

71st Amendment, 1992

- Amend schedule 8
- Included Konkani, Manipuri and Nepali languages in the Eighth Schedule to the Constitution.

73rd Amendment, 1993

- Insert part 9. Insert schedule 11.
- A new Part-IX and 11th Schedule were added in the Indian Constitution to recognize Panchayati Raj Institutions and provisions related to them
- Gave constitutional status to the Panchayati Raj Institutions

74th Amendment, 1993

- Insert part 9A, insert schedule 12, amend article 280.
- A new Part IX-A and 12th Schedule were added to the Indian Constitution
- Provisions for local administrative bodies in urban areas such as towns and cities were added.

86th Amendment, 2002

- Amend articles 45 and 51A.
- Insert article 21A.
- Article 21A deals with Right to Education that "the State shall provide free and compulsory education to all children of the age of six to fourteen years"

- A new Fundamental Duty under Article 51 A was added - "It shall be the duty of every citizen of India who is a parent or guardian to provide opportunities for education to his child or ward between the age of six and fourteen years"

87th Amendment, 2003

- Amend articles 81, 82, 170 and 330.
- 2001 national census population figures were to be used for state-wise distribution of parliamentary seats.

89th Amendment, 2003

- Amend article 338.
- Insert article 338A.
- The National Commission for Scheduled Castes and Scheduled Tribes was bifurcated into The National Commission for Scheduled Castes and The National Commission for Scheduled Tribes.

91st Amendment, 2003

- Amend articles 75 and 164.
- Insert article 361B.
- Amend schedule 10.
- Restricts the size of the Council of Ministers in the Union Government and in a State Government to fifteen percent of the total number of legislative members.

92st Amendment, 2003

- Amend schedule 8.
- Bodo, Dogri, Santali and Maithali were added as official languages to the 8th Schedule
- Total official languages were increased from 18 to 22

94th Amendment, 2006

- Amend article 164.
- To provide for a Minister of Tribal Welfare in newly created Jharkhand and Chhattisgarh States including Madhya Pradesh and Orissa.

97th Amendment, 2012

- Amend Art 19 and added Art 43B and Part IXB
- Co-operative Societies were granted constitutional status
- Right to form cooperative societies made a fundamental right (Article 19)
- A new Directive Principle of State Policy (Article 43-B) to promote cooperative societies
- A new part IX-B was added in the constitution for cooperative societies
- Added the words "or co-operative societies" after the word "or unions" in Article 19(l)(c) and insertion of article 43B i.e., Promotion of Co-operative Societies and added Part-IXB i.e., The Co-operative Societies.
- In July 2021 Supreme Court Struck Part of the amendment as it was not ratified by the states.

99th Amendment, 2012

- Insertion of new articles 124A, 124B and 124C. Amendments to Articles 127, 128, 217, 222, 224A, 231.
- Formation of a National Judicial Appointments Commission.
- The amendment was struck down by the Supreme Court on 16 October 2015.

100th Amendment, 2015

- Amendment of First Schedule to Constitution
- Exchange of certain enclave territories with Bangladesh and conferment of citizenship rights to residents of enclaves conseq uent to signing of Land Boundary Agreement (LBA) Treaty between India and Bangladesh.

101st Amendment, 2017

- Introduction of "The Goods and Services Tax (GST)" and provision of compensation to states for loss of revenue on account of introduction of goods and services tax. Addition of articles 246A, 269A, 279A. Deletion of Article 268A.
- Amendment of articles 248, 249, 250, 268, 269, 270, 271, 286, 366, 368, Sixth Schedule, Seventh Schedule.

102nd Amendment, 2018

- Constitutional status to National Commission for Backward Classes.
- Addition of articles 338B, 342A, and Added Clause 26C. Modification of articles 338, 366

103rd Amendment, 2019

- A maximum of 10% Reservation for Economically Weaker Sections (EWSs) of citizens of classes other than the classes mentioned in clauses (4) and (5) of Article 15, i.e. Classes other than socially and educationally backward classes of citizens or the Scheduled Castes and the Scheduled Tribes.
- Inserted Clause [6] under Article 15 as well as Inserted Clause [6] under Article 16.

104th Amendment, 2020

- To extend the reservation of seats for SCs and STs in the Lok Sabha and states assemblies from Seventy years to Eighty years. Removed the reserved seats for the Anglo-Indian community in the Lok Sabha and state assemblies.
- Amend article 334.

105th Amendment, 2021

- Amended Article 338B, 342A and 366
- To designed to clarify that the states can maintain the "state list" of OBCs.
- To restore the power of the state governments to identify Other Backward Classes (OBCs) that are socially and educationally backward.
- This amendment annulled the Supreme Court judgement of 11 May 2021, which had empowered only the Central government for such identification

APPENDIX-II

A GLIMPSE OF LANDMARK SUPREME COURTJUDGEMENTS IN INDIA

CASE RELATED TO PREAMBLE

In Re: Berubari : It was held that the Preamble is not part of the Constitution. This Judgment was overruled by the 12-judge Bench in the Kesavananda Bharati case, and it was held that the "Preamble is a part of the Indian Constitution"

CASES RELATED TO FUNDAMENTAL RIGHTS

1. **Chanpakam Dorairajan V State of Madras :** The verdict of this case led to the first amendmen[1]t of the constitution. The Supreme Court had struck down the Communal Government Order, which provided Caste based reservation in the Government Jobs and Colleges. The Supreme Court has held that the order violates Article 16 (2) of the Constitution. This case not only protected and defended the Fundamental Rights but also at the same time the Parliament of India reacted to the judgment of the case and thought of amending and modifying the laws which were in conflict with DPSPs. This case led to the First Amendment in the Constitution of India.
2. **Indra Sawhney etc. Vs. Union of India and others :** The apex court examined the scope of Article 16(4) of the Constitution which provides for the reservation of jobs in favour backward classes and held that 'backward classes' mentioned in Article 16(4) can be identified only on the basis of caste and not economic conditions. It upheld the constitutional validity of 27% reservation for the OBCs with certain conditions. The propositions of 50% threshold in reservations, the bar against reservations in certain types of posts and the exclusion of 'creamy layer' were propounded in this case.
3. **M. Nagaraj v. Union of India :** The Court validated Parliament's decision to extend reservations for SC/STs to include promotions (reservation in promotion). However, the Nagaraj judgement laid down three controlling conditions that the State must meet prior to granting a SC/ST a reservation in promotion. First, the State must show the backwardness of the class. Second, it must show that the class is inadequately represented in the position/service for which reservations in promotion will be granted. Finally, it must show that the reservations are in the interest of administrative efficiency.
4. **Janhit Abhiyan v. Union Of India :** The Supreme Court upheld the 103rd Constitutional Amendment providing EWS reservation. With this, the Court extended the net of reservation benefits to include solely economic backwardness.
5. **Shreya Shinghal v. Union of India :** The Supreme Court struck down Section 66A of the Information Technology Act (IT Act) which violated freedom of speech and expression, declaring it to be unconstitutional.

---

[1]The First Constitutional Amendment Act, 1951 was enacted to add Clause 4 to Article 15. Article 15(4) was introduced by the Constitution. So, to enable the state to make any special provisions for the improvement of backward classes.

6. **A.K.Gopalan VS. State of Madras :** The petitioner, detained under the Preventive Detention Act challenged the legality of detention under Art. 32 of the Constitution on the ground that the said Act contravened Arts. 13, 19, 21 and 22 of the Constitution and was, therefore, ultra vires. The S.C. held that Article 22 was a self-contained Code and if personal liberty is taken away by the State in accordance with the procedure established by law i.e. if the detention was as per the procedure established by law, then it cannot be said that the law was violative of provisions contained in Articles 14, 19 and 21 of the Constitution.

7. **Maneka Gandhi v. Union of India :** The view expressed in A. K. Gopalan's case was revisited after about 28 years. The main issues were whether the right to go abroad is a part of the right to personal liberty under Article 21 and whether the Passport Act prescribes a 'procedure' as required by Article 21 of the Constitution. The SC held that the right to go abroad is a part of the right to personal liberty under Article 21. The SC also ruled that the mere existence of an enabling law was not enough to restrain personal liberty. "The procedure prescribed by law has to be fair, just and reasonable, not fanciful, oppressive or arbitrary."

8. **ADM Jabalpur v. Shivakant Shukla (Life & Personal Liberty) :** A Constitution Bench by a majority of 4:1, ruled that while proclamation of emergency is in operation, the right to move High Courts under Article 226 for Habeas Corpus challenging illegal detention by State will stand suspended. The apex Court said "......If extraordinary powers are given, they are given because the Emergency is extraordinary, and are limited to the period of the Emergency."

   The judgment is more recognised for the dissenting opinion of Justice HR Khanna in which he said "*detention without trial is an anathema to all those who love personal liberty... A dissent is an appeal to the brooding spirit of the law, to the intelligence of a future day, when a later decision may possibly correct the error into which the dissenting Judge believes the court to have been betrayed*".

9. **K.S. Puttaswamy (retd.) Vs. Union of India & others (ADM Jabalpur v. Shivkant Shukla Overruled) :** The apex court overruling the majority view expressed in ADM Jabalpur v. Shivkant Shukla held that.. "The view taken by Justice Khanna must be accepted, and accepted in reverence for the strength of its thoughts and the courage of its convictions ...". The Supreme Court held that the privacy is to be an integral component of Part III of the Indian Constitution, which lays down the fundamental rights of the citizens. The Supreme Court also stated that the state must carefully balance the individual privacy and the legitimate aim, at any cost as fundamental rights cannot be given or taken away by law, and all laws and acts must abide by the constitution. The Court also declared that the right to privacy is not an absolute right and any invasion of privacy by state or non-state actor must satisfy the triple test i.e.

   A. Legitimate Aim

   B. Proportionality

   C. Legality

10. **Hussainara Khatoon v. Home Secretary :** The apex observed that although the right to have a speedy trial is not explicitly mentioned as a fundamental right in the Indian Constitution, yet it is implicit in the broad sweep and content of Article 21. Further, the court also pointed out that Article 39A emphasized that free legal services were an inalienable element of reasonable, fair, and just procedure and that the right to free legal services was implicit in Article 21.

11. **Rajagopal v. State of Tamil Nadu :** The right to life as well as liberty guaranteed under Article 21 of our Constitution includes the right to privacy. It is a right to be left alone.

12. **Sheela Barse v. Union of India :** The Court held that the right to legal aid is a Fundamental Right under Article 14 and Article 21 of the Constitution.

AMENDABILITY OF FUNDAMENTAL RIGHTS

1. **Shankari Prasad v. Union of India :** This case dealt with the amendability of Fundamental Rights (the First Amendment's validity was challenged). Th Supreme Court held that the power conferred on Parliament by Art. 368 to amend is a very wide power and include the power to take away the fundamental rights guaranteed by Part III, & that in the context of Art. 13(@) "law" must be taken to mean rules or regulations made in exercise of ordinary legislative power and not amendments to the constitution made in the exercise of constituent power with the result that Art.13(2) does not affect amendments made under Art.368. This view reiterated in ***Sajjan Singh Vs. State of Rajasthan.***

2. **I.C. Golak Nath Vs. State of Punjab :** Overruling Sajjan Supreme Court Singh held that by a majority of six to five the amendment under Article 368 is "law" within the meaning of Article 13(2). It further ruled that Legislature does not enjoy the power to amend Part III of the Constitution to take away or abridge fundamental rights .

3. **His Holiness Kesavananda Bharati Sripadagalvaru v. State of Kerala (Doctrine of Basic Structure) :** Supreme Court held that Constitutional amendment is not "law" within the meaning of Article 13 and that although no part of the Constitution, including Part III comprising of fundamental rights, was beyond the Parliament's amending power, the "basic structure of the Constitution" could not be abrogated even by a constitutional amendment.

4. **Indira Nehru Gandhi Vs. Raj Narain :** The validity of 39th Constitution amendment enacted in 1975 which (Article 39A) sought to place the election of the President, the Vice President, the Prime Minister and the Speaker of the Lok Sabha beyond the scrutiny of the constitutional courts was challenged in this case. The S.C. resorting to the theory of basic structure of the Constitution struck down Clause (4) of Article 329A on the grounds that it was beyond the Parliament's amending power as it destroyed the basic structure of the Constitution.

5. **Minerva Mills Vs. UOI :** Validity of Constitution (42nd ,which inter alia provided Amendment) Act , 1976 for exclusion of judicial review of constitutional amendments and expressly conferred unlimited amendment power to the Parliament, challenged on the ground that they are 'basic structure' of the Constitution. The Court ruled that Parliament's power to make Constitutional amendments is limited which itself is a basic feature of the Constitution. The judgement makes it clear that the Constitution, and not the Parliament is supreme.

6. **IR Coelho's Case :** The supremacy of the Constitution mandates all constitutional bodies to comply with the provisions of the Constitution. Judicial Review is a mechanism for testing the validity of legislative acts through an independent organ, viz. the judiciary is part of basic structure. The Court held that any law inserted in the Ninth Schedule on or after Keshavananda April 24, 1973 (date on which was pronounced) can be subject to judicial review and will be struck down if it violates the basic structure doctrine.

RELATION BETWEEN FUNDAMENTAL RIGHTS & DIRECTIVE PRINCIPLES OF STATE POLICY

Minerva Mill v. Union of India : The Supreme Court held the "Harmony and balance between fundamental rights and directive principle is an essential feature of the basic structure of the constitution". The court also invalidated the provision of 42nd Amendment which under Article 31-C gave pre-eminence to all the directive principles against some of the fundamental rights. Court also held that the social welfare law cannot curtail the fundamental rights.

PUBLIC INTEREST LITIGATION

1. **Mumbai Kamgar Sabha :** This case is considered to be the foundation of public interest litigation in India. In this case Justice V.R. Krishna Iyer speaking for the Court held that "Procedural prescriptions are handmaids, not mistresses, of justice.... Our adjectival branch of jurisprudence, by and large, deals not with sophisticated litigants but the rural poor, the urban lay and the weaker societal segments for whom law will be an added terror.
2. **Sunil Batra v. Delhi Administration & Others :** A landmark decision on prison reforms, in this case the apex Court held that a convict is entitled to the precious right guaranteed by Art. 21 that he shall not be deprived of his life or personal liberty except according to the procedure established by law. The Court ruled that fundamental rights do not flee the person as he enters the prison although they may suffer shrinkage necessitated by incarceration.
3. **Bandhua Mukti Morcha v. Union of India :** In a matter concerning release of bonded labour raised by way of PIL the Supreme Court issued direction for their release.

CASES RELATED TO HUMAN RIGHTS

1. **Common Cause (A Regd. Society) vs. Union :** In 2018 the Supreme Court recognised the right to die with dignity as a fundamental right and prescribed guidelines for terminally ill patients to enforce the right. In 2023 the Supreme Court modified the guidelines to make the right to die with dignity more accessible.
2. **National Legal Services Authority vsUnion Of India & Ors. :** Gender identity is integral to the dignity of an individual and is at the core of "personal autonomy" and "self-determination" and Article 14, 19 and 21 of the Constitution within their sweep include transgender and are not as such limited to male or female gender. Eunuchs, therefore, have to be considered as Third Gender, over and above binary genders under our Constitution and the laws. The apex Court directed the Centre and the State Governments to take steps to treat them as socially and educationally backward classes of citizens and extend all kinds of reservation in cases of admission in education institutions and for public appointments.
3. **Navtej Singh Johar Vs, Union of India :** (decriminalized homosexuality) – The Supreme Court ruled that sexual orientation is an intrinsic element of liberty, dignity, privacy, individual autonomy and equality and that intimacy between consenting adults of the same-sex is beyond the legitimate interests of the state. Section 377 was the product of the Victorian era, with its attendant moral values. Victorian morality must give way to constitutional morality. That insofar as Section 377 criminalises consensual sexual acts of adults in private, is violative of Articles 14, 15, 19 and 21 of the Constitution.

GENDER JUSTICE

1. **Vishaka Vs. State of Rajasthan :** The apex Court issued guidelines that defined sexual harassment at workplace and put the onus on the employers as well as other responsible persons or institutions to provide a safe working environment for women. These guidelines are called 'Vishaka Guidelines'. These were to be considered law until appropriate legislation was enacted.
2. **Shayara Bano vs Union of India And Ors. :** Instant triple talaq is manifestly arbitrary in the sense that the marital tie can be broken capriciously and whimsically by a Muslim man without any attempt at reconciliation so as to save it. This form of Talaq must, therefore, be held to be violative of the fundamental right contained under Article 14 of the Constitution of India.

3. **Joseph Shine vs. Union Of India :** The apex Court struck down Section 497 of IPC which criminalised adultery holding that it is violative of Articles 14, 15 and 21 of the Constitution. The Supreme Court called the law unconstitutional because it "treats a husband as the master". The Court held - "Any provision of law affecting individual dignity and equality of women invites the wrath of the Constitution. It's time to say that the husband is not the master of the wife. Legal sovereignty of one sex over other sex is wrong".

CASES RELATED TO EMERGENCY & CONSTITUTIONAL DEMOCRACY

1. **S. R. In Bommai v. Union of India :** In this judgement, the SC attempted to curb the blatant misuse of Article 356 of the Constitution of India, which allowed President's rule to be imposed in States. The first and most important question which the Supreme Court had to determine was whether the Presidential Proclamation under Article 356 was justifiable and if so to what extent. Answering the question the apex Court held, the Judicial Review will involve three questions only:
   - Is there any material behind the proclamation?
   - Is the material relevant?
   - Was there any mala fide use of power?

   The majority enjoyed by the Council of Ministers shall be tested on the floor of the House. The Court also held that "Secularism" was part of the Indian Constitution before the word "Secular" was added in the preamble. The Court also declared "secularism" as the part of basic structure of the constitution. The Court also declared that "Preamble indicates the basic structure of the constitution".
2. **NOTA CASE :** The Supreme Court dealing with the issue of election reforms held that democracy and free elections are part of the basic structure of the Constitution. In a parliamentary democracy a positive 'right not to vote' is a part of voter's right to expression under Article 19(1)(a) and it has to be recognized and given effect to in the same manner as 'right to vote'. The only way by which it can be made effectual is by providing a button in the EVMs to express that right. Therefore, the voter must be given an opportunity to choose none of the above (NOTA) button, which will indeed compel the political parties to nominate a sound candidate.
3. **Lily Thomas Vs. Union of India :** In this case the Supreme Court in a PIL declared sub-section(4) of Section 8 of the Representation of the People Act, 1951, which allowed convicted members of legislative bodies a 3 month time period for appeal against the conviction and sentencing, as ultra vires the Constitution. The Court ruled that Members of Parliament, Legislative Councils and Legislative Assemblies convicted of crimes where they had been awarded a minimum sentence of 2 years imprisonment would cease to be members of the house to which they are elected from the date of sentencing.

INDEPENDENCE OF JUDICIARY

1. **S.P. Gupta Vs. Union of India & Ors (First Judges Case) :** The apex court held by that the word "consultation" in Article 124(2) and in Article 217(1) of the Constitution does not mean "concurrence" however the "consultation" with the CJI must be full and effective. The apex court rejected the idea that the CJI's opinion should have primacy and held that in the event of a disagreement, the "ultimate power" would rest with the Union Government and not the CJI.

2. **Supreme Court Advocates on Record Association Vs. Union of India (Second Judge's Case) :** This verdict gave birth to the concept of Collegium System. The Court held that there should be a collegium consisting of Chief Justice and two other senior most judges of the Supreme Court for making proposal and appointment of judges. The apex Court held that in the event of conflict between the President and the CJI with regard to appointments of Judges, it was the Chief Justice of India whose opinion would not only have primacy, but would be determinative in the matter.

3. **In Re Special Reference Case (Third Judge's case) :** The only thing that this reference introduced from the Second Judges case was to increase the number of the judges in the collegium. The collegium was now to consist of the CJI and the four other senior most judges of the Supreme Court.

4. **Supreme Court Advocates-on- Record Association Vs. Union of India :** Struck down the Ninety-ninth Constitutional Amendment Act and the NJAC Act as unconstitutional holding that the constitution of the Commission will amount to an infringement of judicial independence and a violation of the separation of powers.

Cases related to Anti-defection law

1. **Kihoto Hollohan vs Zachillhu and Others :** It was held that the decision of the Chairman and the Speaker regarding the disqualification of the members was to be considered valid but subject to judicial reviews of the court. Thus, this case implicitly provided that the decisions of the Speaker of the house were legal and binding but were questionable before the courts.'

2. **G. Vishwanathan v. Speaker, Tamil Nadu Legislative Assembly case :** Members who have publicly expressed opposition to their party or support for another party were deemed to have resigned.

3. **Ravi S Naik v. Union of India :** In the absence of a formal resignation by the member, the giving up of membership can be inferred by his conduct.

Cases related to Environmental Protection

1. **MC Mehta v. Union of India :** The Supreme Court evolved the concept of "Absolute Liability". The Court held that "where an enterprise is engaged in a hazardous or inherently dangerous activity and harm results to anyone on account of an accident in the operation of such hazardous or inherently dangerous activity resulting, for example, in escape of toxic gas the enterprise is strictly and absolutely liable to compensate all those who are affected by the accident.

2. **M.C. Mehta v. Kamal Nath :** The concept of Public Trust Doctrine was laid down. The state is the trustee of all the natural resources, which are meant by nature for public use and enjoyment. These resources cannot be converted into private property. The State being the trustee of natural resources is under the legal obligation to protect such natural resources.

APPENDIX-III

LIST OF ARTICLES

PART I : THE UNION AND ITS TERRITORY

Article 1 - Name and territory of the Union.

Article 2 - Admission or establishment of new States.

Article 2A [Repealed.]

Article 3 - Formation of new States and alteration of areas, boundaries or names of existing States.

Article 4 - Laws made under articles 2 and 3 to provide for the amendment of the First and the Fourth Schedules and supplemental, incidental and consequential matters.

PART II : CITIZENSHIP

Article 5 - Citizenship at the commencement of the Constitution.

Article 6 - Rights of citizenship of certain persons who have migrated to India from Pakistan.

Article 7 - Rights of citizenship of certain migrants to Pakistan.

Article 8 - Rights of citizenship of certain persons of Indian origin residing outside India.

Article 9 - Persons voluntarily acquiring citizenship of a foreign State not to be citizens.

Article 10 - Continuance of the rights of citizenship.

Article 11 - Parliament to regulate the right of citizenship by law.

PART III : FUNDAMENTAL RIGHTS

Article 12 - Definition.

Article 13 - Laws inconsistent with or in derogation of the fundamental rights.

Article 14 - Equality before law.

Article 15 - Prohibition of discrimination on grounds of religion, race, caste, sex or place of birth.

Article 16 - Equality of opportunity in matters of public employment.

Article 17 - Abolition of Untouchability.

Article 18 - Abolition of titles.

Article 19 - Protection of certain rights regarding freedom of speech, etc.

Article 20 - Protection in respect of conviction for offences.

Article 21 - Protection of life and personal liberty.

Article 21A - Right to education

Article 22 - Protection against arrest and detention in certain cases.

Article 23 - Prohibition of traffic in human beings and forced labour.

Article 24 - Prohibition of employment of children in factories, etc.

Article 25 - Freedom of conscience and free profession, practice and propagation of religion.

Article 26 - Freedom to manage religious affairs.

Article 27 - Freedom as to payment of taxes for promotion of any particular religion.

Article 28 - Freedom as to attendance at religious instruction or religious worship in certain educational institutions.

Article 29 - Protection of interests of minorities.

Article 30 - Right of minorities to establish and administer educational institutions.

Article 31 [Repealed.]

Article 31A - Saving of Laws providing for the acquisition of estates, etc.

Article 31B - Validation of certain Acts and Regulations.

Article 31C - Saving of laws giving effect to certain directive principles.

Article 31D [Repealed.]

Article 32 - Remedies for enforcement of rights conferred by this Part.

Article 32A [Repealed.]

Article 33 - Power of Parliament to modify the rights conferred by this Part in their application to Forces, etc.

Article 34 - Restriction on rights conferred by this Part while martial law is in force in any area.

Article 35 - Legislation to give effect to the provisions of this Part.

PART IV : DIRECTIVE PRINCIPLES OF STATE POLICY

Article 36 - Definition.

Article 37 - Application of the principles contained in this Part.

Article 38 - State to secure a social order for the promotion of the welfare of the people.

Article 39 - Certain principles of policy to be followed by the State.

Article 39A - Equal justice and free legal aid.

Article 40 - The organisation of village panchayats.

Article 41 - Right to work, to education and to public assistance in certain cases.

Article 42 - Provision for just and humane conditions of work and maternity relief.

Article 43 - Living wage, etc., for workers.

Article 43A - Participation of workers in the management of industries.

Article 43B - Promotion of co-operative societies.

Article 44 - Uniform civil code for the citizens.

Article 45 - Provision for free and compulsory education for children.

Article 46 - Promotion of educational and economic interests of Scheduled Castes, Scheduled Tribes and other weaker sections.

Article 47 - Duty of the State to raise the level of nutrition and the standard of living and to improve public health.

Article 48 - The organisation of agriculture and animal husbandry.

Article 48A - Protection and improvement of environment and safeguarding of forests and wildlife.

Article 49 - Protection of monuments and places and objects of national importance.

Article 50 - Separation of judiciary from the executive.

Article 51 - Promotion of international peace and security.

PART IVA : FUNDAMENTAL DUTIES

51A Fundamental duties.

PART V : THE UNION

Chapter I: The Executive

The President and Vice-President

Article 52 - The President of India.

Article 53 - The executive power of the Union.

Article 54 - Election of President.

Article 55 - Manner of election of President.

Article 56 - Term of office of President.

Article 57 - Eligibility for re-election.

Article 58 - Qualifications for election as President.

Article 59 - Conditions of the President's office.

Article 60 - Oath or affirmation by the President.

Article 61 - Procedure for impeachment of the President.

Article 62 - Time of holding the election to fill the vacancy in the office of President and the term of office of person elected to fill the casual vacancy.

Article 63 - The Vice-President of India.

Article 64 - The Vice-President to be ex officio Chairman of the Council of States.

Article 65 - The Vice-President to act as President or to discharge his functions during casual vacancies in the office, or during the absence, of President.

Article 66 - Election of Vice-President.

Article 67 - Term of office of Vice-President.

Article 68 - Time of holding the election to fill the vacancy in the office of Vice-President and the term of office of person elected to fill the casual vacancy.

Article 69 - Oath or affirmation by the Vice-President.

Article 70 - Discharge of President's functions in other contingencies.

Article 71 - Matters relating to, or connected with, the election of a President or Vice-President.

Article 72 - Power of President to grant pardons, etc., and to suspend, remit or commute sentences in certain cases.

Article 73 - The extent of executive power of the Union.

Council of Ministers

Article 74 - Council of Ministers to aid and advise the President.

Article 75 - Other provisions as to Ministers.

The Attorney-General for India

Article 76 - Attorney-General for India.

Conduct of Government Business

Article 77 - Conduct of business of the Government of India.

Article 78 - Duties of Prime Minister as respects the furnishing of information to the President, etc.

Chapter II : Parliament

General

Article 79 - Constitution of Parliament.

Article 80 - Composition of the Council of States.

Article 81 - Composition of the House of the People.

Article 82 - Readjustment after each census.

Article 83 - Duration of Houses of Parliament.

Article 84 - Qualification for membership of Parliament.

Article 85 - Sessions of Parliament, prorogation and dissolution.

Article 86 - Right of President to address and send messages to Houses.

Article 87 - Special address by the President.

Article 88 - Rights of Ministers and Attorney-General as respects Houses.

Officers of Parliament

Article 89 - The Chairman and Deputy Chairman of the Council of States.

Article 90 - Vacation and resignation of, and removal from, the office of Deputy Chairman.

Article 91 - Power of the Deputy Chairman or other person to perform the duties of the office of, or to act as, Chairman.

Article 92 - The Chairman or the Deputy Chairman not to preside while a resolution for his removal from office is under consideration.

Article 93 - The Speaker and Deputy Speaker of the House of the People.

Article 94 - Vacation and resignation of, and removal from, the offices of Speaker and Deputy Speaker.

Article 95 - Power of the Deputy Speaker or other person to perform the duties of the office of, or to act as, Speaker.

Article 96 - The Speaker or the Deputy Speaker not to preside while a resolution for his removal from office is under consideration.

Article 97 - Salaries and allowances of the Chairman and Deputy Chairman and the Speaker and Deputy Speaker.

Article 98 - Secretariat of Parliament.

Conduct of Business

Article 99 - Oath or affirmation by members.

Article 100 - Voting in Houses, power of Houses to act notwithstanding vacancies and quorum.

Disqualifications of Members

Article 101 - Vacation of seats.

Article 102 - Disqualifications for membership.

Article 103 - Decision on questions as to disqualifications of members.

Article 104 - Penalty for sitting and voting before making oath or affirmation under article 99 or when not qualified or when disqualified.

Powers, Privileges and Immunities of Parliament and its Members

Article 105 - Powers, privileges, etc., of the Houses of Parliament and of the members and committees thereof.

Article 106 - Salaries and allowances of members.

Legislative Procedure

Article 107 - Provisions as to introduction and passing of Bills.

Article 108 - Joint sitting of both Houses in certain cases.

Article 109 - Special procedure in respect of Money Bills.

Article 110 - Definition of "Money Bills".

Article 111 - Assent to Bills.

Procedure in Financial Matters

Article 112 - Annual financial statement.

Article 113 - Procedure in Parliament with respect to estimates.

Article 114 - Appropriation Bills.

Article 115 - Supplementary, additional or excess grants.

Article 116 - Votes on account, votes of credit and exceptional grants.

Article 117 - Special provisions as to financial Bills.

Procedure Generally

Article 118 - Rules of procedure.

Article 119 - Regulation by law of procedure in Parliament in relation to financial business.

Article 120 - Language to be used in Parliament.

Article 121 - Restriction on discussion in Parliament.

Article 122 - Courts not to inquire into proceedings of Parliament.

Chapter III : Legislative Powers of the President

Article 123 - Power of President to promulgate Ordinances during recess of Parliament.

Chapter IV : The Union Judiciary

Article 124 - Establishment and constitution of Supreme Court.

Article 124A - National Judicial Appointments Commission. (Declared unconstitutional by the Supreme Court, however not repealed by the Parliament)

Article 124B - Functions of Commission.

Article 124C - Power of Parliament to make law.

Article 125 - Salaries, etc., of Judges.

Article 126 - Appointment of acting Chief Justice.

Article 127 - Appointment of ad hoc judges.

Article 128 - Attendance of retired Judges at sittings of the Supreme Court.

Article 129 - Supreme Court to be a court of record.

Article 130 - Seat of Supreme Court.

Article 131 - Original jurisdiction of the Supreme Court.

Article 131A [Repealed.]

Article 132 - Appellate jurisdiction of Supreme Court in appeals from High Courts in certain cases.

Article 133 - Appellate jurisdiction of Supreme Court in appeals from High Courts in regard to Civil matters.

Article 134 - Appellate jurisdiction of Supreme Court in regard to criminal matters.

Article 134A - Certificate for appeal to the Supreme Court.

Article 135 - Jurisdiction and powers of the Federal Court under existing law to be exercisable by the Supreme Court.

Article 136 - Special leave to appeal by the Supreme Court.

Article 137 - Review of judgments or orders by the Supreme Court.

Article 138 - Enlargement of the jurisdiction of the Supreme Court.

Article 139 - Conferment on the Supreme Court of powers to issue certain writs.

Article 139A - Transfer of certain cases.

Article 140 - Ancillary powers of Supreme Court.

Article 141 - Law declared by Supreme Court to be binding on all courts.

Article 142 - Enforcement of decrees and orders of Supreme Court and orders as to discovery, etc.

Article 143 - of President to consult Supreme Court.

Article 144 - Civil and judicial authorities to act in aid of the Supreme Court.

Article 144A [Repealed.]

Article 145 - Rules of Court, etc.

Article 146 - Officers and servants and the expenses of the Supreme Court.

Article 147 - Interpretation.

Chapter V : Comptroller and Auditor-General of India

Article 148 - Comptroller and Auditor-General of India.

Article 149 - Duties and powers of the Comptroller and Auditor-General.

Article 150 - Form of accounts of the Union and of the States.

Article 151 - Audit reports.

PART VI: THE STATES

Chapter I : General

Article 152 - Definition.

Chapter II : The Executive

The Governor

Article 153 - Governors of States.

Article 154 Executive power of State.

Article 155 - Appointment of Governor.

Article 156 - Term of office of Governor.

Article 157 - Qualifications for appointment as Governor.

Article 158 - Conditions of Governor's office

Article 159 - Oath or affirmation by the Governor.

Article 160 - Discharge of the functions of the Governor in certain contingencies.

Article 161 - Power of Governor to grant pardons, etc., and to suspend, remit or commute sentences in certain cases.

Article 162 - Extent of executive power of State.

Council of Ministers

Article 163 - Council of Ministers to aid and advise Governor.

Article 164 - Other provisions as to Ministers.

The Advocate-General for the State

Article 165 - Advocate-General for the State.

Conduct of Government Business

Article 166 - Conduct of business of the Government of a State.

Article 167 - Duties of Chief Minister as respects the furnishing of information to Governor, etc.

Chapter III : The State Legislature

General

Article 168 - Constitution of Legislatures in States.

Article 169 - Abolition or creation of Legislative Councils in States.

Article 170 - Composition of the Legislative Assemblies.

Article 171 - Composition of the Legislative Councils.

Article 172 - Duration of State Legislatures.

Article 173 - Qualification for membership of the State Legislature.

Article 174 - Sessions of the State Legislature, prorogation and dissolution.

Article 175 - Right of Governor to address and send messages to the House or Houses.

Article 176 - Special address by the Governor.

Article 177 - Rights of Ministers and Advocate-General as respects the Houses.

Officers of the State Legislature

Article 178 - The Speaker and Deputy Speaker of the Legislative Assembly.

Article 179 - Vacation and resignation of, and removal from, the offices of Speaker and Deputy Speaker.

Article 180 - Power of the Deputy Speaker or other person to perform the duties of the office of, or to act as, Speaker.

Article 181 - The Speaker or the Deputy Speaker not to preside while a resolution for his removal from office is under consideration.

Article 182 - The Chairman and Deputy Chairman of the Legislative Council.

Article 183 - Vacation and resignation of, and removal from, the offices of Chairman and Deputy Chairman.

Article 184 - Power of the Deputy Chairman or other person to perform the duties of the office of, or to act as, Chairman.

Article 185 - The Chairman or the Deputy Chairman not to preside while a resolution for his removal from office is under consideration.

Article 186 - Salaries and allowances of the Speaker and Deputy Speaker and the Chairman and Deputy Chairman.

Article 187 - Secretariat of State Legislature.

Conduct of Business

Article 188 - Oath or affirmation by members.

Article 189 - Voting in Houses, power of Houses to act notwithstanding vacancies and quorum.

Disqualifications of Members

Article 190 - Vacation of seats.

Article 191 - Disqualifications for membership.

Article 192 - Decision on questions as to disqualifications of members.

Article 193 - Penalty for sitting and voting before making oath or affirmation under article 188 or when not qualified or when disqualified.

Powers, privileges and immunities of State Legislatures and their Members

Article 194 - Powers, privileges, etc., of the Houses of Legislatures and of the members and committees thereof.

Article 195 - Salaries and allowances of members.

Legislative Procedure

Article 196 - Provisions as to introduction and passing of Bills.

Article 197 - Restriction on powers of Legislative Council as to Bills other than Money Bills.

Article 198 - Special procedure in respect of Money Bills.

Article 199 - Definition of "Money Bills".

Article 200 - Assent to Bills.

Article 201 - Bills reserved for consideration.

Procedure in Financial Matters

Article 202 - Annual financial statement.

Article 203 - Procedure in Legislature with respect to estimates.

Article 204 - Appropriation Bills.

Article 205 - Supplementary, additional or excess grants.

Article 206 - Votes on account, votes of credit and exceptional grants.

Article 207 - Special provisions as to financial Bills.

Procedure Generally

Article 208 - Rules of procedure.

Article 209 - Regulation by law of procedure in the Legislature of the State in relation to financial business.

Article 210 - Language to be used in the Legislature.

Article 211 - Restriction on discussion in the Legislature.

Article 212 - Courts not to inquire into proceedings of the Legislature.

Chapter IV : Legislative Power of The Governor

Article 213 - Power of Governor to promulgate Ordinances during recess of Legislature.

Chapter V : The High Courts in The States

Article 214 - High Courts for States.

Article 215 - High Courts to be courts of record.

Article 216 - Constitution of High Courts.

Article 217 - Appointment and conditions of the office of a Judge of a High Court.

Article 218 - Application of certain provisions relating to Supreme Court to High Courts.

Article 219 - Oath or affirmation by Judges of High Courts.

Article 220 - Restriction on practice after being a permanent Judge.

Article 221 - Salaries, etc., of Judges.

Article 222 - Transfer of a Judge from one High Court to another.

Article 223 - Appointment of acting Chief Justice.

Article 224 - Appointment of additional and acting Judges.

Article 224A - Appointment of retired Judges at sittings of High Courts.

Article 225 - Jurisdiction of existing High Courts.

Article 226 - Power of High Courts to issue certain writs.

Article 226A [Repealed..]

Article 227 - Power of superintendence over all courts by the High Court.

Article 228 - Transfer of certain cases to High Court.

Article 228A [Repealed.]

Article 229 - Officers and servants and the expenses of High Courts.

Article 230 - Extension of jurisdiction of High Courts to Union territories.

Article 231 - Establishment of a common High Court for two or more States.

Chapter VI : Subordinate Courts

Article 233 - Appointment of district judges.

Article 233A - Validation of appointments of, and judgments, etc., delivered by, certain district judges.

Article 234 - Recruitment of persons other than district judges to the judicial service.

Article 235 - Control over subordinate courts.

Article 236 - Interpretation.

Article 237 - Application of the provisions of this Chapter to certain class or classes of magistrates.

PART VII : THE STATES IN PART B OF THE FIRST SCHEDULE

Article 238 [Repealed.]

PART VIII : THE UNION TERRITORIES

Article 239 - Administration of Union territories.

Article 239A - Creation of local Legislatures or Council of Ministers or both for certain Union territories.

Article 239AA - Special provisions with respect to Delhi.

Article 239AB - Provision in case of failure of constitutional machinery.

Article 239B - Power of the administrator to promulgate Ordinances during recess of Legislature.

Article 240 - Power of President to make regulations for certain Union territories.

Article 241 - High Courts for Union territories.

Article 242 [Repealed.]

PART IX : THE PANCHAYATS

Article 243 - Definitions.

Article 243A - Gram Sabha.

Article 243B - Constitution of Panchayats.

Article 243C - Composition of Panchayats.

Article 243D - Reservation of seats.

Article 243E - Duration of Panchayats, etc.

Article 243F - Disqualifications for membership.

Article 243G - Powers, authority and responsibilities of Panchayats.

Article 243H - Powers to impose taxes by, and Funds of, the Panchayats.

Article 243-I - Constitution of Finance Commission to review financial position.

Article 243J - Audit of accounts of Panchayats.

Article 243K - Elections to the Panchayats.

Article 243L - Application to Union territories.

Article 243M - Part not to apply to certain areas.

Article 243N - Continuance of existing laws and Panchayats.

Article 243-O - Bar to interference by courts in electoral matters.

PART IXA : THE MUNICIPALITIES

Article 243P - Definitions.

Article 243Q - Constitution of Municipalities.

Article 243R - Composition of Municipalities.

Article 243S -Constitution and composition of Wards Committees, etc.

Article 243T - Reservation of seats.

Article 243U - Duration of Municipalities, etc.

Article 243V - Disqualifications for membership.

Article 243W - Powers, authority and responsibilities of Municipalities, etc.

Article 243X - Power to impose taxes by, and Funds of, the Municipalities.

Article 243 - Finance Commission.

Article 243Z - Audit of accounts of Municipalities.

Article 243ZA - Elections to the Municipalities.

Article 243ZB - Application to Union territories.

Article 243ZC - Part not to apply to certain areas.

Article 243ZD - Committee for district planning.

Article 243ZE - Committee for Metropolitan planning.

Article 243ZF - Continuance of existing laws and Municipalities.

Article 243ZG - Bar to interference by Courts in electoral matters.

PART IXB : THE CO-OPERATIVE SOCIETIES

Article 243ZH - Definitions

Article 243ZI - Incorporation of co-operative societies

Article 243ZJ - Number and term of members of the board and its office bearers.

Article 243 ZK - Election of members of board.

Article 243ZL - Supersession and suspension of the board and interim management.

Article 243ZM - Audit of accounts of co-operative societies.

Article 243ZN - Convening of general body meetings.

Article 243ZO - Right of a member to get information,

Article 243ZP - Returns.

Article 243ZQ - Offences and penalties.

Article 243ZR - Application to multi-state co-operative societies.

Article 243ZS - Application to Union Territories.

Article 243ZT - Continuance of existing laws.

PART X : THE SCHEDULED AND TRIBAL AREAS

Article 244 - Administration of Scheduled Areas and Tribal Areas.

Article 244A - Formation of an autonomous State comprising certain tribal areas in Assam and creation of local Legislature or Council of Ministers or both therefor.

PART XI : RELATIONS BETWEEN THE UNION AND THE STATES

Chapter I : Legislative Relations

Distribution of Legislative Powers

Article 245 - Extent of laws made by Parliament and by the Legislatures of States.

Article 246 - Subject-matter of laws made by Parliament and by the Legislatures of States.

Article 246A - Special provision with respect to goods and services tax.

Article 247 - Power of Parliament to provide for the establishment of certain additional courts.

Article 248 - Residuary powers of legislation.

Article 249 - Power of Parliament to legislate with respect to a matter in the State List in the national interest.

Article 250 - Power of Parliament to legislate with respect to any matter in the State List if a Proclamation of Emergency is in operation.

Article 251 - Inconsistency between laws made by Parliament under articles 249 and 250 and laws made by the Legislatures of States.

Article 252 - Power of Parliament to legislate for two or more States by consent and adoption of such legislation by any other State.

Article 253 - Legislation for giving effect to international agreements.

Article 254 - Inconsistency between laws made by Parliament and laws made by the Legislatures of States.

Article 255 - Requirements as to recommendations and previous sanctions to be regarded as matters of procedure only.

Chapter II : Administrative Relations

General

Article 256 - Obligation of States and the Union.

Article 257 - Control of the Union over States in certain cases.

Article 257A [Repealed.]

Article 258 - Power of the Union to confer powers, etc., on States in certain cases.

Article 258A - Power of the States to entrust functions to the Union.

Article 259 [Repealed.]

Article 260 - Jurisdiction of the Union in relation to territories outside India.

Article 261 - Public acts, records and judicial proceedings.

Disputes relating to Waters

Article 262 - Adjudication of disputes relating to waters of inter-State rivers or river valleys.

Co-ordination between States

Article 263 - Provisions with respect to an inter-State Council.

PART XII : FINANCE, PROPERTY, CONTRACTS AND SUITS A LEVEL

Chapter I : Finance

General

Article 264 - Interpretation.

Article 265 - Taxes not to be imposed save by authority of law.

Article 266 - Consolidated Funds and public accounts of India and of the States.

Article 267 - Contingency Fund.

Distribution of Revenues between the Union and the States

Article 268 - Duties levied by the Union but collected and appropriated by the State.

Article 268A [Repealed.]

Article 269 - Taxes levied and collected by the Union but assigned to the States.

Article 269A - Levy and collection of goods and services tax in the course of inter-state trade or commerce.

Article 270 - Taxes levied and distributed between the Union and the States.

Article 271 - Surcharge on certain duties and taxes for purposes of the Union.

Article 272 [Repealed.]

Article 273 - Grants in lieu of export duty on jute and jute products.

Article 274 - Prior recommendation of President required to Bills affecting taxation in which States are interested.

Article 275 - Grants from the Union to certain States.

Article 276 - Taxes on professions, trades, callings and employments.

Article 277 - Savings.

Article 278 [Repealed.]

Article 279 - Calculation of "net proceeds", etc.

Article 279A - Goods and Services Tax Council.

Article 280 - Finance Commission.

Article 281 - Recommendations of the Finance Commission.

Miscellaneous financial provisions

Article 282 - Expenditure defrayable by the Union or a State out of its revenues.

Article 283 - Custody, etc., of Consolidated Funds, Contingency Funds and moneys credited to the public accounts.

Article 284 - Custody of suitors' deposits and other moneys received by public servants and courts.

Article 285 - Exemption of property of the Union from State taxation.

Article 286 - Restrictions as to imposition of tax on the sale or purchase of goods.

Article 287 - Exemption from taxes on electricity.

Article 288 - Exemption from taxation by States in respect of water or electricity in certain cases.

Article 289 - Exemption of property and income of a State from Union taxation.

Article 290 - Adjustment in respect of certain expenses and pensions.

Article 290A - Annual payment to certain Devaswom Funds.

Article 291 [Repealed.]

Chapter II : Borrowing

Article 292 - Borrowing by the Government of India.

Article 293 - Borrowing by States.

Chapter III : Property, Contracts, Rights, Liabilities, Obligations and Suits

Article 294 - Succession to property, assets, rights, liabilities and obligations in certain cases.

Article 295 - Succession to property, assets, rights, liabilities and obligations in other cases.

Article 296 - Property accruing by escheat or laps or as bona vacantia.

Article 297 - Things of value within territorial waters or continental shelf and resources of the exclusive economic zone to vest in the Union.

Article 298 - Power to carry on trade, etc.

Article 299 - Contracts.

Article 300 - Suits and proceedings.

Chapter IV : Right To Property

Article 300A - Persons not to be deprived of property save by authority of law.

PART XIII : TRADE, COMMERCE AND INTERCOURSE WITHIN THE TERRITORY OF INDIA

Article 301 - Freedom of trade, commerce and intercourse.

Article 302 - Power of Parliament to impose restrictions on trade, commerce and intercourse.

Article 303 - Restrictions on the legislative powers of the Union and of the States with regard to trade and commerce.

Article 304 - Restrictions on trade, commerce and intercourse among States.

Article 305 - Saving of existing laws and laws providing for State monopolies.

Article 306 [Repealed.]

Article 307 - Appointment of authority for carrying out the purposes of articles 301 to 304.

PART XIV : SERVICES UNDER THE UNION AND THE STATES

Chapter I : Services

Article 308 - Interpretation.

Article 309 - Recruitment and conditions of service of persons serving the Union or a State.

Article 310 - Tenure of office of persons serving the Union or a State.

Article 311 - Dismissal, removal or reduction in rank of persons employed in civil capacities under the Union or a State.

Article 312 - All-India services.

Article 312A - Power of Parliament to vary or revoke conditions of service of officers of certain services.

Article 313 - Transitional provisions.

Article 314 [Repeated.]

Chapter II : Public Service Commissions

Article 315 - Public Service Commissions for the Union and for the States.

Article 316 - Appointment and term of office of members.

Article 317 - Removal and suspension of a member of a Public Service Commission.

Article 318 - Power to make regulations as to conditions of service of members and staff of the Commission.

Article 319 - Prohibition as to the holding of offices by members of Commission on ceasing to be such members.

Article 320 - Functions of Public Service Commissions.

Article 321 - Power to extend functions of Public Service Commissions.

Article 322 - Expenses of Public Service Commissions.

Article 323 -Reports of Public Service Commissions.

PART XIVA : TRIBUNALS

Article 323A - Administrative tribunals.

Article 323B - Tribunals for other matters.

PART XV : ELECTIONS

Article 324 - Superintendence, direction and control of elections to be vested in an Election Commission.

Article 325 - No person to be ineligible for inclusion in, or to claim to be included in a special, electoral roll on grounds of religion, race, caste or sex.

Article 326 - Elections to the House of the People and to the Legislative Assemblies of States to be on the basis of adult suffrage.

Article 327 - Power of Parliament to make provision with respect to elections to Legislatures.

Article 328 - Power of Legislature of a State to make provision with respect to elections to such Legislature.

Article 329 - Bar to interference by courts in electoral matters.

Article 329A [Repealed.]

PART XVI : SPECIAL PROVISIONS RELATING TO CERTAIN CLASSES

Article 330 - Reservation of seats for Scheduled Castes and Scheduled Tribes in the House of the People.

Article 331 - Representation of the Anglo-Indian community in the House of the People.

Article 332 - Reservation of seats for Scheduled Castes and Scheduled Tribes in the Legislative Assemblies of the States.

Article 333 - Representation of the Anglo-Indian community in the Legislative Assemblies of the States.

Article 334 - Reservation of seats and special representation to cease after sixty years.

Article 335 - Claims of Scheduled Castes and Scheduled Tribes to services and posts.

Article 336 - Special provision for Anglo-Indian community in certain services.

Article 337 - Special provision with respect to educational grants for the benefit of the Anglo-Indian Community.

Article 338 - National Commission for Scheduled Castes.

Article 338A - National Commission for Scheduled Tribes.

Article 338A - National Commission for Backward Classes.

Article 339 - Control of the Union over the Administration of Scheduled Areas and the welfare of Scheduled Tribes.

Article 340 - Appointment of a Commission to investigate the conditions of backward classes.

Article 341 - Scheduled Castes.

Article 342 - Scheduled Tribes.

Article 342A - Socially and educationally backward classes.

PART XVII : OFFICIAL LANGUAGE

Chapter I : Language of the Union

Article 343 - Official language of the Union.

Article 344 - Commission and Committee of Parliament on official language.

Chapter II : Regional Languages

Article 345 - Official language or languages of a State.

Article 346 - Official language for communication between one State and another or between a State and the Union.

Article 347 - Special provision relating to language spoken by a section of the population of a State.

Chapter III : Language of The Supreme Court, High Courts, Etc.

Article 348 - Language to be used in the Supreme Court and in the High Courts and for Acts, Bills, etc.

Article 349 - Special procedure for enactment of certain laws relating to language.

Chapter IV : Special Directives

Article 350 - Language to be used in representations for redress of grievances.

Article 350A - Facilities for instruction in mother-tongue at the primary stage.

Article 350B - Special Officer for linguistic minorities.

Article 351 Directive for development of the Hindi language.

PART XVIII: EMERGENCY PROVISIONS

Article 352 - Proclamation of Emergency.

Article 353 - Effect of Proclamation of Emergency.

Article 354 - Application of provisions relating to distribution of revenues while a Proclamation of Emergency is in operation.

Article 355 - Duty of the Union to protect States against external aggression and internal disturbance.

Article 356 - Provisions in case of failure of constitutional machinery in States.

Article 357 - Exercise of legislative powers under Proclamation issued under article 356.

Article 358 - Suspension of provisions of article 19 during emergencies.

Article 359 - Suspension of the enforcement of the rights conferred by Part III during emergencies.

Article 359A [Repealed.]

Article 360 - Provisions as to financial emergency.

PART XIX : MISCELLANEOUS

Article 361 - Protection of President and Governors and Rajprakukhs.

Article 361A - Protection of publication of proceedings of Parliament and State Legislatures.

Article 361B - Disqualification for appointment on remunerative political post.

Article 362 [Repealed.]

Article 363 - Bar to interference by courts in disputes arising out of certain treaties, agreements, etc.

Article 363A - Recognition granted to Rulers of Indian States to cease and privy purses to be abolished.

Article 364 - Special provisions as to major ports and aerodromes.

Article 365 - Effect of failure to comply with, or to give effect to, directions given by the Union.

Article 366 - Definitions.

Article 367 - Interpretation.

PART XX : AMENDMENT OF THE CONSTITUTION

Article 368 - Power of Parliament to amend the Constitution and procedure therefor.

PART XXI: TEMPORARY, TRANSITIONAL AND SPECIAL PROVISIONS

Article 369 - Temporary power to Parliament to make laws with respect to certain matters in the State List as if they were matters in the Concurrent List.

Article 370 - Temporary provisions with respect to the State of Jammu and Kashmir.

Article 371 - Special provision with respect to the States of Maharashtra and Gujarat.

Article 371A - Special provision with respect to the State of Nagaland.

Article 371B - Special provision with respect to the State of Assam.

Article 371C - Special provision with respect to the State of Manipur.

Article 371D - Special provisions with respect to the State of Andhra Pradesh.

Article 371E - Establishment of Central University in Andhra Pradesh.

Article 371F - Special provisions with respect to the State of Sikkim.

Article 371G - Special provision with respect to the State of Mizoram.

Article 371H - Special provision with respect to the State of Arunachal Pradesh.

Article 371-I - Special provision with respect to the State of Goa.

Article 371J - Special provision with respect to the State of Karnataka.

Article 372 - Continuance in force of existing laws and their adaptation.

Article 372A - Power of the President to adapt laws.

Article 373 - Power of President to make order in respect of persons under preventive detention in certain cases.

Article 374 - Provisions as to Judges of the Federal Court and proceedings pending in the Federal Court or before His Majesty in Council.

Article 375 - Courts, authorities and officers to continue to function subject to the provisions of the Constitution.

Article 376 - Provisions as to Judges of High Courts.

Article 377 - Provisions as to Comptroller and Auditor-General of India.

Article 378 - Provisions as to Public Service Commissions.

Article 378A - Special provision as to the duration of Andhra Pradesh Legislative Assembly.

Article 379-391 [Repealed.]

Article 392 - Power of the President to remove difficulties.

PART XXII: SHORT TITLE, COMMENCEMENT, AUTHORITATIVE TEXT IN HINDI AND REPEALS

Article 393 - Short title.

Article 394 - Commencement.

Article 394A - Authoritative text in the Hindi language.

Article 395 - Repeals.

APPENDIX-IV

LIST OF SUBJECTS

SEVENTH SCHEDULE (Article 246)

List I – Union List

1. Defence of India and every part thereof including preparation for defence and all such acts as may be conducive in times of war to its prosecution and after its termination to effective demobilisation.

2. 2. Naval, military and air forces; any other armed forces of the Union.

   [1][2A. Deployment of any armed force of the Union or any other force subject to the control of the Union or any contingent or unit thereof in any State in aid of the civil power; powers, jurisdiction, privileges and liabilities of the members of such forces while on such deployment.]

3. Delimitation of cantonment areas, local self-government in such areas, the constitution and powers within such areas of cantonment authorities and the regulation of house accommodation (including the control of rents) in such areas.

4. Naval, military and air force works.

5. Arms, firearms, ammunition and explosives.

6. Atomic energy and mineral resources necessary for its production.

7. Industries declared by Parliament by law to be necessary for the purpose of defence or for the prosecution of war.

8. Central Bureau of Intelligence and Investigation.

9. Preventive detention for reasons connected with Defence, Foreign Affairs, or the security of India; persons subjected to such detention.

10. Foreign affairs; all matters which bring the Union into relation with any foreign country.

11. Diplomatic, consular and trade representation.

12. United Nations Organisation.

13. Participation in international conferences, associations and other bodies and implementing of decisions made thereat.

14. Entering into treaties and agreements with foreign countries and implementing of treaties, agreements and conventions with foreign countries.

15. War and peace.

---

[1]Ins. by the Constitution (Forty-second Amendment) Act, 1976, s. 57 (w.e.f. 3-1-1977).

16. Foreign jurisdiction.
17. Citizenship, naturalisation and aliens.
18. Extradition.
19. Admission into, and emigration and expulsion from, India; passports and visas.
20. Pilgrimages to places outside India.
21. Piracies and crimes committed on the high seas or in the air; offences against the law of nations committed on land or the high seas or in the air.
22. Railways.
23. Highways declared by or under law made by Parliament to be national highways.
24. Shipping and navigation on inland waterways, declared by Parliament by law to be national waterways, as regards mechanically propelled vessels; the rule of the road on such waterways.
25. Maritime shipping and navigation, including shipping and navigation on tidal waters; provision of education and training for the mercantile marine and regulation of such education and training provided by States and other agencies.
26. Lighthouses, including lightships, beacons and other provision for the safety of shipping and aircraft.
27. Ports declared by or under law made by Parliament or existing law to be major ports, including their delimitation, and the constitution and powers of port authorities therein.
28. Port quarantine, including hospitals connected therewith; seamen's and marine hospitals.
29. Airways; aircraft and air navigation; provision of aerodromes; regulation and organisation of air traffic and of aerodromes; provision for aeronautical education and training and regulation of such education and training provided by States and other agencies.
30. Carriage of passengers and goods by railway, sea or air, or by national waterways in mechanically propelled vessels.
31. Posts and telegraphs; telephones, wireless, broadcasting and other like forms of communication.
32. Property of the Union and the revenue therefrom, but as regards property situated in a State subject to legislation by the State, save in so far as Parliament by law otherwise provides.
34. Courts of wards for the estates of Rulers of Indian States.
35. Public debt of the Union.
36. Currency, coinage and legal tender; foreign exchange.
37. Foreign loans.
38. Reserve Bank of India.
39. Post Office Savings Bank.
40. Lotteries organised by the Government of India or the Government of a State.

41. Trade and commerce with foreign countries; import and export across customs frontiers; definition of customs frontiers.
42. Inter-State trade and commerce.
43. Incorporation, regulation and winding up of trading corporations, including banking, insurance and financial corporations, but not including co-operative societies.
44. Incorporation, regulation and winding up of corporations, whether trading or not, with objects not confined to one State, but not including universities.
45. Banking.
46. Bills of exchange, cheques, promissory notes and other like instruments.
47. Insurance.
48. Stock exchanges and futures markets.
49. Patents, inventions and designs; copyright; trade-marks and merchandise marks.
50. Establishment of standards of weight and measure.
51. Establishment of standards of quality for goods to be exported out of India or transported from one State to another.
52. Industries, the control of which by the Union is declared by Parliament by law to be expedient in the public interest.
53. Regulation and development of oilfields and mineral oil resources; petroleum and petroleum products; other liquids and substances declared by Parliament by law to be dangerously inflammable.
54. Regulation of mines and mineral development to the extent to which such regulation and development under the control of the Union is declared by Parliament by law to be expedient in the public interest.
55. Regulation of labour and safety in mines and oilfields.
56. Regulation and development of inter-State rivers and river valleys to the extent to which such regulation and development under the control of the Union is declared by Parliament by law to be expedient in the public interest.
57. Fishing and fisheries beyond territorial waters.
58. Manufacture, supply and distribution of salt by Union agencies; regulation and control of manufacture, supply and distribution of salt by other agencies.
59. Cultivation, manufacture, and sale for export, of opium.
60. Sanctioning of cinematograph films for exhibition.
61. Industrial disputes concerning Union employees.
62. The institutions known at the commencement of this Constitution as the National Library, the Indian Museum, the Imperial War Museum, the Victoria Memorial and the Indian War Memorial, and any other like institution financed by the Government of India wholly or in part and declared by Parliament by law to be an institution of national importance.

63. The institutions known at the commencement of this Constitution as the Benares Hindu University, the Aligarh Muslim University and the [2][Delhi University; the University established in pursuance of article 371E;] any other institution declared by Parliament by law to be an institution of national importance.

64. Institutions for scientific or technical education financed by the Government of India wholly or in part and declared by Parliament by law to be institutions of national importance.

65. Union agencies and institutions for— (a) professional, vocational or technical training, including the training of police officers; or (b) the promotion of special studies or research; or (c) scientific or technical assistance in the investigation or detection of crime.

66. Co-ordination and determination of standards in institutions for higher education or research and scientific and technical institutions.

67. Ancient and historical monuments and records, and archaeological sites and remains, [3][declared by or under law made by Parliament] to be of national importance.

68. The Survey of India, the Geological, Botanical, Zoological and Anthropological Surveys of India; Meteorological organisations.

69. Census.

70. Union Public Service; All-India Services; Union Public Service Commission.

71. Union pensions, that is to say, pensions payable by the Government of India or out of the Consolidated Fund of India.

72. Elections to Parliament, to the Legislatures of States and to the offices of President and Vice-President; the Election Commission.

73. Salaries and allowances of members of Parliament, the Chairman and Deputy Chairman of the Council of States and the Speaker and Deputy Speaker of the House of the People.

74. Powers, privileges and immunities of each House of Parliament and of the members and the Committees of each House; enforcement of attendance of persons for giving evidence or producing documents before committees of Parliament or commissions appointed by Parliament.

75. Emoluments, allowances, privileges, and rights in respect of leave of absence, of the President and Governors; salaries and allowances of the Ministers for the Union; the salaries, allowances, and rights in respect of leave of absence and other conditions of service of the Comptroller and Auditor General.

76. Audit of the accounts of the Union and of the States.

77. Constitution, organisation, jurisdiction and powers of the Supreme Court (including contempt of such Court), and the fees taken therein; persons entitled to practise before the Supreme Court.

---

[2]Subs. by the Constitution (Thirty-second Amendment) Act, 1973, s. 4, for "Delhi University and" (w.e.f. 1-7-1974).

[3]Subs. by the Constitution (Seventh Amendment) Act, 1956, s. 27, for "declared by Parliament by law".

78. Constitution and organisation [4][(including vacations)] of the High Courts except provisions as to officers and servants of High Courts; persons entitled to practise before the High Courts.

79. [5][Extension of the jurisdiction of a High Court to, and exclusion of the jurisdiction of a High Court from, any Union territory.]

80. Extension of the powers and jurisdiction of members of a police force belonging to any State to any area outside that State, but not so as to enable the police of one State to exercise powers and jurisdiction in any area outside that State without the consent of the Government of the State in which such area is situated; extension of the powers and jurisdiction of members of a police force belonging to any State to railway areas outside that State.

81. Inter-State migration; inter-State quarantine.

82. Taxes on income other than agricultural income.

83. Duties of customs including export duties.

84. Duties of excise on tobacco and other goods manufactured or produced in India except— (a) alcoholic liquors for human consumption; (b) opium, Indian hemp and other narcotic drugs and narcotics, but including medicinal and toilet preparations containing alcohol or any substance included in sub-paragraph (b) of this entry.

85. Corporation tax.

86. Taxes on the capital value of the assets, exclusive of agricultural land, of individuals and companies; taxes on the capital of companies.

87. Estate duty in respect of property other than agricultural land.

88. Duties in respect of succession to property other than agricultural land.

89. Terminal taxes on goods or passengers, carried by railway, sea or air; taxes on railway fares and freights.

90. Taxes other than stamp duties on transactions in stock exchanges and futures markets.

91. Rates of stamp duty in respect of bills of exchange, cheques, promissory notes, bills of lading, letters of credit, policies of insurance, transfer of shares, debentures, proxies and receipts.

92. Taxes on the sale or purchase of newspapers and on advertisements published therein.

[6][92A. Taxes on the sale or purchase of goods other than newspapers, where such sale or purchase takes place in the course of inter-State trade or commerce.]

[7][92B. Taxes on the consignments of goods (whether the consignment is to the person making it or to any other person), where such consignment takes place in the course of inter-State trade or commerce.]

[8][92C. Taxes on services.] Offences against laws with respect to any of the matters in this List.

[4]Ins. by the Constitution (Fifteenth Amendment) Act, 1963, s. 12 (with retrospective effect).

[5]Subs. by the Constitution (Seventh Amendment) Act, 1956, s. 29 and Sch., for entry 79.

[6]Ins. by the Constitution (Sixth Amendment) Act, 1956, s. 2.

[7]Ins. by the Constitution (Forty-sixth Amendment) Act, 1982, s. 5.

[8]Ins. by the Constitution (Eighty-eighth Amendment) Act, 2003, s. 4 (which is yet not in force, date to be notified later on).

93. Inquiries, surveys and statistics for the purpose of any of the matters in this List.

94. Jurisdiction and powers of all courts, except the Supreme Court, with respect to any of the matters in this List; admiralty jurisdiction.

95. Fees in respect of any of the matters in this List, but not including fees taken in any court.

96. Any other matter not enumerated in List II or List III including any tax not mentioned in either of those Lists.

List II—State List

1. Public order (but not including 3[the use of any naval, military or air force or any other armed force of the Union or of any other force subject to the control of the Union or of any contingent or unit thereof] in aid of the civil power).

2. [9][Police (including railway and village police) subject to the provisions of entry 2A of List I.]

3. [10]Officers and servants of the High Court; procedure in rent and revenue courts; fees taken in all courts except the Supreme Court.

4. Prisons, reformatories, Borstal institutions and other institutions of a like nature, and persons detained therein; arrangements with other States for the use of prisons and other institutions.

5. Local government, that is to say, the constitution and powers of municipal corporations, improvement trusts, districts boards, mining settlement authorities and other local authorities for the purpose of local self-government or village administration.

6. Public health and sanitation; hospitals and dispensaries.

7. Pilgrimages, other than pilgrimages to places outside India.

8. Intoxicating liquors, that is to say, the production, manufacture, possession, transport, purchase and sale of intoxicating liquors.

9. Relief of the disabled and unemployable.

10. [11]Burials and burial grounds; cremations and cremation grounds.

12. Libraries, museums and other similar institutions controlled or financed by the State; ancient and historical monuments and records other than those [12][declared by or under law made by Parliament] to be of national importance.

13. Communications, that is to say, roads, bridges, ferries, and other means of communication not specified in List I; municipal tramways; ropeways; inland waterways and traffic thereon subject to the provisions of List I and List III with regard to such waterways; vehicles other than mechanically propelled vehicles.

---

[9]Subs. by the Constitution (Forty-second Amendment) Act, 1976, s. 57, for entry 2 (w.e.f. 3-1-1977).

[10]Certain words omitted by s. 57, ibid. (w.e.f. 3-1-1977).

[11]Entry 11 omitted by s. 57, ibid. (w.e.f. 3-1-1977).

[12]Subs. by the Constitution (Seventh Amendment) Act, 1956, s. 27, for "declared by Parliament by law".

14. Agriculture, including agricultural education and research, protection against pests and prevention of plant diseases.
15. Preservation, protection and improvement of stock and prevention of animal diseases; veterinary training and practice.
16. Pounds and the prevention of cattle trespass.
17. Water, that is to say, water supplies, irrigation and canals, drainage and embankments, water storage and water power subject to the provisions of entry 56 of List I.
18. [13]Land, that is to say, rights in or over land, land tenures including the relation of landlord and tenant, and the collection of rents; transfer and alienation of agricultural land; land improvement and agricultural loans; colonization.
21. Fisheries.
22. Courts of wards subject to the provisions of entry 34 of List I; encumbered and attached estates.
23. Regulation of mines and mineral development subject to the provisions of List I with respect to regulation and development under the control of the Union.
24. Industries subject to the provisions of [14][entries 7 and 52] of List I.
25. Gas and gas-works.
26. Trade and commerce within the State subject to the provisions of entry 33 of List III.
27. Production, supply and distribution of goods subject to the provisions of entry 33 of List III.
28. [15]Markets and fairs.
30. Money-lending and money-lenders; relief of agricultural indebtedness.
31. Inns and inn-keepers.
32. Incorporation, regulation and winding up of corporations, other than those specified in List I, and universities; unincorporated trading, literary, scientific, religious and other societies and associations; co-operative societies.
33. Theatres and dramatic performances; cinemas subject to the provisions of entry 60 of List I; sports, entertainments and amusements.
34. Betting and gambling.
35. [16]Works, lands and buildings vested in or in the possession of the State.
37. Elections to the Legislature of the State subject to the provisions of any law made by Parliament.

---

[13]Entries 19, 20 and 29 omitted by the Constitution (Forty-second Amendment) Act, 1976, s. 57 (w.e.f. 3-1-1977).

[14]Subs. by the Constitution (Seventh Amendment) Act, 1956, s. 28, for "entry 52".

[15]Entries 19, 20 and 29 omitted by the Constitution (Forty-second Amendment) Act, 1976, s. 57 (w.e.f. 3-1-1977).

[16]Entry 36 omitted by the Constitution (Seventh Amendment) Act, 1956, s. 26.

38. Salaries and allowances of members of the Legislature of the State, of the Speaker and Deputy Speaker of the Legislative Assembly and, if there is a Legislative Council, of the Chairman and Deputy Chairman thereof.

39. Powers, privileges and immunities of the Legislative Assembly and of the members and the committees thereof, and, if there is a Legislative Council, of that Council and of the members and the committees thereof; enforcement of attendance of persons for giving evidence or producing documents before committees of the Legislature of the State.

40. Salaries and allowances of Ministers for the State.

41. State public services; State Public Service Commission.

42. State pensions, that is to say, pensions payable by the State or out of the Consolidated Fund of the State.

43. Public debt of the State.

44. Treasure trove.

45. Land revenue, including the assessment and collection of revenue, the maintenance of land records, survey for revenue purposes and records of rights, and alienation of revenues.

46. Taxes on agricultural income.

47. Duties in respect of succession to agricultural land. 48. Estate duty in respect of agricultural land.

48. Estate duty in respect of agricultural land.

49. Taxes on lands and buildings.

50. Taxes on mineral rights subject to any limitations imposed by Parliament by law relating to mineral development.

51. Duties of excise on the following goods manufactured or produced in the State and countervailing duties at the same or lower rates on similar goods manufactured or produced elsewhere in India: — (a) alcoholic liquors for human consumption; (b) opium, Indian hemp and other narcotic drugs and narcotics; but not including medicinal and toilet preparations containing alcohol or any substance included in sub-paragraph (b) of this entry.

52. Taxes on the entry of goods into a local area for consumption, use or sale therein.

53. Taxes on the consumption or sale of electricity.

54. [17][Taxes on the sale or purchase of goods other than newspapers, subject to the provisions of entry 92A of List I.]

55. Taxes on advertisements other than advertisements published in the newspapers [18][and advertisements broadcast by radio or television].

56. Taxes on goods and passengers carried by road or on inland waterways.

57. Taxes on vehicles, whether mechanically propelled or not, suitable for use on roads, including tramcars subject to the provisions of entry 35 of List III.

---

[17]Subs. by the Constitution (Sixth Amendment) Act, 1956, s. 2, for entry 54.

[18]Ins. by the Constitution (Forty–second Amendment) Act, 1976, s. 57 (w.e.f. 3-1-1977).

58. Taxes on animals and boats.
59. Tolls.
60. Taxes on professions, trades, callings and employments.
61. Capitation taxes.
62. Taxes on luxuries, including taxes on entertainments, amusements, betting and gambling.
63. Rates of stamp duty in respect of documents other than those specified in the provisions of List I with regard to rates of stamp duty.
64. Offences against laws with respect to any of the matters in this List.
65. Jurisdiction and powers of all courts, except the Supreme Court, with respect to any of the matters in this List.
66. Fees in respect of any of the matters in this List, but not including fees taken in any court.

List III – Concurrent List

1. Criminal law, including all matters included in the Indian Penal Code at the commencement of this Constitution but excluding offences against laws with respect to any of the matters specified in List I or List II and excluding the use of naval, military or air forces or any other armed forces of the Union in aid of the civil power.
2. Criminal procedure, including all matters included in the Code of Criminal Procedure at the commencement of this Constitution.
3. Preventive detention for reasons connected with the security of a State, the maintenance of public order, or the maintenance of supplies and services essential to the community; persons subjected to such detention.
4. Removal from one State to another State of prisoners, accused persons and persons subjected to preventive detention for reasons specified in entry 3 of this List.
5. Marriage and divorce; infants and minors; adoption; wills, intestacy and succession; joint family and partition; all matters in respect of which parties in judicial proceedings were immediately before the commencement of this Constitution subject to their personal law.
6. Transfer of property other than agricultural land; registration of deeds and documents.
7. Contracts, including partnership, agency, contracts of carriage, and other special forms of contracts, but not including contracts relating to agricultural land.
8. Actionable wrongs.
9. Bankruptcy and insolvency.
10. Trust and Trustees.
11. Administrators-general and official trustees.

[19][11A. Administration of Justice; constitution and organisation of all courts, except the Supreme Court and the High Courts.]

---

[19]Ins. by the Constitution (Forty–second Amendment) Act, 1976, s. 57 (w.e.f. 3-1-1977).

12. Evidence and oaths; recognition of laws, public acts and records, and judicial proceedings.
13. Civil procedure, including all matters included in the Code of Civil Procedure at the commencement of this Constitution, limitation and arbitration.
14. Contempt of court, but not including contempt of the Supreme Court.
15. Vagrancy; nomadic and migratory tribes.
16. Lunacy and mental deficiency, including places for the reception or treatment of lunatics and mental deficients.
17. Prevention of cruelty to animals.

[20][17A. Forests. 17B. Protection of wild animals and birds.]

18. Adulteration of foodstuffs and other goods.
19. Drugs and poisons, subject to the provisions of entry 59 of List I with respect to opium.
20. Economic and social planning.

[21][20A. Population control and family planning.]

21. Commercial and industrial monopolies, combines and trusts.
22. Trade unions; industrial and labour disputes.
23. Social security and social insurance; employment and unemployment.
24. Welfare of labour including conditions of work, provident funds, employers' liability, workmen's compensation, invalidity and old age pensions and maternity benefits.
25. [22][Education, including technical education, medical education and universities, subject to the provisions of entries 63, 64, 65 and 66 of List I; vocational and technical training of labour.]
26. Legal, medical and other professions.
27. Relief and rehabilitation of persons displaced from their original place of residence by reason of the setting up of the Dominions of India and Pakistan.
28. Charities and charitable institutions, charitable and religious endowments and religious institutions.
29. Prevention of the extension from one State to another of infectious or contagious diseases or pests affecting men, animals or plants.
30. Vital statistics including registration of births and deaths.
31. Ports other than those declared by or under law made by Parliament or existing law to be major ports.
32. Shipping and navigation on inland waterways as regards mechanically propelled vessels, and the rule of the road on such waterways, and the carriage of passengers and goods on inland waterways subject to the provisions of List I with respect to national waterways.

---

[20]Ins. by the Constitution (Forty–second Amendment) Act, 1976, s. 57 (w.e.f. 3-1-1977).

[21]Ins. by the Constitution (Forty–second Amendment) Act, 1976, s. 57 (w.e.f. 3-1-1977).

[22]Subs. by s. 57, ibid., for entry 25 (w.e.f. 3-1-1977).

33. [23][Trade and commerce in, and the production, supply and distribution of,— (a) the products of any industry where the control of such industry by the Union is declared by Parliament by law to be expedient in the public interest, and imported goods of the same kind as such products; (b) foodstuffs, including edible oilseeds and oils; (c) cattle fodder, including oilcakes and other concentrates; (d) raw cotton, whether ginned or unginned, and cotton seed; and (e) raw jute.]

[24][33A. Weights and measures except establishment of standards.]

34. Price control.

35. Mechanically propelled vehicles including the principles on which taxes on such vehicles are to be levied.

36. Factories.

37. Boilers.

38. Electricity.

39. Newspapers, books and printing presses.

40. Archaeological sites and remains other than those [25][declared by or under law made by Parliament] to be of national importance.

41. Custody, management and disposal of property (including agricultural land) declared by law to be evacuee property.

42. [26][Acquisition and requisitioning of property.]

43. Recovery in a State of claims in respect of taxes and other public demands, including arrears of land-revenue and sums recoverable as such arrears, arising outside that State.

44. Stamp duties other than duties or fees collected by means of judicial stamps, but not including rates of stamp duty.

45. Inquiries and statistics for the purposes of any of the matters specified in List II or List III.

46. Jurisdiction and powers of all courts, except the Supreme Court, with respect to any of the matters in this List.

47. Fees in respect of any of the matters in this List, but not including fees taken in any court.

---

[23]Subs. by the Constitution (Third Amendment) Act, 1954, s. 2, for entry 33.

[24]Ins. by the Constitution (Forty-second Amendment) Act, 1976, s. 57 (w.e.f. 3-1-1977).

[25]Subs. by the Constitution (Seventh Amendment) Act, 1956, s. 27, for "declared by Parliament by law".

[26]Subs. by s. 26, ibid., for entry 42.

APPENDIX-V

SCHEDULES OF INDIAN CONSTITUTION

PURPOSE

1. **Additional Information :** Schedule is an appendix attached to any act, supplementing the legislation with additional information that is not mentioned under the main text of the articles. For Example, Article 1 of the Constitution talks about the states and Union territories i.e., the spirit of the law, but the names of states and union territories cannot be mentioned in the article itself so the schedule acts as an instrument to describe that additional information in a separate column. Hence, it becomes easy for the reader to know what the article talks about and the additional information concerning the article.
2. **Easily amendable :** The objective of the schedule is to make the provisions of the act less complex by separating the legal part from its additional information and hence, also making it concise and easy to comprehend. This separation caused by the schedule also acts beneficially in case of amendments. If there was no such separation, then every time an amendment was to be made in the additional information, an amendment would be required in the article itself which is a difficult procedure.
3. **Improves readability :** It helps improve the ability of the reader to read and interpret the legislation more effectively.
4. **Non-legal information :** The information in the schedules can be of technical as well as administrative in nature. The matter contained in schedule should not be legal but rather about the legal principle mentioned under the main text of the act.
5. **Conciseness :** Schedule forms a separate part for additional information hence making the main text of the act concise.

LIST OF SCHEDULES

1. **First Schedule :** The first schedule contains the list of states and union territories and their territories
2. **Second Schedule :** The second schedule contains provisions of the President, Governors of States, Speaker and the Deputy Speaker of the House of the People and the Chairman and the Deputy Chairman of the Council of States and the Speaker and the Deputy Speaker of the Legislative Assembly and the Chairman and the Deputy Chairman of the Legislative Council of a State, the Judges of the Supreme Court and of the High Courts and the Comptroller and Auditor-General of India.

3. **Third Schedule :** The third Schedule contains the Forms of Oaths or Affirmations.
4. **Fourth Schedule :** The fourth Schedule contains provisions as to the allocation of seats in the Council of States.
5. **Fifth Schedule :** The fifth Schedule contains provisions as to the Administration and Control of Scheduled Areas and Scheduled Tribes.
6. **Sixth Schedule :** The sixth Schedule contains provisions as to the Administration of Tribal Areas in the States of Assam, Meghalaya, Tripura and Mizoram.
7. **Seventh Schedule :** The seventh Schedule contains the Union list, State list and the concurrent list.
8. **Eighth Schedule :** The eighth Schedule contains the list of recognized languages.
9. **Ninth Schedule :** Ninth Schedule contains provisions as to validation of certain Acts and Regulations.
10. **Tenth Schedule :** The tenth Schedule contains provisions as to disqualification on ground of defection.
11. **Eleventh Schedule :** The eleventh Schedule contains the powers, authority and responsibilities of Panchayats.
12. **Twelfth Schedule :** The twelfth Schedule contains the powers, authority and responsibilities of Municipalities.

APPENDIX-VI

TABLE OF PRECEDENCE

The order of precedence of the Republic of India is a list in which the functionaries, dignitaries and officials are listed for ceremonial purposes and has no legal standing and does not reflect the Indian presidential line of succession or the co-equal status of the separation of powers under The Constitution of India. The order is established by the President of India, through the President's Secretariat and is maintained by the Ministry of Home Affairs. It is not applicable for the day-to-day functioning of the Government of India. If there are multiple persons of similar rank, then they will be listed in alphabetical order. The order of precedence between themselves is determined by the date of entry into that position/rank.

1. President
2. Vice-President
3. Prime Minister
4. Governors of States within their respective States
5. Former Presidents; 5A. Deputy Prime Minister
6. Chief Justice of India; Speaker of Lok Sabha
7. Cabinet Ministers of the Union; Chief Ministers of States within their respective States; Deputy Chairman, Planning Commission; Former Prime Ministers; Leaders of Opposition in Rajya Sabha and Lok Sabha; 7A. Holders of Bharat Ratna decoration
8. Ambassadors Extraordinary and Plenipotentiary and High Commissioners of Commonwealth countries accredited to India; Chief Ministers of States outside their respective States; Governors of States outside their respective States.
9. Judges of Supreme Court; 9A. Chairperson, Union Public Service Commission; Chief Election Commissioner; Comptroller & Auditor General of India
10. Deputy Chairman, Rajya Sabha; Deputy Chief Ministers of States; Deputy Speaker, Lok Sabha; Members of the Planning Commission; Ministers of State of the Union {and any other Minister in the Ministry of Defence for defence matters} .
11. Attorney General of India; Cabinet Secretary. Lieutenant Governors within their respective Union Territories.
12. Chiefs of Staff holding the rank of full General or equivalent rank.
13. Envoys Extraordinary and Ministers Plenipotentiary accredited to India.
14. Chairmen and Speakers of State Legislatures within their respective States. Chief Justices of High Courts within their respective jurisdictions.
15. Cabinet Ministers in States within their respective States; Chief Ministers of Union Territories and Chief Executive Councillor, Delhi within their respective Union Territories; Deputy Ministers of the Union.
16. Officiating Chiefs of Staff holding the rank of Lieutenant General or equivalent rank.
17. Chairman, Central Administrative Tribunal; Chairman, Minorities Commission; Chairperson, National Commission for Scheduled Castes; Chairperson, National Commission for Scheduled

Tribes; Chief Justices of High Courts outside their respective jurisdictions; Puisne Judges of High Courts within their respective jurisdictions.

18. Cabinet Ministers in States outside their respective; States Chairmen and Speakers of State Legislatures outside their respective States; Chairman, Monopolies and Restrictive Trade Practices Commission; Deputy Chairmen and Deputy Speakers of State Legislatures within their respective States; Ministers of State in States within their respective States; Ministers of Union Territories and Executive Councilors, Delhi, within their respective Union Territories; Speakers of Legislative Assemblies in Union Territories and Chairman of Delhi Metropolitan Council within their respective Union Territories.

19. Chief Commissioners of Union Territories not having Councils of Ministers, within their respective Union Territories; Deputy Ministers in States within their respective States; Deputy Speakers of Legislative Assemblies in Union Territories and Deputy Chairman of metropolitan Council Delhi, within their respective Union Territories.

20. Deputy Chairmen and Deputy Speakers of State Legislatures, outside their respective states; Ministers of State in States outside their respective States Puisne Judges of High Courts outside their respective jurisdictions.

21. Members of Parliament.

22. Deputy Ministers in State outside their respective States.

23. Army Commanders/ Vice-Chief of the Army Staff or equivalent in other services; Chief Secretaries to State Governments within their respective States; Commissioner for Linguistic Minorities Commissioner for Scheduled Castes and Scheduled Tribes; Members, Minorities Commission; Members, National Commission for Scheduled Castes; Members, National Commission for Scheduled Tribes Officers of the rank of full General or equivalent rank Secretaries to the Government of India (including officers holding this office ex-officio); Secretary, Minorities Commission; Secretary, Scheduled Castes and Scheduled Tribes Commission; Secretary to the President; Secretary to the Prime Minister; Secretary, Rajya Sabha/Lok Sabha; Solicitor General; Vice-Chairman, Central Administrative Tribunal.

24. Officers of the rank of Lieutenant General or equivalent rank.

25. Additional Secretaries to the Government of India; Additional Solicitor General Advocate Generals of States; Chairman, Tariff Commission Charge d' Affairs and Acting High Commissioners a pied and ad interim; Chief Ministers of Union Territories and Chief Executive Councillor, Delhi outside their respective Union Territories; Chief Secretaries of State Governments outside their respective States; Deputy Comptroller and Auditor General; Deputy Speakers of Legislative Assemblies in Union Territories and Deputy Chairman, Delhi Metropolitan Council, outside their respective Union Territories; Director, Central Bureau of Investigation; Director General, Border Security Force; Director General, Central Reserve Police; Director, Intelligence Bureau Lieutenant Governors outside their respective Union Territories; Members, Central Administrative Tribunal; Members, Monopolies and Restrictive Trade Practices Commission; Members, Union Public Service Commission; Ministers of Union Territories and Executive Councillors, Delhi, outside their respective Union Territories; Principal Staff Officers of the Armed Forces of the rank of major General or equivalent rank; Speakers of Legislative Assemblies in Union Territories and Chairman of Delhi, Metropolitan Council, outside their respective Union Territories.

26. Joint Secretaries to the Government of India and officers of equivalent rank. Officers of the rank of Major-General or equivalent rank